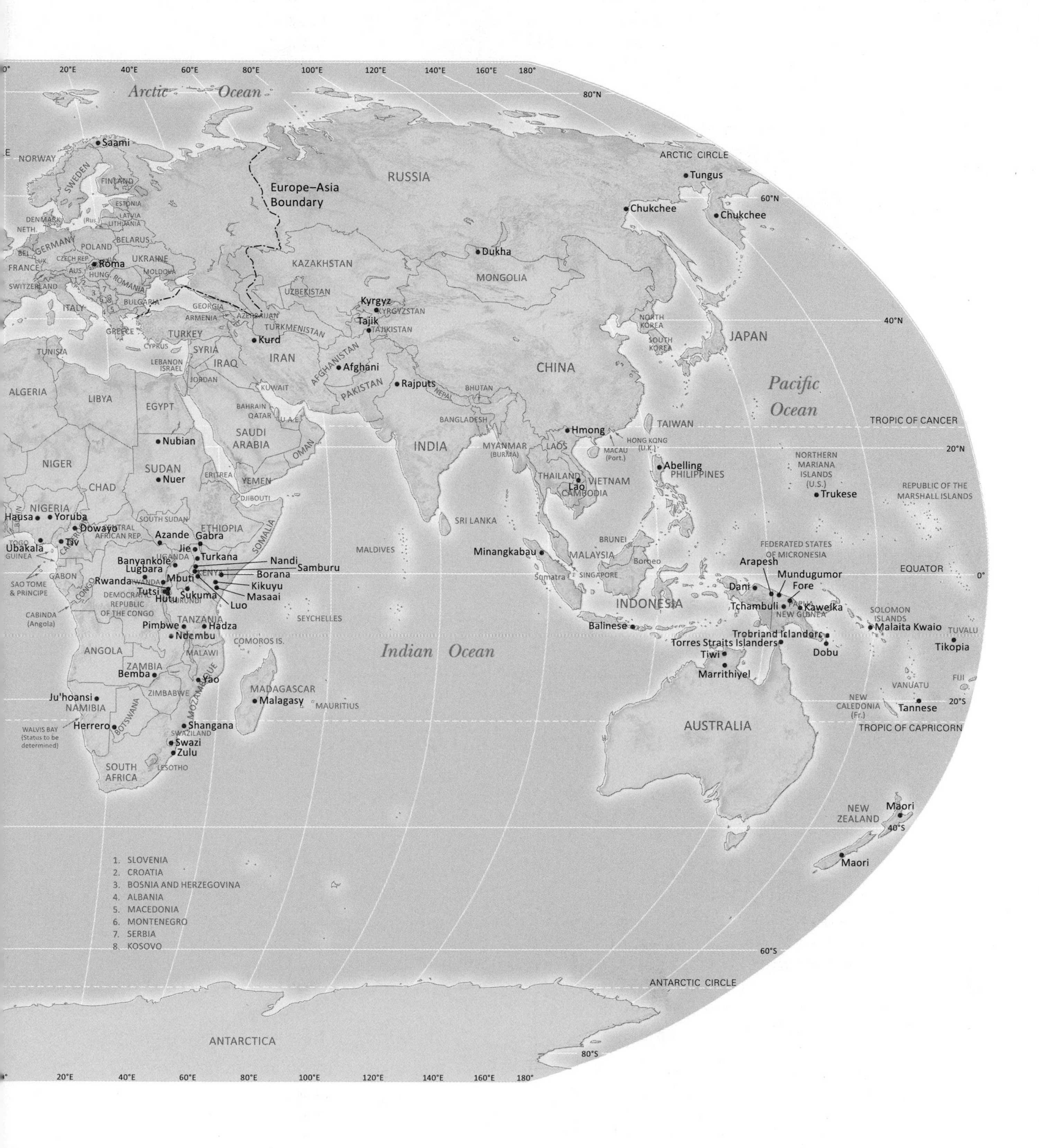
Arctic Ocean
Pacific Ocean
Indian Ocean
RUSSIA
Europe–Asia Boundary
ARCTIC CIRCLE
ANTARCTIC CIRCLE
TROPIC OF CANCER
TROPIC OF CAPRICORN
EQUATOR
NORWAY
SWEDEN
FINLAND
ESTONIA
LATVIA
LITHUANIA
DENMARK
NETH.
GERMANY
POLAND
BELARUS
UKRAINE
MOLDOVA
FRANCE
SWITZERLAND
ITALY
GREECE
TURKEY
CYPRUS
SYRIA
LEBANON
ISRAEL
JORDAN
IRAQ
IRAN
KUWAIT
BAHRAIN
QATAR
U.A.E.
SAUDI ARABIA
OMAN
YEMEN
GEORGIA
ARMENIA
AZERBAIJAN
TURKMENISTAN
UZBEKISTAN
KAZAKHSTAN
KYRGYZSTAN
TAJIKISTAN
AFGHANISTAN
PAKISTAN
INDIA
NEPAL
BHUTAN
BANGLADESH
SRI LANKA
MALDIVES
CHINA
MONGOLIA
NORTH KOREA
SOUTH KOREA
JAPAN
TAIWAN
HONG KONG (U.K.)
MACAU (Port.)
MYANMAR (BURMA)
LAOS
THAILAND
VIETNAM
CAMBODIA
PHILIPPINES
MALAYSIA
BRUNEI
SINGAPORE
Sumatra
Borneo
INDONESIA
PAPUA NEW GUINEA
AUSTRALIA
NEW ZEALAND
NORTHERN MARIANA ISLANDS (U.S.)
REPUBLIC OF THE MARSHALL ISLANDS
FEDERATED STATES OF MICRONESIA
SOLOMON ISLANDS
TUVALU
VANUATU
FIJI
NEW CALEDONIA (Fr.)
TUNISIA
ALGERIA
LIBYA
EGYPT
NIGER
CHAD
SUDAN
SOUTH SUDAN
ERITREA
DJIBOUTI
ETHIOPIA
SOMALIA
NIGERIA
TOGO
GUINEA
CAMEROON
CENTRAL AFRICAN REP.
GABON
CONGO
SAO TOME & PRINCIPE
CABINDA (Angola)
DEMOCRATIC REPUBLIC OF THE CONGO
UGANDA
KENYA
RWANDA
BURUNDI
TANZANIA
SEYCHELLES
COMOROS IS.
MALAWI
ANGOLA
ZAMBIA
ZIMBABWE
MOZAMBIQUE
MADAGASCAR
MAURITIUS
NAMIBIA
BOTSWANA
WALVIS BAY (Status to be determined)
SWAZILAND
LESOTHO
SOUTH AFRICA
ANTARCTICA
Saami
Roma
Tungus
Chukchee
Chukchee
Dukha
Kyrgyz
Tajik
Kurd
Afghani
Rajputs
Hmong
Abelling
Lao
Trukese
Minangkabau
Balinese
Arapesh
Mundugumor
Fore
Dani
Tchambuli
Kawelka
Malaita Kwaio
Trobriand Islanders
Dobu
Torres Straits Islanders
Tiwi
Marrithiyel
Tikopia
Tannese
Maori
Maori
Nubian
Nuer
Hausa
Yoruba
Dowayo
Tiv
Ubakala
Azande
Gabra
Jie
Turkana
Nandi
Samburu
Banyankole
Lugbara
Borana
Mbuti
Rwanda
Tutsi
Hutu
Sukuma
Kikuyu
Masaai
Luo
Pimbwe
Hadza
Ndembu
Bemba
Yao
Malagasy
Ju'hoansi
Herrero
Shangana
Swazi
Zulu
1. SLOVENIA
2. CROATIA
3. BOSNIA AND HERZEGOVINA
4. ALBANIA
5. MACEDONIA
6. MONTENEGRO
7. SERBIA
8. KOSOVO
20°E 40°E 60°E 80°E 100°E 120°E 140°E 160°E 180°
80°N 60°N 40°N 20°N 0° 20°S 40°S 60°S 80°S

CANADIAN EDITION

Cultural Anthropology

An Applied Perspective

Gary Ferraro

Susan Andreatta

Chris Holdsworth
University of Calgary

NELSON

NELSON

Cultural Anthropology, Canadian Edition

by Gary Ferraro, Susan Andreatta, and Chris Holdsworth

VP, Product and Partnership Solutions:
Anne Williams

Publisher, Digital and Print Content:
Leanna MacLean

Marketing Manager:
Ann Byford

Content Development Manager:
Katherine Goodes

Photo and Permissions Researcher:
Mary Rose MacLachlan

Senior Production Project Manager:
Imoinda Romain

Production Service:
MPS Limited

Copy Editor:
Frances Robinson

Proofreader:
MPS Limited

Indexer:
Chris Banta

Design Director:
Ken Phipps

Managing Designer:
Pamela Johnston

Interior Design Modifications:
MPS Limited

Cover Design:
Trinh Truong

Cover Image:
pixdeluxe/Getty

Compositor:
MPS Limited

Printed and bound in Canada
1 2 3 4 20 19 18 17

For more information contact Nelson Education Ltd.,
1120 Birchmount Road, Toronto, Ontario, M1K 5G4. Or you can visit our Internet site at nelson.com

Library and Archives Canada Cataloguing in Publication

Ferraro, Gary P., author
Cultural anthropology : an applied perspective / Gary Ferraro, Susan Andreatta, Chris Holdsworth. — Canadian edition.

Includes bibliographical references and index.
Issued in print and electronic formats.
ISBN 978-0-17-653200-0 (softcover).—ISBN 978-0-17-676769-3 (PDF)

1. Ethnology—Textbooks. 2. Applied anthropology—Textbooks. 3. Ethnology—Canada—Textbooks. 4. Applied anthropology—Canada—Textbooks. 5. Textbooks. I. Andreatta, Susan, author II. Holdsworth, Chris, author III. Title.

GN316.F46 2017 306
C2017-900198-1
C2017-900199-X

ISBN-13: 978-0-17-653200-0
ISBN-10: 0-17-653200-5

To Stefan and Stephanie—aka "The Steffersons"—who embody the values of multiculturalism, cross-cultural understanding, and the insights of cultural anthropology.

GPF

For Tim—Thank you for your love and for understanding the value of anthropological fieldwork.

SLA

For Phyllis for your love and understanding and for Philip, Ann, Lisa, and Heather as you embark upon your careers in this multicultural world.

CJH

Brief Contents

Detailed Contents

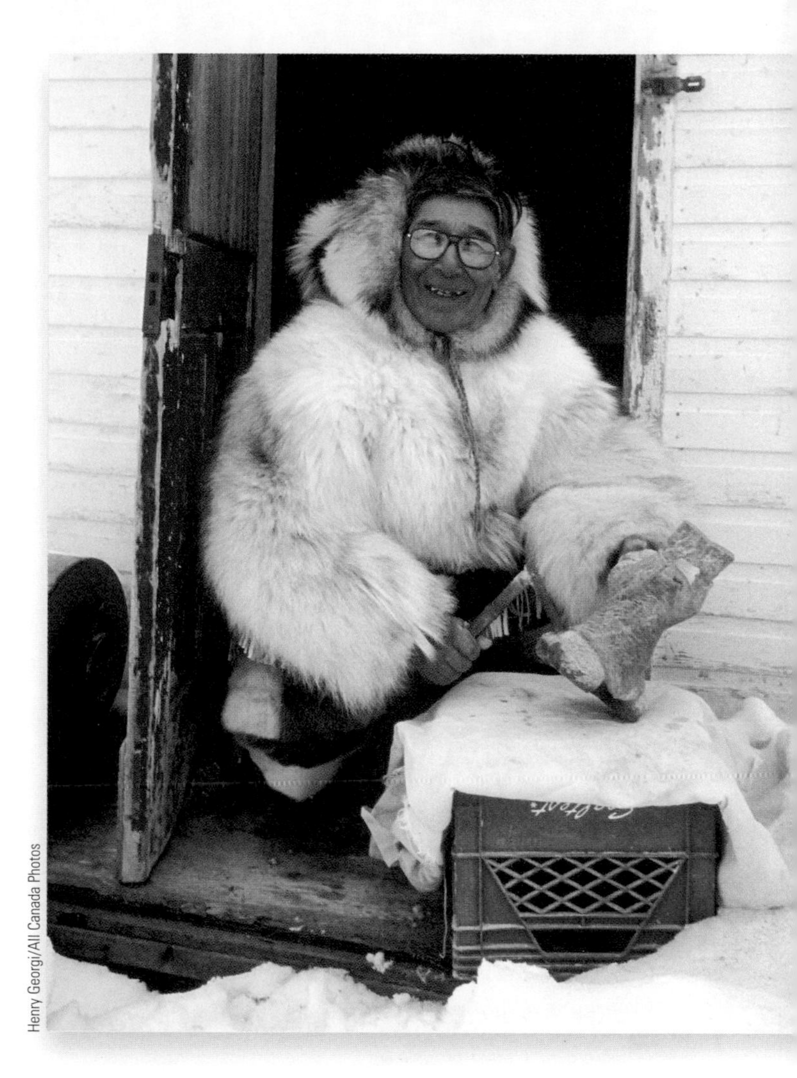
Henry Georgi/All Canada Photos

Dinodia Photos/Alamy Stock Photo

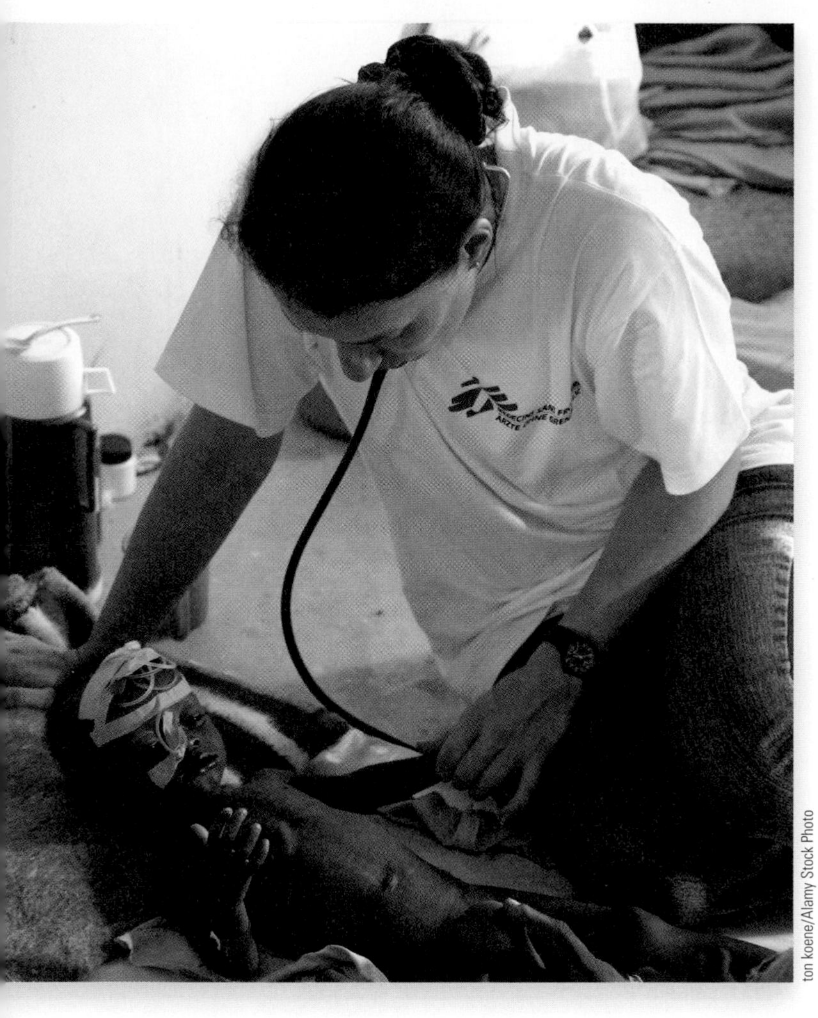
ton koene/Alamy Stock Photo

Strauss/Curtis/Getty Images

Yoshikazu Tsuno/AFP/Getty Images

Jim West/Alamy Stock Photo

CHAPTER 9
Sex and Gender 226

imageBROKER/Alamy Stock Photo

CHAPTER 10

Social Inequality: The Meaning of Difference 260

CHAPTER 11

Political Organization and Social Control 292

Paul Almasy/Corbis/VCG via Getty Images

CHAPTER 12
Religion 322

CHAPTER 13
Art 352

aaron peterson.net/Alamy Stock Photo

Joerg Boethling/Alamy Stock Photo

Feature Contents

STORIES FROM THE FIELD

CROSS-CULTURAL MISCUE

Preface

Cultural Anthropology: An Applied Perspective has been one of the best-selling introductory anthropology textbooks in the United States since 1992. *Cultural Anthropology: An Applied Perspective,* Canadian Edition, retains all the features that made it so successful: its applied approach, its coverage of core concepts and principles, its in-depth case studies of applied anthropology, its cross-cultural miscues, and its easy-to-read style. But much has changed with this Canadian edition. Most of the American examples have been replaced with contemporary Canadian ones, and the work of Canadian anthropologists highlighted. The text also takes an anthropological perspective to issues facing Canada's Indigenous peoples, which are, or should be, a concern for all Canadians.

The world we live in is vastly different from that of a few short years ago. Consequently, the issues anthropologists are interested in and research have changed. This is reflected not only through discussion of methodological innovations, such as multi-sited field research, the use of new technologies, and reflexive and intersubjective approaches, but also in the topics covered. Topics that receive greater attention in this text include human relations with the environment, religious and political conflict, medical anthropology, climate change, the growth of information technologies, international migration, urbanization, development, decolonization, and business anthropology.

As a step toward decolonizing anthropology, the cover of the text does not use an image of an "exotic" person of colour dressed in traditional costume and engaged in a traditional activity. Such images tend to stress inequality, can be dehumanizing, and give students the wrong impression about what anthropology in the 21st century is really all about. This is particularly important given our increasingly multicultural classes. Cultures are also not isolates existing in the ethnographic present. Consequently, one of the themes that runs throughout the text is that cultures are in a constant state of flux and are continually interacting with each other, both locally and globally.

Over the past three decades, anthropology has grown steadily in popularity. In large part, this is because people both inside and outside the discipline have begun to recognize that, in today's globalized, multicultural world, cultural competency is an essential skill. All three authors thus share a vision of the importance of an applied perspective within the discipline and, particularly, the need for an applied focus in introductory level anthropology courses. While we hope students will followup their introductory course with other courses in anthropology, we realize that most will not, and so it is important that whatever profession or career they enter, they can draw upon the lessons of anthropology and apply them in their everyday, personal and professional lives.

Most employers no longer hire on the basis of what a job candidate knows, since much of that knowledge can be acquired while on the job. Instead, they want to know whether the person can add value to the organization. Do they have the skills and competencies needed to be creative and to solve future problems? Whether students work at home or abroad, or whether they work for government, non-governmental organizations, or private enterprise, or whether they work on applied projects that facilitate making a difference in local communities, they will increasingly be interacting with customers, clients, patients, colleagues, students, and others from different cultural backgrounds who will have different ways of thinking and different ways of doing things. In today's global marketplace it is difficult to imagine any job that would not require cross-cultural skills and sensitivities. Even engineers need to understand how culture influences the people they work with and the end-users of the things they design.

Because cultural anthropology has always been the academic discipline best positioned to educate for cultural competency, it only makes sense to make our introductory courses as relevant and as applied as possible. Consequently, we feel that the applied focus of this textbook is particularly germane to today's students. It thus has three primary objectives: (1) to introduce students to the field of social and cultural anthropology by providing a comprehensive overview of the discipline while drawing on rich ethnographic examples; (2) to provide students with an appreciation for the cultural diversity that exists in the world today; and (3) to demonstrate how the theories, insights, and methods of cultural anthropology have been, and can be, applied to contemporary situations. Our hope is that students will gain a level of cultural competency whereby they are able to relate the concepts, findings, methods, and theories of cultural anthropology to their own lives.

The theme of applied anthropology runs throughout this text and thoroughly integrates the application of anthropological theories, methods, and examples to contemporary situations that students are likely to encounter in everyday life. The applied perspective is further highlighted by several other features: chapter-opening case studies, Applied Perspective cases, Cross-Cultural Miscues, Stories from the Field, and Critical Thinking Questions.

Please note that the first and last chapters begin with letters written to students rather than opening scenarios. The opening letter in Chapter 1 tells students essentially what is covered in this preface, since most instructors do not require their students to read the preface. The closing letter in Chapter 14 is designed to introduce students to the capstone chapter, remind them of the importance of the applied features of the text, and show them how anthropological understandings and sensitivities are absolutely essential for the resolution of the human challenges of today.

Pedagogical Features

The Canadian edition of *Cultural Anthropology: An Applied Perspective* contains a number of pedagogical features designed to enhance student learning and illustrate the relevance of cultural anthropology in our everyday lives.

General chapter features include:

- Contemporary examples, most of which are Canadian, illustrate the application of anthropological concepts and methods in the field, workplace, and in one's personal life.
- What We Will Learn introductory statements alert the student to the key concepts of the chapter.
- Real-life, chapter-opening case studies designed not only to catch the student's attention, but also to illustrate the underlying theme of the chapter. In addition, they demonstrate the importance of culture and anthropology in understanding the world around us.
- Concise chapter summaries highlight the key points of the chapter.
- Applied Perspective boxes demonstrate how the methods and insights of cultural anthropology have been applied to the solution of specific societal and cultural problems and challenges. Questions for Further Thought in each box are designed to encourage students to think critically about the broader implications of the applied case.
- Stories from the Field are brief accounts by fieldworkers when they came to a sudden understanding or realization of the value of anthropology or the role of culture.
- Cross-Cultural Miscue boxes demonstrate the misunderstandings and negative consequences of failing to understand cultural differences. They are based on real-life experiences of anthropologists, business people, politicians, and others.
- Ten Critical Thinking Questions at the end of each chapter are designed to make students think about the material covered in the chapter as well as how to apply the knowledge in novel situations.
- A running glossary, a list of key terms, as well as a cumulative glossary familiarize the student with anthropological concepts.

Chapter Highlights

Chapter 1: Anthropology in a Global World

1. Applied Perspective on Transplant Tourism and Advocacy Anthropology
2. Discussion of selective abortion of female fetuses in China, India, and Canada
3. Discussion of the skills anthropology provides for life in the contemporary world

Chapter 2: The Concept of Culture

1. Opening discussion of cultural challenges international students face in adjusting to school and life in Canada
2. Comprehensive coverage of the core attributes and features of culture
3. Discussion about the relationship between culture and identity

Chapter 3: Applied Anthropology

1. An examination of those aspects of anthropology that suit it as an applied discipline
2. Extensive coverage of applying anthropology in five areas: medicine, business, development, the environment, and education
3. Opening study that discusses doing anthropological business research in China

Chapter 4: The Growth of Anthropological Theory

1. Discussion of the Hawthorne Studies, a historical example of Applied Anthropology

2. A comprehensive survey of the theoretical approaches in anthropology along with summaries of key points
3. In-depth discussion of postmodernist anthropology

Chapter 5: Research Methods in Cultural Anthropology

1. Traces the stages of conducting ethnographic fieldwork, including obtaining ethics approval
2. Coverage of new data-gathering techniques, such as the use of new information technologies
3. Discussion of the requirements for conducting ethnographic fieldwork in Canada, including working with First Nations

Chapter 6: Communication and Culture

1. Chapter opening discussion of the loss and revival of indigenous languages in Canada
2. Extensive coverage of non-verbal forms of communication including kinesics, proxemics, paralanguage, and haptic communication
3. Discussion of the relationship between language and social status, gender, nationalism, and identity

Chapter 7: Economics, Adaptation, and Subsistence Patterns

1. Chapter opening discussion of the practice of tipping in Canada
2. A cross-cultural comparison of systems of production, distribution, and consumption
3. Coverage of the major food-getting strategies, from subsistence to market exchange

Chapter 8: Marriage, Family, and Kinship

1. Chapter opening discussion of surrogacy in Canada and the kinship implications
2. A cross-cultural survey of marriage forms, family types, and kinship structures
3. Discussion of the impact of new information technologies on interpersonal relationships

Chapter 9: Sex and Gender

1. Thorough coverage of the cultural construction of gender
2. Discussion of changing gender roles in Canada
3. Coverage of sex-selective abortions in Canada and elsewhere

Chapter 10: Social Inequality: The Meaning of Difference

1. Discussion of class structure in Canada
2. Coverage of Immigration and Discrimination in Canada
3. Discussion of racism in Canada, with particular focus on its impact on Canada's Indigenous peoples

Chapter 11: Political Organization and Social Control

1. Opening study focusing on justice for Indigenous people, with discussion of the R. V. Gladue case
2. Discussion of the impact of the Internet and social media on governments, as well as means of social control
3. How First Nations bands are constituted and how they function

Chapter 12: Religion

1. Discussion of the changing face of religion in Canada
2. Analysis of Islamic Fundamentalism and religious nationalism
3. Extensive coverage of Wicca

Chapter 13: Art

1. Introductory opening covers the repatriation of the G'psgolox totem pole
2. The role of art as a mechanism for social control in complex societies
3. Theoretical discussion of what art is and its place in society

Chapter 14: The Modern World Order

1. Discussion of the forces of globalization today
2. Coverage of the challenges facing the world today and the role of applied cultural anthropology
3. Discussion of the struggle for cultural survival of Indigenous peoples

Instructor Resources

The **Nelson Education Teaching Advantage (NETA)** program delivers research-based instructor resources that promote student engagement and higher-order thinking to enable the success of Canadian students and educators. Visit Nelson's **Inspired Instruction** website at nelson.com/inspired to find out more about NETA.

The following instructor resources have been created for *Cultural Anthropology: An Applied Perspective,* Canadian Edition. Access these ultimate tools for customizing lectures and presentations at nelson .com/instructor.

NETA Test Bank

This resource was written by Deidre Rose, University of Guelph. It includes over 800 multiple-choice questions written according to NETA guidelines for effective construction and development of higher-order questions. Also included are approximately 350 true/false, over 140 short-answer, and approximately 70 essay-type questions.

The NETA Test Bank is available in a new, cloud-based platform. **Nelson Testing Powered by Cognero®** is a secure online testing system that allows instructors to author, edit, and manage test bank content from anywhere Internet access is available. No special installations or downloads are needed, and the desktop-inspired interface, with its drop-down menus and familiar, intuitive tools, allows instructors to create and manage tests with ease. Multiple test versions can be created in an instant, and content can be imported or exported into other systems. Tests can be delivered from a learning management system, the classroom, or wherever an instructor chooses. Nelson Testing Powered by Cognero for *Cultural Anthropology: An Applied Perspective,* Canadian Edition can be accessed through nelson .com/instructor.

NETA PowerPoint

Microsoft® PowerPoint® lecture slides for every chapter have been created by Terry Webb, University of Western Ontario. There is an average of 25 to 30 slides per chapter, many featuring key figures, tables, and photographs from *Cultural Anthropology: An Applied Perspective,* Canadian Edition. NETA principles of clear design and engaging content have been incorporated throughout, making it simple for instructors to customize the deck for their courses.

Image Library

This resource consists of digital copies of figures, short tables, and photographs used in the book. Instructors may use these jpegs to customize the NETA PowerPoint or create their own PowerPoint presentations. An Image Library Key describes the images and lists the codes under which the jpegs are saved.

NETA Instructor Guide

This resource was written by Deidre Rose, University of Guelph. It is organized according to the textbook chapters and addresses key educational concerns, such as typical stumbling blocks student face and how to address them. Other features include important notes about what students will learn in the chapter, why the chapter is important to students, and why they should care; assorted engagement activities that instructors may wish to use in class; and various online activities.

MindTap

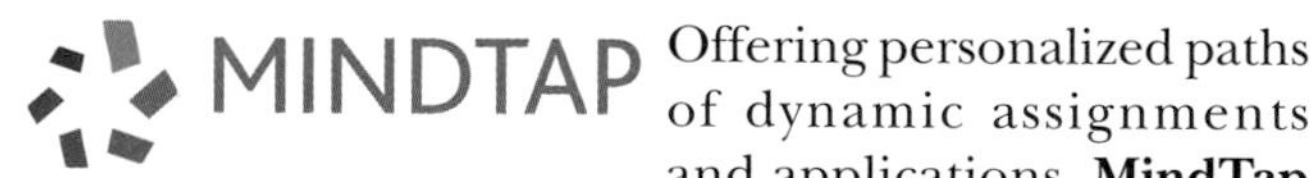

Offering personalized paths of dynamic assignments and applications, **MindTap** is a digital learning solution that turns cookie-cutter into cutting-edge, apathy into engagement, and memorizers into higher-level thinkers. MindTap enables students to analyze and apply chapter concepts within relevant assignments, and allows instructors to measure skills and promote better outcomes with ease. A fully online learning solution, MindTap combines all student learning tools—readings, multimedia, activities, and assessments—into a single Learning Path that guides the student through the curriculum. Activities and assessment were written by Maureen Bracewell, Capilano University. Instructors personalize the experience by customizing the presentation of these learning tools to their students, even seamlessly introducing their own content into the Learning Path.

Acknowledgments

To one degree or another, many people have contributed to this textbook. Some have made explicit suggestions for revisions, many of which have been incorporated into various editions. Others have contributed less directly, yet their fingerprints are found throughout the text. We are particularly grateful to the many colleagues with whom we have studied at Syracuse University (Ferraro), Michigan Sate University (Andreatta), and University of Calgary (Holdsworth). We owe a similar debt to the many colleagues over the years who have shared with us their thinking on anthropological research and teaching. Although there are far too many names to fit into a small preface, they have had an important impact on our careers as anthropologists and thus on the content of this book. They have always responded graciously to our requests for information in their various areas of expertise and have taught us a great deal about teaching introductory anthropology. We are confident that they know who they are and will accept our most sincere gratitude.

We are also grateful to Diana E. French, University of British Columbia Okanagan, and Deidre Rose, University of Guelph, for relating their experiences and contributing to the Stories from the Field boxes.

This textbook has benefitted from excellent editorial guidance and the comments of many reviewers. Their valuable and insightful suggestions strengthened this text. For this Canadian edition we would like to express our gratitude to:

Beryl Amaron, Okanagan College
Anna Boshnakova, Sheridan College/Trafalgar Campus
Jamie Cidro, University of Winnipeg
Diana E. French, University of British Columbia Okanagan
Douglas Hudson, University of the Fraser Valley
Liam Kilmurray, University of Ottawa
Erin McGuire, University of Victoria
Rob Phillips, University of Manitoba
Cathy Prowse, Mount Royal University
Deidre Rose, University of Guelph
Terry Webb, University of Western Ontario

We also want to thank the many unsolicited reviews—both by professors and students—commenting on various aspects of the text over the years. We trust that these reviewers will see that many of their suggestions have been incorporated into this edition. We encourage any readers, professors, or students to send comments, corrections, and suggestions for future improvements via email to choldwor@ucalgary.ca.

We also want to express our deepest gratitude to our many students who have helped us define and refine our anthropological perspectives and, consequently, the concepts and interpretations of this book.

Gary Ferraro
Susan Andreatta
Chris Holdsworth

About the Authors

Gary Ferraro, Professor Emeritus of Anthropology at the University of North Carolina–Charlotte, received his B.A. in history from Hamilton College and his M.A. and Ph.D. from Syracuse University. He has been a Fulbright Scholar at the University of Swaziland in Southern Africa (1979–1980) and again at Masaryk University in the Czech Republic (2003). He has served twice (1983, 2003) as a visiting professor of anthropology in the University of Pittsburgh's Semester at Sea Program, a floating university that travels around the world. He has conducted research for extended periods of time in Kenya and Swaziland and has travelled widely throughout many other parts of the world. He has served as a consultant and trainer for such organizations as USAID, the Peace Corps, the World Bank, IBM, G.E. Plastics, and Georgia Pacific, among others. From 1996 to 2000 he served as the Director of the Intercultural Training Institute at UNC–Charlotte, a consortium of cross-cultural trainers and educators from academia, government, and business, designed to help regional organizations cope with cultural differences at home and abroad. He is the author of

The Two Worlds of Kamau (1978)
The Cultural Dimension of International Business (1990, 1994, 1998, 2002, 2006, 2010, and 2013 with co-author, Elizabeth K Briody)
Anthropology: An Applied Perspective (1994)
Applying Cultural Anthropology: Readings (1998)
Global Brains: Knowledge and Competencies for the Twenty-First Century (2002)
Classic Readings in Cultural Anthropology (2004, 2009, 2012)

Susan Andreatta, Professor of Anthropology at the University of North Carolina–Greensboro, received her B.A. in anthropology and Spanish at the University of Delaware, her M.A. in anthropology from Iowa State University, and her Ph.D. in anthropology from Michigan State University. Andreatta also did a two-year post-doc in England at the University of Hull. During the past 25 years she has conducted fieldwork in Costa Rica, Jamaica, St. Vincent, Barbados, Antigua, Dominica, Mexico, Uganda, China, Peru, and North Carolina. Her theoretical orientation lies in political economy and political ecology as applied to the environment and health. Since 1985 she has participated in a wide range of applied projects, including those that focused on tourism, migration and resettlement, health and nutrition, agriculture, agroforestry, fishing, and marketing of fresh local produce and seafood. Her interests in small family farms, rural communities, fishing communities, and their transformation or resistance to the expansion of agribusiness and the globalization of agriculture have enabled her to work both overseas and domestically. In addition, she has been examining traditional and Western approaches to healthcare in changing economic and political systems. Her work has been published in *Human Organization; Culture and Agriculture; Southern Rural Sociology; Urban Anthropology;* and *Home Health Care Management & Practice.* Andreatta is the Director of Project Greenleaf at University of North Carolina–Greensboro, a project she started in 2001 that provides undergraduate students with hands-on, applied research experiences. She is a past board member and former secretary for the Society for Applied Anthropology (SfAA) as well as a past president of the Society for Applied Anthropology (2007–2009).

Courtesy of Chris Holdsworth

Chris Holdsworth, Senior Instructor of Anthropology at the University of Calgary, received his B.Sc. and M.A. in physical anthropology from the University of Toronto, and his D.Phil. in social and cultural anthropology at the University of Oxford, England. After receiving his M.A., a summer job as a dealer, pit boss, and then assistant casino manager in Canada's first casino in the Yukon Territory, led him on a career path in Canada's fledgling gaming industry. He spent two years as a professional poker player before becoming a gaming consultant, a casino manager, and finally a regulator working with British Columbia's Solicitor General's office to draft the operating procedures and financial controls presently used in all casinos in British Columbia. He then returned to academia and after receiving his D.Phil. for a thesis on the history and philosophy of anthropology, he taught at Goldsmith's College, University of London. When he returned to Canada he was hired as a product manager for a software development company in Calgary on the basis of his knowledge of anthropology, which he applied on a daily basis for several years. He also began teaching marketing research and consumer behaviour as a sessional for the University of Lethbridge, and anthropology for the University of Calgary, where he now devotes his time to teaching. In addition to teaching Introduction to Social and Cultural Anthropology, he also teaches courses in Business Anthropology, Economic Anthropology, the History of Anthropology, Language and Communication, Anthropology of Religion, and Contemporary Indigenous Issues in Canada. His four 20-something children keep him young and help him understand his students.

Inuit elder in traditional clothing works on a soapstone carving in Kimmirut, Baffin Island, Nunavut, Canada.

CHAPTER

1

Anthropology in a Global World

WHAT WE WILL LEARN

- **How anthropology differs from other social and behavioural sciences**
- **What the four-field approach to the discipline of anthropology is**
- **What anthropologists mean by *holism***
- **What is meant by *cultural relativism*, and why it is important**
- **The difference between the *emic* and *etic* approaches**
- **The skills students develop from the study of anthropology**
- **How anthropology can help solve social problems**

A LETTER TO STUDENTS

Greetings! Welcome to the first Canadian edition of *Cultural Anthropology: An Applied Perspective.*

We are proud of this textbook and the difference we believe it will make in your lives. While all introductory textbooks in cultural anthropology are designed to introduce the reader to the content of cultural anthropology, this textbook, with its "Applied Perspective," goes beyond the content of the discipline by showing you how the research findings, theories, methods, and insights of cultural anthropology can be useful in your everyday personal and professional lives.

The study of cultural anthropology is, in other words, far more than the study of the similarities and differences among the thousands of cultures in today's interconnected world; it is far more relevant. The *applied orientation* of this book illustrates (through distinct examples and scenarios) how an understanding of the concepts, theories, and methods of anthropology, as well as the ways people from different cultures, both at home and abroad, think and act helps us in our daily and professional lives by enabling us to interact with people more effectively. Conversely, when we fail to take our cultural environments seriously, we are likely to commit some serious cultural faux pas.

The book's applied orientation is woven into each chapter through three unique features: chapter-opening, real-world scenarios, Applied Perspective features, and Cross-Cultural Miscues. First, an introductory mini case study that is actual, and not hypothetical, begins each chapter and illustrates why it is important to understand the basic concepts in the chapter. The second feature that highlights applied anthropology is the Applied Perspective boxes. These are longer case studies that are based on real anthropological research, and demonstrate how cultural anthropology has been used to solve specific societal problems in such work-related areas as medicine, government, architecture, education, economic development, and business. Finally, the Cross-Cultural Miscues, which appear in each chapter, illustrate the negative consequences of failing to appreciate cultural differences in one's everyday interactions.

This book has a twofold purpose: to introduce you to the basic field of cultural anthropology, and to demonstrate how cross-cultural awareness is extraordinarily relevant in today's highly interconnected world. We also want to alert you to several important features of each chapter that should be taken seriously, as they remind us of the relevance of cultural knowledge to our everyday lives. It is these highly relevant scenarios and examples that you should cite to your parents and friends

who never fail to ask the question, Why are you taking (or worse yet, majoring in) cultural anthropology? Because we all play out our lives in a cultural context and to an increasing degree in a multicultural or cross-cultural context, an understanding of cultural anthropology is extremely important for understanding the behaviour of others, and this can be of value in whatever line of work we might pursue.

We trust that you will find reading about living and working in other cultures, or about anthropology and new product research in the developing world, interesting and thought provoking as you learn about the real impact culture has on your everyday life. ■

What Is Anthropology?

When most Canadians hear the word *anthropologist*, a number of images come to mind. They picture, for example:

- Jane Goodall devoting years of her life to making systematic observations of chimpanzees in their natural environment in Gombe Stream National Park, Tanzania;
- A field anthropologist interviewing exotic tribespeople about their kinship system;
- The excavation of a jawbone that will be used to demonstrate the evolutionary link between early and modern humans;
- A linguist meticulously recording the words and sounds of a First Nation elder speaking a language that has never been written down;
- A cultural anthropologist studying the homeless in Vancouver's lower east side; or
- A team of archaeologists in pith helmets unearthing an ancient temple from a rainforest in Guatemala.

Each of these impressions, to one degree or another, accurately represents the concerns of scientists who call themselves anthropologists. Anthropologists do travel to different parts of the world to study little-known cultures (cultural anthropologists) and languages (anthropological linguists), but they also study subcultural groups within their own cultures. Anthropologists also unearth fossil remains (physical or biological anthropologists) and various artifacts (archaeologists) of individuals who lived thousands and, in some cases, millions of years ago. Even though anthropologists in these subspecialties engage in substantially different types of activities and generate different types of data, they are all directed toward a single purpose: the scientific study of humans, both biologically and culturally, in whatever form, time period, or region of the world they might be found.

Anthropology—derived from the Greek words *anthropos* for human and *logos* for study—is, if we take it literally, the study of humans. To the extent that anthropology raises a wide variety of questions about the human condition, this is an accurate description. And yet this literal definition is not particularly illuminating as a number of other academic disciplines (including sociology, biology, psychology, political science, economics, and history) also study human beings. What is it that distinguishes anthropology from all these other disciplines?

Anthropology is the study of people, their origins, their development, and their contemporary variations. Of all the disciplines that study humans, anthropology is by far the broadest in scope. Anthropology's subject matter includes fossilized skeletal remains of early humans, artifacts and other material remains from prehistoric, pre-contact, and historic archaeological sites, and all the contemporary and historical cultures of the world. The task anthropology has set itself is enormous. Anthropologists strive to understand the biological and cultural origins and evolutionary development of the species. They are concerned with all humans, both past and present, as well as their behaviour patterns, thought systems, and material possessions. In short, anthropology aims to describe, in the broadest sense, what it means to be human (Peacock 1986).

In their search to understand the human condition, anthropologists, drawing on a wide variety of data and methods, have created a diverse field of study. Many specialists in the field of anthropology often engage in research that is directly relevant to other fields. It has been suggested (Wolf 1964) that anthropology spans the gap between the humanities, the social sciences, and the natural sciences. To illustrate, anthropological investigations of Indigenous art, folklore, values, and supernatural belief systems are primarily humanistic in nature; studies of social stratification, comparative political systems, and means of distribution are common themes in sociology, political science, and economics, respectively; and studies of comparative anatomy and radiocarbon dating are central to the natural sciences of biology and chemistry.

The global scope of anthropological studies has increased over the past century. In the early 1900s, anthropologists concentrated on non-Western, preliterate, and technologically simple societies, and were content to leave the study of Western industrial societies to other disciplines such as sociology and economics. In recent decades, however, anthropologists have devoted increasing attention to cultural and subcultural groups in industrialized areas. It is not uncommon for anthropologists today to apply their field methods to the study of the Hutterites of Alberta or multinational corporations in China, or to understanding the impact of a proposed pipeline on First Nations communities in British Columbia. In particular, anthropologists are more and more concerned with how cultures throughout the world are adapting in response to environmental change and to the forces of globalization.

Traditionally, the discipline of anthropology is divided into four distinct branches, or subfields: *physical or biological anthropology*, which deals with humans as biological organisms; *archaeology*, which attempts to reconstruct the cultures of the past, most of which have left no written records; *anthropological linguistics*, which focuses on the study of language in historical, structural, and social contexts; and *cultural anthropology*, which examines similarities and differences among contemporary cultures of the world (see Table 1.1). This scheme was developed in the late 19th century by Franz Boas, the founder of American Anthropology. Most anthropology departments in Canada follow this model, although only about one-third offer instruction in all four fields—many lack linguistics—(Darnell 1998).

All four subfields of the discipline engage in both theoretical research and more practical forms of research designed to solve specific societal problems. This more problem-oriented endeavour is itself comprised of two broad streams: ***applied anthropology***, which involves conducting applied research projects designed to generate policy recommendations for addressing societal problems; and ***practice anthropology***, which involves using already existing anthropological data, methods, theories, and insights on a daily basis. The American Anthropological Association estimates that, today, more than half of all anthropologists work outside academia, practicing anthropology as a profession (Bennett et al. 2006). Such "practice" anthropologists are employed by government as well as by non-government agencies (NGOs), private businesses, research institutions, community and service organizations, and others; many also work as independent consultants. Such anthropologists use their knowledge and skills to develop programs, provide services, inform policies, and assess needs in a host of areas. Many anthropologists argue that applied anthropology should be considered a fifth subfield, but applying anthropological methods, theory, and knowledge is an important aspect of all four branches.

Despite this four-field division, the discipline of anthropology has a long-standing tradition of emphasizing the interrelations among these four subfields. In recent years there has been considerable blurring of the boundaries among the four branches. For example, the specialized area known as medical anthropology draws heavily from both biological and cultural anthropology; educational anthropology addresses issues that bridge the gap between cultural anthropology and linguistics; and sociobiology looks at the interaction between culture and biology. Although cultural anthropology is the central focus of this textbook, a brief discussion of all four branches will provide an adequate description of the discipline as a whole.

applied anthropology The application of anthropological knowledge, concepts, theories, and methods to the solution of specific societal problems.

practice anthropology The use of existing anthropological data, methods, theories, and insights on a daily basis.

TABLE 1.1

Branches of Anthropology

Physical or Biological Anthropology	Archaeology	Anthropological Linguistics	Cultural Anthropology
Paleoanthropology	Historical archaeology	Historical linguistics	Development anthropology
Evolutionary psychology	Prehistoric and pre-contact archaeology	Descriptive linguistics	Psychological anthropology
Human variation	Contract archaeology	Ethnolinguistics	Environmental anthropology
Primatology	Applied archaeology	Sociolinguistics	Medical anthropology
Applied physical anthropology Forensic anthropology Medical anthropology	Cultural resource management	Applied linguistics	Urban anthropology Political anthropology Applied anthropology Business anthropology

Physical or Biological Anthropology

The study of humans from a biological perspective is called ***physical* or *biological anthropology***. Essentially, biological anthropologists are concerned with three broad areas of investigation. First, they are interested in reconstructing the evolutionary record of the human species; that is, they ask questions about the emergence of humans and how we have evolved, both physically and cognitively. This area of biological anthropology is known as ***paleoanthropology***. The second area of concern to biological anthropologists is known as primatology; it focuses on our nearest living relatives, namely apes, monkeys, and prosimians. And the third area, known as human variation, studies how and why the physical traits of human populations vary throughout the world. Unlike comparative biologists, physical anthropologists also study how culture and environment have influenced biological evolution and contemporary variations.

Evolutionary Record of Humans

In their attempts to reconstruct human evolution, paleoanthropologists draw heavily on fossil remains of humans, protohumans, and other primates. Once these fossil remains have been unearthed, the difficult job of comparison, analysis, and interpretation begins. To which species do the remains belong? Are the remains human or those of our prehuman ancestors? If not human, what do the remains tell us about our own species? When did these primates live? How did they adapt to their environment? To answer these questions, paleoanthropologists use the techniques of comparative anatomy, comparing such physical features as cranial capacity, teeth, hands, position of the pelvis, and the shape of the head of the fossil remains with those of humans or other nonhuman primates. Paleoanthropologists also look for signs of culture (such as tools) to help determine the humanity of the fossil remains. For example, if fossil remains are found in association with tools, and if it can be determined that the tools were made by these creatures, then it is likely that the remains will be considered human. A more recent area of concern is evolutionary psychology. Evolutionary psychologists are interested in how human emotional and cognitive capacities evolved as psychological adaptations to ancestral environments.

To fill in the human evolutionary record, biological anthropologists draw on the work of a number of other specialists: paleontologists (who specialize in prehistoric plant and animal life), archaeologists (who study prehistoric and pre-contact material culture), and geologists (who provide data on local physical and climatic conditions).

In addition to reconstructing the human evolutionary record, paleoanthropology has led to various applications of biological anthropology. For example, forensic anthropologists for years have used traditional methods and theories from biological anthropology to help identify the remains of crime and disaster victims. Forensic anthropologists can determine from skeletal remains the age, sex, and stature of the deceased, as well as other traits such as physical abnormalities, traumas (such as broken bones), nutritional history, and evidence of foul play. In 1984 Canadian forensic anthropologist Owen Beattie demonstrated that members of Sir John Franklin's ill-fated 1845 Arctic expedition not only resorted to cannibalism, corroborating Inuit accounts, but also that their judgment may have been impaired due to lead poisoning from their tinned foods (Beattie and Geiger 1988).

Beattie also helped identify victims of the 1994 genocide in Rwanda. In recent years, forensic anthropologists have been called on to testify in murder trials. Between 2002 and 2003, University of Toronto's Tracy Rogers led a team of 25 forensic anthropologists, many of whom were senior undergraduate and postgraduate students, to help identify the skeletal remains and badly decomposed bodies of up to 65 missing women on serial killer Robert Pickton's pig farm in Port Coquitlam, British Columbia (Cameron 2011). See Figure 1.1.

Some applied forensic anthropologists have headed international teams to study the physical remains

University of Toronto Mississauga/Photo by Stephen Uhranoy

FIGURE 1.1 Students in the University of Toronto's Forensic Anthropology Field School, taught by Dr. Tracy Rogers and GIS/Data Librarian Andrew Nicholson, collect crime-scene data taken from a fictional crime scene on the U of T Mississauga campus.

physical or biological anthropology The subfield of anthropology that studies human biological evolution, primates, and contemporary physical variations among peoples of the world.

paleoanthropology The study of human evolution through fossil remains.

of victims of mass human rights abuses and other disasters. For example, forensic anthropologists have worked to identify the remains of victims of Slobodan Milosevic's ethnic cleansing programs in Bosnia and Kosovo during the 1990s, the attack on the World Trade Center on September 11, 2001, and the tragic Lac-Mégantic derailment in Quebec in 2013.

Primatology

Primatologists study the anatomy and social behaviour of such nonhuman primate species as gorillas, baboons, and chimpanzees in their natural habitats (Figure 1.2) in an effort to gain clues about our own evolution as a species. Biological anthropologists do not have the luxury of observing the behaviour of human ancestors from several million years ago; however, by studying contemporary nonhuman primates in similar environments, they can learn how early humans could have responded to certain environmental conditions and changes in their developmental past. For example, the simple yet real division of labour among baboon troops can shed light on role specialization and social stratification in early human societies; and the rudimentary tool-making skills found among chimpanzees in Tanzania may help explain early human strategies for adapting to the environment.

Sometimes the study of *primatology* leads to findings that are both startling and eminently practical. While studying chimps in their natural habitat in Tanzania, primatologist Richard Wrangham noticed that young chimps occasionally ate the leaves of plants that were not part of their normal diet. Because the chimps swallowed the leaves whole, Wrangham concluded that they were not ingesting these leaves primarily for nutritional purposes. Chemical analysis of the leaves by pharmacologist Eloy Rodriquez indicated that the plant contains substantial amounts of the chemical compound thiarubrine A, which has strong antibiotic properties. Wrangham concluded that the chimps were medicating themselves, perhaps to control internal parasites. Seeing the potential for treating human illnesses, Rodriquez and Wrangham applied for a patent. They use part of the proceeds from their new drug to help preserve the chimpanzee habitat in Tanzania. In Wrangham's words, "I like the idea of chimps showing us the medicine and then helping them to pay for their own conservation" (quoted in Howard 1991).

Orangutan Foundation International (OFI)

FIGURE 1.2 **World-renowned Canadian primatologist Biruté Galdikas holds an orphaned adolescent orangutan at the Orangutan International Foundation in Borneo, Indonesia. Galdikas established the centre as a refuge for orphaned orangutans in 1971. The 2011, 3D IMAX film Born to Be Wild chronicles her continuing work with orangutans in the rainforest.**

Physical Variation among Humans

Although all humans are members of the same species considerable physical variation exists among human populations. Some of these differences are based on visible physical traits, such as the shape of the nose, body stature, and skin colour. Other variations are based on less visible biochemical factors, such as blood type and susceptibility to disease.

For the first half of the 20th century, biological anthropologists attempted to document human physical variation by dividing the world's populations into various racial categories. A *race* was defined as a group of people who shared a greater statistical frequency of genes and physical traits with one another than they did with people outside the group. Today, however, no anthropologists subscribe to the notion that races are fixed biological entities whose members all share the same physical features, and most do not consider racial categories to be particularly useful. Today, we know that the amount of genetic variation is much greater within racial groups than between racial groups. In other words, human biological races do not exist. Anthropologists now view race as a social construct whereby people who share similar physical characteristics, especially skin colour, are deemed to belong to a particular category of people. (For more on race and racism, see Chapter 12.)

Although contemporary anthropologists continue to be interested in human physical variation, they have turned their attention to examining how

primatology The study of nonhuman primates in their natural environments for the purpose of gaining insights into the human evolutionary process.

race A social construct whereby people who share similar physical characteristics, especially skin colour, are deemed to belong to a particular category of people.

human physical variations help people adapt to their environment. Biological anthropologists have found that populations with the greatest amount of melanin in their skin are found in tropical regions, whereas lighter-skinned populations generally reside in more northern latitudes. This suggests that natural selection has favoured darker skin in tropical areas because it protects people from dangerous ultraviolet light. In colder climates, people tend to have considerable body mass (less body surface), which is a natural protection from the deadly cold. And sickle cells, found widely in the blood of people living in sub-Saharan Africa, protect people against the ravages of malaria. These three examples illustrate how physical variations can help people adapt to their natural environments. In their investigations of how human biological variations influence adaptation, biological anthropologists draw on the work of three allied disciplines: *genetics* (the study of inherited physical traits), *population biology* (the study of the interrelationships between population characteristics and environments), and *epidemiology* (the study of the causes, occurrence, distribution, transmission, and control of disease in populations over time).

Archaeology

Experts in the field of *archaeology* study the lifeways of people from the past by excavating and analyzing the material culture they have left behind. The purpose of archaeology is to understand cultural adaptations of ancient peoples by at least partially reconstructing their cultures. Because archaeologists concentrate on societies of the past, they are limited to working with material culture including, in some cases, written records. From these material remains, however, archaeologists are able to infer many nonmaterial cultural aspects (ideas and behaviour patterns) held by people thousands, and in some cases millions of years ago.

Archaeologists work with three types of material remains: artifacts, features, and ecofacts. *Artifacts* are objects that have been made or modified by humans and that can be removed from the site and taken to the laboratory for further analysis. Tools, arrowheads, and fragments of pottery are examples of artifacts. *Features*, like artifacts, are made or modified by people, but they cannot be readily carried away from the dig site. One interesting example of an archaeological feature is the fossilized footprints believed to be of a man, woman, and child, along with the remains of an ancient campfire discovered on Calvert Island in British Columbia in 2014. Believed to be more than 13 000 years old, they demonstrate that there is a very long history of human occupation on Canada's west coast (Meissner 2015). Archaeological features include such things as house foundations, fireplaces, postholes, and culturally modified trees. Archaeology graduate student Karen Church, for example, uses remote sensing, geographic information systems (GIS), historical maps, and ethnographic research to explore the ancient trails and other inland archaeological sites of Haida Gwaii. The results of her research are shared with the Haida community and help to better understand the pre-contact lifeway of a Northwest Coast rainforest (Figure 1.3). *Ecofacts* are objects found in the natural environment (such as bones, seeds, and wood) that were not made or altered by humans, but were used by them. Ecofacts provide archaeologists with important data concerning the environment and how people used natural resources.

Courtesy of Karen Church/Photo by James Stanley

FIGURE 1.3 Archaeology graduate student Karen Church examines a culturally modified tree (CMT) on Haida Gwaii, British Columbia. Large Western red cedar trees such as this one were tested to see if they were good candidates for dugout canoes. Other CMT types acted as trail markers in inland areas, planks, house posts, baskets, and even as a source of food and medicine.

genetics The study of inherited physical traits.

population biology The study of the interrelationships between population characteristics and environments.

epidemiology The study of the causes, occurrence, distribution, transmission, and control of disease in populations.

archaeology The subfield of anthropology that focuses on the study of prehistoric, pre-contact, and historic cultures through the excavation of material remains.

artifact A type of material remains made or modified by humans, such as tools and arrowheads.

features Archaeological remains made or modified by people, and that cannot easily be carried away, such as house foundations, fireplaces, postholes, and culturally modified trees.

ecofacts Physical remains that were used by humans, but were not made or reworked by them (e.g., seeds and bones).

Since the overwhelming majority of material possessions do not survive thousands of years under the ground, archaeologists search for fragments of material evidence (such items as projectile points, hearths, beads, and postholes) that will enable them to piece together a culture. A pre-contact garbage dump is particularly revealing because the archaeologist can learn a great deal about how people lived from what they threw away. These material remains are then used to make inferences about the nonmaterial aspects of the culture (i.e., values, ideas, and behaviours) being studied.

By studying the bits and pieces of material culture left behind, within the context of both environmental data and anatomical remains, the archaeologist seeks to determine such things as how the people supported themselves, whether they had a notion of an afterlife, how roles were allocated between men and women, whether some people were more powerful than others, whether the people engaged in trade with neighbouring peoples, and how lifestyles have changed over time.

FIGURE 1.4 Dredge No. 4, owned by the Yukon Consolidated Gold Corporation, dredged for gold on Bonanza and Hunker Creeks in the Yukon Territory between 1913 and 1959. Seasonal flooding, the ravages of weather, and tourists were gradually destroying it until it was restored, stabilized, and made a national historic site in 1997.

Present-day archaeologists work with both historic, prehistoric, and pre-contact cultures. Historic archaeologists help to reconstruct the cultures of people who used writing, and about whom historical documents have been written. Prehistoric archaeology, on the other hand, deals with the vast segment of the human record (several million years) that predates the advent of writing (about 5500 years ago). Pre-contact archaeology can be considered a branch of prehistoric archaeology in that it examines cultures—mostly those in the Americas—before contact with Europeans. It must be remembered, however, that some of these cultures, such as the Mayans, Aztecs, and Incas, did have writing systems. Most Canadian archaeologists deal with pre-contact cultures.

Prehistoric and pre-contact archaeologies have consequently provided us with a much longer time frame than has written history for understanding the record of human development.

The relevance of studying ancient artifacts often goes beyond helping us to better understand the prehistoric and pre-contact past. In some cases, the study of stone tools can lead to improvements in our own modern technology. To illustrate, while experimentally replicating the manufacture of stone tools, archaeologist Don Crabtree found that obsidian from the western part of the United States can be chipped to a sharp edge. When examined under an electron microscope, the cutting edge of obsidian was found to be 200 times sharper than modern surgical scalpels. Some surgeons now use obsidian scalpels because healing is faster and scarring is reduced (Sheets 1993).

Another area of applied archaeology is called ***cultural resource management***. Cultural resource management (CRM) deals with the protection and management of archaeological and historical cultural heritage resources, such as landmarks, historic buildings, artefacts, and archaeological sites (Figure 1.4). A host of international, national, provincial, and even municipal laws protect these resources from being destroyed by any project, such as the construction of highways, pipelines, and office buildings, by requiring archaeological research to be conducted before construction starts. In response to these laws, archaeologists developed the specialty of cultural resource management (also known as *public archaeology* or *contract archaeology*). Cultural resource management has grown so rapidly in recent years that, today, about half of all professionally trained archaeologists work in this field.

Although, archaeology focuses typically on pre-contact and historic peoples, some archaeologists use their techniques to study contemporary societies by studying what they throw away. For example, researchers with the Garbage Project, started by American "garbologist" William Rathje in 1973, excavated landfills (including the Toronto dump) and sorted, weighed, recorded, and analyzed what they found. Like an archaeological excavation of an ancient civilization, garbology can tell the stories of cultures that no longer exist (Harrison 2012).

The results have indicated that we know little about what ends up in our landfills, or their fate underground, and this has important implications

---

cultural resource management A form of applied archaeology that involves identifying, evaluating, and sometimes excavating sites before roads, dams, pipelines, and buildings are constructed.

for urban planners in charge of solid waste facilities. Moreover, this research supported the notion that there is always some discrepancy between what people say they do and what they actually do. When surveyed by questionnaire, 15 percent of Rathje's interviewees claimed to be beer drinkers. Yet analysis of the garbage of these same people revealed that approximately 80 percent of the households consumed beer. This sizeable discrepancy (533 percent) between real and reported behaviour is useful to sociologists, medical anthropologists, and public health officials who need to address issues of health and dietary patterns.

Anthropological Linguistics

The branch of the discipline that studies human speech and language is called *anthropological linguistics*. Although we are not the only species that has systems of symbolic communication, ours is by far the most complex form. In fact, some would argue that language is the most distinctive feature of being human because, without language, we could not acquire and transmit our culture from one generation to the next.

anthropological linguistics The scientific study of human communication within its socio-cultural context.

historical linguistics The study of how languages change over time.

descriptive linguistics The branch of anthropological linguistics that studies how languages are structured.

ethnolinguistics The study of the relationship between language and culture, and how language influences how people perceive and experience the world.

Linguistic anthropology, which studies contemporary human languages as well as those of the past, is divided into four branches: historical linguistics, descriptive linguistics, ethnolinguistics, and sociolinguistics.

Historical linguistics deals with the emergence of language in general, and how languages have diverged over time. By comparing contemporary languages, linguists have been able to identify certain language families and can approximate when two related languages began to diverge from each other. Some of the earliest anthropological interest in language focused on the historical connections between languages. For example, 19th century historical linguists discovered many similarities between most European languages and Sanskrit, one of the official languages of India, and postulated that they all derived from a common source language called proto-Indo-European. You can see some of these similarities in the names for the numbers (Table 1.2).

Today, historical linguistic techniques are used in conjunction with archaeological and biological evidence (e.g., DNA). As an example, Cecil Brown (2006) established the pre-contact linguistic chronology of the common bean in the New World, which both complemented and supplemented archaeological dating techniques.

Descriptive linguistics is the study of sound systems, grammatical systems, and the meanings attached to words in specific languages. Every culture has a distinctive language with its own logical structure and set of rules for putting words and sounds together for the purpose of communicating. In its simplest form, the task of the descriptive linguist is to compile dictionaries and grammar books for previously unwritten languages.

Ethnolinguistics (also known as cultural linguistics) is the branch of anthropological linguistics that examines

TABLE 1.2

The Numbers One to Ten, Plus 100, in Several Indo-European Languages

English	French	German	Latin	Greek	Sanskrit
one	un	eins	ūnus	ena	éka
two	deux	zwei	duo	dio	dvi
three	trois	drei	trēs	tria	trí
four	quatre	vier	quattuor	tesserae	catúr
five	cinq	fünf	quīnque	pente	pañca
six	six	sechs	sex	exi	ṢáṢ
seven	sept	sieben	septem	epta	saptá
eight	huit	acht	octō	octo	aṢṭá
nine	neuf	neun	novem	ennea	náva
ten	dix	zehn	decem	deka	dasa
hundred	cent	hundert	centum	ekato	sata

the relationship between language and culture. In any language, certain cultural aspects that are emphasized (such as types of snow among the Inuit, cows among the pastoral Maasai, or automobiles in North American culture) are reflected in the vocabulary. Moreover, ethnolinguists explore how different linguistic categories can affect how people categorize their experiences, how they think, and how they perceive the world around them. These ideas will be explored in greater detail in Chapter 6.

Sociolinguistics examines the relationship between language and social relations. For example, sociolinguists are interested in investigating how social class, age, gender, and ethnicity influence the choice of words a person speaks, and how people use different forms of a language, depending on the social situation they find themselves in at any given time. For example, conversation between a Canadian university student and a classmate is more likely to be more casual and relaxed than with a professor, grandparent, or a potential employer during a job interview.

Anthropological linguists also engage in applied activities. After describing the structure of a language, descriptive linguists frequently take the next logical step and work with educators to plan effective strategies for teaching English as a second language. Some anthropological linguists serve as consultants to government and educational leaders responsible for setting language policy in a state or country.

Anthropological linguists also work with First Nations people whose languages are spoken by so few people that they are in danger of becoming extinct. Still other applied linguists help design foreign language and culture programs for people who are preparing to live and work abroad. Moreover, linguists such as Deborah Tannen (see Chapter 6) apply their knowledge of gender differences in language to help men and women better understand one another.

Because languages are constantly changing, anthropological linguists also document these changes to show how they reflect changes in a culture as a whole. In recent years anthropological linguists have expanded their research interests to include television advertising, linguistic aspects of popular culture, computer and Internet jargon, and text messaging.

Cultural Anthropology

The branch of anthropology that studies specific contemporary cultures (***ethnography***) and the more general underlying patterns of human culture derived through cultural comparisons (***ethnology***) is called ***cultural anthropology***. Before cultural anthropologists can examine cultural differences and similarities throughout the world, they must first describe the features of cultures in as much detail as possible. These detailed descriptions (ethnographies) are the result of extensive field studies (usually a year or two in duration) in which the anthropologist observes, talks to, and lives with the people he or she is studying.

Anthropologists can obviously not do this alone and require the assistance of local people, who are not only observed and interviewed, but also help the anthropologist learn the language and the proper ways to behave, and also provide information and explanations about what is going on. These people were originally called informants. More recently, however, anthropologists have come to recognize that the production of the ethnography is much more of a collaborative effort, and so they are now often referred to as collaborators, consultants, teachers, or some other term that reflects the nature of the relationship between the anthropologist and the people they work with. Anthropologists have also become much more aware of the fact that the people they study are very cognizant of what is going on in their culture and that they have agency; in the past they were viewed as passive recipients of their own culture. In addition, anthropologists today are much more aware of how their personal social situation and personal experiences influences their research and writing.

The writing of large numbers of ethnographies has provided an empirical basis for the comparative study of cultures. In the process of developing these descriptive accounts, cultural anthropologists provide insights into such questions as, How are the marriage customs of a group of people related to the group's economy? What effect does urban migration have on the kinship system? In what ways have supernatural beliefs helped a group of people adapt more effectively to their environment? Thus, while describing the essential features of a culture, the cultural anthropologist might also explain why certain cultural patterns exist, and how they may be related to one another.

Ethnology is the comparative study of contemporary cultures, wherever they may be found. Ethnologists seek to understand why people differ in both terms of

---

sociolinguistics The study of how language is used in different social contexts.

ethnography The anthropological description of a particular contemporary culture by means of direct fieldwork.

ethnology The comparative study of cultural differences and similarities.

cultural anthropology The branch of anthropology that studies specific contemporary cultures and the more general underlying patterns of human culture derived through cultural comparisons.

ideas and behaviour patterns, and what all cultures have in common with one another. The primary objective of ethnology is to uncover general cultural principles, that is, the "rules" that govern human behaviour. Because all humans have culture and live in groups, there are no populations in the world today that are not viable subjects for the ethnologist. The lives of contemporary Inuit living in the Arctic, Greek peasants, Maasai herdsmen in Tanzania, and slot machine players in Las Vegas have all been studied by cultural anthropologists.

Ethnographers and ethnologists face a daunting task in that they describe and compare the many peoples of the world today. A small number of cultural anthropologists must deal with enormous cultural diversity, numerous features of culture that can be compared, and a wide range of theoretical frameworks for comparing them. To describe even the least complex cultures requires many months of interviewing people and observing their behaviour. Even with this large expenditure of time, rarely do contemporary ethnographers describe total cultures. Instead, they usually investigate a particular aspect or problem in greater depth.

Anthropologists also realize that cultures in today's globalized world do not exist as isolated entities, but are very much interconnected and influence one another. Moreover, societies are comprised of numerous groups, each with their own *subculture*. To understand these subcultures, ethnographers must explore their relationship to the larger dominant culture. Cultures also undergo continual change, and much of contemporary ethnography looks at the forces of change, the impact these forces have on cultures, and how people deal with them.

Areas of Specialization

In recent decades cultural anthropologists have tended to specialize, often identifying themselves with one or more of these five areas of specialization:

1. *Urban anthropology* Since World War II, anthropologists in greater numbers have turned their attention to the study of people in more complex urban social systems. With increasing rural-to-urban migration in many parts of the world, it is becoming more difficult to think of rural populations as isolated, insulated entities. Cultural anthropologists assess the impacts cities have on traditional rural societies, and follow rural people into the cities to see how the two systems interact.

   By focusing on how factors such as size, density, and heterogeneity affect customary ways of behaving, urban anthropologists have, in recent decades, examined such important topics as descriptive accounts of ethnic neighbourhoods, rural-urban linkages, labour migration, urban kinship patterns, social network analysis, emerging systems of urban stratification, squatter settlements, and informal economies. Urban anthropology has also focused on social problems such as homelessness, race relations, poverty, social justice, unemployment, crime, and public health. Some recent studies have described the modern urban subcultures of truck drivers, cocktail waitresses, street gangs, drug addicts, skid-row alcoholics, and prostitutes. Interestingly, few studies have been conducted in the middle-class suburbs, where various forms of social problems are also found.
2. *Medical anthropology* Another area of specialization is medical anthropology, which studies the relationship of biological, environmental, and socio-cultural factors to health, disease, and illness, now and in the past. Medical anthropology includes a variety of perspectives and concerns, ranging from a biological pole at one end of the spectrum to a socio-cultural pole at the other. Medical anthropologists with a more biological focus tend to concentrate on interests such as the role of disease in human evolution, nutrition, growth and development, and *paleopathology* (the analysis of disease in ancient populations). Medical anthropologists with more social or cultural interests focus their studies on *ethnomedicine* (belief systems of ethnic groups about disease, its diagnosis, treatment, and prevention), medical practitioners, and the relationship between traditional and Western medical systems. Contemporary medical anthropology represents both the biological and the socio-cultural approaches, but we should not think of them as separate and autonomous. In practice, theory and data from one approach are often used in the other.

---

subculture A group of people within a larger culture with beliefs and values differing from those of the larger culture.

urban anthropology The study of people in complex urban environments.

medical anthropology The comparative study of the complex relationships between culture, disease, the environment, and biocultural adaptation.

paleopathology The study of disease in prehistoric and pre-contact populations.

ethnomedicine The comparative study of ideas about the causes, diagnosis, treatment, and prevention of disease in different societies.

Medical anthropology, like many other specialty areas, deals with both theoretical and applied questions of research. Because beliefs and practices about medicine, illness, and healing are part of any culture, they deserve the same type of study as other features of culture, such as economics or family patterns. Many medical anthropologists are motivated by the desire to apply theories, methods, and insights to programs designed to improve health services at home and abroad, and to serve as cultural brokers between healthcare professionals and their culturally diverse patients (Figure 1.5).

3. ***Development anthropology*** The aim of most development projects is to alleviate poverty and sustain economic development through improvements in education, health, technology, and agriculture and by providing job training. Although the various institutions, businesses, non-profit organizations, and states administering these projects are well-meaning, many projects fail, often because they work from a Western understanding of problems and solutions. Development anthropologists, on the other hand, use anthropological perspectives and methods, and work within local institutions to understand problems and needs. They are also able to assess the qualitative effects of projects on local communities often ignored by quantitative economic approaches. Many development anthropologists no longer start by asking, "How can I make this large development project successful?" Rather, they ask, "Will this project benefit the target population?" If the answer is yes, then the development anthropologists will likely become involved in various aspects of the project by providing the vital local cultural information needed to make it successful. The criteria for success depend on the benefits for the local populations, such as less poverty, equitable economic growth, environmental protection, and respect for human rights. Increasingly, development anthropologists are becoming more involved in the entire development cycle, which includes project identification, design, budgetary considerations, implementation, and evaluation.
4. ***Environmental or ecological anthropology*** Environmental anthropologists examine how human populations interact with the environment and, by so doing, develop solutions to current and future environmental problems. Environmental anthropologists are concerned with two fundamental questions: What role does the physical environment play in the formation and evolution of cultures? How do specific socio-cultural groups perceive, manage, and modify their environments, particularly in response to changing environmental conditions? Most leading environmental anthropologists have demonstrated repeatedly that culture and environment cannot be treated in isolation because they are so intimately interconnected.

Although contemporary anthropologists are still interested in the relationships between culture and the natural environment per se, they have expanded their research interests to include theories and approaches useful for addressing contemporary problems of environmental degradation. These concerns include, but are not limited to, conflicts over land use, biodiversity conservation, air and water pollution, deforestation, soil erosion, human rights issues, sustainable development, mineral extraction, food security, and the effects of biochemicals on the health of local populations. Often working collaboratively with scholars from many other disciplines, environmental anthropologists assist policy makers and planners by providing valuable insights into the local cultures of the people who are negatively affected by environmental changes.

FIGURE 1.5 Physician and medical anthropologist, Dr. Paul Farmer, examines an AIDS patient at the Partners in Health Hospital in Cange, located in the central plateau of Haiti. For more than two decades, Dr. Farmer has been working with the Haitian people on a successful treatment program for infectious diseases such as tuberculosis and AIDS.

development anthropology The application of anthropological knowledge, theory, perspectives, and methods in projects that improve the well-being of people in marginalized communities.

environmental or ecological anthropology The study of how human populations interact with the environment, and the use of anthropological knowledge and methods to find solutions to human-environmental problems.

Randy Risling/Toronto Star via Getty Images

FIGURE 1.6 **Some applied anthropologists conduct research in multiethnic classrooms such as this music classroom in Vancouver, British Columbia. Their findings enable teachers to better understand the cultural backgrounds of their students.**

CROSS-CULTURAL MISCUE

In April 2009 a seven-year-old First Nations boy at the McKellar Park school in Thunder Bay was having difficulty reading in a computer lab because his long bangs were getting in the way. Seeing this, a teaching assistant took him into the hall, put him on a chair, and with scissors in hand trimmed 10 cm of his hair at the front. The boy normally kept his hair tucked behind his ears and wore it long as a cultural practice as he participated in Indigenous dancing. When it was cut he was not only understandably upset but also felt ashamed.

While such an incident would have been distressing for any parent it was even more disturbing for the First Nation community of Thunder Bay. The evidence suggests that the teaching assistant's intent in cutting the boy's hair was only to help him see better, but for many First Nation elders it reminded them of one of the most humiliating experiences of Residential School. Forced haircuts were usually the first thing that happened to First Nation boys when they entered Residential School, and was one way the schools fulfilled the national policy at the time of assimilation and civilization. Hair has spiritual significance for many First Nations people, and forcibly cutting it crushes dignity and pride in one's culture and beliefs.

The teaching assistant paid a price for her lack of cultural understanding: she was suspended over the incident, although no assault charges were laid (Brown 2009).

Source: From "Teaching aide suspended over hair cut," By Sarah Elizabeth Brown, *The Chronicle Journal - Thunder Bay*, May 22, 2009.

5. *Psychological anthropology* Psychological anthropology looks at the relationship between culture and the psychological makeup of individuals and groups. Psychological anthropologists examine how culture may affect personality, cognition, attitudes, and emotions, focusing on such problems as symbolism, cognition, and consciousness in specific societies. Statistics are widely used, and psychological anthropologists have collaborated with those from other disciplines, such as psychology and linguistics.

These five areas are only a partial list of the specializations within cultural anthropology. Other specialties include agricultural anthropology, legal anthropology, educational anthropology (Figure 1.6), the anthropology of religion, business anthropology, economic anthropology, political anthropology, the anthropology of tourism, the anthropology of work, and nutritional anthropology.

psychological anthropology The study of the relationship between culture and the psychological makeup of individuals and groups.

Guiding Principles

For the past century, cultural anthropology has distinguished itself from other disciplines in the humanities and social sciences by following several guiding principles. Although other disciplines have adopted some of these major themes over the decades, they remain central to the discipline of cultural anthropology.

Holism

A distinguishing feature of the discipline of anthropology is its holistic approach. This means looking at cultures not simply as a collection of parts, but as wholes. For example, even though this book is divided into chapters on religion, economics, kinship, and so on, we cannot fully understand these aspects of culture without looking at the larger picture, since they are all interrelated. The Indian parable about the blind men and the elephant illustrates this concept well. Six blind men each touch a different part of an elephant,

FIGURE 1.7 The blind men and the elephant.

but because they cannot see the whole elephant they misinterpret what they touch (Figure 1.7).

Anthropological *holism* is evidenced in a number of important ways. First, the anthropological approach involves both biological and socio-cultural aspects of humanity. Second, anthropology has the longest possible time frame, from the earliest beginnings of humans several million years ago to the present. Third, anthropology is holistic to the extent that it studies the culture of people wherever they may be found, from East African pastoralists to Korean factory workers. And finally, anthropologists study many different aspects of human experience, including family structure, marital regulations, house construction, methods of conflict resolution, means of livelihood, religious beliefs, language, space usage, and art.

In the past, cultural anthropologists made every effort to be holistic by covering as many aspects of a culture as possible. More recently, however, the accumulated information from all over the world has become so vast that most anthropologists have needed to become more specialized or focused. This is called a *problem-oriented research approach*. For example, anthropologist Karen Hansen looked at the multibillion dollar second-hand clothing business and how it has impacted African economies. Most of us would be surprised to learn that the clothes we donate to charity are often sold and then exported to countries such as Zambia, where they are not only resold as "luxury goods," but also modified to meet Zambian concepts of fashion (Hansen 2000). Despite the recent trend toward specialization, anthropologists continue to analyze their findings within a wider cultural context. Hansen, for instance, showed how second-hand clothing in Zambia was involved in political, economic, and cultural processes.

Comparative Approach

Cross-cultural comparison is an integral part of the development of anthropological theory. By observing the range of possibilities and seeking patterns of similarities and differences between cultures, anthropologists attempt to understand why these similarities and differences exist. Cross-cultural comparison also helps us understand issues facing many cultures worldwide, such as the impact of globalization, environmental changes, and issues regarding human rights and inequality. Comparison of other cultures with our own, which is often done implicitly, also makes it easier to see aspects of our own culture that we frequently take for granted.

Ethnocentrism

The word *ethnocentrism* comes from the Greek words *ethnos*, which means people or nation, *centr*, which means the centre, and *ismos*, which means doctrine, theory, or practice. Ethnocentrism thus literally means looking at the world from the perspective of one's own culture. This provides a narrow view of the world, and often leads to the belief that one's own ideas and ways of doing things are better than others'.

Examples of ethnocentrism are extensive. Most maps are ethnocentric. The world map most of us are familiar with has England in the centre. This is because many of the first world maps were drawn from the perspective of European, and especially British, explorers. If it had been the Australian Aborigines who had been the first to explore and chart the world, the maps we would be familiar with would be like those in Figure 1.8, and globes would have Antarctica and Australia at the top.

Sometimes our own ethno-centrism can startle us when we find ourselves in a different cultural setting. This feeling of disorientation and anxiety that we feel when immersed in another culture is known as *culture shock*.

Ethnocentrism is pervasive throughout the world because most people are raised in a single culture and never learn about other cultures during their lifetime. It is thus only logical that their own way of life—their values, attitudes, ideas, and ways of behaving—seems to be the most natural, while those of others seems wrong or immoral. For example, traditionally the Berewan of Borneo stored the body of a deceased loved one in a glazed jar in their house. Then, after several months, the secretions of the decomposing corpse were collected, mixed with rice, and consumed. While most of us find this practice disgusting, the Berewan were equally horrified by the North American practice of embalming bodies with preservative fluids and displaying the body in an open coffin. The Berewan believe that when a

---

holism A perspective that attempts to study a culture by looking at all parts of the system and how those parts are interrelated.

ethnocentrism The practice of viewing the cultural features of other societies in terms of one's own.

culture shock The feeling of anxiety and disorientation when experiencing a different culture.

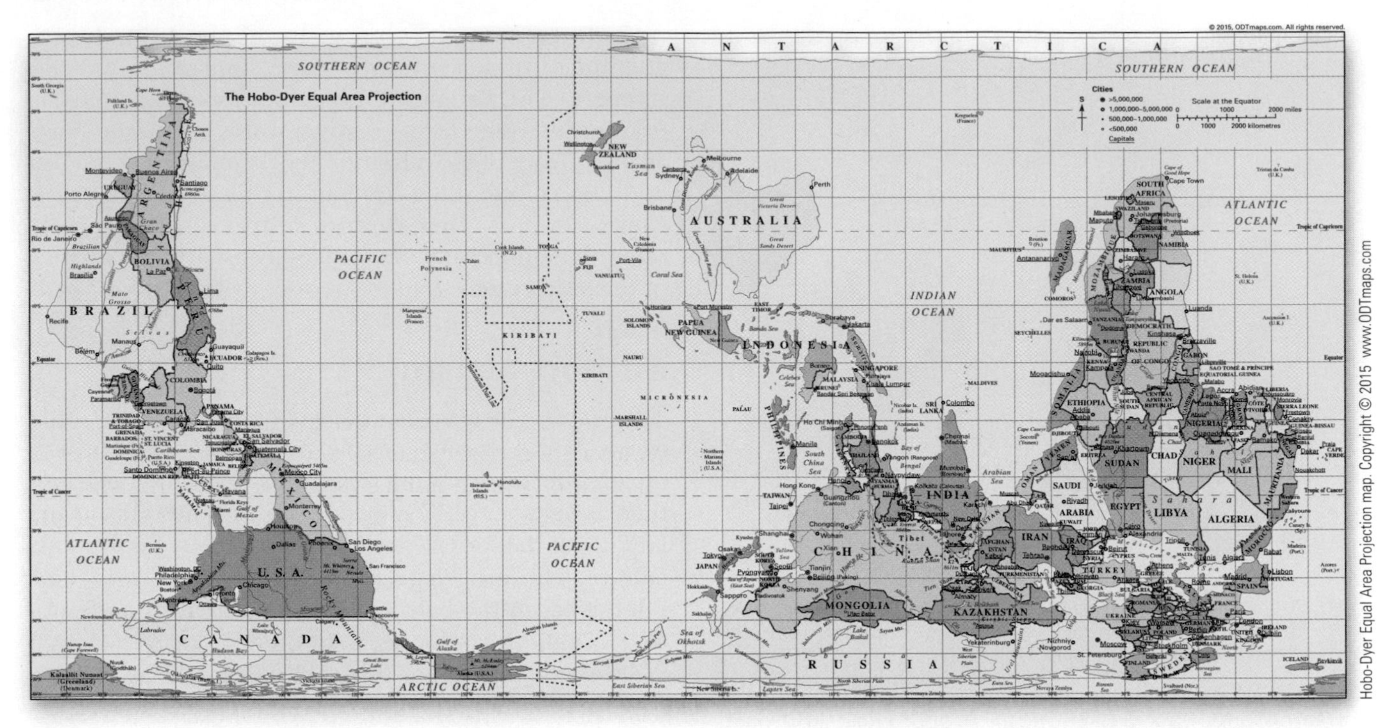

FIGURE 1.8 The Hobo–Dyer equal projection map with Australia at the top presents a different perspective on the world than we are used to.

person dies the soul is divorced from the body, and the process of decay gradually allows the soul to join the ancestors in the land of the dead. Preserving the body, however, delays decomposition and traps the soul of the loved one between the living and the dead, with the potential to reanimate the body (Metcalf 1978).

Our ethnocentrism should not be a source of embarrassment because it is a natural by-product of growing up in any society. In fact, from a functionalist perspective, ethnocentrism may serve the positive societal function of enhancing group solidarity. Ethnocentrism is, however, *the* major obstacle to the understanding of other cultures, which is, after all, a major objective of cultural anthropology. Each of us has a unique perspective on the world stemming from our particular age, gender, class, personal and cultural background, and place in time, and although we cannot eliminate ethnocentrism totally, we can reduce it. By becoming aware of our own ethnocentrism, we can temporarily set aside our own value judgments long enough to learn how other cultures operate.

Cultural Relativism

Anthropologists today recognize a need for dispassionate and objective descriptions of the people they are studying and strive to prevent their own cultural values from colouring the descriptive accounts of the people under study.

Anthropologists try to achieve that level of detachment by practicing ***cultural relativism***. This is the notion that any part of a culture (such as an idea, a thing, or a behaviour pattern) must be viewed and judged in its proper cultural context rather than from the viewpoint of the observer's culture. The cultural relativist asks, How does a cultural item fit into the rest of the cultural system of which it is a part? Cultural relativism rejects the notion that any culture, including our own, possesses a set of absolute standards by which all other cultures can be judged. Cultural relativity is a cognitive tool that helps us understand why people think and act the way they do.

Perhaps a specific example of cultural relativity will help to clarify the concept. Over the years, anthropologists have described a number of cultural practices from around the world that appear to be morally reprehensible to most Westerners. For example, in many Asian cultures, such as China and India, boys are preferred over girls. With ultrasound technology (Figure 1.9) it is now possible to tell the sex of a fetus at an early stage of gestation, and many parents in these societies use this information to selectively abort female fetuses, especially if they already have a girl. Sex-selective abortion is illegal in China and India and many other countries, but the laws are difficult to enforce and often ignored, especially by those with money. Most Canadians find this practice, known as female feticide but sometimes called "gendercide," repugnant and foreign to their values. Sex-selective abortion is not illegal in Canada

cultural relativism The idea that cultural traits are best understood when viewed within the cultural context of which they are a part.

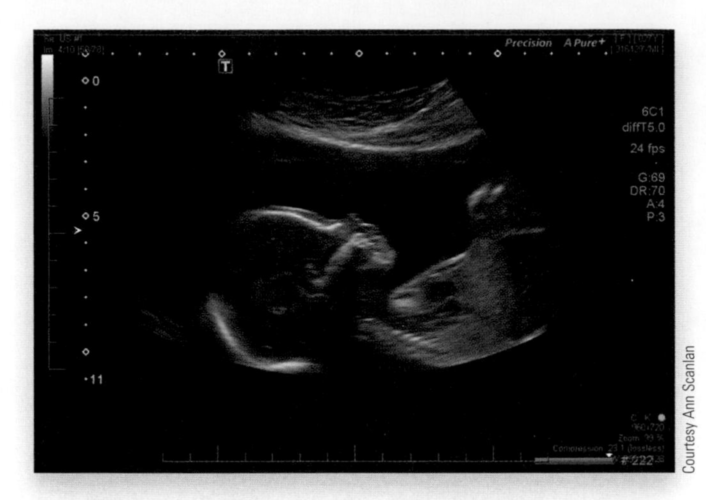

FIGURE 1.9 A healthy second trimester fetus as seen via ultrasound.

Courtesy Ann Scanlan

(or the United States), however, as women in Canada have a right to an abortion without having to state a reason. Abortion is often seen as a private matter, and the freedom of choice is highly valued in Canadian society. But Canada is not immune to this practice. Although most prospective parents want to know if they will be having a boy or a girl, most hospitals will not reveal the sex of a fetus until after 30 weeks gestation—when abortions are very rare. There are many private clinics in Ontario and British Columbia and elsewhere, however, that will tell parents the sex of the fetus during the first trimester. According to a study published in the *Canadian Medical Association Journal*, the normal male:female ratio is 1.05:1, and this ratio remained unchanged for subsequent children of women born in Canada. In contrast, it was higher for Canadian women born in South Korea and China; and for women born in India who already had two children, the ratio was 1.36 (with a 95 percent confidence interval between 1.27 and 1.46), a significant difference (Ray et al. 2012).

If we view such a practice by the standards of our mainstream Canadian culture (i.e., ethnocentrically), we would have to conclude that it is unethical and contrary to our understanding of human rights. But the cultural relativist would look at female feticide in the context of the culture of which it is a part. There is a high cultural motivation in China and India and elsewhere—and among immigrants—to have a boy because male children are seen as providers and carry on the line, while girls can be expensive.

There is a problem with taking the notion of cultural relativism too literally. If cultural relativism is taken to its logical extreme, we would have to conclude that absolutely no behaviour found in the world would be immoral, provided that the people who practice it concur that it is morally acceptable or that it performs a function for the well-being of the society. Practicing cultural relativism, however, does not require that we view all cultural practices as morally equivalent; that is, not all cultural practices are equally worthy of tolerance and respect. To be certain, some cultural practices (such as genocide) are morally indefensible within any cultural context. Also, keep in mind that to practice cultural relativism does not require us to give up our own culture and practice another. In fact, it does not even require we like, or approve of, the other culture. Yet, if our goal is to *understand* human behaviour in its myriad forms, then cultural relativism can help us identify the inherent logic behind certain ideas and customs that, from an ethnocentric perspective, may seem irrational, incomprehensible, or immoral.

This does present a dilemma for the anthropologist, however. If our goal is understanding, how do we stand by as neutral observers when we know people's human rights are being abused? We can understand why parents selectively abort female fetuses, or why desperate people, to feed their families, will sell their organs, or their children into prostitution, but should we not advocate for their rights? When we see a young girl undergo a gruesome operation using primitive tools and without anesthetic to remove her genitals, knowing that it might kill her or lead to physical and psychological problems later in life, we can understand why her parents and her society want her to go through this operation, but should we not do something to stop this practice?

By its very nature, anthropology is involved in the social issues and political and economic struggles of the people they study. Nancy Scheper-Hughes (1992, 17–18), who did her fieldwork in a "favela," or shantytown, in Northeast Brazil, provides a description of this experience:

> "… a fight broke out among Irene Lopes and several women waiting outside the crèche where I was conducting interviews and gathering reproductive histories. When I emerged to see what the commotion was about, the women were ready to turn their anger against me. Why had I refused to work with them when they had been willing to work with me? Didn't I care about them personally anymore, their lives, their suffering, their struggle? Why was I so passive, so indifferent, so resigned…?"*

Anthropologists produce information about other societies that can be used to help or harm them. In the past, colonial administrations used the knowledge of other societies generated by anthropologists to control them politically and economically, and to deny them their rights. In recent years a branch of applied anthropology, known as ***advocacy anthropology***, has arisen whereby anthropologists advocate on behalf of the people they study. The issue goes to the heart of anthropology, and is perhaps most succinctly stated by Peter Kellett (2009, 22):

*Nancy Scheper-Hughes (1992:17-18).

advocacy anthropology A branch of applied anthropology that advocates on behalf of the people studied.

"Is the role of the anthropologist to try to change the world or to 'merely' understand it? Can (and should) anthropologists act as advocates for the rights of people they study, or does this compromise their objectivity?"

Emic versus Etic Approaches

Another feature of cultural anthropology that distinguishes it from other social science disciplines is its emphasis on viewing another culture from the perspective of an insider. For decades anthropologists have made the distinction between the *emic approach* and the *etic approach*, which are terms borrowed from linguistics. The emic approach (derived from the word *phonemic* or meanings of words?) refers to the insider view, which seeks to describe another culture in terms of the categories, concepts, and perceptions of the people being studied. By contrast, the etic approach (derived from the word *phonetic* or sounds of words) refers to the outsider view, in which anthropologists use their own categories and concepts to describe the culture under analysis. For example, Hindus in India do not eat beef. The emic, or insider explanation for this is that cows are sacred. Marvin Harris (1977), however, takes an etic approach: Cows in India are not eaten because they serve a utilitarian function: they bear calves, give milk, serve as draft animals, clean up unwanted vegetation, and their dung is used for fuel.

For the past half century, there has been an ongoing debate among anthropologists as to which approach is more valuable for the scientific study of comparative cultures. The emic and etic approaches are complementary, however, since the ability to understand and interpret other cultures often requires both. Anthropologists will typically emphasize the emic perspective when studying one culture in detail and the etic perspective when making cross-cultural comparisons. The degree to which either of the two perspectives is emphasized will vary from researcher to researcher.

Contributions of Anthropology

One of the major contributions of anthropology to the understanding of the human condition stems from the broad task it has set for itself: examining all aspects of humanity for all periods of time and for all parts of the globe. Because of the magnitude of this task, anthropologists must draw on theories and data from a number of other disciplines in the humanities, the social sciences, and the physical sciences. As a result, anthropology is in a good position to integrate the various disciplines dealing with human physiology and culture.

Enhancing Understanding in a Globalized World

Over the past few decades, the Internet, mobile technology, cheap air travel, lower shipping costs, international migration, and the lowering of tariff barriers have meant that today we live in an increasingly interconnected world. This recent intensification of the flow of people, money, goods, services, and information to all parts of the globe has greatly accelerated culture change, and has made the study of cultures more complex. Increasing numbers of people today are moving outside their own familiar cultural borders, causing dramatic increases in cross-cultural contact and the potential for culture change as well as conflict.

These changes have also changed the focus of cultural anthropology. In the past, anthropologists were often concerned with less technologically advanced cultures. Today, however, the focus has shifted to how these, as well as other societies, deal with the changes. Of particular interest is how local forces interact with global forces to shape identities and change societies economically, politically, and culturally to form new versions of the original culture, a process known as *glocalization*.

Anthropologists are also interested in such questions as, How do people adjust to living in urban environments? What connections do international migrants maintain with their relatives back home? How does their new home influence their cultural traditions? Decolonization and globalization have raised new issues of nationalism, Indigenous rights, as well as issues of health, education, global inequality, and the changing rights and status of women. Through its distinctive methodology of long-term, intensive, participant-observation research, cultural anthropology offers a more in-depth look at how local cultural groups are reacting to the processes of globalization. Cultural anthropologists are interested in knowing what is actually occurring on the ground, and how the local people themselves talk about their life experiences in a time of rapid globalization.

Still another contribution of anthropology is that it helps us better understand ourselves. The early Greeks claimed that the educated person was the person with self-knowledge ("know thyself"). One of the best ways to gain self-knowledge is to know as much as possible about one's own culture, that is, to understand the forces that shape our thinking, values, and behaviours. And the best way of learning about our culture is to

---

emic approach A perspective in ethnography that uses the concepts and categories that are relevant and meaningful to the culture under analysis.

etic approach A perspective in ethnography that uses the concepts and categories of the anthropologist's culture to describe another culture.

glocalization The process whereby the universalizing processes of globalization interact with the particularizing tendencies of local cultures to produce new forms of the original cultures.

examine the similarities and differences between ourselves and others. With its emphasis on the comparative study of cultures, the anthropological perspective should lead us to the conclusion that our culture is just one way of life among many, and that it represents one way among many possible ways to adapt to a particular set of environmental conditions. Through the process of contrasting and comparing, we gain a fuller understanding of other cultures as well as our own, which then allows us to operate more effectively (both personally and professionally) in our increasingly interconnected world.

Transplant Tourism and Advocacy Anthropology

In July 2012, in the first criminal organ-trafficking case in the United States, Israeli immigrant Levy Rosenbaum was sentenced to 2½ years for brokering the sale of three kidneys for transplantation. Customers paid as much as $160 000 for the kidneys, while donors received about $25 000. Although many vilified Rosenbaum for exploiting both the desperate and the destitute, many of his supporters praised him for saving the lives of people dying from kidney disease (Glovin and Voreacos 2012).

Kidney transplantation has become a successful global practice. Surgery in modern, well-equipped hospitals carries minimal risks for donors in good health, and survival rates for recipients have increased markedly over the past few decades. Demand for kidneys, however, far outstrips supply. As of December 31, 2012, there were 3428 patients in Canada waiting for a kidney transplant; 84 patients died in 2012 waiting (CIHI 2014). In the United States, more than 80 000 are waiting for legal organs; many have been on the lists for years, and five to seven die each day (Glovin and Voreacos 2012).

Most countries, as well as the World Health Organization, encourage donation for transplantation. In almost all countries, however, it is illegal to sell a kidney. With thousands of people dying of kidney failure each year, and with no lack of destitute people willing to sell an "extra" kidney for cash—in many cases for only a few thousand, or even a few hundred dollars—the black market in kidneys (and other organs) has become a multi-billion dollar global industry linking hospital administrators, surgeons, brokers, sellers, and recipients worldwide. It has been facilitated by the spread of transplant technology, the growth of the travel industry, and the development of the Internet, which has made web-based matching, anonymous living donation, and information about services easily accessible (Hamlin 2012).

Most of the "donors" live in South America, Southeast Asia, and Africa. Medical anthropologist Nancy Scheper-Hughes (2000, 193) notes that, "In general, the flow of organs follows the modern routes of capital: from South to North, from Third to First World, from poor to rich, from black and brown to white, and from female to male." With the cost of surgery in such countries as India, Thailand, and Mexico often a quarter to a tenth what it is in the West (Hamlin 2012), it is not surprising that organ recipients travel to such countries to receive a kidney, followed by a recuperative vacation. Such transplant tourism raises ethical issues about the exploitation of those disadvantaged individuals selling their kidneys, the neglect they often receive after surgery, and the focus of national governments on activities that increase foreign revenue at the expense of primary healthcare for local residents.

Scheper-Hughes has conducted multi-sited fieldwork in Brazil, China, the United States, and South Africa, and has interviewed everyone from organ donors and recipients, to brokers, transplant surgeons, and hospital administrators. She has interviewed them in research laboratories, dialysis centres, morgues, courts, police stations, and municipal offices, and has even posed "as a kidney buyer in order to understand the misery that prompts a person to bargain over the value of his kidney" (Scheper-Hughes 2009, 14). The biggest issues surround the black market itself and the exploitation of the sellers, almost all of whom sell their organs because of debt and crippling poverty, and who need the money to feed their families or simply to survive. Many see it as exploitation of developing countries by Western developed countries taking advantage of the relationship of inequality. Making the sale and purchase of kidneys illegal, however, raises questions about individual rights—who owns your body, you or the state—and may also prevent people escaping from poverty.

Scheper-Hughes's work on the illegal organ trade has raised other issues of interest to anthropologists. For instance, selling organs and transplanting them into other bodies commoditizes the body and raises issues about how people think about both the sanctity of their bodies and their identity. It also raises issues about cultural definitions of death: are you dead when your heart stops beating, or when your brain stops working. Religious prohibitions against donating organs, whether from living or dead donors, has exacerbated the shortage of kidneys in such places as Saudi Arabia and Israel, leading residents of these countries to travel to Eastern Europe and India for a kidney.

Organ scarcity, long waiting lists, and the expense of dialysis—a treatment that removes impurities from the blood—makes organ donation a concern of governments and policy makers. Dialysis costs the Canadian health system $2.2 billion annually—about $60 000 per person per year. A kidney transplant, on the other hand, costs about $23 000 and $6000 per year in anti-rejection drugs (Picard 2011). Spain, Sweden, Belgium, and Austria have a "presumed consent" policy whereby a person is automatically considered an organ donor in the event of accidental death unless they explicitly state otherwise. Canada has an "informed consent" policy whereby a person states, while still alive, their desire to be a donor.

Scheper-Hughes' work has also raised issues about the nature and ethics of anthropology. Anthropologists hold as their highest ethical principle the duty to protect the people who have helped them in their research, provided them with information, and trusted them. This creates a moral dilemma for the anthropologist when their collaborators are engaged in illegal activities that the

(Continued)

Transplant Tourism and Advocacy Anthropology (*Continued*)

anthropologist may also be morally opposed to. What takes precedence: following a professional code of conduct, or intervening when crimes are committed against vulnerable people? And how ethical is it for anthropologists to gather information under false pretenses, for example, as a buyer of a kidney?

Nancy Scheper-Hughes believes anthropologists should advocate for human rights. To that end, she helped found the Berkeley Organs Watch Project in 1999 to research transnational human organ trafficking networks, and in 2008 investigated an international group of organ sellers in the United States and Israel, leading to multiple arrests by the FBI. She has also acted as an advisor to the European Union, the United Nations, and the World Health Organization, and given expert testimony before the U.S. Congress, the Council of Europe, and the British House of Lords (AAA 2013).

In September 2013 the American Anthropological Association awarded her the first Public Policy Award for her work and research on how organ trafficking has "shaped how governments and international bodies address the issues of illegal transplantation" (AAA 2013). Her work demonstrates the contribution anthropology can make to public policy debates, and how it can influence government decision makers worldwide.

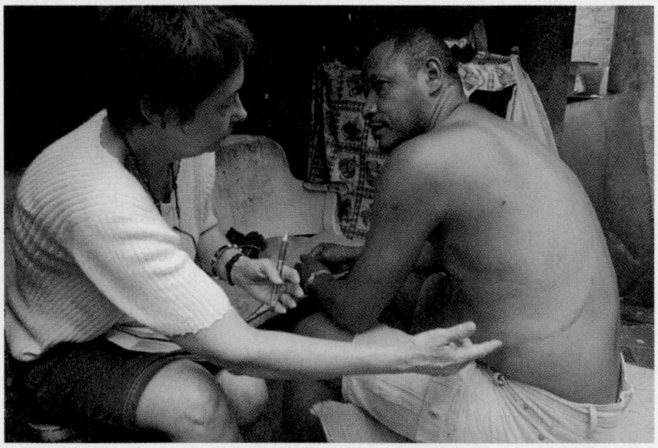

Photo by John Maier/Courtesy of Nancy Scheper-Hughes.

Nancy Scheper-Hughes with Alberty Alfonso da Silva in his mud-walled hut in a slum of Recife, Brazil. Alberty was trafficked in August 2003 to Durban, South Africa, where he sold his kidney to an American kidney patient who was flown in from New York City.

Questions for Further Thought

1. Should people be allowed to sell a kidney, and should the market forces of supply and demand establish the price?
2. If you or a close family member were in need of a kidney, would you travel to a country such as India or the Philippines to receive a kidney sold by someone who needed the money to feed their family?
3. How would you obtain permission to study criminal behaviour?
4. Canada currently has an "opt-in" organ donation system. Should we have a system where we are all automatically presumed to be an organ donor unless we expressly "opt out"?
5. In May 2015 Canadian billionaire and owner of the Ottawa Senators, Eugene Melnyck, underwent a successful liver transplant after making a public plea for a donor. Did Melnyck's financial resources and public image help him "jump the queue"? Has it helped publicize the need for more donors? What would you do if you were in his situation?

The Relevance of Cultural Anthropology

Most anthropology professors will tell you they think every student should take at least an introductory course in anthropology, as cultural anthropology has relevance for all of us, in both our personal and professional lives. Anthropology will broaden your perspective on whatever career you choose, whether it is business, law, psychology, literature, medicine, the sciences, or even engineering. Activities such as taking courses about different cultures, participating in study-abroad programs, internships with international organizations, and living in a university's international residence all combine to enrich our lives, provide insights into the lives of others, and give us a better understanding of world events. Whether you get your news via television, newspapers, the Internet, or your phone, you will find much that resonates with what you learn from anthropology.

Like other social science disciplines, cultural anthropology engages in both basic and applied research. Basic research is dedicated to gaining scientific knowledge for its own sake. Applied research, on the other hand, seeks to gain knowledge for the sake of informing public policy and solving particular societal problems. In other words, the fields of applied (or practicing) anthropology are aimed at putting to use the knowledge and methods anthropology has produced over the years. Interest in applying anthropology has increased over the past several decades. The number of graduate and undergraduate courses in applied anthropology has increased, as has the number of people with masters and doctorate degrees finding employment outside academic settings. Applied and practicing anthropologists usually work in non-academic settings such as government agencies, international development agencies, public health organizations, consulting companies, and for-profit businesses. Anthropologists can do all kinds of jobs; they work as researchers, analysts, policy makers, writers, cultural negotiators, project managers, business consultants, educators, community activists, and so on. Few employment opportunities, however, are targeted specifically at anthropology students. One reason for this is that many people still view anthropology as the study of exotic or primitive cultures. And while there is a growing awareness of the value of anthropology in various fields, it does mean that in applying for jobs it is necessary to stress the skills acquired as an anthropology student. For a list of the types of non-academic careers anthropology students qualify for, see Chapter 3.

Building Skills for a Globalized World

The data, concepts, and insights derived from the study of other cultures can help us better meet our professional goals and lead more satisfying lives in a multicultural society. But the process of studying cultural anthropology is also valuable because of the skills and competencies that it helps develop. Anthropology students gain writing and organizational skills, learn how to conduct interviews and understand social relationships, and acquire observational skills. But there are other skills that go beyond the mere mastery of subject content and method. These skills involve developing a broad perspective, appreciating other points of view, operating comfortably in ambiguous situations, working effectively as part of cross-cultural teams, and becoming emotionally resilient, open-minded, and perceptually aware. These traits are essential for coping with an increasingly interdependent world. And because the study of cultural anthropology involves immersing oneself in other cultures, it is perhaps the best training ground for developing those competencies.

Development of a Broad Perspective

This skill involves seeing the big picture and the interrelatedness of the parts, in other words, holistically. The student of anthropology is continually being asked to analyze a part of a culture in relationship to the whole.

Appreciation of Other Perspectives

A basic anthropological strategy for understanding other cultures is to look at a cultural feature from within its original cultural context, rather than looking at it from the perspective of one's own culture, that is, relatively. Being inquisitive, non-judgmental, and open to new ways of thinking is vital if we are to adapt to ever-changing environments. This involves, essentially, a willingness to learn and postpone making evaluations until more facts are known. Such a capacity also requires suppressing one's ego and letting go of old paradigms. It does not mean giving up one's cultural values, ideas, or ways of doing things in favour of others. But it does entail (at least temporarily) letting go of cultural certainty, learning how other cultures view us, and a willingness to see the internal logic of another culture.

Balance Contradictions

A major requirement for working and living effectively in a global society is the ability to balance contradictory needs and demands rather than trying to eliminate them. Contradictions and conflicts should be seen as opportunities, not as liabilities. Conflicting values, behaviours, and ideas are a fact of life in today's world. The study of cultural anthropology provides insights into the nature of the world's diversity. When anthropology students are exposed to logical alternatives to their own ways of thinking and behaving, they learn to cope with differences and contradictions, and actually use these differences for the sake of achieving synergy.

Emphasis on Global Teamwork

Success in a globalized world requires an emphasis on cultural awareness and cross-cultural teamwork, not just personal awareness and individual mastery. Both private and public institutions are becoming increasingly more global in focus. For example, foreign subsidiaries, joint ventures with foreign firms, and overseas facilities are commonplace in the world of business. Being successful at working within and leading these culturally complex organizations, requires knowledge of the underlying cultural assumptions of the diverse people in those multicultural teams. This skill is especially important in Canada, with its diverse multicultural population. One's colleagues, whether in government, business, or a charitable organization, are likely to come from a variety of cultures, as are the organization's suppliers and customers. There is no academic discipline in higher education today that addresses this competency better than cultural anthropology.

Development of Cognitive Complexity

People today need what is referred to as *cognitive complexity*, which is made up of the twin abilities of differentiating and integrating. Differentiation involves being able to see how a single entity is composed of a number of different parts; integration, on the other hand, involves the capacity to identify how the various parts are interconnected. The cognitively complex person is able to engage in both types of thinking, and can move comfortably between the two. One must be able to focus on the unique needs of the local situation while at the same time understanding how it fits into the operations of the larger society. For example, how would a First Nation community maintain a culturally appropriate curriculum and still meet provincially mandated, educational achievement standards?

Development of Perceptual Acuity

In today's globalized world people need to be perceptually acute. We need to accurately derive meaning from interactions with others from a wide variety of cultures and subcultures. This involves being attentive to both verbal and nonverbal communication by being an active listener, deriving meaning from social context, and being sensitive to the feelings of others and to one's effect on others. Studying other cultures, and particularly living in other cultures, forces the student of anthropology to derive meaning not only from the words exchanged in cross-cultural encounters, but also from the nonverbal cues, the social context, and the assumptions embedded in the other culture.

Thus, a number of skills and capacities considered essential for effective living and working in the 21st century can be mastered while studying cultural anthropology. The comparative study of the world's cultural diversity and shared heritage is the single best way for acquiring these competencies. Even if you do not major in anthropology, however, you can develop these skills by doing what anthropologists do; that is, by throwing yourself into other cultures by travelling and living abroad, either before, during, or after university. In addition, it has become increasingly important for university students to have some type of experiential international learning opportunity during their undergraduate careers. An appreciable number of university graduates (both anthropology and non-anthropology majors) are beginning to realize the value of immersing oneself in a different culture. Students who take a year or two off to travel and work in a culture different from their own, or who enrol in study-abroad programs, find it a way of developing vital global skills. For many it has been a way to leverage their position in the job market when they return home, as many employers are also recognizing the value of this experience.

The Bottom Line: Understanding Other Cultures to Understand Our Own

Although a large part of cultural anthropology involves acquiring information on the world's cultures, it also involves learning about one's own culture. What we know, or think we know, about our own culture is not, however, necessarily perceived in the same way by people from other cultures. In other words, we may see ourselves as holding a particular value or cultural trait, but then we describe that trait in only the most positive ways. Those looking at us from the outside, however, are more likely to see some of the negative implications as well.

These different interpretations of our values by people from other cultures can be illustrated in a number of ways. For example, whereas many people in North America place a high value on individualism and independence, people from other cultures often place a higher value on collectivism, cooperation, and interdependence, and therefore tend to see Westerners as selfish, disloyal, superficial in their relations, and unwilling to meet their social obligations to others and to their society in general. North Americans also tend to be youth-oriented to the extent that young people are held in higher esteem than old people. It is believed that the young are energetic, resourceful, enthusiastic, resilient, forward-thinking, and more tech-savvy than their elders—all traits that are associated with high levels of productivity. This high value on youth, however, is not universally held by many cultures in Asia, Africa, or South America, where older people are afforded the highest status because they are thought to be the wisest, most thoughtful, and most trustworthy segment of society. People from societies who hold elders in the highest esteem cannot understand why North Americans have younger people supervising older people in the workplace, make jokes about older people and the aging process, and generally treat our elders with such disrespect, or perhaps even worse, neglect. In short, they view the emphasis on youth as both immoral and counterproductive because they are not using the wisdom, experience, and competencies of older citizens for the betterment of society.

Thus, if cultural anthropology is to help us function more effectively in an increasingly interconnected world, we will have to focus on accomplishing three tasks: understanding culture-specific information about other cultures, understanding our own culture, and understanding how people from other cultures view us and our cultural patterns.

Summary

1. The academic discipline of anthropology involves the study of the biological and cultural origins of humans. The subject matter of anthropology is wide-ranging and includes fossil remains, nonhuman primate anatomy and behaviour, artifacts from past cultures, past and present languages, and all the prehistoric, pre-contact, historic, and contemporary cultures of the world.
2. As practiced in most universities in Canada and the United States, the discipline of anthropology follows an integrated four-field approach comprising physical or biological anthropology, archaeology, anthropological linguistics, and cultural anthropology. All four subdisciplines have both theoretical and applied components.
3. The subdiscipline of physical or biological anthropology focuses on three primary concerns: paleoanthropology (deciphering the biological record of human evolution through the study of fossil remains), primatology (the study of nonhuman primate anatomy and behaviour for the purpose of gaining insights into human adaptation to the environment), and studies in human physical variations and how biological variations contribute to adaptation to one's environment.
4. The subfield of archaeology has as its primary objective the reconstruction of past cultures, both historic, pre-contact, and prehistoric, from the material objects the cultures leave behind.
5. Anthropological linguistics, which studies both present and past languages, is divided into four major subdivisions: historical linguistics (studying the emergence and historical divergence of languages), descriptive linguistics (analyzing the phonetic and grammar systems in languages), ethnolinguistics (exploring the relationship between language and culture), and sociolinguistics (understanding the relationship between language and social relations).
6. Cultural anthropology focuses on the study of contemporary cultures wherever they are found in the world. One part of the task of cultural anthropology involves describing particular cultures (ethnography), and the other part involves comparing two or more cultures (ethnology). Cultural anthropologists tend to specialize in areas such as urban anthropology, medical anthropology, development anthropology, environmental anthropology, and psychological anthropology, among others.
7. The discipline is holistic (or comprehensive) in four important respects: it looks at both the biological and the cultural aspects of human behaviour; it encompasses the longest possible time frame by looking at contemporary, historic, pre-contact, and prehistoric societies; it examines human cultures in every part of the world; and it studies many different aspects of human cultures.
8. There are essentially two ways to respond to unfamiliar cultures. One way is ethnocentrically, that is, through the lens of one's own cultural perspective. The other way is from the perspective of a cultural relativist, that is, within the context of the other culture. Cultural anthropologists strongly recommend the second mode, although they are aware of certain limitations.
9. Cultural anthropologists distinguish between the emic (insider) approach, which uses native categories, and the etic (outsider) approach, which describes a culture in terms of the categories, concepts, and perceptions of the anthropologist.
10. The study of anthropology is valuable from a number of different viewpoints. From the perspective of the social and behavioural sciences, cultural anthropology is particularly valuable for testing theories about human behaviour within the widest possible cross-cultural context. For the individual, the study of different cultures provides a much better understanding of one's own culture and develops valuable leadership skills. From a societal point of view, the understanding of different cultures can contribute to the solution of pressing societal problems.
11. This textbook takes an *applied* perspective. This means that, in addition to surveying the content material of cultural anthropology, this book takes a number of opportunities to emphasize how the theories, methods, and insights of cultural anthropology can be used to help solve societal problems, both at home and abroad.
12. The discipline of cultural anthropology helps students develop the skills and competencies needed to live in the 21st century. These include developing a broad perspective, cognitive complexity, and perceptual acuity; appreciating other perspectives, balancing contradictions, and emphasizing global teamwork.

Key Terms

advocacy anthropology
anthropological linguistics
applied anthropology
archaeology
artifact
cultural anthropology
cultural relativism
cultural resource management
culture shock
descriptive linguistics
development anthropology
ecofacts
emic approach
environmental or ecological anthropology
epidemiology
ethnocentrism
ethnography
ethnolinguistics
ethnology
ethnomedicine
etic approach
features
genetics
glocalization
historical linguistics
holism
medical anthropology
paleoanthropology
paleopathology
physical or biological anthropology
population biology
practice anthropology
primatology
psychological anthropology
race
sociolinguistics
subculture
urban anthropology

Critical Thinking Questions

1. Compare the concepts of ethnocentrism and cultural relativism. Is there any value in looking at other cultures from an ethnocentric perspective? Are there any drawbacks from taking a culturally relative viewpoint?
2. Why is ethnocentrism the major obstacle to the understanding of other cultures? How might it be overcome?
3. One of the new subspecialties of cultural anthropology is the anthropology of tourism. What type of research do you think an anthropologist who studies tourism typically conducts, and how can the findings from this research be applied to help societies cope with the cultural changes resulting from tourism?
4. How does Anthropology differ from Sociology and the other Social Sciences? How is it similar?
5. The discipline of anthropology studies the human condition from a cultural and a biological perspective. Can you think of some examples of the interrelatedness of culture and biology from your own life?
6. How might migration from a First Nation reserve to a large city affect family relationships? Generate at least three hypotheses.
7. In what ways might a group's religious beliefs impact their ideas about the causes, diagnosis, and treatment of disease?
8. Global warming is occurring in the Arctic at almost twice the global average rate, reducing the hunting season and altering migration patterns of many species. It presents many new social, economic, and political challenges. How can anthropologists work with Indigenous peoples living in the Arctic to adapt to these changes?
9. Since June 2014 the Islamist group ISIS has destroyed many pre-Islamic archaeological sites, most notably the 13th century BCE Assyrian capital of Nimrud, a UNESCO World Heritage site, the ancient city of Hatra, also a UNESCO World Heritage site, both in Iraq; and Palmyra in Syria. Should the destruction of these sites be considered a "war crime" or "cultural cleansing" as some have suggested? Why does ISIS destroy these sites?
10. How might an understanding of social and cultural anthropology be of value to you in your career choice?

Make the Grade with MindTap

Stay organized and efficient with **MindTap**—a single destination with all the course material and study aids you need to succeed. Built-in apps leverage social media and the latest learning technology. For example:

- ReadSpeaker will read the text to you.
- Self-quizzing allows you to assess your understanding.
- Flashcards are pre-populated to provide you with a jump-start for review—or you can create your own.
- You can highlight text and make notes in your MindTap Reader. Your notes will flow into Evernote, the electronic notebook app that you can access anywhere when it's time to study for the exam.

Visit nelson.com/student to start using **MindTap**. Enter the Online Access Code from the card included with your text. If a code card is not provided, you can purchase instant access at NELSONbrain.com.

A Muslim teacher with children in a classroom at an Islamic school in Uttar Pradesh, India

CHAPTER 2

The Concept of Culture

ADJUSTING TO CANADIAN UNIVERSITY CULTURE

Canadian universities attract many international students, and this, coupled with Canada's relatively liberal immigration policies and commitment to multiculturalism, mean that classrooms today contain students from a variety of different cultural backgrounds. This presents a challenge not only to universities and teachers, but also to students who must adjust to cultural differences.

For instance, when marketing student Farrukh Asif Khan arrived in Canada from Hyderabad, India, to attend Algoma University in Sault Ste. Marie, Ontario, she was not only excited about beginning a new chapter in her life, but also nervous about being able to manage on her own. Being Muslim, she was particularly concerned about whether she would be able to find halal meat in Canada. For Sima Marin from Thailand, the challenge was being away from her family and doing her own shopping, cooking, and laundry. "At times," she said, "you realize that even a very very small thing, which you thought was not important, would suddenly seem a thousand times more valuable than you initially thought" (Kidd 2011).

Students coming to Canada face other issues, such as understanding lectures in an unfamiliar language, adjusting to new methods of studying and learning, knowing what is expected of them, making friends, and participating in the social life of the university, not to mention dealing with Canadian winters.

The increase in enrolment of international students in Canadian universities is happening at a time when many students are politically active over such issues as rape culture, racism, sexism, and patriarchy on their campuses. Many Chinese students, such as Canace Zhang, studying sociology at the University of Windsor, have a different perspective on such issues and what is politically correct. While she supports advocacy for women's and LGBT rights, she also finds Canadian students to be hypersensitive and the university's attempts to cater to students as "childish and naïve" (Moir 2016). But she is also reluctant to get involved because, given the repressive regime in China, which blocks certain websites and monitors people's online activities, any public comments or any type of activism can be dangerous.

Canada has an individualist and egalitarian culture that emphasizes equality and personal achievement. This can lead to a competitive educational environment where students are encouraged to participate in class discussions and are often expected to ask questions and even challenge their teachers. China and many other Asian cultures, on the other hand, have a collectivist and more hierarchical culture. Such cultures emphasize the welfare of the family and the group

Dinodia Photos/Alamy Stock Photo

WHAT WE WILL LEARN

- What anthropologists mean by the term *culture*
- How culture informs one's thoughts and behaviours
- How we acquire our culture
- How culture influences biological processes
- The features common to all cultures of the world
- How culture influences our sense of who we are
- How cultures change over time

over the individual, and harmony over competition. Chinese children are also taught from a very young age to respect and honour older people and people in positions of authority, such as parents and teachers.

This means students from China are often reluctant to engage in class discussions and express their thoughts, as they do not want to stand out or bring attention to themselves. They are also less likely to ask questions, as this could be seen as a challenge to their teacher's authority or could cause the teacher embarrassment if they are unable to answer, resulting in both the teacher and the student losing "face" or respect. Not participating in class can often negatively impact grades, which can also cause loss of face. Chinese culture places a high value on education, and poor grades can be seen as shameful as they are letting their family down.

Adjusting to life in Canada can thus often be daunting and may result in culture shock: feelings of disorientation, fear, apprehension, anger, and loneliness experienced when trying to live in a culture different from what one is used to. The culture we are born into shapes our ideas, attitudes, emotions, patterns of behaviour, and our understanding of how the world works. We think of this as natural and normal until we experience another culture. When we go to another country, not only are our friends and family absent, but also many of the common cultural touchstones we use to solve everyday problems, and which we feel comfortable with, can no longer be relied upon. The values and norms of behaviours may be quite different. For instance, as Canadians we learn to speak our minds, be open and forthright, and not to "beat around the bush." This behaviour may be perceived as rude in another culture.

Fortunately for Farrukh, Sima, Canace, and others like them, Canadians in general are very welcoming, supportive, and helpful, and many Canadian universities offer international students programs to help them adjust to life in Canada. The reason many international students struggle with Canadian university life is that they have learned a different set of cultural values and behaviours. In this chapter we will explore what culture is, how we learn it, and how it influences the way we perceive and deal with the world. ■

What Is Culture?

In 2014 Merriam-Webster Dictionary declared "culture" to be the most important word of the year, as more people looked up its definition than any other (Dressler 2015). The term has become ubiquitous in English in such phrases as pop culture, multicultural, corporate culture, and so on. The concept of culture is extremely complex, and we can perhaps gain something of an understanding of that complexity by looking at how the term evolved.

According to the Oxford English Dictionary, the word culture entered the English language from Latin in the mid-1400s, and had the meaning of cultivating the soil or tillage. This meaning is still with us in such terms as agriculture, bacterial culture, and cultured pearls. By the mid-1600s the term had become metaphoric: it was not simply land, animals, and plants that were cultivated, but people. It came to mean cultivation of the mind and the development of manners through education. By 1700 it had taken on the idea that people devoted attention to particular pursuits; that is, they "cultivated" an interest in the arts or the sciences. At about the same time it gained the idea that people who were "cultured" had refined tastes and manners, and had cultivated their artistic and intellectual talents. By the mid-1800s culture had come to be seen as the ideas, customs, and behaviour or way of life that characterized a particular society. In the early 1900s this concept began to be used as a modifier for particular groups of people who subscribed to a particular way of life, and we find such terms as "gun culture," "drug culture," "café culture," "youth culture," and so on. By the mid-1900s this idea was seen as a character of institutions, in the sense of "corporate culture," or "prison culture." More recently it has become objectified such that it is seen as a thing, for example in terms such as "cultural survival," or "culture hero," "culture jamming." Culture can thus live or die or be defended, or interfered with. Most of these senses of the concept are still with us and this brief etymology of the term gives an idea of the complexity of the concept and demonstrates that it is not a static concept but changes and takes on new meanings over time.

Although the concept is used by most of the social sciences today, it has received its most precise and comprehensive definition from the discipline of anthropology. Whereas sociology has concentrated on the notion of society; economics on the concepts of production, distribution, and consumption; and political science on the concept of power; anthropology has focused on the concept of culture. From anthropology's 19th century beginnings, the concept of culture has been central to both ethnology and archaeology, and has been an important concern of physical or biological anthropology. Anthropology, through its constant examining of different lifeways throughout space and time, has done more than any other discipline to refine our understanding of the concept of culture.

The first anthropological definition of culture has been attributed to Edward Burnett Tylor ([1871] 1903, 1) who began his 1871 book *Primitive Culture* with the following definition: "Culture or civilization, taken in its wide ethnographic sense, is that complex whole which includes knowledge, belief, art, morals, law, custom, and any other capabilities and habits acquired my man as a member of society." This is perhaps the most quoted definition of culture in anthropological literature, but it has many features different from more contemporary senses of the term. Tylor made culture synonymous with "civilization in its wide ethnographic sense" to distinguish it from "civilization in the narrow sense." In the 19th century the word "civilization" was more common than the word "culture" and had two basic meanings. Civilization in the narrow sense referred to the culture of civilized people as opposed to that of "barbarians" and "savages." The wide ethnographic sense of civilization, which Tylor made synonymous with culture, was more holistic and referred to the continuum from savagery, to barbarism, to civilization. Thus, the elements are "included" rather than "integrated" and he refers to them being "acquired by man as a member of society," rather than as a member of "a particular" society. Tylor thus did not see culture as characteristic of a particular group of people, an idea common to more recent definitions. There is no idea of cultural relativism in Tylor's definition (Stocking 1989).

Alfred Kroeber and Clyde Kluckhohn (1952) have argued that Tylor was intentionally attempting to establish the discipline of Anthropology by defining its subject matter on the first page of *Primitive Culture*. This is debatable, but "culture" *is* anthropology's guiding theoretical concept. What anthropologists think culture is determines the questions they ask, the methods by which they answer them, and the answers they get. Nineteenth century anthropologists, for instance, thought of culture as something that evolved, and sought, through cultural comparison, to trace its evolution. Early 20th century British anthropologists viewed culture in more relative terms and thought it played a role in human society, and thus looked for its functions. More recently, anthropologists have viewed culture as a symbolic system, and so look for meaning.

Culture Defined

In non-scientific usage, the term culture refers to personal refinements such as classical music, the fine arts, world philosophy, and gourmet cuisine. The "cultured" person thus listens to Bach rather than Justin Bieber, orders escargot rather than poutine when dining out, and attends the ballet instead of professional wrestling. The anthropologist, however, does not distinguish between cultured people and uncultured people. According to the anthropological definition, all people have culture (Figure 2.1). Thus, for the anthropologist, projectile points, creation myths, and mud huts are items of culture as legitimate as a Beethoven symphony, a Group of Seven painting, or a Nickleback concert.

Over the past century, anthropologists have formulated a number of definitions of the concept of culture. In fact, in 1952 Alfred Kroeber and Clyde Kluckhohn (1952) identified more than 160 different definitions. Since then there have been hundreds if not thousands of others. This proliferation of definitions should not however lead to the conclusion that anthropology is a chaotic battleground where no consensus exists among practising anthropologists. While there is certainly some debate about the nature of culture, many of these definitions say essentially the same thing, and build on previous ones, beginning with Tylor's.

Adding to the already sizable number of definitions, we will define the concept of ***culture*** as "everything that people have, think, and do as members of a society." This definition can be instructive because the three verbs (*have, think,* and *do*) correspond to the three major components of culture. That is, everything that people *have* refers to material possessions; everything that people *think* refers to the things they carry around in their heads, such as values, attitudes, beliefs, and ideas; and everything that people *do* refers to behaviour patterns. Thus, all cultures are composed of material objects; values, attitudes, beliefs, and ideas; and patterned ways of behaving. The last part of the definition, "as members of a

---

culture Everything that people have, think, and do as members of a society.

© Danita Delimont/Alamy Stock Photo

Ferenc Szelepcsenyi/Shutterstock.com

FIGURE 2.1 **This Australian aborigine playing the didgeridoo (*top*) has as much culture as the conductor of this symphony orchestra (*bottom*).**

society A community of people who share the same culture.

values What is important to people, and that which they act to acquire or maintain.

attitudes Learned, positive or negative evaluations of an element of culture.

society," means that culture is relative to a community of people, that is, a ***society***.

This is a very broad definition of culture, covering all areas of human experience; and although we compartmentalize these three components, we should not conclude that they are unrelated. In fact, the components are so intimately connected that it is frequently hard to separate them in real life. Thus, we use material things and attribute meaning to them, and people act because of the meanings they hold for them. Because the elements are so interconnected, if we want to understand culture we must take a holistic approach.

To gain a better understanding of these three major components of culture, we need to have a closer look at the material aspects of culture and what they mean, what values, attitudes, beliefs, and ideas are, and the influence they have on behaviour.

Values, Attitudes, Beliefs, and Ideas

Values are abstract concepts of what is important to people in their everyday lives which they act to acquire or maintain. They include such things as freedom, respect, honesty, equality, cleanliness, democracy, and so on. We learn our values as we grow up, and they reflect our sense of good and evil, right and wrong, and justice. Consequently, values may form the basis of laws and customs, and we often make decisions based on them (Nelson 2004). As people age and their life situation changes, and as society changes in response to things such as recession, terrorism, economic growth, so to do people's values (Kahle 1983). Values vary, of course, between individuals, but each society also tends to have a set of common core values that most members share. For example, North Americans tend to place a higher value on youth than old age. Because of this we tend to make jokes about getting old, place our senior citizens in nursing homes, and promote the age-defying properties of many products in advertisements. In Japan, however, age has a higher value, and older people are seen to be wise and are given a great deal of respect. Values are important in understanding culture in that they influence attitudes and behaviour. In many Asian and Middle Eastern cultures, for example, family honour is such a high value that many Canadians find it hard to understand so-called honour killings where a family member is killed because they are thought to have disgraced the family.

Attitudes are evaluations or feelings, either negative or positive, about such things as behaviours, people, objects, ideas, and even ourselves. For instance, people can evaluate such things as public displays of affection, the use of cellphones in restaurants, alcohol, companies, fundamentalist religions, and so on, either negatively or positively. If we have a negative evaluation of ourselves we tend to have low self-esteem. We learn our attitudes as we grow up, and changing them is often difficult and requires a substantial amount of persuasion. This is because attitudes are important to us. They help us make decisions. For instance, if we have a negative attitude toward the use of chemical fertilizers, we will most likely buy organic foods. Our attitude toward a particular political party and its policies will undoubtedly also influence how we vote.

Beliefs have to do with the knowledge of the state of affairs; that is, what one thinks is true. They can range from things such as belief that God (or aliens) exists, or that the war on drugs creates more problems than it solves. *Ideas* are what we think things are or how things work. The idea of a chair, for instance, is a piece of furniture that is used to sit on, and biological evolutionism is an idea about how biological organisms change through time. Anthropologists, in their attempt to understand the similarities and differences between cultures, have been particularly interested in how ideas spread from one culture to another.

Norms

Similar to the way our speech is guided by the grammatical rules of language, which we follow unconsciously, we are also guided in our attitudes and actions by rules, mostly unwritten, about what is appropriate and what is inappropriate in specific situations, and which we also follow unconsciously. These ideas are known as *norms.* Most norms are established by implicit consensus without being openly expressed, and they govern such things as the appropriate ways to dress, speak, greet one another, conduct business, and so on.

Because most of us want to fit in, we are concerned with what others think of us, and often change our behaviours to fit in. To accept and follow the norms is to be accepted by the group. There is often considerable pressure to conform to norms, and failure to follow them can trigger sanctions, ranging from disapproving glances, gossip, and even exclusion from group activities or the group itself. We internalize norms so that we continue to act in compliance with them, and we change our behaviour even in the company of strangers. For example, in an interesting experiment on handwashing in a public restroom, Munger and Harris (1989) discovered that nearly twice as many people (77 percent as opposed to 39 percent) washed their hands after using the facilities when a stranger was present than when no one was present. People were thus willing to change their behaviour and comply with social norms to meet the expectations of others.

Norms also function to co-ordinate interactions with others and to get things done. Because people from the same culture learn essentially the same set of values, rules, and expected behaviours, their lives are made somewhat less complicated because they know, within broad limits, what to expect from one another. In a sense, norms are a form of communication. For example, when we go to the check-out at the grocery store, we first wait for space to open up on the conveyor belt before placing the divider to separate our groceries from the next person in line, and then, when it is our turn, we greet the cashier, wait while he or she scans our items, and then hand over our loyalty card and debit or credit card or cash. There may be slight variations on this; perhaps the cashier bags the groceries or we do, but we know what to do. One of the things we do not do is haggle over the prices. The cashier also follows a script, although in many cases this is proscribed by management. Such a pattern of behaviour is known as a ***schema***, and we follow the pattern routinely and unconsciously. Norms are adaptive in that they help us go about our daily lives with ease and to concentrate on other perhaps more important things.

Our culture exerts a powerful influence on our conduct, often without our even being aware of it. However, to assert that culture *influences* our behaviour is hardly the same as asserting that it *determines* our behaviour. Deviance from the cultural norms is found in all societies. Because individual members of any society maintain, to varying degrees, a free will, they have the freedom to say no to cultural expectations. Unlike the honeybee, which behaves according to its genetic programming, humans can make a range of behavioural choices. Of course, choosing an alternative may result in unpleasant consequences, but all people have the option of doing things differently from what is culturally expected.

People sometimes choose to go against cultural conventions for a number of reasons. In some cases where adherence to a social norm involves a hardship, people may justify their noncompliance by stretching the meaning of the norm. Or sometimes people flout a social norm or custom to make a social statement. Whatever the reason, the fact remains that social norms rarely, if ever, receive total compliance. For this reason, cultural anthropologists distinguish between ideal behaviour (what people are expected to do) and real behaviour (what people actually do).

---

beliefs Ideas about what is true.

ideas Thoughts about what things are or how things work.

norms Ideas about what is appropriate and what is inappropriate behaviour.

schema An organized pattern of behaviour that helps organize our daily lives.

CROSS-CULTURAL MISCUE

When Ayelet Tsabari, an Israeli-born writer, came to Canada in 1998 she was surprised by the strange sight of Canadians automatically forming neat, orderly lines at every Vancouver bus stop. In Israel, everyone jockeys for position based on age, need, level of disability, and how well they can express their urgency. While queuing is the norm in Canada, the United Kingdom, the United States, and other English-speaking nations, and also in Japan, for many people lining up for trains, buses, or to be served in stores, clinics, or government offices is not only unheard of but also baffling. In Russia, India, China, and the entire Middle East, getting on a train or bus can often be a mad scramble. It is not a matter of who was at the stop first but who will be the first on. In these large, densely populated countries with limited resources, being first can be a matter of survival (Figure 2.2 and Figure 2.3).

In Canada it is all about etiquette. Beginning in kindergarten, Canadians are taught not only to line up, but also how close to stand in the line when they leave the classroom. We are also taught that it is impolite to "cut in" or "jump the queue." According to a 2008 Angus Reid survey, queue jumping topped the list of things that enraged Canadians, especially in Alberta where 74 percent of residents said the sight of a queue jumper made their blood boil. Jumping the queue can also have deadly consequences. In 2009, in New York City, a 19-year-old was killed for jumping ahead in line at a falafel stand (Hopper 2014). What this miscue shows is that norms are learned, they enable people to function in their society, they are important to people, and breaking them can have serious consequences.

Laura Pedersen/National Post

FIGURE 2.2 **Torontonians line up at a bus stop. In Canada the etiquette norm is to space oneself from the person next in line and get on the bus in an orderly manner.**

Dhiraj Singh/Bloomberg via Getty Images

FIGURE 2.3 **Commuters board a train at Kurla railway station during the morning rush hour in Mumbai, India, where the norm is to get on public transit as quickly as possible to ensure you get a spot.**

Characteristics of Culture

While culture may consist of material things, our intangible values, attitudes, beliefs, and ideas, as well as the way we behave, it has a number of other characteristics that make it uniquely human. These characteristics are discussed below in some detail and are summarized in Table 2.1.

Culture Influences Biological Processes

Human existence, by its nature, is ***biocultural***; that is, it is the product of both biological and cultural factors. All animals, including humans, have certain biologically determined needs that must be met if they are to stay alive and well. We all need to ingest a minimum number of calories of food each day, protect ourselves from the elements, sleep, and eliminate wastes from our body. It is vital for us to distinguish between these needs and the ways in which we satisfy them. To illustrate, even though all people need to eliminate wastes from the body through defecation, how often, where, in what physical position, and under what social circumstances we defecate are all questions that are answered by our individual culture. In India, less than half the population has access to toilets, resulting in "open defecation," which can lead to the spread of infectious disease. One of the reasons for this practice is poverty, but it is not the only reason. In some parts of India it is a cultural norm and socially accepted (Dinnoo 2014).

biocultural Human existence is the product of both biological and cultural factors.

TABLE 2.1

Features of the Concept of Culture

Culture defined	Culture is everything that people have, think, and do as members of a society.
Culture influences biological processes	Our bodies and biological processes are influenced by culture.
Culture is symbolic	The capacity to use such symbols as language and art (which is the hallmark of humanity) enables people to better understand the world around them.
Culture is learned	Culture is learned by observing others, participating in the culture, and by being taught what things mean and how to behave.
Culture is unconscious	Our own culture is so ingrained in us that we often take it for granted and view our values and behaviour as natural and normal.
Cultures are integrated	The various parts of a culture (i.e., things, ideas, and behaviour patterns) are interconnected to some degree. A change in one part of the culture is likely to bring about changes in other parts of the culture.
Culture is shared	The shared meanings connected to things, ideas, and behaviour patterns make life less ambiguous and more predictable for members of the same cultural group.
Culture and identity	We derive a large part of our sense of identity or who we are from our culture.
Culture is relative	As people share culture as a members of a society, culture is relative, but we must remember that there is a great deal of overlap.
Cultural universals	Despite variations in specific details, all cultures have certain common features, such as systems of governing, patterns of producing and distributing food, forms of enculturation, and family patterns.
Culture is adaptive	Culture enables people to adapt to their environments and thus increase their chances of survival.
Culture is dynamic	The things, ideas, and behaviour patterns of some cultures change constantly through both internal and external processes.

(See Applied Perspective.) Thus, to say that life is biocultural means that our bodies and their accompanying biological processes are heavily influenced by our cultures.

Culture Is Symbolic

Perhaps the most fundamental aspect of culture, and what makes humans unique in the animal world, is the capacity to symbolize. A ***symbol*** is something concrete that stands for or represents something intangible. Symbols can thus be anything we can sense and include, but are not limited to, material objects, behaviours, words, colours, gestures, sounds, and even smells and tastes. The intangible includes values, attitudes, ideas, and beliefs. For instance, countries, religions, companies, sports teams, and so on are really just ideas, and we use flags, icons, and logos to represent them. We cannot see "Canada" but we can see the Canadian flag, which represents everything Canada is.

The key to understanding a symbol is its context. For example, the maple leaf flying at full mast symbolizes ideas of democracy, nationalism, multiculturalism, patriotism, and pride in one's country; flown upside down it symbolizes disrespect; at half-mast it means someone important has died; and draped over a coffin, that the person has died for their country. Symbols are thus ***polysemic***, which means they have many meanings, depending on context.

A classic example of the importance of context in interpreting the meaning of symbols was provided by English philosopher Gilbert Ryle, who asked what the difference is between a wink and a twitch. A twitch, of course, is an involuntary contraction of the eyelid, while a wink is intentional. A twitch does not carry symbolic meaning but a wink does, and it can mean different things depending on whether the person is winking at another on the beach, conversing with friends, practising for a play, and so on. It is the context that allows us to determine the meaning. Symbols can also represent different things to different people from different cultures. For instance, the thumbs up gesture means approval to most Canadians, but is a rude gesture elsewhere.

Symbols are powerful: they move people to act. People will sacrifice their lives for their flag, or rather for what it represents: their country. Marketers in particular have been good at persuading people to buy products not so much for what they do but for what they mean. People will buy a Rolex watch, for instance, not so much because it tells time better than a Casio, but because it symbolizes wealth and status.

The meanings of symbols are also not static but change over time. For example, when Canadians see a swastika, a multitude of ideas and images come to mind, including the Holocaust, Nazism, Adolf Hitler, concentration camps, and goose-stepping storm

symbol Something tangible, such as a material object or behaviour, that represents something intangible, such as a value, attitude, belief, or an organization.

polysemic Having many meanings, for example, symbols.

Open Defecation in India

An estimated 600 million people in India urinate and defecate outdoors wherever they can (Doron and Jeffrey 2014). Worldwide, an estimated 2.5 billion people lacked access to adequate sanitation facilities in 2010 (Budge 2012). When water that has been contaminated by fecal matter is used to irrigate vegetables, it can cause serious gastrointestinal diseases. Children are particularly at risk if they play in areas used for defecation. In India the lack of adequate toilet facilities is largely responsible for the country's high infant and child death rates. And worldwide an estimated 1.5 million children die each year from diarrheal diseases (Budge 2012). Women face more difficulties than men. There are stories of young girls dropping out of school because of the lack of toilets, and yet being in danger of sexual assault when they go to secluded areas to urinate or defecate.

In his 2014 campaign to become Prime Minister of India, Narendra Modi made the country's lack of toilets a prominent issue, arguing that they should come before temples. Modi's assumption was "that once latrines were built, people would flock to use them, just as they flock to temples" (Doron and Jeffrey 2014, 72). The Ministry of Drinking Water and Sanitation thus has a plan to install millions of individual household and public latrines. The lack of adequate toilets is a complex issue, however, and such a "technological" fix is only a partial solution.

The poor in India, as in other developing areas, defecate and urinate where it is convenient and free. This usually means in bushes and fields in rural areas, on vacant land, near railway tracks, along river banks, or other marginal areas in urban areas. In many cases they have little choice; the wealthy can prevent lower class people from using their fields, forcing them to use less hospitable areas. In urban slums there may be no public toilets at all, pay toilets (which are ineffective when people can defecate for free), or there may be one or two latrines for hundreds of people. Using these facilities involves long queues, putting up with foul smells, and thousands of flies. Not surprisingly people prefer to relieve themselves elsewhere.

In some places, open defecation is not seen as a problem to be solved, but rather a resource to be exploited. While some landlords may prevent lower class groups using their land, others welcome them as their bodily excretions help fertilize the soil. Defecation in fields is seen by many villagers in India as proper and pleasurable, and has become a habit. The excrement is moved far from the home and it often provides a welcome chance to meet friends and talk.

Where toilets are installed, cleaning and maintaining them becomes an issue. Who is to do the "dirty" work? Few may have the knowledge to maintain or repair them, so when they become blocked they fall into disrepair and disuse. In private homes, rooms built for a toilet that is unused or unwanted may be converted into a storage area.

The issue is also different in different areas of India. In Kerala, for instance, which has a relatively high population of both Muslims and Christians, it is not as big a problem as elsewhere. Muslim families believe women should be shielded from the view of others, and Christians have had a longer exposure to European ideas of the relationship between sanitation and health. People in Kerala also tend to have higher levels of primary school education and literacy, and are thus more aware of the need for basic sanitary measures. Sanitation-awareness

troopers. The swastika, however, is an ancient symbol and historically has meant good luck, but was appropriated by Hitler's National Socialist (Nazi) party. You might be surprised to learn that several Canadian hockey teams at one time had a swastika emblazoned on their jerseys (Figure 2.4).

It is our capacity to create and give meaning to symbols that help people identify, sort, and classify things, ideas, and behaviours. When people symbolize by using language (the most important human symbolic system), they are able to express experiences that took place at a previous time or suggest events that may happen in the future. Without symbols we would not be able to store the collective wisdom of past generations, and consequently we would be prone to repeating the mistakes of the past. Symbols tie together people who otherwise might not be part of a unified group. The power of our shared symbols becomes clear when we meet others from our own culture in a far-off country. Generally, we are drawn

Fernie and District Historical Society, no. 972

FIGURE 2.4 The Fernie Swastikas women's hockey team 1922–26. Other hockey teams with a "lucky" swastika symbol included the Edmonton Swastikas and The Windsor Swastikas.

campaigns in other areas of India continue to have limited effect due to limited education and understanding of the connections between human excreta, water, disease, and nutrition (Doron and Jeffrey 2014, 72).

India is not the only country facing such problems. Danish graduate student Christopher Furlan (2012), for example, discovered that people in Ghana who had bought a toilet were not necessarily using it but were continuing to defecate outside for a number of reasons, even when this created difficulties and potential embarrassment for them. He discovered that, in many cases, latrines were locked and available only to senior male members of the household; people (especially women) associated the smell and heat from latrines with disease, and saw defecating outside as a healthier option.

PRAKASH SINGH/AFP/Getty Images

Indian residents arrive to defecate in an open field in a village in the Budaun district of Uttar Pradesh.

In 1999, after decades of unsuccessfully attempting to solve the problem of open defecation by constructing latrines and toilets, Indian development consultant Kamal Kar, formed Community-Led Total Sanitation (CLTS) (Budge 2012). Many anthropologists have since become involved in this approach, which is not so much about building toilets or latrines, but about bringing behavioural change by provoking shame and disgust about inadequate sanitation in communities so that they take responsibility for their own sanitation situation and build and pay for their own latrines and toilets (CLTS 2015). The aim of the CLTS website is to provide a global hub and online resource centre to connect practitioners, communities, NGOs, agencies, researchers, governments, donors, and others involved or interested in CLTS.

This applied approach demonstrates that, while open defecation is a problem that affects hundreds of millions of people, the "technical fix" of simply providing a toilet is not necessarily a solution. We need to recognize that many significant and interrelated cultural factors influence whether or not people will actually use them. Furlan (2012) reminds us that people, rather than latrine technologies, should be at the centre of sanitation issues. Toilets need to be economical, socially acceptable, and technologically appropriate. It is also important to understand the local context and practices in attempts to initiate change. What works in India may not work in Ghana or Thailand.

Questions for Further Thought

1. How would you feel about people openly defecating near where you live?
2. What other cultural reasons might there be for people to prefer open defecation to using toilets?
3. What would you recommend policy makers do to improve sanitation?

to them because we share a common set of symbols, for example, language, nonverbal forms of communication, and material culture such as clothing. It is the shared meaning of our symbols that enables us to interact with one another with the least amount of ambiguity and misunderstanding.

The meanings of symbols, however, are arbitrary. There is no objective reason why the meanings we give things have the meanings they do. For example, words are symbols, and there is no objective reason why the sound of the word "cat" in English refers to the animal it does. In Spanish the word is "*gato*," in Icelandic, "*köttur*"; "*myyp*" in Mongolian, and "*o nran*" in Yoruba. It is only by tradition and implicit consensus that speakers of each language agree that a respective sound refers to a furry, domesticated, carnivorous mammal. Because symbolic meanings are arbitrary, we cannot innately know what they mean, or how to behave toward them. This means we have to learn our culture.

Culture Is Learned

During the first half of the 20th century, psychologists, anthropologists, and other social scientists tended to explain human behaviour in terms of various instincts or genetically based propensities. So called Gypsies travelled about because they were thought to have "wanderlust" in their blood; black people were musical because they were believed to have natural rhythm; and some people, owing to their genetic makeup, were supposedly born criminals. Today, anthropology has dismissed this type of biological determinism. Instead, although acknowledging the role of biology, most social scientists support the notion that humans are born with little predetermined behaviour.

If we stop to think about it, a great deal of what we do during our waking hours is learned. Brushing our teeth, eating three meals a day, doing the dishes, attending school, carrying around our cellphones, knowing to stop at a red light, sleeping on a mattress, and waving

Jamie Grill/The Image Bank/Getty Images

FIGURE 2.5 Children learn their culture from their parents and others in their society, as shown here by a mother and daughter practising yoga.

goodbye are all learned responses to our cultural environment (Figure 2.5). In addition to learning which behaviours are appropriate, we also learn which beliefs we should hold, the attitudes we should have, and what things mean. Even though there is an enormous range of variation in cultural behaviour throughout the world, all people acquire their culture by the same process. The process of learning a culture is called ***enculturation***, and it begins the day we are born.

From day one we are immersed in a culture where people have certain things, hold certain values, attitudes, and ideas, and behave in certain ways. If we want to function and be accepted in this society we must learn what these things are and how to behave. There are three primary ways we learn our culture. The first is through observation. We watch what our parents, siblings, friends, and others do and then emulate them. In other words, they set examples, good and bad, for us to follow.

Advertisers capitalize on this process of learning by observation by showing successful happy customers using their products. In this way, the advertisers attempt to persuade us to emulate the success of those customers by buying the product. A commercial for toothpaste, for instance, may show people using the product and then making friends by flashing a smile displaying beautiful teeth, and, since we would like to be accepted, we emulate the characters in the ad and buy the product. Occasionally this backfires. In 2011 the United Kingdom's Advertising Standards Authority (ASA) banned ads by the car maker Citroën showing cyclists not wearing helmets because the ASA argued they might be seen by children and "might encourage younger children to emulate a behaviour prejudicial to their health and safety" (Advertising Standards Authority 2011) (Figure 2.6).

The second way we learn our culture is by participating in it. In other words, we learn it through experience. For instance, when we were young our parents may have taken us grocery shopping with them. Not only were we participating in the activity and observing how our parents selected items from the shelves, placed them on the conveyor belt, and then paid for them, our parents may also have given us the money to pay for the items. In this fashion we learned through participation what it feels like to perform appropriately.

The third way we learn our culture is through being taught it. Our parents, peers, teachers, television, magazines, books, and so on tell us what is important, what attitudes and beliefs we should have, and what behaviour is appropriate. From a young age, for example, we are told to say please and thank you, how to address our elders, that it is wrong to steal, or that God exists.

When we are immersed in a different culture we go through the same process of enculturation. For example, when we begin working for a new company we become immersed in that company's culture and at first do not know which things are appropriate and how to act. To function and be accepted we first begin to observe our colleagues: how do they dress, how do they refer to their bosses; do they use email, text, or telephone to contact them; how do they talk to customers; and so on. And then we emulate them. But we undoubtedly make mistakes. Perhaps we see our colleagues dress in business suits and so dress accordingly, only to feel out of place when on Fridays everyone is dressed casually for casual Fridays. We also participate. We go to meetings, interact with colleagues, partners, customers, and perhaps we shadow someone on a sales trip, or collaborate on some project. And finally, we are

Fred Dufour/AFP/Getty Images

FIGURE 2.6 Advertisements showing cyclist without helmets have been banned in the United Kingdom for fear children might copy them.

enculturation The process by which humans learn their culture.

taught or told what is appropriate. We may be given a manual that outlines company expectations, or perhaps the company has a mentoring program whereby "old timers" tell the newcomers what things mean, and what to wear or not wear, or what is considered appropriate and inappropriate behaviour and language.

When an anthropologist is learning a new culture they are like children. They are immersed in another culture, often knowing little about what is appropriate or what things mean. And they have to be enculturated by the same process as children, whether they are studying a society in the Amazon jungle or the culture of a company. They observe, they participate, and they have someone, an informant or collaborator, who helps them understand the values, attitudes, beliefs, and norms of the culture. The key in all these instances is they learn through total immersion. The difference with anthropologists learning another culture, however, is that they are much more conscious of the process.

Culture Is Unconscious

Most of us begin to say our first words at about one year of age. By the time we are three, we have a vocabulary of several hundred words and, regardless of the language, have mastered its grammar except perhaps for some of the exceptions to the rules. As adults, we put sentences together and make ourselves understood without thinking about the rules of grammar. By three years of age most of us have also learned how to be polite, the proper way to eat our food, what it means to be a boy or a girl, what things are important, and what things mean. In other words, by the time we are three we have learned the basics of our culture. For most of us, however, our memory of when we were three is fragmentary at best. We have internalized our core culture and, just as we speak without being conscious of the grammatical rules of our language, we go about our daily lives without thinking or awareness of the unarticulated rules that govern our behaviour. We have become unconscious to them, taking them for granted.

Culture is so embedded in our psyche that we frequently live out our lives without thinking too much about how our culture influences our thinking and behaviour. How we act and what we think are often so automatic and habitual that we rarely give them any thought at all. Unfortunately, this can lead to the uncritical conclusion that how we live out our lives is natural and normal and really no different from how people from other cultures live out theirs. Because of this we also often think of our culture as being superior. In other words, we begin to be ethnocentric and to judge the ideas, values, and behaviours of others from the standards of our own culture. The job of cultural anthropology is to heighten our awareness of other cultures, as well as our own, in hopes that we will be less likely to take our own culture for granted or as better, and that other cultures are simply different. Learning *not* to take our own culture for granted is the best way to combat ethnocentrism.

Cultures Are Generally Integrated

Cultures should not be thought of as a grocery list of norms, values, and material objects, but as integrated wholes, the parts of which, to some degree, are interconnected with one another. All material things carry often subtle and unconscious meanings for people who act according to what things mean. Thus, we cannot fully understand the material culture without also considering the mental or behavioural aspects. A corporate logo, for example, is a material image that symbolizes the characteristics of the brand, and people often buy, or do not buy, a branded product because of what it means. In a recent experiment, pedestrians in New York City were given the choice of a free T-shirt, one with a Nike logo and the other with a Reebok logo. Most chose the Nike logo. According to Montague (2013), people chose Nike because it meant "high-performance athletics," whereas the Reebok brand lacked the same appealing meaning.

When we view cultures as integrated systems, we can begin to see how particular culture traits fit into the whole system and, consequently, how they tend to make sense within that context.

The study of comparative cultures has taught us that people in different cultures learn different cultural content (the meaning of material items, values, attitudes, ideas, and behavioural patterns), and that they accomplish this with similar efficiency. Culture is not so much a characteristic of individuals per se but of individuals as members of groups. We should not take this to mean, however, that cultures are separate bounded entities with little similarity. Indeed, cultures are more similar than they are different. It is simply that it is the differences that we tend to notice more. For instance, people in predominantly Islamic countries have smartphones, as we do, and use them to maintain relationships with friends and family, coordinate their daily activities, and record memorable moments, as we do. But for many Muslims in the West, as well as in Islamic countries, the cellphone has an additional use and meaning. Many phones now come with a pre-installed app, or an app that can easily be downloaded, that tells Muslims when prayer time is and where Mecca is, and thus in which direction to pray wherever they are. Praying toward the Kaaba, in Mecca, five times a day fulfills one of the five pillars of Islam, and also symbolizes the unity of Muslims worldwide. For many Muslims then, the smartphone also means they can fulfil one of the obligations of their faith. Like the computer, the car, and television, the cellphone is thus more than simply a piece of technology. It is a piece of technology embedded in a social and cultural context from which it derives its meaning.

When describing cultures, anthropologists often identify economic, kinship, social control, marriage, military, religious, aesthetic, technological, and linguistic systems—among others. These various parts of a culture are more than a random assortment of customs, but are to some degree interconnected. Thus, we can speak of cultures as being logical and coherent systems.

The integrated nature of culture enables anthropologists to explain certain socio-cultural facts on the basis of other socio-cultural facts. When we say that cultures are integrated, we are suggesting that many parts not only are connected to one another but also in fact influence one another.

A good example of the integrated nature of culture is provided by Winston Blackmore, who is the religious leader of the polygamous (plural marriage) Mormon fundamentalist community in Bountiful, British Columbia. He has at least 24 wives and anywhere from 67 to 130 children (the reported numbers vary) (Figure 2.7). To get a more comprehensive understanding of polygamy in this context we need to consider it from several aspects. Although from a social aspect polygamy is an uncommon marriage practice in Canada, elsewhere it is the preferred form of marriage. It is, however, currently illegal in Canada, and Blackmore has faced several criminal prosecution charges, which have raised political issues over the ban on polygamy's constitutionality. Some of his defenders say it violates his right under the Charter of Rights and Freedoms to religious freedom. The B.C. government, however, launched constitutional reference cases against him in 2009 and 2014. The first case found that the law did not violate his right to religious freedom, but that the potential harm it could do to women and children was more important and so the case was dismissed. In 2014 the judge concluded that the law does not violate the religious protections in the Charter of Rights and Freedoms (Hutchinson 2014).

While mainstream Mormons abandoned polygamy nearly 150 years ago, the group that Blackmore leads believes that having multiple wives is a commandment from God, and that to achieve salvation a man must marry at least three wives and have as many children as possible. In his community, he, along with his wives, gain prestige by fulfilling their religious obligations. Blackmore's polygamous marriage is also an economic union, and many of his children work for him. In 2013 he was convicted of tax evasion, and in late 2014 the Church of Jesus Christ of Latter-day Saints, who want nothing to do with him, or polygamy, sued him for alleged corporate trademark violation (Keller 2015).

Jonathan Hayward/The Canadian Press

FIGURE 2.7 **Winston Blackmore, the religious leader of the polygamous community of Bountiful, British Columbia. To understand institutions such as polygamy, anthropologists look at it from political, economic, religious, and other aspects.**

The institution of polygamy in Bountiful also raises kinship issues. Blackmore has over 20 sets of in-laws (perhaps a major reason why it is not popular in Canada), and the children from Blackmore's various wives are all half-siblings, who may have competing claims to any inheritance. If the children continue to live in the small community they may have little choice but to marry one another, which could raise medical issues. The point of this example is that, if we want to understand any institution in its context, we must look at it from religious, kinship, political, economic, legal, and other aspects. The concept of integrated cultures is directly related to the concept of cultural relativism (discussed in Chapter 1), which involves viewing any item from within its proper cultural context rather than from the perspective of the observer's culture.

The notion of integrated cultures has important implications for our understanding of culture change. If the parts of any given culture are integrated, then we might expect that a change in one part of the cultural system will bring about changes in other parts of the system. In other words, most changes that occur in cultures tend to be ***linked changes***. The introduction of a single technological innovation may well set off a series of changes in other parts of the culture. To illustrate, since Coca-Cola was introduced into the southern Mexican state of Chiapas in the 1950s, the soft drink has stimulated changes in a number of other features of the local culture. The local power structure has been headed by a family that became the sole distributor of the soft drink nearly a half-century ago. Because this enormously popular carbonated beverage accounts for a large part of the total sales of local shopkeepers, this powerful family distributorship, for all practical purposes, determines who will or will not be a successful retailer in Chiapas. At the same time, Coke has become a major status symbol

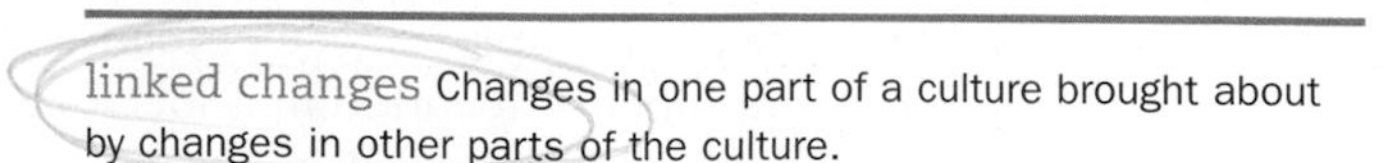

linked changes Changes in one part of a culture brought about by changes in other parts of the culture.

in Chiapas at family celebrations such as baptisms. Serving Coca-Cola has replaced the local alcoholic beverage (called *pox*) as the highest form of hospitality. In fact, the number of servings of Coke offered to a guest is directly proportional to his or her social status. The introduction of Coke into Chiapas has even influenced the state government, which over the past several decades has used Coke in its campaign to curb the consumption of alcohol. Thus, as this example illustrates, a change in one part of the culture system (the introduction of Coke) has been responsible for changes in other parts of the system, namely, the economic power structure, symbols of social status, and the operation of government programs (Borden 2004).

Culture Is Shared

The last phrase in our working definition—*as members of a society*—reminds us that culture is a shared phenomenon. Thus, most people in a society have the same material possessions, share the same ideas about what they mean, have similar attitudes and beliefs, act in similar ways, and participate in the same rituals and ceremonies. Most of us, for example, have smartphones, and we use them to text, arrange meetings, take photos, listen to music, tell time, and so on. Most of us would be lost without them because they mean we can maintain our relationships with friends and family, coordinate our daily activities, and record memorable moments. In other words, the smartphone is a part of the material culture that most of us have, that we use in a similar manner, and that means the same things to most of us.

It is this shared nature of culture that makes our lives less complicated. Because people share a common culture, they are able to predict, within limits, how others will think and behave. For example, when two people meet for the first time in Toronto, it is customary for them to shake hands. If both people grew up in Toronto, neither party will have to wonder what is meant by an outstretched hand. They will know, with nearly absolute certainty, that the extended hand is a nonverbal gesture signifying friendship rather than a sexual advance, a hostile attack, or an attempt to steal one's wallet. It is when we step outside our familiar cultural setting—where meanings are not shared with other people—that misunderstandings occur. In fact, the uncertainty one experiences when trying to operate in an unfamiliar culture often leads to culture shock, a form of psychological distress that can result in depression, overeating, or irritability (see Chapter 5).

The degree to which people within any given society share their culture varies from culture to culture. It was originally thought that people in small-scale societies had the same "cultural stamp," and that they were homogenous in their behaviours and ways of thinking. Even in small-scale societies, however, one can expect to find a certain amount of differentiation based on gender, class, age, religion, or ethnicity. Moreover, societal rules are never adhered to strictly. Although culture exerts a powerful influence, people continue to exercise free will by reinterpreting rules, downplaying their consequences, or disregarding them altogether, such as the Catholic who practises birth control or the person who does not come to a full stop at a stop sign.

In larger, highly complex societies, such as Canada, one is likely to find a number of subcultural groups in addition to the mainstream culture. The use of the terms *subculture* and *mainstream culture* should in no way imply that subcultures are inferior or any less worthy of study. Rather, subcultures are subsets of the wider culture. They share a number of cultural features with the mainstream, but they retain a certain level of cultural uniqueness that sets them apart.

Many societies, such as Canada and the United States, are called ***pluralistic societies*** because they are composed of a number of subcultural groups. Pluralistic societies are not without their difficulties. When different subcultural groups operate with different sets of values and behaviours, misunderstandings (or outright hostilities) are always possible.

Culture and Identity

As culture deals with our deepest values and attitudes, it is intimately tied into our sense of self. We define ourselves in large part by the material items we possess, the values we hold, and the way we behave. We also occupy identities such as age, gender, ethnicity, family, race, and so on. What it means to be each of them is influenced by culture. Each of us belong to these multiple groups simultaneously, and our identity is shaped by the various groups we belong to. One way to look at a society or an organization is as a set of overlapping and nested groups. The larger groups, such as our national, ethnic, religious, age, gender, and kinship groups, tend to have the most influence on our lives, providing us with our core ways of thinking and behaving, as well as our primary sense of identity.

A good example of this is Molson Brewery's 2000 Canadian brand "Joe Rant" beer commercial. In the commercial, Joe, a "typical" Canadian, comes on stage and "rants" about what it means to be Canadian. The script is reproduced below. The ad draws upon major symbolic icons, behaviours, and attitudes that exemplify Canadian identity. The implication is that you can also be truly Canadian by drinking Molson's

pluralistic societies Societies composed of a number of different cultural or subcultural groups.

Canadian beer. The ad was extremely successful, won multiple awards, and increased market share by 2.5 percent, while the competitor brand, Labatt's Blue, lost 2.9 percent market share (MacGregor 2003). It was successful because it appealed to young Canadians who identified with the material items, the symbols, behaviours, and the attitudes experienced by Joe. The commercial also focused on those elements that distinguish Canadians from Americans, while it ignored the vast similarities. What do you identify with in Joes' Rant?

> Hey,
> I'm not a lumberjack, or a fur trader.
> And I don't live in an igloo, or eat blubber, or own a dogsled,
> And I don't know Jimmy, Sally, or Susie from Canada,
> Although I am certain they're really, really nice.
> I have a Prime Minister, not a President.
> I speak English and French, not American.
> And I pronounce it "about" ... not "a-boot."
> I can proudly sew my country's flag on my backpack.
> I believe in peacekeeping not policing;
> Diversity not assimilation;
> And that the beaver is a truly proud and noble animal!
> A tuque is hat; a chesterfield is a couch.
> And it is pronounced ZED not ZEE, ZED!
> Canada is the second largest landmass,
> The first nation of hockey,
> And the best part of North America!
> My name is Joe.
> And I am Canadian.
> Thank you.
> (MacGregor 2003)*

Culture Is Relative

One more point that needs to be made about our definition is that the phrase "as members of a society" implies that the things we have, think, and do are relative to a particular group of people, and are thus culturally relative. While this tends to emphasize the differences between groups, we must remember that there is a great deal of overlap. It is the differences, however, that pose the greatest challenges. Harris and Moran (1987, *x*), for example, have remarked that "the approaches and operations of U.S. and Japanese companies are 95 percent alike but that it is the 5 percent difference that really matters."

Cultural Universals

Since the early 20th century, cultural anthropologists have described the wide variety of cultures found in the contemporary world. As a result, anthropology has been far more effective at documenting cultural differences than at showing similarities among cultures. This preoccupation with different forms of behaviour and different ways of meeting human needs was the result, at least in part, of wanting to move away from the premature generalizing about human nature that was so prevalent a century ago.

This vast documentation of culturally different ways of behaving has been essential to our understanding of the human condition. The significant number of cultural differences illustrates how flexible and adaptable humans are in comparison with other animals because each culture has developed its own set of solutions to the universal human problems facing all societies. For example, every society, if it is to survive, needs a system of communication that enables its members to send and receive messages efficiently. That there are thousands of mutually unintelligible languages in the world today certainly attests to human flexibility. Thus, it is important to bear in mind that, despite their many differences, all cultures of the world share a number of common features (***cultural universals***) because they have all worked out solutions to the whole series of problems that face all human societies.

One of the most fundamental requirements of each society is to see that the basic physiological needs of its people are met. Clearly, people cannot live unless they receive a minimum amount of food, water, and protection from the elements. Every society thus needs to work out systematic ways of producing (or procuring from the environment) absolutely essential commodities and then distributing them to its members. This can be through a capitalist market system based on supply and demand, distribution of food based on kinship, or some other means. Many societies distribute valuable commodities as part of the marriage system, sending considerable quantities of livestock from the family of the groom to the family of the bride. Even though the details of each of these systems of distribution vary greatly, every society has worked out systems of production, distribution, and consumption ensuring that people get what they need for survival. As a result, we can say that every society has an *economic system.*

All societies also need to make provisions for orderly mating and child-rearing that give rise to patterned *systems of marriage and family.* If a society is to endure, it will need to develop a systematic way of passing on its culture from one generation to the next. This universal societal need for cultural transmission leads to some form of *educational system* in all societies. A prerequisite for the longevity of any society is the maintenance of social order; that is, most of the people must obey most of the rules most of the time. This universal societal need to avoid chaos and anarchy leads to a set of mechanisms that coerce people to obey the social norms,

*MacGregor, R. M. (2003). "I am Canadian: National identity in beer commercials." *Journal of Popular Culture* 37(2), 276-286.

cultural universals Those general cultural traits found in all societies of the world.

which we call a *social control system*. Because people in all societies are faced with life occurrences that defy explanation or prediction, all societies have developed systems for explaining the unexplainable, most of which rely on some form of supernatural beliefs such as religion, witchcraft, magic, or sorcery. Thus, all societies have developed a *system of supernatural beliefs* that serves to explain otherwise inexplicable phenomena. And because all societies, if they are to function, need their members to be able to send and receive messages efficiently, they all have developed *systems of communication*, both verbal and nonverbal.

Culture Is Adaptive and Maladaptive

Most living organisms other than humans adapt to their environments by developing physiological features that equip them to maximize their chances for survival. Humans, on the other hand, have relied more on cultural than biological features for adapting to their environments so that they can continue to survive and reproduce. Culture provides humans with an enormous adaptive advantage over all other forms of life. Because culture is learned, humans can produce technological solutions to better adapt to the environment much faster and more efficiently.

Through the invention and use of cultural tools such as spears, arrows, guns, and knives, humans are able to kill and butcher animals even more efficiently than an animal can with its massive jaws and teeth. The discovery of chemical substances such as penicillin, quinine, and the polio vaccine has provided the human species a measure of protection against disease and death. The proliferation of agricultural technology over the past century has dramatically increased humans' capacity to feed themselves. Because humans rely much more heavily on cultural adaptation than on biological adaptation, we are enormously flexible in our ability to survive and thrive in a wide variety of natural environments. Because of the **adaptive nature of culture**, people are now able to live in many previously uninhabitable places, such as deserts, the polar regions, under the sea, and even in outer space.

The notion that culture is adaptive should not lead us to the conclusion that every aspect of a culture is adaptive. It is possible for some features to be adaptively neutral, neither enhancing nor diminishing the capacity of a people to survive. Moreover, it is even possible for some features of a culture to be maladaptive or dysfunctional. To illustrate, the large-scale use of automobiles coupled with industrial pollutants is currently destroying the quality of the air in our environment. If this set of cultural behaviours continues unchecked it could potentially destroy our environment to such an extent that it will be unfit for human habitation. Thus, it is not likely that such a maladaptive practice will persist indefinitely. Either the practice will disappear when the people become extinct, or the culture will change so that the people will survive. Whichever outcome occurs, the maladaptive cultural feature will eventually disappear.

What is adaptive in one culture may be maladaptive or adaptively neutral in another culture. For example, in Canada and North America in general, people are enculturated to be competitive and aggressive in their business dealings, and to express their own point of view. This can be disadvantageous when dealing with Japanese business associates where the goal in negotiations is to achieve consensus and promote harmony, and to be good listeners (Ferraro and Briody 2013).

CROSS-CULTURAL MISCUE

When *National Post* reporter Matthew Coutts was informed by the landlady of his Toronto apartment building that a complaint had been filed against him for an apparently inappropriate hallway interaction with another tenant's wife he was stunned. It was not as if he had uttered some crude sexual comment or made some racial slur, all he had done was say "good morning" on his way to work. The husband was a doctor from the Middle East who felt Coutts had broken a cultural taboo by speaking directly to his wife, while Coutts felt he was simply making a polite neighbourly greeting. The incident resulted in a shouting match and warnings not to repeat his indiscretion. His landlady tried to help by telling Coutts never to speak to his neighbour or even to make eye contact with her.

The incident highlights the fact that living in a multicultural society has become increasingly complicated, and we have to be careful about stereotyping the husband's reaction as a reflection of his culture rather than an individual personality trait. But this example does raise the question about who has made the cultural miscue. Was it Coutts for not being more culturally aware, or was it the husband for not being more understanding of the norms of Canadian cultural etiquette. Should Coutts follow his landlady's advice, or should the husband be more accepting of Canadian cultural practices (Coutts 2009)?

Culture Is Dynamic

Thus far we have presented culture as a combination of things, ideas, and behaviour patterns transmitted from generation to generation through the process of

adaptive nature of culture The implication that culture is the major way human populations adapt or relate to their specific habitat in order to survive and reproduce.

learning. This view of culture, focusing as it does on continuity among the generations, tends to emphasize its static rather than dynamic aspects. And yet a fundamental principle underlying all cultures is that there is nothing as constant as change. Indeed, in one sense, culture can be looked at as an ongoing process; it is always changing and evolving, never static. As the material aspects of culture change, so too do the meanings we attach to them, our ideas and values, and the behaviours we engage in. Some cultures—those that remain relatively insulated from the global economy—change quite slowly, whereas for others change occurs more rapidly. Despite the wide variation in the speed with which cultures change, one thing is certain: No culture remains completely static year after year.

One need not be a scholar of cultural change to notice that cultures have been changing more rapidly with each passing decade. In contrast to our hectic existence, the everyday lives of our grandparents seem simple and slow moving. Today many people are overwhelmed by how quickly their cultures are changing. In 1970, Alvin Toffler (1970) coined the terms *information overload* and *future shock*, which he defined as the psychological disorientation resulting from living in a cultural environment that is changing so rapidly that people feel they are constantly living in the future. Toffler's notion of future shock rings truer than ever before.

Cultural change now occurs at such an accelerated pace that it is often difficult to keep up with the latest developments. The recent revolution in transportation and electronic communications has made the world seem smaller. Today it is possible to fly to the other side of the Earth in about the same time it took our great-grandparents to travel 50 km using a horse and carriage. Via Skype we can communicate face-to-face with relatives, friends, and business associates instantly for free and from anywhere in the world. Indeed, the global exchange of commodities and information is bringing the world's population closer to the notion of living in a global village. Because of this rapid and dramatic increase in our capacity to interact with people in other parts of the world, the likelihood of cultures diffusing (or spreading) has increased dramatically in recent decades.

In a real sense, any ethnographic description of a specific group of people is like a snapshot at one particular time. If the ethnographer studies the same group again five years later, some cultural features undoubtedly will have changed.

invention A new combination of existing cultural features.

innovation A change brought about by the recombination of already existing items within a culture.

cultural diffusion The spreading of a cultural trait (i.e., a material object, idea, or behaviour pattern) from one society to another.

Cultural change is brought about by both internal and external factors. Internal factors include inventions and innovations, as well as new ideas, whereas external factors include cultural diffusion (spreading) between cultures. Although diffusion is responsible for the greatest amount of cultural change, it is important to examine both processes of change in greater detail.

Inventions and Innovations

Any new thing, idea, or behaviour pattern that emerges from within a society is an ***invention*** or an ***innovation***. Some inventions are deliberate and purposeful, whereas others are unconscious and unintentional. Ralph Linton, one of the most prominent scholars of cultural change in the 20th century, suggested that, over the long run, the unconscious inventor has had a greater impact on cultural change than has the conscious inventor. The unconscious or accidental inventor contributes to cultural change without being driven by an unmet societal need, or even realizing that she or he is making a contribution. As Linton (1936, 311) put it, "Their inventions are, as a rule, of little individual importance, but they loom large in the aggregate."

These numerous unintentional inventors sometimes go unnoticed and unrewarded, even though they may be making a significant cumulative contribution to their culture. An example of an unintentional invention—which actually had an important impact—was the scientist at 3M who, while trying to invent a strong adhesive, failed and produced instead a weak adhesive that was ideal for Post-it Notes. Most often it is the deliberate, intentional inventor who is recognized and rewarded. Alexander Graham Bell, for instance, was sufficiently motivated to help people communicate that he invented the telephone, while Canadian Frederick Banting was the first to synthesize insulin to help overcome diabetes. Hundreds of other inventors have come up with new discoveries, gadgets, and ideas because they wanted to do something better or more efficiently. As important as inventions and discoveries are to cultural change, the total number of inventions in any given society is generally quite small.

Cultural Diffusion

Most change is due to external forces. Cultures are not isolates but are integrated into a global system where new ideas and ways of doing things are easily borrowed. The spread of cultural elements from one culture to another is known as ***cultural diffusion*** and takes less effort than invention. It may not even need direct contact. When Europeans first contacted people in the Amazonian jungle, they were already using metal tools that had diffused from the coast into the interior through various trade routes. If every culture had to rely solely on its own inventions, human progress over the centuries would indeed be slow. Cultures have been able to develop rapidly because the process of diffusion has enabled humans to pool their creative/inventive resources.

In precolonial times most sub-Saharan African societies viewed thin women as unattractive, and overweight women as beautiful. But due to the influence of Western ideals, contemporary African women (with the assistance of government health officials) are getting the message that being obese, or even overweight, not only is unhealthy but also will dash whatever hopes they might have of participating in the "Miss Universe" contest held in the major capitals of the world. As one indicator of these changing values, women in Mauritania—where women have routinely been "force fed" to make them more corpulent—are now seen going on power walks at local sports stadiums to lose weight (LaFraniere 2007, 4). Although many Africans continue to hold onto their traditional values, Western values are beginning to take hold through the process of cultural diffusion.

The Process of Diffusion Is Selective

When two cultures come into contact, they do not exchange every cultural item. If that were the case, there would be no cultural differences in the world today. Instead, only a small number of cultural elements are ever diffused from one culture to another. Which cultural item is accepted depends largely on the item's use and compatibility with already existing cultural traits. Cultural diffusion is a selective process. Some things, especially new technologies, are readily accepted by other cultures and spread quickly, while others, such as religious beliefs and values and behaviour patterns spread very slowly. For example, a traditional farmer in Senegal is more likely to be convinced of the advantages of using a tractor over a hoe for plowing his field than he is of substituting Shintoism for his traditional form of ancestor worship. Other variables that influence diffusion include the duration and intensity of contact, the degree of cultural integration, and the similarities between the donor and recipient cultures.

Even when an innovation is consistent with a society's needs, there is still no guarantee that it will be accepted. For example, most people in the United States have resisted adopting the metric system even though making such a change would enable U.S. citizens to interface with the rest of the world more efficiently.

Diffusion Is a Two-Way, Reciprocal Process

We should not assume that cultural items diffuse only from technologically complex societies to simpler societies; cultural traits are diffused in both directions. European contact with native North Americans is a case in point. Even though Europeans introduced much of their culture to native North Americans, the Europeans nevertheless received a number of cultural features in return, including articles of clothing, such as ponchos, parkas, and moccasins; medicines, such as quinine, pain relievers, and laxatives; and food items, such as corn, beans, tomatoes, squash, yams, avocados, and the so-called "Irish" potato.

Cultural Elements May Be Modified

When cultural elements are accepted into a new culture, they are recontextualized and may take on new meanings and uses and undergo changes in form or function. Pizza is a good example of how a cultural item can change form as it diffuses. Pizza, which diffused from Italy to Canada and the United States in the late 19th century, has been modified in significant ways to conform to North American tastes. It is unlikely that its Italian originators would recognize a pizza made of French bread, English muffins, or pita bread, and topped with pineapple, tuna, or jalapeño peppers.

As things move from one culture to another, their meanings may also be reinterpreted as they are integrated into the receiving culture. A good example of this is tobacco. Among many First Nations cultures, tobacco is seen as an offering to the Creator. When Sir Walter Raleigh introduced it into Europe in the 1500s, the context was changed and smoking tobacco became an activity with no religious significance.

Sometimes the reinterpretation process involves a change in the way an item is used. The Maasai of Kenya and Tanzania, for instance, practise the custom of piercing the earlobes and enlarging the hole by inserting increasingly larger round pieces of wood until a loop of skin is formed. Rather than using pieces of round wood for this purpose, at least one group of Maasai have used flashlight batteries discarded by tourists. In this case the form of the batteries is the same, but the function has been changed.

Acculturation is a special type of diffusion that takes place as a result of sustained contact between two societies, one of which is subordinate to the other. Thus, both diffusion and acculturation involve cultural change as a result of contact with another group. But whereas diffusion involves a single trait or a complex set of traits, acculturation involves the widespread reorganization of one or both cultures over a short period of time. Both the dominant and the subordinate culture may experience changes, but the subordinate culture always changes more dramatically. Acculturation

---

acculturation A specific form of cultural diffusion in which a subordinate culture adopts many of the cultural traits of a more powerful culture.

can have a variety of consequences. The subordinate culture may become extinct, it may be incorporated as a distinct subculture of the dominant group, or it may be assimilated (blended) into the dominant group. But whatever form it takes, acculturation is *forced* borrowing under conditions of external pressure.

The concept of acculturation implies that the subordinate group changes voluntarily under the influence of the more dominant culture. In many cases, however, change is forced upon the subordinate culture whereby they have little choice but to accept the worldview, beliefs, and practices of the dominant group. This has now become known as ***cultural hegemony***, although the term was originally used by the Italian Marxist philosopher Antonio Gramsci to show how the ruling capitalist classes dominated the working classes (Lears 1985). Cultural hegemony can lead to the complete loss of culture, which has become known as ***cultural genocide***. A good example of this is the loss of much of the traditional culture of many of Canada's First Nations. Already deprived of most of their land through various treaties and by other means, a federal policy of mandatory assimilation meant that, under the Residential School system, First Nations children were forcibly removed from their communities to attend schools in remote locations. Run by various church organizations, the children were prevented from speaking their own language or practising their own beliefs and customs. Instead, they were required to adopt Euro-Canadian culture and to speak English or French. In its final report on Canada's Residential Schools, the Truth and Reconciliation Commission stated that the Canadian Indian residential school system "can best be described as 'cultural genocide' " (Truth and Reconciliation Commission 2015, 1). Unsurprisingly, many First Nations lost much of their traditional culture, and many of the continuing difficulties First Nations people face is due to this loss. One of their major concerns is to revive and reconnect with their traditional culture, albeit in the contemporary context.

cultural hegemony A process whereby a people are forcibly assimilated by a dominant culture.

cultural genocide A process whereby a people lose their identity as a distinct culture through disposing of their lands and cultural hegemony.

small-scale society A society that has a small population, minimal technology, lacks a written form of their language, has little division of labour, and is not highly stratified.

"Primitive" Cultures

A fundamental feature of the discipline of Cultural Anthropology is its comparative approach. Whether studying religions, economic systems, ways of resolving conflicts, or art forms, cultural anthropologists look at these aspects of human behaviour in the widest possible context, ranging from the most technologically simple foraging societies at one end of the continuum, to the most highly industrialized societies at the other. Societies with simple technologies, once called "primitive," are described by contemporary cultural anthropologists as *preliterate*, *small-scale*, *egalitarian*, or *technologically simple*. Because of the misleading implication that something primitive is both inferior and earlier in a chronological sense, the term *primitive* is not used in this book. Instead, we use the term ***small-scale society***, which refers to societies that have small populations, are technologically simple, lack a written form of language, have little labour specialization, and are not highly stratified. Making such a distinction between small-scale and more complex societies should not be taken to imply that all societies can be pigeonholed into one or the other category. Rather, it is more fruitful to view all the societies of the world along a continuum from most small-scale to most complex.

Summary

1. For the purposes of this book, we have defined the term *culture* as everything that people have, think, and do as members of a society. This includes material items, values, attitudes, and ideas, as well as norms of behaviour.
2. There is considerable pressure to conform to the norms of the society, although people have the freedom to say no to cultural expectations.
3. Certain aspects of culture, such as ideas, beliefs, and values, can affect our physical bodies and our biological processes.
4. Culture consists of arbitrary symbols that gain their meaning from their context. People's interpretation of their meanings influences their behaviour.
5. Rather than being inborn, culture is acquired through a learning process called *enculturation*. People in different cultures learn different things, but people in all cultures learn through observation, participation, and by being taught what things mean and how to behave.
6. We take for granted most aspects of culture, which leads us to take what we think and do as natural

and normal until we experience another culture, and this can result in *culture shock*.

7. A culture is more than the sum of its parts. Rather, a culture should be seen as an integrated system with its parts interrelated to some degree. This cultural integration has important implications for the process of culture change because a change in one part of the system is likely to bring about changes in other parts.
8. Culture is something that is shared by members of the same society. This shared nature of culture enables people to predict—within broad limits—the behaviour of others in the society. Conversely, people become disoriented when attempting to interact in a culturally different society because they do not share the same behavioural expectations as members of that society.
9. As culture deals with our deepest values and attitudes, it is intimately tied into our sense of self.
10. While the phrase "as members of a society" implies that culture is relative to a particular group of people, there is a great deal of overlap between cultures.
11. Although cultures throughout the world vary considerably, certain common features (cultural universals) are found in all cultures. Cultural anthropology—the scientific study of cultures—looks at both similarities and differences in human cultures wherever they may be found.
12. Cultures function to help people adapt to their environments and consequently increase their chances for survival. It is also possible for cultures to negatively alter or even destroy their environments.
13. Cultures—and their three basic components of things, ideas, and behaviour patterns—are constantly experiencing change. Although the pace of culture change varies from society to society, no culture is totally static. Cultures change internally (innovation) and by borrowing from other cultures (diffusion).
14. Cultural diffusion is selective, it is a two-way process, it is likely to involve changes in form or function, some cultural items are more likely candidates for diffusion than are others, and it is affected by other important variables.
15. Acculturation is a form of cultural diffusion whereby a dominant society overwhelms a subordinate one. Cultural hegemony exists when the subordinate group is forced to accept the dominant culture and can result in cultural genocide.
16. Because the parts of a culture are to some degree interrelated, a change in one part is likely to bring about changes in other parts. This insight from cultural anthropology should be of paramount importance to applied anthropologists, who are often involved directly or indirectly with planned programs of cultural change.

Key Terms

acculturation
adaptive nature of culture
attitudes
beliefs
biocultural
cultural diffusion
cultural genocide
cultural hegemony
cultural universals
culture
enculturation
ideas
innovation
invention
linked changes
norms
pluralistic societies
polysemic
schema
small-scale society
society
symbol
values

Critical Thinking Questions

1. Working with fellow students, come up with 20 ways in which the words culture and cultural are used (e.g., multicultural, pop culture). What do these terms imply about the concept of culture?
2. Select a team or a group, or some activity you engage in with others, and list the norms of the group.
3. While we all must eat to survive, what we eat, when we eat, how we eat, how often we eat, where we eat, how much we eat, and so on are all heavily influenced by our culture. Discuss with a fellow student from a culture different from your own the differences in your consumption patterns.
4. How do the values, attitudes, and beliefs of your generation differ from those of your parents' and grandparents' generations?
5. The smartphone is now a ubiquitous part of our material culture. How has it affected our behaviours and the non-material aspects of our culture?

6. Some of the enculturating forces in Western society are media, such as television, movies, news stories, advertisements, and so on. How have they influenced the things you have, how you behave, and your attitudes, beliefs, and values? How has access to Western media influenced other non-Western cultures?
7. What are the cultural symbols that are important to you in terms of your identity as a person of a given gender, age, and ethnicity or nationality?
8. Poaching—the illegal hunting of wild animals—is a worldwide problem that can result in the extinction of endangered species, environmental changes, and the outbreak of diseases, such as Ebola, SARS, and HIV. Motives for poaching vary from providing subsistence and making a livelihood to financial gain and pleasure. How could an anthropologist work with a culture in sub-Saharan Africa to end the practice of killing and consuming chimpanzees, gorillas, and other primates?
9. What elements of mainstream Canadian culture have been borrowed from China, India, and the Middle East?
10. First Nations peoples have lost much of their traditional culture through colonization by Euro-Canadians. How could anthropologists work with them to revive and reconnect with their traditional cultures?

Make the Grade with MindTap

Stay organized and efficient with **MindTap**—a single destination with all the course material and study aids you need to succeed. Built-in apps leverage social media and the latest learning technology. For example:

- ReadSpeaker will read the text to you.
- Self-quizzing allows you to assess your understanding.
- Flashcards are pre-populated to provide you with a jump-start for review—or you can create your own.
- You can highlight text and make notes in your MindTap Reader. Your notes will flow into Evernote, the electronic notebook app that you can access anywhere when it's time to study for the exam.

Visit nelson.com/student to start using **MindTap**. Enter the Online Access Code from the card included with your text. If a code card is not provided, you can purchase instant access at NELSONbrain.com.

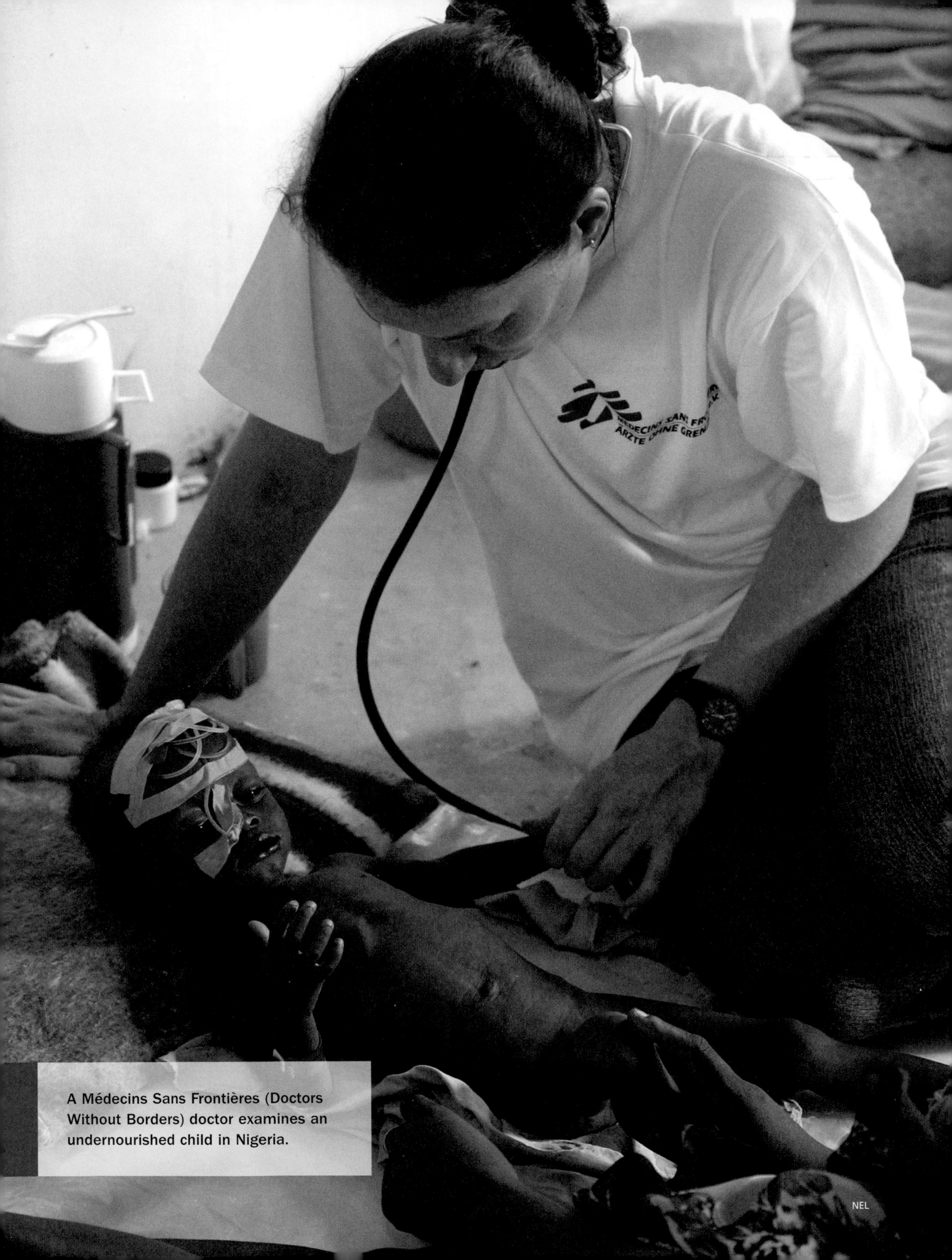

A Médecins Sans Frontières (Doctors Without Borders) doctor examines an undernourished child in Nigeria.

Applied Anthropology

CHAPTER

3

WHAT WE WILL LEARN

- What applied anthropology is
- How applied anthropology differs from ethnographic anthropology
- The value of the anthropological perspective in applied anthropology
- What specialized roles applied anthropologists play
- What job opportunities are available for students of applied anthropology
- How one can apply anthropology in the real world

THE CHINA HOME LEARNING PC

In early 2003, Intel anthropologist Genevieve Bell and her team travelled to China in search of a marketing opportunity. Research had shown that a large number of families with school-aged children were not buying personal computers (PCs) even though they could afford one. Clearly, the standard PC was not meeting their needs.

The team conducted ethnographic research in a number of households with children ages 6 to 12 years. Under China's one-child policy, the top priority of parents—for which they are willing to make great sacrifices—is to ensure that their child receives a good education as this is seen to open up opportunities for them in later life. This means getting good grades in both written and spoken Mandarin Chinese, as well as English. Parents were not buying PCs because they were seen as a distraction and were afraid their child would waste time surfing the Internet or playing games. Immersing themselves in the lives of the families gave the team a good idea of what the parents wanted, what the typical child user was like, and where a PC would be located in the cramped living space of the home or apartment. In order for designers to understand how a young family would interact with and experience a PC in the home, Intel even built a replica of a Chinese apartment, along with a PC and desk.

This knowledge was then translated into a set of six basic engineering requirements: (1) it must have Mandarin Chinese, English, and math content relevant to the school curriculum; (2) it must accommodate reading, writing, and speaking functionality; (3) it must have a keyboard and mouse, as well as a stylus for handwriting; (4) parents must have control so that only Internet sites with educational activities and content could be accessed; (5) it must function as a state-of-the-art PC for parental use; and (6) it had to fit within the physical constraints of a typical Chinese apartment.

In January 2005 the China Home Learning PC was launched. It comes with a physical lock-and-key mechanism so parents can restrict their child's access to educational content. The monitor has two positions: upright for use with a mouse and keyboard, and horizontal for writing with a stylus. Software prompts the child to match handwriting and speech. A Mandarin sentence is played and the child is encouraged to repeat it. His or her words are then matched against ideal pronunciation, and feedback is provided to help the child improve. The product received the China Design Excellence Award in late 2004.

This example shows how ethnographic methods and an understanding of technology in the cultural context in which it is used can be applied to help companies develop not only products that people actually desire and use, but also to reduce the risks of introducing new technology. Intel calls it "People-inspired technology" (D'Hooge 2006). ■

Applying Anthropology

As we pointed out in the first two chapters, cultural anthropologists are inquisitive and curious about people, their way of life, their beliefs and values, the way they do things, and the material objects they make, use, collect, and discard over a lifetime. In general, cultural anthropologists may be considered ethnographic, or descriptive, anthropologists because their interests lie principally in describing another culture. Globalization, however, has accelerated change in many local communities, creating numerous opportunities and also posing many challenges. For example, the expansion of the global economy into China, India, Brazil, Africa, and elsewhere has resulted in increased wealth for some and transformed social relationships. The introduction of new products and ideas has changed people's attitudes and behaviours and, as economies in developing countries engage in greater manufacturing, there have been negative environmental impacts (Copeland-Carson et al. 2012). An increasing number of anthropologists thus apply their anthropological training to the solution of human problems, and conduct research aimed explicitly at practical applications.

These pragmatic anthropologists purposefully conduct field research among populations experiencing serious societal problems and apply anthropological data, concepts, and strategies to the solution of social, economic, environmental, and technological problems, both at home and abroad. They work on such issues as public health, inadequate food production, high infant mortality, political repression, and community development. These practitioners share their applied perspective, which is characterized by ***problem-oriented research*** among the world's contemporary populations.

In other settings, anthropologists with an applied perspective might be employed to develop new products, or organize a vaccination program in a developing country, or facilitate team building in an international corporation. These cultural anthropologists are often referred to as applied anthropologists. Simply put, applied anthropology is the application of anthropological knowledge, concepts, theories, and methods to the solution of specific problems. Some applied anthropologists also have further specializations that they acquired in graduate school while completing advanced degrees.

Some people make a further distinction between applied anthropologists and practicing anthropologists: Applied anthropologists generally work at a university, and also work as consultants for government or nongovernmental agencies, or as principal investigators on their own research. Such applied anthropologists may also work with community partners to establish a community-based research project while also employed at a university. Practicing anthropologists, on the other hand, may be specialists in a topical area of anthropology or a particular methodology, but they use their anthropological knowledge in their places of employment. These applied anthropologists are not employed by a university, rather, they are practitioners applying anthropological concepts and methods where they work and in the jobs they perform. For example, companies such as Intel, Microsoft, and Google all employ applied anthropologists. As noted in the opening vignette, Genevieve Bell (Figure 3.1) heads a team of anthropologists and designers at Intel. To help the company develop new products for their chips (Singer 2014), these anthropologists watch people throughout the world using technology both at home and in public.

As you read through this chapter, we hope you find ways to include anthropological concepts in your careers. No matter what career you chose, however, you can carry your anthropological knowledge with you to help you better interact with people from around the world.

FIGURE 3.1 Genevieve Bell is a Vice President of Intel Labs and Director of User Experience Research. She leads a team of social scientists, designers, engineers, and computer scientists who help shape new Intel products and technologies focusing on people's needs and desires.

---

problem-oriented research A type of anthropological research designed to solve a particular societal problem rather than to test a theoretical position.

Stephen Dorey ABIPP/Alamy Stock Photo

FIGURE 3.2 Medical anthropologists can contribute to food and nutrition programs where they assist in a variety of capacities as researchers and advocates, as in this feeding project in the village of Buli, Malawi.

Data from a recent survey conducted by the American Anthropological Association (AAA) indicate that more than half the anthropologists with doctorate degrees are finding permanent employment outside academia in government, nonprofit organizations, and private sector firms (Fiske et al. 2010). This trend has been accompanied by increases in the number of masters programs in applied anthropology and growing membership in applied anthropology organizations, such as the Society for Applied Anthropology (SfAA) and the National Association for the Practice of Anthropology (NAPA).

The nature of ethnographic research—which involves living with people, sharing their lives, and often befriending them—makes it difficult for cultural anthropologists to ignore the enormity of the problems these societies face on an everyday basis. It should therefore come as no surprise that many cultural anthropologists feel a sense of responsibility for helping to solve—or at least alleviate—some of these pressing social problems (Figure 3.2). The methods, objectives, and time frames of pure ethnographic research and applied anthropology, however, differ. (Table 3.1) As discussed in Chapter 1, some anthropologists consider applied anthropology to be a fifth subfield of anthropology, whereas other anthropologists recognize that applied concepts are embedded in all of anthropology's four major subfields.

Most anthropologists who identify with an applied perspective are cultural anthropologists, but the other three traditional subfields (archaeology, biological or physical anthropology, and linguistics) are certainly involved in their share of applied activities. For example, an archaeologist may develop a career around cultural resource management; a biological anthropologist may be involved in forensic anthropology and work on crime scenes and testify in court, or they may assist in disaster work with DNA analysis and body recovery; and a linguist may work on language preservation among speakers of an endangered language (one with a small number of speakers). Some applied anthropologists share an interest in both biological and cultural anthropology, and may combine these interests in the form of medical anthropology. For example, there are some medical anthropologists who have a degree in nursing or in medicine.

The Anthropological Perspective

The *anthropological perspective*, or the way anthropologists look at and understand peoples and cultures, is invaluable in applications of its concepts and methods to improve the lives of people everywhere. There are several aspects of this perspective that make it valuable.

Holistically. Anthropologists try to see the larger picture and how one aspect of life connects with others. They are thus good at seeing complexity. For example, if an anthropologist is concerned with agricultural practices, he or she would also look at the influence of political policies, family structure, religious beliefs, and so on.

Relativistically. All behaviour takes place within a particular social and cultural context, and can best be understood from within that context. Anthropologists

anthropological perspective The way anthropologists look at and understand peoples and cultures; that is, holistically, relativistically, naturalistically, comparatively, globally, bio-culturally, and reflexively.

TABLE 3.1

Comparison of Ethnographic and Applied Anthropology

	Ethnographic Anthropology	Applied Anthropology
Primary objective	To test hypotheses and describe ethnographic reality	To help solve societal problems
Research methods	Participant observation and interviewing	Rapid ethnographic assessment (see Chapter 5)
Time frame	A year or longer	Several weeks to several months
Collaboration	usually work individually	Usually work as a member of a team

© Cengage Learning

thus attempt to see things from the other's point of view, which is usually different from our own. We want to know the historical and environmental context of the culture, the values and attitudes the people have, what motivates them, what things mean to them, and consequently why they behave the way they do. Once anthropologists know this, they are in a much better position to provide culturally relevant programs.

Naturalistically. Connected with the idea of relativism is the practice of studying people in their natural settings. These settings include hospitals, businesses, local villages, agricultural fields, and so on. This is the essence of ethnographic fieldwork and allows anthropologists to see how people actually interact with one another and use things, and to question them about their thoughts and attitudes.

Comparatively. By looking at how behaviours and attitudes vary from one society to another, we can find general patterns and understand why differences exist, and we can suggest why one approach may work in one culture and not another.

Globally. Anthropologists are interested in cultures everywhere and are particularly interested in how global forces impact local cultures, and how those local cultures adapt to these forces. With this approach anthropologists are better able to understand how any proposed change may impact a culture.

Bio-culturally. Anthropologists recognize that there is a relationship between human biology and culture, and that cultural practices may affect biology. For example, cultures without a history of raising cattle tend to have a higher incidence of lactose intolerance, or an inability to drink milk.

Reflexively. Anthropologists are also aware that their gender, race, or social position may influence not only the data they gather, but also how it is applied. For instance, a female anthropologist may find it easier to provide assistance to children than a male anthropologist might.

Applying the Anthropological Perspective

The work of applied anthropology involves (to varying degrees) three major products: information, policy, and action. The first of these products is the collection of solid sociocultural *information* on the people under study—the so-called project beneficiaries. This information, obtained by conducting research with community partners (see Chapter 5), can range from raw ethnographic data, with different levels of analyses, to general anthropological theories (Figure 3.3). Using research findings as a foundation, the applied anthropologist next develops *policy*, which can be used to help lessen a problem or condition identified during the information gathering phase. Although anthropologists may, in fact, be involved in the policymaking process, it is more likely that they will include the policy implications in their findings, or even make policy recommendations. The final product of the applied anthropologist is a plan of *action*, or intervention, designed to correct the problem or undesirable condition. Thus, as John Van Willigen (2002, 11) reminds us, "information is obtained through research, information is used to formulate policy, and policy guides action."

Neil McAllister/Alamy Stock Photo

FIGURE 3.3 A Darwin Initiative Project employee talks to an Indonesian environmental researcher in Ambeua, Kaledupa Island, Sulawesi, Indonesia.

Examples of Applied Anthropology

As we have seen, applied anthropologists use their knowledge and expertise in a variety of areas, from managing cultural resources (CRM), to healthcare, international development, business, and so on. In this section we will look at five of these areas: medicine, business, development, environment, and education.

Medical Anthropology

Disease, illness, and health are concerns for people everywhere. But ideas about what causes people to become ill and how they deal with illness vary from one culture to another. All cultures have also developed particular institutions and traditions to promote health, and when people become sick they turn to their medical system for help (Erickson 2008). A ***medical system*** consists of ideas about the causes of illness, or ***etiology***; the methods of diagnosis, treatment, and prevention;

medical system The etiology, methods of diagnosis, treatment, and prevention of disease, and the organization of the health system.

etiology Ideas about the causes of disease.

CROSS-CULTURAL MISCUE

In the Democratic Republic of Congo over 930,000 people are infected with HIV, yet only 25 percent of them receive medication. In response to this serious problem, aid agencies have flooded the country with free or low cost condoms, but only 3 percent of young adults in the Congo use them. The aid agencies encourage people to use them by focusing on fear (of getting HIV), fidelity (to protect one's partner), and finance (to remind people who paid for them, i.e., the aid agency) (Figure 3.4). They are marketed with messages to act prudently, such as "Thank you for taking care of yourself and protecting your partner," and are given names such as "Trust," "Prudence," "Vive–Love to Live!" They come in packages with a red ribbon to remind users of HIV or with pictures of a loving couple, and are dispensed from machines that remind people who paid for them. This marketing message and the packaging of condoms was acceptable to the aid agencies' donors and politicians back home, but was simply not getting through to the users.

Amy Lockwood, global development worker and deputy director of Stanford's Center for Innovation in Global Health, points out that fear, fidelity, and finance are not the things people think about when they get a condom. "What is it that you think about just before you get a condom? Sex!" The private companies, on the other hand, which sell condoms for a higher price, use sexual and provocative imagery in their packaging. Even though condom use in the Congo is still low, Lockwood argues that the private companies are winning market share because they understand their customers. The message here is that, if what aid agencies are really trying to do is stop the spread of HIV by getting people to change their behaviour, they must see things from the point of view of the end user, or customer. As Lockwood says, "What are the messages that are going to get them to change their behaviour, it may just save their lives" (Lockwood 2011).

Per-Anders Pettersson/Getty Images

FIGURE 3.4 A 2005 advert for Life Guard condoms on a billboard in Kampala, Uganda. Life Guard condoms are bought by The President's Emergency Plan for AIDS Relief and the Global Fund to Fight AIDS, Tuberculosis and Malaria; and are distributed free of charge with the implicit messages of fear, fidelity, and finance.

Source: From "Selling condoms in the Congo," TedGlobal 2011. Copyright © TED Conferences, LLC.

and the organization of the health practitioners who have the knowledge and skills and culturally recognized training to deliver healthcare. For instance, if you believe you are ill because of sorcery, you may go to a diviner or shaman for a diagnosis, who may then prescribe some sort of counter-magic or herbal remedy, and provide you with an amulet to ward off further attacks. In Canada, the primary healthcare system is based on the ***biomedical model***, in which disease is thought to be due to some infection or genetic disorder that affects the biology of the body, and health is the absence of disease and the normal functioning of the body. If you become ill you are most likely to believe it is because of some bacterial or viral infection, and visit a general practitioner who has graduated from a certified medical school for a diagnosis. He or she may then prescribe antibiotics and suggest a change in your diet to boost your immune system.

The Western biomedical system has a hierarchical structure and reflects our core cultural values of independence, individualism, the scientific method, and capitalism (Erickson 2008, 5). Because of its success in treating the physical body, and because the West has dominated the world through colonization and globalization, the biomedical model has ruled global medical practice since the late 1800s. For the most part, however, the biomedical system rarely considers the psychological, social, spiritual, economic, or political contexts of disease, or the lived experience of the patient (Erickson 2008). The biomedical model also rarely considers the roles that family, religious groups, or community organizations play in patient care. But medical systems, including biomedicine, cannot be understood apart from these things.

Most societies also have more than one medical system—a situation known as ***medical pluralism***. For example, although biomedicine is the primary model in Canada there is also homeopathy, naturopathy,

biomedical model The primary Western medical system in which disease is thought to be due to genetics or infection that affects the biology of the body, and where diagnosis and treatment are performed by highly trained specialists.

medical pluralism A situation in which more than one medical system co-exist.

acupuncture, Ayurvedic (Indian) and Chinese medicine, as well as other "alternative" medicines. The comparative study of these medical systems is known as ethnomedicine, which also includes an understanding of a group's knowledge of the medicinal properties of plants in their environment and their use of drugs, or ***ethnopharmacology***.

One of the distinctions that medical anthropologists make is between ***disease*** and ***illness***: Disease is a biomedical concept and considers the pathogen, such as a virus or bacterium, and the body's response to it. Illness, on the other hand, is a sociocultural concept and relates to a person's perception and experience of being sick, the community's understanding of disease, and the social value associated with being sick. The way that people understand and give meaning to symptoms and illness influences the way they behave toward those who are afflicted. For instance, for centuries in Europe, people with leprosy were thought to be unclean and were ostracized and forced to live in leper colonies. Even today in India and Japan, many people with leprosy are required to live apart from the rest of the population. Social stigma is attached to other diseases such as syphilis, tuberculosis, and HIV/AIDS, often preventing people from seeking medical attention or receiving it. When we understand the cultural perceptions of illness in a specific context, then we can understand illness behaviours and begin to implement change.

Medical anthropology is concerned primarily with comparing the ways societies conceive of and deal with disease, illness, and health, as well as the relationship between patients and healers, and between ill people and others in the family and society. Medical anthropologists are also interested in the complex relationships between culture, economics, politics, disease, the environment, and biocultural adaptation. Consequently, they also investigate the role of demographics, government policies, genetics, and epidemiology, which looks at the causes and patterns of disease transmission in populations. In other words, medical anthropologists are concerned with the context and experience of illness and health (Erickson 2008).

Culture influences a society's medical beliefs and practices, and anthropologists, as well as medical practitioners and healthcare workers, are becoming increasingly aware of the need to understand these influences if they want to alleviate human suffering. As an area of applied anthropology, medical anthropologists are concerned with applying their knowledge and methods to improve the health and well-being, and alleviate the suffering, of people in all societies. ***Applied medical anthropology*** is thus the application of anthropological theories, concepts, and methods in the study of health, illness, and healing to improve the well-being of people everywhere.

Applied medical anthropologists use their knowledge of local medical systems to implement community health programs among ethnic and cultural minorities in Canada, other Western cultures, as well as non-Western societies. They evaluate current methods of healthcare and communities' responses to healthcare practices, and recommend improvements to enhance healthcare delivery. They work with local healthcare providers, whether they are shamans, midwives, traditional healers, or professionally trained doctors. They may also, for instance, examine how men and women, different classes, or different ethnic groups within a society may have differential access to the medical system. Medical anthropologists are thus also concerned with how people access medical care, and seek ways to improve equality of access.

Canadian applied medical anthropologist Wayne Warry, for instance, works with First Nations to evaluate and develop healthcare programs and systems that are culturally specific and appropriate (Warry 2007). Indigenous people in Canada are the poorest group in Canada, having the lowest levels of education, employment, and adequate housing, as well as the highest levels of smoking and substance abuse. They also have the highest rates of diabetes, obesity, chronic respiratory diseases, and suicide. Warry maintains that the remoteness of many communities and the paternalistic attitude and policies of the Canadian government produces challenges to healthcare delivery services, which are largely run by non-Indigenous people. He advocates for greater indigenous management and control over their health services, and argues that many of the issues can be resolved by improving training and educating for First Nations people, who can then provide culturally appropriate healthcare. It is the local communities that have contact with and know people on the reserve, and know what is needed. Warry's work demonstrates that interventions must consider the broader social, cultural, economic, and political contexts. With the aid of applied medical anthropologists such as Warry, First Nations healthcare systems are improving.

Medical anthropology is one of the most rapidly expanding areas of anthropology and spans both the biological and social sciences. Many medical anthropologists come from health professions such as medicine or nursing, whereas others come from backgrounds such as psychology, social work, education, human geography, or sociology. In recent years the number of positions in medical anthropology has been increasing rapidly, and the Society for Medical Anthropology is

---

ethnopharmacology An ethnic group's use of drugs.

disease The body's response to a pathogen.

illness The cultural experience of being sick.

applied medical anthropology The application of anthropological theories, concepts, and methods in the study of health, illness, and healing to improve the well-being of people everywhere.

Ebola Emergency and Anthropology's Response

Ebola is a highly contagious viral disease spread by direct contact with bodily fluids such as saliva, feces, vomit, sweat, and blood, or from contact with items, such as clothing or bedding, that have been contaminated with bodily fluids. Infected people experience headaches, high fever, projectile vomiting, explosive diarrhea, internal and external bleeding, and, in about 50 percent of cases, death. With no cure, medical practitioners can provide little more than palliative care. Efforts are directed to containing its spread, which requires early detection, tracing people who have had contact with infected people, quarantine, and proper disposal of the dead. Understandably, the disease generates a huge amount of fear.

There have been several outbreaks of Ebola since it was first reported in 1976, but the most severe epidemic occurred in early 2014, spreading rapidly through the West African countries of Guinea, Sierra Leone, and Liberia. In August, 2014, as the number of cases began increasing exponentially and to appear in Nigeria, the United States, Spain, and elsewhere, the World Health Organization (WHO) declared it an international public health emergency and called for "a coordinated international response [to] reverse the international spread of Ebola" (WHO 2014a). Politicians, medical and public health practitioners, and non-governmental agencies such as Médecins Sans Frontières (MSF; Doctors Without Borders) rallied to contain the spread. But, according to anthropologist Barry Hewlett, who had worked on an earlier outbreak of Ebola in Uganda (Hewlett and Hewlett 2007), they were doing it wrong because of "the lack of [a] culturally sensitive and appropriate control effort" (Anrys 2014).

Symptomatic individuals were often removed from villages by international healthcare workers dressed in hazmat suits, and family members were seldom told where their relatives were taken or what had happened to them. The last they would see of them was when they were taken to isolation units (Poon 2014), which came to be seen as places of death (Fassassi 2014).

Although mortuary practices vary considerably across the region, for many West African communities death is a journey accompanied by a set of traditional rituals. The body must be washed and touched to say farewell, the deceased's possessions, such as clothing, prepared to accompany them on their journey, and they must be buried with bare hands (Sáez et al. 2014; Fassassi 2014; Sack et al. 2014). These practices served to spread the disease and, to contain it, health authorities in many areas prevented family members from burying their dead and even from attending the funerals (Elliot 2014). Bodies would be zipped up in body bags (Poon 2014), taken away by burial teams consisting of police or military forces—already distrusted by locals with long histories of conflict and resistance with distant central governments (Lydersen 2014)—and then cremated, which precluded closure for families.

Many West Africans also understood the disease through different cultural models, not as a biological phenomenon transmitted by contact with bodily fluids, but the result of sorcery or witchcraft (Poon 2014; Fassassi 2014). They turned to traditional healing techniques and the local community for treatment (Anrys 2014; Nossiter 2014; AAA 2014) rather than healthcare workers who were thought either to be spreading the disease (Anrys 2014) or to be in the body parts business (Poon 2014; Sack et al. 2014). Western governments were thought to have introduced the disease as a form of population control, or to gain access to their land and resources (Grey and Devlin 2015).

Unsurprisingly, many people, suspicious and fearful, vehemently refused to go to treatment centres, hid in the bush, concealed bodies, or resisted handing them over to officials for safe burial (Lydersen 2014; Fassassi 2014). In some cases, road blocks were set up and doctors and health teams attacked, making it impossible for them to retrieve infected people or bodies (Nossiter 2014). In Monrovia, Liberia, a treatment centre was raided, sick people were taken home, and infected blankets and bedding stolen. In another area of Liberia, three journalists and five healthcare workers were killed in their attempts to warn people of the risks of the Ebola virus (Reuters 2014).

The misunderstanding, fear, anger, and resistance made it difficult not only to persuade people that healthcare workers were there to help, and that going to the hospital was in their best interest, but it also led to the rapid spread of Ebola in West Africa. As of February 1, 2015, over 22 000 people had been infected and nearly 9000 people had died from the virus (WHO 2015a).

What Can Anthropologists Do?

The Ebola outbreak is a global crisis, and containing its spread requires both an international effort as well as local knowledge and local action. Most of the issues present cultural challenges that government officials, doctors, and other health practitioners are ill-equipped to handle. Medical anthropologists, on the other hand, are trained to listen to peoples' concerns, see things holistically, take historical and political contexts into consideration, and understand local concepts and practices of illness. Many have worked in the affected areas and know the people, the languages, and the cultures well. There is a clear and definite need for anthropologists with regional experience to get involved. But by the fall of 2014, few were (Abramowitz 2014; Anrys 2014; NPR 2014). The MSF and the U.S. Centers for Disease Control and Prevention (CDC) do not have permanent medical anthropologists on staff, and it was not until the end of 2014 that they began to employ medical anthropologists on the ground. In November, the American Anthropological Association (AAA) established the Ebola Anthropology Emergency Response Network to promote an anthropological response to the outbreak.

So what can medical anthropologists with an understanding of local people and cultures do to help control the spread of Ebola? The AAA, and other anthropologists, have suggested that, among other things, anthropologists can:

- Help medical practitioners understand how local ideas, beliefs, and responses to disease may impact treatment and lead to the spread of the disease, and then help them develop culturally appropriate and effective treatment and prevention methods (Lydersen 2014; AAA 2014);

(Continued)

Ebola Emergency and Anthropology's Response (*Continued*)

John Moore/Getty Images

A woman crawls toward the body of her sister as Ebola burial team members take her sister for cremation in October, 2014 in Monrovia, Liberia. The burial of loved ones is important in Liberian culture, making the removal of infected bodies for cremation all the more traumatic for surviving family members.

- Aid health teams in understanding that how their efforts affect local people may influence treatment and containment, and then develop intervention strategies that are flexible and adaptive to the context (NPR 2014);
- Advise health teams on how to gain the respect of locals (Lydersen 2014); for instance, by attending funerals (Poon 2014);
- Act as intermediaries between health response teams and communities to develop a relationship of trust (Sáez et al. 2014; NPR 2014; AAA 2014);
- Help local communities understand the nature of Ebola and develop the kind of rituals and burial practices that allow the living to express their grief and maintain the dignity of the dead, while preventing the spread of the disease (AAA 2014);
- Help epidemiologists understand how local economic practices, such as cross-border seasonal migrations of wage labourers (AAA 2014), or the practice of moving the corpses of married women in Mende villages back to the village where they were born (Richards and Mokuwa 2014), enables the spread of the disease;
- Help trace individuals who have had contact with infected people (Lydersen 2014);
- Work with local healers, institutions, and community and religious leaders to disseminate information and help institute best practices such as control over quarantines (AAA 2014);
- Persuade officials that local populations should be seen as resources rather than problems, and to enlist them in the fight (AAA 2014);
- Share their networks of local contacts with international relief agencies; and
- Enlist Ebola survivors to show locals that treatment is not a death sentence but can save their lives.

Conclusion

By early 2015, the number of new Ebola cases was in sharp decline in Liberia, Guinea, and Sierra Leone (Onishijan 2015). There are many reasons for this decline. Medical teams have made it a priority to educate locals about the nature of the disease and for the need for safe burials, while respecting traditional burial practices. The biggest reason for the decline, however, is that local residents themselves are changing their approaches and taking precautions (Onishijan 2015). In many communities, chiefs, local elders, and educated youth are establishing and overseeing volunteer Ebola watchdog groups, setting up hand-washing stations, helping health workers keep records of the sick and the dead, enlisting traditional healers and caretaking networks, placing households under quarantine (Onishijan 2015), and innovating alternative burial practices (AAA 2014). In early 2015 people began to speak of beating Ebola.

Questions for Further Thought

1. How can anthropologists help in eliminating other infectious diseases such as HIV/AIDS?
2. What cultural obstacles do medical practitioners face when dealing with infectious diseases?
3. Why is it important to enlist local people to fight such diseases?
4. The most recent global health crisis is the spread of the Zika virus, which is transmitted by infected mosquitos and can result in children being born with microcephaly (small brain). How can anthropologists help medical practitioners as well as affected populations deal with this disease?

now the second largest unit in the AAA (Ember and Ember 2004). Most medical anthropologists in Canada are employed by government and non-governmental organizations, by private companies, or public health agencies rather than in Anthropology departments (Jacklin 2014). Many Anthropology departments in Canada offer courses in medical anthropology and some (McGill University, University of Alberta, University of Manitoba, University of Toronto, University of British Columbia, the University of Saskatchewan, and York University) also have graduate programs.

Business Anthropology

In the early 1980s Japan was a rising economic power. Canadian, American, and European businesses realized that this offered not only new market opportunities for their products, but also new manufacturing and joint venture possibilities. Japan, however, is a collectivist culture, where group harmony and welfare are more important than the concerns of individuals. Canada and the United States, on the other hand, are individualist cultures, where people are encouraged to express their opinions, be self-reliant, and show initiative. Japan is also a culture with a long-term orientation, where businesses focus on long-term goals and how the company will benefit future generations. In Canada the focus is on quick results, deadlines, and short-term goals such as quarterly sales projections (Hofstede et al. 2010). To successfully capitalize on the Japanese market, Western businesses realized they needed to understand Japanese culture. In 1981, *Theory Z* (Ouchi) and *The Art of Japanese Management* (Pascale and Athos) were published to help North Americans do just that (Jordan 2013).

At about the same time, businesses started to realize that their organizations were like small-scale societies with their own unique culture. The term "corporate culture" became a buzzword (Jordan 2013) as managers began to realize that to be successful they needed to think about their organization's culture. They also began to look at using ethnographic methods to develop new products and services. Since then, anthropologists have come to realize that their knowledge of culture and their expertise in ethnographic methods is of value to businesses and other organizations. ***Business anthropology*** is the application of anthropological concepts and methods to help businesses and other organizations solve all kinds of business- and industry-related problems. Business anthropologists are involved in all areas of business operations, including, management, operations, marketing, and human resources. Business anthropology is also one of the most recent and fastest growing areas of anthropology.

There are four main areas where anthropologists' skills and knowledge are being applied to the issues businesses deal with:

1. New product development;
2. Understanding and managing corporate culture;
3. Consumer behaviour; and
4. Conducting business internationally.

1. New Product Development

Companies have traditionally used quantitative marketing research methods such as surveys to develop new products and services. But, unlike ethnographic methods, such methods are conducted out of context of the use situation and provide little information as to what new products are needed, how they would be used, or what they would mean to people. Many companies now hire anthropologists or consulting firms to participate in peoples' daily activities, observe their behaviour as it happens, and use unstructured interviews to gain deeper insights into their customers' needs and ideas, and to develop successful new products and improve existing ones. One difference from academic ethnographic research is that it has to be done rapidly in a matter of weeks. Companies can afford neither the money nor the time to pay for months of fieldwork.

Susan Squires, for instance, by actually sitting at the breakfast table with parents and their children, has not only shed light on new ways of thinking about food consumption in the mornings, but has also led to the development of a successful new breakfast food product (NAPA 2012). Squires learned that breakfast is a hectic time for most U.S. families since, with both parents working, the children have to be dropped off at school early. Often they leave the house by 7:00 a.m. without eating much of anything except perhaps bananas, which are nutritious, portable, disposable, and fun to eat. Mothers believed that breakfast food should be nutritious and free of preservatives; fathers preferred less nutritional "comfort food"; grandparents thought bacon, eggs, and buttered toast made the best breakfast; and children preferred sweetened cereals or pancakes and maple syrup. A new breakfast food product would thus have to meet the needs of a number of family members. It would need to be nutritious, like a banana, portable, disposable, versatile, and fun to eat. Based on her ethnographic research—which determined *actual* eating patterns rather than asking people what they had for breakfast—Squires developed a new breakfast food product designed for the two-parent, working family on the go called Go-Gurt (known as Yoplait Tubes in Canada). The first yogurt served in a tube, Go-Gurt is a healthy (Figure 3.5), high-protein food; it is smooth and creamy and comes in a number of fun and tasty flavours such as Strawberry Splash and Cool Cotton Candy; and had sales of more than $37 million during its first year on the market.

2. Understanding and Managing Corporate Culture

In many ways companies and other organizations are like societies in that each has its own culture. ***Corporate or organizational culture*** consists of the material things in the company such as the products, buildings, furniture, decorations, and so on; the symbolic meanings these things have; the attitudes, values, and beliefs that

---

business anthropology The application of anthropological concepts and methods to help businesses and other organizations improve productivity through understanding and managing culture.

corporate or organizational culture Everything people have, think, and do as members of a company or an organization.

Monkey Business Images/Shutterstock

FIGURE 3.5 By conducting participant-observation research on eating patterns of U.S. families at breakfast time, applied cultural anthropologist Susan Squires contributed to the development of a new breakfast food product called "Go-Gurt" (called "Yoplait Tubes" in Canada).

people in the company hold; and their ways of doing things, or norms. In other words, corporate or organizational culture is everything people have, think, and do as members of a company or organization. Large organizations may also have subcultures.

An organization's culture can work for or against the strategic goals of the company. For instance, a company may value customer service, but if the employees fail to go out of their way to help customers, the company's image and profitability may suffer. Managers are thus learning that, in addition to managing cash, products, and services, they must also manage their company's culture (Ford 2007). Anthropologists are helping companies to manage corporate culture by entering the workplace and watching how people interact with one another and how they work; by listening to what they say about their company, products, and customers; and by conducting formal and informal interviews.

Culture also plays a role in the recruitment process. In multicultural countries such as Canada, potential employees may come from a diversity of cultures. Many, however, may not know how to play the "employment game" (or feel uncomfortable doing so), which involves marketing oneself both on the resume and at the interview. For instance, people from collectivist cultures may have difficulty flaunting their skills or achievements as they have learned that their individual aspirations are less important than those of the group. Others may be also be extremely honest when asked, "Why do you want this job?" The answer, "Because I need the money" may be the truth, but it is not what a potential employer is looking for. It is not in a company's best interests if qualified people with the skills, experience, and knowledge to do the job are bypassed because they are unaware of the cultural norms involved in getting a job. Companies are also starting to realize that having a culturally diverse workforce is an asset since there are variety of ways of tackling problems, and it helps when dealing with a culturally diverse customer base.

Culture also plays a role in mergers and acquisitions. Since companies have different cultures, when one merges or acquires another the two cultures may clash.

3. Consumer Behaviour

In recent years companies have focused their efforts on customers. After all, it is the customers who ultimately pay the bills. This involves providing them with not only the products they want or need, but also understanding how to market to them. Human behaviour, including consumption behaviour, takes place within a particular cultural context and, as Gail Tom reminds us, "to successfully serve the customers in your target market, you must first understand reality as your target market perceives it" (Tom 2001, 1). In other words, businesses need to understand the cultural lens through which consumers assess a company's brands, and the way they make their purchases. People buy things not so much for what they do, but for what they mean (Solomon et al. 2013). For instance, when the first McDonald's franchise opened in Hong Kong in 1975 people flocked to the restaurant, not because the food was different or any better but because to be seen going into McDonald's meant that you were Western and modern (Watson 2005). As with other areas of business anthropology, understanding consumers involves spending time observing them, participating with them, and talking to them to discover their attitudes, values, experiences, and thoughts.

4. Conducting Business Internationally

In today's globalized connected world, conducting business internationally is relatively easy for even the smallest business. But because people from other cultures do not think or behave the way most of us do in Canada, entering into a business relationship with companies in countries such as China, Japan, or India, or selling products or services in these countries, requires an understanding of the cultural differences (Figure 3.6). People interpret products and services, as well as marketing communications, through their own cultural lens. Thus, when products and brands enter a different culture they often take on different uses or meanings. In other words, they become *recontextualized*. For instance, in India refrigerators are a sign of status and many people place them in their living rooms. To accommodate this, Whirlpool produces them in bright colours to suit local taste and culture (casestudyinc.com 2010). As Jordan points out, "the success or failure of . . . a product consumed globally, is best understood in local contexts" (Jordan 2013, 85). This may mean changing the product or changing the way it is marketed. It was not until the technology

recontextualized products Products or brands that take on new meanings and uses in different cultures.

FIGURE 3.6 The study of cultural anthropology prepares people for working in the global economy of the 21st century.

company Philips reduced the size of its coffee makers to fit into the smaller Japanese kitchens that it started to make a profit in the country (Kotler 1986).

Development Anthropology

Access to sufficient, good quality food, water, housing, and education and a healthy environment are essential for both human well-being and sustained development. Development anthropology takes international development and international aid as its primary focus. Within this specialization, the term *development* refers to the social action made by different institutions, business enterprises, states, and independent volunteers who are trying to improve the economic, technical, political, and social life of people throughout the world, especially in impoverished areas. Anthropologists who specialize in development anthropology are often part of multidisciplinary teams, and use anthropological knowledge, theory, perspectives, and methods to help with a project's design, its implementation, or its evaluation.

Development anthropologists tend to be involved in projects that seek to improve the economic well-being of marginalized communities to alleviate poverty and create healthier, more equitable, prosperous societies. Projects are generally aimed at putting people first by focusing on, for example, improving healthcare, providing access to education, creating jobs or new cottage industries, improving the quality of the environment such as with water purification or digging wells for increased water access. Other projects are aimed at agriculture and development for improved food security and food access. The list of possible development projects is endless.

Development anthropologists work both at home and abroad in international development agencies such as the World Bank, the United Nations, the Department of Foreign Affairs, Trade and Development, or Canada's International Development Research Centre (IDRC/CRDI), and their partner organizations. Many are also employed by non-governmental organizations.

Environmental Anthropology

Environmental or ecological anthropology examines relationships between humans and their environment. Everywhere, humans have changed their environment and in turn have been changed by it and adapted to it. Drawing on political ecology (discussed in Chapter 4), this perspective integrates culture, politics and power, globalization, localized issues, and more. Environmental anthropologists thus look at economic activities, social practices, and political policies, on the environment, as well as the impact of the environment on health, and cultural practices. The focus and data interpretation are often used for arguments for and against the creation of policy, and to prevent exploitation and damage of land, water, and forested areas. They are also concerned with peoples' consciousness of their environment, and how this leads to environmental change both locally and globally. The goal of environmental anthropologists is to help solve human-environmental problems and develop healthy sustainable communities.

In the late 1990s, one of the authors of this textbook, Susan Andreatta, studied the impact of the use of agrochemicals (i.e., insecticides, fungicides, and herbicides) on the health of both local farmers and their physical environments (Figure 3.7) in the Caribbean islands of Antiqua, Barbados, and St. Vincent (1998). Andreatta collected her data in 1994–1995 from farm owners, farm labourers, government officials, and international corporations.

Andreatta found that the increased use of chemical biocides was driven by a number of factors: a world marketplace demanding blemish-free fruits and vegetables, international chemical companies wishing to expand their markets into developing countries, growers interested in producing the most marketable produce possible, and a lack of government control of the importation and use of potentially dangerous

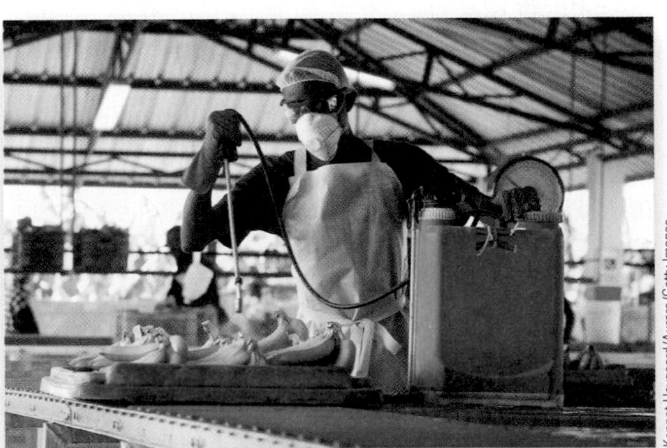

FIGURE 3.7 Co-author Susan Andreatta found that the continued use of insecticides and herbicides on such export crops as bananas had negative health and environmental effects in several Caribbean Islands.

chemical biocides. Andreatta also discovered that the continued use and misuse of agrochemicals over the decades has had harmful consequences for the health of local producers as well as the quality of their physical environments. Because most of the chemical products did not come with mixing instructions, farm workers often used more powerful concentrations of the chemicals than necessary. Moreover, workers often mixed and applied the chemicals without wearing adequate protective clothing. Direct exposure to the biocides used on banana trees caused eye damage, skin rashes, and fingernail loss. The literature on other banana-producing nations, such as Costa Rica, indicates that overexposure or continued exposure to such biochemicals could lead to lower sperm counts and sterility for men, whereas women reported increased reproductive problems, including producing infants with serious birth defects.

The widespread use and misuse of biocides also had major negative effects on the natural environments of these three Caribbean islands. First, the use of biocides on banana crops often contaminated other food crops as well, such as peppers, tomatoes, broccoli, and strawberries. Second, farmers who used biocides were unable to raise chickens because chickens die from exposure to the chemicals. Third, biocides often leached into natural drinking water supplies. And finally, chemical runoff into streams and rivers killed off fish populations, thereby endangering a source of protein in the diets of local populations.

After documenting the risks of agrochemicals on both human and environmental health, Andreatta offered some useful suggestions to help ameliorate some of the more negative consequences of using agrochemicals. To illustrate, there was a pressing need for the departments of agriculture on these three islands to take a more proactive role in regulating both the importation and the use of these biocides. Some products could be banned from entering the country because they are simply too toxic. The governments could require by law that biocide products contain explicit instructions on their packaging for mixing and application. The governments need to ensure that local producers receive adequate training (and perhaps even certification) on the safe use of agrochemicals, including wearing protective clothing, marking recently sprayed fields with appropriate signs or flags, and adhering to a safe reentry schedule.

Educational Anthropology

Educational institutions are one of the primary places where children are enculturated, learning as much or more about themselves as they do about the world. Cultural factors also influence the process of schooling, teaching, and learning. For instance, the value a society places on being male or female may determine who receives an education or to what level. ***Educational anthropology*** is the "application of anthropological concepts and methods to the study of educational institutions and processes" (Ahmad 2008).

Educational anthropologists work with parents, teachers, administrators, and policymakers to find solutions to such educational problems, as educational inequalities, culturally inappropriate materials, and discrimination, by developing curriculum resources, advocating for educational change, and intervening in health and community development (Schensul 2011). Whether assisting immigrant populations or refugees in acculturating to their new home, or children from these same relocated households do better in school, educational anthropologists can help to minimize certain issues that arise from cross-cultural misunderstandings. Educational anthropologists come with diverse backgrounds to be able to address issues of cross-cultural understanding in learning, ethnic identity, ethnic change, and the transmission of cultural knowledge and behaviour between generations. Some educational anthropologists further specialize and get trained in teaching English as a second language (ESL) or in teaching English as another language (EAL).

The Greater Use of Anthropological Knowledge

This book focuses on how anthropological knowledge can be used to solve problems of architects, government officials, businesspeople, medical personnel, educators, foreign aid personnel, court officials, family planners, and others. Although this applied perspective demonstrates how anthropology has contributed to the solution of societal problems, much still needs to be done to increase the extent to which anthropological knowledge can actually be used by policymakers. It is one thing to point out the potential uses of anthropological information, and it is quite another to actually apply that information to make a difference in public policy and the quality of people's lives.

Cultural anthropology as a discipline—and recent research by many of its practitioners—certainly has policy relevance for a number of issues facing Canada and the world. More cultural anthropologists' voices need to be heard and contribute to the pressing policy issues of our time. Drawing on anthropological data and their own analytical skills, many leading anthropologists take on many of the most controversial topics of the day. For example, cultural anthropology, to a greater extent than any other social science, is in the best position to reframe current debates and contribute to public policy on same-sex marriage, terrorism,

educational anthropology The application of anthropological concepts and methods to the study of educational institutions and processes.

STORIES FROM THE FIELD

I was hired as a product manager for a software development company in Calgary on the basis of my knowledge of anthropology, especially for seeing things holistically and for seeing the "other's" point of view, and certainly not for my non-existent technical knowledge. Shortly afterward the company was purchased by a German firm, and unfortunately it went bankrupt two years later due largely to cultural reasons. The German executives insisted on doing things their way, which resulted in a great deal of resistance from the Canadian staff. The company also changed the name of all the products, changing customers' perceptions of them. At about the same time there was a major cultural trend in the computing industry and the company was unable to change fast enough. It was then that I realized that culture can make or break a company.

—Chris Holdsworth, *University of Calgary*

new reproductive technologies, Indigenous peoples' rights, and gender inequality. They also have a good deal to say on other areas of public concern such as globalization, the environment and equitable access to resources, culture wars, nation building and the spread of democracy, migration, family violence, issues of racism, ethnic conflicts, equitable food access, social justice, and poverty. Clearly, cultural anthropologists, with their cross-cultural perspective, are in a unique position to help people from all cultures navigate effectively and humanely through a world that is growing increasingly more interdependent each year.

Career Opportunities in Applied Anthropology

With the cost of a university education continuing to skyrocket, more and more parents are asking their university-aged children why they are majoring in anthropology. Behind such a question, of course, is the more pragmatic question, What kind of job can you get with a bachelor's degree in anthropology? It is important to bear in mind that a bachelor's degree in cultural anthropology is a liberal arts degree, not some type of professional certification. The terms *applied anthropologist* and *cross-cultural expert* are not standard job categories in the online job boards. In today's globalized world there is a growing need for anthropology majors. According to the AAA, "Anthropological study provides training particularly well suited to the 21st century. The economy will be increasingly international; workforces and markets, increasingly diverse; participatory management and decision making, increasingly important; and communication skills, increasingly in demand. Anthropology is the only contemporary discipline that approaches human questions from historical, biological, linguistic, and cultural perspectives" (AAA 2016). Based on U.S. labour statistics, the AAA also claims that employment of anthropologists and archaeologists is expected to grow 19 percent from 2012 to 2022, making it the fastest growth forecast for all occupations. In other words, anthropology is a good career choice.

The reason is not hard to find, as anthropology's unique perspective and training provides students with the skills and insights employers in all areas of the economy are looking for. Anthropology majors are well suited for jobs that require sensitivity to cross-cultural issues, working with people from different cultural backgrounds, an ability to conduct ethnographic research, as well as strong observational and analytic skills combined with good oral and written skills. Anthropology majors also learn to think holistically and deal with complexity, to see the other's point of view, and to think reflexively about problems and issues. They thus gain a deeper understanding of situations and are able to interpret statistical data and use various explanatory models. In a 2009 AAA survey of 758 students who had received an M.A. from a North American institution before 2008, students said that what benefited them most from their degree were the research skills, especially qualitative skills, case studies, and reading and writing skills. Also important were the thesis/research project and the field research opportunities (Fiske et al. 2010).

Today, anthropologists find employment in four main areas: academia, government, non-governmental organizations, and private enterprise. Jobs in academia usually require a Ph.D. and involve teaching, conducting ethnographic research, writing articles and books, and supervising graduate students. While most academic anthropologists are employed in anthropology departments, many also work in other departments or programs such as medicine, education, psychology, international relations, development, design, public health, and community studies. While the academic job market is relatively steady, it is highly competitive; and today more than half of Ph.D. students now find employment in other sectors of the economy (Fiske et al. 2010).

As more and more doctorate-level anthropologists are working in non-academic jobs, employment opportunities for those with less than doctorate training in anthropology are also increasing. Employers in other areas are also starting to realize the value of skills acquired by anthropology majors (Batteau and Morais 2015). This is reflected in articles such as "Ethnography Is the New Core Competence" (Nussbaum 2006); "Getting to Know You: Microsoft dispatches anthropologists into the field to study small businesses like yours. Here's why." (Murphy 2005); and "An Anthropologist Walks into a Bar . . ." (Madsbjerg and Rasmussen 2014); all written in prominent business magazines. Many corporations now hire anthropology majors to conduct market research; improve existing products and services, and develop new ones; to analyze the results of surveys, interviews, and ethnographic research; and to help market products overseas. Governments at the federal, provincial, and municipal level hire anthropologists to help develop policy, plan community initiatives, conduct research and impact studies, and assess cultural resources. And non-profit organizations, such as development and aid agencies, international health organizations, local, community-based organizations, and environmental organizations, are also hiring anthropology majors. As Fiske et al. (2010) note, "Anthropologists are nothing if not flexible in the job market" (Table 3.2).

TABLE 3.2

Anthropology Majors: Descriptions of Their Post-graduate Employment

Education/Outreach	Administration/Management
Archaeology	Ethnography/Cultural anthropology
Cultural resource management (CRM)	Evaluation/Assessment
Historic preservation	Health (international/public health)
Museum/Curation/project design	Environment and natural resources
Community development	Business
Advocacy (human rights/ social justice)	Tourism/Heritage
Human/Social services	Healthcare management/ services/delivery
Computers/Software development/Information technology	Management consulting/ Organizational development/ Training
Design (products and/or services)	Social impact assessment
International development/ affairs	Market research
Forensics	Law/Criminal justice/Law enforcement
Mass communication	Humanitarian efforts

Source: Fiske, Shirley J., Linda A. Bennett, Patricia Ensworth, Terry Redding, and Keri Brondo. 2010. *The Changing Face of Anthropology: Anthropology Masters Reflect on Education, Careers, and Professional Organizations.* AAA/CoPAPIA 2009 Anthropology MA Career Survey. Arlington, VA: American Anthropological Association, www.americananthro.org

Anthropology thus prepares students for a variety of jobs, and is a valuable asset in whatever career is chosen. In the 2009 AAA survey of M.A., graduates over 75 percent said their degree in anthropology played a significant role in their overall career satisfaction (Fiske et al. 2010).

CROSS-CULTURAL MISCUE

If you were to walk on the outskirts of Jakarta (Indonesia's capital), you may be surprised to come across dozens of people stretched out on train tracks in what appears to be a mass suicide (Figure. 3.8), but you would be mistaken. Even though they twitch visibly as an oncoming train approaches and sends an electric current through their bodies, they have no intention of killing themselves and know exactly when to get up.

The poorer members of Jakarta are turning to electric therapy for healthcare. Laying on the tracks is a free way to obtain treatment. Hundreds of people come to lay on the tracks every day, undeterred by warning signs and threatened penalties.

Ethnomedicine is a local approach that people use for healthcare. In this case, electric therapy is used to feel comfort or relief from what ails them. Although there is no scientific evidence that train track electric therapy does any good, users contend it offers pain relief, lowers blood pressure, and helps with diabetes, rheumatism, sleeplessness, and high cholesterol. Medical anthropologists spend a lot time researching local belief systems and health, and have learned that believing in a particular treatment makes a difference in the outcome. Understanding that other cultures have different ways of approaching wellness and healing helps us to recognize that our own culture may have its own *unusual* approaches to healthcare.

Nurcholis/Rex Features/The Canadian Press

FIGURE 3.8 In Rawa Buaya, Jakarta, Indonesia, villagers lie on a railway track and wait for a train to rattle by for electric therapy, believing that the electric current from the track could cure various diseases.

APPLIED PERSPECTIVE

If the Food Won't Kill You, the Cooking Will

Cooking on a cookstove can be hazardous to one's health in many homes around the world. The World Health Organization (WHO) lists indoor household cooking fires as a leading environmental cause of death in the world, with as many as two million deaths annually, which is more deaths than are caused each year by malaria (Martin et al. 2011). Almost half the world's population lives in poverty, and those households generally use biomass (wood, crop residues, charcoal, or dung) or coal as fuel for cooking and heating. Typically, fires fill the homes with dense smoke and sicken those within, especially women and children. Researchers say it is as if those exposed were lifelong tobacco smokers (Martin et al. 2011). Women and children are at higher risk for adverse health outcomes from exposure to the indoor air pollution from these fires because they are at home more, and the women are responsible for cooking meals and heating the home. Men, spouses, and fathers tend to spend more time outdoors, and therefore suffer less from chronic exposure. The two leading causes of death are acute pneumonia in children under five years of age and chronic obstructive pulmonary disease for adults (Martin et al. 2011).

For those households at the bottom of the energy ladder, reliance on biomass fuels and coal contributes to local and regional environmental degradation and deforestation. A 2011 World Bank report underscores the health benefits for a cookstove intervention, and highlights other benefits to the environment and climate. Improved and more efficient stoves reduce fuel use and carbon dioxide emissions; thus interventions would contribute positively to people's health and their surrounding environment.

Past projects for improving stoves or fuels have been around for decades. For any number of reasons, though, a variety of obstacles have interfered with a smooth transition for a technology transfer and adoption. Some challenges stem from lack of the public's awareness of the health-related problems associated with indoor air pollution made from the existing style of cookstoves used by local community members. Another reason great strides have not been made is that there has been limited health research in determining the minimal levels of exposure needed to reduce the health risks associated with the indoor smoke. And lastly, funding a global cookstove project of this magnitude is problematic. The lack of affordable improved stoves or fuels that reduce exposures to safer levels, and the logistics of trying to solve this problem that affects nearly three billion people, make this an enormous and daunting project (Martin et al. 2011).

To address this problem, the United Nations Foundation launched the Global Alliance for Clean Cookstoves. It is a public–private partnership aimed at creating a global market for clean and efficient cookstoves and fuels in the developing world. Their goal is to have 100 million homes adopt the new cookstoves and fuels by 2020 (Global Alliance for Clean Cookstoves 2011, http://cleancookstoves.org). Several small-scale projects have been started in Guatemala and Peru.

There is a role for applied anthropologists to contribute on any number of levels to facilitate this process of efficient cookstove adoption. From a community-based approach, anthropologists could work with community members to better understand the gendered division of labour and technology access and adoption. Women and girls typically gather fuel for home use, sometimes at great distances from their villages, and they may have to travel to places that may not be safe to secure materials for cooking and heating. A more efficient cookstove could reduce the time spent in collecting fuel to burn, saving time and requiring fewer trips.

However, providing just a new cookstove is not enough for successful adoption. Users must receive training on how to use the stove and be taught that fuel saving would follow with proper and sustained use. Most importantly though, promoting changes in the way food is prepared to reduce exposure to poor indoor air requires fundamental understanding of traditions, social interaction, and family dynamics, which vary widely across cultures. Successful implementation will involve women designing the stove, training, use in the home, and follow-up with the community.

Questions for Further Thought

1. Based on this reading, what role do you see for the applied anthropologist in working with people from the United Nations on a cookstove project?
2. What challenges do you see facing the anthropologist involved in this project?
3. What ethical considerations need to be considered with a cookstove project?

Source: © Cengage Learning

Summary

1. Applied anthropology is characterized by problem-oriented research among the world's contemporary populations. Applied anthropologists attempt to apply anthropological data, concepts, and strategies to the solution of social, economic, environmental, and technological problems, both at home and abroad.
2. Applied anthropologists generally work at a university, whereas practicing anthropologists (about 30 percent of all anthropologists with doctorate degrees) work outside academia for governments, businesses, and non-governmental agencies.
3. The anthropological perspective involves looking at issues holistically, relativistically, naturalistically, comparatively, globally, bio-culturally, and reflexively.
4. Applying the anthropological perspective involves collecting sociocultural information on the people under study, and developing policy to help lessen a problem and a plan of action, or intervention, to correct the problem.
5. Applied medical anthropologists are concerned with the ways societies conceive of and deal with disease, illness, and health, as well as the relationship between patients and healers, the structure of the medical system, and the relationships between culture, economics, politics, disease, and the environment. They apply anthropological theories, concepts, and methods to improve the well-being of people everywhere.
6. Business anthropologists use anthropological methods to help businesses develop new products, manage their corporate cultures, understand their consumers, market their products both domestically and internationally, and develop international business relationships.
7. Development anthropologists are involved in a variety of projects, from education to cottage industries and agriculture, in an attempt to improve economic well-being, alleviate poverty, and create healthier, more equitable and prosperous societies.
8. Environmental anthropologists examine the relationships between humans and their environment, and help to solve human-environmental problems.
9. Educational anthropologists work with parents, teachers, administrators, and policymakers to find solutions to educational problems such as educational inequalities, culturally inappropriate materials, and discrimination.
10. In the past several decades there has been significant growth in areas that have attracted applied and practicing anthropologists. These include architecture, environmental studies, fisheries research, geriatric services, the military, tourism, and water resource management.

Key Terms

anthropological perspective
applied medical anthropology
biomedical model
business anthropology
corporate or organizational culture
disease
educational anthropology
ethnopharmacology
etiology
illness
medical pluralism
medical system
problem-oriented research
recontextualized products

Critical Thinking Questions

1. Canada has recently accepted thousands of refugees from Syria. How might an applied anthropologist work with them to adjust to their new lives in Canada?
2. Lack of adequate housing has been an issue for First Nations, Inuit, and Métis people for decades. Many of the homes, particularly in the North, have been built with little consideration of cultural requirements. How might an anthropologist work with an Inuit community, architects, and government agencies to develop housing that meets their needs?
3. Ethnotourism (people travelling to visit and experience Indigenous cultures and societies) is becoming more popular. While it offers economic opportunities, it is also changing these cultures.

How might a small-scale culture be affected, and how might an anthropologist work with them to adjust to changes brought about by tourism?

4. How might the introduction of computers in a small-scale society change people's ideas, attitudes, and behaviours?
5. If you were working with an Indigenous people in rural India to improve irrigation, what questions would you ask?
6. Poliomyelitis is a highly infectious disease that can result in permanent disability and death. Once prevalent throughout the world, it has nearly been eradicated thanks to a polio vaccine. Today it is found only in Afghanistan and Pakistan. How could an anthropologist work with local people in these countries to accept vaccination when they are distrustful of Western doctors?
7. Why is it important in any development project to take a holistic approach?
8. Compare the differences between the concepts of disease and illness.
9. Dishwashers are not a common appliance in Japanese homes. If you were tasked with marketing dishwashers in Japan, how would you conduct the research?
10. How might you apply anthropological knowledge and methods in your career?

Make the Grade with MindTap

Between 1922 and 1924, Canadian anthropologist T. F. McIlwraith spent 11 months in the isolated community of Bella Coola, British Columbia, living among the people now known as the Nuxalk First Nation.

CHAPTER

4

The Growth of Anthropological Theory

WHAT WE WILL LEARN

- What a theory is, and how it can be useful
- Who the important theorists in cultural anthropology have been
- What theories anthropologists have used to explain cultural differences and similarities
- How anthropological theory can be used to help solve societal problems

THE HAWTHORNE STUDIES

In 1924 the electrical engineering company Western Electric, which made equipment for the expanding telephone industry, began a series of experiments to improve productivity at their Hawthorne manufacturing plant outside Chicago. The plant employed nearly 40 000 people, and so any improvement in worker efficiency would increase profits. In one experiment, six young women were placed in a separate room where they could be easily observed and conditions monitored. They were required to assemble relay switches which were then dropped down a chute and automatically counted (photo opposite page). After a weekly baseline of 2400 relays per week was established for the group, the management began changing their working conditions and observed the impact on the women's productivity. For instance, at different times they gave them more breaks, longer breaks, longer lunch times, sent them home earlier, and gave them a per piece wage incentive. In every case, productivity increased. In fact, productivity increased the most when they took away all the changes and went back to the baseline conditions.

These puzzling results led the investigators to interview the women. What they discovered was that the women felt special in being selected for the tests, and so changed their behaviour because they knew they were being observed and wanted to meet what they thought were the observers' expectations. This has become known as the *Hawthorne effect*. The researchers also discovered that the women developed a sense of responsibility to each other, and found the close associations with one another deeply rewarding, even to the point of turning down promotions if it meant leaving the group. This led the researchers to consider such work groups as a small society and, in place of a controlled experiment, they substituted the notion of a social system that needed to be described and understood as a system of informal interconnected relationships.

In a subsequent experiment, 14 men were separated from the rest of their fellow workers in a special room where they were required to wire banks of telephone exchanges. With advice from Harvard anthropologist William Lloyd Warner, who had done field research on Australian Aborigine social structure and relationships among individuals within groups (Mulvaney 1990), the investigations were designed as an anthropological study to gain some insight into worker attitudes, thoughts, and feelings. The bank wiring room, where the observations

Courtesy of McIlwraith family

took place, was thought of as a natural setting, and the group conceived of as a small society. Warner suggested they use participant observation, and so an observer was placed in the group who worked alongside the men and engaged in informal conversation with them as they worked. This observer also took detailed notes informing the researchers about the personal relationships and interactions between the men, as well as comparing what the workers said they were doing with what they actually did.

The men were paid an hourly wage plus a bonus for every unit the group completed above the weekly quota. The investigators hypothesized that the faster workers would encourage the slower ones to work as fast as possible so they would earn more. In fact, the opposite occurred: the slower workers would censure the faster ones by calling them names such as "rate busters," "runts," or "slaves" to bring them into line. The men feared that if they produced above the quota, the higher rate would become the standard, or that some of them would be let go, or that their hourly wage would be reduced. What the investigators had stumbled upon was the informal organization of workers and the power of norms to change workers' behaviour. In this case, the norms of the group worked against the strategic goals of the company; whereas, in the relay assembly room, they worked for the goals of the company (Schwartzman 1993).

The Hawthorne studies were the first time anthropological theory and methods were applied to business to produce an anthropological account of the social organization of an industrial organization. They also demonstrated to management the importance of culture and social relationships in the organization of the company, and that people are motivated by things other than monetary incentives, such as belonging to a group. The Great Depression brought an end to the studies, and anthropologists left the field until near the end of the century. ■

Theories and Hypotheses

As anthropologists began to accumulate data on different cultures during the 19th century, they needed to explain the cultural differences and similarities they found. This desire to account for vast cultural variations gave rise to anthropological theories.

A ***theory*** is a general statement that explains phenomena. Theories also enable us to postulate or predict certain observations. A good theory is one that can both explain and predict. In other words, theories allow us to hypothesize, or make educated guesses, about the way things are. An ***hypothesis*** is thus simply a proposed explanation of phenomena. Hypotheses can be generated by either ***induction*** or ***deduction***. The inductive, or "bottom up," approach involves making observations, looking for patterns, and generating a tentative broader explanation or theory for the observations. The deductive, or "top-down," approach begins with the theory or premise and then, through logical implication or reasoning, generates ideas about what observations are to be expected.

Hypotheses can be tested to either corroborate or contradict the theory by making observations. With induction, observations continue to corroborate the theory until one or more of them contradicts it. With deduction, the hypothesis remains a true explanation until one or more observations contradicts it. In either case, once an observation disconfirms the theory, it must be either revised or abandoned.

Hawthorne effect The phenomenon whereby subjects in behavioural studies change their performance in response to being observed.

theory A general statement that explains observations.

hypothesis An unproven proposition that can provide a basis for further investigation.

induction Deriving a conclusion by making particular observations.

deduction Predicting an observation by reasoning from a general premise.

Testing hypotheses involves asking questions about one's material, and thus guides empirical (hands-on) research.

Anthropological theories attempt to make sense out of a variety of ethnographic information from different parts of the world. An anthropological theory or theoretical framework (also known as school of thought) is necessary because it provides an explanatory framework for the research to be conducted. It answers such questions as, Why do people behave as they do? How do we account for human diversity? In other words, theoretically driven research helps to build new insights into our understanding of people's cultures.

In this chapter we will explore—in roughly chronological order—the major theoretical schools of cultural anthropology that have developed since the mid-19th century. Some of the previous theoretical orientations no longer attract much attention, others have been modified and reworked into something new, and still others continue to command some popularity. It is easy, with the advantage of hindsight, to demonstrate the inherent flaws in some of the early theoretical orientations. We should keep in mind, however, that contemporary anthropological theories that appear plausible today have been built on what we learned from previous ones.

Evolutionism

In the latter half of the 19th century, the Industrial Revolution was literally steaming ahead and improving people's lives. Food was becoming more plentiful, water was getting cleaner, medical care was getting better, people were living longer, and there were more amenities to enjoy. It was also the Age of Empire. The nations of Europe were rapidly carving up the world into colonial empires and, in North America, colonists were pushing their dominion further and further west over the continent. As they did so, they were also encountering people who seemed to be at a far lower stage of development. The prevailing theory was that these so-called savages had fallen from God's Grace and had degenerated from a more civilized state. The ruins of the Romans, Aztecs, Mayans, Egyptians, Babylonians, and so on seemed to support this theory. ***Degenerationism*** seemed counterintuitive, however, to the progress that was so self-evident. Europeans and North Americans at the time wanted not only an explanation for the differences between themselves and the peoples they were encountering, but also an explanation for how their culture had developed. For that they looked to history. In the 19th century, however, history went back only as far as the Greeks, the Egyptians, and the Babylonians. There was no "prehistory."

Around mid-century, archaeologists began to discover stone tools that were thousands of years old, and that were remarkably similar to the stone tools still being made and used by contemporary "savages," such as the Australian Aborigines. The first anthropologists thus assumed that other aspects of contemporary "savage" culture, such as their religious beliefs, kinship structure, political organization, and so on, must also have been similar to that of prehistoric peoples. Contemporary "savages" thus took on a new significance. Previously they had been used in political and religious debates, but now their cultures came to represent the earliest stages of cultural evolution. It is this analogy, which by the way is false, that sparked the growth of anthropology (McGrane 1989).

The basic premise of ***evolutionism*** is that all societies pass through a series of distinct evolutionary stages: from savagery to barbarism to civilization. We find differences in contemporary cultures because they are at different evolutionary stages of development. Savages, for instance, are the most primitive, existing in small bands and hunting and gathering for a living using the bow and arrow. Barbarians have developed pottery, have domesticated animals, and live in larger polygamous horticultural communities. And civilized peoples have developed writing, live in state societies, and are monogamous. This theory, developed by British anthropologist Sir Edward Tylor (1832–1917) (Figure 4.1) in *Primitive Culture* (1871 [1903]) and American anthropologist Lewis Henry Morgan (1818–1881) (Figure 4.2) in *Ancient Society* (1877 [1963]), placed Euro-American cultures at the top of the evolutionary ladder and "less-developed" cultures on the lower rungs. The Australian Aborigines were believed by many to occupy the lowest rung since their culture seemed the most primitive. The evolutionary process was thought to progress from simpler (lower) forms to increasingly more complex (higher) forms of culture. A ***unilinear model*** was assumed whereby all aspects of cultures, and cultures as a whole, would pass through the same set of preordained evolutionary stages.

The evolutionary anthropologists would compare aspects of culture in terms of the degree of complexity and place them in sequence. For instance, Tylor was interested in the evolution of religion and believed that it had evolved from simple animism, or belief in spirits, to polytheism, or many gods, to monotheism, or belief in a single god. For proof of this sequence

---

degenerationism A theory that so-called savage or primitive cultures had degenerated from more civilized cultures because they had fallen from God's Grace.

evolutionism The 19th century anthropological theory that cultures evolved from savagery through barbarism to civilization.

unilinear model A 19th century idea that all cultures passed through the same sequence of stages.

From Popular Science Monthly Volume 26 December 1884 (1884)

FIGURE 4.1 Edward Burnett Tylor (1832–1917), British evolutionary anthropologist sometimes called the "Father of Anthropology."

Schaffer Library, Union College, Schenectady, NY

FIGURE 4.2 Lewis Henry Morgan (1818–1881).

they relied on *survivals*. Survivals were items of culture that had apparently "survived" from an earlier time and now seemed out of place in contemporary society. For instance, Tylor would argue that the phrase "a little bird told me" was a survival from a time when people believed that birds actually spoke.

Sorting cultural phenomena into an evolutionary sequence according to the degree of complexity is a deductive approach. Most evolutionary anthropologists did not do fieldwork, and are often called armchair anthropologists. They would sit at their desks (or armchairs) and glean information from travelogues or the writings of missionaries, colonial administrators, or military personnel. Tylor and Morgan also corresponded with some of these men, sending them questionnaires to complete. The most famous of these questionnaires was *Notes and Queries on Anthropology* (1874), the purpose of which was "to promote accurate, anthropological observation on the part of travellers, and to enable those who are not anthropologists to supply the information, which is needed for the scientific study of anthropology at home" (BAAS 1874, vii).

The evolutionary anthropologists stressed independent invention, claiming that cultural features have arisen in different parts of the world independently of one another as a result, in large measure, of the *psychic unity* of humankind. Humans were seen as essentially rational, that they would contemplate their environmental situation and come up with solutions. Similar environments would thus result in similar solutions. Agriculture was thus invented several times. Tylor, for instance, said that "Civilization is a plant much oftener propagated than developed" (1871 I [1903], 53).

Because they concluded that Western societies represented the highest levels of human achievement, this evolutionary scheme appears terribly ethnocentric by today's standards. Tylor and Morgan have also been criticized for being armchair speculators, putting forth grand schemes to explain cultural diversity based on fragmentary data. Although there is considerable substance to these criticisms, we must evaluate the 19th century evolutionists with an eye toward the times in which they were writing. As David Kaplan and Robert Manners (1986, 39–43) remind us, Tylor and Morgan may have overstated their case somewhat because they were trying to establish what Tylor called "the science of culture," whereby human behaviour was explained in terms of secular evolutionary processes rather than supernatural causes.

survivals Elements of culture that evolutionary anthropologists believed had survived from an earlier period.

psychic unity A concept popular among some 19th century anthropologists who assumed that all people, when operating under similar circumstances, will think and behave in similar ways.

Evolutionism in Brief

- All cultures pass through the same developmental stages in the same order, from simple to complex.
- Evolution is unidirectional and leads to higher (better) levels of culture.

- A deductive and comparative approach is used.
- Survivals provided "proof" that evolution had occurred.
- Evolutionary anthropologists are known as "armchair" anthropologists.
- Evolutionism was ethnocentric.

Diffusionism

As time went on, evidence began to accumulate contradicting evolutionary theory. Folklorist and anthropologist Andrew Lang, for example, commenting on Tylor's idea that monotheism was the most advanced form of religion said, "[t]hat such moral, practically omniscient Gods are known to the very lowest savages – Bushmen, Fuegians, Australians" (Lang 1898, 176). Toward the end of the 19th century, anthropologists suggested that advanced cultural traits in an otherwise "primitive" culture could have been borrowed from more "civilized" societies. The Australian Aborigines, for instance, could have adopted belief in a single god from Christian missionaries. This, of course, complicated outlining the evolution of cultural traits, and so anthropologists began to trace how aspects of culture were borrowed or diffused from one culture to another. ***Diffusionism*** held that humans were essentially uninventive. According to the diffusionists, certain cultural features originated in one or several parts of the world and then spread, through the migration of peoples, trade, or simply through contact, to other cultures.

Initially, this involved looking at the history of cultures and their relationships with other cultures in different regions of the world. In Germany and Austria, Fritz Graebner (1887–1934) and Wilhelm Schmidt (1868–1954) argued that groups of interrelated culture traits formed a ***culture complex*** that developed in a certain area and then diffused outward in a circular fashion known as a ***Kulturkreis***, or culture circle. In England and the United States, archaeologist V. Gordon Childe introduced the idea of ***culture-historical archaeology***. This theory was based on the idea that each society produced its own distinct material culture. As Childe put it, "We find certain types of remains—pots, implements, ornaments, burial rites and house forms—constantly recurring together. Such a complex of associated traits we shall call a 'cultural group,' or just a 'culture.' We assume that such a complex is the material expression of what today we would call 'a people' " (Childe 1929, v–vi). Archaeologists using this concept could then trace the diffusion of culture and the migration of ancient peoples. Thus, for example, the appearance of pottery bowls with unique decorations in neighbouring societies could be explained by diffusion, while the sudden appearance of such bowls in more distant localities was more likely due to migration.

Childe also coined the terms ***Neolithic Revolution*** and ***urban revolution***. The Neolithic Revolution denotes the major cultural changes that occurred in history when hunter-gatherers became sedentary, domesticated plants and animals, and adopted agriculture. The term urban revolution, on the other hand, refers to the cultural changes that resulted from the development of state-level societies and cities (Smith, M. 2009).

Some English diffusionists, particularly Grafton Elliot Smith (1871–1937) and William James Perry (1887–1949), took the concept of diffusion to the extreme. Because mummification, Sun worship, and pyramid building are found in many societies, they suggested that everything found in the world could ultimately be traced back to the early Egyptians (Smith 1915) (Figure 4.3).

Diffusionism had run its course by the early part of the 20th century. To be certain, the diffusionists started with a particularly sound anthropological concept—that is, cultural diffusion—but they either took it to its illogical extreme or left too many questions unanswered. Few cultural anthropologists today would deny the central role that diffusion plays in the process of culture change.

Even though they collected considerable historical data, the diffusionists were not able to answer a number of important questions concerning the process of cultural diffusion. For example, when cultures come into contact with one another, what accounts for the diffusion of some cultural items but not others? What determines the rate at which a cultural item spreads throughout a geographic region? Diffusionists failed to raise certain important questions, such as why certain traits arose in the first place. Despite these limitations they were the first to point out the need to develop theories dealing with contact and interaction among cultures.

Diffusionism in Brief

- All societies change as a result of cultural borrowing from one another.

---

diffusionism The late 19th and early 20th century theory that cultural differences can be explained by the diffusion of cultural traits from one society to another.

culture complex A group of closely related aspects of culture.

Kulturkreis A German and Austrian form of diffusionism whereby culture complexes diffused from several culture centres.

culture-historical archaeology An archaeological theory that separate societies or ethnic groups produce their own unique pattern of material culture that could be used to trace the diffusion of culture or the migration of people.

Neolithic Revolution The period in history when hunter-gathers took up agriculture, resulting in major cultural changes.

urban revolution The cultural changes that resulted from the development of state-level societies and cities.

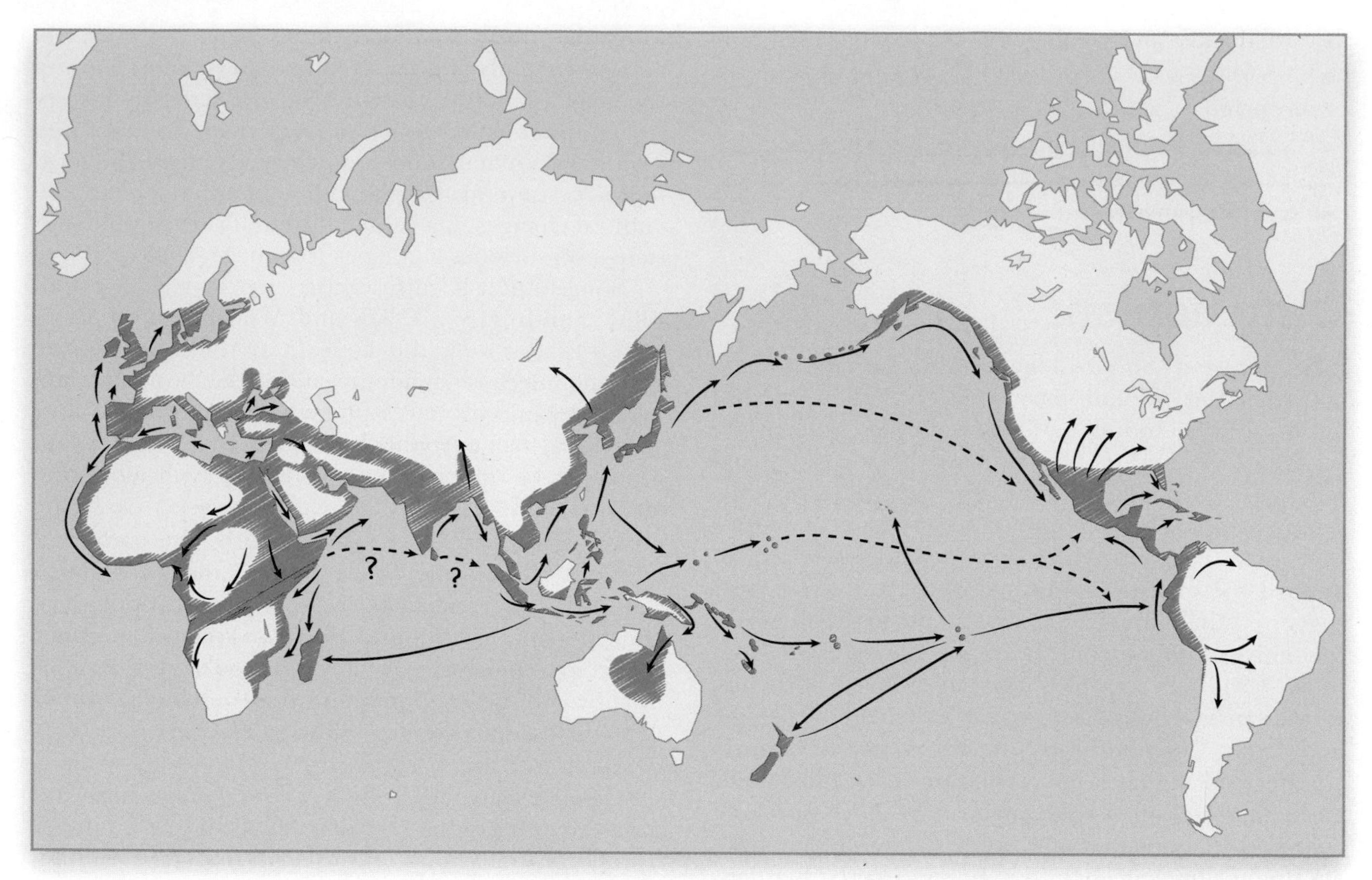

FIGURE 4.3 An attempt to represent roughly the areas directly affected by the "heliocentric" culture-complex, with arrows to indicate the hypothetical routes taken in the migrations of the culture-bearers who were responsible for its diffusion.

Source: From Smith, Grafton Elliot. 1915. *The Migrations of Early Culture*. Manchester University Press. London: Longmans, Green & Co. page 14.

- A deductive approach is used, with the general theory of diffusion being applied to explain specific cases of cultural diversity.
- The theory overemphasized the essentially valid idea of diffusion.

Fieldwork

Because the evolutionists, for the most part, did not do fieldwork, they suffered from a lack of good ethnographic data. They were also under the not-unfounded impression that most of the cultures they were interested in were rapidly disappearing under the onslaught of civilization. It therefore became imperative that they actually go into the field and collect as much data as they could before it was too late. One of the first attempts to do this was the 1898 ***Cambridge Expedition to the Torres Straits***. The Straits lie between Australia and new Guinea.

The expedition consisted of seven members, and from April to November 1898 they spent their time going from one island to another collecting linguistic, biological, psychological, and ethnographic data (Kuklick 2008) (Figure 4.4). In many ways the expedition represented a turning point for British anthropology because anthropologists recognized that this was not the way "to do" anthropology (Stocking 1995). Expeditions were hugely expensive, disruptive, required the use of

Cambridge University Museum of Archaeology and Anthropology

FIGURE 4.4 Members of the 1898 Torres Straits Expedition: standing (*from left to right*): Rivers, Seligman, Ray, Wilkin; seated: Haddon.

Cambridge Expedition to the Torres Straits An 1898 British expedition that investigated the cultures and peoples of the Torres Straits.

FIGURE 4.5 During one of the longest uninterrupted fieldwork experiences on record, Bronislaw Malinowski not only set the standard for conducting fieldwork, but he also developed an important new way of looking at contemporary cultures, known as functionalism.

translators, and only scratched the surface of the available ethnographic material. What was required, they realized, was an intensive type of fieldwork. In 1913, W. H. R. Rivers, one of the expedition leaders, wrote that what was needed was a type of fieldwork "in which the worker lives for a year or more among a community of perhaps four or five hundred people and studies every detail of their life and culture; in which he comes to know every member of the community personally; in which he is not content with generalized information, but studies every feature of life and custom in concrete detail and by means of the vernacular language" (cited in Urry 1993, 28).

Anthropologists began conducting fieldwork in the early 1900s, although most did not live among the people they studied, learn their language, or participate in any meaningful way (Urry 1993). The first British anthropologist to do this in earnest was Polish-born Bronislaw Malinowski (1884–1942; Figure 4.5) who, beginning in 1914, spent two-and-a-half years studying the people of the Trobriand Islands, off the northeast coast of New Guinea. In his book *Argonauts of the Western Pacific* (1922 [1961]) he laid out the method for how to do ethnographic fieldwork. Malinowski insisted on learning the local language and trying to understand a culture from an insider's perspective (emic approach). The goal of the ethnographer, he said, was "to grasp the native's point of view, his relation life, to realize *his* vision of *his* world" (1922 [1961], 25). He had no interest in asking how a cultural item got to be the way it is.

Functionalism

When Malinowski began his fieldwork, evolutionism and diffusionism were still the dominant theories of the day. But because they required cross-cultural comparison, they were of little help to him in making sense of the data he was collecting on a single culture. He did, however, have with him a copy of Émile Durkheim's *The Rules of Sociological Method* (1895). Durkheim, along with Max Weber and Karl Marx, is often considered one of the founding fathers of sociology. All three are also important in the development of anthropological theory. Durkheim was interested in what held societies together. In *The Division of Labour in Society* (1893 [1933]) he argued that small-scale societies were held together by ***mechanical solidarity***. What he meant by this was that everyone was basically the same: they held similar beliefs, followed the same traditions, did similar work, behaved similarly, belonged to the same kinship group, and so on. It was this similarity that provided people with a sense of identity and solidarity. In larger societies, however, society had become differentiated, and labour had become specialized. What held society together was the fact that, to survive, people had to depend upon each other, and this required everyone fulfilling their respective duties and roles in society. He called this ***organic solidarity***.

Durkheim believed that society consisted of social facts. ***Social facts*** were basically institutions such as marriage, the family, kinship group, economics, religion, medicine, and so on. An ***institution*** consisted of a pattern of beliefs and thinking, and roles and behaviours that are relatively stable over time. Like the organs of the body, each also had a separate function. To function properly, however, individuals had to fulfill their roles and duties that were appropriate for that institution. The family, for instance, is an institution where the mother/wife and father/husband, as well as the children, are expected to behave in culturally appropriate ways. In traditional Western culture, for example, the family consisted of a married, opposite-sex couple and their children; the man was the breadwinner and the woman looked after the house and children. By fulfilling these roles, they fulfilled the function of an institution that could perhaps be said to provide for the welfare and education of the next generation. We learn how we are supposed to act and what we are supposed to believe as we grow up, and so institutions channel or shape our thinking and behaviour. This also means that institutions transcend, or are greater than, the individual since they exist before we are born and continue to exist after we die. An implication of this is that they are objective and, by observing the general patterns of beliefs and behaviours, are measurable. For Durkheim this meant that sociology was a science.

Social facts are also thought to have coercive power, and anyone who deviates from fulfilling their institutional

mechanical solidarity The idea that small-scale societies are integrated because its members believe and act similarly.

organic solidarity The idea that complex societies are integrated by the dependence of its members on each other.

social facts The institutions of a society that transcend the individual and have a coercive influence such that people follow the appropriate cultural norms.

institution A pattern of beliefs and behaviours that are relatively stable over time.

obligations is brought back into line through various informal sanctions such as ridicule, ostracism, and so on, or more formal sanctions such as laws. This is necessary because otherwise the institution fails to function properly, which could jeopardize the society as a whole, just as a malfunctioning heart or liver jeopardizes the body as a whole. Institutions were thus integrated and had to be studied in their interrelationships. This gave an order or structure to the society, and also meant society had to be looked at holistically.

Durkheim's ideas about institutions and how they functioned laid the foundation of the theoretical orientation, known as *functionalism*. Believing that little could be learned about the *origins* of culture, Malinowski drew upon Durkheim's ideas and concentrated on exploring how contemporary cultures operated, or functioned. Functionalism assumed that cultures provided various means for satisfying both societal and individual needs. For instance, individuals need food, shelter, sex, etc., and thus the function of horticulture, economics, marriage, etc. is to ensure those needs are met. The society as a whole also needs to ensure people behave, and so the function of law is to keep people in line. According to Malinowski, no matter how bizarre a cultural item might at first appear, it had a meaning and performed some useful function for the well-being of the individual and the society. The job of the anthropologist is to become sufficiently immersed in the culture and language to be able to identify these functions.

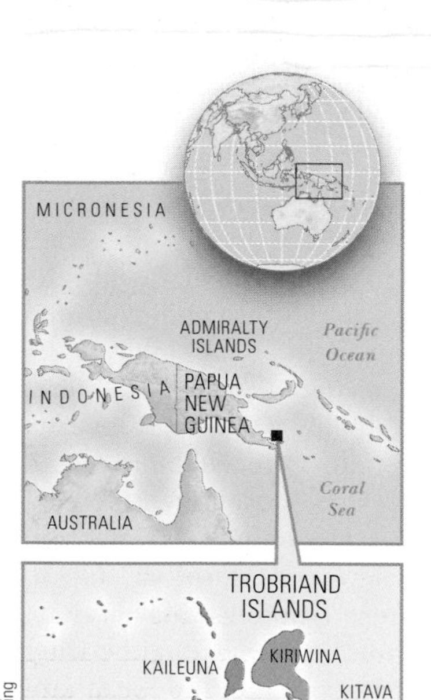

Locator map of Trobriand Islands

Not only do all aspects of a culture have a function, according to Malinowski, they are also interrelated. This functionalist tenet is no better illustrated than in Malinowski's own description of the *kula* ring, which involves the exchange among the Trobriand Islanders of ceremonial necklaces and bracelets as well as everyday commodities across a large number of islands. The *kula* not only provides participants with prestige in obtaining a renowned *kula* item and performs the function of distributing goods within the society, it is also related to many other areas of Trobriand culture, including political structure, magic, technology, kinship, social status, myth, and social control. Even though the exchanges are based on the principle of reciprocity, usually long periods of time elapse between repayments made by trading partners. Alvin Gouldner (1960, 174) suggested that, during these periods, debtors are morally obligated to maintain peaceful relationships with their benefactors. If this is the case, we can see how the *kula* ring maintains peace and thereby functions as a mechanism of social control as well as a medium of material exchange. Thus, by examining a cultural feature (such as the *kula* ring) in greater depth, the ethnographer, according to this functionalist perspective, will begin to see how it is related to many other aspects of the culture, and what it contributes to individuals and society as a whole.

Another form of functionalism was developed by the British anthropologist Alfred Reginald Radcliffe-Brown (1881–1955). Like Malinowski, Radcliffe-Brown held that the various aspects of institutions should be studied in terms of the functions they perform. Whereas Malinowski viewed their functions mostly as meeting the needs of the *individual*, Radcliffe-Brown saw them in terms of contributing to the well-being of the *society*. For Malinowski, the function of the institution of family is to provide for the biological needs of the individual, such as reproduction, education, and care of children. For Radcliffe-Brown, when people fulfil their roles they are maintaining the structure of their society. Because of this emphasis on social functions rather than individual functions, Radcliffe-Brown's theory has taken the name *structural functionalism*.

The functionalist approach, most closely associated with Malinowski and Radcliffe-Brown, is based on two fundamental principles: First, the notion of *universal functions* is that every part of a culture has a function. For example, the function of a hammer is to drive nails into wood; the function of a belief in an omnipotent god is to create solidarity; the function of law is to control people's behaviour; and in Canada the function of shaking hands is to communicate nonverbally one's intentions to be friendly. The second principle, known as *functional unity*, is that a culture is an integrated whole composed of a number of interrelated parts. When one part changes, other parts must also change. A common analogy is that the institutions of a culture, such as religion or marriage, are like the organs of the body. The function of the heart, for instance, is to pump

---

functionalism The theory that social institutions are integrated and function to maintain or satisfy the biological needs of the individual.

structural functionalism A school of cultural anthropology that examines how parts of a culture function for the well-being of the society.

universal functions The functionalist idea that every part of a culture has a particular function.

functional unity A principle of functionalism stating that a culture is an integrated whole consisting of a number of interrelated parts.

blood, which then oxygenates the cells. Ultimately it keeps the body alive. Similarly, social institutions have a specific function to perform and ultimately to ensure that the culture runs smoothly.

A corollary to the principle of functional unity is that, if the parts of a culture are interconnected, then a change in one part of the culture is likely to produce change in other parts. Another corollary is that individuals must be coerced or persuaded into fulfilling their roles through a system of rewards and sanctions.

Functionalists have been criticized for not being able to account for change. Societies are seen as being in harmony, and any change, usually caused by external factors, disrupts the system. Individuals are also seen as little more than puppets whose job is simply to behave according to the dictates of their roles. They are not seen as being in conflict with one another, or rebelling, or contesting things.

Functionalism in Brief

- Through direct fieldwork, anthropologists seek to understand how the parts of contemporary cultures contribute to the well-being of the individual and the society.
- Society is like a biological organism with many interconnected parts.
- With this high level of integration, societies tend to be in a state of equilibrium: a change in one part of the system brings change in other parts.
- The existing institutional structure of any society performs indispensable functions, without which the society could not continue.
- Functionalists have been criticized for not being able to account for change.

Historical Particularism

While Bronislaw Malinowski was putting anthropology on a more empirical footing in the United Kingdom, Franz Boas (1858–1942) (Figure 4.6) was also proceeding inductively by establishing a tradition of first-hand data collection in the United States. In 1883 Boas travelled from his native Germany to Baffin Island, where he spent a year studying the Inuit living as they did and participating in their daily activities. Like Malinowski, Boas was a strong advocate of fieldwork. Both men insisted on learning the local language and trying to understand a culture from an insider's perspective.

Coming from an academic background in physics and geography, Boas was interested in the impact of the Arctic environment on the inhabitants' culture. Beginning in 1886 he began to make frequent trips to study the culture of the Kwakwaka'wakw, or Kwakiutl, and other First Nations in Canada's Pacific Northwest.

Bettmann/Getty Images

FIGURE 4.6 Franz Boas, the teacher of the first generation of cultural anthropologists in the United States, put the discipline on a firm empirical basis.

Boas came to realize that culture helps societies adapt to their environment, and different groups in an area formed culture trait complexes, similar to the idea of the diffusionists. But unlike the diffusionists, Boas and his students were not interested in tracing the origin and development of cultural traits over vast regions, but how they diffused between neighbouring groups and were changed to suit different social and environmental conditions. Boas realized that different societies could have developed similar cultural elements for a number of reasons, such as adaptation to the environment, borrowing, or simply by accident, or even because of human nature. One implication of this was that, to understand any one specific culture, it was also important to know about that culture's particular history; hence the reason why his approach is often called ***historical particularism***.

Boas was appalled by what he saw as speculative theorizing about the origins of culture masquerading

historical particularism A school of anthropology prominent in the first part of the 20th century that insisted on the collection of ethnographic data (through direct fieldwork) before making cross-cultural generalizations.

as science. Rather than dreaming up large, all-encompassing theories to explain why particular societies are the way they are, Boas wanted to put the discipline on a sound footing using an inductive approach; that is, Boas planned to start by collecting specific data and then move on to develop general theories. Boas felt that the enormous complexity of factors influencing the development of specific cultures rendered any type of sweeping generalization, such as those proposed by the evolutionists and diffusionists, totally inappropriate. Thus, he and his followers insisted on a moratorium on theorizing and focused on collecting detailed ethnographic data through fieldwork in particular cultures. Boas believed language influenced the way people perceived their world; thus, it was also essential to understand the language of the people one studied.

Some of Boas's more severe critics claimed that this anti-theoretical stance was responsible for retarding the discipline of anthropology as a science. Yet, in retrospect, most commentators would agree that his experience in the areas of physics and mathematics enabled Boas to bring to the young discipline of anthropology both methodological rigor (such as in the form of systematic and thematic data collection) and a sense of how to define problems in scientific terms. Even though Boas himself did little theorizing, he left the discipline on a sound empirical footing.

The impact Boas had on anthropology is perhaps most eloquently demonstrated by the fact that he trained virtually the entire first generation of U.S. anthropologists. In recruiting graduate students to study anthropology with him at Columbia University, in New York City, Boas, from the beginning, was purposeful about attracting women to the discipline. Ruth Benedict and Margaret Mead are perhaps the most notable. Recognizing that male fieldworkers would be excluded from observing certain aspects of a culture because of their gender, Boas felt that to describe cultures more completely the discipline needed both male and female ethnographers. Today, compared to other academic disciplines, cultural anthropology has been producing more female professionals than male.

At the time Boas was writing, many people thought that race and culture were closely connected. Thus, darker skinned people were thought to have lower mental capacity that resulted in a more primitive culture than lighter skinned people. In his book *Race, Language, and Culture* (1940) he refuted this idea and showed that differences in culture were not due to biology, but that culture could influence biology.

Franz Boas is sometimes called the "Father of American Anthropology." Not only did he establish one of the first anthropology departments in the United States—at Columbia University, New York City, where he trained the first cohort of North American anthropologists—he was also instrumental in establishing the American Anthropological Association, in 1902. Boas insisted on understanding not only the culture of a people but also their archaeology, language, and biology, and so was also responsible for anthropology's four-field model.

Historical Particularism in Brief

- Ethnographic facts must precede the development of cultural theories (induction).
- Any culture is partially composed of traits diffused from other cultures.
- Direct fieldwork is absolutely essential.
- Each culture is, to some degree, unique.
- Ethnographers should use an emic perspective.

Culture and Personality

As early as the 1920s, U.S. anthropologists became interested in the relationship between culture and the individual. A number of Boas's students were asking some theoretically powerful questions: What role do personality variables play in human behaviour? Should personality be viewed as a part of the cultural system? If personality variables are part of culture, how are they causally related to the rest of the system? Wanting to relate some of the insights of Gestalt (the idea that the whole is greater than the sum of its parts) and Freudian psychology to the study of culture, the early psychological anthropologists looked at child-rearing practices and personality from a cross-cultural perspective. They held that child-rearing practices (which are an integral part of a culture) help shape the personality structure of the individual, which in turn influences the culture. Thus, they saw an interactive relationship among child-rearing practices, personality, social structure, and culture. This theoretical approach is called the ***culture and personality*** school, although some now see it as a branch of psychological anthropology, which studies the relationship between culture and personality, emotion, perception, ways of thinking or cognition, and other psychological functions (see Chapter 1).

Ruth Benedict (1887–1948) was one of the earliest anthropologists to suggest that each society produces its own personality characteristics. In *Patterns of Culture* (1934) she claimed that each society unconsciously chooses a limited number of cultural traits, and that individuals within a society internalize those traits through a wide range of enculturation practices. Collectively, Benedict suggested, this results in similar ways of thinking and behaving that form a

---

culture and personality A theoretical school in anthropology that looks at the relationship between culture and personality.

Ruth Benedict and National Character Studies

Shortly after the Japanese attacked Pearl Harbor in December 1941, the U.S. government established the Office of War Information (OWI). One of its goals was to collect information on their enemies, particularly the Japanese, as their culture seemed incomprehensible to most Americans. They had to understand their enemy. As anthropologist Ruth Benedict put it:

> "in the all-out war Japan was fighting we had to know, not just the long history of Japan, not just economic and military statistics; we had to know what their government could count on from the people. We had to try and understand Japanese habits of thought and emotion and the patterns into which these habits fell. We had to know the sanctions behind these actions and opinions." (Benedict 2005 [1946], 4)

The OWI hired Benedict to assist them in this effort but, unable to visit Japan, she conducted "Anthropology at a Distance" and began by interviewing Japanese Americans in internment camps and prisoners of war. She also studied translations of Japanese novels, newspapers, and films. Shortly before the United States dropped the atomic bomb on Hiroshima, she wrote a report entitled "Japanese Behavior Patterns," which after the war was published as *The Chrysanthemum and the Sword* (1946); it became a bestseller in both the United States and Japan.

The report came too near the end of the war to have any impact on it, but Benedict did have an influence on what happened afterward. The Americans had to know what to do with Emperor Hirohito, and what the Japanese people would do under occupation. Conventional wisdom suggested that Japan's highly rigid hierarchical society and worship of the Emperor as a deity made it both incapable of changing and totally unsuited to democratic institutions. Benedict, however, was able to convince those in charge of the occupation that, rather than being stubbornly rigid, Japanese society was actually quite adaptable. She argued that Japan, being a *shame and honour culture*, was perhaps more amenable to change than cultures, such as the United States, that are based on *guilt culture* and absolute standards of good and evil, where social control is achieved by instilling feelings of guilt for behaviour deemed undesirable. In shame and honour cultures, on the other hand, social control is maintained by instilling shame and threatening ostracism from the group. They respond better to externally imposed standards. So, she argued, if the United States wanted to change the behaviour of postwar Japanese, the first step would be to change the standards. In other words, Benedict suggested that change was possible, indeed likely, if the United States were to work within the already existing parameters of Japanese culture rather than trying to change the culture itself.

Benedict also convinced the occupying authorities not to eliminate the institution of the Emperor. Even though the Emperor was a monarch, he would be needed to build solid democratic institutions and a strong free-enterprise economy. Clearly, the Japanese people venerated the Emperor and gave him their unending loyalty, but for centuries the Japanese imperial system had been highly flexible. Advisors to the Emperor, or the Emperor himself, were replaced to reflect changing times. Given this traditional flexibility, Benedict argued that the institution of the Emperor must be preserved in postwar Japan. The fact that the Emperor had been defeated by the Allies could be explained away by having received bad advice from militarists who took Japan down the road to war. So, according to Benedict, the Allies should convince the Emperor to reject militarism (as shameful) and accept democracy (as honourable), and when that happened the Japanese people, with their great loyalty to the Emperor, would gladly follow.

Much to their credit the U.S. occupation authorities heeded Benedict's advice. Not only did the Japanese embrace democratic institutions, but also the economy rebounded and today is one of the largest in the world. The rebuilding of postwar Japan into a democratic nation with a strong economy would very likely not have occurred if the U.S. occupying forces had followed conventional thinking by eliminating the position of the Emperor and forcing the country to accept democratic and capitalistic institutions. Benedict's sensitive study of Japanese culture led her to conclude that conquering military powers would not be able to bring about meaningful social change by force or coercion.

Ruth Benedict's national character approach has been criticized for being stereotypical and for not being based on participatory fieldwork or using the local language. She was right, however, about what the Japanese would do after the war if the Emperor was allowed to stay (Stille 2003).

Benedict's work was not the last time anthropologists have worked for the U.S. military, or indeed the Canadian armed forces. The U.S. military employed anthropologists during the Vietnam War and more recently, in 2005, the U.S. Department of Defense began a program called the Human Terrain System (HTS). This program embedded teams of anthropologists and other social scientists in combat units in Iraq and Afghanistan in order to help military commanders understand the local populations (the human terrain) they were dealing with (Rohde 2007). It has been embroiled in controversy since the beginning. American officers have praised the program, saying that it helped them to see the Afghan perspective and reduce combat operations (Rohde 2007). Anthropologists, on the other hand, have been particularly opposed to it. In 2007 the AAA executive stated that it was an "unacceptable application of anthropological expertise" (Albro et al. 2009, 4) since it conflicted with anthropologists' primary ethical responsibility to protect the people they study. In a later report the AAA executive stated, "When ethnographic investigation is determined by military missions, not subject to external review, where data collection occurs in the context of war, integrated into the goals of counterinsurgency, and in a potentially coercive environment—all characteristic factors of the HTS concept and its application—it can no longer be considered a legitimate professional exercise of anthropology" (Albro et al. 2009, 3).

(*Continued*)

Ruth Benedict and National Character Studies (*Continued*)

Although the program ended in September 2014, after the withdrawal of most U.S. troops from Afghanistan and Iraq, another U.S. Department of Defense project, Project Minerva, is ongoing. Project Minerva provides funding for social science research into areas of strategic importance to the U.S. government. It too is surrounded in controversy.

Questions for Further Thought

1. How would you distinguish between a shame and honour culture and a guilt culture?
2. What other roles can cultural anthropologists play in assisting governments?
3. Is using anthropological knowledge for military purposes an "unacceptable application of anthropological expertise"?

group personality pattern. To illustrate her perspective, Benedict analyzed the basic personality traits of three societies: the Kwakwaka'wakw, or Kwakiutl, of the Pacific Northwest, the Zuñi of the U.S. Southwest, and the Dobu of the South Pacific. She claimed the Kwakiutl were an aggressive people who were prone to excess and competition. In contrast, the Zuñi were described as peaceful, restrained, and distrustful of excesses and disruptive disputes; and the Dobuans as passionate and consumed with jealousy, suspicion, and resentment. Benedict's ideas have been sharply criticized as stereotyping people, and to this day there is little evidence that any society has a modal or group personality.

Margaret Mead (1901–1978) was one of the most prolific writers in the field of culture and personality. After completing her graduate training under Boas at Columbia University, Mead became fascinated with the emotional disruption that seemed to accompany adolescence in the United States. Psychologists at the time maintained that the stress and emotional problems found among U.S. adolescents were a biological fact of life and occurred at puberty in all societies. In 1925 she left for Samoa to try to determine whether the strains of adolescence were universal (i.e., biologically based) or varied from one culture to another. In her first book, *Coming of Age in Samoa* (1928), Mead reported that the permissive family structure and relaxed sexual patterns among Samoans were responsible for a calm adolescence (Figure 4.7). Thus, she concluded that the emotional turbulence found among adolescents in the United States was culturally rather than biologically based because U.S. adolescent sexuality was (at the time) strictly monitored.

From the turbulence of adolescence, Mead next turned to the question of gender roles. Based on her research among the Arapesh, Tchambuli, and Mundugumor of New Guinea, she attempted to demonstrate that there were no universal temperaments that were exclusively masculine or feminine. More specifically, Mead reported that, among the Arapesh, both men and women had what Westerners would consider feminine temperaments (i.e., nurturing, cooperative, non-aggressive, maternal). Both Mundugumor men and women displayed exactly the opposite traits (i.e., ruthless, aggressive, violent

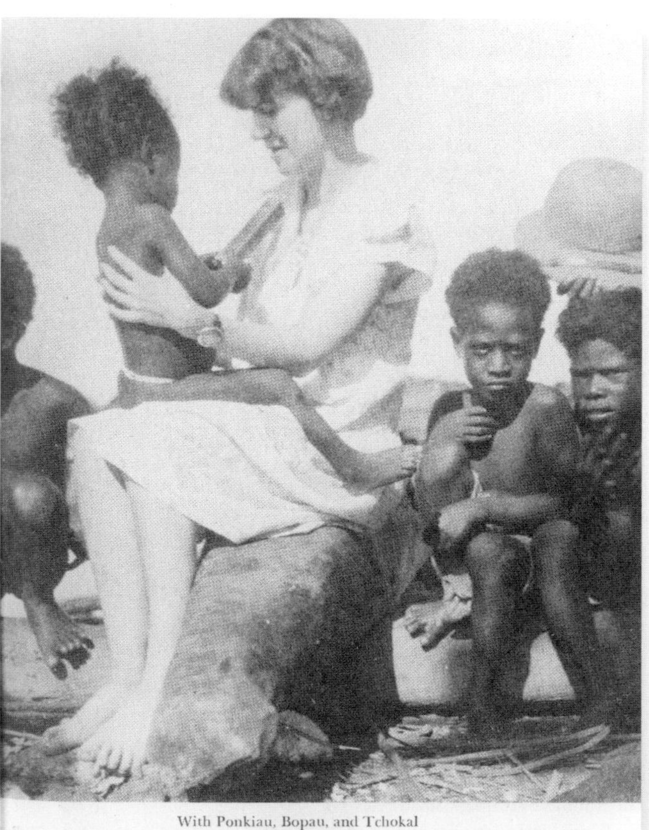

Fotosearch/Getty Images

FIGURE 4.7 **Margaret Mead devoted much of her long and distinguished career in anthropology to the study of how culture affects the process of growing up. Here she is conducting fieldwork in the Admiralty Islands in 1953.**

demeanours), whereas among the Tchambuli there was a complete reversal of the male-female temperaments found in North American culture. Based on these findings, Mead concluded in her *Sex and Temperament in Three Primitive Societies* (1935) that our own Western conception of masculine and feminine is not genetically based but rather is culturally determined.

Culture and Personality in Brief

- Anthropologists explore the relationships between culture and psychological variables such as personality, emotion, and cognition.
- Personality is largely the result of cultural learning, but there is no modal cultural personality type for a particular society.
- Universal temperaments associated with males and females do not exist.

Neoevolutionism and Cultural Ecology

As we have seen, Boas and others were extremely critical of the 19th century evolutionists, in part because they made sweeping generalizations based on inadequate data. Despite these criticisms, no one, including Boas himself, was able to demonstrate that cultures do *not* develop or evolve in certain ways over time.

As early as the 1930s, Leslie White (1900–1975), a cultural anthropologist trained in the Boasian tradition of collecting detailed ethnographic data based on an emic perspective, resurrected the theories of the 19th century evolutionists. Like Tylor and Morgan, White believed that cultures evolve from simple to increasingly more complex forms, and that cultural evolution is as real as biological evolution. It was White's position that Tylor and Morgan had developed a useful theory, but their major shortcomings were that they lacked the data to demonstrate it, and the unilinear model was too sweeping. White's unique contribution to anthropological theory was to suggest the cause (or driving force) of evolution, which he called his "basic law of evolution." According to White (1959), as the amount of energy harnessed annually increases, or as putting energy to work becomes more efficient, a culture evolves.

According to White's ***neoevolutionism*** model, culture evolves when people are able to increase the amount of energy per capita under their control. For most of human prehistory, while people were hunters and gatherers, the major source of energy was human power. But, with the domestication of animals and the invention of agriculture, the steam engine, the internal combustion engine, and nuclear power, humans began to dramatically increase the levels of energy at their disposal. To illustrate, the daily average energy output for a healthy human is a small fraction of a horsepower per day; the amount of energy produced from a kilogram of uranium in a nuclear reactor is approximately 33 billion horsepower! For White, the significant equation was $C = ET$, where C is culture, E is energy, and T is technology. Therefore, White's mathematical equation offers an explanation of the mechanics for cultural evolution: Culture evolves and becomes more complex as the amount of energy harnessed per capita and the level of technology increase.

Another anthropologist who rejected Boas's particularist orientation was Julian Steward (1902–1972). Like White, Steward was interested in the relationship between cultural evolution and the interaction between culture and the environment. He argued that similarities between cultures could be explained as similar solutions to the challenges of similar environments, such as finding enough food and shelter. For example, Steward studied the Shoshone and Paiute of the Great Basin—foraging societies that congregated in winter to collect pinyon (pine) nuts and hunt rabbit and pronghorn, and dispersed in winter to fish for salmon, essentially following the available calories. These societies lived in small mobile and egalitarian groups in which women did the gathering and the men hunted, and the nuclear family was the primary kinship group. Steward concluded that this pattern was an adaptation to the ***carrying capacity*** of their environment, and that "pursuits concerned with the problems of daily existence dominated their activities to an extraordinary degree and limited and conditioned their [social] institutions" (1938, 1-2). He also noted that other groups such as the Australian Aborigines had similar adaptions to similar environments.

He suggested that, given a particular environment and a certain level of technology, a ***cultural core*** of traits and strategies would emerge directly related to exploitation of the environment that would fulfil the basic needs of a society (Figure 4.8). Societies in similar situations would develop similar strategies and form what he called a ***culture type***. Other features, not relevant to adaptation to the environment, such as artistic expression, the specifics of religious beliefs, various traditions etc., that differentiated societies, were the result of historical circumstances, diffusion, and so on.

---

neoevolutionism A 20th century school of cultural anthropology whereby similarities between cultures could be explained by parallel adaptations to similar natural environments.

carrying capacity The maximum population size an environment can sustain, given the food and water resources and technology available.

cultural core The constellation of features most closely related to subsistence activities.

culture type Cultures that shared similar core features.

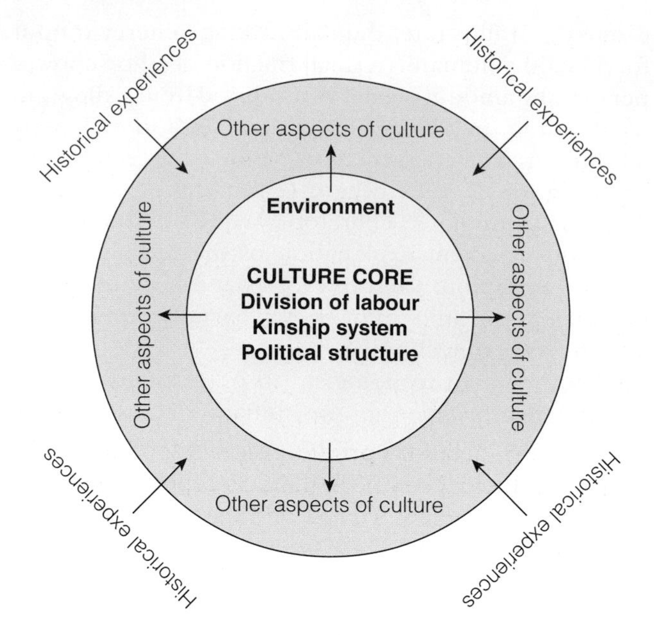

FIGURE 4.8 **Julian Steward argued the environment and technology determined a core of cultural features. Cultures in similar environments developed similar cores (a cultural type), while other aspects varied depending on historical circumstances of the society in conjunction with their cultural core.**

Steward distinguished three basic cultural types: family, multifamily, and state societies, which were later refined to band, tribe, chiefdom, and state.

Steward arranged these cultural types into a hierarchical sequence according to complexity, and held that, by examining sequences of change in different parts of the world, one could identify paths of development and some limited causal principles that would hold true for a number of societies. To test his hypothesis, Steward selected areas of the world that had produced complex societies (civilizations), such as Egypt, the Middle East, Mexico, China, and Peru. In all these cases, Steward tried to show certain recurring developmental sequences, from earliest agriculture up through large, complex, urbanized societies. For example, in all of these areas, people were faced with dry environments that required them to develop methods of irrigation to obtain water for farming. This led to food surpluses, population growth, and, as competition for resources increased, warfare, state societies, and empires. Steward called this ***multilinear evolution***.

Even though environment is a key variable in Steward's theory, he was not an environmental determinist because he recognized the variety of human responses to similar environmental conditions. By focusing on the relationships among people, environment, and culture, Steward was the first and leading proponent of ***cultural ecology***, a theory many anthropologists rely on today as they begin their research on political ecology (discussed later in this chapter). Cultural ecology attempts to discover how people use culture to deal with the basic issues of survival and, more recently, environmental issues such as deforestation, pollution, and climate change. By considering a society's culture, environment, and the consequences of how they deal with these issues, cultural ecologists hope to learn from their successes and their mistakes (Sutton and Anderson 2013). Cultural ecologists are also concerned with the impact cultural activities have on the environment, both minor and catastrophic, which, as Sutton and Anderson (2013) point out, affect human activities in turn. For example, deforestation and conversion of the land into cash crops and pasture can lead to food insecurities, which can in turn result in migration or increase social inequalities and so on.

Neoevolutionism and Cultural Ecology in Brief

- Culture is shaped by environmental conditions.
- Through culture, human populations continuously adapt to techno-environmental conditions.
- Cultures evolve in direct proportion to their capacity to harness energy.

Cultural Materialism

There are two underlying, and opposite, theoretical tendencies in anthropological theory: ***idealism*** and ***materialism***. Idealism is the view that culture is more about what we make of the world—the values, meanings, and ideas we give to it. Thus, if we want to understand people's behaviours and cross-cultural differences and similarities, we should focus on such intangible things such as symbols and morals. Materialism, on the other hand, looks at material phenomena, such as human biological nature and the environment, and how these influence people's ideas and values. The neoevolutionist–cultural ecology school was informed primarily by this perspective and by the 1960s had become generally accepted.

The leading materialist anthropologist was Marvin Harris (1927–2001). His idea of ***cultural materialism*** is a theoretical position based on the concept that material conditions or modes of production determine

---

multilinear evolution The mid-20th century anthropological theory whereby specific cultures evolve independently of all others but follow a similar evolutionary process.

cultural ecology An approach to anthropology that examines the interactions between people who reside in similar environments and their technologies, social structures, and political institutions.

idealism The position that reality is shaped or constructed by ideas.

materialism The position that reality shapes or influences ideas.

cultural materialism An anthropological theory that cultural systems are most influenced by such material things as natural resources, technology and human biology.

human thoughts and behaviour. According to this approach (Harris 1968, 1979a, 1999), the primary task of anthropology is to provide cause and effect explanations for the similarities and differences in thought and behaviour found among human groups. Cultural materialists accomplish this task by studying material constraints that arise from the universal need to produce food, technology, tools, and shelter. These material constraints are distinguished from mental constraints, which include such human factors as values, ideas, religion, and aesthetics, and which follow from the materialist constraints. Harris and cultural materialists see material constraints as the primary causal factors accounting for cultural variations.

For example, in India Hindus typically do not consume beef. Cows are sacred and are often seen roaming the streets, even in large cities (Figure 4.9). The idealist interpretation for this phenomenon is that the behaviour is explained by the belief: cows are sacred so are not eaten and are allowed to roam free. In this case the practice follows from the belief. For Harris, this explanation is insufficient as it must also explain why, in Canada and many Western countries for instance, beef is seen almost as a delicacy. Why do Islam, Judaism, and Christianity not prohibit eating beef? Marvin Harris has a materialist explanation. In a country such as India with a high rural population, cattle provide a useful service: cows are a source of milk, their dung is used as fuel, and oxen (castrated bulls) are used as draft animals. It is therefore ecologically necessary that they are not eaten, and to ensure they are not, they are made sacred. In other words, the material situation is the cause of the belief (Harris 1985). In Europe, however, population density is lower, there are other animals, such as horses, available as draft animals and so there is no need to make them sacred, and thus there is no prohibition against eating them.

Dhiraj Singh/Bloomberg via Getty Images

FIGURE 4.9 Pedestrians walk past cows in the street in the Zaveri Bazaar area in Mumbai, India, February 2015.

Cultural materialists rely heavily on an etic research methodology—that is, one that assumes the viewpoint of the anthropologist rather than the local collaborator. This research strategy uses the scientific method, logical analysis, testing of hypotheses, measurement, and quantification. Using these scientific methods, cultural materialists attempt to explain the similarities and differences among various socio-cultural structures by focusing on material and economic factors. As Harris (1979) argued, codes and rules are not at all helpful in explaining phenomena such as poverty, underdevelopment, imperialism, population explosions, minorities, ethnic and class conflict, exploitation, taxation, private property, pollution, the military-industrial complex, political repression, crime, urban blight, unemployment, and war.

Cultural Materialism in Brief

- Material conditions determine human thoughts and behaviour.
- Theorists take an etic viewpoint, not that of the local informant.
- Anthropology is seen as scientific, empirical, and capable of generating causal explanations.
- Cultural materialism de-emphasizes the role of ideas and values in determining the conditions of social life.

French Structuralism

No single theoretical orientation is as closely associated with a single person as ***French structuralism*** is associated with Claude Lévi-Strauss (1908–2009). Although both Radcliffe-Brown and Lévi-Strauss are called structuralists, their approaches to cultural analysis are vastly different. Whereas Radcliffe-Brown focused on identifying how the parts of a society function as a systematic whole, Lévi-Strauss concentrated on identifying the mental structures that underpin culture and social behaviour. The structure that Lévi-Strauss is concerned with is the structure of the mind, which is then imposed on the world.

Lévi-Strauss argues that one of the basic characteristics of the human mind is that it is programmed to think in ***binary oppositions***, or opposites. All people, he claims, have a tendency to think in terms of pairs of opposites,

French structuralism A theoretical orientation holding that cultures are the product of unconscious processes of the human mind.

binary oppositions A mode of thinking found in all cultures, according to Claude Lévi-Strauss, based on opposites, such as old-young, nature-nurture, and left-right.

such as male–female, hot–cold, old–young, night–day, nature–culture, and right–left. It is this underlying pattern of human thought that gives shape to, and is reflected in, various cultural institutions. Consider, for example, Lévi-Strauss's interpretation of totemism, a belief system found in many parts of the world that states a relationship between social groupings (such as clans or lineages) and aspects of the natural world (such as plants or animals). Lévi-Strauss suggests that totemic beliefs are complex mental devices that enable people to classify the units of their culture and relate them to the natural world. For example, in the northwest of British Columbia there are First Nation groups that label their ancestral lineage as the bear, wolf, and eagle clans.

Cultural differences occur, according to Lévi-Strauss, because these inherent mental codes are altered by environment and history. Although he recognizes these surface differences, Lévi-Strauss suggests that, in the final analysis, the mental structure of all humans is essentially the same. The content of a cultural element may vary from one society to another, but the structure of these elements is limited by the nature of the human mind.

Lévi-Strauss's structuralism has been criticized for being overly abstract. It also fails to consider how cultures change, or the meaning cultural elements have for people, and because his theories are not inclined to empirical testing, many anthropologists have rejected them. He did, however, focus on the grand questions that anthropologists, in their modern-day quest for specialization, have largely abandoned: How does the human mind work? Even with the world's vast cultural variations, is there a psychic unity for all of humankind? Even though French structuralism does not appeal to more empirically oriented anthropologists, Lévi-Strauss has made a major contribution by directing our attention to the relationship between culture and cognition.

French Structuralism in Brief

- It is assumed that the human mind categorizes phenomena in terms of binary oppositions.
- Human cultures are shaped by certain preprogrammed codes of the human mind.
- Theory emphasizes repetitive structures rather than socio-cultural change.
- Rather than examining attitudes, values, and beliefs, structural anthropologists concentrate on what happens at the unconscious level.

CROSS-CULTURAL MISCUE

In an effort to avoid war, James Baker, who in January 1991 was the United States Secretary of State, met with Iraq's foreign minister Tariq Aziz. At the meeting was a half-brother of Saddam Hussein whose job it was to report on the progress of the talks to the Iraqi leader. Baker calmly told Aziz that the United States would attack Iraq if they did not leave Kuwait, which they had invaded and annexed in August 1990. Hussein's half-brother then reported that "the Americans will not attack. They are weak. They are calm. They are not angry. They are only talking." A few days later a U.S. led coalition of 34 nations attacked Iraq with the loss of about 175 000 Iraqi lives. Iraqis focus more on how something is said rather than on what is said. According to Carnevale and Choi (2000), if Baker had shown anger and outrage, possibly by shouting or pounding the table, things may have been different; Iraq may have withdrawn from Kuwait and tens of thousands of lives saved. This example demonstrates that cross-cultural miscues can have serious consequences.

Symbolic Anthropology

In the 1960s and 1970s there was a general re-evaluation of cultural anthropology as a scientific enterprise. Focus shifted from function to meaning, from cultural determinism and constructionism to how individuals shape their culture and experience it. Many anthropologists in both Britain and North America began to move away from materialist interpretations of culture toward more idealist theories, and to view culture as a fundamentally symbolic system in which symbols are used to convey meaning. The job of anthropology was to understand the meaning of symbols—how they are created, used, and experienced. ***Symbolic anthropology*** thus focuses not so much on patterns of behaviour or adaptation to the environment, or on what people do, as on what people think they are doing.

For example, for British anthropologist Victor Turner (1920–1983), symbols are involved in social processes, particularly rituals. Symbols, Turner says, produce action and "groups mobilize around them, worship before them, perform other symbolic activities near them, and add other symbolic objects to them" (1967, 22). In *The Forest of Symbols* (1967) he discusses the role of the mudyi tree (or milk tree) in girls' initiation rituals among the Ndembu, who live in Zambia. The mudyi tree, which exudes a white sap when cut, is regarded as feminine by the Ndembu and represents human breast milk, the mother-infant bond, womanhood, mother's breasts, and the principle of matriliny (descent reckoned through women). When young girls participate in the ritual, the symbols are

symbolic anthropology A theoretical school in anthropology that views the goal of anthropology as the interpretation of symbols.

manipulated, providing them with adult status and creating a bond of solidarity between women.

Another British anthropologist who looked at symbols was Mary Douglas (1921–2007). Douglas argued that symbols not only promote social solidarity but that they are also a form of social control and are important in structuring society (1966). She was particularly interested in the body as a source of symbols and argued that bodily secretions, such as spit, urine, blood, tears, and so on, are seen as polluting and thus a threat to purity. Taboos are established to ensure one is not contaminated by such substances, and other rituals are performed to remove pollution. Douglas also sees these ideas as an organizing principle of society. For instance, in the traditional Indian caste system, high status people are seen as pure and lower caste individuals as impure. The most impure are the Dalits, who are in fact outside the caste system. Because they were seen as impure and polluting, they used to be called "untouchables." If a Brahmin, a high caste individual, touched a Dalit they would have to perform a ritual cleansing. And to ensure higher castes were not polluted, Dalits were required to live on the outskirts of villages and to announce their arrival.

Symbolic Anthropology in Brief

- Culture is a fundamentally symbolic system.
- Symbols are involved in social processes such as ritual.
- People behave according to the meaning of symbols.
- The meaning of a symbol requires the cultural context.
- Symbols are used to structure society and provide a sense of solidarity.

Interpretative Anthropology

Interpretive anthropology, advocated by Clifford Geertz (1926–2006), triggered a major re-evaluation of the anthropological enterprise, and made anthropologists become much more aware of the cultural contexts they worked in, the relationship they had with the people they observed, and the ethnographic accounts they produced. For Geertz, "[t]he concept of culture ... is essentially a semiotic one. ... [M]an is an animal suspended in webs of significance he himself has spun, I take cultures to be those webs, and the analysis of it to be therefore not an experimental science in search of law, but an interpretive one in search of meaning" (Geertz 1973, 5). In other words, culture consists of a complex web of meaning, and the job anthropology is to unravel them, which means anthropology is not a science. Rather than searching for general propositions or laws about human behaviour then, Geertz and fellow interpretive anthropologists took a more descriptive approach by examining how the people themselves (rather than the anthropologist) interpret their own behaviours.

Putu Sayoga/Getty Images

FIGURE 4.10 **Roosters prepare to fight during a cockfight in Bali, Indonesia. Geertz argues that the cockfight is a metaphor for men who fight for status.**

According to Geertz, because cultures are such complex webs of meaning, the job of the anthropologist is to describe, in as much detail as possible, not only the behaviour of people but also the details of the context. Geertz called this "*thick description*." This thick description was necessary in order to first grasp what was going on and then render the ethnography intelligible to outsiders.

The ethnography for Geertz was an interpretation of the interpretations of his cultural collaborators. Trained in the West as observers of foreign cultures, interpretive anthropologists believe they can never adequately describe another culture, but essentially articulate their own culture's response to the "other." For example, Geertz described the Balinese cockfight (Figure 4.10) and argues that it is only a metaphor. It is not the cocks that are fighting but men who vie with one another for status. The wins and losses of the cock fights themselves symbolize other things that happen behind the scenes and involve such things as alliances, and whose bird is supported.

The issue Geertz raised is that if anthropological knowledge is essentially interpretive then it can never be validated. Most of us cannot go to Bali to verify the observations, and since another anthropologist, even if they could go to Bali, would be observing and

interpretive anthropology A theoretical orientation holding that culture is a web of symbols and meaning, and the job of anthropology is to interpret those meanings.

thick description The detailed description of behaviours in ethnographic context.

writing from a different personal background, their interpretations can never be duplicated. In the past, anthropologists would inform their readers about how long they conducted fieldwork, whether it was done in the local language, and the way they took observations. Geertz calls this a demonstration of "being there" (1988), which gave authority to the ethnography. But if the ethnography is just one person's interpretation, it cannot be verified and thus anthropology cannot be a science because it cannot make any statements about culture that are empirically true.

Interpretative Anthropology in Brief

- Culture is viewed as an interconnecting web of meaning, which individuals interpret and which guides their behaviour.
- Interpretive anthropologists use thick description to describe a culture they observe.
- Interpretative anthropologists take an emic approach by examining how the people themselves interpret their own values and behaviours in a given context.

Feminist Anthropology

Feminist anthropology developed alongside the wider women's movement in the 1960s and 1970s and has its roots in psychological anthropology with previous contributions from Mead and Benedict. The feminist critique of anthropology and past theoretical orientations was centred on the fact that anthropology had been androcentric (male-centred). Critics argued that, although some anthropologists were women, the women in those societies studied by anthropologists were often neglected as objects of study or embedded with gender-neutral terms such as "the farmer" or "the peasant," where it could not be discerned if one was speaking about a man or a woman. Even when women were put under the anthropological lens, they were often portrayed as passive objects rather than as prime players in the mainstream of social life. In brief, most anthropologists were men, and they relied on the opinions and ideas of the men—particularly as they related to women—in the cultures they studied.

As a long-overdue corrective to this neglect, marginalization, and misrepresentation of women in anthropology, *feminist anthropology* called for a systematic reanalysis of the role women play in social structure. As recounted by Micaela di Leonardo (1991, 8), feminist anthropologists in the 1970s responded enthusiastically to the challenge of reanalyzing and rewriting previous ethnographies "as if gender really mattered." Feminist anthropologists such as Louise Lamphere (1974), Sherry Ortner (1974), Eleanor Burke Leacock (1978), and Michelle Zimbalist Rosaldo (1974), among others, tried to rectify this male bias by focusing on women's positions, roles, contributions, and experiences within society. Many of the early feminist studies concentrated on explaining female subordination (which some scholars saw as a cultural universal) and inequality. More recent studies, however, have looked at the social construction of gender, work and production, reproduction and sexuality, body image variations between different groups of women, and how gender influences economic, political, and social power (see Lewin 2006).

Although feminist anthropology is diverse in terms of areas of investigation and theoretical indebtedness, two basic features are generally agreed on. First, feminist anthropology takes as a given that gender is an important, albeit previously neglected, variable when studying any aspect of cultural life. That is, just as economics, politics, and religion vary according to status, class, power, and age, they also vary according to gender. Second, there is little or no attempt in feminist anthropology to assume a value-neutral position; it is aimed at consciousness-raising and empowerment of women and, in the words of Stanley Barrett (1996, 164), "unapologetically promotes the interests of women."

The new attention given to women by the feminist anthropologists of the 1960s and 1970s led some anthropologists to return to sites where previous studies had been conducted from a largely male-centric perspective. Annette Weiner (Figure 4.11) is an excellent example. According to Malinowski's (1922) original ethnography, Trobriand men gave gifts of yams at harvest time to their sisters' husbands. Malinowski

Private collection of E. Hutchins, Envelope 46, Roll 7, Image 25. University of California, San Diego

FIGURE 4.11 Feminist anthropologist Annette Weiner with two Trobriand Islanders and harvested yams.

feminist anthropology A theoretical approach that seeks to describe and explain cultural life from the perspective of women.

viewed these gifts as a type of tribute from the girl's family to her husband's family, and thus as a way of consolidating male power, but Weiner (1976) had a different interpretation. She found that, because the yams are given *in the wife's name*, the gift is as much a symbol of the high value placed on women as it is a symbol of power and status for men. Moreover, because Malinowski paid limited attention to the world of women, he failed to record that this gift of yams had to be reciprocated. Rather than reciprocating to his wife's brother, however, the recipient of the yams was expected to give directly to his own wife a unique form of wealth consisting of women's skirts made from banana leaves, which she used in important funeral ceremonies. If the husband failed to provide his wife with these skirts, his own brother-in-law might reduce or eliminate altogether his gift of yams, which would negatively affect the husband's chances of ever elevating his status in becoming a big man. Thus, in her restudy of Trobriand culture, Weiner was able to show that men were much more dependent on women for their status and power than Malinowski's previous description would have us believe.

Over time, feminist anthropology has evolved into gender studies that consider both men and women and from a more balanced perspective. Feminist anthropology not only provided a needed corrective to the male bias in anthropology, but it also alerted anthropologists to the fact that ethnographies were influenced by the anthropologists' gender, status, and Western perspective.

Feminist Anthropology in Brief

- All aspects of culture have a gender dimension that must be considered in any balanced ethnographic description.
- Feminist theory represents a corrective to male bias in traditional ethnographies.
- Feminist anthropologists promote the interests of women.

Political Economy

Although valued by ethnographers in general, a major theoretical framework used by many applied anthropologists is ***political economy***. At the core of political economy theoretical perspectives are the abstract issues of conflict, ideology, and power. Anthropologists whose research relies on this framework do so to explain, in part, the relationship between economic production and political processes. It is often used when there is a hierarchical social order with one group dominating or controlling another within a culture and between cultures. Conceptually it leads to multiscaled research that can start in a local village, connect to a more dominant regional government, and reach all the way to the international arena.

Courtesy of Sydel Silverman Wolf

FIGURE 4.12 Anthropologists such as Eric Wolf and other scholars challenge capitalism for its incquality and the marginalizing effects it has on local people, ethnic minorities, the poor, and the disenfranchised through a political economy perspective.

Political economy scholars challenge capitalism for its inequality and the marginalizing effects it has on local people, ethnic minorities, the poor, and the disenfranchised. To illustrate, Eric Wolf's work, *Europe and the People without History* (1982), provides an in-depth account of the political-economic perspective in anthropology (Figure 4.12). He provides insight into people's responses and resistance to the process of control by élite groups. Other anthropologists have taken a slightly different perspective, detailing how political and economic structures govern a labour force, or worker and capitalist relations, or discussions of war and violence. Anthropologists find political economy helpful to examine the increasing presence of poverty, the limited access to education, healthcare, and growing unemployment. Still others, such as

political economy A perspective that, at its core, examines the abstract issues of conflict, ideology, and power.

Pierre Bourdieu (1977), use the political economy framework to examine the production of cultural meaning and symbols. For Bourdieu, a society's cultural construction of meaning and symbols has political and economic implications, especially when there is conflict over the meanings or when they prove to be provocative in their interpretation. For example, understanding the different positions groups (e.g., governments, different tribes, special interests, etc.) have during a time of war.

Political economy has the potential to be widely used to frame research that focuses on social injustice, human rights, and marginalization, which is appealing to applied anthropologists. Unequal access to power, resources, and capital poses challenges, preventing some people from having a better quality of life than others. For applied anthropologists the political economy perspective guides the research process so as to unravel the political and economic barriers, to confront them, develop a project, get it funded, and implement it. Political economy has applications in business, education, healthcare, development, and urban planning. For example, a medical anthropologist might use a political economy approach to examine malnutrition, unequal access to healthcare, and diseases and illnesses related to poverty, to name a few social issues that receive attention nationally and internationally.

Political Economy in Brief

- Political economy at its core examines the abstract issues of conflict, ideology, and power.
- An ethnographic approach to political economy tends to be descriptive.
- An applied approach using a political economy framework focuses on making a difference for marginalized or disenfranchised groups of people.

Political Ecology

Previous anthropologists who framed their research with a political economy theoretical perspective often were not interested in the environment. Since the late 1970s and 1980s, however, research grounded in political economy began a resurgence by including environmental issues. Simply put, ***political ecology*** is the study of power relations among groups and how they are linked to the biophysical environment at the local, state, national, and international levels. Scholars whose work uses the political ecology perspective examine relationships among political, economic, and social factors with environmental issues and changes within a community and beyond. By paying attention to environmental interests, knowledge, beliefs, values, and practices of social groups, applied anthropologists can differentiate how resources are used, misused, and overused according to ethnicity, gender, and race or other factors.

Historically, political ecology focused on marginalized conditions affecting the developing world. Today, political ecology incorporates political economy into its theoretical construct, and then goes one step further by including the environment along with the political structure or economic systems. Political ecology addresses issues of power and recognizes the importance of explaining environmental impacts on cultural processes as part of the political and economic context. For example, resources (e.g., access to water, fish, soils and land, oil, trees and timber, biodiversity, clean air), especially in the context of wide-ranging ecological settings such as coastal rainforests, deserts, high mountains, glaciers, and urban and rural communities, are particularly complex and get even more complicated when subsequent policy and regulatory actions favour certain groups over others.

For anthropologists who integrate ecological social science with political economy, their work might emphasize topics such as sustainability, conservation, environmental conflict, environmental identities, marginalization, and social movements. The use of political ecology sees environmental degradation as a cause and effect of social marginalization.

Whether we are examining where a new garbage dump or the next hydroelectric dam is to be located, there are those with the power to decide on the future location and those who will be relocated, with or without compensation, or be forced to reside near the smells or potential for flooding. An example of political ecology helps to illustrate how the environment is brought to the forefront of the research. This example also illustrates the multiscalar approach (connecting the local level to the state or region and global levels) frequently used in political ecology. In this case, a hydroelectric dam was constructed in Patagonia, Chile, with the approval of the Chilean government (Figure 4.13). Where the dam was to be constructed, however, would flood the region inhabited by the Mapuche. The Spanish utility company gained permission from the Chilean government to locate a dam for a hydroelectric project along the river where the Mapuche families had resided for centuries. As a cultural practice, the Mapuche also use the river banks to inter their dead; to them the river and adjoining banks were sacred. However, it was necessary for the Spanish hydroelectric company to

---

political ecology A perspective that examines how unequal relations in and among societies affect the use of the natural environment and its resources, especially in the context of wide-ranging ecological settings, and subsequent economic, policy, and regulatory actions.

FIGURE 4.13 A Pehuenche, whose group is part of the Mapuche peoples in the Andes in south central Chile, stands on a hill overlooking the construction site of a US$500 million hydroelectric dam. The hydroelectric dam, once constructed, flooded lands to which the Pehuenche claim historical ownership rights.

STR/Reuters

flood the river to generate the power needed to make electricity. Yet, these decisions destroyed 14 ancient cemeteries and an Indigenous homeland.

In the end, the Mapuche lost their land, their way of life, and their ancestors' remains. Families were relocated into a barren region of Chile where they were without sufficient means to afford the electricity from the newly installed hydroelectric facility. Today, the Spanish electric company owns the hydroelectric dam in southern Chile and sells the electricity to Chileans. Clearly this example illustrates how unequal relations among societies and populations affect the use of the natural resources and the marginalization of those with less access and power.

Political Ecology in Brief

- Political ecology is the study of power relations among groups and how they are linked to the biophysical environment at the local, state, national, and international levels.
- The use of political ecology sees environmental degradation as a cause and effect of social marginalization. Scholars whose work uses the political ecology perspective examine relationships among political, economic, and social factors with environmental issues and changes within a community and beyond.
- Political ecology is used to examine how unequal relations in and among societies affect the use of the natural environment and its resources (e.g., access to water, fish, soils and land, oil, trees and timber, biodiversity, clean air) and marginalization of those with less access.

Postmodernist Anthropology

Modernism arose in Western industrial societies in the late 19th and early 20th centuries with the growth of cities and the expansion of empires. It was characterized by a faith in science and, for many modernists, a rejection of religious beliefs. The 19th and early 20th century founders of anthropology saw anthropology as essentially a scientific discipline and never abandoned such scientific canons as gathering empirical data, testing hypotheses, looking for cause and effect relationships, and adhering to the scientific method. Anthropologists, such as Malinowski for instance, saw themselves as detached scientific observers providing an objective account of the cultures they studied. By spending long periods of time in these cultures, learning the language, and taking a participant observer approach, they were seen as the authorities on "their" cultures and wrote ethnographies that purported to provide a holistic and objective picture of another culture.

Postmodernist anthropology means, literally, after modernist anthropology. It is a rather diffuse concept however, and grew out of a series of internal critiques, especially feminist and interpretative anthropology. In the mid-1980s anthropology seemed to be in a crisis as postmodernist anthropologists began to challenge many of the foundations of the discipline, and especially the idea that anthropology could be scientific, or that it could produce objective knowledge of another culture. Essentially, postmodernists dispute the possibility that anthropology can construct a grand theory of human behaviour. A basic tenet of postmodernism is that the "modernists" were extraordinarily arrogant to think that they could describe, interpret, and give meaning to the lives of people from other cultures. Postmodernists began to examine the nature of fieldwork, how other cultures are represented (especially in the ethnography), the power relationships between the ethnographer and the people being studied, and the influence of the ethnographer's personal experiences and situation (Figure 4.14).

Postmodernism and Fieldwork

Fieldwork, and the ethnography that results from it, have been—and still are—the primary means by which anthropologists gather and present their data. The early ethnographers claimed to provide a holistic view of culture after a year or more of fieldwork. Postmodernists, however, claim—and rightly so—that a complete understanding of another culture by any one

postmodernist anthropology A school of anthropology that advocates the switch from cultural generalization and laws to description, interpretation, and the search for meaning.

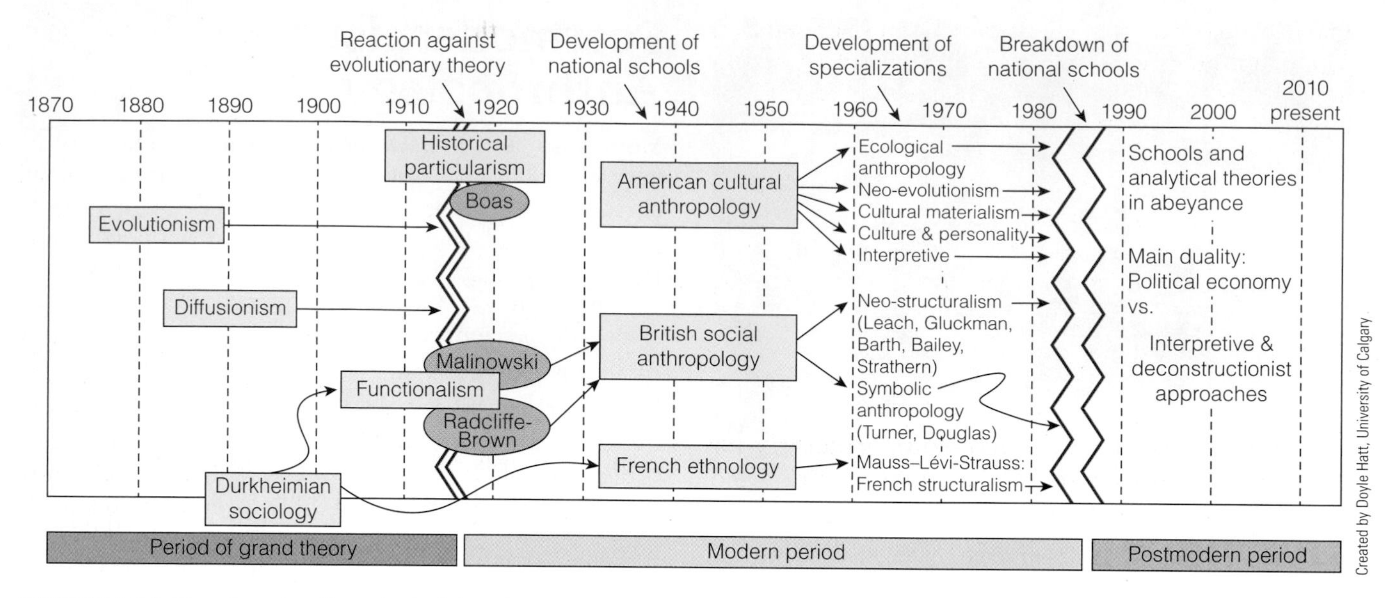

FIGURE 4.14 Time line of anthropological theories.

person in such a short period of time is an impossible task. By necessity, fieldworkers can only be in specific places at specific times and can never see everything. They must also work with collaborators who unavoidably influence what the anthropologist observes and understands. Fieldwork results are also influenced by the anthropologist's gender, age, ethnicity, personal experiences, interests, political views, and so on. Thus, postmodernists argue the particular circumstances of fieldwork and the fieldworkers' own interests and social situation have a major influence on the results they obtain. In other words, the knowledge anthropologists provide is "situated knowledge." Thus, rather than attempting to discover the truth about how the world works through empirical investigations, postmodernists hold that all ethnographic accounts are subjective.

Postmodernism and Ethnography

The ethnography is a written account of other cultures acquired through fieldwork. Modernists claimed these accounts were true and objective; postmodernists dispute this and question how the ethnography was written. Many postmodernists drew upon the works of French philosopher Jacques Derrida, who used literary criticism techniques to deconstruct scientific texts. Postmodernist anthropologists thus began to investigate the literary and rhetorical devices used to persuade people of the truth of the ethnographic data they were describing.

One of the first of these devices is what Geertz (1988) has termed "being there." Most ethnographies provide a brief statement of how long the ethnographer lived with the group they studied, and the extent to which they learned their language and managed to "fit in." This indicates to the reader that the anthropologist is an expert on the culture and so should be believed. But, as noted, simply being there does not make the account objective, as it must always be situated knowledge.

Another rhetorical device is known as the ***ethnographic present***, which is the practice of giving accounts of other cultures and societies in the present tense. It appears as if the cultures described in the ethnography never change, whereas intuitively we know they change just as ours does. Thus, when one reads *Argonauts of the Western Pacific*, for example, it is as if the Trobriand Islanders still live the way Malinowski described them 100 years ago. Johannes Fabian (1983) claims that writing in the present tense denies the other what he calls "coevalness," that is, being in the same time. If the people written about in the ethnography shared the same time as the anthropologist, then the ethnography should be written in the past tense since the events described in the ethnography occurred in the past. Writing in the present tense is an indication that the account is a commentary on the world and thus objective, whereas the past tense signals a historical account and thus is perhaps more humanistic. Fabian maintains the ethnographic present is a rhetorical device that serves to sustain objectivity by keeping the subject (us) and object (them) apart by placing them in different times.

Traditional ethnographies are also often written in the third person (he, she, they), which seems more scientific than the more subjective first person (I) or second person (we). The third person gives the impression that the ethnographer is an omniscient observer,

ethnographic present The practice of giving accounts of other cultures in the present tense.

making objective statements about another culture. The truth, however, is that the collection of anthropological data is a subjective experience and depends to a great extent on the ethnographer's experience and standing and relationships formed in the field. Many postmodern anthropologists see cultural anthropology as more of a humanistic enterprise than a scientific one, having more in common with art and literature than with biology or psychology.

Postmodernism and Power Relationships

Postmodernists claim that the modernists' enterprise for much of the 20th century was based on the privileged status of science (held by most developed countries), and reflected the basic power imbalances between the wealthy colonial countries and those developing countries where much of the anthropological research was conducted. It is nearly impossible, they contend, for predominantly white, male, Western anthropologists to step outside their own culture so as to produce an objective view of another culture. It has been said that Anthropology (at least British social anthropology) is "the child of Imperialism" (Gough 1968) and the "handmaid of colonialism" (Asad 1973). Their membership in a dominant culture gave anthropologists economic and legal advantages and determined the conditions under which fieldwork was conducted. The information they provided was also often used by colonial administrations to pacify, tax, and subjugate people. Upon their return, the anthropologist was often rewarded with a good paying job, essentially acquired through the exploitation of the people who provided the information. In other words, the anthropologist's membership in the dominant group significantly affected the results of his or her research, raising doubts about the claim to scientific independence.

The anthropologist has also been the one to control what information about another culture is made public. For instance, while anthropologists have always worked with informants/collaborators and may, in an attempt to present "the native's point of view," have provided direct quotes from them and others, it has been the anthropologist who chooses which quotes to use, and on what topics, and thus ultimately what readers of the ethnography are presented with.

Instead of the ethnographer being the sole authority, postmodernists call for a collaborative approach. For the postmodernist, written ethnography should have multiple contributors, thereby creating a dialogue between the anthropologist and the people being studied. It involves relinquishing sole authorship to include the voice of the research subjects themselves. This extends to having cultural collaborators review the ethnography before it is published, or even be named as coauthors. Postmodernists contend that only through this dialogical process will meaning and interpretations emerge.

Postmodernism's Impact

Postmodernist anthropology has shown that fieldwork is a subjective experience, that the ethnography uses rhetorical devices to give an illusion of objectivity, and that the anthropological enterprise is based on an unequal power relationship. This has dispelled for many the idea that anthropology can ever be a scientific discipline. One of the impacts of this is that anthropologists are now much more reflexive. ***Reflexive anthropology*** involves not only examining the discipline's biases, ethics, concepts, and goals, but also acknowledging one's own subjectivity in the production of anthropological knowledge. Thus, many ethnologists now typically describe their personal background, how they interacted with the people they studied, their political views, whether they were a member of the society studied, and so on. Many ethnographies are now not so much a description of the society or culture per se as an account of their fieldwork experience. Admittedly, the postmodernist perspective is relativistic and designed to sensitize anthropologists to their own views and values as well as those of the informant. They advocate combining self-knowledge with knowledge of the people under study so that anthropologists learn something about themselves as they are learning about the culture of the local collaborators. In fact, a reading of a postmodernist ethnography usually reveals as much about the anthropologist as it does about the people being studied.

The most radical postmodernists contend that, because objectivity is impossible and all interpretations are relative, generalizations are unwarranted and anthropology should be treated as literature rather than as science. In fact, purists, in the postmodern sense, believe all anthropologists carry with them their own cultural baggage; they would argue that, from the beginning, their research will be subjective in nature. It will be an interpretation from their own cultural lens. Fortunately, few anthropologists today hold such an extreme view, which would in effect reject all past attempts to make generalizations about cultural differences and similarities. Postmodernists have had many heated discussions with their more traditional, scientifically oriented colleagues. However, even their strongest critics should realize that the postmodernists have raised the consciousness of all anthropologists to consider issues such as how we generate knowledge, how we come to know what we think we know, and whose story we are telling in ethnographic accounts: theirs or ours.

---

reflexive anthropology Recognition of anthropology's biases as well as the influence of the anthropologist's own personal situation and experiences in the production of anthropological knowledge.

Postmodernism in Brief

- Postmodernism calls on anthropologists to switch their focus from cultural generalizations and predictable laws to description, interpretation, and the search for individual meaning.
- Ethnographies should be written from several voices: that of the anthropologist along with those of the people under analysis.
- Postmodernism involves being reflexive about concepts and terms used as well as the influences of one's personal situation and experiences on the production of anthropological knowledge.

Theory, Practice, and Praxis

Anthropologists depend on theory at the beginning of their research to be able to frame their research questions, or at the end of the research to interpret their findings and overall to contribute to the body of anthropological knowledge. Descriptive accounts presented by academic ethnographers are important for documenting the rich cultural heritage found around the world. In contrast, applied anthropologists are concerned with producing useful information that raises awareness for contemporary social problems and places those findings within a broader context of implementation (of projects and programs), thus contributing to making policy. These anthropologists emphasize the practical aspects of their work rather than their theoretical contribution. The opposite tendency is true of ethnographic anthropologists, who would prefer to emphasize their theoretical contributions and descriptive analyses over any practical or pragmatic application. Anthropologists working outside of academia altogether (practising anthropologists), as described in Chapter 3, may also have to write for a particular audience such as a client or an employer, or colleagues working for nongovernmental organizations as well as the public who may not know any anthropology. Their work is more general in nature, and a theory-driven or scholarly paper will probably not help them keep their job. Someone working for the World Bank, however, may need to understand kinship and family for their research, but they will probably not be writing about specific marriage patterns and descent groups like an academic anthropologist would.

Praxis in Anthropology

Integrating theory with practice is known as *praxis* and serves as a means to produce new knowledge. Although not always standard practice among some researchers, praxis is frequently used among applied anthropologists when combining their approach in data collection, data analysis, and application to an applied project. Applied business anthropologist Marietta Baba reminds us, "praxis carries with it a strong sense of social critique that we find in political economy and political ecology, where by people with whom anthropologists work may be liberated from the exploitive and alienating circumstances of their lives" (2000, 26). Praxis is an attainable ideal within anthropology that provides a balance that includes theory, method, and application. This balance is important to recognize, especially considering the continuum discussed in Chapter 3 that separates ethnographic theorists on the one hand, from practising anthropologists on the other, where one extreme is mostly theoretical (and no empirical research) and the other mostly practice (and no theory). In striving to combine theory with practice we always need to keep in mind the ethical considerations of our work and the people with whom we consult and interact, especially when engaged in applied research.

praxis Integrating theory with practice; serves as a means to produce new knowledge.

Concluding Thoughts on Anthropological Theory

This chapter was written with subheadings that divide the field of anthropological theory into discrete schools. Table 4.1 summarizes the primary anthropological theories and their proponents. These divisions can serve as a useful device to help track, in general terms and in roughly chronological order, the various emphases that anthropologists have taken since the mid-19th century. It is important to note, however, that we should not think of these different schools (theoretical frameworks) as being superseded by those that came later. In other words, evolutionism was not replaced by American historicism, nor was functionalism replaced by political ecology theories. Moreover, these schools of anthropology are not particularly relevant categories for distinguishing among the different approaches used by contemporary anthropologists. Few anthropologists today would tie themselves to a single school or theoretical orientation such as neoevolutionism, functionalism, cultural materialism, or political ecology.

Contemporary anthropologists tend to be more eclectic and problem oriented, focusing on explaining cultural phenomena while drawing on a wide variety of theories, research methods, and sources of data. Today, it is generally recognized that many of these theoretical schools are not mutually exclusive. It is evident that anthropology is maturing as a discipline when its practitioners reject hard-drawn lines among themselves and thereby enrich one another's thinking.

TABLE 4.1

Anthropological Theories and Their Proponents

School	Major Assumption	Advocates
Evolutionism	All societies pass through a series of stages.	Sir Edward Tylor, Lewis Henry Morgan
Diffusionism	All societies change as a result of cultural borrowing from one another.	Fritz Graebner, Grafton Elliot Smith
Functionalism	The task of anthropology is to understand how parts of contemporary cultures contribute to the well-being of individuals.	Bronislaw Malinowski
Structural Functionalism	Anthropology's task is to determine how cultural elements function for the well-being of the society.	Alfred Reginald Radcliffe-Brown
Historical Particularism	Fieldwork must precede cultural theories.	Franz Boas, Alfred Kroeber
Culture and Personality	Anthropology's task is to show relationships among psychological and cultural variables.	Ruth Benedict, Margaret Mead
Neoevolutionism and Cultural Ecology	Cultures evolve in direct proportion to their capacity to harness energy.	Leslie White, Julian Steward
Cultural Materialism	Material conditions determine human consciousness and behaviour.	Marvin Harris
French Structuralism	Human cultures are shaped by certain preprogrammed codes in the human mind.	Claude Lévi-Strauss
Symbolic Anthropology	Culture is a system of symbols that influence behaviour and are involved in rituals.	Victor Turner, Mary Douglas
Interpretive Anthropology	Human behaviour stems from the way people perceive and classify the world around them.	Clifford Geertz
Feminist Anthropology	Social relationships should be viewed as being gendered.	Louise Lamphere, Sherry Ortner, and Michelle Zimbalist Rosaldo
Political Economy	Economic and political systems are critical to understand conflict, struggle, and power.	Eric Wolf, June Nash, Sidney Mintz, Pierre Bourdieu, Phillipe Bourgois, Marshall Sahlins
Political Ecology	Combining political economy with the environment and resource use.	Eric Wolf, Susan Stonich, Arturo Escobar, Dianne Rocheleau, and Susan Paulson
Postmodernism	Anthropological knowledge is influenced by the circumstances of fieldwork and the anthropologist's background.	James Clifford, George Marcus, Johannes Fabian, James Boon, Michael Fischer

Summary

1. Anthropological theory helps explain the cultural diversity in the world, and provides a set of principles that direct research.
2. The first group of anthropologists used the notion of evolution to account for differences in human cultures. Nineteenth century evolutionists such as Tylor and Morgan suggested that all societies pass through a series of distinct evolutionary stages: from savagery to barbarism and then to civilization. They have been criticized for being overly speculative and ethnocentric in their formulations.
3. The diffusionists explained cultural differences and similarities in terms of the extent of borrowing from contact with other cultures.
4. The British functionalists Malinowski and Radcliffe-Brown were strong advocates of fieldwork, and concentrated on how contemporary cultures functioned to meet the needs of the individual and perpetuate the society. Not only do all parts of a culture serve a function, but also they are interconnected (functional unity) so that a change in one part of the culture is likely to bring about change in other parts.

5. Historical particularists such as Franz Boas insisted on the collection of first-hand empirical data on a wide range of cultures before developing anthropological theories. Boas insisted on a four-field approach and put the young discipline of anthropology on solid scientific footing.
6. The early psychological anthropologists, most notably Benedict and Mead, were interested in exploring the relationships between culture and the individual. By examining the configuration of traits, Benedict described whole cultures in terms of individual personality characteristics. Mead's early research efforts brought her to Samoa to study the emotional problems associated with adolescence, and later to New Guinea to study male and female gender roles.
7. The theory of evolution was brought back into fashion during the 20th century by White and Steward. White held that cultures evolve from simple to complex forms, but for White the process of evolution was driven by his "basic law of evolution" ($C = ET$). Steward's major contribution was the concept of multilinear evolution, a form of evolution of specific cultures that did not assume that all cultures passed through the same stages. Steward also introduced the concept of cultural ecology, formally bringing the environment into the discussion when describing a culture.
8. Led by Marvin Harris, cultural materialists believe that tools, technology, and material well-being are the most critical aspects of cultural systems, and that they influence ideas.
9. Drawing heavily on the models of linguistics and cognitive psychology, Lévi-Strauss maintained that certain codes or mental structures preprogrammed in the human mind are responsible for culture and social behaviour. A fundamental tenet of Lévi-Strauss's theory is that the human mind thinks in binary oppositions: opposites that enable people to classify the units of meaning in their culture and relate them to the world around them.
10. Symbolic anthropologists such as Victor Turner and Mary Douglas saw culture as a system of symbols that were important in structuring rituals.
11. Interpretive anthropologists such as Clifford Geertz conceive of culture as webs of meaning, and the role of the anthropologists as the unravelling of this web and the rendering of meaning into an ethnography intelligible to the anthropological audience.
12. Feminist anthropologists call for a systematic analysis of the role women play in social structure. The feminist critique, by and large, does not embrace positivism, quantitative methods, or a value-neutral orientation.
13. Anthropologists whose research relies on a political economy, theoretical framework do so to explain the relationship between economic production and political processes, especially when there is a hierarchical social order with one group dominating or controlling another within a culture and among cultures.
14. Political ecology is the study of power relations among groups and how they are linked to the biophysical environment at the local, state, national, and international levels. This type of research examines how unequal relations in and among societies affect the use of the natural environment and its resources, especially in the context of wide-ranging ecological settings and subsequent economic, policy, and regulatory actions.
15. Postmodernists argue that anthropology is not about scientific laws but interpretation. They challenge anthropologists to be reflexive about the role that their personal situation and experience plays in influencing the data collected during fieldwork and the construction of the ethnography, arguing that other voices must be present in the text.
16. Integrating theory with practice is known as *praxis* and serves as a means to produce new knowledge. It is an ideal that applied anthropologists strive to achieve in their application of their research.

Key Terms

binary oppositions
Cambridge Expedition to the Torres Straits
carrying capacity
cultural core
cultural ecology
cultural materialism
culture and personality
culture complex
culture-historical archaeology
culture type
deduction
degenerationism
diffusionism
ethnographic present
evolutionism
feminist anthropology
French structuralism
functionalism
functional unity
Hawthorne effect
historical particularism
hypothesis
idealism
induction
institution
interpretive anthropology

Kulturkreis
materialism
mechanical solidarity
multilinear evolution
neoevolutionism
Neolithic Revolution
organic solidarity
political ecology
political economy
postmodernist anthropology
praxis
psychic unity
reflexive anthropology
social facts
structural functionalism
survivals
symbolic anthropology
theory
thick description
unilinear model
universal functions
urban revolution

Critical Thinking Questions

1. Why is theory important to both ethnographic and applied anthropologists, and indeed all anthropologists?
2. Can you identify a particular social problem that an applied anthropologist might want to get involved in and think about what theoretical perspectives would be useful to develop a research proposal?
3. If you were to conduct fieldwork to understand how tourism affects gender relationships, what theoretical perspective or perspectives (if any) do you think would be most useful to you?
4. Why is it important, when studying the history and growth of anthropological theory, to read original works rather than commentaries on them?
5. Is a knowledge of evolutionism and diffusionism of any practical value to anthropologists today?
6. How would a functionalist understanding of marriage differ from an interpretive one?
7. Compare idealist versus materialist approaches to anthropological theory.
8. Is social or cultural anthropology a science?
9. How would a political economist approach an understanding of terrorism?
10. If you were to conduct fieldwork with an Indigenous group, what personal circumstances would influence the information you obtained and the way you presented it?

Make the Grade with MindTap

Stay organized and efficient with **MindTap**—a single destination with all the course material and study aids you need to succeed. Built-in apps leverage social media and the latest learning technology. For example:

- ReadSpeaker will read the text to you.
- Self-quizzing allows you to assess your understanding.
- Flashcards are pre-populated to provide you with a jump-start for review—or you can create your own.
- You can highlight text and make notes in your MindTap Reader. Your notes will flow into Evernote, the electronic notebook app that you can access anywhere when it's time to study for the exam.

Visit nelson.com/student to start using **MindTap**. Enter the Online Access Code from the card included with your text. If a code card is not provided, you can purchase instant access at NELSONbrain.com.

An ethnographer is greeted by an Inuit friend on his arrival at Gjoa Haven, King William Island, Nunavut, Canada.

CHAPTER 5

Research Methods in Cultural Anthropology

FIELDWORK IN TRISTAN DA CUNHA

Tristan da Cunha is the most remote inhabited island in the world. Located in the middle of the South Atlantic Ocean, it was settled in 1816 by the British and remains today as one of the last vestiges of the British Empire. In 1961 the island's volcano erupted and the entire population of 297 was evacuated to England where, because of their previous isolation, unusual dialect, and close biological ties, they were treated as a curiosity by the British press. Numerous reporters interviewed them and featured them in several articles, radio programs, and television shows, portraying them "as either an anthropological 'missing link' or a kind of unique species that had evolved like some of the creatures found on the Galapagos Islands, even referring to them as 'mutant inbreds'" (Day 2008, 48). The British government also had plans to assimilate them into British society, but the Islanders refused to be separated and were eventually all housed together in the married quarters of an air force base until 1963, when they returned home.

Most of the still-living evacuees are now quite elderly, and in 2006 the local Island Council thought it would be a worthwhile project to capture their memories of this period as part of the island's 500th anniversary celebrations (the island was discovered in 1506 by Portuguese explorer Tristão da Cunha). The Council decided to implement an oral history project and invited British social historian, Ann Day, to conduct the interviews over a four-week period. In preparation, Day read newspaper accounts and archival records of the evacuation, which helped to her to formulate her questions for the interviews and she felt ready to start interviewing almost immediately upon arrival. Day had also communicated with the Deputy Head Teacher at the school and the Island Administrator, who had posted a notice about the project on a bulletin board in the administration building; both seemed excited about the project. She assumed from this that "the Tristan community were fully aware of the project and would be willing to share their memories with me, but the reality was very different" (Day 2008, 48). By the fourth day she had found no one willing to participate.

What she discovered was that the experience in Britain had left the Islanders with a strong collective sense of identity that made them wary of outsiders and skeptical of their motives. Her desire to interview them, although intended to benefit their community, was perceived as a threat, making them reluctant

RICHARD OLSENIUS/National Geographic Creative

WHAT WE WILL LEARN

- **The stages cultural anthropologists go through in conducting ethnographic fieldwork**
- **The types of data-gathering techniques cultural anthropologists use**
- **The problems cultural anthropologists face in the field**
- **What culture shock is, and how anthropologists deal with it**
- **The ethical dilemmas anthropologists face when they conduct fieldwork**
- **How fieldwork impacts the anthropologist as well as the people he or she studies**

to participate in the project. She had also assumed that, because the Tristan people spoke English, they would have the same understanding of the term "oral history." Using this term put her at a disadvantage. The term "interview" was also problematic as it brought up negative memories of the evacuation years. Clearly she was going to have to change her approach.

Since the island lacks telephone, email, newspapers, and postal service, the only way to contact people was through word of mouth. The most helpful person was the local doctor (a South African), who was much respected by the Islanders and who took her on his rounds and introduced her to many of the local elders. From there she was able to use a "snowballing" method to reach others. She also realized that to gain the Islander's trust and let them know about her intentions she needed to participate in local social activities, and so began buying groceries at the Island's only shop, using the Internet café, cooking cakes, which she took to the interviews, and knitting squares to contribute to a blanket being made by one woman for children in South Africa. Day also changed her approach by getting to know the people first in an informal way before asking them if they would allow her to come and *talk* to them rather than interview them. Day took a life history approach to the interviews, where she first asked respondents general questions about their childhood memories of Tristan da Cunha, schooling, family life, and so on, before getting to more detailed questions about the evacuation years.

Day's experience highlights the fact that there are complex reasons why people may or may not participate in ethnographic field research. It also demonstrates that personal connections are often helpful, and that participating in the lives of the people one wants to study helps build rapport, trust, and cooperation. A final point Day makes is that her initial desire to conduct the interviews was based on considerations of time and money, but that it was when she was more sympathetic to the needs and understandings of the interviewees that they opened up to her. ■

Ethnographic Fieldwork

A distinctive feature of present-day cultural anthropology is the reliance on ***ethnographic fieldwork*** as the primary way of conducting research and collecting data. Fieldwork is a research method that requires the researcher to be personally immersed in the daily social activities of some group of people while conducting research (Wolcott 2008). Traditionally, this meant total immersion 24-7 for a year or more so that the researcher was able to see the yearly cycle of changes. Today, however, if one is studying a particular occupation, or under a time constraint for example, this is not always possible, although it is still important to spend as much time as possible with the people being studied and participate in their activities. Like any other professionals, cultural anthropologists want to describe the basic subject matter of their discipline. They are interested in documenting the enormous variety of ways of life found among the peoples of the world today. How do people feed themselves? What do different people like to eat? What do they believe? How do they legitimize marriages? In addition to learning the *what* and the *how* of different cultures, cultural anthropologists are also interested in explaining *why* people behave and think the way they do.

As a research strategy, anthropological fieldwork is eminently experiential, which means that researchers collect their primary data by immersing themselves in the cultures they are studying (Figure 5.1): living with the people, learning their language, asking them questions, surveying their environments and material possessions, and spending long periods of time observing their everyday behaviours and interactions in their natural setting. Conducting extended ethnographic fieldwork is how anthropologists gain expertise in the methods of the discipline and produce knowledge of other cultures. It is the core of anthropology and has become a rite of passage for most professional anthropologists; few receive a Ph.D. without doing it.

ethnographic fieldwork The practice whereby an anthropologist is immersed in the daily life of a culture to collect data.

© Gary Ferraro

© J.Enrique Molina/Alamy Stock Photo

FIGURE 5.1 **The study of everyday life in the state of Bahia in Brazil (*top*) presents different problems and challenges to the field anthropologist than does the study of village life in Burkina Faso (*bottom*). For example, the languages are different, as are the climate, dress, and housing.**

Even though anthropologists have routinely conducted fieldwork for most of the 20th century, they did not explicitly discuss their field techniques until the 1960s. A reader had no way of knowing, for instance, how long the anthropologist stayed in the field, how many people were interviewed and observed, how samples were selected, what data-gathering techniques were used, what problems were encountered, or how the data were analyzed. Because the credibility of any ethnographic study depends on its methodology, cultural anthropologists now produce excellent accounts of their own fieldwork experiences and data-collection methods.

By the 1980s anthropologists had begun to involve members of the cultural group they were studying with the project design, data collection, and data analyses. Involving local people in the applied research process is known as ***participatory action research***. This is a critical methodological change in the discipline because it empowers local residents and those participating in research projects to be part of the research design and data-collection process, and not just subjects who were interviewed in a study. Today this method is referred to as ***community-based participatory research (CBPR)***. A CBPR approach is collaborative and involves partners from within a community in all aspects of the research process. Most importantly, CBPR begins with a research topic of importance to the community. By working together and combining knowledge with action, CBPR project goals are aimed at achieving social change equitably.

Some anthropologists have dedicated their research to problem-oriented topics such as reforestation, nutrition, post-disaster events (earthquakes, tsunamis, and hurricanes), and resettlement. For example, Anthony Oliver-Smith has researched disasters and involuntary resettlement for the past 30 years (Figure 5.2). His work has taken in him to Peru, Honduras, India, Brazil, Jamaica, Mexico, Japan, and the United States, where he has assisted in post-disaster recovery and resettlement. After many years in the field that resulted in contributing to policy, Oliver-Smith (2010) observed a change in the voices being heard: that of the victims of the events. He recounts these changes in *Defying Displacement: Grassroots Resistance and the Critique of Development*, in which he describes how societies and cultures are taking

Eddie Gerald/Alamy Stock Photo

FIGURE 5.2 **Rosemie Durandisse stands with one of her children in front of her temporary home, four years after the earthquake in Port-au-Prince Haiti. Anthropologists, such as Anthony Oliver-Smith, research disasters and involuntary resettlement and work with local people to find better alternatives.**

participatory action research A mode of research in which the anthropologist and the community work together to understand the conditions that produce the community's problems and find solutions to those problems.

community-based participatory research (CBPR) A collaboration involving partners from within a community in all aspects of the research process. Most importantly, CBPR begins with a research topic of importance to the community, and works toward achieving social change equitably.

action against development-forced displacement and resettlement. And rather than it being only a negative critique of development, he also reports on new ideas and alternatives to resettlement and displacement, many of which come from the people with whom he has worked.

Why do anthropologists choose primarily to use the ethnographic approach? First, the ethnographic approach takes a holistic view (see Chapter 1). By studying all aspects of a culture, even while focusing on a particular issue, anthropologists are able to place issues in context. Second, the ethnographic approach depends on first-hand, experiential methods, which include face-to-face interactions with people within the culture. This provides a deeper understanding of issues than can be acquired by other methods or from an external perspective.

To get a better handle on a particular culture, an anthropologist begins by listening to stories and other kinds of talk that give insight into the community. Such ***qualitative data*** are gathered from personal interviews, oral histories, observations, and interactions with community members. These data are important to the research process and may be logged in anthropologists' ***field notes*** or digitally recorded and transcribed for later text analyses. Being able to see the patterns in the shared worldviews within a culture provides perspective on the numerical data obtained from gathering quantitative data.

Quantitative data are numerical data such as population trends, morbidity and mortality rates, household and community size, the numbers of births and marriages, landholding size, annual income, education levels, and any other data that can be counted. Quantitative data are used to conduct statistical analyses and are good for comparing groups, for following trends, and for telling us *how many*. For example, quantitative data can tell us whether men's attitudes to say marriage differ from women's, or how many women of childbearing age have children under five years of age who are malnourished. What quantitative methods are poor at, however, is answering the question *why*. Why do men's attitudes differ from women's? Why are so many children under five malnourished? To answer these sorts of questions, qualitative methods are required.

Anthropologists are grounded in ethnography, the methods of gathering, coding, and analyzing data. Applied anthropologists focus their research endeavours on contemporary problems and social issues. Given the nature of their work, applied anthropologists often collaborate on projects with other scientists and community participants to help expedite the fieldwork. They may work as facilitators, assisting in project design, project implementation, or evaluation. They may be interested in such things as the incidence of malnutrition in a village, the rate at which deforestation is taking place in a region, or how a village has been able to retard the spread of HIV/AIDS. Each of these topics requires that the applied anthropologist specializes in something beyond the knowledge of a particular people's culture. Such specializations may include (but are not limited to) nutritional anthropology, environmental anthropology, or medical anthropology, which requires the specialist to undertake additional training in related methods of data collection and analyses. Most important, though, the applied anthropologist's role is to provide a cultural understanding of how a problem came to be and how it may be removed, lessened, or resolved.

qualitative data People's words, actions, records, and accounts obtained from participant observation, interviews, group interviews, and relevant documents.

field notes The daily descriptive notes recorded by an anthropologist during or after an observation of a specific phenomenon or activity.

quantitative data Data that are counted and interpreted through statistical analyses.

CROSS-CULTURAL MISCUE

When Thomas Crampton (2003), correspondent for the *International Herald Tribune* in Hong Kong, visited the rural home of an English-speaking Thai acquaintance from Bangkok, he was treated like a celebrity. Although excited about having the weekend to learn about life in rural Thailand, Crampton was soon taken aback by the barrage of questions he was asked that, by Western standards, would be considered overly personal. Are you married? How much do you earn? How old are you? Particularly puzzling was the question, Would you like a bath? Unfortunately, Crampton did not understand that this is a common Thai greeting.

Wanting to be a good guest, he finally took them up on their offer and retreated to the bathroom, which had a full-sized tub already filled with water. He got in, lathered up, shampooed his hair, and rinsed off. When he finished, he could not find a drain in the tub to let out the dirty, soapy water. Feeling more than mildly perplexed, he scooped out the upper layer of soap scum with a bowl he found in the bathroom until the water looked relatively clean. After concluding that the Thais must have a special system for draining the tub, he dressed and rejoined his hosts.

The next morning Crampton's friend, with a big smile on his face, made a broad scooping motion with the bowl into the tub, used the water to rinse his mouth, and spit it into the drain on the floor. In Crampton's own words, "horror and embarrassment welled up as I learned lesson No. 1 of life in rural Thailand: Do not bathe in the week's supply of drinking water."

Any general discussion of how to do fieldwork is difficult because no two fieldwork situations are the same. The problems encountered while studying the reindeer-herding Chukchee of Siberia are quite different from those faced when studying hard-core, unemployed street people in Vancouver or rural peasant farmers in Peru. Even studies of the same village by the same anthropologist at two different times involve different experiences because, during the period between the two studies, both the anthropologist and the people being studied have changed.

Despite these differences, field anthropologists face some common concerns, problems, and issues. For example, everyone embarking on ethnographic fieldwork must make preparations before leaving home, gain acceptance into the community, select the most appropriate data-gathering techniques, understand how to operate within the local political structure, take precautions against investigator bias, cope with culture shock, learn a new language, and be willing to reevaluate his or her findings in light of new evidence.

Preparing for Fieldwork

Like any scientific enterprise, ethnographic fieldwork makes serious demands on one's time, patience, and sense of humour, and requires a lot of hard work and thoughtful preparation. Any fieldwork project lasting a year or longer may well require a minimum of a year's preparation. For a fieldwork project to be successful, the anthropologist must attend to many essential matters during this preparatory period. First, because it is expensive, it is necessary to obtain funding from a source that supports anthropological research, such as the Social Sciences and Humanities Research Council of Canada (SSHRC), Canadian International Development Agency (CIDA), The Pierre Elliott Trudeau Foundation, or the Wenner-Gren Foundation for Anthropological Research. Financial support (covering living expenses, transportation, and other research- and project-related costs) is awarded on a highly competitive basis to the proposals that have the greatest merit. The SSHRC, for instance, currently has five priority areas for funding: (1) Aboriginal Research, (2) Canadian Environmental Issues, (3) Digital Economy, (4) Innovation, Leadership and Prosperity, and (5) Northern Communities: Towards Social and Economic Prosperity. Even though a proposal may require months of preparation, there is no guarantee that it will be funded, as funds are limited. Proposals that stress the value of the research and are of interest to the funding agencies are more likely to be approved. Most anthropologists spend time writing and submitting more than one grant proposal with the hope at least one will take them to the field. A useful skill for an anthropologist is to know how to write grant proposals to secure funding for the desired projects.

Aldo Pavan/© age fotostock/Alamy Stock Photo

FIGURE 5.3 A dentist's office in Kankan, Guinea. A visit to the dentist before leaving for extended fieldwork is a good idea.

Second, preparation for fieldwork involves taking the proper health precautions. Before leaving home, a fieldworker should obtain all relevant immunizations. For example, a fieldworker travelling to a malaria-infested area must take the appropriate malarial suppressants. It is also prudent to get information about available health facilities ahead of time in case the anthropologist or a family member becomes ill while in the field. A visit to the dentist may also save some grief (Figure 5.3). In a humorous account of his fieldwork among the Dowayo people in northern Cameroon, British anthropologist Nigel Barley (1983) tells of how an abscessed tooth led him to a local dentist, where he contracted viral hepatitis.

Third, if the field research is to be conducted in a foreign country, permission or clearance must be obtained from the host government. Because field projects usually last a year or longer, no foreign government will allow an anthropologist to conduct research without prior approval. Even countries hospitable to Westerners require researchers to spell out the nature of the proposed research in considerable detail. The host government officials often want to ensure that the research will not be embarrassing or politically sensitive, that the findings will be useful, and that the researcher's presence in the host country will not jeopardize the safety, privacy, or jobs of any local citizens. Moreover, host governments often require cultural anthropologists to become affiliated with local academic institutions to share their research experiences with local scholars and students. Sometimes—particularly in developing countries—the approval process can be slow, which is another reason it can take nearly a year to prepare for a long-term field study. Thus, before entering a country, the anthropologist must obtain a long-term visa and research clearance, or permission, from a high level of the national government.

Michael Wheatley/All Canada Photos/Getty Images

FIGURE 5.4 A Salish First Nations canoe leaves Ambleside Beach, West Vancouver, September 2012, for Salish First Nations, Gathering of Canoes to Protect the Salish Sea. Anthropologists wishing to work with Canada's First Nations must agree to the OCAP principles.

In Canada, anthropologists wishing to conduct research with First Nations communities must also respect ***OCAP principles*** if they want community participation (Figure 5.4). OCAP stands for ownership, control, access, and possession. These principles, which most First Nations have adopted, stemmed from a historic failure of researchers looking into the health of First Nations communities to consider the relevance and impact their research had on the communities themselves. Some communities were harmed by participating in some research projects. The OCAP principles are intended to ensure First Nations communities are involved in the collection of data about them, who has access to the information, and how it is used. It is a good example of community-based research as, essentially, they require community members be involved in the design of research projects from the beginning, even before funding is applied for. The principles also ensure that data are collected in a manner that respects the customs and traditions of the people, and are meaningful and of value to the communities who provide the information (Schnarch 2004; Castellano 2004). Some First Nations also have their own ethics policies.

A fourth concern that must be addressed before leaving for the field is proficiency in the local language. An important tradition of anthropological fieldwork is that it should be conducted in the native language. If the anthropologist lacks fluency in the language, he or she should learn it before leaving home. That may not always be possible, however. Dictionaries and grammar books may not exist for languages with few speakers, and finding a native speaker to serve as a tutor while still at home may not be possible. In such cases the ethnographer will have to learn the language after arriving in the field. Building time for learning a new language into the fieldwork timeline is important for the research design, for conducting the research, as well as for funding purposes—and it may, and for good reasons, lengthen one's stay in the field.

Anthropologists should also have some knowledge of the culture they are going to as well as the topic they are interested in researching. In other words, they should conduct a ***literature review***. A literature review is an overview, synthesis, and appraisal of secondary resources about a particular issue or topic. Literature reviews look at the current state of knowledge about a topic and evaluate the strengths and weaknesses of theoretical and methodological contributions. They are an essential part of the research process as they help the anthropologist understand the issues, define the research questions, and find gaps in current knowledge. A literature review is thus essential in the development of the research proposal since it helps to justify the research by showing how one's own fieldwork can contribute to knowledge of the field. Literature reviews also allow the anthropologist to contextualize their research within the academic literature; they thus often form an essential chapter in a Ph.D. thesis.

Finally, the soon-to-be field anthropologist must take care of a host of personal details before leaving home. Arrangements must be made for:

- The care of personal possessions such as houses, cars, and pets;
- What to ship and what to purchase abroad;
- Children's education if families are involved;
- Equipment to purchase and insure, such as cameras, laptops, and recording devices;
- Up-to-date passports and international driving license; and
- A schedule for transferring money between one's bank at home and a convenient bank in the host country.

Despite taking care of all these pre-departure details, nothing can ever really prepare one for the experience of fieldwork itself. Fieldwork can be frustrating and daunting, as well as joyful and immensely rewarding. Nigel Barley (1983), for instance, describes his frustration and unnecessary delays caused by bank officials who required him to fill in countless forms before they would give him his money even before he reached his study location. But he also tells the story of how he thought his

OCAP principles Principles of ownership, control, access, and possession that ensure First Nation communities actively participate in ethnographic research.

literature review An evaluation of previously conducted research on a topic that allows the researcher to develop their own research proposal and situate their findings within the academic literature.

neighbour was suffering from indigestion because of the flatulence and belching coming from her house, only to discover later that it was her goats.

Stages of Field Research

Although no two fieldwork experiences are the same, every study should progress through the same six basic stages:

1. Selecting a research problem
2. Formulating a research design
3. Collecting the data
4. Analyzing the data
5. Interpreting the data
6. Writing up and presenting the results.

Stage 1: Selecting a Research Problem

In the early 20th century, the major aim of fieldwork was to describe a culture in as much ethnographic detail as possible. In recent decades, however, anthropologists have moved away from general ethnographies of particular cultures to research that is focused, specific, and problem-oriented. Rather than studying all the parts of a culture with equal attention, contemporary cultural anthropologists are more likely to examine specific issues dealing with relationships among various phenomena, such as the relationship between gender socialization and employment opportunities, or the relationship between nutrition and food-getting strategies. The shift to a problem-oriented approach lends itself to research that builds on a series of descriptive questions that are progressively more complex to better understand not only *how* and *why* particular problems have come to be, but also *what* may be done about them. The initial stage of selecting a problem often begins with a literature review.

Stage 2: Formulating a Research Design

The ***research design*** is the overall strategy for conducting the research. In the research design stage, the anthropologist must decide how to identify who might be willing to participate in a project, who to talk to, what methods of data collection should be used, how long the research will take, and so on.

Once the anthropologist has settled on a problem and formulated the design for the project, a ***research proposal*** is prepared for funding the research. The proposal details the project's purpose, hypotheses, methodology, and significance. There is a need to be flexible, however, because the techniques originally planned in the research proposal may prove to be inappropriate when actually used in the field. Whatever techniques are finally chosen, a variety of methods will be needed so that the findings from one technique can be used to check the findings from others.

Stage 3: Collecting the Data

Once a series of big-picture questions, driven by theory, have been developed, the next step—collecting data—involves going to the field site and using the appropriate data-gathering techniques. Often multiple data-gathering techniques are relied upon; however, the two principal techniques used are participant observation and semi-structured interviews.

Stage 4: Analyzing the Data

Once data have been collected from any fieldwork experience, the process of analyzing data begins. The fieldworker starts by transcribing recordings of interviews—a long process, as every hour of recorded interview takes several hours of transcription. The information from the surveys is then put into a spreadsheet (e.g., Excel) to be coded in a way that helps identify patterns and trends. For qualitative data, software such as ATLAS.ti helps facilitate the analysis by analyzing and helping to visualize complex phenomena hidden in unstructured data from interviews, video files, photographs, field notes, and so on. An ATLAS .ti app now makes it easier to collect and analyze data in the field. For quantitative data, most anthropologists use the Statistical Package for the Social Sciences (SPSS).

Stage 5: Interpreting the Data

Like any science, the discipline of anthropology does more than simply describe specific cultures. Interpreting data—perhaps the most difficult step—involves explaining the findings. Have the research questions been answered? What patterns and trends emerged from the analyses, and what do they mean? What factors can be identified that will help explain the findings? How do these findings compare with the findings of other, similar studies? How generalizable are the findings to wider populations? Have these findings raised methodological or theoretical issues that have a bearing on the discipline? In applied cultural anthropology, the questions may revolve around how the findings contribute to a project's design, implementation, or evaluation. These are the types of questions anthropologists must answer, usually after returning home from the fieldwork experience.

---

research design The overall strategy for conducting the research.

research proposal A written proposal required for funding anthropological research that spells out in detail a research project's purpose, hypotheses, methodology, and significance.

Stage 6: Writing Up and Presenting the Results

The final stage in the process is writing up the results of the fieldwork experience. This often takes a year or more. Typically, anthropology Ph.D. theses include a literature review, a discussion of the methods of data collection and the influences on the study, as well as the theoretical approach taken. The data are then presented along with an interpretation of them. Typically, the fieldwork provides for numerous, additional, more focused articles published in scholarly journals and presented at conferences.

In describing these six stages of field research, there is a risk of portraying the research process as a neat, precise, and systematic process. In reality, doing fieldwork is messier than is often admitted. The ethnographic books and articles that emerge from field research usually emphasize the orderly, systematic, and scientific aspects of the research process, while downplaying the chaotic aspects such as people not showing up for an arranged interview time, language barriers, or coming down with an illness.

Data-Gathering Techniques

A central problem facing any anthropological fieldworker is determining the most appropriate methods for collecting data. Some people may find data-collection methods, such as filming or interviewing with a digital recorder, objectionable, so that what might work in one culture may be totally inappropriate for a neighbouring culture. It is thus important that anthropologists have a number of options so that they can match the appropriate set of data-gathering techniques to each fieldwork situation.

Participant Observation

Participant observation—as the name implies—means becoming involved in the culture under study while making systematic observations of what people actually do. Anthropologists use this method more than any other single technique, and more extensively than any other social science discipline. When anthropologists participate, they become as immersed in the culture as the local people permit. They share activities, attend ceremonies, eat together, and generally become part of the rhythm of everyday life. H. Russell Bernard (2002, 137) captured the complexity of participant observation:

> It involves establishing rapport in a new community; learning to act so that people go about their business as usual when you show up; and removing yourself every day from cultural immersion so you can intellectualize what you've learned, put it into perspective, and write about it convincingly. If you are a successful participant-observer, you will know when to laugh at what your informant thinks is funny; and when informants laugh at what you say, it will be because you meant it to be a joke.

Guidelines for Participant Observation

From the first day of fieldwork, gaining entry into the community presents some challenges for the participant-observer. The anthropologist typically begins by observing the community before fully participating in all aspects of social life, so as to gradually learn the appropriate behaviour for participating in a local community in a non-obstructive way. Cultural anthropologists in the field can hardly expect to be accepted as soon as they walk into a new community. Under the best of circumstances, the anthropologist, as an outsider, will be an object of curiosity. More often, however, the beginning anthropologist encounters a wide variety of fears, suspicions, and hostilities of the local people that must be overcome. By and large, the anthropologist conducting participant observation fieldwork for the first time has received little instruction in how to cope with these initial problems of resistance. In a sense, it is not really possible to prepare the first-time fieldworker for every eventuality for the obvious reason that no two fieldwork situations, cultures, or ethnographers are the same. Nevertheless, it is possible to offer some general guidelines that apply to most fieldwork situations, and it is helpful to take a cultural anthropology methods course before writing a grant proposal or conducting fieldwork.

Since the anthropologist must have a good working relationship with the people he or she studies, one of the first goals of the researcher is to overcome any apprehension people may have and to gain their trust. In other words, the ethnographer must establish rapport. When Malinowski visited the Trobriand Islands during World War I, he obtained the cooperation of the locals by offering them tobacco (Malinowski 1922). These days, of course, offering people cigarettes to gain their acceptance raises ethical issues, but giving small gifts or paying for information has been a traditional way anthropologists have attempted to establish a working relationship. It is not without issue, however, for not only can giving gifts or hiring a local become expensive, it can also create jealousies and disrupt local economic and personal relationships. Often one of the best ways to gain rapport is simply to pitch in and help, whether that means working in the fields, helping to prepare a meal, aiding in building a latrine, or helping deal with other agencies. For example, Andreatta (one of the authors of this text), when she participated in the Jamaica Agroforestry Project (JAP) in the early 1990s, spent the first months engaging in a number of activities that did not seem particularly scientific, including helping people move

---

participant observation Research that involves living with and observing the people under study.

Observing Shoppers

In 1997, when Paco Underhill wrote the first edition of *Why We Buy: The Science of Shopping* "the academic world knew more about the market place in Papua New Guinea than what happened at your local supermarket or shopping mall. Twentieth century anthropology wasn't about what happened in your own backyard" (Underhill 2009, 4). Things have changed since then, and numerous companies across the globe now hire anthropologists to understand their consumers in their homes, in restaurants, stadiums, airports, hotels, museums, retail environments, and so on. The company Underhill runs, Envirosell, has been observing shoppers for decades, and has helped its clients improve the shopping experience of their customers and, of course, sales.

Underhill says he uses "the tools of urban anthropology... to study how people interact with the retail environment" (2009, 17–18). He hires graduate students, many of whom are anthropology majors, as field researchers to "track" shoppers. Their most important research tool is a track sheet on which they record their observations of almost everything a shopper does in the store. Did the shopper check the price tag? How long did they stay in the store? How long did they look at the product? What route did they take through the store? Did they see the advertising sign? The trackers also record nearly 40 variables about the shopper such as their age, gender, clothing, whether they are carrying anything, whether they are alone or not, and of course, whether they buy anything. Notes are also taken about the environment, such as lighting, the positions of displays, time of day, width of aisles, and so on. All this information is then entered into a database and analyzed. Underhill and his team also videotape customers and train cameras on entrances, aisles, shelves of products, and the cashier area. In some cases they also interview customers to get a better idea of their motivations.

James Leynse/Corbis via Getty Images

Paco Underhill, president of Envirosell, poses with a video camera that his company uses to observe people's behaviour while shopping.

The results of his research have been surprising. Journalists have called one of his more well-known discoveries the "butt-brush effect." After watching customers looking at ties on a tie rack positioned near a main aisle, Underhill noticed that, while they were examining the ties they were occasionally bumped from behind by other customers entering or leaving the store. After a few times, customers, both men and women, would stop looking at the ties and move on without buying. Sales from the tie rack were lower than expected, but when it was moved just off the main aisle, sales increased rapidly and dramatically. Clearly, people do not like to be inadvertently disturbed when examining merchandise.

In another example, his team observed that it was mostly children and the elderly who were purchasing treats for their pets. While adults feed their pets, children and older people like to pamper and spoil them. Pet treats, however, are typically stored on the top shelves of supermarkets, where older people and children often have difficulty reaching them. When Underhill suggested moving them lower where they could be reached, sales went up instantly. While this may seem obvious when pointed out, few people have really observed what customers actually do in stores.

Underhill notes that "stores, banks, restaurants and other such spaces must be friendly to the specifications of the human animal" (2009, 39). People have two hands, most of us favour the right hand, our eyes focus on what is directly in front of us, we walk at a certain pace, and we are influenced by our surroundings. This means that what people see in stores, such as merchandise and signs; what they pick up and put in a basket or cart, or carry; where they go, and whether they do so leisurely or swiftly will be determined by how the retail environment adapts to out biology. Is the promotional sign placed so customers can see it? Is the lighting adequate? Are the racks of merchandise arranged so people can get to them easily? Managers won't know the answers to these questions unless they observe people.

Through his observations, Underhill has discovered there are significant differences between how men and women shop. Men move faster through stores, spend less time looking at items, particularly at items they did not intend to buy, and rarely ask help in finding what they are looking for. Men also usually shop alone, while women are far more likely to shop with a friend. Men are likely to be concerned mostly with functionality in merchandise, whereas for women, aesthetics are often equally as important. For example, "When a man takes clothing into a

(*Continued*)

Observing Shoppers (*Continued*)

dressing room, the only thing that stops him from buying it is if it doesn't fit. Women on the other hand, try things on only as part of the consideration process, and garments that fit just fine may be rejected on other grounds" (2009, 105). "In practical terms," Underhill says, this means that "women demand more of shopping environments than men" and that "retailers must keep all of this in mind when deciding where to sell what" (2009, 126).

Questions for Further Thought

1. If you were to undertake research of customers at Tim Hortons, what sort of information would you track?
2. What cultural influences might there be on the way people shop?
3. How would you observe what people did online?

cattle from one pasture to another, collecting sugarcane tops to feed the cattle during a drought, planting and harvesting pigeon peas, and selling eggs at the farmers market. These activities helped to demonstrate that she was interested in the locals as people rather than merely as sources of information, and offered a way to give back to the people who were sharing information with her. Once the local people got to know and trust Andreatta, they were far more willing to give her the type of realistic cultural information she needed for the project.

Second, when introducing oneself, one should select a particular role and use it consistently. There are a number of ways that a field anthropologist could answer the question: Who are you? (a question that is asked frequently and requires an honest and straightforward answer). For example, Andreatta could have said, with total honesty, that she was a student (she was finishing her doctorate), an anthropologist, a visiting research associate at the University of the West Indies-Jamaica, a teacher, and a number of other things. Yet many of these roles, although accurate, were not particularly relevant to the members of the community where she was working. Even though she was there because she was an anthropologist, that particular role would have little meaning to the local people. So, when asked who she was and what was she doing in Jamaica, Andreatta always said that she was a researcher collecting information on the people's use of natural resources for their animals and for their general well-being—a role that the residents understood.

A third general piece of advice for most fieldworkers is to proceed slowly. Coming from a society that places a high value on time, most North American anthropologists do not take kindly to the suggestion to slow down. After all, because they will be in the field for a limited amount of time, most Western anthropologists think they must make the best use of that time by collecting as much data as they can as quickly as possible. The natural tendency for most Westerners is to want to "hit the ground running." There seems to be so much to learn and so little time. There are compelling reasons for not rushing into asking highly specific questions from day one: because most fieldworkers have such an imperfect understanding of the culture during the initial weeks and months they live in a community, they often do not know enough to even ask the right types of specific questions; and the quality of one's data will vary directly with the amount of social groundwork the anthropologist has been able to lay.

Fourth, the anthropologist must communicate to the local people, in a genuine way, that she or he is like a student, wanting to learn more about a subject on which *they* are the experts. For example, anthropologists are not interested in simply studying the physical environment (rivers, grasslands, livestock, homes, and so on) of a pastoral people, they also want to discover how the people define and value these aspects of their physical surroundings. To assume a student's role, while putting the local informant in the role of the teacher/resident expert, is a helpful way to elicit information. The reason the anthropologist is there is to gather information on the local culture, a subject on which he or she has an imperfect understanding. The local people, on the other hand, certainly know their own culture better than anyone else. When people are put in their well-deserved position of teacher/expert, they are likely to be more willing to share their cultural knowledge.

Advantages of Participant Observation

Using participant observation has certain methodological advantages for enhancing the quality of the data obtained. For example, people in most cultures appreciate any attempt on the part of the anthropologist to live according to the rules of their culture. No matter how ridiculous one might appear at first, the fact that the anthropologist takes an interest in the local culture is likely to improve rapport. And as trust levels increase, so do the quantity and quality of the data an anthropologist is able to obtain.

Another major advantage of participant observation is that it enables the anthropologist to distinguish between normative and real behaviour—that is, between what people *say they do* and what people *actually do*. When an anthropologist conducts an interview, there is no way to know for certain whether people behave as they say they do. The participant-observer, however, has the advantage of seeing actual behaviour rather than relying on hearsay. The participant-observer gains a more accurate picture of the culture by observing what people actually do rather than merely relying on what they say they do.

Disadvantages of Participant Observation

On the other hand, participant observation poses certain methodological problems that can jeopardize the quality of the data. For example, the nature of participant observation precludes a large sample size. Because such studies are both in-depth and time-consuming, fewer people are actually studied than would be if questionnaires or surveys were used. A second problem is that the data are often hard to code or categorize, which makes synthesizing and comparing the data more challenging. Third, participant-observers face special problems when recording their observations because it may be difficult, if not impossible, to record notes while attending a circumcision ceremony, participating in a feast, or chasing through the forest after a wild pig. The more time that passes between the event and its recording in one's field notes, the more details are forgotten. And, finally, a major methodological shortcoming of participant observation is that it can have an obtrusive effect on the people being studied, known as the Hawthorne effect (see Chapter 4)

Table 5.1 summarizes the methodological advantages and disadvantages of participant observation.

Interviewing

In addition to using participant observation, cultural anthropologists in the field rely heavily on ethnographic interviewing. Interviewing is used for obtaining information on what people think or feel (***attitudinal data***) as well as on what they do (***behavioural data***). Even though interviewing is used widely by many disciplines (including sociology, economics, political science, and psychology), the ethnographic interview is unique in three important respects. First, in the ethnographic interview, the interviewer and the participant often speak different first languages. Second, the ethnographic interview is often broad in scope because it elicits information about the entire culture. Third, the ethnographic interview cannot be used alone, but must be used in conjunction with other data-gathering techniques.

Structured, Semi-Structured, and Unstructured Interviews

Ethnographic interviews may be unstructured or structured, depending on the level of control retained by the interviewer. ***Unstructured interviews*** are used most often in the early stages of fieldwork and involve a minimum of control. The interviewer asks open-ended questions on a general topic and allows interviewees to respond at their own pace using their own words. Unstructured interviews have the advantage of allowing respondents to decide what is important to include in their responses, and they also give the anthropologist the flexibility to pursue issues raised by the respondent. In an unstructured interview, for example, the research collaborator might be asked to describe all the steps involved in getting married in her or his culture. It is from the unstructured interview that the anthropologist may narrow in on a line of questioning in a semi-structured interview to obtain more detailed nuanced information from the participant on a specific subject.

In ***semi-structured*** interviews, the anthropologist relies on an ***interview guide*** covering the topics or themes he or she needs to address in a particular order during an interview. An interview guide is simply a list of topics and questions that need to be asked and acts as a framework to guide the interview (Bernard 2002, 205). Semi-structured interviews are flexible to the extent that new ideas can be explored depending on what the interviewee says, and questions can be tailored to suit the context of the interview and to the particular interviewee.

At the other extreme are ***structured interviews***, or surveys, in which the interviewer asks all respondents

TABLE 5.1

Methodological Advantages and Disadvantages of Participant Observation

Advantages	Disadvantages
Generally enhances rapport	Practical only for small sample size
Enables fieldworkers to distinguish actual from expected behaviour	Difficult to obtain standardized comparable data
Permits observation of nonverbal behaviour	Incomplete data resulting from problems recording information
Enables fieldworkers to experience the behaviours being observed	Obtrusive effect on subject matter

attitudinal data Information collected in a fieldwork situation that describes what a person thinks, believes, or feels.

behavioural data Information collected in a fieldwork situation that describes what a person does.

unstructured interview A data-gathering technique in which interviewees are asked to respond to broad, open-ended questions.

semi-structured interview A data-gathering technique relying on an interview guide covering the topics or themes needing to be addressed.

interview guide A list of questions and topics that the anthropologist uses to guide interviews.

structured interview An ethnographic data-gathering technique in which large numbers of respondents are asked a set of specific questions.

the same set of questions, in the same sequence, and, except for open-ended questions, with the same choice of possible answers. Structured interviews have the advantage of producing large quantities of data that are comparable and thus lend themselves well to rapid statistical analyses. Because structured interviews ask questions based on specific cultural information, they are used most commonly late in the fieldwork, if at all, and only after the anthropologist knows enough about the culture to ask highly specific questions. Structured, semi-structured, and unstructured interviews thus have advantages that tend to complement each other.

It is important to be aware of the social situation in which the interview takes place. In other words, what effect does the presence of other people have on the answers given? The social context of the interview became an issue when Andreatta was collecting data while accompanied by a local resident, an adult male and respected farmer of the community. During one of the interviews, the respondent claimed to own a lavish house that was being constructed. The following day when she questioned the farmer who accompanied her, Andreatta learned that the respondent was a property caretaker and not the owner, who was still residing in England. The farmer did not understand why his friend and neighbour chose to lie about what he did and did not own. She never found out exactly why he made up such a tale, but Andreatta determined that the presence of the farmer might have influenced his response. Therefore, from that time on, she conducted the interviews privately and allowed the respected farmer to help arrange the interviews when needed.

Table 5.2 offers guidelines for conducting ethnographic interviews.

Validity of the Data Collected

The cultural anthropologist in the field must devise ways to check the validity of interview data. One way to validate data is to ask a number of different people the same question. If all people answer the question in essentially the same way independently of one another, it is safe to assume that the data are valid. Another method of checking the validity of interview data is to ask a person the same question over a period of time. If the person answers the question differently at different times, there is reason to believe that one of the responses might not be truthful. A third way to determine validity is to compare the responses with people's actual behaviour. As mentioned earlier, what people do is not always the same as what they say they do.

TABLE 5.2

Guidelines for Ethnographic Interviewing

- Obtain informed consent before interviewing; when appropriate get a signature from the respondent.
- Maintain neutrality by not conveying to the interviewee what may be the "desired" answer.
- Pretest questions to make sure they are understandable and culturally relevant.
- Keep the recording of an interview as unobtrusive as possible.
- Make certain that the conditions under which the interviews are conducted do not encourage distortion of the testimony.
- Use simple, unambiguous, jargon-free language. Phrase questions to avoid yes or no responses. For example, ask "What is your favourite food?" rather than "Is pizza your favourite food?"
- Keep the questions and the interview itself short, preferably one page for questions handled in less than an hour.
- Avoid double-barrelled (having two parts to the answer) questions.
- Save controversial questions for the end of the interview.
- Be sensitive to the needs and cultural expectations of the respondents.

Additional Data-Gathering Techniques

Even though participant observation and interviewing are the mainstays of anthropological fieldwork, cultural anthropologists use other techniques for collecting cultural data at various stages of the field study to provide depth and breadth to the data they are collecting. These techniques include census taking, ethnographic mapping, document analysis, collection of genealogies, and photography—although this list is hardly exhaustive.

Census Taking

Early on in the fieldwork, anthropologists usually conduct a census of the area under investigation. Because *census taking* involves the collection of basic demographic data, such as age, occupation, marital status, and household composition, it is generally not threatening to the local people. Because things change in the short and long terms, the census should be updated with new information such as marriages and births as they occur.

Ethnographic Mapping

Used in the early stages of fieldwork, *ethnographic mapping* attempts to locate people, material culture, and environmental features in space (Figure 5.5). Anthropologists often map how people divide up their land, where they live, pasture their livestock, where public and private buildings and public and sacred places are located, and how people position themselves

census taking The collection of demographic data about the culture being studied.

ethnographic mapping A data-gathering tool that locates where the people being studied live, where they keep their livestock, where public buildings are located, and so on to determine how that culture interacts with its environment.

Richard Cummins/Lonely Planet Images/Getty Images

FIGURE 5.5 Ethnographic mapping involves locating buildings and spaces, such as the stores in this street in St. John's, Newfoundland and Labrador, and how people relate to them.

in relation to environmental features such as rivers, mountains, and oceans. We can learn a good deal about a culture by examining how people interact with their physical environment. For instance, anthropologist Nazima Kadir works with various public sector clients to visualize and understand how one of the poorest neighbourhoods in the United Kingdom is organized by walking through the area and photographing every storefront, doctor's office, church, pub, day-care centre, and so on. She then integrates the photos into a digital map whereby her clients, by clicking on parts of the map, can see a photo of the space. This provides them with insights into the challenges facing the community. Her aim is to help her clients develop a communication strategy before any planning or intervention in the community takes place (http://nazimakadir.wordpress.com/2014/01/03/digital-ethnographic-mapping/).

Aerial and panoramic photographs are particularly useful for mapping a community's ecology. Advanced training in geographic information systems (GIS) and remote sensing, or collaborating with a geographer trained in these mapping techniques, offers additional understanding of the people and how they interact with their environment, with space, and with one another. For example, the University of Victoria's Ethnographic Mapping Lab uses GIS and qualitative data analysis to help Indigenous communities map traditional land use and occupancy.

Document Analysis

Cultural anthropologists may supplement the information they collect through interviews and observation by *document analysis*. For example, some anthropologists study personal diaries, colonial administrative records, newspapers, marriage registration data, deeds and property titles, government census information, and various aspects of popular culture, such as song lyrics and television programs. Advantages to using historical documents or reviewing popular culture are that it is neither expensive nor time-consuming, and it is totally unobtrusive in providing the anthropologist with a cultural context for their

Library and Archives Canada

FIGURE 5.6 Demasduit, a Beothuk woman captured by the English in 1819, was one of the last known Beothuk. After learning some English and teaching about 200 words of Beothuk to the settlers, she was released but died the following year of tuberculosis.

research. The study of cultures using such methods, as well as archaeological methods, oral histories, as other sources of information (e.g., paintings, maps, drawings, language, place names) is known as *ethnohistory*. Ethnohistorians are interested not only in the history of existing ethnic groups, but also those that have disappeared.

An excellent example of ethnohistory is Ingeborg Marshall's (1998) study of the Beothuk. The Beothuk lived in Newfoundland and in the late 1490s were perhaps the first group of native North Americans to be contacted by Europeans. The last known full-blooded Beothuk, Shanawdithit, died in 1829 (Figure 5.6). Marshall uses archival material, maps, oral histories, drawings, archaeological data, and other methods to reconstruct an ethnography of the Beothuk.

Collecting Genealogies

In Western societies much of our interaction with people is with non-family members, such as teachers,

---

document analysis Examination of data such as personal diaries, newspapers, colonial records, and so on.

ethnohistory The use of historical documents, oral traditions, as well as other archaeological and ethnographic methods to understand the history of ethnic groups, both past and present.

employers, co-workers, and friends. In small-scale societies, however, people tend to interact primarily with their family and extended familial relations. Collecting information about these relationships is thus especially important in these societies as kinship relationships tend to be the primary social ties (Figure 5.7). One of the earliest techniques used to collect cultural data is the ***genealogical method***, which involves the anthropologist interviewing individuals and asking them such questions as, Who was your father? Where and when was he born? How many brothers and sisters did he have? When did he marry your mother and how was he? Where do your relatives live? How do you refer to, interact with, and treat your relatives? The data are often expressed in a kinship diagram, or genealogy, and from this information the anthropologist can deduce how family members relate to one another, what the gender roles in the community are, who marries whom, and what behavioural expectations exist among different categories of kin. Sometimes the information can also be used to reconstruct past historical events.

genealogical method A technique of collecting data in which the anthropologist writes down all the kin of a research collaborator.

Climate Change: Food and Water Insecurity

Food and water insecurity pose challenges for human health and well-being in many parts of the world. Climatic change combined with uncertain economic, political, and social conditions have made equitable access to nutritious food and potable (drinkable) water a global crisis. Some cultures, however, face these uncertain conditions with regularity. Social scientists want to know how they cope with food or water insecurity, and if it is possible to measure the degree of insecurity. Is there a standard measure that could be used to determine who is at risk? Researchers Hadley and Wutich (2009) conducted a study in Tanzania and Bolivia that focused on developing new measures to answer these questions. Such a tool would be valuable as a way to head off future crises in areas known for food and water shortages.

Applied anthropologists, with their years of experience in community-based research, are uniquely poised to contribute to the growing need for development of locally appropriate tools to measure and monitor levels of community-based food and water insecurities. Food and water insecurity occur when there is insufficient and uncertain access to nutritious food and potable water to maintain a healthy and active lifestyle (Food and Agriculture Organization 2005). Generally, when medical and nutritional anthropologists study these situations they focus on caloric consumption, measurements of actual daily water use, and anthropometric (body) measurements such as weight for age, height for age, and body mass index in their fieldwork. Although these data can provide insights into households or individuals experiencing food insecurity, such quantitative indicators do not measure an individual's *experience* with food insecurity. In other words, previous measures did not illicit how people responded to or felt during those times of food or water shortage; their qualitative responses were not recorded as part of the data set.

Another approach was used in Sen's (1981) research, in which he found that inequitable access to food—rather than the absolute scarcity of food—produced food insecurity. From this economic perspective, a different line of questioning emerged to assess food access. Such questions focused on the distance to food markets, the availability of land or livestock to produce food locally, household income, socio-economic status, and food prices (Hadley and Wutich 2009, 452). A similar economic line for assessing water access tends to examine variables such as the distance to water sources, seasonality in water availability, water expenditures, time spent acquiring water, and storage capacity (Hadley and Wutich, 2009, 452). This economic line of questioning still does not get at how people responded or what they felt when they were unable to easily access food and water.

© Images of Africa Photobank/Alamy Stock Photo

Water is in short supply in many parts of the world. Children are expected to help with water collection and other chores from an early age. These children use their donkeys to transport the water they collect at Lake Langano, Ethiopia.

Hadley and Wutich critiqued these methods because they each missed something. Specifically, the data collected and their analyses were incomplete because they did not help explain the *adequacy* of the quantity of food or water acquired, or the *security* of access to those resources, or how people respond to food and water shortages. Hadley and Wutich (2009) used a different approach to measuring food insecurity that enabled them to focus not only on the physiological demands for food and water, the link between inequalities and access, and subsequent health impacts, but also on a people's culture and individual experience and perceptions to get a complete picture of food and water insecurities and health consequences. Hadley and Wutich (2009) illustrated the need for new models for measuring food or water insecurity in their research from Tanzania and Bolivia.

One example of the use of the genealogical method is how anthropologists discovered the cause of Kuru, a fatal degenerative neurological disorder similar to Creutzfeldt–Jakob disease (the human form of mad cow disease), among the Fore of New Guinea. Curiously, it was primarily women who contracted the disease, and originally it was thought to be hereditary. Prior to the 1960s, the Fore were endocannibals; that is, they ate the bodies of their deceased kin. Significantly, it was primarily women who ate their dead relatives. Men rarely did so and those who did, did not eat the bodies of women. By using the genealogical method and tracing the distribution of Kuru among relatives, anthropologists were able to demonstrate that the disease was not hereditary but cultural in origin. The practice has now ceased but Kuru can have a long incubation period, and every now and then a Fore person who ate a relative when they were young is diagnosed with the disease (Lindenbaum 2008).

Photography

A particularly important aid to the fieldworker's collection of data is photography, both still photography and videography, and ethnographic documentaries. Recent

The Pimbwe of Tanzania are horticulturalists, and the Sukuma of Tanzania are agro-pastoralists. In each of these settings, the data revealed there was a *hunger season*, that is, a period of time when a substantial portion of the population experienced food insecurity. Community members commented that children were the most affected, often going to bed without having eaten. Insecure access to food and the presence of hunger are key dimensions to poverty, but the question remains how to measure food security systematically. The authors first thought to measure when stores ran out of food, thus limiting households' access to food items. They came to realize this measure was useless, especially for those who ran small shops or those employed in something other than farming. In other instances those with larger families depleted their stocks more quickly than those with smaller families or smaller social networks.

In the end, the authors recognized that if they reworded their questions to ask respondents how they acquired food other than through purchasing, and modified the question on food frequency to include local dietary patterns, they would be moving in the right direction and be developing a survey instrument with greater reliability in capturing food insecurity in wet and dry seasons. More importantly, they revealed that the uncertainty and worry that goes with providing food for one's family was the burden carried by all the mothers, which affected their mental health. The seasonally insecure access to food and the uncertainty of not being able to feed their children carried with it a psychosocial burden.

In Bolivia, the authors developed an ethnographically grounded measure for water insecurity. They worked in a semi-arid region of the Bolivian Andes, in a squatters' settlement located on the south side of the city of Cochabamba. Nearly 38 percent of the population is without municipal water service, forcing those households to collect rainwater and surface water, dig wells, or seek out private water sources for cooking, bathing, and cleaning. "Because many of these alternative sources are vulnerable to climatic variability, year-round water insecurity intensifies during the dry season" (Hadley and Wutich 2009, 454).

After spending five months living in the community, the authors learned to use water in culturally appropriate ways. They also identified six categories in which water insecurity affected residents: (1) water quantity, (2) water quality, (3) water acquisition, (4) water conflicts, (5) economic issues, and (6) health outcomes. Using these six domains, they designed a survey that asked questions from each one. To interpret the responses, Hadley and Wutich (2009) had to develop tools to scale the respondents' qualitative responses.

Their research reminds us of the increasing importance of using multiple, integrated methods in applied research. There is no one measure that will work for all conditions when learning about (in)equitable access to food and water, or the effects of chronic shortages. Rural or urban settings, highlands or lowlands, levels of poverty, education, access to employment, gender, age, and household size are only a few of the indicators that influence coping strategies for food or water insecurity. Developing measures that include multidimensional experiences as well as those of psychosocial trauma are necessary for understanding a local context for any kind of policy when facing water and food uncertainty and insecurity. Biological demands of food and water should not be separated from the cultural needs, which are deeply embedded in the cultural system. Anthropological approaches have a great deal to offer in conceptualizing and measuring, and possibly alleviating food and water security in some communities. It is from these varied approaches that we can develop an understanding of how adaptations and coping strategies affect the incidence and experience of food and water security across cultures, and thus a single measure should not be the only measure.

Questions for Further Thought

1. What is the different between quantitative and qualitative data collection?
2. Why is it important to develop a community-based tool to measure food or water insecurity?
3. How does an ethnographic approach inform applied research? Does this mean there is only one way to collect empirical data?

FIGURE 5.7 Ethnographers in the field are interested in studying all segments of a population, including these Salvadorian children and their parents. The anthropologist might want to learn about agricultural production, nutritional intake, education levels, and health status. By collecting data on all family members, and with parental consent, ethnographers can gain a thorough understanding of a culture.

FIGURE 5.8 Photographs taken in the field can serve as probes during an interview as well as useful sources of information. Asking questions about activities or actions can provide insight into gender roles and other appropriate or inappropriate behaviours.

decades have brought a proliferation of ethnographic documentaries portraying a wide variety of cultures from all parts of the world. Although ethnographic documentaries are valuable for introducing anthropology students to different cultures, they also have more specific uses in anthropological research. To illustrate, ethnographic documentaries can be extremely helpful in ***proxemic analysis*** (i.e., the study of how people in different cultures distance themselves from one another in normal interactions) and ***event analysis*** (i.e., documentation of who participates in events such as circumcision ceremonies, marriages, and funerals). Leaving copies of these photographic images with community members, if appropriate, is a way of sharing with the community (Figure 5.8).

proxemic analysis The study of how people in different cultures use space.

event analysis Photographic documentation of events such as weddings, funerals, and festivals in the culture under investigation.

Human Relations Area Files (HRAF) The world's largest anthropological data retrieval system, used to test cross-cultural hypotheses.

Cross-Cultural Comparisons

During the first half of the 20th century, anthropologists amassed considerable descriptive data on a wide variety of cultures throughout the world. Because of these many first-hand ethnographic field studies, sufficient data existed by mid-century to begin testing hypotheses and building theory inductively.

The development of statistical, cross-cultural comparative studies was made possible in the 1940s by George Peter Murdock and his colleagues at Yale University, who developed a coded data retrieval system known as the ***Human Relations Area Files (HRAF)***. Now in electronic form, the eHRAF World Cultures contains vast amounts of ethnographic information covering all

CROSS-CULTURAL MISCUE

When Nancy Scheper-Hughes settled into the west Ireland town of Ballybran in June 1974 for her first, year-long fieldwork experience, the trusting villagers welcomed her into their homes and opened up to her. She wanted to know what was happening among the families and in the schools, churches, pubs, and other spaces in remote Irish country villages that resulted in them having the highest rates of mental illness, particularly schizophrenia, in the world. She believed that by studying "madness" she could learn about Irish society and culture as a whole.

The resulting ethnography, *Saints, Scholars and Schizophrenics: Mental Illness in Rural Ireland* (1979), won the Margaret Mead Award from the Society for Applied Anthropology and has gone through 20 editions. She concluded that "rural Ireland was a place where it was difficult to be 'sane' and where 'normal' villagers could appear more 'deviant'" (Scheper-Hughes 2001, 122) because the traditional subsistence-based peasant economy of rural Ireland was rapidly disappearing due to the cumulative effects of British colonization, the Great Famine, modernization, welfare dependency, and emigration. This resulted in depression, alcoholism, and high rates of psychiatric hospitalization.

In 1999, 25 years later, she returned to the village to visit old friends. She soon discovered, however, that she was not warmly welcomed. Indeed, quite the opposite. After a few weeks' stay she was literally "run out of town." Members of her host family complained to her saying, "Why don't you go home and write about your own troubles. God knows, you've got plenty of them, with school children shooting each other and U.S. planes bombing hospitals in Kosovo. Why pick on us?" and "Who made you such an authority?" And when they said, "admit it. You wrote a book to please yourself at our expense. *You ran us down, girl, you ran us down*.... We warn our village children before they go off to the university in Cork or Dublin to beware books about Ireland written by strangers," she burst into tears (Scheper-Hughes 2000, 119). The villagers complained that she wrote about all their troubles and not about their strengths, about their friendliness, or about their love for "Mother Ireland." Reviews of her book by Irish scholars blasted her book as biased, insensitive, ethnocentric, and that she was tone deaf to the fact that rural Ireland at the time had the lowest incidence of physical assault, rape, adultery, and divorce, that theft was unheard of, and that young women had a great deal of freedom and independence in an otherwise patriarchal society. Another critic described her book as "unethical" since it did not take long for journalists and others to discover that the village of Ballybran was really An Clochan. The last straw, however, was when she was seen taking notes, and was asked to leave the village immediately.

Scheper-Hughes clearly made some mistakes, but she also learned some lessons. The first perhaps was that she was so sure of herself, and lacked the reflexivity to see that her objectives had blinded her to other aspects of what was going on, resulting in glaring omissions, distortions, and a highly subjective interpretation that did "violence to the natives' own understanding of the meaning of their culture and social relations" (p. 127). In other words, the anthropologist engaging in first fieldwork can often be naïve.

Anthropologists also have an ethical obligation to protect the identity of their collaborators by making them anonymous through changing their names, including the villages where they live, but that this is often done poorly and that often it "fools few and protects no one—save, perhaps, the anthropologist's own skin" (p. 128).

aspects of cultural and social life on more than 300 different cultures organized into more than 700 different cultural subject headings. Classified by subject at the paragraph level, the use of the simple coding system enables the cross-cultural researcher to access large quantities of data within minutes for the purpose of testing hypotheses and drawing statistical correlations. Most of the larger universities in Canada have a membership to the service.

Applied Field Methods

As pointed out in Chapter 3, there are fundamental differences in the research conducted by descriptive ethnographers and applied cultural anthropologists. When compared to more descriptive anthropological research, applied research is characterized as (1) more collaborative and interdisciplinary; (2) more inclusive of local people in all stages of the research, including initiating the research; and (3) performed rapidly. Faced with real-time limitations (weeks or months rather than years). Applied anthropologists tend to rely on data-collection techniques that are focused on the problem and expedite the data-collection process, such as survey methods and focus groups (groups of 6 to 10 people convened to discuss a particular topic), to gather a large amount of attitudinal and behavioural data in a relatively short time frame.

Recent Trends in Ethnographic Fieldwork

Despite the quest for scientific objectivity, conducting ethnographic fieldwork is quite different from doing research in a chemistry or biology laboratory. To reflect the "native's point of view," the observer must interact with her or his subjects, which introduces a powerful element of subjectivity. Nowhere is the coexistence of subjectivity and objectivity more evident than in the data-gathering technique of participant observation. Participation implies a certain level of emotional involvement in the lives of the people being studied. Making systematic observations, on the other hand, requires emotional detachment. Thus, by its nature, participant observation carries with it an internal source of tension, because sympathizing with the people one is trying to describe is incompatible with scientific objectivity.

Reflexive Methods

Since the 1970s, however, postmodernists (see Chapter 4) have ushered in a new type of ethnography known as ***reflexive, or narrative ethnography***. Being less concerned with scientific objectivity, narrative ethnographers are interested in co-producing ethnographic knowledge by focusing on the interaction between themselves and their informants (Michrina and Richards 1996). In fact, many if not most ethnographers today use terms such as ***collaborator, research participant, or cultural expert*** rather than ***informant***, recognizing the role of the person who is providing the information to the anthropologist and the production of anthropological knowledge. When dealing with First Nations people, and indeed other cultures, many anthropologists also use the term ***elder*** when appropriate. Elders are influential people in a society who have gained the respect of their community members through the experience and wisdom that comes with age, although not all elders are old, nor are elders always leaders.

Reflexive ethnographies are also conscious reflections on how the anthropologist's own personality and context combine with the personality and context of their culture experts to produce cultural data. This idea originated with the feminist critique of anthropology in the 1960s and 1970s, which challenged the notion that traditional ethnographic research and writing was, or could be, objective. It was argued that ethnographies were written by anthropologists who were mostly male, white, and came from a privileged socio-economic position, and that this had a huge influence, not only on how rapport was established and the data collected, but also on the nature of the knowledge produced. Donna Haraway (1988) has called it ***situated knowledge***. According to Haraway and other postmodernist anthropologists, anthropological knowledge cannot be truly objective because it is always influenced by, among other things, the anthropologist's age, gender, religion, socio-economic status, ethnicity, education, and historical and cultural context. Reflexive or narrative ethnographies thus take the particular situation of the ethnographer into account and attempt to understand how their context influences their research.

This situated perspective also limits what the researcher can learn and how he or she learns it. For example, in many cultures a male ethnographer may find it inappropriate to ask questions publicly or privately of women, and especially single women. In more general terms, an ethnographer might find it nearly impossible to conduct research among a particular group of people because the ethnographer is not the correct gender, age, or ethnicity. Because the anthropologist is positioned, all ethnographies are partial accounts—just views from different perspectives. It also means that many sweeping generalizations about how people in a society think or behave cannot be made. Postmodernist anthropologists also argue that once you understand the limitations you will be better able to represent the research. For instance, once the ethnographer recognizes that he or she is clearly wealthier and more powerful than the people they study, they can better judge whether this influences the relationship and the responses their collaborators provide.

By the 1980s and 1990s it became common practice for anthropologists to write about these limitations and also about how their feelings, experiences, and background, as well as the historical and political context of the people they worked with, influenced their research methods and findings (Salzman 2002). Salzman defines this reflexivity as "the constant awareness, assessment, and reassessment by the researcher of the researcher's own contribution/influence/shaping of intersubjective research and the consequent research findings" (2002, 806).

In her ethnography *The Lubicon Lake Nation*, for example, Dawn Martin-Hill (2008), using Lubicon words and concepts, contrasts the Lubicon people's own understanding of their historical attempts to gain recognition as a distinct people, and a reserve settlement from the federal government, with that of the official colonial version of history. In the first chapter of the book she relates how her position as a Mohawk woman from the Six Nations community in Ontario not only allowed her access to the Lubicon community of Alberta, but also gave her an empathetic

---

reflexive or narrative ethnography An ethnography in which the ethnographer discusses the influence of his or her personal and cultural context on the ethnography, and which are co-produced and focus on the interaction between themselves and their collaborators.

collaborator, research participant, cultural expert, or informant The person in the culture being researched who provides the ethnographer with information.

elder An influential person in a society who is respected for their experience and wisdom.

situated knowledge Anthropological knowledge that is influenced by the anthropologist's age, gender, religion, socio-economic status, ethnicity, education, and historical and cultural context.

understanding of their experience, and particularly the experience of the women: "I am a minority within the majority, I *have* the life experiences that they [her anthropological colleagues] study, examine, and write about but that they do not *live*. This reality has shaped my research at every conceivable level" (2008, 6).

Postmodernist anthropologists also recognize that collaborators are as equally situated as the ethnographer. The anthropological knowledge that comes out of the encounter between them results from their attempts to learn to communicate with one another and through a sharing of ideas about what is going on, or, in other words, through ***intersubjectivity***.

In an effort to reclaim a more "scientific" methodology, Lawrence Kuznar (1996), Marvin Harris (1999), and many others have harshly critiqued these reflexive methods. If these often ferocious debates on methods are taken too literally, people are led to believe that the discipline is in turmoil because it cannot agree on which methodology is the correct one. But, as Ivan Brady (1998) noted, people should avoid drawing absolute lines between subjective and objective ethnographic methods. Instead, contemporary ethnography is moving toward a "methodological pluralism" whereby anthropologists use multiple methods of data collection and analyses to help produce a richer and more accurate description of ethnographic reality.

Autoethnography

One of the newer methods that considers the subjectivity and influence of the ethnographer on the research is ***autoethnography***. Part autobiography and part ethnography, autoethnography is both a method and a genre of anthropological writing. With autoethnography, the anthropologist is the topic of investigation (Ellis and Bochner 2000). He or she engages in what is known as ***systematic sociological introspection*** (Ellis 1991, 45), which involves the ethnographer studying his or her own behaviours, thoughts, and emotions in a given cultural context. The purpose in doing so is to gain insights into the culture being studied as well as the influence of one's own emotions on the conduct of fieldwork and the generation of anthropological knowledge (Ellis et al. 2010). The written account of this experience usually takes the form of a narrative describing events and the ethnographer's role in the story, the thoughts and emotions experienced, and an analysis of what the events and experiences mean.

For example, while anthropologist Edward Hedican (2006) was conducting fieldwork in Northern Ontario, Elijah, a young Anishinaabe Cree, was killed by a Canadian National Railway passenger train. Hedican describes how the experience filled him "with feelings of intense sadness and remorse" but that his "academic training left [him] largely unprepared to deal with the emotional consequences of such an event" (Hedican 2006, 3). Hedican was torn between attending the young man's funeral and gathering ethnographic data, or not attending to respect the family's privacy in a sensitive situation, even though they probably expected him to show up. He saw his decision not to attend as a methodological ethical issue of fieldwork. On reflecting on this incident, he came to realize his lack of control over events and how the emotional conflict he experienced influenced the course of his fieldwork. Hedican urges "that a study of our inner, emotional selves become a necessary aspect of our methodological inquiry, because such emotional introspection is apt to reveal much about how emotional states influence the researchers' processing of information" (Hedican 2006, 6).

Autoethnographers have been criticized for being too focused on themselves, too personal, biased, and not scientific enough. They have also been attacked for not doing enough fieldwork by failing to adequately engage with community members or fully participate in the culture (Ellis 2010). While there is some validity to these criticisms, autoethnography does provide valuable insights, although it should not be seen as a substitute for traditional ethnography.

Life Histories

Similar to the autoethnography is the ***life history or life story*** approach. Although this method has been used for decades, it has gained new momentum with the postmodernist reflexive movement. Although life stories can be acquired through letters, journals, photos, archival materials, and web pages, the primary method is the in-depth interview in which the ethnographer asks collaborators to describe in their own words the story of their lives and to describe what it is like to experience their culture. Life histories, or life stories, tend to emphasize the person's life cycle, how they were socialized, and how they related to key events in their lives and in their culture. An underlying assumption is that their experiences are not necessarily unique and are thus representative of their culture. By discussing their thoughts, motivations, and emotions, and how they experience historical events from their own cultural context, anthropologists hope to not only give their collaborators a voice but, through interpretation

---

intersubjectivity Shared meanings constructed through the interactions of people from different perspectives.

autoethnography An ethnographic method in which the ethnographer attempts to understand another culture through a description and analysis of their own fieldwork experience.

systematic sociological introspection An examination of the ethnographer's emotions, thoughts, and behaviours during fieldwork, and how they impact data collection.

life history or life story The story of a collaborator's life experiences in a culture that provides insight into their culture.

and analysis, also gain an insight into their culture, in particular the life cycle of people living that culture (Reed-Danahay 2001; Harrison 2009).

The life history approach has been used to understand the lives of native North Americans, criminals, transsexuals, heroin addicts, fishermen, factory workers, and women in different societies (Bertaux and Kohli 2009). Perhaps the best known life story, however, is that of Nisa, a 50-something !Kung woman living in northeastern Botswana. In a series of interviews, Nisa told anthropologist Marjorie Shostak (1981), in rough chronological order, about her early memories as a child, her first sexual experience, her marriages, husbands and lovers, about giving birth in the bush, being a mother, grieving the death of her children, and about growing old. Shostak's purpose in obtaining Nisa's story was to discover how the !Kung "felt about their relationships and their lives" (Shostak 1981, 7) and to better understand what it must have been like to be a !Kung woman living in the Kalahari desert in the 1970s.

Multi-sited Fieldwork

Because much of the early fieldwork in anthropology was conducted on islands, cultures were often viewed as isolated, bounded, and unchanging. Cultures, however, have never really been isolated; boundaries have always been fuzzy and change is the only one true constant. With colonization, industrialization, and recent globalization, cultural boundaries are dissipating rapidly, change is occurring at an accelerated pace, and people are moving from their home country or region to another and from rural areas to urban centres. With communication and travel both cheap and easy, people have little problem maintaining ties with one another across continents. The world, in other words, is becoming mobile, transnational, and interconnected. This means that if anthropologists want to know what is going on in a local community, they must also consider what is going on in migrant populations and how local people and activities are influenced by global forces. Anthropological fieldwork has thus had to adapt to these changes by becoming multi-sited (Marcus 1995).

Multi-sited fieldwork looks at how forces of globalization, such as the Internet, tourism, migration, the media, investment by multinational organizations, and so on, influence local communities. It means that, instead of the traditional approach of studying a community in one location, ethnographic research is conducted at more than one site. Most multi-sited research projects focus on the associations and relationships between people that connect the locations (Figure 5.9).

FIGURE 5.9 Children in Montreal from Russian Orthodox origins with traditional Easter Koulitchis cakes brought to church to be blessed. If anthropologists wanted to know how the meanings and practices surrounding these cakes have changed between Russia and Canada, they would need to conduct multi-sited fieldwork.

This often means following migrants, money, handicrafts, jobs, and so on. Typically, anthropologists are interested in how meanings, practices, or other social phenomena change from one location to another, or how they are manifested in the different contexts.

For example, anthropologist Veronica Montes (2013) was interested in whether the migration of men from Guatemala to California influenced their ideas about masculinity, and so conducted participant observation and interviewed people in both locations. In Guatemala, masculinity means being unemotional, non-nurturing, aggressive, and dispassionate, and hiding all emotions other than anger, pride, and independence. In contrast, the men who had migrated to California were much more willing to express emotions such as fear, anxiety, nostalgia, love, and sacrifice. Montes argues that learning to cope with the stresses of leaving their family and loved ones gave both migrant and non-migrant men the opportunity to reflect on their emotional relationship with their family, leading them to reassess

---

multi-sited fieldwork Ethnographic fieldwork conducted in more than one location and united by a common research topic or theme.

their masculinity and embrace a model of masculinity that allowed them to adjust to their new emotional circumstances. She also points out that emotions as well as economics play a role in the decision to migrate.

Cheap international phone calls, cheap air fare, social media sites such as Facebook and Google+, along with applications such as Skype, have also meant that it is easier for the ethnographer, after he or she has left the field, to maintain ties with these disparate communities for follow-up discussions, to fill in gaps in information, or simply to keep up relations.

Multi-sited fieldwork is not without its critics. Doing fieldwork in multiple locations means that it is hard to go into as much depth or have as great a familiarity with a culture than research limited to one location. There is also less time to build personal relationships with collaborators and obtain the insights they offer. Others have argued that multi-sited fieldwork tends to focus more on formal organizations than on how people experience their lives (Coleman and Hellermann 2011).

New Information Technology

Although anthropologists today continue to use traditional data-gathering methods, such as participant observation and interviewing, the revolution in information technology has greatly expanded the toolkit of cultural anthropologists. New tools include, but are not limited to, the following examples:

- *Internet search engines:* Search engines such as Google Scholar and Yahoo! provide a wide variety of data relevant for research in cultural anthropology.
- *Research databases*: Since the mid-1990s, several searchable databases have been established specifically focused on anthropology, such as *Anthropology Index* and *Anthropology Plus,* allowing researchers to find relevant resources. Another useful resource is *Ethnographic Video Online,* which provides streaming videos of classic and contemporary documentaries from hundreds of cultures on dozens of topics. Perhaps the mostly widely used database by anthropologists, however, is JSTOR (Journal Storage), which provides full-text searches of digitized back issues of about 2000 academic journals.
- *Programs for ethnographic analysis:* Since the 1980s, several excellent computer-assisted programs have been developed to facilitate analysis of ethnographic data. ATLAS.ti and NVivo, two such software packages, allow ethnographers to import text-based qualitative data (such as interview transcripts, field notes, and other text-based documents) into their personal computers for easier and more efficient data analysis.
- *Internet reference pages:* Such websites as New York Times, Smithsonian Institution, and Library of Congress are excellent sources of information for conducting research in either ethnography or ethnology.
- *Internet survey research:* Using such sites as Zoomerang and Survey Monkey, cultural anthropologists are able to create survey instruments, invite participants, administer the surveys, and tally and analyze the results. Although these tools do not provide the quality of data derived from actual fieldwork, they enable the researcher to obtain and analyze data without ever having to leave their personal computer.

Mining Social Networking Websites and the Internet for Socio-cultural Data

Some social scientists are beginning to use social networking websites, such as Facebook, Twitter, and LinkedIn, to mine large quantities of socio-cultural data about the adults who frequent these sites. Every day, millions of people throughout the world logon to Facebook.com to troll for friends, share videos, photos, stories, news, and opinions on a variety of topics, and continuously refine and update their public personas for the rest of the world to see. In 2008 Twitter emerged as an online and more rapid way to communicate with one's social network. Each communiqué on Twitter is known as a tweet and is limited to 140 characters. Anyone can follow a Twitter page (unless it is private) or create a personal one to have instant messaging with friends or strangers who join their social network.

Facebook and Twitter have captured the interests of many from around the world. In the aftermath of the 2010 earthquake in Haiti, locals who were able to take photographs on their cell phones let the world know what was happening by logging on to their Facebook accounts and tweeting. The dramatic images informed the world instantly of the devastation that had occurred and helped to mobilize rescue workers from around the world to coordinate with agencies already established in Haiti.

Similarly, the uprisings against dictatorial regimes in the Arab world that began in December 2010 known as the Arab Spring, were coordinated to a large extent through Twitter and Facebook. The texts, tweets, photos, videos, and other communications that flew between people (mostly young people) helped activists bypass state-controlled media and inform others, not only in Arab countries but also throughout the world, about what was happening and about their aspirations.

The virtual world of the Internet has itself become a site for anthropological study. For example, Tom Boellstorff's (2008) *Coming of Age in Second Life: An Anthropologist Explores the Virtually Human* is an ethnography of the virtual world known as Second Life. Using his avatar Tom Bukowski (a digital representation of himself), Boellstorff used participant observation and in-depth interviews of many of the "residents" to provide "an ethnography portrait of the culture of Second Life" (Boellstorff 2008, 7). One of his aims was to demonstrate that ethnographic methods could be used to study virtual worlds.

Choosing a Technique

Which data-gathering technique(s) will be used depends largely on the nature of the problem being investigated. For example, environmental studies on overuse of the commons (shared community lands that are not owned by anyone) may require gathering information on the natural resources used by a community. A medical anthropologist may look to Indigenous (local) practices in healthcare and also may seek out where Western medicine may intersect local practices. And like the other examples, food and agricultural studies are likely to combine a number of methods in addition to participant observation and interviewing.

Another significant factor that influences the choice of techniques is the receptivity of the people being studied. It is important that the anthropologist carefully plan which techniques will be appropriate to use and what types of data to collect, as well as the segments of the population to study. If, after entering the field, the anthropologist finds that a technique is not working, he or she must be sufficiently flexible to revise the research design and creative enough to come up with a workable alternative. Whatever technique is selected, it should be used in conjunction with at least two other techniques. By using multiple techniques, the anthropologist can collect different types of data concerning the same set of issues, using the different sets of data to cross-check their validity.

The Ethics of Fieldwork

Collecting data with or from participants in a field study needs to be carried out ethically. All universities in Canada, because they are publicly funded, must comply with the *Tri-Council Policy Statement: Ethical Conduct for Research Involving Humans (TCPS 2)* 2010. Formulated by the Canadian Institutes of Health Research (CIHR), the Natural Sciences and Engineering Research Council of Canada (NSERC), and the Social Sciences and Humanities Research Council of Canada (SSHRC) (the tri-council), this policy statement ensures that research involving humans is conducted ethically. The underlying principle of the policy is "respect for human dignity." This is expressed through three complementary and interdependent core principles: (1) Respect for Persons, (2) Concern for Welfare, and (3) Justice. Respect for persons means that researchers must respect an individual's autonomy or freedom, including those with diminished autonomy. The welfare of a person means that the research should not impair the quality of a person's life by impacting their "physical, mental and spiritual health, as well as their physical, economic and social circumstances." This means that the research should not impact their membership or social standing in the community, and usually means taking measures to ensure that personal information is kept confidential. Justice means that researchers have an obligation to treat people fairly and without discrimination.

To ensure that these principles are adhered to, all research at Canadian universities, whether funded or not, that involves people must be reviewed and approved by an appropriate University ***Research Ethics Board***. Some journals also require that research has been approved by a research ethic board before they will publish the results.

Anthropologists are also expected to adhere to the code of professional ethics adopted by the AAA (2009), which identifies the following major areas of responsibility:

- *Responsibility to the people studied:* Similar to the TCPS 2, the anthropologist's paramount responsibility is to the people he or she studies. Every effort must be made to protect the physical, psychological, and social well-being of the people under study. The aims and anticipated consequences of the research must be clearly communicated to the research subjects so they can decide for themselves whether they wish to participate in the research. Participation is to be voluntary and should be based on the principle of informed consent. Collaborators should in no way be exploited, and their right to remain anonymous must be protected.
- *Responsibility to the public and to the communities affected by our actions:* Anthropologists have a fundamental responsibility to respect the dignity, integrity, and worth of the communities that will be directly affected by the research findings. More generally, anthropologists have a responsibility to the general public to disseminate their findings truthfully and openly. They are also expected to make their findings available to the public for use in policy formation.
- *Responsibility to the discipline and social science colleagues:* Anthropologists bear responsibility for maintaining the reputation of the discipline and their colleagues. They must avoid engaging in any research of which the results or sponsorship cannot be freely and openly reported. Anthropologists must refrain from any behaviour that will jeopardize future research for other members of the profession.

Research Ethics Board An official group of people that ensures research conducted involving humans is done in an ethical manner.

- *Responsibility to sponsors, employers, and funders:* Anthropologists have a professional responsibility to be honest about their qualifications, capabilities, and purposes. Before accepting employment or research funding, an anthropologist is obligated to reflect sincerely on the purposes of the sponsoring organizations and the potential uses to which the findings will be put. Anthropologists must retain the right to make all ethical decisions in their research, while at the same time reporting the research findings accurately, openly, and completely.
- *Responsibility to one's own and the host governments:* Anthropologists should be honest and candid in their relationships with both their own and the host governments. They should demand assurances that they will not be asked to compromise their professional standards or ethics as a precondition for research clearance. They should not conduct clandestine research or write secret reports.

Ethical Consideration in Private and Public Sectors

With the growth in applied anthropology in recent decades, many cultural anthropologists are finding employment in the private and public sectors. This raises some important ethical dilemmas because, as employees or contractors, applied anthropologists may not have control over their own research. To illustrate, an applied anthropologist may be contracted to improve work processes in a company that could lead to collaborators losing their jobs. They could also be hired to engage in research that could be harmful to a specific population, such as how best to market cigarettes or alcohol. Often the applied anthropologist is prohibited from publishing important scientific findings based on his or her proprietary research because the employing firm felt it might give an advantage to a competitor. Fortunately, these and many other potential conflicts of interest are explicitly covered by the general guidelines of the AAA.

The Pains and Gains of Fieldwork

Unlike many other scientific endeavors, anthropological fieldwork tends to have a powerful impact not only on the community studied but also on the life of the practitioner. Spending a year or longer living and working in an unfamiliar culture is bound to have life-altering consequences; the anthropologist is never quite the same after completing a fieldwork project. The initial feeling of being overwhelmed by the fieldwork situation is more common than most anthropologists are willing to admit.

The anthropologist in the field faces a number of anxiety-producing situations that can result in both stress and growth. For example, cultural anthropologists in the field rarely, if ever, follow their research design step by step in a cookbook fashion. Despite the most meticulous research design and pre-departure preparations, fieldwork is fraught with unanticipated events. From day one, the fieldworker can expect to be surprised, as was the case with Hannah Gill (2004), who went to the Dominican Republic to study the role of religious music in the migration of Dominican families to the United States. She quickly discovered, however, that the community of people she was living with, whose migrant families had moved to the United States, were heavily involved in drug trafficking. "In addition to this unexpected finding" she also discovered that "disputes over drugs that originated in Boston and New York were 'resolved' at home in the Dominican Republic in often lethal ways" (Gill 2004, 2). Risk became a daily part of her fieldwork experience: "on the second day I found myself flattened under a car to avoid getting shot by a woman seeking revenge for her husband's murder in the town market, and on the third day I was sprinting away from a knife fight at a local hang-out" (Gill 2004, 2). Because of this experience, criminal activities became a major focus of her research. It also gave her an insight into the nature of anthropological fieldwork:

> "I became aware that anthropological fieldwork breaks every Western rule of personal safety for women (and men): don't go to unfamiliar places alone, don't trust strangers, don't accept strange drinks or food from strangers, don't be out late at night, and don't make yourself vulnerable by living alone. But rules of personal safety are based on sticking to the familiar—the antithesis of anthropological research. If an anthropologist followed these rules, she would never go anywhere, try anything new, make any friends, or progress in research. Taking risks (or taking advantage of opportunities) and being independent is a crucial aspect of fieldwork, and to gain intimate understandings requires a lot of trust. The researcher must find a middle ground that allows her to take advantage of opportunities without compromising her own safety." (Gill 2004, 3)*

Despite the threat to her personal safety, Gill decided to continue with her research but reduced the risk by taking precautions, such as carrying mace and a "dummy" wallet, by sewing extra pockets into her clothes, by minimizing alcohol consumption, and by planning an exit strategy—street smarts rarely taught in the classroom.

*From Gill, Hannah E. 2004. "Finding a middle ground between extremes: notes on researching transnational crime and violence." Anthropology Matters 6(2).

Culture Shock

Not all introductions to fieldwork are as unsettling as these of course. But even anthropologists whose fieldwork experience is less traumatic encounter some level of stress from culture shock, the psychological disorientation caused by trying to adjust to major differences in lifestyles and living conditions. Culture shock, a term introduced by anthropologist Kalervo Oberg (1960), ranges from mild irritation to out-and-out panic. For example, a person might think the food is strange, people do not keep their appointments, no one likes them, everything seems unhygienic, people do not look them in the eye, and on and on. It is not simply due to adjusting to new foods or about how to obtain basic services, however, it is a general psychological stress that occurs when the anthropologist tries to play the game of life with little or no understanding of the basic rules. The anthropologist, struggling to learn what is meaningful in the new culture, never really knows when she or he may be committing a serious social indiscretion that might severely jeopardize the entire fieldwork project, such as using the wrong hand when giving a gift or sharing food, or speaking out of turn. When culture shock sets in, everything seems to go wrong: someone may become irritated over minor inconveniences; a person may begin to view things critically and negatively.

Even though culture shock manifests itself in many different symptoms, it usually has these characteristics:

- A sense of confusion over how to behave
- A sense of surprise, even disgust, after realizing some of the features of the new culture
- A sense of loss of old familiar surroundings (such as friends, possessions, and ways of doing things)
- A sense of being rejected (or at least not accepted) by members of the new culture
- A loss of self-esteem because the person does not seem to be functioning effectively
- A feeling of impotence at having so little control over the situation
- A sense of doubt when the persons' own cultural values are brought into question

One would hope that undergoing the training to become an anthropologist, and making specific preparations for entering the field, would help to prevent anyone from experiencing extreme culture shock. Nevertheless, every anthropologist should expect to suffer, to some extent, from the discomfort of culture shock. Generally, the negative effects of culture shock subside as time passes, but it is unlikely that they will go away completely.

Biculturalism

Not all the consequences of fieldwork are negative. Culture shock is real and should not be taken lightly. Yet, despite the stress of culture shock (or perhaps because of it), the total immersion experience of fieldwork provides opportunities for personal growth and increased understanding of the nuances of a culture. Spending weeks and months operating in a radically different culture can provide new insights into how the local people think, act, and feel. In the process of learning about another culture, however, people unavoidably learn a good deal about their own culture as well (Gmelch 1994). When learning about another culture in depth, people become bicultural and develop a much broader view of human behaviour. This can be a consequence of successful fieldwork. Richard Barrett (1991, 20–21) captures the essence of this ***bicultural perspective***, which he claims enables cultural anthropologists

> to view the world through two or more cultural lenses at once. They can thus think and perceive in the categories of their own cultures, but are able to shift gears, so to speak, and view the same reality as it might be perceived by members of the societies they have studied. This intellectual biculturalism is extremely important to anthropologists. It makes them continually aware of alternative ways of doing things and prevents them from taking the customs of our own society too seriously.

When speaking of achieving biculturalism, it should not be assumed that the anthropologist, no matter how much fieldwork he or she does, will ever become a native. Roger Keesing (1992) reminds us that, after many fieldwork encounters with the Malaita Kwaio of the Solomon Islands, he still considered himself little more than an informed outsider. Keesing relates a story of his unsuccessful attempts to convince the Malaita Kwaio not to eat a dolphin they had caught because, he argued, it was not a fish but a mammal like us. He used the argument that dolphins, like humans, are warm-blooded and red-blooded, but the Malaita Kwaio were unimpressed. He got their rapt attention when he informed the locals that dolphins should not be eaten because they actually communicate with one another, just as humans do. Keesing was then asked a series of questions he could not answer to their satisfaction: How do you talk to a dolphin? What language do they speak? How can they talk under water? Finally, as his collaborators were cooking the dolphin steaks on the fire, Keesing came to realize a basic fact about anthropological fieldwork: No matter how long one spends studying another culture, the anthropologist is little more than "an outsider who knows something of what it is to be an insider" (1992, 77).

bicultural perspective The capacity to think and perceive in the categories of one's own culture as well as in the categories of a second culture.

Summary

1. Since the beginning of the 20th century, cultural anthropologists have conducted their research in a first-hand manner by means of direct ethnographic fieldwork. Explicit discussion of how anthropologists actually do their fieldwork is a much more recent phenomenon, however.
2. Preparations must be made before any fieldwork experience is begun, including securing research funds; taking adequate health precautions, such as getting immunizations; obtaining research clearance from the host government; gaining proficiency in the local language; and attending to a host of personal matters, such as securing passports and visas, purchasing equipment and supplies, making sure that one's affairs at home are in order, and obtaining ethics approval.
3. Although every fieldwork project in cultural anthropology has its own unique character, all projects go through the same basic stages: selecting a research problem, formulating a research design, collecting the data, analyzing the data, and interpreting the data, and writing up the results.
4. Because no two fieldwork experiences are identical, cultural anthropologists must match the appropriate data-gathering techniques to their own fieldwork situations. Among the tools at the anthropologist's disposal are participant observation, interviewing, ethnographic mapping, census taking, document analysis, the collection of genealogies, and photography.
5. Two general guidelines are applicable to most fieldwork situations. First, when one introduces oneself to the local population, it is important to select a single role and use it consistently. Second, to firmly establish one's credibility with the local people, it is best to proceed slowly.
6. The participant observation technique has certain methodological advantages, including building rapport and allowing the anthropologist to distinguish between real and normative behaviours. Participant observation's shortcomings are that it is time-consuming, poses problems of data comparability, presents difficulties in recording data, and may interfere with the thing that is being studied.
7. Ethnographic interviews, which are particularly useful for collecting both attitudinal and behavioural data, are of three basic types: unstructured, semi-structured, and structured. In unstructured interviews, interviewers ask open-ended questions and permit interviewees to respond at their own pace. In semi-structured interviews, the anthropologist relies on an interview guide covering the topics or themes he or she needs to address. In structured interviews, interviewers ask the same questions of all respondents, in the same order, and under the same set of social conditions.
8. When cultural anthropologists conduct field research in cultures different from their own, they need to be flexible and should always expect the unexpected. Like anyone else trying to operate in an unfamiliar cultural setting, cultural anthropologists are susceptible to culture shock.
9. Recent trends in ethnographic fieldwork include reflexive methods, autoethnography, life history or life story approach, and multi-sited fieldwork.
10. Today, many anthropologists use web-based tools for collecting large amounts of high-quality anthropological data. Social networking sites such as Facebook provide attitudinal and behavioural data from people throughout the world.
11. All anthropologists, be they applied or ethnographic in their approach to fieldwork, are accountable to the people with whom they study. Research must comply with the *Tri-Council Policy Statement: Ethical Conduct for Research Involving Humans (TCPS 2)* 2010 as well as the AAA's code of professional ethics. The published insights from the research should not bring harm to the people who are the subject of the field study or beneficiaries of a project.

Key Terms

attitudinal data
autoethnography
behavioural data
bicultural perspective
census taking
collaborator, research participant, culture expert, or informant
community-based participatory research
document analysis
elder
ethnographic fieldwork
ethnographic mapping
ethnohistory
event analysis
field notes
genealogical method
Human Relations Area Files (HRAF)
intersubjectivity
interview guide
life history or life story
literature review
multi-sited fieldwork
OCAP principles
participant observation
participatory action research
proxemic analysis
qualitative data

quantitative data
reflexive or narrative ethnography
research design
Research Ethics Board
research proposal
semi-structured interview
situated knowledge
structured interview
systematic sociological introspection
unstructured interview

Critical Thinking Questions

1. Why is it necessary for applied anthropologists to have experience in ethnographic methods for their fieldwork?
2. What similarities and differences can you discern in the field methods used by applied and ethnographic anthropologists?
3. If you were to evaluate the success of a project, what criteria would you use for your evaluation?
4. What are the pitfalls and biases associated with participant observation?
5. How might a collaborator's identity be revealed in an ethnography, and what steps would you take to ensure they remain anonymous?
6. What is the difference between anonymity and confidentiality?
7. While the anthropologist's personal circumstances result in situated knowledge, in what ways does a collaborator's personal circumstances result in situated knowledge?
8. Generation Z, that is, those born between 1995 and 2012, tend to skip breakfasts of cereal and toast because it takes too much time to clean up. If you were hired by General Foods to come up with a new breakfast food that would appeal to this generation, how would you go about researching it?
9. Indigenous people's traditional knowledge of the medicinal properties of plants in their environment has been exploited by pharmaceutical companies to develop new drugs. Should Indigenous people be compensated for use of their knowledge and, if so, how?
10. What steps can be taken to overcome culture shock?

Make the Grade with MindTap

Stay organized and efficient with **MindTap**—a single destination with all the course material and study aids you need to succeed. Built-in apps leverage social media and the latest learning technology. For example:

- ReadSpeaker will read the text to you.
- Self-quizzing allows you to assess your understanding.
- Flashcards are pre-populated to provide you with a jump-start for review—or you can create your own.
- You can highlight text and make notes in your MindTap Reader. Your notes will flow into Evernote, the electronic notebook app that you can access anywhere when it's time to study for the exam.

Visit nelson.com/student to start using **MindTap**. Enter the Online Access Code from the card included with your text. If a code card is not provided, you can purchase instant access at NELSONbrain.com.

Whether on computer or a smart phone, our means of communicating with others is changing. What might once have been private information is now shared with many.

Communication and Culture

CHAPTER

6

REVITALIZING FIRST NATIONS LANGUAGES

What do the following languages all have in common: Tsetsaut, Pentlatch, Huron-Wyandot, and Twana? Answer: They are all extinct First Nations languages (UNESCO 2016).

Abenaki, Tagish, Nakoda, Tsuu T'ina, Tsimshian, Xaaydaa Kil, Nuu-chah-nulth, Nicola, Tsetsaut, and many others may soon join them as only a few elders continue to speak them (SIL International 2016). The youngest Tsuu T'ina speaker, for example, is over 60 (Komarnicki 2009), and Kathy Robinson, at 81, is one of the last two fluent native speakers of Tseshaht (pronounced "tsi-sha-aht") on Vancouver Island's west coast (Daigneault 2012).

At the time of contact with Europeans, there were an estimated 450 Indigenous languages and dialects spoken in Canada (Office of the Commissioner of Official Languages, 1992). According to Statistics Canada, however, only 60 were still spoken as of 2011 (Statistics Canada 2012c). More than half are in British Columbia, and all but Inuktitut, Cree, and Anishinaabe, which are widely spoken, are in trouble.

Epidemics (especially smallpox), famine, and innumerable conflicts led to the loss of many of them, but most of have disappeared in the last 150 years or so due primarily to the Indian Residential Schools. From the 1840s until the mid-1970s, approximately 150 000 First Nations children, many as young as five years, were forcibly removed from their families to attend one of the 139 schools in the system (Truth and Reconciliation Commission 2015). The goal of the schools was to assimilate First Nations children into mainstream Canadian culture by separating them from their families, their culture, and their language. Children were often severely punished for speaking their native tongues, which were looked upon as "primitive" at best, and the language of the devil at worst. "'I got slammed right across the face,' says Olive Davis, recalling her first days at the St. Paul Residential School, near Cardston, in the early 1940s" (Komarnicki 2009). Anthropologist Patricia Shaw, who founded UBC's First Nations Languages Program, notes that many of the children entered the Residential Schools speaking only their native language (Thicke 2014), but forced to speak English or French, all but a few lost the ability to speak it. Even after the close of the Residential Schools, many children were bused to schools where the language of instruction was English or French. They then came home to watch TV in English. Little funding was (and is still not) available for materials and instruction in First Nations languages with few speakers. In the 1960s, under the jurisdiction of Child Welfare Services, thousands of Indigenous children were also placed in non-Indigenous foster homes or adopted

Strauss/Curtis/Getty Images

WHAT WE WILL LEARN

- What languages are
- How anthropologists study language and communication
- How languages change
- How people communicate without using words
- How language influences social relationships
- How our social identity shapes our language use and is shaped by it
- How language is politicized
- What the relationship is between language and culture
- How the recent revolution in communication technology has influenced the way people communicate

by non-Indigenous families in what has come to be known as the Sixties Scoop. This further hindered the transmission of Indigenous languages (Baloy 2011).

Of the First Nations people who did retain some of their language, many bought into the ideology that their language was socially inferior, or tied to the past, or backward, and refused to teach it to their children, believing they were protecting them from the shame and pain they experienced in the Residential Schools (Baloy 2011). Others stopped using their traditional tongues, believing them obsolete and that success for their children in Canadian society meant mastering English or French. Today, even if parents do try "to keep the old speech alive, their efforts can be doomed by the influence of films and computer games" (Economist 2008). Many First Nations youth thus see little point in learning the language of their parents and grandparents. The challenge is to convince "today's generation of 'Facebookers' and texters that the native words aren't simply old-fashioned" (Komarnicki 2009).

When First Nations communities no longer speak their native languages, they lose more than the words and a means to communicate. A people's history, values, mythology, music, its knowledge of the environment—its culture—are all contained in the language. More than anything else, perhaps, is the loss of their sense of identity. It is no wonder then that First Nations leaders now see retention of their language as a top priority.

First Nations people, as well as linguistic anthropologists, now realize that a rich cultural heritage is contained in these Indigenous languages and are making efforts not only to preserve them but also to revive them. "There's a sense of desperation, of our data disappearing before our eyes," laments Indigenous language expert Darin Flynn from the University of Calgary (Komarnicki 2009). Revitalizing these languages is an opportunity to reclaim Native heritage, identity, and pride, as well as spirituality, and to reverse the process of colonization and assert sovereignty (Baloy 2011).

Many First Nations peoples, in collaboration with anthropologists and other institutions, are working to record, preserve, and revive these languages. While computers, the Internet, and cellphones may contribute to the current decline of Indigenous languages, they are also essential resources in revitalizing them. One example is the Indigitization project (www.indigitization.ca/), which is a collaborative project between several B.C. First Nations, U.B.C.'s Museum of Anthropology, and other organizations (Indigitization 2015). The aim is to conserve First Nations languages as a resource for future generations through digitizing documents, maps, photographs, as well as the spoken word. Perhaps the most innovative organization is FirstVoices, which uses web-based tools and services to help First Nations people with language archiving, teaching and revitalization. Like Indigitization, FirstVoices helps First Nations upload audio, documents, and images files; it also includes online games to help people learn the languages (FirstVoices 2015). The organization has also developed an app, "FirstVoices Chat," which allows First Nations members to send text messages to each other in their native languages. FirstVoices also runs The Language Tutor, a language program used in several B.C. schools to help parents, teachers, and students learn specific First Nations languages. These programs and apps have encouraged an interest in youth involvement in their language (Daigneault 2012).

Many First Nations are developing their own language education programs. Elder Kathy Robinson, for instance, developed the foundations of the Tseshaht curriculum that is still used at the local Tseshaht community school (Daigneault 2012). Blackfoot elder Alvine Eagle Speaker leads a culture and language class on the Siksika reserve east of Calgary (Figure 6.1). Several universities also now offer courses in First Nations languages.

The key to the retention and revival of these languages lies with the elders. After two years of intensive study learning the language from elders, Michele Johnson, for instance, is sufficiently proficient to teach a community class of adults Nsyilxcən—also known as Okanagan, or Interior Salish—which is on the brink of extinction (Thicke 2014). This master-apprentice approach is only one of the ways First Nations languages are being revived. Other programs bring fluent speakers and learners together in short-term immersion camps where elders teach younger people (Baloy 2011). The goal of these efforts is to create fluent speakers who will pass the language down to their children as a first language. The real test of a language's viability, however, is its use in everyday communication. For a language to survive, people need to speak it with one another.

Leah Hennel/Calgary Herald

FIGURE 6.1 Alvine Eagle Speaker teaches the Blackfoot language to students at Siksika Nation High School, an hour's drive east of Calgary. By the time the students graduate from her classes, they should be able to hold simple conversations in the language.

Concerns over the disappearance of First Nations languages and the attempts to revive them demonstrate the importance of language in people's lives. As we will see in this chapter, language is intimately connected with culture and identity as well as how we think about and perceive the world. ■

Communication, Language, and Culture

The word *communication* comes from the Latin word *communicare*, which means to transmit or impart something—such as information, knowledge, and even diseases—so that it is shared or made common (OED). The word *community* has a similar origin and initially had the idea of joint ownership, but also of participating and sharing things such as fellowship and culture. In other words, community is created through sharing or communicating. As we saw in Chapter 2, the idea of sharing something by a community is essential to the concept of culture, and thus it is important to understand how we communicate or share. We tend to think of communication as synonymous with language since language is by far our most dominant form of communication and is also perhaps what most distinguishes us from other animals. But it is not the only form.

The word language comes from the Latin word *lingua*, which means "tongue" or speech of a particular community. While language is the focus of this chapter, it is only one way we communicate; there are several others. For example, we communicate through music, mathematics, body language, facial expressions, gestures, clothing, and many more ways.

Language and other forms of communication are the way we organize our lives and give meaning to them. It is through language and communication that we persuade others to do things, negotiate contracts, end disputes, fall in love, and so on. Fundamental aspects of any culture, such as religion, family relationships, and the management of technology, would be impossible without a symbolic form of communication. Language is also the way we classify and make sense of the world. The language we speak is one of the primary ways we identify ourselves; in fact, the name of most ethnic groups and countries is intimately connected with the name for the dominant language. Most of us spend much of our daily lives communicating, talking to friends and family, attending lectures, reading, writing, and simply thinking (i.e., talking to ourselves). Language and communication in general are such an

communication The process of sharing information and knowledge through either language or some nonverbal system of meaning.

Masterfile

FIGURE 6.2 When we communicate with others, we are constantly making decisions about the words and gestures we use and how we use them, depending on our relationship with the people we are communicating with and the context in which it takes place.

integral part of the human condition that they permeate everything we do. Anthropologist Edward T. Hall reminds us that, "Communication constitutes the core of culture and indeed of life itself" (Hall, E. T. 1966, 1). It is largely through language that we pass on our cultural heritage and identity from one generation to the next. Language, by also categorizing the world, also acts as a filter for our perceptions and consequently our behaviour. Communication is thus the key to understanding another culture, and it is why anthropologists have always advocated learning the language of the people they study as the first step in understanding them.

Communication also takes place within a specific context. When we communicate we are communicating with individuals whom we may or may not know, with whom we may have a particular personal relationship, who may hold power over us, or who may come from a different background. We also communicate with them in different places, such as the coffee shop, the dinner table, school, in court, online, etc. All these variables require us to make choices when we communicate: do we communicate with words or gestures; do we do it directly or indirectly; are we polite, or can we be impolite; what words should we use; do we simplify our language to make ourselves clear; and so on (Figure 6.2). Many of these decisions are made consciously, but most are made unconsciously. It also means the use of language is highly political.

Today, the Internet, mass media, and new technologies, combined with international travel, migration, and global marketing, mean we are encountering other languages and ways of communicating more than ever before, and also increasing the opportunities for misunderstandings. It is important therefore to understand the nature of language and the fundamental differences between languages. Many languages (e.g., English, Spanish, Chinese) are becoming truly global, while others with fewer speakers are, as we have seen, rapidly disappearing.

The Nature of Language

Language is a symbolic system of sounds that, when put together according to a certain set of rules, conveys meanings to its speakers. The meaning attached to any given word in all languages is arbitrary; that is, there is no objective connection between the sound of a word and the thing it represents. Thus, different languages will have different sounds for the same thing. For instance, the sound of the English word "cow" has no particular connection to the female domesticated ox that is kept to produce milk or beef to which the word "cow" refers. Other languages use different, and equally arbitrary, words to describe the same animal. For instance, the word cow in Spanish is *vaca,* in Yoruba *Maalu,* in Blackfoot *áápotskina,* and in Mohawk *tyonnhonhskwaron.*

CROSS-CULTURAL MISCUE

When Erin Meyer went to her first dinner party in France, she asked her hosts what she thought was an innocent question: "How did the two of you meet?" Her husband, who had more experience, was horrified and later explained "We don't ask that type of question to strangers in France. It's like asking them the colour of their underpants." What Meyer quickly learned was that some topics are appropriate to discuss with people from other cultures while others are not.

Meyer makes the distinction, initially made by the German-American psychologist Kurt Lewin, between a "peach" and a "coconut" culture. Peach cultures, such as the United States and Brazil, are soft on the outside, open and friendly, and more than willing to discuss personal issues with complete strangers, but hard on the inside, and will not discuss much deeper personal questions. Coconut cultures, such as Russia and Germany, on the other hand, are hard on the outside and soft on the inside. People are hard to get to know, smile very little, and are very protective of their personal lives. After time, however, they open up and real deep, long-lasting friendships can form. Misunderstanding can arise when, for example, a peach meets a coconut. A peach's initial friendliness can appear to a coconut as suspicious and, when the peach does not allow for a deeper relationship, as disingenuous or hypocritical (Meyer 2014).

Source: From Meyer, Erin. 2014. "One Reason Cross-Cultural Small Talk Is So Tricky." *Harvard Business Review,* May 30, 2014.

language A symbolic system of arbitrary sounds that, when put together according to a certain set of rules, convey meaning to its speakers.

Anthropological Linguistics

Linguistics is the scientific study of language and, because language is so intimately connected with human nature and culture, anthropologists have always been interested in studying it. Biological anthropologists, for instance, are concerned with the development of the human capacity for language as physically evidenced in fossil remains, and the extent to which other primates are capable of it. Descriptive linguists are interested in the sound and meaning structure of languages, while historical linguists are concerned with how languages have changed over time. Sociolinguists study the relationship between language and society, and in particular how people use language in different social contexts to structure social, political, and economic relationships within a society. Finally, ethnolinguists are concerned with the relationships been language and culture, and especially how languages categorize the world and shape our thoughts and experiences. This chapter focuses primarily on ethnolinguistics and sociolinguistics.

Non-human Primate Language

The call systems of most primates are to a large extent genetically based, and are rigidly inflexible such that each call always has the same form and conveys the same meaning. Chimpanzees and gorillas, however, have a latent capacity to learn language but lack the vocal equipment for speech. In an effort to circumvent this physical limitation, researchers have taught some aspects of American Sign Language to chimpanzees and gorillas with some startling results (Figure 6.3). In four years, Allen and Beatrice Gardner (1969) taught a chimp named Washoe (1965–2007) to use 130 different signs. Of even greater significance is the fact that Washoe was able to manipulate the signs in ways that previously had been thought possible only by humans. For example, Washoe was able to combine several signs to create a new word (having no sign for the word *duck*, she called it *waterbird*), thereby "opening up" her system of communication. In another research effort in nonhuman communication, a gorilla named Koko by age four was able to use more than 250 different signs and, like Washoe, was able to name new objects by combining several different signs.

Susan Kuklin/Science Source

FIGURE 6.3 Joyce Butler of Columbia University shows famous chimpanzee Nim Chimpsky the sign configuration for "drink," and Nim imitates her. Even though Nim has been trained to use sign language, the differences between his form of communication and human language are vast.

Descriptive Linguistics

Descriptive linguistics examines (describes) the structure of a particular language with respect to the ways the systems of sounds and grammar are put together to create meaning. Humans can make an extraordinarily large number of sounds, but no single language uses all possible sounds. English for example, uses a total of 46 sounds.

All languages have rules and principles governing what sounds are to be used and how they are to be combined to convey meaning. The smallest unit of sound is called a *phoneme*. The differences in sound between phonemes create differences in meaning. For example, the only difference in the words "bit" and "pit" is in the difference in sound between the "p" and the "b," but this difference changes the meaning of the words. A *morpheme*, on the other hand, is the smallest unit of speech that conveys meaning. The word "dogs," for instance, contains two morphemes: "dog" which refers to the animal, and "s" which conveys the meaning of plural. Phonemes and morphemes are combined to create words according to a highly complex set of rules that make up the *grammar* of a language. The principles guiding how words are arranged into phrases and sentences is known as *syntax*. Different languages have different sets of rules governing what sounds can be used, how they are to be combined to create words, and how the words are to be arranged to create meaningful communication. Most of us learn these rules by the time we are three, and so apply them unconsciously.

linguistics The scientific study of language.

phoneme The smallest unit of sound that distinguishes meaning in a language.

morpheme The smallest linguistic form that conveys meaning.

grammar The systematic rules by which sounds are combined in a language to enable users to send and receive meaningful utterances.

syntax The linguistic rules, found in all languages, that determine how phrases and sentences are constructed.

MGM/courtesy Everett Collection/via CP Images

FIGURE 6.4 Bob and Doug McKenzie played by Rick Moranis and Dave Thomas in CBC skit known as the *Great White North* in the 1980s. They played upon typical Canadian stereotypes such as wearing toques, drinking beer, eating back bacon, and interjecting the word "eh" after most sentences.

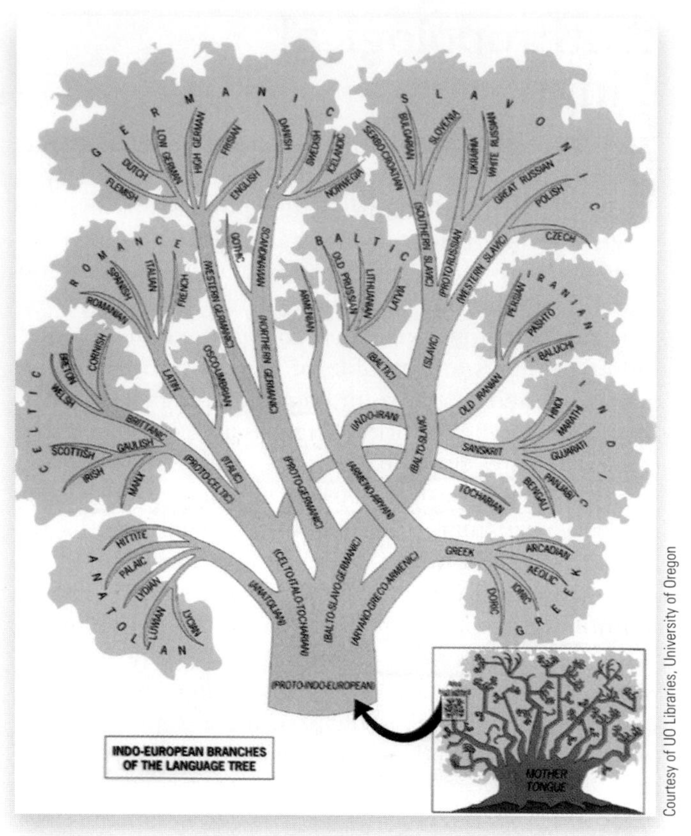

Courtesy of UO Libraries, University of Oregon

FIGURE 6.5 Indo-European branches of the Language Tree.

Historical Linguistics

Like all other aspects of culture, language is constantly changing. The word "eh," for example, was once quintessentially Canadian, its use identifying the speaker as Canadian. Today, however, it is disappearing from Canadian speech and being replaced by "right." Only older Canadians continue to use "eh" (Figure 6.4). Older Canadians also say "I've *got* a dog," while younger Canadians say "I *have* a dog." Other phrases such as "and stuff," "and everything," and "you know" are becoming more popular. The word "really" is being replaced by "very," as in "really big, really fast, and really great," and "I said" is being replaced with "I'm like…" (Spears 2013).

The pronunciation of words, the meanings of words, and the grammar also change over time. They also change for a variety of reasons, and the study of these changes is known as historical linguistics. By studying how languages change over time, and through cross-cultural comparison, historical linguistics can trace the historic relationship of languages to one another (Figure 6.5).

---

speech community People who share a set of norms about how to speak and expectations about how language is used.

Speech Communities

People who share a set of norms about how to speak and expectations about how language is used are known as a ***speech community*** (Yule 2006). Speech communities can be countries, villages, neighbourhoods, social classes, professional groups, or simply a group of friends or an interest group. The longer speech communities are separated from one other, say in different countries or villages, the more likely pronunciation of certain words may gradually change. For instance, English and German, which are both Germanic languages, share a common proto-Germanic ancestor. After the Angles and the Saxons moved from what is now Germany to settle in Great Britain in the 5th century, the pronunciation of certain words changed. For example, in many words the "pf" sound shifted to a "p" sound, and the "s" to a "t" so that we have "apple" and "water" in English and "apfel" and "wasser" in German. With so many other changes, the two speech communities became mutually unintelligible, forming new languages. Linguists have used these sound correspondences to trace the historical relationships between languages.

Changes in the meanings of words can also reflect changing cultural values. For example, the word "gay" originally meant being merry, carefree, and light-hearted (Figure 6.6). By the late 1970s it had come to mean homosexual, and now is used in this sense almost exclusively.

Twining and Company

FIGURE 6.6 As culture changes, many words take on new meanings. The word "gay" for instance originally meant happy and carefree, which is the meaning intended in this 1950s ad for Ovaltine. Today, of course the word gay is used primarily to describe people who are attracted to members of the same sex.

Languages also change due to linguistic borrowing. It is generally thought that languages borrow from one another for two primary reasons: need and prestige. When a language community acquires a new cultural item, such as a concept or a material object, it needs a word to describe it. This explains why different cultures have similar words referring to the same thing, such as automobiles, computers, and coffee. The other reason that words are borrowed from other languages is that they convey prestige to the speakers of the recipient language. To illustrate, the French word *cuisine* (from *kitchen*) was adopted into English because French food was considered more prestigious than English food during the period of French dominance (700 to 950 years ago).

Given the arbitrary nature of languages and the way they change, it should come as no surprise that there is enormous linguistic diversity among human populations. A reasonable estimate is that there are nearly 7000 mutually unintelligible languages (Wilford 2010). It has also been estimated that 95 percent of the world's people speak fewer than 100 of them.

Nonverbal Communication

To comprehend fully how people in any particular culture communicate, we must become familiar with their nonverbal forms of communication in addition to their language. *Nonverbal communication* is important because it carries messages of its own and often helps us to interpret linguistic messages. In fact, it has been suggested that up to 70 percent of all messages sent and received by humans are nonverbal.

Like language, nonverbal forms of communication are arbitrary and have to be learned, and therefore vary from one culture to another. Even though some nonverbal cues have the same meaning in different cultures (for instance using the index finger to point is almost universal), an enormous range of variation in nonverbal communication exists among cultures. As with spoken language, the same message can be sent in a number of different ways by different cultures. The same nonverbal form can also send different messages. For example, whereas in Canada nodding the head up and down means "yes," in Bulgaria, Turkey, Iran, parts of Greece, and elsewhere it means "no." When the Russians, who nod to say "yes," occupied Bulgaria in the 1800s, they disciplined themselves to nod when they meant "no" as the Bulgarians did. Unfortunately, the Bulgarians did not know whether they were "speaking" Bulgarian or Russian (Axtell 1998).

We communicate without words in a number of important ways, including hand gestures, facial expressions, eye contact, touching, space usage, scents, gait, stance, and even our hairstyle and the clothes we wear.

---

nonverbal communication The various means by which humans send and receive messages without using words.

Men and women in most cultures, for instance, communicate their gender by wearing their hair differently and by wearing what are considered men's clothing or women's clothing. A thorough discussion of these and other aspects of nonverbal communication is beyond the scope of this textbook. To convey the importance of this form of human communication we will look briefly at only four types of nonverbal communication: kinesics (body language), paralanguage (the manner of speaking), proxemics (the use of space), and haptic communication (touch).

Kinesics

The study of ***kinesics*** was first developed by American anthropologist Ray Birdwhistell (1952), and refers to the way we move our bodies to communicate with one another. Kinesics is often called "body language." It includes such things as hand gestures, facial expressions, and the way we walk or stand. Like spoken language, these movements carry meaning.

kinesics A form of nonverbal communication involving the interpretation of bodily movement.

Hand Gestures

A major form of kinesics is hand gestures, and we use many of them every day, from cupping our hand behind our ear to communicate that we cannot hear, to raising our hand in class to ask or answer a question. We also wave hello or good-bye, tell people to be quiet by holding our forefinger vertically against our lips, and give the peace sign by holding up our forefinger and middle finger. We send a different message when we flash half of the peace sign. By making a circle with our thumb and forefinger, we communicate that everything is A-OK. Problems may arise with these gestures, however, when we cross cultural boundaries. Although the A-OK sign carries a positive, upbeat message in Canada, it refers to money in Japan, zero (worthless) in France, male homosexuality in Malta, and is an obscenity in parts of South America. Thus, a single hand gesture carries with it many different meanings throughout the world, and to avoid misunderstanding we have to be careful when we use them (Figure 6.7). When U.S. President George Bush Sr. was on a state visit to Australia in 1993, he flashed the "V" for victory sign from his limousine. Unfortunately he flashed it with his palm facing inward, which in Australia means "up yours, mate," and the next day Australian newspaper headlines read, "President Insults Australians" (Axtel 1998).

AFP/Getty Images

The Print Collector/Print Collector/Getty Images

FIGURE 6.7 With his palm outward British Prime Minister Winston Churchill gave the "V" for "victory" sign to the British and allies during World War II. With his palm facing inward he was insulting their enemies. Since the 1960s the "V" sign has been used to symbolize peace.

The best advice when travelling or interacting with people from another culture is to avoid hand gestures.

Facial Expressions

Facial expressions are a nonverbal form of communication important in communicating emotional information. Typically, they are seen to display six basic emotional categories: fear, happiness, sadness, disgust, anger, and surprise (Smith, Marie L. et al. 2005). In *The Expression of the Emotions in Man and Animals*, Charles Darwin (1998 [1872]) argued these emotions were facially expressed in a culturally universal manner; most evidence since then seems to support this view (Ekman 2009). This means that people can correctly recognize the emotions of people from different cultures from their facial expressions, although what causes people to have these emotions will vary from person to person and culture to culture. While some facial expressions are conscious, most are involuntary and unconscious. Because of this they have been used by intelligence and police agencies, as well as poker players, to discover a person's true thoughts and feelings.

The eyes are the most important element in facial expression, and regulate turn taking in conversations, show interest in others, establish connections between people, and command attention; they are also used to flirt (Rothwell 2004). When people are conversing in the West, the norm is to look each other in the eye to indicate that one is paying attention. When people fail to do this, it suggests they either lack self-confidence, are unfriendly, or are lying (Harris P. et al. 2004). Parents, for instance may often tell their children to look them in the eye to judge the truth of what they are saying. Like other aspects of nonverbal communication, facial expressions, and eye contact in particular, can have different rules for how to communicate and different meanings. Staring or gazing at someone can be seen as expected in one society yet threatening in another. Eye contact is often avoided between Muslim men and women, with women lowering their eyes as a sign of respect. In Japan, children are taught to look at their teacher's Adam's apple rather than their eyes, and, as a sign of respect, adults lower their eyes when speaking to a superior (Harris P. et al. 2004, 58). Similarly, in Nigeria, staring at a superior is seen as disrespectful, whereas in Canada and the United States, simply as rude. Widening of the eyes is interpreted as suppressed anger by Chinese but as an expression of astonishment by North Americans (Harris P. et al. 2004, 58).

Posture (Body Stance)

The way people hold their bodies often communicates information about their social status, religious practices, feelings of submissiveness, desires to maintain social distance, and sexual intentions, or inner feelings—to mention several areas. When communicating, people tend to orient their bodies toward others by assuming a certain stance or posture. A person can stand over another person, kneel, or "turn a cold shoulder," and in each case the body posture communicates something different. Again, the meaning attached to different body postures varies from one culture to another and is learned in the same way that other aspects of a culture are internalized. For instance, in Western cultures, sitting with legs crossed indicates confidence, while standing with arms wide apart and hands open indicates openness.

Perhaps one of the most visible and dramatic nonverbal messages sent by posture is submissiveness. In many cultures people show submission to rulers, superiors, or elders by making themselves appear smaller by lowering the body (crouching, cowering, or grovelling), and can include anything from a head nod, to bowing, to complete prostration—lying flat on the floor face down. As part of their religious practices, some Christians kneel, Catholics genuflect, and Muslims perform *sujud*, which involves touching the forehead, nose, both hands, knees, and all toes to the ground simultaneously.

Nowhere is bowing more important to the process of communication today than in Japanese society. Children learn to bow at a young age, and many companies train their employees how to bow properly. Bowing initiates interaction between two Japanese, it enhances and embellishes many parts of the ensuing conversation, and it is used to signal the end of a conversation. Social rank in Japan is extremely important, and so bowing is also used to demonstrate respect (Figure 6.8). Subordinate and younger people generally bow lower

Holos/The Image Bank/Getty Images

FIGURE 6.8 In Japan, bowing shows respect. The depth of the bow and how long it is held depends on social rank. Generally, a lower status person bows lower and longer.

facial expressions A nonverbal form of communication that uses the face to communicate emotional information.

and hold the bow for longer. Bows also tend to be lower and deeper the more formal the occasion. An indication of how pervasive bowing is in contemporary Japan is that some Japanese department stores employ people whose sole function is to bow to customers as they enter the store. In fact, bowing is so ingrained in the Japanese psyche that some Japanese actually bow to invisible partners at the other end of a telephone line.

Paralanguage

Have you ever noticed how journalists giving their reports on the radio or television speak in an unnatural manner? What they are doing is moderating their voice so their accounts sound objective. It is not a monotone, however, since that would make their reports boring. Rather, they modulate the pitch, or sound frequency, of their words up and down in an atypical manner so that they do not convey emotion. When we speak we communicate not only the dictionary, or lexical, meaning of the words, but also our emotional state as well as information about how the words and phrases are to be interpreted. For instance, a person who speaks quickly or whose voice "cracks" while speaking is probably nervous. This additional information is called ***paralanguage*** and is thus an important aspect of human communication. The prefix "*para*" comes from the Greek word for "beside." Thus, paralanguage is communication that is in addition to or accompanies the words themselves. Paralanguage is not so much about *what* people say but *how* they say it. It includes facial or hand gestures (kinesics), such things as gasps and sighs, as well as prosodic features.

Prosodic features are aspects of language concerned with the auditory qualities of speech such as pitch (or intonation), stress, tone, loudness, rhythm, voice quality, duration, and speed. Variations in these prosodic features can reflect such things as the difference between a command, question, or statement, as well as the emotional state of the speaker, or whether the statement is meant to be ironic or sarcastic. For instance, the sentence "people communicate without using words" can be either a statement or a question. In writing, we use a period or a question mark to indicate the difference. In spoken language, however, questions are indicated by raising the pitch or frequency of sound.

Paralanguage is not generally taught in school but is learned before we understand the meaning of words, and can be seen in the way infants (and even some animals) respond to the tone or loudness, or the way things are said. Infants for instance, will often cry when spoken to harshly even though they do not understand the words. For the most part, paralinguistic cues are expressed and interpreted unconsciously. Most of us can tell when someone is being serious or sarcastic because of paralinguistic cues we are generally not conscious of. Paralanguage is also present in written language but, since many social cues are missing, the printed word is depersonalized and limited by the medium of text. For instance, people demonstrate anger or importance by capitalizing everything. And in text messages, we use a range of emoticons "☺" or non-alphabetic characters such as ":-)" to modulate the meaning.

Like other aspects of language, paralanguage is culturally relative and can lead to cross-cultural misunderstandings. Since it is often used to discriminate between subtle or ambiguous situations—for instance telling the difference between a joke, a statement, or sarcasm—effective inter-cultural communication requires not only an understanding of the meaning of words but also the accompanying paralanguage.

Haptic Communication

Haptic communication refers to the ways people interact through touch, and is perhaps the most personal and intimate form of nonverbal communication. Touch communicates positive emotions and is thus the most important nonverbal means of establishing and maintaining relationships (Hertenstein et al. 2006). As relationships move from impersonal to personal, the amount and type of touching increases. In infants, touching transfers the emotional state of the caregiver and is essential for bonding and normal development (Hertenstein et al. 2006).

We communicate through touch in a variety of ways such as patting a person on the head or back, slapping, kissing, punching, stroking, embracing, tickling, holding hands, high fiving, and laying-on of hands. We also use touch to communicate for a variety of reasons. Touching can be sexual or non-sexual (kissing, for example, can be both), or it can be platonic, such as when people hug one another. People also touch one another to show support and concern, or gratitude, to express affection, sexual attraction, or communicate status and power (Henley 1977).

Much of the touching we do is ritualistic. For example, when introduced to someone most Canadians shake hands as a sign of friendship. Other cultures have other forms of greeting that may involve touch; for instance, cheek kissing is common in Europe, the Middle East, and South America. In New Zealand, the traditional Maori greeting is called a *hongi* and involves

---

paralanguage A nonverbal form of communication that accompanies words and helps to convey their meaning as well as expressing the emotional state of the speaker.

prosodic features Auditory qualities of speech, such as intonation, stress, loudness, and rhythm, that help interpret the meaning of words.

haptic communication A form of nonverbal communication that involves touch.

Samir Hussein/WireImage/Getty Images

FIGURE 6.9 Prince William and New Zealand's ex-Governor General Sir Paul Reeves greet each other with a traditional Maori hongi in Wellington in January 2010.

pressing each other's nose and forehead together at the same time (Figure 6.9). We also engage in ritualized touching on departure, which can also involve handshakes or giving each other a hug.

Every culture has a well-defined set of meanings connected with touching and rules about who can touch whom, on what parts of the body, and under what circumstances. For instance, observant Orthodox Jewish men typically do not touch women who are not their wives, including shaking hands with them. Observant Muslim men and women also do not typically shake hands as a sign of modesty and chastity. The refusal of some Jewish and Muslim men to shake hands with women has become a contentious issue for many Western women who feel shocked and personally insulted, seeing it as sex discrimination. To avoid accidentally touching women, some Haredi Jewish (an orthodox group) men have refused to sit next to women on El Al airline flights, claiming it is a strict requirement of their faith. This has caused delays to some flights when the woman refused to move or an alternative seat could not be found (Stone 2014). This raises the issue of whether religious beliefs should trump another's individual rights or discrimination against women when faith cannot be easily accommodated.

Refusal to shake hands is contrary to Western social norms and can sour business deals and create misunderstandings. Touching someone contrary to social norms can also create misunderstandings. For instance, in Thailand, Malaysia, and some other Muslim countries, the head is sacred, and touching someone on the head, especially the heads of children, which in Canada can be seen as a sign of affection, can be seen as rude (P. Harris et al. 2004). Touching someone as a gesture of support can sometimes also be misinterpreted as an unwanted sexual advance. There have been numerous incidents of doctors, teachers, and employers begin accused of sexual assault for touching people against their will.

According to a classic study by Henley (1977), powerful and high status people are more likely to touch than be touched, as they have the privilege to do so, which lower-status people lack. Interestingly though, it is lower status people who initiate a handshake, whereas higher status people are more likely to initiate touches to the arm and shoulders.

Public displays of affection (i.e., touching in public) such as holding hands or walking arm in arm demonstrate to others the nature of the relationship. Cultures also dictate the extent of public touching. In most Western countries, it is acceptable to hold hands and kiss in public. In many Middle East countries, however, kissing in public may contravene decency laws, and there have been several cases where people have been arrested and imprisoned for kissing in public. One man in Saudi Arabia, for instance, was given 90 lashes and sentenced to four months in jail for kissing a woman in a mall (CTV News 2010).

Some cultures have been described as high-touch cultures and others as low-touch. Some studies (Paige et al. 2002) have suggested that Eastern European, Jewish, African, and Arab cultures tend to be high-touch cultures, whereas northern European cultures such as German and Scandinavian cultures tend to be low-touch. The difference between high- and low-touch cultures can be observed in public places, such as subways or elevators. For example, Londoners (from a low-touch culture) travelling in a crowded subway are likely to assume a rigid posture, studiously avoid eye contact, and refuse to even acknowledge the presence of other passengers. The French (from a high-touch culture), on the other hand, have no difficulty leaning and pressing against one another in a crowded Parisian subway.

Proxemics

The term *proxemics* was coined by the cultural anthropologist Edward T. Hall (1966) and refers to the way people perceive and use space. It involves not only how people orient themselves to one another, but also how we organize space in places such as offices, houses, and even cities. Hall identified four types of distance (intimate, personal, social, and public), each with a near, close, and far phase, which people try to maintain between one another. The distances are a reflection of how we

proxemics A form of nonverbal communication that involves how people use space.

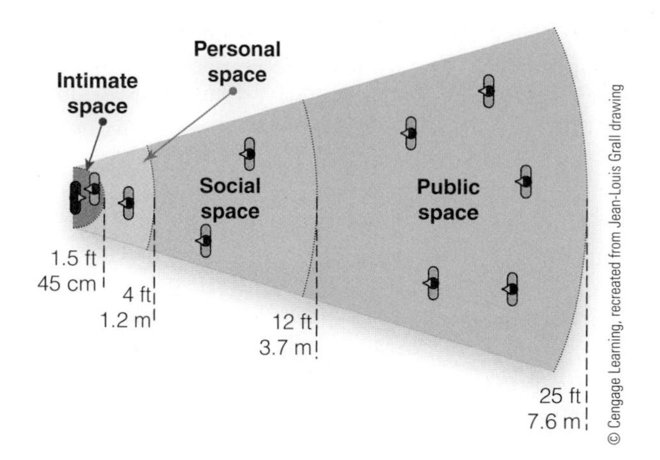

FIGURE 6.10 **Edward T. Hall identified four types of distance: intimate, personal, social, and public, which people try to maintain based on their personal relationships with others.**

perceive and maintain our relationship with others. For most North Americans, the close intimate distance is "the distance of love-making and wrestling, comforting and protecting" (Hall 1966,117); the far phase (15 to 46 cm / 6 to 18 inches) occurs when people are so close that their presence is unmistakable: close enough to smell them, feel their body heat, and hear the sound of their breath. This space is reserved for the people we are closest to: our lovers, family, children, and dearest friends. At times, however, such as when on crowded elevators, trains, or buses, we have little choice but to allow strangers into this space. In these cases we have coping mechanisms such as looking up or down, or closing our eyes and listening to our iPod to deal with this intrusion. Personal space is the immediate bubble of space surrounding us that we feel most comfortable maintaining between friends and acquaintances and varies between 0.5 to 1.2 m (18 inches to 4 feet). When someone we don't know, or don't know very well, invades this space we may feel threatened, angry, anxious, and certainly uncomfortable. Personal space is also related to a person's social status. People with more wealth, prestige, or power tend to have a larger personal space. Social space, about 1.2 to 3.7 m (4 to 12 feet), is used for conversing with strangers or business associates, while public space is the zone reserved for speeches and lectures: 3.6 to 7.6 m (12 to 25 feet) or more (Figure 6.10).

As with other forms of nonverbal communication, the standards for the use of space vary from one culture to another and are thus learned. In many Asian and Arabic speaking cultures, people have a much smaller personal space than most Canadians. These different standards can lead to cross-cultural misunderstandings. When people with different standards invade our personal space we feel uncomfortable and may view them as pushy or aggressive. On the other hand, when we keep our distance from people from cultures with a smaller personal space we are likely to be viewed as aloof and standoffish.

High- and Low-Context Cultures

Anthropologist Edward T. Hall (1976) has also made the distinction between high- and low-context cultures. In ***high-context cultures*** found in Asia, the Middle East, Africa, and South America, communication tends to be ambiguous, implicit, and inexact. How something is said is often more important than what is said. With much less emphasis placed on words, high-context cultures rely heavily on nonverbal cues and social context to derive meaning. Things are often left unsaid as the context or culture (e.g., the location, history, or relationship of the people involved in the interaction) will convey understanding. Communication tends to be more formal as one of the goals in communication is not to offend people, but to give them the opportunity to "save face" and avoid shame. High-context cultures tend to be collectivist, emphasize personal relationships, and strive for harmony and consensus.

In ***low-context cultures***, such as Canada, the United States, and most of Western Europe, however, people strive to communicate in a way that is precise, straightforward, and unambiguous. We are expected to "tell it like it is" and avoid "beating around the bush." Words are taken literally and are more important than how they are said. Low-context cultures tend to be individualist, task- rather than people-focused, and less likely to make decisions for emotional or social reasons.

These differences in linguistic style can result in cross-cultural misunderstandings. Ishii et al. (2003) have shown that North Americans have greater difficulty ignoring the content of a message than ignoring how the message is intoned. However, their findings showed just the opposite for Japanese; that is, the Japanese had greater difficulty ignoring vocal tone than ignoring verbal content. Thus, the North Americans had an attentional bias toward content, whereas the Japanese paid more attention to intonation. This stylistic difference between these two linguistic groups at least partially explains why both sides have a propensity to misunderstand each other. North Americans are often perplexed because they think their Japanese counterparts do not seem to mean the same thing that they mean by the word *yes*. Many Japanese, conversely, feel perplexed by the fact that the Americans just do not seem to get it because they are failing to read the available nonverbal cues such as intonation. The

high-context cultures Cultures in which communication is indirect, relying heavily on the context to convey meaning.

low-context cultures Cultures in which communication is direct and unambiguous, where meaning is conveyed by the words themselves.

indirect style of the Japanese has been known to test the patience of Westerners, who mistakenly interpret it as sneaky and devious. Japanese business people, on the other hand, are often offended by the low-context style of North Americans, which comes across as rude and insensitive. Japanese business people like to establish a relationship before conducting business, whereas businesspeople from low-context cultures like to get "down to business" first.

Silence

Another aspect of indirect versus direct linguistic style is the role of silence in communication. People from high-context societies see silence as useful; they tolerate intermittent periods of silence so as to gain a better understanding of their communication partners. On the other hand, direct communicators, such as the majority of North Americans, avoid silence at all costs. Thus, in some cultures, silence (i.e., whether or not a person actually uses words) is determined by the nature of the social relationship between people and their social context.

In a comparative study of Japanese and American college students, Watanabe (1993) discovered that North American students viewed it important to speak and hold the floor, while the Japanese students saw it as a liability. This has the tendency of North Americans to look down on those who don't strive to speak, when it is really more a difference in what is valued. North Americans tend to value speech, while Japanese tend to value silence (Yamada 1997).

One of the differences between Japanese and North Americans in the way they speak is that Japanese leave longer silent spaces between taking conversational turns. North Americans find this uncomfortable and in business meetings are more likely to jump in, repeating themselves, believing their Japanese colleagues have not understood them (Yamada 1997). The difference between the two is exemplified by differences in proverbs. Proverbs express encoded values and attitudes about appropriate behaviour. Yamada contrasts North American proverbs, such as "The squeaky wheel gets the grease" and "Ask and you shall be heard," with Japanese proverbs, such as "If the bird had not sung it would not have been shot," and "The mouth is the source of calamity" (Yamada 1997, 17). North Americans are thus encouraged to speak, whereas the Japanese are encouraged to be silent.

Sociolinguistics

The language we speak and the ways we speak are the principal means by which interaction with others is organized. Whenever we speak we make choices about the words we use and the way we say them. These choices are, to a large extent, influenced by our relationship to the person or people we are speaking with, as well as the context in which the conversation takes place. For instance, the language a university student might use with a roommate is appreciably different from the language used when talking to grandparents, and the expressions heard in a hockey locker room would hardly be appropriate to use in a job interview. In short, what we say and how we say it are often influenced by variables such as our age, gender, education, ethnicity, relative social status, as well as our goals. Put another way, the language we use sends messages about who we are, where we are from, who we associate with, our social status, our character, and much more. Sometimes this information can be revealed in a single word. As we saw earlier, for instance, someone who uses the word "eh" is probably Canadian.

Most of the choices are made unconsciously. When we are learning our language we learn not only the meaning of words and the grammatical rules, but also the appropriate way to speak to certain people. Conversation is very much about taking turns, and we learn the social cues for when it is our turn to speak and when we have to hand the conversation over to others. Boys and girls learn this differently, and it is part of understanding our gender.

Language and language-use are also political. Most countries have an official language; French and English for example are the official languages of Canada. Some forms of speech, spoken by people from different social classes or from different regions, are also looked down upon or have a different status in society.

The study of the relationship between language and social structure and how language is used in society is known as sociolinguistics. Sociolinguistics covers many areas such as what can we tell about the social relationships between two people from the language they use with each other, the value placed on speaking a particular form of language, and how individuals use language to achieve their personal goals.

Language and Social Status

Analyzing terms of address can be particularly useful in understanding the social relationship between two people. When we address people in English we often use a title, a first or given name, and a last or family name. Professor Elizabeth Green, for example, could be addressed as Dr. Green, Ma'am, Professor, Ms. Green, Elizabeth, darling, Doc, Prof, or Beth, depending on who is doing the addressing and in what circumstances. One would not expect that her mother or husband would refer to her as Ma'am, or that her students would call her Beth. Instead, we would expect that the term of address chosen would appropriately reflect the relative social status and

STORIES FROM THE FIELD

I learned very early in my career not to make assumptions about the languages spoken by the people I was interviewing. I was introduced by one Elder to another in the Tlingit language and then assumed that the interviewee did not speak English. After a painstaking one hour interview involving translations back and forth between Tlingit and English, I asked a final question, "Do you have any photographs?" In perfect English the Elder, with a twinkle in her eye said, "Yes, I have lots and would you like a cup of tea?" Lesson learned.

—Diana E. French, *University of British Columbia Okanagan*

relationship of the two parties. We would also expect that the same person might use different terms of address for Professor Green in different social situations. Her husband might call her Dr. Green when referring to her in the presence of students, Beth at a cocktail party, darling when they are making love, and Elizabeth when engaged in an argument.

In Canadian society, the reciprocal use of first names indicates a friendly, informal relationship between equals. The reciprocal use of titles followed by last names indicates a more formal relationship between people of roughly the same status. And the nonreciprocal use of first names and titles is found among people of unequal social status. Teachers, for example, usually refer to their students by their first name, while students address their teachers using a title (Mr., Ms., professor) and their last or family name. This non-reciprocal use of first name, last name, and title not only reflects and maintains the different power relationships between people, but also is seen as a sign of respect by the lower status person.

Forms of address, as well as other words or phrases that show respect and thus encode social status, are known as ***honorifics***. The most familiar ones in English are Mr., Miss, and Mrs., which reveal not only a person's gender, but in the case of women, their marital status. Many women now prefer the honorific Ms. to avoid this gender bias. Recently, the gender neutral Mx has been gaining wider usage, especially among transgendered individuals who do not identify with any particular gender. In the United Kingdom it is now accepted by banks, universities, on drivers' licences, passports, and other official documents (Paton 2015). The assistant editor of the Oxford English Dictionary (to which the word was added in 2015) noted that its use was an indication of the English language's ability to adapt to changes in society whereby the language does not dictate identity (Paton 2015).

Other honorifics are used to show a person's prestige or position. For instance, among the Coast Salish people on the West Coast, individuals who had demonstrated leadership by gaining and disposing of wealth were referred to with the prestigious title "siem" (Suttle and Lane 1990). In Canada we use honorifics when referring to various politicians. For instance the Prime Minister, Governor General, and Chief Justice of Canada are addressed as "the Right Honourable," while senators and other members of parliament as "Honourable." Honorifics are common in many languages and are extremely important in Chinese, Korean, and Japanese. Japanese has many honorifics that reflect the hierarchical nature of the society. The most common honorific is the suffix –*san*, which is applied to the end of the person's name (e.g., Hayashi-*san*) and is roughly equivalent to Mr., Mrs., or Ms. and is used in both formal and informal situations. Use of honorifics in Japanese is almost mandatory for proper speech, and not using them in conversation is seen as either rude or awkward unless the person one is referring to is one's spouse, child, or very close friend. Honorifics thus not only denote differences in social status but also politeness in Japanese. They also extend beyond forms of address to verbs, nouns, pronouns, and other grammatical elements. In conversation between an older and a younger person, for example, the younger person must use "respectful language," whereas the older person is free to use more casual or familiar forms.

Language and Gender

Men and women use language differently. In conversation, men and women have different communication goals and follow different norms and conventions about what words to use and how they are supposed to behave (Tannen 2006). In other words, men and women, whatever language they speak, have different styles or varieties of speech. These gendered differences in language use are called ***genderlects***.

Men and women differ, for instance, in turn-taking in conversations. Conversation involves one person speaking while another listens, and then switching

honorifics Words or phrases that show respect and thus encode social status.

genderlects Varieties of speech associated with particular genders.

roles. While perhaps self-evident, it usually involves a silent space—but not necessarily—as one person can interrupt another, and there can be a conversational overlap where both interlocutors speak at the same time. While taking conversation turns is universal, how it is done is learned as we acquire proficiency with language, and is thus culturally relative (Stivers et al. 2009).

In an interesting study of the language used by contestants on the popular game show Jeopardy!, Thomas Linneman (2013) discovered that women use a rising, questioning intonation when making statements, known as a "high rising terminal" or ***uptalk***, twice as often as men. Uptalk has become common in North American speech, and Linneman found that men use uptalk more when surrounded by women contestants, and that the more successful men are, the less likely they are to use it. Women, on the other hand, use uptalk more the more successful they are. Linneman suggests that this difference is related to competitiveness and uncertainty, and that women use it as a way to compensate for their success. His study does demonstrate, however, that when people are interacting they are constantly in the process of constructing their genders.

In mixed conversations among North Americans, men tend to interrupt women more, take longer turns speaking, and leave shorter periods of silence between speakers than women. Women, on the other hand, are more likely to listen more and make more supportive minimal responses, such as saying "mm hm" or "uh huh," "yes," "really," and nodding the head. These minimal responses are a form of paralanguage that indicate the listener is actually listening and supporting what the speaker says and have little referential meaning. They are called ***backchannels*** and serve primarily a social function.

These differences between men and women in conversation were originally thought to reflect differences in power relationships between men and women, and are just one way men dominated women and women deferred to men (Zimmerman and West 1975; West 1979). More recent studies, however, have reached different conclusions. While numerous studies have shown that men do indeed interrupt women more, take longer turns speaking, leave shorter periods of silence, and engage in less backchannel communication, the differences can be attributed to a number of other factors besides gender, such as individual style, status, regional and ethnic differences, and the context of the conversation (Tannen 2012).

There are also questions about how interruptions are interpreted and what the intent of the interruption is. Deborah Tannen (2012) points out that taking conversational turns rests on two assumptions: "that speakers agree that conversational space should be filled with talk, and second, that speakers seek the floor. Thus the floor is seen as a prize to be won, and conversation is conceptualized as a competition for that prize, the speaker who gains the floor having won the competition" (Tannen 2012, 145). In other words, interruption has been characterized as intrusive and thus a competition in which the men win and dominate women, whereas the reality may be that the interruption is collaborative (Anderson and Leaper 1998).

Deborah Tannen (1990) argues that these differences should be seen more as different "subcultures" where men have been socialized differently in how to use language. She claims that women engage in "rapport talk" and men use "report talk." Rapport talk seeks to establish connections, negotiate relationships, and reach agreement. Women's speech tends to be cooperative, with women acknowledging one another's contributions and engaging in more active listening. Report talk, in contrast, is a male mode of discourse aimed at providing factual information; that is, it is a report. Report talk is more competitive, less social, more individualistic, and aimed at controlling the flow of talk. In cross-gender conversations, then, men may dominate the conversation but this does not mean they dominate women, as the goals of both men and women are both achieved (Table 6.1).

Julia Wood (1994) suggested that these basic speech differences between men and women in North America

TABLE 6.1

Gender Differences in Communication

Men	Women
report-talk	rapport-talk
converse to establish status and power	converse to establish relationships
emphasize independence	build consensus
competitive	cooperative
focus on facts	focus on feelings
talk for information	talk for interaction
focus on solutions	ask questions
interrupt more	overlap more
talk more	listen more
shorter silent gaps	longer silent gaps
avoid eye contact	use eye contact

uptalk The use of a rising, questioning intonation when making statements.

backchannels Minimal responses to a speaker that serve to continue the conversation or to show agreement.

CROSS-CULTURAL MISCUE

At a weekly cross-cultural banking meeting between two Americans and two Japanese, office manager Claire felt she was being bullied by Vice President Mr. Tanaka. Every time Claire began to speak on her topic of the new distribution of the filling system across divisions, Tanaka would ask her questions usually beginning with "How 'bout..." and "Couldn't you...." This derailed her presentation and took away her right to speak, reducing her to simply answering his questions. Claire viewed this as Japanese male chauvinism. What Claire did not understand, however, was that Tanaka was operating under Japanese communication strategies. She was lower in rank than Tanaka, who felt obliged to assume "the 'responsible' role of carrying the burden of talk" even though Claire was more familiar with the topic. Tanaka would have behaved the same toward a subordinate man. Thus, the issue was not about gender but rank (Yamada 1997, 102–103).

Source: Yamada, Haru. 1997. *Different Games, Different Rules: Why Americans and Japanese Misunderstand Each Other.* New York: Oxford University Press.

result, at least in part, from the childhood games that girls and boys play. On one hand, girls tend to play games that are cooperative, collaborative, and inclusive. There is little incentive to outdo others and there is a strong inclination to be sensitive to others' feelings. Boys, on the other hand, are expected to assert themselves, establish their leadership, and win. By focusing on outcomes, boys' games encourage participants to solve problems, achieve goals, and generally "make things happen." Because of these differences in childhood games and socialization, Wood finds that women talk for the purpose of building and supplementing rapport with others, but men talk to assert themselves; women use self-disclosure as a way of learning about others, but men tend to avoid self-disclosure; women's discourse strives for equality in social relationships, but men's discourse attempts to establish status and power; women often match their experiences with others for the sake of showing understanding and empathy ("I know how you feel"), but men match experiences for the sake of gaining attention ("I can top that"); and finally, women show their support by expressing their understanding, whereas men show their support by giving advice or trying to solve a problem.

These differences in linguistic style between men and women have important implications for everyday interactions. New studies demonstrate that how men and women communicate, even with a mobile phone, shows gender differences that may be cultural. Naomi Baron and her undergraduate research assistant, Elise Campbell (Baron and Campbell 2012), identified gender patterns in a cross-national study of mobile phone use by university students in Sweden, the United States, Italy, Japan, and Korea. Their research indicates "females send more and/or longer texts, or are more likely to use texting, than males." Women's texts also tend to be longer, with more emotional content and more emoticons, while men's texts tend to be short one-sentence messages of a more practical nature. To be certain, any number of important applied uses may be derived from the outcomes of this kind of research, especially for future users and developers of technology, business, and the marketing of products. For example, Apple anticipates the iPad will go gender neutral in the near future and become the global shopping tool for both men and women.

When Is a Language a Language?

Although there is no definitive answer to the question of when a language is a language, one criterion is ***mutual intelligibility***, that is, when speakers readily understand each other. Mutual intelligibility, however, is a matter of degree. For instance, most Americans have little difficulty understanding Canadians and vice-versa, but when Canadians use the following words most Americans have little idea what they mean, or have a different idea of what they mean: mickey, toque, Freezies, donair, pencil crayon, homo milk, Pablum, parkade, Robertson screwdriver, hooped (Hopper 2013b). The word football is another good example; it means different things to Canadians and Americans than to the British. There is no level of intelligibility where one can draw the line between one language and another, although linguists estimate there are roughly 7000 languages spoken in the world today (Ethnologue 2016).

Dialect Continuum

The issue is complicated by a phenomenon known as a ***dialect continuum***. A dialect continuum consists of a chain of neighbouring areas across a wide geographic region where the slight differences in speech between people in adjacent areas are not enough to make them mutually unintelligible; but at opposite ends of the continuum, people's speech is so different that they cannot understand each other. There is thus a continuum of mutually intelligibility where slight differences accumulate so that, at the ends, there are essentially two different mutually unintelligible languages. In other

mutual intelligibility When speakers can readily understand each other, they speak the same language.

dialect continuum A chain of speech variants that are mutually intelligible between adjacent geographic areas, but the ends are mutually unintelligible.

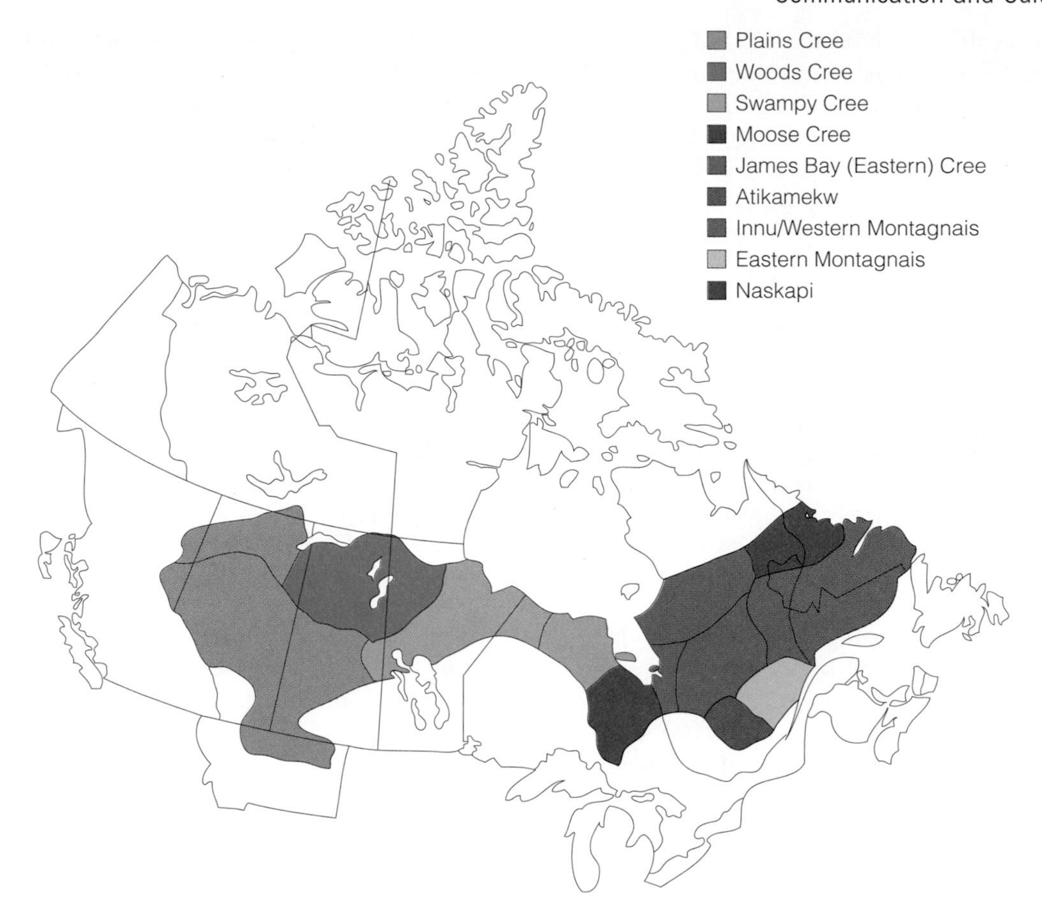

FIGURE 6.11 **The Cree language has the greatest number of speakers of any First Nation language spoken in Canada. A dialect continuum stretches across the country from Labrador to Northern British Columbia. While speakers of Naskapi and Eastern Montagnais dialects would have little difficulty understanding each other, speakers of Naskapi and Plains Cree would.**

Source: Brock University Map Library. Canada (no names). [PDF]. Software Edition. St.Catharines, ON: Brock University Map Library. 2004.

words, one language gradually blends into another over a large geographic area (Figure 6.11). For example, one dialect continuum runs from Portuguese spoken in southern Portugal to Spanish spoken in northern Spain, to French, to Italian, and finally to Romansch spoken in Switzerland (Chambers and Trudgill 1998). Another example is found among the Straits Salishan originally spoken around Juan de Fuca strait. The continuum stretches from Washington State, across to Vancouver Island, and to mainland British Columbia (Montler 1999).

Lingua Francas, Pidgins, Creoles, Mixed Languages, Invented Languages

When speakers are unable to understand one another, they may resort to a third language, a ***lingua franca***, to communicate. English is perhaps the best known lingua franca as it is the language of international business, science, and government. Commercial airline pilots and controllers, for instance, although they may speak any native tongue, use English as a lingua franca. In fact, being able to read, write, and speak English is a job requirement. In the past, where no lingua franca existed but where communication was necessary, such as for trade or colonization, people often resorted to a type of language known as a ***pidgin***, which, with continued interaction over time, may become a lingua franca. Pidgins are built from words from the mother tongues of the speakers and have a basic vocabulary and simplified grammar (R. A. Hall 1966; Morris 2012). They are not spoken by anyone as a native language but are learned as a second language and develop over time simply as a means of communication where no common communication language exists, and usually for limited purposes such as trade.

Where people learn the pidgin language as a mother tongue with a larger vocabulary and fully developed grammatical system which serves many functions, it becomes a ***creole*** language. One of the

lingua franca A common language that people use to communicate when they do not share same native or first language.

pidgin A simplified language used as a means of communication.

creole A pidgin that has become a mother tongue or native language.

most studied creoles is Tok Pisin (Talk Pidgin), spoken in Papua New Guinea. Tok Pisin grew out of a pidgin consisting of English and some of the regional languages when English traders and settlers interacted with the local people (Todd 1990). It is now considered a language of its own, with 122 000 (2004) native speakers (Ethnologue 2016). There is also some debate as to whether English is a creole. Bailey and Maroldt (1977) and Thomason and Kaufman (1988) ague that, when the French Normans, who spoke a Romance language, invaded Britain in 1066 they had to interact with the existing Saxon populace, who spoke a Germanic language. In order to do so, they developed a pidgin language with simplified lexicon and grammar, which eventually developed into modern English.

Chinook Jargon

Another example of a pidgin is Chinook Jargon, spoken in the Pacific Northwest of Canada and the United States. This area is home to many First Nations groups, who historically spoke about 100 different languages (Holton 2004). The language originally developed in order for these diverse groups to communicate and trade with one another (Lang 2008). Although many of the words are borrowed from Chinook—spoken near the mouth of the Columbia River—there are also words from Nuu-Chah-Nulth (Nootka) and other Indigenous languages. When European missionaries, trappers, and settlers moved into the area they also began to use the language, and Chinook Jargon not only picked up some English and French words but also its use increased and it spread further north and south (Lang 2008; Holton 2004). It was widely used by employees of the Hudson's Bay Company in Victoria, British Columbia and also by Franz Boas, who spoke the language to communicate with the people he studied. Several dictionaries were published to help settlers and, by one estimate, there were over 100 000 speakers by 1875 (Holton 2004, Lang 2008). But as the Indigenous population was overwhelmed by white settlers, the need to use it diminished, and because both the U.S. and Canadian governments prohibited children from speaking it at school, it faded from use, although it was still used in church services in British Columbia in the 1970s (Holton 2004). According to Ethnologue (2016) it is nearly extinct. The Confederated Tribes of the Grand Ronde Community of Oregon have programs to revitalize the language, as does the Canadian website chinookjargon.com. The words potlatch and skookum (meaning big, great, or excellent) come from Chinook Jargon.

Mixed Languages

In other contact situations two languages may fuse to form a ***mixed language***, with much of the vocabulary coming from one language and the grammar from another (Meakins 2013). A good example of a mixed language is Michif, the traditional language of Canada's Métis. Most of the nouns in Michif come from French, while the verbs and grammar come mostly from Cree or Ojibwe. It developed before the 1840s as a result of French fur-trading fathers living with mothers who spoke Cree, Ojibwe, or some other First Nation language (Bakker 1997). Originally, the children would have been bilingual, but over several generations their descendants began to express themselves in this new language and also to develop a separate ethnic identity. Today Michif is spoken by fewer than 1000 people, mostly elders, in Métis communities in Alberta, Saskatchewan, Manitoba, and Nunavut, as well as North Dakota (Bakker 1997). It is thus an endangered language and several groups are trying to revitalize it, including the Métis Youth British Columbia (MYBC) and the Métis Nation BC (MNBC) through their website, LearnMichif.com.

Invented Languages

Aside from lingua francas, pidgins, creoles, and mixed languages, people who speak different languages can also communicate using an invented or constructed language. Generally simpler than "natural" languages, there are more than 1000 known (Adams 2011) and they generally fall into two types. An ***international auxiliary language*** (IAL) is used for communication between people lacking a common language. Perhaps the best example is Esperanto, which was developed in the late 19th century by Polish physician L. L. Zamenhof. Zamenhof hoped Esperanto would become a universal language to facilitate world peace (Okrent 2009). Today there are over 100 magazines and thousands of books published in Esperanto; it is used widely on the Internet and, according to the Universal Esperanto Association (UEA 2016), there are several hundred thousand people who have a working knowledge of the language, and its use is growing.

The other type of constructed language is known as an ***artlang***, which, as the name suggests, is created for artistic purposes. To provide a sense of realism and plausibility, many novels, television shows, online games, and movies use artlangs, which are then learned by

mixed language A language that results from the fusion of two languages, in which the grammatical elements come from one and much of the vocabulary from the other.

international auxiliary language An invented language used for communication between people lacking a common language.

artlang A language created for artistic purposes to provide a sense of realism in novels, television shows, online games, and movies.

fans (Okrent 2009). Some examples include Dothraki from *Game of Thrones*, Na'vi spoken by the alien race in the 2009 film *Avatar*, Elvish used in Tolkein's *Lord of the Rings* (Adams 2011; Schreyer 2015), and Kryptonian invented by Canadian linguist Christine Schreyer for the 2013 Superman film *Man of Steel* (Schreyer 2016). The most sophisticated of these artlangs is Klingon (KLI 2016) from the *Star Trek* movies released in the 1980s. The producers used a professional linguist to create an authentic Klingon language, which has its own vocabulary, grammar, figures of speech, and even slang and regional dialects (KLI.org). Klingon is discussed in academic journals and some of Shakespeare's plays and Charles Dickens's *A Christmas Carol* have been translated into it. The Klingon Language Institute is a non-profit organization that "exists to facilitate the scholarly exploration of the Klingon language and culture" (www.kli.org/). Today there are even a few humans who speak Klingon fluently.

Speakers of these constructed languages are different from speakers of "natural" languages in that they tend to be geographically isolated and come from a wide variety of linguistic and cultural backgrounds, but unite to form an online speech community and only rarely get together physically. Schreyer (2015) used anthropological perspectives to survey speakers of Na'vi and discovered that, while they were fans of the movie *Avatar*, they were bigger fans of the language, which was what inspired them to learn it. It takes a big commitment to learn artlangs such as Na'vi, and Schreyer suggests that the ways fans learn it, such as meet-ups over Skype, email, chats, various apps, and the www.learnnavi.org website, can provide valuable ideas to Indigenous communities about how to revitalize their language. She also suggests that these online language communities can offer insights into how new languages work and develop, and how people learn languages. Schreyer discovered that learning Na'vi not only gave speakers a sense of shared community and identity, but also that they were developing social norms and values about the way Na'vi is spoken, which could be valuable for anthropologists in understanding the role of language in culture.

Dialects and Accents

Different groups within a society may also speak slightly different variations of the same language. These differences can be a combination of vocabulary, grammar, and pronunciation, and can be spoken by people from different social classes, ethnic groups, or geographic regions. They constitute a particular pattern of speaking called a ***dialect***. One of these variants often forms the ***standard language***. Standard languages are often the polite form of language spoken by the upper classes in a society, such as with Standard English (SE) spoken in Britain, which is sometimes referred to as "the Queen's English" or "BBC English." In general, the standard language, while not official, is the variety of language spoken in government, business, education, the media, or in public in general.

Standard Canadian English (SCE) is a combination of British English and American English. In Canada there is little difference in speech between people living in Ontario through to those living in British Columbia and forms the basis of SCE. The English spoken in Quebec and the Atlantic provinces, however, differs from it slightly.

French spoken in Canada also has different varieties, depending on where it is spoken. The French spoken in the Maritime Provinces (Acadian French) is different from the Québécois French spoken in Quebec, which forms standard French Canadian. Acadia and Quebec were historically distinct from each other and both evolved from the French colonists to New France, and were influenced by English in different ways and at different times. Both are different from the French spoken in France.

One characteristic of the standard language is that it is spoken with a particular ***accent***. Accent simply refers to the manner of pronunciation of nouns and verbs. It can characterize individuals, regions, countries, social classes, ethnicities, or other social divisions. The standard accent is called the ***received pronunciation*** and is the variant that tends to have the most prestige. As it is the standard, it also often considered to be "accentless" or the "correct" form.

No language, or variant of a language, is better than any other, although those who speak the standard language with the received pronunciation are usually the ones with power and are perceived as being educated. It is the form that receives government and institutional support. Other variants are often looked down upon and have been used as a means of discrimination. Such claims are, however, based on social or political rather than linguistic grounds. That is, minority dialects are often assigned an inferior status by the majority for the purpose of maintaining the political, economic, and social subordination of the minority. One example is Newfoundland English spoken in Newfoundland and Labrador, which differs significantly from SCE. For example, speakers of Newfoundland English will say *me mudder* and *me fadder*, and *b'y*, whereas SCE speakers will use "my mother" and "my father," and "boy." This way of speaking is often seen as "backward" and made of fun of in so-called "Newfie" jokes. The different accent

---

dialect A regional or class variation of a language.

standard language The variety of language spoken in public that receives the most institutional support.

accent The manner of pronouncing words.

received pronunciation The accent of the standard language.

and grammar, however, is a result of English fishermen from Cornwall, Devon, Dorset, and Somerset settling in Newfoundland in the early 1600s, and later immigrants from Ireland and Scotland, whereas most of the rest of English-speaking Canada was settled from other areas of England (Kirwin et al. 1990). In other words, a Newfoundlander accent is not backward or inferior to SCE, just different.

Another example of linguistic discrimination is found in the majority attitudes toward the dialect used by many African Americans in the United States, known as African American Vernacular English (AAVE), Black English, or Ebonics. Clearly such expressions as "You be goin' home," "Don't nobody go nowhere," "chil'ren," "learn me," "drownded," and so on will never be used by major network newscasters, in business, formal education, or government. Although such expressions are often considered to be inferior by speakers of Standard American English (SAE), these forms demonstrate logically consistent grammatical patterns and in no way prevent the expression of complex or abstract ideas. AAVE should not be viewed as simply a series of haphazard mistakes in SAE. Rather, it is a fully efficient language with its own unique set of grammatical rules that are applied consistently (Hecht et al. 1993; Rickford 1999). In other words, AAVE, while perhaps not conducive to success in the world of business, government, or media, is entirely appropriate among friends and family and in more informal contexts (McClendon 2004).

CROSS-CULTURAL MISCUE

When Juliette Giannesini moved to Ottawa from France, she was unsure how to address her French-speaking colleagues. French has two forms of the second person pronoun "you": *vous*, which is the polite and formal form, and *tu*, the informal or familiar form. This is common in many other languages as well. Her colleagues thought she was being a snob when she referred to them with *vous* when she was really just trying to be polite and respectful. Québécois French rarely use *vous*, preferring the informal *tu*. Giannesini quickly learned that, in Canada, people are far more informal than in France (Giannesini 2012). We might also ask how a Québécois would fare if they moved to France and used the more informal *tu*.

Source: Giannesini, Juliette (Zhu). 2012. "Three Faux Pas I (Must Have) Committed When I Came to Canada." Correr Es Mi Destino blog. Posted June 11, 2012.

Diglossia and Code Switching

A linguistic situation such as that where speakers can chose to speak either AAVE or SAE, is an example of ***diglossia***. Diglossia comes from the Greek words for "two" and "language," and refers to situations in which two languages (e.g., French and English) or varieties of the same language (such as standard form, dialect, or pidgin) are spoken by either the same person or community at different times or under different social circumstances.

One form is often associated with literacy, education, business, government, and, to some degree, religion, and is more prestigious, while the other form is associated with the marketplace, instructions given to subordinates, and conversations with friends and relatives, and has less prestige. Speakers familiar with both forms have to decide which form to use, depending on context. When speakers change the way they speak depending on the situation, they are ***code switching***. For many African Americans, being able to code switch is a survival skill, as being able to speak SAE is essential for getting a better education and a good job. At the same time, however, it is also essential to fit in with one's family and peers, and thus speak AAVE.

diglossia The situation in which two languages or forms of the same language are spoken by people in the same language community at different times and places.

code switching Speakers of two or more languages or varieties of one language switch between the two, depending on the social context.

Specialized Vocabularies

Code switching is seen quite dramatically in complex societies made up of a number of special interest groups, each with its own specialized vocabulary. Jean Lave and Etienne Wenger (1991) introduced the concept of "community of practice"—a group of people within a large society who interact regularly around specialized activities. They may be skateboarders, stockbrokers, prostitutes, politicians, truck drivers, or computer geeks. They may spend much time together, or they may have only limited contact with one another. Similarly, members of a community of practice may have contact with one another for decades, or their membership may be much more short-lived. From a linguistic perspective, however, these "communities" develop unique ways of communicating, complete with their own signature expressions.

Language, Nationalism, and Ethnic Identity

In most countries today, more than one language is spoken. India probably has the highest number of languages: the 2001 Census of India discovered 1635 mother tongues, of which 122 were spoken by

10 000 people or more (Government of India). Even in Canada, more than 200 languages were spoken as a home language or mother tongue in 2011 (Statistics Canada 2012c). Although Canada has two official languages (French and English), the country is becoming increasingly diversified linguistically as well as more bilingual. In 2011, 17.5 percent of the Canadian population reported speaking at least two languages at home. In Quebec, the proportion of the population who reported speaking only French at home decreased from 75.1 percent to 72.8 percent between 2006 and 2011. In the rest of Canada, the proportion of the population that reported speaking only English at home declined from 77.1 percent to 74.1 percent between 2006 and 2011. Most of these changes were due to an increase in the number of bilingual speakers as well as a large, increasingly multi-ethnic, immigrant population.

It should be recognized that language plays an important symbolic role in the development of national and ethnic identities. In some situations, powerful political leaders or factions attempt to suppress local languages for the sake of standardization across a nation-state. In other situations, attempts are made to revive a language as a means to galvanize political support for a national cause. And in still others, laws are passed to protect a language and promote its use.

When Tanzania became independent in the 1960s, its leaders were faced with the task of running a country that contained 120 mutually unintelligible languages. To administer a country with such linguistic diversity, the government adopted Swahili as the official national language. This meant that Swahili became the language of instruction in schools, government bureaucracies, and parliament. Although Swahili (an Arabicized Bantu language) is spoken by fewer than 15 million people as a first language, about 150 million people speak it as a second language (Irele and Jeyifo 2010). It has served as a unifying lingua franca for the many linguistic communities throughout Southeast Africa. To be certain, each linguistic group would have preferred to have had its own language declared the official language, but the adoption of Swahili early in Tanzania's history as a sovereign nation enabled the country to standardize its national language and get on with the business of nation building. Swahili is the official language in Tanzania, Kenya, Uganda, and the Democratic Republic of the Congo.

Irish Gaelic has been spoken in Ireland for centuries, but in the late 1500s it began to decline under English Tudor rulers, who viewed it as a threat to their authority and banned its use in government and education. Parents also discouraged its use as speaking Irish was stigmatized; success meant speaking English. By the mid-1800s only a small percentage of Irish people spoke it as a first or native language, most of whom lived in the more remote rural areas. As part of the move to expel the English, however, Irish nationalists saw Irish as an important part of Irish national identity and began to promote the language to counter the spread of English and as part of their effort to galvanize support for their cause. The southern counties of Ireland gained independence from Britain in 1922, and Irish Gaelic is today considered an important part of its heritage and culture. Irish is now the first official language in the Republic of Ireland and is recognized as a minority language in Northern Ireland. Although still spoken by a small percentage of people, considerable efforts are made to promote its use in schools and elsewhere in the country.

Perhaps the best place to look at the relationship between language, identity, and politics is in Canada. In the 1960s and early 1970s, Quebec's Anglophones were perceived as "the oppressors" (Scowen 2007), and there was considerable concern for the future of French language and culture as birth rates declined and immigrants chose to learn English instead of French (Centre for Constitutional Studies 2013). To strengthen the French language and counter the attraction of English, the Quebec government passed Bill 101. *La charte de la langue française* (Charter of the French Language) in 1977 (Scowen 2007). Since then it has been amended several times to reinforce its provisions. Its intention, as stated in the preamble, is to make French "the language of government and the law as well as the normal everyday language of work, instruction, communication, commerce and business." To accomplish this task it places numerous restrictions on the use of English and promotes the use of French. The First article of Bill 101 declares French the official language of Quebec. Although under the Canadian Constitution, court services must also be available in English, all other government administration and health and social services are provided in French. With a few exceptions, all instruction from elementary school through high school must be in French, although learning English as a second language is mandatory from grade one on. French must also be spoken in organizations with 50 or more employees. Labels on consumer products as well as manuals, warranties, instructions, brochures, catalogues, and software must be in French, as well as menus in restaurants. Other languages may be used but cannot be more prominent than French. With a few exceptions, bilingual signs must give prominence to French, and company names must also be in French unless an exemption is granted.

Feeling that their rights had been limited, and that they were being discriminated against, initial reaction to the Bill by many within the Quebec Anglophone community was to leave the province. Although many people within Quebec support the Bill, it has also been resented and ridiculed by both French and English speakers in Quebec. L'Office québécois de la langue

THE CANADIAN PRESS/Graham Hughes

FIGURE 6.12 L'Office québécois de la langue française warned Massimo Lecas, co-owner of Buonanotte restaurant, that there is too much Italian on the menu of his Italian restaurant.

française (OQLF) was created to promote the use of French in everyday use and to see that organizations comply with the terms of Bill 101. The OQLF has been accused of being overzealous in their enforcement and referred to as the "Language police."

In February 2013, a OQLF inspector sent a letter to the owner of Buonanotte, a fashionable Italian restaurant in Montreal, informing him that words such as "pasta," "calamari," "pesce," and "minestrone" on the menu had to be translated into the French equivalents (*pâtes alimentaires, calmar, poisson, soupe aux legumes*) (Figure 6.12). Rather than comply, he went public. Dubbed "Pastagate" by the media, the incident was reported in 350 articles in 14 countries and caused other restaurants to also break the silence (Wyatt 2013). Caffe Conti was told to delete the extra "f" in Caffe, thus forcing it to change its wine glasses engraved with its name; Montreal brasserie Holder was asked to tape over the on/off switch on the microwave, and Joe Beef was told to remove a wall memento from a Prince Edward Island beach that says "exit" (Hamilton 2013). Not only was the OQLF accused of abusing its powers, but also many francophone Quebecers came to realize that strict enforcement of the language law has made the province look ridiculous not only in the rest of Canada but also in the rest of the world (Hamilton 2013).

Endangered Languages

With or without the help of the OQLF, Quebecois French is unlikely to disappear any time soon. As we saw in the initial case study, many First Nations languages are endangered, and many more have disappeared. But they are not the only ones. The 19th edition of *Ethnologue* (2016), which is a catalogue of the world's languages, defines an ***endangered language*** as "a language that is at risk of no longer being used by the younger generation." Generally, but not always, endangered languages are spoken by a relatively few and decreasing number of elders in minority and often marginalized ethnic groups. According to the Endangered Languages Project (2016), there are 74 endangered languages in Canada, almost all of which are Indigenous languages. When the last known speaker of a language dies, it becomes an ***extinct language***. *Ethnologue* estimates that in 2016 there were 7097 living languages worldwide, but that by the end of this century more than half will have become extinct (Simons 2016). That's roughly one every week.

Languages fail to be spoken for a variety of reasons. When people move away from their community or marry someone who does not speak their language, there may be little opportunity to speak it or little incentive to pass it on to their children. Often speakers see little value in maintaining their language when other languages, such as English, Spanish, Russian, Chinese, Indonesian, Arabic, or Hindi, are more widely spoken in the area. When their native tongue is not taught at school or spoken in the playground, when there are no radio, television, movies, newspapers, books, or music produced in their language, or when the language of business and government is not theirs, the prestige and opportunities that come from joining the mainstream language community are very alluring. This is especially true if their language is looked down upon.

In other cases there is overt political pressure for communities to give up their language in favour of the dominant one. We saw this with First Nations languages and Residential Schools, but it is also happening elsewhere. Between 1896 and 1986 for example, it was illegal to speak Hawaiian in public schools in Hawaii (Thurman 2015). And until 2002, Turkish law prohibited the production of Kurdish language newspapers and radio and television shows, and it was illegal to formally teach Kurdish in schools, even though Kurdish is the second most widely spoken language after Turkish (Aslan 2014; Human Rights Organization 1999). Although the situation has improved in Turkey, Kurdish is still prohibited in Syria.

As noted in the opening case study, a community loses much of its history and cultural identity when it loses its language. Anthony Woodbury (n.d.) provides a good description of the importance of language to a community, and what the community loses when its language disappears:

> "Much of the cultural, spiritual, and intellectual life of a people is experienced through language. This ranges from prayers, myths, ceremonies, poetry, oratory, and technical vocabulary to everyday greetings,

endangered language A language that is at risk of disappearing because it is not being used by the younger generation.

extinct language A language of which the last known speaker has died.

leave-takings, conversational styles, humor, ways of speaking to children, and terms for habits, behaviors, and emotions. When a language is lost, all of this must be refashioned in the new language—with different words, sounds, and grammar—if it is to be kept at all. Frequently traditions are abruptly lost in the process and replaced by the cultural habits of the more powerful group. For these reasons, among others, it is often very important to the community itself that its language survive."

Unfortunately, preserving linguistic diversity does not seem to be as important as preserving biodiversity, although it should. When a language disappears we also lose an opportunity to understand the different ways the human mind works and how different people think, perceive the world, and experience life.

The loss of their language is one of the major social issues facing Indigenous groups worldwide. Fortunately, there are a number of programs and organizations that, in collaboration with linguists, anthropologists, and native speakers, are devoted to promoting this cultural and linguistic diversity (see Table 6.2). Not only do these organizations host seminars, workshops, and conferences, but also they all work to preserve, maintain, and revitalize endangered languages by recording, documenting, and teaching them. About two-thirds of the world's languages lack a written form (Eveleth 2014), and so many of these organizations are engaged in developing grammars and dictionaries. Technological advances have made these tasks easier and cheaper, and have involved creating and hosting online texts and grammars, talking dictionaries, as well as other innovative methods such as contests for the best short film in the language, YouTube videos, and smartphone apps (Anderson 2014). One team of translators is translating movies and even Korean television soap operas into Udmurt, a language spoken by 350 000 people in Russia (Eveleth 2014).

Since 1991, independent Canadian anthropologist and linguist Ian Mackenzie has made semi-annual field trips to live among the Penans, a hunting and gathering people who live in Borneo. Mackenzie works with the Penan to record and preserve their language and culture, both of which are endangered. Mackenzie records, in Penan, myths, oral history, and ethnobotany, and has created a dictionary and grammar of Penan, which has about 10 000 speakers, and which is available to Penan speakers on his website (www.rimba.com/penindexf/penindexhapenan.html), along with the first volume of memoirs by a Penan elder. Mackenzie's work was featured in the 2008 film *The Last Nomads*, which records how the Penan have been forced to abandon their nomadic lifestyle and take up farming. The film won the grand prize at the 2008 Banff Mountain Film Festival.

These efforts have had varying degrees of success. Some languages have been revived and even thrive; Irish, Cymraeg (spoken in Wales), Saami (spoken in Sweden, Norway, and Finland and on the Kola Peninsula in Russia), Marrithiyel (spoken in Australia),

TABLE 6.2

Endangered Language Organizations and Programs

Organization	Program	Website
The Long Now Foundation	Rosetta Project	http://rosettaproject.org/
Cambridge Endangered Languages and Cultures Group	Hosts seminars, workshops and conferences	http://groups.ds.cam.ac.uk/celc/
The Living Tongues Institute for Endangered Languages and National Geographic	Enduring Voices	http://livingtongues.org/ http://travel.nationalgeographic.com/travel/enduring-voices/
The Alliance for Linguistic Diversity	Endangered Languages Project[a]	www.endangeredlanguages.com
The Endangered Language Alliance	Arts and culture, outreach and education, language documentation, and revitalization programs	http://elalliance.org
Ethnologue	Languages of the World	www.ethnologue.com
UNESCO	Atlas of the World's Languages in Danger	www.unesco.org/languages-atlas/index.php?hl=en&page=atlasmap&cc2=CA
The Foundation for Endangered Languages	Conferences	www.ogmios.org/index.php
The Foundation for Endangered Languages (FEL) Canada	Indigenous Language Revitalization Program	www.felcanada.org/

[a] *See also* www.endangeredlanguages.com/#/3/22.831/-1.253/0/100000/0/low/mid/high/unknown

Hawaiian, Maori (spoken in New Zealand), and Wôpanâak (spoken in Massachusetts) are a few examples (Thurman 2015). Perhaps the best success story is that of Modern Hebrew, which was on the verge of extinction in the late 19th and early 20th centuries, but is now the mother tongue of 4 million people in Israel (Thurman 2015).

While it may seem obvious, the real key to maintaining or reviving a language is to speak it. The more it is used in everyday life, including such things as texting in the language, the more likely it is to survive. But what is crucial is that speakers see the value in preserving their language and that they pass it on to their children by speaking it at home. If the children do not learn the language it is much more likely to become extinct.

How Language Influences Culture

Another major concern of linguistic anthropology since the 1930s has been whether language influences or perhaps even determines our thoughts and perceptions about the world. Edward Sapir (1929, 209) stated this notion in its most explicit form:

> "Human beings do not live in the objective world alone, nor alone in the world of social activity as ordinarily understood, but are very much at the mercy of the particular language which has become the medium of expression for their society. It is quite an illusion to imagine that one adjusts to reality essentially without the use of language and that language is merely an incidental means of solving specific problems of communication and reflection. The fact of the matter is that the "real world" is to a large extent unconsciously built up on the language habits of the group. No two languages are ever sufficiently similar to be considered as representing the same social reality. The worlds in which different societies live are distinct worlds, not merely the same world."*

The Sapir–Whorf Hypothesis

Drawing on Sapir's original formulation, Benjamin Lee Whorf, a student of Sapir's, extended this idea and argued that, since language influences thoughts and perception, it must also influence behaviour. Whorf noticed that workers often threw cigarette butts and matches into "empty" gasoline drums—a potentially explosive behaviour since the drums still contained vapours and invisible traces of gasoline. Whorf concluded that the men's behaviour resulted from the interpretation, or rather misinterpretation, of the word "empty" (Whorf 1941).

Whorf also conducted ethnolinguistic research among the Hopi of Arizona to determine whether different linguistic structures produced different ways of viewing the world. The Hopi language stresses the intensity, cyclicity, duration, and continuity of events, whereas English stresses boundaries. For instance, English speakers use the word "morning" to define a particular time of day and can speak of a period of 10 days, whereas the Hopi word for morning means "while morning phase is occurring," and 10 days is conceived of as a continuous stream. Whorf hypothesized that this difference influenced their understanding and experience of the world (Whorf 1941). Both Sapir and Whorf were suggesting that language is more than a vehicle for communication; it actually establishes mental categories that predispose people to see and experience things in a certain way and thus behave in a particular fashion. In other words, language is a causal variable in the development of culture. This notion has come to be known as the ***Sapir–Whorf hypothesis***.

Sapir and Whorf suggested that both perception and the resulting behaviour are determined (or at least influenced) by the linguistic categories we use to group some things under. For example, in English and French the single word "uncle" refers to my mother's brother, my father's brother, my mother's sister's husband, and my father's sister's husband. It is likely that I will perceive all these family members as genealogically equivalent, and consequently will behave toward them in essentially the same way. Speakers of Mandarin Chinese, however, must decide whether reference is to their mother's brother or their father's brother, whether it is an uncle by birth or by marriage, and whether the person is older or younger than their mother or father. In other words, Mandarin requires its speakers to think in different ways about their relatives than speakers of English or French, and thus are also likely to behave differently toward them (Chen 2012).

Later scholars focused on two main ideas: first, a theory of linguistic determinism that states that the language you speak *determines* the way you perceive the world around you. Most scholars make a distinction between strong determinism, in which language actually determines thought, and weak determinism, where language simply influences thought. The strong determinism is universally rejected, while the weak form, while accepted by many, remains controversial.

*Sapir, Edward. 1929. Culture, Language, and Personality: Selected Essays, Edited by David G. Mandelbaum. Berekely: University of California Press.

Sapir–Whorf hypothesis The notion that a person's language shapes her or his perceptions and view of the world, and consequently their behaviour.

The second idea is a theory of linguistic relativism that states that each language classifies the world in its own unique or culturally relative way. For instance, the colour spectrum is simply a continuum of wavelengths of light visible to the human eye, yet different languages divide up this spectrum differently. English, for instance, divides the colour spectrum into 11 basic colour terms (black, white, red, green, yellow, blue, brown, purple, pink, orange, and grey), whereas Jalé, which is found in the highlands of Papua New Guinea, has only two, and Tiv, spoken in Nigeria, has three (Berlin and Kay 1969). Just because the language divides up the spectrum differently does not necessarily mean that they perceive the colours differently. Lera Boroditsky reminds us, however, that just because "languages differ from one another in innumerable ways,... does not necessarily mean [people] think differently" (Boroditsky 2011).

Testing the Hypothesis

In a classic test of the Sapir–Whorf hypothesis, Carroll and Casagrande (1960) compared Navajo-speaking children with English-speaking children living on the same reservation. Navajo verbs stress the shape or form of objects, such as long and rigid versus long and flexible. Carroll and Casagrande reasoned that, if asked to choose which two objects went together from a set of three consisting of a yellow stick, a yellow rope, and a blue rope, the Navajo-speaking child would focus on the shape rather than the colour and choose the yellow rope and the blue rope. The English-speaking children, on the other hand, would chose according to colour, that is, the yellow stick and yellow rope. And indeed, this is what happened. The results seemed to support the hypothesis that grammatical differences influenced the way people categorize objects. Carroll and Casagrande also conducted the same test on English-speaking children from Boston, however, and discovered that they too categorized according to form. This suggested to them that the environment may also impact cognitive processes.

More recently, experiments have been conducted to define more accurately this relationship between language and perception. Boroditsky (2009) asks why the Scales of Justice and the Statue of Liberty are depicted as female (Figure 6.13). Indeed, all the virtues (faith, love, justice, liberty, peace, truth, courage, charity, and so on) are usually depicted as female. Could it be that, in Latin and the Romance languages (such as Italian, French,

FIGURE 6.13 Why are the Statue of Liberty, in New York City, and the Statue of Lady Justice, holding the scales of justice, female? Could it be that the virtues of "liberty" and "justice" are feminine nouns in Latin?

and Spanish), the nouns for the virtues are feminine? Boroditsky (2009) has demonstrated that grammatical gender can have significant effects on perception. In many languages, such as the Romance languages, nouns are classified as either masculine or feminine, which means that masculine and feminine nouns are treated differently grammatically. In these languages, speakers must use the proper gender-related pronouns, adjectives, and verb endings, depending on the gender of the noun. For example, in a language that designates the word *sofa* as masculine, to say "my sofa is old" requires that the words *my*, *is*, and *old* be used in their masculine forms to agree with the masculine noun.

In one of many studies, Boroditsky asked German and Spanish speakers to describe the characteristics of objects that have opposite gender assignments. To illustrate, she asked them to describe a key; the word for *key* is masculine in German and feminine in Spanish. In describing a key, German speakers used such words as *heavy*, *hard*, *jagged*, *metal*, and *serrated*; whereas Spanish speakers used such words as *lovely*, *intricate*, *golden*, *little*, *shiny*, and *tiny*. And, when asked to describe an expansion bridge, which is feminine in German and masculine in Spanish, German speakers used such descriptors as *beautiful*, *elegant*, *fragile*, *pretty*, and *slender*; whereas Spanish speakers used such words as *big*, *strong*, *dangerous*, *sturdy*, and *towering*. Boroditsky (2009, 116–129) concluded that "the seemingly arbitrary assignment of gender to a noun, can have an effect on people's ideas of concrete objects in the world." Her study adds to the growing body of evidence demonstrating a close relationship between grammatical structures in language and other aspects of culture, and that the linguistic categories not only

Could Your Language Affect Your Ability to Save Money?

Languages deal with time in two fundamental ways with respect to future-time reference (FTR). In strong-FTR, or "futured" languages such as English, future events are grammatically marked. For instance, in speaking about the weather, English speakers say "It rained yesterday," "It is raining today," and "It will rain tomorrow." In other words, English marks the past, present, and future by a change in verb tense. Other languages make finer distinctions, such as near or recent past and future, and still

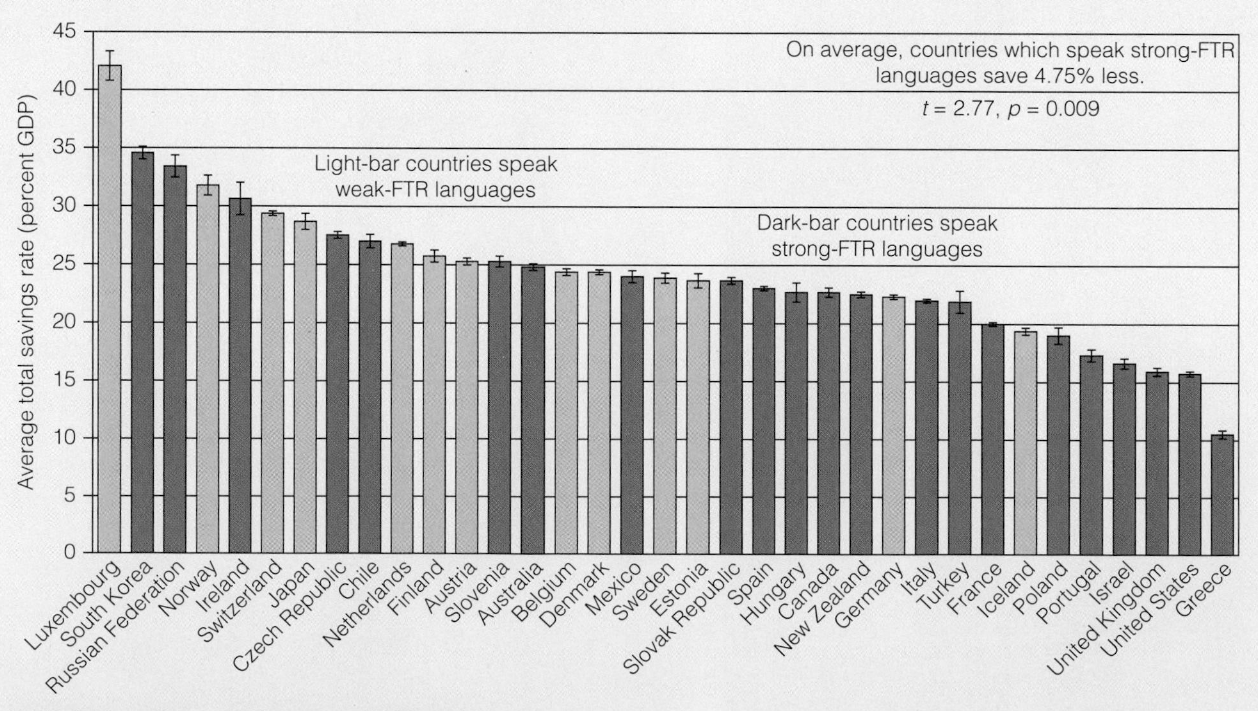

OECD Savings Rates and Language, 1985–2010

Source: From Chen, M. Keith. 2013. "The Effect of Language on Economic Behavior: Evidence from Savings Rates, Health Behaviors, and Retirement Assets". American Economic Review 2013, 103(2): 690–731. (Chen 2013. p. 715). Based on OECD data: OECD Savings Rates and Language, 1985–2010.

influence our thoughts but are also reflected in the material world we create.

The power of language can also be seen in the way people use language to alter other people's perceptions of various things. For example, language can be used to mislead by making things appear better than they actually are. Large organizations, such as corporations and branches of the federal government, are particularly adept at using euphemisms—forms of language that conceal something unpleasant, bad, or inadequate. Corporate structures are *downsized, reengineered,* or *restructured.* And people seeking work in Canada no longer apply for *unemployment* insurance but *employment* insurance.

The problem with the Sapir–Whorf hypothesis—and the reason it remains a hypothesis rather than a widely accepted fact—is causation. Problems arise when attempting to demonstrate that language actually *determines* culture, or vice versa, in any definitive way. What does seem obvious, however, is that all people, being constantly bombarded with sensory stimuli, have developed filtering systems to bring order to all of these incoming sensations. Sapir, Whorf, and more recent scholars have suggested that language provides a set of lenses that highlight some perceptions and deemphasize others. Today, most scholars agree that language does influence perception in certain limited ways. We cannot conclude from this, however, that language forces or coerces people to have particular thoughts or perceptions, or prevents them from thinking in certain ways.

others, such as Chinese, have no tenses at all. In German, a weak-FTR or "futureless" language, speakers, in talking about the weather, say "*Gestern regnete es*" (yesterday it rains), "*Jetzt regnet es*" (now it rains), and "*Morgen regnet es*" (tomorrow it *rains*) (Chen 2013, 694).

Keith Chen, a behavioural economist, wondered whether the way one's language deals grammatically with time influenced how one thought about time, and in particular whether it influenced one's behaviour. He hypothesized that grammatically separating the future and the present makes the future seem more distant for speakers of futured languages. He further hypothesized that this would lead people to think less about the consequences of their present behaviour, and thus "take fewer future-oriented actions" (2013, 691) such as saving, exercising, practising safe sex, or abstaining from smoking. In weak-FTR, or futureless languages, however, he argues that the future appears closer, and thus people are more likely to be concerned for their future and thus exercise, do not smoke, use condoms, and save.

In a statistical comparison of a large number of countries, he found a strong correlation between savings rate and language spoken. Speakers of futureless languages, it appears, save more, as measured by savings rate as a percentage of GDP, than speakers of futured languages. Germans, for instance save 10 percentage points more than the British (Chen 2012).

This could, however, have been due to other cultural or political differences not related to language. What Chen wanted to do was "to determine if differences in language *cause* these differences in behavior" (Chen 2013, 691). To do this he needed to control for some of these other variables, and so found multilingual countries where one of the languages spoken was futured and the other futureless. For instance, in Belgium people speak either French, a futured language, or Dutch, a futureless language, as their mother tongue. He discovered similar situations in Burkina Faso, Ethiopia, Estonia, The Democratic Republic of Congo, Nigeria, Malaysia, Singapore, and Switzerland (2013, 691). Based on data from five international surveys that measured such things as health, ageing, retirement practices, and income, he then matched people in these countries according to race, sex, religion, age, education, marital status income, number of children amongst others. Essentially then, individuals were matched who were born and raised in the same country (and presumably the same culture) and were identical on all these dimensions, except for speaking a future or futureless language.

After controlling for such variables, he discovered that saving rates do appear to be influenced by one's language. Speakers of futured languages do save less than speakers of futureless languages. Moreover, they also smoke more, save less, exercise less, plan less, and over-consume. They tend to have less wealth at retirement and also to be more obese (Chen 2012).

Keith Chen's research seems to lend support to the Sapir–Whorf hypothesis: that language affects how one thinks and consequently how one behaves. The issues he raises are important concerns for governments, who generally are more prosperous when their people save more and are healthy.

Questions for Further Thought

1. How can speakers of future languages be encouraged to save?
2. While there seems to be a strong correlation between language and savings rate, correlation is not causation. What might be some other explanations for the observation? How else might you establish a causal relationship?
3. Chen's research assumes that, because people live in the same country, they share the same culture although speaking different languages. To what extent is this true?
4. How would you research the alternative hypothesis that, because futured languages make a distinction between past, present, and future, speakers are *more* likely to think about the future than speakers of futureless languages?
5. Can you think of an example in English that uses the present tense to reference a future time?

Communication and Technology in Today's World

Students today have learned that if they want to communicate with their grandparents, they phone; if they want to communicate with parents and professors, they email; and if they want to communicate with friends, they either text or go on Facebook. All these forms of communication are at the expense of face-to-face interaction. The revolution in information technology (IT) has had profound consequences on the way humans communicate today. It was not until the 1990s that the Internet and cellphones emerged as the communication technologies of choice. The first social network site was launched in 1997 (Boyd and Ellison 2008), and the number seems to have grown exponentially since then. And it was not until about 2010 that smart phones began to become ubiquitous. When viewed from this narrow time frame, the changes in the number of ways of communicating at our disposal today are truly revolutionary. Space limitations allow only a brief discussion of three closely related technologies and issues: texting, instant messaging, and social media.

Innovations in IT have revolutionized how information is delivered and how we produce and consume it. At the same time they have transformed our social lives and behaviours as citizens (Figure 6.14). A good example of this occurred in San Francisco in September 2013 when Justin Valdez, 20, a student at San Francisco State University, was shot in the back of his head by Nikhom Thephakaysone as he left the San Francisco light-rail train he was riding on. Security camera footage revealed that Thephakaysone had pulled out his gun numerous times, pointed at several passengers, and even wiped his nose with it. None of the other passengers noticed until he fired the gun because they were all too absorbed texting or reading on their cellphones (O'Connor 2013).

As the world becomes increasingly interconnected, information technology is having a profound effect on politics, economics, business, education, kinship, religion, social relationships, and indeed, on all the topics discussed in this textbook. And it is such a new phenomenon that anthropologists and other social scientists are only now beginning to explore the impact it is having, and also how to exploit it. There is a growing body of scholarship that looks at how issues of race, ethnicity, religion, gender, sexuality, and indeed identity, are affected by social network sites. Many questions remain, however, about who is and who is not using social networking sites and why. In particular there is little understanding about how the use of these sites is impacting the lives of people outside the West (Boyd and Ellison 2008). It means, of course, that there is a great deal of ethnographic research that needs to be done, and new methods to access this information are needed, especially since users of many of the sites number in the millions and are located all over the world.

Paul Souders/Getty Images

FIGURE 6.14 People absorbed with their smart phones on public transit such as these passengers in Shanghai, China, are becoming a common sight worldwide. The new technologies are changing the way we relate to others and to our surroundings.

Texting and Instant Messaging

When cellphones evolved from simply a speaking tool to also becoming a writing tool to send text, ***texting*** required multiple key strokes per character, messages were limited to only 160 characters, and people were charged by the word (Crystal 2008). To get around these space and cost restrictions, and to speed up conversations, people resorted to ignoring punctuation, grammar, and capitalization, abbreviating words, and using acronyms such as lol (laughing out loud), bff (best friends forever) brb (be right back) yolo (you only live once), and so on. Texting spread like wildfire, especially among adolescents. The use of text shortcuts, common expressions such as ok, yeah, like, cool, wow, and nope, as well as terms taboo in ordinary speech and writing (e.g., wtf), was seen as an informal, less dignified form of language associated with people of lower class and became known as ***Internet slang*** (Haas et al. 2011). Slang typically originates with youth and, by being up-to-date and using disrespectful forms, results in a subculture giving users a sense of common identity opposed to established authority (Haas et al. 2011). Until recently there was considerable concern by parents, teachers, and academics that texting and Internet slang were creating a generation of young

---

texting The use of cellphones to send text messages to another cellphone.

Internet slang The use of text shortcuts, common expressions, and taboo terms; viewed as a less dignified form of language.

people unable to write proper English (Thurlow 2006). In *Txtng: The gr8 db8,* David Crystal (2008) argues these fears are unfounded because students have to understand language first before they can start playing with it, that using abbreviations and acronyms is nothing new, and that very little Internet slang is used in written work. Since Crystal wrote his book, however, alphabetic keyboards on smartphones, as well as predictive text such as autocorrect, have made the issue less controversial (Haas et al. 2011), although it is a reminder that language continues to evolve. In a sense, texting can be looked at as another form of language and students need to be able to code switch. While it may be acceptable to use Internet slang when texting friends, it is better to use proper English on term papers, or when emailing teachers or professors.

Text messaging is widely used by young people in rural India as a way to circumvent the long-standing traditional barriers against premarital mingling. Young adults in rural India cannot flirt or "cruise for dates" at crowded bars or clubs. Unmarried women are expected to marry young, show no interest in men's flirtatious advances, and marry a person chosen for them by their families. And because most young adults in India live with their families and share rooms with siblings, they have few opportunities to speak privately with a member of the opposite sex. Text messaging offers young Indian singles a way to overcome their awkwardness and lack of experience in interacting with the opposite sex. In other words, singles are able to communicate in private without having to worry about either violating traditional customs or revealing intimate feelings.

Instant Messaging

Text messaging in North America, however, is in decline and being replaced by ***instant messaging*** (IM), which allows users to eliminate the costs associated with texting. Although similar to texting, instant messaging differs in that it is not simply a text message to a phone number, but is the real-time exchange of messages over the Internet, and much of it is to people who are anonymous. Examples include Facetime, Facebook Chat, iMessage, Skype, WhatsApp, and Twitter, all of which have been facilitated by the spread of smart phones. And data use is skyrocketing as more and more people use their smart phones to access the Internet. The network equipment manufacturing company Cisco Systems estimates that mobile data traffic will grow 10-fold from 2014 to 2019, a compound annual growth rate of 57 percent (Cisco Systems 2015). Instant messaging is changing our lives by allowing people to chat to anyone, anywhere, for free. It is also changing the way companies do business, from collaborating on projects between people on different continents, to holding Webinars (web conferences) and focus groups, to chatting with customers about their products and services.

quka / Shutterstock.com

FIGURE 6.15 Social media applications are democratizing the world by allowing people with common interests to connect with one another, wherever they may reside, and share information and images.

Social Media

Social media refers to Internet-based applications that allow users to create and share information and images. Typical applications include blogs (Blogger, Tumblr, Twitter), photo sharing sites (Flickr, Pinterest, Snapchat, Instagram), wikis (Wikipedia, Wikileaks), online role-playing games (Warcraft), virtual worlds (Secondlife .com), video sharing (Youtube.com), crowdsourcing (Kickstarter.com), consumer reviews (Yelp.com), question and answers (Answers.com), social networking (Facebook, LinkedIn, Google+), service sharing (Airbnb, Uber, Craigslist), dating sites (PlentyOfFish, eHarmony, Tinder), and many more (Figure 6.15). Some popular non-English sites include Mixi (Japan), Qzone (China), Renren (China), Sina Weibo (China), Sonico (Latin America), and VK (Russia).

These sites allow users to upload text, video, and audio files in what is known as ***user-generated content***. Many of them also allow individuals to interact with other users to receive, exchange, and share information and to establish relationships. Social media is thus substantially changing the ways in which we communicate and interact with family and friends, with various organizations and communities, as well as with businesses. They provide places where people can exchange information and ideas about their lives, local and world events, products and services, different places, and so. In short, they provide places where information *about everything* can be shared freely. They are democratizing

---

instant messaging The real-time exchange of messages over the Internet.

social media Internet-based applications that allow users to create and share information and images.

user-generated content Text, video, or audio material created and uploaded by users of social media websites.

the Internet. They also allow people with common interests, wherever they may reside, to connect with one another and build relationships as well as reputations. Because of this, social media has become an integral part of our lives and it is changing the way we think about things and the way we behave. In other words, social media is perhaps the most important agent of cultural change in the 21st century.

Social Media and Politics

A good example of the impact social media is having is its role in political change. It was a major organizing tool in the popular uprisings that occurred in many Arabic-speaking countries in the early 2010s. The Arab Spring, as it has become known, began in Tunisia in December 2010, when Mohammed Bouazizi, a poor fruit peddler, burned himself alive in protest over his inability to feed his family. The event was captured by a cellphone and uploaded to Facebook, where it went viral (Shearlaw 2016). The protests then spread to other countries, some of which were successful in overthrowing their existing regimes (Tunisia, Libya, Egypt), while others were not (Bahrain, Syria, Yemen). Social media sites such as Facebook, Twitter, Flickr, blogs, and others were used to report on events, warn people of police and military activities, spread information about medical requirements, coordinate demonstrations, and spread awareness about ongoing events to those involved as well as the rest of the world. As one Egyptian activist tweeted, "We use Facebook to schedule the protests, Twitter to coordinate, and YouTube to tell the world" (Shearlaw 2016). Governments, of course, attempted to block various sites, and in some cases even shut down the Internet entirely. While social media was not the cause of the uprisings, and there is considerable debate about the actual role it played, the Arab Spring does demonstrate how social media can be a powerful political tool.

Another example of the value of social media in coordinating protests is the Idle No More Movement, which began in late 2012 when several First Nations women from Saskatchewan decided they would be "Idle No More" and speak out against Bill C-45, which, among other things, contemplated changes to the *Indian Act*, the *Navigable Waters Protection Act*, the *Environmental Assessment Act*, and the *Fisheries Act* (Graveline 2012). Using Twitter they called on other First Nations people to also speak out and news quickly spread across Canada's Indigenous community through Twitter, Facebook, and other social media networks. Social Media was used to coordinate rallies in Winnipeg, Edmonton, and other major cities. Thousands of Canadians gathered on December 10, 2012, for a national day of action, although the Bill passed two days later. To date, the movement focuses on opposing resource exploitation, particularly on First Nations territory, and protecting water, air, and land resources.

Social Media and Education

Social media and IM are also having an impact on education—but not without controversy. Many high schools block popular social media websites, and some teachers and professors have banned cellphones and laptops from the classroom, seeing them as a distraction that interferes with teaching and learning. Despite these apprehensions, however, students are using social media and will increasingly do so. Many educators now realize that IM and social media applications can be valuable tools to be incorporated into the educational program. Most professors already use YouTube to show short relevant video clips, but others also assign video projects to be uploaded or to develop wikis. Google Docs and similar applications allow students to work collaboratively on group projects, and others allow students not only to connect with their classmates and organize study groups, but also to complete homework and assignments. Twitter and Facebook can be used to encourage students, particularly those who may be shy about discussing things in class, to voice their opinions. There are also other applications, such as Top Hat specifically designed for the classroom, where instructors can interact with students, test comprehension, and keep the class engaged. Social media is such a relatively new phenomenon that educators have only recently begun to tap into its potential.

Online learning is also being revolutionized by massive open online courses (MOOCs), the first of which was run by two instructors from Athabasca University in Alberta in 2008. Such courses allow several thousand students to participate simultaneously using web-based applications. Unlike other online courses, registration is open to anyone, the curriculum is only loosely structured, and learning is a collaborative effort using blogs and other interactive forums where the instructor is more of an observer and facilitator rather than an instructor (Masters 2011).

While social media provides unprecedented access to information, there is also a lot of misinformation, which can spread very quickly with little regard to accuracy or original source. Wikipedia articles, for instance, while they provide basic information on a topic, which for the most part is accurate, are written by unknown individuals, with unknown credentials and unknown motives. The articles are also constantly changing and often poorly referenced. Most professors thus instruct their students not to quote it on assignments.

Information Technology and Social Concerns

Social media sites also raise a number of other issues, including lack of face-to-face social skills, privacy, sexual harassment, cyberbullying, and their use by terrorists.

Sexting and Cyberbullying

A relatively new phenomenon that has arisen since the introduction of smart phones is the exchange of sexually explicit messages and photos, or ***sexting***. Sexting introduces a new element into personal relationships and, although it is not much of an issue between consenting adults, it can become an issue when relationships break down and the images and texts cease to be private. Sexting is also becoming increasingly common among minors, and has led to numerous charges of child pornography.

Unwanted sexting can also lead to ***cyberbullying***, which is the use of text messaging, IM, and social media to harass people and cause harm. In addition to unwanted sexting, cyberbullying can include anything from spreading rumours and gossip, to publishing defamatory materials, to posting and exchanging explicit sexual material without consent, and is a major social concern. Unlike "schoolyard" bullying, cyberbullying is much easier because it is easier to remain anonymous by using temporary email accounts, and pseudonyms on social media sites and instant messaging applications. The impact of cyberbullying on people's lives was highlighted by the suicide in April, 2013, of 17-year-old Rehtaeh Parsons of Dartmouth, Nova Scotia. When Rehtaeh was 15 she was allegedly raped by four teenage boys at a party while she was drunk. Soon after, photos of the incident were circulated among her peers and she was continuously harassed until she committed suicide 17 months later. Her mother blamed the boys for the rape and circulation of the photos, and the relentless bullying that lead to Rehtaeh's decision to kill herself. Her mother set up a Facebook memorial page for Rehtaeh, and her husband started a blog, both of which went viral and eventually led to the Nova Scotia government passing a law to protect people from cyberbullying (Jauregui 2013). An anti-cyberbullying law (Bill C-13) was passed by the Federal government in 2014 to combat online harassment by making it illegal to share "intimate images" of someone without their consent (Puzic 2015).

Privacy Concerns

The readily available information about individuals on social media sites has raised issues about privacy, especially among younger users who are more likely to post personal information. Many sites allow individuals to disclose not only their name but also information about their age and gender, where they live, who they are in relationships with, what their interests are, the activities they are engaged in, and even their personalities. Such information can easily be gathered and exploited without the user's knowledge or consent. Employers will sometimes screen prospective employees by checking their Facebook pages, or use it to delve into the personal lives of existing employees to find reasons for letting them go. A great deal of personal information can also be gathered electronically by various tracking software and used by police and governments to "spy" on their citizens, or by businesses to track consumer trends and provide targeted advertising. Personal information can of course also be exploited by dishonest individuals' intent on identity theft or financial gain. In June 2015 the Canadian government passed the Digital Privacy Act, which strengthens the Personal Information Protection and Electronic Documents Act to protect an individual's privacy more rigorously.

Terrorism

Social media sites and IM are also available to extremist groups such as al-Qaeda and the Islamic State (ISIS) who use it not only to coordinate activities, as was done by activists during the Arab Spring, but also to raise funds and to radicalize and recruit people. Aqsa Mahmood, for example, a British woman living in Syria, uses her blog to appeal to Western women to abandon their homes and families and join ISIS (Petrou 2015). In January 2015, four young men and two women left Canada headed to Syria to join ISIS after exploring ISIS on social media. Two were only 18 and 19 years old and four went to the Collège de Maisonneuve in Montreal (CTV News 2015).

The Digital Divide

More than anything else, the Internet and new cellphone technologies are providing access to information hitherto unavailable. Information about people, products, world events, science and technology, society and culture—in short, about everything. In today's world, however, there is a great ***digital divide*** between those who have access to these technologies and the skills to use them and those who do not. Having access to the digital world is now seen as an equally important component of a community's infrastructure as roads, water, and power; all of which are necessary for sustainable economic growth (McMahon 2014). Most of us rely on these technologies for work, for school, to obtain public services, and to participate online with others. People living in communities without access to this digital infrastructure are thus disadvantaged when it comes to employment, education, medical care, and a host of other services, as well as simply keeping in

---

sexting The exchange of sexually explicit messages and images between cellphones.

cyberbullying The use of text messaging, instant messaging, and social media to harass people and cause harm.

digital divide The differences between those who have access to information technologies and the skills use them and those who do not.

contact with one another. Those who lack access tend to be women, the poor, the uneducated, rural residents, and ethnic minorities.

A digital divide exists in Canada. Many First Nations and Inuit communities, particularly those in rural and remote areas, lack access to broadband services and are thus at an economic disadvantage compared to the rest of Canada. There are several reasons for this. Primarily it is because providing digital services to these communities is uneconomical. Commercial Internet service providers see little profit in building and maintaining infrastructure in these sparsely populated, remote communities, especially since most people living in them are also poor (McMahon et al. 2014). Another reason, however, is that Canada's national digital strategy, launched in 2014 and known as Digital Canada 150 (so named to coincide with Canada's 150th birthday in 2017), is a universal policy that lumps Indigenous and non-Indigenous broadband development needs together as simply "rural and remote," and does not consider the specific needs of Indigenous communities (McMahon and Smith 2010).

To successfully build and maintain an IT infrastructure requires not only qualified IT technicians, web-site developers to support local businesses and services, but also digitally literate people to operate water and power facilities, maintain local information databases, provide online healthcare, teach people Internet skills, and so on (Whiteduck 2010). Several researchers (Whiteduck 2010; McMahon et al. 2014; Bredin 2001) as well as First Nations leaders have argued that the digital infrastructure in Canada must involve these communities in its ownership, development, and management, and that policy must consider the specific economic, cultural, and social contexts and focus on individual community needs, rather than the needs of service providers or government (Whiteduck 2010; McMahon et al. 2014).

One successful model is the Aboriginal Peoples Television Network (APTN). According to the APTN website (http://aptn.ca/) it is "the first and only national Aboriginal broadcaster in the world, with programming by, for and about Aboriginal Peoples" (APTN 2016). Licensed in 1999, APTN gives Indigenous people control over local, regional, and national broadcasting, allowing them to provide culturally relevant radio and television programs (Bredin 2011). Another example is the Kuhkenah Network (K-Net) (Kuhkenah an Oji-Cree term for everyone, everywhere) (http://knet.ca/K-Net), which is based in Sioux Lookout, Ontario, and owned and operated by a tribal council whose members come from several First Nations in the area. Created in 1994 to link high-school students across a vast remote region of northwestern Ontario to provide them with an online bulletin board, email, computer training, and technical support (Bredin 2011), it now offers broadband services, cellular service, and online applications to these communities (McMahon et al. 2014). K-Net provides content that meets the specific social, economic, and cultural needs of their communities. The organization also works with institutions such Confederation College and Brock University to develop and deliver distance education applications (McMahon et al. 2014).

Summary

1. Communication involves the transmission of information and knowledge through either language or some nonverbal system of meaning. Communication constitutes the core of culture and is integral to the human condition. The form and meaning of communication is influenced by context, which means it is the key to understanding another culture. Today, the Internet, mass media, and new technologies, combined with international travel, migration, and global marketing, are changing the way we communicate but also increasing the opportunities for misunderstandings.
2. Language is a symbolic system of arbitrary sounds that, when put together according to a certain set of rules, conveys meanings to its speakers.
3. Biological anthropologists are concerned with how language developed and evolved, and the extent to which other primates are capable of it. Descriptive linguists are interested in the sound and meaning structure of languages; historical linguists with the historical development and relationships of languages; and sociolinguists with how people use language in a given situation or context.
4. The majority of human messages are sent and received without using words. Human nonverbal communication involves, among other forms, body language, hand gestures, facial expressions, the manner of speaking, the use of space, and touch. Like language, they are arbitrary, have to be learned, are culturally variable, and can lead to cross-cultural misunderstandings.
5. Nonverbal forms of communication are better than verbal forms in providing information about our emotional state as well as about how the words and phrases are to be interpreted.
6. In high-context cultures such as those in Asia, the Middle East, Africa, and South America, communication tends to be ambiguous, implicit, and inexact. In low-context cultures, such as in Canada,

people strive to communicate in a way that is precise, straightforward, and unambiguous.

7. The study of the relationship between language and social structure and how language is used in society is known as sociolinguistics. The language we use and the way we speak sends messages about who we are, where we are from, who we associate with, our social status, our character, and much more. The choices we make whenever we speak are influenced by our relationship to the person or people we are speaking with, as well as the context in which the conversation takes place. Forms of address and honorifics demonstrate relative social status.
8. Men and women use language differently. In mixed conversations among North Americans, men tend to interrupt women more, take longer turns speaking, and leave shorter periods of silence between speakers than do women. These differences do not necessarily reflect differences in power relationships between men and women, but different conversational goals. Women engage in "rapport talk" to establish relationships, while men use "report talk" to provide information.
9. One criterion of when a language is a language is mutual intelligibility, but phenomena such as a dialect continuum make it hard in some cases to know where one language ends and another begins.
10. When people do not share the same native or first language, they may use a lingua franca to communicate. If none exists they may use a simplified form of language known as pidgin to communicate. When a pidgin becomes a mother tongue it is known as a creole. A mixed language occurs when the grammatical elements come from one language and the vocabulary from another. Languages to enable mutual understanding have also been invented: Esperanto is an example.
11. Different social groups may speak slightly different variations of the same language, known as a dialect. The variant spoken by people in government, education, business, and the mainstream media is called the standard language, which is also spoken with a particular pronunciation. Other varieties are often viewed as primitive or backward, and those who speak them are often at a social disadvantage.
12. A linguistic situation in which speakers can chose to speak either one language, or variety of a language, or another is called diglossia. Speakers must learn to code switch depending on the context.
13. Language plays an important symbolic role in the development of national and ethnic identities. Quebec's Bill 101 is a good example of this.
14. According to the Sapir–Whorf hypothesis, language influences perception and consequently behaviour. Language, according to Sapir and Whorf, not only is a system of communicating but also establishes mental categories that affect the way in which people conceptualize the real world.
15. The development of the Internet and cellphones has had a profound effect on how humans communicate, which in turn has impacted all aspects of culture. Texting, instant messaging, and social media allow users to receive, exchange, and share information and to establish relationships. These new applications have been used to change political regimes, such as with the Arab Spring, and they are also impacting education. They also raise concerns about privacy, cyberbullying, and their use by terrorists. There is a digital divide between those who have access to these technologies and those who do not, such as the poor, those living in remote areas, and many Indigenous groups, which puts them at an economic disadvantage.

Key Terms

accent
artlang
backchannels
code switching
communication
creole
cyberbullying
dialect
dialect continuum
digital divide
diglossia
endangered language
extinct language
facial expressions
genderlects
grammar
haptic communication
high-context cultures
honorifics
instant messaging
international auxiliary language
Internet slang
kinesics
language
lingua franca
linguistics
low-context cultures
mixed language
morpheme
mutual intelligibility
nonverbal communication
paralanguage
phoneme
pidgin
prosodic features
proxemics
received pronunciation
Sapir–Whorf hypothesis
sexting
social media
speech community
standard language
syntax
texting
uptalk
user-generated content

Critical Thinking Questions

1. How can linguistic anthropologists work with First Nations people to revitalize their languages? Can you think of any ways some of the new technologies may be used to help in this process?
2. What role have different power relationships played in the loss of Indigenous languages?
3. What cultural motives could there be for inventing a language?
4. How do you communicate with classmates whose first language is not the same as yours? How does this differ from the way you communicate with classmates whose first language is the same as yours?
5. How does language influence, or how is it influenced by, issues of class, gender, and ethnicity?
6. How has language changed in your lifetime, and what factors have contributed to these changes?
7. Bill 101 declares French the official language of Quebec, and l'Office québécois de la langue française (OQLF) has gone to great lengths to ensure that is used in everyday situations. How important is French in maintaining Québécois identity, and what impact does Bill 101 and the OQLF have on English-speaking Canadians in Quebec and elsewhere in Canada?
8. How is technology changing the way you communicate with family, friends, and others?
9. How are texting, instant messaging, and social media applications influencing the way you learn? How can instructors use these new technologies to improve their teaching?
10. Second Life (secondlife.com) is a 3-D virtual world where users create avatars (online representations of themselves) that allow them to interact with other players from all over the world. How would you conduct ethnographic research in this virtual world? What questions would you ask, and what insights might such a study provide about the real world?

Make the Grade with MindTap

Stay organized and efficient with **MindTap**—a single destination with all the course material and study aids you need to succeed. Built-in apps leverage social media and the latest learning technology. For example:

- ReadSpeaker will read the text to you.
- Self-quizzing allows you to assess your understanding.
- Flashcards are pre-populated to provide you with a jump-start for review—or you can create your own.
- You can highlight text and make notes in your MindTap Reader. Your notes will flow into Evernote, the electronic notebook app that you can access anywhere when it's time to study for the exam.

Visit nelson.com/student to start using **MindTap**. Enter the Online Access Code from the card included with your text. If a code card is not provided, you can purchase instant access at NELSONbrain.com.

A worker of Japanese automaker Fuji Heavy Industries installs the battery in the company's latest Subaru brand, XV hybrid.

CHAPTER

7

Economics, Adaptation, and Subsistence Patterns

WHAT WE WILL LEARN

- **How anthropologists study economic systems cross-culturally**
- **How resources such as land and property are allocated in different cultures**
- **How technology and environment influence food-getting strategies**
- **How people use culture and produce resources to help them survive in their environment**
- **The different ways societies get their food**
- **How humans distribute the goods they have produced**

THE PRACTICE OF TIPPING

According to Sam Sifton (2011), Per Se is the best restaurant in New York City. It is not cheap though: the menu has a set price of $295 (without wine), and a dinner for two can reach $1000. When the owner decided to add a fixed service charge, similar to those in Europe, there was uproar—it was un-American (Surowiecki 2005). One could add—un-Canadian. Patrons were also upset when the Smoke 'N Water Restaurant, in the Pacific Shores Resort in Parksville, British Columbia, decided in 2014 to automatically tack on an 18 percent service charge to the bill (Coyne 2014).

We like to think that we tip to reward good service, but when there is a set service charge we get upset because the power to decide what to tip is taken away from us. We would like the discretion to tip more or to tip less, depending on the service received, or even to make a symbolic statement for poor service by tipping a cent (or now five cents). The reality though, is that we tip based on the amount of the bill, not the level of service. It takes the same amount of effort to serve a $29.50 meal, or open a bottle of wine that costs $20, as it does to serve a meal that costs $295, or open a $200 a bottle of wine, yet in Canada we are likely to tip somewhere between 15 and 20 percent of the bill (including on the tax) regardless of the service. There is only a weak correlation between the quality of service people receive and the amount they tip, and service is also no better in Canada than in Japan or Australia, where tipping is unusual (Surowiecki 2005).

In North America, tipping is a multi-billion dollar economy, yet it is an anomaly according to economic theory. It is not like buying food at the grocery store, or paying for items at Walmart, where prices are set and we exchange our cash for the products we want. It is not even like buying items at a garage sale where we can bargain over the price. We tip when we don't have to. We are not trying to maximize our economic benefit, because, if we were, we would not tip. We could argue that it is to ensure good service next time, but most of us will tip the same to the people who serve us every week as to the people who serve us at an out-of-town restaurant.

Yoshikazu Tsuno/AFP/Getty Images

Tipping is more similar to what anthropologists call a "gift economy" than a market economy. Tips are essentially gifts. These days most of us pay our restaurant bill (and the tip) by credit or debit card, which means our guests at the dinner table do not know how much we tip. Not too long ago, however, people would try to impress their guests, and the servers, by being a "big tipper." There is a good deal of social pressure to tip, and we feel guilty if we don't tip, or don't tip enough. Tipping in Canada has thus become a social norm.

As with other gifts, we tend to give better gifts to those we like than to those we don't. Servers who cultivate a personal relationship with the customer can increase their tips. Introducing themselves by name, giving each customer a candy at the end of the meal, writing thank you on the back of the bill, squatting by the table to talk to customers, and touching them lightly on the shoulders have all been shown to improve tips (Surowiecki 2005).

This relationship is modified/damaged by the minimum wage laws. In British Columbia and Ontario, employers are allowed to pay liquor servers less than the minimum wage because they receive tips, and, in Quebec, employers can pay below minimum wage to anyone who earns gratuities. Service providers and customers are no longer equal; service providers have become dependent on the customers for a large part of their living, putting the customer in a position of power. It can also put the employer-employee relationship at odds in what economists call the principal-agent problem, where the incentives of the two are different. Consider the bartender who "tops up" your drink in hope of getting a bigger tip. While he or she may receive a bigger tip, it is at the expense of company profits.

Who we tip is also rather arbitrary. Most of us will tip the cab driver who takes us to the airport, and who we will most likely never see again, but not the bus driver who takes us to work every day. We tip restaurant servers, hair dressers, bell hops, blackjack dealers, and bartenders, but not garbage collectors, nurses, fast-food restaurant servers, flight attendants, or the checkout person at Walmart, all of whom provide us with equally valuable services and with whom we may develop a relationship. There are also categories of people we should not tip—the police, government employees, pharmacists—as doing so can be perceived as bribery or corruption. In other countries, however, "tipping" these people is an expected norm.

Knowing who to tip, when to tip, and how much to tip is a piece of cultural etiquette we have to learn, and is culturally relative. There are no universal rules or obligations concerning tipping. In many Asian and European countries, tipping is not the norm, although it is often expected of North American tourists and at some high-end restaurants.

We tend to think of economics as a rational behaviour based on supply and demand, yet this discussion of tipping demonstrates that it involves much more than that. It is not necessarily what we would call "rational," and it involves culturally relative norms of behaviour, attitudes, symbols, personal relationships, relations of power, as well as legal aspects. ■

Economics

The primary biological imperative of any organism, including humans, is to survive. All humans must thus meet certain fundamental material needs such as food, water, and shelter (Figure 7.1). Most animals are biologically equipped to do this, but we humans are not. We would have great difficulty surviving without the support of others. Even people who forage for their food have to rely on other members of their society for survival. And we should remember when we buy that lettuce from the supermarket that there is a long chain of people from the farmer who planted it to the person who stocked it on grocery store shelf, to the salad plate where it is consumed. We rely on the organization of all their efforts, as well as our own, to survive.

In one sense, economics is the core organizing principle of culture. It is essential to our survival that our biological needs for food and water are satisfied before all others. Thus, all societies, whether small-scale or highly complex, face a common challenge: to satisfy the material needs of their members. This simple fact requires that all societies carefully allocate scarce resources, produce needed commodities, distribute their products to the people, and develop efficient consumption patterns. In other words, every society, if it is to survive, must develop organized systems of production, distribution, and consumption. How these systems are organized varies enormously from society to society. Some groups meet most of their material needs with goods procured from hunting and gathering, others from growing food, and others by manufacturing products or providing services that are traded for what is needed.

The word economics (and also ecology) comes from the Greek word *oikos*, which means "house, home, or place to live" (Gudeman and Whitten 1982). While ecology referred to the management of the environment, economics for the Ancient Greeks referred to the management of domestic resources, household members and their activities, as a means to create wealth—what we would perhaps today call "home economics." It was not until the mid-1700s that economics began to be the study of how resources were produced, distributed, and consumed by societies as a whole (OED).

Prabhat Kumar Verma/Pacific Press/LightRocket via Getty Images

FIGURE 7.1 People queueing for food at a temporary shelter in Kathmandu, Nepal, after the 7.8 magnitude earthquake on April 25, 2015, highlights the fact that the first priority for any society is to see that its members' biological needs are met.

A society's economy thus consists of the production, distribution, and consumption of resources. The science of ***economics***, sometimes called formal economics, focuses on how these processes are organized in the industrialized world. This is because its philosophical roots lie in the study of Western industrialized economies. As a result, much of ***formal economic theory*** is based on assumptions derived from observing Western industrialized societies. For example, economic theory is predicated on the notion of supply and demand. When demand for a particular commodity is high and supply low, producers can charge high prices and earn big profits. In a free market, the prospect of high profits attracts other producers who increase supply. The increased competition then brings prices down until some sort of equilibrium is reached and where profit margins are thin. Another assumption of this model is that, when people are exchanging goods and services, they rationally weigh out the costs and the benefits to maximize their material well-being and their profits.

We live in a monetized society, that is, one in which the processes of production, distribution, and consumption are evaluated in terms of money. Dollar figures are applied to what it costs to extract resources, the labour costs involved in converting them into the goods and services that people want, and the transportation costs in getting them into people's hands.

Economists use their theories (based on these assumptions) to predict how people will make certain choices when producing or consuming commodities. Owners of a manufacturing plant, for example, are constantly faced with choices. Do they continue to manufacture only blue jeans, or do they expand their product line to include casual clothes? Do they move some or all of their manufacturing facilities to China, or do they keep them in Toronto? Should they give their workers more health benefits or longer paid vacations? Should they spend more of their profits on advertising or pass on the earnings to the workers? Should they invest more capital on new technology and go green or should they invest more on salaries for the labour force? Western economists assume that all these questions will be answered in a rational way so as to maximize the company's profits and provide

---

economics The academic discipline that studies systems of production, distribution, and consumption, typically in the industrialized world.

formal economic theory Assumptions about economic behaviour based on the experience of Western industrialized economies.

for their shareholders. Similarly, Western economists assume that individuals are motivated by the desire to maximize their material well-being.

As we will see in this chapter, these basic assumptions are not found in all the cultures of the world (including Western societies). For instance, the Trobriand Islanders traditionally grow more yams than they can possibly eat and store them in yam houses, where many are intentionally allowed to rot. They do this to gain prestige and to show others that they are proficient gardeners. Traditionally, the men would also give many of the yams to their sisters' husbands. This is done because the Trobriand Islanders are a matrilineal society where descent is reckoned down through the female line, so that a man's sister's children belong to his lineage and his own children belong to his wife's lineage. Thus, by giving the yams to his sister's husband, he is fulfilling an obligation to his lineage. From a purely formal economic perspective, this behaviour is irrational and the formalist economic model has difficulty explaining these actions.

Economic Anthropology

Economic anthropology goes beyond notions of supply and demand and maximization of profits. It is the cross-cultural comparison of the processes of ***production***, ***distribution***, and ***consumption***, and looks at them in both industrialized and non-industrialized societies alike. These processes do not occur in isolation. They cannot be understood without consideration of religious beliefs, kinship relationships, power differences, political structures, gender ideologies, or other aspects of society and culture. And this means that different societies organize these economic processes differently. Anthropology thus offers a perspective that looks beyond impersonal monetized transactions to the culturally varied ways in which people acquire, distribute, and consume resources. The anthropological approach emphasizes the cultural and social context in which people act, including the importance of social and kinship relationships, the technologies they use, and the ideas and attitudes they have in shaping economic behaviour.

economic anthropology The branch of anthropology that looks at cross-cultural systems of production, distribution, and consumption.

production The process whereby goods are obtained from the natural environment and altered to become consumable goods for society.

distribution How commodities and services, once produced, are distributed among members of the society.

consumption The culturally relative way goods and services are consumed.

allocation of resources A society's regulation and control of such resources as land and water and their by-products.

Production

The initial step in meeting the material needs of any society is to establish a system of allocating the right to use resources to certain people. This depends on the accessibility of environmental resources, the technology and energy resources available for processing them, how the society is organized, and on cultural values, attitudes, and ideas. In few situations, however, can people use resources in exactly the form in which they are found in nature. Animals must be butchered; grains must be ground and cooked; metal ores must be mined, smelted, combined with other chemical elements, and crafted before becoming tools or automobiles; stones must be shaped before they can be put into the wall of a house. This process of obtaining goods from the natural environment and transforming them into usable objects is what economists call production. Production also includes the transformation of one item refashioned into another. For example, water and soda bottles may be converted into articles of clothing such as polar fleece, old tires are ground up and used in road fill or sandals, and scrap metals may become corrugated metal sheets for house siding or roofing.

Allocation of Resources

Every society has access to certain natural resources in its territorial environment, including land, animals, water, minerals, trees, and plants. Even though the nature, number, and amount of these resources vary widely from one group to another, every society has developed a set of rules governing the ***allocation of resources*** and how they can be used. For example, all groups have determined systematic ways for allocating land among their members. In our society, where things are bought and sold in markets, most natural resources are privately owned. Pieces of land are surveyed, precise maps are drawn, and title deeds are granted to those who purchase a piece of property. Small pieces of land generally are held by individuals, and larger pieces of property are held collectively, either by governments (as in the case of roads, public buildings, and parks) or by private corporations on behalf of their shareholders. To be certain, there are limitations on private property ownership in Canada, but the system of resource allocation is based on the general principle of private ownership, whereby an individual or a group of individuals has total or near total rights to a piece of property, and consequently can do with it as they see fit.

In other regions of the world, and in particular where a society bases its subsistence strategy on hunting and gathering, pastoralism, or horticulture, resource allocation is handled differently. The concept of private ownership of land and other natural resources most likely does not factor into their approach to resource allocation. Hunter-gatherers must determine who can hunt animals and collect plants from which areas. Pastoralists need to have some orderly pattern for deciding access to pastureland and watering places. Horticulturalists and agriculturalists must work out ways of acquiring, maintaining, and passing on rights to their farmland.

Units of Production

Like other parts of culture, the way people go about producing is not haphazard or random, but rather is systematic, organized, and patterned. Every society organizes its members into some type of productive unit comprised of people with specific tasks to perform. In industrialized societies the productive unit is the private company that exists for the purpose of producing goods or services. These private firms range from small, individually owned operations to gigantic transnational corporations. Whatever the size and complexity, however, these private companies are made up of employees performing specific roles, all of which are needed to produce the goods and services that are then sold for a profit.

Production in the Household

In most non-industrialized societies, the basic unit of production is the household. In these small-scale societies, most, if not all, of the goods and services consumed are produced by the members of the household. This holds true for small-scale farmers in Western and non-Western cultures, where farming households rely on family labour to produce farm products. The household may be made up of a nuclear family (parents and children) or a more elaborate family structure containing married siblings, multiple wives, and more than two generations. Although household members are most often kin, they can also include nonrelatives. Ancient Greek households, for example, often included slaves. Moreover, some members may not actually live in the household but contribute to its economic well-being while living and working elsewhere. For example, some members of the household may migrate internally or externally to another country to find work or jobs that pay more than they might have earned in their own communities. We see examples of seasonal immigrant workers from Mexico and the Caribbean working in agricultural areas of Canada and the United States. Such family members generally send remittances back home to help provide for the household.

The family household is also more than just a productive unit and is concerned with the emotional, social, psychological, and spiritual needs of its members. It is therefore likely to use some of its resources in economically nonproductive ways. Consequently, the family-based household is less likely than the business firm to use highly productive, progressive, or innovative methods.

Division of Labour

One important aspect of the process of production is the ***division of labour***, that is, the allocation of tasks to be performed by deciding which types of people will perform which categories of work. Every society, whether large or small, distinguishes to some degree between the work that is appropriate for men and women, and for adults and children. Subsistence societies with low population densities and simple technologies are likely to have a division of labour based on little more than gender and age. Most men in these societies engage in essentially the same activities and the same holds true for most women. If specialists do exist, they are usually part-timers engaged in political leadership, ceremonial activities, or specialized tool making. At the other extreme are industrialized societies, where most people are engaged in specialized occupations, such as computer programmer, car mechanic, kindergarten teacher, janitor, accountant, or orthopedic surgeon. One of the major consequences of the transition from hunting and gathering to plant and animal domestication and the growth of industrial societies has been an increased ***labour specialization***. Because intensive agriculture produces food for larger populations, some people were freed to take up tasks not directly involved in food production.

There is also an important distinction between paid and unpaid work. Curiously, those—and generally it is women—who work at home are often classified as unemployed or inactive if the work they are involved in is not remunerated unless performed by a paid domestic (maid). Cleaning, cooking, shopping, doing laundry, caring for children, and other tasks that make a home run smoothly are not jobs that contribute to the household income. There is a higher percentage of economically inactive women in North Africa, the Middle East, and South Asia where there is a higher control over women's activities. For example, in rural Afghanistan women are generally forbidden to work outside their home, let alone be allowed to walk outside unescorted by a male relative. And in many other cultures we see further gender specialization in the work they carry out.

Gender Specialization

Although some roles (jobs) are performed by both women and men throughout the world, many others are associated with one gender or the other. Women generally tend crops, gather wild foods, care for

---

division of labour The assignment of day-to-day tasks to the various members of a society.

labour specialization The extent to which productive activities are divided among the members of a society.

children, prepare food, clean house, fetch water, and collect cooking fuel. Men, on the other hand, hunt, build houses, clear land for cultivation, herd large animals, fish, trap animals, and serve as political functionaries. There are exceptions to these broad generalizations about what constitutes men's and women's work, however. In some parts of traditional Africa, for example, women carry much heavier loads than men, work long hours in the fields, build houses, and even serve as warriors. Not too long ago in Canada, it was only men who were engineers, doctors, and truck drivers, and women were the nurses and teachers. These roles are no longer the exclusive domain of particular genders.

Men and women are often assigned roles for various social, political, or historical reasons. When these factors are inadequately understood, they can appear to be arbitrary. For example, although sewing clothes for the family is thought of as women's work in North America (most men have never operated a sewing machine or made a purchase in a fabric store), among the Ecuadorian men and traditional Hopi of Arizona, it is the men who are the spinners, weavers, and tailors (Figure 7.2).

Age Specialization

In much the same way that societies divide labour on the basis of gender, they also allocate tasks according to age. Often children do not perform certain tasks because they lack the knowledge and physical strength that are needed. In Canada, where formal education routinely lasts through the late teens (and often beyond), young people generally do not engage in much productive work, especially because most of them are not raised in families that depend on what they produce from the land. By way of contrast, children in less industrialized societies, who do not require a formal education to provide for their families, usually become involved in work activities at a considerably younger age. In traditional times, children in Canada and elsewhere were expected to do household chores, help with subsistence farming, and tend flocks of animals; their survival depended on the entire group's effort.

Today, children in many parts of the developing world participate in the market economy, and as a result, an increasing number of children aged 14 years and younger are engaged in wage employment or commercial activity. Poverty is the reason for much of the use of child labour, with children working to help their families, particularly during times of crisis. Children find work, sometime in hazardous conditions and at low pay in agriculture, in industry, possibly in sweatshops, and in the service industry. According to the United Nations, India has become the world capital for child labour, employing more than 55 million children aged 5 to 14, primarily in the garment industry.

Numerous examples of using child labourers are found in Asia, South America, and Africa. To illustrate, children in Kenya are working in light industry, mines (salt and soapstone), plantation agriculture (tea, coffee, sugar, and pineapple), and service areas such as street vendors, domestic servants, scavengers, and bus conductors. In Brazil, children living in favelas (shanty or slum shacked villages) with their families may find themselves living alongside garbage dumps. Hundreds of families who live in and near the dump await the daily arrival of the truck with the city's refuse. Children collect plastics, glass, and other items for home use or sale. The little bit sold helps to put food on the table. Some of the worst forms of child labour worldwide involve slavery, trafficking in children, debt bondage, forcible recruitment for warfare, and prostitution (Figure 7.3).

Pablo Corral V/Corbis/VCG/Getty Images

FIGURE 7.2 Cultures determine which tasks are for men and which are for women. An Ecuadorian man works at a sewing machine, a job usually associated in Canada with women.

© Rob Crandall/SCPhotos/Alamy Stock Photo

FIGURE 7.3 Child workers in the developing world are often subject to unsafe conditions. Workers sew Mango jeans in a garment factory in the city of Shenzhen, China.

Subsistence Strategies

Critical to any culture's survival is meeting the society's basic needs for shelter and access to food and drinkable water. In one form or another, every culture has a system for procuring food: growing it, harvesting it, trading for it, and even shopping for it. The pattern for obtaining one's food is known as a ***subsistence strategy***. Not all food-getting systems or subsistence strategies are equitable. Within societies and between societies, some people have greater access to more food than others. We see examples of extremes in access or lack of access in countries where people are severely malnourished or dying of starvation, whereas in other countries people are dying from obesity due to overconsumption, which has become a global epidemic.

Like other aspects of culture, subsistence strategies vary widely from one society to another and change over time (Figure 7.4). Nevertheless, it is possible to identify five major food-procurement categories found among the world's populations:

1. *Foraging* is living by hunting animals, gathering wild plants, and fishing.
2. *Horticulture* is low-intensity, small-scale cultivation using small fields, plots, or gardens. Horticulturalists rely on human power and simple tools to work small plots of land to produce food primarily for household consumption.
3. *Pastoralism* is a type of animal husbandry. Pastoralists breed and care for domestic and other animals (camels, cattle, goats, horses, llamas, reindeer, sheep, and yaks) and then use their products (such as hair, milk, meat, and blood) either as their major food source or as an item for exchange.
4. *Intensive agriculture* is a large-scale and complex system of farming and animal husbandry. It is a more productive form of cultivation of food plants than horticulture, due to the use of animal or mechanical power, as well as irrigation systems, and fertilizers to produce surpluses.
5. *Industrial agriculture* (agribusiness) is commercial farming on a much larger scale than intensive agriculture. It relies on complex machinery, genetically modified animals and plant seeds, and distribution of products for domestic and export markets. It also is linked to processing systems—the transformation of raw commodities into processed food and nonfood items (i.e., corn fructose used as a flavouring in soft drinks, and corn biomass converted into ethanol, a biodiesel fuel).

As we move forward in this chapter we examine a number of different ways by which societies obtain their food. We also explore the various ways in which food-getting strategies are influenced by technology and the environment, and especially how culture influences what different peoples eat, as well as how they go about getting food in the environment in which they live.

Photo by Universal Images Group via Getty Images

FIGURE 7.4 The Yanomamö, who live in the most inaccessible regions of the Amazon, practise shifting cultivation and supplement their diet with fishing and hunting. This way of life is rapidly disappearing due to disease, disappearance of the rainforest, and run-ins with illegal gold miners. The Horonami Yanomamö Organization claimed 80 Yanomamö were killed by miners in July 2012, although Venezuelan investigators could find no evidence of such a massacre (The Telegraph Sept. 4, 2012).

Human Adaptation

Anthropologists, particularly those specializing in environmental anthropology, have always had an interest in how humans adjust to their natural environments. They want to know how a particular environment influences people and their culture, and conversely how the culture (and people's activities) influences the physical environment (Sutton and Anderson 2009). Some anthropologists refer to this as cultural ecology, or human ecology, first introduced by Julian Steward (see Chapter 4). It is recognized that political and economic systems also influence the manner in which people get their food, how much they have, and where it is from.

When we speak of human adaptation to a particular environment, we are referring to two types of adaptation: *cultural* and *biological*. Cultural responses to cold climates include "technological" solutions such as building fires, using animal skins as clothing and blankets, and seeking refuge from the elements in caves or constructed dwellings. Humans who live in cold climates also engage in certain behaviours that are

---

subsistence strategy **The pattern a society uses to obtain its food.**

adaptive. They tend to eat more food, particularly fats and carbohydrates, especially during the colder months; they engage in greater amounts of activity obtaining food and getting fuel for heat, which increases their internal body temperature; and they curl up when sleeping to reduce the surface area of exposure and resulting heat loss.

Adapting to the Environment

Many small-scale societies have made fitting adaptations to their natural environment without the benefit of modern science and technology. Many groups living in remote parts of the world are so well-adapted to their surroundings that they have been able to manage their essential resources in highly efficient ways for millennia. They often have enormous knowledge of plant life that is useful for eating, building houses, and curing illnesses. They cultivate crops by managing the soil, controlling moisture levels, preventing erosion, attracting certain organisms to reduce pests, and pacing their horticultural activities to correspond to seasonal cycles. In short, they use their accumulated knowledge to maximize the land's productivity and their own long-term benefits.

We should not overly romanticize small-scale societies, however, by thinking that they always live in total harmony with their environments. Some cultures over-farm their soil, overgraze their pastures, pollute their waters, and severely jeopardize both their livelihoods and their environments. This has been particularly true in recent years as many small-scale societies enter modern-market economies, or external pressures force rapid changes that are not sustainable for the culture or the environment. When not dealing with colonial governments, strong world market forces, or pressures from others encroaching on their resource base, however, many small-scale societies develop and maintain a means of survival that is highly adaptive, productive, sustainable, and environmentally friendly.

According to Kevin Krajick (1998), archaeological research in Peru indicates that the Incas used conservation practices such as irrigation canals, terracing, and tree planting to build a highly efficient agricultural system in the Peruvian highlands. Terraces were built by people who hauled soil to the hillsides from the valley and riverbeds below. And the Incas built an extensive canal system that provided water to hillside cultivators from streams and lakes located at higher altitudes. The Incas also practised agroforestry by purposefully planting trees and managing them as part of the agricultural system. Some of the ancient Incan farming practices are being revived for contemporary residents of the area. Since 1995, local Peruvian farmers have rebuilt the terraces, reconstructed the canal system, and put 160 hectares under cultivation (Figure 7.5). One of the major grains produced by the Incas was quinoa. Today quinoa and a variety of Inca potatoes are found in Western supermarkets. Clearly, the Incas had hundreds of years to develop an agricultural system that maximized the utility of the land without degrading it.

Derek Furlong/Robert Harding Picture Library Ltd/Alamy Stock Photo

FIGURE 7.5 Traditional Inca terraces still in use today by local small-scale farmers in Pisac, near Cuzco, Peru, South America.

Today, worldwide consumer appetites for cash crops such as corn, coffee, tea, cocoa, sugar, pineapples, soybeans, tobacco, trees (pine, teak, and neem), and flowers (poppies, roses, and tulips) have led to dramatic changes in traditional subsistence strategies and to the demise of traditional ecosystems all over the globe. Examining the often disastrous effects of industrial agricultural influences has given anthropologists a heightened respect for the ways in which traditional peoples have adapted to their natural environments. Consumer demand for wood furniture has resulted in deforestation of tropical areas and the replanting of plantation monocultured (single species) forests. Drilling for precious metals, minerals, and fossil fuels (coal, gas, and oil) has also led to environmental degradation and the alteration of habitats. In Ecuador, the Huaorani and their neighbours have been fighting to protect their lands from international corporations extracting oil. Even when Western governments have administered their "foreign aid" programs for disaster relief or economic development, inattention to how local people relate to their natural environments has produced unfortunate consequences.

Environment and Technology

Which food-getting strategy is actually developed by any given culture depends, in large measure, on the culture's environment, technology, and way of life. Geographers often divide Earth's land surface into categories, including grasslands, deserts, tropical forests, temperate forests, polar regions, and mountain habitats. Some of these environments are particularly hospitable to the extent that they support a number of modes of food acquisition. Others are more limiting in the types of adaptations they permit. Anthropologists generally agree that the environment does not determine food-getting patterns but rather sets broad limits on the possibilities, especially when we consider that culture defines what is considered a food item. For example, among some cultures in Africa, Asia, and Latin America, insects such as ants, grasshoppers, grubs, locusts, termites, and other larvae are regular fare or snack foods, whereas in other cultures these items are to be avoided. In Uganda after the rains, live, winged termites are sold in the markets because some Ugandans enjoy roasting and eating them (Figure 7.6). In Bali one can sample wingless dragonflies boiled in coconut milk with ginger and garlic.

In part, it is technology that helps people adapt to their specific environment. In fact the human species enjoys a tremendous adaptive advantage over all other species precisely because we have developed a wide range of technological solutions to the problems of survival. In many cases, cultures with complex technologies have gained greater control over their environments and their food supplies. Coupled with technology, it is the knowledge a group has of its environment that is passed down from one generation to the next that facilitates a people's approach to cultural survival.

The specific mode of food getting is influenced by the environment itself and its interface with a people—both their culture and their technology. Environmental factors set an upper limit on the ultimate productivity of any given food-getting system and the size of the population it can support. Cultural ecologists call this limit the environment's carrying capacity (Glossow 1978; Sutton and Anderson 2009).To illustrate, the extent to which a hunting-and-gathering society is able to procure food depends not only on the sophistication of the society's tools but also on the abundance of plant and animal life in the environment and the society's knowledge of what is edible and how to process it into something people can consume. For example, in the Kalahari Desert, in southwest Africa, food and water are sparse and so the Ju/'hoansi who live there live in small family groups of about 30 people. On the other hand, the rich marine environment of Canada's northwest coast supported relatively permanent communities of several hundred or more. Similarly, the productivity of a society based on irrigation agriculture varies according to the society's technology as well as environmental factors, such as the availability of water and the natural nutrients in the water and in the soil.

Yannick Tylle/Corbis/Getty Images

FIGURE 7.6 **Processing grasshoppers for cooking in central Uganda, where they are considered a delicacy as well as being an important source of income. Traditionally, grasshoppers were collected by children and women.**

Major Food-Getting Strategies: Subsistence

The five forms of food procurement (hunting and gathering, horticulture, pastoralism, intensive agriculture, and industrial agriculture) are not mutually exclusive, as most human societies use more than one strategy. Where this is the case, however, one form usually predominates. Moreover, in each category we can expect to find considerable variation, largely because of differences in environment, historical experiences, technology, and cultural preferences. These five categories of food getting are explored in more detail in the following sections.

Foraging Societies

Foraging (also known as hunting and gathering food)—compared to food producing—involves the use of wild plants and animals that already exist in the natural environment. For most of human history, our ancestors hunted, gathered, and fished to survive. That all began to change about 10 000 to 12 000 years ago, when they began to domesticate animals and grow their own food (Smith B. 1998). Today, there are perhaps less than half a million people worldwide who continue to live this way exclusively (Figure 7.7). But because for tens of thousands of years we have lived as hunter-gatherers, this way of life

foraging (hunting and gathering) A form of subsistence that relies on animal, fish, and plant resources found in the natural environment.

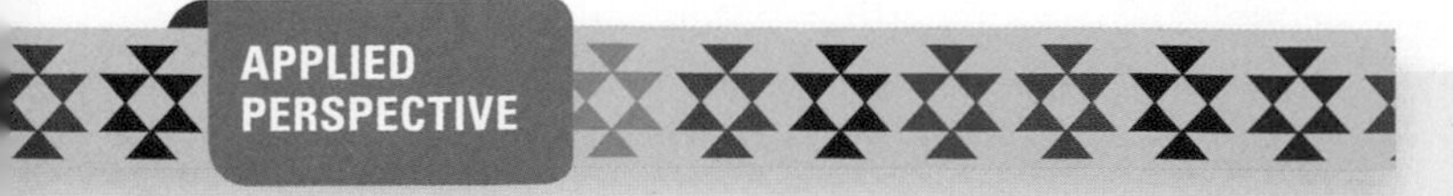

Fighting Hunger with Edible Insects

For decades, people have been fighting hunger. In the 1960s the Green Revolution with its hybrid seeds was supposed to rid the world of poverty and hunger. Today, well into the 21st century, hunger and poverty still abound in all regions of the world. At just over 7 billion, the world's population continues to face finding sustainable protein sources for everyone, especially in light of climate change, water shortages, and other factors impeding food production. At the forefront of many food assistance programs has been the Food and Agriculture Organization (FAO) of the United Nations. Drawing on the work of anthropologists, entomologists (people who study insects), as well as entomophagy—the practice of eating insects—the FAO is working on new initiatives that focus on edible insects (Anthes 2014; Vantomme et al. 2004).

Insects have long been a common food item in many parts of Southeast Asia, Central Africa, and Latin America. It is cultural. Just as escargot (snails) are regular fare in French cuisine, and fish eggs are consumed in many fishing communities as roe, or as caviar (a pricey delicacy in some cultures), insects have met the food needs for many. Some of the more popular of the 1900 edible species of insects include grubs, termites, scorpions, weaver ant larvae, crickets, and meal worms. Insects take up less space, require less water to produce, and produce less waste compared to a cows, pigs, or chickens, and convert plants into protein 12 times more efficiently than cattle. Moreover, they are rich in protein and essential micronutrients such as iron, calcium, and zinc (Anthes 2014; Vantomme et al. 2004). As Schmidt (2011, 16) points out, "bugs are a sustainable, inexpensive source of protein. And raising, harvesting and selling them can be an excellent small-business opportunity for people in the developing world." Indeed, in central Africa, insects are readily available in local markets and sold mostly by women and children (Vantomme et al. 2004).

Eating insects is not new. For example, in the Central African Republic, bush meat, a preferred source of protein, is becoming rare as a result of deforestation and unsustainable hunting practices, and so people are turning to insects such as the caterpillar, the mopane worm, and the Emperor moth as a source of protein. Vantomme et al. (2004) noted that, during the rainy season, caterpillars are gathered by hand by women and children, providing an excellent source of protein, calcium, niacin, and riboflavin. It is customary to eat them stewed, fried, or ground into nutrient-rich flour. Given these valuable micronutrients, children and pregnant or breastfeeding women in Central Africa would consume the mopane worm in some form to combat or ward off malnutrition.

Man holding mopane caterpillars, Kopa, Zambia. A food delicacy, the worms are boiled, dry roasted, and then sold as snacks or for cooking in traditional meals.

has shaped our biology, our culture, and our relation to the environment. Consequently, anthropologists from the very beginnings of the discipline have had an intense interest in foraging strategies.

We must be careful, however, when looking at contemporary foragers as the remaining representatives of an ancient way of life. Things have changed in the past 10 000 years. Contemporary foragers now live in the most marginal environments—deserts, semi-deserts, arctic regions, and dense jungle—where growing food is impossible or impractical. Ten thousand years ago, however, foragers exploited more fruitful environments. All hunter-gatherers are also today in contact with people who follow different subsistence strategies and have interacted for years with neighbouring groups through trade relations,

Given the ease with which these caterpillars are gathered from trees and the ground, they also provide extra income for rural families. Schmidt (2011, 18) reports on one study from Botswana that found "the mopane worm generates about 13 percent of household income for rural families but accounts for only about 6 percent of the labour output. Rural people often sell them to traveling merchants, who then sell them at urban markets."

Scientists, nutritionists, economists, and other development specialists are looking to expand the edible-insect market. There are opportunities in the West for new import-export businesses, but most likely customers would be consuming insects as a luxury item rather than one of necessity. It is easier to expand the edible insect market in developing countries where there is a cultural tradition for entomophagy. One example is from the Philippines, where the mole cricket and June beetle are wreaking havoc in agricultural fields and creating an environmental concern. Scientists are now promoting the idea of harvesting these insects for consumption on a large scale rather than blasting the fields with insecticides. Eating the insects seems to have a greater benefit over the cost of chemically treating the fields. In another case, researchers are looking to expand silkworm farming in Thailand to develop a commercial production of silkworm snacks.

The range of opportunities for development of a new subsistence strategy around edible insects—be they wild caught or farmed raised—has the potential for providing a sustainable protein source and income for many in the developing world. FAO is currently working in Laos, where 40 percent of Lao children are malnourished or stunted by inadequate protein consumption. "Many Lao children and adults also suffer from deficiencies in micronutrients such as iron, iodine and many vitamins" (Schmidt 2011, 19). FAO believes that eating insects in quantity on a regular basis could address all these deficiencies. Lao culture does recognize insects as food, and a high percentage of the population eat them regularly. Currently, FAO trainers teach how to raise and breed crickets, palm weevils, mealworms, and weaver ants for food with an eye toward increasing production to make edible insects more widely available. Laos and Thailand are moving into commercial insect farms as a way to fight poverty, hunger, and malnutrition.

In September 2013, a team of young entrepreneurs from McGill University won the prestigious Hult Prize. The prize is worth one million dollars in start-up funds and was awarded to the team in 2013 that proposed the best solution to the problem of food security for urban slum dwellers. The team's solution was to sell inexpensive cricket farming kits to rural farmers that allow a wide variety of species to be harvested year round. The McGill team then purchases the yield from the farmers, locally processes them into such things as "lime cricket chips," and then sells them to local distributors for delivery in the slums (Rubin 2013).

In the West, where there is no tradition of entomophagy, consumption of insects is a hard sell. Insects are seen as "disgusting" pests, and are associated with garbage, dirt, waste, and disease. One suggestion is to rename them. The U.S. company Six Foods, for example, which sells insects for consumption, calls its waxworms, which eat honeycomb, "honey bugs" (Anthes 2014). There is just something unpalatable about eating "worms." More palatable perhaps than whole insects are products such as cricket flour or cricket tortilla chips. Next Millennium Farms, near Campbellford, Ontario, has been making high-protein cricket flour that has been used in tortilla chips to muffins to energy bars since 2013, and has a hard time keeping up with demand (Faulk 2014).

Food preferences can and do change. Sushi, at one time was just as unpalatable in the West as insects are today, but sushi is now a delicacy. Perhaps insect restaurants are not too far in the future, and indeed there are attempts to introduce insect consumption in Canada. A risotto sprinkled with crickets is available from Atlantic, a restaurant in Toronto (Cuthbert 2015). Today the market for insects for human consumption is about $25 million in North America, and is growing (Faulk 2014). Perhaps in the not-too-distant future we will see as Anthes (2014) suggests "an insect aisle at the supermarket and fast-food restaurants that serve bug burgers.... [and] packages of "beautiful, clean" shrink-wrapped mealworms on display at the meat counter, alongside the steak and chicken." One of the new foods on the midway at the 2015 Calgary Stampede was cockroach pizza (Radke 2015). Awareness, education, and economic opportunities might be all that is needed for a cultural shift that transforms food production and food-eating traditions to one that includes insect farming, harvesting, and consumption.

Questions for Further Thought

1. What could an applied anthropologist contribute to an edible-insect farming program? What cultural information should be considered?
2. If you were a medical anthropologist or a business anthropologist, why would learning about edible insects be useful?
3. Could crickets, caterpillars, and cockroaches become what sushi was 25 years ago?

wage labour, and intermarrying. For decades too they have not lived in a pristine, isolated world. Most switched from stone tools to metal ones centuries ago, and more recently to plastic. Today's hunters and gatherers face rapid change and have not been unaffected by globalization. Instead of living in isolation they are experiencing increased contact with a world of computers, cell-phones, civil wars, and World Bank-sponsored development projects.

Because of the low carrying capacity of the environment in which most food-collecting societies live, population densities are low so that resources are not overexploited. Most foraging and collecting societies are nomadic or semi-nomadic, moving periodically from place to place in search of wild animals and vegetation. Typically, they will exploit the resources near their camp for a few days and then move on. As a general rule, a food-foraging society has open or flexible

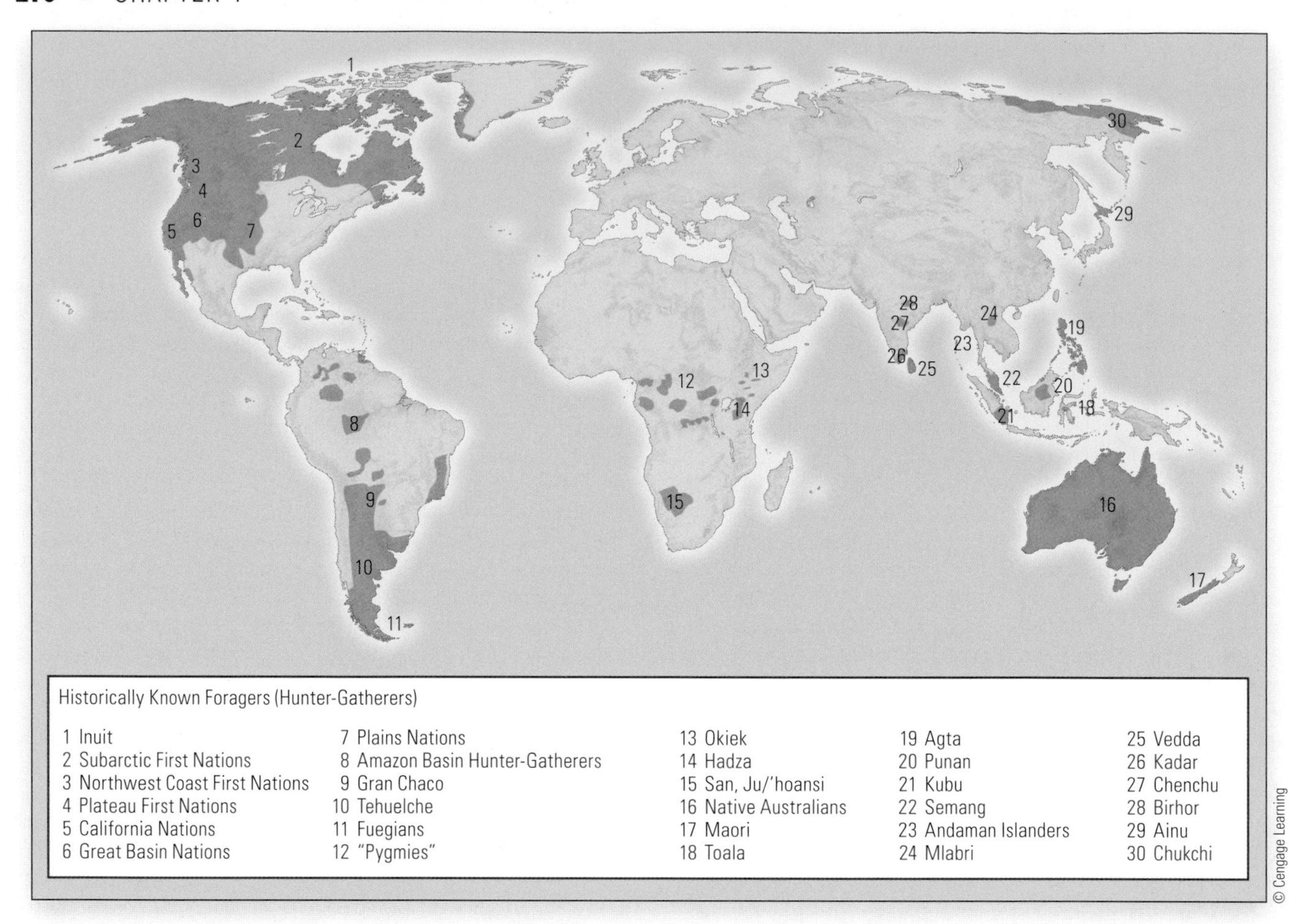

FIGURE 7.7 Historically known foragers.

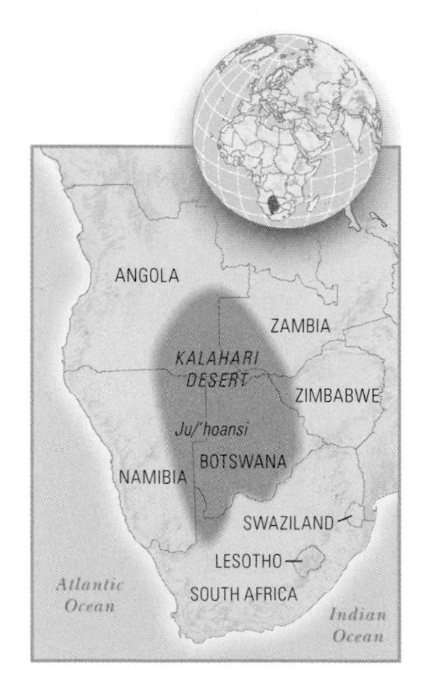

boundaries, as animals are mobile and food and water supplies are unpredictable. The basic social unit among foragers is the family or band—a loose federation of families. These groups tend to be highly fluid in membership, with family members coming and going with considerable regularity.

Because it makes little sense for people to tie themselves exclusively to a single piece of land, most hunting-and-gathering societies do not recognize land ownership in the Western sense of the term. Claiming and defending a particular territory also requires time, energy, and technology that many hunting-and-gathering peoples either do not have or choose not to expend. Thus, there is little conflict and warfare between groups. When they encounter another group they simply move on. Thus, for foraging societies, having flexible territorial boundaries (or none at all) is the most adaptive strategy.

Foragers choose the animal and plant species that tend to maximize their caloric return for the time they spend searching, killing, collecting, and preparing (Smith E. A. 1983; Sutton and Anderson 2009). This theory, known as the *optimal foraging theory*, suggests that decisions to seek out one food source and not others are based on a generally accurate assessment of whether the search is worth the effort. To illustrate, the Ache, a foraging group from Paraguay, prefer to hunt peccaries (wild pigs) rather than armadillos, even though armadillos are easier to find and easier to kill. This is a rational decision, however, because the peccaries produce considerably more calories of food per hour of hunting: 4600 calories per hour for peccaries compared to only 1800 calories for armadillos (Hill et al. 1987).

The association of hunting and gathering with an absence of social, political, and economic complexity is an accurate portrayal of the remaining hunting-and-gathering societies; most are small-scale, with no single individual or group specializing as a hunter of

---

optimal foraging theory A theory that foragers choose those species of plants and animals that maximize their caloric intake for the time spent hunting and gathering.

a particular animal or gathered item. Reciprocity and food sharing are critical to the group's survival.

The introduction of money, commodities, and wage labour expedited the process of culture change for most foragers. For example, by the early years of the 21st century, the Ju/'hoansi's foraging, semi-nomadic way of life had, for all practical purposes, disappeared. Today, most Ju/'hoansi get most of their food by raising small domestic livestock, tending small gardens, participating in government food programs, and purchasing items at food stores. The lands occupied by the Ju/'hoansi are now covered with trading markets, boreholes for water, schools, health clinics, airstrips, and government bureaucrats. And, of course, changes in their means of livelihood have resulted in other, often far-reaching, changes in their way of life (R. B. Lee 2003, 2007; Yellen 1990).

Today the Ju/'hoansi living in //Nhoq'ma village at Nhoma in the Tshumkwe are embarking on eco-tourism and playing host to tourists. Neil Digby-Clarke (2007) reports that the owners of a nearby lodge and safari outfit have developed a close relationship with the Ju/'hoansi (Figure 7.8). In 2000 they entered into an exclusive agreement with the village at //Nhoq'ma, and by 2003 they had built a tent camp for tourists and donated it to the villagers. Digby-Clarke describes the tourist accommodations as "five luxury double tents, complete with en-suite facilities" (Digby-Clarke 2007). The community is able to generate revenue from this arrangement. A number of websites assist tourists making travel arrangements with local safari companies who lead expeditions to Nyae Nyae, where the //Nhoq'ma safari camp is located. There also are several development funds and conservancies established to protect the Ju/'hoansi and their local environment.

Today an exclusive hunting, gathering, and fishing way of life is more of a lifestyle choice for those who continue it. While their parents and grandparents perhaps had little choice but to hunt, gather, and fish for a living, very few continue to live as their immediate ancestors did. Hunting and gathering has become a part-time activity that supplements their diet, although perhaps more so than for the urbanite who obtains a hunting and fishing license or who collects berries to make jam.

Fishing

Although hunting and gathering has been largely replaced by food production, many world economies still depend on fishing. Today's fishing people are equipped with Global Positioning System (GPS) technology to locate large schools of fish, high-tech equipment, and strong synthetic nets invisible to fish. Despite their enormous technological advantages, modern fishing peoples may well become victims of their own success. The rivers, lakes, and oceans of the world, which not too long ago seemed inexhaustible, can produce only a limited number of fish at the current rate of extraction. The Atlantic Ocean is a case in point. After World War II, commercial fishing boats from Europe and Asia began fishing the waters off the coast of Canada and the United States. By the 1960s the cod stock had declined so dramatically from overfishing that the governments of Canada and the United States extended their exclusive fishing rights to 200 nautical miles from shore. Although this kept foreign fishing vessels out of the area, it encouraged the proliferation of domestic fishing. Fishing became excessive, fish stocks shrank, and even future stocks were in jeopardy because fish populations could not sustain themselves. The problem remains today, with too many industrial commercial vessels fishing for a dwindling number of fish. Industrial commercial fishing—the last form of big-time "hunting"—illustrates the traditional dilemma of hunting-and-gathering people. Traditional hunters and fishers are in direct competition with large-scale commercialized fishing outfits for the wild caught, natural resource (Figure 7.9).

FIGURE 7.8 Traditionally, hunters and gatherers of the Kalahari Desert interact with local pastoralists and other neighbouring groups. Today, however, tourists from around the world visit them in their villages in the Kalahari Desert area in Namibia.

FIGURE 7.9 Malagasy fishermen display the fish they sell at Ifaty market, Madagascar. Overfishing by foreign trawlers (both legal and illegal) makes it harder for local people to make a living.

Value is placed on the quantity and frequency of fish caught and traded on an international scale among strangers. As the public demand for wild-caught seafood increases and fishers become more efficient hunters, they run the risk of destroying their food supply and, in the process, eliminating biodiversity and ruining the health of their ecosystem. As with so many aspects of the global economy, overfishing the oceans has had more negative consequences for some segments of the world's population than for others. Because fish populations in the Northern Hemisphere have been drastically reduced by commercial fishing interests in the United States, Japan, Russia, Northern Europe, and Canada, many fishing companies from the developed world have moved south of the equator to the oceans around Africa and South America. Fleets of modern trawlers are now fishing within the 200-mile limits of independent countries. Most are there legally because they pay cash-poor governments for fishing rights. A growing number of commercial fishing companies, however, are harvesting these waters illegally, threatening their livelihoods. The consequence is that people in Regina and Winnipeg can find all their favourite seafood at the supermarket, whereas local fishers in Angola are going out of business and their communities deprived of a sorely needed source of protein (Salopek 2004).

Today's non-food-producing public continues to forage, but in grocery stores and at farmers markets instead of hunting and gathering their own food. Those shoppers are learning to eat in season and eat locally gathered foods. The Oxford English Dictionary added a new entry in 2007—***locavore***, a person who is committed to eating locally in the community or within a narrow radius of where one resides.

Food-Producing Societies

Approximately 10 to 12 000 years ago, humans made a revolutionary transition from hunting and gathering to food production. For reasons that are still unclear, humans began to cultivate crops and keep herds of animals as sources of food. For the first time, humans gained a measure of control over their food supply, no longer having to rely solely on what existed naturally in the environment. This shift from hunting and gathering to producing food, known as the Neolithic Revolution (sometimes called the agricultural or agrarian revolution), occurred independently in several different areas of the world. The earliest known plant and animal domestication occurred around 10 000 years ago in the Middle East in the region referred to as the Fertile Crescent, including parts of Jordan, Israel, Syria, southeastern Turkey, northern Iraq, and western Iran. The first domesticated animal and plant species were dogs, sheep, goats, wheat, and barley. Other early centres of food production also emerged in South and Central America. And by nearly 10 000 years ago, villagers in northern China were raising millet, and people farther south were growing rice (Loewe and Shaughnessy 1999).

That food producing, compared to hunting and gathering, should result in a dramatic increase in population is not difficult to understand. Farmers can increase the food supply, and thus support larger populations, simply by sowing more seeds and managing soil nutrients and irrigation systems. As farmers increased the amount of land under cultivation or cultivated for longer periods of time, they came to rely on their children for help. Children can be taught to perform useful tasks such as weeding fields, scaring off birds or other small animals, and tending flocks, and consequently family size increased.

As populations became larger they also became more sedentary. Cultivators who invest their time and energy in a piece of land, develop the notion of property rights and establish more permanent settlements. This is not meant to imply that all or even most people became tied to the land after the Neolithic Revolution. Many remained hunters and gatherers, some became nomadic or semi-nomadic pastoralists, and still others became horticulturalists. Nevertheless, the Neolithic Revolution initiated the gradual trend toward a more settled way of life.

The cultivation of crops also brought about other important cultural changes. For example, farming can potentially generate more food per unit of land than hunting-and-gathering activities, especially if the farmer has intercropped multiple varieties of seed crops. This may have allowed farmers to store more food for times of scarcity, and trade with others for goods they did not produce, while enabling other members to specialize in non-food-producing activities. The Neolithic Revolution also stimulated a greater division of labour. That is, people could for the first time become specialists, inventing and manufacturing the tools and machinery needed for a more complex social structure. Once some people were liberated from the food quest, they were able to make new farm implements such as the plow, pottery storage containers, metal objects, and the wheel.

These transformations had their downside. Recent discoveries by paleopathologists (physical anthropologists who study disease among ancient peoples) suggest that the transition to early agriculture from a hunting-and-gathering subsistence strategy actually led to a decline in overall health. There are reasons early farmers paid a high price for their new-found, food-getting strategy. First, foragers generally had a more balanced diet (composed of both plants and animal

locavore A person who is committed to eating foods grown locally in the community or within a narrow radius of where they reside.

CROSS-CULTURAL MISCUE

A British fertilizer company from Manchester, England, decided to venture into the potentially lucrative markets of sub-Saharan Africa. After conducting research on locally appropriate fertilizers, the company developed a marketing plan that involved giving, free of charge, hundred-pound bags of fertilizer to selected farmers in certain areas of Kenya. It was thought that those using the free fertilizer would be so impressed with the dramatic increases in crop output that they would spread the word to their friends, family, and neighbours.

Teams of marketers went from hut to hut offering each male head of household a free bag of fertilizer along with an explanation of how to use it. Though polite, every farmer contacted turned down the offer of free fertilizer. The marketing staff concluded that these Kenyan farmers were either not interested in growing more crops or too stupid to understand the benefits of the new product. But both of these conclusions failed to take into account the cultural realities of the small-scale farmers in Kenya. First, company officials tried to convince the village men to accept an agricultural innovation when, in fact, it was the women who were responsible for farming. Failure to understand this basic ethnographic fact did little for their overall credibility. Second, many East Africans have two important beliefs that can help explain their reaction: (1) the theory of limited good, which assumes that there is a finite amount of good in the world (such as fertility), and (2) witchcraft, the notion that evil forces embodied in people can be harmful. Given these two beliefs, the typical east African farmer would never participate in a scheme that promises to produce more crops than any of the neighbours because to do so would open you up to charges of having bewitched the fertility out of other peoples' soil. In short, to continue to grow the same amount as one had in the past is a preferable alternative to being killed for witchcraft.

proteins) than did early farmers, who were often limited in the number of crops planted and time to still hunt and gather items to balance out their diet. Second, if early farmers were dependent on a small number of crops, they ran the risk of serious malnutrition or even starvation if those crops should fail. And finally, the increased population densities caused by the Neolithic Revolution brought people into closer contact with one another and with animals, and consequently made everyone more susceptible to both parasitic and infectious diseases.

Food production also had some dramatic social effects. The egalitarianism of traditional hunting-and-gathering societies was replaced by increasing social inequality and other problems such as poverty, crime, war, aggression, and environmental degradation.

Horticulture

Horticulture—also known as *subsistence agriculture* or *smallholder agriculture*—is small-scale, low-intensity farming on small plots. Horticulturalists use basic hand tools such as the hoe or digging stick rather than plows, draft animals, or other machinery, and purchase little if any fertilizers, seeds, or pesticides. Because horticulturalists produce low yields that are consumed directly by the household, they generally do not generate much of a surplus and thus do not develop extensive market systems. Some horticulturalists keep domesticated food animals, such as pigs or chickens, which are also often raised for prestige. For example, the Swazi of Swaziland in southern Africa keep not only pigs but also a variety of other domesticated animals, including cows, goats, sheep, horses, and donkeys (Kuper 1986). Other horticultural societies, such as the Yanomamö, who live in the Amazon Basin of Venezuela and Brazil are known to supplement their diet with occasional hunting and gathering of wild plants and animals (Chagnon 1992). Still other horticultural groups, such as the Samoans, supplement their crops with protein derived from fishing, whereas the Miskitos, Indigenous people of coastal Nicaragua in Central America, raise small domesticated livestock and fish along with their horticultural practices. Some horticulturalists also produce a small surplus to sell or exchange in local markets for things they cannot produce themselves. In Central America, Mayan horticulturalists augment their crops with fruit-bearing trees such as papaya, avocado, and cacao. On their small-scale plots they plant multiple crops such as corn, beans (using cornstalks as supports), squash, pumpkins, and chili peppers.

In contrast to hunter-gatherers, horticulturalists tend to live on land that is communally controlled, usually by an extended kinship group. Individual nuclear or polygynous families may be granted the use of land by the extended family for growing crops, but the rights are limited. For example, small family units usually retain their land rights for as long as they work the land and remain in good standing with the larger family. Because they do not own the land, however, they cannot dispose of it by selling it. They simply use it at the will of the larger group. Such a method of land allocation makes sense, given their farming technology.

In a typical horticultural society, household members produce most of what they consume; their work includes planting, tending, and harvesting the crops; building houses; preparing and consuming food; procuring firewood and other fuels from the environment; making their own tools; tending some livestock; making their own clothes; and producing various containers for storing and cooking foods. When

horticulture Small-scale crop cultivation characterized by the use of simple technology and the absence of irrigation and fertilizer.

FIGURE 7.10 A young boy from Venezuela assists his family in slash-and-burn agriculture by setting fire to an old garden. The ash from the fire will restore the soil's fertility for the next growing season.

a particular task is too complex to be carried out by a single household, larger groups of family members or neighbours usually join together to help complete the task. The Miskito of the Nicaragua coast call this form of communal labour sharing pana-pana ("hand go and hand come") and use it to prepare their horticultural fields and repair the roofs on their houses.

A major technique of horticulturalists, especially those found in tropical regions of the world, is ***shifting cultivation***, sometimes called *swidden cultivation* or the *slash-and-burn method*. This technique involves clearing the land by manually cutting down the growth, burning it, and planting in the burned area. Even though the ash residue serves as a fertilizer, the soil nutrients are usually depleted within a few years (Figure 7.10). The land is then allowed to lie fallow until the natural vegetation is restored, or it may be abandoned altogether.

The governments of many developing countries are interested in transforming traditional economies, such as those based on slash-and-burn agriculture, into world market economies, thereby attracting foreign capital, providing wage-paying jobs for local people, and raising a country's gross national product. These government officials in parts of Africa, Asia, and South America argue that, by restricting or prohibiting slash-and-burn horticulture altogether, overall productivity will be increased, people will eat better and be healthier, and the export economy will be expanded. A major problem in these efforts to transform traditional horticulture practices, however, has been that government officials often have value assumptions different from the local farmers whose culture they are trying to change. To illustrate, rural horticulturalists in Honduras were asked to shift from subsistence production—growing enough food to feed their family—to the production of chili peppers for the export market. The farmers did not support this initiative because, in their minds, chili peppers did not feed their families. It did not make sense to them to stop producing subsistence crops that fed their families and instead produce cash crops to make money with which they could buy food to feed their families. Outsiders looking on may want to consider what is culturally valued in terms of production per unit of land and the labour used in the process; sometimes what outsiders value or believe is progress is not desired by those residing in the community. Horticulture still exists as a subsistence strategy in South and Central America as well as certain areas of Central Africa, Southeast Asia, and Melanesia.

Today, we find horticulture practised among front and backyard gardeners and those who have transformed their yards into edible landscapes. Relying primarily on one's own labour to plant and harvest for home consumption is providing families with fresh, homegrown produce.

Pastoralism

Like horticulture, ***pastoralism*** first appeared during the Neolithic period. This subsistence pattern is sometimes referred to as ***animal husbandry*** and involves herding, breeding, consuming, and using such domesticated herd animals as camels, cattle, goats, horses, llamas, reindeer, sheep, and yaks. Pastoralism is practised in areas with arable lands for good pasture as well as in areas of the world that cannot support agriculture because of inadequate terrain, soils, or rainfall. These more vulnerable environments may, however, provide sufficient vegetation to support livestock, provided the animals are able to graze over a large enough area. Thus, pastoralism is associated with geographic mobility because herds must be moved periodically to exploit seasonal pastures and water sources (Sutton and Anderson 2009). There are approximately 120 million pastoralists worldwide, 50 million of whom live in sub-Saharan Africa (Rass 2006).

Like hunters and gatherers, nomadic or semi-nomadic pastoralists require extensive territory. For pastoralists to maintain their way of life, they must have access to two vital resources for their livestock: water and pasture. Depending on the local environment,

shifting cultivation (swidden cultivation, slash-and-burn method) clearing the land by manually cutting down natural growth, burning it, and planting in the burned area relatively short periods of cultivation are followed by longer fallow periods.

pastoralism A food-getting strategy based on animal husbandry; found in regions of the world generally unsuited for agriculture.

animal husbandry The herding, breeding, and use of domesticated animals.

MONEY SHARMA/AFP/Getty Images

FIGURE 7.11 Indian nomadic shepherd Maala Ram milks a sheep at his camp on the outskirts of Faridabad some 30 km from New Delhi, India. Nomadic shepherds cover great distances in their yearly trek from the western desert state of Rajasthan in search of pasture for their 2500 sheep. They depend on the sheep to eke out a living by selling the male lambs or sometimes just their wool. While the men take the sheep to graze, the women and children work at various chores, mostly cooking, fetching water, and churning butter.

the availability of these two resources may vary widely. In marginal environments where pasture and water are at a premium, pastoralists need to range over wide territories. In more environmentally friendly regions of the world where grasses and water are more abundant, one is likely to find greater control over land and its resources. In any event, pastoral groups must work out arrangements among themselves and with non-pastoralists to gain access to certain pastureland for their livestock (Figure 7.11).

Variations can be found, but corporate (i.e., non-individual) control of pastures is the general rule among pastoral peoples. At one extreme there are pastoral societies whose entire territory is considered to belong to the society as a whole. In such societies (best represented by East African groups such as the Gabra, Herrero, Turkana, Jie, and Samburu) there are no fixed divisions of land that are used by different segments of the society. At the other extreme we find societies in which the rights to use certain pastures are divided among certain segments of the society. These pastoral societies are most often found in the Eurasian steppes and in the Middle East. And in some pastoral societies, the use of wells or natural watering sources is controlled to some degree by individuals or groups, to the exclusion of others.

Anthropologists differentiate between two types of movement patterns among pastoralists: transhumance and nomadism. *Transhumance* is the seasonal movement of livestock between upland and lowland pastures. Among some pastoral groups there is a base location where the elders, women, children, and lactating animals reside, and a herding camp for adolescent boys and young adult men to raise the non-lactating animals. This division of labour and residence helps to lessen the pressures placed on available pasturelands. *Nomadism* is the migration of whole villages relocating when new pastures are needed for the animals. As Rada and Neville Dyson-Hudson (1980) pointed out, however, the enormous variations even within societies render the distinction between transhumance and nomadism somewhat sterile. For example, following seven Karamojong herds over a two-year period, the Dyson-Hudsons found that "each herd owner moved in a totally different orbit, with one remaining sedentary for a full year and one grazing his herd over 500 square miles" (1980, 18).

Even though anthropologists tend to lump all pastoralists into a single subsistence strategy, pastoralism is not a unified phenomenon. For example, there are wide variations in the ways animals are herded. The principal herd animals are cattle in eastern and southern Africa, camels in North Africa and the Arabian Peninsula, yaks in the Himalayan region, and various mixed herds (including goats, sheep, and cattle) in a number of places in Europe, Asia, Africa, South America, and North America. Reindeer are important for today's Sami people (Lapp) in northern Scandinavia, as well for other groups in the sub-Arctic areas of Eastern Europe and Siberia. The Sami use the reindeer for meat, whereas the Dukha people of northern Mongolia milk and ride their reindeer much as other Mongolians do who raise horses. In addition to variations in the types of animals, other social and environmental factors influence the cultural patterns of pastoral people, including the availability of water and pasturage, the presence of diseases, the location and timing of markets, government restrictions, and the demands of other food-getting strategies (such as cultivation) that the pastoralists may practise.

A general characteristic of nomadic pastoralists is that they take advantage of seasonal variations in pasturage so as to maximize the food supply of their herds. The Kazaks of Eurasia, for example, keep their livestock at lower elevations during the winter, move to the foothills in the spring, and migrate to the high mountain pastures during the summer. Such seasonal movement provides optimal pasturage and avoids climatic extremes that could negatively affect the livestock. Moving their animals at different times of the year avoids overgrazing and enables pastoralists to raise considerably more livestock than they could if they chose not to migrate. Various institutions have evolved to effectively manage rangeland resources to avoid

transhumance The seasonal movement of livestock between upland and lowland pastures.

nomadism The movement pattern of pastoralists involving the periodic migration of human populations in search of food or pasture for livestock.

overgrazing and allow pastures to recover, such as setting aside pasture buffer zones, spacing herds, protecting shade trees, preserving water supplies, and so on. For example, among the Borana, who live in Ethiopia and Kenya, pastures are owned by different clans, and clan leaders form councils that are responsible for managing resources, including grazing zones around homes, use of wells, and setting aside pasture for weak and sick animals, that not only preserve resources but also prevent conflict (WISP 2007).

Pastoralism as a way of life is disappearing in many areas. In Kyrgyzstan and Tajikistan, for instance, environmental degradation, over-grazing, poverty, and changes to pasture tenure regulations have reduced access to better-quality pastures, led to a growing social inequality, and also migration to the city, particularly of young men, which has also increased the workload on women in managing livestock (Kerven et al. 2012). The consensus among anthropologists is that pure pastoralists—that is, those who get all their food from livestock—are either extremely rare or non-existent. Because livestock alone cannot meet all the nutritional needs of a population, most pastoralists need some plants and grains to supplement their diets. Many pastoralists, therefore, either combine the keeping of livestock with some form of cultivation or maintain regular trade relations with neighbouring agriculturalists. Many nomadic pastoralists also produce crafts for sale or trade, occasionally work for the government, or hold other temporary jobs. Thus, although many pastoralists have long engaged in non-pastoral activities, they have always considered animal husbandry as their identity and their livelihood.

It is clear that, in pastoral societies, livestock play a vital economic role not only as a food source but also in other ways. Melville Herskovits (1924), an anthropologist who worked among east African pastoralists, found that cattle served three purposes, from which he derived the term ***cattle complex***. First, cattle were an economic venture with a utilitarian purpose. Cattle were a source of food; their milk, blood, and meat were shared and sold; their dung was used for fertilizer, house building, and fuel; their urine was used as an antiseptic; their bones were used for tools and artifacts; their skins were used for clothing and shelter; and their strength provided a means of transportation or traction. Second, cattle had a social function, played a symbolic role, and were important status symbols: large herds conveyed status to families or enabled sons to secure a wife (or wives). Livestock often influence the social relationships among people in pastoral societies. For example, an exchange of livestock between the families of the bride and the groom in the form of bridewealth (see Chapter 8) is required in many pastoral societies before a marriage is legitimized. In the event of an assault or a homicide, in some societies livestock is given to compensate the victim's family as a way of restoring normal social relations. The sacrifice of livestock at the grave sites of ancestor-gods is a way in which people keep in touch with their deities.

Third, farmers were attached to their cattle; cattle were valued and adorned. These and other social uses of livestock remind us that domesticated animals in pastoral societies not only serve as the major food source but also are intimately connected to other parts of the culture, such as the systems of marriage, social control, and religion.

The Maasai, who occupy the savannah of Kenya and Tanzania, are an excellent example of a pastoral society who have gained the reputation, among Africans and Europeans alike, as quintessential cattle keepers. Numbering between 500 000 and 1 000 000 people, the Maasai traditionally lived mainly from their abundant herds of cattle, goats, and sheep. Like many other pastoralists in the region, the Maasai obtained most of their sustenance in the form of milk and blood from their cows, consuming meat only on ritual occasions. This high-protein diet was occasionally supplemented with grains and honey obtained through trade with neighbouring peoples. It is little wonder that cattle are the major source of wealth among the Maasai, in much the same way that cash is a major concern of Westerners.

The Maasai have traditionally combined their detailed knowledge of the environment (climatic cycles, vegetation, permanent water sources, and the presence of mosquitoes and tsetse flies) with a willingness to remain mobile, flexible, and cooperative. During the dry season, when both wildlife and Maasai pastoralists congregate at the permanent sources of water, a council of elders creates a queuing schedule to ensure that all the animals have access to the water in an orderly fashion. The Maasai reserve a pasture close to the permanent watering areas for young, sick, and lactating animals that cannot travel to more distant pastures. Moreover, because "rainy seasons" sometimes fail to produce adequate water, the Maasai have established a system of "drought insurance," whereby water sources and pastures that never dry up are not used during normal

cattle complex A situation among east African pastoralist cultures in which cattle have both economic and social functions.

times. When a drought occurs, these reserves are opened up as emergency sources of food and water for their cattle.

The Maasai, however, have not only managed but have also actually transformed their environment for the benefit of their livestock in important ways. First, owing to their military prowess, the Maasai were able to prevent the permanent settlement of farmers on the grasslands, thereby preserving the savanna for open grazing. And second, they engaged in the controversial practice of controlled burning of the grasslands for two reasons: first, to destroy the breeding grounds of the tsetse fly, which causes trypanosomiasis ("sleeping sickness," affecting both people and cattle) and second, to stimulate the growth of new, more nutritious grasses. In other words, burning is believed to provide Maasai cattle with better pasturage as well as protect them from disease. Thus, for centuries the Maasai system of cattle keeping has worked effectively for all parties concerned: the Maasai, the abundant wildlife, and the environment itself.

As one of a number of cultures within the east African cattle complex (e.g., the Turkana, Jie, Samburu, among others), the Maasai have experienced enormous socio-cultural changes. With the arrival of colonial governments in the late 19th century, the Maasai found it increasingly difficult to practise their traditional patterns of pastoralism. Beginning in the 20th century, the Maasai lost some of their best dry-season pastures and water supplies to colonial settlers. Since the 1950s large portions of their traditional grazing lands have been appropriated as official game reserves (for encouraging tourism) from which the Maasai and their herds have been excluded. The Maasai are being forced into marginal areas or onto smaller and smaller parcels of land, which resemble cattle ranches. Sandwiched between the fenced fields of cultivators, the Maasai are confined to small landholdings. Gone are the days of moving their herds over vast areas of land. They are becoming permanently settled, investing money in the land (drilling wells), sending their children to school, and engaging in the previously unthinkable practice of selling their livestock for cash.

Today, Maasai herders, still dressed in their traditional red togas, drive pickup trucks, talk on cellphones, and belong to nongovernmental organizations. Many of their traditional houses are now permanent, some women are growing crops, and in some cases the Maasai are keeping chickens, not a traditional herding animal. Today they are becoming integrated into the modern global economy. Some Maasai who live near game reserves are tapping into tourist dollars by selling beaded leather goods, opening up their compounds for "home tours," and performing traditional Maasai dances for Europeans in zebra-striped minivans (Figure 7.12). But Westernization can push only so far before a proud people begin to push back. Believing that they have been evicted from their ancestral land, large groups of Maasai are protesting by driving their herds onto nearby farmland. Maasai are being told by the Kenya government to return to their ranches and accept the fact that their free-roaming life as pastoralists is rapidly coming to an end (Lacey 2004).

William Gray/AWL/Getty Images

FIGURE 7.12 Children learn how to make fire with Maasai pastoralists at a compound in Kenya's Maasai Mara National Reserve. Hosting tourists provides added income.

Intensive Agriculture

Intensive agriculture (intensive cultivation), a more recent phenomenon than horticulture, is the most prevalent subsistence pattern. It relies on large-scale production practices that result in much more food being produced per hectare than with other subsistence patterns, and thus supports larger populations. The development of intensive farming methods began about 5000 years ago as the human population grew beyond the environment's carrying capacity using horticulture and pastoralism.

Intensive agriculture is characterized by the use of the plow, draft animals (or machinery) to pull the plow, fertilizers, irrigation, and other technological innovations that make intensive cultivation much more productive than horticulture. More importantly, the system is designed with the production of a surplus in mind, and as a consequence of increased productivity there is an increase in carrying capacity. A single farmer using a horse-drawn plow, for example, can not only put a larger area of land under production but also, because the plow digs deeper than the hoe or digging stick, can unleash more nutrients from the soil and thereby increase the yield per acre. Applying animal fertilizers (the excrement of the draft animals) enables land to be used year after year rather than having to

intensive agriculture A form of food production that requires intensive working of the land with plows and draft animals and the use of techniques of soil and water control.

leave it fallow to restore its fertility naturally. Irrigation of fields that do not receive sufficient or consistent rainfall is another innovation contributing to increased production from intensive agriculture. Over the past century, large-scale agricultural techniques spread rapidly throughout the world with the introduction of farm machinery, seed varieties, and commercially produced fertilizers, pesticides, and herbicides. This essentially resulted in the industrialization of farming in the richer nations.

There is a price for this greater productivity, however. Because intensive agriculture requires a large investment of both labour and capital, agriculturalists must devote hours of hard work to preparing the land. In hilly areas, the land must be terraced and maintained, and irrigation systems may be developed that involve drilling wells, digging trenches, and building dikes. All these activities increase the land's productivity enormously but are extremely labour intensive. Intensive agriculture, compared to horticulture, also requires a much higher investment of capital in machinery that must be maintained, draft animals (which can become sick and die), and farm inputs such as fuel, fertilizers, and seeds.

In North America, and in most other parts of the industrialized world, resources such as land are allocated according to the principle of private individual ownership (Figure 7.13). Most English-speaking people have no difficulty understanding the concept of private ownership. When we say we "own" a piece of land, the term means that we have absolute and exclusive rights to it. We are able to sell it, give it away, rent it, or trade it for another piece of property if we so choose. The association between private individual land ownership and intensive agriculture is at least partially the result of the possibility of the same person using and taking care of the land year after year, thereby giving the land a permanent and continuous value such that it is in condition to be farmed.

Design Pics/Getty Images

FIGURE 7.13 Property lines are often demarcated using some sort of fencing, such as this one near Canmore, Alberta, to indicate private ownership of where one's property boundary begins and ends.

property rights The Western concept of individual ownership (an idea unknown to some non-Western cultures) in which rights and obligations to land, livestock, or material possessions reside with the individual rather than with a wider group.

This concept of individual ***property rights*** is so entrenched in our thinking and our culture that we sometimes fail to realize that many other cultures do not share this principle with us. Land, animals, and other resources may actually be controlled by the larger kinship group (the lineage or extended family); the individual merely has limited rights to use the resource. This fundamental difference in property allocation is reflected in the local East African language of Swahili, which contains no word that is comparable to the English word *own*. The closest Swahili speakers can come linguistically to conveying the notion of ownership is to use the word *nina*, which means literally "I am with."

Also closely associated with intensive agriculture are both higher levels of productivity and more settled communities. In fact, not until early horticultural societies had developed more intensive forms of agriculture could civilizations exist (i.e., urban societies). In other words, a fully reliable system of food production, brought about by intensive agriculture, is a necessary if not sufficient condition for the rise of civilization. Surplus crops produced by farmers were sold in village markets. Some of these market centres increased in population over time and became towns, and eventually cities.

As farming became more intensive, the specialization of labour became more complex. Under a system of intensive agriculture, some people were liberated to engage in activities other than food production. Many new kinds of occupations emerged such as merchants, craftsmen, professional soldiers, priests, rulers, and bureaucrats. Thus, the intensification of agriculture did not cause, but rather enabled, the development of a more complex division of labour that became differentially valued. Societies became more stratified as a result (i.e., marked by greater class differences), political and religious hierarchies were established to manage the economic surpluses and mediate among the different socio-economic classes, and eventually state systems of government (complete with bureaucracies, written records, taxation, a military, and public works projects) were established. Although the relationship between intensive agriculture and a stratified society is not necessarily a causal one, these structural changes would not have occurred without the development of a reliable system of food production that could sustain a larger population. Intensive agricultural production provided both the opportunity and the commodities, and forever changed the course of history in many parts of the world.

Peasantry

With the intensification of agriculture and the rise of civilization came the development of *peasantry*. Peasant farmers differ from horticulturalists and pastoralists in that they are not isolated or self-sufficient societies. Instead, peasants are tied to the larger unit (the city or state) politically, religiously, and economically. More specifically, peasants are subject to the laws and controls of the state, are influenced by the urban-based religious hierarchies, and exchange their farm surpluses for goods produced in other parts of the state. Peasants usually make up a large percentage of the total population and provide most of the dietary needs of city dwellers.

The intimate relationship peasants have with the cities and the state was succinctly stated by George Foster (1967, 7), who called peasants "a peripheral but essential part of civilizations, producing the food that makes possible urban life, supporting the specialized classes of political and religious rulers and educated elite." Foster's statement is important because it reminds us that the relationship between the peasants and the state is hardly egalitarian. The peasants almost always occupy the lowest stratum of society. Although they supply the rest of the society with its food, peasants have low social status, little political power, and meagre material wealth. The more powerful city dwellers, through the use of force or military power, often extract both labour and products from the peasants in the form of taxation, rent, or tribute.

Industrial Agriculture

As we have seen, the domestication of plants and animals around 10 000 years ago expanded people's food-getting capacity exponentially from what it had been when they relied on hunting and gathering alone. Similarly, the intensification of agriculture brought about by the invention of the plow, irrigation, and fertilizing techniques had revolutionary consequences for food production. A third major revolution in our capacity to feed ourselves occurred with the Industrial Revolution. *Industrial agriculture* relies on technological sources of energy rather than human or animal energy. Water and wind power (harnessed by waterwheels and windmills) were used in the early stages of the industrial period, but today industrial agriculture uses motorized equipment such as tractors and combines powered by fossil fuels and biodiesel. Biochemistry has been applied to modern agriculture to produce fertilizers, pesticides, herbicides, and genetics to produce high-yielding seed varieties, all of which increase agricultural yields of food and nonfood commodities (e.g., cotton and tobacco).

Farmers operating in industrialized societies today have a wealth of new technology at their disposal to increase productivity. Industrial farmers now use the Internet for acquiring a wide range of agricultural information—from equipment sales to pesticide use to marketing opportunities; drones to monitor their crops; recombinant DNA to improve their animal and seed stock; and Global Positioning Systems (GPS) to track harvesting combines in their fields (Friedman 1999). Moreover, new systems of gathering weather information are helping farmers with crop management. Rather than individual farmers having to take weather measurements in their own orchards, fields, and vineyards, precise local information is now available on rainfall, temperature, humidity, and soil water content that comes directly to the farmer's own computer. With such information at their fingertips, farmers are able to assess their risk and react quickly to protect their crops and inform their buyers or consumers as to how their crops are responding.

Within the past several decades, industrial agriculture has witnessed even more changes with the dramatic expansion of agribusiness—large-scale agricultural enterprises involving the latest technology and a sizable salaried workforce. Rather than raise a wide variety of food items for household subsistence, most industrial farmers engage in *monoculture*, the production of a single commodity on vast acreage (Figure 7.14). Some Canadian, U.S., South American, Asian, and African farmers have become experts at

Photo by Dave Olecko/Bloomberg via Getty Images

FIGURE 7.14 **Bill Dillabaugh, a farmer and rancher near Coleville, Saskatchewan, begins to harvest his wheat crop on his 6000-acre farm. Industrialized agricultural production requires heavy machinery and multiple pieces of farm equipment for the annual wheat harvest, a process that is increasingly no longer a family enterprise on some farms.**

---

peasantry Rural people, usually on the lowest rung of society's ladder, who provide urban inhabitants with farm products but have little access to wealth or political power.

industrial agriculture Food production that relies on technological sources of energy rather than human or animal energy.

monoculture The production of a single commodity on vast acreage.

producing single commodities such as corn, soybeans, wheat, tea, coffee, pineapples, and bananas.

A consequence of the rise of agribusiness is the demise of small-scale farms that relied mainly on family labour. As the number of family farms decreases, corporate farms displace farmers in most regions of the world where agriculture and small-scale farmers coexisted. The need for farm labourers—be they displaced farmers or immigrant farm workers—to keep the "new" industrial farm working at optimum efficiency is on the rise. These labourers generally are not family members but rather hired labourers who are paid low wages that often keep them in poverty. Where we find large-scale export agriculture we tend to find transnational corporations controlling the farms and the farming enterprise. The net effect of industrial agriculture has been the loss of food sovereignty and the flow of wealth from poorer nations in the southern hemisphere to rich ones in the northern hemisphere.

Although industrial agriculture has produced farms of enormous size and productivity, these changes have come at a high cost. The machinery and technology needed to run a modern-day agribusiness are expensive. Fuel costs to run the machinery are high. Industrial agriculture has been responsible for considerable environmental degradation. For example, in various parts of the world, the water tables are lower, the ecology of surface water (lakes and rivers) has changed, water fauna have been destroyed by pesticides, aquifers are polluted by pesticides, soil is salinized from over-irrigation, and the air is polluted from crop spraying, and large-scale commercial fishing has decimated fish stocks throughout the world.

Distribution of Goods and Services

Once goods have been produced or procured from the environment, they need to get into people's hands. Although people often consume some of the commodities they produce, surpluses often remain (and remember not all goods consumed are edible; they are consumed by virtue of being used). Systems of exchange are essential for every economy as they allow people to dispose of their surpluses and at the same time maximize the diversity of the goods and services consumed. Goods and services are allocated in all societies according to three different modes of distribution: reciprocity, redistribution, and market exchange (Polanyi 1957).

In Canada, most commodities are distributed according to a free-market exchange system based on the principle of "capacity to pay." People receive money for their labour and then use that money to purchase the goods and services they need or want. Although this is the prevailing type, we can see examples of the other two modes operating in Canada as well. The principle of reciprocity operates, for example, when friends and relatives exchange gifts on birthdays, holidays, and other special occasions. We can see the principle of redistribution at work when people hand over a certain portion of their personal income to the government for taxes, which is then redistributed to public school systems, road maintenance, and other social services. Even though more than one mode of distribution can operate in any given society at the same time, usually one mode predominates.

Reciprocity

Reciprocity is the exchange of goods and services of roughly equal value between two parties without the use of money. Economic anthropologists generally recognize three types of reciprocity, depending on the degree of closeness of the parties involved in the exchange: generalized reciprocity, balanced reciprocity, and negative reciprocity (Sahlins 1972).

Generalized Reciprocity

Generalized reciprocity, which usually occurs among family members or close friends, carries with it the highest level of moral obligation. It involves giving a gift without any expectation of immediate return. Generalized reciprocity is perhaps best illustrated by the giving that takes place between parents and children in our own society. Parents usually give their children as much as they can while their children are growing up: food, toys, educational advantages, a room of their own, and the like, without expecting that their children will repay them at any time in the future. Because of the intimate bonds between parents and children, parents usually provide for their children out of a sense of love, obligation, and social responsibility. In reality, this sense of love and obligation typically becomes a two-way street because children usually come to the assistance of their elderly parents when the parents become too old to care for themselves. Thus, even in this most generalized form of reciprocity, the exchange of goods and services often balances out over the long run.

Even though generalized reciprocity is found in our own society, it is not the predominant form of exchange, as it is in many smaller-scale societies, where the primary unit of economic organization is the family and where material resources may be uncertain.

reciprocity A mode of distribution characterized by the exchange of goods and services of approximately equal value between parties.

generalized reciprocity The practice of giving a gift without expecting a gift in return; creates a moral obligation.

An exchange system based primarily on generalized reciprocity is common among foragers because it contributes to their survival.

For example, in most hunting-and-gathering societies, when a large animal such as a bushbuck is killed, the hunter keeps enough meat for his own immediate family and distributes the rest to his more distant relatives. In warmer regions where there is no means of refrigeration or other way of preserving meat, it makes little sense for the hunter to hoard all the meat himself because it would spoil before it could be eaten. Instead, sharing with others is the expected norm. And, of course, given the uncertainty of hunting, sharing your kill today entitles you to share someone else's kill tomorrow. This form of sharing ensures that no member of the group goes hungry. Such an economic strategy sustains all members by providing a fairly steady supply of meat despite the inconsistent success of most individual hunters. In such societies, generosity is perhaps the highest ideal, and hoarding and stinginess are considered extremely antisocial.

We should not think of generalized reciprocity as being motivated totally by altruism. For all people who live at a subsistence level, maintaining reciprocal exchange relationships is vital to their economic self-interest. At subsistence levels, a person is more dependent on others for her or his material security. In the absence of worker's compensation, employment insurance, and bank loans, people must rely on others when their crops fail or they become too sick to hunt. Subsistence farmers, for example, might not survive without occasional help from their relatives, friends, and neighbours. A farmer may need extra seeds for planting, help with fixing a roof, or extra cash to pay for a child's school fees. The best way of ensuring that these needs will be met is to respond quickly and unselfishly to the requests of others for similar types of assistance.

Balanced Reciprocity

Although we do not always recognize it, reciprocal gift giving in our own society takes a number of different forms. Either consciously or unconsciously, we often give gifts with the expectation of getting something in return. We may expect gratitude, acceptance, friendship, or obligation rather than a material item. For example, when we give a homeless person a loonie or a toonie, the least we expect is a "thank you." When we give our sibling a birthday present, would we not be hurt or disappointed if they did not reciprocate on our birthday? Western industrialized nations do not give millions of dollars in foreign aid to less industrialized nations totally out of a sense of altruism and generosity. Donor nations are looking for something in return, such as access to natural resources, political cooperation, or prestige. When a philanthropist donates millions of dollars to a university, he or she usually expects to have a school or a building named after them. Thus, it appears that, in all societies, including our own, gifts almost always come with strings attached.

Balanced reciprocity is a form of exchange involving the expectation that goods and services of equivalent value will be returned within a specified period of time. In contrast to generalized reciprocity, balanced reciprocity involves more formal relationships, greater social distance, and a strong obligation to repay the original gift. The repayment in balanced reciprocity does not have to be immediate; as Marcel Mauss (1954) suggested, any attempt to repay the debt too quickly can be seen as an unwillingness to be obligated to one's trading partner.

A major economic reason for balanced reciprocity is to exchange surplus goods and services for those that are in short supply. Shortfalls and surpluses can result from different levels of technology, environmental variations, or different production capacities. But whatever the cause, balanced reciprocity enables both parties in the exchange to maximize their consumption.

In Oaxaca, Mexico, balanced reciprocity is illustrated with the exchange of both goods and services. According to social custom, a man is expected to sponsor at least one fiesta celebrating a major saint's day. Such events, involving elaborate food, beverages, and entertainment, are almost always beyond the capability of a man to provide by himself. Consequently the man solicits the help of his relatives, friends, and neighbours, thereby mortgaging his future surpluses. Those who help out expect to be repaid in equivalent amounts when they sponsor a similar fiesta.

Negative Reciprocity

Negative reciprocity is a form of exchange between equals in which the parties attempt to take advantage of one another. It is based on the principle of trying to get something for nothing or to get the better end of the deal. Involving the most impersonal (possibly even hostile) social relations, negative reciprocity can take the form of hard bargaining, cheating, or out-and-out theft. In this form of reciprocity, the sense of altruism and social obligation is at its lowest, and the desire for personal gain is the greatest. Because negative reciprocity is incompatible with close, harmonious relations, it is most often practised between strangers and enemies.

An example of negative reciprocity is provided by the Maasai. According to their creation myth, Ngai (God)

---

balanced reciprocity The practice of giving a gift with the expectation that it will be reciprocated with a similar gift after a limited period of time.

negative reciprocity A form of economic exchange between individuals who try to take advantage of each other.

CROSS-CULTURAL MISCUE

Under the traditional Chinese tradition of *Guanxi*, it is customary to offer gifts in appreciation of business services received. So when Bao Ling Qi applied for a business license to open the Oriental Spa massage parlor in San Mateo County, California, she offered cash, along with several hundred dollars' worth of movie passes and gift cards redeemable at Shell gas stations and Best Buy to the county building inspector and sheriff's investigator (Walsh 2012). County officials, however, did not see these as gifts and charged her with bribery. Her lawyer argued that it was simply a cultural misunderstanding and that she was simply following proper Chinese etiquette and fulfilling an obligation. The court recognized that it was a case of cultural misunderstanding, but still sentenced her to several days in jail and revoked her license. What Bao Ling Qi misunderstood was that, in North America, "gifts" to government officials are unnecessary and may be perceived as bribes. The miscue also highlights the fact that context can determine meaning.

gave all the cattle on Earth to the Maasai, and they have used this myth to justify raiding cattle from neighbouring peoples. If Ngai did indeed give all the cattle to the Maasai, then it logically follows that any non-Maasai in possession of cattle obtained their livestock unlawfully. Maasai have long felt that cattle raids were not stealing but rather reclaiming their God-given property, and obviously they hope the people they "reclaim" them from will not reciprocate.

Redistribution

Another principle of exchange is ***redistribution***, whereby goods are given to a central authority and then given back to the people in a new pattern. The process of redistribution involves two distinct stages: an inward flow of goods and services to a social centre, followed by an outward dispersal of these goods and services back to society. Although redistribution is found in some form in all societies, it is most common in societies that have political hierarchies.

Redistribution can take a number of different forms. In its simplest form, redistribution operates within large families, where family members give their agricultural surpluses to a family head, who in turn stores them and reallocates them back to the individual family members as needed. Among pastoral societies where livestock are shared within the tribe, livestock are raised and used for bridewealth exchanges, which involve the transfer of valuable commodities (often livestock) from the groom's extended family to the bride's extended family as a precondition for marriage (see Chapter 8). In complex societies with state systems of government, such as our own, taxation is a form of redistribution. That is, we give a certain percentage of our earnings to the government in exchange for certain goods and services, such as roads, education, and public health projects. The giving of gifts to charitable organizations (such as the Salvation Army, CNIB, or Goodwill) is also a form of redistribution because benefits are usually given to the poor and homeless.

Chiefly Redistribution or Tribute

In some societies that lack a standardized currency, tribal chiefs are given a portion of food and other material goods by their constituents. The chiefs then give back most of these food items to the people in the form of a feast. This system of ***chiefly redistribution, or tribute***, serves several important social functions at once. In addition to dispensing goods within a society, it affirms both the political power of the chief and the value of solidarity among the people.

Potlatch

Another customary practice that serves as a mechanism of redistribution is the ***potlatch*** found among certain First Nations of Canada's northwest coast (Jonaitis 1991). Traditionally, potlatches were ceremonies in which chiefs or prominent men publicly announced certain hereditary rights, privileges, and high social status within their communities. Perhaps the best-known example of the potlatch was found among the Kwakwaka'wakw of British Columbia, for whom social ranking was of great importance (Rohner and Rohner 1970). Such claims were always accompanied by elaborate feasting and gift giving provided by the person giving the potlatch. In fact, at a potlatch, the host would either give away or destroy all his personal possessions, which could include such articles as food, boats, blankets, pots, fish oil, elaborately engraved copper shields, and various manufactured goods.

The number of guests present and the magnitude of the personal property given away were measures of the host's prestige. The more the host could give away, the stronger was his claim to high social status. In a sense,

---

redistribution A mode of distribution in which goods and services are given by members of a group to a central authority (such as a chief) and then distributed back to the donors.

chiefly redistribution or tribute The practice in which goods (usually food) are given to a chief as a visible symbol of people's allegiance, and then the chief gives the items back to the people (usually in the form of a feast).

potlatch A gift-giving ceremony among First Nations on the northwest coast of Canada and the United States that serves as a mechanism for both achieving social status and distributing goods.

Education Images/UIG via Getty Images

FIGURE 7.15 **Potlatch ceremonies continue to this day among many First Nations on British Columbia's West Coast and serve as a mechanism for both allocating social status and distributing goods.**

the gifts given at a potlatch served as payment to the guests for being witnesses to the host's generosity. In addition to providing a way of allocating social status, the potlatch was an important mechanism for dispersing material goods because each time a person was a guest at a potlatch, he or she returned home with goods. The potlatch was a multifaceted ceremonial activity that also served important socio-political functions. They were often occasions for clans to gather for the purposes of installing new clan leaders, verifying clan claims to certain resources, bestowing clan titles, resolving inter-clan disputes, establishing and reaffirming alliances, and maintaining regional stability (Tollefson 1995) (Figure 7.15).

Potlatches were widely held during the 19th century until missionaries convinced the Canadian government that potlatches were demonic and satanic. As a result, the Canadian government banned them in 1885. Potlatches continued to be held despite the bans, but on a much smaller scale and in secrecy away from non-native eyes. The ban was eventually lifted in 1951 under a revision of the Indian Act. Potlatches are still held today for marriages, funerals, graduations, and so on, although the types of gifts are more contemporary and may include useful household items, native art, and cash (Leung 2007).

All these economic institutions do, in fact, serve as mechanisms for the redistribution of goods and services throughout the societies in which they are practised. But they also serve as ways of allocating social status and prestige. Moreover, many of these systems of redistribution play important ceremonial, political, and integrative roles within the society. That these so-called economic institutions play important societal roles other than economic distribution should serve as a reminder that various domains of culture are interrelated, not separate and isolated.

Market Exchange

The third major mode of distribution is ***market exchange***, whereby goods and services are bought and sold, often through the use of a standardized currency. In market exchange systems, the value of any particular good or service is determined by the market principle of supply and demand. Market exchange tends to be less personal than exchanges based on reciprocity or redistribution, which often involve ties of kinship, friendship, or political relationships. In most cases the exchanges are between individuals who are anonymous to one another. In this respect, market exchanges are predominantly economic in nature because people are more interested in maximizing their profits than in maintaining a long-term relationship or demonstrating their political allegiance to a chief or leader.

The major prerequisite of a market exchange is not whether the exchange is based on currency or barter but rather that the value (or price) of any good or service is determined by the market principle of supply and demand. That is, we can consider an exchange to be based on the market principle when a pig can be exchanged for 10 bushels of corn when pigs are scarce, but bring only 4 bushels of corn when pigs are plentiful.

Market exchange systems are most likely to be found in sedentary societies that produce appreciable surpluses and have a complex division of labour. More labour specialization in a society also contributes to a market exchange system because an "increase in the division of labour brings with it a proliferation of specialized commodities and an increased dependence on market exchange."

Market economies do not always involve money, however. In some small-scale societies, for example, market exchanges may be based on ***barter***, the exchange of one good or service for another without using a standardized form of currency. In a bartering situation, a metalsmith may exchange a plow blade for several bushels of wheat, or an artist and a migrant labourer may swap a piece of sculpture for three days of labour. In Canada and elsewhere, an increasing number of people (such as artists, therapists, and other freelance suppliers) are creating an underground economy by using bartering. A chiropractor, for instance, may exchange his or her services for a meal from the restaurant owner, or for a landscaper to mow the lawn.

Even in the highly complex market economy found in Canada, we find bartering institutions that facilitate the wholesale bartering of goods and services

---

market exchange A mode of distribution in which goods and services are bought and sold, and their value is determined by the principle of supply and demand.

barter The direct exchange of commodities between people that does not involve standardized currency.

between large corporations. By turning over part of its surplus to a bartering corporation, a company that manufactures office furniture can exchange its surplus furniture for items it may need, such as air conditioners, automobile tires, or computers. The Internet and other technological advances have greatly expanded the use of barter, and made it easier for people and companies to find what each other wants. The International Reciprocal Trade Association for instance makes it easier for companies to trade their products worldwide. In 2014 its 400 000 member companies made over 11.3 million inter-exchange barter transactions (a 32 percent increase over 2013) (IRTA 2015).

Standardized Currency

As the range of goods increases, however, it becomes more difficult to find another person who has exactly what you want and wants what you have. Economists call this the *coincidence of wants*. The solution is to have standard currency which everyone wants. A common trait of market economies is the use of *money* for the exchange of goods and services. Money can be defined as a generally accepted medium of exchange that acts as a standard of value. All goods and services can be measured against it to establish their relative worth. Thus, the use of money to purchase items is more flexible than direct exchange of one item for another. Money is also divisible into smaller units, overcoming the problem of barter whereby a farmer's pig, for instance, is worth 10 chickens but he or she only wants 1 chicken. The pig cannot easily be divided. Money also comes in convenient sizes, which allows it to be easily transported; a bag of coins is easier to deal with than a pig. Since money does not perish, unlike most agricultural products, it serves as a store of value, allowing for deferred payment and thus representing a promise to pay in the future with similar value.

Variety of Markets

The extent to which markets are responsible for the distribution of goods and services in any given society varies widely throughout the world. The market economy of Canada and the United States, with their vast networks of commercial interests and consumer products, is one extreme. At the opposite extreme are certain small-scale economies that have little labour specialization, small surpluses, and a limited range of goods and services exchanged in markets.

coincidence of wants The basic problem of barter whereby one exchange partner lacks what the other wants.

money A generally accepted medium of exchange that acts as a standard of value.

Irene Abdou/Alamy Stock Photo

FIGURE 7.16 Women sell greens in the market in the town of Djibo in northern Burkina Faso.

In horticultural societies in South America, such as in Colombia, most of the material needs of a household are met by the productive activities of its members. Whatever surpluses exist are brought to market for sale or exchange, and the profits are used to purchase other goods or needed services or to pay taxes. In such societies the actual location of the market is important because many social functions are performed there in addition to the economic exchange of goods and services. In West Africa, the market is a place where buyers and sellers meet to exchange their surplus goods, but it may also be the place where a person goes to meet a friend, settle a dispute, watch dancing, hear music, pay respects to an important chief, have a marriage negotiated, catch up on the latest news, or see distant relatives (Figure 7.16).

Many societies today find themselves in a transition between these two fundamentally different types of market economies. Of interest is exploring the dynamics of culture change by asking questions such as: How will societies change when individualistic market rationality (individuals wanting more and not less of a good) replaces the values of sharing, personal relationships, and community well-being? Is it possible to hang onto one's traditional core of community values when technologies, including global satellites, cellphones, and the Internet, are used to exchange goods and services? To what extent do people in small-scale societies choose to participate in the global economy? Should a member of the family migrate to another country to seek gainful employment? How might this influence others from the same community to migrate along with the successful individual? And what cultural changes might occur over time as a result of these new international economic ties? These and other questions concerning the impact of global markets on local communities are being posed with increased frequency by anthropologists all over the world.

Informal Economy

This worldwide transition from small-scale to global markets raises the distinction between formal and *informal market economies*. Informal market economies include legal but unregulated producers of goods and services that, for a variety of reasons, escape government control and regulation (taxation, public monitoring, and auditing). The informal economy should not be confused with the *underground economy*, however, which involves illegal activities such as prostitution, drug dealing, human trafficking, and racketeering. Informal economies include some self-employed individuals as well as those employed in homes and at factories operating "under the radar." Workers do not claim income on personal tax forms, nor do employers file employment records. Working conditions, earnings, and safety standards in the informal economic sector are almost always far inferior to those in the formal sector. There is a wide variety of informal economic activities, including house cleaning, garment work done in homes, construction work, gardening, selling crafts or fruit and vegetables on street corners, begging, child care, independent taxi driving, home catering, hair cutting, and other microenterprises.

Economists have recognized these informal economic activities for years, but because they are difficult to track, they are challenging to study. In some parts of the developing world, the informal economy has generated more economic activity than the formal economy. The presence of informal activity has been obvious for decades in many of the megacities of Africa, southern Asia, and South America—where millions of people struggle to survive by hawking single pieces of fruit on the street.

For example, street vendors make up a large part of the informal economy in Central America, where they are often found on busy city street corners. According to Danillo Valladares (2010), women in Guatemala are playing an increasingly large role in the informal economy working as domestics, street vendors, and in-home seamstresses. Working in the informal sector enables women to provide additional income for their families, in part because their own positions do not pay well enough and their husbands also may not bring in enough money. "According to the third regional report on the labour market in Central America and the Dominican Republic produced by the International Labour Organization (ILO) and the Central American Integration System (SICA), 64 percent of women in the labour force in the region work in the informal sector, compared to 50 percent of men in the workforce" (Valladares 2010). Female vendors would love to be employed in jobs that pay a regular wage, social security, and other benefits, but such jobs are not available for everyone, especially for those who lack formal education and skills for the higher paying positions.

---

informal market economies Legal but unregulated exchange of goods and services that escape government control and regulation.

underground economy Illegal market activities such as prostitution, drug dealing, human trafficking, and racketeering.

Summary

1. Economic anthropology involves a cross-cultural examination of how resources are allocated, converted into usable commodities, distributed, and consumed.
2. Economic anthropology goes beyond notions of supply and demand and maximization of profits, it also looks at the roles of religious beliefs, kinship relationships, political structures, gender ideologies, and other aspects of culture.
3. Whereas property rights to land are strongly protected in Canada, many parts of the world do not share the notion of property ownership. Instead of owning something in our sense of the word, people have limited rights and obligations to a particular object, resource, or piece of land.
4. Every society, to one degree or another, allocates tasks according to gender and age. Because the same type of activity (such as weaving) may be associated with either gender in different cultures, the division of labour by gender is sometimes seen as arbitrary.
5. The amount of labour specialization varies from society to society.
6. If any culture is to survive, it must develop strategies and technologies for procuring or producing food from its environment.
7. Although they are not mutually exclusive, five major food-procurement categories are recognized by cultural anthropologists: foraging (hunting and gathering), horticulture, pastoralism, intensive agriculture, and industrial agriculture.
8. The success of various food-getting strategies depends on the interaction between a society's technology and its environment. Although different environments present different limitations and possibilities, it is generally recognized that environments influence rather than determine food-getting practices. The level of technology that

any society has at its disposal is a critical factor in adapting to and using the environment.

9. Hunting and gathering, the oldest form of food getting, relies on procuring foods that are naturally available in the environment. Hunting-and-gathering societies tend to have low-density populations, are nomadic or semi-nomadic, live in small social groups, and occupy remote, marginally useful areas of the world. Hunting and gathering was the only form obtaining food until about 10 000 years ago.
10. Horticulture, a form of small-scale plant cultivation that relies on simple technology, produces low yields with little or no surpluses. Horticulture most often uses the slash-and-burn method of cultivation, which involves clearing the land by burning it and then planting seeds in the fertile ash residue. Most horticulturalists plant multiple varieties of seeds to ensure that there is enough food for their households.
11. Pastoralism, keeping domesticated livestock as a main source of food, is usually practised in areas of the world that are unable to support any type of cultivation. Pastoralism most often involves a nomadic or semi-nomadic way of life, small family-based communities, and regular contact with cultivators as a way of supplementing the diet.
12. Intensive agriculture, a more recent phenomenon than horticulture, uses technology such as irrigation, fertilizers, and mechanized equipment to produce high crop yields capable of supporting large populations. Unlike horticulture, intensive agriculture is usually associated with permanent settlements, cities, high levels of labour specialization, and the production of a surplus to be sold or traded at a market.
13. Industrial agriculture (agribusiness) relies on high levels of technology (such as tractors and combines), high-yielding seeds, a mobile labour force, and a complex system of markets.
14. Goods and services are distributed according to three different modes: reciprocity, redistribution, and market exchange. Reciprocity is the exchange of goods and services of roughly equal value between two trading partners; redistribution, found most commonly in societies with political bureaucracies, is a form of exchange whereby goods and services are given to a central authority and then reallocated to the people according to a new pattern; and market exchange systems involve the use of standardized currencies to buy and sell goods and services.
15. Economic anthropologists generally recognize three types of reciprocity depending on the degree of closeness of the parties: Generalized reciprocity involves giving a gift without any expectation of immediate return; balanced reciprocity involves the exchange of goods and services with the expectation that equivalent value will be returned within a specific period of time; and negative reciprocity involves the exchange of goods and services between equals in which one or both parties try to gain an advantage over the other.
16. Redistribution involves a social centre from which goods are distributed. The potlatch ceremony among the First Nations of Canada's northwest coast is an example of redistribution.
17. Market exchange, based on standardized currencies, tends to be less personal than either reciprocity or redistribution because people in such an exchange are interested primarily in maximizing their profits. As a general rule, the higher the degree of labour specialization in a society, the more complex the system of market exchange.

Key Terms

allocation of resources
animal husbandry
balanced reciprocity
barter
cattle complex
chiefly redistribution or tribute
coincidence of wants
consumption
distribution
division of labour
economic anthropology
economics
foraging (hunting and gathering)
formal economic theory
generalized reciprocity
horticulture
industrial agriculture
informal market economies
intensive agriculture
labour specialization
locavore
market exchange
money
monoculture
negative reciprocity
nomadism
optimal foraging theory
pastoralism
peasantry
potlatch
production
property rights
reciprocity
redistribution
shifting cultivation (swidden cultivation, slash-and-burn)
subsistence strategy
transhumance
underground economy

Critical Thinking Questions

1. As the world's population continues to increase and extreme climatic events are experienced, are traditional subsistence strategies sustainable?
2. How does foraging compare with grocery shopping?
3. Foraging and pastoralist societies are being forced, especially through environmental change and government regulations, to give up their nomadic lifestyle and become sedentary. How can an anthropologist work with such groups to help them make the transition?
4. Although economists tend not to consider it, the gift economy in Canada constitutes a major part of the economy. What are the social norms and customs governing gift exchange in mainstream Canadian society?
5. Raising chickens in inner cities in Canada is catching on; many cities outlaw it, but some, such as Victoria, B.C., permit it, while others are considering it. If you were contracted by your local community to help city officials make their decision, how would you go about researching urban chicken farmers? What data would you need to collect?
6. How do the processes of production, distribution, and consumption of resources differ between cultures where land is privately owned compared to those where land is owned communally?
7. In terms of production, how do gender roles between men and women differ in Canadian society compared to a horticultural society?
8. In many countries, poverty necessitates that children work in order for the family to survive. This is at the expense of their education, which makes it difficult for them to escape their poverty. How could an anthropologist work with these children, their parents, and employers to resolve this dilemma?
9. Insects are an inexpensive source of protein, and cultivating them offers an excellent small-business opportunity for people in the developing world and can thus potentially alleviate both poverty and hunger—provided that people can be persuaded to eat them. How would you work with a local community to change people's negative attitudes toward eating insects?
10. Immigrants to Canada from many poorer nations send money to their relatives back home. What impact might this have on these home communities?

Make the Grade with MindTap

Stay organized and efficient with **MindTap**—a single destination with all the course material and study aids you need to succeed. Built-in apps leverage social media and the latest learning technology. For example:

- ReadSpeaker will read the text to you.
- Self-quizzing allows you to assess your understanding.
- Flashcards are pre-populated to provide you with a jump-start for review—or you can create your own.
- You can highlight text and make notes in your MindTap Reader. Your notes will flow into Evernote, the electronic notebook app that you can access anywhere when it's time to study for the exam.

Visit nelson.com/student to start using **MindTap**. Enter the Online Access Code from the card included with your text. If a code card is not provided, you can purchase instant access at NELSONbrain.com.

Part 5

Record
of Solemnization of
Marriage
This is to certify that

ANDREA LOUISE MARKS *and* LINDSEY MICAELA ROTHSCHILD.
were married on
the 24th day of MAY 2008.
Day, month, year

in the city or town of
WINDSOR, ESSEX COUNTY.
Name of city, town, village

Neil A. Hodges
Signature of person who performed the marriage

Signature of witness

Signature of witness

E0534482

The concepts of marriage and family are changing as gay and lesbian couples marry and have children.

CHAPTER 8

Marriage, Family, and Kinship

WHAT WE WILL LEARN

- What anthropologists mean by the term marriage
- What functions marriage and family systems perform
- Who can marry whom
- What economic considerations are associated with marriage
- How modern family structures have changed
- What anthropologists mean by the term kinship
- The different ways in which cultures categorize kin
- What descent groups are and what their various functions are
- How matrilineal and patrilineal systems of kinship differ
- How new reproductive technologies are changing our understanding of marriage, family, and kinship

NEW REPRODUCTIVE TECHNOLOGIES AND PARENTHOOD

When Winnipeg couple Mike Olson and Lisa Seel were unable to conceive naturally, Seel's sister, Averill Stephenson, offered to act as a surrogate mother. She soon became pregnant with twin boys (Bosanac 2013), but Olson and Seel have no legal right to the twins. Manitoba law assumes that the woman who delivers the child is the biological mother, and her husband the father regardless of who supplied the egg or the sperm (Bosanac 2013). According to the law, Lisa Seel is the aunt whereas biologically she is the mother since it was her ovum. The law thus uses a different concept of biological and is failing to keep up with new realities.

More open-minded attitudes toward gender identities and same-sex marriages in Canada, the United States, and Europe, along with new advances in reproductive and transplant technologies, are forcing us to question traditional concepts of marriage, family, and kinship.

The first "test tube" baby was born in July 1978, and since then there have been an estimated 5 million babies born through in vitro fertilization (IVF) (Kirkey 2013), a process whereby an egg is fertilized by a sperm outside the body (in a "test tube"), and then the embryo implanted into either the egg donor's uterus or that of another woman. **Surrogacy** involves agreeing to become pregnant, usually through artificial insemination or surgical implantation, and to carrying the fetus to term for another person. It is becoming big business. There are numerous agencies in Canada and elsewhere helping people to create a family.

For many people, surrogacy offers a faster, cheaper, and easier way to start a family than adoption. And in some cases the only way. Adoption can take 5–10 years and can cost $100 000 or more; the prospective parents have to go through a rigorous screening process with no guarantee of success. Many prospective adoptees are also older, may have suffered from neglect or abuse, may be physically or mentally disabled, or have medical problems (Surrogacy in Canada Online 2015). Finding a surrogate mother, however, can take only a few weeks, since Canada's fertility treatment industry is largely unregulated and does not require prospective parents be screened. Moreover, if the eggs and sperm come from one or both parents, then the child is genetically related to them. And although not cheap, surrogacy can be cheaper than adoption. When Kate from Vancouver, for example, discovered she could not have children, she contacted an Ontario agency who found a surrogate mother within three months and charged her $3000 (Blackwell 2012b).

---

surrogacy Carrying a fetus to term for another person.

Surrogate expenses typically total about $15 000 (Blackwell 2012b), although Surrogacy in Canada Online estimates $60 000 be budgeted for gestational surrogacy to pay for clinic, lawyer, social worker, and surrogate mother's expenses.

In many countries surrogacy is illegal. In Israel, commercial surrogacy is legal, but not between relatives due to religious reasons and over concerns about incest. In the United States some states (e.g., California) recognize surrogacy, while others do not (e.g., New York) (Surrogacy in Canada Online 2015). In Canada it is legal under the 2004 Assisted Human Reproduction Act (Parliament of Canada 2004), but like Australia and the United Kingdom, it is illegal for people to sell their eggs or sperm, to pay a surrogate, or to advertise such services. Consequently, eggs and sperm must be donated, and surrogates must offer their services for altruistic reasons, in what is called "altruistic surrogacy" (Surrogacy in Canada Online 2015). Most surrogate mothers are therefore relatives of the person they are acting as a surrogate for. The intent of the Act is to prevent eggs, sperm, and embryos from being considered commodities. Surrogates can, however, be reimbursed for reasonable expenses. What are "reasonable" expenses is open to debate, however, and has allowed agencies to flourish (Blackwell 2012b).

Canada's fertility industry is booming. In the past few years, demand for IVF treatments has increased several-fold and now comes not only from infertile heterosexual couples, but also from same-sex couples, single men, single women, and transsexual people. One Vancouver clinic estimates that, in the 1980s, 95 percent of the clients were heterosexual couples, but that by 2006 about a third wanting donated sperm were lesbian couples, and a third single women. One estimate is that close to 25 percent of clients at some clinics are gay, lesbian, or transsexual (Blackwell 2012c). Demand far outstrips the world supply, and agencies are constantly on the lookout for new surrogates (Blackwell 2012b).

Many people are thus looking to countries such as Mexico and especially India for surrogate mothers. For instance, in 2012 a gay couple from Quebec used a surrogate mother from Mexico who underwent IVF with a donated egg and sperm from one of the fathers. She gave birth to triplets (Blackwell 2014). In same-sex situations then, children have either two mothers or two fathers.

Next time you are in the park and see a man with a beard breastfeeding don't be surprised. When Mr. Hope, a Toronto musician who was born female, was in her 20s she underwent sex-reassignment surgery to become a man. The surgery did not, however, involve removing her uterus (a hysterectomy) (Blackwell 2012a). When Mr. Hope and his partner, also a transsexual, decide they wanted to start a family, a Toronto fertility clinic artificially inseminated him, and he gave birth by Caesarean section in late 2011 (Blackwell 2012a, 2012c). This example makes us think about whether we should continue to use the term "pregnant woman" and instead use "pregnant person." In this situation Mr. Hope is, in a sense, both mother and father. In male-to-female sex reassignment surgeries, transsexuals are often still able to produce sperm, which can be used in fertility treatments (Blackwell 2012c).

With the desire to be a parent so strong, many are taking unconventional paths to form a family. When Emily Jordan was diagnosed with cervical cancer and had to undergo a radical hysterectomy, it meant she and her husband, Mike, could not have children of their own—or so they thought. Although lacking a uterus in which a baby could grow, Emily's ovaries were intact. The embryo, created from one of her eggs and sperm from her husband, was implanted into a surrogate mother—Emily's own 53-year-old mother, Cindy Reutzel (Figure 8.1). On August 30, 2012,

Reutzel gave birth to Elle Cynthia Jordan, who was thus both her daughter and her granddaughter (Irvine 2012). Because they came from the same womb, Emily and her daughter Cindy are also sisters, but because Emily donated the egg she is also the mother. And Mike is both the father and brother-in-law.

In rare cases women are born without a uterus but, since 2000, several uterus transplants have been performed. The intent behind these operations is that the recipient be able to carry a fetus to term in the transplanted uterus. In 2013 Swiss doctors transplanted a uterus into an unidentified patient who the following year was implanted with an embryo fertilized by her husband's sperm and her own egg (her ovaries were functioning), and she gave birth to a boy in September 2014. The person who donated the uterus, however, was the patient's mother (R. Smith 2014). In this case, the woman is the mother since her son was conceived with her egg and she also gave birth to him, but since he also emerged from same uterus she herself did, she could be considered his sister.

AP Photo/Sitthixay Ditthavong

FIGURE 8.1 Emily Jordan (*left*) and her pregnant mother Cindy Reutzel. After Jordan underwent a radical hysterectomy, she and her husband took up an offer from Reutzel to act as their surrogate.

Canadians are very motivated to start families and will go to great lengths and expense to have children. Fifty years ago adoption was open only to heterosexual couples. Same-sex couples could not marry let alone have children. And single people still have difficulty adopting. With today's new technologies, more options than adoption are available, and not only for heterosexual couples but also for gay and lesbian couples, single men and women, and transsexuals. These changes have not gone uncontested and raise numerous ethical, legal, religious, and human rights issues. Should the laws of supply and demand be allowed to operate and payment be allowed for donating eggs and sperm or for acting as surrogate mothers, or should people's motives be entirely altruistic? Contrary to the evidence, many people believe gay and lesbian couples, individuals, and transsexuals make poor parents or are poor role models for children, and thus should not be allowed to use the services of a surrogate mother. The reality is that those who opt to use surrogates have probably put considerably more thought into being parents than many who have children by natural means.

As with other issues, to understand the impact new technologies are having on marriage, the family, and kinship, we must take a holistic approach and look at the issue from various aspects. Surrogacy is becoming a global enterprise so anthropologists must look at how it is impacting people in countries such as India. In particular we should look at economic considerations. In 2011 Quebec decided to fund in vitro fertilization under Medicare, which has led to more than a doubling of IVF patients as cost barriers have come down (Blackwell 2012c).

These new attitudes and technologies are making us rethink the concept of the family and terms such as mother, father, sister, and aunt. They remind us that these ideas are fluid since children can be genetically related to both parents, or one parent, or neither. We must cease thinking entirely in biological terms and should perhaps focus more on social terms. ■

Kinship, Marriage, and Family

It has been said that there are two kinds of people in the world: those to whom we are related, and those to whom we are not. The difference is important as we behave differently toward our relatives than toward strangers. Imagine, for instance, that you receive a request to stay with you for a few days from a distant cousin whom you have never met or had anything to do with. You are more likely to agree to the request than if it came from someone completely unrelated to you. Both are essentially strangers, but we have a sense of obligation to our cousin, whereas not to the non-relative. Of course, who we consider to be our relatives varies from one culture to another, as does the nature of the relationship. Brad Pitt and Barak Obama, for instance, are ninth cousins (Buckman 2009) (Figure 8.2), but it is unlikely they see themselves as relatives. For most Western cultures, kinship is not as important as it is in small-scale cultures, and although we may interact with more distant relatives at social occasions, for the most part we have little to do with them on a day-to-day basis.

One way to look at kinship is as a process. And it all begins with marriage. People get married and by doing so increase their social network. And then they have children. When they do, they also create aunts and uncles, brothers and sisters, grandparents and cousins, i.e., a kinship system.

Many young couples today face new challenges in the globalized and biotech world. Pressure to get an education and establish a career delays marriage for many. Marrying later in life has contributed to a range of fertility problems for some men and women. In other instances, couples elect to have smaller families or are forced to have only one child, making the sex of the child for some an important issue. Biotechnology is providing new avenues for applied anthropologists specializing in marriage and family planning, and changing notions of family, marriage, and kinship. This chapter examines the process of marriage throughout the world that leads to the formation of a variety of families and larger kinship groups.

In all societies people recognize certain groups of people who are considered marriageable, and the relatives who make up the basic social group, generally called the family. This is not to imply, however, that all societies

Han Myung-Gu/WireImage

Michael B. Thomas/AFP/Getty Images

FIGURE 8.2 Brad Pitt and Barak Obama are ninth cousins. They share a common ancestor born in 1690. It is unlikely that they consider themselves as "kin," although in some societies they might.

view the family in the same way. In fact, humans have developed a wide variety of family types. To many middle-class Canadians, the family includes a husband and wife and their children. To an East African herdsman, however, the family includes hundreds of kin related through both blood and marriage, whereas among the Hopi, the family is made up of a woman and her husband and their unmarried sons and married daughters, along with the daughters' husbands and children.

Marriage and the Family

For years, anthropologists have attempted to arrive at definitions for the terms marriage and family that will cover all known societies. They have also often debated whether families and the institution of marriage are universals. For our purposes ***marriage*** is defined as a socially approved union between two or more adult partners that regulates the sexual and economic rights and obligations between them. It usually involves an explicit contract or understanding, and is entered into with the assumption that it will be permanent. A ***family*** is a social unit consisting of both adults and children who recognize certain rights and obligations toward one another. It is characterized by economic cooperation, adults who maintain a socially approved sexual relationship, the reproduction and raising of children, and a common residence. As with most definitions there are exceptions to the terms.

Socially Approved

In all societies, being married, whatever form marriage may take, is the expected norm for adults. There is also usually an ideal form that most people approve of. Other forms, if they are considered "marriage," are disapproved of. In Canada and the United States, for instance, people living together, that is, living ***common law***, have traditionally been stigmatized. In the United States until the 1960s, for example, couples could not rent a hotel room or take out a mortgage unless they were legally married. People who took up this lifestyle were "living in sin." This phrase indicates that, for many people, marriage is a deeply religious concern. For Roman Catholics, marriage is a sacrament, that is, when God is thought to be present. While about 75 percent of couples who do get married are married in a religious ceremony, the number of civil weddings is increasing. Much of the opposition to changing the definition of marriage to include same sex couples, comes from people opposed to it for religious reasons.

But times are changing. As religion becomes less important in the lives of many Canadians, and as society becomes more secular generally, the stigma attached to living together without being married is disappearing. The result is an increase in the number of common law unions. In 1981, 93.7 percent of people in couples in Canada were married, while only 6.3 percent were living common-law. By 2011 only 80.1 percent of couples were married and (19.9 percent) were common-law partners (Milan 2013).

Surprisingly, common-law unions are more popular now with older Canadians than with younger people. Of all those living common law in 2011, less than a quarter (23.7 percent) were in their 20s, while almost half (49.6 percent) were in their 40s or older. This may reflect a growing acceptance of this form of arrangement by older people. The fastest growth of common-law unions is in the 65–69 year-old age group, which increased by two-thirds between 2006 and 2011 (Milan 2013).

While people are increasingly choosing to live common law as opposed to getting married, a lot of Canadians are shunning the institution of marriage and cohabitation altogether. In 1981 about one-quarter (26 percent) of young adults aged 25–29 years had not been married. In 2011 that figure had increased to almost three-quarters (73.1 percent). More than 50 percent of Canadians in their early 30s also remained unmarried in 2011 (Milan 2013). This change is due in part to an increase in the average age at marriage, and not only to more people living common law, but also to more people deciding to live a single life. This also has the effect of reducing the number of families, and also the size of those families.

Same-Sex Unions

Until recently, most Westerners assumed that marriage took place only between men and women. Until 2005 the Canadian government defined marriage as the "lawful union of one man and one woman." Under the equality rights provision of the *Canadian Charter of Rights and Freedoms*, however, this was seen to be discriminatory. Thus, since July 2005, marriage in Canada has been defined as the "lawful union of two persons to the exclusion of all others." Replacing "one man and one woman" with the words "two persons" permits same-sex marriages. It is also important to note, however, that it is still a "lawful union." In other words, marriage in Canada is a legal institution and thus is legitimated and protected, and accorded the same rights as heterosexual unions. The phrase "to the exclusion of all others," ensures that it is a monogamous union and not polygamous, which is still illegal in Canada.

---

marriage A socially approved union between two or more adult partners that regulates the sexual and economic rights and obligations between them.

family A social unit consisting of adults, who maintain a socially approved sexual relationship, and children, and is characterized by economic cooperation and the reproduction and raising of children in a common residence.

common law People living together as a couple without being legally married.

Michael Kovac/Getty Images for EJAF

FIGURE 8.3 **David Furnish and Elton John with their sons Elijah and Zachary. Same-sex marriage became legal in the United Kingdom in March 2014. Furnish and John were married in December 2014 on the ninth anniversary of their civil partnership. Elijah and Zachary were born in California from the same surrogate mother.**

Although the issue remains hotly contested, many other Western countries now recognize the legitimacy of same-sex marriages. Same-sex marriage became legal in Ireland, which has a high percentage of Catholics, through a referendum in May 2015, and in the United States in June 2015. In Canada, the number of same-sex couples, whether married or not, has been increasing rapidly. In 2006 only 16.5 percent of same-sex couples were married; by 2011 it had nearly doubled to 30 percent (Milan 2013) (Figure 8.3).

In other societies, same-sex marriages have been acceptable traditionally. Among the Nandi of Kenya, for example, only men can hold and manage property and livestock. If a woman becomes a widow she can hold property in trust for her sons, but not for her daughters, as this is considered inappropriate. But if she is childless, or has only girls, any property she may have would be passed down to the sons by other wives of her deceased husband or to his brothers. To resolve this problem, the woman can take on the role of a man (adopts male gender). She is expected to dress as man, do men's work, and has the rights and privileges of a man, such as the right to speak in public meetings. She also has the right—in essence by becoming a female husband—to marry. By paying bridewealth she can marry another woman (often a girl who has become pregnant by a man who refused to marry her) and arrange for this wife to bear sons through consorts. The female husband becomes the social and legal father of the wife's children. More importantly, since she is technically a man in Nandi eyes, she can hold property and pass it down to her sons. It is also important to note that these arrangements are not sexual but economic, the female husband does not have sexual intercourse with her wife nor, since she is considered a man, with other men (Oboler 1980). Nandi female husbands demonstrate how people can use the institution of marriage to resolve issues within their own cultural context. Same-sex marriage is not recognized in Kenya, however; but in October 2011, the High Court of Kenya upheld the validity of a traditional Nandi woman-to-woman marriage as it is a traditional cultural practice and protected under the 2010 Kenyan Constitution (Canning 2011).

Sexual Relations

Marriage, according to our definition, is a socially legitimate sexual union. Sexual relations outside marriage in many societies, but not all, are often disapproved of, with both partners ideally expected to be virgins when they marry and to remain faithful once married. When two adults marry, it is implied that they are having a sexual relationship or that the society permits them to have one if they desire it. Although this is generally true, we should bear in mind that this social legitimacy is not absolute; there may be specified periods during which sexual relations with one's spouse are taboo. To illustrate, in many societies, sexual relations between spouses must be suspended during periods of menstruation and pregnancy. After a child is born, women in many societies are expected to observe a ***postpartum sex taboo*** lasting, in some cases, until the child is weaned, which can be as long as several years. As William Stephens (1963, 10) suggested, "There may be other sex taboos in honor of special occasions: before a hunting trip, before and after a war expedition, when the crops are harvested, or during various times of religious significance." Given this wide range of occasions when sex with one's spouse is prohibited, it is possible that, in some societies, husbands and wives are prevented from having sexual relations for a significant segment of their married lives.

There are also instances where there is no intent of the partners having sexual relations, for instance in a so-called "marriage of convenience" where the marriage is contracted for economic, political, or personal reasons rather than love or forming a long-lasting relationship. Marrying a Canadian citizen by a non-Canadian does not confer Canadian citizenship on the spouse. And marrying a Canadian for the sole purpose of immigrating to Canada or to gain citizenship is illegal. Such "marriage fraud" has become a problem and, to prevent it, the Canadian government passed new regulations on October 25, 2012, whereby immigrants must live with their sponsors for two years to show they have a genuine relationship before they can gain permanent residence status in Canada (Citizenship and Immigration Canada 2015b).

postpartum sex taboo The rule that a husband and wife must abstain from any sexual activity for a period of time after the birth of a child.

Age at Marriage

Part of our definition states that marriage is a union between adults. When a person is considered an adult and thus eligible to marry, however, varies from one culture to another. Customary age of marriage may also differ from the legal age of marriage. In Bangladesh, for example, the legal age of marriage is 18, yet in 1993–1994 the median age of first marriage for girls (i.e., when 50 percent of all women are married) was 14.1 years—one of the lowest in the world (Sing and Samara 1996) (Figure 8.4). By 2012, the median age had increased to 15 (Hoq 2012). Sing and Samara (1996) discovered that, in Bangladesh, Guatemala, India, and Yemen, 60–82 percent of all women had married by age 20. Men generally marry later than women throughout the world.

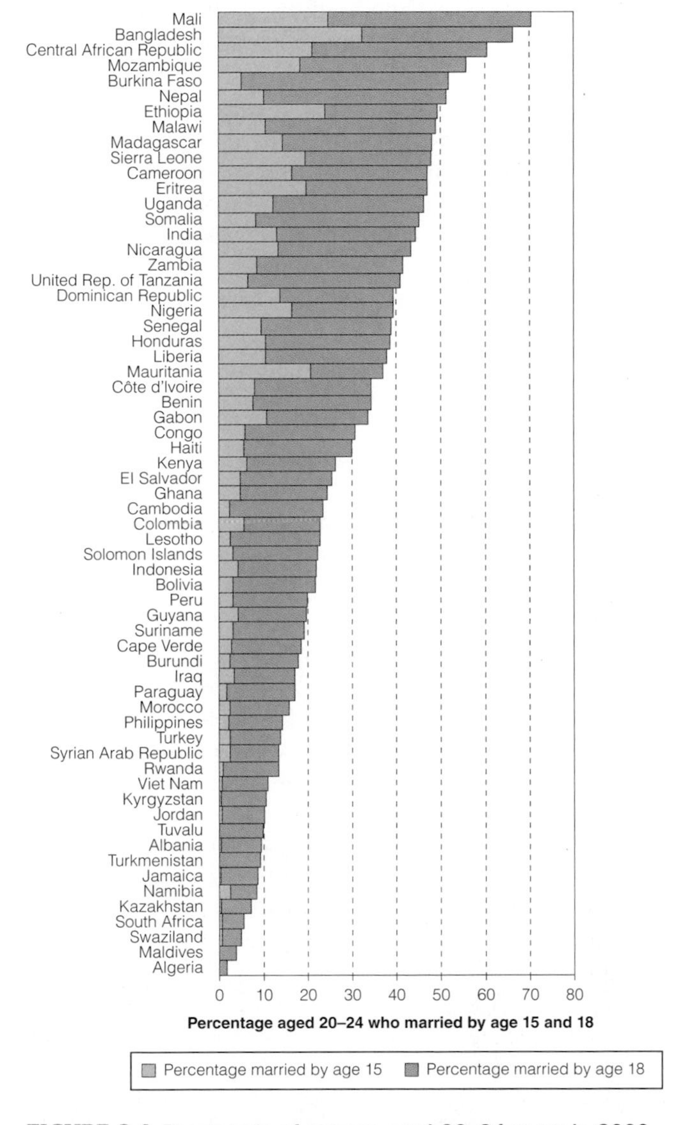

FIGURE 8.4 **Percentage of women aged 20–24 years in 2000–2010 who had married by ages 15 and 18 in countries where the minimum legal age at marriage without parental consent is 18 years or over.**

Source: MEASURE DHS, ICF Macro (2011). DHS Reports, accessed from http://www.measuredhs.com/publications on 20 December 2011; UNICEF (2011). Multiple Indicator Cluster Surveys - Available reports/datasets by country, accessed from http://www.childinfo.org/mics_avail- able.html on 20 December 2011; United Nations, Department of Economic and Social Affairs, Population Division (2011). World Fertility Policies 2011 (United Nations publication, Sales No. E.11.XIII.5).

An early age at marriage was also common in Europe: in the 1400s, the legal age of marriage for girls was 12—usually after their first menstruation. One of the driving forces of an early marriage age for girls is poverty. Parents not only benefit from having one less mouth to feed, but in some cases can also benefit from a dowry. Girls are also married for political reasons as well as simply tradition. Early age at marriage is also more common in rural than urban areas, and in poorer districts than wealthier ones. When girls marry young they also have children at a young age, which poses greater risks both for the mother and the child, and leads to high rates of maternal and infant mortality as well as sexually transmitted diseases such as HIV (ICRW 2015). Women who marry young are also more likely to care for their children at the expense of their education and employment opportunities (Sing and Samara 1996), which only perpetuates the cycle of poverty. The more education women have, the less likely they are to get married at an early age, and the more likely they are to find employment (Sing and Samara 1996). Girls who marry young also find it difficult to form an identity outside their husband's. If they marry after 20, they have more of an opportunity to develop independence. Marriage breakdown for young single mothers can thus cause social and economic hardship.

Many of these marriages of young girls are arranged and so the girls have little choice in whether to marry or not. Often the men they are married to are considerably older than they are. Once married, they are also more likely to be physically and sexually abused. For example, when Nujood Ali, who comes from a poor and broken family in Yemen, was 8 years old her father arranged a marriage to Faez Ali Thamer, a man more than three times her age who physically and sexually abused her (Figure 8.5). When Nujood was 10 she managed to escape and made her way to Sana'a (the capital of Yemen) where she demanded a judge grant her a divorce. She also filed a case against her father. Nujood's husband rejected her demand for a divorce, claiming it was his right to keep her as his wife, and under Yemeni law he has not committed a crime. While there have been recommendations to make 18 the minimum age for marriage for both men and women in Yemen, the Yemeni Jurisprudence Committee has claimed that, under Islam, there is no basis to impose such a law. Nujood Ali is not alone. A 2006 study revealed that 52.1 percent of Yemeni girls were married at a young age, the average age being 14.7 years. The average marriage age also varies from one geographical area to another. In one region, for instance, the average age was 8, and in another 10 (Forward 2008).

KHALED FAZAA/AFP/Getty Images

FIGURE 8.5 Yemeni child bride Nujood Ali (*third from left*), 10 years old, at her family's house with her siblings in the suburbs of Sana'a, Yemen. Nujood broke tribal tradition to demand a divorce from a man nearly three times her age in a marriage arranged by her father.

In Canada the legal age of marriage in all the provinces and territories is either 18 or 19, except in Quebec, where it is 16. People can get married between the ages of 16 and 18, but require parental consent or the consent of the courts. Marriage for girls under 16 requires court approval and a physician's certificate showing that she is pregnant or the mother of a living child.

Everywhere in the developing world, however, women and men are getting married at later ages (United Nations Department of Economic and Social Affairs 2011). In the 1960s and 1970s, the average for first marriages in Canada was about 23 for women and 25 for men. In 2008, women were getting married for the first time at 29.6 years of age, and men at 31.0 years (Milan 2013).

Permanence

Another qualification to our definition involves the permanence of the marital union. Often, as part of the marriage vows recited in Western weddings, spouses pledge to live together in matrimony "until death do us part." Even though it is difficult to ascertain a person's precise intentions or expectations when entering a marriage, an abundance of data suggest that the permanence of marriage varies widely, and in no societies do all marriages last until death. Statistics Canada ceased collecting statistics on divorce in 2008 but, at that time, 41 percent of marriages ended in divorce before the 30th anniversary and it was 48 percent overall; that is, nearly half of all marriages ended in divorce. High divorce rates often indicate that fewer people are available to care for their aging parents, thus putting more strain on healthcare. Schools also use divorce-rate data to estimate the level of services they need to provide, and it also affects rates of household formation and thus the need for housing, taxed income, and social services.

Impermanent marriages can also be found in smaller-scale societies. In short, when it comes to the permanence of marriage, there is always a discrepancy between ideal expectations and actual behaviour.

In the industrialized world, the incidence of divorce has increased dramatically over the past hundred years, and most industrialized nations have legal procedures for dissolving marriages. To illustrate, Canada experienced a tenfold increase in the rate of divorce between 1890 and 1980. A number of factors have been cited for the initial dramatic rise of divorce in Canada. First, industrialization and urbanization modified the functions of the family. When the basic unit of production changed from the family farm to the factory, the economic ties holding the family together were weakened. And as people had more disposable income, the notion of recreation and leisure time changed from family-based activities to attendance at paid events, such as movies and concerts. The rise of individualism and the pursuit of personal happiness have also led some people to spend less time with family members and made some less willing to make sacrifices for the good of the family. The emphasis that Western culture puts on romantic love as the basis for marriage also makes marriages vulnerable when sexual passion subsides. There is also much less stigma attached to divorce today than a century ago. In the 1950s, a divorced couple was looked upon with pity, if not contempt, for not being able to "save their marriage." Finally, divorce in Canada today is relatively easy to obtain. No longer must a spouse prove infidelity or physical abuse. Today, a wife or husband seeking to end a marriage simply needs to claim only that the marriage has "failed" or that there are "irreconcilable differences." As one law professor commented, "It is easier to walk away from a marriage than from a commitment to purchase a new car" (quoted in Etzioni 1993) (Figure 8.6).

epa european pressphoto agency b.v./Alamy Stock Photo

FIGURE 8.6 Like many marriages in Western society, the marriage of Katie Holmes and Tom Cruise ended in divorce after five years of marriage.

CROSS-CULTURAL MISCUE

Marriage in every society contains certain structural stresses and strains between partners. This holds true for spouses who share a common cultural background, but it is even more challenging in so-called "mixed marriages," where the partners were raised in different cultures or subcultures. Anthropologist Edward T. Hall, an expert in nonverbal forms of communication, tells the story of a mixed marriage in the United States in which the wife was so concerned about marital problems that she consulted a psychiatrist. Her husband, raised in a reserved family in New England, was taught to keep a tight rein on his emotions and to respect the privacy of others. His wife, by way of contrast, was raised in a large, boisterous Italian American family, where the family members were warm, loud, emotional, volatile, demonstrative, and physical. Coming from two such different family backgrounds, each with its own way of expressing caring and emotions, this husband and wife faced some serious communication problems arising from different expectations. According to Edward and Mildred Hall (2009, 23):

> When the husband came home after a hard day at the office, dragging his feet and longing for peace and quiet, his wife would rush to him and smother him. Clasping his hands, rubbing his brow, crooning over his weary head, she never let him alone. But when the wife was upset or anxious about her day, the husband's response was to withdraw completely and leave her alone. No comforting, no affectionate embrace, no attention—just solitude. The woman became convinced her husband didn't love her, and, in desperation, she consulted a psychiatrist. Their problem wasn't basically psychological but cultural.

Just as all cultures have established a variety of ways of legitimizing marriages, they also have many ways of dealing with separation and *divorce*, the formal dissolution of a marriage. Divorce arrangements found in the many cultures of the world vary widely according to the reasons for divorce and how easy or difficult it may be to get divorced. As a general rule, divorce rates are lower in societies that have strong kinship ties. By way of contrast, in foraging societies, such as the Ju/'hoansi, divorce is quite easily accomplished. Such nomadic or semi-nomadic societies generally lack large, formal, social groups beyond the nuclear family that could complicate divorce proceedings.

Although marriages break down in all societies, some societies are reluctant to officially sanction divorce; only the Vatican and the Philippines forbid it. By way of contrast, a Hopi woman from Arizona could divorce her husband quite easily by simply putting his belongings outside the door.

Marriage and the Family: Functions

Marriage serves several important functions for societies. One function is to create fairly stable relationships between men and women (and same-sex unions) that regulate sexual mating and reproduction. Because humans are continually sexually receptive and (in the absence of contraceptives) heterosexual intercourse often leads to reproduction, it is imperative that societies create and maintain unions that will regulate mating, reproduction, and child rearing in a socially approved manner.

A second social function of marriage is to provide a mechanism for regulating the sexual division of labour that exists to some extent in all societies. For reasons that are both biological and cultural, men in all societies perform some tasks and women perform others. To maximize the chances of survival, it is important for a society to arrange the exchange of goods and services between men and women. Heterosexual and same-sex marriage usually brings about domestic relationships that facilitate the exchange of these goods and services.

Third, marriage creates family relationships that can provide for the material, educational, and emotional needs of children. Unlike most other animal species, human children depend on adults for the first decade or more of their lives for their nourishment, shelter, and protection. Moreover, human children require adults to provide the many years of cultural learning they need to develop into fully functioning members of the society. Even though it is possible for children to be reared largely outside a family unit, in most societies, marriage creates a set of family relationships that provide the material, educational, and emotional support children need for their maturation.

Mate Selection: Who Is Out of Bounds?

Every society has established rules that regulate sexual intercourse. The most common form of prohibition is mating with certain types of kin who are defined

divorce The legal and formal dissolution of a marriage.

by the society as being inappropriate sexual partners. The prohibition on mating with certain categories of relatives is known as the *incest taboo*. Following the lead of Robin Fox (1967), we distinguish between sexual relations and marriage. Incest taboos are prohibitions against having sexual relations and are different from rules prohibiting marrying certain relatives, although the two often coincide; that is, those relatives you are forbidden to have sex with, you are also forbidden to marry.

The most universal form of incest taboo involves mating between members of the immediate (nuclear) family—that is, mothers and sons, fathers and daughters, and brothers and sisters—although there are several notable yet limited exceptions. For political, religious, or economic reasons, for example, members of the royal families among the ancient Egyptians, Incas, and Hawaiians were permitted to mate with and marry their siblings, although this practice did not extend to the ordinary members of those societies. Queen Cleopatra of Egypt, for instance, married, in turn, each of her brothers, Ptolemy XII, Ptolemy XIII, and Ptolemy XIV. The incest taboo and the prohibition against marriage invariably extends beyond the scope of the immediate or nuclear family, however. In most countries, Canada included, people are legally allowed to marry (and have sexual relations with) their first cousins; China, the Philippines, Bulgaria, and some U.S. states are exceptions. In some non-Western societies, the incest taboo may extend to large numbers of people on one side of the family but not on the other. And in still other societies, a man is permitted (even encouraged) to marry the daughter of his mother's brother (a first cousin) but is strictly prohibited from marrying the daughter of his mother's sister (also a first cousin). Thus, although it seems clear that every society has incest taboos, the relatives that make up the marriageable group vary from one society to another. Given that incest taboos are found throughout the world, anthropologists have long been interested in explaining their origins and persistence. A number of possible explanations have been suggested.

Preferential Cousin Marriages

A common form of preferred marriage is *preferential cousin marriage*, which is practised in one form or another in many regions of the world. Some kinship systems distinguish between two different types of first cousins: cross cousins and parallel cousins. This distinction rests on the gender of the parents of the cousin. *Cross cousins* are children of siblings of the opposite sex—that is, one's mother's brothers' children, and one's father's sisters' children. *Parallel cousins*, on the other hand, are children of siblings of the same sex (the children of one's mother's sisters and one's father's brothers). One way to think of this is to recognize that, in Western society, when women get married they usually take their husband's last name. Thus, the children of your father's sister (your aunt) would have a different last name than you, as your aunt would have changed her name at marriage. These are your cross cousins. The children of your father's brother, however, have the same last name as you, and so are your parallel cousins.

In societies that make such a distinction, parallel cousins, who are considered family members, are called "brother" and "sister," and thus are excluded as potential marriage partners. However, because one's cross cousins are not thought of as family members, they are considered by some societies as not just permissible marriage partners, but often preferred ones.

The most common form of preferential cousin marriage is between cross cousins because such a union strengthens and maintains the ties between kin groups established by the marriages that took place in the preceding generation. That is, in the system of cross-cousin marriage, a man originally marries a woman from an unrelated family, and then their son marries his mother's brother's daughter (cross cousin) in the next generation. Because a man's wife and his son's wife come from the same family, the ties between the two families tend to be solidified.

A much less common form of cousin marriage is between parallel cousins. Found among some Arabic-speaking societies of the Middle East and North Africa, it involves the marriage of a man to his father's brother's daughter. Because parallel cousins belong to the same group, such a practice can prevent the fragmentation of family property and facilitate arranged marriages.

Inbreeding Theory

A popular theory that attempts to explain the existence of the incest taboo focuses on the potentially harmful effects of inbreeding on the family. This inbreeding theory holds that mating between close kin, who are likely to carry the same harmful recessive genes, tends to produce a higher incidence of genetic defects that result in higher mortality rates. We share half our genes with our parents and our siblings, and so if both carry a copy of a recessive gene there is a 25 percent chance that any children resulting from such a union will have two copies. Cousins have one-eighth of their genes in common and although offspring from cousin-cousin matings

---

incest taboo The prohibition of sexual intimacy between close relatives.

preferential cousin marriage A preferred form of marriage between either parallel or cross cousins.

cross cousins Children of one's mother's brothers or father's sisters.

parallel cousins Children of one's mother's sisters or father's brothers.

do result in increased genetic defects, the incidence is not that different from marrying unrelated people. Most people are thus unlikely to make the connection between birth defects and cousin marriage, although they might between closer relatives.

Just because there is a taboo, however, it is unlikely to be the main reason preventing the vast majority of people from engaging in incest. Occasionally we hear in the news of someone who has been charged with incest, but the fact that it makes the news suggests its rarity, and so we must look elsewhere for an answer.

Family Disruption Theory

A second theory centres on the negative social consequences of incest and holds that mating between a mother and son, father and daughter, or brother and sister would create such intense jealousies within the nuclear family that the family would not be able to function as a unit of economic cooperation and socialization. For example, if adolescents were permitted to satisfy their sexual urges within the nuclear family unit, fathers and sons and mothers and daughters would be competing with one another and, consequently, normal family role relationships would be seriously disrupted. The incest taboo, according to this theory, originated as a mechanism to repress the desire to satisfy one's sexual urges within the nuclear family.

In addition to causing disruption among nuclear family members through sexual competition, incest creates the social problem of *role ambiguity*. For example, if a child is born from the union of a mother and her son, the child's father will also be the child's half-brother, the child's mother will also be the child's grandmother, and the child's half-sister will also be the child's aunt. These are just some of the bizarre role combinations created by such an incestuous union. The 1947 song *I'm My Own Grandpa*, by Dwight Latham and Moe Jaffe, illustrates these ambiguities. Because different family roles, such as brother and father, carry with them vastly different rights, obligations, and behavioural expectations, the child will have great difficulty deciding how to behave toward immediate family members. Does the child treat the male who biologically fathered him or her as a father or as a brother? How does the child deal with the woman from whose womb he or she sprung—as a mother or as a grandmother? Thus, the incest taboo can be viewed as a mechanism that prevents this type of role ambiguity or confusion.

Theory of Expanding Social Alliances

Incest avoidance can also be explained in terms of positive social advantages. By forcing people to marry out of their immediate family, the incest taboo functions to create a wider network of interfamily alliances, thereby enhancing cooperation, social cohesion, and survival. Each time one of your close relatives marries a person from another family, it creates a new set of relationships with people toward whom your family is less likely to become hostile. This theory holds that it makes little sense to marry someone from one's own group with whom one already has good relations. Instead, there is more to be gained socially by expanding one's networks outward, which helps to create a more peaceful society by increasing one's allies.

Childhood Familiarity Theory

According to the childhood familiarity theory, children who are brought up together, whether related or not, are not sexually attracted to one another. In other words, people do not commit incest with family members simply because they have no interest in doing so. Originally proposed by anthropologist Edward Westermarck, the theory has received some ethnographic support. Prior to the 1970s, children born on Israeli kibbutzim (collective agricultural communities) were separated from their parents at a very young age and raised together with other children of their same age. They even slept in the same dormitories with minimal contact with their parents. Surveys discovered that virtually none of these children married one another (Smith, D. L. 2007).

Exogamy and Endogamy

Beyond this notion of incest, people in all societies are faced with rules either restricting their choice of marriage partners or strongly encouraging the selection of certain people as highly desirable mates. These are known as rules of *exogamy* (marrying outside a certain group) and *endogamy* (marrying within a certain group) (Figure 8.7).

In societies such as Canada and the United States, the exogamous group extends only slightly beyond the nuclear family; that is, marrying one's first cousin is considered inadvisable (if not illegal in some places) and disapproved of, but beyond that one can marry other, more distant relatives. In societies based on unilineal descent groups (see below), however, the exogamous group is usually the lineage, which can include hundreds of people, or even the clan, which can include

role ambiguity Confusion about how one is expected to behave within the family.

exogamy A rule requiring marriage outside a specified social or kinship group.

endogamy A rule requiring marriage within a specified social or kinship group.

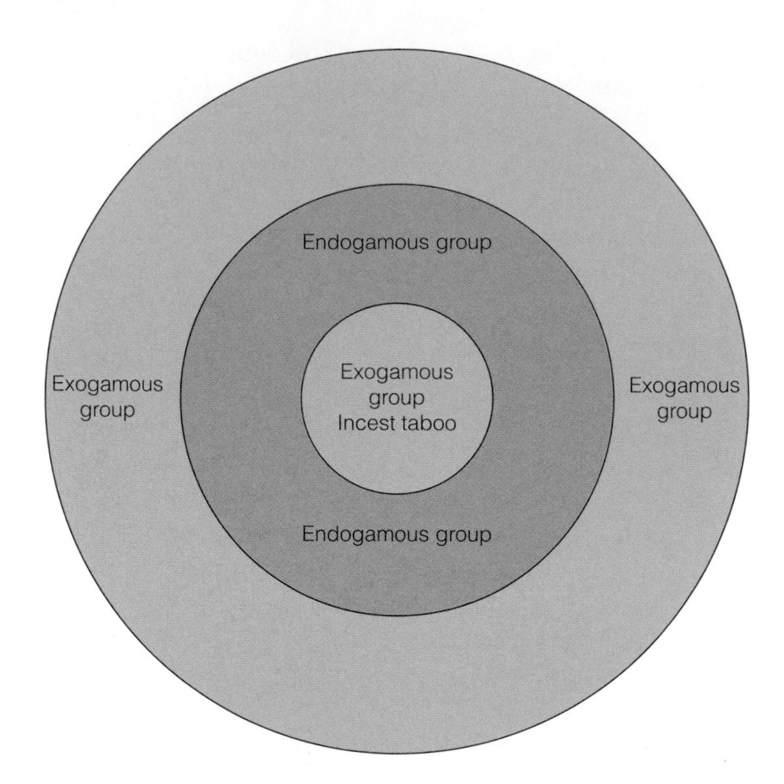

FIGURE 8.7 **People should marry those in the endogamous group (i.e., people like themselves) and not people in the exogamous group (i.e., the immediate family and people who are unlike themselves).**

thousands of people who are unmarriageable. Thus, when viewed cross-culturally, rules of exogamy based on kinship do not appear to be based on the closeness of blood ties.

In contrast to exogamy, which requires marriage outside one's own group, the rule of endogamy requires a person to select a mate from within one's own group. Hindu castes in traditional India are strongly endogamous, believing that to marry below one's caste would result in serious ritual pollution. Caste endogamy is also found in a somewhat less rigid form among the Rwanda and Banyankole of eastern central Africa. In addition to being applied to caste, endogamy may be applied to other social units, such as to the village or local community, as was the case among the Incas of Peru, or to racial groups, as was practised in the Republic of South Africa for much of the 20th century.

Even though there are no strongly sanctioned legal rules of endogamy in Canada, there is a certain amount of marrying within one's own group based on class, ethnicity, religion, and race (Figure 8.8). This general de facto endogamy found in Canada results from the fact that, generally, people have infrequent social contacts with people from different backgrounds. Wealthy families live in wealthier neighbourhoods, belong to the same organizations, and send their children to private schools, while those less well-off live in poorer parts of the city, belong to the same organizations (but generally different ones than wealthier people), and send their children to public schools. This general social segregation by class, coupled with parental and peer pressure to "marry your own kind," results in a high level of endogamy in complex Western societies such as Canada.

epa european pressphoto agency b.v./Alamy Stock Photo

FIGURE 8.8 **Robert DeNiro and his wife Grace Hightower. At one time in the United States, interracial marriage was illegal.**

The Role of Romantic Love and Courtship

Romantic love has been a major reason for marriage in Western cultures for generations (Figure 8.9). Most 19th and 20th century anthropologists, however,

Guido Mieth/Moment/Getty Images

FIGURE 8.9 Romantic love has been a major reason for marriage in Western cultures for generations.

tended to overlook romantic love in the non-Western world because it was not supposed to exist. In fact the "conventional wisdom" among most social scientists until quite recently was that romantic love was a luxury that only affluent societies had the time and energy to engage in. However, the findings of cross-cultural research have found that, even though many non-Western people may not base a marriage on romantic love, they certainly have the notion of romantic love (Jankowiak and Fischer 1992).

The critical question all cultures must answer is, To what extent do the people *themselves* decide whom they shall marry? The ethnographic possibilities range from permissive societies that allow sexual experimentation, "dating," and courtship by early adolescents to societies in which the groom does not see the face of his bride, and vice versa, until the official wedding ceremony.

The Trobriand Islanders of Papua New Guinea are on the permissive end of the continuum. According to Annette Weiner (1988), Trobriand boys and girls begin playing erotic games with one another when they are seven or eight years old. By the early to mid-teens, they begin experimenting with sexual partners with no expectation of any committed relationship on the part of either party. Adolescents are free to pursue these liaisons because they do not sleep in their parents' houses but rather with their peers in boys houses or girls houses. Even though adolescents do engage in some productive work, they are largely left to pursue freely their own relationships and adventures. Girls are every bit as assertive and proactive as boys in their acceptance or rejection of lovers. Thus, traditional Trobriand courtship practices and experimenting with heterosexual relationships are not that different from the types of "virtual courtships" young adults in Canada and the United States engage in today through such websites as Facebook, Twitter, LinkedIn, Pinterest, and Tinder.

At the opposite end of the continuum, where any contact between unmarried men and women is forbidden, is Saudi Arabia—perhaps the most socially conservative Islamic country in the world. Until young adults marry, they are expected to live in their parental home, which is segregated by gender, with boys living in one part of the house and girls in another. The males in a typical Saudi household do everything in their power to protect the reputations of their unmarried sisters by rigidly enforcing the prohibition against any type of social contact between unmarried people. If they fail to protect their sisters and daughters from heterosexual contact from outside the family, the honour of the entire family will be jeopardized. Thus, marriages are arranged between men and women who often have never seen, or spoken to, one another. There should be no social contact between the prospective bride and groom even during the months between the signing of the marriage contract and the wedding ceremony. As with any set of cultural practices anywhere in the world, however, the extent to which *all* young adults adhere to these rigid standards of no social contact is not 100 percent.

Most young people in the world today live in cultures that fall somewhere between these two extremes. Moreover, many of these cultures, owing to modern communication and transportation technology, are experiencing rapid socio-cultural change. For example, cellphones and text messaging now permit both men and women to circumvent the traditional prohibitions against premarital social interaction.

Arranged Marriages

In Western societies, with their strong emphasis on individualism, mate selection is largely a decision made jointly by the prospective couple. Aimed at satisfying the emotional and sexual needs of the individual, the choice of mates in Western society is based on such factors as physical attractiveness, emotional compatibility, and romantic love. Even though absolute freedom of choice is constrained by such factors as social class, ethnicity, religion, and race, individuals in most contemporary Western societies are free to marry anyone they please.

In many societies, however, the interests of the families are so strong that marriages are ***arranged***. Negotiations are handled by family members of the prospective bride and groom, and for all practical purposes, the decision of whom one will marry is made primarily by one's parents or other influential relatives. In certain cultures, such as parts of traditional Japan, India, and China, future marriage partners are betrothed while they are still children. In one extreme example—the Tiwi of North Australia—females are

arranged marriage A marriage in which the selection of the spouse is outside the control of the couple.

CROSS-CULTURAL MISCUE

Medical anthropologist Geri-Ann Galanti (1991) tells of a tragic incident that resulted from a U.S. physician working in Saudi Arabia failing to understand the culture of one of his patients. An 18-year-old Bedouin girl from a remote village was brought in to the hospital with a gunshot wound in the pelvis. When the doctors took X-rays to determine the extent of the girl's injury, they discovered, much to their surprise, that she was pregnant. Because Bedouin girls receive no sex education, the girl was unaware that she was pregnant.

Three doctors were involved in the case: a U.S. neurosurgeon who had worked in the region for several years, a European gynecologist who had worked in the Middle East for a decade, and a young internist from the United States who had just arrived in the area. They all realized that the girl's pregnancy presented a real problem because tribal custom punishes out-of-wedlock pregnancies with death.

To save the girl's life, the physicians decided to send her to Europe for a secret abortion, telling her parents that her gunshot wound needed special treatment available only in Europe. The young U.S. physician was hesitant to make such a recommendation, but the other two doctors, more experienced in Middle Eastern cultures, convinced him of the seriousness of the situation. They explained that a pregnant unmarried girl was a terrible slur on the reputation of the men of the family, who were responsible for her protection. Her pregnancy was a sure sign that they had not done their job. The only way that the family could restore its honour would be to put the girl to death.

The young American reluctantly agreed not to tell the parents, but at the last minute changed his mind because he could not be deceitful. He told the girl's father as she was being wheeled to the airplane. The father immediately grabbed the girl off the stretcher, rushed her to his car, and drove away. Several weeks later the hospital staff learned that the girl had been killed by her family. The family's honour had been restored, but the ethnocentric internist had a nervous breakdown and returned to the United States.

betrothed or promised as future wives before they are born (Robinson 1997). Because the Tiwi believe that females are liable to become impregnated by spirits at any time, the only sensible precaution against unmarried mothers is to betroth female babies before birth or as soon as they are born.

Arranged marriages are based on the cultural assumption that, because marriage is a union of two kin groups rather than merely two individuals, it is far too significant an institution to be based on something as frivolous as physical attractiveness or romantic love.

Pep Roig/Alamy Stock Photo

FIGURE 8.10 Arranged marriages are often found in societies that have elaborate social hierarchies; perhaps the best example is Hindu India.

Arranged marriages are often found in societies that have elaborate social hierarchies; perhaps the best example is Hindu India (Figure 8.10). Indeed, maintaining the caste system in India depends largely on a system of arranged marriages. Indian arranged marriages are further reinforced by other traditional Indian values and beliefs. Fathers, it was traditionally held, sinned if they failed to marry off their daughters before puberty. Both parents in India shared the common belief that they were responsible for any sin the daughter might commit because of a late marriage. For centuries, Hindu society has viewed females as lustful beings who tempt males with their sexual favours. Thus, a girl had to be married at an early age to protect both herself and the men who might become sinners. And, if girls were to become brides before reaching adolescence, they could hardly be trusted to select their own husbands.

Anthropologist Serena Nanda (1992) reminds us that arranging marriages in India is serious business and should not be taken frivolously. In addition to making certain that a mate is selected from one's own caste, parents must be careful to arrange marriages for their children that take into consideration such factors as level of education, physical attractiveness, compatibility with future in-laws, and level of maturity. Requiring seriousness, hard work, and patience, an arranged marriage may take years to bring about, as one of Nanda's Indian informants explains, "This is too serious a business. If a mistake is made we have not only ruined the life of our son or daughter, but we have spoiled the reputation of our family as well. And, that will make it much harder for their brothers and sisters to get married" (1992, 142).

Indian couples were once introduced by family members who spent months, even years, researching potential partners. Today these matchmaking kinsmen are being rendered obsolete by an explosion of matrimonial websites. Would-be brides and grooms from India (as well as Indians living abroad) can go to websites with URLs such as Asianmatches.com, Suitablematch.com, and Matrimonials.com where they can search for the ideal partner according to language, religion, caste, level of education, occupation, and even height, complexion, or astrological sign. By participating in these electronic matchmaking services, Indian young people are essentially agreeing with the traditional notion of arranged marriages but are asking for (and getting) more input in the process. The effect of this is to diminish the importance of caste in India. These new high-speed matrimonial websites greatly expand the pool of potential candidates, increase the amount of information that is available for prescreening, and allow the bride and groom more time to make up their minds. Traditional Indian parents are willing to move from the traditional arranged marriage to what might be called "assisted marriage" largely because they are more efficient and are likely to lead to what both parents and children want: strong, long-lasting marriages between compatible partners and compatible families. In fact, many parents today are searching these matrimonial websites themselves on behalf of their unmarried sons and daughters.

Arranged Marriages in Canada

Even though mate selection in North America generally is a matter of individual choice, many singles are not opposed to seeking help. Whereas Indians use the Internet to find potential marriage partners, the matchmaking services used by North Americans focus on dating, romance, and finding the right relationship, with marriage as a more distant goal. The number of websites devoted to matchmaking has exploded in the last few years. Online dating services, which have millions of subscribers and generate hundreds of millions of dollars in revenue each year, have become a normal part of the singles scene for people of all ages.

Dating in Canada has also changed with the times. Due possibly to busy and overly complicated lives and schedules, people find that their life-partner is not always their high-school or university sweetheart, someone from church, from work, or a pick-up from the bar scene. Some adults seeking love and romance and marriage partners are using a type of matchmaking service known as speed dating. Speed dating involves organized venues where people can meet a lot of eligible singles in one evening. Events are controlled with rules and time, people have an opportunity to meet and greet for a few minutes and then move onto another person. At the end of the event, people share their real identity or not, giving their contact information only to those they may be interested in for a longer meeting.

Many matchmaking services, including speed dating, specialize in a variety of demographics, such as nationality (Russia, China, Colombia), ethnicity (Latino, African American), religion (Catholic, Jewish, Hindu, Muslim), sexual orientation (gay, lesbian, straight), or lifestyle preference (vegetarians, Harley-Davidson enthusiasts, farmers, pet lovers, yoga practitioners, or singles with sexually transmitted diseases). There are even matchmaking services today that specialize in helping subscribers find their political soul mates. These matchmaking site services also provide opportunities for husbands and wives to seek out extramarital relations.

All these recent matchmaking services—both electronic and more personal—are noticeably different from the traditional forms of matchmaking, which were largely in the hands of family members. Nevertheless, these new mechanisms for arranging marriages fit in nicely with the pressures of the modern world. Young people, particularly those trying to manage their careers, simply do not have the time or are not interested in cruising singles bars in hopes of finding the right partner.

The Levirate and Sororate

According to the *Old Testament*, "If brothers are living together and one of them dies without a son, his widow must not marry outside the family. Her husband's brother shall take her and marry her and fulfill the duty of a brother-in-law to her... The first son she bears shall carry on the name of the dead brother so that his name will not be blotted out from Israel" (Deuteronomy 25:5-6).

This custom, whereby a widow is expected to marry the brother (or some close male relative) of her dead husband, is known as ***levirate***. Any children fathered by the woman's new husband are usually considered

levirate The practice of a man marrying the widow of his deceased brother.

A Crisis of Births: Family Making in Italy

Some parts of the world are experiencing a crisis of overpopulation. Worldwide, the figures calculate fertility rates at 3.1 births per women, yet globally they range from 1 to 7. Some campaigns attempting to reduce their national population explosion have taken on aggressive family-planning policies such as those that limit the number of children per household (China) or use coercive measures to reduce births through sterilization (India).

Western Europe, however, is experiencing a crisis of underpopulation and doing so without family-planning initiatives. Demographers and politicians worried about nationalism along with social and economic issues drew media attention for some time on the region's low fertility rates. Anthropologist Elizabeth Krause conducted her fieldwork in central Italy during the height of the media blitz that encouraged families to become larger. In her ethnographic account, Krause (2005) explores the phenomenon of making smaller families and the implication it has on society, politics, and culture in *A Crisis of Births: Population and Family-Making in Italy*. What Krause discovered is that the small family had become a symbol of the postwar era for upwardly mobile and modern Italians where the average family now has one child. The birth of 1.4 children per couple is below the rate of 2.1 children per household necessary for population stability, and has become a national problem that demographers, politicians, and policymakers want to fix (Krause 2005).

Krause relied on ethnographic methods such as interviewing, gathering oral histories, and participant observation; she also conducted archival and media research while she lived in an industrial-agricultural province in Tuscany for two years with her husband and her five-year-old daughter. She had a number of questions guiding her research, but one underlying theme she explored was what contributed to Italy's declining fertility rate? In her research she wanted to understand "what happens when a whole society's pattern of making families changes dramatically" (Krause 2005, xiii)?

During the course of her two years, she worked in a family-operated workshop for a sweater factory, sewing on buttons. In this capacity, getting involved in the community, meeting locals as a local, she was able to get a real appreciation of the life of working-class families and family-making from different social and economic classes. It is from this ethnographic experience that she was able to articulate how economics and family influence gender roles, division of labour, the concept of work, immigration, racism, nationalism, as well as emotions, feelings, expectations, and ultimately family making. History played a critical role in her experience because the older generation of

Cultura Creative (RF)/Alamy Stock Photo

Family having a picnic at the beach.

Italians have a different perspective on family and family size than that of the younger generations. She found that low fertility is much about struggles over male and female relations. It is about men and women carving out new identities in what it means to be Italian, European, and modern.

From an applied perspective, Krause's research findings could contribute to demographers' and politicians' approaches to future family-planning initiatives, and create family policies to mitigate the low birth rate. She points out, "Family-making is not merely about reproducing babies, but also about producing the material goods and wages, as well as the care and nurturing, that make for a viable family" (Krause 2005, 67). Demographers and politicians who fear that immigrants will reproduce at a more rapid rate and alter the old social and class structures of Italian society are clearly missing the contemporary Italian cultural context (that of smaller families) that figures prominently into current family-making beliefs and practices.

Questions for Further Thought

1. Why is Italy experiencing a low birth rate?
2. How does the trend of people going from having large families to having small families play out at different levels of society?
3. What would be necessary to construct an effective pro-family campaign?

to belong legally to the dead brother rather than to the actual father. Because the bride marries into her husband's family and essentially severs her ties with her original family, such a custom serves as a form of social security for the widow and her children. It also preserves the rights of the husband's family to her future children. The levirate is found in patrilineal societies (those societies made up of a man, his sons, and the sons' wives and children) and is closely associated with placing a high value on having male heirs.

It is practised in a wide variety of societies in Oceania, Asia, Africa, and India, and was practised by ancient Hebrews.

In India, widows are not always supported by their dead husband's families. It has been estimated (Damon 2007) that over 44 million widows in India live in abject poverty because their husband's families have chosen not to support them. These widows cannot return to their natal or birth families because they severed those ties when they married. Thus, facing a type of "social death," these Indian widows are at the mercy of inadequate support provided by either the government or local Hindu temples.

The *sororate* is essentially the opposite of the levirate and comes into play when a wife dies. It is the practice of a widower marrying the sister of his deceased wife. If the deceased wife has no sibling, her family is under a general obligation to supply some equivalent relative as a substitute. For example, in societies that practise the sororate, a widower may receive as a substitute wife the daughter of his deceased wife's brother.

Levirate and sororate demonstrate the fact that marriages are not simply contracts between individuals but between groups of people. When the contract is broken the terms still have to be fulfilled, and this usually means producing children to carry on the lineage.

A Nuer woman whose husband has died also remains subject to a legal contract and is obligated to continue his bloodline (Figure 8.11). Rather than marry the deceased man's brother or close relative, however, she remains married to his ghost. Under such *ghost marriage* arrangements, the children she bears by other men belong to her deceased husband's lineage. Also under Nuer tradition, when a woman marries, any wealth she may have becomes the property of her husband at marriage. One way to retain it is to marry a deceased man's ghost. Since Nuer men are often considerably older than women when they marry, they often die before their wives, and so almost half the marriages in Nuer society are ghost marriages.

Art Directors & TRIP/Alamy Stock Photo

FIGURE 8.11 Nuer mother and child, South Sudan. If a Nuer woman's husband dies she can remain married to his ghost, and any children she bears by other men belong to her deceased husband's lineage.

Number of Spouses

In much the same way that societies have rules regulating whom one may or may not marry, they have rules specifying how many mates a person may or should have. Cultural anthropologists have identified three major types of marriage based on the number of spouses permitted: *monogamy* (the marriage of one person to one other at a time), *polygyny* (the marriage of a man to two or more women at the same time), and *polyandry* (the marriage of a woman to two or more men at the same time). Polyandry and polygyny are two types of *polygamy*, which simply means having two or more spouses at the same time.

Another type of arrangement, sometimes called group marriage, is *polyamory*, or "many loves." The Canadian Polyamory Advocacy Association (CPAA) defines polyamory as "having more than one intimate relationship at a time with the knowledge and consent of everyone involved" (CPAA 2010). This can involve various combinations of adults. The most common polyamorous relationships involve one man and two women, or two men and one woman, although it can involve more people. Polyamory is not illegal in Canada so long as the arrangement is not formalized. The CPAA advocates for the same rights as other married Canadians in terms of tax laws, insurance, property ownership, and custody of children. Although multiple-partner relationships are not new, they have only recently come into vogue, partly because of the sexual revolution of the 1960s and 1970s and the generally greater social acceptance of same-sex marriage. It was not until 2006 that the term entered the Oxford English Dictionary (Bennett 2009). According to *Newsweek* there are about 500 000 people in the United States in polyamorist relationships (Bennett 2009).

---

sororate The practice of a woman marrying the husband of her deceased sister.

ghost marriage A form of marriage common among the Nuer whereby a woman remains married to her deceased husband's ghost.

monogamy The marital practice of having only one spouse at a time.

polygyny The marriage of a man to two or more women at the same time.

polyandry The marriage of a woman to two or more men at the same time.

polygamy Having two or more spouses at the same time.

polyamory Intimate relationships between three or more people at the same time.

Monogamy

Monogamy is so widespread and rigidly adhered to in Canada that most people have great difficulty imagining any other marital alternative. Any person who chooses to take more than one marriage partner at a time is in direct violation of conventional norms, most religious standards, and the law.

Many societies that practise monogamy circumvent the notion of lifelong partnerships by either permitting extramarital affairs (provided they are conducted discreetly) or practising ***serial monogamy*** (taking a number of different spouses one after another rather than at the same time). Serial monogamy is common in Canada, the United States, and Western Europe.

Polygyny

The majority of world cultures, however, practise polygyny. It remains a preferred form of marriage throughout Asia, Africa, and the Middle East. There is also evidence to support the idea that polygyny played a significant role in the West by virtue of the numerous references to polygyny in the *Old Testament*.

To suggest that approximately 70 percent of the world's *cultures* practise polygyny is not to say that 70 percent of the world's *population* practises polygyny (Figure 8.12). Many cultures that practise polygyny are small-scale societies with small populations. Moreover, even in polygynous societies, the majority of men at any given time still have only one wife. Even in societies where polygyny is most intensively practised, we would not expect to find more than 35 percent of the men actually having two or more wives. Polygyny in these societies is the *preferred* or *ideal*, not the usual, form of marriage. It is something that men strive for but only a minority of men actually achieve. In other words, while polygyny may be the ideal, the statistical reality is that most marriages are monogamous.

Syamsul Bahri Muhammad/ZUMAPRESS/Newscom

FIGURE 8.12 Polygyny is practised in many parts of the world. A member of Malaysia's Ikhwan Polygamy Club poses for a family photograph during a Maulidur Rasul gathering in Rawang outside Kuala Lumpur with two of his three wives and five of his six children.

There are a number of reasons most men in polygynous societies never acquire more than one wife. First, marriage in many polygynous societies requires the approval (and financial support) of large numbers of kinsmen, and this support is not always easy to obtain. Second, in some polygynous societies it is considered inappropriate for men of low rank to seek additional wives, thereby restricting a certain segment of the males in the society to monogamy. And third, being the head of a polygynous household, which invariably carries high prestige, is hard work. The management of two or more wives and their children within a household requires strong administrative skills, particularly if relations between the wives are not congenial. Societies are also under increasing pressure to accept the socially dominant values of the West and Christian churches have continuously opposed polygyny.

Having two or more wives in a polygynous society is usually a mark of prestige or high status. The late King Sobhuza II of Swaziland (1899–1982), for instance, was estimated to have had more than a hundred wives. In many societies polygyny is a symbol of prestige for older men. Having multiple wives means wealth, power, and high status for both the polygynous husband and the wives and children (Deng 2009); that is, a man's status increases when he takes additional wives, and a woman's status increases when her husband takes additional wives. For this reason, women in some African societies actually urge their husbands to take more wives.

Sometimes a man takes multiple wives because the society views them as economic and political assets. Each wife not only contributes to the household's goods and services but also produces more children, who are valuable economic and political resources.

While not all women may agree with polygyny, there is evidence to suggest that polygyny remains popular among women in many parts of the world (Kilbride 1997; Mulder 1992; Shahd 2005). There are also advantages from the woman's perspective. In polygynous societies it is easier for all women to get married. They can share the domestic duties, including looking after children, and they can offer each other respite from the husband. It is also true that men in polygynous societies view the practice even more positively than women. Opposition to polygyny usually comes from younger, better-educated women who prefer monogamy (or remaining single) to polygyny.

serial monogamy The practice of having a succession of marriage partners, but only one at a time.

Despite the advantages, living in a polygynous household has drawbacks. Even though men desire multiple wives, they recognize the potential pitfalls. A major problem is jealousy among the wives, who often compete for the husband's attention, sexual favours, and household resources. In fact, in some African societies, the word for *co-wife* is derived from the root word for *jealousy*.

Even though competition among wives in polygynous societies can threaten domestic tranquility, there are ways to minimize the friction. First, wives will be less jealous if they have a hand in selecting subsequent wives. Some societies practise a form of polygyny called ***sororal polygyny***, in which a man marries sisters or other female relatives. It is possible that sisters may be less likely to feel jealous of one another when they become wives. Second, wives in many polygynous societies are given their own separate living quarters. As Paul Bohannan and Philip Curtin (1988) remind us, because women may have more difficulty sharing their kitchens than their husbands, jealousy can be minimized by giving each wife her own personal space. Third, dissension is lessened if the rights and obligations among the wives are clearly understood. Fourth, potential conflict among wives can be reduced by establishing a hierarchy among the wives. Because the senior wife often exerts considerable authority over more junior wives, she can run a fairly smooth household by adjudicating the various complaints of the other wives.

Not only can the jealousies among wives be regulated, but some ethnographic reports from polygynous societies also reveal considerable harmony and cooperation among the wives. Sometimes co-wives become companions and allies because they are all "outsiders" to the husband's kin group.

Although Canada is adamantly monogamous, polygyny does exist in the community of Bountiful, British Columbia, among members of the Fundamentalist Church of Jesus Christ of Latter-day Saints (FLDS Church), which broke away from the Church of Jesus Christ of Latter-day Saints in 1890 when they outlawed polygyny. Officially, polygyny is prohibited by the Government of Canada, but because Canada's anti-polygamy laws are thought to be inconsistent with the Canadian Charter's right to religious freedom it is generally not prosecuted. There is nothing inherently immoral or exploitive about the practice of having more than one wife at a time. However polygyny, as practised in Canada, has come under fire recently because of certain abuses to the practice. Winston Blackmore, one of the leaders of the group has 24 wives and about 130 children, and claims polygyny is a sacred religious belief. He was charged with polygamy in 2009 in what was set to be a Charter test case but which was thrown out on a technicality (Figure 8.13). He was charged with polygamy again in August 2014, but this time for also marrying girls as young as 15 and 16 and for the harm it does to women and children.

JOHN LEHMANN/Globe and Mail/CP Images

FIGURE 8.13 Winston Blackmore of Bountiful, British Columbia, with four of his 24 wives, has been charged with polygamy.

The case had yet to be heard before the Supreme Court of British Columbia as of this writing. In a 2011 reference case, the judge found that women in polygamous relationships were at greater risk of physical and sexual abuse and psychological harm than women in monogamous relationships (Hutchinson 2014).

Polyandry

Polyandry is the marriage of a woman to two or more men at the same time and is a much rarer form of plural marriage than polygyny. ***Fraternal polyandry***, the most common form, is where the husbands are brothers. Among those societies that have traditionally practised polyandry, it is for all practical purposes a thing of the past. Perhaps the last places where it is found are in the remote villages of the Himalayas. The practice is seen as an economic solution to small plots of land carved out of the mountainside. To divide the

sororal polygyny A form of polygynous marriage whereby a man marries his wife's sisters or other female relatives.

fraternal polyandry The marriage of one woman to one or more men who are brothers.

property among sons at the death of a father would leave each family with plots of land too small on which to survive. Polyandry also serves as a form or birth control. Whether a woman has one husband or several, there is limit to the number of children she can bear. Polyandrous families rarely have more than six or seven children (Polgreen 2010).

In these sorts of marriages, it is not only the wife that is shared but everything. The children call the eldest brother, father and the younger brothers, uncle, regardless of who is the biological father. It is the wife who decides who the real father is, and the children know who he is. Although the community in the Lahaul Valley is patrilineal, polyandry gives women considerable sway over what goes on in the household (Polgreen 2010).

This form of marriage is rapidly disappearing in the face of technological advances, economic growth, and globalization. Cars, cellphones, satellite TV, and broadband Internet are bringing the outside world to these villages. Children are now going to school and men leave the villages for work elsewhere, reducing the need for brothers to share a wife (Polgreen 2010).

Economic Considerations of Marriage

Most societies view marriage as a binding contract between at least the principal partners, and in many cases between their respective families. Such a contract includes the transfer of certain rights between the parties involved: rights of sexual access, legal rights to children, and rights of the spouses to each other's economic goods and services. Often the transfer of rights is accompanied by the transfer of some type of economic consideration. These transactions, which may take place either before or after the marriage, can be divided into four categories: bridewealth, bride service, dowry, and reciprocal exchange.

Bridewealth

Bridewealth is the compensation given upon marriage by the family of the groom to the family of the bride as a normal part of the marriage process. The bridewealth exchange serves to ratify the marriage between the two families and is practised in many regions of the world, but most widely in Africa.

Bridewealth is paid in a wide variety of currencies, but in almost all cases the commodity used for payment is highly valued in the society. For example, cattle are given by the pastoral Maasai, Samburu, and Nuer of eastern Africa (Figure 8.14), and pigs among the Kawelka of New Guinea.

bridewealth The transfer of goods from the groom's lineage to the bride's lineage to legitimize marriage.

ton koene/Alamy Stock Photo

FIGURE 8.14 Among the Maasai of Kenya and Tanzania, cows are used as the medium of exchange in marriage transactions.

Bridewealth is significant for two reasons. First, the economic stakes are so high that the bride and groom are under enormous pressure to make the marriage work. Early Christian missionaries, viewing bridewealth as a form of wife purchase, argued that it was denigrating to women and repugnant to the Christian ideal of marriage. Many colonial administrators, taking a more legalistic view, saw bridewealth as a symbol of the inferior legal status of women in traditional societies. Both of these negative interpretations of bridewealth led to vigorous yet unsuccessful attempts to stamp out the practice. Anthropologists view bridewealth as security or insurance for the good treatment of the wife; as a mechanism to stabilize marriage by reducing the possibility of divorce; as a form of compensation to the bride's lineage for the loss of her economic potential and her childbearing capacity; as a symbol of the union between two large groups of kin; as a mechanism to legitimize traditional marriages in much the same way that a marriage license legitimizes Western marriages; and as the transference of rights over children from the mother's family to the father's family. It is now generally held that a comprehensive understanding of the practice of bridewealth is impossible without recognizing its economic as well as its noneconomic functions.

Bridewealth payments are essentially a payment for her to bear children. The larger the bridewealth payment, the more complete the transfer of rights over children from the bride's lineage to the groom's lineage. If a marriage is subsequently dissolved, the bridewealth payment may have to be returned to the groom's lineage, which could be a problem if it has already been allocated to a wide range of the bride's kin. Thus, relatively large bridewealth payments, coupled with wide lineage involvement, promote greater marriage stability.

Since the mid-20th century, bridewealth has become "monetized"; that is, money is becoming the typical medium of exchange. The transition from subsistence-based to cash-based economies has profoundly affected traditional bridewealth practices. Because traditional bridewealth solidifies long-term ties between two entire lineages, the bride and groom do not benefit directly from the exchange. However, when bridewealth becomes tied to money that can be earned by the individual prospective groom, the close interdependence of family members (and their sanctioning of the marriage) becomes much less important. Today, a growing number of wage-earners in societies that practise traditional bridewealth are becoming independent of their kinship group when it comes time to get married.

Increasingly, young girls of poor rural families, and in particular girls younger than 18 years of age, are being married off to lessen the burden on their families. These early marriages are referred to as "child-drought brides" and are found in Africa, India, the Philippines, and other parts of the world. It is reported that, in Kenya, families were selling their daughters into marriage, sometimes for as little as $168.00. Marrying their young daughters freed the families from feeding, clothing, and educating them; it was the parent's attempt to ease their economic burden brought on by drought. Yet marrying young puts the adolescent girls at greater risk for exposure to HIV and AIDS, at-risk pregnancies, spending more time caring for the household (gathering wood and water and collecting food or food aid), and less time in getting an education.

Bride Service

In small-scale societies that cannot accumulate capital goods, men often give their labour to the bride's family instead of material goods in exchange for wives. In some cases, ***bride service*** is practised to the exclusion of property transfer; in other cases it is a temporary condition and the transfer of some property is expected at a later date. When a man marries under a system of bride service, he often moves in with his bride's family, works or hunts for them, and serves a probationary period of several weeks to several years.

Bride service is likely to be found in nomadic foraging societies such as the traditional Ju/'hoansi of southwestern Africa. According to Janice Stockard (2002), Ju/'hoansi men select husbands for their daughters based largely, but not exclusively, on the hunting skills of the prospective groom. Suitors must demonstrate considerable hunting expertise before they are eligible to marry because the father-in-law will depend on the daughter's husband to provide him with adequate supplies of meat through a prolonged period of bride service.

Dowry

In contrast to bridewealth, a ***dowry*** is goods or money transferred from the bride's family to the groom or the groom's family as a precondition for a marriage. The recipient of the goods varies from one culture to another. In some societies the dowry is given to the groom, who then has varying rights to dispose of it.

More often than not, the dowry is not given to the husband but is something that the bride brings with her into the marriage. In traditional society in Cyprus, the dowry often consisted of a house or other valuable property. If the husband mistreated his wife or if the marriage ended in divorce, the woman was entitled to take the dowry with her. The dowry in this sense, much like bridewealth, functioned to stabilize the marriage by providing a strong economic incentive not to break up.

In certain European countries, where it is still practised to some extent today, substantial dowry payments have been used as a means of upward mobility, that is, as a way to marry a daughter into a higher-status family.

In India, dowry is still an important component of marriage. If the in-laws and husbands are not satisfied with the amount received by the bride's family, she may be harassed and physically abused, in some cases resulting in what is known as ***dowry death***. Dowry deaths are the deaths of women who are murdered or driven to suicide by their husbands and in-laws as a means to increase the amount of a bride's dowry her family must pay, or to obtain the wife's dowry.

Since 1961, dowries have been banned in India under various acts, such as the Dowry Prohibition Act (1961) and its revised version of 1983. Since the passing of the Protection of Women from Domestic Violence Act in 2005, women can put a stop to harassment for dowry extortion. Nevertheless, next to rape, dowry deaths remain one of the top acts of violence against women in India (Figure 8.15). Bedi (2012) reports that in 2010 there were 8391 dowry death cases

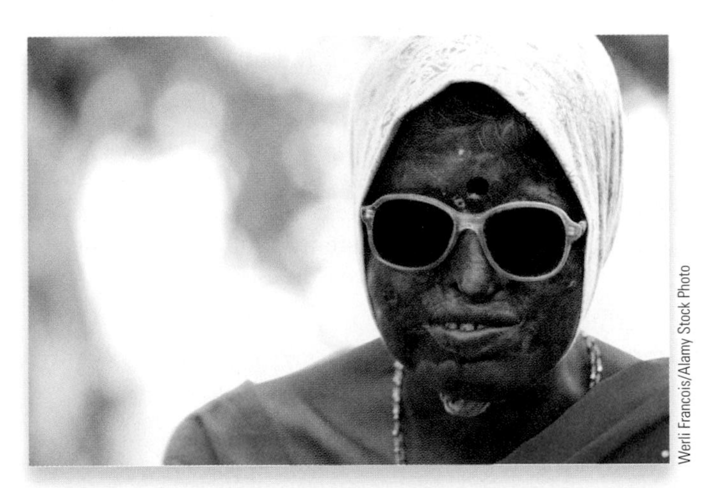

Werli Francois/Alamy Stock Photo

FIGURE 8.15 **In order to obtain his wife's dowry, a husband may set his wife on fire in a so-called "cooking accident." Dowry deaths remain one of the top acts of violence against women in India.**

bride service Work or service performed for the bride's family by the groom for a specified period of time either before or after the marriage.

dowry Goods or money transferred from the bride's family to the groom or the groom's family to legalize or legitimize a marriage.

dowry deaths Deaths of young women either murdered or driven to suicide in an effort to obtain a dowry.

documented across India. A decade earlier there were 6695 cases reported. For 2010 it means a bride was burned nearly every hour, on average. The increase may, however, be due a greater willingness to report these deaths, which implies that the numbers may be an underestimate.

Residence Patterns: Where Do Wives and Husbands Live?

When two people marry in North American, it is customary for the couple to take up residence in a place of their own, apart from the relatives of either spouse. This residence pattern is known as ***neolocal residence*** (i.e., a new place). As natural as this may seem, by global standards it is an atypical residence pattern, practised by only a few of the world's societies. The remaining societies prescribe that newlyweds will live in the same household with (or close to) relatives of the wife or the husband.

Most residence patterns fall into one of the five types presented below.

- ***Patrilocal residence***. The married couple lives with or near the relatives of the husband's father.
- ***Matrilocal residence***. The married couple lives with or near the relatives of the wife.
- ***Avunculocal residence***. The married couple lives with or near the husband's mother's brother.
- ***Ambilocal (bilocal) residence***. The married couple has a choice of living with either the relatives of the wife or the relatives of the husband.
- ***Neolocal residence***. The married couple establishes an independent place of residence away from the relatives of either spouse.

To a significant degree, residence patterns are linked to the types of kinship systems found in any society. For example, there is a reasonably close correlation between patrilocal residence and patrilineal descent (tracing one's important relatives through the father's side), and between matrilocal residence and matrilineal descent (tracing one's important relatives through the mother's side).

Like most other aspects of culture, these five residence patterns are ideal types. Consequently, how people actually behave—in this case, where they reside—does not always conform precisely to these ideals. Sometimes normative patterns of residence are altered or interrupted by events such as famines or epidemics that force newlyweds to live in areas that will maximize their chances for survival or their economic security. To illustrate, during the recession of 2008/2009, the normal neolocal pattern of residence in Canada and the United States was disrupted when many young married adults moved in to live with one set of parents to save money.

Family Structure

Cultural anthropologists have identified two fundamentally different types of family structure: the nuclear family and the extended family. The ***nuclear family*** is based on marital ties and consists of wife, husband, and children; and the ***extended family***, a much larger social unit, is based on blood ties among three or more generations of kin.

The Nuclear Family

Consisting of husband and wife, or partners, and their children, the nuclear family is a two-generation family formed around the marital union. In Canada and most Western countries, it is seen as the ideal form, and most legislation concerning the family (e.g., taxation) is based on this form. Even though the nuclear family is, to some degree, part of a larger family structure, it remains an autonomous and independent unit (Figure 8.16). That is, the everyday needs of economic support, child care, and social interaction are met within the nuclear family itself, rather than by a wider set of relatives. The nuclear family is most likely to be found in societies with the greatest amount of geographic mobility, such as in Canada. Because one's profession largely determines where one will live, adults in Canada often live considerable distances from their parents or other extended family members. In societies based on the nuclear family, it is customary for married couples to live apart from both sets of parents (neolocal residence). This tends to isolate both spouses from their relatives, and forces the couple to rely on each other more than in other types of families. It also means that parents are unavailable to look after children or the sick and elderly, so these functions are often delegated to outside agencies such

---

neolocal residence A residence pattern in which the married couple has its own place of residence apart from the relatives of either spouse.

patrilocal residence A residence pattern in which the married couple lives with or near the relatives of the husband's father.

matrilocal residence A residence pattern in which the married couple lives with or near the relatives of the wife.

avunculocal residence A residence pattern in which the married couple lives with or near the husband's mother's brother.

ambilocal (bilocal) residence A residence pattern in which the married couple may choose to live with either the relatives of the wife or the relatives of the husband.

nuclear family The family unit composed of wife, husband, and children.

extended family The family that includes in one household relatives in addition to a nuclear family.

Angelika Schwarz/E+/Getty Images

FIGURE 8.16 **Consisting of husband and wife, or partners, and their children, the nuclear family is a two-generation autonomous and independent unit.**

as daycares, babysitters, and seniors homes. Generally, parents are not actively involved in mate selection for their children, in no way legitimize the marriages of their children, and have no control over whether their children remain married.

The nuclear family also goes through a life cycle: a couple get married, have children, then become empty nesters when the children leave home, and then ends with the death of the couple. This situation does not arise in extended families, where it continues on after the death of its senior members.

The nuclear family is also found in societies located at the other end of the technological spectrum. In certain foraging societies the nuclear family is the basic food-collecting unit. These nuclear families remain highly independent foraging groups that fend for themselves and have developed a family structure that is well-adapted to a highly mobile life. Thus, both Canadian society and some small-scale, food-collecting societies have adopted the nuclear family pattern because of their need to maintain a high degree of geographic mobility.

Although the independent nuclear family is perhaps the ideal in Canada, it is no longer the norm. Parents with children made up just 39.2 per cent of families in 2011, and a rising proportion of those parents were not officially married. In 2011 there were more adults living alone in Canada (27.6 percent; a 300 percent increase from 1961) than as part of a couple with children (26.5 percent). Lone-parent families represented 16.3 percent of all census families in 2011—almost double the number from 1961 (8.4 percent). About 80 percent of single-parent families are headed by women. Moreover, the size of the family has decreased as well: from 3.9 people in 1961 to 2.9 in 2011 (Milan 2013).

There are several explanations for the recent decline of the nuclear family in Canada. In the early 1960s people married at an early age and had fairly large families. The development of the birth control pill, "no fault" divorce, as well as the increase in number of women in higher education and in the work force, have all led to people delaying marrying and having fewer children (Statistics Canada 2012a). The increasing cost of maintaining the ideal middle-class household that includes the parents, children, a three- or four-bedroom house, a golden retriever, and an SUV has caused some couples to opt for remaining childless altogether. The rising divorce rate in Canada has also contributed to the increase in non-nuclear families in recent decades. Households have been declining in size as people have fewer children or no children at all.

The Extended Family

Extended families consist of two or more nuclear families that are linked by blood ties. Most commonly this takes the form of a married couple living with one or more of their married children in a single household and under the authority of a family head. Such extended families, which are based on parent-child linkages, can be either patrilineal (a man, his sons, and the sons' wives and children) or matrilineal (a woman, her daughters, and her daughters' husbands and children). It is also possible for extended families to be linked through sibling ties, consisting of two or more married brothers and their wives and children (Figure 8.17).

When a couple marries in a society with extended families, the newlyweds are not expected to establish a separate and distinct family unit. Instead, the young couple may, for example, take up residence in the homestead of the husband's father, and the husband continues to work for his father, who also runs the household. Moreover, most of the personal property in the household is not owned by the newlyweds but is controlled by the husband's father. In the event that the extended family is large, it may be headed by two or more powerful male elders who run the family in much the same way that a board of directors runs

Images of Africa Photobank / Alamy Stock Photo

FIGURE 8.17 **Extended families consist of two or more nuclear families that are linked by blood ties. Most commonly this takes the form of a married couple living with one or more of their married children in a single household or through sibling ties, consisting of two or more married brothers and their wives and children.**

a corporation. Eventually the father (or other male elders) will die or retire and allow younger men to assume positions of leadership and power within the extended family. Unlike the nuclear family, which lasts only one generation, the extended family is a continuous unit that can last an indefinite number of generations. As the old die off, they are replaced through the birth of new members.

In extended family systems, marriage is viewed more as bringing a daughter into the family than acquiring a wife. In other words, a man's obligations of obedience to his father and loyalty to his male kin are far more important than his relationship to his wife. When a woman marries into an extended family, she most often comes under the control of her mother-in-law, who allocates chores and supervises her domestic activities.

In some extended-family systems, the conjugal relationship is suppressed to such an extent that contact between husband and wife is kept to a minimum. Among the Rajputs of northern India, for example, spouses are not allowed to talk to each other in the presence of family elders. Public displays of affection between spouses are considered reprehensible; in fact, a husband is not permitted to show open concern for his wife's welfare. Some societies take such severe measures to subordinate the husband-wife relationship because it is feared that a man's feelings for his wife could interfere with his obligations to his own blood relatives.

Modern-Day Family Structure

Most Western societies are seeing a progressive nuclearization of the family in the face of modernization. In fact, the concept of family is changing with increased acceptance of same-sex marriage and same-sex couples adopting children on the rise. Yet, that is only one modification in the modern family.

The challenging economic time from 2009 to the present has made it more difficult for young adults, especially those who are recent university graduates, to find employment that allows them to start out on their own. Moving in with relatives, especially parents, has helped fuel the largest increase in the number of Canadians and Americans living in multigenerational households (composed of two or more generations) in modern history. It has provided a financial lifeline for many households.

A number of factors are responsible for this rise in the number of multigenerational households, including the high unemployment rate, the high cost of housing, the rising cost of living, and growing expenses for child and elder care. But there are more positive explanations as well. Traditionally, immigrant families in Canada maintain extended kinship ties to support family, and also have family traditions for staying together while they acculturate in Canada.

One non-traditional form of the family that has been on the rise in the past half-century in Canada is families made up of unwed single mothers and their children. While raising children as an unwed mother in Canada is not easy, it is not a lifestyle choice that is reviled by the rest of society, nor does the government discriminate against it. In Korea, however, there are few unwed mothers raising their children because they are so thoroughly ostracized by their society. According to one commentator (Choe 2009, 6), unwed mothers are ostracized "to such an extent that Koreans often describe things as outrageous by comparing them to 'an unmarried woman seeking an excuse to give birth.' " This social stigma puts enormous pressure on unwed pregnant women in Korea to either have an abortion or give the child up for adoption. To illustrate, 96 percent of all unwed pregnant Korean women end their pregnancies in abortion, and the great majority of those children who are born (the remaining 4 percent) are given up for adoption (Choe 2009, 6).

Kinship and Descent

For much of the 20th century, cultural anthropologists spent a disproportionate amount of time and energy describing kinship systems. The importance of understanding the role of kinship in social organization was first recognized by W. H. R. Rivers during the Cambridge Expedition to the Torres Straits in 1899. He revolutionized ethnography with his genealogical method in which he argued the first step an anthropologist should take is to make a chart of who is related to whom (Figure 8.18).

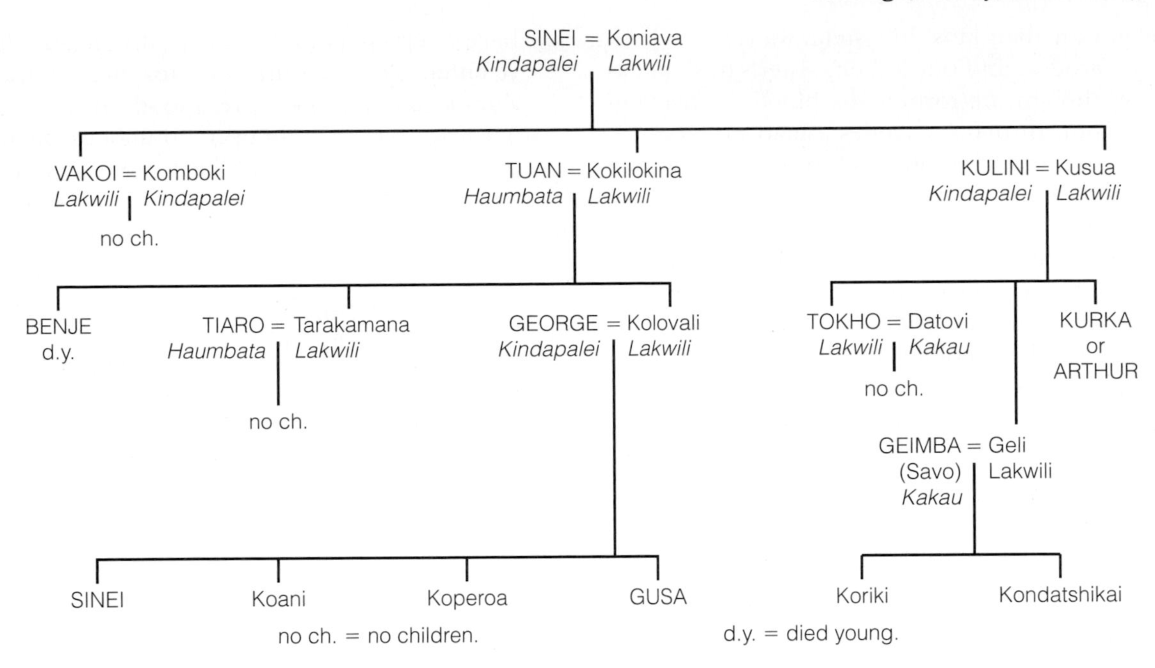

FIGURE 8.18 **W. H. R. Rivers revolutionized ethnography by encouraging anthropologists to begin by interviewing local people about their kin, and then diagramming the relationships. This is the kinship diagram from his informant living in the Solomon Islands (Rivers 1910).**

Source: Adapted from Rivers, W.H.R. 1910: The genealogical method of anthropological inquiry (*Sociological Review*, III, pp.1–12)

Cultural anthropologists, although interested in all societies of the world, have until fairly recently concentrated on studying small-scale societies in which kinship relations tend to be all-encompassing. In highly urbanized, technological societies, fewer social relationships are based on kinship. In Canada, for example, social relationships that are essentially political, economic, recreational, or religious are usually not played out with kin. But even in Canada, where kinship ties are sometimes overshadowed by non-kinship ties, kin relations are usually more long term, intense, and emotionally laden than are relations with non-kin. By way of contrast, in small-scale, non-Western, preliterate, and technologically simple societies, kinship is at the heart of the social structure.

Whether we are considering small- or large-scale societies, kinship systems are important because they provide a plan for aligning people and resources in strategic ways. They set limits on sexual activity and on who can marry whom, they establish the parameters of economic cooperation between men and women, they determine where a person will live and where and with whom they will work, and they provide a basis for proper child rearing. Moreover, kinship systems often provide a mechanism for inheriting property and for sharing certain pieces of property (such as land or cattle) that cannot be divided without being destroyed. Beyond the limits of the immediate family unit, kinship systems extend one's relationship to a much wider group of people. To illustrate, membership in a small, local group of kin enables an individual to draw on more distant kinsmen for protection or economic support during difficult times. Also, when small family groups are confronted with large-scale projects, they often recruit cooperative labour from among already existing groups of extended kinsmen.

Kinship Defined

Kinship refers to the relationships that are based on blood or marriage. Those people to whom we are related through birth or blood are our ***consanguineal relatives***; those to whom we are related through marriage are our ***affinal relatives***. Each society has a well-understood system of defining relationships between these different types of relatives. Every society, in other words, defines the nature of kinship interaction by determining which kin are more socially important than others, the terms used to classify various types of kin, and the expected forms of behaviour between them. Although the systems vary significantly from one society to another, relationships based on blood and marriage are culturally recognized by all societies.

All kinship systems are founded on biological connections. Family and kinship groups would not exist if men and women did not mate and have children. However, kinship systems involve more than biological relationships. Each society classifies its kin according to a set of cultural rules that may or may not account for biological factors. For example, according to the

kinship Relationships between people based on blood or marriage.

consanguineal relatives One's biological or blood relatives.

affinal relatives Kinship ties formed through marriage (i.e., in-laws).

mainstream Canadian kinship system, we refer to both our father's brother and our father's sister's husband as uncles even though the former is a blood relative and the latter is not. In many societies a man refers to his father's brother and his mother's brother (both blood relatives) by different terms and is expected to behave differently toward the two. This distinction between the biological and cultural dimensions of kinship can be seen in Canadian society when we refer to our adopted children as sons and daughters (with all of the rights and obligations that biological children have) even though they have no genetic connection.

The term *fictive kinship* is used for people who are not related by either blood or marriage. Fictive kinship can take a number of different forms. For example, the process of adoption creates a set of relationships between the adoptive parents and child that have all the expectations of relationships based on descent or marriage. Often close friends of the family are referred to as aunt or uncle, even though they have no biological or marital relationship. University fraternities and sororities, some religious groups, and members of the same ethnic group use kinship terminology (such as brothers and sisters) to refer to their members. The godparent–godchild relationship, which carries with it all sorts of kinship obligations, also often involves people who do not share blood or marriage connections. These examples should remind us that it is possible to have kinship-like relationships (complete with well-understood rights and obligations) without having an actual biological or marital connection.

The *biological* meaning of kinship is powerful. This is particularly true when determining legal parenthood. For example, surrogate mothers who have borne children for other women have had some success in the courts in reclaiming those children purely on the basis of being the biological mother. And biological fathers who have abandoned their families have returned to claim custody of their children solely on the basis of biological paternity. In some parts of the world, however, the *social* component of kinship is given far more weight than in Canada. For the Zumbagua of highland Ecuador, parenthood is not established solely and automatically on the basis of either giving birth or being the biological father. Rather, it involves a relationship that must be *achieved* over a relatively long period of time. According to Mary Weismantel (1995, 698):

> Among the Zumbagua, if the biological father's role ends after conception, or if the mother's role ends shortly after birth, these biological parents have a very weak claim to parenthood should they re-enter the child's life at a later time. Thus, the Zumbagua notion of parenthood involves *working* at nurturing the child over a number of years; mere conception or childbirth alone does not, in and of itself, give a man or a woman the right to claim parenthood of a child.

Thus, the Zumbagua place a higher priority on social parenthood that is earned than is found in mainstream Canadian society, which places a higher value on genetically based parenthood. In fact the Zumbaguan notion of nurturing is taken quite literally, defined as actually *feeding or sharing food with* the child. In a sense, food is what binds parents to children because, according to Weismantel (1995, 695), "Those who eat together in the same household share the same flesh."

There are additional ethnographic examples in which kinship is socially constructed rather than universally defined. For example, some Indigenous cultures in South America believe in "partible paternity"—the notion that a child can have more than one biological father. In other words, it is believed that all men who have sex with a woman during her pregnancy actually contribute to the formation of the fetus. When the baby is born, the mother names the men whom she identifies as fathers, who then are expected to assume social responsibility for the child. Kinship categories such as father or parent can thus be defined differently in various cultures.

Using Kinship Diagrams

Although kinship systems are found in every society, the definitions of the relationships between kin vary widely from one group to another. In different societies, people with the same biological connection may be defined differently, labelled differently, and expected to behave differently toward one another. And, as we shall see, societies can choose from a vast array of possibilities. Before sorting out the complexities of different kinship systems, we will introduce some symbols that cultural anthropologists use in analyzing kinship systems.

As a way of simplifying kinship systems, anthropologists use kinship diagrams rather than relying on verbal explanations alone. In this standardized notational system, all kinship diagrams are viewed from a central point of reference (called ***EGO***), the person from whose

fictive kinship Relationships among individuals who recognize kinship obligations even though the relationships are not based on either consanguineal or affinal ties.

EGO The person in kinship diagrams from whose point of view relationships are traced.

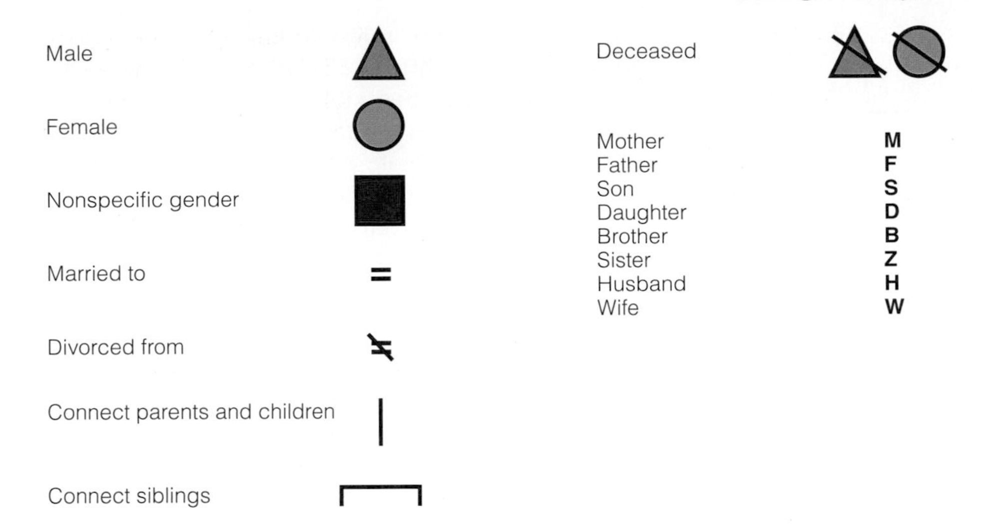

FIGURE 8.19 Kinship diagram symbols.

point of view we are tracing the relationship. All kinship diagrams use the symbols shown in Figure 8.19.

Starting with our point of reference (EGO), we can construct a hypothetical kinship diagram, as in Figure 8.20. We refer to all of the people in the diagram with the following terms:

1. Father's sister's husband (FZH)
2. Father's sister (FZ)
3. Father's brother's wife (FBW)
4. Father's brother (FB)
5. Father (F)
6. Mother (M)
7. Mother's sister (MZ)
8. Mother's sister's husband (MZH)
9. Mother's brother (MB)
10. Mother's brother's wife (MBW)
11. Father's sister's son (FZS)
12. Father's sister's daughter (FZD)
13. Father's brother's son (FBS)
14. Father's brother's daughter (FBD)
15. Brother (B)
16. Sister (Z)
17. Mother's sister's son (MZS)
18. Mother's sister's daughter (MZD)
19. Mother's brother's son (MBS)
20. Mother's brother's daughter (MBD)

Principles of Kinship Classification

These biological relationships are called ***kin types*** and are universal. Anthropologists use them to refer to any individual in any kinship chart. ***Kin terms***, on the other hand, refer to the labels that different cultures place on the kin types (Table 8.1). No kinship system in the world uses a different kin term for every kin type. Instead, all kinship systems group relatives into certain categories, refer to them by the same term, and expect people to behave toward them in a similar fashion. How a particular society categorizes relatives depends on which principles of classification it uses. Some kinship systems are more categorical and use different principles to group certain relatives together, while others are more descriptive and separate them, as discussed in the following subsections.

---

kin types Universal terms anthropologists use to refer to particular individuals in a kinship system.

kin terms The names cultures give to particular categories of relatives.

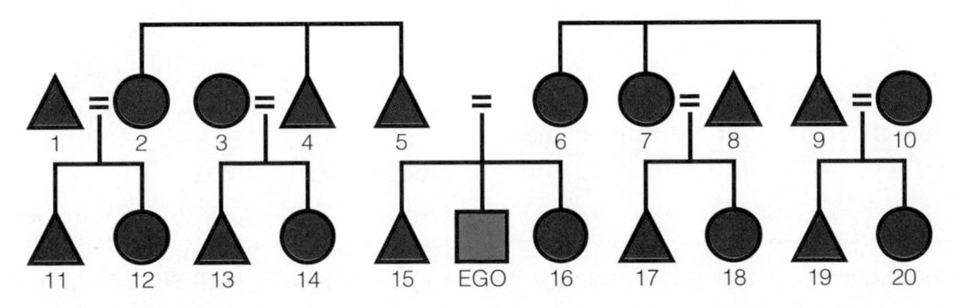

FIGURE 8.20 Generic kinship diagram.

TABLE 8.1

English Kin Terms and Kin Types

Kin Term	Kin type
Mother	M
Father	F
Sister	Z
Brother	B
Daughter	D
Aunt	MZ, FZ
Uncle	FB, MB
Niece	ZD, BD
Nephew	ZS, BS
Cousin	MBD, MBS, MZD, MZS, FZD, FZS, FBD, FBS
Grandmother	MM, FM
Grandfather	MF, FF

Generation

In some kinship systems distinctions between kin depend on generation. Mothers, fathers, and their siblings are always found in the first ascending generation, immediately above EGO; sons, daughters, nieces, and nephews are always one generation below EGO in the first descending generation; grandmothers and grandfathers are always two generations above EGO; and so forth. Although this seems like the natural thing for most Canadians, some societies have kinship systems that do not confine a kin category to a single generation. It is possible, for example, to find the same kin category in three or four different generations. The Haida of British Columbia use the same kinship term to refer to one's father's sister, father's sister's daughter, and father's sister's daughter's daughter.

Sex or Gender

Some kinship terms ignore gender distinctions while in other systems terms are separated by gender. In the English system, for example, kin categories such as brother, father, father's brother, son, and grandfather are always males; sister, mother, mother's sister, daughter, and grandmother are always females. The one area where we do not distinguish on the basis of gender is for cousins.

Lineality versus Collaterality

Lineality refers to kin related in a single line, such as son, father, grandfather. *Collaterality*, on the other hand, refers to kin related through a linking relative, such as the relationship between EGO and his or her parents' siblings. Whereas the principle of lineality distinguishes between father and father's brother, the principle of collaterality does not. That is, in some societies, EGO uses the term *father* to refer to both his or her father and his or her father's brother; similarly, EGO's mother and her sisters may be referred to by the single term *mother*.

Consanguineal versus Affinal Kin

Some societies make distinctions in kinship categories based on whether people are related by blood (consanguineal kin) or through marriage (affinal kin). The mainstream Canadian kinship system uses this principle of classification at some levels but not others. To illustrate, we distinguish between sons and sons-in-law and between sisters and sisters-in-law. But in EGO's parents' generation, we fail to distinguish between mother's brother (a blood relative) and mother's sister's husband (an affinal relative), both of whom we call *uncle*.

Relative Age

In certain kinship systems, relative age is a criterion for separating different types of relatives. In such societies a man or woman uses one kinship term for younger brother or sister and another term for older brother or sister. These different terms based on relative age carry with them different behavioural expectations. Often a person is expected to act toward his or her older sibling with deference and respect while behaving much more informally toward their younger sibling.

Sex of the Connecting Relative

Some societies distinguish between different categories of kin based on the sex of the connecting (or intervening) relative. To illustrate, a mother's brother's daughter (20 in Figure 8.20) and a mother's sister's daughter (18) (who are both called *cousins* in the Western system) are given two different kinship terms. Similarly a father's brother's daughter (14) and a father's sister's daughter (12) are given different kinship terms. One category of cousins (12 and 20) are called *cross cousins*, and the other (14 and 18) are called *parallel cousins*. According to this principle, these first cousins are considered to be different by virtue of the sex of their parents.

Social Condition

Distinctions among kin categories can also be made based on a person's general life condition. According to this criterion, different kinship terms are used for a married brother and a bachelor brother, or for a living aunt and one who is deceased.

lineality Kin relationships traced through a single line, such as son, father, and grandfather.

collaterality Kin relationships traced through a linking relative.

Side of the Family

A final principle has to do with using different kin terms for EGO's mother's side of the family and EGO's father's side of the family. The kinship system used in Canada makes no such distinction: we have aunts, uncles, cousins, and grandparents on both sides of our family. In societies that use this principle of classification, different terms are used to refer to a mother's brother and a father's brother.

Different Systems of Classification

Every society has a coherent system of labelling various types of kin. In any given system, certain categories of kin are grouped together under a single category, whereas others are separated into distinct categories. Mainstream Canadian society groups together under the general heading of "aunt" our mother's sisters, father's sisters, mother's brothers' wives, and father's brothers' wives. Similarly, we lump together under the heading of "uncle" our father's brothers, mother's brothers, father's sisters' husbands, and mother's sisters' husbands. In contrast, other societies might have separate terms for all eight of these categories of kin. Whatever system of classification is used, however, cultural anthropologists have found them to be both internally logical and consistently applied. Even though individual societies may have their own variations, six basic classification systems have been identified: Eskimo, Hawaiian, Iroquois, Omaha, Crow, and Sudanese. We will describe two of these classification systems—the Eskimo (which serves as the basis for the mainstream Canadian kinship system) and the Iroquois—in greater detail.

Eskimo System

The ***Eskimo (Inuit) system*** of kinship classification is associated with descent reckoned down both the male and female lines (see Figure 8.21). The major feature of this system is that it emphasizes the nuclear family by using separate terms (such as mother, father, sister, brother) that are not used outside the nuclear family. Beyond the nuclear family, many other relatives (such as aunts, uncles, and cousins) are lumped together. This emphasis on the nuclear family is related to the fact that societies using the Eskimo system lack large descent groups such as lineages and clans. Moreover, the Eskimo system is most likely to be found in societies (such as Canada and certain food-collecting societies) in which economic conditions favour an independent nuclear family.

Iroquois System

In the ***Iroquois system***, EGO's father and father's brother are called by the same term, and EGO's mother's brother is called by a different term (see Figure 8.22). Likewise EGO's mother and mother's sister are lumped together under one term, and a different term is used for EGO's father's sister. Thus, a basic distinction of classification is made between the sex of one's parents' siblings (i.e., mother's brothers and sisters, and father's

Eskimo (Inuit) system The kinship system most commonly found in Canada; it is associated with bilateral descent.

Iroquois system A kinship system associated with unilineal descent in which the father and father's brother are called by the same term, as are the mother and the mother's sister.

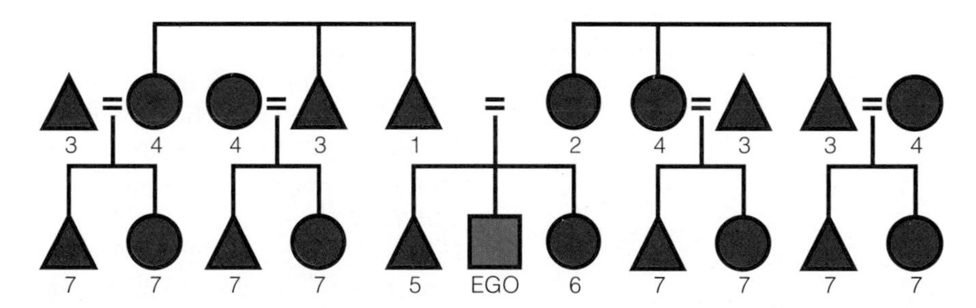

FIGURE 8.21 Eskimo kinship system. (*Note:* Symbols with the same numbers below them are referred to in the same way by EGO.)

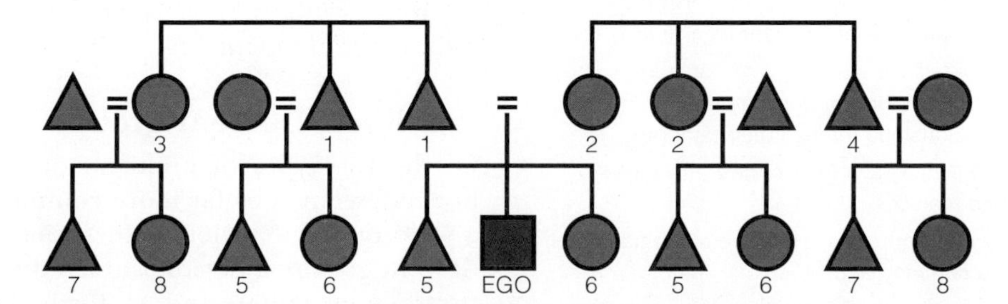

FIGURE 8.22 Iroquois kinship system (*Note:* Symbols with the same numbers below them are referred to in the same way by EGO.)

Source: Based on © 1995 Brian Schwimmer, Department of Anthropology, University of Manitoba

brothers and sisters). Within EGO's own generation, EGO's own siblings are given the same term as the parallel cousins (children of one's mother's sister or father's brother), and different terms are used for cross cousins (children of one's mother's brother or father's sister). Thus, the terminological distinction made between cross and parallel cousins is logical, given the distinction made between the siblings of EGO's parents. The Iroquois system emphasizes the importance of unilineal descent groups by distinguishing between members of one's own lineage and members of other lineages.

The Formation of Descent Groups

As we have seen, kinship systems play an important role in helping people sort out how they should behave toward various relatives. In anthropological terms, ***kinship systems*** encompass all blood and marriage relationships, which helps people distinguish among different categories of kin, creates rights and obligations among kin, and serves as the basis for the formation of certain types of kin groups.

Anthropologists also use the narrower term ***descent*** to refer to the rules a culture uses to establish affiliations with one's parents. These rules of descent often provide the basis for the formation of social groups. These social groups, or descent groups, are collections of relatives (usually descendants of a common ancestor) who live out their lives in close proximity to one another. In fact, in those societies that have descent groups, the group plays a central role in the lives of its members.

Rules of descent may be divided into two distinct types. Under ***unilineal descent***, people trace their ancestry through either the mother's line or the father's line, but not both. Unilineal groups that trace their descent through the mother's line are called ***matrilineal descent groups***, those tracing their descent through the father's line are called ***patrilineal descent groups***. The second type of descent is known as ***cognatic* (or *multilinear*) *descent***, which is traced through both females and males and includes double descent, ambilineal descent, and bilateral descent. Descent in mainstream North America is traced according to the bilateral principle (see below).

Approximately 60 percent of all kinship systems are based on the unilineal principle. Unilineal descent groups are clear-cut, unambiguous social units. Because a person becomes a member of a unilineal descent group at birth, there is no confusion about who is a group member and who is not, and a person has no questions about her or his rights of inheritance, prestige, and social roles. For societies that rely on kinship groups to perform most of their social functions (such as marriage, dispute settlement, and religious ceremonies), unilineal descent groups, with their clear-cut membership, provide a social organization with unambiguous roles and statuses.

Anthropologists distinguish between two different types of kinship groups that are based on the unilineal principle, lineages and clans. A ***lineage*** is a unilineal descent group in which members can trace their ancestry back (step by step) to a common founder. When descent is traced through the male line, the groups are known as patrilineages; when it is traced through the female line, they are known as matrilineages. A ***clan***, on the other hand, is a group of kin whose members believe they are all related to a common ancestor, but are unable to trace the genealogical connections step by step. The clans of Scotland and those of First Nations on Canada's west coast are good examples of clans.

When clans and lineages are found together, the clan is usually made up of a number of different lineages. In some societies, clans are close-knit groups, much like lineages, whose members have a high degree of interaction with one another. More commonly, however, clan members are widely dispersed geographically and only rarely get together for clan-wide activities. Unlike lineages, which serve as corporate functioning groups, clans tend to be larger and more loosely structured categories with which people identify. Because clan members may not know each other personally they often use symbols, such as tartans or totem animals, to indicate group identity.

Patrilineal Descent Groups

Of the two types of unilineal descent groups, patrilineal descent is by far more common and is found in a wide range of societies. In societies with patrilineal descent groups, a person is related through the father, the father's father, and so forth. In other words, a man, his own children, his brother's children (but not his sister's children), and his son's children (but not

---

kinship systems Those relationships found in all societies that are based on blood or marriage.

descent A person's kinship connections traced back through a number of generations.

unilineal descent Descent traced through either a male line or female line but not both.

matrilineal descent group A form of descent in which people trace their primary kin connections through their mothers.

patrilineal descent group A form of descent in which people trace their primary kin relationships through their fathers.

cognatic (multilinear) descent A form of descent traced through both females and males.

lineage A unilineal descent group whose members can trace their line of descent back to a common ancestor.

clan A unilineal descent group whose members claim a common ancestry even though they cannot trace step by step their exact connection to that ancestor.

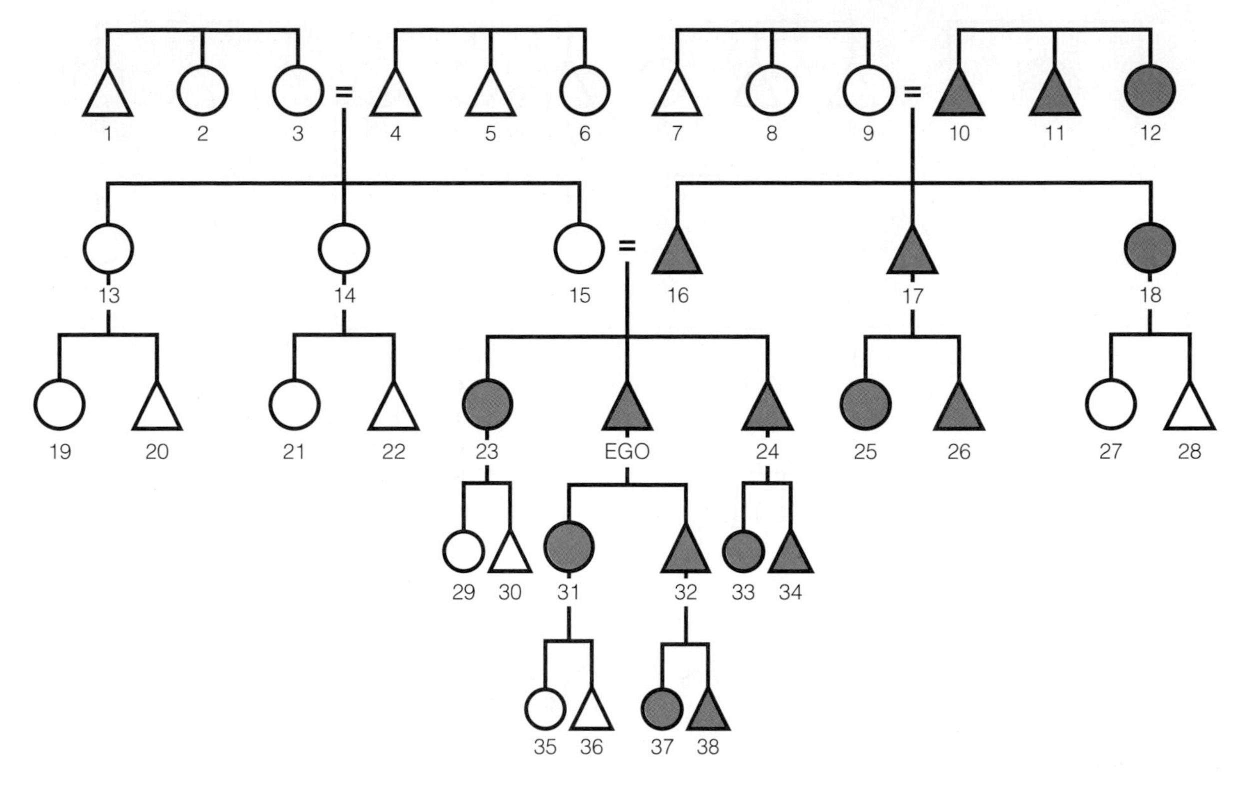

FIGURE 8.23 Patrilineal descent from a male EGO's perspective. In a patrilineal descent system, a person is connected to relatives of both sexes related through males only. Sons and daughters belong to their father's descent group, as do the father's sons' children but not the father's daughters' children.

his daughter's children) are all members of the same descent group (Figure 8.23). Females must marry outside their own patrilineage, and the children a woman bears belong to the husband's lineage rather than to her own. The principle of patrilineal descent is illustrated in Figure 8.23.

China is by far the largest patrilineal society in the world. The traditional Chinese family, at least ideally, was made up of the patrilineage, comprising a man, his wife or wives, his sons, daughters-in-law, grandchildren, and great-grandchildren. When a son reached marriageable age, the extended family provided a wife for him. In most cases the wives came from other unrelated families, but sometimes Chinese couples adopted unrelated infant girls for the express purpose of providing a future bride for one of their sons, a practice known as *sim-pua*. A family with many sons became large by producing many children. The residence pattern was patrilocal, in which the wives lived with and became part of the husband's lineage and produced children for it. The extended family typically occupied a set of buildings forming a single estate. As in any patrilineal society, inheritance passed from the father to his son(s) and grandson(s).

In Canada, the United States, and much of Western Europe, parents are expected to give priority to the needs of their children. But in the traditional Chinese family, the reverse is true: It is the children who have the major obligation to the family. Children must show deference, respect, and obedience to their parents for as long as the parents are alive. Children are obligated to provide for the comfort of their aging parents and, even after their death, must attend to the parents' spiritual needs through ceremonies of ancestor worship. And sons are under constant pressure to perpetuate their father's lineage by producing sons of their own. The male members of the families are responsible for maintaining the ancestral tablets, kept in the family shrine and on which all the names of the family are carefully recorded. A man takes seriously the place of his name in the family tablets as a way of connecting himself to his ancestors and his descendants.

Matrilineal Descent Groups

In a matrilineal kinship system, a person belongs to the mother's group (Figure 8.24). A matrilineal descent group comprises a woman, her siblings, her own children, her sisters' children, and her daughters' children. Matrilineal descent groups make up about 15 percent of the unilineal descent groups found among contemporary societies, including some First Nations (such as the Haudenosaunee (Iroquois), Tsimshian, and the Haida Gwitchin), the Truk and Trobriand Islanders of the Pacific, and the Bemba, Ashanti, and Yao of Africa.

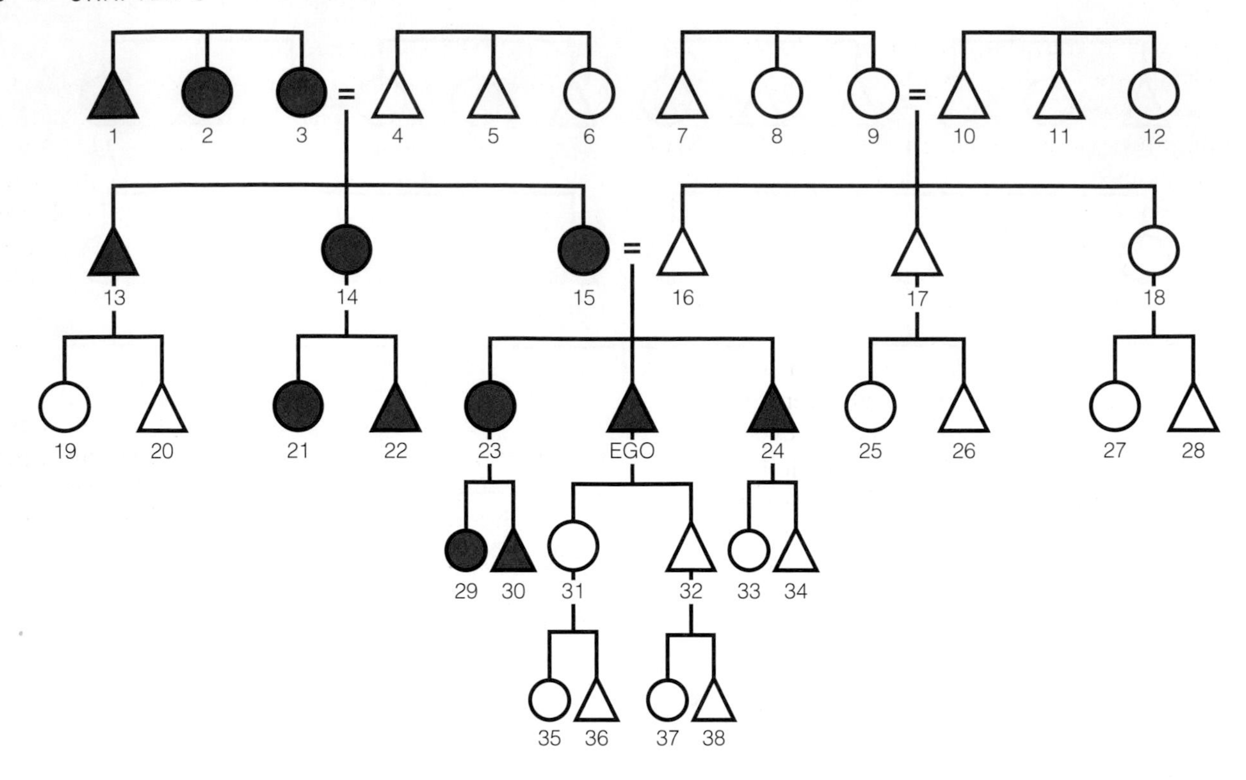

FIGURE 8.24 **Matrilineal descent from a male EGO's perspective. Note that brother and sister are always in the same descent group. Also note that, in this case, EGO's children are not in his descent group but that his sister's children are.**

Source: Based on © 1995 Brian Schwimmer, All rights reserved, Department of Anthropology, University of Manitoba

It is important not to confuse matrilineal descent with *matriarchy*—a situation known only in myth—in which the women in a society have greater authority and decision-making prerogatives than the men. In most cases where matrilineal descent is practised, men retain the lion's share of the power and authority. Men hold the political offices, and it is men, not women, who control property. In matrilineal societies, both property and political office pass from one man to another, but through a woman. To illustrate, whereas in a patrilineal society a man passes his property and hereditary political office to his own son, in a matrilineal society property and office pass from a man to his sister's son. In fact, in a matrilineal society, the most important male relationship a man has is with his sister's son (or mother's brother). The principle of matrilineal descent is illustrated in Figure 8.24.

The Corporate Nature of Unilineal Descent Groups

Because unilineal descent groups clearly define who is a member and who is not and also endure over time, they are good examples of corporate entities that play a powerful and multifaceted role in the lives of individual members. The term corporate is used because in many ways unilineal descent groups act like companies or corporations. We can cite six indicators of the corporate nature of unilineal descent groups:

1. Unilineal groups such as lineages often shape a person's identity. When a stranger asks the simple question, "Who are you?," lineage members are likely to respond, "I am a member of such and such a lineage," rather than, "I am John Smith." Lineage members, in other words, see themselves first and foremost as members of the kinship group rather than as individuals.
2. Unilineal descent groups regulate marriage. Because unilineal descent groups are exogamous, they may involve thousands of people. Moreover in most unilineal descent groups, large numbers of kin on both the bride's and the groom's side of the family must give their approval before marriages can take place.
3. Property (such as land and livestock) is usually regulated by the descent group, rather than controlled by the individual. The group allocates specific pieces of property to individual members for their use. This control of economic resources by the descent group requires the group to help young adults get established economically, pay bridewealth, and support group members during times of crisis.
4. Unilineal descent groups function politically to the extent that lineage elders have the right to settle disputes within their lineage (albeit usually without

matriarchy A system of governance whereby women rule over men or are empowered to make decisions over men.

the power to impose a settlement) and may act as intermediaries in disputes with opposing descent groups.

5. Unilineal descent groups often have their own set of religious deities, and in many cases those deities are deceased family members. When a respected lineage or clan elder dies, he is not buried and forgotten but often is elevated to the status of "ancestor-god." Because it is believed that these deceased ancestors can both protect and curse the living group members, living elders periodically perform religious or supernatural ceremonies to appease the ever-vigilant ancestor-deities.
6. Even the criminal justice system in societies with unilineal descent groups has a strong corporate focus. For example, if a member of lineage (a) assaults a member of lineage (b), the entire lineage (b) will seek compensation from or revenge on lineage (a). The assaulter would not be held solely accountable for her or his individual actions, but rather the group (the lineage or clan) would be culpable.

The corporate nature of unilineal descent groups is no better illustrated than in the strong bonds of obligations that exist among members. The kinship group provides a firm base of security and protection for its individual members. If crops fail, an individual can always turn to her or his unilineal descent group members for assistance; in the event of any threat from outsiders, a person may expect support and protection from members of her or his own descent group. The strength of these bonds of obligation depends on the closeness of the ties. Mutual assistance is likely to be taken seriously among lineage members, less so among clan members.

Multilineal Descent Groups

Approximately 40 percent of the world's societies have kinship systems that are not based on the unilineal principle. These multilineal descent groups are classified into three basic types: double descent, ambilineal descent, and bilateral descent.

Double Descent

With *double descent* (or double unilineal descent), kinship is traced both matrilineally and patrilineally. In such societies an individual belongs to both the mother's and the father's lineages. Descent under such a system is, however, matrilineal for some purposes and patrilineal for others. For example, movable property such as small livestock or agricultural produce may be inherited from the mother's side of the family, whereas non-movable property such as land may be inherited from the father's side. Double descent is rare.

Ambilineal Descent

In societies that practise *ambilineal descent*, parents have a choice of affiliating their children with either kinship group. Compared with unilineal systems, which restrict one's membership to either the mother's or the father's group, ambilineal systems are more flexible because they allow for individual choice concerning group affiliation. Decisions are usually taken for economic or political reasons.

Bilateral Descent

In societies (such as mainstream Canadian society) that practise *bilateral descent*, a person is related equally to both the mother's and the father's sides of the family (Figure 8.25). A bilateral system tends to be symmetrical to the extent that what happens on one side of the kinship diagram also happens on the other side. In other words, the grandparents, aunts, uncles, and cousins are treated equally on both sides of the family.

The kinship group recognized in a bilateral system is known as the *kindred*—a group of closely related relatives connected through both parents to one living relative (or to EGO). Unlike unilineal descent, which forms discrete, mutually exclusive groups, bilateral systems give rise to a situation in which no two individuals (except siblings) have the same kindred. The kindred is not a group at all, but rather a network of relatives. It has no founding ancestor, precise boundaries, or continuity over time. In short, because kindreds are not corporate groups, they cannot perform the same functions—such as joint ownership of property, common economic activities, regulation of marriage, or mutual assistance—as unilineal groups. An individual can mobilize some members of his or her kindred to perform some of these tasks, but the kindred does not function as a corporate entity. About the only time the kindred get together is for funerals and weddings. Because descent is reckoned down both lines, the kindred has very little generational or horizontal depth. That is, people find it difficult to trace their relatives back more than two or three generations; few know who their great-great-grandparents were. Consequently they also don't know who their third cousins are.

double descent A system of descent in which individuals receive some rights and obligations from the father's side of the family and others from the mother's side.

ambilineal descent A form of descent in which a person chooses to affiliate with a kin group through either the male or the female line.

bilateral descent A type of kinship system in which individuals emphasize both their mother's kin and their father's kin relatively equally.

kindred All the relatives a person recognizes in a bilateral kinship system.

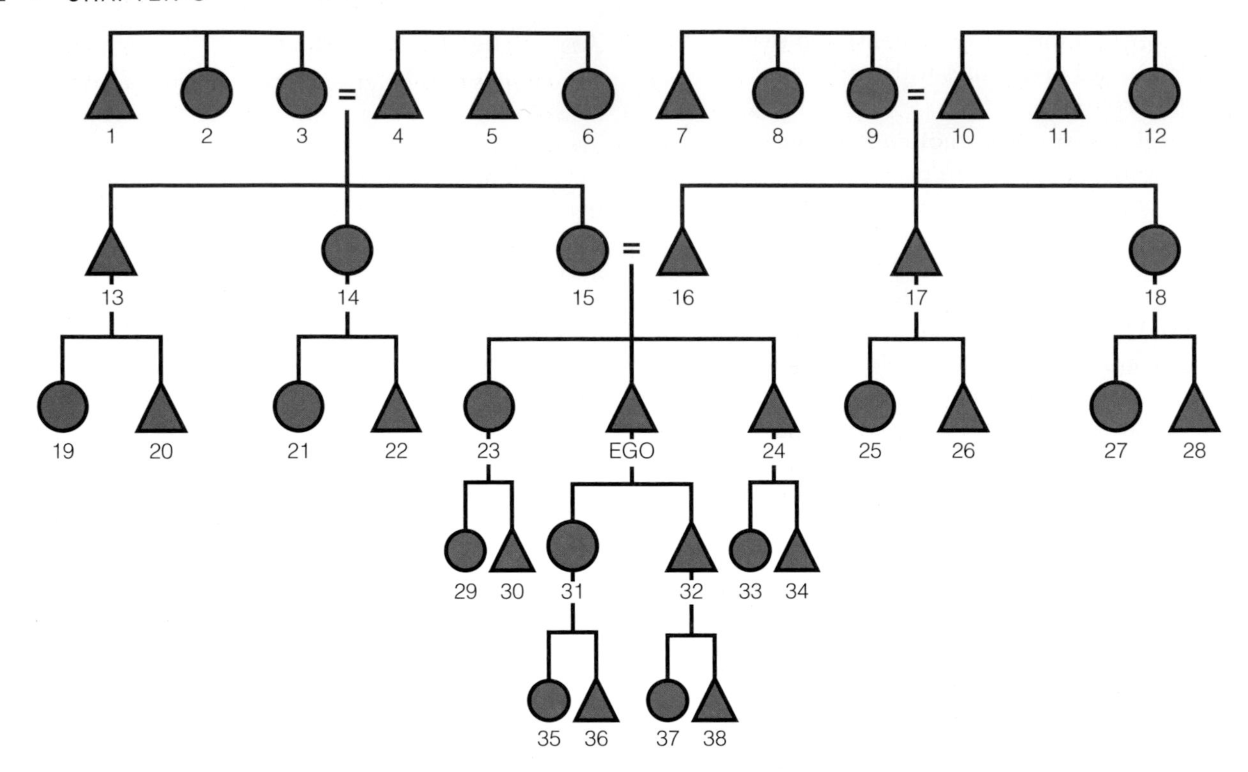

FIGURE 8.25 Bilateral kinship system. In this diagram, everyone on both the mother's and the father's sides of the family is related to EGO equally.

Source: Based on © 1995 Brian Schwimmer, All rights reserved, Department of Anthropology, University of Manitoba

This type of loosely structured network of relatives (kindred) works particularly well in Western societies that highly value individuality, personal independence, and geographic mobility. Although the kindred in bilateral societies establishes a fairly wide set of relationships with mutual obligations, those ties are rather loosely defined and amorphous. The looseness of the ties thus allows for greater autonomy from the demands of kin. In other words, the typical North American can be more economically and geographically mobile if fewer people can make kinship demands on his or her time and resources.

Bilateral descent is also adaptive for small-scale foraging societies, such as the Ju/'hoansi of Botswana and Namibia, but for different reasons than found in economically complex societies. In small-scale societies that are geographically mobile and have scarce resources, bilateral descent enables people to make claims on a large set of kin who may be dispersed over a wide area. This is adaptive because kin may be asked for help, particularly in hard times.

Kinship and the Modern World

With the explosion in information technology in the past two decades, we now have databases that enable us to explore how we are connected to others. For example, in 2011 researchers at Facebook analyzed 69 billion connections and found that 99.6 percent of Facebook users are connected by five degrees (six steps) and that 92 percent are connected by only four degrees of separation (five steps).

In addition to making kinship connections in the present, we are also developing powerful tools for accessing our genealogical histories. Unless they are born into a family that has kept careful records of its history, most people have little knowledge of their ancestors beyond three or four generations. However, within the last few years it has become possible for people to reconstruct their genealogies many generations into the past. The Internet now has a number of online sites that enable people to find information about long-forgotten family members. The site with the largest family database in the world is Ancestry.com, which for a fee provides access to more than 11 billion digitized records on immigration, births, marriages, and deaths. Moreover, the database includes more than 400 historical newspapers as well as thousands of family histories and biographies from Canada, the United States, and Great Britain dating back to the mid-1500s. All these documents have been scanned into this company's database, allowing subscribers to find information on a particular relative.

Kinship systems and relationships are never as neat and tidy in real life as they are in theory. Exceptions to the rules and aberrant forms of individual behaviour can be found in any system. Moreover, kinship systems are constantly experiencing changes through contact with external forces such as industrializing economies, decolonization, missionary intrusions, and cultural diffusion in general.

Of all aspects of human societies, kinship systems represent the most intimate, intense, and long-lasting set of social relationships a person will experience. Based as they are on birth and marriage, they create social ties that are often close and emotional. Kinship groups often involve strong bonds of obligation, security for their members, and moral coercion to adhere to social norms. We cannot assume, however, that these well-integrated kinship groups remain unchanged in the face of external pressures such as urban migration, poverty, unemployment, and a host of other hardships.

Some social scientists have suggested that people living in Western societies with thriving market-driven economies have essentially outsourced many of their traditional kinship roles and obligations to professional service providers for a fee. We now employ wedding planners to design and execute a wedding celebration that had, in previous times, been the job of parents and close relatives; nannies now care for small children while both parents go off to work; "love coaches" advise their clients (many of whom are online daters) how to write a profile that will attract the kind of people they want to meet; etiquette counsellors are hired to teach children how to behave in polite society because parents do not have time in their day to do it themselves; the highly emotional and exhausting work of caring for one's aging parents is now being done by a rapidly growing industry of elder-care providers; and perhaps the most dramatic form of outsourcing of kinship roles is surrogate motherhood, whereby a woman carries and delivers a child for another couple or person. All these social services, and many others too numerous to include here, are examples of how roles traditionally performed by kin are now being handled by professionals who, to one degree or another, are giving not only their time and expertise to their clients, but also the emotional energy required for doing their jobs well. Whatever the causes of this trend of outsourcing kinship roles and obligations, we must conclude that the nature and emotional content of kinship interaction in Canada and other industrialized nations is changing rapidly and in some dramatically new ways. The task of understanding kinship systems in recent years has been made all the more difficult by such complex phenomena as transnational adoptions, gay and lesbian families, and new ***reproductive technologies*** at our disposal. For example, when the baby is born to a surrogate mother, the question arises, Who is the mother? Is it the woman who donated the egg (the genetic mother)? Is it the woman who carried the child and gave birth (the gestational mother)? Or is it the woman who will raise the child (nurturing/social mother)? A number of difficult court cases have dealt with disputes involving children conceived through various reproductive technologies, as we saw in the opening discussion. These new technologies have created challenges for our legal system, our ethical and moral standards, and our basic vocabulary of kinship.

The high cost of acquiring a child through the process of maternal surrogacy in Canada is driving many childless couples to seek a surrogate mother in India, where it is far cheaper. The commercialization of making babies (particularly across international borders) raises troubling ethical and legal questions. For example, what obligations does a couple have to the birth mother after the child is born? What control during the nine-month pregnancy period should the contracting parents have over the birth mother? And what happens if the child is born with serious birth defects?

In 2014, a Thai surrogate for parents from Australia gave birth to twins, a boy and a girl. The Australian parents took the girl but left the boy with the surrogate in Thailand because he had Down syndrome and the surrogate mother refused an abortion (Blackwell 2014). In another instance, however, a gay couple whose surrogate mother gave birth to triplets, one of whom had Down syndrome, decided to keep the infant (Blackwell 2014).

To avoid such problems, contracts are usually drawn up that establish the rights and responsibilities of all parties, and deal with issues such as confidentiality, parental rights, the reimbursement of expenses, and surrogate mother prenatal obligations (Surrogacy in Canada Online 2015). They can impose severe financial penalties on surrogate mothers who refuse the parents' requests (Blackwell 2014).

And, as Ellen Goodman (2008, 13) points out, how different is this whole process from buying and selling babies (i.e., trafficking in newborns)? Quite apart from how one might answer these ethical questions, one thing is certain: The availability of these new reproductive technologies is making it increasingly difficult to define what we mean by kinship connections.

---

reproductive technologies Recent developments, such as in vitro fertilization, surrogate motherhood, and sperm banks, that make the reckoning of kin relationships more complex.

Summary

1. Recognizing the difficulties inherent in such definitions, anthropologists define family as a social unit whose members cooperate economically, manage reproduction and child rearing, and most often live together. Marriage, the process by which families are formed, is a socially approved union between adult partners.
2. Every culture has a set of rules (incest taboos) regulating which categories of kin are inappropriate

partners for sexual intercourse. The explanations for this universal incest taboo include the inbreeding theory, the family disruption theory, the theory of expanding social alliances, and the childhood familiarity theory.

3. Cultures restrict the choice of marriage partners by such practices as exogamy, endogamy, arranged marriages, preferential-cousin marriage, the levirate, and the sororate.
4. In many cultures, romantic love is not a major criterion for selecting a spouse. Courtship practices found throughout the world vary widely, from being virtually non-existent at one extreme to permissive at the other.
5. All societies have rules governing the number of spouses a person can have. Societies tend to emphasize monogamy (one spouse at a time), polygyny (a man marrying more than one wife at a time), or polyandry (a woman marrying more than one husband at a time).
6. In many societies, marriages involve the transfer of some type of economic consideration in exchange for rights of sexual access, legal rights over children, and rights to each other's property. These economic considerations involve such practices as bridewealth, bride service, dowry, and reciprocal exchange.
7. The formation of families functions to reduce competition for spouses, regulates the sexual division of labour, and meets the material, educational, and emotional needs of children.
8. Just as all societies have customary ways of establishing marriages, they also have ways of dissolving them. As a rule, divorce rates are lower in societies that have strong kinship groups and systems of bridewealth.
9. Cultural anthropologists distinguish between two types of family structure: the nuclear family, comprising the wife, husband, and children; and the extended family, a much larger social unit, comprising relatives from three or more generations.
10. All societies have guidelines regarding where a married couple should live after they marry. Residence patterns fall into five different categories: The couple can live with or near the relatives of the husband's father (patrilocal), the wife's relatives (matrilocal), the husband's mother's brother (avunculocal), the relatives of either the wife or the husband (ambilocal), or the husband and wife can form a completely new residence of their own (neolocal).
11. Although kinship relations are more important in some societies than others, kinship is the single most important aspect of social structure in all societies. Kinship is based on both consanguineal (blood) relationships and affinal (marriage) relationships. Most societies recognize some type of fictive kinship, whereby kinship terms and obligations are applied to people who have no biological connection.
12. A fundamental feature of all kinship systems is that they group relatives into certain categories, call them by the same name, and expect people to behave toward these relatives in similar ways. How a particular culture categorizes its relatives varies according to different principles of classification. These principles are based on criteria such as generation, gender, lineality, consanguineality, relative age, sex of the connecting relative, social condition, and side of the family.
13. There are six primary types of kinship systems based on how the society distinguishes different categories of relatives: Eskimo, Hawaiian, Iroquois, Omaha, Crow, and Sudanese.
14. Many societies have sets of rules, called rules of descent, that affiliate people with different sets of kin. Patrilineal descent affiliates a person with the kin group of the father, matrilineal descent affiliates a person with the kin group of the mother, and ambilineal descent permits an individual to affiliate with either the mother's or the father's kin group.
15. Patrilineal descent groups, which are more common than matrilineal, are found in most areas of the world. In a patrilineal system, a man's children belong to his lineage, as do the children of his son, but not the children of his daughter. Women marry outside their own lineage.
16. In matrilineal systems, a woman's children are affiliated with her lineage, not her husband's. Because the mother's brother is the social father of the woman's children, the relations between husband and wife in a matrilineal system tend to be more fragile than in patrilineal societies.
17. In societies that trace their descent unilineally (through a single line), people identify themselves with a particular lineage (a set of kin who can trace their ancestry back through known links) and clans (a group claiming descent but unable to trace all the genealogical links).
18. Bilateral descent, which is found predominantly among foraging and industrialized societies such as Canada's, traces one's relatives on both the mother's and the father's sides of the family equally. Bilateral systems, which are symmetrical, result in the formation of kindreds, which are more like loose kinship networks than permanent corporate functioning groups.
19. Reproductive technologies (such as in vitro fertilization and surrogate motherhood) that have become available in recent decades raise legal, ethical, and definitional questions about the nature of kinship.

Key Terms

affinal relatives
ambilineal descent
ambilocal (bilocal) residence
arranged marriage
avunculocal residence
bilateral descent
bride service
bridewealth
clan
cognatic descent
collaterality
common law marriage
consanguineal relatives
cross cousins
descent
divorce
double descent
dowry
dowry deaths
EGO
endogamy
Eskimo (Inuit) system
exogamy
extended family
family
fictive kinship
fraternal polyandry
ghost marriage
incest taboo
Iroquois system
kindred
kinship
kinship systems
kin terms
kin types
levirate
lineage
lineality
marriage
matriarchy
matrilineal descent group
matrilocal residence
monogamy
neolocal residence
nuclear family
parallel cousins
patrilineal descent group
patrilocal residence
polyamory
polyandry
polygamy
polygyny
postpartum sex taboo
preferential cousin marriage
reproductive technologies
role ambiguity
serial monogamy
sororal polygyny
sororate
surrogacy
unilineal descent

Critical Thinking Questions

1. Is marriage becoming outdated?
2. Most Westerners marry for love and, traditionally, non-Westerners marry for economic or kinship reasons. Yet this is changing with more people in non-Western cultures marrying for romantic reasons. Why is this happening?
3. How is the nuclear family well-suited to a highly mobile culture?
4. In Canada people are increasingly marrying and cohabiting with people from different religious, social, racial, and ethnic backgrounds. What might be some of the reasons for this?
5. Currently, polygamy is illegal in Canada, but in the near future it may be challenged on Constitutional grounds and may become legal. If this happens, how will it affect the legal definition of marriage, and how might it affect marriage patterns in Canada?
6. Design a research project to examine the economic aspects of marriage in a small horticultural village in India or China.
7. If you wanted to know how enculturation practices between same-sex and heterosexual marriages differ in your community, how would you go about the research? What questions would you want your collaborators to answer?
8. Interview a classmate and draw their kinship diagram to the level of grandparents and first cousins. How would you draw situations such as twins, multiple spouses, and half-brothers and -sisters?
9. In what ways is biotechnology reshaping marriage practices and family structure?
10. What are the complex legal and ethical issues that surrogate motherhood raises?

Make the Grade with MindTap

Stay organized and efficient with **MindTap**—a single destination with all the course material and study aids you need to succeed. Built-in apps leverage social media and the latest learning technology. For example:

- ReadSpeaker will read the text to you.
- Self-quizzing allows you to assess your understanding.
- Flashcards are pre-populated to provide you with a jump-start for review—or you can create your own.
- You can highlight text and make notes in your MindTap Reader. Your notes will flow into Evernote, the electronic notebook app that you can access anywhere when it's time to study for the exam.

Visit nelson.com/student to start using **MindTap**. Enter the Online Access Code from the card included with your text. If a code card is not provided, you can purchase instant access at NELSONbrain.com.

Female construction workers carry bricks on their heads at a high-rise construction site in Mandalay, Myanmar.

9

CHAPTER 9

Sex and Gender

WHAT WE WILL LEARN

- What the difference is between sex and gender
- How gender is shaped by ideology and how it is culturally constructed
- How we learn out gender identity
- How ideas about gender roles and gender relations vary across cultures
- How cultures can have more than two genders
- How transgender people are challenging society's ideas and expectations of normality
- How the sexual practices of Western and non-Western peoples vary
- How subsistence strategies influence gender roles and gender relations
- How gender roles are changing in Canada
- How gender inequality affects women and society
- The effects gender-based violence has on both women and men, and society in general

BILLY TIPTON

Dorothy Lucille Tipton was born December 29, 1914, in Oklahoma City, Oklahoma, but after her parents divorced she was raised by her aunt in Kansas City, Missouri. Something of a musical prodigy, her passion was jazz, and Kansas City was a centre for it in the 1920s and 1930s. Dorothy also played the piano and saxophone, but when she tried to join the high school band, she was rejected because she was a girl. Contemporary jazz originated in African American communities in the late 1800s and early 1900s, and particularly in 1910s New Orleans, where performers played primarily in brothels and bars. Jazz was not only the domain of African Americans at the time, but also, "unless you were an attractive 'girl singer' . . . it was strictly for men" (Spokesman-Review 1989). It was certainly not a career for a respectable, middle-class, white woman.

But it was the career Dorothy Lucille Tipton wanted, so, at the age of 18, she bound her breasts, cut her hair, dressed as a man, and became Billy Lee Tipton. It was a deception that was to last for more than 50 years, until her death in 1989.

During the late 1930s and early 1940s, Billy toured with several bands throughout the U.S. Midwest, playing in various nightclubs. In 1954 he formed his own band—the Billy Tipton Trio—which was moderately successful and recorded several records (Figure 9.1). Even though the band stayed in the same hotel room and even slept in the same bed, he managed to keep his secret. His drummer later remarked "I never suspected a thing [although] Tipton, with a baby face and a high singing voice, looked too feminine to be a man" (Los Angeles Times 1989). In 1958 he settled in Spokane, Washington, where he became somewhat of a local celebrity, playing in a downtown night-club and later running a booking agency for musicians before he retired in the 1970s.

Women were attracted to Tipton's "boyish good looks and his meticulous style of dress" (Middlebrook 1999), and although he was never officially married (or divorced), Billy lived with five women during his life who called themselves Mrs. Tipton. In 1962 he "married" Kitty Oakes. They were together for several years, adopted three boys, and lived the typical suburban life, joining the local parent-teacher association and enrolling the boys in the Boy Scouts. Tipton and Oakes separated in 1979 and Billy moved into a trailer where he lived until his death 10 years later.

imageBROKER/Alamy Stock Photo

FIGURE 9.1 The Billy Tipton Trio: from left to right: Ron Kilde, Billy Tipton, and drummer Dick O'Neil.

Billy died on January 21, 1989, from a bleeding ulcer. After carrying him to the bathroom that morning, his son William called 911. When the paramedics arrived and opened his pajamas to administer CPR they asked William "did your father have a sex change?" It came as a complete shock to the musicians he played with, his three sons, and also to Kitty Oakes that Billy was biologically female.

The story was sensational news, and the day after his funeral the local paper went public with the headline "Jazz Musician Spent Life Concealing Fantastic Secret" (Spokesman-Review 1989). It was soon picked up by various tabloids, magazines, TV stations, and national and international newspapers.

How did Billy manage to maintain his secret from so many people for so many years? To begin with, he always acted in a professional and gentlemanly manner. He also always locked the door to the bathroom where he washed and dressed. He told his "wives" that he had been in a horrendous car accident that disfigured his genitals and broke his ribs—hence the bindings and the reason he was not physically intimate with his "wives" (Blecha 2005; Middlebrook 1999). No marriage or divorce was ever recorded for William L. or Billy Lee Tipton, and although he had a social security number he refused to use it to claim benefits and thus ended his life destitute. He also never visited a doctor, refusing even when he was deathly ill.

It is unfortunate that Dorothy Tipton's need to hide her biological sex so she could do what she wanted to do most probably led to her death and to her life ending in poverty. Attitudes toward gender roles have fortunately changed since the 1940s, and few professions in the West are restricted by gender.

Billy Tipton's story exemplifies the difference between sex and gender. Billy was born biologically female, but hid that fact by binding her breasts, never seeing a doctor, never officially getting married, never applying for social assistance, and by never being intimate with his partners. As his biographer remarked, for 40 years Billy looked in the mirror and was the only one who knew that he had the physical body of a female (Middlebrook 1999). He covered that body with the cultural symbols of masculinity: his haircut, his dress, his occupation, his mannerisms, and his name. Most people cover their biological bodies—their sex—with the culturally specific symbols deemed appropriate for their sex, that is, masculine symbols for a male and feminine symbols for a female. Because of this, we tend to see gender differences and gendered behaviour as intimately connected with anatomical sex differences. If sex equalled gender, however, Dorothy/Billy Tipton would never have been able to pull the deception off. ■

Sex Is Biological and Gender Is Cultural

Understanding sex and gender as a specialization within anthropology can play an important role in applied anthropology and applying anthropological concepts to real-world contemporary issues. For example, having an understanding of the principal ways in which a gendered approach to social inquiry can be applied to the design, implementation, monitoring, and evaluation of development projects is of considerable importance, especially when unequal rights between men and women are present in a culture. Combining gender perspectives and participatory practices that include both men and women with other forms of technical expertise can be extremely useful in development work. This chapter introduces some terms and concepts related to sex, gender, and sexuality to provide a context for how they may be used in an applied perspective.

One need not be a particularly keen observer to recognize that human males and females differ physically in important ways. At the most basic level, biology informs us that sex is where males and females differ genetically, with females having two X chromosomes and males having both an X and a Y chromosome. This results in significant physiological differences in humans such that our species is *sexually dimorphic*. Biology and evolutionary theory help to explain why males on average are taller and have considerably greater body mass than females, as well as the differences between internal sex organs, external genitalia, breast size, hormone levels, body hair, and muscle-to-fat ratios (Brettell and Sargent 2005). Some males have greater physical strength because of their larger hearts and lungs and greater muscle mass. There are also behavioural differences linked to biological differences, but there is considerable disagreement on the extent to which they actually cause differences in behaviour (Brettell and Sargent 2005; Eliot 2010).

From 1 in 1500 to 1 in 2000 children are born with atypical genitalia or with both male and female reproductive organs (ISNA 2008a). These *intersex* individuals may have XXY chromosomes, may have some cells XX and some XY, or they may be XX or XY. As Anne Fausto-Sterling reminds us, "A body's sex is simply too complex. There is no either/or. Rather, there are shades of difference" (2000, 2). Intersex individuals have faced considerable discrimination, including denial of citizenship rights, selective abortion, infanticide, as well as cosmetic surgeries "normalizing" their genitals to either male or female without their consent (ISNA 2008b).

One of the more controversial examples of an intersex person is Caster Semenya from South Africa, who won the gold medal in the women's 800 m event in the 2009 World Championships in Athletics. With a rather male physique and features, deep voice, and perhaps (some thought) was too fast to be female, her sex was questioned and she was required to undergo "gender testing" before she was allowed to compete again (Figure 9.2). The International Association of Athletics Federations (IAAF) have never made the outcome of the tests public due to patient confidentiality, but leaked results confirmed that Semenya was raised as a girl but had no ovaries or uterus, and both external female genitalia and undescended testes (Hurst, 2009). The IAAF eventually cleared her to race as a woman and restored her medals and record. What is at stake, however, is not just the gold medal, but her identity as a woman. What is brought into question is what it means to be male and female from a physical and a cultural perspective.

Mike Hewitt/Getty Images

FIGURE 9.2 South African athlete Caster Semenya competing in the Women's 800 m semifinal at the 2012 Olympic Games in London, United Kingdom.

sexually dimorphic The physiological differences in form between males and females.

intersex Individuals with sex characteristics that do not allow them to be identified as male or female.

Gender Is Cultural

Human sexual dimorphism means that the largest physical difference between people in any society is that between males and females. Ever since Charles Darwin published *The Descent of Man and Selection in Relation to Sex* in 1871 (2004) scientists have asked what these differences mean and their social, cultural, and political significance. Until the late 1960s and early 1970s, it was for the most part taken for granted that differences between men and women, and the roles they played in society, were due to biological differences, and that they were natural and normal. The civil rights movement in the United States, and protests against U.S. Social policy at this time, however, raised awareness of women's inequality. Women were paid less, were overworked at home, and had less access to resources, power, and privilege in a society dominated by men. Recognition of this oppression led North American society to question "the assumptions about the biological differences between men and women that restricted women's opportunities, and more and more women began to fight against the social injustices that plagued their lives" (Mascia-Lees and Black 2000, 7).

Our gender has perhaps more impact on our lives than any other characteristic, permeating almost everything we do and our sense of who we are, and what others expect of us. As Eliot (2010) points out, among other things it influences our future relationships, personality, skills, career, and health. Boys in North America, for instance, are four times more likely to have major learning and development disorders such as autism, attention deficit disorder, and dyslexia; 73 percent more likely to die in accidents; twice as likely to be the victim of violent crime (except sexual assault); and three times more likely to succeed at killing themselves. Girls, on the other hand, are twice as likely to suffer from depression, anxiety, and eating disorders, be the victims of sexual assault, and are twice as likely to *attempt* suicide (Eliot 2010).

Anthropologists also began to realize that they had paid little attention to gender or the importance of women in their investigations. Malinowski, for instance, spoke almost exclusively to men and presented a male-centric view of the Trobriand Islanders. Ethnographers also demonstrated that the definition of femaleness and maleness varied widely from society to society. Because of significant cultural variability in behaviours and attitudes between the sexes, most anthropologists and other social scientists now make a distinction between *sex* and *gender*. Sex refers to the biological or genetic differences (between "male" and "female"), while gender refers to the way the sexes are "perceived, evaluated, and expected to behave" (between "men" and "women") (Schlegel 1990, 23). In other, words, gender is what culture makes of sex.

To say that gender is the way that the sexes (including intersex individuals) are perceived, refers to the characteristics of women and men, what they are like, and what it means to be a man or a woman. The phrase "expected to behave" refers not only to the different norms women and men follow but also the culturally appropriate roles they play. How the sexes are evaluated refers to the value a culture places on being a man or a woman, and consequently how that influences each gender's access to the culturally valued resources of wealth, power, and prestige.

Although the use of the term gender acknowledges the role that culture plays, it is not always possible to determine the extent to which culture or biology determines behavioural or attitudinal differences between the sexes. What we can say, however, is that biological differences influence (or set broad limits on) social definitions of maleness and femaleness to varying degrees. To illustrate, the fact that only women can give birth provides a basis for a particular set of attitudes and behaviours for women, and this results in some cultures socializing women to be nurturing and to have life-giving qualities. Likewise, because of their greater body mass, men in some cultures are encouraged to be courageous, aggressive, and warlike. Nevertheless, as we will see, many different social definitions of *masculinity* and *femininity* can be found throughout the world.

Gender Ideology

Ideas about what the genders are like, how they should behave, the appropriate roles they should play, and how they should relate to one another are called *gender ideology*. It can be defined as a system of thoughts, attitudes, and values that legitimizes gender roles, statuses, and customary behaviour. Gender ideology often stems from religious teachings. For example, according to one version of the Biblical story of creation, God formed Eve from Adam's rib as a "help mate" for him. They lived happily in the Garden of Eden and could eat the fruit from any tree except from the tree of knowledge of good and evil, which, if they did so, was punishable by death. The devil, disguised as a snake, tricked Eve, however, into eating from the tree, and she then offered the fruit to Adam. God's punishment was to create enmity between them and to expel them from

sex The biological or genetic differences between males and females.

gender The way the sexes are perceived, evaluated, and expected to behave.

masculinity The social definition of maleness, which varies from culture to culture.

femininity The social definition of femaleness, which varies from culture to culture.

gender ideology A system of thoughts, attitudes, and values that legitimizes gender roles, statuses, and customary behaviour.

the Garden of Eden. Eve's punishment was to experience pain in childbirth and to be ruled over by Adam, while Adam had to toil in the fields until he died. This story, believed for centuries by millions, tells both men and women that women are gullible and can't be trusted; that they are responsible for man's suffering; that they are secondary to men; and that women are to obey men. Other religions also contain ideas about what men and women are like and how they should behave and relate to one another. The Quran, for instance, says that men are the protectors of women (4:34), and that women must not reveal their "adornments" to men except to close male relatives (24:31). Gender ideology thus plays a significant role in the way men and women are supposed to behave and relate to one another.

The Cultural Construction of Gender

The brains of boys and girls at birth are different: they mature at different rates, process sensory information differently, and operate at different activity levels, and these differences do influence later behaviour to a small extent (Eliot 2010). But the brain is very plastic and changes and adapts or is "rewired" in response to our experiences. It is much more plastic when we are young. Thus, for instance, learning another language is effortless for us as young children, but is far more difficult once we are past adolescence. Eliot (2010) points out that every task we do—"reading, running, laughing, calculating, debating, watching TV, folding laundry, mowing grass, singing, crying, kissing, and so on—reinforces active brain circuits at the expense of other inactive ones" (Eliot 2010, 6). Since girls and boys spend so much time doing different things and have such different experiences, by the time they are adults their brains have been rewired differently. In other words, the differences in behaviour between men and women are reflected in biological differences in the brains of men and women. But the cause is due not so much to genetics as it is to different cultural experiences. In a sense, girls and boys are immersed from birth into two different subcultures: a masculine one and a feminine one. As Eliot (2010, 8) puts it, "growing up as girl or a boy is a lot like being immersed in one of two different languages from birth."

Thus, the differences between men and women are biological. However, they are, with minor exceptions, not predetermined biological facts at birth, but the result of different cultural experiences wiring the brain differently. There are at least three implications of this. First, the behaviour of girls and boys will be different in different cultures because the experiences of growing up a girl or a boy in different cultures will be different. Second, we can "re-wire" our brains as adults, although, like learning a language, it will be much harder. This is important for people undergoing sex reassignment surgery. And third, we can change the behaviour of girls and boys by changing their experiences. While this last point may sound like social engineering, it is an important consideration given that gender has such an impact on our lives. If social equality is desirable, then perhaps the experiences we give our children should be gender neutral.

As the ideas about what the genders are like and how they are evaluated and expected to behave vary from one culture or society to another and are thus culturally relative, we can talk about the ***cultural construction of gender***. To say that gender is culturally constructed does not mean, however, that biological differences are unimportant, or that individuals cannot manipulate the meanings of the characteristics.

In a cross-cultural study of 30 societies, including Canada, Pakistan, New Zealand, Nigeria, and Venezuela, Williams and Best (1994) asked university students to indicate which psychological characteristics (e.g., aggressive or emotional) from a list of 300 they thought were best associated with men, with women, or with both equally (Table 9.1). There was remarkable agreement across cultures, and while this does require some explanation, it does not mean that these characteristics are linked to biology, as they also found that children did not begin to learn these associations until they were about five years old. Williams and Best also discovered that the self-concepts young men and women had of themselves only slightly matched the stereotype characteristics. In other words, there is a host of psychological characteristics which are, for the most part, arbitrarily associated with one sex or the other. Different cultures attribute the characteristics differently, and thus the associations have to be learned. Since we learn these associations as we grow up, it makes them seem normal and natural.

These characteristics are ***gender stereotypes***, which are oversimplified conceptions held by many members of a society about the characteristics of men and women. They are important to understand in applied anthropology as they can have an impact on health-care delivery and other development projects. For instance, cross-culturally, women are twice as likely to be diagnosed with depression, even though they may have the same symptoms as men, because they are viewed as being more emotional (WHO 2001). Men, on the other hand, are more likely to be diagnosed with alcohol dependence because substance abuse is seen as a "male" issue. The World Health Organization has called for health policies that are gender sensitive

---

cultural construction of gender The ways a culture shapes individuals so they conform to that culture's concept of gender.

gender stereotypes Oversimplified conceptions about the characteristics of men and women.

TABLE 9.1

The 100 Items of the Pancultural Gender Adjective Checklist

Male-Associated		Female-Associated	
active	loud	affected	modest
adventurous	obnoxious	affectionate	nervous
aggressive	opinionated	appreciative	patient
arrogant	opportunistic	cautious	pleasant
autocratic	pleasure-seeking	changeable	prudish
bossy	precise	charming	self-pitying
capable	progressive	complaining	sensitive
coarse	quick	complicated	sentimental
conceited	rational	confused	sexy
confident	realistic	curious	shy
courageous	reckless	dependent	soft-hearted
cruel	resourceful	dreamy	sophisticated
cynical	rigid	emotional	submissive
determined	robust	excitable	suggestible
disorderly	serious	fault-finding	talkative
enterprising	sharp-witted	fearful	timid
greedy	show-off	fickle	touchy
hard-headed	steady	foolish	unambitious
humorous	stern	forgiving	unintelligent
indifferent	stingy	frivolous	unstable
individualistic	stolid	fussy	warm
initiative	tough	gentle	weak
interests wide	unfriendly	imaginative	worrying
inventive	unscrupulous	kind	understanding
lazy	witty	mild	superstitious

Source: Williams, J. E., and D. L. Best 1994. p. 193.

and that consider gender-specific risk factors and access to healthcare services, as well as gender-awareness training for healthcare providers (WHO 2001).

How Gender Is Learned

In most societies the initial assignment of gender is made at birth based on the infant's genitals: it is either a boy or a girl. Generally, infants with ambiguous genitalia are either pigeonholed into a boy or girl gender, undergo surgery to "correct" their gender, or in some societies killed. Soon after birth a gender is assigned, the infant is given a boy's name or a girl's name, and the process of gender socialization begins. Children learn and internalize the behaviour appropriate for their gender, what emotions they can and cannot express, what clothes they should wear, what games they should play, how they should speak, what occupations they should enter, and how they should interact with others of their own gender and with those of the opposite gender. Children's understanding of their own gender begins to develop at about two years of age (Kosslyn and Rosenberg 2011). They learn their gender from parents, peers, teachers, workmates, books, movies, advertisements, and so on (Figure 9.3). Once children realize they belong to one gender group they actively look to these people and other sources as cues to how they should behave in a manner appropriate for their gender (Martin and Ruble 2004). They also tend to evaluate their own group positively and make assumptions about the differences (Martin and Ruble 2004). In other words they develop a ***gender identity***.

Gender is also big business. Walmart, Toys"R"Us, and most other stores that sell toys have gender-coded aisles. The girls' aisle sells Barbies, baby dolls with all the accessories, easy-bake ovens, and little vacuum cleaners,

gender identity The gender a person identifies with among the range of culturally appropriate possibilities.

Darrow, Whitney Jr. 1970. *I'm Glad I'm a Boy! I'm Glad I'm a Girl!* New York: Windmill Books/Simon and Schuster.

FIGURE 9.3 Children learn their gender and gender roles from a variety of sources, including images in books such as Whitney Darrow Jr.'s book *I'm Glad I'm a Boy! I'm Glad I'm a Girl!* (1970). While it has been called one of the most sexist books ever printed, it was most likely meant as a satire, as Darrow was a satirical cartoonist for the *New Yorker*.

makeup kits, and so on; all of which encourage girls to become mothers, homemakers, and beauty queens with the focus on relationships. The boys' aisle is lined with action figures, superhero outfits, lightsabers, tool kits, footballs and hockey equipment, cars, trucks, and so on, encouraging them to be tough and individualistic with a focus on things rather than relationships. Although there is a movement to sell more gender-neutral toys, or at least not separate toys by gender, surveys have shown that "the pink aisle has gotten much more pink over the years" (Dockterman 2014).

Ideas about gender are present in advertisements, magazines, movies, books, television shows, and elsewhere and serve to reinforce gender stereotypes. In *The Simpsons*, for example, Marge is the homemaker and looks after the children, while Homer works, fulfilling the breadwinner-homemaker model. In such Walt Disney Productions films as *Pocahontas*, *Snow White and the Seven Dwarfs*, *Cinderella*, *Sleeping Beauty*, *The Little Mermaid*, *Beauty and the Beast*, *Mulan*, *Tarzan*, and *The Princess and the Frog*, the female characters are portrayed as beautiful, thin, submissive, highly emotional, often domestic, who focus on family and relationships, and aspire to find their prince. The male characters, on the other hand, are handsome, athletic, brave, authoritative, and born leaders who save the day. In *Mulan* (1998), about a girl who disguises herself as a man and goes off to fight, the hero sings a song entitled "I'll Make a Man out of You." He begins by asking "Did they send me daughters, when I asked for sons?" implying that the boys he has been sent to train are more like girls. To be men, they must be swift, forceful, strong, and mysterious. These films, which cater to younger audiences, provide models for children who emulate the qualities and behaviours of the character that they most identify with.

Mainstream Canadian culture recognizes two genders, masculine and feminine. Social communication requires that we know the gender of the person we are interacting with. Occasionally, however, we encounter people whose gender is not immediately clear and we may often feel uncomfortable because we do not know how to respond appropriately. When individuals do not fit into the binary gender categories or follow the established gender norms, we see them as being abnormal or even curable, and they often face social exclusion or discrimination. To make it easier to know the gender of the person we are interacting with, a number of cultural cues are used, such as clothing, makeup, hairstyle, perfume/cologne, language, and so on. These cues can be manipulated to present as the opposite gender, as with Billy Tipton, and they also change over time. In the 1950s and 1960s women wore skirts and dresses, and it was the men who wore the pants. Now jeans have become ubiquitous. Women were the only ones to wear earrings or carry handbags; now many men do. We normally think of high heels as a strictly women's fashion, signifying femininity and glamour, but originally it was the men who wore high heels. High heels were essential for good horsemanship in Persia (now Iran). When soldiers stood up in the stirrups they would use the heel to brace themselves so they could use their bow and arrow. By the 1500s high-heeled boots found their way to Europe as a symbol of status and masculinity and only afterward were adopted by women (Kremer 2013) (Figure 9.4).

Gender identities can also change when people are unable to fulfill the roles typical for their gender. For example, in many First Nations communities, a man's traditional role was to protect the family and community, and through hunting, fishing, and trapping provide for them.

Image copyright © 2016 Bata Shoe Museum, Toronto, Canada (photo: Ron Wood)

FIGURE 9.4 High heels were once a popular men's fashion, as seen in this boy's shoe from the mid-1600s. The height of the heel and the impracticality of the shoe was an indication of the child's status.

Men were also often the artisans, manufactured snowshoes, canoes, and other equipment, and were also the healers, singers, and dancers. Since contact, however, and the loss of most of their lands, maintaining these roles and consequently their identity has posed a tremendous challenge. As one Métis elder from the Big River area in Northern Saskatchewan has commented, "The role of men was protector and provider, but how can he protect if he has nothing to protect? How can he provide when he doesn't have the ability to provide and that's taken away from him by law? How can he be with his son, when they've taken him and put him into residential school or into foster care?" Without role models and mentors to teach young boys how to hunt, trap, and fish, the traditional male identity is lost. A Mohawk elder writes that many fathers don't know how to be fathers: "They only know how to make babies, but they don't know how to nurture them. They don't know how to show them compassion. And to make babies is great, but if you can't feed them and you can't give them spiritual teachings and wellbeing, then that's criminal" (OFIFC 2013).

Gender Cross-Culturally

That gender is culturally constructed means that not only must it be learned but also that it is not static and is constantly changing; what it means to be a man or a woman, and the roles men and women play in society are not the same today as they were 50 years ago. It also means there can be no universal meaning to the categories "woman" or "man." What it means to be a man or a woman in a particular society will thus be relative to that society.

Margaret Mead's (1935) classic study of sex and temperament in three New Guinea cultures illustrates the range of gender variation found among the Arapesh, Mundugumor, and Tchambuli. Mead found that, among the Arapesh, both men and women were cooperative, nonaggressive, and responsive to the needs of others—all traits that most Westerners would consider to be feminine. In contrast, both genders among the Mundugumor were expected to be fierce, ruthless, and aggressive.

Among the Tchambuli, there was a complete reversal of the male–female temperaments considered usual in Western society; that is, females were the dominant, impersonal partners who were aggressive food providers, whereas males were less responsible, more emotionally dependent, more preoccupied with art, and spent more time styling their hair and gossiping about the opposite sex. Mead argued that if those temperaments that we regard as traditionally feminine (i.e., nurturing, maternal, and passive) can be held as a masculine ideal in one group and can be frowned on for both sexes in another, then we no longer have a basis for saying that masculinity and femininity are biologically based. Although Mead's work has been criticized in recent years for its subjectivity, it nevertheless demonstrates the enormous variability in gender roles across cultures.

Third Genders

A third implication of the cultural construction of gender is that cultures do not have to be restricted to two genders; they could have more than two. Some cultures not only accommodate the ambiguities of these gender alternatives, they also see them as legitimate or, in some cases, powerful.

Two-Spirited People

Third-gender or *transgender* individuals are well-established in Indigenous North American cultures. Over 150 Indigenous American groups have provided a third gender as a legitimate social alternative (Roscoe 1998). Such people were not only accepted, but as they had both masculine and feminine characteristics, were also seen as gifted, or powerful and often became the healers in their societies. In most cases, people adopted a transgender identity through spiritual calling, individual inclination, or parental selection—where parents were involved in selecting their child's sexual orientation. Most were biologically male but dressed and behaved and took the roles of women, although in some societies females became hunters, warriors, and chiefs and constituted a fourth gender.

Early Christian explorers, settlers, and missionaries equated these genders with sexuality, that is, that they engaged in homosexual activities, which was seen not only as unnatural but also sinful. The Jesuits and early French explorers in Canada told stories of transgender men "given to sodomy" and "Hunting Women" with wives (Copley 2009). By the late 1800s mention of them in Canada had all but disappeared (Copley 2009). Whereas they were once respected and honoured in their societies, over time as a result of colonization and the religious teachings in the residential schools, that respect turned to *homophobia*, or fear and hatred of homosexuals, and they faced discrimination not only by their own communities but also by mainstream North American culture.

Anthropologists and other scholars referred to them as *berdache*, a French term that originally came from the Persian, and means "male prostitute" or "kept boy" (Jacobs et al. 1997). Many Native North Americans and anthropologists consider the term derogatory and inappropriate. In 1990 at the first, First Nations/Native American gay and lesbian conference in Winnipeg, the term *two-spirit* was coined

transgender Individuals whose gender expression or identity does not conform to the norms for their sex.

homophobia Fear and hatred of homosexuals.

two-spirit First Nations and Native American individuals who possess both masculine and feminine characteristics, and hold a respected place in their communities.

(Jacobs et al. 1997). Two-spirit better captures the fact that they possess both masculine and feminine characteristics. Two-spirited people include gay and lesbian First Nations/Native American individuals, transsexual and transgender people, as well as the traditional multiple gender categories (Jacobs et al. 1997). The decision by First Nations to use the term was also a political act. It was a deliberate attempt to distance themselves from non-First Nations gay and lesbians (Jacobs et al. 1997). It is also a sign of reclaiming their historical identity (Cameron 2005) and adopting a term for themselves that has meaning for them, that ties them to their cultural traditions, and that validates and socially recognizes them.

The journey has not been easy, however. In 2005, Vancouver fashion designer Tyler-Alan Jacobs, who identifies as two-spirit, was beaten so badly the right side of his face was caved in and his eye dislocated (Klassen 2014) (Figure 9.5). Although he had the support of his family for pursuing a traditionally female occupation and dressing more like a woman, he was beaten numerous times by members of his band, where homophobia (fear and hatred of homosexual people) was rampant. Off-reserve two-spirit people are also subject to racial discrimination for being Indigenous. The Greater Vancouver Native Cultural Society is one organization that helps two-spirit youth gain pride in their identity as both First Nations and gay (Klassen 2014).

Courtesy of Tyler-Alan Jacobs

FIGURE 9.5 Coast Salish fashion designer, Tyler-Alan Jacobs, identifies as two-spirit. His designs pair modern designs with patterns of traditional native regalia. In 2005 Jacobs was beaten nearly to death after coming out as gay in his community.

Hijras

Another example of a third gender are the ***hijras*** of India and Pakistan. Of the roughly two million hijras living in India (Nelson 2014) most are born male or with ambiguous genitalia. They have existed in India for over 2000 years. The notion of a combined male/female role is a major theme in Hindu art, religion, and mythology and many worship the Hindu goddess, Bahuchara Mata, who had cursed a robber with impotence unless he worshiped her by dressing and acting like a woman. There are also many Muslim hijras.

Most present themselves as being "like women," and dress in saris, wear women's jewellery, makeup, and hairstyles; they even walk and carry themselves as women do. Many hijras live in close communities with gurus (teachers) because they have been alienated by their families and society. Many hijras also undergo an emasculation rite involving voluntary castration but without the reconstruction of a vagina. Thus, they are neither male nor female but truly a third gender (Figure 9.6).

Pep Roig/Alamy Stock Photo

FIGURE 9.6 This hijra who presents himself as being "like a woman" is an example of the socially constructed basis for gender.

hijra A third gender found in India and Pakistan.

The term hijra has been translated by the word "eunuch" but this is seen as derogatory, and more recently they have preferred the term transgender. Because they do not fit the traditional binary gender model, however, they are often viewed as social deviants and have faced social stigma, harassment, and discrimination in obtaining healthcare, housing services, education, employment, and their legal rights. Unable to attend university, vote, or obtain a proper job, many find employment in the sex trade or resort to aggressive begging.

They are also seen as being very potent people, having the power to bless and to curse. They thus also attend weddings and newborn naming ceremonies, singing and dancing and giving their blessings. Most couples and parents pay up for fear of being cursed.

In recent decades hijras have been lobbying for their rights and a few have run for political office. In June 2015 Manabi Bandopadhyay became the principal of Krishnagar Women's College in West Bengal—the first transgender person to hold such a post (Dasgupta 2015).

The situation for hijras and other transgender people in India began to improve in April 2014, when the Supreme Court of India passed the Rights of Transgender Persons Bill (Mahapatra 2014), giving them and other transgender people the same rights as men and women by recognizing them as a third gender. The court also designated them as an "Other Backward Caste" (OBC)—a categorization the Indian government applies to groups they see as socially and economically disadvantaged. As an OBC, quota systems must be established for them in education and government positions. The Act also means that they cannot be discriminated against on the basis of their transgender status when applying for social benefits, to educational institutions, or employment. It also means that all important forms and documents (e.g., applications for a bank account), voter cards, and passports, must now include a third gender option. Previously, they had to write male or female against their gender. The Court also required the establishment of social welfare schemes to attend to their medical requirements and a public awareness campaign to erase social stigma. States must also construct special public toilets for third genders in public areas such as hospitals and government departments. In addition, they have the right to adopt a child and get married. The Bill has been seen as an advance for human rights.

Transgender in Western Countries

India is not the only country to recognize the rights of transgender people. In September 2011, Australia allowed its citizens to select a third option, "x," in the gender category in their passport without, as previously, providing proof of gender reassignment surgery (Agence France-Presse 2011). It resolves the issue of people being detained at airports because the gender listed on their passport does not match their physical appearance. In February 2015, Citizenship and Immigration Canada permitted transgender individuals to change the gender on their citizenship certificate without undergoing sex reassignment surgery (Strapagiel 2015). British Columbia, Alberta, Manitoba, Ontario, and Nova Scotia already allow people to change their gender on their birth certificate without surgery (Quan 2015). Although this is not recognition of a third gender, it does recognize a person's right to define their own gender identity.

While gay and lesbian people usually identify as male or female, transgender people challenge society's ideas and expectations of normality. Acceptance of transgender individuals has been helped recently, however, by popular movies such as the 2015 film *The Danish Girl*, which is loosely based on a true story about one of the world's first gender reassignment surgeries in the 1920s, and by prominent transgendered people such as Canadian model Jenna Talackova, Bruce Jenner, and Laverne Cox openly discussing their transgender identity and the issues they face. In 2012 Jenna Talackova challenged the *Miss Universe Canada* contest after being disqualified as a contestant because she was born male (Figure 9. 7). Bruce Jenner became the "world's

THE CANADIAN PRESS/Aaron Vincent Elkaim

FIGURE 9.7 Canadian model Jenna Talackova was initially disqualified from the 2012 Miss Universe Canada pageant because she was transgender. Talackova was born male but underwent sex reassignment surgery when she was 19.

greatest athlete" by winning the men's decathlon at the 1976 Olympics in Montreal. In July 2015, however, in the cover story for *Vanity Fair* magazine he announced his transition from male to female and his name change to Caitlyn. Jenner has also appeared in the TV series *Keeping Up with the Kardashians* and stars in the reality TV series *I am Cait*, which is about her transition. Laverne Cox plays a transgender woman in jail for credit-card fraud in the popular Netflix series *Orange Is the New Black*. Cox was also on the cover of the June 9, 2014, issue of *Time* magazine. In their various interviews and the stories they tell about the bullying and the shame they experience in their struggles to establish their identity, as well as the shock and adjustments their friends and family go through, helps to humanize them and demystifies the differences (Bissinger 2015; Associated Press 2015; Steinmetz 2014). The result has been a major shift in awareness about the nature of gender in general, and the rights of transgender people in particular.

As society becomes more accepting of transgender people's right to express their identity, official policies are changing to accommodate them. The Toronto District School Board (TDSB), for instance, has had guidelines in place to accommodate transgender students since 2011 (Boesveld 2014a). And the Vancouver School Board (VSB) updated its sexual orientation and gender identities' policy in 2014 (McParland 2014). Other school boards are also revising their policies in an attempt to be more inclusive by making provisions for transgender students to use washrooms and participate in sex-segregated activities that best correspond to their gender identity (Boesveld 2014a; McNaughton and O'Toole 2012). These changes have not gone unopposed, as many board members and parents fear their children's privacy would be invaded, that it would allow men to use women's bathrooms, change rooms, and showers, and create gender confusion (Posadzki 2014). Policies are also designed to promote equality and protect transgender individuals from violence and discrimination in the schools (McNaughton and O'Toole 2012; McParland 2014).). The TDSB guidelines, for instance suggest using non-masculine/feminine pronouns "Zhe" and "Hir" (McNaughton, and O'Toole 2012), while the VSB prefers the gender-neutral third person pronouns "xe" or "xem" and "xyr" (McParland 2014).

The issue of transgender rights is especially controversial when it comes to teachers. In 2008, Jan Buterman, who identified as a woman, taught a variety of subjects as a substitute teacher for the Greater St. Albert Catholic School Board in Alberta. Over the summer, however, she underwent sex reassignment surgery and returned as a man in the fall. Mr. Buterman was subsequently fired and took the case to the Alberta Human Rights Commission on the grounds of gender discrimination (Gerson 2014). The school board denied it had discriminated against him, arguing that gender reassignment was inconsistent with the teachings of the Catholic Church (McKay-Panos 2015), which is that gender is God-given at birth and cannot be changed. While this may seem like a clear case of discrimination, where the decision to fire someone should be based on their ability to teach, it is complicated by the fact that religious schools also have a right to their beliefs. Mr. Buterman's case challenges firmly held beliefs but poses a bigger challenge perhaps for religious transgender people who must choose between their religious community and living openly as who they are. In 2014, Mr. Buterman made a settlement with the school board (McKay-Panos 2015).

Growing up Gender Neutral

The greater awareness of gender as a cultural construction that may constrain the development of a child's gender identity has led to a growing movement toward raising children as gender neutral or gender fluid. For instance, in *Gender Neutral Parenting: Raising kids with the freedom to be themselves*, Lucas-Stannard (2012) provides guidelines for parents on how to raise their children in a gender-neutral environment. And in *Chasing Rainbows: Exploring Gender Fluid Parenting Practices* (Friedman and Green 2013), the contributors discuss ***gender fluid*** parenting approaches, whereby children are given the freedom to explore and express their gender identities unconstrained by the binary of male and female, by giving them the freedom to choose the clothes they wear, the toys they play with, the books they read, the language they use, and the activities they engage in.

Chasing Rainbows was inspired by a Toronto couple who decided in 2011 not to reveal the sex of their third child, Storm, and to raise him or her as genderless. It sparked an international debate and a deluge of criticisms. People said they were conducting a social experiment of nurture that would marginalize their child and subject him or her to a life of bullying; that it would confuse the child about his or her gender; and even that it was child abuse. Storm's parents, however, believe that by raising their child in a gender-neutral environment, they are giving him/her the freedom to be who they are without constraining them by social norms about male and female (Poisson 2011, 2013).

Storm's parents have decided to educate their children at home, in large part because much of the teasing and bullying begins when they enter school. At the Egalia "gender-neutral" pre-school in Stockholm,

gender fluid A gender identity that can vary between male and female or some non-binary identity over time and in different circumstances.

Sweden, however, the goal is to allow children to develop without the social expectations based on their sex. To do this, teachers refer to the children by their first names or use the genderless pronoun "hen"; choose books that exclude traditional gender roles and characterizations (no Sleeping Beauty or Cinderella); and place traditional boy's and girl's toys side-by-side and encourage the children to play with whatever toy they want (Hebblethwaite 2011).

CROSS-CULTURAL MISCUE

Keizo Ogawa, plant manager of Kasugai USA, a Japanese multinational firm located in the United States, was utterly shocked when he received a letter from Katherine Smithfield's lawyer accusing him of sexual harassment (names are pseudonyms). Previously, Smithfield had managed to persuade workers not to unionize and she met frequently with Ogawa to inform him of union activities. As a reward for her "loyalty" to the company she was promoted to a supervisory position. Ogawa also took Smithfield to dinner on several occasions and also gave her gifts. Although he did not ask for sexual favours, Smithfield saw this as sexual harassment. Ogawa said he also gave gifts to other good employees and that this was Japanese custom. Smithfield also claimed Ogawa attempted to massage her injured knee on one occasion, and that he also called her at home daily while she was off work. Ogawa responded that he was a martial arts instructor and was demonstrating a Japanese method of relieving pain and that it was also Japanese custom to call on employees who were ill to show their concern. Smithfield complained that Ogawa frequently called her into his office and closed the door and shut the blinds, which Ogawa responded by saying that he was either talking about something confidential or giving her constructive criticism and did not want to embarrass her in front of others.

Lawyers familiar with the case advised upper management that Ogawa would have little chance of winning a jury trial as he would look nervous and, in characteristically Japanese style, would cast his eyes down, making him look guilty. Smithfield received a $70 000 out-of-court settlement and Ogawa, humiliated, was recalled to Japan, where he become suicidal once the "scandalous news" reached his wife and parents. Ogawa's miscue was that he did not realize that his customary behaviours could be interpreted in North America as an invasion of privacy or sexual harassment. The company culture also changed and became more formal, and management altered some of its policies; doors were always to be left open and blinds never shut (Hamada 1995).

Human Sexuality

Anthropologists have a long history of documenting the sexual practices of Western and non-Western peoples and have been amassing and incorporating data on these practices into their ethnographic accounts. Over many decades anthropologists and other social scientists have broadened their understanding of ***human sexuality*** and provided multicultural perspectives.

There is wide interest in human sexuality. Culture teaches us what kind of sexual feelings and practices are normal and natural in one's society, and goes so far as to prescribe which ones are deviant, inappropriate, and unlawful. To be sure, gathering ethnographic information on human sexuality is a delicate subject. First, because sexual activity in all societies is a private matter, it remains, to a large degree, off limits to anthropological observation. Second, when anthropologists have interviewed people about sexuality, they tend to confine their questions to more objective matters such as number of sexual partners, frequency of sexual intercourse, and acceptance of premarital sexual activity. Anthropologists today look back at findings from research on human sexuality conducted before the 1970s and recognize a strong male bias because most anthropologists were males who had access to predominantly male informants. Fortunately, times have changed: in more recent ethnographic studies, both sexes are portrayed with greater representation and a more balanced picture of human sexuality is presented.

Perhaps the most fundamental generalization that has emerged is that human sexuality varies widely from culture to culture. In other words, we find enormous variations throughout the world in the sexual behaviours permitted or encouraged before marriage, outside marriage, and within marriage. This cross-cultural variation in human sexuality raises interesting theoretical and methodological questions, especially for how one may go about organizing fieldwork or developing applied health-related projects to address the transmission of HIV and AIDS.

Although no society fails to regulate sexual conduct, some societies are permissive whereas others are more restrictive. Some cultures have serious sanctions against premarital sex, and others treat it much more casually. Of course for the anthropologist, this begs the question of why cultures have these polar opposite attitudes toward premarital sex and experimentation. Is there a functional or utilitarian reason for controlling or not controlling sexual behaviour? Perhaps something inherent in a culture determines how one individual or group controls the sexual actions of another. Before embarking on one's research topic or applied project, anthropologists must be sensitive to the conduct in a particular culture. A few examples will help to illustrate the variation.

human sexuality The sexual practices of humans, usually varying from culture to culture.

Barry Kusuma/Photolibrary/Getty Images

FIGURE 9.8 According to Karl Heider (2006), the Dani do not have sexual relations during the first two years of marriage. Here they lay meat on the grass to be stone grilled, a tribal tradition.

One society with limited sexual expression is the Dani of New Guinea, who appear to be uninterested in sexual behaviour (Figure 9.8). According to Karl Heider (2006), the Dani do not have sexual relations during the first two years of marriage and they adhere to a four- to six-year period of postpartum sexual abstinence; that is, husband and wife abstain from any sexual activity for four to six years after the birth of a child. Although many societies prescribe abstinence after the birth of a child, usually for several weeks or several months, in some societies, it lasts until the child is weaned, which may take several years. Not only do the Dani practise these long periods of abstinence, they appear to have no other sexual outlets, such as extramarital sexual activity or homosexuality. Nor do Dani adults seem to be bothered by these periods of abstinence because the Dani people learn that low sexual expressiveness is a cultural norm.

At the other extreme are societies in which people are expected to have a great deal of sexual experience before marriage. Among such Oceanian societies as the Trobriand Islanders, the Tikopia, and the Mangaians of Polynesia, premarital sex is not only permitted but also encouraged; indeed it is viewed as a necessary preparatory step for marriage. Young boys and girls in these societies receive sex education at an early age and are given permission to experiment during their adolescent years. Premarital lovers are encouraged, and in some societies in the Pacific, trial marriages are actually permitted.

The Ju/'hoansi of southwestern Africa believe that sexual activity is a natural, and indeed essential, part of life. Ju/'hoansi adolescents are permitted to engage in both ***heterosexual*** and ***homosexual*** play, and discreet extramarital sexual activity is condoned. Conversations among women about their sexual exploits are commonplace, as is sexually explicit joking between men and women. According to Marjorie Shostak (1981, 31), sexual activity is considered essential for good mental and physical health. As one woman put it, "If a girl grows up without learning to enjoy sex, her mind doesn't develop normally . . . and if a woman doesn't have sex her thoughts get ruined and she is always angry."

Sexual behaviour in Canada and the United States tends to be on the more permissive end of the continuum. Much of this can be attributed to the so-called ***Sexual Revolution*** of the 1960s to the 1980s, when traditional sexual norms were challenged, morals were relaxed, and sexual freedoms increased. Previously, many sexual practices, such as viewing pornography and premarital sex, were considered unacceptable, and some behaviours, such as homosexuality, were even criminalized (Allyn 2000). As society became more secular during this time, censorship of art, music, literature, and film all decreased, allowing people to view explicit sexual material. Freedom to explore sexuality was also made easier with improvements in contraception, especially "the pill," intrauterine devices (IUD), and the legalization of abortion. Many feminists of the time saw these developments as a step toward "women's liberation," whereby they had the freedom to explore their own sexuality. The Sexual Revolution resulted in more permissive attitudes toward the expression of sex and sexuality.

It is generally accepted that today, young people become sexually active and engage in more frequent sexual activity at an earlier age than in previous generations. About 50 percent of both girls and boys in Canada have experienced sexual intercourse by age 17 (Sears et al. 2007), although the percentage of 18/19 year-olds who have ever had intercourse is declining (about 65 percent in 2005) (McKay and Bissell 2010). Because the chances for unwanted pregnancies and sexually transmitted diseases are high among sexually active adolescents, Health Canada has recognized the importance of promoting sexual health and awareness, and sex-health education is now mandated in all Canadian provinces and territories (Sears et al. 2007).

Homosexuality

The range of openness and restrictiveness among societies in terms of heterosexual relationships to some degree also holds true for same-sex relationships. Some

heterosexual Having a sexual attraction to people of the opposite sex.

homosexual Having a sexual attraction to people of the same sex.

Sexual Revolution The period during the 1960s to the 1980s when conservative Western norms about sexual practices were challenged, resulting in more permissive attitudes toward sex and sexuality.

CROSS-CULTURAL MISCUE

From June 19 to June 28, 2015, Toronto hosted the 35th Gay Pride Festival (Figure 9.9). The festival began in 1981 as a way for the LGBTQ (Lesbian, Gay, Bisexual, Transgender, Gay) community to raise awareness that they have been, and in some cases still are, denied their civil rights, and to take pride in their identity. The 2015 festival was designated a WorldPride event and drew over a million visitors and participants. It culminated in the Pride parade on June 28 and involved 12 500 marchers and over 200 000 onlookers. The parade was attended by federal NDP Leader Thomas Mulcair, federal Liberal Leader Justin Trudeau, Ontario Premier Kathleen Wynne (who is the first openly gay government leader in Canada), and Toronto mayor John Tory (former mayor Rob Ford never attended). Notable by his absence, however, was former Prime Minster Stephen Harper. Harper never attended any of the parades or made a brief supportive statement while he was in power. Making an appearance at the parade has come to be seen as a show of support for the LGBTQ community, and sends a big message about where politicians stand. One headline read "*Harper skips biggest gay pride celebration in Canada, while Mulcair and Trudeau show support.*" Harper received a fair amount of criticism from the LGBTQ community as well as their supporters for his absence, some of whom noted that he was critical of gay marriage and seemed to be out of touch with the average Canadian. There is growing popular support for the community. Perhaps, for politicians, it is well to remember that LGBTQ people also vote (Dinshaw 2015).

nisargmedia.com/Shutterstock.com

FIGURE 9.9 A participant in the 35th annual Pride Parade held in Toronto June 28, 2015—two days after the U.S. Supreme Court allowed gay marriage in all states. The parade promotes equality of rights for Canada's LGBTQ (lesbian, gay, bisexual, transgender, queer) community and celebrates sexual and gender diversity.

people in societies based on Judeo-Christian-Islamic beliefs, however, consider homosexuality a violation of natural law. Such societies take a ***heteronormative*** perspective, that is, that heterosexuality is the norm. This perspective thus equates sex with gender. Societies that incorporate this religious thinking into their political process have laws that criminalize homosexual conduct or limit certain rights between same-sex couples, while those that do not are more liberal in their attitudes toward homosexual behaviour. Countries such as Canada, the United States, and Great Britain for example, allow homosexual relationships and same-sex marriages, while homosexuality is punishable by death in Saudi Arabia, Iran, Nigeria, Sudan, and some other Muslim countries. According to a 2013 Pew Research Center poll, the overwhelming majority of people in predominantly Muslim countries felt homosexuality should be rejected. Most Western countries were more tolerant. Eighty percent of Canadians felt homosexuality should be accepted by society. Younger respondents were even more tolerant and in general the world is becoming more tolerant of homosexual relationships (Pew Research Center 2013). To be sure, the gay and lesbian community in Canada continues to suffer discrimination and hate crimes, but the decriminalization of homosexuality in 1969, the redefinition of marriage in 2005 (see Chapter 8), as well as the election of openly gay politicians such as Kathleen Wynne, the Premier of Ontario, have increased acceptance of the diversity in sexual orientation. One reflection of this occurred in 2015 in Vancouver, Victoria, and Kelowna, as well as other cities in British Columbia and elsewhere in Canada, when, as a demonstration of their communities' spirit of inclusiveness and acceptance they painted some pedestrian crossings in the colours of the rainbow (Takeuchi 2015). This spirit of acceptance is also reflected in the attempts by Canadian high-school students to establish ***gay-straight alliance***s (GSAs)—support groups where LGBTQ youth can meet with straight friends. In March 2015, over objections by Catholic school boards, the government of Alberta made it easier for students to establish these groups by making it mandatory for schools to establish these

heteronormative The view that heterosexuality is the norm.

gay-straight alliance School support groups where LGBTQ youth can meet with straight friends.

GSAs on school property if requested by students. The Act to Amend the Alberta Bill of Rights to Protect Our Children also strikes out the word "sex," replacing it with "sexual orientation, sex, gender identity, or gender expression." Parents also no longer have the right to take their children out of classes that discuss sexual orientation (Ibrahim and Kleiss 2015).

In societies that are more supportive of same-sex activity, there is a wide range of socially acceptable behaviour, and this variability makes it difficult to determine how prevalent the actual practice of homosexuality is in different societies. In more open societies, which are generally tolerant of same-sex relationships, homosexuals tend to be fairly open about their behaviour. In societies where homosexual activity is stigmatized or punished, most homosexuals do not manifest their sexual orientation as openly. Yet the incidence of homosexual activities in both restrictive and open societies may be the same; the only difference is the extent to which it is freely discussed and lived.

When living in countries that have greater sexual freedom, gays, lesbians, and bisexuals from the Middle East practise their homosexuality more openly and without fear of reprisals. For example, the large Muslim population in Berlin has the opportunity to attend an event called Gayhane, a monthly dance club event for Arab and Turkish gays and lesbians (Kulish 2008). This event allows gays and lesbians from the Middle East to merge their cultural and sexual identities. These immigrants may still face discrimination in Berlin for both their ethnicity and their sexual orientation, but at least they are not being put to death "in the worse, most severe way" for their homosexual lifestyles.

So we are left with a big question: Why do some countries have sexual freedom and others do not? At the simplest level, one can say it is because of culture. However, we need to broaden this notion of culture to include religion and politics. For example, in some societies it is their interpretation of their religion or belief system that governs their sexual behaviours. In societies that link their belief system with their political system, it is possible to establish laws governing sexual behaviour and sexuality. Nevertheless, there is no clear pattern to answer why it is culturally permissible to engage in homosexual acts in one country and it is unlawful in another, and the degree to which a crime of engaging in a homosexual act is punished.

Gender Roles

All societies make distinctions between what men and women are expected to do. ***Gender roles*** include the kinds of work assigned to men and women, the familial roles that people play, the leadership positions assigned to men and women both inside and outside the home, and the roles men and women are assigned in ritual practices. In some societies, gender roles are rigidly defined, but in others the roles of men and women overlap considerably. Yet, despite the near-universality of the division of labour by gender, cultures of the world share some general patterns in the ways in which they divide tasks between women and men. In most cases men engage in warfare, trap and kill large animals, work with hard substances such as wood and stone, clear land, build houses, and fish at sea. Women, on the other hand, are more likely to tend crops, gather wild fruits and plants, trap and kill small animals (including fish in lakes and streams), prepare food, care for children, collect firewood, clean house, launder clothing, and carry water. Child care is an overwhelmingly female activity, although in some cases men make substantial contributions. In addition, a number of tasks are performed by both men and women. These include tending small domesticated animals, making utilitarian products (pottery, baskets, and the like), milking animals, planting and harvesting crops, and collecting shellfish.

Gender and Subsistence

In many hunting-and-gathering societies, women's and men's interdependent contributions to their households are reflected in relatively equal social relations and social status. The roles performed by men and women are different, but their relative statuses are not. Because constant migration makes it difficult to accumulate possessions, foraging societies tend to have little private property, and thus sharp status distinctions are minimized for both men and women. Among some societies, however, male dominance is more apparent. In horticultural societies, control over the distribution of produce and goods influences gender status. In societies that are generally egalitarian, women exert their rights to make decisions concerning economic activities. In horticultural economies, women perform most of the farm work, including planting and tending crops and harvesting. In addition, women gather a wide assortment of fruits, nuts, and tubers and are responsible for domestic tasks and child care. Men's subsistence roles include preparing the farm fields and garden plots, as well as hunting and fishing to supplement the basic plant diet. Trading with other native peoples for luxury and utilitarian items is also the work of men. Both women's and men's work is highly valued and socially recognized.

Anthropologists who study pastoral societies, especially in Africa, have found that they tend to have strong patriarchal social and political organization in which men control access to the lands and herds. Men own the animals, particularly cattle, which are the basis

---

gender roles Expected ways of behaving based on a society's definition of masculinity and femininity.

Combat as a Rite of Passage in the Canadian Military

Canadian anthropologist Anne Irwin (2012) notes that combat service has often been looked at as a rite of passage whereby young boys are transformed into men who are strong, competent, authoritarian, and emotionally in control. Rites of passage have traditionally been analyzed using Arnold van Gennep's (1977) and Victor Turner's (1977) three-phase model in which initiates first undergo a process of separation from their original state, then enter a liminal period characterized by shared experiences and a sense of community, and are finally reintegrated into society with a new status. Irwin employs this model to understand the gender transformation of Canadian soldiers who have experienced combat in Afghanistan. In the initial separation phase, the soldiers receive their desert camouflage uniforms, get their hair cut very short, have their photo taken, which is used in a press release in case they are killed, and are then deployed (sent) to Afghanistan. The military operations while away represent the liminal phase, and their return to Canada the reintegration phase. She argues, however, that combat transforms them into old men and yet at the same time they remain boys—"a hybrid that could be termed 'old young men' " (p. 61).

In early 2006, the First Battalion of the Princess Patricia's Canadian Light Infantry, part of the regular Canadian Forces, was deployed to southern Afghanistan, and Irwin went them. She had been studying the Battalion for a number of years and had already spent several months in the field with them as they trained for their missions. But this time they were going on a combat mission. Irwin travelled with Charlie Company, which consisted of about 85 soldiers, only three of whom were women. The soldiers she studied were in their late teens and early twenties—the youngest and most inexperienced soldiers—on their first tour of duty. She used primarily participant observation to conduct her research, living in close contact with the troops, eating the same food, wearing the same combat uniform and body armour, and, short of actual combat, participating in their experiences.

Photo by Cpl Ian Coon/Courtesy of Anne Irwin

Canadian anthropologist Anne Irwin in entry hatch of a light armoured vehicle (LAV) while conducting fieldwork in Afghanistan.

Irwin defines combat as times when the soldiers are "outside the wire." The "wire" refers to the concertina wire surrounding and protecting Kandahar Air Field. Being outside the wire can involve actively fighting the enemy, being on patrol, or a range of activities such as travelling in a vehicle that could trigger an IED (improvised explosive device) and cause loss of life and threat of ambush. In all situations outside the wire there is an ever-present danger, and the soldiers needed to be prepared both physically and psychologically to fight. Irwin notes that every member of the Company who served outside the wire during the 2006 tour considered him- or herself to have "done a combat tour" (p. 69). Life outside the wire involved sleep deprivation, uncertainty and unpredictability, and an "ordeal to endure and survive" (p. 73). It also brought the soldiers closer together; they would talk unashamedly about losing control of their bodily functions or vomiting before, during, or after a firefight, and they easily displayed signs of affection and grief.

Upon their return to Canada, after they had turned in their weapons, ammunition, and body armour, they were reunited at the base with their families—the period of reintegration. Many of the mothers said they hardly recognized their sons since they had physically changed so much; they looked like old men rather than adults. Many had lost 25–35 pounds and many were also marked with physical scars from combat, as well as psychological wounds that made sleep difficult. Many returning soldiers also limited their close relationships to the soldiers they had experienced combat with since their friends and families could not understand what their combat experience was like. "All of these factors," Irwin says, "combined to give the impression of old age, both physically and emotionally" (p. 74). On the other hand, they seemed to be "mired in a perpetual adolescence" (p. 74) as they continued to refer to themselves as "the boys," were naïve about financial matters, had never taken out a bank loan, and had never lived anywhere else but with their parents, or in the army barracks where they had always been told what to do, which diminished "their sense of autonomy and agency" (p. 75)—a sign of adulthood.

Irwin's work with the Canadian military during combat demonstrates that gender is often constructed through circumstances. What it means to be a soldier and a man is, in part shaped by not only their shared experiences but also sharing their experiences.

Questions for Further Thought

1. How does Irwin's work influence the way we think of war and masculinity?
2. How might an understanding of how gender is constructed during combat be useful to the Canadian military?
3. What ethical and methodological issues do anthropologists face studying the military in active duty?
4. How does the work of anthropologists differ from journalists covering the Canadian military during times of war?

Ton Koene/Getty Images

FIGURE 9.10 Women and children can milk the livestock in Ngoiroro, Kenya, a village of 200 inhabitants belonging to the Maasai Tribe. The Maasai live very close to their animals.

of both subsistence and ideology. The people think of themselves as pastoralists with male pursuits, male interests, and male norms. For example, to be a Maasai (cattle herders of Kenya and Tanzania) is to be a pastoralist. Maasai men, therefore, fit this ideal, but Maasai women are marginalized because they are not herders. If women share in the identity of the Maasai, it is as wives of men and mothers of sons, whom they socialize into the male-centred ideal (Figure 9.10).

Among pastoral groups, young girls are socialized to be helpers to their mothers, who are subordinate to their husbands. Within pastoral groups, girls are thought to be the weaker sex and taught to obey, respect, and submit to men. Men achieve their status by taking care of the livestock and protecting the community. Pastoral women and girls continue to be subjected to gender discrimination because they are not viewed as "real" pastoralists. Moreover, their health status and social status are adversely affected because they are not able to fully participate in their communities. Women and girls have limited access to healthcare and education, high mortality rates, low life expectancies, and insufficient medical information and access to family planning and reproductive healthcare and other public services.

Agrarian states are complex societies with centralized political systems that maintain some degree of control over local areas within the state. Their economies are based on intensive farming and the production of a surplus that is sold for profit or cash, which is used to support a ruling elite. Generally, such complex societies segment the population into classes that occupy different positions in society with different occupations and different standards of living. Frequently, such societies are (or were) characterized by male dominance in gender relations. As in other types of societies, however, the degree of male dominance varies widely. Contributing factors to the variation in male dominance are economics, politics, and history, as well as kinship and marriage patterns and family structure. Recent shifts in the political economy of agricultural production, however, are keeping some male farmers at home while their female partners or spouses are employed off the farm. The off-farm earnings may provide needed income for the farm, access to health insurance, and cash when everyone is waiting for the harvest to get to market. In other contexts, farmers are being displaced from their land and likewise their agrarian mode of production, which makes both genders more vulnerable to economic uncertainties (Wright 2006).

There are some notable exceptions to the general rule that men engage in roles that demand maximum physical strength. In certain parts of East Africa, women routinely carry enormous loads of firewood on their backs for long distances. Not only is this a normative practice but, among some groups, also a woman's femininity is directly related to the size of the load she is able to carry (Figure 9.11).

It appears that the wide range of variation in gender roles and subsistence activities requires anthropologists to ask pertinent questions related to culture and subsistence before designing, implementing, or evaluating any project. Surveying what women's and men's roles are, as well as observing what people of all age groups and socio-economic classes are doing in everyday life, are relevant in planned changed initiatives. Experienced field researchers will tell you there is a difference from what people say they do and what they actually do on a day-to-day basis.

Child Rearing for Men and Women

Although exceptions do not invalidate the general rule, some authors (Burton et al. 1977; Mascia-Lees and Black 2000) have argued that the division of labour by gender is more the result of constraints

HOANG DINH NAM/AFP/Getty Images

FIGURE 9.11 An H'mong woman carrying firewood to her home in the northern mountainous province of Ha Giang, Vietnam. Images such as this are common in rural areas of Africa, Asia, and elsewhere.

women face as a result of childbirth and infant care than of differences in strength. This brings us to another argument often used to explain this nearly universal type of gender division of labour: Women do the things they do because those tasks are compatible with pregnancy, breastfeeding, and child care. Unlike certain male tasks, such as hunting and warfare, women's tasks can be done without jeopardizing their own and their children's safety and without having to stray too far from home. This theory suggests that pregnant women would be at a marked disadvantage in running after game; lactating mothers would need to interrupt their tracking and hunting activities several times a day to nurse their children; and, given the danger involved in hunting, small children accompanying their mothers would not be safe. Judith Brown (1970) was the first to hypothesize that women tend to concentrate on tasks that are compatible with child care (i.e., nursing and looking after children). Women's tasks can be interrupted without reducing efficient performance, pose limited threat to the safety of small children, and can be performed in or near the home.

Although this theory is sensible and no doubt can account for some of the division of labour by gender, it also does not tell the whole story. A number of ethnographic studies from around the world since the late 1970s have seriously questioned this connection between female reproductive and childcare roles and the division of labour. To illustrate, some researchers (Burton et al. 1977) have argued that, although pregnancy and breastfeeding do limit work roles for women, a woman's economic (work) obligations sometimes take precedence over childcare considerations. In other words, a woman may make alternative childcare arrangements to engage in some type of work outside the home. This is done in parts of the developing world, where women leave their small children in the care of older siblings or other adults. And in Canada, working mothers leave their infants at professional daycare centres. In addition, others (Raphael and Davis 1985) have found that women often purposefully choose supplemental feeding rather than breastfeeding for their children because of work considerations.

There are societies where fathers play an active role in child care. For example, according to Ziarat Hossain and colleagues (1999), Navajo fathers invest about 60 percent as much time as mothers in direct caregiving tasks. The father role has shifted primarily from an economic provider to a more balanced partner, including playing, emotional bonding, and child rearing. Fathers' investment in child care varies tremendously across families, depending on cultural values (Lamb 1997).

Other research indicates, however, that the father does play an important role in his children's life by disciplining, teaching, playing with, and providing economically for his children (Hauswald 1987). The father provides a strong role model, especially for his male children, and the availability and involvement of other adult family members in child care suggest that Navajo child rearing takes place within an extended family network system.

Gender Roles in Canada

When we think of traditional gender roles in Canada, two words usually come to mind: ***breadwinner*** and ***homemaker***. According to this traditional view, men, who are often characterized as logical, competitive, goal-oriented, and unemotional, were responsible for the economic support and protection of the family. Women, on the other hand, with their warm, caring, and sensitive natures, were expected to restrict themselves to child rearing and domestic activities: preparing meals, cleaning the house, working in the kitchen, and doing a variety of other tasks that helped to support the household.

The family of the breadwinning father and the stay-at-home mother has almost disappeared. Since the 1960s, when more women entered the workforce, opportunities for women as well as their desire to remain employed after having children gradually increased. This was especially true in the 1980s when women reentered the workforce after having children. The number of dual income Canadian families nearly doubled in the 40 years between 1974 and 2014, from 36 to 69 percent (Boesveld 2015a). This shift changed the dynamics of the household. Men are now not only doing the laundry, cooking, and grocery shopping, they are also taking care of the children (Figure 9.12). This has also impacted the way companies market their products, with many men now portrayed performing domestic duties in advertisements, and stores catering to men shoppers by supplying taller carts and moving sale items higher on the shelves (Boesveld 2015a). Women, on the other hand, are now taking responsibilities for financial management.

Between 1976 and 2010, female breadwinners increased from 8 to 31 percent (Milligan 2013). Today, both men and women are in the paid labour force, with approximately 75 percent of men and 70 percent of women in Canada participating (OECD 2014) (the OECD average is 58 percent). It is important to point out that employed married women, particularly those with children, often carry a double

breadwinner A traditional North American gender role that views males as being responsible for the economic support and protection of the family.

homemaker A traditional North American gender role that views females as responsible for child rearing and domestic activities.

JLP/Corbis/Glow Images

FIGURE 9.12 Traditional gender roles are changing in Canada as more and more men stay home, look after the children, and do the housework.

workload by being both wage-employed and primarily responsible for housework and child care. According to the "Better Life Index" published by the Organization for Economic Co-operation and Development (OECD), men spend 160 minutes per day on household chores such as cooking, cleaning, laundry, and looking after the children, which is above the OECD average. Women, on the other hand, spend 254 minutes (about 60 percent more time) (Figure 9.13). It should be noted, however, that this is below the OECD average.

While men are taking responsibility for more of the household work, one reason the inequitable division still exists is that traditional beliefs and expectations about the appropriate roles of men and women persist. Men are still seen to be the providers, and women are still seen to be responsible for the care of children (Ranson 2010). Plan International discovered that 24 percent of Canadian adults and 31 percent of Canadian boys aged 12 to 17 thought that a woman's primary role was to look after the home and feed her children (Abma 2011), while 43 percent of adults and 48 percent of Canadian adolescents felt the man should be earning an income to provide for their families. Ironically, however, 96 percent of teens felt there should be equal opportunities for boys and girls.

The number of stay-at-home dads has also increased in the past 40 years, from 2 to 11 percent (Boesveld 2015a). This has changed not only the perception of stay-at-home dads, it has also spawned a number of websites for them. Sites such as Dadstayshome.com and Fatherville.com provide blogging opportunities and supportive information on topics such as time management, how to talk with children to facilitate learning, part-time work that can be done from home, and effective parenting strategies for stay-at-home dads. New forms of language and gender communication are found in social media, as they help with parenting as well as in everyday life.

Another characteristic of the wage sector of the Canadian economy is its high rate of *occupational segregation* along gender lines. Despite decades of legislation aimed at reducing gender discrimination in the workplace, the majority of both men and women continue to work in gender-segregated occupations. The majority of women in Canada work as secretaries, hairdressers, sales clerks, food service workers, health-care personnel, and childcare workers—all relatively low-paying jobs. Canadian men earn 19 percent more than women (OECD 2014). More than 90 percent of nurses, 80 percent of librarians and elementary and middle school teachers are women. At the other end of the spectrum, women made up only 4.6 percent of chief executive officer (CEO) positions in Standard and Poor's list of top 500 companies in 2014 (Catalyst 2015). In addition, men tend to dominate board, executive, and management positions, even in areas where a majority of the workers are women. Despite these data illustrating occupational segregation, in the past several decades women have made considerable inroads into some high-status professions such as medicine.

More women are also finding employment with the military in combat roles, traditionally dominated by men. Canada is, in fact, a leader in the proportion of women in its military, which opened all military occupations to women in 1989, with the exception of submarine service (which opened to women in 2000) (National Defence and the Canadian Armed Forces 2014). As of January 2014, 14.8 percent of positions in the Canadian Armed forces were held by women (National Defence and the Canadian Armed Forces 2014). Men, on the other hand, are not taking up roles as nurses, preschool teachers, or administrative assistants—traditionally held by women—to the same extent.

---

occupational segregation The separation of different occupations in a society.

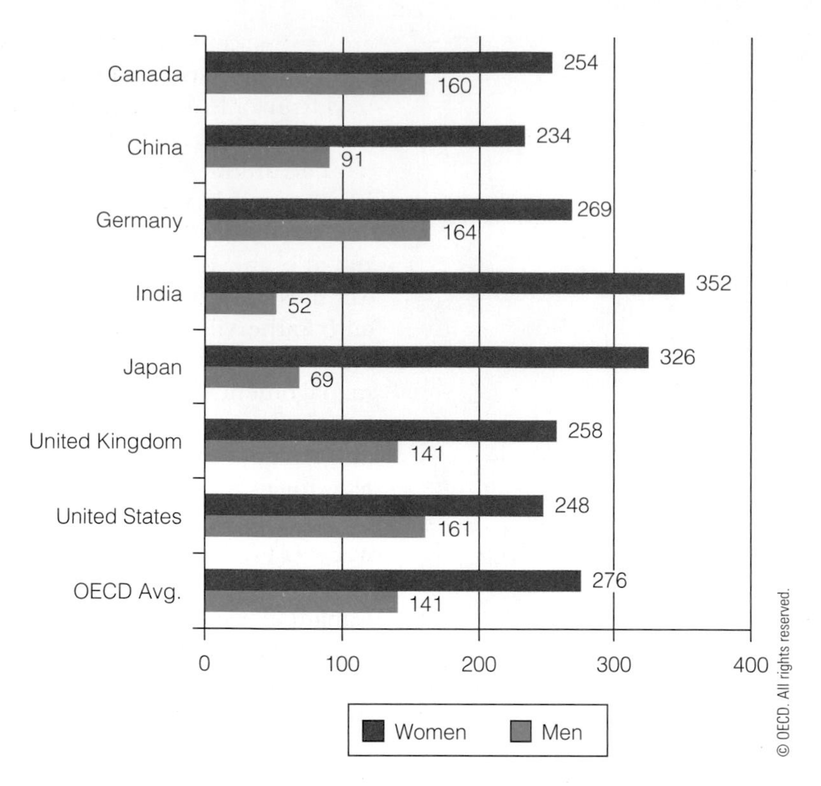

FIGURE 9.13 Minutes spent in unpaid work by gender per day in select countries.

Gender Stratification

The status of women varies from one society to another. In some East African pastoral societies, women are in a clearly subordinate position in their social relationships with men. In other societies, such as the Ju/'hoansi, relationships between the genders are more egalitarian. Social scientists generally agree that *gender stratification* exists to some degree in all societies; however, there is considerably less agreement about how one measures the relative status of men and women, because gender stratification involves a number of different components that may vary independently of one another such as economics, political power, prestige, autonomy, and ideological dimensions. To illustrate, when considering the relative status of women in any society, one needs to look at the roles women play, the value society places on their contributions, their legal rights, whether and to what degree they are expected to be deferential to men, their economic independence, and the degree to which they decide on the major events of their lives, such as marriage, profession, and childbearing, among others.

While there have been strides to improve the situation for women in most countries since the turn of the century, many women are still mired in poverty and remain subservient to men. In Afghanistan for instance, life expectancy for women is about 42 years, which is less than that for Afghani men, and about 20 years shorter than the global average. The death rate from childbirth is one of the highest in the world, as is the fertility rate of 6.6 children per woman on average. The high birth rate makes it difficult for women to get an education, which reduces economic opportunities, and so most women live in poverty. The literacy rate for women is less than 13 percent, about half what it is for men. Most women work in agriculture or look after the home as cultural practices limit job opportunities outside the home. Violence against women is endemic, and 60 to 80 percent are forced into marriage in childhood (Morgan 2008). Despite these conditions, in 2012 a new code of conduct was authorized, which is considered a step backward for women because it prohibits them from going out in public without a male guardian. Women's groups in and outside Afghanistan have complained that this is a major setback for improving the living conditions for women. There is still a need for greater access to education and healthcare for Afghan women. Organizations such as Revolutionary Association of the Women in Afghanistan (RAWA), Afghanistan Women Council (AWC), Women for Afghan Women (WAW), and the Afghan Women's Writing Project are just a few of the organizations working toward addressing basic human rights for Afghan girls and

---

gender stratification The hierarchical ranking of members of a society according to gender.

Mark Pearson/Alamy Stock Photo

FIGURE 9.14 Burkas and veils remain common attire for women in rural and urban areas of Afghanistan. These women receive cold relief supplies to help them in the severe winter in northern Afghanistan.

women, and fighting against gender-based violence. These organizations work to enable women to be represented in all areas of life: political, social, cultural, and economic (Figure 9.14).

Among the Minangkabau of West Sumatra, Indonesia, females and males interact more like partners than competitors. The foundation of gender relationships among the Minangkabau is their central philosophical notion of *adat:* People, animals, and wildlife should be nurtured so that society will be strong. This emphasis on nurturing tends to favour cooperation and the maternal in everyday life rather than competition and male dominance. According to Peggy Sanday (2004), on ceremonial occasions women in Minangkabau society are addressed by the term reserved for the mythical queen, and symbolically the maternal is viewed as the spiritual centre and the original foundation of the society. Moreover, women exert considerable power in everyday social life. Women control land inheritance, husbands reside in their wife's residence, and in the event of divorce, the husband gathers his belongings and leaves. Neither men nor women rule in Minangkabau society because decision making is based on consensus and cooperation (Figure 9.15).

Despite such examples as the Minangkabau, we find that women, to one degree or another, tend to be excluded from the major centres of economic and

Jane Sweeney/Lonely Planet Images/Getty Images

Purepix/Alamy Stock Photo

FIGURE 9.15 Among the Minangkabau of West Sumatra (*left*), decision making between wives and husbands is relatively equal and cooperative. Because of gender ideology, this boy in Rajasthan, India (*right*), is more likely to receive medical attention than his sister.

political power and control in most societies. Although the number of women heads of state varies each year, in most years there are fewer than 10. Canada has had only one woman prime minister, Kim Campbell, who served from to June to November 1993, a little more than four months. The roles women play also invariably carry with them fewer prerogatives and lower prestige than male roles. This gender asymmetry is so pervasive that some anthropologists have attributed it to biological differences between men and women, such as greater size, strength, and physical aggressiveness. Ernestine Friedl (1978), however, argued that men tend to dominate not because of biological traits but rather because they control the distribution of scarce resources. Irrespective of who produces the goods, Friedl contended that the people *controlling* the allocation of resources (usually men) possess the currency needed to create and maintain powerful political alliances and obligations. By using examples from a number of societies, Friedl demonstrated how men dominate in those societies in which women have little or no control over the allocation of scarce resources and, conversely, how women with some control of resources have achieved greater equality.

Gender inequality, however, is not a unified phenomenon; it takes many different forms in different societies. There has always been sexual violence directed against women, during both war and peace time (Brettell and Sargent 2005; Rylko-Bauer et al. 2009). Sometimes the acts of aggression and domination have been individual (rape) and sometimes collective (gang rape). Sometimes these acts have been organized and other times they have been spontaneous. However, this inequity is not a new phenomenon. The record of sexual violence is at times disguised as prostitution, which remains today a huge global industry. In post-industrial countries, gender inequity is creating disparities in access to formal education, employment, healthcare, and finances.

The cost of gender stratification is high for both men and women, with perpetuation of inequality in the workplace as well as at home. One can recognize that the culturally constructed male and female roles and statuses in Canada have negative consequences. For example, men in Canada have higher mortality rates than women at all ages and for most of the 15 leading causes of death. They abuse their bodies with drugs, alcohol, and tobacco more than women. And men engage in certain professions that carry higher risks, such as mining, construction, and deep-sea fishing. In addition to living up to culturally defined notions of masculinity, many men engage in high-risk (health-reducing) behaviours. In a survey of Canadian adolescents, 45 percent said that to be a man you needed to be tough; 38 percent of adults agreed that toughness was a sign of masculinity (Abma 2011). The pressure to be a tough, competitive winner can lead a man to take on more than he can handle, thereby resulting in excessive stress. And when things do not go well, a growing sense of failure can lead to what Terrence Real (2001) calls "covert depression," a form of depression that often goes undiagnosed because it is largely repressed. Adult males in Canada rarely seek help for stress, depression, and other emotional problems because to do so would be to admit weakness.

Women continue to adapt to the changing times. They are making choices that influence their home and family life as well as their place in the workforce. For example, Canadian women are marrying later in life, staying in school longer, delaying childbirth, and having fewer children than in previous years. More women are choosing to continue working while also balancing the traditional parenting role. Gender discrimination persists and at its worst is coupled with fighting battles for equal pay for equal work. Although working women still face the demands of a heavy workload, balancing family, jobs, and possibly sexual harassment at the workplace, they have made great strides in the workplace. Nevertheless, we should see continued efforts for gender equity by both men and women, at home *and* in the workplace. In the next several sections we examine gender differences between men and women with respect to education, employment, finance, and reproductive health.

Education

Women throughout the world have made progress toward equal educational enrolment, but huge gaps remain. There are more illiterate women than men in every major region of the world. Two-thirds of all the illiterate people in the world today are women (about 500 million) (UNESCO 2014). More than 70 percent of women aged 25 and older in sub-Saharan Africa, southern Asia, and western Asia are illiterate (UNESCO 2014). Even though world literacy has been on the rise in recent decades, it has risen faster for men than for women, thereby widening the gender gap. In developing countries such as Pakistan, India, Yemen, and Afghanistan, the large literacy gap between men and women is most often related to poverty and access to education. Where there are high levels of poverty coupled with gender discrimination, women and girls are the ones who are marginalized.

Perhaps one of the best examples of the discrimination against women is that of Pakistani school girl Malala Yousafzai, who was shot in the head by the Taliban while on her way to school in October 2012 (Figure 9.16). The assassination attempt was because she campaigned for girls' rights to be educated—she had won the 2011 International Children's Peace Prize. On October 10, 2014, she and Indian children's rights advocate Kailash Satyarthi were awarded the Nobel Peace Prize "for their struggle against the suppression of children and young people and for the right of all children to education" (Nobelprize.org 2014). Yousafzai was not only the first Pakistani to win the Peace Prize, but at 17 she was also the youngest. Perhaps the struggle she and many young

ODD ANDERSEN/AFP/Getty Images

FIGURE 9.16 **Seventeen-year-old Pakistani schoolgirl Malala Yousafzai receives the Nobel Peace Prize, December 10, 2014. She had been shot by the Taliban for fighting for the right of girls to an education.**

girls like her face is best summed up in the speech she gave at the United Nations in July 2013:

> Dear sisters and brothers, we realize the importance of light when we see darkness. We realize the importance of our voice when we are silenced. In the same way, when we were in Swat, the north of Pakistan, we realized the importance of pens and books when we saw the guns. The wise saying, "The pen is mightier than the sword": It is true. The extremists are afraid of books and pens. The power of education frightens them. They are afraid of women. The power of the voice of women frightens them. This is why they killed fourteen innocent students in the recent attack in Quetta. And that is why they kill female teachers. That is why they are blasting schools every day because they were and they are afraid of change and equality that we will bring to our society. And I remember that there was a boy in our school who was asked by a journalist, Why are the Taliban against education? He answered very simply by pointing to his book. He said, "A Talib doesn't know what is written inside this book." Yousafzai (2013)*

Employment

The percentage of women in the world's workforce has increased in the past several decades, largely because of economic necessity. However, the majority of the world's women, particularly in developing countries, are concentrated in the lowest-paid occupations and receive lower pay and fewer benefits than men. Women are also more likely to work part-time, have less seniority, and occupy positions with little or no upward mobility. Moreover, an increasing number of women in Asia, Africa, and South America are being pushed into the informal economy characterized by the small-scale, self-employed trading of goods and services. Some of the activities associated with the informal economy—such as street vending, beer brewing, and prostitution—are outside the law. All of this has led to the impoverishment of women worldwide, a phenomenon known as the ***feminization of poverty***. In some regions, women provide 70 percent of agricultural labour, produce more than 90 percent of the food (Nhanenge 2011), and yet are nowhere represented in their government's budget deliberations. Overall, the number of women living in poverty increased disproportionately to the number of men during the past decade, in part from the growing number of female-headed households. Moreover, the increasing feminization of poverty was particularly acute in poorer, developing countries and for minority women living in wealthier, more industrialized nations.

A good example of the feminization of poverty are the maquiladora workers of Mexico. Maquiladoras are assembly and manufacturing plants most of which are located close to the U.S./Mexico border. Many of the car parts, cellphones, laptops, and other electronic devices sold under famous brand names of multinational corporations are assembled in maquiladoras (Bacon 2015). Most maquiladoras are foreign owned and, after the signing of the North American Free Trade Agreement (NAFTA) in 1994, their numbers skyrocketed. Today they employ hundreds of thousands of workers, most of whom are women, and most of whom have migrated from small villages and rural areas in central and southern Mexico into the cities of the north. Young women are preferred because they can work longer hours, are more patient, and are more dexterous than men (Kopinak 1995). Working conditions are often unsafe, workers are constantly harassed, and there is no job security. They are also tightly controlled, and any attempt to organize is suppressed, which is a selling point to foreign investors (Bacon 2015). The biggest attraction for multinational companies, however, is the low wages. In 2013, for instance, the minimum wage in Juárez, a city across the Rio Grande from El Paso, Texas, was less than 65 pesos (about US$4.00) per day (Bacon 2015). A typical wage for a woman is about 600 pesos per week, yet food alone for a family costs about 700–800 pesos per week. Many homes are made from cardboard and castoff wooden pallets from factories, which poses a serious fire hazard, and most also lack running water, electricity, and sewers (Bacon 2015). To survive, many women work double and triple shifts, and if they

*Yousafzai, Malala. 2013. "Malala Yousafzai's speech at the Youth Takeover of the United Nations". A world at school.

feminization of poverty **The fact that women make up the largest proportion of world's poor.**

complain the overtime is cut off. Activism in the 1990s led to women being murdered at an increasing rate. In 2010, 247 women in Juárez were killed (Bacon 2015).

In Canada more women than men (59 percent v. 48 percent) complete university or obtain further education after high school (OECD 2014). However, they tend to focus on the arts and social sciences rather than the physical sciences, technology, engineering or mathematics—the so-called STEM disciplines—which pay more. And although an increasing number of women are entering professions that require advanced education, such as law, medicine, and engineering, occupations associated with low prestige and low income still have higher proportions of women. According to the company GoldieBlox, only 14 percent of engineers are women, in large part because gender socialization results in girls losing interest in STEM subjects by the age of eight because construction toys are seen as "boys" toys (Goldieblox.com). Goldieblox is trying to change this by providing stories about Goldie—who acts as a role model for girls—and construction sets that tap into girls' strong verbal and spatial skills while giving them the tools to build and create things.

Poverty in the Canada has become "feminized" just as it has in other parts of the world. For example, more than half of all female-headed families with children are living below the poverty line, a poverty rate that is approximately four times higher than the poverty rate for two-parent families. The feminization of poverty is particularly acute when we look at minorities. Although the total poverty level for all families headed by single women was 30 percent, when the statistic is broken down a different picture emerges. A number of factors have contributed to the feminization of poverty in Canada in recent decades. These include the continued involvement of women in low-paying jobs; the additional responsibilities for child rearing, which many men do not have; the relative dearth of women in political and policy-making positions; and women's limited access to education, skills training, financial credit, and healthcare.

Reproductive Health

A third area in which the world's women have not fared as well as men is in access to healthcare, and for many women it is access to reproductive healthcare. Although most women in the developed world control the number of children they have, in some parts of the world there is pressure to have small families, such as in parts of Europe and China (Krause 2005). In other parts of the world there is pressure to have large numbers of children, and women on average have four or five children. In certain countries with particularly high birthrates (such as Niger, Mali, Uganda, Zambia, Burkina Faso, Somalia, Malawi), the average woman bears more than seven children in her lifetime (CIA World Factbook 2012; Holloway 2007; MacFarquhar 1994). Pregnant women in developing countries face risks that include malnutrition and a lack of trained medical personnel to deal with high-risk pregnancies. In fact, it has been estimated that pregnant women in developing countries are 80 to 600 times more likely to die of complications from pregnancy and birthing than are women in the industrialized world (Holloway 2007).

A related health issue for women is the extent to which gender inequalities make them more vulnerable to HIV and AIDS. Women's economic dependence on men, as well as the threat of violence against wives and girlfriends, makes them less able to protect themselves. In many parts of the world, it is unacceptable for a woman to say no to unwanted or unprotected sex. Adding to the problem is the sex-trade industry. Poverty has forced many women in African communities and elsewhere to put themselves at great risk of contracting HIV and AIDS by engaging in the sex trade for financial gain to support their families. In other instances women and girls enter or are forced into unfaithful marriages or other unsafe relationships with men whose sexual behaviour has either already made them HIV-positive or puts them at greater risk to contract the disease.

Among societies where polygyny is common, there are higher risks for contracting HIV and AIDS. Polygyny in and of itself is not the culprit however; when a man engages in sexual activity unknowingly with a woman who is HIV-positive and subsequently passes on the infection to his other wives, the rate increases. A study conducted in Zambia (Urdang 2001) revealed how vulnerable wives can be to HIV and AIDS and other diseases transmitted sexually by their husbands. Less than one in every four women, according to the study, believed that they could refuse to have sex with their husbands, even if the husband had been unfaithful and was infected. Similarly, anthropologist Richard Lee (2007) attributes the low incidence of HIV and AIDS among the Ju/'hoansi of Namibia and Botswana to, among other factors, the traditional high status of women and their relative gender equality. Because the typical Ju/'hoansi wife tends to be relatively empowered, she is more likely to insist that her husband wear a condom and, should he refuse, to not have sex with him. In addition, social customs are so restrictive in some countries that often young women are denied access to information about the dangers of HIV and AIDS and how best to protect themselves.

Finance

The women of the world are also at a disadvantage in obtaining credit from financial institutions (Waring 1989, 2004). According to World Bank estimates, 90 percent of the more than a half billion women living in poverty around the world do not have access to credit. Small loans of $100 would go a long way in helping women to start their own small businesses, which could substantially improve their economic conditions. But both private lenders and aid organizations, by and large, have not made even this level of credit available to women. A notable exception is the Grameen Bank (which means "village bank") in Bangladesh. Founded by Muhammad Yunus, it is the world's best-known micro-lender, which since 1983 has made small-business loans to the poorest segments of Bangladesh society. Since then, many other banks have introduced *microcredit*, although with some misgivings as the relative administration costs are high. The community development bank makes loans to impoverished people without requiring collateral. Loans are given primarily to women, who use them to turn their operations into viable businesses to pull themselves out of poverty. Extending this type of credit to impoverished women has proven to be an excellent investment. World Bank data show that women repay their loans in 98 percent of the cases, compared with 60 to 70 percent for men. The World Bank has also found that credit given to women has a greater impact on the welfare of the family because women tend to spend their money on better nutrition and education for their children—areas given lower priority by male borrowers. According to Yunus, the main reason for providing loans to women is

> "that a woman was a "better fighter" against poverty than a man. A woman went to greater lengths to improve her children's nutrition and health and educate her daughters. Simply put, she used the loans more effectively. In the past few years, the field of development has come to a similar conclusion, with many aid workers asserting that the best way to fight poverty is to strengthen the positions of women and girls." (Bornstein 2012)

Progress toward Equality for Women

Thus, it is clear that women throughout the world continue to carry a heavy burden of inequality. Although they make up half the world's population, women do approximately two-thirds of the work, earn one-tenth of the world's income, and own less than one percent of the world's property. Even in the wake of some political and economic advances, women in many parts of the world are falling further behind their male counterparts. Moreover, gender inequality does not necessarily depend on how wealthy a country is. Some developing countries have done much better at narrowing the gender gap than have some wealthy, industrialized nations. In terms of women's participation in politics and jobs, for example, Costa Rica has made considerably better progress than Italy or France, whereas Poland is ahead of Japan.

As part of the Human Development Index (HDI), the United Nations developed an indicator of progress toward equality for women called the Gender Inequality Index (GII) which assesses gender inequality in over 150 countries in three main areas: (1) political participation and decision-making power (i.e., parliamentary seats), (2) economic status as measured by participation in the work force, and (3) reproductive health as measured by maternal death rates and adolescent birth rates (United Nations Development Programme 2013). The higher the GII value the greater the difference between men and women. The index sheds light on the status of women and also provides insights into areas where improvement is needed. As is apparent in Table 9.2, Western European nations have the lowest scores, reflecting the highest degree of gender equality, whereas African countries have the lowest scores. Note Canada ranks 24th and the United States 47th.

TABLE 9.2

Countries with the Highest and Lowest Ranks on the Gender Inequality Index (GII) 2013

Country	GII 2013	Rank
Slovenia	0.021	1
Switzerland	0.03	2
Germany	0.046	3
Sweden	0.054	4
Denmark	0.056	5
Austria	0.056	6
Netherlands	0.057	7
Italy	0.067	8
Norway	0.068	9
Belgium	0.068	10
Canada	0.136	24
Côte d'Ivoire	0.645	143
Central African Republic	0.654	144
Liberia	0.655	145
Mozambique	0.657	146
Congo (DRC)	0.669	147
Mali	0.673	148
Afghanistan	0.705	149
Chad	0.707	150
Niger	0.709	151
Yemen	0.733	152
World	0.45	

Source: Based on United Nations Development Programme: Human Development Reports. Table 4: Gender Inequality Index (2013) http://hdr.undp.org/en/content/table-4-gender-inequality-index Countries with the Highest and Lowest Ranks on the Gender Inequality Index 2013.

microcredit Small loans at low interest rates, and without collateral, to people (mostly women) in developing nations to help them start small businesses.

Gender-Based Violence

Sex-Selective Abortions

In many parts of the world, such as India and China, the ideological devaluation of women is evident even before birth. The birth of a son is often cause for rejoicing, but the birth of a daughter is met with silence. In some patriarchal societies, such as China, boys are more highly valued because with a patrilineal kinship system that requires male heirs they will continue the lineage. This is especially true in rural areas, where land inheritance is important for male children (Yardley 2005). Girls, on the other hand, will produce children for their husband's lineage. Because parents often assume that sons will provide for them in their old age, they are much more likely to give sons preferential treatment for health, education, and careers. To ensure that they have at least one male child some parents in these cultures practice ***sex-selective abortion***.

The preference for sons in China and India has created a lopsided ratio of boys to girls. Historically, the sex ratio at birth has been 1.05 boys for every girl (105 boys for every 100 girls). In 2014, however, it was 1.12 in India, 1.11 in China, and 1.07 in South Korea (CIA World Factbook, Country Comparison: Birth Rate). According to Mara Hvistendahl (2012), approximately 163 million girls were not born worldwide since the 1970s due to sex-selective abortions.

Hindu society in northern India is among the most highly stratified along gender lines of any society in the world. India as a whole, and particularly northern India, has enormously skewed sex ratios as a result of the widespread neglect of girls in terms of healthcare and nutrition (Khanna 2010). Sunil Khanna (2010) reports that, in his home country of India, gender bias against girls leads to significant differences in weight-for-age statistics for boys and girls younger than five years of age. In this part of the world, sons are more highly valued than daughters as sons pass down the family name and support the parents in old age. Sons add prestige and status to the family by becoming economic and political assets. "Sons receive . . . better education, healthcare and opportunities for growth in life" (Khanna 2010, 69). Daughters, on the other hand, are viewed as economic liabilities because families have to save for their wedding dowries and daughters move away to the husband's family. This is especially true for wealthy families who do not want to see the dowry go to a lower class husband and can afford the cost of an abortion (Arsenault 2011). Girls born to poorer families are also more likely not to be aborted due to the expense (Arsenault 2011).

Sex ratios have become even more unbalanced in recent years with the widespread use of ultrasound equipment to determine sex prenatally. Ultrasound enables determination of the sex of a fetus with about 99 percent accuracy (Ray et al. 2012). Although the practice of sex-selective abortions is illegal in India (and also China), and ultrasound technicians are forbidden from disclosing the sex of a fetus (Laforet 2011), the law is generally flouted. The desire for a son is so strong that the termination of female fetuses has reduced the female population of some rural villages by nearly 25 percent. And even for those girls who are born, they are often neglected, tend to be chronically malnourished, and are less likely to be taken to a health centre (Arsenault 2011). In a population of almost 200 million in Uttar Pradesh, India's most populous state, men outnumber women by nearly 10 million. In some villages in Punjab, there are no girls under age five, and in some areas there are 700 girls per 1000 boys (Arsenault 2011).

The skewed sex ratio is becoming a social problem in India and China, and elsewhere, as the shortage of women means many men are unable to find wives and are thus unable to become the head of a household. There are growing concerns of increased abuse and violence toward women as well as sex trafficking (Arsenault 2011; Laforet 2011). One solution may be to direct the "excess" males into the military, especially poor men who cannot afford a wife.

Easy access to abortion and advances in ultrasound technology have also made it easier for some immigrant groups in Canada to terminate female fetuses in favour of males (Vogel 2012). The sex ratio of live births to Indian-born and Korean-born mothers, for instance, is significantly skewed in favour of boys (Ray et al. 2012; Choe 2007). The ratio is higher for women whose first child, or first two children, are girls. For Chinese, Korean, and Vietnamese immigrants who already have two daughters, the ratio is 1.39, and for Indians the ratio is 1.90—almost two boys born for every girl (Almond et al. 2009). There have been calls to change the law so that physicians and ultrasound technicians do not disclose the sex of a fetus until after 30 weeks' gestation (Kale 2012; Vogel 2012).

Although it has been illegal in Canada since 2004 to selectively abort a fetus based on sex, it is legal in the United States, and many couples wanting to have a boy, travel to the States for an abortion. Sex-selective abortion is also creating a moral dilemma for physicians who must decide between discouraging sex-selective abortions and their obligations to their patients (Vogel 2012). Many women also have little choice but to have a male child and are pressured into having an abortion by their husbands.

---

sex-selective abortion The abortion of a fetus, usually female, based on its sex.

Female Genital Mutilation/Cutting

Another graphic form of gender exploitation is female genital cutting (FGC), also known as *female genital mutilation (FGM)* and female circumcision. The three terms refer to operations in which a girl's genitalia (labia and clitoris) are either partially or completely surgically cut away. It is usually performed on young girls between infancy and age 15 years, and is done largely for cultural reasons. Parents who have the operation carried out on their daughters prefer the term "cutting" as the term "mutilation" is ethnocentric and judgmental. They do not see it as mutilation of their daughters. The practice is justified by traditionalists on the grounds of protecting a girl's chastity and thus the family's honour, promoting cleanliness, repressing a girl's sexual desires, and reducing the likelihood of rape. In some sense it can be looked at as a rite of passage for young girls to prepare them for womanhood and marriage. Many of these justifications stem from gender ideologies about what women are like, what is feminine and modest, and what is proper sexual behaviour. Although no religious text requires FGC, many religious leaders, as well as community leaders, promote it as a means to fulfill gender ideologies. There is thus a great deal of pressure to conform and continue the practice. In some societies, girls are considered unmarriageable if they have not undergone the procedure.

The term "circumcision" implies that it is little different from male circumcision, which involves removal of the foreskin, and thus hides the physical and psychological severity of the operation, and the term is now little used. The term "mutilation" is preferred by advocates of women's and human rights to reflect the brutality of the operation. These operations are typically performed by traditional circumcisers with crude and unsterile instruments, without benefit of anesthesia, and with little or no protection against infection. There is a trend, however, to have FGM carried out by healthcare providers (WHO 2014b).

The practice is customary in large parts of Africa and the Middle East, and has been condemned by international medical and human rights groups. It has long been known that the operation itself poses severe medical risks for women. With no benefit to a woman's health, there is, in other words, an increasing amount of evidence from many sources that millions of girls worldwide continue to be subjected to unnecessary pain, hemorrhaging (bleeding), psychological trauma, infection, death, and compromises to their reproductive health to an extent that their brothers are not.

Long-term effects can include infertility, recurring bladder and urinary tract infections, and the need for further surgeries. With infibulation, the most extreme form of FGM, the vaginal opening is sealed or narrowed and needs to be repeatedly cut open for sexual intercourse and childbirth. Since the only function of the clitoris is for sexual stimulation, its removal precludes much of the physical pleasure of sexual intercourse, and can thus be seen as a means to control women's sexuality. FGM also increases the risk of complications in childbirth. A large-scale medical study (Rosenthal 2006) concluded that FGM raises the likelihood that mothers or their newborns will die during childbirth by 50 percent. The World Health Organization estimates (2014) that more than 125 million young girls have been cut in the 29 countries where it is regularly practised, and that 3 million young girls are at risk annually (WHO 2014b) (Figure 9.17). Performed on young girls who have little or no say in the matter, FGM is recognized as an extreme form of discrimination against women and a violation of basic human rights to health, freedom from inhuman treatment, and to life.

In 2008 and 2012, WHO and the UN respectively passed resolutions to ban FGM (WHO 2014b). And although the number of young girls who undergo the procedure is declining, it is still a serious issue, and not only in Africa and the Middle East but also in Canada where it is illegal. Canada is home to tens of thousands of immigrants from countries where FGM is practised, and there is evidence that it is practised across Canada and that in some cases, young girls are sent out of the country to have the operation (OHRC n.d.).

Male Circumcision

Male circumcision is also a sensitive and controversial issue that, worldwide, is carried out on about one-third of boys, usually shortly after birth (WHO 2015b). The vast majority of male circumcisions are done for cultural and religious reasons, especially in Muslim countries and Israel, where it is routine. In other countries it is often performed for hygienic reasons; circumcised boys also are less likely to contract urinary infections. The few circumcisions performed later in life are usually done for medical reasons. The Canadian Pediatric Association (CPA) recommends against routine circumcision as the pain caused to a small baby, as well as bleeding and the chance of disfiguring the penis, outweigh its benefits. Only about 1 percent of circumcisions performed by a surgeon in a hospital result in complications but, like FGM, many

---

female genital mutilation (FGM) An operation, usually done with crude instruments, in which a girl's genitalia (labia and clitoris) are either partially or completely surgically cut away.

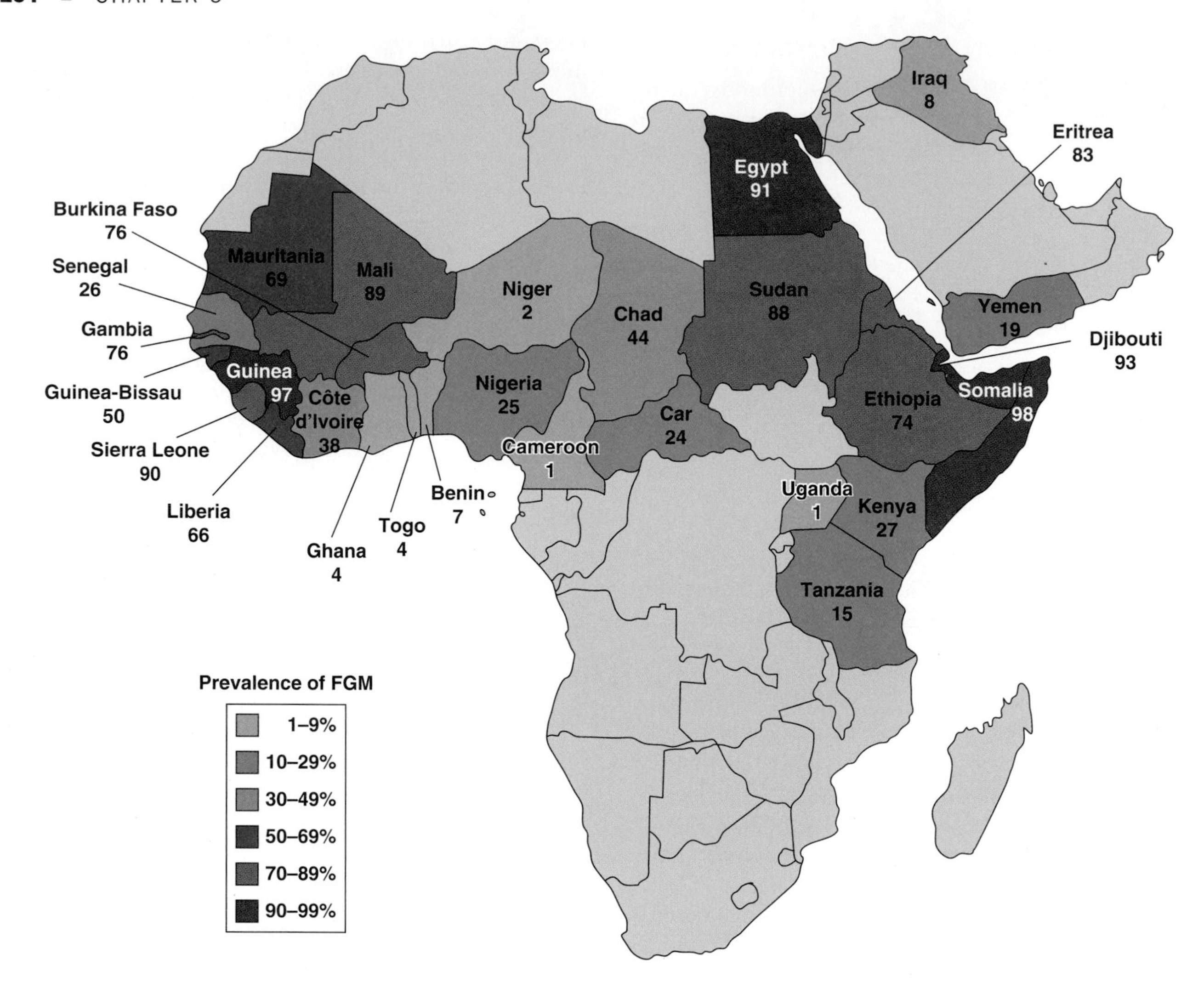

FIGURE 9.17 Prevalence of female genital mutilation (FGM) for women aged 15–49 years.

Source: UNICEF "The state of the world's children 2015: Executive Summary", November 2014, table 9, pp. 84–89, © United Nations Children's Fund (UNICEF) November 2014.

operations are performed by religious practitioners. In 2003 a five-week-old baby in British Columbia bled to death after being circumcised, and in 2013 a 22-day-old Ontario boy also bled to death after a circumcision performed at Toronto's North York General Hospital (Blackwell 2015). In 2015, the CPA reviewed its position, although it did not change it, as research has shown that circumcision reduces the risk of HIV infection in men in sub-Saharan Africa by 50 to 60 percent. The World Health Organization now advocates scaling up voluntary medical male circumcisions in countries in East and Southern Africa, and would like to see 80 percent of men circumcised as an HIV preventative measure (WHO 2015b). Between 2010 and 2014, the annual number of circumcisions increased by 750 percent in this area. In Canada, however, the chance of HIV infection is extremely low, and so parents must still weigh the costs and benefits of circumcising their newborn boys.

gender-based violence Acts of violence committed against people simply because of their gender.

Gender-Based Violence in Western Society

So far in this chapter we have seen examples of violence directed against women for refusing to have sex, a young girl shot because she stood up for her rights to an education, women forced to have abortions because the fetus was not male, and young girls' genitals cut away to ensure their chastity and family honour. Such acts against women are examples of ***gender-based violence*** in that they are committed against them simply because they are women. Other examples include forced marriage, sexual harassment, domestic abuse, honour killings, dowry deaths, and forced prostitution. Many of these acts, especially rape, sexual assault, and spousal abuse, often go unreported because they are widely tolerated in society, because they are taboo subjects, or because there may be stigma attached to being a victim.

Murdered and Missing First Nations, Métis, and Inuit Women

According to an RCMP report, nearly 1200 First Nations, Métis, and Inuit women have gone missing or were murdered between 1980 and 2012 (RCMP 2014). By some estimates, however, the number may be higher because of underreporting of missing women in remote areas (Kirkup 2016). Many of these missing and murdered women events occurred in Vancouver's Downtown Eastside, and along a 720 kilometre section of Highway 16 between Prince George and Prince Rupert, British Columbia, known as the Highway of Tears. According to police records, between 1969 and 2011, 19 young women, more than half of whom were First Nations, Métis, or Inuit, have gone missing or have been murdered on this stretch of highway, although some organizations estimate the number to be twice as high (HRW 2013). First Nations, Métis, and Inuit women are overrepresented among Canada's murdered and missing women. While they constitute only 4.3 percent of the female population in Canada, they represent 25 percent of murder victims and are more than three times as likely to be victims of violence than are non-Indigenous women (RCMP 2014).

Critics charge the government and police with systemic racism, arguing that they are not as concerned with the deaths and disappearances of Indigenous women because they are marginalized, and that if they had been white, the cases would have been more adequately investigated. The RCMP report, however, indicates that the solve rate for missing and murdered women is the same for Indigenous and non-Indigenous women—nearly 90 percent. One study has shown that media articles about missing white women received front page coverage and were four times longer on average than those about missing Indigenous women. Moreover, depictions of Indigenous women lacked the personal details found when discussing missing and murdered white women that allowed readers to sympathize with them. Indigenous women were described simply as "shy," "nice," "caring," and "pretty," and portrayed as victims of poverty, often addicted to drugs, and for choosing a lifestyle that put them at risk (Gilchrist 2010)—in other words, blaming the victim. Much of the cause for the disproportionate statistics has to do with the history of colonization and the Residential School experience of Canada's Indigenous peoples. The legacy of this experience, among other things, has been high-unemployment, substance abuse, poverty, and violence. First Nations, Métis, and Inuit are more than twice as likely as non-Indigenous people to report spousal violence in the previous five years; this is particularly true for Indigenous women (Burczycka 2016). Indigenous people are also more likely to experience abuse as children, which has been show to contribute to spousal violence later in life (Burczycka 2016).

In December 2015 the Canadian government launched an inquiry on murdered and missing First Nations, Métis, and Inuit women, which was one of the recommendations of the Truth and Reconciliation Commission (TRC 2015). While the focus is on the women, Adam Jones (2015) reminds us that First Nations, Métis, and Inuit men are also overrepresented as victims and perpetrators of violence relative to non-Aboriginal men, and should not be forgotten.

Honour Killings

Canada and other Western countries are, of course, not immune to this sort of violence. Some of the violence toward women is the result of immigrants to Canada bringing their cultural values and traditions with them. One example of this is a so called "***honour killing***," which is the killing of a family member, usually a young girl or woman, for an act that is seen to bring dishonour or shame to the family. Dishonour usually results from a violation of cultural norms of sexual modesty or disobedience to the senior male of the family. Breaking these norms provides the justification for killing family members, which is thought to remove the shame and restore honour. Honour killings are not uncommon in countries such as Pakistan, Afghanistan, Iraq, Iran, Turkey, Syria, and Albania (Muhammad 2010). In these traditionally male-dominated cultures, women are expected to be subservient and obedient to their fathers and husbands, and their behaviour, especially sexual behaviour, is tightly controlled. Failure to comply can be met with extreme violence, including murder, punishment for which may be light or non-existent as the penal codes in some countries, such as Iraq and Iran, make an exception for murder conducted in the name of honour, thus condoning it (Muhammad 2010). It can be for such things as refusing an arranged marriage, dressing immodestly, dating someone without permission or who is unsuitable, getting involved with feminist politics, adultery, having sex outside marriage, homosexuality, and even being raped. In 2004, for instance, a 14-year-old St. John's, Newfoundland, rape victim was strangled to death by her father and brother, supposedly for tarnishing the family name (Leader-Post (Regina) 2007).

A good example of an honour killing, which attracted international attention, is the murder of four female members of the Shafia family, who came to Canada from Afghanistan in 2007. In 2012, Mohammad Shafia, his wife Tooba, and their son Hamed were convicted of first-degree murder and sentenced to life imprisonment for killing Shafia's three daughters, Zainab, 19, Sahar, 17, and Geeti, 13, as well as Shafia's first wife, Rona (Figure 9.18). The four were found dead in Shafia's Nissan Sentra at the bottom of a canal in Kingston, Ontario. Shafia was apparently enraged by his teenage daughters' disobedience, dressing immodestly, and their pursuit of a Western

---

honour killing Killing of a family member, usually a young girl or woman, for acting in a way thought to dishonour the family.

FIGURE 9.18 **Mohammad Shafia, front left, Tooba Yahya, front right, and their son Hamed Shafia, back left, are escorted at the Frontenac County courthouse in Kingston, Ontario. They were convicted of murdering the couple's three daughters and another family member.**

lifestyle. The two oldest sisters also had boyfriends. Rona supported the girls and also wanted a divorce because she was abused and humiliated (Tripp 2015).

It should be noted that honour killings constitute only a small fraction of the number of domestic murders in Canada. Only about one per year on average can be classified as an honour killing (Rajiva and Khoday 2014). They become newsworthy, however, because in a relatively egalitarian and individualist society such as Canada it is difficult for most of us to understand honour as a justification for murdering a family member. It should also be noted that the term "honour killing" is controversial as it can stereotype particular ethnic groups, obscures the fact that family homicides occur in all communities, and because offenders may use the concept of dishonour as justification in the hopes of a reduced sentence (Muhammad 2010).

Misogyny

Violence against women in Canada seems to have become more prominent and more violent in recent decades. For example, on December 6, 1989, prospective student Marc Lépine entered the École Polytechnique, an engineering school in Montreal, and shot and killed 14 women and 4 men before committing suicide. Lépine moved among the classrooms and corridors intentionally targeting women, claiming he was "fighting feminism" (Buchignani 1989). Now known as the Montreal Massacre, it is memorialized on December 6 as the National Day of Remembrance and Action on Violence Against Women. Canadians are encouraged to observe a minute of silence and wear a white ribbon as a symbol of support for violence against women on this day.

While part of the explanation for Lépine's actions may be due to his personal circumstances—his father despised women and physically abused both him and his mother (Weston and Aubry 1990)—it is perhaps also a reflection of the ***misogyny*** (hatred of women) present in Western culture. Lépine blamed feminists for ruining his life, and some of his actions may be explained as a general backlash against the feminist movement, which some see as eroding male patriarchy and causing ***misandry***, or hatred of men (Nathanson and Young 2006).

Another good example of this misogyny is the harassment of independent online video game developer Zoë Quinn and her supporters by anonymous persons using the Twitter hashtag #GamerGate. In August 2013 Quinn began being harassed for developing the video game *Depression Quest*, which features a man attempting to deal with his depression. A large number of others joined in on the harassment using various online forums, and soon Quinn was receiving death threats and threats of rape, which eventually forced her to flee her home. When female supporters came to her defence they too were harassed with rape and death threats. Nicknamed Gamergate it eventually became international news in 2014.

Video games have been a traditional domain of young men; young men have been the developers; young men the ones who play them; and young men the protagonists in the games. Many of these games perpetuate gender stereotypes of both men and women and take a misogynist view. For example, *Grand Theft Auto V*, rated one of the best video games ever, has been criticized for its violence and its stereotypical representation of men and misogynist depiction of women. One reviewer of the game said "GTA V has little room for women except to portray them as strippers, prostitutes, long-suffering wives, humourless girlfriends and goofy, new-age feminists we're meant to laugh at" and that "characters constantly spout lines that glorify male sexuality while demeaning women, and the billboards and radio stations of the world reinforce this misogyny, with ads that equate manhood with sleek sports cars while encouraging women to purchase a fragrance that will make them 'smell like a bitch'" (Petit 2013). While the people involved in Gamergate harassment are undoubtedly few in number, a recent poll found that 25 percent of men in the United States hold sexist attitudes (Maxwell et al. 2016).

Today, almost half of all video games are now played by women (Sinclair 2014). More and more women are also developing them, creating female protagonists and making them less violent. This wider audience has also led many to criticize the stereotypes, particularly of women. For example, in a series of YouTube videos entitled *Tropes vs. Women in Video Games*, Canadian feminist Anita Sarkeesian examines such tropes (figures of

---

misogyny Hatred of women.

misandry Hatred of men.

speech/stereotypes) as "Women as Reward," "Women as Background Decoration," and "Damsel in Distress" in video games. Sarkeesian was also targeted in Gamergate, and these changes in video gaming and criticisms are central to Gamergate harassers who fear the games will be desexualized and marketed to women, and that in the interests of being politically correct will take the fun out of them (Dewey 2014; Weinman 2014). On the one side of Gamergate then, are independent game-makers and critics, mostly feminists, who want greater inclusion in gaming, and on the other hand, a group of antifeminists, mostly men, defending their right to play violent and sexist games, although in a threatening manner. *MacLean's* magazine called Gamergate a culture war (Weinman 2014) between two groups attempting to establish their identities through a shared cultural space.

Misandry and Violence against Men

While numerous studies have examined misogyny in popular culture, few have looked at the negative portrayal of men. In *Spreading Misandry*, Paul Nathanson (2001) shows how men are represented in television shows, movies, comic books, commercials, and even greeting cards as inherently violent and evil, and that when women are portrayed as evil, their behaviour is usually shown to be the result of mistreatment by men so we can understand it and sympathize with them. Men are also often portrayed as stupid and incompetent. In the popular family sitcom cartoon *The Simpsons*, for instance, Homer is made out to be a buffoon and Bart a troublemaker, whereas Marge and Lisa, and even Maggie, are seen as sensible and coming to their rescue. Similarly, in *Family Guy*, Peter is the joker always getting into trouble and is rescued by Lois. It should also be noted that both of these shows perpetuate the traditional breadwinner/homemaker model. Both Homer and Peter work, or have schemes to provide for their families, whereas Marge and Lois both look after the home and family.

The feminist movement of the 1970s exposed the biases involved in an androcentric, or male-centred, view of the world, and much of the subsequent scholarship has been a necessary corrective to this view. Nathanson and Young (2006) argue, however, that it has gone too far, resulting in a ***gynocentric view*** of the world that has been promoted in schools and universities for decades. They also argue that this view not only ignores men's needs and problems, but also that this bias has become established in public policy and received official status in law. The result is an institutionalized double standard that favours women, such as affirmative action for women.

This gynocentric view has led the media, activists, and academics to focus on violence toward women while the physical and mental consequences of violence toward men are trivialized (Nathanson 2001). Hatred and violence are not restricted to any gender, however, and the reality is that, while men are overrepresented as perpetrators of violence, they are also overrepresented as victims. In a 2010 US survey, 80 percent of homicide victims and almost two-thirds of robbery victims were men (Young C. 2014). According to Statistics Canada, between 2009 and 2014, equal proportions of men and women reported being victims of spousal violence (defined as physical and/or sexual violence committed by the victim's former or current partner), although violence against women tends to be more severe (Burczycka 2016). This statistic may seem surprising as the common perception is that women are the primary victims of spousal abuse. Men may even be underrepresented as they are less likely to report domestic violence than women (Burczycka 2016). Other studies have shown that men and women are equally responsible for initiating the violence, so it is unlikely the proportion of men reporting abuse is due to women resorting to violence in self-defence (Fiebert 2011). Most of the studies and programs that look for the causes and solutions to domestic violence, however, focus on the violence toward women. Policy is also focussed on women, and the protections afforded to victims of violence are mostly available to women. While there are dozens of agencies and shelters dedicated to female victims of domestic violence in Canada, the Canadian Association for Equality (CAFE) (2016) could find only one for men: the Men's Resource Centre in Winnipeg (http://equalitycanada.com/) (Figure 9.19). While violence against women is a serious global and domestic problem, what CAFE, Nathanson, and Young are saying is that violence against men is also a serious issue that should not be overlooked. Violence in the home has a huge impact on the health and economic well-being of both men and women, and their children as well as society (Widom et al. 2014). By understanding why these attitudes and behaviours occur and continue to persist and be tolerated, anthropologists can heighten awareness and make recommendations for change.

FIGURE 9.19 The Canadian Association for Equality billboard, displayed at a prominent intersection in Toronto in 2015, highlights the fact that men are also victims of spousal violence.

---

gynocentric view A view of the world from a female perspective.

Summary

1. The word *sex* refers to the biological differences between males and females, while *gender* refers to the way members of the two sexes are perceived, evaluated, and expected to behave. Although biology sets broad limits on definitions of gender, there is a wide range of ideas about what it means to be feminine or masculine.
2. Humans are sexually dimorphic, and the differences between men and women have been used to justify appropriate roles for the genders and discrimination, especially against women.
3. Ideas about what men and women are like, how they are supposed to behave, and how they are to relate to one another are informed by a gender ideology. Gender ideology is important in formulating policies and in development projects.
4. We learn our gender and form a *gender identity* from our parents, our peers, and from cultural context. Cues about what is appropriate for our gender are contained in books, toys, movies, advertisements, songs, and so on.
5. Gender is culturally constructed, meaning that it is culturally relative. There can be no universal meaning to the categories "woman" or "man." What it means to be a man or a woman in a particular society will thus be relative to that society.
6. Because gender is culturally constructed, there can be more than one gender. Two-spirit people in First Nations/Native American societies, and the hijra of India and Pakistan are examples of third genders. Transgender people in Canada and elsewhere are challenging society's ideas and expectations of normality and binary gender categories, even while they face discrimination.
7. There are considerable differences in degrees of permissiveness, but all societies regulate the sexual conduct of their members. Some societies are sexually restrictive, whereas others, such as Canada, permit frequent sexual activity between men and women.
8. In general terms, there is considerable uniformity in sex roles throughout the world. Men engage in warfare, clear land, hunt animals, build houses, fish, and work with hard substances; women tend crops, prepare food, collect firewood, clean house, launder clothes, care for children, and carry water.
9. The status of women is multidimensional, involving such aspects as the division of labour, the value placed on women's contributions, economic autonomy, social and political power, legal rights, levels of deference, and the extent to which women control the everyday events of their lives.
10. Hunting-and-gathering societies are the most egalitarian, while agricultural societies are the most stratified in their approach to men and women. In most critical areas, women tend to be subordinate to men in nearly all societies of the world.
11. Gender ideology is used in most societies to justify universal male dominance. Deeply rooted values about the superiority of men, the ritual impurity of women, and the pre-eminence of men's work are often used to justify the subjugation of women.
12. In North America the traditional roles of *breadwinner* and *homemaker* are no longer accurate, as many households are dual income and both contribute to looking after the children and housework, although women continue to do more unpaid labour than men. This in part is because gender role ideology is still prevalent. *Occupational segregation* along gender lines still exists, although it is also changing.
13. There has been a trend in recent decades toward the feminization of poverty around the world as a result of unequal access to education and the higher paying skilled jobs. This is the result of unequal educational opportunities for women, their concentration in the lowest-paid occupations, their unequal access to healthcare, and that fact that they are at a disadvantage in obtaining credit from financial institutions.
14. In some societies gender ideologies are so extreme that females suffer serious negative consequences, such as lack of education, economic dependence on men, pressure to have many children, greater risk of HIV and AIDS, and poverty.
15. The ideological devaluation of women has led to violence against women, including sex-selective abortions, female genital mutilation, and honour killings.
16. First Nations, Métis, and Inuit women have a higher risk of being the victims of violence than non-Indigenous women.
17. While the focus tends to be on women as the victims of violence, it should not be forgotten that men are also victims of violence.

Key Terms

breadwinner
cultural construction of gender
female genital mutilation (FGM)
femininity
feminization of poverty
gay-straight alliance
gender
gender-based violence
gender fluid
gender identity
gender ideology
gender roles
gender stereotypes
gender stratification
gynocentric view
heteronormative
heterosexual
hijra
homemaker
homophobia
homosexual
honour killing
human sexuality
intersex
masculinity
microcredit
misandry
misogyny
occupational segregation
sex
sex-selective abortion
sexually dimorphic
Sexual Revolution
transgender
two-spirit

Critical Thinking Questions

1. If gender is culturally constructed, is it possible to have a genderless or gender-neutral society? If so, what would it look like and is it desirable?
2. What are the symbolic markers of gender in your culture?
3. How do you think things such as toys, movies, magazines, books, advertisements, and so on, have shaped your understanding of your own gender identity?
4. To what extent does biology play a role in the ways the genders are perceived, evaluated, and expected to behave?
5. If you were hired to work on a local development project, what cultural understandings about sex and gender would you want to know before you started?
6. If you were employed at large accounting firm with upper management responsibilities, how might you ensure sexual harassment among your colleagues is avoided?
7. How have gender roles changed in Canada in recent years? Why are men overrepresented in the STEM fields?
8. How is the relative status of the genders measured?
9. Should physicians and ultrasound technicians disclose the sex of a fetus before 30 weeks gestation?
10. At the end of 2015 the Canadian government launched an inquiry that looks exclusively into murdered and missing Indigenous women. How would people respond if it announced it would focus only on missing and murdered Indigenous men?

Make the Grade with MindTap

Stay organized and efficient with **MindTap**—a single destination with all the course material and study aids you need to succeed. Built-in apps leverage social media and the latest learning technology. For example:

- ReadSpeaker will read the text to you.
- Self-quizzing allows you to assess your understanding.
- Flashcards are pre-populated to provide you with a jump-start for review—or you can create your own.
- You can highlight text and make notes in your MindTap Reader. Your notes will flow into Evernote, the electronic notebook app that you can access anywhere when it's time to study for the exam.

Visit nelson.com/student to start using **MindTap**. Enter the Online Access Code from the card included with your text. If a code card is not provided, you can purchase instant access at NELSONbrain.com.

A favela slum in front of corporate towers in São Paulo, Brazil

CHAPTER

10

Social Inequality: The Meaning of Difference

WHAT WE WILL LEARN

- How anthropologists measure social inequality
- How egalitarian, rank, and stratified societies differ from one another
- How class systems differ from caste systems
- How socially mobile Canadians are
- How race is culturally constructed and how the concept of race developed
- What the distinction is between race and ethnicity
- What racism is and the ways it is exhibited
- The extent to which racism exists in Canada
- How the Indian Act and the Indian Residential School experience have impacted Canada's Indigenous peoples

BLACK LIKE ME

Through participant observation, anthropologists experience other cultures with the goal of understanding how "the other" experiences and makes sense of life from their perspective; "to grasp the native's point of view, his relation to life, to realize *his* vision of *his* world," as Malinowski put it (1922 (1961), 25). But anthropologists can't really get "inside the skin" of "the other" and really experience life from the perspective of "the other." Or can they? One person who tried was John Howard Griffin (1920–1980) (Figure 10.1).

Griffin was a writer, and in 1959 he wanted to understand what it really felt like to experience *racial segregation* as a black man living in the southern United States. Jim Crow laws, which were in effect in the old Confederate states from 1890 to 1965, mandated that the daily public lives of blacks and whites were to be kept separate. Blacks and whites went to separate schools, ate in different restaurants, drank from different water fountains, sat in different areas of buses and movie theatres, went to different beaches, and even used separate vending machines. As long as public facilities provided to blacks and whites were equivalent, segregation was legal according the American Constitution under a doctrine known as "separate but equal." It was, of course, a myth. Most of the money was spent on whites, and all the best facilities were reserved for whites; those for blacks were considerably inferior. Intellectually, one can imagine that such discrimination was unpleasant, but no white researcher was ever going to find out what the experience was really like.

So, under the supervision of a dermatologist, Griffin took drugs and spent several hours a day under an ultraviolet light to darken his skin. The transformation was remarkable; even his close friends failed to recognize him at first. When he looked in the mirror he came face-to-face with the self as "other," saying "the transformation was total and shocking. I had expected to see myself disguised, but this was something else. I was imprisoned in the flesh of an utter stranger, an unsympathetic one with whom I felt no kinship. All traces of the John Griffin I had been were wiped from existence" (2010 (1961), 10). He then walked out into the streets of New Orleans, and for the next six weeks travelled through Louisiana, Mississippi, Alabama, and Georgia. The black people he met accepted him as black, as did the white people he

John Michaels/Alamy Stock Photo

© Don Rutledge

FIGURE 10.1 John Howard Griffin (*left*) in New Orleans in 1959.

encountered. *Black Like Me* (1961), his book about his experiences, has become a classic of American literature.

What shocked him more than his appearance was the way he was treated. When he tried to buy a bus ticket, the woman behind the counter refused to give him his change and eventually threw the ticket and his change on the floor. On the bus, he offered the seat next to him to a white woman. The other black passengers stared at him in amazement as they realized no white woman would sit next to a black man. When he was about to get off at his stop, the driver slammed the door in his face and refused to let him off for eight blocks. On a long distance bus ride the whites were let off to stretch their legs and to relieve themselves; the blacks were not. At one point he tried to use a rundown outhouse but was forced to walk 10 blocks to find a toilet he could use. He applied for several jobs, but even though he was well-dressed and well-spoken no one would hire him, assuming he was incompetent and unintelligent.

Occasionally, white men would pick him up hitchhiking, only to ask about his sex life. Working under the stereotypical assumption that he, like all black men, was consumed by primitive sexual urges and possessed oversized genitals, they wanted to engage their prurient interests. One even asked to see his penis.

What troubled him most, however, was the "hate stare" and the word "nigger," which followed him everywhere. What Griffin experienced was the reality of segregation and racism: the prejudice and hatred, the constant threat of physical violence, and the poverty it all led to. Not only was it humiliating and dehumanizing, but he also realized that many black Americans had bought into the segregation and racism, believing they were inferior and deserving of the treatment they received. His biographer noted that "what he learned was that 'blackness' was not a color but a lived experience" (Bonazzi 2010).

Reflecting on his experience in a later book, Griffin (2011, 82) wrote:

> Everything is different. Everything changes. As soon as I got into areas where I had contact with white people, I realized that I was no longer regarded as a human individual. Surely one of the strangest experiences a person can have is suddenly to step out into the streets and find that the entire white society is convinced that an individual possesses qualities and characteristics which that person knows he does not possess. I am not speaking here only of myself. This is the mind-twisting experience of every black person I know.

Not every white person treated Griffin with contempt. And he finds the blacks he encountered, who accepted and trusted him because he was black, and told him things he would not otherwise have been told, were warm, friendly, and helpful, and even put him up in their homes. Ultimately he realizes that neither race understands the other.

Black Like Me was instrumental in raising the awareness of whites in America of the experience of racism. Reaction to his book, and the more than 1200 lectures he subsequently delivered (Bonazzi 2010), was mostly positive. He was,

however, also burned in effigy in Montgomery, Alabama, and he received so much hate mail and threatening phone calls that he had to move with his family to Mexico (Bonazzi 2010).

Griffin's story gets to the heart of what racism is: he was judged not for who he was, but for the colour of his skin. His unique experience gave him insight into two worlds and he discovered that, for the most part, both black and white are kind, hospitable, and giving; they both deal with the struggles of daily life: caring for their children, putting food on the table and a roof over their heads, finding places to relieve themselves, and so on. In other words, his story is not just about racism. It is about human nature. It reminds us of the need for understanding, and that the only real difference between groups of people is that the meaning of difference has been translated into inferiority and thereby the denial of rights.

Griffin's story also raises the question of how far race relations have come in the United States. In June 2015, a gunman walked into Emanuel African Methodist Episcopal Church in Charleston, South Carolina, during Bible study and killed nine people for no other reason than that they were black. This was after several incidents in the United States when unarmed black men were killed by white police. One would like to think that these are isolated incidents and that the widespread vehement racism that Griffin experienced is a thing of the past.

His story also reminds us that racial segregation still exists in the world today, and that Canada has its own history of racial segregation. Until the late 1960s, most First Nations people were confined to reserves, and the continued existence of reserves is a reminder that race-based segregation still exists in Canada (Musto 1990). Under the Residential School system, First Nations children were forcibly sent to schools in remote locations. In some areas, First Nations people, along with some immigrants to Canada, were considered second-class citizens and were also required to use separate facilities. ■

Dimensions of Difference and Social Inequality

Human relationships are often shaped by the differences, either real or imagined, between groups of people. To one degree or another, all societies differentiate among their members, and these differences can become the basis for social inequalities. In every society, people are socially differentiated on the basis of criteria such as physical appearance, ethnicity, profession, family background, gender, ideology, age, or skill in performing certain kinds of economic or political roles. An important distinguishing characteristic of societies is the degree to which these differences are translated into differential access to wealth, power, and prestige. Societies confer a larger share of these rewards on those who possess the most admired characteristics. Scholars generally agree that all complex societies are stratified; that is, these societies make distinctions among certain groups or categories of people that are hierarchically ranked relative to one another. Anthropologists do not find clear-cut social strata in many of the simpler societies of the world, yet even these societies have role and status differences.

Anthropologists are interested in the inequalities that exist in societies because the evaluations people make of others are based, to a large extent, not on who they are as individuals, but on the fact that they are members of a particular group or groups. Anthropologists investigating inequality today are interested in how existing patterns of inequality are maintained and reproduced (Béteille 1998), as

racial segregation The practice of keeping the daily public lives of different races separate.

J.P. Moczulski/Globe and Mail/The Canadian Press

FIGURE 10.2 **According to *Forbes Magazine* (2015), David Thomson and his family, with a fortune worth $25.5 billion as of August 2015, was the richest person in Canada, and the 25th in the world. He owns the Reuters international news agency.**

well as the experience of inequality and its impact on people's lives.

Max Weber (1946) delineated *social inequality* as the differential or unequal access to the culturally valued resources of wealth, power, and prestige. First, people are distinguished from one another by the extent to which they have accumulated economic resources, or *wealth*. The forms wealth may take vary from one society to the next. For the Mexican farmer, wealth resides in the land; for the Samburu of East Africa, a man's wealth is measured by the number of cows he has; and in Canada, most people equate their wealth with income earned in wages, property, stocks, bonds, equity in a home, or other resources that have a cash value (Figure 10.2).

The extent of economic inequality varies from society to society. In foraging societies there are virtually no differences in wealth. In terms of their material possessions and well-being, all people in egalitarian societies are virtually indistinguishable. By way of contrast, enormous differences in wealth exist in capitalistic societies such as Canada, the United States, and Mexico. The range of wealth in Mexico, for example, runs from the unemployed father in Mexico City who sells his blood to feed his children, to Carlos Slim Helu, a self-made telecommunications mogul, who from 2010 to 2013 was the richest man in the world, with a total net worth over $70 billion.

A second dimension of social inequality, according to Weber, is *power*, which can be defined as the ability to achieve one's goals and objectives by controlling or influencing the behaviour of others. Power is often closely correlated with wealth because economic success, particularly in Western societies, increases one's chances of gaining power. Nevertheless, wealth and power do not always coincide. In certain parts of the world, power can be based on factors other than wealth, such as specialized knowledge or eloquence as a speaker. In such cases, the wealth or material possessions of the powerful and the not-so-powerful may not differ significantly.

The third dimension of social stratification, according to Weber's formulation, is *prestige:* the social esteem, respect, or admiration that a society confers on people. Because favourable social evaluation is based on the norms and values of a particular group, sources of prestige again vary from one culture to another. For example, among most First Nations, prestige comes with age. Elders are listened to because their experience has provided them with wisdom, which also gives them power.

Not surprisingly, physicians, corporate presidents, scientists, and top-ranking government officials enjoy high levels of occupational prestige, whereas garbage collectors, day labourers, and janitors are at the low end of the prestige scale. Essentially, four factors separate the occupations at the top from those at the bottom. The occupations at the top end offer higher salaries, require more education, offer greater autonomy (less supervision), and require more abstract thinking and less physical labour.

We should keep in mind that, although wealth, power, and prestige are often correlated, they can also operate independently. Consider that it is possible to possess both power and wealth while having little prestige, as is the case with leaders of organized crime. Canada has a Parliamentary Poet Laureate, whose job is "to encourage and promote the importance of literature, culture and language in Canadian society" by, among other things, "writ[ing] poetry, especially for use in Parliament on important occasions" (Parliament of Canada. 2016). While he or she may have a lot of respect, they get paid little and have little power.

Types of Societies

Following the lead of Morton Fried (1967), most anthropologists distinguish three types of societies based on levels of social inequality: egalitarian, rank, and stratified societies.

Egalitarian Societies

Egalitarian societies have few or no individuals or groups with greater access to wealth, power, or prestige; they are usually found among food collectors, such as the Ju/'hoansi of the Kalahari region (Figure 10.3), the

social inequality Unequal access to the culturally valued resources of wealth, power, and prestige.

wealth The material objects that have value in a society.

power The ability to achieve one's goals by influencing the behaviour of others.

prestige Social honour or respect within a society.

egalitarian society A society that recognizes few differences in status, wealth, or power.

Martin Harvey/Peter Arnold/Getty Images

FIGURE 10.3 Small-scale foraging societies, such as the Ju/'hoansi of Namibia, tend to be egalitarian.

Hadza of Tanzania, and the Mbuti of the Democratic Republic of the Congo. These cultures have economies based on reciprocity, and have little or no political role specialization. Even though certain individuals in an egalitarian society may be highly esteemed for their skills or knowledge or character, they are not able to transform their special skills into wealth or power. No matter how much or how little respect an individual in an egalitarian society may have, he or she is neither denied the right to practise a certain profession nor subject to the control of others. Moreover, whatever esteem an individual manages to accrue is not transferable to his or her heirs. There are logical reasons unequal access to wealth, power, and prestige would be discouraged among nomadic foragers. First, the nomadic existence inhibits the accumulation of large quantities of personal possessions. Second, because foragers do not hold claims to territory, individuals can forage in whatever areas they please. Third, because food cannot be refrigerated it is shared. Generosity in such societies is expected, and attempts to accumulate possessions, power, or prestige are ridiculed.

Rank Societies

In *rank societies*, many of which are found in Oceania, certain groups enjoy higher prestige, even though power and wealth are equally distributed; they are usually found among chiefdoms, have economies based on redistribution, and exhibit limited political role specialization. High-prestige positions such as chief or "big man"—which are largely hereditary—establish a ranking system that distinguishes among various levels of prestige and esteem. In fact, kinship plays an important role in rank societies. Because some clans or lineages may be considered aristocratic, their members qualify for certain titles or high-status positions. For example, in the Trobriand Islands, which has four ranked clans, the paramount chief comes from the highest ranking clan (Malinowski 1922). Other kin groups are rank-ordered according to their genealogical proximity to the aristocratic kin groups. Thus, the number of high-status positions in ranked societies is limited, and the major criterion for allocating such positions is usually genealogical.

Even though the chiefs in a rank society possess great prestige and privilege, they generally do not accumulate great wealth; their basic standard of living is not noticeably different from that of an ordinary person. Chiefs usually receive gifts of tribute from members of other kin groups, but they rarely keep them for their personal use. Instead, they give them all away through the process of redistribution (see Chapter 7). In many rank societies, chiefs are considered to own the land but not in the Western sense of the term. The chief certainly has little power to keep anyone from using the land. The chief may control land to the extent that he encourages people not to neglect either the land or their obligation to contribute to the chief's tribute. But the chief has little real power or control over the land. He maintains his privileged position as "big man" not by virtue of his capacity to impose his will on others but through his generosity.

Stratified Societies

Stratified societies manifest the greatest degree of social inequality in all three forms of social rewards. They are found in societies with large populations, have market economies, and are associated with state systems of government. Stratified societies consist of levels called *strata*, which are relatively permanent horizontal layers separating people according to the differential access they have to wealth, power, and prestige (Figure 10.4). Stratified societies differ in terms of the number and size of strata, the ideology that supports them, and the extent to which the levels are permeable. What they have in common is that social inequality is built into the structure of the society.

The political, economic, and social inequality in stratified societies is both permanent and formally recognized by the members of the society. Some people—and entire groups of people—have little or no access to the basic resources of the society. Various groups in stratified societies, then, are noticeably different in social position, wealth, lifestyle, access to power, and standard of living. The unequal access to rewards found in stratified societies is generally thought to be inheritable from one generation to the next.

rank society A society in which people have unequal access to prestige and status but not unequal access to wealth and power.

stratified society A society with a large population that is divided into several levels based on the degree of social inequality.

strata Relatively permanent levels in societies separating people according to their access to wealth, power, and prestige.

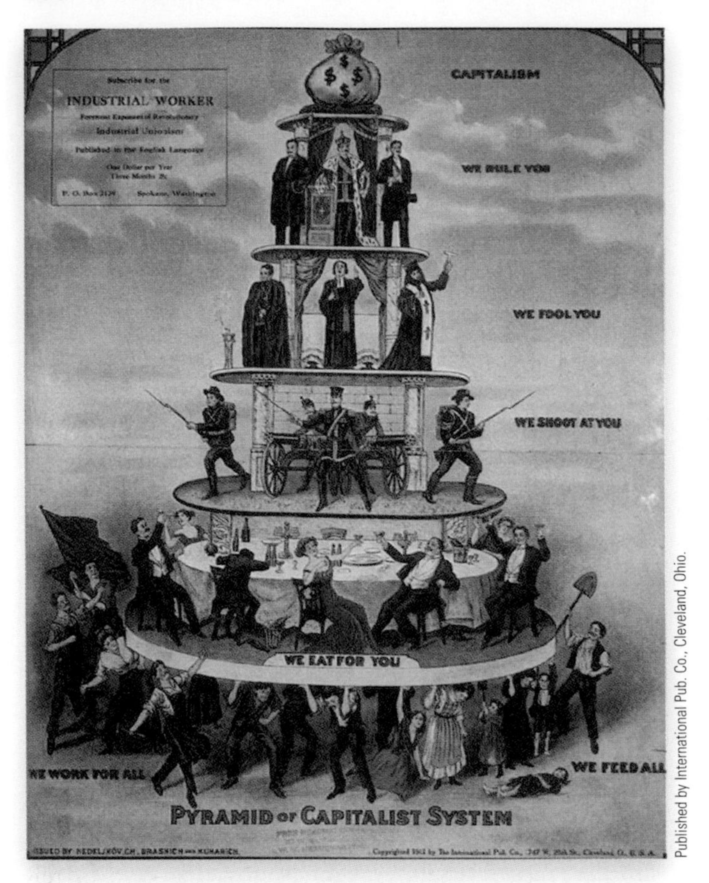

Published by International Pub. Co., Cleveland, Ohio.

FIGURE 10.4 Workers of the World poster from 1911. Stratified societies differ in terms of the number and size of strata, the ideology that supports them, and the extent to which the levels are permeable.

Rather than thinking of these three types of societies as discrete and mutually exclusive, it is more accurate to view them as points on a continuum, ranging from egalitarian societies (the least amount of social inequality) to stratified societies (the greatest degree of social inequality). As societies become more specialized, the system of social stratification also becomes more complex. Different occupations or economic interest groups do not have the same access to wealth, power, and prestige but rather are ranked relative to one another. As a general rule, the greater the role specialization in a society, the more complex is its system of stratification.

social mobility The ability of people to change their social position within the society.

class A ranked group within a stratified society characterized by achieved status and considerable social mobility.

caste A ranked group within a rigidly stratified society in which membership is ascribed at birth and social mobility is almost non-existent.

achieved status The status an individual acquires during the course of her or his lifetime.

ascribed status The status a person has by virtue of birth.

open society A society in which there are no formal barriers preventing people from rising in the social hierarchy.

closed society A society in which there are formal barriers preventing people from moving up the social hierarchy.

Class versus Caste

Social scientists generally recognize two different types of stratified societies: those based on class and those based on caste. The key to understanding this fundamental distinction is *social mobility*. In *class* systems, a certain amount of upward and downward social mobility exists. In other words, an individual can change his or her social position dramatically within a lifetime. Through diligence and hard work, an individual could go from rags to riches. Conversely, a person born to millionaire parents could wind up as a homeless street person (Newman 1988). People in *caste* societies, on the other hand, have little or no social mobility. Membership in a caste is determined by birth and lasts throughout one's lifetime. Whereas members of a class society are able to elevate their social position by marrying into a higher class, caste systems, except for rare exceptions, are strictly endogamous, allowing marriages only within one's own caste.

Another important distinction is how statuses (positions) within each type of society are allocated. Class systems are usually associated with an *achieved status*, whereas caste systems are associated with an *ascribed status*. An achieved status is one that a person has attained as a result of her or his personal effort, such as graduating from college, marrying someone, or securing a particular job. The dominant ideology of Canadian society is that if a person works hard they can move up the social hierarchy regardless of their situation at birth. In other words, everyone has an equal opportunity to be successful; there are no formal barriers preventing people of a particular age, gender, ethnicity, race, or physical disability from working to the best of their abilities and getting ahead. Such societies are known as *open societies*. Although *ideally* there may be equality of opportunity, the reality is that many people remain in the class into which they are born, and marry within that class as well.

In contrast, a person born into an ascribed status has no control over it. Sex, race, and age are examples of ascribed statuses. These societies are *closed societies* since their ascribed status prevents them from advancing or acquiring more wealth, power, and prestige. In caste societies a person's status in the social hierarchy is ascribed to them at birth.

It is important to bear in mind that stratified societies cannot all be divided neatly into either class or caste systems. In general, class systems are open to the extent that they are based on achieved statuses and permit considerable social mobility; caste systems tend to be closed to the extent that they are based on ascribed statuses and allow little or no social mobility, either up or down. We must also realize, however, that class and caste systems overlap. In other words, most stratified societies contain elements of both class and caste. Rather than think in either–or terms, we should think in terms of polarities on the ends of a continuum, with all stratified societies found falling somewhere between these two ideal polarities, depending on the amount of social mobility permitted in each.

Class Societies

For social and economic theorist Karl Marx, classes were groups of people who share common economic interests and perform the same function in relation to the organization of production. Capitalist society was divided into two major classes: the proletariat, or working class, who owned and sold their labour and strove to maximize wages and benefits, and the bourgeoisie, or capitalists, who owned the means of production and strove to make a profit at the expense of the workers; they thus had differential access to resources and power. This system is maintained by an ideology that masks this system of exploitation. When the working class become conscious that they are being exploited, however, they cease to be a class *of* itself and become a class *for* itself, and are able to collectively pursue their common class interests. Marx believed that history was the result of class confrontations and struggles, whereby the different classes clash in pursuit of their own interests. Only then, Marx believed, could the proletariat overthrow the existing social relationships and create a classless society.

The boundaries between social strata in a class society are not, however, as rigidly drawn as Marx makes out, and in many ways the structure should be looked at as a continuum. A social class is a segment of the population whose members have similar levels of wealth, power, and prestige. People in the upper classes tend to have more of all three. Members of the same social class also share similar experiences, educational backgrounds, political views, memberships in organizations, occupations, values, lifestyles, tastes, attitudes, the form of language spoken, the clothes worn (e.g., blue collar versus white collar), how long they live, and consumption patterns. In other words, different classes tend to have different cultures, or rather subcultures. In addition, studies of social class have shown, not surprisingly, that members of a social class tend to associate more often with one another than with people in other classes. They thus also have a similar self-image.

Canada is a good example of a class society. Although where the line between classes is drawn is relatively arbitrary, social scientists tend to identify social classes based on education, power, and especially income and net worth. Typically, Canadian society is divided into upper class, middle class, working class, and lower class (Macionis and Gerber 2013). The upper class, perhaps 3 to 5 percent of the Canadian population, is either "old money," where people have inherited their wealth, or they are the "nouveau riche" (newly rich) and have earned it, usually through starting highly successful businesses. The upper class tend to send their children to private schools, shop at high-end stores, and are more likely to vote conservative.

The middle class, perhaps 40 to 50 percent of Canadians, earn somewhere between $50 000 and $100 000 and tend to be professionals, upper management, or highly skilled trades people (Macionis and Gerber 2013). Because of its large size, this class tends to be not only ethnically diverse but also influences Canadian culture as a whole. It also has a huge impact on Canadian politics, and it is this class that Canadian politicians try to appeal to.

The working class, about one-third of the population, work as unskilled labourers, have lower levels of education, and little accumulated wealth. Because of their lack of higher education, members of this group tend to have little social mobility. Vulnerable to downturns in the economy, working-class people are subject to layoffs during recessions and justifiably feel threatened by the increasingly globalized economy, in which many jobs are going to workers abroad.

The lower class are the poorest segment of the Canadian population—about 20 percent—and barely earn a living at unskilled, low-paying, unpleasant, and often temporary jobs with little security and frequently no benefits; they often require social assistance to survive. Proportionally, more visible minorities and First Nations, Métis, and Inuit fall into this class, which also includes homeless people. Because the boundaries are arbitrary, different scholars may set boundaries differently or will divide Canadian society into fewer strata, or may include subclasses (e.g., upper middle class). The Canadian social hierarchy can also be divided into quintiles, or fifths. The top quintile, for example, represents the top 20 percent of the Canadian population earning the most.

Social Mobility in Canada

In September 2011, several hundred demonstrators occupied Zuccotti Park in New York City's financial district to protest global social and economic inequality in what came to be called Occupy Wall Street. Within weeks, thanks to Twitter, Facebook, Tumblr, and other social media, the "Occupy Movement" had spread to hundreds of cities worldwide, including most major cities in Canada (van Stekelenburg 2012). Protesting against the control and exploitation of the poor by multinational corporations, and especially financial institutions, demonstrators set up temporary camps in parks and on university campuses around the world. Although the movement lasted only a few months and was a failure according to one of the founders of the movement (White 2016), it did raise awareness of the inequality that exists in the world.

STORIES FROM THE FIELD

During the first weeks of my fieldwork in Dominica, an island in the Eastern Caribbean, I learned about the strict greeting protocols and importance of mutual recognition on the island. It was not unusual for strangers to greet me with "good morning" or "good afternoon" and I would respond in kind. One afternoon a man was chasing after me calling out "Becky! Becky!" Since my name is not Becky it took me a while to realise that he was calling out to me. I turned and explained to him that he must have me confused with someone else, "My name is Dee," I said, "not Becky." He looked perplexed, pointed at me repeatedly saying, "Look, of course you are Becky." After a few minutes an older woman approached and chased him off, explaining that he was "a beggar." A few weeks later when I heard someone refer to a light-skinned friend as "Becky." I asked why he was calling his friend Becky. "No, his "ti nom" (nickname) is "bèkè." We call him that because he has light skin." Bèkè, I learned, is Kwéyol (Creole) for a white, or light-complected, person and connotes wealth and privilege. Some people use it exclusively to refer to people born in the Caribbean region. The man was pointing to my arms to indicate that of course I was white/light-skinned and was perplexed by my denial of what, to him, was obvious.

—Deidre Rose, *University of Guelph*

One of the slogans of the movement, "We are the 99%," referring to the common people and opposed to the 1 percent of the world's wealthiest people, has endured, and highlights the differences in income between the rich and the poor. According to one estimate, worldwide, the 1 percent of the population possesses about 40 percent of the global wealth (van Stekelenburg 2012). Other scholars have asserted that, "the richest 1% now has more wealth than the rest of the world combined" (Lambert and McInturff 2016). In Canada, the average income of the 99 percent in 2007 was about $44 000, while the average of the top 1 percent was over $400 000, almost 10 times more (Paradis 2012). Moreover, between 2009 and 2010, the income of the 100 richest Canadians increased by 27 percent, while the average Canadian's income increased by only 1.1 percent (Paradis 2012).

These figures do not, however, consider the source of people's income; nor, because they are snapshots of income distribution at one point in time, do they take account of social and economic mobility (Grubel 2016). Common perceptions about income inequality in Canada are that the wealth of the 1 percent was obtained through exploitation of the poor, that "the rich get richer while the poor get poorer," and that the poor are trapped in their poverty. The reality, however, is that there is a high degree of economic mobility in Canada. Using data from Statistics Canada that tracked the changes in income of nearly 25 000 individuals over a 19-year period, from 1990 to 2009, Lammam et al. (2012) found that, while the rich are getting richer, so are the poor, and even more so than the rich. While individuals may start out in the lowest quintile, in subsequent years they move into higher income brackets and are replaced by new entrants into the workplace such as young people starting out in their careers, or new immigrants to Canada who typically have lower than average incomes for some time after their arrival (Grubel 2016).

At the beginning of their careers the majority of Canadians earn relatively low incomes, being paid near minimum wages at part-time and temporary jobs. As they gain more education and acquire job-related skills and life experience, however, their incomes increase and they move up the quintile ladder. Peak earning years occur in their 50s, after which it declines as they retire, although so do expenses as the children have left home and the mortgage has been paid off. Table 10.1 shows that, over

TABLE 10.1

Movement into Different Quintiles by Individuals (%) between 1990 and 2009

Where They Started (quintiles in 1990)	Where They Ended Up (percentage in each quintile in 2009)				
	Lowest	Second	Third	Fourth	Highest
Lowest	13	21	24	21	21
Second	9	21	27	23	19
Third	7	13	29	32	20
Fourth	6	8	15	35	36
Highest	7	6	7	16	64

Source: Lammam, Karagebovic, and Veldhuis. 2012: Table 7 p. 27

a 19-year period, 87 percent of people who started off in the lowest quintile moved up, including 21 percent of whom moved into the highest quintile. It also shows that over a third who started in the highest quintile dropped into a lower quintile over the same time period.

According to this study, only 13 percent remained in the lowest quintile or were permanently poor. The reasons for their failure to move up are varied and complex. They may not have finished high school or learned a trade; they may have been single parents for a considerable period; or they may suffer from physical or mental disabilities (Grubel 2016). Many may also live in areas with few employment opportunities, which is the case for many of Canada's Indigenous peoples.

Lammam et al.'s study shows that there is considerable income mobility in Canadian society, both up and down, and that our socio-economic status changes over our lifetimes. Moreover, these changes are due not so much to luck or historical or family circumstances, as to individual effort and perseverance.

The same cannot, however, be said of many other countries. The degree to which inequality is transmitted from generation to generation, that is, the degree to which children end up in the same socio-economic class as their parents or move out of that class, is known as intergenerational mobility. It depends on a number of factors in addition to hard work, including such things as demographics, family background, single parenthood, parenting skills, and time devoted to children (Corak 2012). Children from parents with higher incomes have greater opportunities than children from parents with lower incomes. Parents are more likely to have a better education, and have links and contacts in the community that can help their children obtain jobs, which will improve their future career prospects. Public policy also plays a part. In societies where education is compulsory for grade school, opportunities are equalized to a greater extent.

Canada actually has one of the highest levels of intergenerational mobility. In fact, Canadian society is more than three times as mobile as the United States (Corak 2012). In Canada, children are more likely to be living with both biological parents than in the United States, where there are more births to younger and less-educated mothers. In Canada, there is also a greater participation of mothers in the workforce as well as greater provision for child care. Child benefits as well as parental benefits are more generous in Canada than in the United States, where maternity benefits are much more limited. In other words, the public programs offered by the Canadian government are of relatively more benefit to the less well off, and allow for greater class mobility.

The situation in Canada and the United States contrasts starkly with other countries, however, where there are large income inequalities and little economic mobility. The rural population in China and the Indigenous populations in countries such as Peru, Brazil, and Chile, for example, as well as many Indigenous people in Canada, have limited opportunities to participate fully in the labour market, resulting in permanent income inequalities that divide society into relatively impermeable classes (Corak 2012).

Poverty in Canada

According to Food Banks Canada (2016), over 850 000 Canadians, over a third of them children, use a food bank each month. Approximately 13 percent of Canadians live with *food insecurity*, meaning they lack access to adequate, safe, good quality, and nutritious food necessary for an active healthy life. In 2015, 1.7 million different individuals were assisted by a food bank—and the number is growing. On any given night in Canada, approximately 35 000 Canadians are also homeless and have to find accommodation in shelters, with friends, in cars, or sleep out in the open (Table 10.2). According one study, during the course of a year over

food insecurity Lack of access to adequate, safe, good quality, and nutritious food necessary for an active healthy life.

TABLE 10.2

Homelessness in Canada in 2014

Category of Homelessness	Living Situation	Annual Number
Unsheltered	Sleeping rough, out of doors	5 000
Emergency Sheltered	■ Homeless emergency shelters ■ Violence against women shelters	180 000
Provisionally Accommodated	■ In institutional settings (prison, hospital) ■ In interim housing ■ Temporarily with friends or relatives, with no immediate prospect of housing	50 000
	Total	235 000

Source: Stephen Gaetz, Tanya Gulliver, & Tim Richter (2014): The State of Homelessness in Canada: 2014. Toronto: The Homeless Hub Press. Table 2, p. 42. http://www.homelesshub.ca/sites/default/files/SOHC2014.pdf.

© Benedicte Desrus/Alamy Stock Photo

FIGURE 10.5 **Scavengers dig for food waste to eat and items to sell at the Dandora dumpsite outside Nairobi, Kenya. The 30 acre site receives 2000 tonnes of unfiltered garbage daily, including hazardous chemical and hospital wastes, which, although a means of survival, is also harmful to their health.**

235 000 different Canadians experience a period of homelessness (Gaetz et al. 2014). Poverty is a global problem: it robs people of their dignity, prevents them from reaching their potential, shortens their lives, and costs societies billions (Figure 10.5). With so much wealth in the world it is also seen by many as inherently unjust. Policy makers throughout the world, as well as many national and international organizations, are devoted to eliminating it.

There are two ways to measure poverty: absolutely and relatively. ***Absolute poverty*** refers to inadequate access to the necessities of life, such as food, clothing, and shelter, to achieve a minimum level of physical well-being. Most people, when they think of poverty, think of it in absolute terms as a condition of serious deprivation, where people often go hungry, live in squalid conditions, or are homeless. ***Relative poverty***, on the other hand, refers to a situation in which some members of society are less well-off compared to other members of society. Relative poverty focusses more on one's relative position in the distribution of income than on the necessities of life. It defines the poor as lacking the things and opportunities considered normal by the society in which they live (Adamson 2012). Since it is relative, it always exists; as the average standard of living rises so does the poverty line. Measures of relative poverty tend to be higher than is needed to fulfill absolute needs. Canada does not have an official absolute ***poverty line***, that is, the threshold of income below which the basic necessities of life cannot be met.

The Canadian government does, however, calculate a measure of relative poverty: the Low Income Measure (LIM) in which the cut-off for poverty is half the median income. As a measure of relative poverty, LIM has widespread agreement and is used to make international comparisons (Adamson 2012). Sarlo (2013) argues that such relative poverty lines measure inequality rather than poverty, and that if our real concern is with exclusion and marginalization we should focus on absolute poverty rather than relative poverty. He also makes the point that an absolute measure is a better statistic to use in establishing policy and to see how the country is doing to really alleviate poverty. Consequently, he has developed a Basic Needs poverty line based on the income needed by a family of four (two adults and two children) to acquire a basket of basic necessities. According to this statistic, the basic needs poverty line for a household of four persons in 2009 was about $24 300, although with various child and tax benefits the actual income earned by the household to escape absolute poverty is approximately $15 200. Below this level of income, a family of four in Canada would have difficulty meeting its basic needs. Using this measure, the percentage of people living in absolute poverty in Canada declined from 6.7 percent in 1996 to 4.8 percent in 2009 (Lammam and MacIntyre 2016). Poverty has also decreased using a relative statistic, from 15.2 percent in 1996 to 9.7 in 2013 (Lammam and MacIntyre 2016). Some of this decrease can be attributed to public programs to alleviate poverty such as employment insurance, child benefits, tax credits, and government pension programs.

Relative measures of poverty are also used to make international comparisons, which can result in the misleading perception that there is greater poverty in rich countries such as Canada than in others where there may be little difference between the rich and the poor (i.e., low inequality) but where there is a high percentage of people living in absolute poverty. For example, according to a 2012 UNICEF report, Canada has a higher level of relative poverty than Cyprus, Slovenia, the Czech Republic, Ireland, Malta, and Slovakia, among others (Adamson 2012). Thus, a family living at the relative poverty line in Canada might have double the income of a family living at the median income in a country such as Hungary, Poland, or Portugal. Using a relative measure of poverty results in the poverty line of the 10 richest countries being higher than the median incomes of the 10 poorest countries (Adamson 2012). In other words, if the goal is to eradicate poverty worldwide, it is perhaps better to

absolute poverty The condition in a given society in which people lack the income required to access the necessities of life, such as food, clothing, and shelter, to achieve a minimum level of physical well-being.

relative poverty The condition in a given society in which people lack the minimum income required to obtain the society's normal standard of living.

poverty line The threshold of income below which the basic necessities of life cannot be met, or which is deemed adequate in a given country.

use absolute measures. The problems with relative measures have led to a call to supplement relative measures with an absolute measure of poverty (Adamson 2012).

For most low income people in Canada, poverty is a temporary situation; between 2002 and 2007, the average time spent in low income was 2.4 years (Lammam and MacIntyre 2016). Certain groups of people, however, are at greater risk of living in chronic poverty. They include those with less than high-school education, single parent families, persons with physical or mental disabilities, new immigrants, and Canada's Indigenous peoples (Sarlo 2013; Lammam and MacIntyre 2016).

According to a study by the Canadian Centre for Policy Alternatives and Save the Children, 50 percent of First Nations children live below the poverty line (Macdonald and Wilson 2013). And according to Whitzman (2010) nearly three-quarters of single Indigenous mothers live below the poverty line. While these figures use the relative LIM statistic, there is no denying that a large proportion of First Nations people live with chronic poverty in appalling conditions on reserves, and suffer from health issues, suicides, addictions, and violence. A great deal of this stems from the experiences of residential schools, which is discussed below.

Homelessness in Canada

Perhaps the most visible sign of poverty in Canada is *homelessness* (Figure 10.6). Homelessness can be defined as a situation in which an individual or family lack permanent, stable housing. It has been a significant and visible problem in Canada, particularly in inner city areas since the withdrawal of the federal government's investment in affordable housing in the 1990s, along with cuts to pensions and social assistance (Gaetz et al. 2014; Stock 2016).

A national survey by the Salvation Army (2011) found that about 40 percent of Canadians believe that those living rough on the streets do so out of choice. This may be true for a tiny percentage of homeless people, but the vast majority find themselves homeless for a host of reasons, many beyond their control; given the chance, they would move into permanent housing. Research on the causes of homelessness suggests that the primary reason for it is lack of affordable housing. Individuals and families paying more than 50 percent of their income on rent are at risk of homelessness. But other risk factors, such as discrimination because they belong to a marginalized group such as LGBTQ, First Nations, or a racialized minority, may also lead to homelessness. In addition, individuals with mental health issues, addictions, or a history of family violence may find it difficult to obtain a job, and thus housing. Homelessness is thus not simply about individuals but is a result of a society's response to marginalized populations (Gaetz et al. 2014; Stock 2016). While the causes of homelessness are varied, the solution is fairly simple: more affordable housing.

Frank Gunn/The Canadian Press

FIGURE 10.6 **A homeless man sleeps in front of the head offices of Canada's five major banks at the corner of King and Bay Streets in Toronto.**

One of the newest and most successful programs to find housing for homeless people is called Housing First (HF). The first step in getting people off the streets and out of homeless shelters is to move them into their own apartments. After that, other matters, such as health issues, finding employment, help with addictions, and counselling, are addressed to assist them to reintegrate into the community (Stock 2016).

About half the homeless population are males aged 25–55, while a significant number are also youth. Canada's Indigenous peoples are also overrepresented in the homeless population in most urban communities in Canada. In Winnipeg, for example, where approximately 10 percent of the general population are either First Nations, Métis, or Inuit, they comprise

homelessness A situation in which an individual or family lack permanent, stable housing.

anywhere from 55 to 70 percent of the homeless population (Gessler and Maes 2011). First Nations, Métis, and Inuit people also tend to be homeless for longer periods and experience more episodes of homelessness (Stock 2016).

One reason for the overrepresentation of First Nations people is that housing on reserves is often inadequate in terms of both quantity and quality. Houses on many reserves and in northern communities often lack drinkable water, proper sanitation, and adequate heating. Commonly, houses are poorly built, in need of major repairs, suffer from mould, are fire traps, and because they are not designed to meet the needs of larger families are often overcrowded. In addition, people living on these reserves and in these communities are often extremely poor, have high levels of unemployment, low levels of education achievement, suffer food insecurity, and have chronic health issues. It is perhaps not surprising then, that many leave for urban areas in search of better education and employment opportunities. Unfortunately, many of them, when they arrive in the city, lack the education, skills, and social contacts to find employment or a place to live. Moreover, due to the experiences of racism and the history of colonialism, many First Nations people feel uncomfortable working with non-Indigenous organizations, especially when the services offered may not be culturally appropriate (Stock 2016).

Status Symbols

Unlike race, where physical characteristics are used to categorize people, with social classes physical characteristics provide no clue as to what class a person belongs to. When it comes to class we are all basically anonymous. For many upper class people, however, it is important to let others know where they are situated in the social hierarchy. To do this they use ***status symbols***, which are cultural items that convey a person's status. Typically, we think of them as prestigious branded items such as the Rolex watch, the Bugaboo stroller, Louis Vuitton handbag, or the Mercedes, Bentley, or Rolls Royce parked in front of the triple garage door. All of them say to others "I can afford it" (Figure 10.7). Of course, for those who cannot afford these things, there are always counterfeit knockoff items that allow people to represent themselves as belonging to the upper class.

Status symbols change over time and as they become more ubiquitous they lose their ability to convey status. For example, in the 1500s when tea and sugar were being introduced into Britain, sugar was so expensive only the aristocracy could afford it, and black teeth became a status symbol. In the 1700s only the wealthy could afford sugar and tea, but they were still so expensive that they would lock them away in special canisters

status symbol Cultural item that conveys a person's status.

Raymond Boyd/Michael Ochs Archives/Getty Images

FIGURE 10.7 New Mercedes CLS Class cars sell for over $75 000 and are viewed as status symbols in many Western cultures.

and only drank tea with sugar when entertaining guests to impress (Mintz 1986). As the price of sugar dropped over time it ceased to be a symbol of high status and instead became symbolic of the working classes, as sugar constituted 25 percent of their daily caloric intake (Mintz 1986). When cellphones first appeared they were large and heavy, cost several thousand dollars, and conveyed high status until they became cheap. The iPhone when it first came on the market was also a status symbol.

Status symbols are culturally relative and do not always have to display position in the social hierarchy, nor do they have to be material items. For example, in many societies young boys who go through a rite of passage may be scarred to indicate to the rest of their society that they are now men.

Caste Societies

In contrast to class societies, those based on caste rank their members according to birth. Membership in castes is unchangeable; people in different castes are segregated from one another; social mobility is virtually non-existent; and marriage between members of different castes is strictly prohibited. Castes, which are usually associated with specific occupations, are ranked hierarchically.

Caste societies, wherever they may be found, have certain characteristics in common. First, caste membership is directly related to economic issues such as occupation, workloads, and control of valuable resources. The higher castes have a monopoly on high-status occupations, control the allocation of resources to favour themselves, and avoid engaging in difficult or low-status work. Second, members of the same caste share the same social status, residential and social segregation from other castes, and uniformity of lifestyles. Third, caste exclusiveness is further enhanced because each caste has its own set of rituals, which tend to intensify

CROSS-CULTURAL MISCUE

Johanna was an anthropology student on a fieldschool training program in Barbados, and was staying with a local family in the village of Pelican Hill when, one day, her homestay mother told her she had to move out. Johanna had been seeing a Rastafarian named Joseph who lived about an hour from town with a small group of Rasta who lived in caves, wore no clothes, and lived off the land. More importantly, some villagers had seen Johanna spending time with him. Rumours circulated that she had been bathing naked with the Rastas, and must also be a drug addict. The villagers viewed the Rastas as lazy marijuana smokers who stole from local gardens. Her homestay mother told her that, while Johanna would soon go home, she would have to remain in Pelican Hill and did not want her children to associate with the Rastas, and that Johanna's continued presence would ruin her reputation. Through the intercession of George Gmelch, her field supervisor, her homestay mother allowed her to stay, but the villagers stopped talking to her and local road workers harassed her and treated her as a sex object.

Coming from a society where class was unimportant, Johanna assumed that the Barbadian villagers were fairly homogeneous, and failed to realize the importance of social class in small-scale societies. The local villages had stereotyped views of the Rastafarian community, and she had violated local norms about which class of people it was acceptable to associate with. Gmelch also points out that Johanna failed to "understand the ethos and workings of life in a small-scale, face-to-face society where people pay close attention to the actions of neighbours, where gossip is recreation, and where, with the slightest provocation, rumour can affect a family's reputation (Gmelch 1995, 19). When conducting fieldwork it is important to be sensitive to how others view your actions.

group awareness and identity. Fourth, the higher castes are generally most interested in maintaining the caste system for the obvious reason that they benefit from it the most.

Caste societies can be found in a number of regions of the world, such as among the Rwandans in Central Africa, which consist of the Tutsi, who consider themselves the most superior, the Hutu, who outnumbered the Tutsi, and the Twa the smallest of the three groups (Maquet 1962). Traditional Japanese society was also a caste society with the emperor and nobles at the top, below which were four groups, or castes: samurai (who served the nobles), peasants, craftsmen, and merchants (Howell 2005). South Africa under Apartheid can also be consider a caste society. In all these cases the groups were largely endogamous and mobility between them was very limited.

Hindu Caste System

The best-known—and certainly the best-described—example of the caste system is in Hindu India. Hinduism's sacred Sanskrit texts rank all people into four categories, or castes, called *varnas*, which are also associated with certain occupations. Even though local villagers may not always agree about who belongs to which *varna*, most people accept the categories as fundamentally essential elements of their society.

According to a Hindu myth of origin (see Mandelbaum 1970), the four major *varnas* originated from the body of Purusha the primeval or cosmic man. The highest caste, the Brahmins (priests and scholars), came from his mouth; the Kshatriyas (warriors, kings, and governors) emanated from his arms; the Vaishyas (tradesmen, farmers, artisans) came from his thighs; and the Shudras (labourers and servants) sprang from his feet. Each of these four castes is hierarchically ranked according to its ritual purity (Figure 10.8).

Below these four castes—and technically outside the caste system—is still another category, called ***Dalit***, which means literally the *crushed* or *oppressed* people. The Indian government refers to them as Scheduled Castes. The Dalits, who comprise about 20 percent of India's population (Government of India 2011), used to be referred to as untouchables and were confined to the lowest and most menial types of work, such as cleaning latrines, sweeping streets, or disposing of animal carcasses (Figure 10.9). They are considered so impure that contact with them by members of the four legitimate castes is polluting and has to be avoided. To avoid contact, the other castes take elaborate precautions to prevent contamination, or perform elaborate rituals to purify themselves if accidental contact does occur. Contact is avoided by so-called ***untouchability practices*** such as segregation in housing and in schools, denial of access to temples, communal water taps, and healthcare. These practices have kept most Dalits in a state of poverty.

---

varnas Caste groups in Hindu India that are associated with certain occupations.

Dalit The lowest strata in Indian society, technically outside the caste system and formerly called untouchables.

untouchability practices Practices such as segregation and denial of access to community resources, which separate the Dalits from other caste groups.

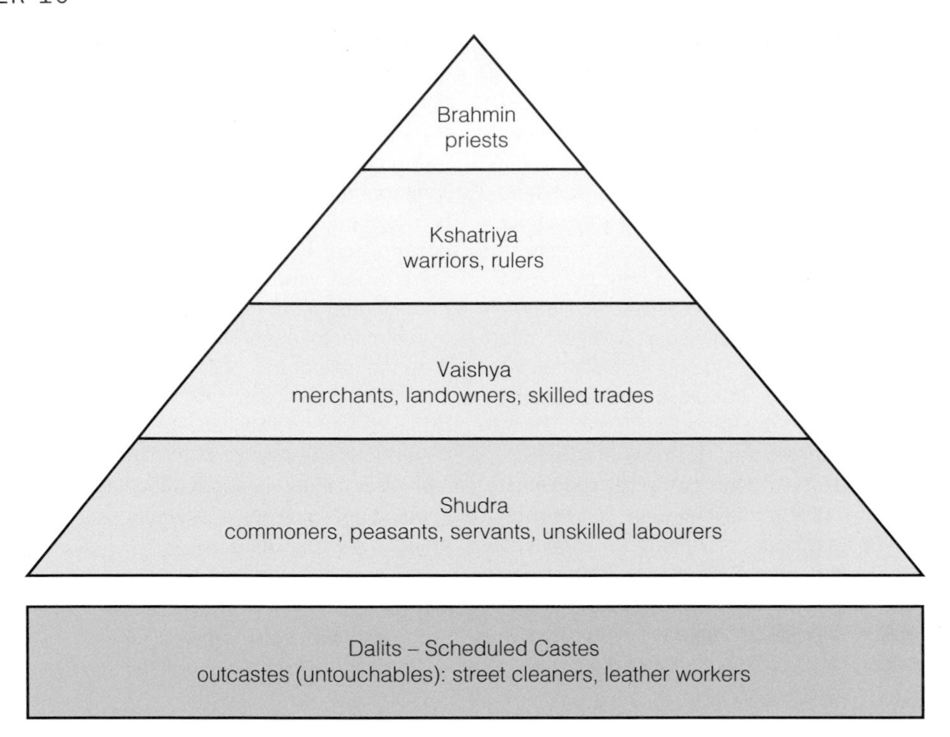

FIGURE 10.8 Hindu caste system.

FIGURE 10.9 The Dalits of India, such as these street cleaners, engage in only the lowest status jobs.

Dalit children are still segregated from higher castes in many schools (CHR&GJ and HRW 2007) and are often subjected to corporal punishment by their teachers and abuse from non-Dalit students. The Center for Human Rights and Global Justice and Human Rights Watch (CHR&GJ and HRW 2007, 13) point out that many

> higher-caste community members...perceive education for Dalits as both a waste and a threat. Their hostility toward Dalits' education—which includes discrimination against Dalit teachers—is linked to the perception that Dalits are not meant to be educated, are incapable of being educated, or if educated, would pose a threat to village hierarchies and power relations.

CHR&GJ and HRW (2007, 111) also note that residential segregation is still the norm rather than the exception:

> Under-educated, severely impoverished, and brutally exploited, Dalits struggle to provide for even their most basic daily needs. Dalits must also endure daily threats to their physical security from both state and private actors. The violence by upper-caste groups against Dalits have two major causes: the "untouchability" and discrimination upper-caste community members practise on a daily basis and the desire of upper-caste community members to protect their own entrenched status by preventing Dalit development and the fulfillment of Dalits' rights.

Traditionally, all of Hindu India was hierarchically ranked according to the four basic castes. In practice, however, each of these four categories is further subdivided and stratified. To add to the complexity of the Indian caste system, the order in which these subcastes are ranked varies from one region to another. These local subgroups, known as *jati*, are local family groups that are strictly endogamous. All members of a jati who share a common social status are expected to behave in ways appropriate for that jati. A person's jati commands his or her strongest loyalties, serves as a source of social support, and provides the primary basis for personal identity. Thus, the jati is the important social entity in traditional Hindu society.

Although the prohibitions against social intercourse among castes are rigidly defined, the amount of interdependence among local castes should not be overlooked. This interdependence is largely economic in nature rather than social. In fact, one of the basic features of caste in traditional India is that each jati is associated with its own occupation that provides goods or services for the rest of the society. Certain lower-caste jati (such as barbers and potters) provide vital services for the upper castes from which they receive food and animal products. Thus, despite the extreme social segregation among the castes in India, there is considerable economic interrelatedness, particularly at the village level.

Even though intercaste mobility has always been limited in India, there have been increasing instances in recent years of people moving up the caste ladder. The process, known as *Sanskritization*, involves taking on the behaviours, practices, and values associated with the Brahmin caste, such as being a vegetarian, giving large dowries for daughters, and wearing sacred clothing associated with Brahmins. According to Pauline Kolenda (1978), people accomplish this type of upward mobility by acquiring considerable wealth and education, migrating to other parts of the country, or becoming political activists. The process of Sanskritization is motivated less by the desire to imitate higher caste values and behavioural patterns than it is an expression of dissatisfaction with the lack of social mobility and socioeconomic deprivations of the caste system.

One aspect of Sanskritization is known as *hypergamy*, or "marrying up." Most people marry within one's social class or caste, often simply because people tend to associate with people of the same class. However, through hypergamy women can marry into a higher social status. By marrying their daughters into a powerful or influential higher caste family, people can raise their social status and increase their opportunities. Hypergamy offers people in rural India, for instance, a chance to move to the city. By sending the bride's younger siblings to the city where there are better jobs and opportunities, the entire family can benefit (Barber 2004). It does, however, usually come at the cost of a big dowry.

Caste still plays an important part in the lives of many Indians, especially in rural areas. But things are changing. In urban areas the traditional caste system's influence is diminished, and people have greater freedom to choose whom they marry or to choose their own career. Modernization has also resulted in the emergence of many new occupations, such as computer engineer, airplane pilot, newscaster, and so on, that are not linked to the traditional caste occupations. Companies, especially multinational corporations, are also more likely to hire and promote based on qualifications and merit rather than caste affiliation.

The Constitution of India, which came into effect in January 1950, outlawed untouchability practices and Dalits now receive preferential treatment through a quota system whereby positions in higher education and government jobs are reserved for them. Discrimination and harassment of Dalits still continues, however, and acts such as the Scheduled Castes and Tribes (Prevention of Atrocities) Act, 1989, which were meant to prevent atrocities against them, have been largely ineffective. The Center for Human Rights and Global Justice and Human Rights Watch (2007) point out that, despite the legislation, many Dalits still face a "lifetime of discrimination, exploitation and violence, including severe forms of torture perpetrated by state and private actors" (p. 2), and that the police have done little to protect them, and in many cases are the perpetrators. Thus, although government jobs are reserved for them, they are often assigned jobs as sweepers or other traditional Dalit occupations (CHR&GJ and HRW 2007).

European Roma

Numbering between seven and nine million people, the Roma (derogatorily called gypsies) of present-day Europe are a migratory version of Indian Dalits. Linguistic and genetic evidence indicates that the Roma originated on the Indian subcontinent about a thousand years ago as low-caste Hindus and subsequently migrated westward, through Persia, into the Balkans, and eventually throughout all of Europe. Wherever they arrived in Europe, they were met with hostility and discrimination. In Romania they were enslaved for nearly 500 years, whereas elsewhere in Europe they were either expelled or subjected to forced labour. It is estimated that during World War II the Nazis murdered several hundred thousand Roma as part of their deliberate program of genocide. Under the Communist regimes of Eastern Europe, Roma experienced serious restrictions

---

jati Local subcastes found in Hindu India that are strictly endogamous.

Sanskritization A form of upward social mobility found in contemporary India whereby people born into lower castes can achieve higher status by taking on some of the behaviours and practices of the highest (Brahmin) caste.

hypergamy The practice of marrying someone from a higher social strata.

Thomas Trutschel/Photothek via Getty Images

FIGURE 10.10 Shabby huts of a Roma settlement on May 28, 2015, in Belgrade, Serbia. More than 300 Roma live here in inhumane conditions.

of cultural freedom. For example, the Romany language and Romany music were banned from public performance in Bulgaria, and in Czechoslovakia Romany women were sterilized as part of a state policy of ethnic cleansing.

Most Roma live in inadequate housing in squatter settlements without potable water, proper sewage treatment, garbage collection, or reliable electricity (Figure 10.10). Hatred and discrimination against the Roma are widespread across Europe; in one study 77 percent of Slovaks said they had hostile feelings toward them (Scheffel 2004). They also tend to have low levels of education and high levels of unemployment. In the town of Sivinia, Slovakia, Roma and ethnic Slovak children are physically separated at school and follow two different education streams (Scheffel 2004). In an unusual multinational initiative, however, 12 central and southeastern European countries with significant Roma populations (Albania, Bosnia and Herzegovina, Bulgaria, Croatia, Czech Republic, Hungary, Macedonia, Montenegro, Romania, Serbia, Slovakia, and Spain) have pledged to close the gap in welfare and living conditions between the Roma and non-Roma populations. Started in 2005, the initiative—called "Decade of Roma Inclusion"—provides state funds to improve housing, employment, health, and education among Roma populations. Although the eight participating governments are appropriating sizable funds to provide more and better social services, reports of systematic discrimination against the Roma are still commonplace. For example, in eastern Slovakia the Roma continue to live in deplorable conditions, with four of every five adults suffering the effects of poverty, unemployment, and alcoholism. Residents of one Slovakian town (Ostrovany) have erected a seven-foot-high concrete wall separating their homes from a Roma ghetto (Bilefsky 2010). It will be interesting to see whether a multinational (or regional) approach to eliminating a long-standing underclass of people will be successful.

CROSS-CULTURAL MISCUE

Most Canadians, when they need to take a taxi, typically get in the back seat if they are alone or as part of a couple. If there are more people it is the last person who sits in the passenger seat next to the driver. Cab drivers also prefer this for safety reasons. If you follow this norm in Australia and New Zealand, however, you are likely to be taken the long route to your destination or have the cab driver make some snide comment, as it is considered rude to sit in the back seat if you are alone. In Australia, proper etiquette is to sit up front next to the driver. Australians pride themselves on being a classless society, and sitting in the back implies that you are somehow better than the driver, who then becomes like a chauffeur. A single woman getting in the back also implies that they expect the driver to molest them. So, if you don't want to be called a rude Canadian (or American), get in the front seat of cabs in Australia and New Zealand (and also Scotland and the Netherlands).

Race and Ethnicity

We all know people look different and we have no difficulty telling whether a person, or their ancestors, come from China, India, Norway, or Kenya. Our judgement would be based largely on the colour of their skin, the shape of their eyes and nose, their type of hair, and also perhaps the clothes they wear or the way they speak. We may even refer to them as Asian, South East Asian, European, and African. But are these differences racial differences? And what if we compared people from India and Pakistan, Norway and Germany, China and Korea, or Kenya and Tanzania? There are physical and cultural differences between each of these pairs but are they races? Until the mid-20th century most North Americans considered Irish and Italian to be distinct races (Chen and Hamilton 2012). What is race? And how many races are there—if any?

Over the past few decades we have heard about racial and ethnic differences leading to inequality, discrimination, antagonism, and conflict in various parts of the world. Race is thus one of the most controversial issues today, scientifically, socially, and politically. Even anthropologists cannot agree on what it is.

Biologists use the concept of race to refer to a geographically and hence reproductively isolated population of a species. It is often used synonymously with the term subspecies. Given enough time and continued isolation, they would develop into separate species. Human populations, however, have never been reproductively isolated long enough to have developed into biological races. For the most part, whenever groups of people have encountered one another they have interbred. Most anthropologists today thus do not consider

Immigration and Discrimination in Canada

Canada is a land of immigrants. Except for about four percent of the population who are Indigenous, most Canadians or their not-too-distant ancestors, have all come from somewhere else. Canada has one of the most liberal immigration policies in the world, and numerous surveys have shown that most people are in favour of maintaining or increasing Canada's emphasis on immigration (Reitz and Banerjee 2007). Prior to 1970 most new immigrants to Canada came from Europe. In the 1970s, however, the pattern changed and, increasingly, people arriving in Canada came from Asia, Southeast Asia, and Africa. In the 1970s, 51.8 percent of new immigrants were visible minorities; in the 1980s this figure was 65.4 percent; and in the 1990s, 75 percent (Reitz and Banerjee 2007). In 1971, the *Multicultural Policy of Canada* made Canada the first country in the world to adopt multiculturalism as an official policy (CRRF 2014), even though at the time less than one percent of the population were a visible minority (Reitz and Banerjee 2007). Today, that figure sits at 20 percent (CRRF). Most new immigrants now come from China, India, the Philippines, and Africa, and settle in the major cities, especially Toronto and Vancouver.

The result is that Canada is now a racially and ethnically diverse society—a truly multicultural society. Multiculturalism can be viewed as a project where the goal is to respect and accommodate diversity in ways that promote equality and justice (Kivisto 2012). According to a survey by the Canadian Race Relations Foundation (CRRF)—a charitable organization "dedicated to the elimination of racism and all forms of racial discrimination in Canadian society"—Canadians overwhelming support multiculturalism and hold human rights, freedom, and equality as their most important values (CRRF 2014). Most Canadians like to think of themselves as living up to those values and as a welcoming and accepting of new people. And most believe racial discrimination in Canada is minimal (Reitz and Banerjee 2007).

But are Canadians that accepting, and do immigrants have the same rights and freedoms and equal opportunities that most have? In June 2015, eight bus stop benches in Nanaimo, British Columbia, featuring Chinese real estate agents were spray painted with such hateful phrases as "Go away" and "Not Welcom [sic]." One bench had a swastika painted over a photograph of the realtor (Bassi 2015). In January 2016, Calgary schools were defaced with anti-Muslim graffiti, and in March 2016, several Syrian refugees were attacked with pepper spray at a welcome event in Vancouver (Kanji 2016). While perhaps isolated events, 64 percent of respondents to the CRRF (2014) poll said that cultural practices had to be compatible with Canadian laws and norms, and nearly half (46 percent) said the government should discourage these practices. One-third said that religious dress such as burqas, hijabs, and turbans should be prohibited in public places and security settings (CRRF 2014). In sum, most Canadians expect newcomers to adapt to Canadian norms, so it appears they are not that accepting after all. In the Ethnic Diversity Survey conducted by statistics Canada in 2002, recent immigrants were asked if they had, within the past five years, "experienced discrimination or been treated unfairly by others in Canada because of your ethnicity, race, skin colour, language, accent, or religion?" (Reitz and Banerjee 2007). Over one third (35.9 percent) said yes and reported experiences of discrimination. The highest rate was for Blacks, at 49.6 percent (Reitz and Banerjee 2007).

Between July 2014 and July 2015, police in London, United Kingdom, reported 816 assaults on Muslims, an increase of 70 percent from the year before (Kanji 2016). There also seems to be a "growing number of extremists lashing out publicly at Muslim immigrants" (Patriquin 2016); one study discovered at least 100 right-wing extremist groups in Canada, which are more active than previously thought and many with ties to European groups (Perry and Scrivens 2016).

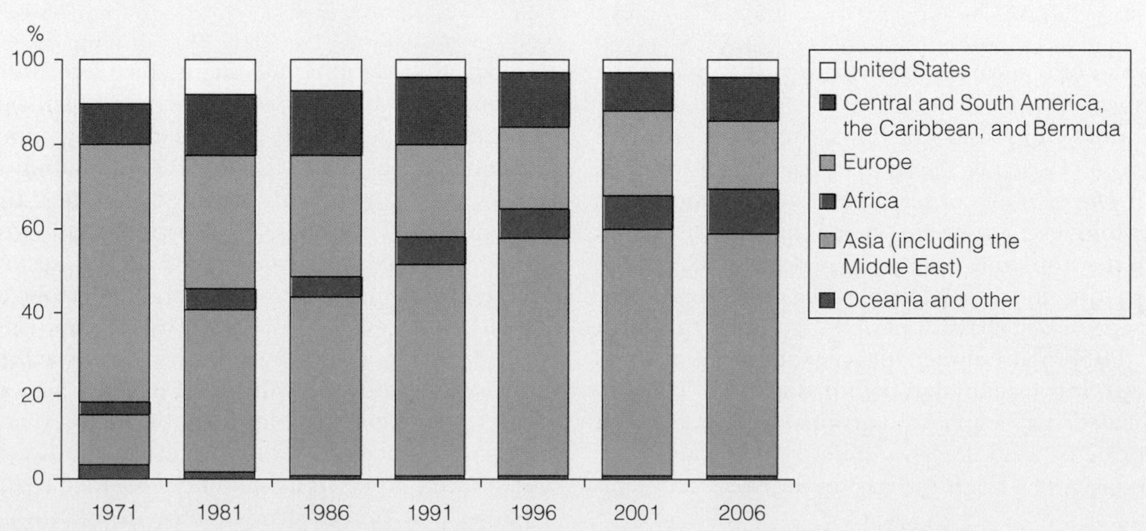

Region of birth of recent immigrants to Canada, 1971 to 2006

Source: Statistics Canada, Censuses of Population, 1971 to 2006. "Figure 2 Region of birth of recent immigrants to Canada, 1971 to 2006."

(*Continued*)

Immigration and Discrimination in Canada (*Continued*)

In addition to ethnic and racial discrimination, new immigrants to Canada also face a number of hurdles of a more structural nature that make them one of the poorest segments of Canadian society. The poverty rate for visible minorities in Canada is nearly twice that of the general population (Reitz and Banerjee 2007). The biggest issue for new immigrants is finding adequate employment. When they come to Canada, many are highly skilled and find their education qualifications and skills are not accepted, while those of native-born Canadians are. In regulated industries, such as engineering, medicine, and pharmacy, or skilled trades such as plumbing and electrical work, standards and entry into the profession are controlled by provincial and territorial laws as well as professional governing bodies, which set standards and require practitioners to obtain licenses or certificates (Hall and Sadouzai 2010). Civil engineers, for example, must be licensed to sign a construction plan. New Canadians find it difficult to find employment in these higher paying occupations, as well as government positions. Many find upon arrival that their educational qualifications from some of the best universities in the world are not accepted. They then spend upward of five years to acquire the proper certification at a high cost, while earning little, only to find that they lack significant Canadian experience (Narang 2012).

This is in addition to other hardships faced by new immigrants. Many have little or no income, no credit history, have difficulty finding housing, lack a social support network, and are ineligible for state benefits (Koning and Banting 2013). The result is that many doctors, engineers, chartered accountants, and other well-educated professional people pick up "survival jobs" as janitors, grocery clerks, taxi drivers, hospital porters, casino workers, and so on (Narang 2012). Many work in these jobs for years simply hoping for a better life for their children. Many leave. One study found that 40 percent of immigrants who entered Canada as skilled workers left the country within their first 10 years—half of those within the first year (Roy 2012).

Reitz and Banerjee (2007) point out that when diversity results in inequality, it not only undermines the sense of fairness and inclusion in society but also weakens cohesion in society and commitment to common values and amicable social relations, which affects the country's ability to pursue common objectives. Although not reflected so much in violent conflict as in other countries, it is evident in such things as a lack of a Canadian identity, sense of belonging (especially for visible minorities), lack of participation in decision-making, low voter turnout, low life satisfaction and trust, and low uptake of Canadian citizenship (Reitz and Banerjee 2007). This also extends to second generations.

How can anthropology be applied to make it easier for new immigrants to Canada, especially visible minorities, to integrate into Canadian society and feel more accepted? To begin with, anthropologists can make policy recommendations on such things as immigration, employment, human rights, housing, and multiculturalism. Multiculturalism is the centrepiece of interethnic relations, but its focus is broad and lacking in detail and specific goals and objectives (Reitz and Banerjee 2007).

Questions for Further Thought

1. How has immigration transformed Canada into an ethnically diverse nation?
2. What is the value of having a multicultural society?
3. What are the challenges facing new immigrants as well as the country as whole in creating an inclusive and equal society?
4. What policy recommendations would you make to meet these challenges?

races, in the biological sense of distinct divisions of the human species, to exist.

This does not, and has not, however, stopped people from classifying the human species into groups based on ***phenotype***, or observable characteristics, such as skin colour, eye colour and shape, hair texture, nose shape, and so on, and calling them "races." Generally speaking, the more noticeable the difference the more it is used to classify people. Because the most obvious difference between people other than sex is skin colour, it is usually skin colour that is the primary basis of classifying people into groups called races. But to select one or a few highly visible traits to categorize people is not a very scientific way to understand human biological variability. A major problem with racial classifications is that the criteria for classification are arbitrary. For example, instead of using skin colour, we could easily divide the world's population into two major races: those with attached earlobes and those with detached earlobes, or into right- and left-handed races. If people were categorized according to earlobe shape rather than skin colour, they would be assigned to different categories. Each physical trait is biologically determined by genes that vary *independently of one another.* Therefore, having dark skin in no way determines what your eye colour will be, or whether you are right- or left-handed. As the American Anthropological Association noted in its statement on race (AAA 1998), "These facts render any attempt to establish lines of division among biological populations both arbitrary and subjective."

phenotype Observable physical characteristics.

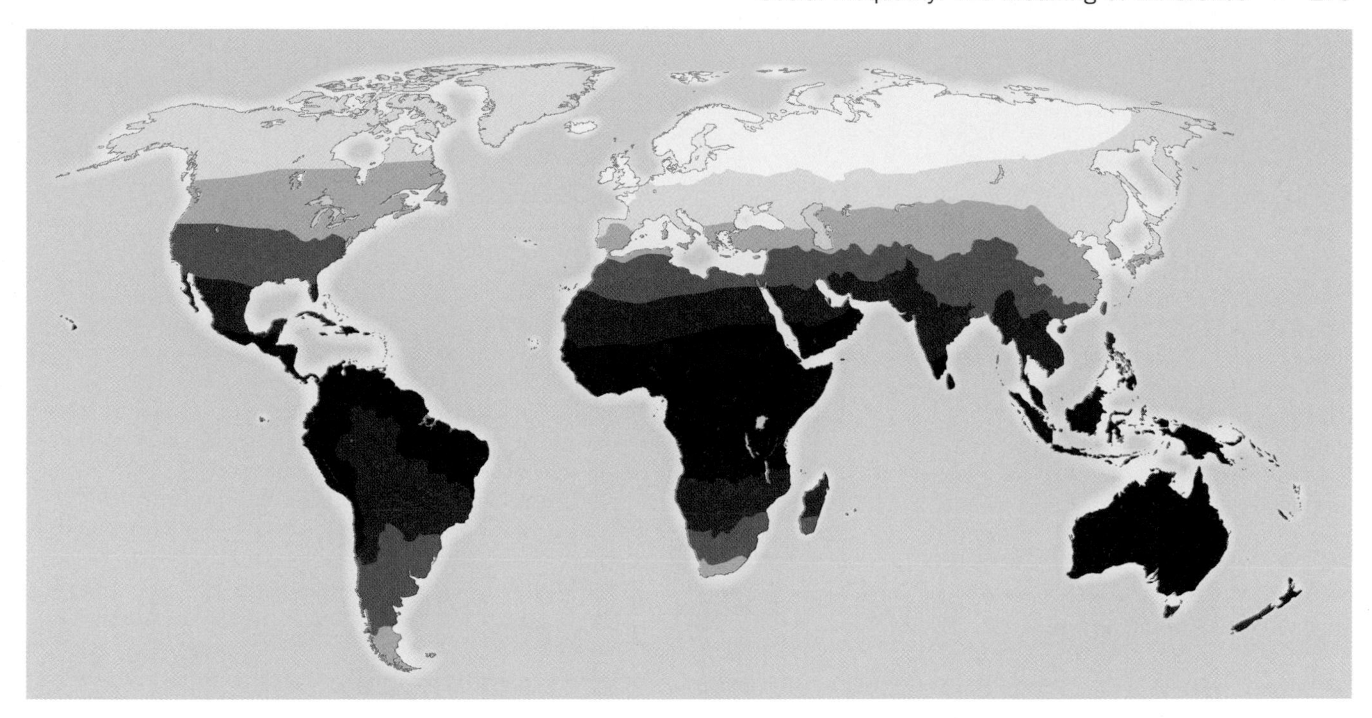

FIGURE 10.11 **Map of Indigenous skin colours. Skin colour is an adaptation to the amount of ultraviolet light.**

Source: Emmanuelle Bournay, UNEP/GRID-Arendal of Vital Ozone Graphics, http://www.grida.no/graphicslib/detail/skin-colour-map-indigenous-people_8b88.

Most phenotypic traits exist because they are adaptive. Skin colour, for instance, is a function of the amount of the pigment melanin produced in a lower layer of the skin. People with dark skin have more of the pigment than people with light skin. Melanin is produced in organelles called melanocytes, and ultraviolet radiation causes them to produce more melanin, causing the skin to darken. Melanin absorbs and disperses the radiation and is thought to protect the skin from radiation damage and thus reduce the risk of skin cancer (Brenner and Hearing 2008). Many studies have shown that darker-skinned people have lower rates of skin cancer than lighter-skinned people (Brenner and Hearing 2008).

The skin is also where vitamin D is produced—also under the stimulation of ultraviolet radiation. Dark skin, however, interferes with this process. There are few sources of vitamin D in people's diets, except for fish and eggs, and so adequate sunlight is essential. Vitamin D is necessary, however, for proper bone development as it helps them absorb calcium. People with vitamin D deficiency may suffer from a range of conditions impairing their health, including rickets, a debilitating disease where the bones do not mineralize properly and become soft and that can lead to skeletal deformities. In children, rickets can lead to pelvic deformities that can impair reproduction (Yuen and Jablonski 2010). This means that people with dark skin in higher latitudes, where there is less ultraviolet radiation, are at an adaptive disadvantage compared to people with light skin. It is now generally accepted that vitamin D deficiency has provided a selective pressure for lighter skin. In other words, lighter skin was selected for in northern latitudes as it allows for the production of vitamin D and prevents rickets, whereas in southern latitudes darker skin is more adaptive as it absorbs ultraviolet radiation and prevents skin cancer. If we look at a map of skin colour distribution we can see that there is a continuum from the darkest skin in the tropics to the lightest skin in the northern latitudes (Figure 10.11). This raises the question of deciding where to draw the line between one race and another. Whatever decision is made, however, it will be arbitrary. It also means potentially there could be hundreds of races if one decided to base them on finer shades of colour.

There are also far more differences between people that are unobservable than observable. If we compare a map of the distribution of blood type O (Figure 10.12) with that of skin colour (Figure 10.11), we see that there is no correlation between the two, which there should be if human races were as distinct as many assume. Most human variation is within "races" rather than between them. Only about 6 to 10 percent of the variation is between groups (Jorde and Wooding 2004). In another words, if you took a group of people selected from a single continent it would account for about 90 percent of the total genetic variation, whereas only 10 percent more variation would be accounted for if you took a collection of people from Europe, Asia, and Africa (Jorde and Wooding 2004).

Basing race on skin colour also leaves open the question of how to classify the increasing number of "multiracial" people. Most people, for instance, would say that the pro-golf player Tiger Woods is African American or black. Yet, from his mother's side Tiger Woods is one-quarter

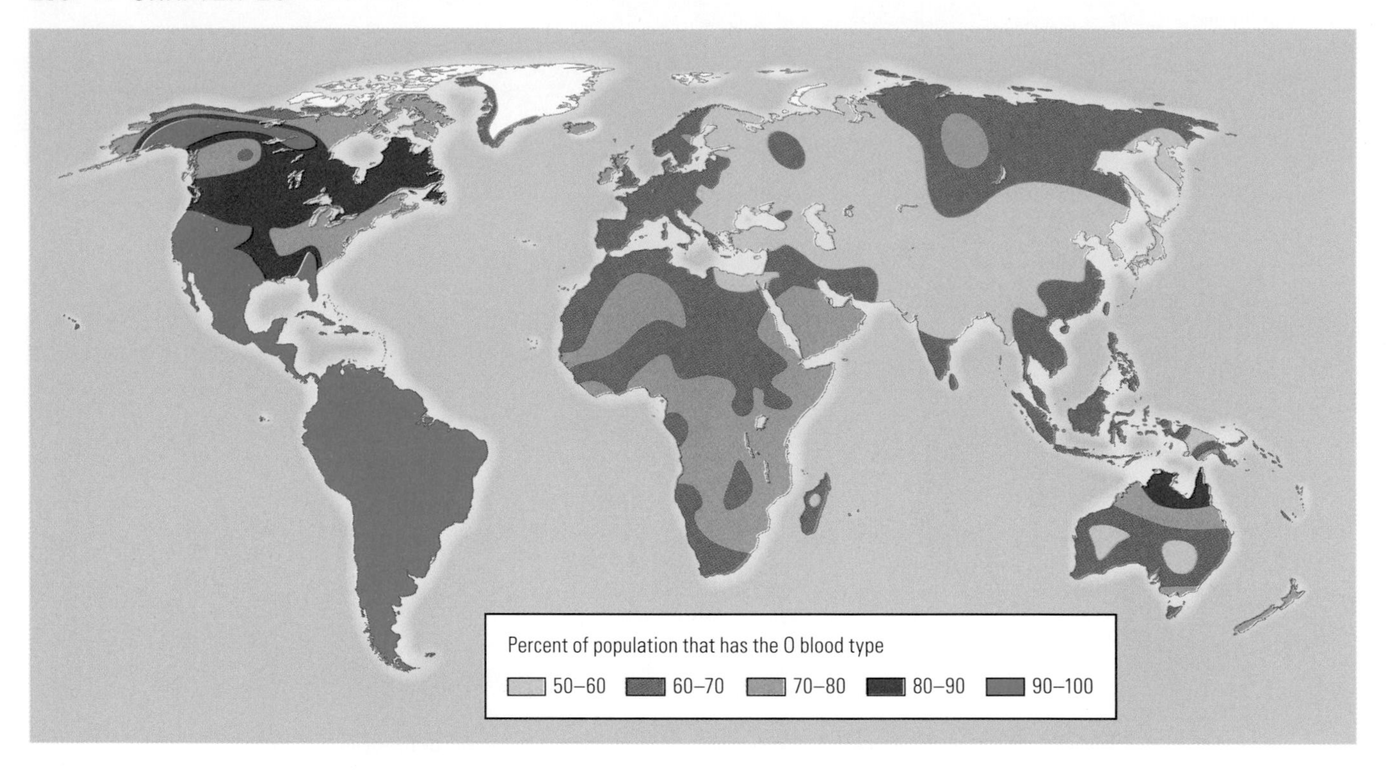

FIGURE 10.12 Distribution of blood group O. Compare this with the map of the distribution of skin colour.

Source: From Mourant, A.E. Ada C. Kopec Kazimiera Domaniewska-Sobczak. 1976. The Distribution of the Human Blood Groups and Other Polymorphisms, published by Oxford University Press. CC BY 2.5.

Chinese and one-quarter Thai, and from his father's side he is one-quarter African American, one-eighth Native American, and one-eighth Dutch (New Netherland Institute). He refers to himself as "Cablinasian": "Ca" for Caucasian, "bl" for black, "in" for American Indian, and the rest Asian. Similarly, U.S. President Barak Obama, who is often referred to as America's first African American or black president, comes from a mixed racial background. His father is Kenyan, of the Luo tribe, while his mother's ancestry is English, Scottish, Irish, German, Welsh, Swiss-German, and French. Technically, one could say he is biracial—half black and half white. But why is he referred to as black?

In the United States, even though a person may appear to be white, they only need to have one ancestor who was black to be considered black. In the southern United States, it was important, under slavery and later under the Jim Crow segregation laws, to know what race a person belonged to. Given the wide range of skin colour, however, it was not always easy to tell, and so some states adopted what came to be known as the "***one-drop rule***" (Figure 10.13). If you had one drop of "black blood" then you were considered black (Davis 2001). For example, in 1982, Susie Phipps discovered that her birth certificate indicated that she was "colored" yet she had lived her life as a white person. She sued the state of Louisiana to have it changed to "white," but it turned out she was the great-great-great-great-granddaughter of a black slave who had married a Frenchman. According to a 1972 Louisiana state law, any one with at least 1/32 "Negro blood" was black. Thus she was legally black and lost the case (Brown 2010). Anthropologists refer to this as ***hypodescent***, which is the assignment of a child from a mixed race, ethnic group, or other social group to the inferior or lower status group (Harris 1964).

The point of the one drop of blood rule was to exclude blacks from voting and running for political office, to determine who was eligible to ride in train seats reserved for whites, and to prevent ***miscegenation***, or interracial marriages and interbreeding (Davis 2001). It was not until 1967 that it was legal in the United States to marry someone of a different race, and not until 2000 that children of such marriages were allowed to self-designate on the U.S. national citizenship registry (Roth 2005). The "one-drop rule" has become enshrined in U.S. law and is used by judges and affirmative action groups to promote policies of inclusion through legislation, and even the white supremacist group the Ku Klux Klan uses it to determine who is black (Davis 2001). Race is entered on U.S. Standard Certificate of live birth, although there are no guidelines as to how race is determined. Some state courts have upheld the rule.

one-drop rule A rule, and in many U.S. States a law, that if a person had one ancestor who was black, typically one great-great-great-great-grandparent, then they too were considered black.

hypodescent The assignment of a child from a mixed race, ethnic group, or other social group to the inferior or lower status group.

miscegenation The marriage or interbreeding of people considered to be of different races.

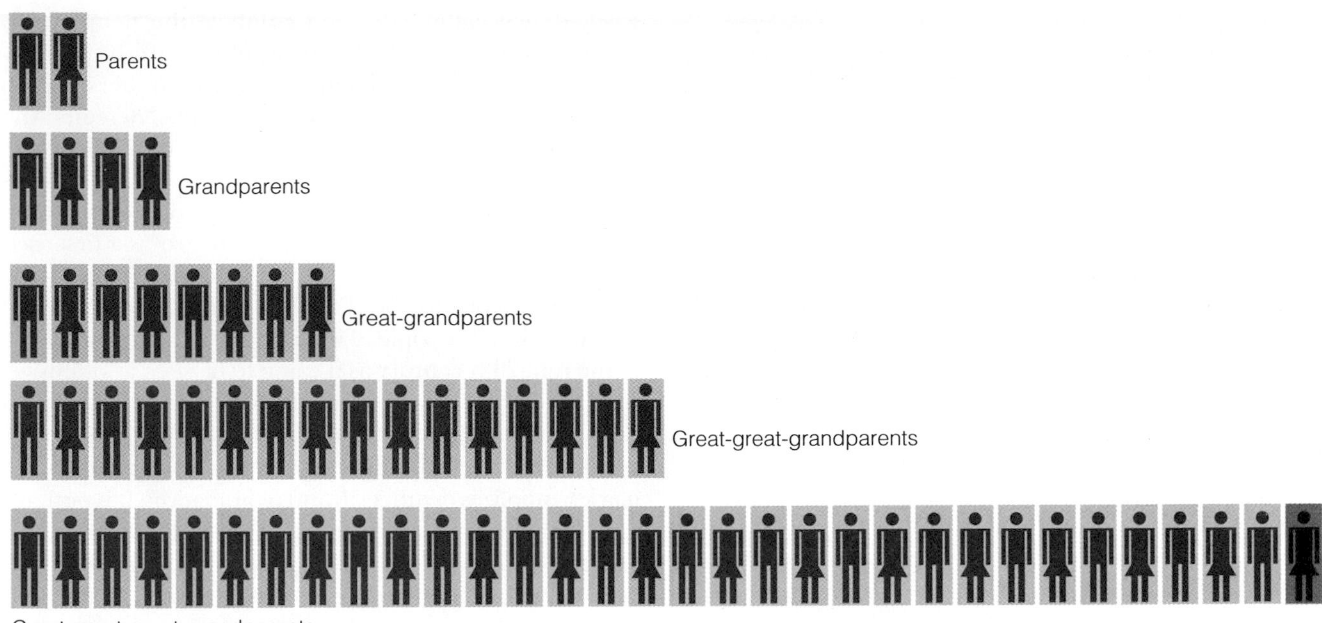

FIGURE 10.13 **According to the "one-drop rule," even if only one of your great-great-great-grandparents was black, then so are you.**

In other words, a person in the United States is both legally and socially defined as black.

Many anthropologists and other scientists have not abandoned the concept of race as it does have some practical applications (Whitmarsh and Jones 2010). This is particularly true when looking at issues of race and health. Many studies have shown a correlation between race and certain medical conditions. Indigenous people in Canada, for instance have higher rates of diabetes, cancer, high blood pressure, and other conditions than non-Indigenous people, and although most of these differences can be attributed to culture, some scientists attribute them to race (Abu El-Ha 2007). Forensic anthropologists also find it useful to classify skeletons according to race (Whitmarsh and Jones 2010; Brown 2010).

From the above discussion it should be clear that defining race is anything but clear. It should also be clear, however, that societies do classify people into categories, usually based on skin colour, and call them "races," although such terms as "black," "white," "Asian," "Hispanic," and so on, do not refer to genetically distinct branches of the human species. The American Anthropological Association considers them to be the product "of historical and contemporary social, economic, educational, and political circumstances" (AAA 1998). What matters is not so much the physical differences between groups of people per se, but what those differences mean, and how people relate to them. Racial groups are assigned significance by society and by governments, and the categorizations are important in people's lives, shaping both private and public interactions. Race is thus the institutionalization of physical difference.

A Brief History of Race and Racism

A better understanding of what race is and what it is not can be obtained by looking briefly at the history of the concept. While the ancient Greeks associated physical differences with cultural differences, and saw themselves as the first among civilized nations, they did not link these differences with skin colour (Brown 2010). Thus, they viewed the light-skinned people to the north as barbarians, while they granted civilized status to the Nubians (Sanjek 1998). The Nubians lived along the southern Nile valley and were perhaps the darkest-skinned people the Greeks knew. The Greek historian Herodotus called them "the tallest and most attractive people in the world" (Sacks and Brody 2005, 66). Medieval Europeans viewed humans as being arrayed in a great chain of being, and ranked different groups of people into higher and lower groups. These groups were seen as unchangeable and as God's divine plan. But again, the categories were not linked with skin colour.

The modern idea of race began to emerge in the early 1500s as Europeans began to explore and colonize the world and encounter and interact on a large scale with people with different skin colours. In the mid-1500s people were categorized into groups according to skin colour, and each "race" was thought to have a specific temperament: The Indigenous peoples of the Americas, with red skin, were savage and warlike; Africans, with black skin, were lethargic and slow witted; yellow-skinned Asians were cunning and devious; while white-skinned Europeans were reflective and rational (Brown 2010).

In the 1700s the differences between such "races" became a focus of scientific interest. In 1735 the Swedish naturalist Carolus Linnaeus the father of taxonomy,

Ann Ronan Pictures/Print Collector/Getty Images

FIGURE 10.14 **Johann Friedrich Blumenbach theorized that humans could be divided into five racial types: American, Mongolian, Caucasian, Ethiopian, and Malayan. This view was widely accepted from the late 1700s until the mid-20th century.**

set out to scientifically classify all the plant and animal species in the world using a binomial system of naming. Based primarily on skin colour, and also linked with temperamental characteristics, he classified humans into four groups or subspecies of descending behaviours and abilities: Europeans (whites), Asians (yellows), Indians (reds), and Africans (blacks) (Brown 2010). In 1779 German naturalist and anthropologist Johann Friedrich Blumenbach expanded on the work of Linnaeus using skull measurements, and divided the human species into five races: Caucasian, Mongolian, Malayan, Ethiopian, and American. His scheme acted as the standard of racial classification for nearly 200 years (Figure 10.14).

When the Europeans encountered "the other" they did not do so on equal terms. They were far superior technologically and militarily, which allowed them to easily defeat, subjugate, and colonize the people they encountered. In 1532, for example, Spanish conquistador Francisco Pizarro, along with 168 soldiers and 50 horses, and armed with cannons and guns, defeated the Incan emperor Atahuallpa and his army of 80 000 at the Battle of Cajamarca (Diamond 1997).

What struck the Europeans most forcefully were differences in skin colour. The word "negro" was first used in the mid-1500s and was derived from the Spanish and Portuguese word for black (OED), and came to refer to all dark-skinned people. The term fell out of general use in the mid-20th century as it came to be seen as offensive. Black and white are emotionally loaded concepts in most European languages, especially English. They are polar opposites: white symbolizes goodness and purity, while black symbolizes death, evil, and degradation. It is perhaps not surprising that, coupled with their military advantage and the colour of their own skin, that Europeans viewed themselves as endowed with superior intellectual and moral characteristics, and the people they encountered as inferior. By the late 1600s the superiority of Europeans was evident in all colonial societies.

A common belief at the time was that the races were immutable, or unchanging, and that they thus had separate origins, a view known as *polygenesis*. *Monogenesis*, on the other hand, was the idea that there was a single origin but that the races had degenerated into their current states. Polygenesis, in part, justified the enslavement of the dark-skinned races by the lighter-skinned European races. Slavery was widespread before 1500 but for the most part the slaves were physically indistinguishable from their owners. Most slaves came from within their own society or from neighbouring groups, which meant that, when freed, they could easily blend in with the rest of the population, unlike the African slaves imported into the Americas and Europe (Sanjek 1998).

One of the main polygenesists was Samuel Morton. By the 1840s Morton had collected nearly 700 skulls of known racial origin (Brace 2005). He went about measuring the cranial capacity of each of the skulls by plugging up all the holes, filling the skulls with lead shotgun pellets, and then pouring the pellets into a beaker to obtain the cranial capacity in cubic centimetres. His results indicated that the Africans and Australian Aborigines had the lowest cranial capacity and Europeans the highest, with the other races in between (Gould 1981). The obvious implication was that the larger the cranial capacity, the larger the brain, and thus the more intelligent. Paleontologist Stephen Jay Gould later reanalyzed Morton's skulls and at first got opposite results before realizing that, in his desire to prove Morton wrong, he had biased his results. When he measured the skulls without knowing their racial identity he found that the measurements overlapped.

Morton's work provided what was thought of as scientific proof of the biological inferiority of certain races. It was this sort of evidence that fuelled the *eugenics*

polygenesis The theory that human races have multiple origins.

monogenesis The theory that human races have a single origin.

eugenics Ideas and practices aimed at improving the genetic quality of a population.

movement. Eugenics is a set of ideas and practices aimed at improving the genetic quality of a population. It involves promoting increased reproduction by people with desired traits (e.g., intelligence) by providing them with incentives, and attempts to limit the reproduction of people with undesirable traits (low intelligence, criminals, people with deformities and disabilities, or simply undesirable groups) through such things as forced sterilization or prohibition on certain groups marrying. The term was coined by British anthropologist, geneticist, and statistician Francis Galton, who also coined the phrase "nature versus nurture." During the early decades of the 20th century eugenics was an academic discipline, and many governments, including Canada, not only funded research but also carried out eugenics programs. For instance, between 1928 and 1972, 2835 people were sterilized, many against their will, under the 1928 Alberta Sexual Sterilization Act. In the latter years nearly 25 percent of those sterilized were Indigenous people (Grekul et al. 2004; Grekul 2011). British Columbia had a similar program. Several U.S. states also passed sterilization laws. California alone sterilized 20 000 people between 1909 and the 1960s (Stern 2005). The eugenics movement was most associated with Nazi Germany and the Holocaust, where nearly six million Jews were murdered. After World War II the idea was generally abandoned.

Many anthropologists in the late 19th and early 20th centuries thought that biological race, language, and culture were intimately connected. It was Franz Boas who perhaps did the most to dispel this idea. By using biological anthropology techniques he demonstrated that the head shape among Eastern European and Western European immigrants, who were subject to a quota system, were not due to race, or language, but were separate (Boas 1912; Sanjek 1998). By the 1960s the idea that one could divide the human species into five or any number of races came under attack in anthropology, and that racial categories were arbitrary and that race was a cultural construct (Sanjek 1998).

Race and Intelligence

It is quite apparent that some people are smarter than others, but is intelligence linked to race? The concept of race has been used to suggest that non-Caucasians are biologically inferior to Caucasians in terms of ability, character, and particularly intelligence. Before the 1920s it was generally thought, even among those in the scientific community, that intelligence, or one's innate, mental ability, varied according to race. Most researchers, however, do not put much stock in intelligence tests as measures of some innate level of genetic intelligence. The AAA (1998) in its statement on race and intelligence affirmed that intelligence is not biologically determined by race. Intelligence tests are, however, accurate measures of how well an individual has mastered his or her mainstream cultural knowledge, or at least the cultural knowledge deemed important by those middle- and upper-middle-class psychologists who construct the test questions. Middle- and upper-class children, in other words, who share a cultural background with the authors of the tests are likely to achieve higher scores than children who do not. The result of including such culture-bound questions on the test is that the lower-class child loses several points of intelligence and his or her wealthier classmate gains several points. Yet this is hardly a measure of innate brain power. Rather it simply reflects that these two groups of children learned different cultural content, even though they could have learned it with relatively equal efficiency.

Despite this, the connection between intelligence and race continues to be controversial. In a provocative paper, which initiated much of the current debate on race and intelligence (Hunt and Carlson 2007), American psychologist Arthur Jensen (1969) argued that supplementary education programs for black and disadvantaged children had failed because the differences between black and white children were due to genetics. In 2007 James Watson, one of the co-discoverers of the structure of DNA, said in an interview in *The Sunday Times Magazine* that he was "inherently gloomy about the prospect of Africa" because "all our social policies are based on the fact that their intelligence is the same as ours—whereas all the testing says not really" (Dean 2007). The reaction from the scientific community was swift. His talk at the London's Science Museum the following day was cancelled and he lost his job at the Cold Spring Harbor Laboratory.

As we have seen, genetic differences resulting in skin colour differences do not map neatly onto genetic differences resulting in different hair type, eye colour, or skull measurements. The same is true for intelligence. Whatever genes result in intelligence (and whatever that may be), they vary independently of skin colour.

Ethnicity

Ethnicity is sometimes confused with race. Whereas race involves physical traits, ***ethnicity*** involves cultural traits that are passed on from generation to generation. Ethnicity is thus an identity that is based on a person's cultural heritage, the language spoken, the religion and traditions followed, and can include a person's race. Ethnicity, however, is also based on self-identification. A person born in Canada to Chinese parents, who speaks Chinese, eats Chinese food, and follows Chinese traditions, may very likely consider themselves to be Chinese. But if they grow up in Canada speaking English or French, eating Canadian food, and following Canadian traditions, they may identify themselves as simply Canadian.

---

ethnicity The linguistic and cultural characteristics and heritage a person identifies with.

An *ethnic group* is a group of people who perceive themselves as sharing many of the same cultural features and heritage. Ethnic group members have a sense of ethnic identity whereby they define themselves and members of their group as "us" and everyone else as "them."

Although the Canadian government does not collect information on "race," or "ethnicity" (It claims to have stopped collecting information on ethnicity in 2009, although the 2011 National Household Survey (NHS) does ask about a person's ethnic or cultural origins.), it does collect information on *visible minorities,* who are "persons, other than aboriginal peoples, who are non-Caucasian in race or non-white in colour" (Employment Equity Act). Under the Canadian Constitution Act, 1982, Aboriginal peoples are defined as Indians, Inuit, or Métis. On the long-form census, respondents are asked to check whether they are white, south Asian (e.g., East Indian, Pakistani, Sri Lankan), Chinese, Black, Filipino, Latin American, Arab, Southeast Asian (e.g., Vietnamese, Cambodian, Malaysian, Laotian), west Asian (e.g., Iranian, Afghan), Korean, Japanese, or Other, in which case they have to specify. The point of collecting this information is "to support programs that promote equal opportunity for everyone to share in the social, cultural, and economic life of Canada" (Employment Equity Act).

More than 200 ethnic groups were reported on the 2011 NHS, which also includes First Nations, Métis, and Inuit, as well as European groups such as the English, French, Scottish, and Irish. Over 19 percent, or about 1/5th of respondents, identified themselves as belonging to a visible minority group, two-thirds of whom were born outside Canada (Statistics Canada 2013b). Due to the changing patterns of ethnic immigration over time, coupled with the original Indigenous diversity, Canada has become a truly *multicultural society*, that is, a society consisting of people from different ethnic, religious, and racial backgrounds.

The Canadian government sees multiculturalism as a national asset that "encourages racial and ethnic harmony and cross-cultural understanding," where "Canadians are free to choose for themselves, without penalty, whether they want to identify with their specific group or not." And while it promotes the idea that "all citizens can keep their identities, can take pride in their ancestry," it also advocates a sense of belonging (Citizenship and Immigration Canada 2015b). So while it celebrates cultural diversity, it simultaneously encourages newcomers to integrate. Multiculturalism is not without its critics, however, who argue that it creates ethnic enclaves whereby many new immigrants settle among others from their ethnic group, which encourages them to maintain their differences rather than developing a shared Canadian identity (Todd 2010). Others claim that by embracing a multiplicity of identities Canada has no core cultural identity (O'Connor 2012).

ethnic group A group of people who share many of the same cultural features and heritage.

visible minorities People in Canada, other than Aboriginal (Indigenous) peoples, who are non-Caucasian in race or non-white in colour.

multicultural society A society consisting of people from different ethnic, religious, and racial backgrounds.

discrimination The practice of treating individuals differently simply based on the group (e.g., gender, sex, age, ethnic group) they belong to.

Discrimination, Racialism, and Racism

Discrimination

Discrimination is the practice of treating individuals differently based on the age, sex, race, or ethnic or religious group they belong to rather than to individual merit. Although technically a neutral concept, discrimination has taken on a negative connotation. Generally, it means denying or restricting members of one group equal access to the opportunities and privileges (i.e., wealth, power, and prestige) reserved for another.

Many governments recognize this is as unjust and have passed legislation making discrimination an offence. In Canada it is known as equal opportunity. The purpose of Canada's Human Rights Act (1985), for instance, is to ensure

> that all individuals should have an opportunity equal with other individuals to make for themselves the lives that they are able and wish to have and to have their needs accommodated, consistent with their duties and obligations as members of society, without being hindered in or prevented from doing so by discriminatory practices based on race, national or ethnic origin, colour, religion, age, sex, sexual orientation, marital status, family status, disability or conviction for an offence for which a pardon has been granted.*

The purpose of the Employment Equity Act (1995) is to

> achieve equality in the workplace so that no person shall be denied employment opportunities or benefits for reasons unrelated to ability and, in the fulfilment of that goal, to correct the conditions of disadvantage in employment experienced by women, aboriginal peoples, persons with disabilities and members of visible minorities by giving effect to the principle that employment equity means more than treating persons in the same way but also requires special measures and the accommodation of differences.**

*Canadian Human Rights Act (R.S.C., 1985, c. H-6)

**Employment Equity Act (S.C. 1995, c. 44)

Employers normally hire according to qualifications, but if all else is equal, then they should hire someone from one of the above groups, and may hire only Aboriginal people if the "employer is engaged primarily in promoting or serving the interests of aboriginal peoples" (Employment Equity Act).

In an effort to right past injustices and reverse social inequalities, some governments pass legislation and/or establish quotas that can lead to ***reverse discrimination***, where the dominant group is denied access to opportunities and privileges in favour of the subordinate group. Examples of reverse discrimination when it comes to employment may include hiring or promoting women solely on the basis of gender, or hiring a non-white person regardless of experience or qualifications.

An example of reverse discrimination occurred in November 2005, when the deputy minister of Canada's Public Works instructed managers in an email to temporarily hire only visible minorities, women, Aboriginal people, and the disabled, and not to hire "Caucasian males" as the department had failed to meet its targeted employment-equity goals (World Net Daily 2005). Another example of reverse discrimination nearly occurred in Nova Scotia in 2011 when Carole Nixon, a white Anglican minister, was hired as executive director of the Africville Heritage Trust. Africville was an African Nova Scotian community in Halifax settled by former U.S. slaves in the 1800s. The community was neglected by the city and residents struggled with poor health conditions and poverty as their houses continued to deteriorate (Figure 10.15). In the mid-1960s the city evicted the residents, relocated them to better housing, and bulldozed Africville. Africville has become a symbol of black Canadians' identity and their fight against racism. In 1996 it was designated a National Historic Site, and in 2010 the Africville Heritage Trust was established (Africville Genealogical Society 2010). The Trust was set up to establish a memorial, and some members of Nova Scotia's black community were outraged that a white person had been hired for the position. A town meeting was organized, calling for her resignation, and a flyer distributed demanding the Trust cancel her appointment. Nixon had a certificate in black history from the University of Toronto plus other experience that made her the best qualified candidate (Mellor 2011). The six members of the trust's board of directors who were representatives of the Africville community, did not give in to the demands of the community. Nixon kept her job. Reverse discrimination of members of majority groups is equally unjust and unfair as it is to individuals of minority groups. Both ignore individual characteristics and qualifications.

Photographer: Bob Brooks. Reference no.: Bob Brooks NSARM accession no. 1989-468 vol. 16 /negative sheet 6 image 31/Nova Scotia Archives

FIGURE 10.15 Africville residents did not receive the water and sewer services provided to other Halifax residents. The city demolished the community in the mid-1960s.

Racialism

Race is the idea that the human species can be systematically classified into discrete groups based on physical characteristics. A closely related concept is ***racialism***. Racialism is the idea that race determines specific characteristics and capacities such as intelligence, moral habits, and cultural characteristics, and that some races are superior to others. In other words, racialism leads to racial stereotypes. First Nations people, for instance, are often negatively stereotyped as alcoholics, drug addicts, and as "wards of the state" (Loppie et al. 2014). Unfortunately, these demeaning stereotypes are often perpetuated by the media and internalized and accepted as true by First Nations people, which lowers their self-esteem and damages their sense of identity (Harding 2006).

Racism

Racism is a type of discrimination whereby people are treated differently based on the race they are deemed to belong to. Racism is thus based on the racialist belief that one race is better than another and uses this belief to discriminate against the inferior or lower status group. Racism is made evident in the hatred, prejudice, antagonism, and fear of members of one group toward members of another. It has significant material effects on people's lives, and is manifested by attempts, whether overt or covert, by some members of the superior group to keep the subordinate group from obtaining the wealth, power, and prestige reserved for their group.

Perhaps the person who best understood what racism is and its impact on people's lives was civil rights activist Martin Luther King Jr. who, in his famous "I have a Dream"

---

reverse discrimination Treating members of the dominant group differently in an effort to remedy previous discrimination against members of subordinate groups.

racialism The idea that race determines specific characteristics and capacities such as intelligence, and that some races are superior to others.

racism A type of discrimination whereby people are treated differently based on the race they belong to.

speech, said: "I have a dream that my four children will one day live in a nation where they are not judged by the colour of their skin but by the content of their character" (King 1963). Racialism thus ascribes a person's character, values, convictions, morals, and ideology to their genetic heritage (i.e., race)—something they can do nothing about—while racism discriminates against them because they are different from the society's dominant group.

More than anything else, perhaps, racism is an experience. While anthropologists can understand the causes and implications of racism, it is hard for them to experience racism unless they really become "the other," as John Griffin's story demonstrates. Racism is acutely felt by Canada's Indigenous peoples. In one study, 38 percent of First Nations adults claimed they had experienced at least one instance of racism in the past year (Loppie et al. 2014).

Structural Racism

Racism is also exhibited in a subtle form called *structural racism*, whereby the institutions and systems of society are structured such that they privilege the dominant group while the subordinate group is disadvantaged or discriminated against. In other words, racism is built into the structure of the society. For example, in areas such as education, housing, law, employment, and so on, it is the dominant group in society that has the power to make and enforce decisions, has access to the resources, sets the norms of behaviour, and provides the accepted view of reality. For instance, the Canadian justice system is structured so that it favours mainstream Canadian society, and discriminates against marginalized groups. In 2013, 23.1 percent of inmates in Canadian federal prisons were either First Nations, Métis, or Inuit, yet they constitute only 4.3 percent of the Canadian population (Office of the Correctional Investigator 2013). It is even higher for Indigenous women, who represent more than a third (33.6 percent) of all federally sentenced women in Canada. In some prisons in Manitoba and Saskatchewan, two-thirds of the prisoners are Indigenous. Not only is the incarceration rate for Indigenous adults about 10 times higher than for non-Indigenous adults, but also it is increasing. There are a number of reasons for this, but as a judgement in one case noted, "The excessive imprisonment of aboriginal people is only the tip of the iceberg insofar as the estrangement of the aboriginal peoples from the Canadian criminal justice system is concerned. As this Court recently noted (...), there is widespread bias against aboriginal people within Canada, and... [t]here is evidence that this widespread racism has translated into systemic discrimination in the criminal justice system" (The Supreme Court of Canada R. v. Gladue 1999).

structural racism Where the institutions and systems of society are structured such that the subordinate group is disadvantaged or discriminated against.

racial profiling The discriminatory practice of targeting a person for reasons of safety, security, or public protection based on a stereotype of their race, ethnicity, religion, or place of origin.

Racial Profiling

One aspect of racism is known as *racial profiling*, a discriminatory practice whereby a person is targeted for reasons of safety, security, or public protection based on a stereotype of their race, ethnicity, religion, or place of origin (OHRC 2003). The most visible forms of racial profiling occur when a person is stopped by the police and questioned, searched, or arrested on suspicion of committing some offence solely on the basis of their race or ethnic group. It can, however, involve other actions, for example refusing to serve a customer, hire a person, or rent someone an apartment based on beliefs about the ethnic group they belong to.

In many cities in Canada, police routinely stop people and ask them to volunteer personal information about their age, gender, race, ethnicity, where they live, and who they associate with. People have a right to refuse to give this information but, once provided, it is stored in police databases. Police claim the process, known as carding, helps them fight crime, but it has received a great deal of negative publicity because visible minorities seem to get disproportionately carded (Soupcoff 2015). An analysis of 1.7 million contact cards completed by Toronto police officers between 2003 and 2008 indicated that black people in Toronto are three times more likely to be stopped and "carded" by police than white people (Rankin 2010). Other ethnicities were also targeted disproportionately.

First Nations people in Canada also seem to be the victims of racial profiling. The Ontario Human Rights Commission heard numerous stories of First Nations people stopped and questioned by storekeepers, security guards, transit employees, and police for no other reason than that they were Indigenous. One story, for instance, involved a First Nations man out walking with his friend one morning when he was stopped and accused by police of stealing the bicycle he had with him because he could not produce a bill of sale. The result of such racial profiling is not only fear, humiliation, and frustration in trying to obtain some service, but also lack of trust and hatred toward police officers, and a belief that all police officers are racists (OHRC 2003).

Ethnic Cleansing and Cultural Genocide

Racism can perhaps be viewed as a continuum. At one end it is expressed in the form of insults, workplace discrimination, and violence; Indigenous men for instance are two to three times more likely to experience violence from others than non-Indigenous men (Brownridge 2010). At a more extreme level is *ethnic cleansing*, which is the systematic and forced removal of an ethnic or religious group from a given geographic area, usually by a more powerful group in order to make it religiously and/or ethnically homogenous. Ethnic cleansing itself can take many forms. It can involve forcible migration of people out of a territory or intimidation so they leave, by confiscating their lands, and destroying their homes, places of worship, businesses, and so on. Good examples of this are the expulsion of Jews and Christians from many countries in the Middle East, and more recently the forced migration of many different ethnic groups from Syria. Ethnic cleansing can also involve cultural genocide, or ethnocide, where the language, traditions, spirituality, and culture is systematically suppressed and extinguished so that the group is assimilated into the majority or mainstream population. Perhaps the best example of this is the attempted assimilation of Canada's First Nations people through the use of Indian Residential Schools (discussed below). At its most extreme, ethnic cleansing involves *genocide*, whereby an entire group of people is exterminated. The best known examples are the extermination of Jews in Europe during World War II by Nazi Germany, the murder of Armenians in what is now Turkey by the Ottoman Empire during World War I, and the massacre of nearly 1 000 000 Tutsis by Hutus, in Rwanda in 1994. Canada also has a history of genocide. In the mid-1700s Edward Cornwallis, the founder of Halifax, placed a bounty of 10 guineas on the scalps of every Mi'kmaq man, woman, or child (O'Connor 2011). And Jeffrey Amherst, after whom Amherst Nova Scotia is named, is implicated in the distribution of blankets infected with smallpox to the Indigenous peoples around Fort Pitt (now Pittsburgh) in 1763 (Fenn 2000).

Residential Schools and Cultural Genocide

From the 1880s until 1996, when the last government-run Indian Residential School, the Gordon Residential School in Saskatchewan, closed, the federal government, in collaboration with various churches, operated 139 Indian Residential Schools (INAC 2016a). The purpose of these schools was to get First Nations children to abandon their Indigenous identity and assimilate into the dominant Euro-Canadian Christian society (Truth and Reconciliation Commission 2015). They operated under the assumption that European civilization and Christianity, which were essentially the same thing, were superior to Indigenous culture and religion, which were deemed as savage and brutal. As Indian Affairs Deputy Minister Duncan Campbell Scott said in 1920, "our object is to continue until there is not a single Indian in Canada that has not been absorbed into the body politic, and there is no Indian question, and no Indian Department" (Truth and Reconciliation Commission 2015). As the Truth and Reconciliation Commission note, this is a good definition of cultural genocide.

First Nations children, as well as a many Inuit and Métis children, were taken from their families, often forcibly, to live in residential schools most of which were situated in remote locations. When children first entered a school, their heads were shaved and they were given a number that was sewed into all the clothes issued to them by the school to replace their traditional clothing (Truth and Reconciliation Commission 2015). Siblings were separated and they were forbidden to speak their mother tongue; traditional spiritual practices were banned, as were their cultures in general. Buildings were often cold, draughty, poorly built, and poorly maintained; the staff were poorly trained and underqualified; the food was meagre and of poor quality; daily life was highly regimented and discipline was harsh. The teachers as well as the curriculum materials demeaned and denigrated their culture; some books referred to First Nations people as "redskins" and the women as "squaws." Many children were neglected as well as abused, emotionally, physically, and sexually. The First Nations children were thought to have a low mental capacity and so educational expectations were low. From 1940–41 to 1959–60, 41.3 percent of children in Grade 1 were not promoted to Grade 2 (Truth and Reconciliation Commission 2015); few made it to Grade 12. Because most of the schools were underfunded, they attempted to be financially self-sufficient and operated on a half-day system where half the day was spent on lessons—with a heavy emphasis on religion—and half the day on vocational training; boys' work focused on agricultural jobs and girls' on domestic chores. The children were also exposed to fatal diseases such as tuberculosis, and many died. The Truth and Reconciliation Commission was created as part of the Indian Residential Schools Settlement Agreement, which resolved the class action suits brought against the federal government and the churches by survivors of Residential Schools for the abuses they received.

The immediate result of the Residential School experience was loss of language and loss of Indigenous spirituality, loss of culture, and overall a loss of their identity. Graduates of the schools also lost not only the skills necessary for their traditional economy, but also the skills required to obtain wage labour; many could barely read or write. While the apologies given by the various churches, and in 2008 by Prime Minister Stephen Harper, along with compensation for abuses, and the work of the TRC go a long way to help heal the damage done, it will take decades

---

ethnic cleansing The systematic and forced removal of an ethnic or religious group from a given geographic area in order to make it religiously and/or ethnically homogenous.

genocide The systematic murder of an entire group of people.

to overcome the inter-generational trauma caused by the Indian Residential School experience. With one foot in mainstream culture and one in their traditional culture, survivors belong to neither. Receiving abuse rather than love they also did not acquire the parenting skills to raise their own children, but taught them what they knew. Much of the violence, the poverty, the mental and physical health problems, and the substance abuse that Canada's Indigenous people face today are a direct result of the Residential School experience. It is thus not surprising that they are overrepresented in the criminal justice system and among the homeless, and that they mistrust the government and are reluctant to deal with non-First Nation associations.

The Indian Act

Racism stereotypes people and then treats them as if they meet the stereotype. A good example is the Indian Act of 1876. In his 1876 annual report of the Department of the Interior, the minister, David Laird, in proposing the Indian Act (Laird 1876, 12-13), said

> Our Indian legislation generally rests on the principle, that the aborigines are to be kept in a condition of tutelage and treated as wards or children of the State. ...the true interests of the aborigines and of the State alike require that every effort should be made to aid the Red man in lifting himself out of his condition of tutelage and dependence, and that is clearly our wisdom and our duty, through education and every other means, to prepare him for a higher civilization by encouraging him to assume the privileges and responsibilities of full citizenship.*

This clearly paternalistic statement rests on the stereotype that Canada's Indigenous peoples were like children. It is also aimed at assimilating them into mainstream society by eliminating their culture. In 1876 most people did not see the Indian Act as racist, after all it was considered the "***white man's burden***" to help them reach and enjoy the benefits of a civilized state. The reality was that it assumed control over the lives of First Nations people and still does. Under the Act, including its many amendments, First Nation peoples were not allowed to practise ceremonies such as the Potlatch or Sundance, had to ask permission before appearing in traditional costume in any public show or exhibition, and were prevented from raising funds to process a legal claim against the government. The Indian Act also dictated how First Nations were to run elections for their chiefs, how they could spend their money, and who could and who could not live on reserves. The Act also gave the government the power to expropriate portions of a reserve for roads, railways, or agriculture; move communities if they were too close to towns; and dictated when they could sell their produce and at what price. Until 1960, the Indian Act also denied First Nation people the right to vote, or sit on juries, unless they voluntarily gave up their Indian status.

To administer the Act, Indian agents were appointed to oversee affairs on reserves. They had considerable power to regulate the lives of First Nations people. They could determine who was an Indian and member of a band and entitled to the benefits, acted as the justice of the peace, forced parents to give up their children to send them to Residential Schools, suppressed religious practices, restricted people to the reserves unless they were given a pass, and took over much of the decision-making power of bands. It is not surprising that they were widely despised; it was not until 1969 that Indian Agents ceased to exist (Cumming and Ginn 1986).

The Indian Act is a good example of the power of the state to define who a person is. According to the Act, an Indian is "a person who pursuant to this Act is registered as an Indian or is entitled to be registered as an Indian." Beginning in the mid-1800s Indian agents made lists of First Nations people and the bands they belonged to in order to determine who was eligible for treaty and other benefits. In 1951 the government created a national register from these lists, which is now maintained by Indigenous and Northern Affairs Canada (INAC). Such "Registered Indians," also referred to as a "Status Indians," are entitled to a range of programs and services unavailable to non-status persons offered by federal agencies and provincial governments (INAC 2016b). For instance, those with status receive on-reserve housing as well as education benefits. Registered Indians also do not pay federal or provincial taxes on personal property on the reserve, or income tax on money earned on the reserve (INAC 2016b). To make it easier to obtain these services, INAC issues a status card to those desiring one (Figure 10.16).

Deciding who is eligible to be registered has changed several times. For decades, a status woman who married a non-status man lost her status, as did any children born after marriage—a process called ***enfranchisement***. A status man, on the other hand, did not lose his status if he "married out" (i.e. if he married a non-status woman), although he could lose it if he managed to enter a professional occupation. Under the Constitution Act of 1982, however, enfranchisement became illegal as it was discriminatory to women. In 1985 *Bill C-31, An Act to Amend the Indian Act*, reinstated

*Employment Equity Act (S.C. 1995, c. 44)

white man's burden The 19th century belief that it was the white man's obligation to raise so-called "savages" to a civilized cultural state.

enfranchisement The loss of Indian status.

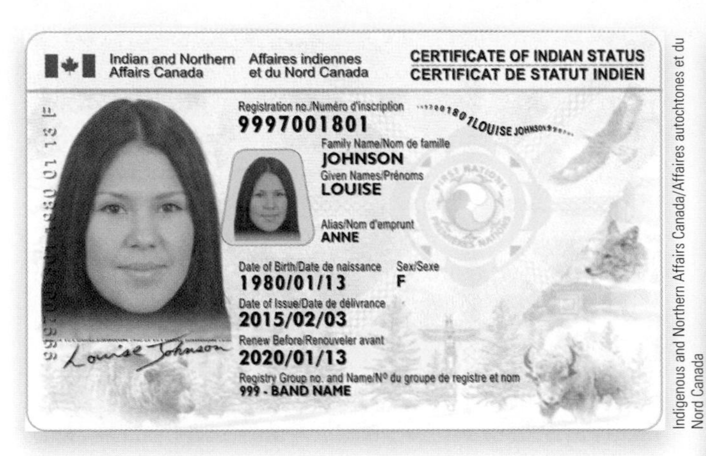

Indigenous and Northern Affairs Canada/Affaires autochtones et du Nord Canada

FIGURE 10.16 Certificate of Indian Status issued by Indigenous and Northern Affairs Canada to any person who desires one and is on the department's list of registered Indians.

Nathan Denette/The Canadian Press

FIGURE 10.17 Houses on the Attawapiskat reserve in Northern Ontario. Many homes in First Nation communities are overcrowded and suffer from mould. About 40 percent of homes on reserves need major repairs.

status to those women who had been enfranchised and also dictated that children born to parents and grandparents both of whom had "married out" could not obtain status. This still proved to be discriminatory, however, since the grandchildren of women who regained their status did not have status, whereas the grandchildren of their brothers did. This was rectified by Bill C-3, the *Gender Equity in Indian Registration Act*, which came into effect in 2011.

There have been several attempts to abolish the Indian Act, the most well-known was made in 1969 by Jean Chrétien, then Minister of the Department Indian Affairs and Northern Development (DIAND) (now Indigenous and Northern Affairs Canada (INAC)). Recognizing the discriminatory nature of the Act, his infamous "White Paper" proposed, among other things, abolishing the Act and Indian Status, dissolving DIAND, settling all outstanding land claims, and converting the reserves to private property (Chrétien 1969). Ironically, most of the opposition to the White Paper came from First Nations leaders, who viewed its abolition as the final step in assimilation. Harold Cardinal (1969) in a response to the paper wrote, "In spite of all government attempts to convince Indians to accept the white paper, their efforts will fail, because Indians understand that the path outlined by the Department of Indian Affairs…, leads directly to cultural genocide. We will not walk this path" (p. 139).

While the Indian agents have gone and many of the Indian Act's more discriminatory paragraphs repealed, it remains a racist piece of legislation in that it defines a certain group of people based on their ancestry, and denies them certain rights available to the rest of the population. While First Nations people may not have to pay income tax on income earned while on the reserve, or pay sales tax on items purchased on the reserve, they are also unable to own their houses on the reserve, which means they are unable to use their homes or the land they are on as collateral for bank loans, which in turn means they cannot borrow to invest in businesses or to improve their houses (Figure 10.17). The result is that the standard of living for many First Nations people, especially those living on reserves (a little less than half), is far lower than that of most Canadians. Generally, First Nations Métis and Inuit people have lower life expectancy, higher rates of crime and unemployment, fewer high school graduates, and lower incomes than the non-Indigenous population.

Human Nature

We are all born with the same essential human nature: we all have the same wants, needs, hopes, and desires, but within specific cultural contexts. At the same time, however, we are physically and culturally different, and it is impossible not to notice these differences. It is also perhaps human nature to identify with those who seem most like us. What we make of the differences and how we behave to others who are unlike us, however, is learned. In Chapter 2 we learned that our understanding of the world and our behaviour are shaped by our observation of others, by being taught what is appropriate by our parents, peers, the media, and society in general, and by simply being immersed and participating in our culture. If our culture and society teaches us that people unlike us are inferior to us, and are to be mistreated or denied the same rights as us, then we are very likely to be prejudicial and our actions unjust unless we focus on the fact that "the other" is in essence just like us. As Bonazzi (2010) said in his commentary to *Black Like Me*, "extrinsic differences separate us instead of the deeper commonalties that should unite us—survival and basic needs, raising families, creating art, desiring peace, risking love, daring to hope, enduring pain, and dying—everything that makes us human" (p. 210).

Summary

1. Differences between people are the basis for social inequalities. Social inequality can be measured by the degree to which societies distribute wealth, power, and prestige among the different groups. Anthropologists distinguish three types of societies based on levels of social inequality: egalitarian, rank, and stratified societies.
2. Egalitarian societies are unstratified in that they allocate wealth, power, and prestige fairly equally. In rank societies, which are partially stratified, people have equal access to power and wealth but not to prestige. The most completely stratified societies are those based on classes or castes and that have unequal access to wealth, power, and prestige. The strata vary in the number, size and permeability of strata and the supporting ideology.
3. Stratified societies range from open class societies, which permit high social mobility, to more rigid caste societies, which allow for little or no social mobility. Class societies are associated with achieved status—positions that the individual can choose or at least have some control over. Caste societies such as found in India, on the other hand, are based on ascribed statuses into which one is born and which cannot change.
4. Canada is a good example of a class society. An open society, most people in Canada move up in class through their lifetimes. First Nations people are overrepresented among the poor and homeless, and have limited opportunities to participate fully in the labour force due to a history of colonization.
5. Poverty can be measured in absolute or relative terms. A significant proportion of Canadians are poor and suffer from food insecurity and are homeless. The causes, and solutions of poverty and homelessness are varied.
6. Many upper class people use status symbols to indicate their status. Status symbols are culturally relative and change over time.
7. Hindu India is often cited as the most extreme form of caste society in the world. Social boundaries among castes are strictly maintained by caste endogamy and strongly held notions of ritual purity and pollution. The Indian caste system, which has persisted for two thousand years, has created an ideology enabling the upper castes to maintain a monopoly on wealth, status, and power, although modernization is breaking down the system.
8. The Dalits are outside the caste system and used to be called untouchables because they were thought to be the most polluting. Dalits continue to be discriminated against, especially in rural areas.
9. Race is a classification of people based on physical traits, especially skin colour. Skin colour is an adaptive response to ultraviolet radiation. Attempts to classify people into races are based on arbitrary criteria. Consequently, the concept of race is not particularly meaningful from a scientific standpoint, although it is important because people's ideas of racial differences have led to powerful systems of stratification and discrimination.
10. Despite the long-term use of intelligence tests, there is no convincing research to suggest that some populations are genetically more intelligent than any others.
11. Ethnicity is an identity based on a person's cultural heritage, language, and traditions and also on self-identification. Canada is multicultural society in that it consists of people from different ethnic, religious, and racial backgrounds.
12. Discrimination is the practice of treating individuals differently based on the group they belong to. Racialism is the idea that the human species is not only divided into races but also that race also determines specific characteristics and capacities such as intelligence, moral habits, and cultural characteristics, and that some races are superior to others. Racism is a type of discrimination whereby people are treated differently based on the race they are deemed to belong to.
13. Structural racism is a form of racism where the institutions and systems of society are structured such that it privileges the dominant group while discriminating against the subordinate group. Racial profiling is a discriminatory practice whereby a person is targeted for reasons of safety, security, or public protection based on a stereotype of their race, ethnicity, religion, or place of origin. Cultural genocide involves the systematic suppression of a group's language, traditions, spirituality, and culture so that they are assimilated into the majority. Canada's Indian Residential Schools are a good example of cultural genocide.
14. Since 1876 the Indian Act has been used to discriminate against First Nations people who are one of the poorest groups in Canada.

Key Terms

absolute poverty
achieved status
ascribed status
caste
class
closed society
Dalit
discrimination
egalitarian society
enfranchisement
ethnic cleansing
ethnic group
ethnicity
eugenics
food insecurity
genocide
homelessness
hypergamy
hypodescent
jati
miscegenation
monogenesis
multicultural society
one-drop rule
open society
phenotype
polygenesis
poverty line
power
prestige
proletariat
racialism
racial profiling
racial segregation
racism
rank society
relative poverty
reverse discrimination
Sanskritization
social inequality
social mobility
status symbol
strata
stratified society
structural racism
untouchability practices
varnas
visible minorities
wealth
white man's burden

Critical Thinking questions

1. John Griffin's story was a unique experiment that is unlikely to ever be repeated. What ethical issues does it raise for anthropologists?
2. What barriers to equality of access to wealth, power, and prestige can you identify for certain segments of the Canadian population such as women, immigrants, and First Nations people? What would it take to eliminate some of these barriers?
3. What impact is globalization having on India's caste system?
4. To what extent is the concept of "race" a useful anthropological concept?
5. How can anthropologists work with law enforcement agencies, Canada's Indigenous peoples, and other marginal groups in Canada to eliminate racial profiling?
6. Economic inequality is generally seen as unjust, and national and international policies and programs are designed to eliminate it. In a capitalist society, such as Canada's, where for the most part there is equality of opportunity, and where people who get a good education and work hard can move up the economic ladder, economic inequality inevitably results. Hunger, homelessness, ill health, and severe deprivation of any kind are problems, but why is inequality per se a problem or unjust?
7. The causes of poverty and homelessness are complex and varied and consequently there can be no one solution to the problems. How can anthropologists contribute to an understanding of the causes of poverty and their solution?
8. Race is generally considered a cultural construct. How have "Indigenous people," "Canadians," and "whites" been culturally constructed?
9. How do First Nations people experience racism? What impact does it have on their lives? And how can anthropologists work with First Nations to deal with the experience of racism?
10. Should the Indian Act, and Indian status, be eliminated? What impact would it have?

A Hausa chief from western Nigeria in traditional regalia.

CHAPTER

11

Political Organization and Social Control

WHAT WE WILL LEARN

- What the different types of political organization are
- How First Nations bands are constituted and how they function
- How state systems of government vary
- How nation-states deal with different ethnic groups within their borders
- How the Internet and modern technologies have impacted state societies
- How societies maintain social order and control
- What systems of justice are and the difference between retributive and restorative justice
- What the causes of war are

R. V. GLADUE

On September 16, 1995, Jamie Tanis Gladue, a Cree living in Nanaimo, British Columbia, was at home celebrating her 19th birthday with family and friends. She had been drinking heavily and had a blood-alcohol content more than twice the legal driving limit when she got into an argument with her common-law husband, Reuben Beaver, suspecting he was having an affair with her older sister. The argument ended when Gladue stabbed Beaver in the chest with a large knife, killing him. She pled guilty to manslaughter, and at sentencing the judge took into consideration several mitigating factors: she had no criminal record; had a hyperthyroid condition, which caused her to overreact to emotional situations; Beaver had been verbally and physically abusive to her; while on bail she had attended alcohol abuse counselling and completed her Grade 10; and she showed remorse. The judge sentenced her to three years in prison, of which she served six months followed by an electronic monitoring program (CanLii 1999).

Gladue appealed her sentence to the Supreme Court of Canada, partly on the grounds that the judge had failed to adequately consider her circumstances as an Aboriginal offender under Section 718.2(e) of the *Criminal Code* of Canada (CanLii 1999). Section 718.2(e), which came into effect in 1996, reads as follows: "all available sanctions other than imprisonment that are reasonable in the circumstances should be considered for all offenders, with particular attention to the circumstances of aboriginal offenders." R. v. Gladue was the first case in Canada to test this section of the *Criminal Code* and has widespread implications for justice for First Nations, Métis, and Inuit people in Canada. Although the Supreme Court upheld the sentence, feeling it was appropriate and that a re-sentencing hearing would not have been in the interests of justice or the community, the Court also unanimously concluded that the trial judge had made a mistake in believing the section did not apply because Gladue was not living on a reserve. The Court also felt it necessary to clarify section 718.2(e) (CanLii 1999).

The provision was designed to address the problem over overrepresentation of First Nations, Métis, and Inuit people in Canada's prisons (CanLii 1999). In 2014, they comprised 22.8 percent of the incarcerated population (Office of the Correctional Investigator 2014) yet only about 4 percent of the Canadian population. What section 718.2(e) means is that, when striving to determine a sentence

Paul Almasy/Corbis/VCG via Getty Images

for Indigenous offenders, judges must also consider "(a) the unique systemic or background factors which may have played a part in bringing the particular aboriginal offender before the courts; and (b) the types of sentencing procedures and sanctions which may be appropriate in the circumstances for the offender because of his or her particular aboriginal heritage or connection" (CanLii 1999).

In passing sentence, judges must therefore consider two things: the impact of larger background influences on the offender in committing the crime, and cultural factors in sentencing. The Supreme Court later said, "To be clear, courts must take judicial notice of such matters as the history of colonialism, displacement and residential schools and how that history continues to translate into lower educational attainment, lower incomes, higher unemployment, higher rates of substance abuse and suicide and, of course, higher levels of incarceration for Aboriginal Peoples" (CBC News 2012a). Particular attention to these circumstances, many of which were discussed in the previous chapter, needs to be made in the interest of fairness since they are different from those influencing non-Indigenous offenders. In practice, this means a case-specific, pre-sentence report, called a *Gladue report*, is prepared that details the systemic or background factors that may have influenced the offender, as well as relevant cultural factors pertinent to sentencing. Much of the report is often based on representations from the Indigenous offender's community and is made available to the judge when determining the appropriate sentence. Sentencing requires that judges consider culturally appropriate alternatives to imprisonment, with prison being the last resort (Figure 11.1).

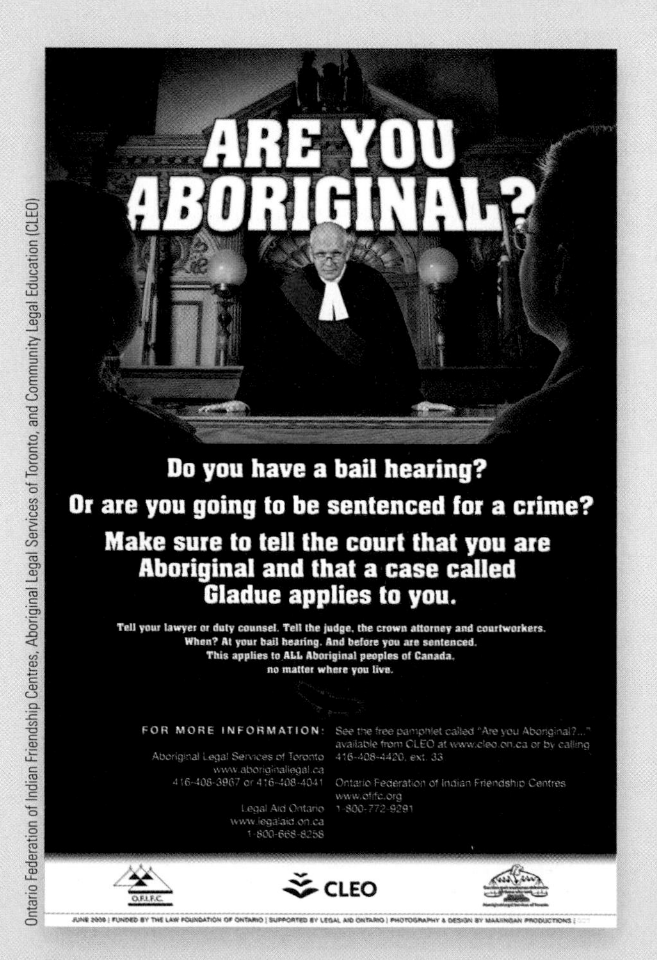

FIGURE 11.1 The Ontario Federation of Indian Friendship Centres, Aboriginal Legal Services of Toronto, and CLEO (Community Legal Education Ontario) poster informing Aboriginals of their Gladue rights.

Ontario Federation of Indian Friendship Centres, Aboriginal Legal Services of Toronto, and Community Legal Education (CLEO)

The Canadian justice system tends to be adversarial and punitive, and traditional sentencing goals focus on deterrence, denunciation, and separation, and secondarily on rehabilitation (CanLii 1999). While Indigenous ideas of justice and sentencing vary considerably across Canada, they generally tend to take a more restorative approach to sentencing. For many First Nations peoples, crime is perceived as a broken relationship with the community, the victim's family, and the perpetrator. Sentencing is more about healing, restitution, and reintegration into the community. Prison may thus not be the most appropriate sanction. Where no alternatives exist, judges must consider the length of the jail term, which in some circumstances may be less than that imposed on a non-Indigenous offender for the same offence (CanLii 1999).

The Gladue case means that, under Section 718.2(e) of the Criminal Code, First Nations, Métis, and Inuit offenders can have a Gladue report prepared and the systemic background influences on them taken into consideration during sentencing. This has, however, led to charges of reverse discrimination, a two-tier justice system, and race-based justice in that it is seen to favour Indigenous offenders over non-Indigenous offenders (Gunter 2012; CBC News 2015). The purpose of the section, however, "is to treat aboriginal offenders fairly by taking into account their difference" (CanLii 1999). The R. v. Gladue case illustrates the different conceptions and approaches to crime and punishment and the Canadian government's attempt to apply culturally appropriate justice. ■

Political Organization and Social Control

All societies, if they are to remain viable over time, must maintain social order. Every society must develop a set of customs and procedures for making and enforcing decisions, resolving disputes, and regulating the behaviour of its members. Every society must make collective decisions about its environment and its relations with other societies, and about how to deal with disruptive or destructive behaviour on the part of its members. These topics are generally discussed under headings such as political organization, law, power, authority, social control, and conflict resolution. In addition to exploring all these subjects, this chapter deals with the cultural arrangements by which societies maintain social order, minimize the chances of disruption, and cope with whatever disruptions do occur (Kurtz 2001; Lewellen 2003).

When most Canadians think of politics or political structure, a number of familiar images come to mind:

- Political leaders such as prime ministers, presidents, premiers, mayors, or MLAs
- Complex bureaucracies employing thousands of civil servants
- Legislative bodies ranging from the smallest town council to the House of Commons
- Formal judicial institutions that comprise municipal, provincial, and federal courts
- Law enforcement bodies such as local police departments, the RCMP, and the armed forces
- Political parties, nominating conventions, and secret-ballot voting

All these are formal mechanisms that our society uses for making and enforcing political decisions, as well as coordinating and regulating people's behaviour. Some small-scale societies in the world have none of these things—no elected officials, legislatures, judges, formal elections, armies, or bureaucracies. We should not conclude from this, however, that such societies lack any form of ***political organization*** if by political organization we mean a set of customary procedures that accomplish decision making, conflict resolution, and social control.

Types of Political Organization

The term political organization refers to the ways in which power is distributed within a society to control people's behaviour and maintain social order. All societies are organized politically, but the degree of specialization and the formal mechanisms vary considerably from one society to another. Societies differ in their political organization based on three important dimensions:

- The extent to which political institutions are distinct from other aspects of the social structure; for example, in some societies, political structures are barely distinguishable from economic, kinship, or religious structures
- The extent to which legitimate ***authority*** is concentrated in specific political roles
- The level of ***political integration***, that is, the size of the territorial group that comes under the control of the political structure

These three dimensions have been used by anthropologists to classify societies into four fundamentally different types of political structure: band societies, tribal societies, chiefdoms, and state societies (Service 1978). Although some societies do not fit neatly into a single category, this fourfold scheme can help us understand how different societies administer themselves and maintain social order.

Although our discussion of all four types of political organization are written using the "ethnographic present," we need to remember that there are no pure bands, tribes, or chiefdoms in the world today. Rather, these non-state forms of political organization have had more complex state political systems superimposed upon them.

Band Societies

The least complex form of political arrangement is the band, characterized by small, usually nomadic populations of food collectors. Although band size can range from 20 to several hundred individuals, most bands are made up of between 30 and 50 people. The actual size is directly related to the carrying capacity of their environment. Although bands may be loosely associated with a specific territory, they have little concept of individual property ownership and place a high value on sharing, cooperation, and reciprocity. ***Band societies*** have little role specialization and are highly egalitarian in that few differences in status, power, and wealth can be observed. Because this form of political organization

---

Gladue report A pre-sentencing report providing an account of the historical and cultural influences on a First Nations, Métis, or Inuit offender used in considering sentencing.

political organization The ways in which power is distributed within a society to control people's behaviour and maintain social order.

authority The power or right to give commands, take action, and make binding decisions.

political integration The process that brings disparate people under the control of a single political system.

band societies Societies lacking formal political structure and where decisions are often embedded in the family; typically egalitarian, hunting-and-gathering societies.

Nigel Pavitt/Getty Images

FIGURE 11.2 The Hadza, who live around Lake Eyasi and the Serengeti Plains of Tanzania, live in bands of 20–30 people and still follow a traditional hunting and gathering lifestyle. Here a Hadza hunter wearing a baboon skin returns to camp with a haunch of impala over his shoulder.

is so closely associated with a foraging technology, it is generally thought to be the oldest form of political organization (Figure 11.2).

Band societies share four traits:

- Because bands are composed of a relatively small number of people who are related by blood or marriage, a high value is placed on "getting along" with one another.
- Band societies have the least amount of political integration; that is, the various bands are independent of one another and are not part of a larger political structure.
- In band societies, political decisions are often embedded in the wider social structure. Because bands are composed of kin, it is difficult to distinguish between purely political decisions and those that we would recognize as family, economic, or religious decisions.
- Leadership roles in band societies tend to be informal. There are no specialized political roles or leaders with designated authority. Instead, leaders in foraging societies are often, but not always, older men respected for their experience, wisdom, good judgment, and knowledge of hunting.

The Ju/'hoansi of the Kalahari, who until the mid-1970s lived primarily as foragers (Smith et al. 2010; Lee 2012), exemplify a band society with a headman. Although the position of headman is hereditary, his actual authority is quite limited. The headman coordinates the movement of his people and usually walks at the head of the group. He chooses the sites of new encampments and has first pick of location for his own house site. But beyond these limited perks of office, the Ju/'hoansi headman receives no other rewards. He is not responsible for organizing hunting parties, making artifacts, or negotiating marriage arrangements. These activities fall to the individual members of the band. The headman is not expected to be a judge of his people. Moreover, his material possessions are no greater than any other person's.

With the growth of nation-states, few true band societies still exist. The Ju/'hoansi now live in settled communities near water resources and combine food production with some foraging and money earned through wage labour or selling crafts (Biesele and Hitchcock 2011).

Indian Act Band

A distinction needs to be made between a band society and an *Indian Act band*, usually referred to as simply a band. A band is defined by Canada's Indian Act as "a body of Indians (*a*) for whose use and benefit in common, lands, the legal title to which is vested in Her Majesty, have been set apart before, on or after September 4, 1951, (*b*) for whose use and benefit in common, moneys are held by Her Majesty, or (*c*) declared by the Governor in Council to be a band for the purposes of this Act" (Indian Act 1985). In other words, a band is an administrative and legal unit that manages reserves and funds provided to them by the federal government. A *reserve* is "a tract of land, the legal title to which is vested in Her Majesty, that has been set apart by Her Majesty for the use and benefit of a band" (Indian Act 1985). Indigenous and Northern Affairs Canada (INAC), and in many cases the bands themselves, maintain a list of people who belong to the band. Roughly 40 percent of First Nations people currently live on reserves (Milke 2013b).

The functioning of the band, including its governance, is controlled by the Indian Act. Bands have their own governing band council consisting of a chief and a minimum of two and a maximum of 12 counsellors who are elected by band members. The band councils run the day-to-day business of the band, which can include such things as providing education, household services, building maintenance, fire services, and passing and enforcing bylaws. While, technically, band council resolutions have to be approved by the Minister of INAC, the current policy is to give them a great deal of autonomy.

Bands may administer multiple reserves. For instance, in Alberta there are 140 reserves but only 45 First Nations, and in British Columbia, 1606 reserves

Indian Act band An administrative and legal unit that manages Indian reserves and First Nations funds.

reserve A tract of land, the legal title to which belongs to the federal government, that has been set aside for the use and benefit of a band.

and about 200 First Nations (about one-third of all First Nations in Canada) (AANDC 2010). For the most part, bands correspond to First Nation communities of which there were 617 as of April 2015. First Nations people "refers to Status and non-status 'Indian' peoples in Canada." First Nations and bands are not equivalent, however. For example, in Alberta, the Saddle Lake Cree Nation and the Whitefish Lake (Goodfish) First Nation are administered separately but are considered one band (INAC 2010).

Bands may also form an association called a *tribal council*. While lacking the administrative power of bands, tribal councils provide member bands with advice and help deliver services. Member bands usually speak the same language and have the same culture. For example, the Nuu-chah-nulth Tribal Council (NTC) on Vancouver Island's west coast consists of 14 Nuu-chah-nulth First Nations who share a common language and culture. The NTC represents its member Nations' common interests and provides advice and assistance with such services as child welfare, economic development, education, employment training, financial administrative support, and so on, to nearly 9500 individual members (Nuu-chah-nulth Tribal Council 2015).

Tribal Societies

Whereas band societies are usually associated with food collecting, *tribal societies* are found most often among food producers (horticulturalists and pastoralists). Because plant and animal domestication is far more productive than foraging, tribal societies tend to have populations that are larger, denser, and more sedentary than bands. Tribal societies are similar to band societies in several important respects however. Both are egalitarian to the extent that there are few marked differences in status, rank, power, and wealth. In addition, tribal societies, like bands, have local leaders (and they are usually men) but no centralized leadership. Leadership in tribal societies is informal and not vested in a centralized authority. A man is recognized as a leader by virtue of certain personality traits such as wisdom, integrity, intelligence, and concern for the welfare of others. Although tribal leaders often play a central role in formulating decisions, they cannot force their will on a group. In the final analysis, most decisions are arrived at through group consensus.

The major difference between tribes and bands is that tribal societies have certain *pan-tribal mechanisms* that cut across and integrate all the local segments of the tribe into a larger whole. These mechanisms include tribal associations such as clans, age grades, and secret societies. Pan-tribal associations unite the tribe against external threats. These integrating forces are not permanent political fixtures however. Usually the local units of a tribe operate autonomously. The integrating mechanisms come into play only when an external threat arises. When the threat is eliminated, the local units return to their autonomous state. Even though these pan-tribal mechanisms may be transitory, they nevertheless provide wider political integration in certain situations than would ever be possible in band societies. For example, clan elders, although they do not hold formal political offices, usually manage the affairs of their clans (e.g., settling disputes between clan members) and represent their clans in dealings with other clans.

The pastoral Nuer of South Sudan, first described in detail by Evans-Pritchard (1940), are a good example of a tribal form of political organization. Although accurate figures are hard to come by, the Nuer today number approximately 1.8 million (CIA World Factbook 2015b, South Sudan). Traditionally, they have no centralized government and no government functionaries with coercive authority. Of course, there are influential men but their influence stems more from their personal traits than from the force of elected or inherited office. The Nuer, who are highly egalitarian, do not readily accept authority beyond the elders of the family. Social control among the Nuer is maintained by segmentary lineages in that close kin are expected to come to the assistance of one another against more distantly related people (Figure 11.3).

Tony Karumba/AFP/Getty Images

FIGURE 11.3 A man from the Nuer tribe grooms community-owned cattle at dawn in ash to keep pests away at a smoky traditional cattle camp (South Sudan February 2015). Cattle are traditionally a source of enmity between the main tribes of Dinka and Nuer, who for generations have raided each other's lands, and fought and killed for possession due to the respect and prestige that owning numerous head of cattle is perceived to carry.

tribal council An association of Indian Act bands that lacks official administrative power but that provides member bands with various services and assistance.

tribal societies Small-scale societies that have local informal leaders but no centralized leadership.

pan-tribal mechanisms Mechanisms such as clans, age grades, and secret societies found in tribal societies that cut across kinship lines and integrate all the local segments of the tribe into a larger whole.

The term "tribe" has carried with it a generally negative connotation in the West for several centuries. During the colonial period of the 19th century, the term "tribal," often equated to "uncivilized," was used to disparage any group with no centralized hierarchical authority. Anthropologists do not associate the term *tribal society* with anything negative. Rather, the term is used to describe a group of ethnically homogeneous people capable of coordinating political action yet lacking a centralized bureaucracy. Awareness of negative stereotyping of tribal societies is important because Westerners often speak of "ancient tribal hatreds" (caused by inherent cultural differences) when, in fact, present-day intertribal hostilities often result from the intervention of other cultures. Negative stereotyping can lead us to misunderstand the nature of contemporary ethnic or tribal conflicts in places such as Somalia, the former Yugoslavia, and Iraq (see Whitehead and Ferguson 1993).

Chiefdoms

As societies become more complex, with larger and more specialized populations, more sophisticated technology, and growing surpluses, their need for more formal and permanent political structures increases. In such societies known as ***chiefdoms***, political authority is likely to reside with a single individual, acting alone or in conjunction with an advisory council.

Chiefdoms differ from bands and tribes in that chiefdoms integrate a number of local communities in a more formal and permanent way. Unlike bands and tribes, chiefdoms are made up of local communities that differ from one another in rank and status. Based on their genealogical proximity to the chiefs, nobles and commoners hold different levels of prestige and power. Chiefships are often hereditary, and the chief and his or her immediate kin constitute a social and political élite. Rarely are chiefdoms totally unified politically under a single chief; more often they are composed of several political units, each headed by its own chief (Figure 11.4).

The traditional, hereditary chief system is still active in the Gitxsan Nation in British Columbia. The Gitxsan Nation is comprised of more than 50 Houses, or Wilps, which are the primary social, economic, and political unit. The Gitxsan is a matrilineal society, and each Wilp consists of between 20 and 250 people closely related through their mothers. Each Wilp also has its own territory, oral history, and hereditary chief who performs planning and administrative duties on behalf of its members (Gitxsan.com 2016). In 2014 there was a split among the hereditary chiefs over the Prince Rupert Gas Transmission gas pipeline, several kilometres of which would run through Gitxsan territory. About half the chiefs were in favour of the pipeline, while half were opposed to it, primarily for environmental reasons (Hoekstra 2014).

Robert Estall photo agency/Alamy Stock Photo

FIGURE 11.4 Shangana (also known as Tsonga) warriors, who live in Mozambique and South Africa, gathered around their chief.

Chiefdoms also differ from tribes and bands in that chiefdoms are centralized and have permanent officials who have higher rank, power, and authority than others in the society. Unlike a band or tribal headmen or headwomen, chiefs usually have considerable power, authority, and, in some cases, wealth. Internal social disruptions are minimized in a chiefdom because the chief usually has authority to make judgments, punish wrongdoers, and settle disputes. Chiefs often have the authority to distribute land to loyal subjects, recruit people into military service, and recruit labourers for public works projects.

Chiefs are also intimately related to the economic activities of their subjects through the redistributive system of economics (see Chapter 7). Subjects give food surpluses to the chief (not uncommonly at the chief's insistence), which he or she then redistributes through communal feasts. This system of redistribution through a chief serves the obvious *economic* function of ensuring that no people

chiefdom A form of political organization in which political authority is likely to reside with a single individual or chief and his or her advisors.

in the society go hungry. It also serves the important *political* function of providing the people with a mechanism for expressing their loyalty and support for the chief.

Within the past 130 years, a number of societies with no former tradition of chiefs have had chiefships imposed on them by European colonial powers. As the European nations created their colonial empires during the 19th century, they created chiefs (or altered the nature of traditional chiefs) to facilitate administering local populations. For example, the British created chiefs for their own administrative convenience among chiefless societies in Nigeria, Kenya, and Australia. These new chiefs—who were given salaries and high-sounding titles such as "Paramount Chief"—were selected primarily on the basis of their willingness to work with the colonial administration rather than any particular popularity among their own people. In some cases these new chiefs were held in contempt by their own people because they were collaborators with the colonial governments, which were often viewed as repressive and coercive.

Canadian Chiefs

In Canada, many chiefs were created to facilitate administering local populations without a former tradition of chiefs. Today, election of band chiefs and counsellors is controlled by the Indian Act. They are elected democratically every two years by band members who are registered on the band list and over 18 years old, but do not have to live on the reserve. Candidates for chiefs, however, as well as those nominating them, do need to be band members or resident on the reserve. As of 2015, only about 40 percent of bands follow the election rules dictated by the Indian Act. About 55 percent of bands follow what is known as "custom election" (AANDC 2015), which also falls outside the Indian Act electoral rules, allowing them to select their leaders according to traditional customs, which thus vary from one First Nation to another (Milke 2013a).

Custom election has proved controversial in that, in some cases, elections are not that traditional and can be undemocratic. For instance, in the Red Sucker Lake First Nation, in northern Manitoba, candidates for chief must be married, and in the Garden Hill First Nation, also in Manitoba, they must not only be married but must also be over 50, while counsellors must be over 40. First Nations are still subject to the Charter of Rights and Freedoms but, if they can demonstrate that a rule existed prior to European contact, they may be allowed to continue with customs such as electing only men, or having hereditary chiefs (Boesveld 2014b). It should be noted that the chief of a First Nation band really refers to the chief counsellor. As of April 2015, First Nations have another way to elect officials. Under the First Nations Election Act (2015), First Nations that choose to opt into the Act can, among other things, elect officials for four instead of two years, and coordinate elections with up to six other First Nations. This Act, which was developed in collaboration with First Nations, also removes the role of the Minister in cases of appeals and is an attempt to allow First Nations bands to develop longer-term planning and investments, which hopefully will lead to increased economic development.

The remaining 5 percent of First Nations are self-governing and are not governed by the Indian Act. Since 1995 the Canadian government, in cooperation with provincial and territorial governments, has entered into self-government agreements with a number of First Nations, and is continuing to do so. Most of these agreements are the result of comprehensive land claims negotiations and each is unique, taking into consideration the particular historical, cultural, economic, and political circumstances of each First Nation. Once the agreement has been signed, self-governing First Nations cease to be an Indian Act band, allowing them to determine their own political, economic, and social development. Self-governing First Nations are free to manage their own lands and resources, and typically develop their own constitution, school boards with relevant curricula, health and social services, economic plans, relevant legislation, and local tax schemes.

For example, the Nisga'a Nation became a self-governing First Nation in May 2001 with the signing of the Nisga'a Final Agreement—the first treaty signed in British Columbia since Treaty 8 in 1899. It had taken the Nisga'a 113 years of lobbying and negotiating. The Nisga'a had claimed approximately 24 000 square kilometres of traditional territory but settled for 1930 square kilometres of provincial crown land plus 62 square kilometres of Indian reserve land. This land is held in fee simply, that is, the same way most Canadians own their land, although they also have rights to the subsurface and natural resources. They also received $190 million, which is used to deliver programs and services and transition the Nisga'a into the new form of self-governance. The Nisga'a Lisims Government is a representational democracy and can make laws governing Nisga'a citizenship, property, health services, education, housing, resource management, and social services. The Lisims government can also provide policing, correctional, and court services. Federal and provincial laws still apply to Nisga'a citizens and others on Nisga'a lands, however, and they must also now pay income tax and sales tax. The Nisga'a Lisims government also has the power to tax Nisga'a citizens on Nisga'a lands in much the same way municipalities tax their residents (Hoffman and Robinson 2010). The Nisga'a Final Agreement is, as the title suggests, final, which means that they have relinquished all claims to the remainder of their traditional territory. These lands can now be leased or sold by the province without contest or legal recourse by the Nisga'a. The terms of this treaty are similar to most self-governing agreements signed subsequently.

CROSS-CULTURAL MISCUE

As we saw in Chapter 6 on communication, bowing is a means of showing respect and communicating status, especially in countries such as Japan. Subordinate people generally bow lower than superior people. As arguably the most powerful man in the world, President Barak Obama should not have had to bow to anyone. However, he seemed to have developed a habit of bowing resulting in a great deal of media criticism. He bowed to the Queen of England, the mayor of Tampa, Mexico's President Felipe Calderon, Cuban President Raul Castro, Chinese President Hu Jintao, a Republican (Obama is a Democrat), and in April 2014 to ASIMO, a Japanese humanoid robot (Ohlheiser 2014). The most notorious occasions, however, occurred in 2009, when he bowed to Saudi King Abdullah and to Japanese Emperor Akihito. The press claimed that, as the head of a democratic nation that values equality, he should not have bowed to heads of state from repressive regimes such as Saudi Arabia. And by bowing as a sign of deference to Akihito that he was humiliating not only himself but also his country. He also shook hands with Akihito at the same time which was also a breach of etiquette. As one commentator noted, "the president of the United States is the leading political figure in the world. He must command respect. Let others bow to him" (Koffler 2012).

State Societies

The state system of government is the most formal and most complex form of political organization. A ***state*** can be defined as a hierarchical form of political organization that governs many communities within a large geographic area, where it has a monopoly on the use of force. States collect taxes, recruit labour for armies and civilian public works projects, and have a monopoly on the right to use force. They are large bureaucratic organizations made up of permanent institutions with legislative, administrative, and judicial functions (Figure 11.5). Whereas bands and tribes have political structures based on kinship, state systems of government organize their power on a supra-kinship basis. That is, a person's membership in a state is based on his or her place of residence and citizenship rather than on kinship affiliation.

The authority of the state rests on two important foundations. First, the state holds the exclusive right to use force and physical coercion. Any act of violence not expressly permitted by the state is illegal and consequently punishable by the state. Thus, state governments make written laws, administer them through various levels of the bureaucracy, and enforce them through mechanisms such as police forces, armies, and armed forces reserves. The state needs to be continuously vigilant against internal and external threats to usurp its power through rebellions and revolutions. Second, the state maintains its authority by means of ideology. For the state to maintain its power over the long run, there must be a philosophical understanding among the citizenry that the state has the legitimate right to govern. In the absence of such an ideology, it is often difficult for the state to maintain its authority by means of coercive force alone.

jiawangkun/Shutterstock

FIGURE 11.5 State systems of government are characterized by a high degree of role specialization and hierarchical organization. Many of the specialized political roles are played out in legislative bodies, such as the House of Commons in Ottawa.

State systems of government, which first appeared about 5500 years ago, are found in societies with complex socio-economic characteristics. They are maintained by intensive agriculture, which is required to support a large number of non-food-producing bureaucrats. This efficient food-production system gives rise to cities, considerable labour specialization, and a complex system of internal distribution and foreign trade. Because the considerable surpluses produced by intensive agriculture are not distributed equally among all segments of the population, state societies are socially stratified. That is, forms of wealth such as land and capital tend to be concentrated in the hands of an élite, who often use their superior wealth and power to control the rest of the population. Moreover, the fairly complex laws and regulations needed to control a large and heterogeneous population give rise to the need for some type of writing, accounting, record keeping, and a system of weights and measures.

State systems of government are characterized by a large number of ***specialized political roles***. Many people are required to carry out specific tasks such as law enforcement, tax collection, dispute settlement, recruitment of labour, and protection from outside invasions. These political and administrative

---

state A particular type of political structure that is hierarchical, bureaucratic, centralized, and has a monopoly on the legitimate use of force to implement its policies.

specialized political roles Specific tasks expected of a person or group, such as law enforcement, tax collection, dispute settlement, recruitment of labour, and protection from outside invasions.

functionaries are highly specialized and work full time to the extent that they do not engage in food-producing activities. These permanent political functionaries, like the society itself, are highly stratified, or hierarchical. At the apex of the administrative pyramid are those with the greatest power—kings, prime ministers, presidents, governors, and legislators—who enact laws and establish policies. Below them are descending echelons of bureaucrats responsible for the day-to-day administration of the state. As is the case in our own form of government, each level of the bureaucracy is responsible to the level immediately above it.

The Modern Nation-State

In recent times the word state has been combined with the word *nation* to form the entity called a *nation-state*. Although these two words are often used interchangeably in everyday conversation, they are two quite distinct concepts. On the one hand, a nation is a group of people who share a common identity, culture, history, and often religion. A nation is thus synonymous with "ethnic group." In fact, the word "ethnic" comes from the Greek word *ethnos*, which means "nation." A state, on the other hand, is a particular type of political structure distinct from a band, tribal society, or chiefdom. Thus, Canada's First Nations are nations in that they share a common culture, language, and identity, but they are not states. When combined, the term nation-state refers to a group of people sharing a common cultural background, living in a particular geographic area, and unified by a political structure that they all consider legitimate. Thus, a nation-state is a socio-cultural entity as well is a political community that has legitimacy over a defined territory that it protects. Nation-states can also establish relationships with other nation-states and can be thought of as synonymous with countries.

The ideal of a nation-state is where the cultural and political boundaries coincide. The reality, however, is that few (if any) of the nearly 200 nation-states in the world today actually fit the definition. This is largely because few nation-states have populations with homogeneous cultural identities but rather are *polyethnic*. For example, the country of Great Britain, which has existed for centuries, comprises England, Wales, Northern Ireland, and Scotland. We sometimes refer to Great Britain as England, but the Welsh, Irish, and Scotch clearly do not regard themselves as English in terms of language, tradition, or ethnicity. Many of the newly independent African nation-states represented in the United Nations since the 1960s have enormous ethnic heterogeneity. To illustrate, the country of Tanzania comprises approximately 120 different ethnic groups, all of which speak mutually unintelligible languages. Thus, even after a half-century of living in a nation-state, the people of Tanzania tend to identify themselves more as Maasai, Wazaramo, or Wachagga than as Tanzanians.

The modern nation-state arose, for the most part, in the 19th and early 20th centuries with the decline of monarchies and the colonization of the world by European countries. They divided the world into political and geographic nation-states with little regard for ethnic groups. For example, Yugoslavia was created after World War I and consisted of more than 20 ethnic groups. After the fall of the Berlin Wall in 1989 and the disintegration of the USSR in 1991, conflict broke out between many of these groups, resulting in the formation of seven new nation-states: Serbia, Montenegro, Kosovo (not universally recognized), Slovenia, Macedonia, Croatia, and Bosnia and Herzegovina.

Nations can also be spread out across nation-states. Thus, for example, the Kurds, while they comprise a nation, live in the nation-states of Turkey, Iran, Iraq, and Syria (Figure 11.6). A major challenge for some contemporary state governments is that they contain within their boundaries ethnic populations that are seeking statehood or expanded autonomy. A particularly good example are the 12 million Kurds living in southern Turkey, who have been struggling for an independent state since the formation of modern Turkey in 1923. Because the Kurds make up approximately 20 percent of Turkey's population and occupy an area that controls the headwaters of the Tigris and Euphrates Rivers, the Turkish government is not interested in granting the

FIGURE 11.6 Kurdish areas in the Middle East.

---

nation A group of people who share a common identity, history, and culture.

nation-state A socio-cultural entity as well as a political community that has legitimacy over a defined territory.

polyethnic People from many ethnic backgrounds living within the same nation-state or geographic area.

Kurds independence. For decades, the Turkish government has used political repression as the major strategy for dealing with what they call the "Kurdish problem." Not only have Kurds been oppressed and denied basic civil liberties, but so have non-Kurdish Turks who speak out in favour of Kurdish independence. And yet the Kurds of Turkey represent only one of many groups that are involved in intrastate conflicts. Others include Palestinians in Israel, Chechens in Russia, and the Kayapo of Brazil.

In the West, nation-states are becoming increasingly heterogeneous as globalization has resulted in accepting immigrants and refugees from numerous ethnic backgrounds. Canada for instance consists of more than 200 ethnic groups, including First Nations (Statistics Canada 2013a). The challenge of nation-states, since they are polyethnic, is to create a sense of belonging or allegiance to the larger political and geographic entity that overrides the importance of ethnic identity. In other words, one of the biggest challenges nation-states face is to create a sense of nationalism or national identity. Failure can result in hostility toward immigrants and internal conflict. The key perhaps is to develop both respect for ethnic differences and also a strong sense of citizenship.

Variations in Political Structures

In the preceding sections, we have looked at four fundamentally different types of political systems. This fourfold scheme, although recognized by some anthropologists, is not universally accepted. For example, in a classic study of political systems in Africa, Meyer Fortes and E. E. Evans-Pritchard (1940) distinguished between only two types of structures: state systems and *acephalous societies* (literally, headless societies). Others (Cohen and Eames 1982) recognize three major forms of political structure: simple, intermediate, and complex. Such differences in the way that various ethnologists have conceptualized political structures should serve as a reminder that all these schemes are ideal types. That is, not all the societies in the world fit neatly into one box or another. Instead of discrete categories, in reality, there is a continuum, with bands (the simplest form) at one extreme and states (the most complex form) at the other. Thus, whether we use two, three, or four major categories of political organization, we should bear in mind that the political systems of the world vary along a continuum on a number of important political dimensions. As we move from bands through tribes and chiefdoms to states, gradations occur in terms of (a) level of political integration, (b) the extent to which political institutions are distinct from family or religious institutions, and (c) the extent to which legitimate authority is concentrated in purely political roles.

Types of State Societies

States can take many different forms and can vary from democratic to autocratic to totalitarian in nature. In an *autocratic state* the political system is controlled by an absolute leader who denies popular participation in the process of governmental decision making. In a *totalitarian state* the state recognizes no limits to its authority and strives to regulate every aspect of public and private life wherever feasible.

In a *representative democracy* the ultimate power rests with the citizens, who periodically elect members of their society to represent them in some form of assembly such as a parliament, senate, legislature, or congress. On decisions that could have a potentially large impact on citizens, some governments may go directly to the people for a decision in a *referendum* in which the citizens are asked to vote on a particular proposal. For example, in 1980 and 1995 the Quebec government went directly to the people of the province to determine whether to remain in Canada or not. Similarly, the British people were asked in 2016 whether or not to leave the European Union. Voters in the Greater Vancouver Metropolitan region were asked in 2015 whether they were for or against a 0.5 percent sales tax increase to fund transportation improvements; they voted against the increase.

Not everyone has *suffrage*, or the right to vote, however. Every state restricts eligibility to vote according to age. In Canada, for instance, one must be 18 years or older to vote in federal elections, although in other countries the minimum voting age ranges from 16 to 21. Many countries also restrict the right to vote by sex, race, religion, ethnicity, education, land ownership, and other criteria. For example, First Nations members could not vote in Canadian federal elections until 1960 without giving up their status, and not until 1970 in Quebec provincial elections. At one time or another in Canada, Doukhobors, Chinese, Japanese,

acephalous societies Societies that have no political leaders such as a presidents, kings, or chiefs.

autocratic state A form of government controlled by a leader who holds absolute power and denies popular participation in decision making.

totalitarian state A political system in which the state recognizes no limits to its authority and strives to regulate every aspect of public and private life wherever feasible.

representative democracy A form of government in which power rests with the citizens, who periodically elect members of their society to some form of assembly to represent them in decision making.

referendum A direct vote by the electorate on a particular proposal.

suffrage The right to vote.

When You Sing It Now, Just Like New

Although we normally think of cultural anthropologists as being both researchers and university professors, they are, with increasing frequency, venturing outside academia to apply their cultural insights to real-world situations. Some cultural anthropologists are working with First Nations to get the Canadian government to live up to the terms of treaties.

The Dane-zaa (previously Beaver Indian) live in four communities in the Peace River area of northeastern British Columbia. Although today they live in a world of computers, smart phones, pick-up trucks, and pipelines, traditionally they lived a semi-nomadic lifestyle, moving seasonally between the Rocky Mountains and the plains area of Alberta, hunting moose and other game, and harvesting plants and berries. When Rocky Mountain Fort was established south of Fort St. John, British Columbia, in 1794 they became involved in the fur trade, and in 1900, as prospectors moved through their land on their way to the Klondike goldfields, their leaders signed Treaty 8. The treaty promised them 128 acres of reserve land for each band member (Ridington 2011), and in 1914 the Fort St. John Band (now the Doig River and Blueberry River bands) was allotted a reserve at Gat Tah Kwậ (Montney) (Virtual Museum of Canada 2015). There was a discrepancy, however, between the number of people who were given land and the number of people who were actually members of the band. So, in 2000, the Doig River and Blueberry River First Nations began negotiations with the federal government to rectify the situation. They also turned to anthropologist Robin Ridington and his wife for assistance.

Ridington, professor emeritus at the University of British Columbia, has spent nearly 50 years working with the Dane-zaa. When he began his long-term fieldwork they still lived a semi-nomadic way of life, with hunting and trapping providing most of their food and income. He was particularly drawn to the songs and stories of the elders, using them to understand the Dane-zaa's relationship with their environment and their social organization. He was surprised to find that many of the stories passed down to them provided an accurate oral history of events going back over 150 years to the early days of the fur trade (Ridington 2011). One story told of trading dried bison meat (pemmican) with the white traders at Fort St. John for such things as sugar and tea. Historical records confirm that the traders at Rocky Mountain Fort depended heavily on Dane-zaa hunters, who brought in the bison that at that time roamed the plains in the Peace River area.

The stories Ridington recorded with Dane-zaa Dreamer Charlie Yahey in the 1960s and 1970s were passed down to him from previous ancestors. It was very much a collaborative effort, and Charlie Yahey knew when he was making the recordings that his songs and stories would be important to the Dane-zaa in the future. Dane-zaa songkeepers continue to pass down Dreamers' songs from their ancestors, which now reach out to present generations, connecting them with their ancestors and traditional way of life. Charlie Yahey's songs, as well as those of others, also contained a great deal of genealogical information.

Many of the recordings proved valuable in the Dane-zaa's treaty entitlement claims. The Dane-zaa had an accurate and detailed knowledge of their kinship because they knew the names and stories of their ancestors' lives. Ridington used this knowledge, along with genealogies he collected in the 1960s, to create an accurate census of band members in 1914. The names of ancestors also consistently appeared in baptismal records, and the government claims adjudicators accepted the validity of the ethnographic evidence without question. The research uncovered a large number of people who were unaccounted for, and so the Dane-zaa were entitled to additional reserve land. The songs and stories, as well as photographs, continue to be valuable in other Dane-zaa land claims, and have been made available to present Dane-zaa communities as well as others in a digital archive made available from the B.C. Museums association (www.virtualmuseum.ca/sgc-cms/expositions-exhibitions/danewajich/english/index.html).

Dane-zaa oral tradition describes how the creator drew a cross on the surface of a primordial body of water and sent muskrat down to bring back the first dirt. He placed the dirt at the centre of the cross, and from this small beginning, he made the world. The last Dreamer, Charlie Yahey (1881–1976), played a drum to illustrate his story.

Questions for Further Thought

1. How else may Dane-zaa songs and stories be valuable?
2. In what ways could anthropologists work with First Nations people in their dealings with provincial and federal governments?
3. What knowledge and experience might be incorporated in contemporary songs and stories?

Mennonites, and Hutterites have also been prohibited from voting. It was not until 1918 that women were allowed to vote in federal elections and not until 1940 in Quebec provincial elections. In December 2015, women were allowed for the first time to stand as candidates and vote in local municipal elections in Saudi Arabia. Female candidates had to be represented by a man or speak behind a partition when campaigning, however, and registered women voters had to be driven to the "women only" polling stations by men as they are still not allowed to drive in that country (BBC News 2015a).

In democracies, people generally have a high degree of equality and freedom compared to other forms of states. Enforcement of decisions by the majority, however, can lead to what is sometimes called the "tyranny of the majority," whereby the minority are forced to conform, which may negatively impact minority groups who can be oppressed or discriminated against. Thus, for instance, laws against same-sex marriage prevent homosexual couples from enjoying the benefits available to heterosexual couples. To protect the rights of citizens, some countries have a written *constitution*—a set of laws that provides the basic rules and principles by which a state is structured and governed, and in many cases protects the rights of its citizens. Canada's constitution, which came into effect in April 1982, is the country's supreme law; all other legislation must be in accordance with its rules and principles. The Constitution also establishes the federal, territorial, and provincial levels of government, as well as the relation between the House of Commons and the Senate. Canada's constitution also contains the Canadian Charter of Rights and Freedoms, which outlines the rights and freedoms of all Canadian citizens and others living in Canada. Among other things, it guarantees freedom of religion, movement, opinion, expression, and peaceful assembly.

The Canadian Constitution also protects historic Aboriginal rights that were recognized by the Royal Proclamation of October 7, 1763, as well as any rights and freedoms that were acquired (or may be acquired) through various treaties and land claims agreements. These include such things as fishing, logging, and hunting rights, as well as a right to land and any rights acquired through self-government agreements.

constitution A set of laws that provide the basic rules and principles by which a state is structured and governed, and in many cases protects the rights of its citizens.

monarchy A form of nation-state in which the power rests with a single individual or family within which power is inherited.

dictatorship A nation-state in which one individual holds power.

theocracy A nation-state in which ultimate power rests with a deity or God.

In contrast to a democracy, in a *monarchy*, power is held by a single individual—or monarch—or a royal family. Traditionally, most monarchs inherited their position, which lasts until they die or abdicate. Saudi Arabia is a monarchy run by the Al Saud royal family. Brunei, Morocco, and Swaziland are also monarchies in which the monarchs have considerable power. Until the end of the 19th century most states in Europe were monarchies, although most have now either disappeared or the monarch has become a symbolic figurehead with limited powers, such as Queen Elizabeth II. The Queen is the head of the state of Great Britain as well as Canada and, technically, all new legislation must receive her royal assent before it becomes law. The Queen, however, is not the head or leader of the government: the prime minister is. In a republic, such as the United States, the president is both head of state and the head of government.

In a *dictatorship* one individual holds absolute power to make laws. Dictatorships are usually repressive and brutal; individual citizens have few freedoms, elections are suspended, and opponents repressed or eliminated. Many dictators come to power through use of the military in a military coup. Dictatorships are also often totalitarian in that the state tries to control all aspects of people's lives. Some examples of dictatorships include Adolph Hitler in Nazi Germany, Joseph Stalin in Communist Russia, Fidel Castro in Cuba, Kim Jong-un in North Korea, and Robert Mugabe in Zimbabwe.

In a *theocracy* ultimate power rests with a deity or God. The actual decisions are made by a group of religious leaders who administer what they believe to be the laws and decisions of their God. The best example of a theocracy is Iran, or more precisely, The Islamic Republic of Iran. In Iran the head of state or supreme leader is a religious scholar who appoints heads to various government positions. The government implements Islamic law, or Sharia, as the basis of the legal system, and all institutions operate in accordance with Islamic principles and customs.

The Islamic State of Iraq and the Levant (ISIL), also known as Islamic State of Iraq and Syria (ISIS), became infamous in the early 2010s for seizing large areas of Iraq and Syria, as well as for mass killings, abductions, beheadings, and the destruction of ancient cultural heritage sites, in addition to the 2015 terrorist attack in Paris and the 2016 attack in Brussels. In June 2014, ISIS proclaimed the establishment of a worldwide Islamic State (IS) or "caliphate," which is to be governed by its interpretation of Sharia law (BBC News 2015b). IS also claims religious, political, and military authority over Muslims worldwide, and demands that they swear allegiance to its leader Abu Bakr al-Baghdadi, considered the religious successor to the Islamic prophet, Muhammad, and also move to territory it controls (Mortada 2014).

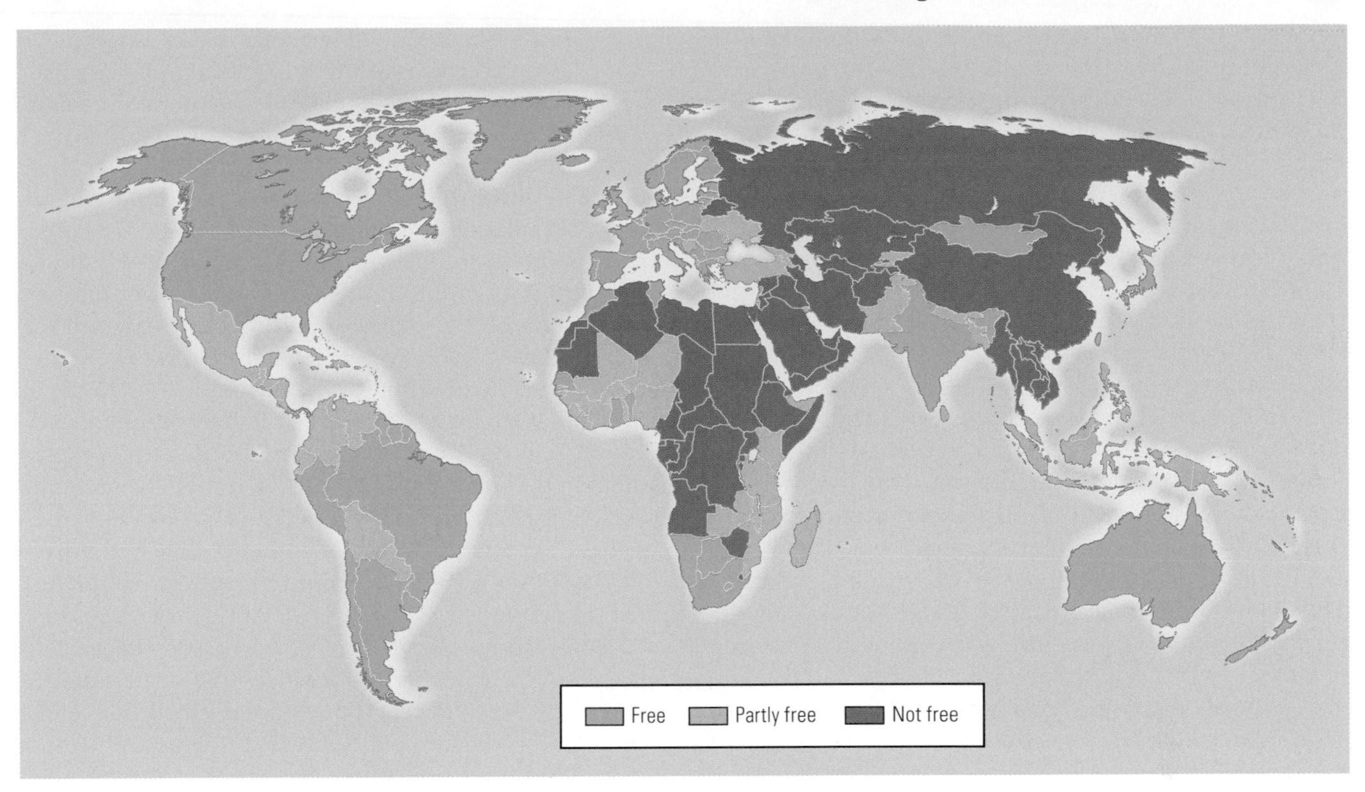

FIGURE 11.7 **Between 2006 and 2015, almost twice as many countries declined as gained in freedom. Most of the reversals were in freedom of expression, civil society, and the rule of law.**

Source: https://freedomhouse.org/report/freedom-world/freedom-world-2016.

Changing State Systems of Government

The global historical trend during the past several decades has been toward democracy and away from autocracy. According to Freedom House (www.freedomhouse.org) (an organization that tracks political trends throughout the world), by the end of 2014, just 89 of the world's 195 countries were electoral democracies (46 percent of the world's population). While this is up from 66 countries in 1987, it represents a decline from the previous few years. For the ninth year in a row, global political rights and civil liberties declined, and almost twice as many countries declined as gained in freedom (from 61 to 33). Democratic ideals, they note, are under more threat today than in the past 25 years (Puddington 2015). Several countries continue to flout democratic values. Russia, for instance, invaded Ukraine in 2014 and seized the Crimea in violation of international agreements. Most of the reversals, however, were in freedom of expression, civil society, and the rule of law. Governments also increased surveillance on its citizens, placed restrictions on Internet access, and limited personal freedom, including the ability to make choices about education, employment, and travel. Terrorist activity, especially by ISIL in Iraq, Syria, and elsewhere, has brutally restricted people's freedom and resulted in millions of refugees. Freedom House also assigns each nation of the world to one of three categories: free, partly free, and not free (Figure 11.7).

Information Technology, Social Media, and Politics

As information technology has developed dramatically in recent years, proponents claim it is leading to new forms of democracy. To be certain, the Internet is the most important information technology since the printing press. Theoretically, it makes it possible for anyone to have free access to information, for opposition parties to spread their agendas, and for formerly oppressed people to connect with others to present a united front against those who would exploit them. In short, the Internet is a democratizing technology that has the *potential* to serve as a powerful tool to fight political repression, racism, and economic exploitation by allowing people to express their concerns.

Even in China, which has a tight control on the Internet and social media, people are using it to fight for injustice and against corruption and expose the truth. For example, in 2009, when a local Communist Party official demanded sex from 21-year-old waitress and manicurist Deng Yujiao at the spa where she worked, she refused. When he tried to force himself on her she fought back and ended up killing him with a pedicure knife. Government authorities charged her with murder and tried unsuccessfully to suppress the news. The incident spread quickly online, however, and not only was she hailed as a heroine, but also people became angry at the abuse of power by local officials, and at the economic circumstances that required her to work in sleazy establishments. To avoid riots the government dropped the charges (MacKinnnon 2012). Previously, Deng Yujiao would have simply disappeared, with few knowing what happened to her.

For the Internet to be a democratizing force, it must be accessible to all people, not just those who can afford the technology. Although the Internet may permit the sending of uncensored information, it can at the same time be used by oppressive governments to create new possibilities for surveillance and sabotage. The Communist Party of China (CCP) attempts to regulate access and what its citizens do online by censoring online speech, blocking selected websites, and filtering for key words (such as Tiananmen) entered into search engines that may incite people. China's censorship of the Internet has come to be called "The Great Firewall of China."

The Internet has also allowed governments to spy on and gain information about the activities of its citizens. Most people were unware that the United States collected information on hundreds of millions of emails and instant messages, and tracked the online activity of millions of its citizens until Edward Snowdon, former Central Intelligence Agency (CIA) and National Security Agency (NSA) employee, leaked details of the government's surveillance activities to the press in 2013.

Today, repressive regimes such as China and Iran censor information, suppress free speech and political dissent, and maintain surveillance on Internet users. As Kline (2011) points out, such authoritarian governments have good reason to fear such things. In 2010 the wave of revolutionary demonstrations that swept across much of North Africa and the Middle East, known as the Arab Spring, was organized, to a large extent, using the Internet and social media and brought down the governments of Tunisia, Egypt, Yemen, and Libya (see Chapter 6). Uprisings in other countries were unsuccessful. Even democratic countries are increasing censorship. Turkey blocks access to YouTube and other search engines and Australia requires Internet service providers (ISPs) to block over 500 sites—mostly child pornography sites, and also some religious sites and YouTube videos (Kline 2011). While censorship of child pornography sites may be praiseworthy, censorship tends to expand over time. The USA has also seized Internet sites and blocked others, and there have been attempts to force ISPs to install surveillance equipment and provide personal information on their subscribers in an attempt to crack down on crime (Kline 2011). Attempts to censor the Internet will most likely fail, as there are many technologies, such as proxy servers and virtual private networks, or people purposefully misspelling words or writing in code, that allow them to get around government surveillance and controls.

A good example of this is the 2014 Umbrella Revolution in Hong Kong, known as such because protestors used umbrellas to ward off tear gas, and the umbrella quickly became a symbol of the movement. When the United Kingdom returned Hong Kong to mainland China in 1997, part of the agreement was that the Chinese government would not interfere in its affairs and would allow the city to remain democratic under a policy known as "one country, two systems." In 2014, however, Beijing mandated that candidates for Hong Kong's chief executive position would first have to be approved by the CCP. Tens of thousands of people came out in protest and occupied central Hong Kong for weeks. Concerned that knowledge of such protests would reach the mainland and incite dissent, the CCP began to arrest sympathizers and censor news. In addition to Twitter, Facebook, and YouTube, which were already blocked, China also blocked access to Instagram (because protestors were uploading and sharing images) and Weibo, China's version of Twitter (Parker 2014) (Figure 11.8).

In the past, such protests would have been a local Hong Kong story, and few people in mainland China would have seen images or had any knowledge of events. Suppression of Internet sites and censorship have certainly given most Chinese people a distorted view of their own society as well as the larger world. But in 2014, as Emily Parker (2014) writes, "In the social-media age, protests are no longer 'local.' "

Paula Bronstein/Getty Images

FIGURE 11.8 Pro-democracy protestors open their umbrellas as a sign of solidarity in Hong Kong in October 2014. The "Occupy Central" civil disobedience movement began in response to China's decision to allow only Beijing-vetted candidates to stand in the city's 2017 election for the top civil position of chief executive.

People worldwide see and hear what is happening and can lend their support on Facebook and other platforms. Social media played a big part in organizing the protests, with people sending images and information over many different platforms to avoid police. Protestors used the texting app WhatsApp to exchange information, and those who used an app called FireChat were successful in communicating via Bluetooth, or cellphone radio, which does not require an Internet connection thus preventing them being cut off from the Internet.

The Internet and Electoral Processes

In those nation-states that have relatively unencumbered access to information, the Internet is significantly influencing the political and electoral processes. Within the past decade, political campaigns have become more sophisticated in taking advantage of what the Internet has to offer. Politicians have access to computer-generated mailing lists, enabling them to target voters. They can become much more efficient in raising campaign funds by using computer programs to identify potential donors. The Internet is also a cost-effective way of disseminating information (and "misinformation") about a candidate, as well as recruiting and mobilizing supporters, volunteers, and campaign funds. Moreover, a candidate's website allows for two-way communication with the voter, establishing an avenue for instant feedback on issues. And, with the explosive popularity of such personal networking sites as Facebook, LinkedIn, Twitter, and blogs, circulating political information and educating the voting public have become enormously more efficient and participatory. In the past, an election could be (and usually was) decided by the number and effectiveness of the TV commercials a candidate could purchase. Such a system clearly worked to the advantage of those candidates who had the most money. With the widespread accessibility of the Internet, however, candidates can get their message across for a fraction of the cost of TV ads.

Perhaps one of the best examples of the use of the Internet and social media to win an election is that of Calgary's mayor Naheed Nenshi. A month before the election in 2010, Nenshi, a Mount Royal University business professor, was in third place with 8 percent of the popular vote, far behind the leading, and better funded, two candidates, who held 42 percent and 28 percent (Braid 2010). Nenshi came from behind to win the election with 40 percent of the vote in large part because of his skill in capitalizing social media. Whereas the other candidates used the Internet and social media to post news releases and answer people's questions, Nenshi used it to talk with the people more directly, spending at least an hour in the evening Tweeting and commenting on Facebook (Braid 2010). He even used an iPhone app to stay in contact with his supporters. Unsurprisingly, he appealed to young urban voters most familiar with social media (Visser 2015). Pollsters were taken by surprise by the win as many voters were between 18 and 30—a demographic unreachable by traditional polling methods because they do not own landlines (Di Cintio 2012). His win made headlines all around the world, not only because he is Canada's first Muslim mayor of a major city in what is sometimes considered Canada's most conservative city, but also because of his use of new technologies (Kaufmann 2010). His campaign is being looked at as a model on how to use Facebook, Twitter, YouTube podcasts, and blogs in political campaigning (Braid 2010). Nenshi won a landslide re-election in 2013 with 74 percent of the vote, and in 2015 was named the world's top mayor (Visser 2015).

Social Control

Whatever form of political organization is found in a society, it must inevitably address the issue of *social control*. In other words, every society must ensure that most of the people behave in appropriate ways most of the time. Every society has defined what it considers to be normal, proper, or expected ways of behaving. These expectations, known as social norms (see Chapter 2), serve as behavioural guidelines that help the society work smoothly. To be certain, social norms are not adhered to perfectly, and in fact there is a certain amount of deviance from them in all societies. Social norms take a number of different forms, ranging from etiquette to formal laws, and some are taken more seriously than others and are more rigidly enforced. To illustrate, although it is customary in Canada for people to shake hands when being introduced, a person's refusal to do so does not constitute a serious violation of social norms. The person who does not follow this rule of etiquette might be considered rude but would not be arrested. On the other hand, some social norms (such as those against forgery or murder) are taken seriously because they are considered absolutely necessary for the survival of the society.

All social norms, whether trivial or serious, are sanctioned; that is, societies develop patterned or institutionalized ways of encouraging people to conform to the norms. These *sanctions* are both positive and

social control Mechanisms found in all societies that function to encourage people to maintain social norms.

sanctions Any means used to enforce compliance with the rules and norms of a society.

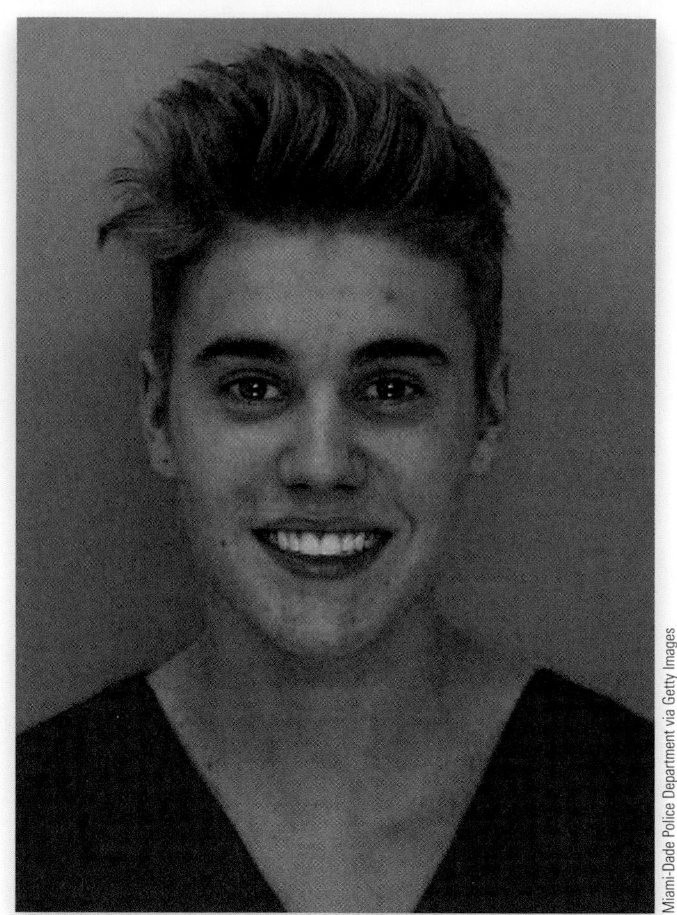

FIGURE 11.9 All societies control behaviour with both positive sanctions (rewards) and negative sanctions (penalties). On the left, Canadian film director Atom Egoyan displays his Order of Canada medal, awarded for bringing recognition to the Canadian film industry. On the right is Canadian singer Justin Bieber's mugshot after he was charged with drunk driving, resisting arrest, and driving without a valid license in Miami, January 2014.

negative: people are rewarded for behaving in socially acceptable ways or punished for violating the norms. ***Positive sanctions*** range from a smile of approval to being made a member of the Order of Canada. ***Negative sanctions*** include everything from a frown of disapproval, to fines, prison, and, in some jurisdictions, the death penalty (Figure 11.9).

Social sanctions may also be formal or informal, depending on whether a formal law (legal statute) has been violated. To illustrate, if a person in a restaurant is talking in a voice that can be easily overheard by people at nearby tables, he or she will probably receive stares from the other diners. But if they start yelling at the top of their lungs in the restaurant, they will probably be arrested for disturbing the peace or disorderly conduct. The difference, of course, is that in the first case the person is not breaking the law, but in the second case they are.

There is thus a continuum of the formal–informal dimension of social norms and sanctions in Canadian society and they are always changing. For example, in July 2015 three Waterloo sisters were stopped by police for cycling topless and told to cover up because it was the law (Boesveld 2015b). It wasn't. Women in Ontario have had the right to go topless since 1996 (Kheiriddin 2015), as they do in British Columbia and elsewhere. In other provinces they are likely to be charged with public indecency. Under the *Criminal Code* of Canada (Section 173) it is illegal to perform an indecent act in a public place. What is indecent is open to interpretation, however, and recently the interpretation of this moral law has become more liberal. Since 2014 a "Free the Nipple" campaign has been gathering momentum to bring awareness to the "double standard" whereby men are allowed to go shirtless but women are expected to cover their breasts. In other countries, such as France, where there is a greater acceptance of female toplessness,

positive sanctions Mechanisms of social control for enforcing a society's norms through rewards.

negative sanctions Punishments for violating the norms of a society.

CROSS-CULTURAL MISCUE

Conrad Black is a media baron born into a wealthy Canadian family in 1944. His company, Hollinger International, controlled *The Daily Telegraph*, *The Jerusalem Post*, *The Chicago Sun-Times*, as well as over 400 smaller newspapers across North America. In 1998 he started the *National Post* as competition for *The Globe and Mail*. He has also written several history books and currently writes a column for the *National Post* and hosts *The Zoomer*, a contemporary affairs program for baby boomers on Vision TV. In 1990, in recognition of his service to Canada, he was appointed an Officer of The Order of Canada, one of Canada's most prestigious medals of honour. In 2001, Queen Elizabeth made him a life peer with the title Baron Black of Crossharbour (a suburb of London), which entitled him to sit in the British House of Lords. His peerage was blocked, however, by Prime Minister Jean Chrétien on the basis that Canadian citizens could not accept foreign peerages, so Black renounced his Canadian citizenship.

His real troubles started in 2000, however, when Hollinger International sold its Canadian newspaper chain to CanWest Media and he received $74 million not to compete, half of which he funnelled into another company to avoid taxes. Directors of Hollinger International later claimed he and an associate were paying themselves unauthorized salaries and that the sale of Hollinger was for personal benefit and funds should have gone to shareholders. In 2004 Black was forced to resign from the board of Hollinger and the next year he was arrested and charged with fraud and obstruction of justice by the U.S. Securities and Exchange Commission (SEC). In 2007 he was convicted and sentenced to six and a half years in prison (CTV News 2007). His conviction also meant he was expelled from the House of Lords. In 2011, on appeal, all but one fraud charge was dropped, leaving only an obstruction of justice charge and a fine of $125 000 from the SEC. Black went back to prison for another 13 months, was released in 2012, and then deported to Canada (Tedesco 2015). Because he had renounced his citizenship, however, he required a special permit to stay in the country. Regaining his citizenship may be problematic as Canada's immigration laws prohibit granting citizenship to foreign convicted criminals. To make matters worse, in 2014 the Tax Court of Canada deemed him a Canadian resident in 2002, claiming he owed $5.1 million in back taxes. He was also removed from the Order of Canada (CBC News 2014).

Black (2011) has never acknowledged any crime and has compared the U.S. justice system to that of North Korea (Johnson 2012). He has also said, "I do not accept that these charges in this manner have any validity and they certainly would not have occurred in this country. In this country, there would have been no prosecution and no conviction" (Johnson 2012). Conrad Black's miscue was not understanding the justice system in the United States and not appreciating the value countries place on citizenship and honours awarded to its citizens. Unfortunately he felt the impact of sanctions.

the trend is to cover up and only 2 percent of women under 35 report that they sunbathe semi-nude, citing not only concerns of skin cancer but also fear that a photo of them will find its way to their Facebook wall (Kheiriddin 2015).

Just as the types of social norms found in any society vary, so do the mechanisms used to encourage people to adhere to those norms. State societies, such as Canada's, have a wide variety of formalized mechanisms to keep people's behaviour in line, including written laws, judges, bureaucracies, prisons, and police forces. Most of our "proper" behaviour, however, is probably caused by less formal, and perhaps less obvious, mechanisms of social control. In band and tribal societies that lack centralized authority, informal mechanisms of social control may be all that exist. In fact, people deviate from what is considered to be acceptable behaviour considerably less in most band societies than in societies that have more formal, elaborate, and complex forms of political organization.

Compared to complex state organizations, bands and tribes have little that appears to be *governmental* in the Western sense of the term. These small-scale political systems have been described as *acephalous* societies, or "tribes without rulers" (Middleton and Tait 1958). In the absence of formal governmental structures, how do these acephalous societies maintain social order? The following three subsections examine mechanisms of social control that are found (a) universally in all types of societies, from band through state systems; (b) only in small-scale societies such as bands and tribes; and (c) only in complex, heterogeneous, and hierarchical state systems.

Mechanisms of Social Control

Public Opinion

One of the most compelling reasons for not violating social norms is ***public opinion***, or social pressure. In general, people from all parts of the world wish to be accepted by the other members of their society. Most people fear being rejected or criticized by

public opinion What the general public thinks about an issue, which, when brought to bear on an individual, can influence his or her behaviour.

their friends or neighbours. This strong desire to be liked is reflected in comments such as "Don't do that! What will the neighbours think?" Of course, it is impossible to determine how many people are deterred from violating social norms by fear of negative public opinion. At the same time, societies use social pressure (or what is called "strategic embarrassment") deliberately to keep people in line. Indeed gossip, ostracism, rumour, sarcasm, and derision are powerful corrective measures for reforming social behaviour. For example, some city and provincial governments in Canada print the names of delinquent dads on websites in an attempt to embarrass them into paying their child support. In the past, in Europe and in North America, people were often shamed and humiliated publicly by being locked into the village stocks (hinged wooden boards in which the person's feet are locked in place), where passers-by could mock them. Today, of course, shaming is made public via the Internet and social media.

Supernatural Belief Systems

A powerful mechanism of social control in all types of societies is supernatural belief systems—belief in supernatural forces such as gods, witches, and sorcerers. People will refrain from antisocial behaviour if they believe that some supernatural force will punish them for it. Of course it is impossible to determine how many norms are *not* violated because people fear supernatural retribution, but we have to assume that the belief in supernatural sanctions acts as a deterrent to some degree. Nor is it necessary to prove that the gods, for example, will punish the social deviants. If people believe that "god will get them" for doing something wrong, the belief itself is usually enough to discourage the deviant behaviour. This is certainly the case in Western religions (Judeo-Christian) that teach about atonement for one's sins and heaven and hell, which are the ultimate positive and negative sanctions. In small-scale societies there are other forms of supernatural belief systems (such as ancestor worship, sorcery, and witchcraft) that are equally effective social mechanisms for controlling people's behaviour.

Belief in *witchcraft*, which is common in some small-scale societies and even among some people in larger societies, illustrates how people are discouraged from engaging in socially deviant behaviour. In many societies in which witchcraft is practised, people reject the idea that misfortunes are the result of natural causes. If crops fail or large numbers of people die, the usual explanation is that someone has been practising witchcraft. In such societies the risk of being accused of witchcraft strongly encourages conformity. For example, the Ibibio of Nigeria believe that witchcraft is responsible for all diseases. Problems during childbirth, for instance, are seen as the result of witches punishing the mother or father for breaking such taboos as committing adultery, or in the case of AIDS, for having unprotected and illicit sex. Because of Ibibio belief, they are more likely to ignore modern healthcare facilities and resort almost exclusively to the use of traditional medicine and faith healing to appease the witches (Ajala 2010). As Evans-Pritchard (1937) pointed out long ago, witchcraft is very much about social relationships as it concerns hatred, envy, greed, jealousy, and evil intentions between people. To avoid this, people are encouraged to maintain good relations.

Oaths and Ordeals

Another way of resolving conflicts—particularly when law enforcement agencies (such as governments) are not especially strong—is through religiously sanctioned methods such as oaths and ordeals. An *oath* is a formal declaration to some supernatural power that what you are saying is truthful or that you are innocent. Although they can take many different forms, oaths almost always are accompanied by a ritual act, such as smoking a peace pipe, signing a loyalty document, or swearing on the Bible. Because some believe that to swear a false oath could lead to supernatural retribution, oaths can be effective in determining guilt or innocence.

An *ordeal* is a means of determining guilt by submitting the accused to a dangerous test. If the person passes the test, it is believed that a higher supernatural force or entity has determined the party's innocence; if he or she fails, then they have been found guilty. In some African societies, an accused person is expected to plunge his hand into a pot of boiling water, lift out a hot stone, and then put his hand into a pot of cold water. The hand is then bandaged and examined the following day. If the hand is blistered, the accused is deemed guilty; if not, his innocence is proclaimed. To Westerners steeped in the principles of the physical sciences, such an approach to determining guilt or innocence seems mystical at best. But there is often more information being gathered than meets the untrained eye. For example, those in charge of conducting the ordeal prepare the accused psychologically to take the

---

witchcraft The practice of an inborn, involuntary, and often unconscious capacity to cause harm to other people.

oath A declaration to a god to attest to the truth of what a person says.

ordeal A painful and possibly life-threatening test inflicted on someone suspected of wrongdoing to determine guilt or innocence.

proceedings seriously. They explain in considerable detail how the ordeal works; they may put their own hands in the water briefly to show how the innocent are protected from blistering. During these preliminaries to the actual physical ordeal, the person administering the ordeal is looking for nonverbal behaviours of the suspect that may indicate probable guilt: signs of excessive anxiety such as muscle tension, perspiration, or dilation of the pupils. Based on an assessment of these nonverbal signs of anxiety, the ordeal administrator may alter such factors as the length of time the suspect's hand stays in the water, which, in turn, may affect the outcome of the ordeal.

Corporate Lineages

Corporate lineages (whose members can number in the hundreds) play an important role in most small-scale societies and are kinship groups whose members often live, work, play, and pray together. Property is controlled by the lineage, people derive their primary identity from the group, and even religion (in the form of ancestor worship) is a lineage matter. Acting like a small corporation, the lineage has a powerful impact on the everyday lives of its members and can exert considerable pressure on people to conform to the social norms.

One means by which a corporate lineage exerts control over its members is economic. All important property, such as land and livestock, is controlled by the elders of the corporate lineage. Often property is allocated on the basis of conformity to societal norms. Those who behave as the society expects them to behave are likely to receive the best plots of land and use of the best livestock. Conversely, those who violate social norms are likely to be denied these valuable economic resources.

Marriage in corporate lineage societies also plays a role in social control. Marriage in such societies is regarded primarily as an alliance between two lineages—that of the bride and that of the groom—and only secondarily as a union between two individuals. In many cases the marriage is legitimized by bridewealth (the transfer of property, often livestock, from the kin group of the groom to the kin group of the bride; see Chapter 8). When a man wants to get married, he is usually unable to pay the bridewealth himself as he lacks personal control over property. Like the rest of his relatives, he has limited rights and obligations to property such as cattle. If marriage-cattle are to be transferred, the prospective groom must convince a number of his kin to give up their limited use of cows. If the prospective groom has a reputation for violating the social norms, it is unlikely that the permission to transfer the cows will be given. Thus, the members of a corporate lineage, through their collective capacity to control marriage, have considerable power to coerce people to behave appropriately.

Intermediaries

Some societies use *intermediaries* to help resolve serious conflicts. The Nuer of the African Sudan are a case in point (Evans-Pritchard 1940). Even though the Nuer political system is informal and decentralized, one role in the society—the Leopard-Skin Chief—is, to a degree, institutionalized. In the absence of any formal system of law courts to punish serious crimes such as murder, the Leopard-Skin Chief serves as a mediator between the victim's family and the family of the murderer. When a homicide occurs, the murderer, fearing the vengeance of the victim's family, takes sanctuary in the home of the Leopard-Skin Chief. In an attempt to prevent an all-out feud, the Leopard-Skin Chief attempts to negotiate a settlement between the two families. His role is to work out an equitable agreement whereby the murderer's family will compensate the victim's family with some form of property settlement (e.g., 40 head of cattle) for the loss of one of its members. These animals will be used as bridewealth for the lineage to obtain a wife for one of its members. It is thought that the sons from such a marriage will fill the void left by the murder victim.

If either side becomes too unyielding, the Leopard-Skin Chief can threaten to curse the offending party. He does not decide the case, however. Rather, he is only an intermediary, with no authority to determine guilt or force a settlement between the parties. Intervening on behalf of the public interest, he uses his personal and supernatural influence to bring the disputing parties to some type of settlement of their dispute.

Age Organizations

In some acephalous societies, *age organizations* serve as effective means of social control. Societies with age organizations have particular groups of people passing periodically through distinct age categories (see Figure 11.10). This shows the basic distinction between *age sets* and *age grades*. An age set is a group of people (usually

---

corporate lineages Kinship groups whose members engage in daily activities together.

intermediaries Mediators of disputes among individuals or families within a society.

age organizations A type of social organization wherein people of roughly the same age pass through different levels of society together; each ascending level, based on age, carries with it increased social status and rigidly defined roles.

age sets Groups of people roughly the same age who pass through various age grades together.

age grades Permanent age categories in a society through which people pass during the course of a lifetime.

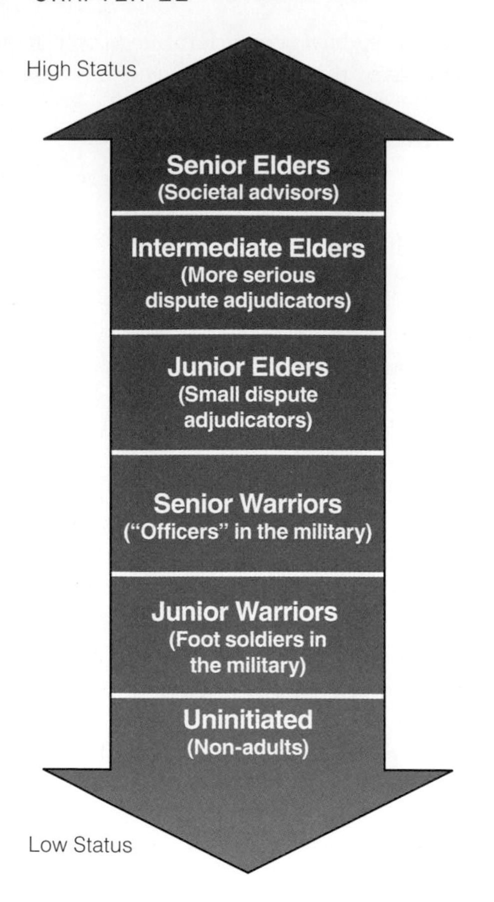

FIGURE 11.10 The general structure of an age-graded society.

men) initiated during a periodic ceremony and having a strong sense of group identity with one another. An age set lasts from its inception, usually when most members are late adolescents, until its last member has died. Age sets pass (as a group) through successive categories called age grades, such as warriors, elders, or various subdivisions within these grades. Each age grade is associated with a well-understood set of social roles (i.e., they perform exclusive functions) and statuses (i.e., higher prestige is associated with higher age). To illustrate this distinction further, an age set is analogous to a group of students who go through university together. The academic years through which they pass are comparable to the age grades. Thus, we can speak of a particular age set occupying the senior warrior grade at a particular moment.

Age organizations control behaviour in significant ways. First, because they establish a clear set of roles and statuses, there is little room for infringing on the authority or domain of others. There is little incentive, in other words, to try to usurp the authority of those above you for the simple reason that if you live long enough, you will eventually have that authority by virtue of your own advanced age.

Second, individuals enter the age-set system at the lowest echelon through the process of initiation. These rites of passage are almost always preceded by intense periods of training in the norms and values of the society. This socialization teaches the soon-to-become adults not only the expected behaviours but also the penalties for deviation and why the behaviours should be followed.

Third, the bonds of camaraderie among members of the same age set are usually so strong that age sets tend to take on the characteristics of a corporate group. Age-set members who experienced their initiation ceremonies together support one another throughout the remainder of their lives in much the same way as do members of the same lineage. Unlike lineages, though, age sets are neither self-perpetuating nor property owning, but they exert the same type of pressure toward conformity as lineages do.

Social Media Shaming

Social media shaming involves shaming a person online by using social networking services such as Facebook to publicly humiliate them. Social media gives people a voice where they can express their opinions and shame others into changing their behaviour and complying with social norms. Politicians' abuse of power and privilege and their secrets can be exposed and they can be shamed. There are countless examples—from getting people to stop watering their gardens during water bans in Vancouver, to getting neighbours to weed their lawns in Ontario.

Occasionally, social media shaming goes international; for example, when Minnesota dentist Walter Palmer and his guides lured Cecil the lion out of a Zimbabwe game preserve in July 2015 so that he could shoot him legally, he was persecuted mercilessly on social media. Not only was his house vandalized but he also received death threats and had to close his website and his practice (Ferreira 2015). In this case it seems social media shaming has led to ***vigilantism***, which is circumventing the law and punishing someone, and attempting to effect justice based on one's own ideas of justice.

In another example, Justine Sacco, who was a senior director of corporate communications at InterActiveCorp (IAC), was on a flight from New York to Cape Town, South Africa, in December 2013, to visit family. While waiting for her connecting flight in London, England, she tweeted as a joke to her 170 followers, "Going to Africa. Hope I don't get AIDS. Just kidding. I'm white!" By the time she arrived in South Africa she was the number one trending topic on Twitter, with 15 000 follows, had lost her job, and was met at the airport by dozens of reporters. Thousands of

social media shaming Publicly humiliating a person online using social networking services such as Facebook to get them to conform to social norms.

vigilantism Taking the law into one's own hands and punishing others according to one's own ideas of justice.

people were upset at what they considered a disgusting, racist tweet and flaunting her privileged status, which angered people and they were determined to punish her for it. While it was probably not meant as a racist comment (Ronson 2015b), it was certainly a poor choice of words. The notoriety she received from the tweets, many more offensive than hers, destroyed her life. Not only did it take her months to obtain another job, but it also took a heavy emotional toll. It also made Google somewhere between $120 000 and $468 000 as Sacco's name was Googled 1 220 000 time in the last 10 days of December 2013 (Ronson 2015b).

Incidents such as these raise numerous questions. Why do we, as a culture, publically shame people online to the point of ruining someone's life because of an unthinking comment or unfortunate phraseology, perhaps taken out of context? In Sacco's case the punishment certainly did not fit the crime. The anonymity of the Internet makes us forget that real people are the targets. Ronson (2015a, 2015b) argues that we like to surround ourselves with like-minded and like-feeling people and attack those who think and feel differently. Attacking Sacco showed they were compassionate and cared about people dying of AIDS in Africa. Ronson (2015b) also notes that this is not only undemocratic but also that "our desire to be seen to be compassionate is what led us to commit this profoundly un-compassionate act." Moreover, and ironically, while the Internet gives people a voice, the fact that what we say can go global in minutes means the best survival strategy is often to remain silent. Unfortunately, this may curtail dialogue on important but sensitive issues such race and gender, especially if speaking up may mean losing one's job. In short, in our efforts to shame people into changing their behaviour, we must consider whether we are doing more harm than good.

It is not just individuals who can be publically shamed into changing their behaviour. In June 2015, in response to an online petition and complaints on Twitter from SumOfUs, an international corporate watchdog group, Tim Hortons pulled ads on its in-store televisions (Tims TV) for Enbridge, the oil and gas company seeking to build the Northern Gateway Pipeline. It backfired. Thousands began boycotting Tim Hortons and signed petitions arguing that the company should not have capitulated so easily, and that pulling the ads was an attack not only on the Canadian energy industry but also the thousands of Canadians employed by Enbridge. Even some politicians got in on the action (Krugel 2015). Companies have to be on their toes more so now than ever before. Any disgruntled customer can complain online anonymously about the quality of a company's goods and services, its values, and the causes it supports.

Organizations are also being punished by various Internet hacker groups for behaviour the group finds unacceptable. Ashley Madison, for example, is a Canadian online dating service catering to married people who want to have an adulterous affair. In July 2015, hackers accessed the company's database and released the names, addresses, emails, and sexual fantasies of 30 million customers worldwide to punish both the company and its mostly male customer base for what they considered unethical or amoral behaviour (Lamont 2016). The fallout has been a few suicides and countless broken relationships. It is also a reminder to all of us that what we do online does not necessarily stay online.

The group Anonymous, which is a loosely organized, international group of computer hackers, has been responsible in recent years for a number of attacks on government agencies, religious groups, and corporations. Generally, the group stands for freedom of the Internet and against injustice. Most of the attacks involve a distributed denial-of-service (DDoS) whereby the organization's website is so overwhelmed by requests that it has to shut down. In other cases, Anonymous hackers break into the databases of organizations, threatening to release secret or personal information unless their demands are met. For instance, in the Rehtaeh Parson's case discussed in Chapter 9, Anonymous threatened to publicize the names of the alleged rapists, which since they were minors at the time were protected under the *Criminal Code* of Canada (CBC News 2013). In July 2015, the group hacked into CSIS, Canada's spy agency, and twice released confidential information about foreign stations and the foreign activities as a vendetta against the government's failure to arrest the RCMP officer responsible for the fatal shooting of one of its members in British Columbia (Humphreys 2015a and 2015b). Dalhousie University in Halifax was also the victim of DDos attack in April 2016, in retaliation for what the group claimed was a failure by the school and police to take action over an alleged frat-house rape (Humphreys 2016).

Courts and Codified Laws

As previously noted, *all* societies use informal mechanisms of social control to some degree. Often, however, these informal mechanisms are insufficient to maintain the desired level of conformity to the norms. Violation of social norms often results in disputes among people in the society. When such disputes become violent conflicts (such as theft, assault, or homicide), we call them ***crimes***. Because societies face the possibility of violent conflict erupting among their members, they need to develop explicit mechanisms to address and, it is hoped, resolve the conflicts.

Although no society in the world is free from crime, the incidence of crime varies considerably from society

---

crime Harm to a person or property that society considers illegitimate.

to society. It appears that crime is more likely to occur in large, heterogeneous, stratified societies than in small-scale societies. For example, the crime rate in Canadian cities is far greater than in rural areas. Several logical arguments support these findings. First, in small-scale societies, people have little or no anonymity, which makes getting away with a crime more difficult. Second, because people in small-scale societies know most of the other people, they are more likely to be concerned with negative public opinion. Third, the heterogeneous character of populations in large-scale, complex, state societies means that there are many groups with different, and sometimes conflicting, interests. Finally, the fact that large-scale societies are almost always stratified into classes or castes means that the lower strata of the population may feel blocked from upward mobility and consequently may be more likely to want to violate the rights of those in the more privileged strata.

A characteristic of state systems of government is that they possess a monopoly on the use of force. Through a system of codified laws, the state both forbids individuals from using force and determines how it will use force to require citizens to do some things and prevent them from doing others. These laws, which are usually in written form, are established by legislative bodies, interpreted by judicial bodies, and enforced by administrators. When legal prescriptions are violated, the state has the authority, through its courts and law enforcement agencies, to fine, imprison, or even execute the wrongdoer. To suggest that the state has a monopoly on the use of force does not mean that only the government uses force. State systems of government constantly have to deal with unauthorized uses of force, such as crime (violent disputes between individuals or groups), ***rebellion*** (attempts to displace the people in power), and ***revolution*** (attempts to overthrow the entire system of government).

The system of codified laws used to resolve disputes and maintain social order in complex societies is different from other types of social norms. Legal anthropologist E. Adamson Hoebel (1972) identified three basic features of ***law***. Although his definition of law goes beyond the type of law found in Western societies, it certainly holds true for that type of law as well.

1. Law involves the legitimate use of physical coercion. Law without the force to punish or deprive is no law at all, although in most cases force is not necessary because the threat of force or compulsion acts as a sufficient deterrent to antisocial behaviour (Figure 11.11).
2. Legal systems allocate official authority to privileged people who are able to use coercion legitimately.
3. Law is based on regularity and a certain amount of predictability; that is, because laws build on precedents, new laws are based on old ones.

rebellion An attempt within a society to disrupt the status quo and redistribute the power and resources.

revolution An attempt to overthrow the existing form of political organization, the principles of economic production and distribution, and the allocation of social status.

law Codified rules enforced through the legitimate use of physical coercion.

Steve Duguay/AFP/Getty Images

FIGURE 11.11 By means of codified laws, state systems of government maintain a monopoly on the use of force. Here a student is arrested by the Montreal police during a protest over tuition fee increases in 2012.

Legal systems in complex societies have objectives different from systems of conflict resolution found in other societies. The objective of the Nuer Leopard-Skin Chief, for example, was to compensate the victim and to re-establish harmony among the disputants, and consequently peace within the community. In contrast, law enforcement and conflict resolution in complex societies tend to emphasize punishment of the wrongdoer, which often takes the form of incarceration or, in some cases, death. In other words, the legal system is not aimed at either compensating the victim or reintegrating the offender back into the community.

The incompatibility of customary law and Western law presented some legal challenges for newly independent countries beginning in the early 1960s. When Western governments administered colonies in the 19th and 20th centuries, they invariably imposed their own laws on the local people, which were often at odds with local customary laws. As the colonial period came to an end during the 1960s and 1970s, many newly independent governments needed to develop legal systems based on their own customs and traditions rather than on those of the former colonial powers. For many newly independent governments, this proved to be a formidable task, given their considerable ethnic diversity.

One such former colony was the country of Papua New Guinea, which won its independence in 1975. With a population of 3.5 million, Papua New Guinea was made up of approximately 750 mutually unintelligible languages and at least that many customary legal systems (Scaglion 1987, 98). The government of this newly independent country was faced with the daunting task of identifying the legal principles of these diverse customary legal systems and reconciling them into a new national legal system. To accomplish this, the parliament established the Law Reform Commission, which sponsored the Customary Law Project (CLP). Headed by legal anthropologist Richard Scaglion, the CLP conducted research on local customary law to determine how, and to what extent, it might serve as the basis for a national legal system.

Collecting this database of customary law (made up of hundreds of detailed case studies) made two important practical contributions to the emerging legal system of Papua New Guinea. First, this legal database was immediately useful to lawyers in searching out legal precedents for their ongoing court cases. Second, the database helped to identify, and subsequently alleviate, certain problems arising from a conflict between customary law and the existing national legal system. To illustrate, in the area of family law, polygyny was perfectly permissible under customary law but was strictly forbidden under existing statutory law. Drawing on the legal database of case studies, the Law Reform Commission, in conjunction with the legislative and judicial branches of the government, drafted and passed a family bill that formally recognized the legality of customary marriages and provided for polygyny under certain circumstances.

Justice Systems

The idea of *justice* is an enduring topic of debate among philosophers, theologians, legislators and social scientists. Justice, in the context of a legal system, can be defined simply as doing what is right. Doing what is right, however, is culturally relative. It is not simply about fairness, although this is how most of us think of it. Whether at work, in the courtroom, or out in the world, we all want to be treated fairly. We do not want to be judged or treated differently based on our gender, faith, age, wealth, or the colour of our skin. This idea of justice is typical of individualist cultures where everyone is "equal before the law." In Canada, this principle is enshrined in the Charter of Rights and Freedoms. In other cultures, however, treating people in ways we would consider unfair or unjust may be what is right. For instance, under Sharia law, which is the legal system based on Islam and which governs all aspects of Muslim life in many countries, women's lives and those of non-Muslims are considered to be worth only half the value of a Muslim man's life. While we may consider this unjust, Sharia law is based on the Quran and the sayings, practices, and teachings of the Prophet Mohammed, and is thus right under Islam.

We also think the administration of justice requires consideration of the motivations and circumstances of wrongdoers. Should a person who steals a loaf of bread because their family is starving receive the same punishment as someone who steals for gain?

Justice can also be retributive or restorative. ***Retributive justice***, which is common in Western cultures, focusses on revenge and punishment of the wrongdoer. For the victims of crimes, justice involves seeing that crimes do not go unpunished and that the offender is appropriately punished—that the punishment "fits the crime." Little thought is given, however, to reparations for the victim(s), although it may also involve some form of monetary compensation. ***Restorative justice***, on the other hand, is about resolving conflict, healing the harm done, and restoring harmonious relationships, although punishment is not precluded. Victims and the community as a whole often take an active role in the restorative justice process, and offenders are encouraged not only to take responsibility for their actions but also to understand the harm they have done to their victims and to make reparations.

The justice system can be looked at as consisting of at least seven elements: ideology, a code, policing, judgement, sanctions, prevention, and institutions.

1. The basis of the system is ideology and it underpins all the other elements. What are a society's ideas about right and wrong? When is an act a crime? How are wrongdoers to be judged? Is the sanction meant to protect the community, teach the individual, and heal broken relationships, or is it for retribution? Is everyone equal before the law? Is the accused innocent until proven guilty, or guilty until proven innocent?
2. A society's ideology of justice is translated into, and embedded in, informal and formal codes of appropriate behaviour, or, in other words, into social norms and laws.
3. Policing is about monitoring. It involves scrutinizing the behaviour of others to see if they are following the social norms and laws, accusing wrongdoers, and perhaps detaining them.
4. Judgement is about how the guilt or innocence of alleged wrongdoers is determined. Methods can vary considerably, from consensus opinion, ordeals, trial by jury, and so on.

---

justice Doing what is right in the context of a legal system.

retributive justice A system of justice that focusses on revenge and punishment of the wrongdoer.

restorative justice A system of justice that focusses on resolving conflict, healing, and restoring harmonious relationships whereby offenders are encouraged to take responsibility for their actions and also to understand the harm they have done to their victims.

5. Sanctions are about determining what to do with wrongdoers. Should they be shamed, ostracized, banished, required to provide service to the community, made to confront their victims, make reparations, fined, imprisoned, physically maimed, put to death?
6. Prevention involves stopping people from offending and reoffending. This can involve punishment as a deterrent—making the wrongdoer aware of the harm he or she has caused—or healing broken relationships. Prevention may also involve understanding and getting at the root causes of wrongdoing and then intervening. Do people break laws and norms because of poverty, substance abuse, poor parenting, and so on?
7. Finally, throughout this process there are individuals and institutions, such as shamans, elders, police, lawyers, lawmakers, judges, courts, prisons, and social services, involved in administering justice.

Correctional Service Canada | Service correctionnel Canada

FIGURE 11.12 Pê Sâkâstêw Centre in Maskwacis (formerly Hobbema), Alberta, is a minimum security prison for Indigenous offenders. The prison promotes Indigenous culture in a process to heal and reintegrate offenders into society.

Retributive versus Restorative Justice in Canada

As noted in Chapter 10, Indigenous people in Canada are overrepresented in the criminal justice system. Relative to non-Indigenous people, they are not only more likely to be in conflict with the law, imprisoned, serve longer sentences, and reoffend, they are also more likely to be the victims of crime. One of the reasons for the overrepresented is, according to the Royal Commission on Aboriginal Peoples (1996), "The fundamentally different world views of Aboriginal and non-Aboriginal people with respect to such elemental issues as the substantive content of justice and the process of achieving justice" (p. 309). The Canadian justice system is based on Biblical notions of retribution—an eye for an eye. The laws and the system of justice themselves are, for the most part, administered by representatives of the state such as police officers, judges, and prison wardens. There are over 600 First Nations in Canada, each with its own ideas about justice, which, for the most part are based on restorative justice.

Generally, First Nations people view justice more in spiritual terms and broken relationships that need to be healed than as a contravention of some law that needs punishment. The Indigenous justice system tends to be less confrontational, involves the victims and community, and strives for harmony (Myers 2008; Friedrichs 2006; Hansen 2009). Under the Canadian justice system, resolution of wrongdoing follows the sequence of arrest, court appearance, sentencing, and fine or incarceration, or both. Many First Nations people, however, have a poor understanding of their rights, court procedures, or the adversarial nature of the system, and so are more likely to be arrested, tried, found guilty, and sent to prison.

Ideological differences and approaches to justice are not the only reason why First Nations, Inuit, and Métis people are overrepresented in the Canadian justice system. At a more fundamental level, the overrepresentation is, among other things, the result of greater levels of poverty, poor education, unemployment, physical and sexual abuse, violence, dysfunctional families, substance abuse, and lack of identity. Most of these things can be directly related to colonization and especially to the experience and legacy of the Residential Schools.

Through various government inquiries, reports, and Supreme Court decisions, the Canadian government is beginning to realize its system of justice does not meet the needs and experiences of Indigenous people. Consequently, it is attempting to make the system more responsive to First Nations, Inuit, and Métis concerns, needs, and cultures by involving Indigenous people more in law enforcement, the courts, in sentencing, in corrections, and in prevention solutions (Figure 11.12). One initiative, for instance, is the First Nations Policing Policy (FNPP). Begun in 1991, the goal of the policy is to provide police services to First Nations through negotiated agreements for police services that meet the particular needs of each community. Most of the police officers are of Indigenous descent. The Aboriginal Justice System (AJS), also started in 1991, aims to support Aboriginal communities in taking greater responsibility for the administration of justice and to help reduce crime through various programs managed by First Nations and innovations in sentencing, for example sentencing or healing circles.

Sentencing Circles

Sentencing circles began in the early 1900s in the Yukon Territorial Court and are generally seen as a culturally sensitive approach to justice. Their goal is not so much to punish the wrongdoer as much as it is to have the offender face their victim(s), understand the harm they have done, and restore harmony between the wrongdoer, their victim(s), and the community. They involve the community hearing the evidence of an alleged crime and seeking input from all who have been affected by the crime: the victim, the defendant, family members, elders, the chief, and any other interested members of the community. A judge, who has the final word on sentencing, is also present. Members sit in a circle and discuss the offence, the offender, his or her circumstances, the impact the offence has had on the community, and a suitable sentence. Most sentencing circles, but not all, deal with minor offences and the sentences tend to involve community service. Sentencing circles are controversial in that, in some instances, victims have been coerced into participating and sentences are seen as light.

Warfare

Just as societies have ways of regulating the social relationships of people within their own society, they also have mechanisms for managing external relationships with other groups, be they states, tribes, bands, clans, or lineages. One such mechanism of social control outside one's own group or society is *warfare*, which we can define as systematic, organized, and institutionalized fighting between different groups. As with most other aspects of culture, there is enormous cultural variability in the extent to which societies use warfare, or other forms of large-scale violence, as a way of resolving conflicts and controlling people's behaviour. In some small-scale societies, warfare as we know it is virtually non-existent; at the other end of the spectrum are societies such as the United States, which participated in World War II at a cost of hundreds of thousands of lives and nearly $3 trillion.

It is often stated that warfare has been around as long as there have been people. Although it is probably true that violence has occurred on occasions throughout human prehistory, warfare began about 10 000 years ago. Most prehistorians agree that warfare as we know it was unknown before the invention of food-production techniques. Before food production, foraging societies had little motivation for engaging in warfare. They had no centralized governments that could finance and coordinate the relatively large numbers of people needed for military campaigns; the absence of food surpluses precluded prolonged combat; because foraging societies did not control land or territorial boundaries, one of the major motivations of warfare simply did not exist; and because they are usually composed of small exogamous bands, people are unlikely to become hostile toward other bands into which their relatives have married.

With the arrival of food production 10 000 years ago, populations became more sedentary, people began to claim rights over specific pieces of land, and the world experienced its first population explosion. If farmers and pastoralists, by the nature of their means of livelihood, experience significant population growth and land scarcity, they are more likely to resort to warfare as a solution to the problem of resource depletion. They will, in other words, resort to warfare to procure rights to other people's land and scarce resources.

Even though small-scale warfare was a possibility 10 000 years ago, war increased in scale with the rise of state societies about 5500 years ago. The formation of large, hierarchically organized states allowed the creation of significant military organizations. In fact, some have argued that state systems of government could not exist without powerful armies to both protect and control their populations. Since the emergence of those early states, the sophistication of military organization and technology has increased steadily over the centuries. The 20th century witnessed an incredible escalation in the power of warfare throughout the world. Not only does humankind now possess the technological capacity to totally annihilate itself within a matter of hours, but technology has also resulted in the killing of large segments of civilian populations. Modern warfare is likely to produce more civilian than military casualties.

States have always spied on one another to gain political or military advantage, but the Internet has taken espionage to another level. By using hackers to infiltrate enemy computer networks (as well as those of their allies), governments can now obtain not only classified or secret information, but they also, because we have become so dependent on computers and the Internet, have the ability to "shut down" much of the infrastructure of enemy states.

The Causes of War

For decades, anthropologists and other social scientists have been fascinated with the question, What causes war? A number of anthropologists over the past 30 years have addressed this question in their examination of the Yanomamö peoples of the Amazon region of Brazil and Venezuela because of their institutionalized warfare and their reputation for fierceness. The Yanomamö were one of the last Amazonian peoples to be contacted by outsiders when, in 1964, anthropologist Napoleon Chagnon began more than 25 fieldwork visits of living with and documenting

---

warfare Institutionalized, armed conflict between nation-states or other politically distinct groups.

their social behaviour, movements, and warfare. Since then more than 30 anthropologists have conducted fieldwork among them (Chagnon 2013). Chagnon claims that the Yanomamö live in a state of chronic warfare and are in a barely detectible transition from primitive to complex, and thus are a perfect group to understand the origins of war (Chagnon 2013). He attempted to explain their system of warfare on the basis of their social structure, namely their acephalous political structure and their competition for women, and that political and personal security was the overwhelming driving force in human social and cultural evolution (1983, 1992, 2013). Marvin Harris (1979b, 1984), a cultural materialist (see Chapter 4), offered a materialist explanation, namely, that Yanomamö warfare is the result of shortages of protein. The most recent entry in the debate is anthropologist R. Brian Ferguson (1995), who claims that the Yanomamö have had direct or indirect contact with Westerners for centuries and go to war over the scarcity of metal tools.

Thus, we have three anthropologists attempting to explain Yanomamö warfare using three different sets of causal factors. That three scholars can come up with three different primary causes for Yanomamö warfare illustrates the complexity of trying to understand warfare. In all likelihood, warfare among the Yanomamö is a multidimensional phenomenon, with all three causal factors valid to some degree.

If we try to search for the causes of war in general, the task becomes even more daunting. When considering warfare (for all time) in both small-scale societies and modern nation-states, we can identify four general factors that contribute to warfare:

1. *Social problems.* When internal social problems exist, political leaders may turn the society's frustrations toward another group. The outsiders may be portrayed as having more than their share of scarce resources or even as causing the social problems. It matters little whether this blame is justified; what is important is that people are convinced that other groups are the cause of their problems. When that happens, one group can declare war on another. Examples of this factor are when the Yanomamö go to war with neighbouring villages over scarce metal tools, and when Adolf Hitler moved his troops into neighbouring European countries to acquire more "living room" for the German people.
2. *Perceived threats.* In some cases, societies go to war when they think their security or well-being is in jeopardy. During the 1960s, the people of North Vietnam were willing to wage war because they felt that their security was threatened by the long-term influence of the French and Americans in the southern part of Vietnam. The Americans, on the other hand, felt, either rightly or wrongly, that Vietnam, and indeed all Asia, was being threatened by the presence of a godless, Communist regime; if South Vietnam fell to the Communists, it would start a domino effect that would eventually threaten the entire free world.
3. *Political motivations.* Sometimes governments wage war to further their own political objectives. The brief wars (or "military actions") that the United States initiated in Haiti, Grenada, Panama, and Somalia were motivated by the desire to show sufficient power to enforce its political will.
4. *Moral objectives.* It is difficult to think of any war in human history that has been waged without moral urgency. Even when wars are waged primarily for political or economic reasons, those who commit their soldiers to battle justify their actions on some moral grounds. Europeans waged the Crusades against the Islamic infidels because they were convinced that God was on their side. Interestingly, if we read accounts of those same wars written by Islamic historians, it is the European Christians who were godless. Both sides justified waging wars for generations on the basis of moral correctness.

It is possible, even likely, that more than one of these factors operate at the same time. To illustrate, the U.S. Congress authorized the use of military action in Iraq in 2003 based on the perceived threat that Saddam Hussein had stockpiles of chemical and biological weapons and intended to sell them to the terrorists who were responsible for the September 11, 2001, attacks. After the weapons of mass destruction and the links to al-Qaeda failed to materialize, the U.S. government argued that its preemptive war in Iraq was justified on political grounds; that is, establishing one democratic regime in the region would cause democracy to spread throughout the Middle East. In addition, the government used the moral justification by arguing that Hussein needed to be overthrown because he was an evil dictator responsible for many atrocities perpetrated against his own people. Thus, in this example, three of the four factors contributing to warfare (listed previously) have been used at one time or another to justify the war in Iraq.

Summary

1. All societies have political systems to manage public affairs, maintain social order, and resolve conflict. The study of political organization involves topics such as the allocation of political roles, levels of political integration, concentrations of power and authority, mechanisms of social control, and means for resolving conflict.
2. Anthropologists generally recognize four levels of political organization based on amounts of political integration and specialization of political roles: bands, tribes, chiefdoms, and states.
3. Societies based on bands have the least political integration and role specialization. They are most often found in foraging societies and are associated with low population densities, distribution systems based on reciprocity, and egalitarian social relations.
4. Historically related to the concept of a band society in Canada is the Indian Act band, which is an administrative unit that manages Indian reserves. The structure and functioning of such bands is governed by the Indian Act.
5. Tribal organizations are most commonly found among horticulturalists and pastoralists. With larger and more sedentary populations than are found in band societies, tribally based societies have certain pan-tribal mechanisms that cut across a number of local segments and integrate them into a larger whole.
6. Chiefdoms have a more formal and permanent political structure than is found in tribal societies. Political authority in chiefdoms rests with a single individual, acting either alone or with the advice of a council. Most chiefdoms, which tend to have quite distinct social ranks, rely on feasting and tribute as a major way of distributing goods.
7. In Canada, election of chiefs to a First Nations band is controlled by the Indian Act, although many bands now engage in traditional custom elections and, most recently, some First Nations, such as the Nisga'a, have signed self-governing agreements.
8. State systems—with the greatest amount of political integration and role specialization—are associated with intensive agriculture, market economies, urbanization, and complex social stratification. States, which first appeared about 5500 years ago, have a monopoly on the use of force and can make and enforce laws, collect taxes, and recruit labour for military service and public works projects.
9. A major challenge for many nation-states today is that they contain within their boundaries distinct ethnic populations that seek independence or greater autonomy, as illustrated by the French in Canada and the Kurds in Turkey.
10. Modern nation-states take many forms, including representational democracies, in which power rests with the people; monarchies, in which power is in the hands of an individual or royal family; dictatorships, in which the leader has absolute power; and theocracies, in which the ultimate power rests with God.
11. During the past several decades, there has been a general trend toward democracy and away from autocracy, although that trend has reversed during the period of 2006 to 2015.
12. The Internet and social media are powerful tools to fight political repression, racism, and economic exploitation and many states are trying to control them. They are also influencing political and electoral processes.
13. In the absence of formal mechanisms of government, many band and tribal societies maintain social control by means of informal mechanisms such as socialization, public opinion, corporate lineages, supernatural sanctions, and age organizations.
14. Social media is a new powerful force not only to control people's behaviour by shaming them publically online, but also can go too far and ruin people's lives.
15. In addition to informal means of control, state societies also use a system of codified laws and a court system to resolve disputes and maintain social order.
16. A justice system consists of an ideology, a code, policing, judgement, sanctions, prevention, and institutions. Retributive justice focusses on revenge and punishment of the wrongdoer, while restorative justice focusses on resolving conflict, healing, and restoring harmonious relationships.
17. A society will go to war when it (a) blames another society for its own social problems, (b) believes that it is threatened, (c) wants to further its own ends, or (d) is defending a moral position.

Key Terms

acephalous societies
age grades
age organizations
age sets
authority
autocratic state
band societies
chiefdom
constitution
corporate lineages
crime
dictatorship
First Nations
Gladue report
Indian Act band
intermediaries

justice
law
monarchy
nation
nation-state
negative sanctions
oath
ordeal
pan-tribal mechanisms
political integration
political organization
polyethnic
positive sanctions
public opinion
rebellion
referendum
representative democracy
reserve
restorative justice
retributive justice
revolution
sanctions
social control
social media shaming
specialized political roles
state
suffrage
theocracy
totalitarian state
tribal council
tribal societies
vigilantism
warfare
witchcraft

Critical Thinking Questions

1. In sentencing First Nations offenders, judges are required to pay "particular attention to the circumstances of aboriginal offenders." Gladue reports detailing these circumstances are often prepared. A major intent of this provision is to take into consideration the impact of colonization and especially the impact of Residential Schools on First Nations people. It has, however, led to accusations of a two-tier justice system. Is it right to take the historical and specific background of First Nations offenders into consideration when sentencing?
2. Do you think there is more social deviation in small-scale societies or in larger, more complex societies? Why or why not?
3. During the colonial period many societies, including many First Nations, with no former tradition of chiefs have had chiefships imposed on them by European colonial powers. What has been the impact on these societies, and how can anthropologists work with them to overcome this particular legacy?
4. What advantages and disadvantages do you see to First Nation bands following custom election rules?
5. What benefits are there to First Nations, and to Canada as a whole, when self-governing agreements are signed? What role is there for anthropologists in this process?
6. A major challenge for states containing numerous ethnic groups is to create a unified national identity while the ethnic populations themselves are seeking independence or expanded autonomy. Using a specific example, discuss how anthropologists can work with either an ethnic group to gain more autonomy, or with the state government to forge a common identity.
7. Can you think of an example of public shaming not mentioned in the text? How does it compare with shaming in small-scale societies?
8. How do the rights of Indigenous people in Canada compare with the rights of Indigenous people in Australia, New Zealand, and the United States?
9. The Canadian justice system is primarily one of retribution, whereas the justice system of most Indigenous groups is restorative, and is a major reason why First Nations people are over-represented in the criminal justice system. How can anthropologists work with the Canadian government and First Nations to reconcile these differences?
10. What advantages are there for First Nations communities to be policed by members of their own communities?

Make the Grade with MindTap

Stay organized and efficient with **MindTap**—a single destination with all the course material and study aids you need to succeed. Built-in apps leverage social media and the latest learning technology. For example:

- ReadSpeaker will read the text to you.
- Self-quizzing allows you to assess your understanding.
- Flashcards are pre-populated to provide you with a jump-start for review—or you can create your own.
- You can highlight text and make notes in your MindTap Reader. Your notes will flow into Evernote, the electronic notebook app that you can access anywhere when it's time to study for the exam.

Visit nelson.com/student to start using **MindTap**. Enter the Online Access Code from the card included with your text. If a code card is not provided, you can purchase instant access at NELSONbrain.com.

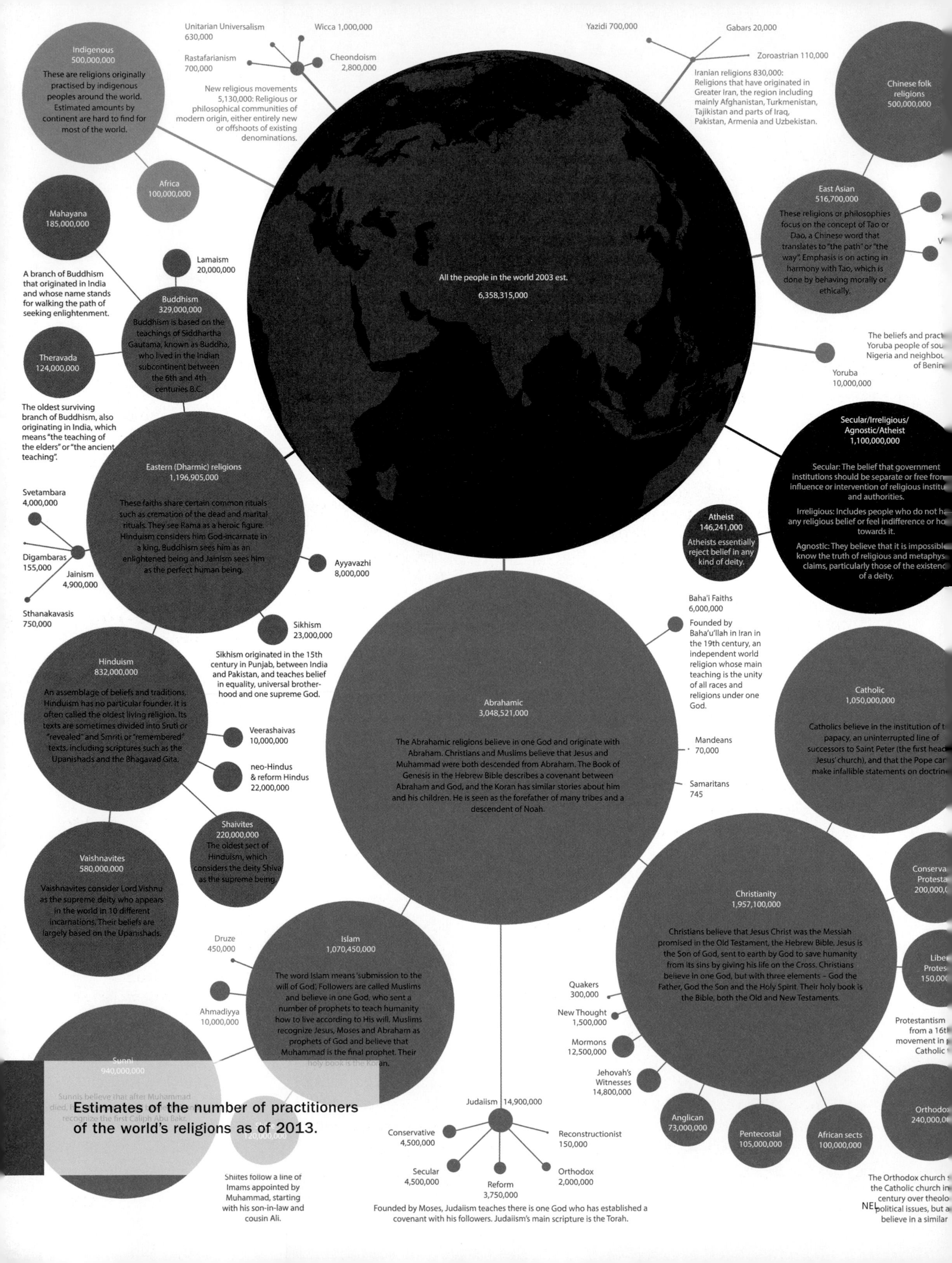

Indigenous
500,000,000
These are religions originally practised by indigenous peoples around the world. Estimated amounts by continent are hard to find for most of the world.
Africa
100,000,000
Unitarian Universalism
630,000
Wicca 1,000,000
Rastafarianism
700,000
Cheondoism
2,800,000
New religious movements
5,130,000: Religious or philosophical communities of modern origin, either entirely new or offshoots of existing denominations.
Yazidi 700,000
Gabars 20,000
Zoroastrian 110,000
Iranian religions 830,000: Religions that have originated in Greater Iran, the region including mainly Afghanistan, Turkmenistan, Tajikistan and parts of Iraq, Pakistan, Armenia and Uzbekistan.
Chinese folk religions
500,000,000
East Asian
516,700,000
These religions or philosophies focus on the concept of Tao or Dao, a Chinese word that translates to "the path" or "the way". Emphasis is on acting in harmony with Tao, which is done by behaving morally or ethically.
All the people in the world 2003 est.
6,358,315,000
Mahayana
185,000,000
A branch of Buddhism that originated in India and whose name stands for walking the path of seeking enlightenment.
Lamaism
20,000,000
Buddhism
329,000,000
Buddhism is based on the teachings of Siddhartha Gautama, known as Buddha, who lived in the Indian subcontinent between the 6th and 4th centuries B.C.
Theravada
124,000,000
The oldest surviving branch of Buddhism, also originating in India, which means "the teaching of the elders" or "the ancient teaching".
Yoruba
10,000,000
Secular/Irreligious/Agnostic/Atheist
1,100,000,000
Atheist
146,241,000
Atheists essentially reject belief in any kind of deity.
Eastern (Dharmic) religions
1,196,905,000
These faiths share certain common rituals such as cremation of the dead and marital rituals. They see Rama as a heroic figure. Hinduism considers him God-incarnate in a king, Buddhism sees him as an enlightened being and Jainism sees him as the perfect human being.
Svetambara
4,000,000
Digambaras
155,000
Jainism
4,900,000
Sthanakavasis
750,000
Ayyavazhi
8,000,000
Sikhism
23,000,000
Sikhism originated in the 15th century in Punjab, between India and Pakistan, and teaches belief in equality, universal brotherhood and one supreme God.
Hinduism
832,000,000
An assemblage of beliefs and traditions, Hinduism has no particular founder. It is often called the oldest living religion. Its texts are sometimes divided into Sruti or "revealed" and Smriti or "remembered" texts, including scriptures such as the Upanishads and the Bhagavad Gita.
Veerashaivas
10,000,000
neo-Hindus
& reform Hindus
22,000,000
Shaivites
220,000,000
The oldest sect of Hinduism, which considers the deity Shiva as the supreme being.
Vaishnavites
580,000,000
Vaishnavites consider Lord Vishnu as the supreme deity who appears in the world in 10 different incarnations. Their beliefs are largely based on the Upanishads.
Baha'i Faiths
6,000,000
Founded by Baha'u'llah in Iran in the 19th century, an independent world religion whose main teaching is the unity of all races and religions under one God.
Abrahamic
3,048,521,000
The Abrahamic religions believe in one God and originate with Abraham. Christians and Muslims believe that Jesus and Muhammad were both descended from Abraham. The Book of Genesis in the Hebrew Bible describes a covenant between Abraham and God, and the Koran has similar stories about him and his children. He is seen as the forefather of many tribes and a descendent of Noah.
Mandeans
70,000
Samaritans
745
Catholic
1,050,000,000
Christianity
1,957,100,000
Christians believe that Jesus Christ was the Messiah promised in the Old Testament, the Hebrew Bible. Jesus is the Son of God, sent to earth by God to save humanity from its sins by giving his life on the Cross. Christians believe in one God, but with three elements – God the Father, God the Son and the Holy Spirit. Their holy book is the Bible, both the Old and New Testaments.
Druze
450,000
Ahmadiyya
10,000,000
Islam
1,070,450,000
The word Islam means 'submission to the will of God'. Followers are called Muslims and believe in one God, who sent a number of prophets to teach humanity how to live according to His will. Muslims recognize Jesus, Moses and Abraham as prophets of God and believe that Muhammad is the final prophet. Their holy book is the Koran.
Sunni
940,000,000
Shiites follow a line of Imams appointed by Muhammad, starting with his son-in-law and cousin Ali.
Quakers
300,000
New Thought
1,500,000
Mormons
12,500,000
Jehovah's Witnesses
14,800,000
Anglican
73,000,000
Pentecostal
105,000,000
African sects
100,000,000
Judaism 14,900,000
Conservative
4,500,000
Reconstructionist
150,000
Secular
4,500,000
Reform
3,750,000
Orthodox
2,000,000
Founded by Moses, Judaism teaches there is one God who has established a covenant with his followers. Judaism's main scripture is the Torah.

Estimates of the number of practitioners of the world's religions as of 2013.

CHAPTER

12

Religion

WHAT WE WILL LEARN

- What religion is
- How anthropologists study religion
- The problems involved in defining religion
- The functions religion performs for the individual and for the society
- The difference between magic, witchcraft, and religion
- The different forms religion takes among the societies of the world
- What rites of passage are
- How and why new religious movements emerge
- What Wicca is and why it is one of the fastest growing religions in North America
- The state of religion in Canada
- How religions are changing in the age of globalization
- The impact of Islamic Terrorism and Islamophobia on society

ST. JOSEPH, THE UNDERGROUND REAL ESTATE AGENT

Margaret Seymour's house in Barrie, Ontario, had been on the market for four months with no interest from buyers. Desperate to move, she buried a figurine of St. Joseph, said a prayer, and the next day her house sold (Lewis 2009). Similarly, Stephen Weir and his wife were also having trouble selling their Toronto home in a down market. The day after they buried St Joseph, they too had an offer on their house. Weir told his story to a colleague and his wife also buried St Joseph. The next day they had not one but two offers on their Oakville home (Weir 2013). And every time Calgary realtor Gizella Davis puts up a for sale sign she also buries St. Joseph (Lewis 2009).

In the Roman Catholic faith, St. Joseph, the Earthly father of Jesus, is the patron saint of homes, families, workers, and more recently, it seems, of real estate agents. Patron saints in the Catholic tradition are thought to intercede, or intervene, on behalf of those who pray to them. Saints are often the patrons of places, and St. Joseph, along with St. Jean de Brébeuf, is also the patron saint of Canada. Although not sanctioned by the church, tradition has it that if the faithful bury a small statue of St Joseph, he will "lend a divine hand in helping to find a willing buyer" (Lewis 2009) for their house. For him to work his magic, however, he has to be buried upside down with his feet facing the heavens.

Many people believe this tradition started in the mid-1500s when St. Teresa of Avila in Spain buried a medallion of St. Joseph and prayed to him to help her religious community obtain more land for a convent (Catholic Faith Store). The medals later evolved into figurines. Others believe that when Brother André Bessett wanted land on Mount Royal in Montreal to build an oratory (a small chapel) in the late 1800s, the landowners refused to sell, but when he planted a medallion of St. Joseph the owners relented and sold him the land (Madigan 2010). None of these stories are present in the academic literature, however, and so it is more likely "retrofitting lore to a custom" (Madigan 2010). Whatever the real history, the tradition of burying a plastic St. Joseph seems to date from the late 1970s to the mid-1980s in both Canada and the United States.

The ritual has become so widespread that many religious goods and church supply stores even offer home sale kits for about $10 and are having difficulty keeping them in stock (Figure 12.1). Most kits are available online and include a four-inch plastic statue of St. Joseph, a protective plastic burial bag, a prayer card, and an instruction booklet. More expensive kits may also include the 2003 book *St. Joseph, My Real Estate Agent* by Stephen Binz, and a larger,

Paul Velgos/iStock/Getty Images Plus

FIGURE 12.1 Some Catholics believe that burying a figurine of St. Joseph upside down next to the "for sale" sign will help sell their home.

better-quality figurine. One site also offers a free listing on the St Joseph's Homeseller Listing website: www.stjosephstatue.com/homes/main.php.

Instructions on how to bury St. Joseph vary: upside down in the front yard facing the house; facing away from the house; near the "for sale" sign; in the backyard in a flower bed; exactly 12 inches deep, and so on. If you live in a condominium, no problem, bury St. Joseph in a flower pot. Most importantly, however, is to say a devotional prayer once he is buried, asking for his help. After the house sells, he should be dug up and given a place of honour in the new home. Of course, to sell your home it also helps to fix up the property, stage it properly for prospective buyers, and set the price at current market value.

The practice of burying a St. Joseph statue has many characteristics of religion that we will explore in this chapter. People often turn to their religious beliefs in times of uncertainty and when they feel powerless. Burying him and praying to him to intercede is not only a sign of faith but also provides people with a semblance of control. It also has many elements of what anthropologists consider to be magic, that is, manipulating something physical to achieve a goal through supernatural means. It is also a ritual that must be done in a prescribed way if it is to work. If the house fails to sell, then the most likely explanation is that the ritual was not performed correctly. The practice is also a good example of how new rituals are developed and change over time to suit current social and cultural contexts. ■

The Anthropological Study of Religion

Anthropologists are unconcerned with the truth of a particular belief or religion but understand the "facts" of religion in context, accepting that they are true for the adherents. We accept that the world's people inhabit are just as real and vivid for them as they are for us. Even though they may seem strange from our standpoint, by understanding religions in context from an emic perspective, anthropologists attempt to avoid ethnocentrism.

As with other aspects of culture, anthropologists also look at religion holistically. Religion is viewed not as a separate sphere but as interconnected with such other dimensions of culture as gender, kinship, economics, political organization, and so on. Religion is a social and political force both within Canada and globally, and influences such issues as same-sex marriage, abortion, polygamy, the environment, healthcare, education, and justice. Religions are also never static, and so anthropologists are also in interested in how and why they change. They are interested in the rise of fundamentalism, and why new religions arise where and when they do. In addition to these concerns, anthropologists are also interested in the effects of globalization and the Internet on religious beliefs, and the role of religion in political struggles around the world.

Beginning in the 19th century, religion was studied from a scientific rather than simply a theological perspective. Edward Burnett Tylor, for instance, was interested in how religion originated and evolved. He argued that "primitive" people observed two phenomena of experience: the difference between a live body and a dead one, and the visions of humans that appear in dreams and trances. To reconcile these two things they, according to Tylor, posited the existence of a spirit or soul that inhabits and breathes life into, or animates, all living things and even inanimate objects such as stones, weapons, mountains, and rivers. For Tylor, this was the earliest form of religion, which he called *animism*, from the Latin word *anima*, which means soul or breath, and that he defined as "belief in spiritual beings" (1871 (1958) Vol I p. 383).

Animistic beliefs are common in societies such as foragers, horticulturalists, and even followers of neo-pagan religions, where people see themselves as part of nature. Animists have a much closer connection to their spirits and gods than monotheists (believers in a single god), and they can turn them to help in the hunt or to help heal the sick. Spirits are thought to have an interest in human affairs, some with good and some with evil intentions. Tylor believed that animism evolved into *polytheism*, or belief in many gods, and eventually into monotheism, the belief in a single god. Even *monotheists*, however, believe in multiple spiritual beings, such as angels and demons and the devil, but only one is all-powerful.

Tylor's successor at Oxford, R. R. Marett (1914), argued that early humans, before they posited the existence of supernatural beings, first had an emotional reaction of "awe" to such natural phenomena as thunderstorms, earthquakes, rainbows, floods, and so on. This reaction was "pre-animistic" and Marett suggested that, before primitive people came up with the idea of a spirit, they first believed in the existence of some impersonal personal power called *mana*. Mana is a Melanesian term first described by English missionary Robert Codrington, who defined it as "a force altogether distinct from physical power, which acts in all kinds of ways for good and evil, and which it is of the greatest advantage to possess or control" (Codrington 1891, 118).

Scottish social anthropologist, James George Frazer, in his influential work *The Golden Bough* (1894), argued that "primitive" peoples were concerned primarily with practical problems such as getting enough food to eat, curing illnesses, and defeating their enemies. Because human beings face important life problems that cannot all be resolved through the application of science and technology alone, Frazer argued that they attempted to overcome these human limitations by manipulating supernatural forces, in other words, by *magic*. Magic, is the manipulation of nature using supernatural methods, such as spells, incantations, and *rituals*, to achieve some goal. Frazer believed there were two basic types of magic: imitative, or sympathetic magic, and contagious magic. With *imitative magic* there is believed to be a mystical connection between the image or likeness of something and the thing itself. Sticking pins into a "voodoo doll" that resembles or represents one's enemy to cause them pain in the part of the body stuck

De Agostini/C. Marchelli/Getty Images

FIGURE 12.2 Archers, dogs, and a hoofed animal in cave paintings in Tassili n'Ajjer, Algeria World Heritage Site. By depicting a successful hunt, was the artist practising imitative magic?

by the pin is a good example of imitative magic. There is some suggestion that paleolithic hunters who drew images of a successful hunt on cave walls may perhaps have been trying to control the outcome of a hunt through imitative magic (Figure 12.2). With *contagious magic* there is believed to be a supernatural connection between the whole and the part, or between things that were once in contact, and that what is done to the part affects the whole. Sorcerers, for example, are sometimes thought to perform spells on the finger nail clippings, hair, or clothing of their victims to harm them. Frazer believed that magic progressed to religion and then to science.

In *The Elementary Forms of Religious Life*, French sociologist Émile Durkheim ([1912] 2001) argued that religion enables people to transcend their individual identities and see themselves as part of a larger collective. Durkheim's goals were to describe and explain religion in "its most primitive and simple form" (p. 1), and to understand how people categorized things

---

animism The belief that animals, plants, and inanimate objects are animated by spirits.

polytheism The belief in many gods.

monotheism The belief in a single all-powerful god.

mana An impersonal and powerful supernatural force that can reside in people, animals, plants, and objects.

magic The manipulation of nature using supernatural techniques to accomplish specific aims.

rituals A set of behaviours using words, gestures, and objects, performed in a prescribed sequence and manner.

imitative magic Performing a magical ritual on the likeness of someone or event to influence the real person or event.

contagious magic Performing a magical ritual on something that has been in contact with someone to influence that person.

in relation to religious beliefs. Durkheim believed the most "primitive," or rather "elementary," form of religion was that of the Australian Aborigines who practised *totemism*. Totemism is a mystical or spiritual relationship between an animal or plant (the totem) and a group of people or kinship group, which also serves as the symbol or emblem for the group.

Durkheim also believed societies divided the world into two ideal categories: the *sacred* and the *profane*. The profane refers to the everyday world of mundane existence and routine experience where nothing is special. It is the utilitarian and secular world of work necessary for survival. The sacred, however, is beyond the everyday, and beyond empirical nature and knowledge acquired by the senses. The sacred can be objects (e.g., books, amulets, totems), places (e.g., mosques, shrines), times (e.g., Friday or Sunday), people, or anything else set aside from the ordinary as special. One tells the difference between the two by the way people behave toward them. Toward the sacred, or in the presence of sacred things, people behave reverently and with respect. For example, when people go to church they often dress in their Sunday best. People often perform *purification rituals* to keep the two worlds separate. For example, before Muslims pray or handle the Qur'an, a ritual washing known as *wudu* should be performed to remove any uncleanliness (Figure 12.3). Wudu typically involves washing the hands and both arms up to the elbows, as well as the face and feet up to the ankles, in a prescribed manner. Ritual washing does not mean the body is necessarily physically dirty, but rather impure. Another example is baptism, which many Christians see as a form of ritual purification that washes away original sin.

Durkheim defined religion as "a unified system of beliefs and practices relative to sacred things, that is to say, things set apart and forbidden—beliefs and practices which unite into one single moral community called a Church, all those who adhere to them" ([1912] 2001: 47). Magic, for Durkheim, was a problem since it was not part of a community but was performed for selfish and potentially evil purposes, and thus did not bind the group together. Religion, on the other hand, was something social, in fact for Durkheim, religion was divinized or made god-like: "If religion has given birth to all that is essential in society," he said, "it is because the idea of society is the soul of religion" ([1912] 2001): 419).

FIGURE 12.3 A Pakistani Muslim performs wudu before congregational prayers.

British social anthropologist Bronislaw Malinowski (1962) was critical of Durkheim's theory of religion and took a functionalist perspective, making a clear distinction between the functions of science, magic, and religion. Science, he argued, involves observation of natural processes and careful reasoning about the world, and is necessary for survival. Magic, on the other hand, gives people a sense of control; it steps in, he said, "wherever man cannot control hazard by means of science. It flourishes in hunting and fishing, in times of war and in seasons of love, in the control of wind, rain and sun, in regulating all dangerous enterprises" (1962, 261). Religion, according to Malinowski, has both psychological and sociological functions. By providing answers to such things as what happens after death, religion reduces anxiety and provides a feeling of peace and well-being; it helps people cope with reality. It also has a social function by providing people with a moral code about how to behave, as well as sanctions for not following cultural norms. By participating in rituals, religion also gives people a sense of community.

---

totemism A mystical or spiritual relationship between an animal or plant (the totem) and a group of people or kinship group.

sacred The aspect of such things as places, times, objects, and people that is beyond sensation that makes them special and thus worthy of great respect.

profane The utilitarian and secular world of work and routine experience.

purification rituals A ritual performed to remove uncleanliness before worship or coming in contact with something sacred.

wudu The Islamic purification ritual of washing parts of the body before prayer or before handling the Qur'an.

Another social scientist who analyzed religion as it relates to economic institutions was Max Weber. In his classic study, *The Protestant Ethic and the Spirit of Capitalism*, Weber (1958 [1904]) claimed that the Protestant faith supported the rise of capitalism in Western societies. According to traditional Catholic teachings, money and its pursuit were seen as leading people away from a good Christian life. With the Protestant Reformation, which began in the early 1500s, however, Protestants came to view hard work as fulfilling one's religious obligations, and the rewards of wealth as proof of genuine faith. The growth of the capitalist system was thus a result of changes in religious belief.

American anthropologist Clifford Geertz (1966) defines a religion as "(1) a system of symbols which acts to (2) establish powerful, pervasive, and long-lasting moods and motivations in men by (3) formulating conceptions of a general order of existence and (4) clothing these conceptions with such an aura of factuality that (5) the moods and motivations seem uniquely realistic" (p. 4). Geertz's definition is important because it emphasizes the important roles of symbols and emotion in religion. By taking a more emic approach, it also avoids the dichotomy between the natural and supernatural and points out that much of human action is motivated by religious beliefs.

Defining Religion

As we can see from the above, definitions of ***religion*** vary enormously, as do its forms, but all are alike to the extent that they view a belief in the supernatural as it's most essential characteristic. For our purposes in this chapter, we shall define religion as a system of beliefs and practices involving supernatural beings and forces directed at helping people make sense of the world and solve important problems.

Anthropologists have long observed that all societies have a recognizable set of beliefs and behaviours that can be called religious. But religions entail more than belief in the supernatural. They are also systems of symbols and contain a moral code. Most religions also make a distinction between the sacred and profane, provide adherents with a sense of identity, help reduce stress and anxiety, involve altered states of consciousness, have rituals, contain stories or myths about how humans and the world came to be, have specially skilled individuals, and involve magic and witchcraft.

To be sure, nonreligious people can be found in all societies. But when we claim that religion (or a belief in the supernatural) is universal, we are referring to a cultural phenomenon rather than an individual one.

Because religion, in whatever form it may be found, is often taken seriously and passionately by its adherents, there is a natural tendency for people to see their own religion as the best or the only true religion while viewing all others as inferior. Westerners often use science, logic, and empirical evidence (e.g., through the study of Biblical texts) to bolster and justify their own religious practices. The central issue for anthropologists is not to determine which religion is better or more correct, but rather to identify the various religious beliefs in the world as well as how they function, to what extent they are held, and the degree to which they influence human behaviour.

Problems of Defining Religion

While defining religion in terms of the "supernatural" has value as a working definition, it is important to recognize that it implies a distinction between the natural and the supernatural worlds, which we in the West make but many other societies do not. For many peoples the physical world is permeated with the spiritual or "supernatural." People may make a distinction between humans and spirits and use magic to achieve their goals, but these beings and processes are simply part of their everyday world of experience. Magical rituals are just as normal and natural a way to achieve goals as hard labour. If we refer to a society's beliefs in witchcraft as a belief in "supernatural" forces when they do not see it as supernatural, then we are being ethnocentric.

Defining religion is also difficult because anthropologists disagree on how to distinguish between religious and nonreligious phenomena. Religion is so thoroughly embedded in the culture that it is difficult to distinguish religious behaviour from economic, political, or kinship behaviour. Because many small-scale, less-specialized societies do not divide human behaviour into the same categories used in Western society, it is often difficult for Westerners to recognize those aspects of human behaviour that we think of as religious. To illustrate, when a Kikuyu elder sacrifices a goat at the grave of an ancestor-god, is he engaging in religious behaviour (he is calling for the ancestor-god to intervene in the affairs of the living), economic behaviour (the meat of the sacrificed animal is distributed to and eaten by members of the kinship group), or kinship behaviour (kin have a chance to express their group solidarity at the ceremonial event)? Such a ritual sacrifice performs all these functions at the same time (Figure 12.4).

Another difficulty in defining religion and the supernatural is that different societies have different ways of distinguishing between the natural world and the supernatural world. In our society, we reserve the term supernatural for phenomena we cannot explain

religion A system of beliefs and practices involving supernatural beings and forces that functions to provide meaning, peace of mind, and a sense of control over unexplainable phenomena.

Jacob Maentz/Getty Images

FIGURE 12.4 The Abelling Tribe in the Philippines believe that Anitos (spirits) will reveal their future to them by inhabiting the body of a tribe elder for a given time. For this to happen, a pig is sacrificed and the elders drink the blood of the dying pig. In this state, important decisions are made for the tribe. The pig sacrifice thus not only fulfills a religious function, but also an economic one since the pig will be eaten, as well a political function.

through reason or science. Other societies may also divide the world into natural or supernatural arenas, but may divide it up differently. For example, the Shoshone, who traditionally were foragers living in the desert areas of Nevada and Utah, believed in the existence of a creature called a water baby. Water babies lived near springs and rivers, were about the size of a human infant, and made a sound like a baby crying. Hearing a water baby cry, some young mothers would try to quiet it by picking it up and nursing it. The water baby would then attach itself to her breast and suck all the blood from her until she died (Crapo 2003). Most of us would probably classify water babies as supernatural creatures and as part of their religious beliefs. The Shoshone, however, classify them along with the other animals in their environment such as snakes and mountain lions, and not with the supernatural creatures that they also recognize. As Crapo points out, if we were to classify this belief as religious, we would be ethnocentric since they do not classify water babies as being supernatural. If, on the other hand, we took a culturally relative stance and classified them as part of their traditional environmental knowledge, we would be put in the awkward position of placing them alongside other animals when we know that they, like vampires, do not really exist.

Another source of confusion when we try to define religion is our inability to separate supernatural beliefs from other aspects of culture. People often claim to be acting in the name of their religion, but in fact they are using their religion to support or reject other (nonreligious) features of their culture. For example, we often think of such policy issues as opposition to abortion, gay marriage, Darwin's theory of evolution, and stem-cell research as being part of the philosophy of evangelical Christianity. Instead, these are social issues that many evangelicals tend to support by citing their own interpretations of scripture. But it is certainly possible—and definitely demonstrable—to believe in the central core of evangelical Christianity (e.g., personal conversion and the full authority of the Bible) without rejecting abortion, Darwinian evolution, or gay marriage.

Functions of Religion

Anthropological studies of religion are no longer dominated by the search for origins. More recent studies have focused on how religious systems function for both the individual and the society as a whole. Because religious systems are so universal, it is generally held that they must meet a number of important needs at both personal and societal levels. Yet, it should be obvious to most religious practitioners that supernatural powers do not always work as effectively as the practitioners think they should. For example, we may pray to God for the recovery of a sick friend, but the friend dies nevertheless; a ritual specialist conducts a rain dance, but it still does not rain; or the living relatives sacrifice a goat at the grave site of the ancestor-god but still are not spared the ravages of a drought. Although supernatural beings and forces may not always perform their requested functions (i.e., bring about supernatural events), they do perform less obvious functions for both the individual and the society as a whole. These latent functions, as they are called by Robert Merton (1957), fall into two broad categories: social and psychological.

Social Functions of Religion

One of the most popular explanations for the universality of religion is that it performs important functions for the overall well-being of the society of which it is a part. Three such social functions of religion are social control, conflict resolution, and reinforcement of group solidarity.

Social Control

One important social function of religion is its use as a mechanism of social control. Through both positive and negative sanctions, religion tends to maintain social order by encouraging socially acceptable behaviour and discouraging socially inappropriate behaviour. Every religion, regardless of the form it takes, is an ethical system that prescribes proper ways of behaving. When social sanctions (rewards and punishments) are backed with supernatural authority, they become more compelling. Biblical texts, for example, are explicit about the consequences of violating the Ten Commandments. Because of their strong belief in ghostly vengeance, the Lugbara of Uganda scrupulously avoid engaging in any antisocial behaviour that would provoke the wrath of the ancestor-gods.

Religious beliefs and behaviours serve as mechanisms of social control for reasons other than fear of divine retribution. Michael McCullough and Brian Willoughby (2009) have investigated the notion that a sincere belief in religion gives people greater internal control, resistance to temptation, and hence obedience to societal norms. A review of the scholarly research over the past century reveals that devoutly religious people generally are more successful in school, live longer, and have more satisfying marriages. But McCullough and Willoughby were interested in learning whether these findings could be explained by an increase in self-control. They found that brain-scan studies reveal that praying, reading holy texts, and meditating (three religious activities) stimulate two parts of the brain associated with self-regulation of attention and emotions. In another study, conducted in 2003, people who were subliminally exposed to religious words, such as God and Bible, were slower to recognize words associated with temptation, such as alcohol and pornography. Although McCullough and Willoughby reviewed research conducted largely on Western and Christian populations, evidence from research conducted in the non-Western world is consistent with their main conclusions that there is a close correlation between religious beliefs and practices on the one hand, and self-control, conscientiousness, and adherence to social norms on the other.

From an anthropological perspective, it is irrelevant whether supernatural forces really do reward good behaviour and punish bad behaviour. Rather than concern themselves with whether and to what extent supernatural forces work the way they are thought to, anthropologists are interested in whether and to what extent people actually believe in the power of supernatural forces. After all, it is belief in the power of the supernatural sanctions that determines the level of conformity to socially prescribed behaviour.

Conflict Resolution

Another social function of religion is the role it plays in reducing the stress and frustrations that often lead to social conflict. In some societies, for example, natural calamities such as epidemics or famines are attributed to the evil deeds of people in other villages or regions. By concentrating on certain religious rituals designed to protect themselves against outside malevolence, people avoid the potential disruptiveness to their own society that might occur if they took out their frustrations on the evildoers. Moreover, disenfranchised and powerless people in stratified societies sometimes use religion as a way of diffusing the anger and hostility that might otherwise be directed against the entire social system. To illustrate, in his study of separatist Christian churches in the Republic of South Africa, Bengt Sundkler (1961) showed how small groups of black South Africans—who until recently were systematically excluded from the power structure by Apartheid—created the illusion of power by manipulating their own religious symbols and forming their own unique churches. By providing an alternative power structure, these breakaway Christian churches served to reduce conflict in South Africa by diverting resentment away from the wider power structure.

Reinforcement of Group Solidarity

A third social function of religion is to intensify the group solidarity of those who practise it. Religion enables people to express their common identity in an emotionally charged environment. Powerful social bonds are often created among people who share the experiences of religious beliefs, practices, and rituals. Because every religion or supernatural belief system has its own unique structural features, those who practise it share in its mysteries, whereas those who do not are excluded. In short, religion strengthens a person's sense of group identity and belonging. And of course, as people come together for common religious experiences, they often engage in other nonreligious activities as well, which further strengthens the sense of social solidarity.

Psychological Functions of Religion

In addition to promoting the well-being of the society, religion functions psychologically for the benefit of the individual. Anthropologists have identified two fundamentally different types of psychological functions of religion: a cognitive function, whereby religion provides a cognitive framework for explaining parts of our world that we do not understand; and an emotional function, whereby religion helps to reduce anxiety by prescribing some straightforward ways of coping with stress.

Cognitive Function

In terms of its cognitive and intellectual functions, religion is psychologically comforting because it helps us explain the unexplainable. Every society must deal with imponderable questions that have no definitive logical answers: When did life begin? Why do bad things happen to good people? What happens to us when we die? Where did we come from? What is our relationship to nature? Even in societies such as our own—where we have, or think we have, many scientific answers—many questions remain unanswered. A medical pathologist may be able to explain to the parents of a child who has died of malaria that the cause of death was a bite by an infected anopheles mosquito. But that same pathologist cannot explain to the grieving parents why the mosquito bit their child and not the child next door.

Religion can provide satisfying answers to such questions because the answers are based on supernatural authority.

Unlike any other life form, humans have a highly developed desire to understand themselves and the world around them. But because human understanding of the universe is so imperfect, religion provides a framework for giving meaning to events and experiences that cannot be explained in any other way. Religion assures its believers that the world is meaningful, that events happen for a reason, that there is order in the universe, and that apparent injustices will eventually be rectified. Humans have difficulty whenever unexplained phenomena contradict their cultural *worldview*. One of the functions of religion, then, is to enable people to maintain their worldview even when events seem to contradict it.

Emotional Function

The emotional function of religion is to help individuals cope with the anxieties that often accompany illnesses, accidents, deaths, and other misfortunes. Because people never have complete control over the circumstances of their lives, they often turn to religious ritual in an attempt to maximize control through supernatural means. In fact, the less control people feel they have over their own lives, the more they are likely to practise religion. The fear of facing a frightening situation can be at least partially overcome by believing that supernatural beings will intervene on one's behalf; a person can reduce shame and guilt by becoming humble and pious in the face of the deities; and during times of bereavement, religion can be a source of emotional strength (Figure 12.5).

People perform religious rituals as a way of invoking supernatural beings to control the forces over which they feel they have no control. This takes different forms throughout the world. To illustrate, the Trobriand Islanders perform magico-religious rituals for protection before a long voyage; to protect their gardens, men in parts of New Guinea put leaves across their fences, believing that the leaves will paralyze the arms and legs of any thief who raids the garden; and in Nairobi, Kenya, some professional football teams reportedly hire their own ritual specialists to bewitch their opponents. In addition to providing greater peace of mind, such religious practices may actually have a positive, indirect effect on the events they are intended to influence, even if their witchcraft does not work. For example, hockey players are likely to play more confidently if they believe they have a supernatural advantage. NHL hockey players stop shaving when their team enters the Stanley Cup playoffs. Shaving before being eliminated or winning the Stanley Cup is taboo and sure to result in a loss. The "playoff beard" is thus a form of magic, whereby players try to control the outcome of their games. While it is unlikely to really do so, it is a reminder to the players that they are a team and in the playoffs together, which gives them confidence. This ability to act with confidence is a major psychological function of religion.

Mathew Lodge/lodgephoto.com/Alamy Stock Photo

FIGURE 12.5 The iron cross found among the rubble of the World Trade Center, after the terrorist attacks of September 11, 2001, became a religious symbol of faith and hope. It was a time of uncertainty after the attack and church attendance, according to a PEW poll, almost doubled as people turned to their faith to relieve anxieties, although it has since fallen back to pre-9/11 levels (PEW 2003).

Religion, Magic, Sorcery, and Witchcraft

Anthropologists who study supernatural beliefs cross-culturally have long been fascinated by the relationship between religion and magic. Whereas some anthropologists have emphasized the differences between these two phenomena, others have concentrated on their similarities. It is important to examine both the

worldview A society's knowledge, beliefs, and perspective on the world.

Burial and Belonging

Death is a very emotional time when those left behind must not only mourn the departed and come together to fill the void, but also dispose of the body. Although every society has public mortuary ceremonies, or funerals, whereby the dead are necessarily disposed of, the actual ritual practices vary considerably. Religious beliefs often dictate how the body is to be treated after death.

In Islamic mortuary rituals, for example, after a person dies their body is ritually washed and then covered with a white cotton or linen shroud, followed by a prayer. Islamic religious law (Sharia law) requires that the body is buried; cremation is forbidden. Typically, autopsies and embalming are also not performed, unless absolutely necessary, as the body is believed to experience pain. The body is also buried as soon after death as possible, usually within 24 hours, as it is thought the soul is unable to leave the body until it is buried (Balkan 2015). This means the person is usually buried where they die. To transport the body to another town or country would delay burial and may necessitate embalming. Preferably, bodies should be buried without a coffin and in cemeteries or sections of cemeteries reserved for Muslims, as being buried with people of other faiths is looked down upon. Finally, the deceased is laid to rest on their right side with their head facing Mecca and should remain undisturbed forever.

In Germany, federal laws make fulfilling these religious obligations difficult. In most German states, bodies must be buried in a coffin and the family must wait at least 48 hours after death before burial, unless there is a risk from infectious disease. Mandatory autopsies are also required when the cause of death is unknown. There are also few Islamic burial grounds and cemeteries in Germany, and less than 1 percent have sections reserved for Muslims (Balkan 2015). Burial plots, which cannot always be aligned toward Mecca, are leased, and after 20 years the lot must be renewed, otherwise the corpse is exhumed and another body interred in the grave.

Because state law prevents the fulfillment of many Islamic mortuary practices, it can be distressing for the nearly three million Muslims living in Germany, two-thirds of whom are from Turkey (CIA World Factbook 2015a: Germany). Migrant populations face a difficult decision when family members die: should they bury the person in the country they have migrated to, or should the body be repatriated to their homeland. If it is buried in Germany, they will be unable to fulfil their religious obligations to the dead, yet if it is shipped back home they may also be unable to fulfil their religious obligations because burial will be delayed and the body may have to be embalmed.

In the early 1990s only 2 percent of Turkish-German Muslim migrants living in Berlin were buried in the city; most were repatriated to their homeland. Twenty years later, however, 20–30 percent of Turkish-Germans were buried locally, while 70–80 percent were returned to Turkey for burial (Balkan 2015). Anthropologist Osman Balkan looked at Turkish Muslims living in Berlin and wanted to understand how they dealt with the dilemma of fulfilling competing religious obligations and state laws. How did they decide where to bury their dead, especially when a 2006 survey indicated 87 percent of Turkish-German Muslims believed that a religious ceremony was important? To find the answer to this and other questions, Balkan conducted participant observation with Turkish Muslim migrant communities living in Berlin, and especially those working in the Islamic funeral industry.

What he discovered was that burial laws and practicalities that make a proper Islamic funeral all but impossible were of secondary importance in decisions about where to bury a body. Most important were family ties, ideas about the soil, and about being part of a community. Migrants asked themselves where they belonged: do they belong to the land they left or the land they have come to. When people are buried they literally become part of the land. And where they are buried becomes transformed into "hallowed" or sacred ground. For the bereaved, where one's ancestors are buried provides a sense of connection and attachment with the place, and thus a sense of identity and citizenship. As Balkan argues, while graves are the end of the journey for migrants, they are a beginning for their descendants. When they are buried in Germany, their children and grandchildren can visit their graves, and this was a decisive factor in German Turkish migrants' decision to be buried in Germany. Those opting to be buried in Turkey, on the other hand, believed it was important for their children and grandchildren "to maintain a connection to their ancestral soil." Another factor in the decision to repatriate bodies was the sense of exclusion many felt from Germany society due to the lack of accommodation for Islamic burials. As time passes, however, and the third generation of immigrants choose to be buried in Germany, they cease to be immigrants and start to lose their connection to their ancestral homeland.

While this suggests that religious traditions may be more flexible than assumed, the fact remains that state laws still frustrate Muslims' attempts to achieve a proper Islamic burial, and most

robertharding/Alamy Stock Photo

Old Muslim cemetery in Istanbul, Turkey. Turkish migrants to Germany must decide whether to be buried in Germany or in their homeland.

(*Continued*)

Burial and Belonging (*Continued*)

still repatriate the remains of their kin. Balkan found that many of his respondents were intimidated by state authorities and were reluctant to express their concerns or raise objections. As more Muslim migrants settle in Germany and other European countries, issues about burial practices are likely to increase. It will thus become important for Germany to accommodate different mortuary practices and provide suitable burial grounds if the country is to provide immigrants with a sense of belonging and citizenship.

Questions for Further Thought

1. How important is it for you to fulfill religious obligations when disposing of deceased relatives?
2. Should the laws of Germany or other non-Muslim countries be changed to accommodate different cultural practices concerning the dead?
3. What Canadian laws might prevent Muslims from feeling included in Canadian society?

similarities and the differences because, even though religion and magic can be found operating separately, often they are combined. Religion and magic share certain features. Because both are systems of supernatural belief, they are not susceptible to scientific verification. In other words, whether religious or magical practices actually work cannot be empirically demonstrated. Rather, such practices must be accepted as a matter of faith. Moreover, both religion and magic are practised—at least in part—as ways of coping with the anxieties, ambiguities, and frustrations of everyday life.

On the other hand, magic and religion differ in important respects. First, religion deals with the major issues of human existence, such as the meaning of life, death, and one's spiritual relationship with deities. In contrast, magic is directed toward specific, immediate problems, such as curing an illness, bringing rain, ensuring safety on a long journey, or even winning a hockey game (Figure 12.6). Second, religion uses prayer and sacrifices to appeal to or petition supernatural powers for assistance. Magicians, on the other hand, believe they can control or manipulate nature or other people by their own efforts. Third, religion by and large tends to be a group activity, whereas magic is more individually oriented. Fourth, whereas religion is usually practised at a specified time, magic is practised irregularly in response to specific and immediate problems. Fifth, religion usually involves officially recognized functionaries such as priests, imams, and rabbis, whereas magic is performed by a wide variety of practitioners who may or may not be recognized within the community as having supernatural powers.

Despite these five differences, elements of religion and magic in actual practice are usually found together. In any religion, for example, there is a fine line between praying for God's help and coercing or manipulating a situation to bring about a desired outcome, such as burying a statue of St. Joseph. Also, it is not at all unusual for a person to use elements of both religion and magic simultaneously. To illustrate, a soldier about to enter combat may ask for divine protection through prayer while carrying a lucky rabbit's foot (a magical charm).

FIGURE 12.6 **Magical rituals are common in sports, especially hockey. In the 1952 Stanley Cup playoffs, fans threw an octopus onto the ice, claiming it symbolized the eight wins the Detroit Red Wings needed to win the Stanley Cup. They won 8-0, and so fans still throw octopuses onto the rink so they will win (Scaringi 2014).**

Magic involves the manipulation of supernatural forces for the purpose of intervening in a wide range of human activities and natural events. Magic is used ritualistically in some societies to ensure the presence of game animals, to bring rain, to cure or prevent illness, or to protect oneself from misfortune. Magic, however, can also be (and often is) directed to cause evil. In some societies it is believed that certain people called sorcerers use supernatural powers to bring harm to people.

Sorcery

Sorcery often involves the use of materials, potions, and medicines, and is the deliberate use of supernatural powers to bring about harm. Some societies have specialized practitioners of sorcery, but in other societies anyone can practise sorcery. Sorcerers are generally believed to direct their malevolence purposefully against those they dislike, fear, or envy rather than acting randomly or capriciously. In any given society, hostile relations can occur among people who have some relationship to one another—such as outsiders who marry into a local village, rivals for a father's inheritance, wives in a polygynous household, men who are competing for a political office, or even rivals in competitive sports. People are therefore likely to attribute their own personal misfortune to the sorcery of some rival who might gain from harming them. Thus, accusations of sorcery are patterned to the extent that they reflect the conflicts, rivalries, and antagonisms that already exist among the people in any given society.

Witchcraft

Whereas sorcery involves using material substances and incantations to cause harm to people, witchcraft is the inherent power of people to cause misfortune or death by supernatural means (Evans-Pritchard 1937). It relies solely on psychic power, that is, thoughts and emotions. In other words, witches can turn their jealousy, envy, anger, and hatred into evil deeds simply by thinking evil thoughts. How witches are conceptualized varies from society to society, but they are generally seen as being unaware that it is their willpower that is causing them to bewitch people. Consequently, when a person is accused of being a witch, they invariably deny it. Anthropologists are not concerned with the reality or actual performance of witchcraft, but with the beliefs underlying social and psychological factors and the social consequences (Niehaus 2012).

Witchcraft is the epitome or embodiment of a society's conception of evil. Whatever a society values—success, health, good relations, love—witchcraft opposes it. Witches cause the crops to fail, football (soccer) teams to lose, neighbours to fight, and people to have accidents, get sick, and die. Implicit in the idea of witchcraft is that there is no such thing as bad luck. Something, that is, witchcraft, made it happen. In a famous example, Evans-Pritchard (1937) describes how the Azande, who live in southern Sudan, explain what happens when a granary collapses. The Azande are horticulturalists growing mostly maize and millet, which they store in huts, or granaries, on wooden stilts to keep animals out. The granaries also provide great places for shade. Unfortunately, termites eat away at the supports and occasionally a granary will collapse, and occasionally someone will be sitting under it and will be hurt. The Azande have two explanations for the collapse. The first is scientific and explains *how* it collapsed—because the termites ate away the supports. But this cannot explain *why* it collapsed. Why did it have to collapse when someone was sitting under it? The answer is witchcraft. The Azande's theory of witchcraft thus does not exclude empirical knowledge about cause and effect, it simply supplements it.

Most Azande are also Christian, but there is no contradiction between their faith in Christianity and their belief in witchcraft. World religions provide answers to such questions as where did I come from? How should I behave and relate toward my neighbour? and What happens after I die? But they cannot answer the question "why me"? Why did *I* get sick? Why did *my* child die? Why did *I* forget the answer on the anthropology exam? The most likely answer is witchcraft.

It is not surprising perhaps that societies that believe in witchcraft are afraid of it—it is the source of all the bad that happens. The real victims of witchcraft, however, are not those who believe they are bewitched (although from an emic perspective they are), but those accused of practising witchcraft. They tend to be the powerless—the poor, the elderly, the disabled, children, women, and the marginalized. You don't accuse the witchdoctor (a person who detects witches and heals the harm done by witchcraft), the pastor, the police chief, or the headman, or other people in power who can retaliate. Because witches are by definition evil, accusers are always on the side of right and good. Punishment of witches varies from society to society, and can range from apologies to banishment to death.

Fear of witchcraft as well as fear of being accused of witchcraft can be seen as forms of social control. Fearing that their actions may result in retaliatory witchcraft, people tend to avoid behaviour that would make others angry, envious, or jealous. At the same time, being aware that any misfortune that occurs to others may result in accusations of witchcraft also constrains behaviour that might be construed as envious or jealous or hostile. Belief in witchcraft and witchcraft accusations are thus effective sanctions to control disruptive behaviour. Witchcraft beliefs have also been seen as a levelling mechanism, as any success or advancement over others may result in jealousy and envy in others and thus bewitchment, while success can be seen as being achieved by the use of witchcraft and thus attract accusations. The result is that wealth tends to be equally balanced.

While Evans-Pritchard's work was conducted over 80 years ago witchcraft is still an ever-present fear among many cultures in Africa, Melanesia, the Americas, Asia, and the Pacific (Niehaus 2012). It is also a serious social problem. Between 2005 and 2011, approximately 3000

sorcery The performance of certain magical rites for the purpose of harming other people.

CROSS-CULTURAL MISCUE

Saudi Arabia, one of the wealthiest most prosperous countries in the Middle East and whose citizens enjoy a high standard of living, are technologically savvy, and have embraced globalization, still frequently executes people for the crime of witchcraft. The Saudi government enforces Sharia law, a strict legal system of crime and punishment based on literal interpretations of the Qur'an as well as other writings. Any belief in a god or power other than "the one true God Allah," or practices such as witchcraft, fortune telling, using charms, or casting spells, is seen as blasphemous and subject to severe punishment. Judges, usually religious clerics, have a great deal of discretion in interpreting Sharia law, determining what constitutes witchcraft and in delivering sentences. Witchcraft and sorcery are taken seriously. The *Harry Potter* series is banned in Saudi Arabia because it is full of magic and sorcery (Miller 2011), and being bewitched has been used as a legitimate defence in some court cases (Miller 2011). Saudi Arabia's religious police, the Committee for the Promotion of Virtue and the Prevention of Vice (CPVPV), enforces Sharia law and, in 2009, a new Anti-Witchcraft Squad was created to investigate witchcraft accusations as well as other magical practices (Miller 2011). Many people in the Kingdom, including foreigners, have been put to death by beheading (Human Rights Watch 2009).

If Ali Sabat had known how serious witchcraft was taken by Saudi Arabian authorities, he may not have made his pilgrimage to Medina in May 2008. Sabat was a host on a popular Lebanese, call-in, satellite television station show called *The Hidden*. Seen by many as a psychic, he frequently gave advice about people's lives and made predictions about the future. Recognized by the religious police, he was arrested in his hotel room, and in November 2009, was sentenced to death by beheading for practising witchcraft (Human Rights Watch 2009). The only evidence against him were the TV programs, which were available in Saudi Arabia. After pressure from human rights groups and the Lebanese government, Sabat was released in 2012. That same year, however, the religious police arrested 215 people suspected of being magicians (Muhammad 2013).

Others are not so lucky. Egyptian pharmacist Mustafa Ibrahim was executed in 2007 for using sorcery to separate a married couple. And several Indonesian guest workers, mostly domestic servants, are facing the death penalty in Saudi Arabia for witchcraft. Many of the charges are due to cultural misunderstandings where a folk heirloom they have brought with them is seen by their hosts as an object of witchcraft. In other cases their hosts may have accused them of witchcraft if they complained about working conditions or ill-treatment (Schulson 2014).

people, about 500 a year, were killed in Tanzania after being accused of being witches (Huffington Post 2012; BBC News 2014). In 2014, police charged 23 people for killing 7 villagers suspected of witchcraft. The victims, most of whom were women over 60, were attacked with machetes and burned alive (BBC News 2014). Women are often targeted if they have red eyes, which is thought to be a sign of witchcraft but is really the result of burning cow dung (Huffington Post 2012). Illnesses such as AIDS, cancer, and Ebola are often thought to be caused by witchcraft and have hindered control and relief efforts.

Children are also often targeted. Between 2006 and 2009, between 25 000 and 50 000 children in the Democratic Republic of Congo were thrown out of their homes, accused of witchcraft, and about 1000 killed (Christianity Today 2009). Some have also been subjected to painful exorcisms to rid them of the witchcraft by unscrupulous pastors who provide their services for a fee (Houreld 2009). And in Ghana, so many women have been exiled after being accused of being a witch that several "witch camps" now exist consisting of only women "witches" (Whitaker 2012).

myth A religious or sacred story that explains how the world, people, or some event, phenomenon, or practice came to be.

Myth and Worldview

When we hear the word ***myth*** we often think of stories or ideas that are widely believed to be true but are in fact false. For example, many people believe that we use only 10 percent of our brains. This can be called a myth because the truth is we use most of our brains most of the time. We may also think of myths as the stories of gods and terrifying creatures, and supernatural events told by the Ancient Greeks or some "primitive" tribe. We call them myths because we do not believe them to be true. But when we refer to stories from the Bible or Qur'an as myths, many Christians and Muslims may be offended. The word myth comes from the Greek word *mythos*, which simply means story. When anthropologists use the word myth, they refer to sacred stories that relate to a culture's worldview. Anthropologists do not pass judgment on whether they are true or false. What is important is that the adherents themselves believe them since it is this belief that influences their values, attitudes, and actions.

The topics of myths often include gods and goddesses and other supernatural beings and events that occurred in the remote past. They are a religion's stories about how the world came to be, about how humans and their institutions originated, and about

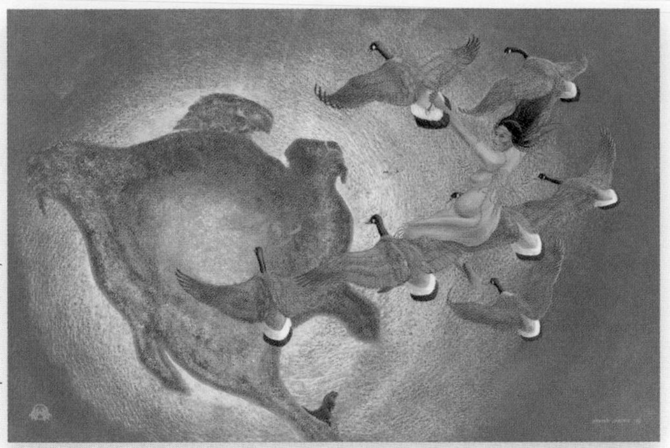

FIGURE 12.7 *Sky Woman Descending Great Turtle Island* (Arnold Aron Jacobs (Onondaga Nation, Turtle Clan) 1981).

how humans should relate to each other and the world around them. In other words, myths provide societies with a worldview. For instance, much of the Christian story of creation tells of how God created the Earth, humans, and the creatures of the world, and then gave humans dominion or control over the world and the creatures in it. This story has been used to justify Christian ideas of ownership of the land and animals. It is different from the worldview of other religions. For example, according to the Haudenosaunee (Iroquois) creation story, Sky Woman fell from the sky and was rescued by birds that gently lowered her onto the back of giant sea turtle (Figure 12.7). The other animals then brought Earth from the bottom of the sea, placing it on the back of the great sea turtle, which began to grow and create Turtle Island, or what we now know as North America. In the Haudenosaunee story, the land is not owned and animals are seen as providers for humans, and who give themselves to hunters. In general, First Nations, Métis, and Inuit worldviews, identity, and spirituality are intimately connected with the land and the spirits that exist in all living things (Fonda 2011).

Types of Religious Organization

Like other aspects of culture, religion takes a wide variety of forms throughout the world. To bring some measure of order to this vast diversity, it is helpful to develop a typology of religious systems based on certain common features. One commonly used system of classification—suggested by Anthony Wallace—is based on the level of specialization of the religious personnel who conduct the rituals and ceremonies. Wallace (1966) identified four principal types of religious organization based on what he calls cults. Wallace uses the term cult in a general sense to refer to forms of religion that have their own set of beliefs, rituals, and goals. This analytical and non-judgmental use of the term *cult* should not be confused with the more popular, and pejorative, definition used to refer to an antisocial religious group that brainwashes its members. The four types of religious organization Wallace identified are individualistic cults, shamanistic cults, communal cults, and ecclesiastical cults.

Wallace's four types correspond roughly to different levels of socio-economic organization. In a general way, individualistic and shamanistic cults are usually associated with food-foraging societies, communal cults are usually found in horticultural and pastoral societies, and ecclesiastical cults are characteristic of more complex industrialized economies. However, this association between types of religious organization and socio-economic types is only approximate at best because there are some notable exceptions. For example, certain Plains First Nations and some Indigenous Australians had communal forms of religion even though they were foragers and lived in bands. See Table 12.1 for a summary of the characteristics of the four types of religious organizations.

cult A religious group that has its own set of beliefs, practices, and rituals.

TABLE 12.1

Characteristics of the Four Types of Religious Organizations

Type	Role Specialization	Subsistence Pattern	Example
Individualistic	No role specialization	Food foraging	Crow vision quest
Shamanistic	Part-time specialization	Food foraging, pastoralism, and horticulture	Tungus shamanism
Communal	Groups perform rites for community	Horticulture and pastoralism	Totemistic rituals
Ecclesiastical	Full-time specialization in hierarchy	Industrialism	Christianity and Buddhism

Source: Adapted from Anthony F. C. Wallace, *Religion: An Anthropological View* (New York: Random House, 1966).

Individualistic Cults

Individualistic cults are the most basic type of religious structure and have no full-time religious specialists. Each person has a relationship with one or more supernatural beings whenever he or she has a need for control or protection. Even though no known societies rely exclusively on individualistic cults, some small-scale band societies practise this type of organization as a predominant mode.

Shamanistic Cults

Shamanistic cults are found in Arctic and Subarctic regions, Siberia, Tibet, Mongolia, parts of Southeast Asia, and widely throughout the South American rain forests. *Shamans* are part-time religious specialists who are thought to have supernatural powers by virtue of birth, training, or inspiration. They use these powers for healing, divining, and telling fortunes during times of stress, usually in exchange for gifts or fees. Shamanistic cults represent the simplest form of religious division of labour because, as Anthony Wallace (1966, 86) reminds us, "The shaman in his religious role is a specialist; and his clients in their relation to him are laymen." The term shaman, derived from the Tungus-speaking peoples of Siberia (Service 1978), encompasses many different types of specialists found throughout the world, including medicine men and women, diviners, spiritualists, palm readers, and magicians (Figure 12.8). At least as many women as men practise shamanism throughout the world.

Shamans are generally believed to have access to supernatural spirits that they contact on behalf of their clients. The reputation of a particular shaman often rests on the power of the shaman's "spirit helpers" (usually the spirits of powerful, agile, and cunning animals) and her or his ability to contact them at will. Shamans usually contact their spirits while in an altered state of consciousness brought on by smoking, taking drugs, drumming rhythmically, chanting, or dancing monotonously. Once in a trance, the shaman, possessed by a spirit helper, becomes a medium or spokesperson for that spirit. While possessed, the shaman may perspire, breathe heavily, take on a different voice, and generally lose control over his or her own body.

In shamanistic societies it is believed that everyday occurrences are intimately connected to events in the spirit world. The shaman's role is to enter an altered state of consciousness, allow his or her soul to travel to the spirit world, seek out the causes of earthly problems, and then coerce, beg, or fight with the spirits to intervene on behalf of the living. Traditional Inuit shamanism provides a good example of how shamans are thought to work. Traditionally, most Inuit believed that water mammals were controlled by an underwater female spirit called Nuliajuk or Sedna who occasionally withheld animals when Inuit hunters behaved immorally (Figure 12.9). One of

Karel Navarro/AP Photo/The Canadian Press

FIGURE 12.8 A shaman holds up coca leaves during a ritual for good luck in 2012 in Lima, Peru.

John Sylvester/Alamy Stock Photo

FIGURE 12.9 Sculpture of Sedna, Inuit goddess of the sea, Nuuk, Greenland.

individualistic cult The least complex type of religious organization in which each person is his or her own religious specialist.
shamanistic cult A type of religious organization in which part-time religious specialists called shamans intervene with the deities on behalf of their clients.
shaman A part-time religious specialist who is thought to have supernatural powers by virtue of birth, training, or inspiration.

the most challenging tests for an Inuit shaman was to travel to the watery underworld to convince the spirit to release the seals and walruses so they could be hunted again.

Perhaps the most famous shaman in the anthropological literature is Quesalid, a Kwakwaka'wakw shaman from Vancouver Island described by Claude Lévi-Strauss (1963). Quesalid, who was most likely Boas's primary informant George Hunt (Whitehead 2000), was skeptical of shamans and so to expose their tricks he became an apprentice. One trick he learned was to hide a tuft of bird down in his mouth, bite his inner lip so the down became bloody, and then discreetly pretend to suck it out of his patients, presenting the bloodied "worm" as proof that he had extracted the illness from them. Although he knew he was deceiving his patients and intended to expose other shamans as fakes, he was surprised when his patients got better. Quesalid knew the healing ritual was a deception, but his healing powers became legendary and he gained a reputation as a powerful shaman. He also knew that his patients believed in him and over time he came to believe in his ability to cure them. As Lévi-Strauss put it, "Quesalid did not become a great shaman because he cured his patients; he cured his patients because he had become a great shaman" (1963, 180). Levi-Strauss also points out that the society his patients belonged to also believe in the effectiveness of shamanism. The example of Quesalid has been used in theories of medicine to demonstrate the role of symbols and belief in healing (Whitehead 2000).

Communal Cults

Communal cults involve a more elaborate set of beliefs and rituals and operate at a higher level of organizational complexity. Groups of ordinary people (organized around clans, lineages, age groups, or secret societies) conduct religious rites and ceremonies on behalf of the larger community. These rites, which are performed only occasionally or periodically by non-specialists, are considered to be absolutely vital to the well-being of both individuals and the society as a whole. Even though these ceremonies may include specialists such as shamans, orators, or magicians, the primary responsibility for the success of the ceremonies lies with the non-specialists, who return to their everyday activities at the conclusion of the ceremony. Examples of communal cults are the ancestral ceremonies among the traditional Chinese, puberty rites found in sub-Saharan African societies, and totemic rituals practised by the Indigenous peoples of Australia.

Communal rituals fall into two broad categories: rites of passage, which celebrate the transition of a person from one social status to another, and rites of solidarity, which are public rituals that foster group identity and group goals and have explicit and immediate objectives, such as calling on supernatural beings or forces to increase fertility or prevent misfortune. We will explore rites of passage later in the chapter.

CROSS-CULTURAL MISCUE

Anna Hackman (2011) could not sell her Vancouver home for two years despite lowering the price several times. Her mistake, living on the West Coast, was not to consider *feng shui*. After she hired a *feng shui* consultant to rearrange some of the furniture and clear the energy in the house from the previous owners, however, she had two offers. Feng shui, which combines the words for wind and water (Boyce 2014), concerns the mystical forces or energy in the universe called *qi* (chi), which create a harmonious and healthy environment. To improve one's quality of life in a building, the chi must flow easily. This involves the proper placement of windows, doors, fireplaces, staircases, mirrors, and so on. For example, the back door should not be visible from the front door or the chi will flow straight through the house, and a mirror should not face the front door as it will reflect the chi back out of the house (Boyce 2014). With other properties, bad chi becomes more difficult to overcome, for example, being on the fourth floor of an apartment building (four sounds like the word for "death" in Chinese).

In Metro Vancouver, immigration from Asian countries, particularly mainland China, Taiwan, and Hong Kong, where feng shui has been an important factor in design for decades, is a significant driver in choosing and purchasing a home and in new house construction (Gold 2012). Nearly one-third of buyers of existing homes and two-thirds of new home buyers in Vancouver may be influenced by feng shui (Bloomberg Business 2011). It is partly because of this that house prices in Vancouver are now more expensive than San Francisco, London, and New York (Bloomberg Business 2011).

Developers and builders these days must take feng shui into consideration when designing a new building. And it is not only Chinese home buyers who are concerned about feng shui principles. Johnson Li, a feng shui master who charges thousands of dollars for his services, says many of his clients are Westerners and East Indians who realize that feng shui will not only increase the value of their home but also make it easier to sell (Gold 2012). Sales of homes can be improved by minor renovations and rearranging furniture, but the best way to ensure your home is built properly or sells is to hire a feng shui master, who often has the power of veto and will probably have the last word on whether your house sells (Gold 2012).

---

communal cult A type of religious organization in which groups of ordinary people conduct religious ceremonies for the well-being of the total community.

Ecclesiastical Cults

The most complex form of religious organization, according to Wallace, is the ecclesiastical cult, which is found in societies with state systems of government. There are examples of ecclesiastical cults in societies that have a pantheon of several high gods (such as traditional Aztecs, Incas, Greeks, and Egyptians) and in those with essentially monotheistic religions (such as Buddhism, Christianity, Islam, and Judaism). Ecclesiastical cults are characterized by full-time professional clergy who are formally elected or appointed and devote all or most of their time to performing priestly functions. Unlike shamans, who conduct rituals during times of crisis or when their services are needed, these full-time religious specialists conduct rituals that occur at regular intervals.

In addition, these specialists are usually part of a hierarchical or bureaucratic organization. Often, but not always, these clerical bureaucracies are either controlled by the central government or closely associated with it. In many ecclesiastical cults, the prevailing myths and beliefs are used to support the supremacy of the ruling class. For example, Queen Elizabeth is Head of the Commonwealth as well as Supreme Governor of the Church of England, although her roles nowadays are more a formality.

In societies with ecclesiastical cults, there is a clearly understood distinction between laypersons and religious specialists. Laypersons are responsible primarily for supporting the bureaucracy through their labour and their financial contributions. The specialists are responsible for conducting religious rituals on behalf of the lay population, either individually or in groups. Whereas the specialists serve as active ritual managers, the lay population participates in rituals in a generally passive fashion (Figure 12.10).

Marcia Chambers/dbimages/Alamy Stock Photo

FIGURE 12.10 This Anglican priest from Quebec City is a full-time religious specialist who works within a hierarchical religious organization.

Rites of Passage

Rites of passage are ceremonies that mark a change in a person's social position and also help them through the transformation. These ritualistic ceremonies, which have religious significance, help both individuals and society deal with important life changes such as birth, adolescence, marriage, and death. They include naming ceremonies, initiation rites in which young boys and girls become young men and women, marriage ceremonies, and funerals. Rites of passage are more than ways of recognizing certain transitions in a person's life, however. When a person marries, for example, he or she not only takes on a new status but also creates an entire complex of new relationships with new rights and obligations. Rites of passage, then, are important public rituals that recognize a wider set of altered social relationships.

Rites of passage were first analyzed by Arnold van Gennep in 1908 (1960), who considered initiation rites to be the most typical rite of passage and who said that, in whatever culture they may be found, they have three distinct ritual phases: separation, transition, and incorporation. The first phase, separation, is characterized by the stripping away of the old status and may employ symbols that represent a death to the previous state. In the transitional phase, which van Gennep called the liminal phase, from the Latin word for threshold, because the individual is on the threshold of a new state; the initiate is cut off from the old status but has not yet achieved the new status. As British anthropologist Victor Turner (1967a) later said, they are "Betwixt and Between." The third and final phase involves the ritual incorporation of the individual into the new status. This stage often involves a ceremony in which

---

ecclesiastical cult A highly complex religious organization in which full-time clergy are employed.

rite of passage A ritual that celebrates the transition of a person from one social status to another.

the initiate may receive a new set of clothes or be physically marked in some way, such as by circumcision, tattooing, or scarification. These markings indicate to the person, and to the community, that they have gone through the ritual and now have the rights and obligations that go with their new position and must be treated as such. Ethnographic data from all over the world have supported van Gennep's claim that all rites of passage involve these three phases.

In the transition stage initiates are prepared for a new social status or role. Because it is associated with danger and ambiguity, they often endure certain unpleasant ordeals while removed from normal, everyday life for a certain period of time. Turner's analysis of this stage has been very fruitful as a model for understanding how society is structured and individual identity shaped. In this transitional stage, where the responsibilities of old statuses and the social inequalities have been stripped away, there is a condition Turner called ***communitas***, which is Latin for community. Because all the initiates go through the ritual together there is a sense of equality, fellowship, and comradery, where old relationships outside the ritual situation no longer apply and new relationships can be formed.

Also in the liminal phase, initiates receive the skills and knowledge to be successful in the next state. The liminal phase can last anywhere from a few minutes to years. In one sense, we could consider university students in a liminal phase of a rite of passage. Students are no longer high school students, nor are they graduates, but spend four years in which communitas exists and where they acquire the skills and knowledge required for life after graduation.

A good example of a secular rite of passage is the basic training provided by the Canadian Armed Forces. All new recruits, both men and women, who come from all socio-economic and ethnic backgrounds, must complete basic training. In the separation phase, recruits are sent to the Canadian Forces Leadership and Recruit School in Saint-Jean-sur-Richelieu, Quebec. Here they exchange their civilian clothes for a cadet uniform and receive the regulation haircut. Over the course of 14 weeks they not only receive physical training, but also gain the knowledge and skills which are necessary to succeed in the military. For example, they learn the structure of the military, first aid, how to march, how to handle weapons, and to use a map and compass. As the Canadian Forces website states, "Basic training will teach you a new way of life" (www.Forces.ca). At the end of basic training they undergo a graduation ceremony where they receive a new uniform marking their transition from civilian to military personnel. People who go through basic training together often form close and long-lasting personal relationships.

Another example of a rite of passage is the ***quinceañera***, which is a celebration for young girls in Latin American cultures when they turn 15, marking their transition into womanhood (Figure 12.11). The quinceañera is one of the most meaningful and distinctive rituals marking Mexican culture. The word itself comes from the Spanish quince, "fifteen," and años, "years" (Voices 2002). Traditionally, it begins with a Catholic Mass before the altar of the Virgin of Guadalupe. The girl, dressed in a pink gown, processes down the aisle with her father along with seven girls and seven boys (sometimes 14 couples) who then part, leaving her at the altar. Here she is presented to the community and thanks God for her blessings and for the guidance she has received (Davalos 1996). She also receives a religious medal blessed by the priest and presented to her by her godparents.

Hill Street Studios/Blend Images/Getty Images

FIGURE 12.11 Hispanic girl celebrating quinceañera with a priest in a Catholic Church.

Traditionally, young girls also received instruction from their mother as well as the priest on the roles and responsibilities of being a woman. By going through the ceremony she becomes ready to take on the responsibilities of womanhood, including marriage, and those who know her treat her differently afterward. More specifically, however, she becomes a Catholic woman and

---

communitas The situation during the liminal phase of a rite of passage characterized by equality and fellowship.

quinceañera A rite of passage for young girls in Latin American cultures when they turn 15 years of age marking their transition into womanhood.

a Mexican woman (Davalos 1996). The quinceañera is thus also a celebration of cultural identity. The ancient Aztec and Mayan cultures had ceremonies preparing young women for their roles in society, and many claim the quinceañera combines the Spanish-Catholic tradition of presenting marriageable daughters to society with Indigenous traditions (Davalos 1996).

Although quinceañeras have other meanings today, they are still celebrations of womanhood, and have become lavish affairs costing tens of thousands of dollars. Girls now wear an elaborate gown, a jewelled tiara, and her first pair of high heels and the celebration involves an immense cake and a live band (Voices 2002). They have become big business.

Rites of Solidarity

The other type of communal cult is directed toward the welfare of the community rather than the individual. These *rites of solidarity* permit a wider social participation in the shared concerns of the community than is found in societies with predominantly shamanistic cults. A good example of a cult that fosters group solidarity is the ancestral cult, found widely throughout the world. Ancestral cults are based on the assumption that, after death, a person's soul continues to interact with and affect the lives of her or his living descendants. In other words, when people die, they are not buried and forgotten but rather are elevated to the status of ancestor-ghost or ancestor-god. Because these ghosts, who are viewed as the official guardians of the social and moral order, have supernatural powers, the living descendants practise certain communal rituals designed to induce the ancestor-ghosts to protect them, favour them, or at least not harm them.

Religion: Continuity and Change

By examining the various functions of religion, we can see that religion is a conservative force in a society. In a general sense, religions support the status quo by keeping people in line through supernatural sanctions, relieving social conflict, and providing explanations for unfortunate events. Moreover, some of the major world religions, through both philosophical convictions and political interpretations, have tended to retard social change. To illustrate, orthodox Hindu beliefs, based on the notion that one's present condition in life is determined by deeds in past lives, have had the effect of making people so fatalistic that they accept their present situations as unchangeable. Such a worldview is not likely to bring about major revolutions or even minor initiatives for change.

Revitalization Movements

Under certain circumstances, religion can play an important role in transforming a society. Occasionally, societies have experienced such high levels of stress and strain that the conservative functions of religion could not hold them together. Instead, new religions arose to create a new social order. These religious movements, with their aim of breathing new life and purpose into the society, are called *revitalization movements* (Wallace 1966). They tend to arise during times of cultural stress brought about by rapid change, foreign domination, or perceived deprivation. Because these conditions are often, but not always, associated with colonialism, many revitalization movements have appeared in societies that have been under colonial domination.

Despite considerable differences in the details surrounding various revitalization movements, Wallace suggests that most follow a fairly uniform process. Starting from a state of equilibrium in which change occurs, although slowly, a society is pushed off balance by forces such as conquest, social domination, warfare, or some natural disaster. These conditions lower the self-esteem of an increasing number of individuals and place them under intolerable stress, and they may become apathetic or violent, or turn to substance abuse. People become disillusioned with their faith and the cultural values that sustained them, leading to a cultural disorganization (e.g., higher crime rates and a general increase in antisocial behaviour). When the social fabric deteriorates sufficiently, revitalization movements are likely to appear in an effort to bring about a more satisfying society. Some movements call for a return to the better days of the past; others seek to establish a completely new social order.

Revitalization movements have been found in many parts of the world, including among Indigenous American groups. The tragic suffering of Indigenous Americans since their earliest contact with Europeans resulted in a number of revitalization movements.

Handsome Lake

One of the earliest Indigenous American revitalization movements was started by Handsome Lake (Deardorff 1951; Parker 1913) among the Seneca of New York State. By 1800, the Seneca had lost much of their land to colonists, who held them in contempt because they sided with the British during the American Revolution. The Seneca were confined to reservations, and their numbers severely reduced by European diseases such as

---

rite of solidarity A ceremony performed for the sake of enhancing social integration among a group of people.

revitalization movement A religious movement designed to bring about a new way of life within a society.

measles and smallpox. Once a proud nation of warriors, hunters, and traders, by the early 1800s the Seneca were defeated, dehumanized, and demoralized. Alcoholism became rampant and conflicts and accusations of witchcraft increased.

From this state of cultural disorganization came a prophet, Handsome Lake, who was visited by the corn, squash, and bean spirits who, in a series of visions, told him to stop drinking. Handsome Lake instituted other important cultural changes as well. For example, he urged his followers to adopt European agricultural practices involving both men and women working in the fields, which traditionally was solely women's work. In the Seneca family, he emphasized the priority of the conjugal unit of husband and wife over the larger matrilineage. Divorce, which had been common in traditional Seneca society, was no longer permitted. Thus, Handsome Lake's revitalization movement led to far-reaching cultural changes. The Seneca became models of sobriety, their family structure was altered, they initiated new farming practices, and they changed the traditional division of labour between men and women. The spirits warned that the Seneca would suffer a great catastrophe (such as fire, destruction, and death) if they did not mend their ways. Most of the prescriptions set down by Handsome Lake constituted a new set of moral principles and rules of behaviour. Followers of the new religious movement were expected to stay sober, be peaceful, and lead pure and upright lives. The Handsome Lake movement evolved into the Longhouse Religion, which is still practised among some member of Six Nations Reserve in Ontario (Cave 2006; Myers 2006).

The Ghost Dance Religion

The best known revitalization movement in North America is the Ghost Dance Religion. Traditionally, the Nations of the Great Plains considered the buffalo to be sacred and were dependent on the millions of them that roamed the plains for their survival. The buffalo provided not only most of their food, but also their hides were used for robes, blankets, and shelter, and even their dung was used for fuel. In the late 1860s, however, a steady stream of settlers on their way to California began moving through the Plains Nations' territory, followed soon after by the railways and the whiskey traders. Conflict was perhaps inevitable and there were numerous massacres; most committed by the military. The U.S. government required the Nations to sign treaties, most of which required settling on reservations and taking up agriculture, and most of which the U.S. government subsequently broke by failing to live up to the treaty terms or to provide land to homesteaders. The Plains are also unsuitable for agriculture and so, starving, many groups left the reservations to hunt buffalo. The final solution to the so-called "Indian Problem" was to kill the buffalo, which were slaughtered in the tens of thousands, their carcasses simply left to rot. Although exact figures are hard to come by, there were an estimated 40 to 60 million buffalo on the Plains around 1800 (Shaw 1995); by the late 1880s there were little more than 1000.

The disappearance of the buffalo also meant the disappearance of the Plains Nations' traditional way of life. Disillusioned, starving, decimated by disease and conflict with the U.S. military, many became violent or turned to alcohol. In January 1889, however, things changed. A Nevada Paiute prophet named Wovoka (also called Jack Wilson) had a vision, apparently during a solar eclipse, whereby the living would be reunited with the ancestors, the buffalo would return, there would be no sickness, disease, or old age, and the white man would leave. For the prophecy to come true, however, followers had to stop fighting one another, not steal or lie, love one another, and make peace with the white man (Mooney 1897). They also had to dance for five successive nights, when dancers would then drop from exhaustion and have similar visions (Figure 12.12). Other groups in the area sent members to investigate the prophecies and within a year the Ghost Dance Religion, which was an attempt to revitalize Plains Nations cultures, had spread to most of the Plains Nations, adapting to specific circumstances as it went (Kehoe 2006).

The movement alarmed both settlers and the U.S. military in the area, whose basic strategy had been to divide and conquer. With all the Nations drumming, chanting, and dancing as part of the Ghost Dance ritual it seemed as though all the Nations were uniting. The U.S. authorities thus banned it, although most groups defiantly continued to practise it. On December 28, 1890, Big Foot, a Lakota Chief, along with his band of about 350 Lakota, surrendered to the U.S. military, establishing a camp at Wounded Knee Creek. The next day, as the Lakota were being disarmed, a single shot,

FIGURE 12.12 Ogalala Sioux Ghost Dance, Pine Ridge Native American Reservation, South Dakota. Illustration by Frederic Remington, 1890.

according to one report, was fired and the soldiers opened fire killing over 150 Lakota, mostly women and children; 25 cavalry were also killed. After Wounded Knee the Ghost Dance Religion went underground for fear of reprisals. And although it lingered on in places into the 20th century, and still survives as the New Tiding religion among the Dakota of Saskatchewan, Wounded Knee effectively put an end to the Ghost Dance (Kehoe 2006).

Cargo Cults

Another type of revitalization movement is known as a *cargo cult*. Over 200 of them have been recorded since the late 1700s (Trompf 2015), although most appeared during and after World War II on the islands of Melanesia. Their characteristic features are the delivery of consumer goods (i.e. cargo) as well as a return to traditional customs (*kastom*) denied them by outsiders (Trompf 2015). Many also involve a messianic (messiah or prophet-like) figure who would deliver the cargo and the promised return to a golden age.

As with other revitalization movements, the societies on these islands underwent a period of considerable stress. Missionaries and colonial administrators banned many of the traditional customs such as kava drinking (a mild narcotic drink), ritual dancing, and polygamy, and forbade working and any amusement on Sundays (Raffaele 2006). The South Pacific was also a major theatre of World War II in the early 1940s. The Americans needed not only a military force in the tens of thousands but also the infrastructure and supplies to support it. This meant building docks, landing strips, roads, bridges, field offices, hospitals, and so on, and delivering vast quantities of supplies such as canned food, clothing, medicine, radios, weapons, refrigerators, sewing machines, and other equipment, as well as luxuries such as cigarettes, beer, chocolate bars, and, of course, Coca-Cola, much of which was air dropped. The islanders, whose numbers were often swamped by those of the occupying service personnel, were often hired as labourers and guides and received many of the manufactured items as gifts. It seemed as if a time of plenty had arrived. And then the war ended; the Americans left and the islands returned to colonial administrations.

The cargo cults arose in an attempt to return to that time of plenty. Having a limited understanding of how modern manufacturing processes and global distribution networks worked, however, presented a problem: how to get the planes to land and offload their cargo. For many, the appearance of planes delivering consumer goods was little short of miraculous. So, to lure planes into landing on their islands, many islanders built model airplanes positioned on landing strips complete with bamboo control towers and signal fires and torches to light up the runway. Cargo cult followers were also familiar with the efficacy of ritual and so many mimicked the mysterious rituals they had observed the newcomers doing, by marching, writing incomprehensible signs on paper, and talking into wooden radios with coconut headsets on.

Most of the cargo cults have disappeared—after all, the cargo never came—but not all. On Tanna Island, Vanuatu, with a population of about 30 000 (Tabani 2009), the John Frum Movement endures. At the heart of the movement is a figure named John Frum, who not only was a man like any other but also a spirit who overwhelms other traditional spirits (Tabani 2009). Followers believe John Frum will not only return with cargo, but also will lead them back to their traditional ways before the British. One of the current leaders has said that John Frum told them to "throw away [our] money and clothes, take our children from their schools, stop going to church and go back to living as kastom people. We should drink kava, worship the magic stones and perform our ritual dances" (Raffaele 2006). The Tannese then began throwing their money into the sea, stopped working, and killed their pigs in a big feast awaiting John Frum's return. This was a major concern for the colonial administrators, who arrested the leaders but only succeeded in making them martyrs (Raffaele 2006). The time of plenty came in 1942, when thousands of Americans encamped on the island. Today John Frum followers worship the Red Cross (from the time of war hospitals), and on February 15, the day John Frum is supposed to return, they march in formation, carry bamboo rifles, raise the American flag, wear old U.S. uniforms, and paint "USA" on their chests (Figure 12.13).

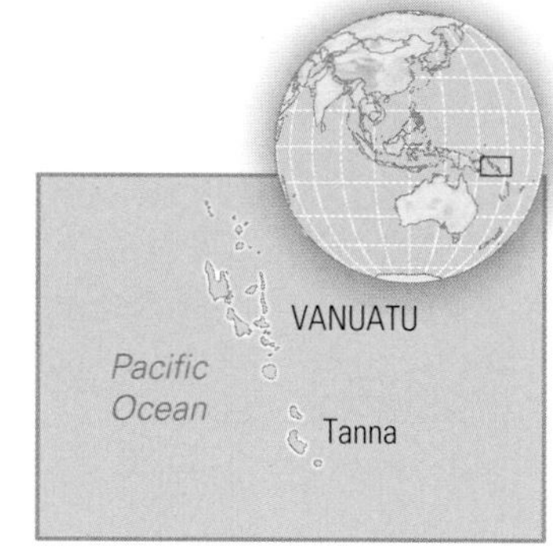

Many anthropologists (e.g., Kaplan 1995) have been critical of the term "cargo cult" in that the focus is on "cargo" when for the groups themselves it is more about returning to traditional custom or "kastom." Kaplan suggests that the term reflects Western concern with the irrational and exotic, and really says more about "us" than "them." Tabani (2009) argues that, given the context of colonial and post-colonial domination and their focus on reviving "kastom," cargo cults should be looked at more as a strategy of resistance that looks to return not only to a golden age of tradition but also to a new golden age of plenty brought about by cultural heroes like John Frum. By continuing to drink kava and practise their traditional dances they were expressing their opposition to the missionaries and colonial governments.

cargo cult A Melanesian revitalization movement characterized by rituals intended to bring material goods, that is, cargo.

Thierry Falise/LightRocket via Getty Images

FIGURE 12.13 Young Melanesian men on the island of Tanna, Vanuatu, with "USA" painted on their chests in red, march on February 15th to celebrate John Frum Day. They believe that by following the rituals observed by the Americans during WWII that John Frum will deliver trade goods.

Peter Worsley (1957) has argued that they should be looked at as politico-religious movements and a form of "proto-nationalism."

Wicca

One of the most recent, and perhaps most studied, new religious movements is ***Wicca***, sometimes referred to as modern-day witchcraft. The term is derived from the Old English word for witch, although Wiccans should not be confused with the Hallowe'en witches, who stem from the late Medieval European witch hunts of the 1400s to 1600s. Nor should they be confused with contemporary witches in Africa and elsewhere. Most Wiccans see Wicca as a revival or reconstruction of ancient pagan (non-Christian) beliefs and practices, many of which are focused on respect for, and being in tune with, nature. Wicca is also a type of ***duotheism*** in that most adherents worship a male horned god associated with nature and animals, as well as a mother goddess associated with fertility and springtime. Some Wiccans also accept the existence of other, lesser spiritual beings. Wicca can thus be described as a duotheistic, neo-pagan, nature-centred religion.

It is also a reconstructed religion. Most Wiccans trace the origin of Wicca to Gerald Gardner, a British civil servant who claimed that he had been inducted into a witch's coven (a local association of witches) that, because of persecution, had practised in secret for centuries. Whether or not this is true is questionable, but in the early 1950s Gardner drew on old Celtic beliefs, Greek and Roman ideas, and other pre-Christian religions to write several books about the history and practice of Wicca. These books form the basis of the modern faith (Clifton 2006).

The Wiccan Rede, or primary moral edict, is "an it harm none, do what ye will." This is generally taken to mean that people have the freedom to do whatever they like so long as they do not harm anyone (including themselves), for everything one does, good or bad, will come back to them three times over. The pentagram (a five pointed star within a circle) is a symbol of faith worn by many Wiccans. The points of the star represent the five elements: spirit, air, water, earth, and fire, which respectively symbolize spiritual love, the mind, the cycle of life, motherhood, and passion. Wiccans also use magic, or rather "magick," as a tool for personal growth and transformation, but for many practitioners it lacks a supernatural element (York 2005) (Figure 12.14). Wiccan festivals, or sabbats, are connected with the yearly agricultural cycle and the solar year. Many of the rituals are performed in a circular fashion such as handfasting, the Wiccan marriage ceremony (Gallagher 2005). The media have sensationalized some of the Wiccan practices such as performing rituals in the nude, or "skyclad," and the Great Rite, which involves sexual intercourse. Most Wiccans, however, perform their rituals fully clothed and the Great Rite is performed symbolically whereby an *athame* (dagger) is thrust into a chalice.

Although some Wiccans are organized into local groups called covens, most of which can trace their lineage back to ones created by Gardner, the majority of Wiccans engage in solitary practice, learning about Wicca through books and these days via the Internet. This makes the faith open to individual interpretation and practice. Wicca also lacks any sacred text such as the Bible or Qur'an, as well as any established hierarchy. In other words, Wicca lacks ***dogma***; there are no authoritative rules or teachings that must be followed

---

Wicca A duotheistic, neo-pagan, nature-centred religion.

duotheism Belief in two gods.

dogma Authoritative rules or teachings established by religious authorities that must be followed or taken as true.

Scott Olson/Getty Images

FIGURE 12.14 Wiccan high priestess Virginia Powell participates in a Wicca lunar ritual in the temple at the Witch School in Hoopeston, Illinois.

or taken as true. Wicca is thus a very flexible and adaptable religion and very accepting of alternative lifestyles and minorities.

In the early 1960s Wicca spread to North America, where it grew rapidly. Much of its success can be attributed to the profound social changes occurring at this time related to what has been called the *counter-culture* movement (Clifton 2006). Young baby boomers (children born post World War II: 1946–1964) were disillusioned with the status quo and the values and norms of the "Establishment" (i.e., those in power). Discontent with the overt sexism and racism in society fuelled the growth of the civil rights movement; increasing pollution led to a concern for nature and the beginnings of the environmental movement; the development of the birth control pill resulted in the so-called sexual revolution, where women were "liberated" and both men and women were free to experiment with sex and social relationships, contrary to established morals; and the Cold War, the development of the hydrogen bomb, and the Vietnam War led to peace movements such as "Ban the Bomb." The 1960s was also the age of Rock and Roll, hippies, and experimentation with new hallucinogenic drugs such as LSD. American psychologist and philosopher Timothy Leary enticed people to "turn on, tune in, drop out." The hypocrisy, dogmatism, and patriarchal nature of mainstream religion turned people away from them, although not necessarily from spirituality (Pike 2004). Disenchanted, many people adopted Eastern religions such as the International Society for Krishna Consciousness (Hare Krishna) and Transcendental Meditation (promoted by the Beatles), as well as neo-pagan religions such as Wicca.

Wicca's lack of dogma and hierarchy, its concern for nature and equality, the fact that it has a goddess, which is empowering for women (Griffin 2005), and can be practised on an individual level tapped into most of these counter-culture trends and meant that Wicca was, and still is, successful in attracting adherents. Wicca has evolved since the 1960s and is now divided into several traditions. Although precise figures are hard to come by, it is perhaps the fastest growing religion in percentage terms in Canada, Britain, and the United States (Jensen and Thomson 2008). According to the Canadian 2001 census (the last year Statistics Canada kept records on religion), the number of neo-pagans (of which Wicca is only one) increase by 281 percent from 1991.

Many devout Christians equate Wicca with medieval witchcraft and view it as devil-worship; however, it is gaining more social acceptance. For example, the University of Victoria administration approved anthropologist Heather Botting as a Wiccan chaplain—the first of any university in the world—and has been marrying Wiccans since 1995, when the B.C. government recognized the right of Wiccan chaplains to legally conduct marriages (Todd 2003). Pagan Pastoral Outreach is a pagan organization based in Ontario that has worked with Correctional Services Canada since 2002 to provide chaplaincy services to Wiccan inmates, helping them hold Wiccan rituals and sabbat observances, as well as providing consultation services and courses on Wicca (Gagnon 2008). Wicca is also now recognized by the Department of National Defence, Canada, which permits pagans to take time off to celebrate their holidays (James 2014).

Globalization of World Religions

In much the same way that markets have been globalizing over the past decade, the revolution in information and communication has had far-reaching effects on the various ecclesiastical religions of the world. For much of the 20th century, most North Americans who identified with a particular religion followed a fairly straightforward set of religious beliefs and practices.

counter-culture A subculture in which the norms and values are opposed to those of mainstream society.

People practised Islam, Christianity, Buddhism, or Judaism, and it was relatively easy to predict what set of beliefs they held. Today, however, many people are practising a hodgepodge of beliefs. It has been reported (Lamont-Brown 1999) that as many as 40 million people in Japan are now practising "new religions," which involve blending the two major religions in Japan (Buddhism and Shintoism) with elements of Confucianism, shamanism, animism, ancestor worship, Protestantism, and Catholicism.

The blending of religions is known as *syncretism* and was common throughout the 19th and 20th centuries, when colonizing nations imposed their religious beliefs on the societies they colonized. Many societies, for instance, while they may have adopted Christianity, still believe in witchcraft. While Christianity may provide a moral code and answer some of the larger questions, such as what happens when they die, it cannot answer such questions as why accidents happen, or why they get sick, whereas witchcraft can.

This cross-fertilization of religious beliefs and practices is a dilemma for many leaders of world religions, who see this intermingling as a threat to their identity. The process of globalization will no doubt continue well into the future, however, throwing culturally and religiously different peoples together. If living in close proximity to people of different faiths actually threatens one's religious identity, the likely response will be to build walls around religious communities and systematically exclude non-believers. There are some people of faith, however, who are embracing living in close proximity to newly arrived immigrant groups that practise different religions from their own.

Another major change in the mosaic of world religions is that, owing to decades of Christian proselytizing, the geographic distribution and centres of power in some world religions such as Christianity are actually changing. Over the past half-century, Christianity has experienced a major shift in power and influence, from the long-established churches of Europe and North America to the so-called "Global South" (Africa, South America, and south Asia). For decades, European Christian churches have been losing membership and have faced considerable difficulties recruiting priests. This is particularly true of Roman Catholicism, which is the world's largest Christian denomination. Catholic Church membership in the developing world, however, has been booming during this same period. For example, although there are 277 million Catholics presently living in Europe (24 percent), there are 483 million living in Latin America (41 percent), 177 million living in Africa (15 percent), and 138 million living in south Asia (12 percent). This demographic shift in the past 60 years is particularly problematic because, although most Catholics live outside of Europe, the Church itself has been run like a European mini-state. Moreover, until the election of Pope Francis of Argentina in 2013, there had never been a non-European Pope in the history of the Church. This is because, even though Europe is home to less than a quarter of all Catholics, 62 percent of the Cardinals, who actually elect the Pope, are from Europe. With the major demographic centre of gravity of Catholicism shifting from Europe to the "Global South," there is an ongoing debate among Roman Catholics as to whether the Pope should represent those parts of the world where most Catholics reside or where the spiritual vision of the Church originated and developed over most of its history (Donadio and Povoledo 2013).

In some countries the nonreligious changes occurring in the global economy are bringing about fundamental changes in their own traditional religious practices. To illustrate, although Indians have practised yoga for centuries, many middle-class Indians, whose contemporary jobs are putting increased pressure on their time, feel that the practice of traditional yoga is too complex and time-consuming. Today, followers of Swami Ramdev practise a form of "yoga lite" with 12 000 of their closest friends in Jawaharlal Nehru Stadium in New Delhi, India. By concentrating on breath control, which is only one aspect of traditional yoga, the Swami claims that practitioners of his "yoga made easy" will remain healthy in mind and body. This is an appealing message for people caught up in the pressures of the modern global economy (Kumar 2005).

We have heard a good deal in recent years about the outsourcing of manufacturing and high-tech jobs from Canada and the United States to India. Less known, however, is that because of a shortage of priests in North America, local Catholic parishes are sending Mass Intentions (requests for masses said for a sick relative, the remembrance of deceased kin, or a prayer offering for a newborn) to India. Catholic priests in India (who have more time than North American priests and need the money) are now conducting masses on behalf of North American Catholics after receiving requests via email (Rai 2004).

Religion in Canada

Religious affiliation and conviction in Canada is changing dramatically. In general, the number of people attending religious services has been declining for several decades. This is particularly true for younger people. In 2005 only 16 percent of people aged 15–24 said they attended a religious service at least once a week (Lindsay 2008). This is due in large part to an increasing number of people who claim no religious affiliation—about 25 percent of the Canadian population (Figure 12.15).

---

syncretism The blending of religions.

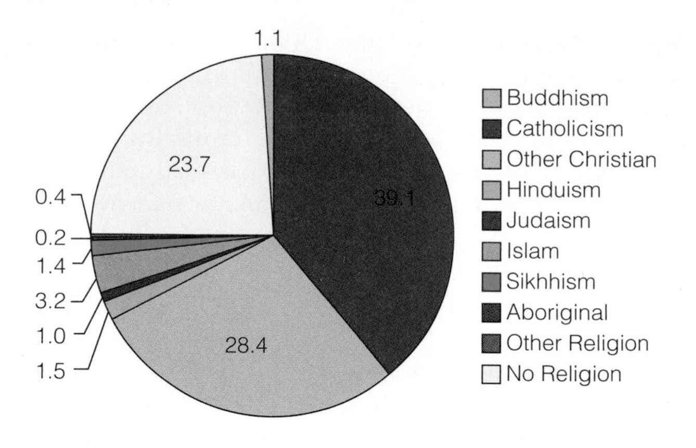

FIGURE 12.15 Religion in Canada in percentages, 2011.

Source: 2011 National Household Survey: Immigration, place of birth, citizenship, ethnic origin, visible minorities, language and religion. http://www.statcan.gc.ca/daily-quotidien/130508/dq130508b-eng.htm?HPA

Faced with an aging population, shrinking congregations, and declining donations, many churches, particularly mainstream Protestant churches, have trouble paying their expenses and have had to either close or amalgamate. For instance, the average age of members of the United Church of Canada, once a "pillar of Canadian society" is 65 (Wente 2012), and it is closing about 50 churches a year (Brown 2015; Hopper 2013a). Canadian society has also changed. With the need for two incomes, there is less time to go to church; Sundays are for shopping, sports, and household chores.

Protestant faiths were sustained by immigration from Europe until the 1970s, when immigration patterns changed. Today, about 20 percent of immigrants to Canada come from South America or the Philippines and bring their Catholic faith with them, as do Muslims, Sikhs, and Buddhists (Brown 2015).

The other Christian groups that are doing well and are attracting younger people are ***proselytizing*** and ***evangelical*** churches. Proselytizing is an attempt to convert people to one's religion, and evangelical refers to those Christian denominations that believe in receiving salvation, being "born again," and in the literal interpretation of the Bible. In Vancouver, where half the people claim to have no religion, up to 2000 people fill the 85 000-square-foot Broadway Church's pews every Sunday morning (Hopper 2013a). The Pentecostal church boasts six screens, casually dressed preachers, sermons interspersed with movie clips, and a full-sized rock band. Sermons are simultaneously translated into Korean, Mandarin, and Cantonese, and if a person misses the sermon there is always the podcast (Hopper 2013a). Broadway Church is one of Canada's 22 mega-churches hosting over 2000 people per week. Others include Calgary's First Alliance Church, Springs Church in Winnipeg (with 7500 people attending per week), and Église Nouvelle Vie in Longueuil, Quebec (Hartford Institute for Religious Research 2015). Catch the Fire Ministries, near Toronto's Pearson International Airport, is a network of churches that began in Toronto in January 1994; its worship centre seats over 3000. By September 1995, it had a yearly attendance of over 600 000. Catch the Fire Ministries now has churches and missions all over the world (Catch the Fire 2015).

Churches such as these are easily accessible and provide podcasts, modern websites, as well as lots of parking, gymnasiums, coffee bars, childcare, family services, and so on. Because they are entrepreneurial, modern, friendly, relaxed, and easy to understand, they attract the "connected," contemporary worshipper and are thus growing rapidly (Hopper 2013a). In 1970 there were about 50 million Pentecostals, while today there are about 280 million worldwide (Lewis 2011). The Charismatic Catholics, which have adopted Pentecostal-style worship, have increased similarly, from about 13 million in 1970 to 305 million today (Lewis 2011).

proselytizing Attempting to convert people to one's religion.

evangelical Christian denominations that believe in receiving salvation, being "born again," and the literal interpretation of the Bible.

religious fundamentalism A religious movement characterized by a return and strict adherence to the fundamental principles of the religion, and often involving a literal interpretation of religious texts, as well intolerance of other faiths.

The Rise of Fundamentalism

Much has been written in the past several decades about a worldwide shift toward ***religious fundamentalism***. Religious fundamentalists feel threatened by an increasingly modern, scientific, secular world. They want to separate themselves from today's modernists, whose original religious principles, they believe, have been corrupted through neglect and compromise. The use of the Islamic term jihad (meaning struggle) should in no way suggest that religious fundamentalism includes only Islamic fundamentalism. In fact, religious fundamentalism includes any group that purposefully chooses to separate itself from the larger religious group from which it arose. Such groups seek to separate themselves from both foreign religions and compromised versions of their own religion. Thus, we see Islamic fundamentalists who, rejecting foreign and modern ideas, advocate a return to Islamic culture, strict principles based on Islamic law (Sharia), a literal interpretation of the Qur'an, and close fellowship among Muslims.

Likewise, Christian fundamentalists, wanting to return to a previous and less-corrupted form of their own religion, insist on interpreting scripture as infallible, historically accurate, and literally true. Moreover, like any other form of religious fundamentalism, Judaic fundamentalists see themselves as distinct from the corruptions of the modern world and hold their own sacred scriptures as divinely inspired, infallible,

© Rolin Riggs/The New York Times/Redux

FIGURE 12.16 The merging of religion and nationalism occurs not only in Middle Eastern countries. On July 4, 2006, this Statue of Liberation Through Christ was consecrated at a fundamentalist church in Memphis, Tennessee, to demonstrate the congregation's belief that Christianity is the foundation of American society.

and unchangeable. What all fundamentalist groups have in common is that they all draw most of their converts from among members of their own religion—a religion that, the fundamentalists claim, has strayed from its original principles and practices.

Islamic Fundamentalism and Religious Nationalism

An extremely significant trend in global religion today is ***religious nationalism***. This movement, which can be found in countries that represent a number of different religious traditions, rejects the idea that religion and government should be separate. Instead, religious nationalism calls for a merger of traditional religious beliefs with government institutions and leaders (Figure 12.16).

Nowhere is religious nationalism more evident than in the Middle East. Islamic nationalism—perhaps the most visible form of religious nationalism—combines fundamentalist religious orthodoxy with contemporary political institutions. The alignment of Islam with contemporary political Arab nationalism stems from the 1967 Arab–Israeli war. Israel's thorough defeat of Syria, Egypt, and Jordan in just five days left many Arabs feeling that something was wrong in the Arab world. From the late 1960s onward, many Arabs have restructured their sense of nationalism within the religious framework of Islam. Their religion has become a vibrant source of national identity as well as an alternative solution to their political, economic, and military problems. In the early 1980s, Islamic nationalism experienced some significant victories over the non-Arab, non-Islamic world. For example, Hezbollah forced the United States from Beirut, the Israelis were driven out of Lebanon, and Russia finally limped out of Afghanistan. As Islamic nationalism flexed its muscles, it sent a clear message to others both in the Arab world and beyond: Islam is a powerful force and can be mobilized to challenge what it sees as foreign influence and oppression. Islamic nationalism also represents a rejection of what is seen as the often-exploitive government and economic systems (such as capitalism and democracy) that Middle Eastern peoples have endured over the decades.

In its more extreme form, religious nationalism, which takes on the character of a religious war, can pose a real threat to the rest of the world. Secular nationalistic movements, such as those found in Western democracies, have goals and objectives with imposed time limits. For example, secular nationalists promise their followers that if they do certain things now, they will live for a long time in a peaceful world. Religious nationalism, on the other hand, promises its followers endless rewards; for example, if you martyr yourself in the struggle against the infidels, you will immediately enter paradise and stay there forever. That, needless to say, poses some real challenges for those defined as infidels.

A distinction needs to be made between an ***Islamist*** and an ***Islamic terrorist***, or extremist. An Islamist supports and may advocate for a government that operates according to Islamic laws. Most Islamists who promote this form of government promote it through peaceful means, seeing violence as incompatible with Islam. Islamic terrorists, however, want to achieve an Islamic state through violent means (Doughart and Saeed

religious nationalism A trend toward merging traditional religious principles with the workings of government.

Islamist A person who advocates for or supports a government that operates according to Islamic laws.

Islamic terrorist A person who advocates for or supports, through violent means, a government that operates according to Islamic laws.

World History Archive/Alamy Stock Photo

FIGURE 12.17 Abu Bakr al-Baghdadi, leader of the Islamic State of Iraq and the Levant (ISIL), an Islamic extremist group in western Iraq, Libya.

al-Mutar 2012). And it is the actions of this group that result in Islamophobia.

Perhaps the biggest challenge faced today by religious nationalism is that posed by the terrorist group Islamic State of Iraq and the Levant (ISIL). Sometimes referred to as ISIS (Islamic State of Iraq and Syria), their goal is to establish, through force, a caliphate—an Islamic government lead by a leader of the entire Muslim community—spanning the entire world (Withnall 2014) (Figure 12.17). Nearly 60 countries are fighting this group, which the United Nations holds responsible for innumerable human rights abuses, war crimes, and ethnic cleansing.

Islamic Terrorism and Islamophobia

A phobia can be defined as an exaggerated, often irrational, fear of something, such as a fear of closed spaces, heights, or spiders. Recent years have witnessed the rise of ***Islamophobia***, "an exaggerated fear, hatred, and hostility toward Islam and Muslims" (Wajahat et al. 2011). The fear is perhaps not hard to understand. The attacks on the World Trade Center on September 11, 2001 (9/11), the suicide bombing of a double-decker bus in London on July 7, 2005 (7/7), the shooting of corporal Nathan Cirillo at the war memorial on Parliament Hill, Ottawa, in October 2014, and the bombings in Paris in November 2015, and Brussels in March 2016 by groups such as ISIS, al-Qaida, Boko Haram (Nigeria), and al-Shabab (Somalia) have almost all been done in the name of Islam. The fact that most attacks have occurred in countries such as Syria and Iraq, and against other Muslims, and that numerous Islamic religious leaders have condemned them as the acts of murderers, makes little difference to the increased sense of insecurity in many Western countries.

Islamophobia An exaggerated fear, hatred, and hostility toward Islam and Muslims.

Islamophobia is a fear fuelled by lack of knowledge. Despite efforts by many Muslim organizations to raise awareness of Islam, few Canadians and Americans know even the basic tenets of the faith. It is also not simply about fear, but also about hatred. The insecurity and fear is thus also felt by many Muslims living in Western countries, and it is increasing (Ali-Karamali 2012).

Most people are aware that the attacks are committed by a tiny fraction of Muslims who have a distorted view of Islam, and that there is little to fear from Islam or from Muslims. But the fear has led to negative stereotypes. Islam is perceived as a religion that preaches violence, and Muslims as suspicious and untrustworthy (Doughart and Saeed al-Mutar 2012; Ali-Karamali 2012). According to one poll, over 54 percent of Canadians have an unfavourable view of Islam, and the figure is increasing (Geddes 2013). Islam has also become equated with race; Muslims are seen as having not simply a particular religious belief, but also as belonging to a racial group. These stereotypes have resulted "in bias, discrimination, and the marginalization and exclusion of Muslims from social, political, and civic life" (Wajahat et al. 2011).

The discrimination takes many forms, from Donald Trump's pre-election promise to ban Muslims from entering the United States, to pulling men off planes for having an Arabic name, to hate crimes such as painting "Die Bombers" and "ISIS Go Home" in large letters on a school wall in Ottawa (Helmer 2016), to burning mosques in the United States. The National Council of Canadian Muslims tracks anti-Muslim incidents reported across Canada and notes that the number of incidents is increasing (NCCM 2016).

Western countries such as Denmark, Great Britain, and the Netherlands, are also reconsidering their immigration policies with respect to Muslims (Doughart and Saeed al-Mutar 2012). In 2009, nearly 60 percent of Swiss voters voted in favour of banning minaret construction. France has banned wearing the niqab (a cloth that covers the entire body and face except for the eyes) in public. And in Canada, the Parti Québécois, under Pauline Marois, before they were defeated in 2014, also attempted to ban services to women wearing the niqab when applying for government services. The Conservative government under former prime minister Harper appealed a Supreme Court decision to allow women to wear it during citizenship ceremonies. The Liberals, under Justin Trudeau, dropped the appeal (Mas and Crawford 2015). Over 80 percent of Canadians, including many Muslims however, agree with the ban on face-coverings (Beeby 2015).

Canada is a multicultural, tolerant society that values freedom of religion and opposes discrimination. There is a fear, however, that any criticism of Muslims or Islam will result in charges of Islamophobia, racial profiling, or religious discrimination. Accusations of Islamophobia have thus unfortunately stifled serious intellectual and academic discussion about the shortcomings of Islam (Doughart and Saeed al-Mutar 2012). Criticism of Islam is not Islamophobia any more than criticism of Christianity is Christophobic. As Doughart and Saeed al-Mutar (2012) point out, "freedom of belief, if it is to have universal and consistent meaning, must include the freedom to criticize beliefs and believers—a concept that is foreign to the social and political worldview of Islam."

Religious Change and Technology

Although religious evangelists have used the radio to convert non-believers to Christianity, it was not until the 1970s that television greatly increased their ability to gain converts, raise funds, and spread their influence. In fact, television was such a powerful medium that many televangelists became superstars with their own broadcasting empires, news exposure, and political influence. In the United States evangelists such as Jerry Falwell, Billy Graham, Oral Roberts, Pat Robertson, and Robert Schuller recruited thousands by promising personal salvation, material success, and physical health. Their messages resonated particularly with those who were poor, undereducated, underemployed, sick, elderly, or those who were fearful of crime, changing sexual values, and anything foreign. Through their on-air fundraising, many televangelists built multimillion-dollar media empires.

In Canada, 100 Huntley Street, which began in 1977, is the country's longest-running daily television show and the sixth longest in the world (100 Huntley Street 2015). It airs on Global TV every morning and is also broadcast in the United States. The show attempts to attract people to Christianity by providing testimonials from leaders, celebrities, and everyday people "who have had life-changing encounters with God" (100 Huntley Street 2015).

Today's religious organizations have their own websites and chat rooms. It is now possible to spread your own religious ideas cheaply, instantaneously, and all over the world. In much the same way that radio and television extended the reach of religious ideas, the Internet has enabled religion to expand beyond the walls of a church. A good example of this is the online virtual world of Second Life (see Chapter 5). One Evangelical church based in Oklahoma even broadcasts its weekly sermon to its virtual church in Second Life (Crabtree 2007). Players have also set up virtual synagogues, churches, Buddhist temples, and mosques where people can join a community and participate in rituals. For instance, Beth Brown, an Orthodox Jew living in Dallas, Texas, meets online with her mother, who lives in New York City, every Friday night to light virtual Shabbat candles. Other Second Lifers have formed study groups and prayer sessions and they establish relationships with fellow believers from all over the world (Grossman 2007). As with so many aspects of life today, the Internet brings together people who share common religious traditions who may be spread across the globe. There are matchmaking websites designed for particular religions as well. For example, Jewish singles can log onto www.Jdate.com, Christians can visit www.Christiansingles.com, and www.Eharmony.com appeals to those of a more "new age" religious persuasion.

Summary

1. The anthropological study of religion concentrates on describing the various systems of religious belief, how they function, how they are interconnected with other dimensions of culture, and the degree to which they influence human behaviour.
2. Nineteenth-century anthropologists were interested in how religion evolved. Tylor thought it evolved from animism to polytheism and monotheism, while Frazer thought magic evolved into religion and then science.
3. Anthropologists such as Durkheim and Malinowski were concerned with the functions religion served for the society and the individual, while Clifford Geertz saw religion as a system of symbols.
4. Although people in all cultures have supernatural beliefs, these beliefs take widely varying forms from society to society. It is difficult to define supernatural belief systems cross-culturally because different societies have their own ways of distinguishing between the natural and the supernatural.
5. Religion performs certain social functions. It enhances the overall well-being of the society by serving as a mechanism of social control, helping to reduce the stress and frustrations that often lead to social conflict, and intensifying group solidarity.
6. Religion also performs certain psychological functions, such as providing emotional comfort by helping to explain the unexplainable, and helping a person cope with the stress and anxiety that often accompany illness or misfortune.
7. Religion differs from magic in that it deals with big issues such as life, death, and god, whereas magic deals with more immediate and specific problems. Whereas religion asks for help through prayer, magic is a direct attempt to control nature by manipulating supernatural forces.

8. Whereas sorcery involves the deliberate use of certain material substances to cause people misfortune, witchcraft is an inborn and generally involuntary capacity to work evil.
9. Witchcraft is a serious problem in many African, Melanesian, Asian, and South American societies, where many people suspected of being witches have been killed.
10. Myths are stories believed to be true by adherents and explain things such as how humans came to be and how they are supposed to behave and relate to the world; they provide a worldview.
11. Following the scheme suggested by Wallace, the four distinctive types of religious organization are individualistic cults, shamanistic cults, communal cults, and ecclesiastical cults. These types correspond roughly with increasing levels of socioeconomic complexity.
12. The individualistic cult is associated with food foraging societies and is characterized by an absence of religious specialists.
13. Shamanistic cults involve the least-complex religious division of labour. Shamans are part-time religious specialists who, it is believed, help or cure their clients by intervening with supernatural powers while in an altered state of consciousness.
14. In communal cults, ordinary people conduct religious ceremonies for the well-being of the community. Rites of passage are examples of communal cult ceremonies.
15. Ecclesiastical cults, which are found in societies with state systems of government, are characterized by full-time professional clergy who are usually organized into a hierarchy.
16. Rites of passage are ceremonies that mark a change in a person's social position and also help them through the transformation. They typically involve three phases: separation, transition, and incorporation.
17. Revitalization movements—religious movements aimed at bringing new life and energy into a society—usually occur when societies are experiencing rapid cultural change, foreign domination, or perceived deprivation. Handsome Lake and the Ghost Dance Religion are two examples of revitalization movements.
18. Cargo cults are a type of revitalization movement found in Melanesia characterized by delivery of consumer goods and a return to traditional customs, and may involve a messianic figure. The John Frum Movement on Tanna Island, Vanuatu, is an example.
19. Wicca, or modern-day witchcraft, is a duotheistic, neo-pagan, nature-centred religion that is gaining in popularity in North America.
20. Religious affiliation and conviction in Canada is declining rapidly, although Catholicism, Islam, and other Eastern religions are growing through immigration. Pentecostal churches are also gaining in popularity.
21. A significant trend in global religion today is the rise of religious fundamentalism and religious nationalism. Found most prominently in the Islamic world and also among North American Christians, religious nationalism aims to merge traditional religious beliefs with contemporary political institutions.
22. Islamophobia is increasing in Western countries, resulting in discrimination and marginalization of Muslims from social, political, and civic life. Fear of being labelled Islamophobic is restricting discussion and criticism of Islam.
23. New technologies are changing the way religion is delivered and accessed.

Key Terms

animism
cargo cult
communal cult
communitas
contagious magic
counter-culture
cult
dogma
duotheism
ecclesiastical cult
evangelical
imitative magic
individualistic cult
Islamic terrorist
Islamist
Islamophobia
magic
mana
monotheism
myth
polytheism
profane
proselytizing
purification ritual
quinceañera
religion
religious fundamentalism
religious nationalism
revitalization movement
rite of passage
rite of solidarity
ritual
sacred
shaman
shamanistic cult
sorcery
syncretism
totemism
Wicca
worldview
wudu

Critical Thinking Questions

1. In what ways do people in your culture try to control events through supernatural means?
2. What role does religion play in Canada with regard to issues such as assisted suicide, abortion, family, appropriate dress, birth control, gay marriage, and so on?
3. Arnold van Gennep suggested that all rites of passage have three distinct phases. Can you identify these phases in certain rites of passage that people in your culture typically go through?
4. What religious or magical icons do you or your friends wear, have in their cars or homes (if any), and what do they mean to you, your family, and your friends?
5. Is it rational to believe in witchcraft? Are there different types of logic that may be called upon to explain circumstances?
6. How do religious texts or myths explain or reinforce existing social hierarchies? Can you think of any examples?
7. All religions are concerned with sex and gender: where men and women came from, what men and women are like, how they are supposed to behave, and how they are supposed to relate to one another. Compare the way two religions approach sex and gender.
8. What are the differences and similarities between Christian fundamentalism and Islamic fundamentalism?
9. If scientific explanation replaces religious beliefs, how can we explain the growing popularity of new religions, such as neo-paganism, and the rise of fundamentalism in many parts of the world, including North America?
10. Religion provides important functions such as group cohesion solidarity, social control, and conflict resolution as well as cognitive and intellectual functions. Can these functions be achieved online? What other functions may religion online serve?

Make the Grade with MindTap

Stay organized and efficient with **MindTap**—a single destination with all the course material and study aids you need to succeed. Built-in apps leverage social media and the latest learning technology. For example:

- ReadSpeaker will read the text to you.
- Self-quizzing allows you to assess your understanding.
- Flashcards are pre-populated to provide you with a jump-start for review—or you can create your own.
- You can highlight text and make notes in your MindTap Reader. Your notes will flow into Evernote, the electronic notebook app that you can access anywhere when it's time to study for the exam.

Visit nelson.com/student to start using **MindTap**. Enter the Online Access Code from the card included with your text. If a code card is not provided, you can purchase instant access at NELSONbrain.com.

Agawa Rock red ochre pictographs in Lake Superior National Park, believed painted by Ojibwa artists in 1600s and 1700s.

Art

CHAPTER

13

THE G'PSGOLOX TOTEM POLE

In 1862 a smallpox epidemic swept through the First Nations of British Columbia's northwest coast, killing nearly 90 percent of the population in a matter of days. For example, the population of four Haisla villages located approximately 600 km northwest of Vancouver, fell from about 3500 to 57 (Jessiman 2011). Sometime afterward, Chief G'psgolox of the Haisla Eagle clan, who had lost his wife and children to the epidemic, wandered into the forest where he encountered the spirit Tsooda, who gave him a spiritual experience in which he was re-united with his family. In 1872, to commemorate the spirit encounter and the loss of his children, Chief G'psgolox commissioned a 9 m high mortuary totem pole to be built and erected in the village where his children died. Totem poles incorporate traditional art forms such as symbolic figures and crests that represent the clan of the owner. They are thus not simply an art form but part of the owner's identity and heritage.

On top of G'psgolox's totem pole was Tsooda, wearing a revolving hat; below him was a carving of Asoalget, a mythical grizzly bear that represented spiritual power. For 57 years the pole sat at the entrance of the seasonal village, but in 1929, when the villagers returned from a fishing trip they found the totem pole had vanished. In the 1980s, with the help of photographs taken by Frank Swannell in the early 1900s, the Haisla First Nation began looking for it. In 1990 they found it in the Museum of Ethnography in Stockholm, Sweden.

After the collapse of the Northwest Coast First Nations populations in the late 1800s and early 1900s, Christian missionaries entered many villages and convinced converts to destroy totem poles, as they were viewed as objects of heathen worship. Over several decades, hundreds of totem poles, along with other art objects such as masks, headdresses, rattles, baskets, coppers, and so on, found their way into the hands of private collectors and museums in Canada, the United States, and Europe. Some objects were purchased, but many were simply removed without permission from villages that were seasonally vacant or abandoned. This is what seems to have happened to the G'psgolox pole.

In 1929, with the help of the local Indian agent, and permission from the federal Department of Indian Affairs, the pole had been sold (although no receipt has ever been found) to the Swedish Consul in Prince Rupert, British Columbia. While the villagers were away, the totem pole was sawed off at the base and shipped to the Museum of Ethnography in Stockholm, where it lay out of sight in an unheated storeroom until 1980, when it was re-erected in a purpose-built, climate-controlled hall in the museum.

It was obvious that the G'psgolox family totem pole was stolen, and in 1991 the great-great-granddaughter of G'psgolox, along with other members of the

aaron peterson.net/Alamy Stock Photo

WHAT WE WILL LEARN

- **How anthropologists define art**
- **How art in small-scale societies differs from art in complex societies**
- **How forms of art reflect other aspects of a culture**
- **What the various functions of art are in society**
- **How anthropologists look at art forms such as music, dance, and film**
- **How the symbolic meaning and function of graffiti and tattoos have changed over time**
- **How art is changing in the age of globalization**

Haisla Nation, went to Sweden to ask for its return. Negotiations to have the pole repatriated began in 1994. The museum and the Swedish government agreed to return it, but insisted that the pole be housed in a climate-controlled museum. Totem poles typically last about 80 years, after which they are traditionally left to rot where they fall, eventually returning to the earth. Some Haisla Nation members wanted the pole to be returned to the earth as should have happened, while others wanted it preserved as part of their history and to teach their children. As a compromise, two exact replicas of the pole were carved by the grandson of the original carver. The first was carved at the Museum of Ethnography, where visitors could watch it being carved (Figure 13.1). The second was erected on the site of the original pole, where it will be allowed to stand until it decays. In July 2006, the original G'psgolox totem pole was returned to Kitimaat, British Columbia, the home of the Haisla Nation, where it waits until the funds can be raised to build a dedicated heritage facility.

© Carl Staffan Holmer

FIGURE 13.1 Replica of the G'psgolox pole at the Museum of Ethnography in Stockholm.

The G'psgolox totem pole demonstrates the relation between art and other aspects of society, especially kinship and identity. It also raises questions about ownership and the meaning of cultural items in museums and art galleries. While the pole was seen by many in the West as an art object, in its original context it had a function; that is, it was a mortuary statue much like a gravestone, and marked an important event. There are countless First Nation artifacts and art objects in museums and private collections around the world, some of which were obtained legitimately, others under more dubious circumstances. Both Canada and Sweden signed the UNESCO 1970 Convention on the Means of Prohibiting and Preventing the Illicit Import, Export and Transfer of Ownership of Cultural Property, which attempts to protect cultural property from theft and return such property that has been stolen. Unfortunately, it only covers the return of cultural items stolen after 1970. ■

The Role of Art

Artistic expression is one of the most distinctive human characteristics. No group of people known to cultural anthropologists, either in the past or today, spends all its time in the utilitarian pursuit of meeting basic survival needs. In other words, people do not hunt, grow crops, make tools, and build houses purely for the sake of sustaining themselves and others. After their survival needs are met, all cultures, even technologically simple ones, decorate their storage containers, paint their houses, embroider their clothing, and add aesthetically pleasing designs to their tools. They compose songs, tell riddles, dance creatively, paint pictures, make films, and carve masks. All these endeavours reflect the human urge for self-expression and aesthetic pleasure. It would be hard to imagine a society without art, music, dance, and poetry. As the study of cultural anthropology reminds us, artistic expression is found in every society, and aesthetic pleasure is felt by people everywhere (Coote and Shelton 1992). Art, however, not only provides us with pleasure but it also has a function, and so anthropologists interested in art also focus on its role in society and especially in

Agencja Fotograficzna Caro/Alamy Stock Photo

FIGURE 13.2 **The 11.1 cm high Venus of Willendorf (Austria), carved about 25 000 years ago, is one of the oldest known representations of the human body. Its purpose is unknown but some researchers speculate that she symbolized fertility.**

its role in constructing a cultural identity. In 2008, at Hohle Fels cave in Germany, a small 6 cm figurine of a woman carved from a mammoth's tusk was discovered (Figure 13.2). Over 35 000 years old (Curry 2012), it is the oldest of hundreds of similar Venus figurines found from southern France to Siberia (Vandewettering 2015). Most of the figurines are of the female form and were made by foragers. This latest discovery has reignited debate about the origins of art and its functions (Curry 2012).

What Is Art?

For centuries, people from a variety of disciplines—including philosophers, anthropologists, politicians, art historians, and professional artists themselves—have proposed definitions of art. George Mills (1957, 17) suggested that "definitions (of art) vary with the purposes of the definers." To illustrate, the artist might define art in terms of the creative process, the politician's definition would emphasize the communicative aspects of art that could mobilize public opinion, the art historian or knowledgeable collector would focus on the emotional response art produces, and the cultural anthropologist might define art in terms of the role or function it plays in religious ceremonies. Nevertheless, despite these diverse definitions, any definition of art, if it is to have any cross-cultural comparability, must include five basic elements:

1. The artistic process should be creative, playful, and enjoyable and need not be concerned with the practicality or usefulness of the object being produced.
2. From the perspective of the consumer, art should produce some type of emotional response, either positive or negative.
3. Art should be ***transformational***. An event from nature, such as a cheetah running at full speed, may be aesthetically pleasing in that it evokes a strong emotional response, but it is not art. It becomes art only when someone transforms the image into a painting, dance, song, or poem.
4. Art should communicate information by being representational. In other words, once the object of art is transformed, it should make a symbolic statement about what is being portrayed.
5. Art implies that the artist has developed a certain level of technical skill not shared equally by all people in a society. In fact, the word art comes from the old French word for skill. Some people have more highly developed skills than others because of the interplay of individual interests and opportunities with genetically based acuities (Figure 13.3).

© Paa Joe, Ghana, Africa late 20th to early 21st century. Lion-shaped coffin, 2001. Mint Museum, Charlotte, NC.

FIGURE 13.3 **This lion-shaped coffin (constructed of wood, enamel, raffia, and fabric) is the creation of Ghanaian artist Paa Joe.**

transformational The quality of an artistic process that converts an image into a work of art.

Centuries of debate have failed to produce a universally agreed-on definition of art. Although we will not presume to establish a universal definition, it will be useful, for the purposes of this chapter, to suggest a working definition based on the five elements just listed. Thus, *art* is both the process and the product of applying certain skills to any activity that transforms matter, sound, or motion into a form that is deemed aesthetically meaningful to people in a society.

By using these five features, we can include a wide variety of artistic activities in our definition. In all societies people apply imagination, creativity, and technical skills to transform matter, sound, and movement into works of art. The various types of artistic expression include the graphic or plastic arts, such as painting, carving, weaving, basket making, and sculpting of clay, metal, or glass; the creative manipulation of sounds and words in such artistic forms as music, poetry, and folklore; and the application of skill and creativity to body movement that gives rise to dance. It should be pointed out that these three neatly defined categories of artistic expression sometimes include forms that are not familiar to Westerners. To Westerners, the graphic and plastic arts include such media as painting and sculpture, but in the non-Western world, people may also include the Nubians' elaborate body decoration (Faris 1972) and Navajo sand painting (Witherspoon 1977). Moreover, some activities that, in our own society, have no particular artistic content may be elevated to an art form in other societies.

The Japanese tea ceremony is an excellent case in point. In Japan, the manner of preparing and serving green tea is all choreographed from how the table is laid out, the tea brewed, the table prepared, and the tea scooped into the cup. The tea ceremony is not about drinking tea, but is an aesthetic or artistic performance (Figure 13.4).

Every society has a set of standards that distinguish between good art and bad art, or between more and less satisfying aesthetic experiences. In some societies, such as our own, what constitutes good art is determined largely by a professional art establishment made up of art critics, museum and conservatory personnel, professors of art, and others who generally make their living in the arts. Other societies may not have professional art establishments, and their artistic standards tend to be more democratic in that they are maintained by the general public. Thus, the decoration on a vase, the rhythm of a song, the communicative power of a dance, and the imagery of a painting are subject to the evaluation of artists and non-artists alike.

art The process and the product of applying certain skills to transform matter, sound, or motion into a form that is deemed aesthetically meaningful to people in a society.

Digital Vision/Photodisc/Getty Images

FIGURE 13.4 In the Japanese tea ceremony, the preparation and presentation of green tea is viewed as an art form.

Differences in Art Forms

Many Western people view art from other, less-complex societies as being "primitive" because it does not adhere to our culture's notion of what constitutes good art. The art of less-complex societies is often thought of as childlike, or instinctive, or having an emotional connection with nature. Western art is displayed in museums and galleries with the name of the artist prominently featured. When we visit exhibitions of Indigenous American, African, or Polynesian art in Western museums, however, the artist is often not even identified by name. Instead, the viewer is given a rather elaborate description of where the piece comes from, the materials and techniques used to make it, the function it performs, how it might reflect other aspects of the local culture, such as religious beliefs, and the name of the Western collector who purchased it. According to Sally Price (2001), this practice of identifying the collector rather than the artist is a not-so-subtle way of saying that the value of the art object is determined more by who bought it than by who made it.

This practice of treating art objects in small-scale societies as ethnographic artifacts rather than works of art made by individual artists with actual names is changing, albeit slowly. This is a radical departure from traditional museum practice, which scholars and curators hope will become routine museum practice in the not-too-distant future. Few (if any) art scholars and curators would argue that Indigenous artists should be kept in anonymity because their artistry is inferior to Western art. Rather, the process of identifying Indigenous artists is a long and arduous process requiring enormous amounts of time, energy, and research. But as more and more museums throughout the world begin to engage in this attribution research, art researchers will be able to build on each other's work, thereby speeding up the process of identifying artistic authorship. With the many financial and staffing challenges facing museums today, this process of identifying Indigenous artists will not be completed overnight. But it appears that the traditional practice of keeping Indigenous artists anonymous is slowly being reversed (Dobrzynski 2011).

Despite attempts by art historians to perpetuate the use of the term *primitive*, we do not use it in this book because of its misleading connotations of both inferiority and evolutionary sequencing. Instead we use the term *small-scale* to describe egalitarian societies that have small populations, simple technologies, and little specialization of labour.

One difference stems from the lifestyles and settlement patterns found in these logically opposite types of societies. Because small-scale societies tend to be foragers, pastoralists, or shifting cultivators with nomadic or semi-nomadic residence patterns, the art found in these societies must be highly portable. It is not reasonable to expect people who are often on the move to develop an art tradition comprising large works of art, such as larger-than-life sculptures or large painted canvases. Instead, art in small-scale societies is limited to forms that people leave behind on rock walls or cliffs, or forms that they can take with them easily, such as performing arts (song, dance, and storytelling); body decoration, such as jewellery, body painting, tattooing, and scarification; and artistic decorations on practical artifacts such as weapons, clothing, and food containers.

The second significant difference between the art of small-scale societies and complex societies stems from their different levels of social differentiation (i.e., labour specialization). As societies began to develop increasingly more specialized roles about 10 000 years ago, some segments of the population were freed from the everyday pursuits of providing food. The subsequent rise of civilizations was accompanied by the emergence of full-time specialists, such as philosophers, intellectuals, literati, and aesthetic critics, whose energies were directed, among other things, at distinguishing between good art and bad art. The standards of aesthetic judgment have become much more explicit and elaborately defined by specialists in more complex societies (Figure 13.5). To be certain, small-scale societies have aesthetic standards, but they are less elaborate, more implicit, and more widely diffused throughout the entire population.

FIGURE 13.5 Spider sculpture in front of the National Gallery of Canada, Ottawa, Canada. In complex societies, artistic standards are defined by such full-time specialists as art curators, brokers, critics, and scholars, many of whom are associated with museums and art galleries.

A third major contrast arises from differences in the division of labour. As a general rule, as societies become more specialized, they also become more highly stratified into classes with different levels of power, prestige, and wealth. The aesthetic critics responsible for establishing artistic standards in complex societies are invariably members of the upper classes or are employed by them. Thus, art in complex societies becomes associated with the élite. Not only are those who set the standards often members of the élite, but also art in complex societies often is owned and controlled by the upper classes. Moreover, in some complex societies, art both glorifies and serves the interests of the upper classes. In contrast, because small-scale societies are more egalitarian, art tends to be more democratic in that all people have roughly equal access to it.

This notion that, in complex societies, unlike more small-scale societies, the upper classes have greater control over and access to art is particularly evident in Canada. If the directors of museums, symphonies, opera companies, or ballet companies want to raise money, they are not likely to go canvassing in working-class or lower-class neighbourhoods. Moreover, it is the upper and upper-middle classes that are most likely to be season ticket holders for such performances, not the lower classes or even middle classes.

In addition to these three fundamental differences, art in small-scale societies is often embedded to a greater degree in other aspects of the culture. Although we can observe connections between art and, say, religion in our own society, in small-scale societies art permeates many other areas of culture. In fact, because art is such an integral part of the *total* culture, many small-scale societies do not even have a word for

Paul Chesley/Getty Images

FIGURE 13.6 The art form of sand painting among the Navajo of New Mexico is intimately connected with their traditional systems of healing and religion.

art. That is, because art pervades all aspects of people's lives, they do not think of art as something separate and distinct. One such example, sand painting as practised in Navajo culture, is as much religion, myth, and healing as it is art. According to Dorothy Lee (1993, 13), Navajo sand paintings (Figure 13.6) are created as part of a ceremony that includes, myth, ritual, and a series of sacred songs sung over a sick person. The art is in the ceremony, and when it is over the painting is destroyed as it has fulfilled its function.

Because art in small-scale societies is embedded in most other areas of the culture, one is likely to see artistic expressions throughout many realms of peoples' everyday lives. This is not the case in more highly differentiated and stratified societies, which have institutions such as museums and private galleries where art is viewed, appreciated, understood, discussed, and, in some cases, bought and sold. Most people who pay admission to an art museum in North America are doing so to view the artistic exhibits, learn more about them, and experience the feelings they engender. Likewise, when people enter a private art gallery, they are interested not only in seeing and experiencing the works shown, but also in possibly purchasing the works of art. In other words, in most complex societies people go to places that are essentially single-purpose venues (such as museums, galleries, theatres, and opera houses) to see, experience, or trade in artistic objects.

In some parts of the world, it is possible to see how the political system of a society is reflected in its art. Anthropologist Christopher Steiner (1990) has shown how one form of artistic expression—body decoration—reflects the different political structures in Melanesia and Polynesia. A prominent form of political leadership in Melanesia is big men. In the absence of permanent political offices or hierarchies, big men earn their authority by working hard to attract a large number of followers. Because big men can lose their followers, the system of political leadership in Melanesia is very fluid, always subject to change. In Polynesia, on the other hand, leadership is based on centralized chiefdoms with permanent (usually hereditary) authority. The differences in the political structures of these societies are reflected in their forms of bodily adornment. Melanesians decorate their bodies with paints—a temporary medium that can be washed off or lost in much the same way that a big man can lose his high status if he loses the support of his followers. In contrast, Polynesians use tattoos to reflect their more centralized and permanent hereditary offices, as well as their high status.

The Functions of Art

The fact that artistic expression is found in every known society suggests that it functions in some important ways in human societies. The various functions of art can be divided into two basic types: how artistic elements function for the psychological well-being of the individual, and how they function for the well-being and continuity of the society as a whole.

Emotional Gratification for the Individual

Quite apart from whatever benefits art may have for the total society, it is generally agreed that art is a source of personal gratification for both the artist and the viewer. It would be hard to imagine a world in which people engaged only in pursuits that met their basic survival needs. Although people devote most of their time and energy to meeting those needs, it is equally true that all people derive some enjoyment from art because it provides at least a temporary break from those practical (and often stressful) pursuits. After the crops are harvested, the African horticulturalist has time to dance, tell stories, and derive pleasure from making or viewing pieces of art. Likewise, as a diversion from their workaday lives, many Westerners seek gratification by attending a play, a concert, a museum, or going to a movie. No doubt, it was this personal gratification derived from art that prompted Richard Selzer (1979, 196) to comment, "art... is necessary only in that without it life would be unbearable."

The psychologically beneficial functions of art can be examined from two perspectives: that of the artist and that of the beholder. For the artist, the creative process releases emotional energy in a concrete or visible way, that is, by painting, sculpting, writing a play, performing an interpretive dance. Artists, at least in the Western world, are viewed as living with a creative tension that, when released, results in a work of art. This release of creative energy also brings pleasure to the artist to the

CROSS-CULTURAL MISCUE

Over the decades, the fresco *Ecce Homo* (Behold the Man)—an early 20th century painting of Jesus wearing a crown of thorns—painted by Elias Garcia Martinez on a wall in the Sanctuary of Mercy Church in Borja, northeastern Spain, had deteriorated considerably from humidity. It was badly in need of restoration, and although some funds had been donated to repair it, local artist 83-year-old Cecilia Giménez was so upset about its worsening condition that she decided to restore it herself (National Post Staff 2012). Her "restoration," however, has been described as an "amateurish, almost cartoon-like portrait" (CBC News 2012b), "a child's finger-painting" (National Post Staff 2012), and as "a crayon sketch of a very hairy monkey in an ill-fitting tunic" (BBC News 2012) (Figure 13.7). Although not very valuable, the painting did have local sentimental value (National Post Staff 2012; BBC News 2012). So botched was her job that restoration is now impossible (Carvajal 2014). Her miscue was not understanding that art restoration is an art in itself. News of her mistake made international headlines and went viral on social media.

Initially, Cecilia was devastated and ashamed at being branded a "crazy old woman." Since then, however, her restoration has become a tourist magnet for the town of Borja, with a population of about 5000. By the end of 2014 the image had attracted more than 150 000 tourists from around the world who each paid a euro to see it (Carvajal 2014). Her rendering of "Ecce Homo" has become a pop art icon, and local restaurants, which had been struggling during the recession, have filled up; nearby vineyards have vied with each other to put the painting on their wine labels; the portrait has had a part in a movie where two thieves try to steal it; and the town has used the image on their Christmas lottery tickets. In addition, a nearby art museum has seen annual visits increase from 7000 to 70 000 (Carvajal 2014). Thus, what was an artistic disaster turned out to be an economic miracle.

Cesar Manso/AFP/GettyImages

FIGURE 13.7 Elias Garcia Martinez's "Ecce Homo" at the Borja church, Spain, as "restored" by 83-year-old Cecilia Giménez.

extent that she or he derives satisfaction from both the mastery of techniques and the product itself.

From the perspective of the viewer, art can evoke pleasurable emotional responses. For example, works of art can portray events, people, or deities that conjure up positive emotions. The symbols used in a work of art can arouse a positive emotional response. The viewer can receive pleasure by being dazzled by the artist's virtuosity. These pleasurable responses can contribute to the mental well-being of art viewers by providing a necessary balance with the stresses in their everyday lives.

However, it is also possible for art to have the opposite effect by eliciting negative emotions. The artistic process, if not successful from the artist's point of view, can result in increased frustrations and tension. Moreover, any art form is capable of eliciting disturbing or even painful emotions that can lead to psychological discomfort for the viewer.

Social Integration

In addition to whatever positive roles it may play for the individual, art functions to sustain the longevity of the society in which it is found. As anthropologists remind us, art is connected to other parts of the social system. One need only walk into a church, synagogue, or temple to see the relationship between art and religion. Moreover, art has been used in many societies to evoke positive sentiments for systems of government and individual political leaders.

Through various symbols, art communicates a good deal about the values, beliefs, and ideologies of the culture of which it is a part. The art forms found in any given society reflect the major cultural themes and concerns of the society. To illustrate, prominent breasts on females are a major theme in much of the wood sculpture from West Africa. This dominant theme reflects an important social value in those West African societies: the social importance of having children. Much of the art in Renaissance Europe reflected religious themes central to Christianity. Thus, certain forms of graphic arts function to help integrate the society by making the dominant cultural themes, values, and beliefs more visible. By expressing these cultural themes in a tangible way, art ultimately functions to strengthen people's identification with their culture by reinforcing those cultural themes.

The intimate interconnectedness of art and religious life is well-illustrated in Bali (Indonesia), a culture with a long and rich tradition of dance and music. The large number of ceremonies that occur annually on the Bali-Hindu calendar involve elaborate displays and performances designed to attract the gods and please the people. Various life cycle events such as births and funerals are celebrated by special orchestras with music and dance. Some musical instruments, thought to be the gift of the gods, are considered so sacred that they can only be displayed, not actually played. According to one Balinese expert, "Music and dance are spiritual musts. The arts are an invitation for the gods to come down and join the people. There is a very physical contact with the unseen, with the ancestors... that makes the people in the village very happy" (Charle 1999, 28).

Art helps to strengthen and reinforce both social bonds and cultural themes. For example, cultural values are passed on from generation to generation using the media of song and dance. As part of the intense education in African bush schools, various forms of dance are used to teach proper adult attitudes and behaviours to those preparing for initiation.

The role of music in education is well illustrated by Bert, Ernie, Kermit, and the other characters of *Sesame Street,* who sing about values such as cooperation, acceptable forms of conflict resolution, the fun of learning, and race relations. Music also can be used to solidify a group of people. Any history of warfare is woefully incomplete without some mention of the role that martial music played to rally the people against the common enemy.

Sometimes art can be a social integrator in a community by bridging differences among subgroups based on race, class, religion, or ethnicity. To illustrate, Belfast, the capital of Northern Ireland, is a deeply divided city where several 4 m high walls topped with razor wire separate neighbouring Catholics and Protestants. There are, however, cross-community initiatives to bring the walls down and also to bring people together. One of these initiatives is to use the walls for publically commissioned art. There are over 2000 paintings on the walls in Belfast, which are a mixture of political murals, graffiti, and commissioned art. The murals depict aspects of the history and culture of Belfast and Northern Ireland that reflect important community values. The murals help provide a sense of identity and belonging. In the past they were intended to incite hatred and divide communities. Today many are intended to bring communities together. One mural, based on Picasso's *Guernica,* was painted by two artists, one a Catholic the other a Protestant, and is a step in uniting the two communities (Mcloughlin 2014) (Figure 13.8). Today, thousands of tourists come to Belfast to visit the murals scattered throughout the city.

FIGURE 13.8 This mural on Falls Road, Belfast, based on Picasso's *Guernica*, was painted by a Catholic and a Protestant artist and helps unite the two communities.

Social Control

A popular perception of artists and their works in the Western world is that they are visionary, nonconformist, and often anti-establishment. Although this is often true in contemporary Western societies, much art found in other societies (and indeed in our own Western tradition in past centuries) functions to reinforce the existing socio-cultural system. For example, art can help instill important cultural values in younger generations, coerce people to behave in socially appropriate ways, and buttress the inequalities of the stratification system in a society.

First, art can serve as a mechanism of social control. Art historians generally recognize that art has a strong religious base, but they have been less cognizant of the role art plays in other cultural domains. A notable exception is Roy Sieber (1962), an art historian who has demonstrated how wooden masks serve as agents of social control in several tribal groups in northeastern Liberia. It was generally believed by the Mano, for example, that the god-spirit mask embodied the spiritual forces that actually control human behaviour. The death of a high-status man was marked by a wooden death mask carved in his honour. A crude portrait of the deceased, the death mask was thought to be the ultimate resting place of the man's spirit.

Through the medium of these pieces of art, the spirits were thought to be able to intervene in the affairs of the living. Specifically, the masks played an important role in the administration of justice. When a dispute arose or a crime was committed, the case was brought before a council of wise and influential men who reviewed the facts and arrived at a tentative decision. This decision was then confirmed (and given supernatural force) by one of the judges who wore the death mask, thus concealing his own identity. Therefore, in addition to whatever other functions these artistically carved masks played among the Mano, they served as mechanisms of social control within the criminal justice system.

Art also plays an important role in controlling behaviour in more complex societies. In highly stratified societies, state governments sponsor art to instill obedience and maintain the status quo. In some early civilizations, for example, state-sponsored monumental architecture—such as pyramids, ziggurats, and cathedrals—was a visual representation of the astonishing power of both the gods and the rulers. Most people living in these state societies would think twice before breaking either secular or religious rules when faced with the awesome power and authority represented in these magnificent works of art.

Particularly in modern times, the state may use art to control (or at least influence) people's behaviour in more subtle ways. For example, in present-day China, the music played on state-controlled radio is purposefully chosen to soothe rather than to provoke. In keeping with its desire to build a "harmonious society," Chinese authorities play only light and upbeat music, with such themes as romance, diligence, and "it's not so bad being poor but happy." You will hear no angry rap music, protest songs, or heavy rock tunes on state-monopolized radio in China today. For the Chinese, the purpose of music is to lull the masses into passivity, rather than to arouse any negative or inharmonious sentiments (French 2007).

Preserving or Challenging the Status Quo

By serving as a symbol for social status, art contributes to the preservation of the status quo. To one degree or another, all societies make distinctions between different levels of power and prestige. As societies become more highly specialized, systems of stratification become more complex, and the gap widens between the haves and the have-nots. Power is expressed in different ways throughout the world, including the use of physical force, control over political decisions, and accumulation of valuable resources. One particularly convincing way to display one's power is symbolically through the control of valuable items in the society. The accumulation of such practical objects as tools would not be a particularly good symbol of high prestige because everyone has some and because one hardly needs an overabundance of everyday practical objects to meet one's own needs. The accumulation of art objects, however, is much more likely to serve as a symbol of high prestige because art objects are unique, not commonly found throughout the society, and often priceless.

Art is associated with status symbols in many societies that have ranked populations. For example, virtually all the art in ancient Egyptian civilizations was the personal property of the pharaohs. The high status of the hereditary king of the Ashanti of present-day Ghana is symbolized by a wide variety of artistic objects, the most important of which is the Golden Stool.

Art is a force for preserving the status quo, but it is also often used in the opposite way, as a vehicle of protest, resistance, and even revolution. A number of artists have attempted, through their own artistic media, to raise the consciousness of their oppressed countrymen and women to bring about changes in the political and social structure. For example, Marjorie Agosin (1987) documented the case of the Chilean *arpilleristas,* who told the story of political oppression on scraps of cloth. These courageous artists were considered such a threat to the established government that they were eventually banned in their own country. In Chile during the Augusto Pinochet regime, local artists painted murals under the cover of night depicting scenes of government oppression, only to have them removed by the military police the next morning.

For more current, and dramatic, examples of how various art forms have been used to challenge the status quo, we have only to turn to the revolutions going on in the Middle East, known as the "Arab Spring." Fed up with corrupt governments, widespread injustice, growing economic inequality, and little freedom of

STORIES FROM THE FIELD

My fieldwork centred around two popular theatre troupes operating in Dominica in the late 1990s. Both groups used theatre and theatrical workshops to raise awareness and provide education about HIV and AIDS. The first group, Dominica's Movement for Cultural Awareness (MCA), used an interactive street theatre performance. The production phase included touring the island and conducting workshops with community members, healthcare experts, and cultural workers from MCA. The second stage involved putting selected skits into a coherent play. The third step was to perform the production for a wider audience. The success was that people who would not otherwise access information about this (at the time) stigmatized virus, were able to learn while out for a night of entertainment.

—Deirdre Rose, *University of Guelph*

expression, people have taken to the streets in Tunisia, Egypt, Libya, Bahrain, and Syria since 2010. Dictators have been overthrown, government toppled, and in some cases civil wars have raged. But what all these recent revolutions have in common is that artists, particularly musicians and graphic artists, have played a key role in mobilizing popular support.

Before the Arab Spring, heavy metal bands kept a low profile in all Islamic countries, playing their music largely on the Internet rather than in live public concerts. Most of the hard rock and rave musicians, who were considered by the government to be satanic, lived in fear of the secret police. Playing popular music in public was certainly a risky business for most pop singers, particularly if the lyrics were in Arabic.

But this veil of timidity and caution was shattered by an unlikely, little known rapper in Tunisia by the name of Hamada Ben Amor, aka El Général, a 21-year-old musician who lived in Tunis with his parents. Several months before the revolution broke out in Tunisia, El Général uploaded on to Facebook his in-your-face rap creation titled "President, Your Country," with lyrics that captured the mood of the country:

> My president, your country is dead/
> People eat garbage/
> Look at what is happening/
> Misery everywhere/
> Nowhere to sleep/
> I'm speaking for the people who suffer/
> Ground under feet.*

This single musical event was the shot heard around the Middle East. Within hours the song was being listened to by people all across North Africa. It was broadcast by the Tunisian TV network and al Jazeera. And although El Général's MySpace page and cellphone were shut down almost immediately by a nervous dictatorship, this musical act of defiance was seen by many observers as the start of the revolt in Tunisia, and indeed the entire Arab Spring itself. Such is the power of music to bring about a radical and dramatic shift in the status quo (Morgan 2011).

Graphic and Plastic Arts

Graphic and plastic arts include a number of forms of expression and a wide variety of skills. Although the Western notion of ***graphic arts*** and ***plastic arts*** usually refers to painting, sculpture, printmaking, and architecture, the anthropological definition also includes such art forms as weaving, embroidery, tailoring, jewellery making, and tattooing and other forms of body decoration. In some societies, one form of art, such as woodcarving, may be highly developed and others, such as painting or metalworking, may be non-existent.

The analysis of these art forms is further complicated because different cultures use different materials and technologies depending, in part, on what materials are available locally. Whereas First Nations of the Pacific Northwest are well-known for their carvings of wood, other cultures use horn, bone, ivory, or soapstone. In some small-scale societies, the nature of people's ceramic art is determined by the availability of locally found clays. Often the level of technology influences whether a culture uses metals such as gold, silver, and bronze in its art traditions.

Not only do different art traditions draw on different materials, techniques, and media, but the nature of the creative process can also vary cross-culturally. To illustrate, in the Western tradition, the practice of commissioning a piece of art is quite common. For a fee, portrait artists use their creative talents to paint realistic (and usually flattering) likenesses of their prominent clients. However, it is not likely that a client could commission an Inuit artist to carve a walrus from a piece of ivory. According to the Inuit notion of the creative process, that would be much too willful, even heavy handed. Whereas the Western artist is solely responsible for painting the canvas or molding the clay in a total act of will, the Inuit carver never forces the ivory into any uncharacteristic shapes. The Inuit artist does not create but rather helps to liberate what is already in the piece of ivory. Edmund Carpenter (1973, 59) describes the Inuit's notion of the role of the artist:

> As the carver holds the unworked ivory lightly in his hand, turning it this way and that, he whispers, "Who are you! Who hides there!" And then, "Ah, Seal!" He rarely sets out to carve, say, a seal, but picks up the ivory, examines it to find its hidden form and, if that's not immediately apparent, carves aimlessly until he sees it, humming or chanting as he works. Then he brings it out: seal, hidden, emerges. It was always there: he did not create it, he released it; he helped it step forth.*

Of all the various forms of art in the world, the graphic and plastic arts have received the greatest amount of attention from cultural anthropologists. This is understandable because the graphic and plastic arts, produce objects that are tangible and can be removed

*Source: Hamada Ben Amor, aka El Général

*Source: Slobin, Mark, and Jeff T. Titon. 1984. "The Music Culture as a World of Music." In *Worlds of Music: An Introduction to the Music of the World's Peoples.* Jeff T. Titon et al., eds., pp. 1–11. London: Collier Macmillan Publishers.

graphic arts Forms of art that include painting and drawing on various surfaces.

plastic arts Artistic expression that involves molding certain forms, such as sculpture.

from their cultural contexts, displayed in museums, and compared with relative ease. Moreover, a painting or a sculpture has a permanence of form not found in music, dance, or drama. Two forms of art that have fascinated anthropologists for decades for their symbolic meanings and roles in society are graffiti and tattoos.

Graffiti

We are all familiar with the often profane, racist, and sexist comments and images written on bathroom stalls, with a person's name and date written on some monument or tree, and the walls of buildings, bridges, railway cars, letter boxes, and other public areas defaced by scribbled comments and huge bubble letters. But we are also familiar with the beautiful wall murals painted in public spaces. All of these can be considered ***graffiti***, a form of art, communication, and public culture consisting of writing or drawings on public walls or other public surfaces. Graffiti is a worldwide phenomenon that has been around for centuries; there are numerous examples from Ancient Egypt, Greece, and Rome. Most cities view it as vandalism and thus illegal. Consequently, graffiti artists, or vandals (depending on one's view), must not only work hurriedly, but also remain anonymous.

Graffiti is sometimes referred to as a form of public art and, while many murals and some pieces, do have an aesthetic quality, it is hard to imagine offensive racist comments spray-painted over a park bench or black and white scribblings that deface property as art. Because graffiti encompasses such a variety of forms it raises the question whether it is art or vandalism. The answer is that some graffiti is art and some is not, but where it is located and whether it is illegal or not is not relevant. If spray-painted drawings or initials are not intended as art, take no talent to produce, have no meaning other than to communicate identity and are not aesthetically pleasing, then they are perhaps not art. But if they are aesthetically pleasing, were intended as art by their creator, and are recognized by art by both art critics and the public, then graffiti is art.

Types of Graffiti

The most basic type of graffiti is ***signature graffiti***, which is a representation of the self to the public and simply declares "I was here." The signature is the extent of the work (Gauthier 2001). Signature graffiti consists of three types: ***tags***, ***throw ups***, and ***pieces***. A tag is a graffiti writer's nickname and can consist of initials, a symbol, or cartoon-like characters, and are the most common form of signature graffiti as they are quick to produce, monochrome, and highly stylized. Because most are not aesthetically pleasing, are not meant as art and they deface property, most people do not consider them art. Throw ups are enlarged versions of tags consisting of big coloured-in bubble letters. Pieces (short for masterpiece (Green 2014)) are an even larger version and consist of exaggerated 3-D letters or symbols or more elaborate images (Gauthier 2001).

Signature graffiti began with tags in the ghettos and subways of New York City in the mid-to-late 1960s and early 1970s (Ley and Cybriwsky 1974; Gauthier 2001), and was associated with street gangs, and as the visual aspect of hip hop. Hip hop is a subculture that emerged in New York City in the early 1970s among African American, Latino, and Caribbean youth and involves rap music, break dancing, deejaying, and graffiti (Chang and Herc 2005).

With the development of spray paint, styles evolved from simple tags to other, more aesthetically pleasing forms including ***stencil graffiti***, which emerged in the 1980s. Stencil graffiti involves cutting out shapes and designs in a rigid material such as cardboard, and then placing the stencil on a wall and spray-painting over it. Stencil graffiti is popular with graffiti artists as it can be put up quickly and reduces the chances of getting caught. Unlike tags, however, which are often done on the spur of the moment on any convenient surface, stencil graffiti requires considerable imagination, forethought, and planning. Not only must the artist plan the piece but must also decide where to paint it. Perhaps the most famous stencil graffiti artist is British artist Banksy, who came to world attention in 2003 with an image on the West Bank wall in Gaza Strip criticizing Israel's policies toward Palestine (Green 2014) (Figure 13.9). His unique style involving humorous images and slogans combined with political and social commentary on war, capitalism, and government earned him a place on *Time* magazine's list of the 100 most influential people in 2010 (Ellsworth-Jones 2013). Banksy's work has appeared in Britain, the United States, and throughout Europe, and his prints command thousands of dollars (Green 2014). Banksy continues to conceal his identity even though he has written a book, made an Academy Award-nominated documentary film, and moved from urban walls to

---

graffiti A form of art, communication, and public culture consisting of writing or drawings on public walls or other public surfaces.

signature graffiti A type of graffiti consisting of tags, throw ups, and pieces where the signature or nickname constitutes the extent of the inscription.

tags Graffiti writers' nicknames, consisting of monochrome, and highly stylized initials, symbols, cartoon-like characters, or unique styles.

throw ups Enlarged versions of tags consisting of big coloured-in bubble letters.

pieces Larger versions of tags consisting of exaggerated 3-D letters or symbols.

stencil graffiti A form of graffiti in which shapes and designs are cut into a rigid material to create a stencil, which is then placed on a wall and spray-painted over.

FIGURE 13.9 **Banksy's original poster-style graffiti is often used to make political statements, as does this one near the Separation Wall in Bethlehem, Israel, in 2013.**

paint on canvas (Ellsworth-Jones 2013). Banksy is also largely responsible for transforming graffiti and street art into a form of high art (Schacter 2008).

The Functions of Graffiti

Anthropologists have had a fascination with graffiti since the 19th century for what it reveals about the lifestyles, languages, and cultures of societies both past and present. Graffiti artists, for instance, have their own social hierarchy. Artists who simply tag are most likely to be viewed as vandals and their work removed as soon as possible, whereas those who put up pieces, since they take more time and are thus riskier, are more likely to gain respect and their work thought of as "graffiti art." Those who tag in the riskiest places such as on police cars (with the police in the car) or even on airplanes have been called "graffiti kings" (Ley and Cybriwsky 1974).

Graffiti also serves many functions. At its simplest it stands as a record of a person's presence at a particular moment. For instance, two miles into the Cave of the Mammoths in South Dakota, across an 11 000-year-old image of a bison is inscribed in enormous letters "Boutier 1906" (Rose 1987). Signature graffiti can also serve as a form of self-expression, or desire to be recognized, or as a rebellion against authority.

In some inner city areas in the United States, graffiti can be seen as an indicator of the relationship between social and spatial order. For instance, it has been used to mark gang territory, make claims to neighbourhoods, and identify areas of ethnic conflict related to social change (Ley and Cybriwsky 1974). Graffiti has also been used to make political comments from statements about culture and society (such as those made by Banksy), to the offensive racist slurs on bus benches in Vancouver and schools in Toronto (see Chapters 9 and 11). Such cases are a representation of social attitudes and, in contrast to signature graffiti, are often anonymous and legible.

Many cities view graffiti as vandalism and eyesores that suggest an area of neglect and decay, which encourages crime (Green 2014). Montreal's official position on graffiti writing is "that it is overall a destructive and filthy practice, and that the people who produce it are vandals and should be treated as criminal" (Gauthier 2001, 273). A number of cities, however, have begun capitalizing on graffiti art, protecting some of it (some of Banksy's work has been protected) and commissioning murals, which not only beautify the city but also can give it a certain character (McAuliffe 2012). Chemainus, British Columbia, on Vancouver Island has become well-known for its murals and attracts thousands of tourists each year.

Tattoos

Tattoos are a form of body art involving implanting ink, or some other substance such as charcoal, ashes, or gunpowder, into the lower levels of the skin. With graffiti, the canvas is a wall, the artwork is public, impermanent, and done with a spray can. With tattoos, on the other hand, the canvas is the body, the artwork private, permanent, and the artist's "brush" is a needle. Anthropologists are interested in the symbolic meaning of tattoos, their function and role in society, and what they say about a culture's conception of the body. They vary from crude prison tattoos, elaborate cultural designs, small commercially reproducible designs called flash drawings, to larger original designs that illustrate the tattooist's personal style and artistic talent. The word "tattoo" comes from the Polynesian word *tatau* (Atkinson 2003; Fedorenko et al. 1999). They have been known for thousands of years and in hundreds of societies worldwide. The oldest example of tattooing is that of a tattooed man discovered in 1991 embedded in a melting glacier in the Alps (Spindler 1994). Called Ötzi he has 61 tattoos and lived about 5250 years ago (Scallan 2015; Deter-Wolf et al. 2016).

Shifting Contexts and Meanings of Tattoos

The history of tattooing is one of shifting contexts, symbolic meanings, and functions. One of the earliest uses of tattoos in the Western world was for

---

tattoos A form of body art involving implanting ink or some other substance into the lower levels of the skin.

identification. Roman soldiers were forcibly tattooed, as were deserters, gladiators, slaves, and criminals. The Greeks also tattooed criminals, referring to the marks as *stigma* (Atkinson 2003). Such tattoos are a form of social control and stigmatize those wearing them as deviant. Many countries, England, the United States, Japan, France, China, and others, have used tattoos to brand individuals as criminal or deviant (Atkinson 2003). In the 800s the Catholic Church banned the use of all tattoos, seeing it as a pagan practice and the art disappeared in Europe (Mayor 1999) until contact between Europeans and Polynesians in the 1700s. Copying the art from the Polynesians, many British sailors tattooed themselves so that, in the case of shipwreck, their bodies could be identified and given a Christian burial (Spindler 1994), bringing both the word and the practice back to Europe. The tradition of getting tattoos not only is still common among sailors today, but also with armed personnel in many countries to indicate their military units, battles, or kills.

By the late 1800s tattooing had become fashionable as a status symbol among the upper classes in North America and Europe. The invention of the electric tattoo machine in the early 1900s, however, meant that tattooing was easier and cheaper and thus available to the lower classes, and so conveyed a different status (Irwin 2001). Until the 1950s and 1960s about the only people who got tattoos were criminals, prostitutes, and bikers, and so tattooing in the West became associated with deviant subculture groups and criminal activities (Copes and Forsyth 1993; DeMello 2000; Atkinson 2003). Even psychologists described tattooing as a sign of deviancy and personality disorders (Copes and Forsyth 1993). Tattoos were thus not simply symbolic of a rejection of mainstream culture but also of Otherness (Atkinson 2003).

In the 1960s, however, a transformation in tattooing occurred with the counter-culture movement (Kwong 2012). Tattoo studios were more sterile and featured tattoo artists with formal training in art school and graphic design, who began producing custom designs and works of art (Copes and Forsyth 1993; Atkinson 2003). The 1960s through to the 1980s thus witnessed a resurgence of interest in tattooing. Tattoos were popularized and made more acceptable by reality TV programs such as *L.A. Ink* and the tattoo competition series *Ink Master* (Kwong 2012), and by athletes, rock stars, and celebrities, such as Cher and Johnny Depp openly displaying their tattoos. Even Barbie has a tattoo (Kuntzman 1999).

The 1990s was a transitional period when the symbolic meanings and stigma attached to tattoos changed from deviancy to acceptability. Parents disapproved of tattoos, judging them on the older conceptions; tattoo studios were thought of as unclean, unhygienic places where their children could contract diseases or infections, and tattoos themselves as a status risk as their children would be associated with undesirable social groups, which would threaten their financial future (Irwin 2001). Their children, however, were lining up to get tattooed. Since the early 1990s tattooing has been part of mainstream Western fashion, particularly among the youth (Copes and Forsyth 1993; Irwin 2001). It is now a booming trade. In the early 2000s there were only 15 studios in the Toronto Yellow Pages, but by 2012 there were 40, with perhaps a 100 more not listed (Kwong 2012). Several studies have shown that anywhere from 30 to 40 percent of people in North America have one or more tattoos, more so among the young, and that the number is increasing (Laumann and Derick 2006; Kwong 2012). In 2016 the U.S. food retailer Whole Foods, announced that its new "365" chain of smaller stores would also house tattoo parlours as one way to attract Millennials (Wahba 2016).

The Functions of Tattoos

People get tattoos for many reasons. Some get tattoos to symbolize their belonging or identification with particular groups, such as religious organizations, military units, or gangs. The Yakuza–Japanese crime syndicates–for example, have full-body tattoos, and the Russian Mafia are also well-known for their extensive tattoos. Tattoos are also common among prisoners and mark the person wearing them as a convict or an ex-convict to the outside world. Within the prison they are not only used to express class and ethnicity, but also allow prisoners to join the convict community; without tattoos they often feel isolated (DeMello 1993).

Many societies in South America and Asia, see tattoos as having magical properties (Krutak 2012). Before European contact, Hawaiians used tattoos to protect themselves from harm (Atkinson 2003). In Thailand, yantra tattoos, consisting of geometrical and animal shapes, are administered by Buddhist monks and are thought to protect the wearer from evil spirits and bring good luck by harnessing the power of Buddha himself (Krutak 2012).

Tattoos can also mark status, as with the traditional ***Tā moko*** tattoos among the Māori of New Zealand (Figure 13.10). Tāmoko (or simply Moko) tattooing involves chiselling into the skin rather than using a needle. In Maori culture, the head is thought to be the seat of a person's spiritual being and power and is thus sacred (King and Friedlander 1992; DeMello 2000) and subject to *tapu* (taboo); neither hands nor food could touch it (NZETC 2015). The Moko tattoos

---

Tā moko Traditional tattoos of Māori men and women, indicating the wearer's lineage, social position, and tribal affiliations.

Mint Images/Getty Images

FIGURE 13.10 Māori man with traditional Moko facial tattoos, Rotorua, New Zealand. The Moko tattoos signal status and ancestry, the bulging eyes indicate ferocity, and the stuck out tongue that he is going to eat you after he has killed you. In recent years there has been a renewed interest in Moko, by both Māori men and women as a sign of their identity.

George H. Wilkins/Library and Archives Canada/PA-165665

FIGURE 13.11 An Inuit woman with facial tattoos and beaded parka, Nunavut, between 1903 and 1904.

only increase the power and sacredness (Newell and King 2006). They are also thought to make the wearer more attractive (Media New Zealand 2016). Usually received during a rite of passage from childhood to adulthood, only the highest status Māori received Moko. Women received the tattoos on their lips and chins while men traditionally received the marks on their faces, buttocks, and thighs. The Moko tell the story of the wearer's lineage, social position, and tribal affiliations (Atkinson 2003; Media New Zealand 2016). The practice disappeared in the mid-1800s and many Māori now wear Moko as a symbol of their identity as a Māori and an expression of cultural pride (Media New Zealand 2016).

Historically, the Inuit also had a tradition of tattooing but, forbidden by Christian missionaries who saw it as a shamanistic practice that contradicted Catholicism and Protestantism, the art was almost forgotten (Freeman 2016). Young girls received tattoos on their hands and face after their first period to mark the transition into womanhood (Figure 13.11). Subsequent tattoos marked significant life events such as the birth of a child (Oudshoorn 2016; Freeman 2016). Inuit filmmaker *Alethea Arnaquq-Baril in her film Tunniit: Retracing the Lines of Inuit Tattoos,* traces the history of traditional Inuit women's face tattoos before getting tattooed herself as a way to reconnect with her traditions and her ancestors (Arnaquq-Baril 2015). Tattoos, she notes, were a physical embodiment of their spirituality, culture, and identity as an Inuit woman (Oudshoorn 2016; Freeman 2016).

Many societies use tattoos as part of a rite of passage, including Western societies. Tattoos are sometimes used to mark a rite of passage such as graduating from high school or university. Sometimes they mark a significant event in a person's life, such as having a child, getting married, or ending a relationship (Fedorenko et al. 1999). Many people view tattoos as a symbol of liberation, independence, and freedom, especially from parental constraints, and will get tattoos on moving out of home (Irwin 2001). For others, tattoos are meant to reflect some aspect of their personality. For instance cartoon characters may illustrate their sense of humour, flowers or birds their gentleness. For others the tattoo is meant to inspire them, such as a Greek or Latin saying (e.g., *carpe diem* (seize the day)), or to remind them about what is important to them, such as a religious symbol or phrase from the Bible, or a yin-yang symbol to represent their involvement in martial arts. Others get them as they feel it provides them with a sense of identity and individuality (Fedorenko et al. 1999). Whatever the reason for getting a tattoo, they are an integral part of self-definition, and people are making an investment in art that will last a lifetime and that hopefully will be appreciated for as long.

Music

We often hear the expression "music is the universal language." By this people mean that, even if two people do not speak each other's language, they can at least appreciate music together. But like so many popular sayings, this one is only partially true. Although all people do have the same physiological mechanisms for hearing, what a person actually hears is influenced by his or her culture. Westerners tend to miss much of the richness of Javanese and Sri Lankan music because they have not been conditioned to hear it. Whenever we encounter a piece of non-Western music, we hear it (process it) in terms of our own culturally influenced set of musical categories involving scale, melody, pitch, harmony, and rhythm. And because those categories are defined differently from culture to culture, the appreciation of music across cultures is not always ensured. To illustrate this point, Mark Slobin and Jeff Titon (1984, 1) tell a story about a famous Asian musician who attended a symphony concert in Europe during the mid-19th century:

> Although he was a virtuoso musician in his own country, he had never heard a performance of western music. The story goes that after the concert he was asked how he liked it. "Very well," he replied. Not satisfied with this answer, his host asked (through an interpreter) what part he liked best. "The first part," he said. "Oh, you enjoyed the first movement?" "No, before that!" To the stranger, the best part of the performance was the tuning up period.*

Ethnomusicology

The cross-cultural study of music is known as ***ethnomusicology*** and involves the cooperative efforts of both anthropologists and musicologists (Nettl and Bohlman 1991). Ethnomusicology has made rapid progress as a result of developments in high-quality recording equipment needed for basic data gathering. Slobin and Titon (1984) identified four major concerns of ethnomusicology:

1. *Ideas about music.* How does a culture distinguish between music and non-music? What functions does music play for the society? Is music viewed as beneficial or harmful to the society? What constitutes beautiful music? On what occasions should music be played?
2. *Social structure of music.* What are the social relationships between musicians? How does a society distinguish between various musicians on the basis of such criteria as age, gender, race, ethnicity, and education?
3. *Characteristics of the music itself.* How does the style of music in different cultures vary (scale, melody, harmony, timing)? What different musical genres are found in a society (lullaby, sea chantey, hard rock, and so on)? What is the nature of musical texts (words)? How is music composed? How is music learned and transmitted?
4. *Material culture of music.* What musical instruments are used in a culture? Who makes the musical instruments, and how are they distributed? How are musical tastes reflected in the instruments used?

Christine Osborne/World Religions Photo Library

FIGURE 13.12 Ethnomusicologists are interested in studying both the music of this gamelan orchestra in Bali, Indonesia, and how the music reflects the wider culture of which it is a part.

As these areas of interest indicate, ethnomusicology is concerned with both the structure and techniques of music and the interconnections between music and other parts of the culture (Figure 13.12). Yet, during the course of cross-cultural studies of music, ethnomusicologists have been torn between two approaches. At one extreme, they have searched for musical universals—elements found in all musical traditions. At the opposite extreme, they have been interested in demonstrating the considerable diversity found throughout the world. Bruno Nettl (1980, 3) describes this tension: "In the heart of the ethnomusicologist there are two strings: one that attests to the universal character of music, to the fact that music is indeed something that all cultures have or appear to have... and one responsive to the enormous variety of existing cultures."

*Source: Slobin, Mark, and Jeff T. Titon. 1984. "The Music Culture as a World of Music." In *Worlds of Music: An Introduction to the Music of the World's Peoples.* Jeff T. Titon et al., eds., pp. 1–11. London: Collier Macmillan Publishers.

ethnomusicology The study of the relationship between music and other aspects of culture.

TABLE 13.1

Comparison of Music between Egalitarian and Stratified Societies

Egalitarian Societies and Simple Economics	Stratified Societies and Complex Economics
Repetitious texts	Non-repetitious texts
Slurred articulation	Precise articulation
Little solo singing	Solo singing
Wide melodic intervals	Narrow melodic intervals
Non-elaborate songs (no embellishments)	Elaborate songs (embellishments)
Few instruments	Large number of instruments
Singing in unison	Singing in simultaneous intervals

All ethnomusicologists—whether their background is in music or cultural anthropology—are interested in the study of music in its cultural context. Alan Lomax (1968) conducted one of the most extensive studies of the relationship between music and other parts of culture. Specifically, he found some broad correlations between various aspects of music and a culture's level of subsistence. Foraging societies were found to have types of music, song, and dance that were fundamentally different from those of more complex producers. By dividing a worldwide sample of cultures into five different levels of subsistence complexity, Lomax found some significant correlations. For example, differences emerged between egalitarian, small-scale societies with simple subsistence economies and large-scale, stratified societies with complex systems of production (see Table 13.1).

Dance

Dance has been defined as purposeful and intentionally rhythmical, nonverbal, body movements that are culturally patterned and have aesthetic value (Hanna 1979, 19). Although dance is found in all known societies, the forms it takes, the functions it fulfills, and the meanings attached to it vary widely from society to society. In some societies dance involves considerable energy and body movement, whereas in other societies, it is much more restrained and subtle. Because the human body is capable of a wide variety of postures and movements, which body parts are active and which postures are assumed differ from one dance tradition to another. In some African societies (such as the Ubakala of Nigeria) drums are a necessary part of dance, whereas in others (such as the Zulu) they are not. Dancing alone is the expected form in some societies, but in others it is customary for groups to dance in circles, lines, or other formations. Yet, whatever form dance takes in any culture, it remains a persuasive form of communication that blends body movements with both emotions and cognition. As Judith Hanna (2005, 11) reminds us, "Both dance and verbal language have vocabulary (locomotion and gestures in dance), grammar (ways one movement can follow another), and semantics (including symbolic devices and spheres for encoding feelings and ideas)."

Moreover, the relative value of dance as an art form varies widely from one society to another. To illustrate, the government of Cuba supports dance in a number of visible ways, making Cuba one of the great dance nations of the world. Cuba is the venue for a number of important international dance festivals and, in fact, many world-class dancers go to Cuba to study dance. The professional dancers of the Ballet Nacional de Cuba enjoy high status at home and international acclaim when performing abroad. And free dance education is available to any child from kindergarten through university. The overwhelming majority of adults in Canada have never attended a fully staged ballet, a contemporary dance performance, or even a ballroom dance competition. Despite the fact that the physical conditioning required of professional dancers often exceeds that of other professional athletes, dance in Canada is generally thought of as a female, or an effeminate, profession.

Functions of Dance

As with other forms of artistic expression, the functions of dance are culturally variable. Dance is likely to function in different ways both between and within societies. Dance often performs several functions simultaneously within a society, but some functions are more prominent than others. To illustrate, dance can function psychologically by helping people cope more effectively with tensions and aggressive feelings; politically by expressing political values and attitudes, showing allegiance to political leaders, and controlling behaviour; religiously by various methods of communicating with supernatural forces; socially by articulating and reinforcing relationships among members of the society; and educationally by passing on cultural traditions, values, and beliefs from one generation to the next.

Dance and Other Aspects of a Culture

Lomax (1968) demonstrated quite graphically how dance is connected to other aspects of a culture. Specifically, his research shows how dance reflects

dance Intentional, rhythmic, nonverbal body movements that are culturally patterned and have aesthetic value.

Jerry Kobalenko/Getty Images

FIGURE 13.13 **Inuit couple in traditional caribou skins drum dancing and singing, Devon Island, Nunavut.**

and reinforces work patterns. By examining more than 200 films, he was able to find a number of similarities between work styles and dance styles. The traditional Inuit provide an interesting—and not atypical—example. For the Inuit, dancing consists of solo performances where many of the postures and motions in Netsilingmiut (Netsilik) dance are the ones that are necessary for successful seal hunting in an Arctic environment. The Netsilingmiut seal hunter may wait patiently and silently for hours over a hole in the ice before a seal appears. When it does, the hunter's harpoon flies instantly and powerfully in a single stroke diagonally across the chest. Thus, the stylistic movements found in Netsilingmiut dance are essentially identical to those used in their everyday hunting activities. The qualities of a good hunter—speed, strength, accuracy, and endurance—are portrayed and glorified in dance (Figure 13.13). In other words, as part of their leisure activity, hunters, through the medium of dance, re-dramatize the essentials of the everyday subsistence activities that are so crucial for their survival.

CROSS-CULTURAL MISCUE

When Ann Philbin, director of the Hammer Museum in Los Angeles, was over for dinner at American comedian Steve Martin's one evening, she saw a "fantastic," very stylized painting of trees with a lake behind it hanging on his wall. Curious, she asked Martin who the painter was. Her response, when he told her it was Lawren Harris, was "Who's that?" Perhaps an odd comment from someone familiar with the art world, but then Philbin is American and Harris was Canadian. There is big gap in America's artistic knowledge when it comes to Canadian art. Lawren Harris was a core member of the Group of Seven—a group of Canadian landscape painters in the 1920s and early 1930s who pioneered a uniquely Canadian style of painting. Harris is arguably Canada's greatest painter, known for his stark landscapes of the Canadian North and Arctic. When Steve Martin bought the piece he too thought Harris was an unknown artist. Martin, who has collected art for decades, now owns three of his paintings.

An artist's fame depends not simply on the quality of his or her art, however, but as Martin put it a "loving curator is an asset to an artist." Harris's work is visually striking, but he is virtually unknown in America because he has not been promoted. Martin is trying to change that, and his goal is to get Americans to love Harris as much as he does. Recently he has visited several art museums in Canada asking them to loan him their paintings by Harris. In conjunction with Philbin, the Hammer Museum, and the Art Gallery of Ontario, he is co-curating an exhibit "The Idea of the North: The Paintings of Lawren Harris," in 2016 (Tucker 2015).

Film

When Canadians think of film as an art form, they usually think of Hollywood and filmmaking legends such as Steven Spielberg, Robert Altman, and George Lucas. However, many countries in all parts of the world have long and rich traditions of filmmaking as an art form. For example, Ingmar Bergman in Sweden, Sergei Eisenstein in Russia, and Akira Kurosawa in Japan all made world-class films during the 20th century. The continent of Africa (from Cape Verde to Cape Horn) possesses a rich tradition of filmmaking; since 1987 the Mogadishu Pan-African and Arab Film Symposium has supported its own annual international film festival in Mogadishu, Somalia, exclusively for African films.

The latest territory to receive critical acclaim for filmmaking is Nunavut. Until recently the only connection between the Inuit and filmmaking was Robert Flaherty's documentary *Nanook of the North*, a silent film about the Inuit, made in 1922. Eight decades later an Inuit filmmaker named Zacharias Kunuk, using all Inuit actors and crew, made a feature-length film in Inuktitut, the language of the Inuit. The film, *Atanarjuat: The Fast Runner*, while providing ethnographic insights into traditional Inuit culture, is more than just another documentary about a vanishing way of life. Based on an ancient Inuit folk epic, *Atanarjuat* uses Inuit actors to tell a powerful and compelling story in the ancient words of their traditional language. Shot over a period of six months, the film portrays the movement of the seasons, which so thoroughly influence Inuit daily life. Capturing on camera a number of different hues of black and white, Kunuk manages to reveal complex psychological motives behind the actions of his mythical characters, whose story up until now had always been conveyed in oral tradition. *Atanarjuat* won the "Best

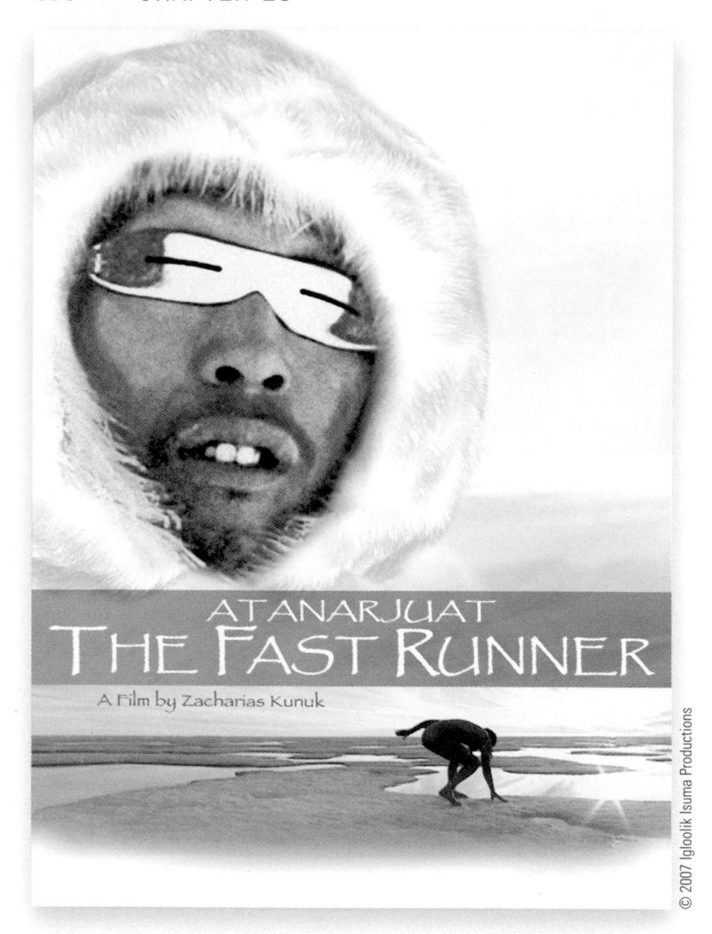

FIGURE 13.14 Winner of numerous awards, *Atanarjuat* is Canada's first feature-length fiction film written, produced, directed, and acted by Inuit.

First Feature Film" award at the Cannes International Film Festival in 2001 (Figure 13.14).

While Hollywood studios have been making big-budget films for decades, filmmakers in Mumbai, India (colloquially known as "Bollywood"), have made far more films than Hollywood over the decades and have won the hearts and minds of a much larger audience. Bollywood films are devoured not only by a potential audience of a billion people at home, but also by the millions of Indians living in Canada, the United States, the United Kingdom, Europe, the Middle East, and elsewhere. These films have been dubbed into other languages, including French, Russian, and Mandarin Chinese. They provide the primary form of entertainment for probably half of the world's population.

The popularity of Bollywood films rests on their story lines, which have been called "pre-cynical" (Mehta 2004). Unlike their Hollywood counterparts, which tend to be edgy and ambiguous when dealing with such topics as love, family, and patriotism, Indian films are melodramatic and always celebrate true love, courage, devotion to country, and, above all, motherhood. Moreover, every Bollywood film is a musical that lasts as long as three and a half hours, with as many as a dozen "big production" song-and-dance numbers. Even though many Canadians have heard of these Indian-made films, few have actually seen one, unless they happen to be Indians living in Canada. For most Canadians these films are too corny, illogical, and too sedate for men, who prefer to watch things being blown up.

Art: Continuity and Change

Like all other aspects of culture, the various forms of expressive arts (graphic and plastic arts, music, dance, and film) are subject to both internal and external forces of change. Anyone who has ever taken a course on the history of art, for example, knows that unique schools of painting (with their own distinctive styles, materials, and themes) emerge, become prominent, and eventually die out and become part of history. To illustrate, Canada's Group of Seven artists painted landscapes of the Canadian Shield and boreal forest using simplified layouts and bright colours. This style was prominent in the 1920s and 1930s but has since been superseded by other styles.

Rapid and dramatic changes occurred in the art world even before the term *globalization* became fashionable. Nowhere is this truer than in the area of glass sculptural art during the last half-century. In the early 1960s, advances in small-furnace technology—along with the pioneering efforts of Harvey Littleton in the United States and Erwin Eisch in Germany—brought the art of glassmaking out of the factory and into the artist's studio. In a little more than four decades, many new techniques of glass blowing, casting, constructing, and lamp-working diffused rapidly throughout the world in the 1960s, thus producing a worldwide art movement that now numbers more than 5000 studio glass artists.

The growth of the glass art movement over the past four decades is noteworthy not only for its scale and global distribution, but also because of its prominence in the art world and in the marketplace.

The possibilities today for quick and widespread cultural diffusion, and the accompanying cross-fertilization of artistic traditions, are increasing. Art exhibits now travel around the world rather than remaining in galleries or museums for decades on end as they did in the past. Similarly, in the area of music, both rock stars and symphony orchestras go on world tours, performing in front of audiences all over the globe. It is not unusual today for Celine Dion to perform in South Africa, the Chicago Symphony to perform in Bangkok, or Lady Gaga to perform in Copenhagen. And it is not just Western music that is being exported and diffused to other parts of the world; there is considerable flow in the opposite direction. In recent decades

Art and Anthropology

The Museum of Contemporary Art in Montreal was started by the Québec government in 1964, and today its permanent collection of nearly 7600 pieces is Canada's largest collection of contemporary works by artists from Quebec, Canada, and around the world. Its mission is to promote contemporary art to the Canadian population. To do this, it offers visitors a free magazine *Musée Magazine*, containing articles on current and upcoming exhibitions, a calendar of events, and stories on a variety of topical subjects related to the Museum. It also provides a visitor-friendly atmosphere, including presentations on various collections, tours for school and university groups, multimedia events such as performances, contemporary music, video, and film, as well as educational day camps tailored to the attendees' level (Montreal Museum of Contemporary Art 2015).

The success of the Museum has not been accomplished without research however. Much of the research on museums and art galleries focuses on the educational role of the institution and its function in society, rather than on how visitors examine and experience exhibits (vom Lehn 2006). And, of course, the more visitors enjoy the experience the more likely they are to return, as well as tell others. Visitors to art galleries and museums range from elementary school children, to university students, senior citizens, tourists, as well as artists. Each group has different interests, needs, perceptions, and preferences. To be successful, therefore, an institution must cater to them all. The best way to perhaps understand their varied needs and improve their experiences is through ethnography. Ethnographers ask questions such as, Who are the people we need to listen to and pay attention to? How do they conceive of and give meaning to art? What are the places, and spaces, and times, that are important to people, and how do these things influence their relationships to the exhibits and to their experience?

With three graduate students, Carol Duhaime, Annamma Joy, and Christopher Ross conducted a two-year team ethnographic study of the Montreal Museum of Contemporary Art. They not only observed people as they interacted with the exhibits, museum employees, other visitors, and the various spaces within the Museum, they also interviewed curators, visitors, and artists. Their argument was that people's early experiences with art and museums, either positive or negative, shape their enduring attitudes and interactions with the exhibits as well as their experience. Their goal was to understand the various needs, interests, and expectations of the various groups so that they could improve their experience and ultimately increase attendance.

One definition of art is that art is that which is displayed in an art gallery or museum. In other words, the very fact that something is on display in an art museum authenticates it as art for patrons. A good example is the work of Damien Hirst, perhaps Britain's wealthiest artist, renowned for displaying animals cut in half and preserved in formaldehyde. Other displays have consisted of half-full coffee cups, empty beer bottles, ashtrays filled with cigarette butts, empty candy wrappers, and so on. Because they are put on display in an art museum, they are considered art, whereas in another context they would be considered rubbish. In fact, that is exactly what one cleaning man thought of such a display at the Mayfair Gallery in London who cleaned up the exhibit, estimated to be worth hundreds of thousands of dollars, and threw it in the garbage (Hoge 2001).

Hemis/Alamy Stock Photo

An exhibition by Francine Savard in Montreal's Museum of Contemporary Art.

Although the Museum of Contemporary Art gave meaning to the items on display as art objects, what they meant to visitors varied and each wanted something different from their visit. Visitors who were artists had a sophisticated understanding of the art work they were viewing and wanted information on the materials used, the colour schemes, the artists interpretations, and so on. Other visitors, particular older patrons, were more interested in the gift shops and café and where the washrooms were than the exhibits themselves. Exhibits that the Museum considered important were given a greater status by their location and were more popular. Patrons were also provided with self-guided tours with radio transmitters. These proved more popular with tourist visitors. Duhaime et al. (1995) argued that the Museum could serve their visitors better, and increase attendance, by providing experiences tailored to each group. For artists, they could provide detailed information about each piece, while ensuring adequate signage to direct others to the café, gift shop, and toilets. Duhaime et al.'s study thus provided a holistic approach to understanding and enhancing visitors' experiences.

Questions for Further Thought

1. How do the different groups who visit the gallery define art?
2. What are the various reasons why people consume art?
3. If you were asked to increase attendance at an art gallery near you who would you talk to and what would you ask them?

we have seen recording artist Paul Simon collaborate with Ladysmith Black Mambazo, a singing group from South Africa, and Sting record fusion music with Cheb Mami from Algeria. Perhaps an even less likely collaboration is between Jaz Coleman, lead singer for the British rock group Killing Joke, and Māori singer and poet Hinewehi Mohi. According to anthropologist Renata Rosaldo, "Cultural artifacts flow between unlikely places, and nothing is sacred, permanent, or sealed off" (Jenkins 2001, 89).

Also, we are beginning to see how a particular society adopts new art forms from other parts of the world and infuses them with its own traditional cultural content. *Indian Idol*, like its U.S. counterpart, involves a talent competition between unknown Indian singers of Western pop music. A new and popular TV show produced in Abu Dhabi, United Arab Emirates (U.A.E), uses the same glamorous sets and big-budget productions, but rather than scantily clad singers competing with Western love ballads, the contestants compete in an elaborate style of Bedouin poetry popular among the Gulf States but virtually unknown in the rest of the Arab world (Fattah 2007). Not only has the success of the show (titled *Poets of Millions*) spawned similar shows in other Islamic countries such as Egypt and Lebanon, but also it is catapulting the U.A.E. to cultural leadership in the Arab world. No longer is the U.A.E. considered to be an ultraconservative, oil-wealthy country with no popular culture of its own. Today the U.A.E. is transforming its traditional art forms and dialects into forms that can be understood and appreciated in other parts of the Arab world and beyond. And interestingly, this repackaging of traditional art from the U.A.E. for both internal and external consumption is occurring in a country that is planning to spend $10 billion to build and operate branches of the Guggenheim and the Louvre museums.

Summary

1. Although there is no universal definition of *art*, for the purposes of this chapter we define *art* as the process and products of applying certain skills to any activity that transforms matter, sound, or motion into a form that is deemed aesthetically meaningful to people in a society. The creative process of making art should be enjoyable, produce an emotional response, be transformational, convey a message, and involve a certain level of skill on the part of the artist.
2. In contrast to the art found in more complex societies, the art of small-scale societies is often more integrated with other aspects of society. Art objects in small-scale societies are often treated as ethnographic artifacts rather than works of art made by individual artists with actual names attached, although this is changing.
3. For the individual, art provides emotional gratification to both the artist and the beholder. From a social perspective, various forms of art strengthen and reinforce both social bonds and cultural themes, promote social control, and serve as a symbol of high status.
4. The Western notion of graphic arts and plastic arts usually refers to painting, sculpture, print making, and architecture; the anthropological definition also includes such art forms as weaving, embroidery, tailoring, jewellery making, and tattooing and other forms of body decoration.
5. Graffiti is a form of art, communication, and public culture consisting of writing or drawings on public walls or other public surfaces and encompasses a variety of forms, which raises the question as to whether it is art or vandalism. Graffiti is also used for political and social commentary. Anthropologists are interested in graffiti for what it reveals about the lifestyles, languages, and cultures of societies.
6. Tattoos are a form of body art with many symbolic meanings and functions. Originally, people with tattoos were stigmatized as deviants but gained increasing acceptability in the 1990s to become part of mainstream culture. Tattoos have been used for identification purposes, in rites of passage, and to symbolize status and belonging, and are an integral part of self-definition and identity.
7. Ethnomusicologists study the relationship between music and other aspects of culture, the functions of music, the social relationships between musicians and society, how the style (scale, melody, harmony, timing) of music varies between cultures, and the musical instruments used.
8. Dance is purposeful and intentionally rhythmical nonverbal body movements that are culturally patterned and have aesthetic value. Dance is intimately connected to other aspects of culture, as illustrated by Brazilian capoeira (Kourlas 2010), a dance form with ties to religion, martial arts, and social commentary.
9. Like all other aspects of culture, forms and styles of art change over time. Despite the Internet and the information technology revolution (which has accelerated the sharing of art across cultures), cultures do not appear to be surrendering their unique forms of artistic expression.

Key Terms

art
dance
ethnomusicology
graffiti
graphic arts
pieces
plastic arts
signature graffiti
stencil graffiti
tags
Tā moko
tattoos
throw ups
transformational

Critical Thinking Questions

1. Does your conception of art vary from the working definition given in this chapter?
2. Thousands of works of art have been taken from various cultural groups throughout the world over the past several centuries, and remain the property of Western museums. Should these works of traditional art be returned or should they remain in the Western museums?
3. How can political leaders use art to motivate people or change their behaviour? Should anthropologists apply their knowledge of art to help them?
4. What role do the various forms of art play in shaping a peoples' identity?
5. Do graffiti artists have the right to create images, however beautiful, on public and private property without permission?
6. Body piercings, other than earlobes, are a relatively recent phenomenon in Western society. Is body piercing an art form? What symbolic meanings are attached to body piercing? What functions might they serve? What do body piercings say about Western conceptions of the body. How do other societies view body piercing?
7. What role does art play in religion?
8. Tourists bring home millions of souvenirs and art objects every year. How would an anthropologist study the relationship between art and tourism?
9. How might Indigenous groups use their traditional art to increase global awareness of the issues they face? Is there any role for anthropologists in this endeavour?
10. Has the Internet led to new forms of art? Has it affected the way we think about art or its role in society?

Make the Grade with MindTap

Stay organized and efficient with **MindTap**—a single destination with all the course material and study aids you need to succeed. Built-in apps leverage social media and the latest learning technology. For example:

- ReadSpeaker will read the text to you.
- Self-quizzing allows you to assess your understanding.
- Flashcards are pre-populated to provide you with a jump-start for review—or you can create your own.
- You can highlight text and make notes in your MindTap Reader. Your notes will flow into Evernote, the electronic notebook app that you can access anywhere when it's time to study for the exam.

Visit nelson.com/student to start using **MindTap**. Enter the Online Access Code from the card included with your text. If a code card is not provided, you can purchase instant access at NELSONbrain.com.

Women in Tamil Nadu, India, are making bricks the traditional way in front of wind turbines used for generating electricity.

The Modern World Order

CHAPTER

14

A CLOSING LETTER TO STUDENTS

Congratulations on working your way through this textbook! We opened Chapter 1 with a letter to you explaining the nature of the book's "Applied Perspective" and what you might hope to gain from it. We said that this is not only a comprehensive textbook introducing you to the field of cultural anthropology, but it is also designed to show you how the research findings, theories, methods, and insights of cultural anthropology can be useful in your everyday personal and professional lives. The real-life relevance of cultural anthropology has been highlighted through real (not hypothetical) chapter-opening scenarios, boxed "Applied Perspective," and "Cross-Cultural Miscue" case studies.

Now that you have had a term to familiarize yourself with both the comprehensiveness and relevance of cultural anthropology, we want to conclude the book with this capstone chapter. This final chapter focusses on the present-day world order and how it has emerged over the course of the past 500 years. We also identify some of today's major global challenges, including (but not limited to) overurbanization in Africa, Asia, and Latin America; environmental degradation; the spread of world health pandemics; the rise of militant religious fundamentalism; and the widening gap between the rich and the poor. And finally, we will explore how cultural anthropologists are contributing to the resolution of many of these global challenges.

As we have seen, anthropological insights can be helpful (and in many cases essential) in solving social problems. Basic cultural information certainly is useful to help us avoid breakdowns in communication when interacting with people from different cultural or subcultural backgrounds, both at home and abroad. In addition, cross-cultural competency can be valuable in meeting your professional objectives, whether you choose a career in medicine, business, education, law, architecture, counselling, public administration, criminal justice, marketing, or just about any other area we could imagine. Anthropologists are making a difference by drawing on the same data, insights, methods, and theories that you have been studying this term!

The purpose of this letter is to make sure that you have fully understood how important cultural anthropology can be to the future of your personal lives, your neighbourhoods, your towns, your provinces, your country, and the planet itself.

Joerg Boethling/Alamy Stock Photo

WHAT WE WILL LEARN

- **What is meant by the term *globalization***
- **How the period of colonization has shaped the contemporary world order**
- **What the impact of decolonization has been on Indigenous peoples and how they are dealing with it**
- **What the forces of globalization are today and the impact they are having on societies**
- **What contributions anthropologists have made to the solution of such global challenges as income inequity, human justice violations, and the refugee crisis**
- **Whether economic development programs always help the people they are intended to benefit**
- **What multiculturalism is and why is it the world's best hope for the future**

Not only is it important to appreciate the importance of cultural anthropology, but you should also know it well enough to be able to communicate it to your parents and friends (who still may be wondering why you are not taking only courses in business management and finance), and also to your future employers, no matter what field you actually enter. ■

The Growth of the Modern World Order: Colonialism and Globalization

As we have seen throughout this book, culture is an ever-changing, dynamic phenomenon. This holds true both for the general outlines of world cultures over time and for the thousands of distinct cultures that exist throughout the world today. Cultures change internally by means of inventions and innovations, and they change from outside forces through the process of borrowing and cultural diffusion. They change in response to changing technologies, economies, demographics, natural environments, values, and ideologies. Although it is true that no cultures stay frozen in time for long periods, the *pace* of change varies from one society to another and from one historical period to another. Today, however, ***globalization*** is rapidly changing all societies. Globalization can be defined as the process of forging international, political, economic, religious, and socio-cultural interconnections and interdependencies. The processes of globalization have affected all cultures, both negatively and positively. Anthropologists have been interested in global interactions and the spread of culture since the late 19th century, well before the term "globalization" appeared (Hahn 2008). In this chapter we will look at the drivers of globalization and, more importantly, the impact that it is having on the world's peoples and their cultures.

Globalization and Colonization

In a sense, globalization began when humans first developed culture. Whenever one group of people encountered another, they sometimes fought but more often they exchanged ideas, material things, and people. A good example of this is the Neolithic trade in obsidian. Obsidian is a black volcanic glass that was greatly desired before the use of metals because of its ability to make extremely sharp tools. Trace elements within obsidian provide it with a "fingerprint" that allows tools made from it to be traced to their source (Figure 14.1). Peter Watson (2005) suggests that obsidian may have been traded around the eastern Mediterranean nearly 150 000 years ago. Obsidian artifacts nearly 15 000 years old from a single source in modern-day Turkey have been found throughout Europe, the Mediterranean, the Middle East, and even as far as Iraq (Williams-Thorpe 1995).

Most scholars, however, trace the beginning of true globalization to the early 1500s, when European nations began to explore and colonize the world. Technological advances in navigation, ship building, cartography, and warfare enabled European explorers, merchants, missionaries, and armed forces to venture all over the globe. European countries created global empires by expanding not only their own territorial borders but also by increasing their control and domination over societies in distant lands and continents through the use of armed forces, police, administrators, and settlers (Nunes 1987). European ***colonialism*** over the past 500 years has created a worldwide system of interconnected nation-states, and commercial enterprises and opportunities to expand their economic and cultural influence to all corners of Earth.

Nathan Benn/Corbis Documentary/Getty Images

FIGURE 14.1 **Neolithic obsidian tools such as these from a single source in Turkey have been found throughout the Mediterranean.**

globalization The process of forging international, political, economic, religious, and socio-cultural interconnections and interdependencies.

colonialism The political, economic, and socio-cultural domination of a territory and its people by a foreign nation.

The primary motivation for European expansion was the desire to obtain wealth, either through theft, which was the primary method of Spanish and Portuguese colonists, or through trade, which was the preferred method of the British, Dutch, and French. It involved the modification of political and economic systems by European powers as well as the exploitation of Indigenous peoples. A secondary goal was to Christianize and, what was thought to be essentially the same thing, to civilize the people they encountered.

European powers, especially Britain, France, Portugal, Germany, Spain, Belgium, and Holland, solidified their influence worldwide through the process of colonization. To one degree or another, colonization by European countries was imperialistic; that is, it involved empire-building through state expansion of both territories and commerce. European colonies were of three types, depending on their basic purpose. In the first type, European countries acquired colonies primarily for the sake of exploiting their local economic resources (such as gold, copper, silver, and spices) needed to drive the Industrial Revolution. With these ***colonies of exploitation***, the Indigenous peoples were not displaced or destroyed but used as a source of cheap labour and markets for their finished products. Most South American, African, and Southeast Asian colonies were of this type. A second type of European colony was acquired to gain maritime areas and thereby control trade. For example, the Dutch settled Cape Town, South Africa, in the 19th century as a restocking area and safe haven for the long trade voyages between Holland and the Far East. And third, some Europeans established ***settlement colonies*** where large numbers of settlers displaced the Indigenous groups through warfare, disease, or murder to become the majority population. Eventually these colonies, through reform or revolution, became politically independent of their mother country. Canada, Australia, New Zealand, the United States, Argentina, and Chile are examples. The original Indigenous populations of these countries remain marginalized, their land appropriated, and, to a large extent, their cultures assimilated into the mainstream culture.

In all three types of colonies, European powers exercised total, or near total, control over the political, commercial, and social systems of the colonial territories. The extent to which these state societies coerced the conquered peoples to give up their Indigenous cultures varied from culture to culture and through time.

European colonization during the 19th century involved the actual possession and administration of foreign territories by European governments (Figure 14.2). This period had perhaps the most influence on our present world order. Many of the European colonial powers amassed great wealth and political power as a direct result of obtaining, controlling, and exploiting their colonial territories. In fact, the acquisitions of wealth and influence during the 19th century created the world economic order of the 20th. And most of these former European colonial powers—even though they granted independence to most of their colonies decades ago—have retained their economic and political influence into the 21st century.

Although colonization proved exceedingly beneficial for the economic and political ascension of the European colonial powers, the Indigenous populations paid a high price:

- Many colonies were acquired by military force, including violence and slaughter if people resisted colonial rule.
- During the earlier stages of colonization (the 17th and 18th centuries), Indigenous African people were sold like chattel in the trans-Atlantic slave trade.
- Natural resources, which belonged to Indigenous peoples, were simply taken from the colonies for the benefit of European industrialization.
- The best land was often appropriated for European settlers, and many Indigenous peoples were thrown off their ancestral (and often sacred) lands.
- Many Indigenous peoples were stripped of their traditional livelihoods, forced to work for low wages to produce commodities desired by European colonialists, and then taxed to help pay for the colonial system that was exploiting them.
- This exploitation of natural and human resources led to a permanently stratified social structure, with European settlers and colonial administrators at the top and Indigenous peoples at the bottom.
- Many societies in settlement colonies lost their languages, traditions, cultures, and identities.

When many colonies won their political independence after World War II, the local populations were poor, unhealthy, severely undereducated, and undercapitalized. At the time, the former colonies were euphemistically referred to as "newly independent but underdeveloped nation-states." These nation-states continue to be among the poorest nations in the world, while the economic gap between the former colonies and the former colonizers has become increasingly wide. To illustrate, according to *World Finance*, of the 20 poorest countries in the world in 2015, 17 were former African colonies of Britain, Belgium, Germany, France, Portugal, and Italy (Pasquali 2015). The other 15 percent of the world's poorest countries, although not in

---

colonies of exploitation European colonies where local economic resources were expropriated, and the Indigenous peoples used as cheap sources of labour.

settlement colonies European colonies where large numbers of settlers displaced the Indigenous groups to become the majority population, marginalizing the Indigenous peoples.

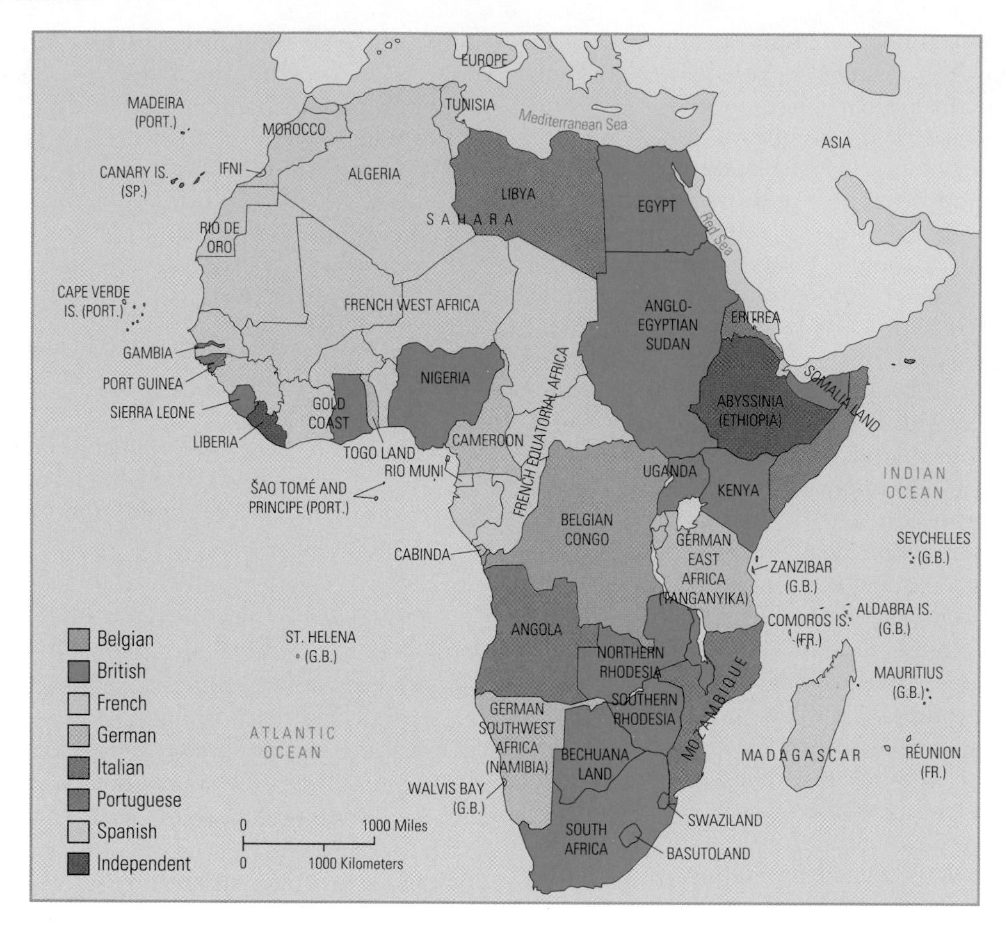

FIGURE 14.2 Except for Liberia (which gained independence from the United States in 1847) and Ethiopia, all of Africa was colonized by European powers by 1914.

sub-Saharan Africa, had, in one way or another, a colonial experience in their histories. The relative wealth of Canada, the 20th wealthiest country in the world in 2015 with a per capita income of $45 981.99, compared to the Central African Republic, the poorest country in the world with a per capita income of $639.94, makes a dramatic statement about the general gap in wealth and power between the colonies of exploitation and the colonies of settlement.

The end of colonial rule brought a host of other serious problems, including severe poverty, high rates of unemployment, substance abuse, political corruption, rapid population growth, underfunded educational systems, human rights abuses, environmental degradation, rapid urbanization, violent civil wars, inadequate housing, and medical pandemics. Enormous disparities can also be seen in non-economic measures. To illustrate, the life expectancy for men and women was 82 years in Canada in 2012 (Statistics Canada 2012b), but only 58.6 in Burkina Faso in 2013 (www.worldlifeexpectancy.com). In 2015 the infant mortality rate in Mali was 96 per 1000 live births, whereas in Canada it was only 4 (World Bank 2015).

modernization theory The idea that differences in economic development may be explained by inherent socio-cultural differences between the rich and the poor.

Theories of Global Inequality

Modernization Theory

How did the contemporary world become so uneven in terms of economic development? Social scientists have offered differing interpretations, but they usually boil down to one of two competing theories. One broad theory explains these vast differences in economic development in terms of the inherent socio-cultural differences between the rich and the poor. Often called *modernization theory*, this model is based on a dichotomy of traditional versus modern, and serves not only as an attempted description of reality but also as a planning strategy for bringing about economic development in less-developed nations. The modern nations are associated with high levels of technology, industrialization, scientific rationality, formal education, efficient bureaucratic governments, strong market economies, punctuality, religious pluralism, low birth and death rates, upward mobility based on merit, rapid change, plans for the future, and a decline in the extended family. Traditional nations, on the other hand, have fewer of these characteristics. Modernization theory posits that, for developing nations to become developed, they must engage in activities that will make them more like the developed nations. In short, they need to become more modern by taking on more of the "modern" characteristics listed.

The modernization theory of economic development suffers from several ethnocentric assumptions. First, modernization theorists assume that all people in the world ought to gladly embrace all of the economic, cultural, and social changes inherent in "becoming modern." Second, they clearly overestimate the extent to which some non-Western people resist modernization, in large part because they ignore the many creative adaptations these people have made for centuries. Third, and perhaps most important, proponents of modernization theory assume that traditional people will be better off if they become modern. Because becoming modern is progressive, it is widely held that it must be beneficial. Modernization theorists assume that the advantages of becoming modern—such as higher incomes and standards of living—are universally beneficial. Even though becoming modern may also involve giving up one's traditional culture, modernization theorists see that as a small price to pay in exchange for the obvious benefits.

World Systems Theory

The other major theory to explain the disparities between rich and poor has been called the *world systems theory*, which was developed primarily by American sociologist and historian Emmanuel Wallerstein in the 1970s (Wallerstein 2011[1974]). Wallerstein's basic argument is that all the nations of the world are connected in a systematic political and economic network of exchange whereby the wealthy nations exploit the poorer ones. He divides the world into three areas: *core*, *periphery*, and *semi-periphery*. The core refers to the wealthy developed countries (such as the United States, Canada, the United Kingdom, Australia, France, and Germany), which have high levels of skill, advanced technologies, and produce capital-intensive complex consumer products. The periphery are the developing nations, especially those in Sub-Saharan Africa, and supply raw materials, agricultural products, and cheap, unskilled labour. The semi-periphery are the industrializing nations between the core and periphery and include countries such as China, Brazil, Indonesia, Mexico, and Eastern Europe. The semi-periphery countries not only export natural resources and agricultural products but also manufacture and export a variety of industrial goods (Figure 14.3).

Exchange between the core and periphery is not conducted on an equal basis. Periphery nations are forced to sell their labour and products at low prices, and buy products from the core nations at high prices. The core nations also benefit from the migration of skilled people from the periphery who move to the core countries to improve their lives. The semi-periphery also benefit from unequal relations with the periphery, although the core, again through unequal exchange relations, benefits from them. The periphery are thus exploited by both the semi-periphery and the core, which is not only in control of the system, but also is the chief beneficiary.

Rawpixel.com/Shutterstock

FIGURE 14.3 This Indigenous Sri Lankan woman is picking tea that may eventually find its way to a grocery store shelf in Canada.

According to Wallerstein this system arose in the 1500s and 1600s with the colonization by Western European nations of the rest of the world, particularly Africa, Asia, and South America, and the rise of capitalism. This process gave the West an advantage in the world economy over the colonized as the network of capitalist economic exchange expanded. By the 19th century almost the entire world was part of one economic world system.

Neocolonialism

While the old colonial empires have gone, and direct military and political control has ended, many scholars contend that the relationship of political and economic dependency and exploitation is still maintained in a new,

---

world systems theory The idea that the nations of the world are connected in a systematic political and economic network of exchange whereby the wealthy nations exploit the poorer ones.

core Wealthy, technologically advanced nations that produce and exchange capital-intensive, complex, consumer products.

periphery Poor, developing nations that provide raw materials, agricultural products, and cheap, unskilled labour.

semi-periphery Industrializing nations between the core and periphery that not only export natural resources and agricultural products but also manufacture and export a variety of industrial goods.

more indirect, form of colonialism. ***Neocolonialism*** is the idea that developed countries and post-colonial powers maintain the political and economic dependency and exploitation of former colonies and less developed countries through economic, financial, and trade policies that favour themselves. While local peoples are no longer the subjects of the colonial power, their labour and the country's resources are still exploited and so are unable to break out of the relationship of dependency. The idea arose in the early 1960s when African states were quickly gaining independence (Yew 2002). Kwame Nkrumah, the first prime minister of newly independent Ghana, argued that such states were only theoretically independent, but in reality their economic systems and political policies were still being controlled by outsiders (Nkrumah 2004 [1965]). Although popular until the early 2000s, more recent scholarship questions the extent to which former colonialists exerted control over their former colonies (Maekawa 2015), and others that the relationship between developed and developing nations is far more complex (Fieldhouse 1999).

Neocolonialists (e.g., Woddis 1967; Nwokeji 2002) argue that there are three primary agents responsible for maintaining this dependency (Yew 2002): powerful developed countries and former colonialists such as the United Kingdom and the United States; international financial organizations, such as the International Monetary Fund (IMF) and the World Bank (WB); and multinational corporations such as Walmart and Coca-Cola. The IMF, WB, and other international financial agencies extend loans to developing nations, which are needed for development. The loans are advanced, however, on condition that the developing nations agree to restructuring programs, usually involving privatization, democracy, and improvement on human rights issues. The result, neocolonialists argue, is that the developing nations become mired in debt and the programs actually lower living standards, resulting in deteriorating health, education, and infrastructure, so that rather than poverty being alleviated, it is increased. In a similar fashion, developed nations provide developing nations with aid and loans on condition that certain restructuring takes place, and again usually involving trade policies that are favourable to them. ***Multinational corporations*** are thought to exploit the resources and raw materials of post-colonial peoples, pay low wages, show little concern for the environment of the host nation, and make few investments in it. The overall result is increasing poverty and environmental damage. Some multinational corporations are wealthier than the countries in which they operate and have considerable economic and political clout. In return for a promise to hire locals and bring in much needed capital, local governments will often grant these corporations favourable terms such as reduced taxes and relaxation of business regulations, building codes, and environmental controls.

Critics of the idea of neocolonialism argue that it tends to blame the failure of nations to develop on oppressive Western political and economic policies, while apportioning little blame to the poor economic planning and corruption of developing countries themselves (Fieldhouse 1999). Others argue that the continued relationship between some of the colonists and their former colonies was economically beneficial (Maekawa 2015; Fieldhouse 1999). Neocolonialism also has difficulty explaining the economic successes of Asia. According to the World Health Organization, the economic, health, and education situation in many countries in Africa has improved in recent years.

Decolonization

After World War II the colonial powers began a process of ***decolonization***, granting their former colonies independence. Decolonization is the dismantling of colonial empires by the withdrawal of colonial powers from their colonies, and the acquisition of self-determination and government in the newly independent states. In many cases this process has been accomplished smoothly with a peaceful handover of power, as it was when Great Britain handed Hong Kong back to China in 1999; and it has been done with much bloodshed through a war of independence. The first country to gain independence from its colonial rulers was the United States of America in 1776. Most of South and Central America gained independence in the 19th century, but it was not until after World War II that states in Africa, Asia, and elsewhere were decolonized. The reason for decolonization at this time was primarily economic. The colonies were simply too expensive to administer, and the benefits, such as cheap labour and cheap goods, could be obtained without the need for a colonial presence. From the colonizers perspective, decolonization was thus a process of unburdening. Today the process is almost complete. With the exception of the Western Sahara, only a few small island states remain under colonial administration and most of those have chosen to remain as colonies.

This is not to say, however, that the numerous Indigenous populations within these newly independent

---

neocolonialism The idea that developed countries and post-colonial powers maintain political and economic dependency and exploitation of former colonies and less-developed countries through economic, financial, and trade policies that favour themselves.

multinational corporations Companies that have operations in two or more countries.

decolonization The dismantling of colonial empires by the withdrawal of colonial powers from their colonies, and the acquisition of self-determination and government in the newly independent states.

states have been decolonized. Many, if not most, remain in a state of colonization relative to the nation-states in which they find themselves. Colonialism was and is not simply political or economic; it is also cultural. More recently, the Indigenous populations in these countries have begun a process of *cultural decolonization*. Colonization involved not only political and economic domination, but also raising the colonizers' ideas, values, and culture above the colonized. It meant domination of Indigenous languages, traditions, cultures, as well as minds. As we have seen with Indigenous people's experience in Canada's Residential Schools, they and their cultures were usually seen as primitive, backward, and disgusting, and they were prevented from speaking their languages and following their traditions. Through the Indian Act they were prevented from administering their own affairs. Many of Canada's First Nations lost their languages and cultures, and with them their identities and ways of thinking and being. In essence, colonization was an attempt to replace Indigenous identities with that of the colonizer. Cultural decolonization is thus a much more difficult process than political decolonization. Politicians and troops can be removed in a few years, but cultural decolonization takes much longer (Nunes 1987). It involves freeing the mind from the ideologies and cultures of the colonizers that made them feel inferior, and reclaiming their traditional cultures and identities (Hack 2008).

Indigenous people everywhere are rediscovering and reviving their lost cultures. In Chapter 6 we saw this in the attempts by First Nations to revive their languages and in Chapter 13 with the revival of traditional tattooing among the Inuit and the Māori. Indigenous artists are also using film to recreate the feeling of the past, and Nunes (1987) discusses how Indigenous writers in former Portuguese colonies are rewriting their histories.

Cultural decolonization is more, however, than simply reviving lost or disappearing languages, ceremonies, and traditions. It also involves substituting colonial values, ethics, and ideologies for traditional, Indigenous ones. It means regaining an identity, which in itself requires regaining the authentic spirituality and ways of thinking and feeling of a person from the original culture. All this must be done within a contemporary context. The way of life of a Cree from the 18th century is irrevocably lost, but that does not mean the spirituality and way of thinking has to be. To culturally decolonize, Indigenous peoples need to reconstruct the past, for it is a key to understanding the present. This means tapping into the knowledge of elders, looking at historical records, repatriating cultural items in museums, studying old ethnographies, and more. Anthropologists are well-positioned to help in this process. Indigenous peoples must also understand their colonizers, both in the past and the present, and how Western ideologies and practices have influenced their own (Nunes 1987). To remove themselves from cultural dependency also requires self-determination and control over their culture and future. First Nations and other Indigenous and marginalized groups must also protect their culture from cultural appropriation.

Cultural Appropriation

In 2007, the United Nations, "Concerned that Indigenous peoples have suffered from historic injustices as a result of, *inter alia* [among other things], their colonization and dispossession of their lands, territories and resources, thus preventing them from exercising, in particular, their right to development in accordance with their own needs and interests," approved the UN Declaration on the Rights of Indigenous Peoples (United Nations 2008). According to Article 31.1:

> Indigenous peoples have the right to maintain, control, protect and develop their cultural heritage, traditional knowledge and traditional cultural expressions, as well as the manifestations of their sciences, technologies and cultures, including human and genetic resources, seeds, medicines, knowledge of the properties of fauna and flora, oral traditions, literatures, designs, sports and traditional games and visual and performing arts. They also have the right to maintain, control, protect and develop their intellectual property over such cultural heritage, traditional knowledge, and traditional cultural expressions.*

Violation of this Declaration is often referred to as *cultural appropriation*, which can thus be defined as the taking, adopting, and using the elements of one culture, such as ideas, symbols, knowledge, artifacts, practices, and other components, by members of another. It is generally perceived of as taking items and ideas from small marginalized groups by members of larger dominant groups who have little knowledge or understanding of the history, culture or spirituality of the groups from which the elements are taken. Implicit in this concept are two other ideas: cultural borrowing and exploitation. Anthropologists have been interested in cultural borrowing and exchange since the 19th century and recognize it as a major element in the process of cultural change and development. Without one culture borrowing items and ideas from another, and re-contextualizing them, humanity would be worse off. The concept of cultural appropriation emerged

*Source: United Nations 2008. United Nations Declaration on the Rights of Indigenous Peoples. Article 31.1.http://www.un.org/esa/socdev/unpfii/documents/DRIPS_en.pdf

cultural decolonization The process of the colonized freeing their minds from the ideologies and cultures of the colonizers and reclaiming their traditional cultures and identities.

cultural appropriation Taking, adopting, and using the elements of one culture by members of another.

in academia in the late 1970s and 1980s as part of the scholarly critique of colonialism (Young 2015). In recent years, however, the idea of cultural appropriation has become controversial and problematic, and the focus has shifted to exploitation.

Exploitation involves taking advantage of others. Appropriation in this sense involves taking something from another culture, without authorization and for one's own gain, which can be either financial or a means to maintain an unequal relationship. Appropriation as exploitation involves a power imbalance wherein members of dominant groups take from marginalized minority groups, and especially Indigenous peoples. The distinction between appropriation as borrowing versus appropriation as exploitation raises an ethical dilemma. At what point does borrowing, which is acceptable, become exploitation, which is not? When is cultural borrowing appropriate and when does it become cultural appropriation?

Perhaps one of the reasons for the dilemma comes from the history of colonialism. Western society generally wants to divorce itself from its exploitative and racist past, as it should. But, in our desire not to be seen as exploitative or racist, we have developed a norm where we try to be politically correct, not offend anyone, and not engage in cultural appropriation. Anyone who is thought to breach this norm is vilified in the media, on the Internet, and in social media. At the same time, the colonized Indigenous and marginalized groups whose cultures were demeaned and exploited, are struggling to reclaim their cultural heritage and maintain their identity. They thus have a vested interest in preventing any further real cultural appropriation.

Opponents of Cultural Appropriation

There are both proponents and opponents of cultural appropriation, and it is worthwhile to examine both sides of the debate. Opponents of cultural appropriation focus on "exploitation." One of the arguments against it is that it ignores intellectual property rights. A good example of this was found in U.K. fashion designer Kokon To Zai's (KTZ) fall 2015 catalogue. A $900 sweater was displayed with an unusual pattern of geometric figures and hands placed directly over the chest, which CBC North producer Salome Awa recognized as a nearly exact duplicate of a garment made by her great-great-grandfather, the shaman Qingailisaq (Hopper 2015) (Figure 14.4). KTZ admitted that the designer had seen it in a museum display and copied it.

Mystic Seaport Collection/Accession Number: 1966.339.68

Victor VIRGILE/Gamma-Rapho via Getty Images

FIGURE 14.4 The Inuit shaman Qingailisaq and a suspiciously similar sweater design from the U.K. firm KTZ.

KTZ subsequently removed it from the catalogue and issued an apology. It is this type of cultural appropriation or exploitation that the Declaration on the Rights of Indigenous Peoples is primarily meant to protect.

Opponents also argue that cultural appropriation oppresses minority groups, disparages their culture, strips them of their identity, reinforces stereotypes, and can also be seen as racist (Nittle 2015). In other words, little has changed since colonial times. For example, Victoria's Secret recently outfitted runway model Karlie Kloss in a fringed suede bikini, a feathered head dress, and turquoise jewellery, a "sexy Indian" costume (Avins 2015). At the very least it was insensitive, but others saw it and similar examples as disrespectful, tasteless, stereotypical, and offensive, if not racist. Oppression is more acutely felt when the items appropriated have spiritual significance and are used out of context, with little understanding of their meaning (Nittle 2015). Perhaps the best known example of this is the use of First Nation icons and derogatory names to represent various sports teams. For example the Ottawa football team, the Nepean Redskins changed its name to the Nepean Eagles in 2014 after complaints that the name was racist (Lofaro 2014).

Another example of how cultural appropriation can cause offense are two murals by English artist George Southwell under the dome of the Parliament Buildings in Victoria, British Columbia. One mural, entitled *Labour*, depicts bare-breasted Salish women participating in the construction of Fort Victoria by hauling logs and fish, while *Justice* shows an Indigenous man being punished before a colonial judge. In 2001, several First Nations in British Columbia wrote a letter to the provincial government saying the murals were "highly offensive, demeaning, and degrading to First Nations people in the province" of British Columbia (Young 2005). Labour is offensive because it is seen as a misrepresentation of Indigenous culture, and stereotypes them, while Justice is offensive as it depicts the Salish as subservient to European colonists, and is a metaphor for the oppression of Indigenous peoples (Young 2005). An advisory panel recommended the removal and preservation of the murals, as the government should not cause offence and shame (Vancouver Sun 2007).

Water lies at the heart of all development. As it becomes scarce, its overuse and competition over allocation of resources, which cross international boundaries, for drinking, agriculture, recreation, and electricity generation will increasingly cause social and political conflict. For many, the overuse or misuse of water has been regarded as an ecological problem, while its allocation a policy and political problem. Rather than conduct an in-depth examination of a particular cultural group, the traditional ethnographic approach, Veronica Stang (2009) realized that, to resolve conflicts and develop more ecologically and socially sustainable forms of water use, ethnographic studies should focus on water itself and look at the ways various cultures and their formal and informal institutions and structures use water in everyday life. Policy also needed to consider the ways different groups conceived of water and its uses, and the way they controlled it.

Proponents for Cultural Appropriation

Proponents for cultural appropriation focus on "borrowing" rather than exploitation, and argue that the cross-fertilization of ideas is not only positive but also inevitable (Avins 1015). Most of the elements in the world today, from food, music, clothing, art, and even mathematics and politics, are the result of cultural appropriation as borrowing (McParland 2015). Proponents argue that it is done with good intent in the sense that "imitation is the highest form of flattery." Borrowers see the value in other designs and ideas and borrow out of admiration (McWhorter 2014). For instance, Europeans realized that Inuit clothing, such as parkas and mukluks, was a better way to keep warm in cold climates than overcoats and wool sweaters, and that the kayak was a good way to navigate open waters. While this is cultural appropriation in that these elements have been "borrowed," they have not been appropriated in the sense of exploitation in that the Inuit have not lost out because of it, nor has it stereotyped them or taken away from their identity. As Hopper (2015) points out, the Inuit generally have no problem with people paddling kayaks or wearing parkas. Proponents point out that cultures also adapt and change what they borrow. For example Hot Yoga as practised in Canada is not the same as Yoga that came from India, and the pizza at Pizza Hut is not the same as that which originated in Italy, any more than the taco at Taco Bell is the same as the taco that originated in Mexico. Proponents also argue that all cultures are the product of cultural appropriation, and that it is a mutually beneficial two-way street; that we are all better off. The Inuit have realized that rifles and snowmobiles make hunting more efficient than dog sleds and bows and arrows.

Resolving Cultural Appropriation

The concept of cultural appropriation was primarily a topic of academic discourse until about 2013, when it entered the more public domains of the Internet and social media. At this time almost every act of cultural appropriation was seen as exploitation or racist, failing to distinguish it from cultural appreciation and the benign borrowing from the truly exploitative. As one journalist has put it, "the hunt for wrongdoing has gone run amok. . . . Nothing is too petty for the new culture cops" (Young 2015). For instance, in 2013, pop star Miley Cyrus was accused of cultural appropriation by twerking (dancing in a sexually provocative way) during recorded and live performances. The twerk is a dance style with roots in the African American community (Nittle 2015). Several white celebrities have also been accused of cultural appropriation and of stealing cherished icons of identity from the subjugated black culture for braiding their hair in cornrows (Abdul-Jabbar 2015). And after Justin Bieber shared photos of his 2016 new look—blond dreadlocks—he was publically accused of culturally appropriating the hairstyle as well as racism (Ahsan 2016). But perhaps the most absurd accusation of cultural appropriation occurred in November 2015, when student leaders at the University of Ottawa halted yoga classes over concerns that the classes were not sensitive enough to yoga's cultural roots. The story became international news and was ridiculed with comments that applying the same principle would also mean cancelling all algebra classes, since it has Islamic origins, and jazz and rock 'n' roll, since they evolved from African American music (Duffy 2015).

The result of this type of social control is that fear of being accused of cultural appropriation has inhibited the cross-fertilization of ideas. If no borrowing can occur because of fear, then Indigenous cultures become frozen, which only enhances stereotypes (Scafidi 2005). Cathy Young (2015) discusses a young woman she met who questioned whether she should pursue a graduate degree in Chinese Studies because she doubted whether it was morally permissible for a white person. Clearly a balance is needed. On the one hand, we do not want to perpetuate power imbalances, demean, mock, or stereotype other cultures; and on the other, we want to encourage empathy, respect, diversity, and interest in other cultures and facilitate the exchange of ideas, styles, and traditions.

There are a few principles that can be applied to help discover whether the cultural appropriation is appropriate or not. The intent of the appropriation must be considered. Is it meant to appropriate for profit, are the designs or ideas more an inspiration or is it more a question of theft? What are the perceived power dynamics between the cultures; what are the social and historical relations between them? Does the appropriation maintain any power imbalance? Is someone losing out because of the appropriation? Does the element being borrowed have sacred or religious meaning for the group it is appropriated from? Does the element borrowed stereotype or demean the culture from which it is taken? It is also important to ask who is making the accusation of cultural appropriation. In many cases it is not someone from the culture who makes the accusation that something has been appropriated.

Cultural Repatriation

During the colonial period, and even afterward, Westerners not only forced Indigenous peoples to assimilate and denigrated their cultures, they also appropriated many art objects, cultural items, and even the people themselves. Some were bought and some were stolen. Since the 1990s, however, Indigenous people, in a desire to reclaim their cultural heritage, and with a renewed strength and determination, are standing up to Western administrations and asking for them back. One aspect of cultural decolonization is the ***repatriation***, or return, of cultural heritage items, including art, artifacts, and human remains, to their former owners or their descendants. Repatriating their heritage is one way Indigenous or colonized peoples are reclaiming their culture, spirituality, and identity. In a spirit of reconciliation, many Western countries, although not all, are cooperating with the return of cultural artifacts to their original homes. Below we discuss three examples: the return of Residential School art to its creators; the return of mummified heads of Māori warriors from Scotland; and the return of blood taken from the Yanomamö in the 1960s.

Residential School Art

Between 1958 and 1960, children at the Alberni Indian Residential School were, contrary to normal practice, told by the art teacher Robert Aller to "draw whatever your heart feels" (Lagasse 2014). Using their own cultural symbols and working from their own Indigenous perspective, they painted everyday scenes that reflected their culture and way of life (Steel 2013; Hunter 2013). Aller kept the paintings and after his death in 2008 they were donated to the University of Victoria. The curator of the collection of 47 paintings, visual anthropologist Andrea Walsh, worked with elders from Coast Salish communities, to track down about half of the artists so they could be reunited with their art (Steel 2013; Hunter 2013). The reunion of the artists with their artworks has been part of the healing process for the Residential School survivors and their children. The Truth and Reconciliation Commission held an exhibition of the artworks in Victoria in April 2012, and they are now in the *We Are All One* exhibit at the Alberni Valley Museum until the Nuu-chah-nulth build a museum or cultural centre of their own.

Mokomokai

When Europeans first contacted the Māori of New Zealand in the late 1700s, they were fascinated with their Moko tattoos. As we saw in Chapter 13, Moko tattoos

repatriation The return of cultural heritage items including art, artifacts, and human remains to their former owners or their descendants.

not only symbolized a man's status and ancestry but they were also the embodiment of his spirit and power. Traditionally, the Māori preserved the tattooed heads (*mokomokai)* of their relatives, which were treated with utmost respect and tenderness and kept for decades in ornately carved boxes, being brought out only for sacred ceremonies (Macrae 2014; NZETC 2015). Mokomokai were also made by decapitating enemies and rival chiefs. Their preserved heads, could then be mocked or ransomed to other tribes (NZETC 2015). Access to European guns provided some Māori groups with a military advantage over their enemies and so, to obtain mokomokai and to satisfy European curiosity, they began hunting down and decapitating their enemies and exchanging the tattooed heads for muskets and ammunition, which only increased their ability to kill their enemies.

In the 1820s the going rate was one musket for four heads (PBS 2003). Demand was so high that some mokomokai were created by tattooing slaves and then taking their heads (Yates 2013). By one estimate, over 18 500 Māori were killed in the so-called Musket Wars (Macrae 2014). The sailors, whalers, and traders who bought the mokomokai would then sell them for a profit, although at one point supply outstripped demand, and at £2 each they were within range of the middle classes (Dunbabin 1923). Such a gruesome trade was unproblematic for the Europeans as all Māori were viewed as subhuman (Atkinson 2003). The Governor of New South Wales outlawed the trade in 1831 (Macrae 2014; Yates 2013) although it continued for some time afterward, but not before fear of being killed for their tattoos put an effective end to the practice of Moko.

The preserved heads were shipped back to Great Britain as souvenirs and curios, where they ended up in various museums and private collections. More than 200 mokomokai are estimated to be in various museums worldwide (NZETC 2015). The American Museum of Natural History in New York has at least 39, purchased from a collector in the early 1900s (Yates 2013). Nine Mokomokai found their way to the Aberdeen University Museum (The Scotsman 2007). The Māori, with support from the New Zealand government, are trying to bring them home. Because the Moko tattoos indicate tribal affiliation, many of their descendants can be identified who can give their ancestors a traditional burial and pay them the respect they deserve once they are returned. The mokomokai in Aberdeen were retuned in 2007 (The Scotsman 2007), but the ones in the Museum of Natural History have not been returned.

Yanomamö Blood

In 1967, anthropologist Napoleon Chagnon and geneticist James Neel took samples of blood from several hundred Yanomamö of Venezuela and Brazil without their informed consent. The Yanomamö did not know how to refuse, nor did they know why the samples were taken or what would happen to them (Elizondo 2009). In 2000, investigative journalist Patrick Tierney accused Chagnon of unethical behaviour for bribing the Yanomamö with pots and pans and steel tools such as machetes to give up their blood (Tierney 2000). Tierney's accusations became widely known, and in 2001 Yanomamö leaders, many of whom had their blood taken when they were children, requested the return of the blood. The frozen samples were being held in four university labs and at the National Cancer Institute in the United States, and were intended to be used for scientific research. The various institutions were happy to return the blood but claim they were hampered by Brazilian administrators concerned about the biohazard risks. Robert Borofsky (2005) claims the blood was not being returned because it might be useful in some future genome project. The issue raised debate among anthropologists about ethics in the field and especially the extent to which they really care for the welfare of the people they study as opposed to their concern for advancing their own interests. According to Yanomamö beliefs, blood is a sacred vital force and the dead cannot rest until all traces of a person are disposed of; only then can their soul leave the world of the living (Adams 2010). In 2015, 2693 samples were returned to the Yanomamö and emptied into the river in a ceremony presided over by shamans from the community where many of the samples were collected (Survival International 2015) (Figure 14.5).

DEA/C. Dani I. Jeske/DeAgostini/Getty Images

FIGURE 14.5 In 2015, blood taken from Yanomamö in 1967 was given back to them and returned to the river in a ceremony presided over by a shaman.

The Forces of Globalization Today

The process of globalization was slow at first but picked up speed in the mid-1800s with new forms of transportation, such as the train and steamship, and communication, such as the telegraph. It slowed down a little with the two world wars and the Depression of the 1930s, but since the end of the World War II globalization has been accelerating at an ever increasing pace, and especially after the 1980s with the development of computers, cellphones, and the Internet. Today, except for perhaps the remotest, largely uninhabited areas of the world, everyone is within range of a cellphone network.

According to classic economic theory, when demand for a product or service is high and supply low, producers can charge high prices and thus make large profits. In a free market, however, the prospect of high profits attracts more producers, who rush in to meet the demand. The increasing supply and competition, however, result in a decrease in prices and lower profits such that an equilibrium is reached whereby the cost of producing, distributing, and marketing the goods supplied is only slightly below what they are sold for. Thus, in highly competitive consumer markets such as we find in Canada, the United States, and Europe, profit margins are thin. Companies do not like this; after all, a company cannot survive if is not profitable in the long term, and so they seek other ways to increase profits. It is hard, however, in Western countries to make a profit when sales of many consumer goods are linked to the increase in population. For example, it is hard to increase the sales of toothpaste or refrigerators in Canada without an increase in population. There are really only three major ways companies can increase profits.

The first is to improve existing products and services or, better yet, develop new ones. This is why we constantly see "new and improved" written on the packages of many existing products, and why we are seeing new products on the shelves each year. In 2010 *Forbes Magazine* estimated that, globally, there are about 250 000 new products launched each year (Wong 2010). Developing new products is not cheap, however, for not only is research and development expensive, but there is also no guarantee of success; 85–95 percent of new products fail in the first year (Wong 2010).

The second way to increase profits is to find totally untapped markets. For this reason Western companies are always looking to sell their products in Asia, South America, Africa, and elsewhere. But it is not a one-way process. Canada is an untapped market for many goods produced elsewhere. Take an inventory of the products in your pantry and you will find that very few are produced in Canada.

The third way to increase profits is to reduce the cost of goods sold, and for almost any product, the highest contributor to the cost is the labour that goes into it. The solution is to produce products in low-wage countries such as India, China, Bangladesh, Brazil, and elsewhere. And it is for this reason that companies will establish manufacturing plants in these countries and outsource services to them. It is thus no surprise that many of the cars we buy come from Japan, the laptops from China, or our clothes from Indonesia, and that when we call customer service the person answering the phone is in Mumbai (Figure 14.6).

Joerg Boethling/Alamy Stock Photo

FIGURE 14.6 **The next time you call customer service it may be answered by one of these women in Kolkata, India.**

The result of this is that businesses will always develop new products, seek new markets, and hire cheap labour. In doing so they are contributing to global economic integration. Trade liberalization agreements such as the North American Free Trade Agreement (NAFTA) between Canada, the United States, and Mexico, a similar agreement in South America known as Mercosur, the European Economic Community (EEC), and most recently the 2015 Trans-Pacific Partnership (TPP) between 12 Pacific Rim nations, are all designed to promote freer trade and make it easier for money, goods, and people to cross borders.

The processes of globalization have been helped by improvements in technology, transportation, and communication. Transportation costs, by air, sea, and rail have all fallen dramatically over the past few decades, making it not only cheaper for goods to be shipped internationally but also for people to travel. Inexpensive travel makes distance increasingly irrelevant and allows personal contact on a regular basis. And it is only going to increase. Boeing estimates that the number of kilometres travelled by passengers annually will increase from 6 billion kilometres in 2014 to 18 billion in 2034 (Boeing 2015). Moreover, the travellers are becoming more diverse; most of this growth will come from Asia, China, and the Middle East (Figure 14.7). The result of people travelling overseas on holiday, or settling in other countries and returning for frequent visits has led to the global spread of ideas and cultural practices.

Ideas and practices are spread not only by the physical movement of people but also by cheap communication costs and technologies. With applications such as Skype, WhatsApp, Messenger, and email, people can stay in contact for free. The Internet, movies,

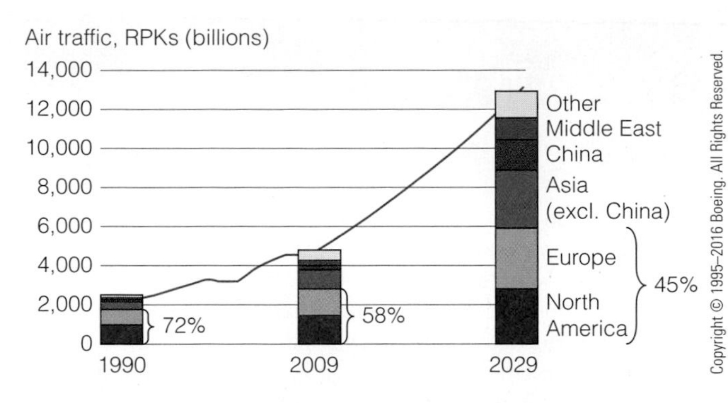

FIGURE 14.7 According to airplane manufacturer Boeing Corporation, air travel is set to triple in the next 20 years, with most travellers coming from Asia, China, and the Middle East (Boeing 2015).

television, radio, and mass marketing have also led to the dissemination of ideas to the "remotest" areas of the world. People in non-Western countries see and learn about different values, attitudes, and lifestyles, and it is changing the way they think and behave. When people in non-Western countries see the relative comfort that Westerners have, it is perhaps only natural that they too desire the material aspects.

Marshall McLuhan, a Canadian who analyzed the impact of mass media on society, coined the term "global village." The term captures in many ways the situation today. Global forces are shaping local village communities while, at the same time, cheap instantaneous communication, intercontinental travel, and highly integrated economic and political networks are increasingly giving the world a village-like character.

The Effects of Globalization

A good example of the impact globalization has on local cultures is anthropologist Tanja Winther's (2008) study of how the introduction of electricity in a village in Zanzibar, East Africa, changed peoples' everyday lives.

One of the first things she noticed was that people's time management changed. Women, for instance, began to cook only two meals a day instead of three because they wanted to watch television at night. Social relationships also changed. Instead of men and women spending time separately in the evening they now sit together

CROSS-CULTURAL MISCUE

In 2000, only 10 million Chinese travelled abroad. By 2012 that figure had risen to 83 million (Cripps 2013). In 2013 they spent $129 billion, a 26 percent increase from the previous year (UN World Tourism Organization 2014), overtaking Americans and Germans as the biggest international tourism spenders. Chinese tourists tend to buy branded luxury items such as Gucci handbags, Dior perfume, and Rolex watches rather than souvenirs (European Travel Commission 2012). With increasing wealth and favourable exchange rates, over 100 million Chinese today travel annually, and by 2020 that figure is set to double (Webb 2014). Many of them are unhappy, however, with the service they receive when travelling. Many complain they are not treated the same way Westerners are, and are made to feel like second-class people even though they may spend a lot of money (Cripps 2013). Most places, for instance, do not accept Chinese credit cards and so they have to pay cash. A study of Chinese bloggers by the European Travel Commission and World Tourism Organization (2012) discovered that most Chinese tourists viewed Europe as a place of "high prices, inconvenience and inadequate service" (p. 27).

Hotels, restaurants, tourist groups, and luxury stores in particular are scrambling to make them feel welcome and comfortable and are adapting their offerings. Some hotels now provide a pair of slippers and a tea kettle, have Chinese TV channels in the guest rooms, and serve Chinese breakfast including congee and dim sum (European Travel Commission 2012). Many restaurants have menus in Chinese and provide chopsticks, while many businesses have hired Chinese-speaking staff.

While Western businesses have been slow to cater to the Chinese tourist, some of the blame for the way they feel is due to their own misunderstanding of Western cultural norms. For instance, many Chinese tourists complain about waiting in line for things in the West, while in China if they do not scramble for things they may miss out. The majority of Chinese tourists also do not plan well enough ahead so that at high class restaurants, which require booking weeks in advance, they are unable to get in and so feel frustrated and discriminated against (Cripps 2013). They are also under the stereotype that, in the West, money can get anything. Many demonstrate a cultural insensitivity and are unaware that tipping is expected in most restaurants, that it is rude to cut in line, and unacceptable to ask that meal times be extended to after hours (Thompson 2013). There are also numerous accounts of Chinese tourists behaving badly and doing such things as spitting, littering, ignoring traffic laws, being loud, dressing inappropriately, and letting their children defecate and urinate in public (Webb 2014). Understandably, these things are seen as inappropriate by their hosts, but then travelling abroad is a new experience for most Chinese and they need to learn, just as the "Ugly American" tourist 20 years ago had to learn, that their behaviour and ignorance of local customs are seen as rude. Travel is a way for people of different cultures to get to learn about and understand one another, but it takes time.

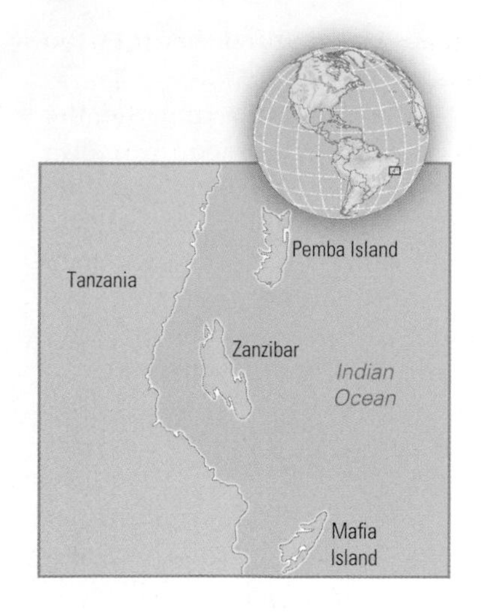

with neighbours and extended family in the same room watching TV. This also cuts down on marital intimacy and it appears that the birth rate is declining. People are getting less sleep than previously and this has caused them to become more quarrelsome. Older people, however, find the community safer in the evening and young girls are able to attend night classes. Because electricity is expensive some men are considering taking more than one wife or not getting married at all.

The long-term effects of globalization on the cultures of the world have yet to be fully realized. Some early scholars (Jameson 1990; Robertson 1992) suggested that globalization will eventually lead to the formation of a single global culture. They argued that the rapid flow of money, commodities, and information to every corner of the world, if allowed to continue unchecked, would eradicate cultural differences. In recent years, however, an alternative view has emerged to suggest that globalization, rather than totally changing cultures, can stimulate local cultures to redefine themselves in the face of these external forces. In other words, local cultures, although changing some features, will reaffirm much of their uniqueness while entering into a dialogue with global forces.

It is certainly true that some languages and cultures are becoming virtually extinct, but at the same time other cultures and ethnic groups are experiencing a resurgence. It is important to recognize that states formed by merging a number of ethnic entities together also have the tendency to eventually come apart. The best contemporary example of this is the Soviet Union, established in 1945 from 15 constituent republics (Armenia, Azerbaijan, Belarus, Estonia, Georgia, Kazakhstan, Kyrgyzstan, Latvia, Lithuania, Moldova, Russia, Tajikistan, Turkmenistan, Ukraine, and Uzbekistan). When this strongly centralized federal union collapsed in 1991, all 15 republics, with their own distinctive languages and cultures, became independent nations. The 1990s also saw the breakup of Yugoslavia into several nation-states. Today this tendency for pluralistic societies to fragment can be seen among the Kurds in Turkey and Iraq, the Basques and Catalonians in Spain, the Tibetans in China, the Scots in Great Britain, and of course many Quebecois in Canada. Thus, it seems unreasonable to expect that the world, through the process of globalization, is moving relentlessly toward a single, culturally homogeneous nation-state.

CROSS-CULTURAL MISCUE

After Lillie Marshall's three-month teaching position at the Total Child School Reading Club in Ghana came to an end, the children in the class decided to give her a gift to say thank you (Marshall 2010). The 40 children were crammed onto their wooden benches watching intently as their teacher presented Lillie with a sparkling red and silver wrapped package. Excitedly, she ripped open the wrapping paper eager to see what the gift was—a beautiful gold, purple, yellow, and green *kente* pattern fabric. "It is the most perfect gift ever," she said, holding back the tears. But when she looked at the children's faces they appeared shocked and horrified. In the West it is rude for recipients not to unwrap presents in front of us as we like to see the surprise on their faces when they open them. She later learned that, in Ghana, it is rude to open gifts in front of people. It made no sense to the children to wrap the gift only to have her open it right there. If the children had wanted her to see it, they would not have wrapped it. By opening it she had ruined the surprise. Lillie should have taken it home and opened the gift there.

Global Challenges and the Role of Applied Cultural Anthropology

As we have tried to show throughout this text, the discipline of anthropology looks at humans, wherever they may be found, from earliest prehistory to the present. Because of the enormous time frame it has carved out for itself, anthropology is able to observe both long-term and short-term socio-cultural trends. Cultural anthropologists are constantly looking at more recent and, by definition, more short-term socio-cultural trends and developments. These include post-World War II trends such as world immigration patterns; the rise of religious fundamentalism; rapid urbanization in Africa, Asia, and Latin America; the spread of world health pandemics such as AIDS; environmental degradation; and the widening gap between the rich and the poor throughout the world.

The former colonies are not alone in facing the many daunting challenges mentioned previously. To one degree or another, these are *global problems* for all nations, rich and poor alike. This is not to suggest that people from affluent nations are suffering the consequences of these global problems as much as people from poor nations do, but wealthy nations have a real stake in helping to ameliorate these pressing issues. Unless some of the more egregious inequities and injustices between rich and poor nations are addressed, the affluent nations will continue to grapple with political instability, global pandemics, and military interventions. The problems that face former colonies and other poor nations are global issues that cannot be ignored by any nation because they affect the sustainability of humankind.

Today's world poses a number of major challenges. These include, but are not limited to, global health problems, the widening gap between poor and wealthy nations (and between poor and wealthy people *within* nations), demographic shifts both between and within nation-states, environmental destruction, the depletion of the world's natural resources, the need for cleaner and more sustainable sources of energy, children's need for quality education and healthcare, and the injustices inflicted on the world's Indigenous peoples and other vulnerable populations. In one way or another, many of these global issues are both interrelated and have their origins in 19th and 20th century industrialization and colonialism. For the remainder of this chapter, we want to look at three of these major global challenges in some detail: (1) the global refugee crisis, (2) sustainable economic development in the developing world, (3) the cultural survival of Indigenous populations. We will describe each of these global problem areas in its contemporary context and then discuss how anthropologists have addressed (and are addressing) these challenges in their research and policy recommendations.

In keeping with the theme of this textbook, we want to reiterate that cultural anthropologists bring a good deal to the table in addressing today's global challenges. First, because cultural anthropologists rely so heavily on direct research (participant-observation) at the grassroots level, they are in the best position to observe the impact of global changes on people's lives. In other words, unlike economists, anthropologists are studying the real consequences of colonialism, industrialization, and rapid globalization for real people rather than focusing on such impersonal "leading indicators" as GNP and demographic shifts. Second, because anthropologists take a holistic approach, they tend to look for those interconnections between the parts of local societies that other specialists (such as agronomists, development planners, and other social scientists) might miss. Third, because anthropologists work from a comparative and cross-cultural perspective, it is likely that they will be aware of how similar peoples in different parts of the world are dealing with these global challenges. And finally, *applied* cultural anthropologists in particular, owing to their collaborative orientation, make excellent members of interdisciplinary development teams.

The Refugee Crisis

In recent years one of the biggest concerns of nations around the world, including Canada, is the number of refugees fleeing the conflict in Syria and elsewhere. The United Nations High Commissioner for Refugees (UNHCR) estimates that, by June 2014, there were more than 60 million refugees and internally displaced people worldwide—the largest number since World War II (UNHCR 2015). They include Syrians fleeing war in Syria and Iraq, Christians and other religious groups escaping persecution in much of the Middle East, Pakistan, Nigeria, and Sudan, and others escaping conflict in Republic of Congo, Afghanistan, Somalia, the Central African Republic, and Ukraine. Not all refugees have managed to reach safety.

In the face of armed conflict, oppression, and persecution, people flee. People also move to escape poverty, seeking to improve their lives and the lives of their children. At the same time, birth rates in many Western countries are below replacement levels and many developed nations have relaxed immigration policies in order to maintain economic growth. Canada, for instance, admitted over 260 000 migrants and refugees into the country in 2014 (Citizenship and Immigration Canada 2015a) and has averaged over 250 000 for the past few years. Borders have also become more porous, especially in Europe, where people can move freely among 22 of the 26 member states of the European Union once they have crossed an external border of one of them. One of the results of globalization is the movement of millions of people around the world, particularly from East to West, from poor to rich. This ***diaspora*** has led to enclaves of ethnic groups and communities each with their own, political, social, and cultural concerns.

It is important to make a distinction between a ***migrant*** and a ***refugee***. A migrant is a person who moves from one nation to another. Migrants move for a variety of reasons such as for study or to be with family; those who move to improve their living conditions or job opportunities are ***economic migrants***. For example, Canadian farmers regularly hire temporary migrant workers from Mexico and Central America to help harvest crops. Nations usually place quotas on the number of migrants allowed into the country based on certain criteria such as age, education, health, and relationship to others already in the country. Economic migrants is an umbrella term and also includes refugees. A refugee is a person who has fled their home country seeking refuge in another because of conflict in their homeland, or because they fear they may be killed, imprisoned, or persecuted

---

diaspora The dispersion of a group of people from their original homeland.

migrant A person who moves from one nation to another.

refugee A person who has fled their home country seeking refuge in another because of conflict in their homeland, or because they fear they may be killed, imprisoned, or persecuted because of their race, religion, nationality, political views, or membership in a particular ethnic or social group.

economic migrants People who move from one nation to another to improve their living conditions or job opportunities.

because of their race, religion, nationality, political views, or membership in a particular ethnic or social group. Under the 1951 UN Refugee Convention, signing countries are legally obliged to shelter refugees and are not permitted to expel them or return them to where their life or freedom would be threatened (UNHCR 2011). Many refugees spend years in "temporary" refugee camps that provide little more than food and shelter and basic sanitation, hoping to return when conditions in their homeland change.

At this time the biggest concern is for those fleeing the conflict in Syria. The reasons for the conflict in Syria are many and complex. Hokayem (2013) identifies five of them. First is the breakdown of the relationship between the government and the people. For 40 years the Assad regime had kept ethnic, religious, and political differences in check through repression. The civil war started in March 2011 as part of the Arab Spring popular uprisings across the Arab world in reaction to dictatorial administrations. Second is the struggle for regional dominance in the area between Saudi Arabia, Iran, and other countries. Third is the growing split between Sunni and Shia Muslims. This split is political and spiritual and is the result of a dispute over the succession after the death of the Prophet Muhammad in 632. Sunnis believe that a member of Muhammad's original Quraysh tribe should have been the next leader, while Shia (or Shiite) believe Muhammad's successor should have been his son-in-law and cousin. Sunni Muslims constitute about 87–90 percent of the world's 1.7 billion Muslims, and are the majority in Egypt, Saudi Arabia, and most other Muslim countries. Shia Muslims constituted 10–13 percent of the world's Muslim population, and are the majority in Iran, Iraq, Yemen, Bahrain, Azerbaijan, and Lebanon. Followers of each branch view adherents of the other branch as if they were non-believers, and it is probably the most important split in the Middle East today. The fourth reason for the conflict in Syria is the rise of radical Islamists who want to create an Islamic state based on Sharia law. And fifth is the increased desire within Syria and elsewhere of ethnic groups, most notably the Kurds, who wish to have their own nation-state.

By the end of 2015 the war had claimed 300 000 lives and displaced 15 million people; 11 million (about half the Syrian population) have fled their homes and moved somewhere else in Syria, while 4 million have fled to other countries (Eakin and Roth 2015). Most leave by foot or car with little more than the clothes they wear, fleeing to Turkey, Lebanon, Jordan, Greece, and elsewhere. Thousands have died along the way, most notably those whose small overcrowded boats capsized while attempting to cross the Mediterranean Sea (Figure 14.8). Most of the refugees live in camps, where diseases such as tuberculosis and measles are increasing and where most children do not go to school (Eakin and Roth 2015).

World leaders remain divided on how best to respond to the crisis. While Turkey, Greece, Macedonia,

Paula Bronstein/Getty Images

FIGURE 14.8 Syrian refugees arriving on the eastern coast of Lesbos. More than 400 migrants and refugees landed every day in 2015 on Lesbos Island, pushing to its limit the authorities' capability to process them.

and Jordan struggle with the sheer number of refugees, Germany has announced it would take 800 000, while the United States little more than 2000. Between December 2015 and the end of April 2016, Canada settled more than 27 000 Syrians and plans to welcome thousands more (Zilio 2016). According to one poll, over two-thirds of Canadians support the government's response to the Syrian refugee crisis, while there are concerns that there may not be enough resources to support their resettlement (Zilio 2016). About 30 percent of Canadians, however, oppose the government's response, arguing that the screening process is too short, which could permit terrorists to enter the country; that resources should be spent on Canadians, and that refugees would take away jobs.

Refugees and Anthropology

Refugees are often portrayed by governments as numbers and as problems to be solved (Kose et al. 2004), whereas anthropologists see them as human beings with their own issues, histories, cultures, identities, and personal experiences. Anthropologists have been interested in forced migrants and refugees for decades, and it is now a major area within anthropology. We want to know why people move, what happens to them when they arrive at their host countries, how it has impacted their sense of identity, how they draw upon their culture and community to survive, and much more. Anthropologists also want to know what the impact is on the home country, and how relationships with the people they have left behind are maintained and change. There are also questions about how they are integrated into their host societies, and how those societies in turn are impacted (Kose et al. 2004). From an applied perspective, anthropologists what to know how they can work with refugees and migrants to improve their lives, how anthropology can inform policy and practice, and how they can advocate for refugees' needs and rights.

Sustainable Economic Development for Marginalized Peoples

Today's countries can be divided into roughly two broad categories: the haves and the have-nots. This dichotomy is sometimes characterized as the industrialized versus the non-industrialized worlds, or the developed versus the developing worlds. There is considerable disagreement about the reasons for these differences, but no one can deny the vast differences in material wealth between the richest nations (such as Canada, Norway, Switzerland, the United States, and Sweden) and the poorest nations (such as Liberia, Burundi, Niger, and the Democratic Republic of the Congo).

The Impact of Development

A current debate in development anthropology revolves around the question of whether rising incomes and standards of living always have a positive effect on all parties concerned. Modernization theorists answer this question affirmatively, but a number of studies over the past several decades have strongly suggested that economic growth and development do not always improve people's lives. Some have even suggested that economic progress (as defined by rising wages, increased GNP, and so on) has actually lowered the quality of life for many non-Western people (Bodley 2007, 2008). Despite the best intentions of international development agencies, multimillion-dollar foreign aid projects have often resulted in greater poverty, longer working hours, overpopulation, poorer health, more social pathology, and environmental degradation.

Contrary to conventional thinking, many of the anticipated benefits of economic development have turned out to be illusory or detrimental. Attempts to engage non-Western people in programs of planned economic development often result in an increase in the incidence of disease for four reasons. First, many of the more modern lifestyles that people adopt bring new diseases associated with the industrialized world. For example, as early as the 1970s, Charles Hughes and John Hunter (1972) and Ian Prior (1971) found that rapid cultural change was followed by dramatic increases in the incidence of diseases such as diabetes, heart disease, obesity, hypertension, gout, and high blood pressure in areas where these conditions previously had been unknown. Second, the incidence of certain bacterial or parasitic diseases increases precipitously in areas experiencing rapid cultural change. To illustrate, the construction of dams and irrigation systems in the Sudan as part of the Azande development scheme created ideal breeding conditions for the snail larva that causes schistosomiasis, one of Africa's most deadly diseases. Third, environmental degradation caused by drilling for oil and gas, mining, and industrial pollution present a host of health threats to people in developing nations. As Alicia Fentiman (2009) has suggested, Nigerian fishing people in the Niger Delta face contaminated drinking water, skin disorders from bathing in oil-polluted water, and respiratory diseases from oil flairs as a direct result of oil drilling by the Shell Oil Company. And fourth, health problems in the developing world are further aggravated by the rapid urbanization that often accompanies economic development. People crowding into cities looking for employment have more exposure to contagious diseases, which are made even worse by poor nutrition and unsanitary living conditions.

Programs of economic development often lead to changes in people's dietary habits. In some cases, these dietary changes are voluntary to the extent that some new foods associated with powerful outsiders are status symbols. But more often than not, diets change because of circumstances associated with the objectives of economic development that are beyond the control of the local people. For example, in an attempt to grow more cash crops (which help to raise wages and bring in foreign exchange capital), non-Western people often divert time and energy from growing their normal subsistence crops. The result is that they spend much of their hard-earned cash on foods that are both costly and nutritionally inferior to feed their families.

This was the case among Brazilian farmers who made the transition from growing food crops to growing sisal, a cash crop used in the production of rope (Gross and Underwood 1971). Although the farmers spent most of their income on food, they could not provide adequate nutrition for their families. The study showed that the children of sisal workers were particularly at risk for their physical and mental development and overall health because most of the food went to the adults so they could maintain the strength needed for their strenuous work.

People also eat food that is worse for them than their traditional diets. Often these foods, purchased rather than homegrown, are low in minerals, vitamins, fibre, and protein, but high in sugar, sodium, and saturated fats, leading to an increased incidence of nutrition-related diseases: for example, the lack of protein may cause kwashiorkor (protein malnutrition), a leading cause of death in Africa and other parts of the developing world. The marked increase in sugar consumption by non-Western people has led to both a rapid and dramatic deterioration of dental health (Bodley 2008) and an alarmingly high rate of obesity among the world's poor (Figure 14.9).

Economic development programs can have had deleterious effects on sizable segments of the target populations. Not only is health negatively affected, but other unfortunate (and usually unanticipated) consequences also occur. The natural environment is often degraded, families break down, social problems increase, and support systems disintegrate. In most cases economic development brings with it higher productivity, lower prices for goods and services, and a rising standard of living; however, higher productivity may lead to fewer jobs as a result of automation or outsourcing. Automobiles in developing countries get better and more affordable,

imageBROKER/Alamy Stock Photo

FIGURE 14.9 Obesity is becoming a major worldwide epidemic, even among the relatively poor peoples of the world. These obese women in a fast food restaurant at the Central Market, San José, Costa Rica, remind us that obesity is no longer a medical problem exclusive to Westerners.

but as cars become more desirable, the roads become jammed with traffic, air pollution increases, and people waste more time stuck in traffic. Economic development brings higher living standards, but stress, anxiety, and clinical depression become more prevalent.

Not all these stories of development are bad, however. Quinoa is a grain-like crop grown in the Andean regions of Peru, Bolivia, Ecuador, and Columbia and is usually harvested by hand (Figure 14.10). Because it is high in protein and essential amino acids, it has become known as a "superfood" and is becoming increasingly popular in Canada, the United States, Europe, and China. Skyrocketing demand has made it extremely expensive; prices tripled between 2006 and 2013 (Collyns 2013) and almost doubled, from $120 per pound to $200 per pound, between July and August 2013 (Harvey 2013). A number of articles have suggested that it has become so expensive that the local people who grow it, and traditionally consumed it as a staple, can no longer afford to eat it and so rely on less nutritious foods such as pasta and rice, and imported junk foods. The demand has led to an increasing quinoa monoculture at the expense of a more diverse range of crops. Indeed, Bolivian production expanded from 240 square miles of farmland in 2009 to 400 square miles in 2012 (Harvey 2013). The increasing demand for quinoa has been cited as an another example where Western consumers are causing poverty and poor health in less-developed countries—or at least that is what some headlines have suggested (Blythman 2013; Collyns 2013).

George Steinmetz/Getty Images

FIGURE 14.10 Bolivian woman harvesting quinoa.

The reality, however, is that the demand has benefitted Andean peoples more than it has harmed them. While it is true that prices have risen and more land is devoted to gowning quinoa, anthropologist Pablo Laguna, who has studied quinoa's influence on local communities and worked with farmers in Bolivia for years, says that they are "quite enthusiastic" about the rise in quinoa's popularity (Harvey 2013). As the price increases, farmers plant more of the crop and make more money (Aubrey 2013). They also typically set aside a portion of the quinoa they grow for themselves. Under Fair Trade agreements their incomes have increased substantially and they are actually adding variety to their diets by eating more vegetables and meat than before because they can now afford to. Laguna says it has increased life-expectancy by about six years since 1995 (Harvey 2013). He also claims they turn to Western diets of processed foods not because they have to but because they have become status symbols (Harvey 2013). The Bolivian government claims that annual consumption of quinoa has quadrupled in recent years, and they are promoting it to combat malnutrition (Collyns 2013) and integrating it into school lunches and meals for the armed forces and pregnant women (Harvey 2013). Bolivia is the poorest country in South America and quinoa cultivation is beginning to lift the farming communities of Bolivia out of extreme poverty.

To be certain, there are segments of non-Western populations that benefit from programs of economic development, but large numbers wind up worse off than they would have been if the development efforts had never begun. To point out these negative consequences, however, is not to suggest that we should abandon foreign assistance or development programs, or stop trying to increase people's access to material resources. The negative results occur most often when development programs are introduced without the full participation and understanding of the people they are designed to help. They are, in other words, "top-down" programs that fail to involve the local people in planning and administration and, perhaps more wrong-headed, fail to ask the appropriate questions about the cultures of the people who are the prospective beneficiaries of the program.

Specifically, what socio-cultural information can anthropologists provide to assist economic development efforts? For example, if a development agency wants to resettle a group of nomadic cattle herders onto farmland so that they can become agriculturalists, the agency will need to know the answers to a number of *cultural* questions to assess (a) how best to meet the program's objectives or (b) whether they should attempt the project at all. To illustrate, the following questions about nomadic pastoralists—routinely asked by anthropologists—are but a few of the many that need answers:

- How are resources shared and distributed in the community?
- What material goods are highly valued, and how are they related to other nonmaterial aspects of the culture?
- How is labour divided according to age and gender?
- Do household tasks change according to the season of the year?
- What is the composition of the family (the basic economic unit)?
- Are there significant differences in family composition throughout the society?
- How stratified (in terms of wealth, power, and prestige) is the society?
- How is decision-making power distributed? Are some groups or individuals systematically excluded from positions of power?

If we take seriously the notion of the systemic nature of culture, then we must assume that a change in one part of the system is likely to bring about changes in other parts. It is only when development planners understand the nature of those parts, and how they are interrelated, that they can anticipate what some of the negative consequences may be and thus take steps to mitigate or avoid them. And because cultural anthropologists are the ones *on the ground* studying the cultures of those local populations targeted for sustainable development projects, it is only logical that anthropologists be intimately involved in the design, administration, and evaluation of sustainable development projects.

The literature on development anthropology is filled with examples of *good* development projects and *bad* ones or—put another way—those that have been largely beneficial to local people and those that have caused more harm than good. As a general rule, good programs of sustainable economic development are those that are initiated from within the country and culture(s) rather than imposed by some well-meaning, but often short-sighted, international development agencies such as the World Bank.

One recent sustainable economic development program was started by the not-for-profit organization called PhytoTrade Africa, established in 2002 as a trade association for natural products (i.e., products derived from indigenous plants and used in the food, drink, and cosmetic industries) in southern Africa (Cox 2008). PhytoTrade Africa's purpose is to alleviate poverty, protect biodiversity, and develop economically successful industries that are ethical, environmentally friendly, and sustainable. The organization accomplishes its goals in three key ways: by identifying and developing new products, by developing world markets for these new products, and by nurturing local African harvesters and producers.

One of the major products PhytoTrade has identified and is bringing to world markets is the harvestable fruit of the baobab tree, which grows naturally and abundantly throughout southern and eastern Africa (Figure 14.11). PhytoTrade partners with local fruit distribution companies (such as the Baobab Fruit Company of Senegal) that agree to purchase their fruit only from those local suppliers who meet their health and processing standards. Thus, local individuals and families harvest the baobab fruit and sell it for a fair market price to local or regional distribution companies.

The fruit of the baobab tree is becoming a popular food product because it has a number of desirable features. Traditionally, it was used as a highly nutritious and tasty snack for children; a dietary supplement for pregnant women; medicine to relieve stomach aches, fevers,

FIGURE 14.11 PhytoTrade Africa is a company that is starting local sustainable industries using the fruit from baobab trees such as this one in Botswana.

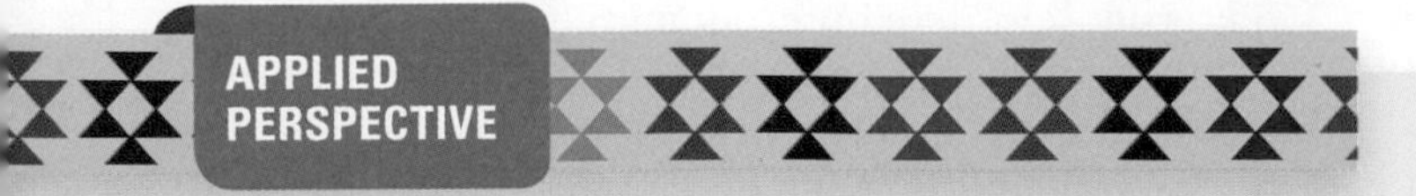

The Nicaragua Grand Canal Project

The centuries-old dream of building a canal through Central America and thus avoiding the long sea voyage around South America or South Africa was realized in 1914 with the opening of the Panama Canal. But the canal is now over 100 years old and, with the increase in global trade in recent decades, it is unable to handle the growing volume, resulting in congestion and delays. It is also too shallow to accommodate the world's nearly 1000 container megaships, which will increase to about 3000 by 2019 (Llana 2006). Such megaships sailing from the east coast of North America to Japan could save about $2 million and 34 days round-trip per ship (Llana 2006). The increasing ship size and the fact that global maritime trade is expected to increase substantially over the coming decades makes a compelling argument for a second, larger, canal.

In June 2013, the Nicaraguan government of Daniel Ortega approved construction of a 259 kilometre canal running through the country from the Atlantic to the Pacific to rival the Panama Canal. The Nicaragua Interoceanic Grand Canal, as it sometimes called, would handle ships twice the size of those currently using the Panama Canal and nearly double the traffic (Llana 2006). One of the largest civil works projects in history, it is estimated to cost $40–$50 billion and take five years to build. It is being financed by the Hong Kong Nicaragua Canal Development Investment Company (HKND), which is headed by Chinese billionaire Wang Jing. In addition to the canal, the project also involves building two port facilities, an international airport, a dam and hydroelectric facility to generate power to operate the locks, a bridge for the Pan-American Highway, numerous road improvements, and a reservoir called Lake Atlanta to provide water for one of the canal's locks (HKND 2015a). The route was approved in July 2014, and a ground-breaking ceremony was held in December 2014, although little construction had taken place as of November 2015. On November 5, 2015, the Nicaraguan government approved the Environmental Impact study, opening the way for construction to begin in earnest (HKND 2015b).

The project, if it is completed, will have a major impact on world trade and especially on the six million people of Nicaragua. Nicaragua is the second poorest country in Central America after Honduras (Pasquali 2015), with an unemployment rate among Indigenous people of nearly 85 percent (Watts 2015). HKND estimates that the project will triple the size of the economy and generate 50 000 jobs, half of which will be filled by Nicaraguans (HKND 2015a), thus helping to enhance the overall living standards of the Nicaraguan people and pulling the country out of poverty (Watts 2015; HKND 2015c). An opinion poll conducted in March 2015, found that 83 percent of Nicaraguans support the project, while only 16 percent are opposed to it (HKND 2015a).

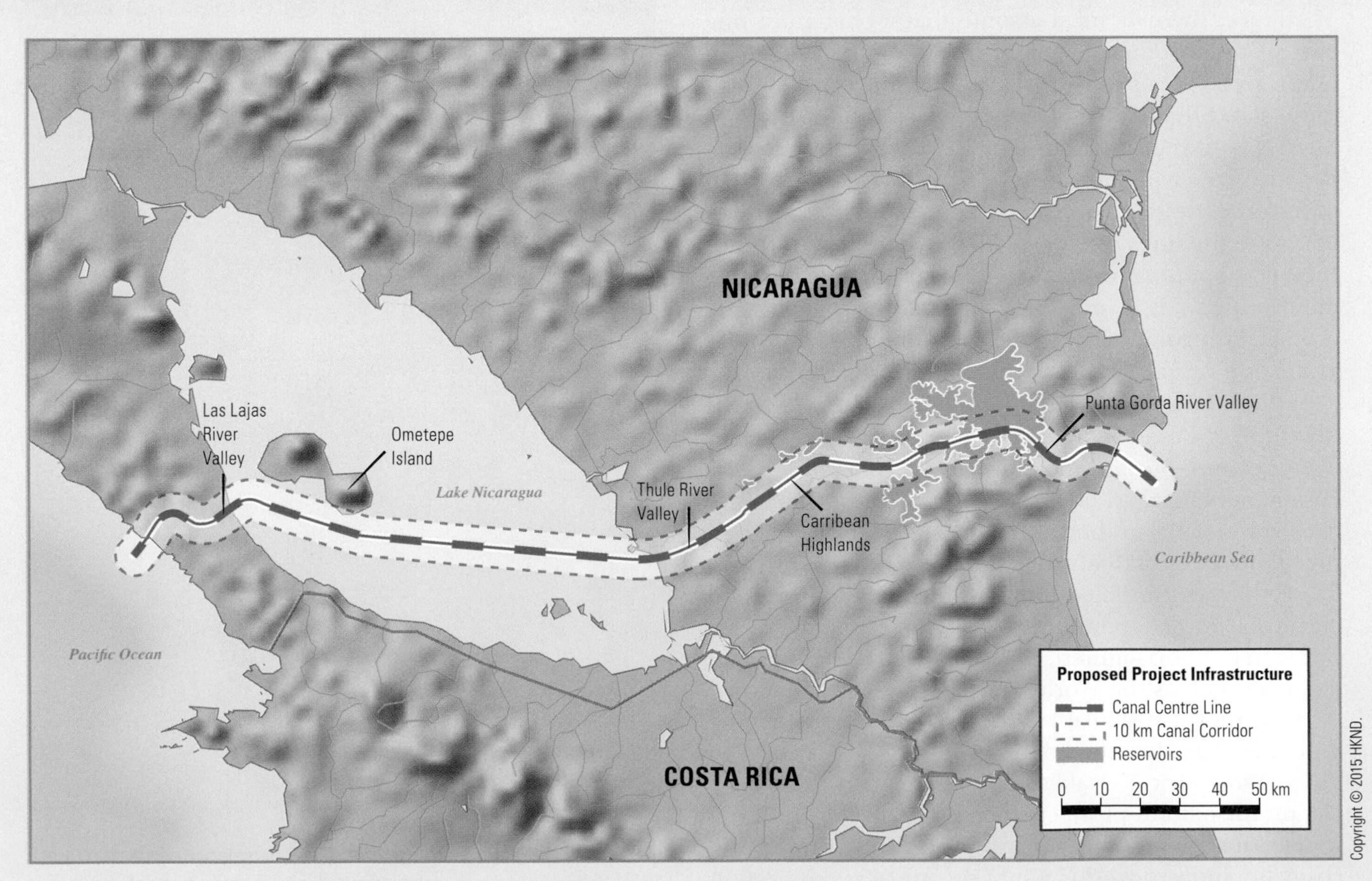

The proposed route of the Nicaragua Canal

A project of this size does not, however, come without controversy. Approval was given without assessment of the environmental and social impacts and without consulting the people it will most affect. One of the biggest issues is the environmental impact it will have on Lake Nicaragua, the largest and most important freshwater reservoir in Central America (Watts 2015). The plan calls for dredging the lake and there are concerns about stirring up toxic wastes, irreparably damaging fragile ecosystems, destroying wetlands and tropical forests, introducing invasive species, and polluting the lake (Herrera 2013). The planned route covers the historic homelands of seven Indigenous peoples (Kjaerby 2015), as well as several peoples of African descent known as "ethnic communities." Many of these peoples depend on the resources of Lake Nicaragua and surrounding forest for their survival (Llana 2006). Unsurprisingly, support for the project by those most affected is only 42 percent (HKND 2015a).

The HKND contract also gives the company the right to expropriate land for the canal. Farmers in local villages claim up to 120 000 people could be displaced by the plans (Ward 2015), while the 2015 Environmental and Social Impact Assessment (ESIA) estimates 30 000 residents need to be relocated (HKND 2015a). This will involve moving 277 villages and completely relocating the Rama, an Indigenous community with only about 2000 people (Kjaerby 2015). Activist and anthropologist Jennifer Goett (2013) notes that people do not know how their livelihoods will be impacted, or what will happen to them, and are afraid that compensation for their property will not match current market value. If they do not have title to the land, which many do not, they will receive little or no compensation (Kjaerby 2015; HKND 2015a). The canal will necessarily involve the forced relocation of people and major disruption of their lives, and will require "reinvention of self and community that is far more profound than what we face under the 'normal' pace of rapid social and cultural change" (Oliver-Smith 2010, 3).

Understandably, the Nicaragua Interoceanic Grand Canal project faces significant opposition from the Indigenous peoples and ethnic communities facing expropriation, or directly affected by the canal, who have been organizing and vigorously protesting against the project (Ward 2015). Most of the opposition concerns the legality of the contract and the fact that the decision was made without an environmental impact study, without consultation or informed consent, and without any legal obligation to compensate or resettle the displaced people—yet it threatens the environment, livelihood, and existence of tens of thousands of people. By protesting against their government and HKND, the Indigenous people of Nicaragua are placing themselves in the middle of global development politics, which tends to favour the Western ideal of progress (Oliver-Smith 2010).

Development projects, such as the Nicaragua Grand Canal, typically favour national and global interests over people at the local level who are most affected by them. Oliver-Smith (2005) points out that "reigning development models, promoting large-scale infrastructural projects, transform social and physical environments and espouse the concept of "the greatest good for the greatest number" while attempting to safe-guard local rights and well-being. Although the record has yet to reflect it, such a position assumes that the less powerful will eventually benefit from the project through well-designed and implemented resettlement programs" (p. 214). Thus, while they hold out the promise of economic growth and improvement in the general welfare, such projects often leave local peoples "displaced, disempowered and destitute" (Oliver-Smith 2010, 2).

French anthropologist Pierre Bourdieu has said that "those who have the good fortune to be able to devote their lives to the study of the social world cannot stand aside, neutral and indifferent, from the struggles in which the future of that world is at stake" (Bourdieu 2003, 11). So what role can anthropologists play in the struggles faced by Nicaragua's Indigenous peoples? Indeed, should they get involved? Peter Kellett asks some pointed questions: "Is the role of the anthropologist to try to change the world or to 'merely' understand it? Can (and should) anthropologists act as advocates for the rights of people they study, or does this compromise their objectivity?.... Should the anthropologist act to try to improve the circumstances of local people? Should the anthropologist act as intermediary and voice on behalf of local people, particularly when requested to do so? Should anthropologists engage as active agents of change?" (Kellett 2009, 1–2). There are no easy answers to these questions.

Advocacy anthropology is a type of applied anthropology in which anthropologists proactively use their knowledge and

Inti Ocon/AFP/Getty Images

Many Indigenous people depend on Lake Nicaragua for their livelihood, which may end if the canal is built, and are opposed to its construction.

(*Continued*)

The Nicaragua Grand Canal Project (*Continued*)

skills to represent, defend, and advocate for the rights of the disempowered or marginalized people they study. While it is unethical to assist governments and corporations to achieve their goals if they cause harm to people (and we should ask ourselves whether we can stand aside when we see the people we study being harmed), it is not always clear whether, and to what extent, such plans harm people. On the one hand, building the Nicaragua Canal will cause massive social dislocations, but on the other, there appear to be clear economic benefits, and not all people are opposed to the canal.

Anthropologists are in a unique position in that they possess knowledge of the Indigenous peoples and how development projects will affect them, and at the same time they generally have a better understanding of global economics and politics than do Indigenous peoples. Perhaps the anthropologist's role should be to educate governments about how their plans will impact their own people and make recommendations. At the same time, perhaps their role is to educate the people they study and help equip them with the knowledge and skills to make changes or engage in self-advocacy. Or perhaps it is the job of the anthropologists to inform the public of the situation and the plight of the people they study. Finally, perhaps anthropologists should become involved in the issues surrounding the construction of the canal and advocate for Indigenous rights. To date, few anthropologists have; although anthropologist Jennifer Goett (2013) is attempting to raise funds to help mount a legal defence through the crowdfunding site Indiegogo.

Questions for Further Thought

1. What development projects in Canada currently impact the lives of Canada's Indigenous peoples, and how?
2. Should anthropologists advocate for the rights of the people they study and, if so, what should they do?
3. How will the Indigenous people affected by the Nicaraguan Grand Canal adapt to being forcibly relocated or their environment irrevocably changed, and what role can anthropologists play to assist them?

and malaria; and, when hydrated, a refreshingly tangy drink similar to lemonade. It is exceptionally nutritious, containing high levels of antioxidants, essential minerals such as calcium, potassium, iron, and magnesium, and twice as much vitamin C as an orange. Today, baobab fruit powder (which is just one form of the product) is being used in a wide variety of food and drink products sold internationally, including smoothies, juices, breakfast cereals, cereal bars, snacks, ice cream, yogurt, jams, sauces, marinades, specialty teas, and health supplements.

All of these features make the new African baobab fruit industry a highly successful effort at sustainable economic development. Most importantly, it is a homegrown development project using local resources and giving the target population a real stake in creating and maintaining profitable employment. Because the major product of the development project (fruit from baobab trees) has played both economic and spiritual roles in the traditional culture, local harvesters protect their sacred baobab trees as well as earn a good livelihood from them. From an anthropological perspective, this project is culturally sensitive because local people are using their own resources, labour, and work procedures to earn a reasonable income. And, as a bonus, it is enabling the African harvesters and entrepreneurs to provide a highly nutritious food product to the rest of the world.

Indigenous population People who are the original inhabitants of a region, identify with a specific cultural heritage, and play little significant role in government.

Cultural Survival of Indigenous Peoples

In recent years, cultural anthropologists have become increasingly concerned with a particular type of cultural change—namely, the rapid disappearance of Indigenous populations of the world. An ***Indigenous population*** is a group of people who (a) are the original inhabitants of a region; (b) identify with a specific, small-scale cultural heritage; and (c) have no significant role in the government (Bodley 2008, 4). Classic examples of Indigenous peoples are the hundreds of small-scale cultures in Asia, Africa, and the Americas that came under the influence of colonial powers during the past several centuries.

Many anthropologists are concerned about the survival of these Indigenous peoples, not because they are the subject of much anthropological research, but because their disappearance is a basic human rights issue. A growing number of cultural anthropologists feel strongly that Indigenous populations over the past several centuries have been negatively affected by the onslaught of civilization. Cultural patterns—and in some cases the people themselves—have been eradicated as a direct result of civilization's pursuit of "progress" and economic development.

A number of anthropologists, historians, and journalists have documented specific examples of the demise of Indigenous populations over the course of the past 150 years. In fact, one anthropologist, John Bodley (2007, 2008), has devoted much of his career reminding us how the spread of civilization and industrialization has resulted in the creation of millions of "victims of progress" throughout the non-Western world. These tragic consequences, all done in the name of civilization, economic development, and progress, have included everything from the annihilation of the entire population of Tasmania in the 19th century to the introduction of measles and influenza to the Indigenous peoples of the Amazon when the government built roads through the Brazilian frontier.

Anthropologists believe that one of the most dramatic examples of the degradation of Indigenous peoples is in the Brazilian Amazon, where Indigenous groups are being swept away by the relentless movement of resettlement and economic development. To illustrate, during the 1960s an Cinta Larga village in Brazil was attacked by a gang of gunslingers allegedly hired by a large Brazilian corporation that wanted them off the land. Shelton Davis (1977) described the Massacre at Parallel Eleven, in which hired hit men attempted to wipe out the village and its inhabitants by throwing dynamite from a low-flying airplane. During the 1970s the threats to Indigenous peoples, although not quite so blatantly genocidal, were no less devastating. By building roads through the Amazonian frontier, the Brazilian government introduced diseases such as influenza and measles to the Indigenous peoples of the region. By the beginning of the 1990s, tens of thousands of gold prospectors had invaded the territory of the Yanomamö (Figure 14.12), extracting millions of dollars' worth of gold from the land and leaving the Yanomamö ravaged by disease (Brooke 1990).

FIGURE 14.12 In 2007 this leader of a group of Yanomamö from the Amazon region presented to German Chancellor Merkel a letter urging Germany to sign Convention No. 169 concerning protecting the rights of Indigenous and tribal peoples living in independent countries.

The 21st century has presented additional challenges to the cultural survival of Indigenous peoples. To illustrate, the Tikuna community in western Brazil (close to the border with Colombia and Peru) has become an important link in drug trafficking. Some young Indigenous Tikuna men, working as drug "mules," use their knowledge of the rivers and dense rain forest to carry cocaine into Brazil's substantial drug market. Unfortunately, not only are a growing number of Tikuna men working in the illicit drug trade, but also many have become addicted to both cocaine and alcohol. In addition to facing unemployment, disease, poor healthcare, substance abuse, and the destruction of their natural environment, contemporary Tikunas are struggling to keep some vestiges of their traditional culture (Barrionuevo 2008).

Not only do cultural anthropologists document the demise of Indigenous peoples, but many also use their specialized knowledge to help these endangered cultures survive against the homogenizing effects of globalization. In one of the most urgent forms of applied anthropology, a number of cultural anthropologists in recent years have contributed to the efforts of Cultural Survival, Inc., a non-profit organization that supports projects on five continents that was designed to help Indigenous peoples survive the changes brought about by contact with industrial societies. In partnership with Indigenous peoples, Cultural Survival advocates for native communities, whose rights, cultures, and dignity are threatened, by (a) strengthening their languages and cultures, (b) educating their communities about their rights, and (c) fighting marginalization, discrimination, and exploitation.

Cultural Survival works to guarantee the land and resource rights of tribal peoples while supporting economic development projects run by the people themselves. As part of their work with Cultural Survival, cultural anthropologists have conducted research on vital cultural issues, served as cultural brokers between the Indigenous peoples and government officials, and published literature informing the public about the urgency of these survival issues. To help support its work, Cultural Survival has maintained, for more than three decades, the premier databank for anthropological and social scientific information on the Indigenous peoples of the world. This vast collection of literature is available free of charge from the Cultural Survival website (www .culturalsurvival.org). *Cultural Survival Quarterly*, the organization's major publication, is an award-winning periodical specializing in articles written by anthropologists and non-anthropologists, with a number of pieces written by Indigenous peoples themselves. A periodic newsletter, *Cultural Survival Voices*, is circulated to more than 350 Indigenous organizations worldwide, providing them with the practical information they need to protect their cultures and native territories.

At any given time, Cultural Survival has a number of ongoing projects around the world. One such project entails working with Panama's largest Indigenous group, the Ngobe, whose homeland is being threatened by a hydroelectric dam (Lutz 2007, 2008).

Numbering about 170 000 people, the Ngobe, who occupy a remote area in western Panama, have traditionally supported themselves by subsistence agriculture and fishing. In the past several years, however, a U.S. construction company, in partnership with the Panamanian government, has started building a major hydroelectric dam on the river that runs through the Ngobe homeland. It has been estimated that the new dam will swallow up the homes and lands of more than a thousand people. Other Ngobe, who will not lose their land, will become even more isolated by losing their transportation routes. Moreover, the dam will disrupt the migration of several fish species that make up a significant portion of the Ngobe diet.

Even though a new hydroelectric dam will provide a much-needed supply of "clean" energy, the Ngobe case has become a human rights battleground largely because of the heavy-handed way the U.S. company and the government of Panama have treated the Ngobe people. Many of the Ngobe, under enormous pressure to sell their lands to the government, put their thumb-prints on sales contracts that they could not read and did not understand. In other cases, people's homes were destroyed and their lands confiscated in the absence of even bogus contracts. When the local people staged a peaceful protest against the dam project in January 2008, government police in riot gear attacked the protesters with clubs; by the end of the day they had arrested 54 people, including 13 children and 2 infants. After this incident, the construction site was cordoned off to any outsiders who sought to meet with the Ngobe.

Organizations such as Cultural Survival—and its local Panamanian partner, the Alliance for Conservation and Development (ACD)—are intensifying their efforts to block the dam project until these blatant human rights injustices have been resolved. The ACD has been pressing the government to legally justify its cordoning off of Ngobe property. It is also conducting workshops for Indigenous peoples on their legal rights as Panamanian citizens and, more practically, on how to file legal complaints with their government. The dam was completed, however, over the protests of the Ngobe people, environmentalists, and human rights advocates in Panama, and despite precautionary measures taken by the Inter-American Commission on Human Rights. In early June 2011, the construction company began filling the reservoir, which flooded the homes of the Ngobe who had refused to negotiate a settlement with the company. Recently, the Ngobe people and the various opponents of the dam had cause to celebrate when Panama's National Public Service Authority (ASEP) decided to prevent AES Corporation from building a second dam on the Changuinola River.

Multiculturalism

If, as we suggested previously in this chapter, the many cultures of the world are not becoming a single homogeneous mega-culture, then what is the most sensible foreign policy strategy for interacting with other peoples of the world? Rather than deliberately trying to eradicate cultural differences, a more workable approach is some type of ***multiculturalism***, that is, an official policy that recognizes the worth and integrity of different cultures at home and abroad. Such an approach, which has been operating effectively in

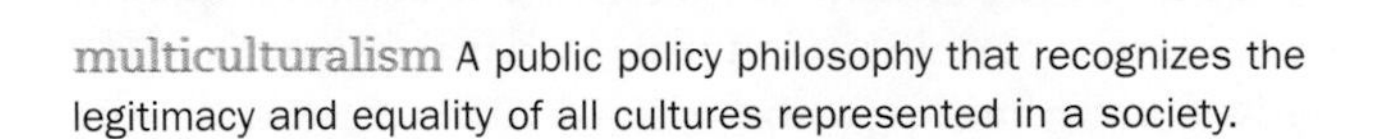

multiculturalism A public policy philosophy that recognizes the legitimacy and equality of all cultures represented in a society.

Canada for generations, requires the basic anthropological understanding that culturally different people are not inherently perverse or immoral. Rather, it is possible to live together in peaceful coexistence, provided we understand the logic of culturally different peoples and are willing to negotiate with them in good faith and without exploitation.

At the least, multiculturalism requires an awareness that people from other cultures who do not share our cultural assumptions, probably do not sympathize with some of our behaviours, ideas, and values. For example, living in a culture that highly prizes individualism, most middle-class Canadians see themselves as strong, competitive, assertive, and independent achievers. People with a more collective value orientation, in contrast, view North Americans in far less flattering terms as self-absorbed greedy materialists with hardly a shred of altruism.

Multiculturalism remains the best hope for enabling all people to have the security, prosperity, and freedom they desire and deserve. And yet multiculturalism should not be seen as a totally selfless and altruistic philosophy. Rather it should be considered a win-win opportunity.

Summary

1. Globalization can be defined as the process of forging international, political, economic, religious, and socio-cultural interconnections and interdependencies.
2. Most scholars trace the beginning of globalization to the early 1500s, when European nations began to explore and colonize the world, increasing their control over societies in distant lands through technological advances in navigation, ship building, cartography, and warfare.
3. European colonization, involving the actual possession and administration of foreign territories, proved exceedingly beneficial for the economic and political growth of the European colonial powers, but the Indigenous populations paid a high price.
4. Modernization theory posits that, for developing nations to become developed, they must engage in activities and acquire the characteristics that will make them more like the developed nations.
5. World systems theory posits that the world is divided into three areas, core, periphery, and semi-periphery to create a systematic political and economic network of exchange whereby the wealthy nations exploit the poorer ones.
6. Neocolonialism is the idea that, after former colonies gain independence, the developed countries continue to maintain political and economic dependency and exploitation of former colonies and less developed countries through economic, financial, and trade policies that favour themselves.
7. Decolonization is the dismantling of colonial empires by the withdrawal of colonial powers from their colonies, and the acquisition of self-determination and government in the newly independent states. Cultural decolonization is the process of the colonized freeing their minds from the ideologies and cultures of the colonizers and reclaiming their traditional cultures and identities.
8. As part of the cultural decolonization process, Indigenous groups try to prevent further cultural appropriation. The distinction between appropriation as borrowing and as exploitation raises ethical dilemmas and has become a big issue on social media. Another aspect of decolonization is the repatriation of cultural items taken from Indigenous peoples.
9. The processes of globalization are primarily economic and have been helped by lower costs and improvements in technology, transportation, and communication.
10. It is unreasonable to expect that the world, through the process of globalization, is moving relentlessly toward a single, homogeneous culture. Local cultures are modifying global forces to generate new cultural identities.
11. The basic trends of the post–World War II era that concern anthropologists are world immigration patterns; the rise of religious fundamentalism; rapid urbanization in Africa, Asia, and Latin America; the spread of world health pandemics such as AIDS; environmental degradation; and the widening gap between the rich and the poor throughout the world.
12. One of the biggest concerns facing the world today is the increasing number of refugees fleeing persecution and conflict in Syria and elsewhere. The study of refugees and migrants is now a major area within anthropology.
13. A major concern of anthropology in the past half-century has been sustainable economic development for the poor and marginalized peoples of the world. Because anthropologists study the alleged beneficiaries of economic development projects in a face-to-face way, they are in the best position to

ascertain whether the projects are actually helping the local populations.

14. Cultural anthropologists, through such organizations as Cultural Survival, work to help Indigenous populations survive the onslaught of civilization and "economic progress."
15. With the world and all its 5000-plus cultural groups becoming increasingly interconnected, all nations must become more multicultural; that is, they must become more adept at understanding and dealing with people from different cultural traditions. If the world is to successfully meet the challenges of this century, people can no longer afford to have an us-versus-them mentality because resolving our problems depends on cross-cultural understanding. And there is no academic discipline better equipped to provide cross-cultural understanding than anthropology.

Key Terms

colonialism
colonies of exploitation
core
cultural appropriation
cultural decolonization
decolonization
diaspora
economic migrants
globalization
Indigenous population
migrant
modernization theory
multiculturalism
multinational corporations
neocolonialism
periphery
refugee
repatriation
semi-periphery
settlement colonies
world systems theory

Critical Thinking Questions

1. What examples of globalization can you cite that affect the way all people live their lives today that did not exist 25 years ago? Be specific.
2. Does the core need the periphery to remain underdeveloped?
3. One of the effects of globalization is global warming. How has this affected Indigenous populations living in the Arctic?
4. What socio-cultural information can anthropologists provide to assist economic development efforts?
5. Many migrants come to Canada from Central America and elsewhere to help farmers with their crops because they can earn more than at home. Much of the money they make is sent back to family they have left behind. How would you research the impact of economic migration on the migrants themselves, their families, and societies left behind?
6. How can anthropologists work with Syrian refugees and other agencies to help them adapt to life in Canada?
7. When is cultural borrowing appropriate, and when is it inappropriate?
8. What strategies are Indigenous peoples using to decolonize?
9. Why might it be important to an Indigenous group to have their cultural objects returned to them?
10. In 2006 the Grameen Bank and its founder Muhammad Yunus received the Nobel Peace prize for helping poor people in developing countries escape poverty through microloans. Since then there have been several suggestions that Walmart also receive the Nobel Peace prize for helping poor people in developing countries escape poverty. Should it?

Make the Grade with MindTap

Stay organized and efficient with **MindTap**—a single destination with all the course material and study aids you need to succeed. Built-in apps leverage social media and the latest learning technology. For example:

- ReadSpeaker will read the text to you.
- Self-quizzing allows you to assess your understanding.
- Flashcards are pre-populated to provide you with a jump-start for review—or you can create your own.
- You can highlight text and make notes in your MindTap Reader. Your notes will flow into Evernote, the electronic notebook app that you can access anywhere when it's time to study for the exam.

Visit nelson.com/student to start using **MindTap**. Enter the Online Access Code from the card included with your text. If a code card is not provided, you can purchase instant access at NELSONbrain.com.

Glossary

absolute poverty The condition in a given society in which people lack the income required to access the necessities of life, such as food, clothing, and shelter, to achieve a minimum level of physical well-being.

accent The manner of pronouncing words.

acculturation A specific form of cultural diffusion in which a subordinate culture adopts many of the cultural traits of a more powerful culture.

acephalous societies Societies that have no political leaders such as a presidents, kings, or chiefs.

achieved status The status an individual acquires during the course of her or his lifetime.

adaptive nature of culture The implication that culture is the major way human populations adapt or relate to their specific habitat in order to survive and reproduce.

advocacy anthropology A branch of applied anthropology that advocates on behalf of the people studied.

affinal relatives Kinship ties formed through marriage (i.e., in-laws).

age grades Permanent age categories in a society through which people pass during the course of a lifetime.

age organizations A type of social organization wherein people of roughly the same age pass through different levels of society together; each ascending level, based on age, carries with it increased social status and rigidly defined roles.

age sets Groups of people roughly the same age who pass through various age grades together.

allocation of resources A society's regulation and control of such resources as land and water and their by-products.

ambilineal descent A form of descent in which a person chooses to affiliate with a kin group through either the male or the female line.

ambilocal (bilocal) residence A residence pattern in which the married couple may choose to live with either the relatives of the wife or the relatives of the husband.

animal husbandry The herding, breeding, and use of domesticated animals.

animism The belief that animals, plants, and inanimate objects are animated by spirits.

anthropological linguistics The scientific study of human communication within its socio-cultural context.

anthropological perspective The way anthropologists look at and understand peoples and cultures; that is, holistically, relativistically, naturalistically, comparatively, globally, bioculturally, and reflexively.

applied anthropology The application of anthropological knowledge, concepts, theories, and methods to the solution of specific societal problems.

applied medical anthropology The application of anthropological theories, concepts, and methods in the study of health, illness, and healing to improve the well-being of people everywhere.

archaeology The subfield of anthropology that focuses on the study of prehistoric, pre-contact, and historic cultures through the excavation of material remains.

arranged marriage A marriage in which the selection of the spouse is outside the control of the couple.

art The process and the product of applying certain skills to transform matter, sound, or motion into a form that is deemed aesthetically meaningful to people in a society.

artifact A type of material remains made or modified by humans, such as tools and arrowheads.

artlang A language created for artistic purposes to provide a sense of realism in novels, television shows, online games, and movies.

ascribed status The status a person has by virtue of birth.

attitudes Learned, positive or negative evaluations of an element of culture.

attitudinal data Information collected in a fieldwork situation that describes what a person thinks, believes, or feels.

authority The power or right to give commands, take action, and make binding decisions.

autocratic state A form of government controlled by a leader who holds absolute power and denies popular participation in decision making.

autoethnography An ethnographic method in which the ethnographer attempts to understand another culture through a description and analysis of their own fieldwork experience.

avunculocal residence A residence pattern in which the married couple lives with or near the husband's mother's brother.

backchannels Minimal responses to a speaker that serve to continue the conversation or to show agreement.

balanced reciprocity The practice of giving a gift with the expectation that it will be reciprocated with a similar gift after a limited period of time.

band societies Societies lacking formal political structure and where decisions are often embedded in the family; typically egalitarian, hunting-and-gathering societies.

barter The direct exchange of commodities between people that does not involve standardized currency.

behavioural data Information collected in a fieldwork situation that describes what a person does.

beliefs Ideas about what is true.

bicultural perspective The capacity to think and perceive in the categories of one's own culture as well as in the categories of a second culture.

bilateral descent A type of kinship system in which individuals emphasize both their mother's kin and their father's kin relatively equally.

binary oppositions A mode of thinking found in all cultures, according to Claude Lévi-Strauss, based on opposites, such as old-young, nature-nurture, and left-right.

biocultural Human existence is the product of both biological and cultural factors.

biological anthropology *See* **physical anthropology or biological anthropology.**

biomedical model The primary Western medical system in which disease is thought to be due to genetics or infection that affects the biology of the body, and where diagnosis and treatment are performed by highly trained specialists.

breadwinner A traditional North American gender role that views males as being responsible for the economic support and protection of the family.

bride service Work or service performed for the bride's family by the groom for a specified period of time either before or after the marriage.

bridewealth The transfer of goods from the groom's lineage to the bride's lineage to legitimize marriage.

business anthropology The application of anthropological concepts and methods to help businesses and other organizations improve productivity through understanding and managing culture.

Cambridge Expedition to the Torres Straits An 1898 British expedition that investigated the cultures and peoples of the Torres Straits.

cargo cult A Melanesian revitalization movement characterized by rituals intended to bring material goods, that is, cargo.

carrying capacity The maximum population size an environment can sustain, given the food and water resources and technology available.

caste A ranked group within a rigidly stratified society in which membership is ascribed at birth and social mobility is almost nonexistent.

cattle complex A situation among east African pastoralist cultures in which cattle have both economic and social functions.

census taking The collection of demographic data about the culture being studied.

chiefdom A form of political organization in which political authority is likely to reside with a single individual or chief and his or her advisors.

chiefly redistribution or tribute The practice in which goods (usually food) are given to a chief as a visible symbol of people's allegiance, and then the chief gives the items back to the people (usually in the form of a feast).

clan A unilineal descent group whose members claim a common ancestry even though they cannot trace step by step their exact connection to that ancestor.

class A ranked group within a stratified society characterized by achieved status and considerable social mobility.

closed society A society in which there are formal barriers preventing people from moving up the social hierarchy.

code switching Speakers of two or more languages or varieties of one language switch between the two, depending on the social context.

cognatic descent A form of descent traced through both females and males.

coincidence of wants The basic problem of barter whereby one exchange partner lacks what the other wants.

collaborator, research participant, cultural expert, or informant The person in the culture being researched who provides the ethnographer with information.

collaterality Kin relationships traced through a linking relative.

colonialism The political, economic, and socio-cultural domination of a territory and its people by a foreign nation.

colonies of exploitation European colonies where local economic resources were expropriated, and the Indigenous peoples used as cheap sources of labour.

common law People living together as a couple without being legally married.

communal cult A type of religious organization in which groups of ordinary people conduct religious ceremonies for the well-being of the total community.

communication The process of sharing information and knowledge through either language or some nonverbal system of meaning.

communitas The situation during the liminal phase of a rite of passage characterized by equality and fellowship.

community-based participatory research (CBPR) A collaboration involving partners from within a community in all aspects of the research process. Most importantly, CBPR begins with a research topic of importance to the community, and works toward achieving social change equitably.

consanguineal relatives One's biological or blood relatives.

constitution A set of laws that provide the basic rules and principles by which a state is structured and governed, and in many cases protects the rights of its citizens.

consumption The culturally relative way goods and services are consumed.

contagious magic Performing a magical ritual on something that has been in contact with someone to influence that person.

core Wealthy, technologically advanced nations that produce and exchange capital-intensive, complex, consumer products.

corporate lineages Kinship groups whose members engage in daily activities together.

corporate or organizational culture Everything people have, think, and do as members of a company or an organization.

counter-culture A subculture in which the norms and values are opposed to those of mainstream society.

creole A pidgin that has become a mother tongue or native language.

crime Harm to a person or property that society considers illegitimate.

cross cousins Children of one's mother's brothers or father's sisters.

cult A religious group that has its own set of beliefs, practices, and rituals.

cultural anthropology The branch of anthropology that studies specific contemporary cultures and the more general underlying patterns of human culture derived through cultural comparisons.

cultural appropriation Taking, adopting, and using the elements of one culture by members of another.

cultural construction of gender The ways a culture shapes individuals so they conform to that culture's concept of gender.

cultural core The constellation of features most closely related to subsistence activities.

cultural decolonization The process of the colonized freeing their minds from the ideologies and cultures of the colonizers and reclaiming their traditional cultures and identities.

cultural diffusion The spreading of a cultural trait (i.e., a material object, idea, or behavior pattern) from one society to another.

cultural ecology An approach to anthropology that examines the interactions between people who reside in similar environments and their technologies, social structures, and political institutions.

cultural expert *See* **collaborator, research participant, cultural expert, or informant.**

cultural genocide A process whereby a people lose their identity as a distinct culture through disposing of their lands and cultural hegemony.

cultural hegemony A process whereby a people are forcibly assimilated by a dominant culture.

cultural materialism An anthropological theory that cultural systems are most influenced by such material things as natural resources, technology and human biology.

cultural relativism The idea that cultural traits are best understood when viewed within the cultural context of which they are a part.

cultural resource management A form of applied archaeology that involves identifying, evaluating, and sometimes excavating sites before roads, dams, pipelines, and buildings are constructed.

cultural universals Those general cultural traits found in all societies of the world.

culture Everything that people have, think, and do as members of a society.

culture and personality A theoretical school in anthropology that looks at the relationship between culture and personality.

culture complex A group of closely related aspects of culture.

culture-historical archaeology An archaeological theory that separates societies or ethnic groups produce their own unique pattern of material culture that could be used to trace the diffusion of culture or the migration of people.

culture shock The feeling of anxiety and disorientation when experiencing a different culture.
culture type Cultures that shared similar core features.
cyberbullying The use of text messaging, instant messaging, and social media to harass people and cause harm.

Dalit The lowest stratum in Indian society, technically outside the caste system and formerly called *untouchables*.
dance Intentional, rhythmic, nonverbal body movements that are culturally patterned and have aesthetic value.
decolonization The dismantling of colonial empires by the withdrawal of colonial powers from their colonies, and the acquisition of self-determination and government in the newly independent states.
deduction Predicting an observation by reasoning from a general premise.
degenerationism A theory that so-called savage or primitive cultures had degenerated from more civilized cultures because they had fallen from God's Grace.
descent A person's kinship connections traced back through a number of generations.
descriptive linguistics The branch of anthropological linguistics that studies how languages are structured.
development anthropology The application of anthropological knowledge, theory, perspectives, and methods in projects that improve the well-being of people in marginalized communities.
dialect A regional or class variation of a language.
dialect continuum A chain of speech variants that are mutually intelligible between adjacent geographic areas, but the ends are mutually unintelligible.
diaspora The dispersion of a group of people from their original homeland.
dictatorship A nation-state in which one individual holds power.
diffusionism The late 19th and early 20th century theory that cultural differences can be explained by the diffusion of cultural traits from one society to another.
digital divide The differences between those who have access to information technologies and the skills use them and those who do not.
diglossia The situation in which two languages or forms of the same language are spoken by people in the same language community at different times and places.
discrimination The practice of treating individuals differently simply based on the group (e.g., gender, sex, age, ethnic group) they belong to.
disease The body's response to a pathogen.
distribution How commodities and services, once produced, are distributed among members of the society.
division of labour The assignment of day-to-day tasks to the various members of a society.
divorce The legal and formal dissolution of a marriage.
document analysis Examination of data such as personal diaries, newspapers, colonial records, and so on.
dogma Authoritative rules or teachings established by religious authorities that must be followed or taken as true.
double descent A system of descent in which individuals receive some rights and obligations from the father's side of the family and others from the mother's side.
dowry Goods or money transferred from the bride's family to the groom or the groom's family to legalize or legitimize a marriage.
dowry deaths Deaths of young women either murdered or driven to suicide in an effort to obtain a dowry.
duotheism Belief in two gods.

ecclesiastical cult A highly complex religious organization in which full-time clergy are employed.
ecofacts Physical remains that were used by humans, but were not made or reworked by them (e.g., seeds and bones).
ecological anthropology *See* **environmental or ecological anthropology**.
economic anthropology The branch of anthropology that looks at cross-cultural systems of production, distribution, and consumption.
economic migrants People who move from one nation to another to improve their living conditions or job opportunities.
economics The academic discipline that studies systems of production, distribution, and consumption, typically in the industrialized world.
educational anthropology The application of anthropological concepts and methods to the study of educational institutions and processes.
egalitarian society A society that recognizes few differences in status, wealth, or power.
EGO The person in kinship diagrams from whose point of view relationships are traced.
elder An influential person in a society who is respected for their experience and wisdom.
emic approach A perspective in ethnography that uses the concepts and categories that are relevant and meaningful to the culture under analysis.
enculturation The process by which humans learn their culture.
endangered language A language that is at risk of disappearing because it is not being used by the younger generation.
endogamy A rule requiring marriage within a specified social or kinship group.
enfranchisement The loss of Indian status.
environmental or ecological anthropology The study of how human populations interact with the environment, and the use of anthropological knowledge and methods to find solutions to human-environmental problems.
epidemiology The study of the causes, occurrence, distribution, transmission, and control of disease in populations.
Eskimo (Inuit) system The kinship system most commonly found in Canada; it is associated with bilateral descent.
ethnic cleansing The systematic and forced removal of an ethnic or religious group from a given geographic area in order to make it religiously and/or ethnically homogenous.
ethnic group A group of people who share many of the same cultural features and heritage.
ethnicity The linguistic and cultural characteristics and heritage a person identifies with.
ethnocentrism The practice of viewing the cultural features of other societies in terms of one's own.
ethnographic fieldwork The practice whereby an anthropologist is immersed in the daily life of a culture to collect data.
ethnographic mapping A data-gathering tool that locates where the people being studied live, where they keep their livestock, where public buildings are located, and so on to determine how that culture interacts with its environment.
ethnographic present The practice of giving accounts of other cultures in the present tense.
ethnography The anthropological description of a particular contemporary culture by means of direct fieldwork.
ethnohistory The use of historical documents, oral traditions, as well as other archaeological and ethnographic methods to understand the history of ethnic groups, both past and present.
ethnolinguistics The study of the relationship between language and culture, and how language influences how people perceive and experience the world.

ethnology The comparative study of cultural differences and similarities.
ethnomedicine The comparative study of ideas about the causes, diagnosis, treatment, and prevention of disease in different societies.
ethnomusicology The study of the relationship between music and other aspects of culture.
ethnopharmacology An ethnic group's use of drugs.
etic approach A perspective in ethnography that uses the concepts and categories of the anthropologist's culture to describe another culture.
etiology Ideas about the causes of disease.
eugenics Ideas and practices aimed at improving the genetic quality of a population.
evangelical Christian denominations that believe in receiving salvation, being "born again," and the literal interpretation of the Bible.
event analysis Photographic documentation of events such as weddings, funerals, and festivals in the culture under investigation.
evolutionism The19th century anthropological theory that cultures evolved from savagery through barbarism to civilization.
exogamy A rule requiring marriage outside a specified social or kinship group.
extended family The family that includes in one household relatives in addition to a nuclear family.
extinct language A language of which the last known speaker has died.

facial expressions A nonverbal form of communication that uses the face to communicate emotional information.
family A social unit consisting of adults, who maintain a socially approved sexual relationship, and children, and is characterized by economic cooperation and the reproduction and raising of children in a common residence.
features Archaeological remains made or modified by people, and that cannot easily be carried away, such as house foundations, fireplaces, postholes, and culturally modified trees.
female genital mutilation (FGM) An operation, usually done with crude instruments, in which a girl's genitalia (labia and clitoris) are either partially or completely surgically cut away.
femininity The social definition of femaleness, which varies from culture to culture.
feminist anthropology A theoretical approach that seeks to describe and explain cultural life from the perspective of women.
feminization of poverty The fact that women make up the largest proportion of world's poor.
fictive kinship Relationships among individuals who recognize kinship obligations even though the relationships are not based on either consanguineal or affinal ties.
field notes The daily descriptive notes recorded by an anthropologist during or after an observation of a specific phenomenon or activity.
food insecurity Lack of access to adequate, safe, good quality, and nutritious food necessary for an active healthy life.
foraging (hunting and gathering) A form of subsistence that relies on animal, fish, and plant resources found in the natural environment.
formal economic theory Assumptions about economic behaviour based on the experience of Western industrialized economies.
fraternal polyandry The marriage of one woman to one or more men who are brothers.
French structuralism A theoretical orientation holding that cultures are the product of unconscious processes of the human mind.
functionalism The theory that social institutions are integrated and function to maintain or satisfy the biological needs of the individual.
functional unity A principle of functionalism stating that a culture is an integrated whole consisting of a number of interrelated parts.

gay-straight alliance School support groups where LGBTQ youth can meet with straight friends.
gender The way the sexes are perceived, evaluated, and expected to behave.
gender-based violence Acts of violence committed against people simply because of their gender.
gender fluid A gender identity that can vary between male and female or some non-binary identity over time and in different circumstances.
gender identity The gender a person identifies with among the range of culturally appropriate possibilities.
gender ideology A system of thoughts, attitudes, and values that legitimizes gender roles, statuses, and customary behaviour.
genderlects Varieties of speech associated with particular genders.
gender roles Expected ways of behaving based on a society's definition of masculinity and femininity.
gender stereotypes Oversimplified conceptions about the characteristics of men and women.
gender stratification The hierarchical ranking of members of a society according to gender.
genealogical method A technique of collecting data in which the anthropologist writes down all the kin of a research collaborator.
generalized reciprocity The practice of giving a gift without expecting a gift in return; creates a moral obligation.
genetics The study of inherited physical traits.
genocide The systematic murder of an entire group of people.
ghost marriage A form of marriage common among the Nuer whereby a woman remains married to her deceased husband.
Gladue report A pre-sentencing report providing an account of the historical and cultural influences on a First Nations, Métis, or Inuit offender used in considering sentencing.
globalization The process of forging international, political, economic, religious, and socio-cultural interconnections and interdependencies.
glocalization The process whereby the universalizing processes of globalization interact with the particularizing tendencies of local cultures to produce new forms of the original cultures.
graffiti A form of art, communication, and public culture consisting of writing or drawings on public walls or other public surfaces.
grammar The systematic rules by which sounds are combined in a language to enable users to send and receive meaningful utterances.
graphic arts Forms of art that include painting and drawing on various surfaces.
gynocentric view A view of the world from a female perspective.

haptic communication A form of nonverbal communication that involves touch.
Hawthorne effect The phenomenon whereby subjects in behavioural studies change their performance in response to being observed.
heteronormative The view that heterosexuality is the norm.
heterosexual Having a sexual attraction to people of the opposite sex.
high-context cultures Cultures in which communication is indirect, relying heavily on the context to convey meaning.
hijra A third gender found in India and Pakistan.
historical linguistics The study of how languages change over time.
historical particularism A school of anthropology prominent in the first part of the 20th century that insisted

on the collection of ethnographic data (through direct fieldwork) before making cross-cultural generalizations.

holism A perspective that attempts to study a culture by looking at all parts of the system and how those parts are interrelated.

homelessness A situation in which an individual or family lack permanent, stable housing.

homemaker A traditional North American gender role that views females as responsible for child rearing and domestic activities.

homophobia Fear and hatred of homosexuals.

homosexual Having a sexual attraction to people of the same sex.

honorifics Words or phrases that show respect and thus encode social status.

honour killing Killing of a family member, usually a young girl or woman, for acting in a way thought to dishonour the family.

horticulture Small-scale crop cultivation characterized by the use of simple technology and the absence of irrigation and fertilizer.

Human Relations Area Files (HRAF) The world's largest anthropological data retrieval system, used to test cross-cultural hypotheses.

human sexuality The sexual practices of humans, usually varying from culture to culture.

hunting and gathering *See* **foraging (hunting and gathering).**

hypergamy The practice of marrying someone from a higher social strata.

hypodescent The assignment of a child from a mixed race, ethnic group, or other social group to the inferior or lower status group.

hypothesis An unproven proposition that can provide a basis for further investigation.

idealism The position that reality is shaped or constructed by ideas.

ideas Thoughts about what things are or how things work.

illness The cultural experience of being sick.

imitative magic Performing a magical ritual on the likeness of someone or event to influence the real person or event.

incest taboo The prohibition of sexual intimacy between close relatives.

Indian Act band An administrative and legal unit that manages Indian reserves and First Nations funds.

Indigenous population People who are the original inhabitants of a region, identify with a specific cultural heritage, and play little significant role in government.

individualistic cult The least complex type of religious organization in which each person is his or her own religious specialist.

induction Deriving a conclusion by making particular observations.

industrial agriculture Food production that relies on technological sources of energy rather than human or animal energy.

informal market economies Legal but unregulated exchange of goods and services that escape government control and regulation.

informant *See* **collaborator, research participant, cultural expert, or informant.**

innovation A change brought about by the recombination of already existing items within a culture.

instant messaging The real-time exchange of messages over the Internet.

institution A pattern of beliefs and behaviours that are relatively stable over time.

intensive agriculture A form of food production that requires intensive working of the land with plows and draft animals and the use of techniques of soil and water control.

intermediaries Mediators of disputes among individuals or families within a society.

international auxiliary language An invented language used for communication between people lacking a common language.

Internet slang The use of text shortcuts, common expressions, and taboo terms; viewed as a less dignified form of language.

interpretive anthropology A theoretical orientation holding that culture is a web of symbols and meaning, and the job of anthropology is to interpret those meanings.

intersex Individuals with sex characteristics that do not allow them to be identified as male or female.

intersubjectivity Shared meanings constructed through the interactions of people from different perspectives.

interview guide A list of questions and topics that the anthropologist uses to guide interviews.

invention A new combination of existing cultural features.

Iroquois system A kinship system associated with unilineal descent in which the father and father's brother are called by the same term, as are the mother and the mother's sister.

Islamic terrorist A person who advocates for or supports, through violent means, a government that operates according to Islamic laws.

Islamist A person who advocates for or supports a government that operates according to Islamic laws.

Islamophobia An exaggerated fear, hatred, and hostility toward Islam and Muslims.

jati Local subcastes found in Hindu India that are strictly endogamous.

justice Doing what is right in the context of a legal system.

kindred All the relatives a person recognizes in a bilateral kinship system.

kinesics A form of nonverbal communication involving the interpretation of bodily movement.

kinship Relationships between people based on blood or marriage.

kinship systems Those relationships found in all societies that are based on blood or marriage.

kin terms The names cultures give to particular categories of relatives.

kin types Universal terms anthropologists use to refer to particular individuals in a kinship system.

Kulturkreis A German and Austrian form of diffusionism whereby culture complexes diffused from several culture centres.

labour specialization The extent to which productive activities are divided among the members of a society. *See also* **division of labour**.

language A symbolic system of arbitrary sounds that, when put together according to a certain set of rules, convey meaning to its speakers.

law Codified rules enforced through the legitimate use of physical coercion.

levirate The practice of a man marrying the widow of his deceased brother.

life history or life story The story of a collaborator's life experiences in a culture that provides insight into their culture.

lineage A unilineal descent group whose members can trace their line of descent back to a common ancestor.

lineality Kin relationships traced through a single line, such as son, father, and grandfather.

lingua franca A common language that people use to communicate when they do not share same native or first language.

linguistics The scientific study of language.

linked changes Changes in one part of a culture brought about by changes in other parts of the culture.

literature review An evaluation of previously conducted research on a topic that allows the researcher to develop their own research proposal and situate their findings within the academic literature.

locavore A person who is committed to eating foods grown locally in the community or within a narrow radius of where they reside.

low-context cultures Cultures in which communication is direct and unambiguous, where meaning is conveyed by the words themselves.

magic The manipulation of nature using supernatural techniques to accomplish specific aims.
mana An impersonal and powerful supernatural force that can reside in people, animals, plants, and objects.
market exchange A mode of distribution in which goods and services are bought and sold, and their value is determined by the principle of supply and demand.
marriage A socially approved union between two or more adult partners that regulates the sexual and economic rights and obligations between them.
masculinity The social definition of maleness, which varies from culture to culture.
materialism The position that reality shapes or influences ideas.
matriarchy A system of governance whereby women rule over men or are empowered to make decisions over men.
matrilineal descent group A form of descent in which people trace their primary kin connections through their mothers.
matrilocal residence A residence pattern in which the married couple lives with or near the relatives of the wife.
mechanical solidarity The idea that small-scale societies are integrated because its members believe and act similarly.
medical anthropology The comparative study of the complex relationships between culture, disease, the environment, and biocultural adaptation.
medical pluralism A situation in which more than one medical system co-exist.
medical system The etiology, methods of diagnosis, treatment, and prevention of disease, and the organization of the health system.
microcredit Small loans at low interest rates, and without collateral, to people (mostly women) in developing nations to help them start small businesses.
migrant A person who moves from one nation to another.
misandry Hatred of men.
miscegenation The marriage or interbreeding of people considered to be of different races.
misogyny Hatred of women.
mixed language A language that results from the fusion of two languages, in which the grammatical elements come from one and much of the vocabulary from the other.
modernization theory The idea that differences in economic development may be explained by inherent socio-cultural differences between the rich and the poor.
monarchy A form of nation-state in which the power rests with a single individual or family within which power is inherited.
money A generally accepted medium of exchange that acts as a standard of value.
monoculture The production of a single commodity on vast acreage.
monogamy The marital practice of having only one spouse at a time.
monogenesis The theory that human races have a single origin.
monotheism The belief in a single all-powerful god.
morpheme The smallest linguistic form that conveys meaning.
multiculturalism A public policy philosophy that recognizes the legitimacy and equality of all cultures represented in a society.
multicultural society A society consisting of people from different ethnic, religious, and racial backgrounds.
multilinear evolution The mid-20th century anthropological theory whereby specific cultures evolve independently of all others but follow a similar evolutionary process.
multinational corporations Companies that have operations in two or more countries.
multi-sited fieldwork Ethnographic fieldwork conducted in more than one location and united by a common research topic or theme.
mutual intelligibility When speakers can readily understand each other, they speak the same language.
myth A religious or sacred story that explains how the world, people, or some event, phenomenon, or practice came to be.

narrative ethnography *See* **reflexive or narrative ethnography**.
nation A group of people who share a common identity, history, and culture.
nation-state A socio-cultural entity as well as a political community that has legitimacy over a defined territory.
negative reciprocity A form of economic exchange between individuals who try to take advantage of each other.
negative sanctions Punishments for violating the norms of a society.
neocolonialism The idea that developed countries and post-colonial powers maintain political and economic dependency and exploitation of former colonies and less-developed countries through economic, financial, and trade policies that favour themselves.
neoevolutionism A 20th century school of cultural anthropology whereby similarities between cultures could be explained by parallel adaptations to similar natural environments.
Neolithic Revolution The period in history when hunter-gathers took up agriculture, resulting in major cultural changes.
neolocal residence A residence pattern in which the married couple has its own place of residence apart from the relatives of either spouse.
nomadism The movement pattern of pastoralists involving the periodic migration of human populations in search of food or pasture for livestock.
nonverbal communication The various means by which humans send and receive messages without using words.
norms Ideas about what is appropriate and what is inappropriate behaviour.
nuclear family The family unit composed of wife, husband, and children.

oath A declaration to a god to attest to the truth of what a person says.
OCAP principles Principles of ownership, control, access, and possession that ensure First Nation communities actively participate in ethnographic research.
occupational segregation The separation of different occupations in a society.
one-drop rule A rule, and in many U.S. States a law, that if a person had one ancestor who was black, typically one great-great-great-great-grandparent, then they too were considered black.
open society A society in which there are no formal barriers preventing people from rising in the social hierarchy.
optimal foraging theory A theory that foragers choose those species of plants and animals that maximize their caloric intake for the time spent hunting and gathering.
ordeal A painful and possibly life-threatening test inflicted on someone suspected of wrongdoing to determine guilt or innocence.
organic solidarity The idea that complex societies are integrated by the dependence of its members on each other.
organizational culture *See* **corporate or organizational culture**.

paleoanthropology The study of human evolution through fossil remains.

paleopathology The study of disease in prehistoric and pre-contact populations.

pan-tribal mechanisms Mechanisms such as clans, age grades, and secret societies found in tribal societies that cut across kinship lines and integrate all the local segments of the tribe into a larger whole.

paralanguage A nonverbal form of communication that accompanies words and helps to convey their meaning as well as expressing the emotional state of the speaker.

parallel cousins Children of one's mother's sisters or father's brothers.

participant observation Research that involves living with and observing the people under study.

participatory action research A mode of research in which the anthropologist and the community work together to understand the conditions that produce the community's problems and to find solutions to those problems.

pastoralism A food-getting strategy based on animal husbandry; found in regions of the world generally unsuited for agriculture.

patrilineal descent group A form of descent in which people trace their primary kin relationships through their fathers.

patrilocal residence A residence pattern in which the married couple lives with or near the relatives of the husband's father.

peasantry Rural people, usually on the lowest rung of society's ladder, who provide urban inhabitants with farm products but have little access to wealth or political power.

periphery Poor, developing nations that provide raw materials, agricultural products, and cheap, unskilled labour.

phenotype Observable physical characteristics.

phoneme The smallest unit of sound that distinguishes meaning in a language.

physical anthropology or biological anthropology The subfield of anthropology that studies human biological evolution, primates, and contemporary physical variations among peoples of the world.

pidgin A simplified language used as a means of communication.

pieces Larger versions of tags consisting of exaggerated 3-D letters or symbols.

plastic arts Artistic expression that involves molding certain forms, such as sculpture.

pluralistic societies Societies composed of a number of different cultural or subcultural groups.

political ecology A perspective that examines how unequal relations in and among societies affect the use of the natural environment and its resources, especially in the context of wide ranging ecological settings, and subsequent economic, policy, and regulatory actions.

political economy A perspective that, at its core, examines the abstract issues of conflict, ideology, and power.

political integration The process that brings disparate people under the control of a single political system.

political organization The ways in which power is distributed within a society to control people's behaviour and maintain social order.

polyamory Intimate relationships between three or more people at the same time.

polyandry The marriage of a woman to two or more men at the same time.

polyethnic People from many ethnic backgrounds living within the same nation-state or geographic area.

polygamy Having two or more spouses at the same time.

polygenesis The theory that human races have multiple origins.

polygyny The marriage of a man to two or more women at the same time.

polysemic Having many meanings, for example, symbols.

polytheism The belief in many gods.

population biology The study of the interrelationships between population characteristics and environments.

positive sanctions Mechanisms of social control for enforcing a society's norms through rewards.

postmodernist anthropology A school of anthropology that advocates the switch from cultural generalization and laws to description, interpretation, and the search for meaning.

postpartum sex taboo The rule that a husband and wife must abstain from any sexual activity for a period of time after the birth of a child.

potlatch A gift-giving ceremony among First Nations on the northwest coast of Canada and the United States that serves as a mechanism for both achieving social status and distributing goods.

poverty line The threshold of income below which the basic necessities of life cannot be met, or which is deemed adequate in a given country.

power The ability to achieve one's goals by influencing the behaviour of others.

practice anthropology The use of existing anthropological data, methods, theories, and insights on a daily basis.

praxis Integrating theory with practice; serves as a means to produce new knowledge.

preferential cousin marriage A preferred form of marriage between either parallel or cross cousins.

prestige Social honour or respect within a society.

primatology The study of nonhuman primates in their natural environments for the purpose of gaining insights into the human evolutionary process.

problem-oriented research A type of anthropological research designed to solve a particular societal problem rather than to test a theoretical position.

production The process whereby goods are obtained from the natural environment and altered to become consumable goods for society.

profane The utilitarian and secular world of work and routine experience.

property rights The Western concept of individual ownership (an idea unknown to some non-Western cultures) in which rights and obligations to land, livestock, or material possessions reside with the individual rather than with a wider group.

proselytizing Attempting to convert people to one's religion.

prosodic features Auditory qualities of speech, such as intonation, stress, loudness, and rhythm, that help interpret the meaning of words.

proxemic analysis The study of how people in different cultures use space.

proxemics A form of nonverbal communication that involves how people use space.

psychic unity A concept popular among some 19th century anthropologists who assumed that all people, when operating under similar circumstances, will think and behave in similar ways.

psychological anthropology The study of the relationship between culture and the psychological makeup of individuals and groups.

public opinion What the general public thinks about an issue that, when brought to bear on an individual, can influence his or her behaviour.

purification ritual A ritual performed to remove uncleanliness before worship or coming in contact with something sacred.

qualitative data People's words, actions, records, and accounts obtained from participant observation, interviews, group interviews, and relevant documents.

quantitative data Data that are counted and interpreted through statistical analyses.
quinceañera A rite of passage for young girls in Latin American cultures when they turn 15 years of age marking their transition into womanhood.

race A social construct whereby people who share similar physical characteristics, especially skin colour, are deemed to belong to a particular category of people.
racialism The idea that race determines specific characteristics and capacities such as intelligence, and that some races are superior to others.
racial profiling The discriminatory practice of targeting a person for reasons of safety, security, or public protection based on a stereotype of their race, ethnicity, religion, or place of origin.
racial segregation The practice of keeping the daily public lives of different races separate.
racism A type of discrimination whereby people are treated differently based on the race they belong to.
rank society A society in which people have unequal access to prestige and status but not unequal access to wealth and power.
rebellion An attempt within a society to disrupt the status quo and redistribute the power and resources.
received pronunciation The accent of the standard language.
reciprocity A mode of distribution characterized by the exchange of goods and services of approximately equal value between parties.
recontextualized products Products or brands that take on new meanings and uses in different cultures.
redistribution A mode of distribution in which goods and services are given by members of a group to a central authority (such as a chief) and then distributed back to the donors.
referendum A direct vote by the electorate on a particular proposal.
reflexive anthropology Recognition of anthropology's biases as well as the influence of the anthropologist's own personal situation and experiences in the production of anthropological knowledge.
reflexive or narrative ethnography An ethnography in which the ethnographer discusses the influence of his or her personal and cultural context on the ethnography, and which are co-produced and focus on the interaction between themselves and their collaborators.
refugee A person who has fled their home country seeking refuge in another because of conflict in their homeland, or because they fear they may be killed, imprisoned, or persecuted because of their race, religion, nationality, political views, or membership in a particular ethnic or social group.
relative poverty The condition in a given society in which people lack the minimum income required to obtain the society's normal standard of living.
religion A system of beliefs and practices involving supernatural beings and forces that functions to provide meaning, peace of mind, and a sense of control over unexplainable phenomena.
religious fundamentalism A religious movement characterized by a return and strict adherence to the fundamental principles of the religion, and often involving a literal interpretation of religious texts, as well intolerance of other faiths.
religious nationalism A trend toward merging traditional religious principles with the workings of government.
repatriation The return of cultural heritage items including art, artifacts, and human remains to their former owners or their descendants.
representative democracy A form of government in which power rests with the citizens, who periodically elect members of their society to some form of assembly to represent them in decision making.
reproductive technologies Recent developments, such as in vitro fertilization, surrogate motherhood, and sperm banks, that make the reckoning of kin relationships more complex.
research design The overall strategy for conducting the research.
Research Ethics Board An official group of people that ensures research conducted involving humans is done in an ethical manner.
research participant *See* **collaborator, research participant, cultural expert, or informant.**
research proposal A written proposal required for funding anthropological research that spells out in detail a research project's purpose, hypotheses, methodology, and significance.
reserve A tract of land, the legal title to which belongs to the federal government, that has been set aside for the use and benefit of a band.
restorative justice A system of justice that focusses on resolving conflict, healing, and restoring harmonious relationships whereby offenders are encouraged to take responsibility for their actions but also to understand the harm they have done to their victims.
retributive justice A system of justice that focusses on revenge and punishment of the wrongdoer.
reverse discrimination Treating members of the dominant group differently in an effort to remedy previous discrimination against members of subordinate groups.
revitalization movement A religious movement designed to bring about a new way of life within a society.
revolution An attempt to overthrow the existing form of political organization, the principles of economic production and distribution, and the allocation of social status.
rite of passage A ritual that celebrates the transition of a person from one social status to another.
rite of solidarity A ceremony performed for the sake of enhancing social integration among a group of people.
ritual A set of behaviours using words, gestures, and objects, performed in a prescribed sequence and manner.
role ambiguity Confusion about how one is expected to behave within the family.

sacred The aspect of such things as places, times, objects, and people that is beyond sensation that makes them special and thus worthy of great respect.
sanctions Any means used to enforce compliance with the rules and norms of a society.
Sanskritization A form of upward social mobility found in contemporary India whereby people born into lower castes can achieve higher status by taking on some of the behaviours and practices of the highest (Brahmin) caste.
Sapir–Whorf hypothesis The notion that a person's language shapes her or his perceptions and view of the world, and consequently their behaviour.
schema An organized pattern of behaviour that helps organize our daily lives.
semi-periphery Industrializing nations between the core and periphery that export natural resources and agricultural products but also manufacture and export a variety of industrial goods.
semi-structured interview A data-gathering technique relying on an interview guide covering the topics or themes needed to be addressed.
serial monogamy The practice of having a succession of marriage partners, but only one at a time.

settlement colonies European colonies where large numbers of settlers displaced the Indigenous groups to become the majority population, marginalizing the Indigenous peoples.
sex The biological or genetic differences between males and females.
sex-selective abortion The abortion of a fetus, usually female, based on its sex.
sexting The exchange of sexually explicit messages and images between cellphones.
sexually dimorphic The physiological differences in form between males and females.
Sexual Revolution The period during the 1960s to the 1980s when conservative Western norms about sexual practices were challenged, resulting in more permissive attitudes toward sex and sexuality.
shaman A part-time religious specialist who is thought to have supernatural powers by virtue of birth, training, or inspiration.
shamanistic cult A type of religious organization in which part-time religious specialists called shamans intervene with the deities on behalf of their clients.
shifting cultivation (swidden cultivation, slash-and-burn method) Clearing the land by manually cutting down natural growth, burning it, and planting in the burned area.
signature graffiti A type of graffiti consisting of tags, throw ups, and pieces where the signature or nickname constitutes the extent of the inscription.
situated knowledge Anthropological knowledge that is influenced by the anthropologist's age, gender, religion, socio-economic status, ethnicity, education, and historical and cultural context.
small-scale society A society that has a small population, minimal technology, lacks a written form of their language, has little division of labour, and is not highly stratified.
social control Mechanisms found in all societies that function to encourage people to maintain social norms.
social facts The institutions of a society that transcend the individual and have a coercive influence such that people follow the appropriate cultural norms.
social inequality Unequal access to the culturally valued resources of wealth, power, and prestige.
social media Internet-based applications that allow users to create and share information and images.
social media shaming Publicly humiliating a person online using social networking services such as Facebook to get them to conform to social norms.
social mobility The ability of people to change their social position within the society.
society A community of people who share the same culture.
sociolinguistics The study of how language is used in different social contexts.
sorcery The performance of certain magical rites for the purpose of harming other people.
sororal polygyny A form of polygynous marriage whereby a man marries his wife's sisters or other female relatives.
sororate The practice of a woman marrying the husband of her deceased sister.
specialized political roles Specific tasks expected of a person or group, such as law enforcement, tax collection, dispute settlement, recruitment of labour, and protection from outside invasions.
speech community People who share a set of norms about how to speak and expectations about how language is used.
standard language The variety of language spoken in public that receives the most institutional support.
state A particular type of political structure that is hierarchical, bureaucratic, centralized, and has a monopoly on the legitimate use of force to implement its policies.
status symbol Cultural item that conveys a person's status.
stencil graffiti A form of graffiti in which shapes and designs are cut into a rigid material to create a stencil, which is then placed on a wall and spray-painted over.
strata Relatively permanent levels in societies separating people according to their access to wealth, power, and prestige.
stratified society A society with a large population that is divided into several levels based on the degree of social inequality.
structural functionalism A school of cultural anthropology that examines how parts of a culture function for the well-being of the society.
structural racism Where the institutions and systems of society are structured such that the subordinate group is disadvantaged or discriminated against.
structured interview An ethnographic data-gathering technique in which large numbers of respondents are asked a set of specific questions.
subculture A group of people within a larger culture with beliefs and values differing from those of the larger culture.
subsistence strategy The pattern a society uses to obtain its food.
suffrage The right to vote.
surrogacy Carrying a fetus to term for another person.
survivals Elements of culture that evolutionary anthropologists believed had survived from an earlier period.
swidden cultivation *See* **shifting cultivation**.
symbol Something tangible, such as a material object or behaviour, that represents something intangible, such as a value, attitude, belief, or an organization.
symbolic anthropology A theoretical school in anthropology that views the goal of anthropology as the interpretation of symbols.
syncretism The blending of religions.
syntax The linguistic rules, found in all languages, that determine how phrases and sentences are constructed.
systematic sociological introspection An examination of the ethnographer's emotions, thoughts, and behaviours during fieldwork, and how they impact data collection.

tags Graffiti writers' nicknames, consisting of monochrome, and highly stylized initials, symbols, cartoon-like characters, or unique styles.
Tā moko Traditional tattoos of Māori men and women, indicating the wearer's lineage, social position, and tribal affiliations.
tattoos A form of body art involving implanting ink or some other substance into the lower levels of the skin.
texting The use of cellphones to send text messages to another cellphone.
theocracy A nation-state in which ultimate power rests with a deity or God.
theory A general statement that explains observations.
thick description The detailed description of behaviours in ethnographic context.
throw ups Enlarged versions of tags consisting of big coloured-in bubble letters.
totalitarian state A political system in which the state recognizes no limits to its authority and strives to regulate every aspect of public and private life wherever feasible.
totemism A mystical or spiritual relationship between an animal or plant (the totem) and a group of people or kinship group.
transformational The quality of an artistic process that converts an image into a work of art.

transgender Individuals whose gender expression or identity does not conform to the norms for their sex.
transhumance The seasonal movement of livestock between upland and lowland pastures.
tribal council An association of Indian Act bands that lacks official administrative power but that provides member bands with various services and assistance.
tribal societies Small-scale societies that have local informal leaders but no centralized leadership.
tribute *See* **chiefly redistribution or tribute.**
two-spirit First Nations and Native American individuals who possess both masculine and feminine characteristics, and hold a respected place in their communities.

underground economy Illegal market activities such as prostitution, drug dealing, human trafficking, and racketeering.
unilineal descent Descent traced through either a male line or female line but not both.
unilinear model A 19th century idea that all cultures passed through the same sequence of stages.
universal functions The functionalist idea that every part of a culture has a particular function.
unstructured interview A data-gathering technique in which interviewees are asked to respond to broad, open-ended questions.
untouchability practices Practices such as segregation and denial of access to community resources, which separate the Dalits from other caste groups.
uptalk The use of a rising, questioning intonation when making statements.
urban anthropology The study of people in complex urban environments.
urban revolution The cultural changes that resulted from the development of state-level societies and cities.
user-generated content Text, video, or audio material created and uploaded by users of social media websites.

values What is important to people, and that which they act to acquire or maintain.
varnas Caste groups in Hindu India that are associated with certain occupations.
vigilantism Taking the law into one's own hands and punishing others according to one's own ideas of justice.
visible minorities People in Canada, other than Aboriginal (Indigenous) peoples, who are non-Caucasian in race or non-white in colour.

warfare Institutionalized, armed conflict between nation-states or other politically distinct groups.
wealth The material objects that have value in a society.
white man's burden The 19th century belief that it was the white man's obligation to raise so-called "savages" to a civilized cultural state.
Wicca A duotheistic, neo-pagan, nature-centred religion.
witchcraft The practice of an inborn, involuntary, and often unconscious capacity to cause harm to other people.
world systems theory The idea that the nations of the world are connected in a systematic political and economic network of exchange whereby the wealthy nations exploit the poorer ones.
worldview A society's knowledge, beliefs, and perspective on the world.
wudu The Islamic purification ritual of washing parts of the body before prayer or before handling the Qur'an.

References

100 Huntley Street. 2015. http://www.100huntley.com/about. Accessed October 1, 2015.

AAA (American Anthropological Association). 1998. *Statement on "Race."* May 17, 1998. http://www.aaanet.org/stmts/racepp.htm. Accessed August 10, 2015.

——. 2009. *Code of Ethics of the American Anthropological Association.* http://s3.amazonaws.com/rdcms-aaa/files/production/public/FileDownloads/pdfs/issues/policy-advocacy/upload/AAA-Ethics-Code-2009.pdf.

——. 2013. *Bulletin, September 11: Anthropology Group Names First Public Policy Award Winner.* http://s3.amazonaws.com/rdcms-aaa/files/production/public/FileDownloads/pdfs/cmtes/ppc/upload/COPP-AiPP-2013-Award.pdf. Accessed May 9 2014.

——. 2014. *Strengthening West African Health Care Systems to Stop Ebola: Anthropologists Offer Insights.* http://www.aaanet.org/about/Governance/upload/AAA-Ebola-Report.pdf. Accessed February 1, 2015.

——. 2016. *Advance Your Career.* http://www.americananthro.org/AdvanceYourCareer/Content.aspx?ItemNumber=1783. Accessed February 1, 2015.

AANDC (Aboriginal Affairs and Northern Development Canada). 2010. *About British Columbia First Nations.* https://www.aadnc-aandc.gc.ca/eng/1100100021009/1314809450456. Accessed October 24, 2016.

——. 2014. *First Nations in Alberta.* https://www.aadnc-aandc.gc.ca/DAM/DAM-INTER-AB/STAGING/texte-text/fnamarch11_1315587933961_eng.pdf. Accessed October 24, 2016.

——. 2015. *Fact Sheet–Understanding First Nation Elections.* https://www.aadnc-aandc.gc.ca/eng/1323193986817/1323194199466. Accessed October 24, 2016.

Abdul-Jabbar, Kareem. 2015. Cornrows and Cultural Appropriation: The Truth about Racial Identity Theft. *Time* (August 26). http://time.com/4011171/cornrows-and-cultural-appropriation-the-truth-about-racial-identity-theft/.

Abma, Derek. 2011. "Many Canadian Youths Believe in Old-Fashion Gender Roles: Study." *National Post,* September 22.

Abramowitz, Sharon. 2014. "Ten Things That Anthropologists Can Do to Fight the West African Ebola Epidemic." *Somatosphere,* September 26. http://somatosphere.net/2014/09/ten-things-that-anthropologists-can-do-to-fight-the-west-african-ebola-epidemic.html. Accessed February 1, 2015.

Abu El-Ha, Nadia. 2007. "The Genetic Reinscription of Race." *Annual Review of Anthropology* 36: 283–300.

Adams, Guy. 2010. "The Tribe that Won Its Blood Back." *The Independent,* May 25). http://www.independent.co.uk/news/world/americas/the-tribe-that-won-its-blood-back-1981974.html.

Adams, Michael. 2011. *From Elvish to Klingon: Exploring Invented Languages.* Oxford: Oxford University Press.

Adamson, Peter. 2012. "Measuring Child Poverty: New League Tables of Child Poverty in the World's Rich Countries." *Innocenti Research Centre. Report Card 10.* United Nations Children's Fund (UNICEF), May.

Advertising Standards Authority. 2011. *ASA Adjudication on Citroen UK Ltd.* http://asa.org.uk/Rulings/Adjudications/2011/4/Citroen-UK-Ltd/TF_ADJ_50261.aspx#.VTAOLJPLIZ8. Accessed January 23, 2016.

Africville Genealogical Society. 2010. *The Spirit of Africville.* Halifax: Formac Publishing.

Agence France-Presse. 2011. "Male, Female, or Neither? Australian Passports Offer Third Gender Option." *National Post,* September 15.

Agosin, Marjorie. 1987. *Scraps of Life: Chilean Arpilleras.* Toronto: William Wallace Press.

Ahmad, Maqbool. 2008. *Comprehensive Dictionary of Education.* New Delhi: Atlantic.

Ahsan, Sadaf. 2016. "Justin Bieber Has Dreadlocks: Fashion Faux Pas or Cultural Appropriation?" *National Post,* April 6.

Ajala, Aderemi Suleiman, and E. N. Ediomo-ubong. 2010. "It's My Stepmother: Witchcraft, Social Relations, and Health Security in Ibibio, South-South Nigeria." *Anthropos* 105 (2): 455–70.

Albro, Robert, James Peacock, Carolyn Fluehr-Lobban, Kerry Fosher, Laura McNamara, George Marcus, David Price, Laurie Rush, Jean Jackson, Monica Schoch-Spana, Setha Low. 2009. *AAA Commission on the Engagement of Anthropology with the US Security and Intelligence Communities (CEAUSSIC): Final Report on the Army's Human Terrain System Proof of Concept Program.* Washington, D.C: American Anthropological Association.

Ali-Karamali, Sumbul. 2012. "Opinion: American Muslims Live in Fear 11 Years after 9/11." *CNN,* September 11th, 2012. http://inamerica.blogs.cnn.com/2012/09/11/opinion-american-muslims-live-in-fear-11-years-after-911/?hpt=us_bn1.

Allyn, David. 2000. *Make Love, Not War: The Sexual Revolution: An Unfettered History.* Little, Brown.

Almond, Douglas, Lena Edlund, and Kevin Milligan. 2009. *O Sister, Where Art Thou? The Role of Son Preference and Sex Choice: Evidence from Immigrants to Canada.* Working Paper 15391, October. Cambridge, MA: National Bureau of Economic Research. http://www.nber.org/papers/w15391. Accessed July 20, 2015.

Anderson, G. 2014. "Saving Endangered Languages Before They Disappear." *Solutions* 2 (5): 76–83.

Anderson, K. J., and C. Leaper. 1998. "A Meta-Analysis of Gender Effects on Conversational Interruptions: Who, What, Where, when, and How." *Sex Roles* 39: 225–52.

Andreatta, Susan L. 1998. "Agrochemical Exposure and Farmworker Health in the Caribbean: A Local/Global Perspective." *Human Organization* 57 (3): 350–58.

Anrys, Stefaan. 2014. "Mistakes in Fighting Ebola Repeated All Over Again, Says Pioneer." *Mondiaal Nieuws,* August 5. http://www.mo.be/en/interview/mistakes-fighting-ebola-repeated-all-over-again-says-pioneer. Accessed Feb. 1, 2015.

Anthes, Emily. 2014. "How Insects Could Feed the World. *The Guardian,* October 30, 2014. https://www.theguardian.com/news/2014/oct/30/-sp-how-insects-could-feed-the-world. Accessed October 15, 2016.

APTN (Aboriginal People's Television Network). 2016. *About: World's First Independent National Aboriginal Broadcaster.* http://aptn.ca/. Accessed June 15, 2016.

Arnaquq-Baril, Alethea. 2015. Tunniit: Retracing the Lines of Inuit Tattoos. Unikkaat Studios. http://www.unikkaat.com/projects/tunniit-retracing-the-lines-of-inuit-tattoos/. Accessed June 1, 2016.

Arsenault, Chris. 2011. "Millions of Aborted Girls Imbalance India." *Aljazeera.com,* October 30. http://www.aljazeera.com/indepth/features/2011/10/2011104153855249 23.html. Accessed July 20, 2015.

Asad, Talal. 1973. *Anthropology & the Colonial Encounter.* Ithaca, NY: Cornell University Press.

Aslan, Senem. 2014. *Nation Building in Turkey and Morocco.* Cambridge, UK: Cambridge University Press.

Associated Press. 2015. "Bruce Jenner Opens up About His Gender Identity: 'My Brain Is More Female than Male.'" *National Post,* April 24.

Atkinson, Michael. 2003. *Tattooed: The Sociogenesis of a Body Art.* Toronto: University of Toronto Press.

Aubrey, Allison. 2013. "Your Love of Quinoa Is Good News for Andean Farmers." *NPR org.* July 17, 2013. http://www.npr.org/sections/thesalt/2013/07/16/202737139/is-our-love-of-quinoa-hurting-or-helping-farmers-who-grow-it.

Avins, Jenni. 2015. "The Dos and Don'ts of Cultural Appropriation." *The Atlantic,* October 20, 2015. http://www.theatlantic.com/entertainment/archive/2015/10/the-dos-and-donts-of-cultural-appropriation/411292/

Axtell, Roger E. 1998. *Gestures: The Do's and Taboos of Body Language Around the World.* New York: John Wiley.

BAAS. 1874. *Notes and Queries on Anthropology for the Use of Travellers and Residents in Uncivilized Lands.* British Association for the Advancement of Science. London: Edward Stanford.

Baba, Marietta L. 2000. Theories of Practice in Anthropology: A Critical Appraisal. *NAPA Bulletin* 18 (1): 17–44.

Bacon, David. 2015. "The Maquiladora Workers of Juárez Find Their Voice." *The Nation*, November 20, 2015.
Bailey, Charles J., and Karl Maroldt. 1977. "The French Lineage of English." In *Pidgins – Creoles – Languages in Contact*, edited by Jürgen Meisel. *Tubinger Beitrage zur Linguistik* 75. Tübingen: TBL Verlag-Narr.
Bakker, Peter. 1997. "A Language of Our Own: The Genesis of Michif, the Mixed Cree-French Language of the Canadian Métis." *Oxford Studies in Anthropological Linguistics 10*. New York: Oxford University Press.
Balkan, Osman. 2015. "Burial and Belonging: Islamic Burial in Germany." *Studies in Ethnicity and Nationalism* 15 (1): 120–34.
Baloy, Natalie J. K. 2011. "We Can't Feel Our Language." *American Indian Quarterly* 35 (4): 515–48.
Barber, Jennifer. 2004. "Community Social Context and Individualistic Attitudes toward Marriage." *Social Psychology Quarterly* 67 (3): 236–56.
Barley, Nigel. 1983. *The Innocent Anthropologist: Notes from a Mud Hut.* London: Penguin.
Baron, Naomi S., and Elise M. Campbell. 2012. "Gender and Mobile Phones in Cross-national Context." *Language Sciences* 34: 13–27.
Barrett, Richard A. 1991. *Culture and Conduct: An Excursion in Anthropology*, 2nd ed. Belmont, CA: Wadsworth.
Barrett, Stanley. 1996. *Anthropology: A Student's Guide to Theory and Methods.* Toronto: University of Toronto Press.
Barrionuevo, Alexei. 2008. "A Tribe in Brazil Struggles at the Intersection of Drugs and Cultures." *New York Times*, December 6. http://www.nytimes.com/2008/12/07/world/americas/07tikunas.html?_r=0. Accessed January 23, 2015.
Bassi, Jett. 2015. "'Go away': Chinese ads defaced with racist messages in Nanaimo." *CTV Vancouver Island*, June 15. http://vancouverisland.ctvnews.ca/go-away-chinese-ads-defaced-with-racist-messages-in-nanaimo-1.2424140. Accessed August 12, 2015.
Batteau Allen W., and Robert J. Morais. 2015. "Standards of Practice for Ethnography in Industry." *EPIC: Advancing the Value of Anthropology in Industry*, March 31, 2015. https://www.epicpeople.org/standards-of-practice-for-ethnography/
BBC News. 2012. "Spanish Fresco Restoration Botched by Amateur." (August 23). http://www.bbc.com/news/world-europe-19349921. Accessed January 21, 2016.
——. 2014. "Tanzania Arrests 23 over Killing of Seven 'Witches.'" (October 10). http://www.bbc.com/news/world-africa-29572974. Accessed March 10, 2016.
——. 2015a. "Saudi Arabia's Women Vote in Election for First Time."(December 12). http://www.bbc.com/news/world-middle-east-35075702. Accessed January 15, 2016.
——. 2015b. "What Is 'Islamic State'?" (December 2). http://www.bbc.com/news/world-middle-east-29052144. Accessed January 15, 2016.
Beattie, Owen, and John Geiger. 1988. *Frozen in Time: Unlocking the Secrets of the Franklin Expedition.* New York: Dutton.
Bedi, Rahul. 2012. "Indian Dowry Deaths on the Rise." *The Telegraph*, February 27.
Beeby, Dean 2015. "Poll Ordered by Harper Found Strong Support for Niqab Ban at Citizenship Ceremonies." *CBC News*, September 24, 2015.
Benedict, Ruth. 1934. *Patterns of Culture.* Boston: Houghton Mifflin.
——. [1946] 2005. *The Chrysanthemum and the Sword.* Boston: Houghton Mifflin.
Bennett, Jessica. 2009. "Polyamory: The Next Sexual Revolution?" *Newsweek, July* 28, 2009. http://www.newsweek.com/polyamory-next-sexual-revolution-82053. Accessed October 15, 2016.
Bennett, Linda, T. J. Ferguson, J. Anthony Paredes, Susan Squires, Judy Tso, and Dennis Wiedman. 2006. "Final Report: Practicing Advisory Work Group (PAWG)." October 25, 2006. Arlington, VA: American Anthropological Association.
Berlin, B., and P. Kay. 1969. *Basic Color Terms. Their Universality and Evolution.* Berkeley: University of California Press.
Bernard, H. Russell. 2002. *Research Methods in Cultural Anthropology.* Newbury Park, CA: Sage Publications.
Bertaux, Daniel, and Martin Kohli. 2009. "The Life Story Approach: A Continental View." In *The Life Story Approach Volume 1*, edited by B. Harrison, 42–65. London: Sage.
Béteille, André. 1998. "Inequality." In *Encyclopedia of Social and Cultural Anthropology*, edited by Alan Barnard and Jonathan Spence, 302–305. New York: Routledge.
Biesele, Megan, and Robert K. Hitchcock. 2011. *The Ju/hoan San of Nyae Nyae and Namibian Independence: Development.* New York: Berghahn Books.
Bilefsky, Dan. 2010. "Walls, Real and Imagined, Surround the Roma in Slovakia." *New York Times*, April 3: A–4.
Binz, Stephen. 2003. *St. Joseph, My Real Estate Agent: Patron Saint of Home Life and Home Selling.* Cincinnati: St. Anthony Messenger Press.
Birdwhistell, R. L. 1952. *Introduction to Kinesics: An Annotation System for Analysis of Body Motion and Gesture.* Washington, DC: Department of State, Foreign Service Institute.
Bissinger, Buzz. 2015. "Caitlyn Jenner Talks About Her Mother's Reaction and Transgender Fans." *Vanity Fair*, June 2015. http://www.vanityfair.com/hollywood/2015/06/caitlyn-jenner-photos-interview-buzz-bissinger. Accessed March 20, 2016.
Black, Conrad. 2011. "I Stand before the Court." *National Review*, June 30. http://www.nationalreview.com/article/270751/i-stand-court-conrad-black.
Blackwell, Tom. 2012a. "Bearded and Breastfeeding—The Story of a Pregnant Man." *National Post*, February 5.
——. 2012b. "Canada's Murky Legal World of Surrogate-Consultants and Human-Egg Buyers." *National Post*, March 9.
——. 2012c. "Who Decides the Makings of a Modern Family?" *National Post*, February 3.
——. 2014. "Surrogacy Isn't Always a Horror Story: How One Canadian Couple Took the Birth of a Down Syndrome Child in Stride." *National Post*, August 6.
——. 2015. "Ontario Newborn Bleeds to Death after Family Doctor Persuades Parents to Get Him Circumcised." *National Post*, October 26.
Blecha, Peter. 2005. "Tipton, Billy (1914–1989): Spokane's Secretive Jazzman." *HistoryLink* File #7456. HistoryLink.org, September 17. http://www.historylink.org/index.cfm?DisplayPage=output.cfm&file_id=7456. Accessed June 30, 2015.
Bloomberg Business. 2011. "Chinese Spreading Wealth Make Vancouver Homes Pricier than NYC." *Bloomberg Business*, May 16. http://www.bloomberg.com/news/articles/2011-05-16/chinese-spreading-wealth-make-vancouver-homes-pricier-than-nyc.
Blythman, Joanna. 2013. "Can Vegans Stomach the Unpalatable Truth about Quinoa?" *The Guardian*, January 16. http://www.theguardian.com/commentisfree/2013/jan/16/vegans-stomach-unpalatable-truth-quinoa.
Boas, Franz. 1912. "Changes in the Bodily Form of Descendants of Immigrants." *American Anthropologist (n.s)* 14 (3) July–Sept: 530–62.
——. 1940. *Race, Language, and Culture.* Chicago: University of Chicago Press.
Bodley, John. 2007. *Anthropology and Contemporary Human Progress.* Lanham, MD: AltaMira Press.
——. 2008. *Victims of Progress*, 5th ed. Lanham, MD: AltaMira Press.
Boeing. 2015. "Long-Term Market Current Market Outlook 2015–2034." http://www.boeing.com/commercial/market/long-term-market/traffic-and-market-outlook/. Accessed November 9, 2015.
Boellstorff, Tom. 2008. *Coming of Age in Second Life: An Anthropologist Explores the Virtually Human.* Princeton: Princeton University Press.
Boesveld, Sarah. 2014a. "The End of Gender? North American Society May Be Ready for More Shades in between Male and Female." *National Post*, May 30.
——. 2014b. "Traditional Values Cited as Woman Separated from her Husband Barred from Running for First Nation Chief." *National Post*, January 24.
——. 2015a. "Men Had to Step Up." *National Post*, June 25.
——. 2015b. "Ontario Sisters to Protest after Being Stopped by Police during Topless Bike Ride." *National Post*, July 29. http://news.nationalpost.com/news/canada/ontario-sisters-to-protest-after-being-stopped-by-police-during-topless-bike-ride
Bohannan, Paul, and Philip Curtin. 1988. *African and Africans.* Prospect Heights, IL: Waveland Press.
Bonazzi, Robert. 2010. Afterword to *Black Like Me* (50th Anniversary Edition), by John Howard Griffin. New York: Signet.
Borden, Teresa. 2004. "In Chiapas, Cola Is Eng." *Atlanta Journal Constitution*, April 14: F–1.

Bornstein, David. 2012. "An Attack on Grameen Bank, and the Cause of Women." *New York Times,* August 22. *http://opinionator.blogs.nytimes.com/2012/08/22/an-attack-on-grameen-bank-and-the-cause-of-women/*. Accessed July 20, 2015.

Boroditsky, Lera. 2009. "How Does Our Language Shape the Way We Think?" In *What's Next: Dispatches on the Futures of Science,* edited by Max Brockman, 116–29. New York: Vintage Books.

——. 2011. "How Language Shapes Thought: The Languages We Speak Affect Our Perceptions of the World." *ScientificAmerican.com,* February: 63–65. https://psych.stanford.edu/~lera/papers/sci-am-2011.pdf.

Borofsky, Robert. 2005. *Yanomami: The Fierce Controversy and What We Can Learn from It.* Book 12 of the California Series in Public Anthropology. Berkeley: University of California Press.

Bosanac, Alexandra. 2013. "Winnipeg Couple Became Parents through Surrogacy—But Not in the Eyes of Canadian Law." *National Post,* May 10.

Bourdieu, Pierre. 1977. *Outline of a Theory of Practice.* Cambridge, UK: Cambridge University Press.

——. 2003. *Firing Back: Against the Tyranny of the Market 2.* London and New York: Verso.

Boyce, Susan M. 2014. "Dismiss Feng Shui at Your Peril." *REW.ca,* August 25. http://www.rew.ca/news/dismiss-feng-shui-at-your-peril-1.1347493.

Boyd, Danah M., and Nicole B. Ellison 2008. "Social Network Sites: Definition, History, and Scholarship." *Journal of Computer-Mediated Communication* 13: 210–30.

Brace, C. Loring. 2005. *"Race" Is a Four-Letter Word: The Genesis of the Concept.* New York: Oxford University Press.

Brady, Ivan. 1998. "Two Thousand and What? Anthropological Moments and Methods for the Next Century." *American Anthropologist* 100 (2): 510–16.

Braid, Don. 2010. "Nenshi Capitalizing on Social-Media Buzz." *Calgary Herald,* September 26.

Bredin, Marian. 2001. "Bridging Canada's Digital Divide: First Nations' Access to New Information Technologies." *The Canadian Journal of Native Studies* XXI (2): 191–215.

——. 2011. "Producing Aboriginal Television in Canada: Obstacles and Opportunities." In M. Bredin, S. Henderson, and S. Matheson, eds. *Canadian Television: Text and Context.* Waterloo, ON: Wilfrid Laurier University Press: 73–94.

Brenner, Michaela, and Vincent J. Hearing. 2008. "The Protective Role of Melanin against UV Damage in Human Skin." *Photochemistry and Photobiology* 84 (3): 539–49.

Brettell, Caroline B., and Carolyn Sargent. 2005. *Gender in Cross-Cultural Perspective,* 4th ed. Upper Saddle River, NJ: Prentice Hall.

Brooke, James. 1990. "Brazil Blows up Miners' Airstrip, Pressing Its Drive to Save Indians." *New York Times,* May 23.

Brown, Cecil. 2006. "Prehistoric Chronology of the Common Bean in the New World: The Linguistic Evidence." *American Anthropologist* 108 (3): 506–16.

Brown, Chris. 2015. "Keeping Faith: The Changing Face of Religion in Canada." *CBC News,* May 17. http://www.cbc.ca/news/canada/keeping-faith-the-changing-face-of-religion-in-canada-1.3071353.

Brown, Judith. 1970. "A Note on the Division of Labor by Sex." *American Anthropologist* 72 (5): 1073–78.

Brown, Paul F. 2010. "Race and Racism." In *21st Century Anthropology: A Reference Handbook,* edited by James H. Birx, 1: 65–75. Los Angeles: Sage.

Brownridge, D.A. 2010. "Intimate Partner Violence against Aboriginal Men in Canada." *Australian and New Zealand Journal of Criminology* 43 (2): 223–37.

Brown, Sarah Elizabeth. 2009. "Teaching Aide Suspended over Hair Cut." *The Chronicle Journal,* May 22.

Buchignani, Walter. 1989. "Amid the Tragedy, Miracles of Survival." *The Gazette,* Montreal, December 8.

Buckman, Rebecca. 2009. "How Brad Pitt and Barack Obama Are Related." *Forbes.com,* May 14. http://www.forbes.com/2009/05/14/ancestry-genealogy-internet-technology-internet-ancestry.html.

Budge, Fiona. 2012. "The Power of Shit: Reflections on Community-Led Total Sanitation in Nepal." *Medische Antropologie* 24 (2): 301–20.

Burczycka, Marta. 2016. "Family Violence in Canada: A Statistical Profile, 2014; Section 1: Trends in Self-Reported Spousal Violence in Canada, 2014." *Statistics Canada.* http://www.statcan.gc.ca/pub/85-002-x/2016001/article/14303/01-eng.htm

Burton, M. L., L. A. Brudner, and D. R. White. 1977. "A Model of the Sexual Division of Labor." *American Ethnologist* 4 (2): 227–52.

Cameron, Michelle. 2005. "Two-Spirited Aboriginal People: Continuing Cultural Appropriation by Non-Aboriginal Society." *Canadian Woman Studies/Iles Cahiers De La Femme* 24 (2,3): 123–27.

Cameron, Stevie. 2011. *On the Farm: Robert William Pickton and the Tragic Story of Vancouver's Missing Women.* Toronto: Vintage Canada.

Canadian Association for Equality (CAFE). 2016. (http://equalitycanada.com/). Accessed June 1, 2016.

Canadian Encyclopedia, The, s.v. "medical anthropology." http://www.thecanadianencyclopedia.ca/en/article/medical-anthropology/

Canadian Human Rights Act. 1985. Justice Laws Website, Government of Canada. http://laws-lois.justice.gc.ca/eng/acts/h-6/.

Canadian Institutes of Health Research, Natural Sciences and Engineering Research Council of Canada, and Social Sciences and Humanities Research Council of Canada, December 2010. *Tri-Council Policy Statement: Ethical Conduct for Research Involving Humans.*

CanLii (The Canadian Legal Information Institute). 1999. *R. v. Gladue,* [1999] 1 SCR 688, 1999 CanLII 679 (SCC). http://www.canlii.org/en/ca/scc/doc/1999/1999canlii679/1999canlii679.html.

Canning, Paul. 2011. "Traditional Same-Sex Marriage Approved by Kenyan Court." *Care2.com,* October 28. http://www.care2.com/causes/traditional-same-sex-marriage-approved-by-kenyan-court.html.

Cardinal, Harold. 1969. *The Unjust Society.* Edmonton: M.G. Hurtig Publishers.

Carnevale, Peter J., and Dong-Won Choi. 2000. "Culture in the Mediation of International Disputes." *International Journal of Psychology* 35 (2): 105–10.

Carpenter, Edmund. 1973. *Eskimo Realities.* New York: Holt, Rinehart & Winston.

Carroll, J. B., and J. B. Casagrande. 1958. "The Function of Language Classification in Behavior." In E. E.Maccoby, T. R. Newcomb, and E. L. Hartley (eds.), *Readings in Social Psychology,* 3rd ed. New York: Holt, Rinehart & Winston.

Carvajal, Doreen. 2014. "A Town, if Not a Painting, Is Restored." *New York Times,* December 14. http://www.nytimes.com/2014/12/15/world/a-town-if-not-a-painting-is-restored.html.

Casagrande, Joseph B. 1958. "The Southwest Project in Comparative Psycholinguistics: A Preliminary Report." *In Men and Cultures: Selected Papers of the Fifth International Congress of Anthropological and Ethnological Sciences,* edited by Anthony F. C. Wallace, 777–82. Philadelphia: University of Pennsylvania Press.

Casestudyinc.com. 2010. "Glocalization Examples—Think Globally and Act Locally." *Casestudyinc.com,* February 10. http://www.casestudyinc.com/glocalization-examples-think-globally-and-act-locally. Accessed February 28, 2015.

Castellano, Marlene Brant. 2004. "Ethics of Aboriginal Research." *Journal of Aboriginal Health*1 (1): 98–114.

Catalyst. 2015. "*Women CEOs of the S&P 500.*" New York: Catalyst, April 3. http://www.catalyst.org/knowledge/women-ceos-sp-500. Accessed July 20, 2015.

Catch the Fire. 2015. Catchthefire.com. http://catchthefire.com/About/History. Accessed October 1, 2015.

Catholic Faith Store. http://www.catholicfaithstore.com/. Accessed October 1, 2015.

Cave, Alfred A. 2006. *Prophets of the Great Spirit: Native American Revitalization Movements in Eastern North America.* Lincoln, NE: University of Nebraska Press.

CBC News. 2011. "Indonesians Lie on Train Rails for 'Therapy.'" *CBC News,* August 2. http://www.cbc.ca/news/health/indonesians-lie-on-train-rails-for-therapy-1.1044184. Accessed February 28, 2015.

——. 2012a. "Aboriginal History Must Factor in Sentences, Supreme Court Says." *CBC News,* March 23. http://www.cbc.ca/news/canada/north/aboriginal-history-must-factor-in-sentences-supreme-court-says-1.1197090. Accessed September 28, 2015.

——. 2012b. "Woman Ruins Spanish Fresco in Restoration Attempt." *CBC News,* August 22. http://www.cbc.ca/news/world/woman-ruins-spanish-fresco-in-restoration-attempt-1.1173998.

——. 2013. "'Anonymous' Won't Release Names of Rehtaeh Parsons Suspects." April 12, 2013. http://www.cbc.ca/news/canada/nova-scotia/anonymous-won-t-release-names-of-rehtaeh-parsons-suspects-1.1365232. Accessed October 15, 2016.

——. 2014. "Conrad Black Removed from Order of Canada." *CBC News*, January 31. http://www.cbc.ca/news/canada/conrad-black-removed-from-order-of-canada-1.2519299

——. 2015. "Father of Saskatoon Crash Victim Sarah Wensley Still Seeking Justice, Accountability." *CBC News*, May 13. http://www.cbc.ca/news/canada/saskatoon/father-of-saskatoon-crash-victim-sarah-wensley-still-seeking-justice-accountability-1.3072142

Centre for Constitutional Studies. 2013. Bill 101. http://ualawccsprod.srv.ualberta.ca/ccs/index.php/ab/496-bill-101?highlight=WyJiaWxsIDEwMSJd. Accessed June 15, 2015.

Chagnon, Napoleon A. 1983. *Yanomamo: The Fierce People*, 3rd ed. New York: Holt, Rinehart & Winston.

——. 1992. *Yanomamo: The Last Days of Eden*, 5th ed. San Diego: Harcourt Brace Jovanovich.

——. 2013. *Noble Savages: My Life among Two Dangerous Tribes—the Yanomamo and the Anthropologists*. New York: Simon & Schuster.

Chambers, J. K, and Peter Trudgill. 1998. *Dialectology*. Cambridge, UK: Cambridge University Press.

Chang, Jeff, and DJ Kool Herc. 2005. *Can't Stop Won't Stop: A History of the Hip-Hop Generation*. New York: Macmillan.

Chaplin, George 2004. Geographic Distribution of Environmental Factors Influencing Human Skin Coloration. American Journal of Physical Anthropology 125:292–302.

Charle, Suzanne. 1999. "A Far Island of Cultural Survival." *New York Times*, July 25, section 2: 1, 28.

Chen, Jacqueline M., and David L. Hamilton. 2012. "Natural Ambiguities: Racial Categorization of Multiracial Individuals." *Journal of Experimental Social Psychology* 48: 152–64.

Chen, M. Keith. 2012. "Could Your Language Affect Your Ability to Save Money?" *TEDGlobal*, June. http://www.ted.com/talks/keith_chen_could_your_language_affect_your_ability_to_save_money. Accessed June 15, 2015.

——. 2013. "The Effect of Language on Economic Behavior: Evidence from Savings Rates, Health Behaviors, and Retirement Assets." *American Economic Review* 103 (2): 690–731.

Childe, V. Gordon. 1929. *The Danube in Prehistory*. Oxford: Oxford University Press.

Choe, Sang-Hun. 2007. "South Korea, Where Boys Were Kings, Revalues Its Girls." *New York Times*, December 23.

——. 2009. "Group Resists Korean Stigma for Mothers on Their Own." *New York Times*, October 8: 6.

CHR&GJ and HRW (Center for Human Rights and Global Justice and Human Rights Watch). 2007. *Hidden Apartheid: Caste Discrimination against India's "Untouchables"; Shadow Report to the UN Committee on the Elimination of Racial Discrimination*. www.hrw.org/sites/default/files/reports/india0207webwcover_0.pdf

Chrétien, Jean. 1969. *Statement of the Government of Canada on Indian Policy*. Ottawa: Queens Printer.

Christianity Today. 2009. "Kolwezi: Accused of Witchcraft by Parents and Churches, Children in the Democratic Republic of Congo Are Being Rescued by Christian Activists." *Christianity Today*, September.

CIA World Factbook. 2012. Country Comparison: Birth Rate. https://www.cia.gov/library/publications/resources/the-world-factbook/rankorder/2054rank.html. Accessed July 20, 2015.

——. 2015a. "Germany." https://www.cia.gov/library/publications/the-world-factbook/geos/gm.html. Accessed October 1, 2015.

——. 2015b. "South Sudan. https://www.cia.gov/library/publications/the-world-factbook/geos/od.html. Accessed August 30, 2015.

CIHI (Canadian Institute for Health Information). 2014. *Canadian Organ Replacement Register Annual Report: Treatment of End-Stage Organ Failure in Canada, 2003 to 2012.*

Cisco Systems. 2015. "VNI Mobile Forecast Highlights, 2014 – 2019." http://www.cisco.com/assets/sol/sp/vni/forecast_highlights_mobile/index.html. Accessed June 15, 2015.

Citizenship and Immigration Canada. 2015a. "Facts and Figures 2014 – Immigration Overview: Permanent Residents." http://www.cic.gc.ca/english/resources/statistics/facts2014/permanent/01.asp. Accessed November 9, 2015.

——. 2015b. "Marriage Fraud. http://www.cic.gc.ca/english/information/protection/fraud/marriage.asp

Clifton, Chas S. 2006. *Her Hidden Children: The Rise of Wicca and Paganism in America*. Walnut Creek, CA: AltaMira Press.

CLTS (Community-Led Total Sanitation). 2015. http://www.communityledtotalsanitation.org/. Accessed April 23 2015.

CNN. 2007. "Shunned from Society, Widows Flock to City to Die." *CNN.com*, July 5. http://www.cnn.com/2007/WORLD/asiapcf/07/05/damon.india.widows/index.html#cnnSTCText. Accessed October 15, 2016.

Codrington, R. H. 1891. *The Melanesians: Studies in Their Anthropology and Folklore*. Oxford: Clarendon Press.

Cohen, Eugene N., and Edwin Eames. 1982. *Cultural Anthropology*. Boston: Little, Brown.

Coleman, Simon, and Pauline von Hellermann. 2011. "Introduction: Queries, Collaborations, Calibrations." In *Multi-Sited Ethnography: Problems and Possibilities in the Translocation of Research Methods* (Routledge Advances in Research Methods). New York: Routledge.

Collyns, Dan. 2013. "Quinoa Brings Riches to the Andes." *The Guardian*, January 14. http://www.theguardian.com/world/2013/jan/14/quinoa-andes-bolivia-peru-crop

Coote, Jeremy, and Anthony Shelton, eds. 1992. *Anthropology, Art, and Aesthetics*. Oxford: Clarendon Press.

Copeland-Carson, Jacqueline, Mary Odell Butler, and Christina Wasson. 2012. "Introduction: Global-Local Connections: The View from Applied Anthropology." In Wasson, Christina Mary Odell Butler, Jacqueline Copeland-Carson, eds. *Applying Anthropology in the Global Village*. Walnut Creek, CA. Left Coast Press: 1–20.

Copes, John H., and Craig J. Forsyth. 1993. "The Tattoo: A Social Psychological Explanation." *International Review of Modern Sociology* 23 (2): 83–89.

Copley, Hamish. 2009. "The Disappearance of the Two-Spirit Traditions in Canada." *The Drummer's Revenge*, August 11. https://thedrummersrevenge.wordpress.com/2009/08/11/the-disappearance-of-the-two-spirit-traditions-in-canada/. Accessed July 20, 2015.

Corak, Miles. 2012. "Inequality from Generation to Generation: The United States in Comparison" (working paper). Ottawa: University of Ottawa. http://nws-sa.com/rr/Inequality/inequality-from-generation-to-generation-the-united-states-in-comparison-v3.pdf

Corbett, Sara. 2008. "Can the Cellphone Help End Global Poverty?" *New York Times Magazine*, April 13: 34–41.

Coutts, Matthew. 2009. "Hallway Culture Clash." *National Post*, 22 May.

Cox, Hillary. 2008. "The Tree of Life." *Cultural Survival Quarterly* 32 (4).

Coyne, Andrew. 2014. "A Tipping Point Has Been Reached." *National Post*, June 3.

CPAA (Canadian Polyamory Advocacy Association). 2010. "What Is Polyamory?" http://polyadvocacy.ca/what-is-polyamory/. Accessed October 15, 2016.

Crabtree, Shona. 2007. "Finding Religion in Second Life's Virtual Universe." *Washington Post*, June 16.Crampton, Thomas. 2003. "Cultural Gaffes: Bathing Rituals in Thai Village Aren't Always What They Seem." *International Herald Tribune*, September 27. http://www.iht.com/articles/2003/09/27rbath_ed3_php.

Crapo, Richley H. 2003. *Anthropology of Religion: The Unity and Diversity of Religions*. Boston: McGraw-Hill.

Cripps, Karla. 2013. "Chinese Tourism: The Good, the Bad and the Backlash." CNN, April 12. http://www.cnn.com/2013/04/09/travel/chinese-tourism-impact/.

CRRF (Canadian Race Relations Foundation). 2014. *Report on Canadian Values*, November 19.

Crystal, David. 2008. *Txtng*: The gr8 db8. *New York*: Oxford University Press.

CTV News. 2007. "Black Guilty on 4 Charges, Including Obstruction." *CTV News*, July 13. http://www.ctvnews.ca/black-guilty-on-4-charges-including-obstruction-1.248554.

——. 2010. "Man Gets Jail, 90 Lashes for Kiss in Saudi Arabia Mall." *CTV News*, June 10. http://www.ctvnews.ca/man-gets-jail-90-lashes-for-kiss-in-saudi-arabia-mall-1.521030. Accessed June 15, 2015.

——. 2015. "6 Young People from Montreal Leave to Join ISIS." *CTV News*, February 26. http://www.ctvnews.CA/canada/6-young-people-from-montreal-leave-to-join-isis-1.2255229.

Cumming, Peter A., and Diana Ginn. 1986. "First Nations Self-Government in Canada." *Nordic Journal of International Law* 55 (1-2): 86–116.

Curry, Andrew. 2012. "Truth and Beauty: The Discovery of a 40,000-Year-Old Figurine Reignites Debate among Archaeologists about the Origin–and True Purpose–of Art." *Smithsonian* 42 (11): 28.

Cuthbert, Pamela. 2015. "Are Those Edible Bugs Actually Sustainable?" *Macleans*, January 17. http://www.macleans.ca/society/life/factory-farmed-insect-how-vulgar/. Accessed October 15, 2016.

Daigneault, Anna Luisa. 2012. "Hishuk Ish Tsawalk: Everything Is One." *The Dominion: News from the Grassroots*, April 6. http://www.dominionpaper.ca/articles/4417. Accessed June 15, 2015.

Damon, Arwa. 2007. "Shunned from Society, Widows Flock to City to Die." *CNN*, July 5. http://www.cnn.com/2007/WORLD/asiapcf/07/05/damon.india.widows/index.html?_s.

Darnell, Regna. 1998. "Toward a History of Canadian Departments of Anthropology: Retrospect, Prospect and Common Cause." *Anthropologica* 40 (2): 153–68.

Darrow, Whitney Jr. 1970. *I'm Glad I'm a Boy! I'm Glad I'm a Girl.* New York: Windmill Books/Simon and Schuster.

Darwin C. [1872] 1998. *The Expression of the Emotions in Man and Animals*, 3rd ed., edited by P. Ekman. London: Harper Collins; New York: Oxford University Press.

Darwin, Charles. [1871] 2004. *The Descent of Man and Selection in Relation to Sex.* London: Penguin Classics.

Dasgupta, Priyanka. 2015. "India Gets Its First Transgender College Principal." *The Times of India*, May 27. http://timesofindia.indiatimes.com/india/India-gets-its-first-transgender-college-principal/articleshow/47436427.cms. Accessed July 20, 2015.

Davalos, Karen Mary. 1996. "'La Quinceañera': Making Gender and Ethnic Identities." *Frontiers: A Journal of Womens Studies* 16 (2/3): 101–27.

Davis, F. James. [1991] 2001. *Who Is Black?: One Nation's Definition.* 10th Anniversary edition. University Park, PA: Pennsylvania State University Press.

Davis, Shelton H. 1977. *Victims of the Miracle: Development and the Indians of Brazil.* Cambridge, UK: Cambridge University Press.

Day, Ann A. 2008. Reappraisal of Insider-Outsider Interviewing: The Tristan Da Cunha Oral History Project. *Oral History* 36 (1): 45–55.

Dean, Cornelia. 2007. "Nobel Winner Issues Apology for Comments about Blacks." *New York Times*, October 19.

Deardorff, Merle. 1951. "The Religion of Handsome Lake." In *Symposium on Local Diversity in Iroquois Culture*, edited by W. N. Fenton, Bulletin 149. Washington DC: Bureau of American Ethnology.

DeMello, Margo. 1993. "The Convict Body: Tattooing among Male American Prisoners." *Anthropology Today* 9 (6): 10–13.

——. 2000. *Bodies of Inscription: A Cultural History of the Modern Tattoo Community.* Durham, NC: Duke University Press.

Deng, Francis. 2009. *The Man Called Deng Majok: A Biography of Power, Polygyny, and Change.* Trenton, NJ: Red Sea Press.

Deter-Wolf, Aaron, Benoît Robitaille, Lars Krutak, and Sébastien Galliot. 2016. "The World's Oldest Tattoos." *Journal of Archaeological Science: Reports* 5: 19–24.

Dewey, Caitlin. 2014. "The Only Guide to Gamergate You Will Ever Need to Read." *Washington Post*, October 14. https://www.washingtonpost.com/news/the-intersect/wp/2014/10/14/the-only-guide-to-gamergate-you-will-ever-need-to-read/

D'Hooge, Herman. 2006. "Case Study: The China Home Learning PC." *EDN Network Magazine*, May 23. http://edn.com/electronics-news/4321057/Case-study-the-China-Home-Learning-PC. Accessed February 28, 2015.

Diamond, Jared. 1997. *Guns, Germs, and Steel: The Fates of Human Societies.* New York: W. W. Norton & Company.

Di Cintio, Marcello. 2012. "Politics 2.0—Naheed Nenshi and the Power of Social Engagement." *Reader's Digest Canada*, May 2012. http://www.readersdigest.ca/features/hot-topics/politics-20-naheed-nenshi-and-power-social-engagement?page=0,2.

Digby-Clarke, Neil. 2007. "Marginalised Ju/'hoansi San at Nhoma Overcome Recent Setbacks." *Namibia Economist.* http://www.economist.com Accessed January 4, 2008.

di Leonardo, Micaela. 1991. *Gender at the Crossroads of Knowledge: Feminist Anthropology in the Postmodern Era.* Berkeley, CA: University of California Press.

Dinnoo, Shannti. 2014. "Why Do Millions of Indians Defecate in the Open?" *BBC News*, June 17.

Dinshaw, Fram. 2015. "Harper Skips Biggest Gay Pride Celebration in Canada, while Mulcair and Trudeau Show Support." *National Observer*, June 29. http://www.nationalobserver.com/2015/06/29/news/harper-skips-biggest-gay-pride-celebration-canada-while-mulcair-and-trudeau-show. Accessed July 20, 2015.

Dobrzynski, Judith H. 2011. "Honoring Art, Honoring Artists." *New York Times*, February 3. http://www.nytimes.com/2011/02/06/arts/design/06names.html?_r=0

Dockterman, Eliana. 2014. "The War on Pink: GoldieBlox Toys Ignite Debate over What's Good for Girls." *Time Magazine*, February 2. http://time.com/3281/goldie-blox-pink-aisle-debate/http://time.com/3281/goldie-blox-pink-aisle-debate/

Donadio, Rachel, and Elisabetta Povoledo. 2013. "Successor to Benedict Will Lead a Church at a Crossroads." *New York Times*, February 11. http://www.nytimes.com/2013/02/12/world/europe/with-popes-resignation-focus-shifts-to-a-successor.html.

Doron, Assa, and Robin Jeffrey. 2014. "Open Defecation in India." *Economic and Political Weekly xlix* (49): 72–78.

Doughart, Jackson, and Faisal Saeed al-Mutar. 2012. "Opinion: Stop Calling Criticism of Islam 'Islamophobia.'" *National Post*, September 2,. http://news.nationalpost.com/holy-post/opinion-stop-calling-criticism-of-islam-islamophobia. Accessed October 15, 2016.

Douglas, Mary. 1966. *Purity and Danger: An Analysis of the Concepts of Pollution and Taboo.* London: Routledge.

Dressler, William W. 2015. "'Culture'….. Again." *Anthropology News*, January.

Duffy, Andrew. 2015. "University of Ottawa Students Derided for Cancelling Yoga Classes over Fears of Cultural Appropriation." *National Post*, November 22.

Duhaime, Carol, Annamma Joy, and Christopher Ross. 1995. "'Learning to See': A Folk Phenomenology of the Consumption of Contemporary Art. In *Contemporary Marketing and Consumer Behavior: An Anthropological Sourcebook*, edited by John F. Sherry, 351–98. Thousand Oaks, CA: Sage Publications.

Dunbabin, T. 1923. "A Strange Trade—Deals in Māori Heads; Pioneer Artists." *Sydney Sun*, January 21.

Durkheim, Émile. [1895] 1982. *The Rules of Sociological Method*, edited by Steven Lukes, translated by W. D. Halls. New York: Free Press.

——. [1912] 2001. *The Elementary Forms of Religious Life*, edited by Carol Cosman. Oxford: Oxford University Press.

——. 1933. *The Division of Labor in Society*, translated by G. Simpson. New York: Macmillan.

Dyson-Hudson, Rada, and Neville Dyson-Hudson. 1980. "Nomadic Pastoralism." *Annual Review of Anthropology* 9: 15–61.

Eakin, Hugh, and Alisa Roth. 2015. "Chapter One: The Displaced. Introduction." In *Flight from Syria: Refugee Stories* (ebook), edited by Hugh Eakin, Lauren Gelfond Feldinger, Stephen Franklin, Joanna Kakissis, Alia Malek, Holly Pickett, Alisa Roth, Alice Su, Selin Thomas, Kem Knapp Sawyer. Washington, DC: Pulitzer Center.

Economist, The. 2008. "Endangered Languages: When Nobody Understands." *The Economist*, October 23.

Ekman, Paul. 2009. "Darwin's Contributions to Our Understanding of Emotional Expressions." *Philosophical Transactions: Biological Sciences* 364 (1535): 3449–51.

Eliot, Lise. 2010. *Pink Brain, Blue Brain: How Small Differences Grow into Troublesome Gaps—and What We Can Do about It.* New York: Mariner Books.

Elizondo, Gabriel. 2009. "Bitter Fight over Brazilian Blood: Why the Yanomami Tribe Want Blood Samples Taken by US Scientists Back." *Al Jazeera*, January 28. http://english.aljazeera.net/news/americas/2009/01/2009127195645873350.html

Elliot, Danielle. 2014. "Chasing Ebola." *The Atlantic*, September 23. www.theatlantic.com/health/archive/2014/09/chasing-ebola/380456/. Accessed February 1, 2015.

Ellis, C. 1991. "Sociological Introspection and Emotional Experience." *Symbolic Interaction*, 14 (1): 23–50.

Ellis, Carolyn, Tony E. Adams, and Arthur P. Bochner. 2010. "Autoethnography: An Overview." *Forum Qualitative Sozialforschung / Forum: Qualitative Social Research*, 12 (1):

Art. 10. http://nbn-resolving.de/urn:nbn:de:0114-fqs1101108.

Ellis, Carolyn, and Arthur P. Bochner. 2000. "Autoethnography, Personal Narrative, Reflexivity: Researcher as Subject." In *The Handbook of Qualitative Research*, 2nd ed., edited by N. Denzin and Y. Lincoln, 733–68. Thousand Oaks, CA: Sage.

Ellsworth-Jones, Will. 2013. "The Story Behind Banksy." *Smithsonian Magazine*, February 2013. http://www.smithsonianmag.com/arts-culture/the-story-behind-banksy-4310304/#EeigihLMryd6o6Qd.99

Ember, Carol R, and Melvin Ember. 2004. Preface to *Encyclopedia of Medical Anthropology: Health and Illness in the World's Cultures*. Springer Science+Business Media. Netherlands.

Employment Equity Act. 1995. Justice Laws Website, Government of Canada. http://laws-lois.justice.gc.ca/eng/acts/E-5.401/.

Endangered Language Project. 2016. Languages: Canada. http://www.endangeredlanguages.com/lang/country/Canada. Accessed October 20, 2016.

Erickson, Pamela L. 2008. *Ethnomedicine*. Long Grove, IL: Waveland Press.

Ethnologue: Languages of the World. 2016. https://www.ethnologue.com/language/tpi. Accessed June 15, 2016.

Etzioni, Amitai. 1993. "How to Make Marriage Matter." *Time* 142 (10): 76.

European Travel Commission and World Tourism Organization. 2012. "Understanding Chinese Outbound Tourism: What the Chinese Blogosphere Is Saying about Europe." Madrid: UNWTO.

Evans-Pritchard, E. E. 1937. *Witchcraft, Oracles and Magic among the Azande*. Oxford: Clarendon.

——. 1940. *The Nuer*. Oxford: Oxford University Press.

Eveleth, Rose. 2014. "Saving Languages through Korean Soap Operas." *The Atlantic*, September 23. http://www.theatlantic.com/international/archive/2014/09/saving-languages-through-korean-soap-operas/380537/

Fabian, Johannes. 1983. *Time and the Other: How Anthropology Makes Its Object*. New York: Columbia University Press.

Faris, James C. 1972. *Nuba Personal Art*. Toronto: University of Toronto Press.

Fassassi, Amzath. 2014. "How Anthropologists Help Medics Fight Ebola in Guinea." *SciDev.Net*, September 24. http://www.scidev.net/global/cooperation/feature/anthropologists-medics-ebola-guinea.html. Accessed February 1, 2015.

Fattah, Hassan M. 2007. "A Familiar Set Helps to Create a New Cultural Market." *New York Times*, August 2: A-4.

Faulk, Frank. 2014. "Cricket Farmer Says Crop Could Help Solve World Food Shortage." *CBC News*, November 30. http://www.cbc.ca/news/business/cricket-farmer-says-crop-could-help-solve-world-food-shortage-1.2847289. Accessed October 15, 2016.

Fausto-Sterling, Anne. 2000. *Sexing the Body: Gender Politics and the Construction of Sexuality*. New York: Basic Books.

Fedorenko, Janet S., Susan C. Sherlock, and Patricia L. Stuhr. 1999. "A Body of Work: A Case Study of Tattoo Culture." *Visual Arts Research* 25 (1): 105–14.

Fenn, Elizabeth A. 2000. "Biological Warfare in Eighteenth-Century North America: Beyond Jeffery Amherst." *The Journal of American History* 86 (4): 1552–80.

Fentiman, Alicia. 2009. "The Anthropology of Oil: The Impact of the Oil Industry on a Fishing Community in the Niger Delta." In *World in Motion: The Globalization and the Environment Reader*, edited by Gary M. Kroll and Richard Robbins, 32–44. Lanham, MD: AltaMira Press.

Ferguson, R. Brian. 1995. *Yanomami Warfare: A Political History*. Santa Fe, NM: School of American Research Press.

Ferraro, Gary P., and Elizabeth K. Briody. 2013. *The Cultural Dimension of Global Business*, 7th ed. Boston, MA: Pearson Education.

Ferreira, Victor. 2015. "Minnesota Dentist Who Killed Cecil the Lion Is on the Lam after Social Media Users Issue Threats against His Life." *National Post*, July 29.

Fiebert, Martin S. 2011. *References Examining Assaults by Women on Their Spouses or Male Partners: An Annotated Bibliography*. http://web.csulb.edu/~mfiebert/assault.htm. Accessed March 16, 2016.

Fieldhouse, D. K. 1999. *The West and the Third World: Trade, Colonialism, Dependence and Development*. Oxford: Blackwell.

First Nations Election Act. 2015. Indigenous and Northern Affairs Canada. https://www.aadnc-aandc.gc.ca/eng/1323195944486/1323196005595. Accessed June 1, 2016.

FirstVoices. http://www.firstvoices.com/. Accessed June 15, 2015.

Fiske, Shirley J., Linda A. Bennett, Patricia Ensworth, Terry Redding, and Keri Brondo. 2010. *The Changing Face of Anthropology: Anthropology Masters Reflect on Education, Careers, and Professional Organizations*. AAA/CoPAPIA 2009 Anthropology MA Career Survey. Arlington, VA: American Anthropological Association.

Fonda, M. 2011. "Introductory Essay: Traditional Knowledge, Spirituality and Lands." *The International Indigenous Policy Journal* 2 (4): 1–5.

Food and Agriculture Organization (FAO). 2005. *The State of Food Insecurity in the World*. Rome: Food and Agriculture Organization.

Food Banks Canada. 2015. https://www.foodbankscanada.ca/. Accessed June 1, 2016.

Forbes. 2015. "The World's Billionaires." *Forbes*. http://www.forbes.com/billionaires/list/#version:static. Accessed August 10, 2015.

Forces.ca. http://www.forces.ca/en/home.

Ford, Linda. 2007. *The Fourth Factor: Managing Corporate Culture*. Indianapolis, IN: Dog Ear Publishing.

Fortes, M., and E. E. Evans-Pritchard. 1940. *African Political Systems*. London: Oxford University Press.

Forward. 2008. "Yemen: Parliament Refuses to Legislate Minimum Age for Marriage," *Forward*, April 16. http://www.forwarduk.org.uk/292-2/. Accessed May 9, 2015.

Foster, George M. 1967. *Tzintzuntzan: Mexican Peasants in a Changing World*. Boston: Little, Brown.

Fox, Robin. 1967. *Kinship and Marriage: An Anthropological Perspective*. Baltimore: Penguin Books.

Frazer, George. 1894. *The Golden Bough: A Study in Comparative Religion*. London: Macmillan and Co.

Freeman, Na'ama. 2016. "Symbolism in Inuit Tattooing." *Culture*, February 15. http://www.mcgilldaily.com/2016/02/symbolism-in-inuit-tattooing/. Accessed June 1, 2016.

French, Howard W. 2007. "The Sound, Not of Music, but of Control." *New York Times*, October 25. www.nytimes.com/2007/10/25/world/asia/25shanghai.html.

Fried, Morton H. 1967. *The Evolution of Political Society: An Essay in Political Anthropology*. New York: Random House.

Friedl, Ernestine. 1978. "Society and Sex Roles." *Human Nature* 1 (4): 68–75.

Friedman, May, and Fiona Joy Green, eds. 2013. *Chasing Rainbows: Exploring Gender Fluid Parenting Practices*. Bradford, ON: Demeter Press.

Friedman, Thomas L. 1999. *The Lexus and the Olive Tree*. New York: Farrar, Straus and Giroux.

Friedrichs, D. 2006. "Restorative Justice and the Criminal Enterprise," In *Handbook of Restorative Justice*, edited by D. Sullivan and L. Tifft. New York: Routledge.

Furlan, Christopher Peter. 2012. "Commoditizing Shit: An Anthropological Guide to Combating Health Problems with Business." *Danida Research Portal*. http://drp.dfcentre.com/project/commoditizing-shit-anthropological-guide-combating-health-problems-business. Accessed April 23 2015.

Gaetz, Stephen, Tanya Gulliver, and Tim Richter. 2014. *The State of Homelessness in Canada: 2014*. Toronto, ON: The Homeless Hub Press.

Gagnon, Mirelle. 2008. "Old Structures, New Faces: The Presence of Wicca and Neopaganism in Canadian Prison Chaplaincies." In *Religion and Diversity in Canada*, edited by Lori Gail Beaman and Peter Beyer, 149–74. Brill NV, Leiden, the Netherlands: Brill Academic Publishers.

Galanti, Geri-Ann. 1991. *Caring for Patients from Different Cultures: Case Studies from American Hospitals*. Philadelphia: University of Pennsylvania Press.

Gallagher, Ann-Marie. 2005. *The Wicca Bible: the Definitive Guide to Magic and the Craft*. New York: Sterling Publishing.

Gardner, R. Allen, and Beatrice T. Gardner. 1969. "Teaching Sign Language to a Chimpanzee." *Science* 165 (3894): 664–72.

Gauthier, Louise. 2001. "Confessions of an Ethnographer: Reflections on Fieldwork with Graffiti Writers in Montreal." *Anthropologica* 43 (2): 273–76.

Geddes, John. 2013. "Canadian Anti-Muslim Sentiment Is Rising, Disturbing New Poll Reveals." *Macleans Magazine*, October 3. http://www.macleans.ca/politics/land-of-intolerance/

Geertz, Clifford, 1966. "Religion as a Cultural System." In *Anthropological Approaches to the Study of Religion*, edited by Michael Banton, 1–46. ASA Monographs, 3. London: Tavistock Publications.

——. 1973. *The Interpretation of Cultures*. New York: Basic Books.

——. 1988. *Works and Lives: The Anthropologist as Author*. Stanford, CA: Stanford University Press.

Gerson, Jen. 2014. "Case Could Set Precedent for Transgendered People." *National Post,* May 12.

Gessler, Suzanne, and Christina Maes. 2011. *The Winnipeg Street Health Report 2011.* Winnipeg, MB: Main Street Project.

Giannesini, Juliette (Zhu). 2012. "Three Faux Pas I (Must Have) Committed when I Came to Canada." *Correr Es Mi Destino blog*, June 11. http://correresmidestino.com/faux-pas-part-one/. Accessed June 15, 2015.

Gilchrist, Kristen. 2010. "'Newsworthy' Victims? Exploring Differences in Canadian Local Press Coverage of Missing/Murdered Aboriginal and White Women." *Feminist Media Studies* 10 (4): 373–90.

Gill, Hannah E. 2004. "Finding a Middle Ground between Extremes: Notes on Researching Transnational Crime and Violence. *Anthropology Matters Journal* 6 (2).

Gitxsan.com. 2016. "The Traditional System Today." *Gitxsan.com.* http://www.gitxsan.com/about/our-way/traditional-system/. Accessed June 1, 2016.

Global Alliance for Clean Cookstoves. 2011. http://cleancookstoves.org/. Accessed March 5, 2015.

Glossow, Michael. 1978. "The Concept of Carrying Capacity in the Study of Cultural Process." In *Advances in Archaeological Theory*, edited by Michael Schiffler, 32–48. New York: Academic Press.

Glovin, David, and David Voreacos. 2012. Kidney Broker Sentenced to Prison as Donor Recalls Doubts. *Bloomberg News,* July 12. http://www.bloomberg.com/news/2012-07-11/n-y-man-gets-30-month-term-in-first-u-s-organ-case.html.

Gmelch, George. 1994. "Lessons from the Field." In *Conformity and Conflict,* 8th ed., edited by James P. Spradley and David McCurdy, 45–55. New York: HarperCollins.

——. 1995. "Nice Girls Don't Talk to Rastas: Status and Sensibilities in a Caribbean Village." *Anthropology Today*, 11 (1): 17–19.

Goett, Jennifer. 2013. "Monkey Point Legal Defense Fund." *Indiegogo.* https://www.indiegogo.com/projects/monkey-point-legal-defense-fund#/. Accessed November 9, 2015.

Gold, Kerry. 2012. "Feng Shui a Mystic Force in Vancouver Real Estate." *The Globe and Mail,* September 8.

Goldieblox.com. http://www.goldieblox.com/pages/about. Accessed June 1, 2016.

Goodman, Ellen. 2008. "Outsourcing Childbirth." *Charlotte Observer,* April 12: 13A.

Gough, Kathleen. 1968. "Anthropology and Imperialism." *The Monthly Review,* April: 12–27.

Gould, Stephen J. 1981. *The Mismeasure of Man.* New York: W. W. Norton & Company.

Gouldner, Alvin. 1960. "The Norm of Reciprocity: A Preliminary Statement." *American Sociological Review* 25: 161–78.

Government of India, Ministry of Home Affairs, Office of the Registrar General & Census Commissioner, India. 2011. Census of India. http://www.censusindia.gov.in/Census_Data_2001/Census_Data_Online/Language/gen_note.html. Accessed June 15, 2015.

Graveline, Fyre Jean. 2012. "Idle No More: Enough Is Enough!" *Canadian Social Work Review /Revue canadienne de service social* 29 (2): 293–300.

Green, Madeleynn. 2014. "A Beautiful Mess: The Evolution of Political Graffiti in the Contemporary City." *Cornell International Affairs Review* 8 (1).

Grekul, J., A. Krahn, and D. Odynak. 2004. "Sterilizing the "Feeble-Minded": Eugenics in Alberta, Canada, 1929-1972." Journal of *Historical Sociology* 17 (4): 358–84.

Grekul, Jana Marie. 2011. "A Well-Oiled Machine: Alberta's Eugenics Program, 1928-1972." *Alberta History* 59 (3): 16–23.

Grey, Mark, and Michele Devlin. 2015. Ebola and Localizing the "Global Other" in the United States. *Somatosphere,* January 16. http://somatosphere.net/2015/01/ebola.html. Accessed February 1, 2015.

Griffin, John Howard. [1961] 2010. *Black Like Me: 50th Anniversary Edition.* New York: Signet.

——. 2011. *Prison of Culture: Beyond Black Like Me.* San Antonio, TX: Wings Press.

Griffin, Wendy. 2005. "Witchcraft and Neopaganism." In *Witchcraft And Magic: Contemporary North America*, edited by Helen A. Berger, 55–80. Philadelphia, PA: University of Pennsylvania Press.

Gross, Daniel, and Barbara A. Underwood. 1971. "Technological Change and Caloric Costs: Sisal Agriculture." *American Anthropologist* 73 (3): 725–40.

Grossman, Cathy Lynn. 2007. "Faithful Build a Second Life for Religion Online: A Peek inside Second Life." *USA Today*, March 3.

Grubel, Herbert G. 2016. *Income Mobility: The Rich and Poor in Canada.* Vancouver, BC: Fraser Institute.

Gudeman, Stephen F., and Norman E. Whitten, Jr. 1982. "Introduction." *American Ethnologist* 9 (2): 223–29.

Gunter, Lorne. 2012. "Lorne Gunter: The Two Colours of Canadian Justice." *National Post*, January 4.

Haas, Christina, Pamela Takayoshi, Brandon Carr, Kimberley Hudson, and Ross Pollock. 2011. "Young People's Everyday Literacies: The Language Features of Instant Messaging." *Research in the Teaching of English* 45 (4): 378–404.

Hack, Karl A. 2008. "Decolonization." In *International Encyclopedia of the Social Sciences*, 2nd ed., edited by William Darity, Jr., (2): 255–57. Detroit: Macmillan Reference.

Hackman, Anna. 2011. "Green Feng Shui: Health and Harmony for Homes and Businesses." *Green Talk*, September 8. http://www.green-talk.com/green-feng-shui-health-and-harmony-for-homes-and-businesses/

Hadley, Craig, and Amber Wutich. 2009. "Experience-Based Measures of Food and Water Security: Biocultural Approaches to Grounded Measures of Insecurity." *Human Organization* 68 (4): 451–60.

Hahn, Hans Peter. 2008. "Diffusionism, Appropriation, and Globalization. Some Remarks on Current Debates in Anthropology." *Anthropos* 103.2008: 191–202.

Hall, Edward T. 1966. *The Hidden Dimension.* New York: Anchor Books.

——. 1976. *Beyond Culture.* New York: Anchor.

Hall, Edward T., and Mildred R. Hall. 2009. "The Sounds of Silence." In *Classic Readings in Cultural Anthropology*, edited by Gary Ferraro, 18–26. Belmont, CA: Wadsworth.

Hall, Peter V., and Tulin Sadouzai. 2010. "The Value of 'Experience' and the Labour Market Entry of New Immigrants to Canada." *Canadian Public Policy / Analyse de Politiques* 36 (2): 181–98.

Hall, R. A. Jr. 1966. *Pidgin and Creole Languages.* Ithaca, NY: Cornell University Press.

Hamada, Tomoko. 1995. "Inventing Cultural Others in Organizations: A Case of Anthropological Reflexivity in a Multinational Firm." *Journal of Applied Behavioral Science* 31 (2): 162–85.

Hamilton, Graeme. 2013. "Even Francophones Are Waking up to Quebec's Language Folly." *National Post, February* 28.

Hamlin, Lois. 2012. "Patients Without Borders: The Rise of Surgical Tourism." *AORN Journal* 95 (4): 524–34.

Hanna, Judith Lynne. 1979. To Dance *Is Human: A Theory of Nonverbal Communication.* Austin, TX: University of Texas Press.

——. 2005. "Dance Speaks Out on Societal Issues." *Anthropology News* 46 (4): 11–12.

Hansen, John George. 2009. "Decolonizing Indigenous Restorative Justice Is Possible." *The Quint* 1 (2): 15–71.

Hansen, Karen Tranberg. 2000. Salaula: *The World of Secondhand Clothing and Zambia.* Chicago, IL: University of Chicago Press.

Haraway, Donna. 1988. "Situated Knowledges: The Science Question in Feminism and the Privilege of Partial Perspective." *Feminist Studies* 14 (3): 575–99.

Harding, R. 2006. "Historical Representations of Aboriginal People in the Canadian News Media." *Discourse & Society* 17 (2): 205–35.

Harris, Marvin. 1964. *Patterns of Race in the Americas.* New York: Doubleday.

——. 1968. *The Rise of Anthropological Theory.* New York: Thomas Y. Crowell.

——. 1977. *Cannibals and Kings: The Origins of Culture.* New York: Random House.

——. 1979a. *Cultural Materialism: The Struggle for a Science of Culture.* New York: Random House.

——. 1979b. "The Yanomamo and the Cause of War in Band and Village Societies." In *Brazil: Anthropological Perspectives: Essays in Honor of Charles Wagley,* edited by M. Margolis and W. Carter, 121–32. New York: Columbia University Press.

——. 1984. "A Cultural Materialist Theory of Band and Village Warfare: The Yanomamo Test." In *Warfare, Culture, and*

Environment, edited by R. B. Ferguson, 111–40. Orlando, FL: Academic Press.
——. 1985. *Good to Eat: Riddles of Food and Culture.* New York: Simon and Schuster.
——. 1999. *Theories of Culture in Postmodern Times.* Walnut Creek, CA: AltaMira Press.
Harris, Philip Robert, and Robert T. Moran. 1987. *Managing Cultural Differences.* Houston, TX: Gulf Publishing Company.
Harris, Philip Robert, Robert T. Moran, Sarah Virgilia Moran. 2004. *Managing Cultural Differences: Global Leadership Strategies for the 21st Century,* 6th ed. New York: Routledge.
Harrison, Barbara. 2009. Editors' Introduction to "Researching Lives and the Lived Experience." In *Life Story Research Volume I,* edited by Barbara Harrison, 3–13. Sage Benchmarks in Social Research Methods. London: Sage.
Harrison, Jeff. 2012. "William L. Rathje: 1945–2012." *University Communications,* June 5. The University of Arizona: The College of Social & Behavioral Sciences. http://web.sbs.arizona.edu/college/news/william-l-rathje-1945-2012. Accessed April 3 2014.
Hartford Institute for Religious Research. 2015. *Megachurches of Canada.* http://hirr.hartsem.edu/megachurch/canadian-megachurches.html. Accessed September 30, 2015.
Harvey, Jade Adia. 2013. "The Quinoa Controversy: The Implications of the Growing Popularity of a Bolivian Grain." *The Yale Globalist,* December 24. http://tyglobalist.org/in-the-magazine/glimpses/the-quinoa-controversy-the-implications-of-the-growing-popularity-of-a-bolivian-grain/.
Hauswald, Lizabeth. 1987. "External Pressure/Internal Change: Child Neglect on the Navajo Reservation." In *Child Survival,* edited by Nancy Scheper-Hughes, 145–64. Dordrecht, Netherlands: D. Reidel Publishing Company.
Hebblethwaite, Cordelia. 2011. "Sweden's "Gender-Neutral" Pre-school." *BBC News,* July 8. http://www.bbc.com/news/world-europe-14038419.
Hecht, Michael L., Mary Jane Collier, and Sidney Ribeau. 1993. *African American Communication: Ethnic Identity and Cultural Interpretation.* Thousand Oaks, CA: Sage Publications.
Hedican, Edward J. 2006. "Understanding Emotional Experience in Fieldwork: Responding to Grief in a Northern Aboriginal Village." *International Journal of Qualitative Methods* 5 (1): 1–8.
Heider, Karl. 2006. *The Dugum Dani: A Papuan Culture in the Highlands of West New Guinea.* Piscataway, NJ: Aldine Transaction.
Helmer, Aedan. 2016. Graffiti on Islamic School a Hate Crime, Police Say. *Ottawa Citizen,* April 11. http://ottawacitizen.com/news/local-news/graffiti-on-islamic-school-a-hate-crime-police-say/.
Henley, N. M. 1977. *Body Politics: Power, Sex, and Nonverbal Communication.* Englewood Cliffs, NJ: Prentice Hall.
Herrera, Julia Rios. 2013. "Environmentalists Warn of Nicaragua Canal Disaster." *Archaeology News Network,* June 15. http://archaeologynewsnetwork.blogspot.ca/2013/06/environmentalists-warn-of-nicaragua.html#.Vjzc1b_1Isl. Accessed November 9, 2015.
Herskovits, Melville. 1924. "A Preliminary Consideration of the Cultural Areas in Africa." *American Anthropologist* 26 (1): 50–63.
Hertenstein, Matthew J., Julie M. Verkamp, Alyssa M. Kerestes, and Rachel M. Holmes. 2006. "The Communicative Functions of Touch in Humans, Nonhuman Primates, and Rats: A Review and Synthesis of the Empirical Research." *Genetic, Social, and General Psychology Monographs* 132 (1): 5–94.
Hewlett, Barry, and Bonnie Hewlett. 2007. *Ebola, Culture, and Politics: The Anthropology of an Emerging Disease.* Belmont, CA: Wadsworth.
Hill, Kim, Hillard Kaplan, Kristen Hawkes, and Magdalena Hurtado. 1987. "Foraging Decisions among Ache Hunter-Gatherers: New Data and Implications for Optimal Foraging Models." *Ethology and Sociobiology* 8: 1–36.
HKND. 2015a. "Canal de Nicaragua Environmental and Social Impact Assessment: Executive Summary." *Company News* http://hknd-group.com/portal.php?mod=view&aid=243.
——. 2015b. "Environmental Permit Granted for Nicaragua Interoceanic Canal, Canal Development Moving Forward Firmly." *Company News,* November 6. http://hknd-group.com/portal.php?mod=view&aid=296. Accessed November 9, 2015.
——. 2015c. "HKND Committed to Build the Canal in Compliance with International Best Practices." *Company News,* October 12. Accessed November 9, 2015.
Hoebel, E. Adamson. 1972. *Anthropology: The Study of Man,* 4th ed. New York: McGraw-Hill.
Hoekstra, Gordon. 2014. "Gitxsan Displeased with Pipeline Offer Made Directly to Hereditary Chiefs." *Vancouver Sun,* July 20.
Hoffman, Ross, and Andrew Robinson. 2010. "Nisga'a Self-Government: A New Journey Has Begun." *The Canadian Journal of Native Studies* XXX (2): 387–405.
Hofstede, Geert, Gert Jan Hofstede, and Michael Minkov. 2010. *Cultures and Organizations: Software of the Mind,* 3rd ed. McGraw-Hill.
Hoge, Warren. 2001. "Art Imitates Life, Perhaps Too Closely." *New York Times,* October 20.
Hokayem, Emile. 2013. *Syria's Uprising and the Fracturing of the Levant* (Adelphi Book 438). The International Institute for Strategic Studies (IISS) (June 3).
Holloway, Kris. 2007. *Monique and the Mango Rains.* Long Grove, IL: Waveland Press.
Holton, R. James. 2004. *Chinook Jargon: The Hidden Language of the Pacific Northwest.* San Leandro, CA: Wawa Press.
Hopper, Tristin. 2013a. "Church for People Who Aren't into Church: Protestant Mega-congregations Packing the Pews in Canada." *National Post,* December 27. http://news.nationalpost.com/holy-post/protestant-megachurches-surging-in-canada-even-as-secularism-grows-and-most-sunday-attendance-plummets.
——. 2013b. "From "Toque" to "Mickey," Ten Canadianisms That Leave Other English Speakers Utterly Confused." *National Post,* December 26.
——. 2014. "Line up, Eh!" *National Post,* July 26.
——. 2015. This Is What Actual, Real-Life Cultural Appropriation Looks Like. *National Post,* December 17.
Hoq, Mohammad Nazmul. 2012. "Regional Differentials of Age at First Marriage among Women in Bangladesh." *Asian Journal of Applied Science and Engineering* 2 (3): 76–83.
Hossain, Ziarat, Beverly Chew, Sheryl Swilling, Sally Brown, Marcia Michaelis, and Sheila Philips. 1999. "Fathers' Participation in Childcare within Navajo Indian Families." *Early Child Development and Care* 154: 63–74.
Houreld, Katharine. 2009. "Churches Denounce African Children as 'Witches.'" *Huffington Post,* October 18. http://www.huffingtonpost.com/huff-wires/20091018/af-nigeria-child-witches/. Accessed October 15, 2016.
Howard, Beth. 1991. "Ape Apothecary: Self-Prescribing Chimps Lead Researchers to Nature's Medicine Cabinet." *Omni* 13: 30.
Howell, David L. 2005. *Geographies of Identity in Nineteenth-Century Japan.* Berkeley, CA: University of California Press.
Huffington Post. 2012. "3,000 Lynched in Tanzania for "Witchcraft" in Past Six Years. *Huffington Post,* May 29. http://www.huffingtonpost.com/2012/05/29/tanzania-witchcraft-3000-lynchings-witches_n_1553448.html.
Hughes, Charles C., and John M. Hunter. 1972. "The Role of Technological Development in Promoting Disease in Africa." In *The Careless Technology: Ecology and International Development,* edited by M. T. Farvar and John P. Milton, 69–101. Garden City, NY: Natural History Press.
Human Rights Organization. 1999. IX. *Restrictions on the Use of the Kurdish Language.* https://www.hrw.org/reports/1999/turkey/turkey993-08.htm. Accessed June 1, 2016.
HRW (Human Rights Watch). 2013. *Those Who Take Us Away: Abusive Policing and Failures in Protection of Indigenous Women and Girls in Northern British Columbia, Canada.* https://www.hrw.org/sites/default/files/reports/canada0213webwcover_0.pdf. Accessed June 1, 2016.
Human Rights Watch. 2009. *Saudi Arabia: Witchcraft and Sorcery Cases on the Rise.* November 24. http://www.hrw.org/news/2009/11/24/saudi-arabia-witchcraft-and-sorcery-cases-rise
Humphreys, Adrian. 2015a. "Anonymous Leaks Another High-Level Federal Document as Part of Vendetta against Government." *National Post,* September 26.
——. 2015a. "Anonymous Releases Hacked CSIS Document after Member's Death, Threatens to Leak 'Stunning Secrets'" *National Post,* July 28.

——. 2016. "Dalhousie Is Under Fire: Anonymous Attacks Websites over Claimed Inaction after Alleged Frat-House Rape." *National Post*, April 17.

Hunt, Earl, and Jerry Carlson. 2007. "Considerations Relating to the Study of Group Differences in Intelligence." *Perspectives on Psychological Science* 2 (2): 194–213.

Hunter, Justine. 2013. "Rediscovered Art by Residential-School Pupils Paints a Portrait of Survival." *The Globe and Mail*, March 27.

Hurst, Mike. 2009. "Caster Semenya Has Male Sex Organs and No Womb or Ovaries." *The Daily Telegraph*, September 11. http://www.dailytelegraph.com.au/sport/semenya-has-no-womb-or-ovaries/story-e6frexni-1225771672245.

Hutchinson, Brian. 2014. "Charges Laid against Bountiful Leader Winston Blackmore after Judge Rules Charter Should Not Protect Polygamists." *National Post*, August 14.

Hvistendahl, Mara. 2012. *Unnatural Selection: Choosing Boys over Girls, and the Consequences of a World Full of Men.* New York: PublicAffairs; reprint edition May 1.

Ibrahim, Mariam, and Karen Kleiss. 2015. "Gay-Straight Alliances Now Mandatory in Alberta: We're No Longer that Redneck, Roughneck Province." *National Post*, March 11.

ICRW. 2015. *International Center for Research on Women "Child Brides.* http://www.icrw.org/what-we-do/adolescents/child-marriage. Accessed May 9 2015.

Immigration, Refugees and Citizenship Canada. 2012. *Canadian Multiculturalism: An Inclusive Citizenship.* http://www.cic.gc.ca/english/multiculturalism/citizenship.asp. Accessed June 1, 2016.

INAC (Indigenous and Northern Affairs Canada). 2010. *First Nations in Alberta.* http://www.aadnc-aandc.gc.ca/eng/1100100020670/1100100020675. Accessed August 30, 2015.

——. 2013. *Aboriginal Demographics from the 2011 National Household Survey.* https://www.aadnc-aandc.gc.ca/eng/1370438978311/1370439050610. Accessed August 30, 2015.

——. 2016a. *Indian Residential Schools.* https://www.aadnc-aandc.gc.ca/eng/1100100015576/1100100015577. Accessed October 24, 2016.

——. 2016b. *Indian Status.* https://www.aadnc-aandc.gc.ca/eng/1100100032374/1100100032378. Accessed October 24, 2016.

Indian Act, R.S.C. 1985, c. I-5, section 2(1). Ottawa: Government of Canada.

Indigitization. 2015. *Indigitization—Toolkit for the Digitization of First Nations Knowledge.* http://www.indigitization.ca/. Accessed June 15, 2015.

Irele, Abiola, and Biodun Jeyifo. 2010. *The Oxford Encyclopedia of African Thought, Volume 1.* New York: Oxford University Press.

IRTA (International Reciprocal Trade Association). 2015. http://www.irta.com/.

Irvine, Martha. 2012. "U.S. Grandmother Gives Birth to Her Own Grandchild; Acts as Surrogate for Daughter" *National Post*, September 7.

Irwin, Anne. 2012. "There Will Be a Lot of Old Young Men Going Home: Combat and Becoming a Man in Afghanistan." In *Young Men in Uncertain Times*, edited by Vered Amit and Noel Dyck, 59–78. New York: Berghahn Books.

Irwin, Katherine. 2001. "Legitimating the First Tattoo: Moral Passage through Informal Interaction." *Symbolic Interaction* 24 (1): 49–73.

Ishii, Keiko, Jose Alberto Reyes, and Shinobu Kitayama. 2003. "Spontaneous Attention to Word Content versus Emotional Tone: Differences among Three Cultures." *Psychological Science* 14 (1): 39–46.

ISNA (Intersex Society of North America). 2008a. *How Common Is Intersex?* http://www.isna.org/faq/frequency. Accessed July 20, 2015.

——. 2008b. *What Is Intersex?* http://www.isna.org/faq/what_is_intersex. Accessed July 20, 2015.

Jacobs, Sue-Ellen, Wesley Thomas, and Sabine Lang. 1997. Introduction *to Two-Spirit People: Native American Gender Identity, Sexuality, and Spirituality*, edited by Sue-Ellen Jacobs, Wesley Thomas, and Sabine Lang. Urbana–Champaign, IL: University of Illinois Press.

James, Richard. 2014. *Legal Status of Wicca & Paganism in Canada.* Wiccan Church of Canada. http://www.wcc.on.ca/legal.html. Accessed June 1, 2016.

Jameson, Frederic. 1990. *Postmodernism, or the Cultural Logic of Late Capitalism.* Durham, NC: Duke University Press.

Jankowiak, W. R., and E. F. Fischer. 1992. "A Cross Cultural Perspective on Romantic Love." *Ethnology* 31 (2): 149–56.

Jauregui, Andres. 2013. "Rehtaeh Parsons, Canadian Girl, Dies After Suicide Attempt; Parents Allege She Was Raped by 4 Boys." *The Huffington Post*, April 9. http://www.huffingtonpost.com/2013/04/09/rehtaeh-parsons-girl-dies-suicide-rape-canada_n_3045033.html

Jenkins, Henry. 2001. "Culture Goes Global." *Technology Review* 104 (6): 89.

Jensen, Arthur. 1969. "How Much Can We Boost IQ and Scholastic Achievement?" *Harvard Educational Review* 39 (1 Winter).

Jensen, Gary F., and Ashley Thompson. 2008. "Out of the Broom Closet: The Social Ecology of American Wicca." *Journal for the Scientific Study of Religion* 47 (4): 753–66.

Jessiman, Stacey R. 2011. "The Repatriation of the G'psgolox Totem Pole: A Study of Its Context, Process, and Outcome." *International Journal of Cultural Property* 18 (3): 365–91.

Johnson, Andy. 2012. "Conrad Black Dismisses Convictions, Likens U.S. to North Korea." *CTV News*, October 23. http://www.ctvnews.ca/world/conrad-black-dismisses-convictions-likens-u-s-to-north-korea-1.1007116.

Jonaitis, Alldona, ed. 1991. *Chiefly Feasts: The Enduring Kwakiutl Potlatch.* Seattle: University of Washington Press.

Jones, Adam. 2015. "Aboriginal Men Are Murdered and Missing Far More than Aboriginal Women. A Proper Inquiry Would Explore Both." *National Post*, April 27.

Jordan, Ann T. 2013. *Business Anthropology*, 2nd ed. Long Grove, IL: Waveland Press.

Jorde, Lynn B, and Stephen P. Wooding. 2004. "Genetic Variation, Classification and 'Race.'" *Nature Genetics* 36 (11): S28–S33.

Justice Laws Website. 2016. *Constitution Act, 1982.* http://laws-lois.justice.gc.ca/eng/const/page-15.html. Accessed February 2, 2016.

Kadir, Nazima. *Ethnographic Mapping.* http://nazimakadir.wordpress.com/2014/01/03/digital-ethnographic-mapping/. Accessed May 30, 2014.

Kahle, L. R. 1983. *Social Values and Social Change: Adaptation to Life in America.* New York: Praeger.

Kale R. 2012. "It's a Girl!"—Could Be a Death Sentence." *CMAJ* 184: 387–88.

Kanji, Azeezah. 2016. "The Disturbing Movement against Syrian Refugees in Canada." *The Toronto Star*, March 10. https://www.thestar.com/opinion/commentary/2016/03/10/the-disturbing-movement-against-syrian-refugees-in-canada.html.

Kaplan, David, and Robert Manners. 1986. *Culture Theory.* Englewood Cliffs, NJ: Prentice Hall.

Kaplan, Martha. 1995. *Neither Cargo nor Cults: Rituals Politics and the Colonial Imagination in Fiji.* Durham, NC: Duke University Press.

Kaufmann, Bill. 2010. "Nenshi Win Makes Ripples around the World." *Calgary Sun*, October 19.

Keesing, Roger. 1992. "Not a Real Fish: The Ethnographer as Inside Outsider." In *The Naked Anthropologist: Tales from Around the World*, edited by Philip DeVita, 73–78. Belmont, CA: Wadsworth.

Kehoe, Alice Beck. 2006. *The Ghost Dance: Ethnohistory and Revitalization*, 2nd ed. Long Grove, IL: Waveland Press.

Keller, James. 2015. "Polygamous Leader in B.C. Ordered to Stop Using Names Linked to Mormons." *Globe and Mail*, January 14.

Kellett, Peter. 2009. "Advocacy in Anthropology: Active Engagement or Passive Scholarship?" *Durham Anthropology Journal* 16 (1): 22–31.

Kerven, Carol, Bernd Steimann, Chad Dear, and Laurie Ashley. 2012. "Researching the Future of Pastoralism in Central Asia's Mountains: Examining Development Orthodoxies." *Mountain Research and Development* 32 (3): 368–77.

Khanna, Sunil K. 2010. *Fetal/Fatal Knowledge: New Reproductive Technologies and Family-Building Strategies in India.* Belmont, CA: Wadsworth.

Kheiriddin, Tasha. 2015. Full Comment: "Tasha Kheiriddin: Bare Boobs Will Not Make a Better World." *National Post*, July 30.

Kidd, Arwen. 2011. "Study Destination Canada: How to Beat Culture Shock Blues." *Canada Bound*, August 31. http://canadaboundimmigrant.com/education/article.php?id=516

Kilbride, Philip L. 1997. "African Polygyny Family Values and Contemporary Change." In *Applying Cultural Anthropology: An Introductory Reader*, edited by Aaron

Podolefsky and Peter Brown, 201–208. Mountain View, CA: Mayfield.

King, M., and M. Friedlander. 1992. *Moko: Māori Tattooing in the 20th Century*, 2nd ed. Auckland: David Bateman.

King, Martin Luther, Jr. 1963. "I Have a Dream by Martin Luther King, Jr; August 28, 1963." *The Avalon Project: Documents in Law, History and Diplomacy*. Yale Law School, Lillian Goldman Law Library. http://avalon.law.yale.edu/20th_century/mlk01.asp. Accessed August 10, 2015.

Kirkey, Sharon. 2013. "Woman Will Attempt to Carry a Child in Her Mother's Transplanted Womb in Groundbreaking Medical Procedure." *National Post*, August 30.

Kirkup, Kristy. 2016. "Number of Missing, Murdered Indigenous Women 'Way Bigger than 1,200,' Minister Says." *National Post*, February 15.

Kirwin W. J., G. M. Story, and J. D. A. Widdowson, eds. 1990. *Dictionary of Newfoundland English*, 2nd ed. Toronto, ON: University of Toronto Press.

Kivisto, Peter. 2012. "We Really Are All Multiculturalists Now." *The Sociological Quarterly* 53 (1): 1–24.

Kjaerby, Claus. 2015. "Nicaragua." In *The Indigenous World 2015*. Copenhagen: International Work Group For Indigenous Affairs: 97–106.

Klassen, Kelsey. 2014. "Two Spirits, One Struggle: The Front Lines of Being First Nations and Gay." *Westender*, July 30. http://www.westender.com/news-issues/two-spirits-one-struggle-the-front-lines-of-being-first-nations-and-gay-1.1269015. Accessed June 1, 2016.

KLI (Klingon Language Institute). 2016. http://www.kli.org/about-klingon/klingon-history/. Accessed June 1, 2016.

Kline, Jesse. 2011. "Internet Freedom Is under Threat Worldwide." *National Post*, July 2.

Koffler, Keith. 2012. "Obama Has Bowed Eight Times as President." *White House Dossier*, June 20. http://www.whitehousedossier.com/2012/06/20/obama-bowed-eight-times-president/.

Kolenda, Pauline M. 1978. *Caste in Contemporary India: Beyond Organic Solidarity*. Prospect Heights, IL: Waveland Press.

Komarnicki, Jamie. 2009. "Vanishing Voices." *Calgary Herald*, October 10.

Koning, Edward A., and Keith G. Banting. 2013. "Inequality below the Surface: Reviewing Immigrants' Access to and Utilization of Five Canadian Welfare Programs." *Canadian Public* Policy/Analyse de Politiques 39 (4): 581–601.

Kopinak, Kathryn. 1995. "Gender as a Vehicle for the Subordination of Women Maquiladora Workers in Mexico." *Latin American Perspectives* 22: 30–48.

Kose, Khalid, Pnina Werbner, and Len Ang. 2004. "Cultural Research and Refugee Studies: New Knowledge, Methodologies, and Practical Implications; A Panel Commentary." *Social Analysis: The International Journal of Social and Cultural Practice* 48 (3): 59–65.

Kosslyn, S. M., and R. S. RosenBerg. 2011. *Introducing Psychology*. Boston: Pearson.

Kotler, Philip. 1986. "Global Standardization—Courting Danger." *Journal of Consumer Marketing* 3 (2): 13–15.

Kourlas, Gia. 2010. "Playing Games with an Afro-Brazilian Leap into the Capoeira Circle." *New York Times*, March 25.

Krajick, Kevin. 1998. "Green Farming by the Incas?" *Science* 281: 323–29.

Krause, Elizabeth. 2005. *A Crisis of Births: Population Politics and Family-Making in Italy*. Belmont, CA: Wadsworth.

Kremer, William 2013. "Why Did Men Stop Wearing High Heels?" *BBC World Service News Magazine*, January 24. http://www.bbc.com/news/magazine-21151350.

Kroeber, Alfred L., and Clyde Kluckhohn. 1952. "Culture: A Critical Review of Concepts and Definitions." *Papers of the Peabody Museum of American Archaeology and Ethnology* 47 (1).

Krugel, Lauren. 2015. "Tories versus Timmies after Doughnut-and-Coffee Chain Pulls Enbridge Ads." *National Post*, June 5.

Krutak, Lars. 2012. *Spiritual Skin: Magical Tattoos and Scarification*. Munich: Editions: Reuss.

Kuklick, Henrika. 2008. *A New History of Anthropology*. Oxford: Blackwell.

Kulish, Nicholas. 2008. "Gay Muslims Pack a Dance Floor of Their Own." *New York Times*, January 1: A-4.

Kumar, Hari. 2005. "India's Harried Elite Now Turns, and Twists, to Yoga Lite." *New York Times*, February 1: A-4.

Kuntzman, Gersh. 1999. "It's Been 40 Years Coming and Now . . . Barbie's New, Improved and Tattooed." *New York Post*, February 4. http://nypost.com/1999/02/04/its-been-40-years-coming-and-now-barbies-new-improved-tattooed/.

Kuper, Hilda. 1986. *The Swazi: A South African Kingdom*, 2nd ed. New York: Holt, Rinehart & Winston.

Kurtz, Donald V. 2001. *Political Anthropology: Power and Paradigms*. Boulder, CO: Westview Press.

Kuznar, Lawrence. 1996. *Reclaiming a Scientific Anthropology*. Thousand Oaks, CA: Sage Publications.

Kwong, Matt. 2012. "Tattoo Culture Making Its Mark on Millennials." *CBC News*, September 19. http://www.cbc.ca/news/canada/tattoo-culture-making-its-mark-on-millennials-1.1149528.

Lacey, Marc. 2004. "Tribe, Claiming Whites' Land, Confronts Kenya's Government." *New York Times*, August 25: A-l.

Laforet, John. 2011. "The 'Missing' Generation of Girls." *The Huffington Post*, November 11. http://www.huffingtonpost.ca/john-laforet/female-feticide_b_1078348.html. Accessed July 20, 2015.

LaFraniere, Sharon. 2007. "In Mauritania, Seeking to End an Overfed Ideal." *New York Times*, July 4: A-4.

Lagasse, Katerina. 2014. "Art in the Alberni Residential School—"You Can't Separate (the Students) Again." *Unsettling*, November 24. https://unsettling2014.wordpress.com/2014/11/24/art-in-the-alberni-residential-school-you-cant-separate-the-students-again/. Accessed June 1, 2016.

Laird, David. 1876. *Annual Report of the Department of the Interior for the Year Ended 30th June, 1875*. Minister, Department of the Interior (Sessional Papers No. 9). Ottawa: Parliament of Canada.

Lamb, M. E. 1997. "The Development of Father-Infant Relationships." In *The Role of the Father in Child Development*, edited by M. E. Lamb, 104–20. New York: Wiley.

Lambert, Brittany, and Kate McInturff. 2016. *Making Women Count: The Unequal Economics of Women's Work*. Canadian Centre for Policy Alternatives and Oxfam Canada.

Lammam, Charles, Amela Karabegović, and Niels Veldhuis. 2012. *Measuring Income Mobility in Canada (Studies in Economic Prosperity)*. Vancouver, BC: Fraser Institute.

Lammam, Charles, and Hugh MacIntyre. 2016. *An Introduction to the State of Poverty in Canada*. Vancouver, BC: Fraser Institute.

Lamont, Tom. 2016. "Life after the Ashley Madison Affair." *The Guardian*, February 28. https://www.theguardian.com/technology/2016/feb/28/what-happened-after-ashley-madison-was-hacked.

Lamont-Brown, Raymond. 1999. "Japan's New Spirituality." *Contemporary Review*, August: 70–73.

Lamphere, Louise. 1974. "Strategies, Conflict, and Cooperation among Women in Domestic Groups." In *Women, Culture, and Society*, edited by Michelle Zimbalist Rosaldo and Louise Lamphere. Stanford, CA: Stanford University Press.

Lang, Andrew. 1898. *The Making of Religion*. London: Longmans, Green, and Co.

Lang, George. 2008. *Making Wawa: The Genesis of Chinook Jargon*. Vancouver: UBC Press.

Laumann, Anne E., and Amy J. Derick. 2006. "Tattoos and Body Piercings in the United States: A National Data Set." *Journal of the American Academy of Dermatology* 55 (3): 413–21.

Lave, Jean, and Etienne Wenger. 1991. *Situated Learning: Legitimate Peripheral Participation*. Cambridge, UK: Cambridge University Press.

Leacock, Eleanor Burke. 1978. Women's Status in Egalitarian Society: Implications for Social Evolution. *Current Anthropology* 19 (2): 235–59.

Leader-Post, The (Regina). 2007. "Cultural 'Honour' Killing Brought to Canada. *The Leader-Post (Regina)*, June 11. http://www.canada.com/vancouversun/story.html?id=d05e437f-4661-4965-9455-ff30c6b9d4a5&k=20265. Accessed June 1, 2016.

Lears, T. J. Jackson. 1985. "The Concept of Cultural Hegemony: Problems and Possibilities." *American Historical Review* 90 (3): 567–93.

Lee, Dorothy. 1993. "Religious Perspectives in Anthropology." In *Magic, Witchcraft, and Religion: An Anthropological Study of the Supernatural*, 3rd ed, edited by Arthur C. Lehmann and James E. Myers, 10–17. Mountain View, CA: Mayfield.

Lee, Richard B. 2003. *The Dobe Ju/'hoansi*, 3rd ed. Belmont, CA: Wadsworth.

——. 2007. "The Ju/'hoansi at the Crossroads: Continuity and Change in the Time of AIDS." In *Globalization and Change in 15 Cultures: Born in One World, Living in Another*, edited by George Spindler and Janice Stockard, 144–71. Belmont, CA: Wadsworth.

——. 2012. *The Dobe Ju/'hoansi*, 4th ed. Case Studies in Cultural Anthropology, edited by Janice E. Stockard and George Spindler. Belmont, CA: Wadsworth Publishing.

Leung, Clint. 2007. *The Northwest Coast Native American Potlatch Ceremony*. http://ezinearticles.com/?expert=Clint_Leung. Accessed June 19, 2010.

Lévi-Strauss, Claude. 1963. "The Sorcerer and His Magic." In *Structural Anthropology*, Vol. 1: 167–85. London: Peregrine.

Lewellen, Ted. 2003. *Political Anthropology: An Introduction*, 3rd ed. New York: Praeger.

Lewin, Ellen, ed. 2006. *Feminist Anthropology: A Reader*. Malden, MA: Blackwell Publishing.

Lewis, Charles. 2009. "Charles Lewis: Bury St. Joseph, Sell Your Home." *National Post*, April 23.

——. 2011. "At the World's Hottest Church." *National Post*, December 23. http://news.nationalpost.com/holy-post/at-the-worlds-hottest-church.

Ley, David, and Roman Cybriwsky. 1974. "Urban Graffiti as Territorial Markers." *Annals of the Association of American Geographers* 64 (4): 491–505.

Lindenbaum, Shirley. 2008. "Understanding Kuru: The Contribution of Anthropology and Medicine." In *The End of Kuru: 50 Years of Research into an Extraordinary Disease. Philosophical Transactions: Biological Sciences* 363 (1510; Nov. 27): 3715–20.

Lindsay, Colin. 2008. "Canadians Attend Weekly Religious Services Less Than 20 Years Ago." *Statistics Canada*. http://www.statcan.gc.ca/pub/89-630-x/2008001/article/10650-eng.htm.

Linneman, Thomas J. 2013. "Gender in Jeopardy! Intonation Variation on a Television Game Show." *Gender & Society* 27 (1): 82–105.

Linton, Ralph. 1936. *The Study of Man*. New York: Appleton-Century-Crofts.

Llana, Sara Miller. 2006. "Megaships May Displace Boats in Lake Nicaragua." *USA Today*, November 26. http://usatoday30.usatoday.com/news/world/2006-11-26-nicaragua-canal_x.htm

Lockwood, Amy 2011. Ted Talk. July 2011. https://www.ted.com/talks/amy_lockwood_selling_condoms_in_the_congo. Accessed February 28, 2015.

Loewe, Michael, and Edward L. Shaughnessy. 1999. *The Cambridge History of Ancient China*. Cambridge, UK: Cambridge University Press.

Lofaro, Tony. 2014. "Nepean Football Club Goes with Eagles for Its New Name." *Ottawa Citizen*, January 12. http://ottawacitizen.com/news/local-news/nepean-football-club-goes-with-eagles-for-its-new-name/. Accessed October 15, 2016.

Lomax, Alan. 1968. *Folk Song Style and Culture*. Washington, DC: American Association for the Advancement of Science.

Loppie, Samantha, Charlotte Reading, and Sarah de Leeuw. 2014. *Aboriginal Experiences with Racism and Its Impacts*. Prince George, BC: National Collaborating Centre for Aboriginal Health.

Los Angeles Times. 1989. "'Dad' to Adopted Sons: Jazz Player Billy Tipton Kept Her Secret to the End." *Los Angeles Times*, February 1. http://articles.latimes.com/1989-02-01/news/mn-1454_1_billy-tipton.

Lucas-Stannard, Paige. 2012. *Gender Neutral Parenting: Raising Kids with the Freedom to be Themselves*. Pleasant Grove, UT: Verity Publishing.

Lutz, Ellen L. 2007. "Dam Nation." *Cultural Survival Quarterly* 31 (4).

——. 2008. "Panama Dam Construction Steps up the Pace." *Cultural Survival Quarterly* 32 (1).

Lydersen, Kari. 2014. "Ebola Teams Need Better Cultural Understanding, Anthropologists Say." *Discover Magazine*, December 9. http://blogs.discovermagazine.com/crux/2014/12/09/ebola-cultural-anthropologists/#.VNU35i7LkVc. Accessed Feb 1, 2015.

Macdonald, David, and Daniel Wilson. 2013. *Poverty or Prosperity: Indigenous Children in Canada*. Canadian Centre for Policy Alternatives and Save the Children. https://www.policyalternatives.ca/sites/default/files/uploads/publications/National%20Office/2013/06/Poverty_or_Prosperity_Indigenous_Children.pdf

MacFarquhar, Emily. 1994. "The War against Women." *U.S. News & World Report*, March 28: 42–48.

MacGregor, R. M. (2003). "I Am Canadian: National Identity in Beer Commercials." *Journal of Popular Culture* 37 (2): 276–86. Copyright © 2003, John Wiley and Sons.

Macionis, John J., and Linda M. Gerber. 2013. *Sociology, Eighth Canadian Edition*. Toronto: Pearson Canada.

MacKinnnon [sic], Rebecca. 2012. "Rebecca MacKinnnon [sic]: China's 'Networked Authoritarianism.'" *National Post*, January 28.

MacRae, Meghan. 2014. "Mokomokai: The Preserved Heads of Māori Tribespeople." *Cvltnation.com*, November 25. http://www.cvltnation.com/mokomokai-the-preserved-heads-of-Māori-tribespeople/. Accessed June 1, 2016.

Madigan, Brian, 2010. "Need an Agent? Why Not Choose St. Joseph?" *Active Rain blog*. http://activerain.com/blogsview/1581759/need-an-agent–why-not-choose-st–joseph-.

Madsbjerg, Christian, and Mikkel B. Rasmussen. 2014. "An Anthropologist Walks into a Bar ...." *Harvard Business Review*. https://hbr.org/2014/03/an-anthropologist-walks-into-a-bar/. Accessed September 25, 2016.

Maekawa, Ichiro. 2015. "Neo-Colonialism Reconsidered: A Case Study of East Africa in the 1960s and 1970s." *The Journal of Imperial and Commonwealth History* 43 (2): 317–41.

Mahapatra, Dhananjay. 2014. "Supreme Court Recognizes Transgenders as 'Third Gender.'" *The Times of India*, April 15. http://timesofindia.indiatimes.com/india/Supreme-Court-recognizes-transgenders-as-third-gender/articleshow/33767900.cms. Accessed July 20, 2015.

Malinowski, Bronislaw. 1922. *Argonauts of the Western Pacific*. New York: Dutton.

——. 1962. *Sex, Culture, and Myth*. New York: Harcourt, Brace and World.

Mandelbaum, David G. 1970. *Society in India*, Vol. 1. Berkeley: University of California Press.

Maquet, Jacques J. 1962. *The Premise of Inequality in Ruanda: A Study of Political Relations in a Central African Kingdom*. London: Oxford University Press.

Marcus, George E. 1995. "Ethnography in/of the World System: The Emergence of Multi-Sited Ethnography." *Annual Review of Anthropology* 24: 95–117.

Marett, Robert. 1914. *The Threshold of Religion*. London: Methuen.

Marshall, Ingeborg. 1998. *A History and Ethnography of the Beothuk*. Montreal: McGill-Queen's University Press.

Marshall, Lillie. 2010. "How I Offended an Entire Class through Cultural Ignorance." *Around the World "L."com*. http://www.aroundtheworldl.com/2010/03/22/how-i-offended-an-entire-class-through-cultural-ignorance/. Accessed November 9, 2015.

Martin, Carol Lynn, and Diane Ruble. 2004. "Children's Search for Gender Cues: Cognitive Perspectives on Gender Development." *Current Directions in Psychological Science* 13 (2): 67–70.

Martin, William J. II, Roger I. Glass, John M. Balbus, and Francis S. Collins. 2011. "Public Health: A Major Environmental Cause of Death." *Science* 334 (6053): 180–81. DOI: 10.1126/science.1213088.

Martin-Hill, Dawn. 2008. *The Lubicon Lake Nation*. Toronto: University of Toronto Press.

Mas, Susana, and Alison Crawford. 2015. "Justin Trudeau's Government Drops Controversial Niqab Appeal." *CBC News*, November 16.

Mascia-Lees, Frances, and Nancy Johnson Black. 2000. *Gender and Anthropology*. Prospect Heights, IL: Waveland Press.

Masters, K. 2011. "A Brief Guide to Understanding MOOCs." *The Internet Journal of Medical Education* 1 (2). http://print.ispub.com/api/0/ispub-article/10995.

Mauss, Marcel. 1954. *The Gift*, translated by I. Cunnison. New York: Free Press.

Maxwell, Angie, Pearl Ford-Dowe, Rafael Jimeno, Todd Shields. 2016. "Is There a War on Women? Attitudes about Women in the Workplace and in Politics: A Report from the 2012 Blair Center-Clinton School Poll." *Blair Center-Clinton School Poll*. http://blaircenterclintonschoolpoll.uark.edu/6759.php. Accessed March 16, 2016.

Mayor, Adrienne. 1999. "People Illustrated: In Antiquity, Tattoos Could Beautify, Shock, or Humiliate." *Archaeology* 52 (2 March/April).

McAuliffe, Cameron. 2012. "Graffiti or Street Art? Negotiating the Moral Geographies of the Creative City." *Journal of Urban Affairs* 34 (2): 189–206.

McClendon, Garrard. 2004. *Ax or Ask? The African American Guide to Better English.* Mcclendon Report.Com.

McCullough, Michael E., and Brian L. B. Willoughby. 2009. "Religion, Self-Regulation, and Self-Control: Associations, Explanations, and Implications. *Psychological Bulletin* 139 (1): 69–93.

McGrane, Bernard. 1989. *Beyond Anthropology: Society and the Other.* New York: Columbia University Press.

McKay, Alexander, and Mary Bissell. 2010. *Sexual Health Education in the Schools: Questions & Answers*, 3rd ed. Ottawa: SIECCAN Sex Information and Education Council of Canada.

McKay-Panos, Linda. 2015. "Settlement Agreements Can Pose Challenges for Human Rights Commissions." *ABlawg University of Calgary Faculty of Law*, March 12. http://ablawg.ca/2015/03/12/settlement-agreements-can-pose-challenges-for-human-rights-commissions/.

Mcloughlin, Darren. 2014. "International Wall of Art on Belfast Peace Line Is a Modern Day Berlin Wall." *UntappedCities.com*, April 2. http://untappedcities.com/2014/04/02/international-wall-of-art-on-belfast-peace-line-is-a-modern-day-berlin-wall/. Accessed October 20, 2015.

McMahon, Rob. 2014. "From Digital Divides to the First Mile: Indigenous Peoples and the Network Society in Canada." *International Journal of Communication* 8: 2002–26.

McMahon, Rob, Michael Gursten, Brian Beaton, Susan O'Donnell, and Tim Whiteduck. 2014. "Making Information Technologies Work at the End of the Road." *Journal of Information Policy* 4: 250–69.

McMahon, Rob, H. E. Hudson, and L. Fabian. 2014. "Indigenous Regulatory Advocacy in Canada's Far North: Mobilizing the First Mile Connectivity Consortium." *Journal of Information Policy* 4: 228–49.

McMahon, Rob, and Richard Smith, 2010. "Ensuring Aboriginal Involvement in Canada's National Digital Strategy." *Digital Canada 150.* https://www.ic.gc.ca/eic/site/028.nsf/eng/00448.html. Accessed June 1, 2016.

McNaughton, Graeme, and Megan O'Toole. 2012. " 'Zhe' & 'Hir': Toronto School Board Guidelines on Gender Identity Allow for Non-masculine/Feminine Pronouns." *National Post*, October 4.

McParland, Kelly. 2014. "Vancouver School Board Gender Policy Allows 'Xe' or 'Xem' in Place of 'He' or 'Her.' " *National Post*, June 17. Accessed June 1, 2016.

——. 2015. Kelly McParland: "'Appropriating' Cultures Is What Canada Is All About." *National Post*, November 24.

McWhorter, John. 2014. "You Can't 'Steal' a Culture: In Defense of Cultural Appropriation." *The Daily Beast*, July 15. http://www.thedailybeast.com/articles/2014/07/15/you-can-t-steal-a-culture-in-defense-of-cultural-appropriation.html.

Mead, Margaret. 1928. *Coming of Age in Samoa.* New York: Morrow.

——. 1935. *Sex and Temperament in Three Primitive Societies.* New York: Morrow.

Meakins, Felicity. 2013. "Mixed languages." In *Contact Languages: A Comprehensive Guide*, edited by Peter Bakker and Yaron Matras, 159–228. Berlin: Mouton de Gruyter.

Media New Zealand. 2016. "Ta Moko—Significance of Māori Tattoos." http://media.newzealand.com/en/story-ideas/ta-moko-significance-of-maori-tattoos/. Accessed May 24, 2016.

Mehta, Suketu. 2004. "Bollywood Confidential." *New York Times Magazine*, November 14: 60ff.

Meissner, Dirk. 2015. "Footprints Found on a Remote B.C. Island Could Be 13,000 Years Old—the Oldest in North America." *National Post*, June 23.

Mellor, Clare. 2011. "Africville Trust Hiring Prompts Some Anger." *The Chronicle Herald*, September 15.

Merton, Robert K. 1957. *Social Theory and Social Structure.* Glencoe, IL: Free Press.

Metcalf, Peter A. 1978. Death Be Not Strange. *Natural History* 87: 6–12.

Meyer, Erin. 2014. "One Reason Cross-Cultural Small Talk Is So Tricky." *Harvard Business Review*, May 30. https://hbr.org/2014/05/one-reason-cross-cultural-small-talk-is-so-tricky/.

Michrina, Barry P., and Cherylanne Richards. 1996. *Person to Person: Fieldwork, Dialogue, and the Hermeneutic Method.* Albany, NY: State University of New York Press.

Middlebrook, Diane Wood. 1999. *Suits Me: The Double Life of Billy Tipton.* Boston: Houghton Mifflin Company.

Middleton, John, and David Tait, eds. 1958. *Tribes without Rulers: Studies in African Segmentary Systems.* London: Routledge & Kegan Paul.

Milan, Anne. 2013. "Marital Status: Overview, 2011." *Statistics Canada.*

Milke, Mark. 2013a. "Aboriginal People Do Better off Reserve." *Winnipeg Free Press*, January 14. http://www.winnipegfreepress.com/opinion/analysis/Aboriginal-people-do-better-off-reserve-186812201.html. Accessed October 24, 2016.

——. 2013b. *Increasing Number of Aboriginals Choose Not to Live on Reserves.* Vancouver, BC: Fraser Institute.

Miller, David E. 2011. "Saudi Arabia's 'Anti-Witchcraft Unit' Breaks Another Spell." *Jerusalem Post*, July 20. http://www.jpost.com/Middle-East/Saudi-Arabias-Anti-Witchcraft-Unit-breaks-another-spell.

Milligan, Kevin. 2013. "What the Data Shows about Female Breadwinners in Canada." *Maclean's*, June 10.

Mills, George. 1957. "Art: An Introduction to Qualitative Anthropology." *Journal of Aesthetics and Art Criticism* 16 (1): 1–17.

Mintz, Sidney W. 1986. *Sweetness and Power: The Place of Sugar in Modern History.* London: Penguin Books.

Moir, Matt. 2016. "The World of Political Correctness, According to Chinese Students." *Highbrow Magazine*, January 31. http://www.highbrowmagazine.com/5588-world-political-correctness-according-chinese-students. Accessed October 13, 2016.

Montague, Ty. 2013. "Would You Wear That Company's T-Shirt in Public?" *HBR Blog Network*, July 8.

Montes, Veronica. 2013. "The Role of Emotions in the Construction of Masculinity: Guatemalan Migrant Men, Transnational Migration, and Family Relations." *Gender & Society* 27: 469–90.

Montler, Timothy. 1999. "Language and Dialect Variation in Straits Salishan." *Anthropological Linguistics*, 41 (4): 462–502.

Montreal Museum of Contemporary Art (Musée d'art contemorain de Montréal). 2015. http://www.macm.org/en/. Accessed October 20, 2015.

Mooney, James. 1897. *The Ghost-Dance Religion and the Sioux Outbreak of 1890.* US Bureau of American Ethnology, 1892-3 Annual Report, 1897.

Morgan, Andy. 2011. "From Fear to Fury: How the Arab World Found Its Voice." *The Guardian*, February 27. http://www.theguardian.com/music/2011/feb/27/egypt-tunisia-music-protests.

Morgan, Clara. 2008. *Afghanistan: The Status of Women.* (Parliamentary Information and Research Service (PRB 07-34E)).Ottawa: Library of Parliament InfoSeries.

Morgan, Lewis H. 1963. *Ancient Society.* New York: World (orig. 1877).

Morris, Mike. 2012. *Concise Dictionary of Social and Cultural Anthropology.* West Sussex: John Wiley & Sons.

Mortada, Radwan. 2014. "What Does ISIS' Declaration of a Caliphate Mean?" *Al-Akhbar English*, June 30.

Mourant, A.E. Ada C. Kopec Kazimiera Domaniewska-Sobczak. 1976. The Distribution of the Human Blood Groups and Other Polymorphisms (2nd Revised edition).Oxford. Oxford University Press.

Muhammad, Amin A. 2010. *Preliminary Examination of So-called "Honour Killings" in Canada.* Ottawa: Department of Justice.

Muhammad, Fatima. 2013. "Calls for Reforms in Hai'a Functioning." *Saudi Gazette*, May 08. http://www.saudigazette.com.sa/index.cfm?method=home.regcon&contentid=20130508164754.

Mulan. 1998. Directed by Tony Bancroft and Barry Cook. "I'll Make a Man out of You," by Matthew Wilder and David Zippel. Performed by Donny Osmond and Disney Studio Chorus. Produced by Walt Disney Feature Animation and Walt Disney Pictures, DVD.

Mulder, Monique B. 1992. "Women's Strategies in Polygynous Marriage." *Human Nature* 3(1): 45–70.

Mulvaney, D. J. 1990. "Warner, William Lloyd (1898–1970)." *Australian Dictionary of Biography.* National Centre of Biography, Australian National University.

Munger, Kristen, and Shelby J. Harris. 1989. "Effects of an Observer on Handwashing in a Public Restroom." *Perceptual and Motor Skills* 69 (3): 733–34.

Murphy, Richard McGill. 2005. "Getting to Know You: Microsoft Dispatches Anthropologists into the Field to Study Small Businesses Like Yours." *Money.cnn.com.* http://money.cnn.com/magazines/fsb/fsb_archive/2005/06/01/8261971/. Accessed September 25, 2016.

Musto, R.J. 1990. "Indian Reserves: Canada's Developing Nations." *Canadian Family Physician*, January 36: 105–16.

Myers, Brendan. 2008. *Aboriginal Policing Update*, 2008. Public Safety Canada. http://www.publicsafety.gc.ca/cnt/rsrcs/pblctns/brgnl-plcng-pdt-2008/index-en.aspx.

Myers, Merlin G. 2006. *Households and Families of the Longhouse Iroquois at Six Nations Reserve*. Lincoln: University of Nebraska Press.

Nanda, Serena. 1992. "Arranging a Marriage in India." In *The Naked Anthropologist*, edited by Philip DeVita, 137–43. Belmont, CA: Wadsworth.

NAPA (National Association for the Practice of Anthropology). 2012. practicing anthropology.org. Accessed February 28, 2015.

Narang, Devanshu. 2012. "Experiences of an Immigrant to Canada." *The Times of India*, February 29. http://timesofindia.indiatimes.com/nri/citizen-journalists/citizen-journalists-reports/devanshu-narang/Experiences-of-an-immigrant-to-Canada/articleshow/12080183.cms.

Nathanson, Paul. 2001. *Spreading Misandry: The Teaching of Contempt for Men in Popular Culture*. Montreal and Kingston: McGill-Queen's University Press.

Nathanson, Paul, and Katherine K. Young. 2006. *Legalizing Misandry: From Public Shame to Systemic Discrimination against Men*. Montreal and Kingston: McGill-Queen's University Press.

National Association of Practicing Anthropologists (NAPA). 2012. "American Breakfast and the Mother-in-Law: How an Anthropologist Created Go-Gurt." http://www.practicinganthropology.org/learn/?storyid=4.

National Defence and the Canadian Armed Forces. 2014. "Women in the Canadian Armed Forces Backgrounder." March 6 / Project number: BG-14 006. http://www.forces.gc.ca/en/news/article.page?doc=women-in-the-canadian-armed-forces/hie8w7rm. Accessed July 20, 2015.

National Post Staff. 2012. "Good Deed" by Rogue Restoration Pensioner Ruins 19th-Century Spanish Fresco." *National Post*, August 22. http://news.nationalpost.com/news/good-deed-by-rogue-restoration-pensioner-ruins-19th-century-spanish-fresco.

NCCM (The National Council of Canadian Muslims). 2016. *Tracking Anti-Muslim Incidents Reported across Canada*. The National Council of Canadian Muslims. http://www.nccm.ca/map/#.

Nelson, Dean. 2014. "Eunuchs Sanctioned as Third Sex in India." *National Post*, April 16.

Nelson, K. A. 2004. "Consumer Decision Making and Image Theory: Understanding Value-Laden Decisions." *Journal of Consumer Psychology* 14 (1-2): 28–40.

Nettl, Bruno. 1980. "Ethnomusicology: Definitions, Directions, and Problems." In *Music of Many Cultures*, edited by Elizabeth May, 1–9. Berkeley: University of California Press.

Nettl, Bruno, and Philip V. Bohlman, eds. 1991. *Comparative Musicology and Anthropology of Music*. Chicago: University of Chicago Press.

Newell, Jenny, and Jonathan King. 2006. "Human Remains from New Zealand: Briefing Note for Trustees." London: The British Museum.

Newman, Katherine S. 1988. *Falling from Grace: The Experience of Downward Mobility in the American Middle Class*. New York: Free Press.

New Netherland Institute. "Tiger Woods [1975]." *Exploring America's Dutch Heritage*. http://www.newnetherlandinstitute.org/history-and-heritage/dutch_americans/tiger-woods/. Accessed August 10, 2015.

Nhanenge, Jytte. 2011. *Ecofeminism: Towards Integrating the Concerns of Women, Poor People, and Nature into Development*. Lanham, MD: United Press of America.

Niehaus, Isak. 2012. "Witchcraft." *Oxford Bibliographies*. http://www.oxfordbibliographies.com/view/document/obo-9780199766567/obo-9780199766567-0029.xml DOI: 10.1093/obo/9780199766567-0029. Accessed June 1, 2016.

Nittle, Nadra Kareem. 2015. "What Is Cultural Appropriation and Why Is It Wrong?" *About.com*, June 22. http://racerelations.about.com/od/diversitymatters/fl/What-Is-Cultural-Appropriation-and-Why-Is-It-Wrong.htm. Accessed June 1, 2016.

Nkrumah, Kwame. [1965] 2004. *Neo-Colonialism: The Last Stage of Imperialism*. London: Panaf Books.

Nobelprize.org. 2014. "The Nobel Peace Prize 2014." *Nobelprize.org*. http://www.nobelprize.org/nobel_prizes/peace/laureates/2014/.

Nossiter, Adam. 2014. Fear of Ebola Opens Wary Villages to Outsiders in Guinea. *NYTimes.com*, November 16. http://www.nytimes.com/2014/11/17/world/africa/fear-of-ebola-opens-wary-villages-to-outsiders-in-guinea.html?_r=2. Accessed February 1, 2015.

NPR. 2014. The Experts the Ebola Response May Need: Anthropologists. *NPR News*, September 28. http://www.npr.org/blogs/goatsandsoda/2014/09/28/351845664/the-experts-missing-from-the-ebola-response-anthropologists. Accessed February 1, 2015.

Nunes, Maria Luisa. 1987. *Becoming True to Ourselves: Cultural Decolonization and National Identity in the Literature of the Portuguese-Speaking World*. (Contributions to the Study of World Literature, Number 22). New York: Greenwood Press.

Nussbaum, Bruce. 2006. "Ethnography Is the New Core Competence." *Bloomberg.com*. http://www.bloomberg.com/news/articles/2006-06-18/ethnography-is-the-new-core-competence/. Accessed September 25, 2016.

Nuu-chah-nulth Tribal Council. 2015. http://www.nuuchahnulth.org/tribal-council/welcome.html. Accessed August 30, 2015.

Nwokeji, G. Ugo. 2002. "African Economies in the Years of Decolonization." In *The End of Colonial Rule: Nationalism and Decolonization*, edited by Toyin Falola. *Africa* 4: 131–57. Durham, NC: Carolina Academic Press.

NZETC (New Zealand Electronic Text Collection). 2015. *Mokomokai: Preserving the Past*. http://nzetc.victoria.ac.nz/tm/scholarly/tei-TeIMoko.html. Accessed June 1, 2016.

Oberg, Kalervo. 1960. "Culture Shock: Adjustments to New Cultural Environments." *Practical Anthropology* July/August: 177–82.

Oboler, Regina Smith. 1980. "Is the Female Husband a Man? Woman/Woman Marriage among the Nandi of Kenya." *Ethnology* 19 (1 Jan): 69–88.

O'Connor, Joe. 2011. "School Drops Halifax Founder's Name over Mi'kmaq Complaints." *National Post*, July 5.

——. 2012. "Multiculturalism in Its Controversial Glory: Is Canada a 'Country without a Core Culture?'" *National Post*, October 24.

O'Connor, Lydia. 2013. "San Francisco Train Passengers Too Distracted by Phones to Notice Shooter's Gun in Plain Sight." *The Huffington Post*, October 10.

OECD Economic Surveys: Canada. 2014. OECD Better Life Index: http://stats.oecd.org/Index.aspx?DataSetCode=BLI. Canada data set: http://www.oecdbetterlifeindex.org/countries/canada/. Accessed July 20, 2015.

OED Online version (June 2013) *Culture*. Oxford: Oxford University Press.

Office of the Commissioner of Official Languages. 1992. *Our Two Official Languages over Time*. Ottawa, ON: Office of the Commissioner of Official Languages.

Office of the Correctional Investigator. 2013. *Backgrounder: Aboriginal Offenders–A Critical Situation*. http://www.oci-bec.gc.ca/cnt/rpt/oth-aut/oth-aut20121022info-eng.aspx. modified 2013-09-16. Accessed August 10, 2015.

——. 2014. *Annual Report 2013-2014 of the Office of the Correctional Investigator*. Ottawa: Queen's Printer.

OFIFC (Ontario Federation of Indian Friendship Centres). 2013. *Bidwewidam Indigenous Masculinities Identities and Mino-Bimazaadiziwin*. Toronto: OFIFC. www.IndigenousMasculinities.com.

Ohlheiser, Abby. 2014. "A Not-So-Brief List of All the Things President Obama Has Bowed To." *The Wire*, April 24. http://www.thewire.com/politics/2014/04/a-not-so-brief-list-of-all-the-things-president-obama-has-bowed-to/361160/

OHRC (Ontario Human Rights Commission). n.d. *4. FGM in Canada*. http://www.ohrc.on.ca/en/policy-female-genital-mutilation-fgm/4-fgm-canada. Accessed July 20, 2015.

——. 2003. *Paying the Price: The Human Cost of Racial Profiling*. http://www.ohrc.on.ca/en/paying-price-human-cost-racial-profiling.

Okrent, Arika. 2009. *In the Land of Invented Languages: Esperanto Rock Stars, Klingon Poets, Loglan Lovers, and the Mad Dreamers Who Tried to Build a Perfect Language*. New York: Random House.

Oliver-Smith, Antony. 2005. "Applied Anthropology and Development-Induced Displacement and Resettlement." In

Applied Anthropology: Domains of Application, edited by Satish Kedia and John Van Willigen, 189–220. Westport, CT: Prager Publishers.

——. 2010. *Defying Displacement: Grassroots Resistance and the Critique of Development.* Austin, TX: University of Texas Press.

Onishijan, Norimitsu, 2015. "As Ebola Ebbs in Africa, Focus Turns from Death to Life." *NYTimes.com*, January 31. http://www.nytimes.com/2015/02/01/world/as-ebola-ebbs-in-africa-focus-turns-from-death-to-life.html?action=click&contentCollection=International%20Business&module=RelatedCoverage®ion=Marginalia&pgtype=article. Accessed February 1.

Ortner, Sherry B. 1974. "Is Female to Male as Nature Is to Culture? In *Woman, Culture, and Society*, edited by M. Z. Rosaldo and L. Lamphere, 68–87. Stanford, CA: Stanford University Press.

Ouchi, William G. 1981. *Theory Z.* New York: Avon Books.

Oudshoorn, Kieran. 2016. "Filmmaker Alethea Arnaquq-Baril Had Feared Doc Would Spark Copycat Tattoo Trend among Non-Inuit." *CBC News*, January 9. http://www.cbc.ca/news/canada/north/film-inuit-tattoos-1.3396160.

Paige, R. M., A. D. Cohen, B. Kappler, J. C. Chi, and J. P. Lassegard. 2002. *Maximizing Study Abroad: A Student's Guide to Strategies for Language and Culture Learning and Use.* Minneapolis and St. Paul, MN: University of Minnesota: Center for Advanced Research on Language Acquisition.

Paradis, Gilles. 2012. "Occupy Wall Street, Bay Street and the Street Nearest You." *Canadian Journal of Public Health* 103 (2): 83.

Parker, Arthur C. 1913. *The Code of Handsome Lake, the Seneca Prophet.* Albany: New York State Museum Bulletin, No. 163.

Parker, Emily. 2014. "Social Media and the Hong King Protests." *The New Yorker*, October 1.

Parliament of Canada. 2004. *Assisted Human Reproduction Act.* http://www.parl.gc.ca/HousePublications/Publication.aspx?DocId=2331611&Language=e&Mode=1&File=22.

——. 2016. *Parliamentary Poet Laureate, the.* http://www.parl.gc.ca/About/Parliament/Poet/index-e.html. Accessed November 10, 2016.

Pascale, R., and A. Athos. 1981. *The Art of Japanese Management.* London: Penguin.

Pasquali, Valentina. 2015. "The Richest Countries in the World." *Global Finance*, November 6. https://www.gfmag.com/global-data/economic-data/richest-countries-in-the-world?page=12. Accessed November 9, 2015.

Paton, Callum. 2015. "Mr, Mrs, Miss . . . and Mx: Transgender People Will Be Able to Use New Title on Official Documents." *Mailonline*, May 3. http://www.dailymail.co.uk/news/article-3066043/A-new-title-transgender-people-join-Mr-Mrs-Miss-used-driving-licences-bank-details-government-departments.html. Accessed June 1, 2016.

Patriquin, Martin. 2016. "The Angry, Radical Right." *MacLean's Magazine*, January 21. http://www.macleans.ca/politics/the-angry-radical-right/.

PBS. 2003. *Skin Stories: The Art and Culture of Polynesian Tattoo: History of Tattoo.* http://www.pbs.org/skinstories/history/newzealand.html. Accessed June 1, 2016.

Peacock, James L. 1986. *The Anthropological Lens.* Cambridge, UK: Cambridge University Press.

Perry, Barbara, and Ryan Scrivens. 2016. "Uneasy Alliances: A Look at the Right-Wing Extremist Movement in Canada." *Studies in Conflict & Terrorism (Special Issue: Measurement Issues in the Study of Terrorism)* 39 (9): 819–41.

Petit, Carolyn. 2013. "Grand Theft Auto V Review: City of Angels and Demons." *Gamespot*, September 16. http://www.gamespot.com/reviews/grand-theft-auto-v-review/1900-6414475/.

Petrou, Michael. 2015. "What's Driving Teen Girls to Jihad?" *Macleans*, March 7. http://www.macleans.ca/society/teen-girl-jihadists/.

PEW (Pew Research Center). 2003. *PEW Poll: Two Years after 9/11, Growing Number of Americans Link Islam to Violence.* Washington, DC: PEW Research Center. http://www.pewforum.org/2003/09/10/poll-two-years-after-911-growing-number-of-americans-link-islam-to-violence/. Accessed October 15, 2016.

Pew Research Center. 2013. *The Global Divide on Homosexuality.* http://www.pewglobal.org/2013/06/04/the-global-divide-on-homosexuality/. Accessed July 20, 2015.

Picard, André. 2011. "Transplant Waiting Lists and Dialysis Costs Grow as Kidney Supply Lags Behind. *The Globe and Mail*, January 20.

Pike, Sarah M. 2004. *New Age and Neopagan Religions in America.* New York: Columbia University Press.

Poisson, Jayme. 2011. "Parents Keep Child's Gender Secret." *Toronto Star*, May 21.

——. 2013. "Remember Storm? We Check in on the Baby Being Raised Gender-Neutral." *Toronto Star*, November 15.

Polanyi, Karl. 1957. "The Economy as Instituted Process." In *Trade and Market in the Early Empires*, edited by Karl Polanyi, Conrad Arensberg, and Harry Pearson, 243–70. New York: Free Press.

Polgreen, Lydia. 2010. "One Bride for 2 Brothers: A Custom Fades in India." *NY Times*, July 17. http://www.nytimes.com/2010/07/17/world/asia/17polyandry.html?_r=0

Poon, Linda. 2014. Why Anthropologists Join an Ebola Outbreak Team. *NPR (National Public Radio) Shots - Health News*, April 2. http://www.npr.org/blogs/health/2014/04/02/298369305/why-anthropologists-join-an-ebola-outbreak-team. Accessed February 1, 2015.

Posadzki, Alexandra. 2014. "Unisex School Bathrooms Sparks Vancouver Debate about Gender Identity, Parental Rights." *The Globe and Mail*, June 13.

Price, Sally. 2001. *Primitive Art in Civilized Places.* Chicago: University of Chicago Press.

Prior, Ian. 1971. "The Price of Civilization." *Nutrition Today* 6 (4): 2–11.

Puddington, Arch. 2015. *Freedom House 2015. Freedom in the World 2015. Discarding Democracy: Return to the Iron Fist.* Washington, DC: Freedom House.

Puzic, Sonja. 2015. "Anti-cyberbullying Law, Bill C-13, Now in Effect." *CTVNews.ca*, March 9. http://www.ctvnews.ca/politics/anti-cyberbullying-law-bill-c-13-now-in-effect-1.2270460.

Quan, Douglas. 2015. "B.C. Human Rights Tribunal to Consider Striking Gender Designation from Birth Certificates." *National Post*, May 25.

Radke, James. 2015. "2015's New Midway Foods Are Waiting for You – The Midway Champion!!" *Calgary Stampede.com*, April 30. http://blog.calgarystampede.com/2015/04/30/2015s-new-midway-foods-are-waiting-for-you-the-midway-champion/

Raffaele, Paul. 2006. "In John They Trust." *Smithsonian Magazine*, February. http://www.smithsonianmag.com/history/in-john-they-trust-109294882/#zZSPXZ5ulY20YCxD.99.

Rai, Saritha. 2004. "Short on Priests, U.S. Catholics Outsource Prayers to Indian Clergy." *New York Times*, June 13: 13.

Rajiva, Mythili, and Amar Khoday. 2014. "Peddling the Margins of Gender-Based Violence: Canadian Media Coverage of Honour Killings." In *Within the Confines: Women and the Law in Canada*, edited by Jennifer M. Kilty, 174–202. Toronto: Women's Press.

Rankin, Jim. 2010. "When Good People Are Swept up with the Bad." *The Star*, February 6. http://www.thestar.com/news/gta/2010/02/06/when_good_people_are_swept_up_with_the_bad.html.

Ranson, Gillian. 2010. *Against the Grain: Couples, Gender, and the Reframing of Parenting.* Toronto: University of Toronto Press.

Raphael, D., and F. Davis. 1985. *Only Mothers Know: Patterns of Infant Feeding in Traditional Cultures.* Westport, CT: Greenwood Press.

Rass, N. 2006. *Policies and Strategies to Address the Vulnerability of Pastoralists in Sub-Saharan Africa.* Rome: Pro-Poor Livestock Policy Initiative, Food and Agriculture Organisation of the United Nations.

Ray, Joel G., David A. Henry, and Marcelo L. Urquia. 2012. "Sex Ratios among Canadian Liveborn Infants of Mothers from Different Countries." *CMAJ* 184: E492–E496.

RCMP (Royal Canadian Mounted Police). 2014. *Missing and Murdered Aboriginal Women: A National Operational Overview.* http://www.rcmp-grc.gc.ca/wam/media/460/original/0cbd8968a049aa0b44d343e76b4a9478.pdf.

Real, Terrence. 2001. "Men's Hidden Depression." In *Men and Masculinity*, edited by Theodore F. Cohen. Belmont, CA: Wadsworth.

Reed-Danahay, Deborah. 2001. "Autobiography, Intimacy and Ethnography." In *Handbook of Ethnography*, edited by Paul Atkinson, 407–426. London: Sage.

Reitz, Jeffrey G., and Rupa Banerjee. 2007. "Racial Inequality, Social Cohesion and Policy Issues in Canada." In *Belonging? Diversity, Recognition and Shared Citizenship in Canada*, edited by Keith G. Banting and Thomas J. Courchene, 489–546. Montreal: McGill-Queen's University Press.

Reuters. 2014. "Eight Bodies Found after Attack on Guinea Ebola Education Team." *Reuters.com*, September 18. http://www.reuters.com/article/2014/09/18/us-health-ebbola-guinea-idUSKBN0HD2JE20140918. Accessed February 1, 2015.

Richards, Paul, and Alfred Mokuwa. 2014. "Village Funerals and the Spread of Ebola Virus Disease." *Cultural Anthropology*, October 7. http://www.culanth.org/fieldsights/590-village-funerals-and-the-spread-of-ebola-virus-disease. Accessed February 1, 2015.

Rickford, John R. 1999. "Suite for Ebony and Phonics." In *Applying Anthropology: An Introductory Reader*, 5th ed., edited by Aaron Podolefsky and Peter J. Brown, 176–80. Mountain View, CA: Mayfield.

Ridington, Robin. 2011. "When You Sing It Now, Just Like New." *Anthropology and Humanism* 36 (1): 18–24.

Rivers, W. H. R. 1910. "The Genealogical Method of Anthropological Inquiry." *The Sociological Review III*: 1–12.

Robertson, Roland. 1992. *Globalization: Social Theory and Global Culture.* London: Sage.

Robinson, Gary. 1997. "Families, Generations, and Self: Conflict, Loyalty, and Recognition in an Australian Aboriginal Society." *Ethos* 25 (3): 303–32.

Rohde, David. 2007. "Army Enlists Anthropology in War Zones." *New York Times*, October 5. http://www.nytimes.com/2007/10/05/world/sia/05afghan.html?_r=0/. Accessed October 14, 2016.

Rohner, Ronald P., and Evelyn C. Rohner. 1970. *The Kwakiutl: Indians of British Columbia.* New York: Holt, Rinehart & Winston.

Ronson, Jon. 2015a. "How One Stupid Tweet Blew up Justine Sacco's Life." *New York Times Magazine*, February 12. http://www.nytimes.com/2015/02/15/magazine/how-one-stupid-tweet-ruined-justine-saccos-life.html. Accessed August 30, 2015.

——. 2015b. "When Online Shaming Spirals out of Control." *Ted Talk*, July. https://www.ted.com/talks/jon_ronson_what_happens_when_online_shaming_spirals_out_of_control/transcript?language=en. Accessed August 30, 2015.

Rosaldo, Michelle Zimbalist. 1974. "Women, Culture, and Society: A Theoretical Overview." In *Women, Culture, and Society*, edited by Michelle Zimbalist Rosaldo and Louise Lamphere. Stanford, CA: Stanford University Press.

Roscoe, William. 1998. *Changing Ones: Third and Fourth Genders in Native North America.* New York: Palgrave Macmillan.

Rose, Phyllis. 1987. "Graffiti in the Cave of the Mammoths." *The Iowa Review* 17 (3): 133–35.

Rosenthal, Elisabeth. 2006. "Genital Cutting Raises by 50% Likelihood Mothers or Their Newborns Will Die, Study Finds." *New York Times*, June 6. http://www.nytimes.com/2006/06/02/world/africa/02mutilation.html.

Roth, W. 2005. "The End of the One-Drop Rule? Labeling of Multiracial Children in Black Intermarriages." *Sociological Forum* 20 (1): 35–67.

Rothwell, J. Dan. 2004. *In the Company of Others: An Introduction to Communication.* New York: McGraw-Hill.

Roy, Baisakhi. 2012. "Why Some Immigrants Leave Canada." *Canadian Immigrant*, April 11. http://canadianimmigrant.ca/community/integration/why-some-immigrants-want-to-leave-canada/.

Royal Commission on Aboriginal Peoples (RCAP). 1996. *Bridging the Cultural Divide: A Report on Aboriginal People and Criminal Justice in Canada.* Ottawa: Canada Communication Group Publishing.

Rubin, Josh. 2013. "McGill Students Awarded $1-Million Hult Prize for Plan to Transform Insects into Food (Including 'Lime Cricket Chips')." *National Post*, September 24.

R. v. Gladue, [1999] 1 S.R.C. 688, par. 61 and 64. Supreme Court of Canada.

Rylko-Bauer, Barbara, Linda Whiteford, and Paul Farmer. 2009. *Global Health in Times of Violence.* Santa Fe, NM: SAR Press.

Sack, Kevin, Sheri Fink, Pam Belluck, and Adam Nossiter. 2014. "How Ebola Roared Back." *NYTime.com*, December 29. http://www.nytimes.com/2014/12/30/health/how-ebola-roared-back.html?_r=0. Accessed February 1, 2015.

Sacks, David, and Lisa R. Brody. 2005. *Encyclopedia of the Ancient Greek World* (revised edition). New York: Facts on File.

Sáez, Almudena Marí, Ann Kelly, and Hannah Brown. 2014. "Notes from Case Zero: Anthropology in the Time of Ebola." *Somatosphere* September 16. http://somatosphere.net/2014/09/notes-from-case-zero-anthropology-in-the-time-of-ebola.html. Accessed Feb 1, 2015.

Sahlins, Marshall. 1972. *Stone Age Economics.* Chicago: Aldine-Atherton.

Salopek, Paul. 2004. "Southern Seas: The New Wild West." *Charlotte Observer*, September 5: P-1.

Salvation Army. 2011. "Canada Speaks: Exposing Persistent Myths about the 150,000 Canadians Living on the Streets." *The Dignity Project.* Toronto: Salvation Army. http://salvationarmy.ca/DPresources/CanadaSpeaks_report_May2011.pdf. Accessed June 1, 2016.

Salzman, Philip Carl. 2002. "On Reflexivity." *American Anthropologist, New Series* 104 (3 Sep.): 805–13.

Sanday, Peggy R. 2004. *Women at the Center: Life in a Modern Matriarchy.* Ithaca, NY: Cornell University Press.

Sanjek, Roger. 1998. "Race." In *Encyclopedia of Social and Cultural Anthropology*, edited by Alan Barnard and Jonathan Spence, 462–65. New York: Routledge.

Sapir, Edward. 1929. "The Status of Linguistics as a Science." *Language* 5: 207–14.

Sarlo, Christopher. 2013. *Poverty: Where Do We Draw the Line?* Vancouver, BC: Fraser Institute. November. https://www.fraserinstitute.org/sites/default/files/Poverty-where-do-we-draw-the-line.pdf.

Scafidi, Susan. 2005. *Who Owns Culture? Appropriation and Authenticity in American Law* (Rutgers Series: The Public Life of the Arts). New Brunswick, NJ: Rutgers University Press.

Scaglion, Richard. 1987. "Customary Law Development in Papua New Guinea." In *Anthropological Praxis*, edited by Robert Wulff and Shirley Fiske, 98–107. Boulder, CO: Westview Press.

Scallan, Marilyn. 2015. "Ancient Ink: Iceman Otzi Has World's Oldest Tattoos." *Smithsonian Science News*, December 9.

Scaringi, Kevin. 2014. "NHL Superstitions: The Best Rituals in Hockey." *Discount Hockey*, June 24. http://discounthockey.com/blogs/news/14760907-nhl-superstitions-the-best-rituals-in-hockey.

Schacter, R. 2008. "An Ethnography of Iconoclash: An Investigation into the Production, Consumption and Destruction of Street-Art in London." *Journal of Material Culture* 13 (1): 35–61.

Scheffel, David Z. 2004. "Slovak Roma on the Threshold of Europe." *Anthropology Today* 20 (1): 6–12.

Schensul, Jean J. 2011. "Building and Applied Education Anthropology beyond the Academy." In *A Companion to the Anthropology of Education*, edited by Bradley A. U. Levinson and Mica Pollock, 112–34. London: Blackwell Publishing.

Scheper-Hughes, Nancy. [1979] 2001. *Saints, Scholars, and Schizophrenics: Mental Illness in Rural Ireland, Twentieth Anniversary Edition, Updated and Expanded.* Berkeley, CA: University of California Press.

——. 1992. *Death without Weeping: The Violence of Everyday Life in Brazil.* Berkeley, CA: University of California Press.

——. 2000. The Global Traffic in Human Organs. *Current Anthropology* 41 (2): 191–224.

——. 2009. "The Ethics of Engaged Ethnography Applying a Militant Anthropology in Organs-Trafficking Research." *Anthropology News*, September, 13–14.

Schlegel, Alice. 1990. "Gender Meanings: General and Specific." In *Beyond the Second Sex: New Directions in the Anthropology of Gender*, edited by Peggy Reeves Sanday and Ruth Gallagher Goodenough, 23–41. Philadelphia: University of Pennsylvania Press.

Schmidt, Sarah. 2011. "Extra Crunch with Lunch." *World Ark Magazine* Fall: 14–21. http://www.nxtbook.com/nxtbooks/heifer/worldark_2011fall/index.php?startid=3#/16/. Accessed October 15, 2016.

Schnarch, Brian. 2004. "Ownership, Control, Access, and Possession (OCAP) or Self-Determination Applied to Research: A Critical Analysis of Contemporary First Nations Research and Some Options for First Nations Communities." *Journal of Aboriginal Health* 1 (1 January): 80–95.

Schreyer, Christine. 2015. "The Digital Fandom of Na'vi Speakers." In "Performance and Performativity in Fandom," edited by Lucy Bennett and

Paul J. Booth. *Transformative Works and Cultures*, no. 18.

——. 2016. *Kryptonian*. http://www.christineschreyer.ca/Kryptonian.html. Accessed June 1, 2016.

Schulson, Michael. 2014. "Will Saudi Arabia Execute Guest Workers for 'Witchcraft'?" *The Daily Beast*, March 29. http://www.thedailybeast.com/articles/2014/03/29/indonesia-workers-in-saudi-arabia-are-on-trial-for-witchcraft-some-facing-the-death-penalty.html.

Schwartzman, Helen B. 1993. *Ethnography in Organizations* (Qualitative Research Methods Volume 27). Newbury Park: Sage Publications.

Scotsman, The. 2007. "No Place Like Home." *The Scotsman*, February 1. http://www.scotsman.com/lifestyle/culture/art/no-place-like-home-1-681191#ixzz48poDBfpJ.

Scowen, Reed. 2007. *Time to Say Goodbye: Building a Better Canada without Quebec*. McClelland & Stewart.

Sears, Heather A., Mary G. Simmering, and Brad A. MacNeil. 2007. "Canada." In *Encylopedia of Adolescence Vol 1 A-J*, edited by Jeffrey Jensen Arnett, 140–56. New York: Routledge.

Selzer, Richard. 1979. *Confessions of a Knife*. New York: Simon & Schuster.

Sen, Amartya. 1981. *Poverty and Famines: An Essay on Entitlement and Deprivation*. Oxford: Clarendon Press.

Service, Elman R. 1978. *Profiles in Ethnology*, 3rd ed. New York: Harper & Row.

Shahd, Laila S. 2001. "An Investigation of the Phenomenon of Polygyny in Rural Egypt." *Cairo Papers in Social Science* 24 (3, Fall). Cairo: American University in Cairo Press.

Shaw, James H. 1995. "How Many Bison Originally Populated Western Rangelands?" *Rangelands* 17 (5): 148–50.

Shearlaw, Maeve. 2016. "Egypt Five Years On: Was It Ever a "Social Media Revolution?" *The Guardian*, January 26. http://www.theguardian.com/world/2016/jan/25/egypt-5-years-on-was-it-ever-a-social-media-revolution.

Sheets, Payson D. 1993. "Dawn of a New Stone Age in Eye Surgery." In *Archaeology: Discovering Our Past*, 2nd ed., edited by Robert J. Sharer and Wendy Ashmore. Mountain View, CA: Mayfield.

Shostak, Marjorie. 1981. *Nisa: The Life of a !Kung Woman*. Cambridge, UK: Harvard University Press.

Sieber, Roy. 1962. "Masks as Agents of Social Control." *African Studies Bulletin* 5 (11): 8–13.

Sifton, Sam. 2011. "A Critic Selects a Last Meal." *New York Times*, October 11. http://www.nytimes.com/2011/10/12/dining/reviews/per-se-nyc-restaurant-review.html?WT.mc_id=GN-D-I-NYT-MOD-MOD-M223-ROS-1011-PH&WT.mc_ev=click&_r=0

SIL International. 2016. http://www.sil.org/

Simons, Gary. 2016. "Welcome to the 19th Edition." *Ethnologue*, February 22. https://www.ethnologue.com/ethnoblog/gary-simons/welcome-19th-edition. Accessed June 1, 2016.

Sinclair, Brendan. 2014. "Women Increasing Representation among US Gamers–ESA." *GamesIndustry.biz*, April 24. http://www.gamesindustry.biz/articles/2014-04-24-women-increasing-representation-among-us-gamers-esa.

Sing, S., and R. Samara. 1996. "Early Marriage among Women in Developing Countries." *International Family Planning Perspectives* 22: 148–57, 175.

Singer, Natasha. 2014. "Intel's Sharp-Eyed Social Scientist." *The New York Times*, February 15. http://www.nytimes.com/2014/02/16/technology/intels-sharp-eyed-social-scientist.html. Accessed January 8, 2015.

Slobin, Mark, and Jeff T. Titon. 1984. "The Music Culture as a World of Music." In *Worlds of Music: An Introduction to the Music of the World's Peoples*, edited by Jeff T. Titon et al., 1–11. London: Collier Macmillan Publishers.

Smith, Bruce. 1998. *The Emergence of Agriculture*. New York: Scientific American Library.

Smith, David Livingstone. 2007. "Beyond Westermarck: Can Shared Mothering or Maternal Phenotype Matching Account for Incest Avoidance?" *Evolutionary Psychology* 5 (1): 202–22.

Smith, E. A. 1983. "Anthropological Applications of Optimal Foraging Theory: A Critical Review." *Current Anthropology* 24: 625–51.

Smith, Eric Alden, Kim Hill, Frank W. Marlowe, David Nolin, Polly Wiessner, Michael Gurven, Samuel Bowles, Monique Borgerhoff Mulder, Tom Hertz, and Adrian Bell. 2010. "Wealth Transmission and Inequality among Hunter-Gatherers." *Current Anthropology* 51 (1): 19–34.

Smith, Grafton Elliot. 1915. *The Migrations of Early Culture. A Study of the Significance of the Geographical Distribution of the Practice of Mummification as Evidence of the Migrations of Peoples and the Spread of Certain Customs and Beliefs*. London: Longmans, Green & Co.

Smith, Marie L., Garrison W. Cottrell, Frédéric Gosselin, and Philippe G. Schyns. 2005. "Transmitting and Decoding Facial Expressions." *Psychological Science* 16 (3 March): 184–89.

Smith, Michael E. 2009. "V. Gordon Childe and the Urban Revolution: A Historical Perspective on a Revolution in Urban Studies." *Town Planning Review* 80: 3–29.

Smith, Rebecca. 2014. "Woman Becomes First to Give Birth from Transplanted Womb—Using One Donated from Her Own Mother." *The Telegraph*, October 3.

Solomon, Michael R., Judith L. Zaichkowsky, and Rosemary Polegato. 2013. *Consumer Behaviour: Buying, Having, and Being*, 5th ed. Don Mills, ON: Pearson Education Canada.

Soupcoff, Marni. 2015. "Marni Soupcoff: The Definitive Guide to the Controversial Police Practice of 'Carding.'" *National Post*, September 28. http://news.nationalpost.com/full-comment/marni-soupcoff-the-definitive-guide-to-the-controversial-police-practice-of-carding.

Spears, Tom. 2013. "Don't Tell Bob and Doug: 'Eh' Is on the Decline." *National Post*, December 18.

Spindler, K. 1994. *The Man in the Ice*. New York: Harmony Press.

Spokesman-Review, The. 1989. "Jazz Musician Spent Life Concealing Fantastic Secret." *The Spokesman-Review* January 31. https://news.google.com/newspapers?nid=1314&dat=19890131&id=FlxWAAAAIBAJ&sjid=5O8DAAAAIBAJ&pg=7025,9288586&hl=en.

Stang, Veronica. 2009. *Gardening the World: Agency, Identity, and the Ownership of Water*. New York: Beghahn Books.

Statistics Canada 2009. Censuses of population, 1971 to 2006: Figure 2 Region of birth of recent immigrants to Canada, 1971 to 2006. http://www12.statcan.ca/census-recensement/2006/as-sa/97-557/figures/c2-eng.cfm

Statistics Canada. 2012a. *Fifty Years of Families in Canada: 1961 to 2011: Families. Households and Marital Status, 2011 Census Population*. Ottawa: Government of Canada. http://www12.statcan.gc.ca/census-recensement/2011/as-sa/98-312-x/98-312-x2011003_1-eng.cfm?wbdisable=true#wb-info

——. 2012b. *Life Expectancy at Birth, by Sex, by Province. Ottawa: Government of Canada.* http://www.statcan.gc.ca/tables-tableaux/sum-som/l01/cst01/health26-eng.htm. Accessed October 15, 2016.

——. 2012c. *Linguistic Characteristics of Canadians Language, 2011 Census of Population*. http://www12.statcan.ca/census-recensement/2011/as-sa/98-314-x/98-314-x2011001-eng.pdf

——. 2013a. *2011 National Household Survey: Immigration, place of birth, citizenship, ethnic origin, visible minorities, language and religion.* Ottawa: Government of Canada. http://www.statcan.gc.ca/daily-quotidien/130508/dq130508b-eng.htm. Accessed August 30, 2015.

——. 2013b. *Immigration and Ethnocultural Diversity in Canada: National Household Survey, 2011*. Ottawa: Government of Canada. http://www12.statcan.gc.ca/nhs-enm/2011/as-sa/99-010-x/99-010-x2011001-eng.pdf. Accessed October 24, 2016.

Steel, Deborah. 2013. "Residential School Childhood Artwork Repatriated by Adult Survivors." *Alberni Valley News*, April 3. http://www.albernivalleynews.com/news/201349521.html.

Steiner, Christopher B. 1990. "Body Personal and Body Politic: Adornment and Leadership in Cross-Cultural Perspective." *Anthropos* 85: 431–45.

Steinmetz, Katy. 2014. "The Transgender Tipping Point: America's Next Civil Rights Frontier." *Time*, May 29.

Stephens, William N. 1963. *The Family in Cross-Cultural Perspective*. New York: Holt, Rinehart & Winston.

Stern, Alexandra. 2005. *Eugenic Nation: Faults and Frontiers of Better Breeding in Modern America*. Berkeley: University of California Press.

Steward, Julian H. 1938. *Basin-Plateau Aboriginal Sociopolitical Groups*. Smithsonian Institution Bureau of American Ethnology Bulletin 120. Washington, DC: United States Government Printing Office.

Stille, Alexander. 2003. "Experts Can Help Rebuild a Country." *New York Times*, July 19: A-15, A-17. http://www.nytimes.com/2003/07/19/arts/experts-can-help-rebuild-a-country.html

Stivers, T., Enfield, N. J., Brown, P., Englert, C., Hayashi, M., Heinemann, T., Levinson, S. 2009. "Universals and Cultural Variation in Turn-Taking in Conversation." *Proceedings of the National Academy of Sciences* 106 (26).

Stock, Matthew. 2016. *Ending Homelessness? A Critical Examination of Housing First in Canada and Winnipeg.* Canadian Centre for Policy Alternatives Manitoba Office.

Stockard, Janice E. 2002. *Marriage in Culture.* Fort Worth, TX: Harcourt College Publishers.

Stocking, George. 1989. "Paradigmatic Traditions in the History of Anthropology." In *Companion to the History of Modern Science*, edited by G. N. Cantor et al. London: Routledge.

Stocking, George W. 1995. *After Tylor: British Social Anthropology 1888–1951.* Madison, WI: University of Wisconsin Press.

Stone, Jon. 2014. "Groups of Ultra-Orthodox Jewish Men Keep Delaying Flights by Refusing to Sit Next to Women." *The Independent*, December 30.

Strapagiel, Lauren. 2015. "Transgender Canadians Can Now Self-Identify on Citizenship Documents without Sex -Reassignment Surgery." National Post, April 28. http://news.nationalpost.com/news/canada/federal-government-quietly-eases-requirements-for-canadians-seeking-to-change-gender-on-citizen-certificate.

Sundkler, Bengt. 1961. *Bantu Prophets of South Africa*, 2nd ed. London: Oxford University Press.

Surowiecki, James. 2005. "Check, Please." *New Yorker*, September 5. http://www.newyorker.com/magazine/2005/09/05/check-please-3

Surrogacy in Canada Online. 2015. http://www.surrogacy.ca/. Accessed May 9, 2015.

Survival International. 2015. "Brazil: Blood Samples Returned to Yanomami after Nearly 50 Years." *Survival International*, April 13. http://www.survivalinternational.org/news/10727. Accessed June 1, 2016.

Suttles, Wayne P., and Barbara Lane. 1990. "Southern Coast Salish." In *The Northwest Coast, Handbook of North American Indians, Vol. 7*, edited by Wayne P. Suttles. Washington: Smithsonian Institution.

Sutton, Mark Q., and E. N Anderson. 2009. *Introduction to Cultural Ecology*, 2nd ed. Lanham, MD: AltaMira Press.

——. 2013. *Introduction to Cultural Ecology*, 3rd ed. Walnut Creek, CA: AltaMira Press.

Tabani, Marc. 2009. "Dreams of Unity, Traditions of Division: John Frum, "Kastom" and Inter-Manipulation Strategies as Cultural Heritage on Tanna (Vanuatu)." *Paideuma: Mitteilungen zur Kulturkunde* 55: 27–47.

Takeuchi, Craig. 2015. "LGBT in B.C.: Kelowna Unveils Rainbow Crosswalks." *The Georgia Straight*, August 6. http://www.straight.com/blogra/503896/lgbt-bc-kelowna-unveils-rainbow-crosswalks.

Tannen, Deborah. 1990. *You Just Don't Understand: Women and Men in Conversation.* New York: Morrow.

——. 2006. "Language and Culture." In *An Introduction to Language and Linguistics*, edited by Ralph W. Fasold and Jeff Connor-Linton. Cambridge, UK: Cambridge University Press.

——. 2012. "Turn-Taking and Intercultural Discourse and Communication." In *The Handbook of Intercultural Discourse and Communication*, edited by Christina Paulston, Scott Kiesling, and Elizabeth Rangel, 135–57. Chicester, UK: John Wiley & Sons.

Tedesco, Theresa. 2015. "Conrad Black Expressed Interest in Any Dailies that Postmedia May Have Had to Sell." *Financial Post*, March 27. http://business.financialpost.com/news/fp-street/conrad-black-expressed-interest-in-any-dailies-that-postmedia-may-have-had-to-sell

Thicke, Lori. 2014. "Vanishing Voices." *Trek Magazine*, December. http://trekmagazine.alumni.ubc.ca/2014/december-2014/features/vanishing-voices/

Thomason, Sarah G., and Terrence Kaufman. 1988. *Language Contact, Creolization and Genetic Linguistics.* Chicago: University of Chicago Press.

Thompson, Chuck. 2013. "China Tourism Surge: Readers' Emotional Responses." *CNN*, April 12. http://edition.cnn.com/2013/04/10/travel/china-tourist-reaction/index.html

Thurlow, Crispin. 2006. "From Statistical Panic to Moral Panic: The Metadiscursive Construction and Popular Exaggeration of New Media Language in the Print Media." *Journal of Computer Mediated Communication* 11 (3): 667–701.

Thurman, Judith. 2015. "A Loss for Words: Can a Dying Language Be Saved?" *The New Yorker. Annals of Conservation*, March 30. http://www.newyorker.com/magazine/2015/03/30/a-loss-for-words

Tierney, Patrick. 2000. *Darkness in El Dorado: How Scientists and Journalists Devastated the Amazon.* New York: W. W. Norton & Company.

Todd, Douglas. 2003. "University of Victoria Chaplain Marks Solstice with Pagan Rituals." *Vancouver Sun*, December 22. http://vancouversun.com/news/staff-blogs/pagans-celebrate-solstice-with-yule-rituals.

——. 2010. "Growing Ethnic Enclaves Hurt Sense of Canadian 'Belonging.'" *Vancouver Sun*, September 11.

Todd, Loreto. 1990. *Pidgins and Creoles*, 2nd ed. New York: Routledge.

Toffler, Alvin. 1970. *Future Shock.* New York: Random House.

Tollefson, Kenneth D. 1995. "Potlatching and Political Organization among the Northwest Coast Indians." *Ethnology* 34 (1): 53–73.

Tom, Gail. 2001. *Understanding Consumer Behavior: Marketing Lessons Learned from Understanding the Consumer.* Cincinnati: South Western Educational Publishing.

Tripp, Rob. 2015. "Shafia Parents and Son, Convicted in Honour Killing of Four Family Members, Seek New Trial." *National Post*, October 13.

Trompf, Garry W. 2015. "New Religious Movements in Oceania." *Nova Religio: The Journal of Alternative and Emergent Religions* 18 (4): 5–15.

Truth and Reconciliation Commission of Canada. 2015. *Honouring the Truth, Reconciling for the Future: Summary of the Final Report of the Truth and Reconciliation Commission of Canada.* Ottawa: Government of Canada.

Tucker, Rebecca. 2015. "Group of Seven Painter Lawren Harris Gets an Unlikely Champion Down South—Steve Martin." *National Post*, October 9. http://news.nationalpost.com/arts/group-of-seven-painter-lawren-harris-gets-an-unlikely-champion-down-south-steve-martin.

Turner, Victor. 1967a. "Betwixt and Between: The Liminal Period in Rites de Passage." In *The Forest of Symbols: Aspects of Ndembu Ritual.* Ithaca, NY: Cornell University Press: 93–111.

——. 1967b. *The Forest of Symbols.* Ithaca, NY: Cornell University Press.

——. 1977. *The Ritual Process: Structure and Anti-Structure.* Ithaca, NY: Cornell University Press.

Tylor, Edward Burnett. [1871] 1903. *Primitive Culture: Researches into the Development of Mythology, Philosophy, Religion, Language, Art, and Custom*, 4th ed. London: John Murray.

UEA (Universal Esperanto Association). 2016. *An Update on Esperanto.* http://uea.org/info/en/ghisdate_pri_esperanto. Accessed June 1, 2016.

Underhill, Paco. 2009. *Why We Buy: The Science of Shopping Updated and Revised for the Internet, the Global Consumer and Beyond.* New York: Simon and Schuster Paperbacks.

UNESCO. *Atlas of the World's Languages in Danger.* http://www.unesco.org/languages-atlas/index.php?hl=en&page=atlasmap

——. 2016. *Atlas of the World's Languages in Danger.* (Canada:) http://www.unesco.org/languages-atlas/index.php?hl=en&page=atlasmap&cc2=CA. Accessed June 1, 2016.

UNESCO Institute for Statistics. 2014. "International Literacy Data 2014." http://www.uis.unesco.org/literacy/Pages/literacy-data-release-2014.aspx.

UNHCR. 2011. *The 1951 Convention Relating to the Status of Refugees and Its 1967 Protocol.* Geneva, Switzerland: UNHCR. http://www.unhcr.org/about-us/background/4ec262df9/1951-convention-relating-status-refugees-its-1967-protocol.html

——. 2015. *UNHCR Global Trends: Forced Displacement in 2014.* Geneva, Switzerland: UNHCR. http://www.unhcr.org/statistics/country/556725e69/unhcr-global-trends-2014.html?query

United Nations. 2008. *United Nations Declaration on the Rights of Indigenous Peoples.* United Nations.

United Nations Department of Economic and Social Affairs, Population Division. 2011. *Population Facts December 2011.*

United Nations Development Programme: Human Development Reports. 2013. Table 4: Gender Inequality Index. http://hdr.undp.org/en/content/table-4-gender-inequality-index. Accessed July 20, 2015.

UN World Tourism Organization. 2014. "International Tourism Generates US$

1.4 Trillion in Export Earnings." *UN World Tourism Organization Press Release PR14034*, May 14.
Urdang, Stephanie. 2001. "Women and AIDS: Gender Inequality Is Fatal." *Women's International Network News* 27 (4 Autumn): 24.
Urry, James. 1993. *Before Social Anthropology: Essays on the History of British Anthropology.* Chur, Switzerland: Harvard Academic.
Valladares, Danillo. 2010. "Central America: Women Eke Out a Living in Informal Economy." *Interpress Service*, February 16. http://www.ipsnews.net/2010/02/central-america-women-eke-out-a-living-in-informal-economy/. Accessed May 3, 2015.
Vancouver Sun. 2007. "Paintings Considered Insensitive and Racist." *Vancouver Sun*, February 13.
Vandewettering, Kaylea R. 2015. "Upper Paleolithic Venus Figurines and Interpretations of Prehistoric Gender Representations." *PURE Insights* 4: Article 7.
van Gennep, Arnold. [1908] 1960. *The Rites of Passage.* Chicago: University of Chicago Press.
——. 1977. *The Rites of Passage.* London and Henley: Routledge and Kegan Paul.
Van Stekelenburg, Jacquelien. 2012. "The Occupy Movement: Product of This Time." *Development* 55 (2): 224–31.
Vantomme, P., D. Göhler, and F. N'decker-Eziangba. 2004. "Contribution of Forest Insects to Food Security and Forest Conservation: The Example of Caterpillars in Central Africa." *Wildlife Policy Briefing* 3 (January).
Van Willigen, John. 2002. *Applied Anthropology: An Introduction*, 3rd ed. Westport, CT: Bergin & Garvey.
Virtual Museum of Canada. 2015. Dane Wajich. http://www.virtualmuseum.ca/sgc-cms/expositions-exhibitions/danewajich/english/. Accessed August 27, 2015.
Visser, Josh. 2015. "Naheed Nenshi Crowned 'King of all Mayors' with a Sweet-Looking Tiara." *National Post*, February 5.
Vogel, Lauren. 2012. "Sex Selection Migrates to Canada." *CMAJ* 184 (3): 492–96.
Voices. 2002. "Quinceañera! A Celebration of Latina Womanhood." *Voices: The Journal of New York Folklore* 28 (Fall-Winter). http://www.nyfolklore.org/pubs/voic28-3-4/onair.html. Accessed October 15, 2016.
vom Lehn, Dirk. 2006. "Embodying Experience: A Video-Based Examination of Visitors' Conduct and Interaction in Museums." *European Journal of Marketing* 40 (11/12): 1340–59.
Wahba, Phil. 2016. "Whole Foods May Add Tattoo Parlors to Lure Millennials." *Fortune*, February 16. http://fortune.com/2016/02/16/whole-foods-tattoos/.
Wajahat Ali, Eli Clifton, Matthew Duss, Lee Fang, Scott Keyes, and Faiz Shakir. 2011. *Fear, Inc.: The Roots of the Islamophobia Network in America.* Washington, DC: Center for American Progress. https://cdn.americanprogress.org/wp-content/uploads/issues/2011/08/pdf/islamophobia.pdf.
Wallace, Anthony F. C. 1966. *Religion: An Anthropological View.* New York: Random House.
Wallerstein, Immanuel. [1974] 2011. *The Modern World-System I: Capitalist Agriculture and the Origins of the European World-Economy in the Sixteenth Century.* Berkeley, CA: University of California Press.
Walsh, Austin. 2012. "Cultural Misunderstanding Closes Massage Parlor: Supervisors Shut Down Business over Gifts Perceived as Bribes." *Redwood City-Woodside Patch*, June 28. http://patch.com/california/redwoodcity-woodside/cultural-misunderstanding-closes-massage-parlor. Accessed April 24, 2015.
Ward, Alexander. 2015. "Mass Protests in Nicaragua as Farmers Claim Planned Canal Will 'Sell Country to the Chinese.'" *The Independent*, June 14. http://www.independent.co.uk/news/world/americas/mass-protests-in-nicaragua-as-farmers-claim-planned-canal-will-sell-country-to-the-chinese-10318705.html.
Waring, Marilyn. 1989. *If Women Counted: A New Feminist Economics.* New York: HarperCollins.
——. 2004. *Counting for Nothing: What Men Value and What Women Are Worth.* Toronto: University of Toronto Press.
Warry, Wayne. 2007. *Ending Denial: Understanding Aboriginal Issues.* Peterborough, ON: Broadview Press.
Watanabe, Suwako. 1993. "Cultural Differences in Framing: American and Japanese Group Discussions." In *Framing in Discourse*, edited by Deborah Tannen, 176–208. New York: Oxford University Press.
Watson, Peter. 2005. *Ideas: A History of Thought and Invention from Fire to Freud.* New York: HarperCollins Publishers.
Watts, Jonathan. 2015. "Land of Opportunity—and Fear—along Route of Nicaragua's Giant New Canal." *The Guardian*, January 20. http://www.theguardian.com/world/2015/jan/20/-sp-nicaragua-canal-land-opportunity-fear-route.
Webb, Nicole. 2014. "Chinese Tourists Behaving Badly." *Mintmochamusings.com*, May 8. http://mintmochamusings.com/chinese-tourists/. Accessed November 9, 2015.
Weber, Max. [1904] 1958. *The Protestant Ethic and the Spirit of Capitalism.* New York: Charles Scribner's Sons.
——. 1946. *From Max Weber: Essays in Sociology*, edited and translated by Hans Girth and C. Wright Mills. New York: Oxford University Press.
Weiner, Annette. 1976. *Women of Value, Men of Renown.* Austin, TX: University of Texas Press.
——. 1988. *The Trobrianders of Papua New Guinea.* New York: Holt, Rinehart & Winston.
Weinman, Jamie. 2014. "How a Gamer Fight Turned into an All-out Culture War." *Maclean's*, December 8. http://www.macleans.ca/society/technology/gamergate-how-a-gamer-fight-turned-into-an-all-out-culture-war/.
Weir, Stephen. 2013. "St Joseph's Mojo Moves Homes in Strange Ways." *Huffington Post*, January 18.
Weismantel, Mary. 1995. "Making Kin: Kinship Theory and Zumbagua Adoptions." *American Ethnologist* 22 (4): 685–709.
Wente, Margaret. 2012. "The Collapse of the Liberal Church." *The Globe and Mail*, July 28. http://www.theglobeandmail.com/globe-debate/the-collapse-of-the-liberal-church/article4443228/.
West, Candace. 1979. "Against Our Will: Male Interruptions of Females in Cross-Sex Conversation." Language, Sex, and Gender: Does La Difference Make a Difference?: Result of a Workshop. *Annals of the New York Academy of Sciences* 327: 81–96. doi: 10.1111/j.1749-6632.1979.tb17755.x.
Weston, Greg, and Jack Aubry. 1990. "The Making of a Massacre: The Marc Lépine Story Part I." *The Ottawa Citizen*, February 7.
Whitaker, Kati. 2012. "Ghana Witch Camps: Widows' Lives in Exile." *BBC News Magazine*, September 1.
White, Leslie. 1959. *The Evolution of Culture.* New York: McGraw-Hill.
White, Micah. 2016. *The End of Protest: A New Playbook for Revolution.* Toronto: Knopf Canada.
Whiteduck, Judy. 2010. "Building the First Nations E-Community." In *Aboriginal Policy Research Volume VI: Learning, Technology, and Traditions.* Toronto: Thompson Educational Publishing: 95–103.
Whitehead, Harry. 2000. "The Hunt for Quesalid: Tracking Lévi-Strauss' Shaman." *Anthropology & Medicine* 7 (2): 149–68.
Whitehead, Neil L., and R. Brian Ferguson. 1993. "Deceptive Stereotypes about Tribal Warfare." *Chronicle of Higher Education*, November 10: 48.
Whitmarsh, Ian, and David S. Jones (eds.). 2010. *What's the Use of Race?: Modern Governance and the Biology of Difference.* Cambridge, UK: MIT Press.
Whitzman, Carolyn. 2010. "Making the Invisible Visible: Canadian Women, Homelessness, and Health outside the 'Big City.'" In *Finding Home: Policy Options for Addressing Homelessness in Canada*, edited by J. David Hulchanski, Philippa Campsie, Shirley Chau, Stephen Hwang, and Emily Paradis. Toronto: University of Toronto. www.homelesshub.ca/FindingHome.
WHO (World Health Organization). 2001. "Gender Disparities in Mental Health." *Department of Mental Health and Substance Dependence.*
——. 2014a. "8 August Statement on the 1st Meeting of the IHR Emergency Committee on the 2014 Ebola Outbreak in West Africa." *WHO Media Centre.* http://www.who.int/mediacentre/news/statements/2014/ebola-20140808/en/. Accessed February 1, 2015.
——. 2014b. "Female Genital Mutilation. Fact sheet N 241." *WHO Media Centre.* http://www.who.int/mediacentre/factsheets/fs241/en/. Accessed July 20, 2015.
——. 2015a. "Ebola Data and Statistics." *WHO Data.* http://apps.who.int/gho/data/node.ebola-sitrep.quick-downloads?lang=en. Accessed February 1, 2015.
——. 2015b. "Voluntary Medical Male Circumcision for HIV Prevention in 14

Priority Countries in East and Southern Africa: Progress Brief." WHO reference number: WHO/HIV/2015.21. *WHO Programmes*. http://www.who.int/hiv/pub/malecircumcision/brief2015/en/. Accessed June 1, 2016.

Whorf, Benjamin L. 1941. "The Relation of Habitual Thought and Behavior to Language." In *Language, Culture and Personality: Essays in Memory of Edward Sapir*, edited by Leslie Spier, A. Irving Hallowell, and Stanley S. Newman, 75–93. Menasha: Sapir Memorial Fund.

Widom, Cathy Spatz, Sally Czaja, and Mary Ann Dutton. 2014. "Child Abuse and Neglect and Intimate Partner Violence Victimization and Perpetration: A Prospective Investigation." *Child Abuse and Neglect* 38 (4): 650–63.

Wilford, John Noble. 2010. "Hunting One Language, Stumbling upon Another." *The New York Times*, October 12. http://www.nytimes.com/2010/10/12/science/12language.html?_r=0. Accessed October 15, 2016.

Williams, J. E., and D. L. Best. 1994. "Cross-Cultural Views of Women and Men." In *Psychology and Culture*, edited by W. J. Lonner and R. Malpass, 191–96. Boston: Allyn & Bacon.

Williams-Thorpe, O. 1995. "Obsidian in the Mediterranean and the Near East: A Provenancing Success Story." *Archaeometry* 37 (2): 217–48.

Winther, Tanja. 2008. *The Impact of Electricity. Development, Desires and Dilemmas*. Oxford: Berghahn.

WISP (World Initiative for Sustainable Pastoralism). 2007. *Pastoralists as Shrewd Managers of Risk and Resilience in the Horn of Africa*. Policy Brief No. 4. http://cmsdata.iucn.org/downloads/pastoralists_as_shrewd_managers_of_risk_and_resilience.pdf. Accessed October 15, 2016.

Witherspoon, Gary. 1977. *Language and Art in the Navajo Universe*. Ann Arbor, MI: University of Michigan Press.

Withnall, Adam. 2014. "Iraq Crisis: Isis Declares Its Territories a New Islamic State with 'Restoration of Caliphate' in Middle East." *The Independent*, June 30.

Woddis, Jack. 1967. *An Introduction to Neo-Colonialism*. New York: International Publishers.

Wolcott, Harry F. 2008. *Ethnography: A Way of Seeing*. Walnut Creek, CA: AltaMira Press.

Wolf, E. 1964. *Anthropology*. Englewood Cliffs, NJ: Prentice Hall.

Wolf, Eric. 1982. *Europe and the People without History*. Berkeley, CA: University of California Press.

Wong, Elaine. 2010. "The Most Memorable Product Launches of 2010." *Forbes*, December 3. http://www.forbes.com/2010/12/03/most-memorable-products-leadership-cmo-network.html

Wood, Julia T. 1994. "Gender, Communication, and Culture." In *Intercultural Communication: A Reader*, 7th ed., edited by Larry Samovar and Richard Porter, 155–65. Belmont, CA: Wadsworth.

Woodbury, Anthony. n.d. "What Is an Endangered Language?" *Linguistic Society of America*. http://www.linguisticsociety.org/content/what-endangered-language. Accessed June 1, 2016.

World Bank. 2015. "Mortality Rate, Infant (per 1,000 Live Births)" *The World Bank Data*. http://data.worldbank.org/indicator/SP.DYN.IMRT.IN. Accessed November 9, 2015.

World Life Expectancy. 2015. "Burkino Faso." *World Health Rankings*. http://www.worldlifeexpectancy.com/burkina-faso-life-expectancy. Accessed November 9, 2015.

World Net Daily. 2005. "Help Wanted: Must Not Be White, Male." *World Net Daily*, November 19. http://www.wnd.com/2005/11/33501/#uWiussgHxqIII9d5.99.

Worsley, Peter. 1957. *The Trumpet Shall Sound: A Study of "Cargo Cults" in Melanesia*. New York: Schocken Books.

Wright, Melissa W. 2006. *Disposable Women and Other Myths and Global Capitalism*. New York: Routledge.

Wyatt, Nelson. 2013. "Quebec's "Pastagate" PR Nightmare: Story Gets 60 Times More Coverage outside Province than Marois Investment Trip." *National Post*, February 26.

Yamada, Haru. 1997. *Different Games, Different Rules: Why Americans and Japanese Misunderstand Each Other*. New York: Oxford University Press.

Yardley, Jim. 2005. "Fearing Future, China Starts to Give Girls Their Due." *New York Times*, January 31: A-3.

Yates, Donna. 2013. "Toi Moko." *Trafficking Culture: Researching the Global Traffic in Looted Cultural Objects*, October 30. http://traffickingculture.org/encyclopedia/case-studies/toimoko/. Accessed June 1, 2016.

Yellen, John. 1990. "The Transformation of the Kalahari !Kung." *Scientific American*, April: 96–104.

Yew, Leong. 2002. "Neocolonialism." *Postcolonial Web.org*. http://www.postcolonialweb.org/poldiscourse/neocolonialism1.html. Accessed June 1, 2016.

York, Michael. 2005. "New Age and Magic." In *Witchcraft and Magic: Contemporary North America*, edited by Helen A. Berger, 28–54. Philadelphia, PA: University of Pennsylvania Press.

Young, Cathy. 2014. "The Surprising Truth about Women and Violence." *Time*, June 25. http://time.com/2921491/hope-solo-women-violence/.

——. 2015. "To the New Culture Cops, Everything Is Appropriation." *Washington Post*, August 21. https://www.washingtonpost.com/posteverything/wp/2015/08/21/to-the-new-culture-cops-everything-is-appropriation/.

Young, James O. 2005. "Profound Offense and Cultural Appropriation." *The Journal of Aesthetics and Art Criticism* 63 (2): 135–46.

Yousafzai, Malala. 2013. "Malala Yousafzai's Speech at the Youth Takeover of the United Nations." *A World at School*. https://secure.aworldatschool.org/page/content/the-text-of-malala-yousafzais-speech-at-the-united-nations/. Accessed July 20, 2015.

Yuen, A. W. C., and N. G. Jablonski. 2010. "Vitamin D: In the Evolution of Human Skin Colour." *Medical Hypotheses* 74 (1): 39–44.

Yule, G. 2006. *The Study of Language*, 3rd ed. Cambridge, UK: Cambridge University Press.

Zilio, Michelle. 2016. "Not Enough Resources for Syrian Refugees in Canada: Poll." *The Globe and Mail*, May 8. http://www.theglobeandmail.com/news/politics/not-enough-resources-for-syrian-refugees-in-canada-poll/article29935148/

Zimmerman, Don H., and Candace West. 1975. "Sex Roles, Interruptions, and Silences in Conversation." In *Language and Sex: Difference and Dominance*, edited by Barrie Thorne and Nancy Hebley, 105–29. Rowley, MA: Newbury House.

Index